APB No.	Date Issued	Title
21	Aug. 1971	Interest on Receivables and Payables
22	Apr. 1972	Disclosure of Accounting Policies
23	Apr. 1972	Accounting for Income Taxes—Special Areas
24	Apr. 1972	Accounting for Income Taxes—Equity Method Investments
25	Oct. 1972	Accounting for Stock Issued to Employees
26	Oct. 1972	Early Extinguishment of Debt
27	Nov. 1972	Accounting for Lease Transactions by Manufacturer or Dealer Lessors
28	May 1973	Interim Financial Reporting
29	May 1973	Accounting for Nonmonetary Transactions
30	June 1973	Reporting the Results of Operations
31	June 1973	Disclosure of Lease Commitments by Lessees

SFAC No.

Financial Accounting Standards Board (FASB),
Statement of Financial Accounting Concepts (1978–85)

SFAC No.		
1	Nov. 1978	Objectives of Financial Reporting by Business Enterprises
2	May 1980	Qualitative Characteristics of Accounting Information
3	Dec. 1980	Elements of Financial Statements of Business Enterprises
4	Dec. 1980	Objectives of Financial Reporting by Nonbusiness Organizations
5	Dec. 1984	Recognition and Measurement in Financial Statements of Business Enterprises
6	Dec. 1985	Elements of Financial Statements (a replacement of *FASB Concepts Statement No. 3*, incorporating an amendment of *FASB Concepts Statement No. 2*)

SFAS No.

Financial Accounting Standards Board (FASB), *Statements of Financial Accounting Standards* (1973–88)

SFAS No.		
1	Dec. 1973	Disclosure of Foreign Currency
2	Oct. 1974	Accounting for Research and Development Costs
3	Dec. 1974	Reporting Accounting Changes in Interim Financial Statements (an amendment of *APB Opinion 23*)
4	Mar. 1975	Reporting Gains and Losses from Extinguishment of Debt
5	Mar. 1975	Accounting for Contingencies
6	May 1975	Classification of Short-Term Obligations Expected to Be Refinanced
7	June 1975	Accounting and Reporting by Development Stage Enterprises
8	Oct. 1975	Accounting for the Translation of Foreign Currency Transactions and Foreign Currency Financial Statements
9	Oct. 1975	Accounting for Income Taxes—Oil and Gas Producing Companies (an amendment of *APB Opinions 11 and 23*)
10	Oct. 1975	Extension of "Grandfather" Provisions for Business Combinations (an amendment of *APB Opinion 16*)
11	Dec. 1975	Accounting for Contingencies—Transition Method (an amendment of *FASB Statement 5*)
12	Dec. 1975	Accounting for Certain Marketable Securities
13	Nov. 1976	Accounting for Leases
14	Dec. 1976	Financial Reporting for Segments of a Business Enterprise
15	June 1977	Accounting by Debtors and Creditors for Troubled Debt Restructurings
16	June 1977	Prior Period Adjustments
17	Nov. 1977	Accounting for Leases—Initial Direct Costs
18	Nov. 1977	Financial Reporting for Segments of a Business Enterprise—Interim Financial Statements
19	Dec. 1977	Financial Accounting and Reporting by Oil and Gas Producing Companies
20	Dec. 1977	Accounting for Forward Exchange Contracts
21	Apr. 1978	Suspension of the Reporting of Earnings per Share and Segment Information by Nonpublic Enterprises
22	June 1978	Changes in the Provisions of Lease Agreements Resulting from Refundings of Tax-Exempt Debt
23	Aug. 1978	Inception of the Lease
24	Dec. 1978	Reporting Segment Information in Financial Statements that Are Presented in Another Enterprises's Financial Report
25	Feb. 1979	Suspension of Certain Accounting Requirements for Oil and Gas Companies (an amendment of *FASB Statement 19*)
26	Apr. 1979	Profit Recognition on Sales-Type Leases of Real Estate (an amendment of *FASB Statement 13*)
27	May 1979	Classification of Renewals or Extension of Existing Sales-Type or Direct Financing Leases (an amendment of *FASB Statement 13*)
28	May 1979	Accounting for Sales with Leasebacks (an amendment of *FASB Statement 13*)
29	June 1979	Determining Contingent Rentals (an amendment of *FASB Statement 13*)
30	Aug. 1979	Disclosure of Information about Major Customers (an amendment of *FASB Statement 14*)
31	Sept. 1979	Accounting for Tax Benefits Related to U.K. Tax Legislation Concerning Stock Relief
32	Sept. 1979	Specialized Accounting and Reporting Principles and Practices in AICPA Statements of Position and Guides on Accounting and Auditing Matters (an amendment of *APB Opinion 20*)
33	Sept. 1979	Financial Reporting and Changing Prices Illustrations of Financial Reporting and Changing Prices, *Statement of Financial Accounting Standards 33*

SAFS No.	Date Issued	Title
34	Oct. 1979	Capitalization of Interest Cost
35	Mar. 1980	Accounting and Reporting by Defined Benefit Pension Plans
36	May 1980	Disclosure of Pension Information (an amendment of *APB Opinion 8*)
37	July 1980	Balance Sheet Classification of Deferred Income Taxes (an amendment of *APB Opinion 11*)
38	Sept. 1980	Accounting for Preacquisition Contingencies of Purchased Enterprises (an amendment of *APB Opinion 16*)
39	Oct. 1980	Financial Reporting and Changing Prices: Specialized Assets—Mining and Oil and Gas (a supplement to *FASB Statement 33*)
40	Nov. 1980	Financial Reporting and Changing Prices: Specialized Assets—Timberlands and Growing Timber (a supplement to *FASB Statement 33*)
41	Nov. 1980	Financial Reporting and Changing Prices: Specialized Assets—Income-Producing Real Estate (a supplement to *FASB Statement 33*)
42	Nov. 1980	Determining Materiality for Capitalization of Interest Cost (an amendment for *FASB Statement 34*)
43	Nov. 1980	Accounting for Compensated Absences
44	Dec. 1980	Accounting for Intangible Assets of Motor Carriers (an amendment of Chapter 5 of *ARB 43*, and an interpretation of *APB Opinions 17* and *30*)
45	Mar. 1981	Accounting for Franchise Fee Revenue
46	Mar. 1981	Financial Reporting and Changing Prices: Motion Picture Films
47	Mar. 1981	Disclosure of Long-Term Obligations
48	June 1981	Revenue Recognition When Right of Returns Exists
49	June 1981	Accounting for Product Financing Arrangements
50	Nov. 1981	Financial Reporting in the Record and Music Industry
51	Nov. 1981	Financial Reporting by Cable Television Companies
52	Dec. 1981	Foreign Currency Translation
53	Dec. 1981	Financial Reporting by Producers and Distributors of Motion Picture Films
54	Jan. 1982	Financial Reporting and Changing Prices; Investment Companies
55	Feb. 1982	Determining Whether a Convertible Security Is a Common Stock Equivalent
56	Feb. 1982	Designation of AICPA Guide and SOP 81-1 on Contractor Accounting and SOP 81-2 on Hospital-Related Organizations as Preferable for Applying *APB Opinion 20*
57	Mar. 1982	Related Party Disclosures
58	April 1982	Capitalization of Interest Cost in Financial Statements that Include Investments Accounted for by the Equity Method
59	April 1982	Deferral of the Effective Date of Certain Accounting Requirements for Revision Plans of State and Local Government Units
60	June 1982	Accounting and Reporting by Insurance Enterprises
61	June 1982	Accounting for Title Plant
62	June 1982	Capitalization of Interest in Situations Involving Certain Tax-Exempt Borrowings and Certain Gifts and Grants
63	June 1982	Financial Reporting by Broadcasters
64	Sept. 1982	Extinguishment of Debt Made to Satisfy Sinking Fund Requirements
65	Sept. 1982	Accounting for Certain Mortgage Bank Activities
66	Oct. 1982	Accounting for Sales on Real Estate
67	Oct. 1982	Accounting for Costs and Initial Rental Operations of Real Estate Projects
68	Oct. 1982	Research and Development Arrangements
69	Nov. 1982	Disclosures about Oil and Gas Producing Activities (an amendment of *FASB Statements 19, 25, 33,* and *39*)
70	Dec. 1982	Financial Reporting and Changing Prices: Foreign Currency Translation (an amendment of *FASB Statement 33*)
71	Dec. 1982	Accounting for the Effects of Certain Types of Regulation
72	Feb. 1983	Accounting for Certain Acquisitions of Banking or Thrift Institutions (an amendment of *APB Opinion 17*, an interpretation of *APB Opinions 16* and *17*, ad an amendment of *FASB Interpretation 9*)
73	Aug. 1983	Reporting a Change in Accounting for Railroad Track Structures (an amendment of *ABP Opinion 20*)
74	Aug. 1983	Accounting for Special Termination Benefits Paid to Employees
75	Nov. 1983	Deferral of the Effective Date of Certain Accounting Requirements for Pension Plans of State and Local Governmental Units (an amendment of *FASB Statement 35*)
76	Nov. 1983	Extinguishment of Debt (an amendment of *APB Opinion 26*)
77	Dec. 1983	Reporting by Transferors for Transfers of Receivables with Recourse
78	Dec. 1983	Classification of Obligations that Are Callable by the Creditor (an amendment of *ARB 43*, Chapter 3A)
79	Feb. 1984	Elimination of Certain Disclosures for Business Combinations by Nonpublic enterprises (an amendment of *APB Opinion 16*)
80	Aug. 1984	Accounting for Futures Contracts
81	Nov. 1984	Disclosure of Postretirement Health Care and Life Insurance Benefits

VOLUME 1 CHAPTERS 1-14

INTERMEDIATE ACCOUNTING

◆

Revised Edition

THOMAS R. DYCKMAN
Ann Whitney Olin Professor of Accounting
Cornell University

ROLAND E. DUKES
University of Washington

CHARLES J. DAVIS
California State University—Sacramento

GLENN A. WELSCH
James L. Bayless Chair for Free Enterprise Emeritus
The University of Texas at Austin

IRWIN

Homewood, IL 60430
Boston, MA 02116

Senior sponsoring editor: Ron M. Regis
Developmental editor: Cheryl D. Wilson
Project editor: Margaret Haywood
Production manager: Ann Cassady
Designer: Laurie Entringer
Art manager: Kim Meriwether
Compositor: Better Graphics, Inc.
Typeface: 10/12 Times Roman
Printer: Von Hoffmann Press

ISBN: 0-256-11305-X

Library of Congress Cataloging-in-Publication Data

Intermediate accounting / Thomas R. Dyckman . . . [et al.].—Rev. ed.
    p.   cm.
   ISBN 0-256-10738-6   ISBN 0-256-11306-8 (Volume I, Chapters 1–14)
   1. Accounting.   I. Dyckman, Thomas R.
 HF5635.I529 1992b
 657′.044—dc20   91–16245

Printed in the United States of America
2 3 4 5 6 7 8 9 0 VH 8 7 6 5 4 3 2

To our wives and families:
Ann, Daniel, James, Linda, David
Phyllis, Peter, Anna
Susan, Nicole, Michael

ABOUT THE AUTHORS

Thomas R. Dyckman, Ph.D., is Ann Whitney Olin Professor of Accounting and Quantitative Analysis and Associate Dean for Academic Affairs at Cornell University's Johnson Graduate School of Management. In addition to teaching accounting and quantitative analysis, he is a program coordinator of Cornell's Executive Development Program. He earned his doctorate degree from the University of Mighigan.

A former member of the Financial Accounting Standards Board Advisory Committee, Professor Dyckman is presently a member of the Financial Accounting Foundation which oversees the FASB. He was president of the American Accounting Association in 1982 and received the association's *Outstanding Educator Award* for the year 1987. He also received the AICPA's *Notable Contributions to Accounting Literature Award* in 1966 and 1977.

Professor Dyckman has extended industrial experience that includes work with the U.S. Navy and IBM. He has conducted seminars for the University of California Management Development Program and the Credit Bureau Executives' Program, as well as for Ocean Spray, Goodyear, Morgan Guaranty, GTE, Southern New England Telephone, and Goulds Pumps.

Professor Dyckman has coauthored several books and written over 50 journal articles on topics from financial markets to the application of quantitative and behavioral theory to administrative decision making. He has been a member of the editorial boards of *The Accounting Review, The Journal of Finance and Quantitative Analysis, The Journal of Accounting and Economics* and *The Journal of Management Accounting Research.*

Roland E. (Pete) Dukes, Ph.D., is professor of accounting at the University of Washington where he teaches intermediate and advanced financial accounting at the undergraduate and graduate levels. He has served as chairman of the department of accounting since 1983. He received his doctorate from Stanford University.

A member of the American Accounting Association, Professor Dukes has chaired the Annual Meeting Technical Program Planning Committee, the Doctoral Consortium Committee, and the Notable Contribution to Accounting Literature Committee. He has also served as a Distinguished Visiting Faculty for the Doctoral Consortium, as Director of the Doctoral Consortium, and as the Puget Power Affiliate Program Professor of Accounting at the University of Washington from 1986 to 1990.

Professor Dukes has published numerous articles in accounting journals, including *The Accounting Review, Journal of Accounting Research,* and the *Journal of Accountancy*. He has served on the editorial boards of *The Accounting Review, Journal of Accounting Research,* and *Journal of Accounting Literature*. He has been a consultant to the Financial Accounting Standards Board, and authored the *FASB Research Report* which investigated the effect of *SFAS No. 8* on security return behavior. Professor Dukes also has served as a consultant to the Securities and Exchange Commission and to industry and government.

Charles J. Davis, Ph.D., C.P.A., is professor and chair of the department of accountancy at California State University, Sacramento. He received his doctorate in accounting from the University of Illinois at Urbana.

Professor Davis has taught in the areas of financial and managerial accounting and auditing at both the intermediate and advanced levels. He has also been active in CPA review programs. Professor Davis received excellence in teaching awards from both the University of Illinois at Urbana and California State University, Sacramento. In addition, he has been active in student accounting groups on campus.

Professor Davis has written journal articles in accounting and related business fields that appear in *Advances in Accounting, Issues in Accounting Education,* and *Journal of Accounting and Public Policy,* and in several health-care fiscal management journals. He serves on the editorial review board of *Advances in Accounting*. He worked as a staff auditor for Peat, Marwick, Mitchell and Company and has served as a consultant to industry and government. Professor Davis is a member of the American Accounting Association.

PREFACE

◆

PHILOSOPHY AND PURPOSE

◆

Financial reporting plays a unique role in the process of allocating resources in our economy. The subject matter of this text, *Intermediate Accounting,* Revised Edition, is the development of the principles underlying that reporting process.

This revision represents a major reorganization and rewriting effort. Our aim is to improve the text as a learning tool while continuing the comprehensiveness and technical quality of previous editions.

The text is completely current as to the date of publication, and includes discussion of the most recent FASB statements. In particular, we have incorporated FASB *Statement Nos. 102* and *104* concerning the statement of cash flows, *Statement No. 105* on financial instruments, *Statement No. 106* on postemployment benefits other than pensions, and the latest pronouncements on accounting for income taxes into the text. Every attempt has been made to assure the accuracy of this material.

Each of us has taught intermediate accounting for many years. In doing so, we have developed an awareness of the issues and applications most difficult for the student to master and have exercised special care in those areas to make the presentation as clear, understandable, and stimulating as possible.

Before embarking on this revision, we surveyed the marketplace to solicit views on topics to be included in the intermediate accounting course, chapter sequencing, desirability of real-world examples, and degree of comprehensiveness. The answers to our surveys and questionnaires were exceptionally helpful in providing overall direction for this revision. In addition, the panel of 30 reviewers were a tremendous source of information about the market and our proposed changes in pedagogy. The insights and recommendations of these reviewers helped shape the final form and substance of the text.

Objectives and Overall Approach of the Revised Edition This revised edition has several objectives. The primary objective is to provide comprehensive coverage of financial accounting topics, both application and rationale. The text emphasizes the reasons for specific accounting principles, along with clear discussions and illustrations of their applications. We believe that continual integration of theory and practice is the most efficient way to present the subject matter. When the student discovers there is a reason for a procedure, much less is relegated to pure memorization. Consequently, this text does not rely on large and complex exhibits as the sole explanation for accounting procedures.

A secondary objective is to bring the subject to life and increase the student's interest in the material. To accomplish this, we have greatly increased the text's real-world emphasis. The text has literally hundreds of examples of real-world reporting and frequent discussions of the financial reporting experiences of actual firms.

Throughout the text, we discuss the process by which specific accounting principles are developed, thus reinforcing the real-world nature of financial reporting standards. The impact of lobbying and the need for compromise by the FASB is discussed in several chapters affected by the more controversial pronouncements. One aim of this emphasis is to develop the student's ability to critically evaluate particular reporting standards. We want the student to address the question: Is a particular accounting principle successfully fulfilling the primary objective of financial statements, namely to provide information useful for decision making? A second aim is to acquaint the student with the political setting in which standard-setting takes place.

The topical sequencing of material within each chapter is designed to present the important reporting issues and the reasons financial statement users and preparers are concerned about them. This approach leads to a discussion of the current GAAP solution to the issue with appropriate rationale. In the more controversial areas, we consider other potential solutions and why these may have been rejected by the relevant rule-making body. As a result, the student is frequently reminded of the dynamic and interactive nature of the standard-setting process and the inherent difficulties facing standard setters in reaching a consensus.

We also emphasize the areas for which the accounting standards provide a choice from among several alternative methods. In related discussions, the text probes the incentives for choosing from among alternative accounting methods.

Curriculum Concerns This revision is responsive to the concerns of the Accounting Education Change Commission. These concerns suggest a new orientation for accounting education. With this new direction, students should be encouraged "to learn how to learn." Curricula should emphasize the underlying concepts, rather than memorization of rules and regulations. The focus is on the process of inquiry in which the student learns to identify problem situations, to search for relevant information, to analyze and interpret the information, and to reach a well-reasoned conclusion.

With these goals in mind, this revised edition frequently asks questions and presents important contemporary issues in a manner that compels the student to think about the appropriate solution to a reporting problem. We believe that the discussions of the more controversial and involved issues will lead the student to his or her own position on the issues. To this end, the text often focuses on the process of inquiry, rather than encouraging memorization of the standards and procedures. What information would the user find more helpful in making decisions? What would the student do in this situation?

We view the current GAAP solutions to reporting problems as one step in the continuing evolutionary process of attempting to provide the most cost-effective and useful information possible. The text involves the student in that process. For example, many of the cases require students to identify and solve unstructured problems and to consider multiple data sources. Our computerized end-of-chapter items encourage interaction and help the student learn by doing. In addition, by weaving theory and application together throughout the text, students are encouraged to apply their knowledge to new situations.

Writing Style and Exposition The text mixes a clear, direct, and concise writing style with an active voice to maintain the positive flow of the material and the student's attention. The text is well outlined and provides considerable structure and good transition between topics. We have clarified and simplified many of the application examples without sacrificing completeness.

The text makes generous use of outlining by using distinctive captions to provide a chronological structure for the reader. We have attempted to minimize the number of pages without any visual "break." We believe that frequent use of examples, headings and new pedagogical devices increases understandability and ease of reading, while maintaining the student's

interest. A greater use of visual aids is apparent in this edition. Furthermore, the new pedagogical features enhance the learning experience for students.

An increased use of summary tables and exhibits helps to synthesize the more complex areas, and gives the student an opportunity to evaluate progress. Many of the exhibits and illustrations were class-tested to fine tune them.

To increase the conversational tone and use of current terminology, certain terms were changed. For example, "balance sheet" replaces "statement of financial position," "income statement" replaces "statement of income," and "payment" replaces "rent" in present value discussions. *Statements of Financial Accounting Standards* are referred to as *SFAS*s. Also, in the text and the end-of-chapter material, the revised edition uses actual year designations such as 1991, rather than 19A, for increased realism.

The text assumes completion of the basic college-level introductory course in financial accounting and is intended primarily for schools covering intermediate accounting in two semesters or three quarters. For example, one logical sequencing for a two semester course is Chapters 1–14 in the first course, followed by Chapters 15–26. By quarter: Chapters 1–8, Chapters 9–16, and Chapters 17–26. This text covers material that is a foundation for a later course in advanced financial accounting and for graduate courses.

REVISION APPROACH AND ORGANIZATION
◆

Financial accounting is concerned with measurement of economic attributes and their recognition in asset, liability, owners' equity, and income statement accounts. Income determination and disclosure also are important focuses of financial reporting. The revised edition reflects a new sequencing of chapters. After considering the conceptual framework of the FASB and a review of the accounting process, the chapters in this book are grouped into modules corresponding to the major balance sheet account classifications, in natural balance sheet order. Within each is a consideration of the related income and disclosure issues. The text concludes with a series of chapters on specialized accounting topics. These chapter groupings are:

	Part	Chapters
I	Foundation and Review	1–6
II	Asset Recognition and Measurement	7–14
III	Liabilities	15–19
IV	Owners' Equity	20–22
V	Special Topics	23–26

Changes in Chapter Order The revised edition significantly changes chapter sequencing. The major changes in chapter order are:

Chapter 2, "The FASB's Conceptual Framework of Accounting" (Chapter 6 in the previous edition) now appears earlier. We believe this is preferable because it allows the instructor to discuss theory before covering the financial statements in the review chapters. The reviewers responded to this major organizational change very favorably.

Chapter 7, "Revenue and Expense Recognition" (Chapter 13 in the previous edition) appears as the first chapter in the section of the text devoted to asset measurement. The chapter ties back to the conceptual framework (when to recognize assets), thereby linking theory with the practical issues of when to record revenues and expenses. The earlier presentation also allows the instructor to cover certain topics without first having to explain recognition criteria.

Chapter 14, "Investments: Temporary and Long Term" (Chapter 18 in the previous edition) is now sequenced as part of the asset section of the text. This grouping allows completion of revenue recognition issues (in this chapter, for intercompany investments) before taking up accounting issues related to liabilities.

Chapter 17, "Accounting for Income Taxes" (Chapter 23 in the previous edition) is now sequenced as part of the liability section of the text. In this way, the liability issues are completed before turning to owners' equity.

Chapter 22, "Earnings per Share" (part of Chapter 22 in the previous edition) is now a stand-alone special topics chapter given the overall importance and complexity of the topic.

Chapter 25, "Financial Statement Analysis and Changing Prices" (part of Chapter 22 and Chapter 25 in the previous edition) are now combined in the revised edition. Adjustments for the effect of changing prices are no longer required, yet many financial statement users continue to make such adjustments when analyzing statements. Hence, adjusting for price-level changes is treated as part of financial statement analysis.

Chapter 26, "Special Topics: Segment Reporting, Interim Reporting, and Disclosures" is a new chapter that combines parts of chapters from the previous edition along with new material on disclosure issues from the FASB.

Flexibility in Use

In reordering the chapters, we had definite objectives in mind. The topical chapters are grouped to provide a more clear and logical transition within major parts of the text. The commonality of issues and principles within each part reinforces similar principles and enhances their understanding.

However, instructors are not bound by this order. For example, some instructors prefer to cover current liabilities immediately after current assets. This text provides the flexibility to accomplish this and virtually any other ordering desired. The chapters following Chapter 6 are topical in nature, and all rely on the first five chapters for conceptual grounding, and the "big-picture" review in Chapters 3 through 5. Given that the topical chapters are self-contained, a considerable degree of flexibility in chapter sequencing is maintained.

Also, use of appendixes increases the flexibility of topical coverage for the instructor. This additional flexibility is important given the ever-increasing scope of topics in the intermediate accounting course.

Real-World Emphasis

This text makes extensive use of financial reporting examples from actual companies when discussing specific reporting areas. We also make frequent use of the AICPA's *Accounting Trends and Techniques* for information on trends in financial reporting. In addition, many references to reporting decisions and consequences from actual businesses are taken from *The Wall Street Journal, Forbes, Financial Executive,* and many other sources. The Sherwin-Williams Company graciously permitted us to reproduce their entire 1990 financial statements and accompanying notes.

Using actual companies in examples helps show how reporting is done in practice. References to well-known corporations capture and hold the student's interest and reflect the tremendous variety of current accounting practices. The real-world examples also help to convince the student of the importance of many abstract concepts and procedures.

Ethics

A topic of continuing interest in business schools, ethical issues are treated in several chapters through an ethics case in the end-of-chapter material. Ethics cases are included in Chapters 3, 6, 8, 9, 11, 12, 16, 19, 23, and 24. Portions of the AICPA Code of Professional Conduct are reproduced in an appendix to Chapter 1. In addition, implicit references are made to the ethics of financial reporting throughout the text.

End-of-Chapter Materials

Numerous changes and revisions were made to this material. Older and more repetitive items were deleted, and many new items were added. These additions supplement the already considerable inventory of homework assignments. CPA examination questions continue to be used in this edition; many were updated.

The **questions** at the end of each chapter provide a context for in-class discussion; **exercises** are generally structured applications of specific issues in the chapter; **problems** generally are longer and less structured applications of one or more specific issues in the chapter; and **cases** often require the student to integrate several issues in the chapter and provide an opinion on a reporting problem or situation.

The cases and some problems provide an opportunity for students to practice their analytical and written communication skills. Furthermore, they frequently place the student in an unstructured setting requiring a broad view to be taken of a business reporting problem. The context in which financial reporting is used must be considered in these instances.

To help the instructor choose appropriate items, each exercise, problem, and case is titled to indicate the primary issue involved. In addition, each is keyed to one or more learning objectives to allow instructors to select those areas they wish to emphasize.

The quantity and variety of items, both in substance and level of difficulty, allows an instructor to vary the homework items from term to term. The end-of-chapter material was checked for accuracy by faculty colleagues.

NEW PEDAGOGICAL FEATURES
♦

Several new pedagogical features have been added to the revised edition. They are designed to make learning easier and, in general, to make this text more user-friendly.

Learning Objectives

Done in list form, a set of proactive learning objectives opens each chapter to provide the student with learning goals and a preview of upcoming topics.

Introductions

Immediately after the list of learning objectives are the introductions or ''stage setters'' that discuss events and reporting by actual companies relevant to the chapter and provide a transition to the upcoming chapter topics. These introductions are attention-grabbing and help the reader understand the significance of the area about to be studied.

Concept Reviews

Throughout the chapters, usually at the end of major sections, students are asked to respond to a brief list of questions. These questions are answerable directly from the text and help students check their understanding of the section's basic concepts or message. These questions also provide a break from the reading and reinforce the major ideas. In addition, the concept reviews give the readers an idea of how well they comprehended the material before moving ahead. The questions are analogous to a short quiz after a lecture on a particular part of a chapter. The answers to the concept review questions are provided at the end of the solutions manual for the convenience of the instructor.

Summary of Key Points

Each chapter concludes with a recap of the main ideas presented. The summaries are now done in list format rather than a paragraph style. The list format better highlights the chapter's content by making the most important ideas more easily identifiable. Each point is keyed to the relevant learning objective.

Review Problem with Solution

Immediately after the summary of key points, a review problem illustrates several of the chapter's main concepts, followed by the solution. The review problems also provide additional practice for the student and a self-test for evaluating progress.

Key Terms

Just before the end-of-chapter material, a list of the chapter's most important new terms appears. Page references indicate where the terms were defined and initially discussed. The key terms are printed in a second color for emphasis allowing the student to easily locate them, and to review their meanings in the context of the chapter.

Comprehensive Problems

In many chapters, one or more problems in the end-of-chapter material cover several of the chapter's learning objectives. Their objective is to integrate the more important ideas into a single situation. They are identified by this symbol in the margin:

Ethics Case

Many chapters include a case in the end-of-chapter material that emphasizes the ethical implications of particular actions and reporting decisions. The student often is placed in a situation requiring a decision that has ethical ramifications. These cases are identified by this symbol in the margin:

Sherwin-Williams Cases

Many chapters also include a case based on the 1990 annual statements of the Sherwin-Williams Company. This case provides an up-to-date application of the chapter material to an actual company. These problems are identified by the Sherwin-Williams logo.

Spreadsheet Applications Template Software (SPATS)

Many chapters include problems and exercises solvable on a computerized spreadsheet. Templates are provided for these problems. A spreadsheet symbol in the margin identifies these problems.

KEY CHAPTER REVISIONS
◆

The changes to the revised edition were very extensive. The following list highlights major revisions made in each chapter.

Chapter 1, "The Environment of Accounting"
* The basic accounting model has been moved to Chapter 3.
* The 1988 RJR Nabisco takeover is used to illustrate the value and limitations of financial reporting.
* Portions of the AICPA's Code of Profesisonal

Conduct are reproduced to provide fundamental ethics coverage.

Chapter 2, "The FASB's Conceptual Framework of Accounting"
* The environment in which the FASB functions and the political nature of the standard-setting process are emphasized.
* The major parts of the *Statements of Financial Accounting Concepts,* as they reflect the development of accounting principles, are discussed in chronological order.
* The historical development of the conceptual framework highlights the nature of the standard-setting process.

Chapter 3, "Review: The Accounting Information Processing System"
* The more general systems approach to the accounting cycle is discussed in the chapter, while an appendix that includes **acetate transparencies** illustrates the worksheet.
* Greater emphasis is placed on adjusting and reversing entries.
* A new discussion comparing two methods of recording operating cash flows that precede recognition of revenue and expense helps the student to understand adjustments and reversals.

Chapter 4, "Review: The Income Statement and the Statement of Retained Earnings"
* New and detailed discussion of the measurement and reporting guidelines for discontinued operations results in comprehensive coverage of this topic.
* The coverage of intraperiod tax allocation parallels the greater emphasis on items below income from continuing operations.
* The new emphasis on the issue of current operating performance versus the all-inclusive approach to income measurement complements the discussion of comprehensive income.

Chapter 5, "Review: The Balance Sheet and the Statement of Cash Flows"
* The balance sheet and statement of cash flows of Merck and Company are used to present and illustrate many of the concepts in this chapter.
* The various valuation approaches used in the balance sheet, the usefulness of the balance sheet, and the limitations of the balance sheet are stressed.
* Both the direct and indirect forms of the statement of cash flows are discussed and illustrated.

Chapter 6, "Interest: Concepts of Future and Present Value"
* Symbols for future and present value calculations are now more user-friendly.

- Use of summary tables and time-line exhibits simplifies the presentation.
- The interest tables now appear in an appendix.

Chapter 7, "Revenue and Expense Recognition"
- The earlier coverage of revenue recognition will assist the discussion of asset recognition in later chapters.
- The fundamental concepts of revenue and revenue recognition are emphasized throughout the chapter.
- The conceptual discussion leads to the general criteria for revenue recognition.

Chapter 8, "Cash and Receivables"
- Three formats for bank reconciliations are covered and greater emphasis is placed on proof of cash.
- The in-depth discussion on using receivables for financing reflects the complexities in this area.
- New coverage of notes receivable exchanged for cash and other privileges demonstrates the variety of uses for notes and resulting accounting issues.

Chapter 9, "Inventory Measurement, Cost of Goods Sold, and DV LIFO"
- Coverage of consignments is expanded.
- The chapter now distinguishes between cost-flow assumptions under both the periodic and perpetual systems.
- A new section on inventory pools emphasizes the importance of cost-benefit concerns in this area.

Chapter 10, "Alternative Inventory Valuation Methods"
- The LCM material has been rewritten to clarify the calculation process and includes additional situations.
- There is new coverage of the use of LCM in reporting income taxes.
- The discussion of the gross margin and retail methods is rewritten to emphasize calculational steps.

Chapter 11, "Operational Assets: Acquisition, Disposal, and Exchange"
- The discussion of the issue of what to capitalize includes the FASB exposure draft on donations.
- The substantially greater emphasis on capitalization of interest includes both theory and application.
- A generalized approach to valuing property acquired in an exchange helps to simplify this area.

Chapter 12, "Operational Assets: Depreciation and Impairment"
- Considerably greater emphasis is placed on the nature of depreciation, incentives for choice of method, and what depreciation means to the financial statement user.
- Depreciation policy is discussed in terms of its effect on dividend policy and cash flows.

- A section on impairment of value considers the decade-long trend of corporations to take large write-offs of operational assets.

Chapter 13, "Intangible Assets and Natural Resources"
- The accounting for all intangibles other than goodwill, research and development, and computer software costs is reorganized.
- In-depth treatment of goodwill estimation emphasizes concepts and examples.
- The oil and gas controversy complements a complete discussion of accounting for natural resources.

Chapter 14, "Investments: Temporary and Long Term"
- Changing between the cost and equity method is discussed and illustrated.
- Consolidations discussion is shorter and has been moved to an appendix.
- Also moved to an appendix are special purpose funds, cash surrender value of life insurance, and future contracts.

Chapter 15, "Short-Term Liabilities"
- New coverage of bonus payments is added.
- The chapter now includes refinancing of short-term debt and the reporting of debt as short term.
- The sections on taxes collected for third parties, property taxes, and conditional payments are extensively revised.

Chapter 16, "Long-Term Liabilities"
- Greater emphasis is placed on theory discussion and the rationale for FASB positions on such controversial topics as troubled debt restructuring, debt extinguishment, and valuation of debt issued with equity securities.
- There is new coverage of troubled debt restructure, which now appears in an appendix.
- The FASB's financial instruments project is discussed in terms of project financing relationships, unconditional purchase obligations, zero-coupon bonds, and creative financial instruments.

Chapter 17, "Accounting for Income Taxes"
- Accounting for operating losses precedes interperiod tax allocation.
- The latest Exposure Draft for income taxes is incorporated in the body of the text. The more complex procedures for determining the amount of deferred tax assets are covered in the appendix.
- The coverage in the chapter is complete and flexible so that the instructor can choose to focus on the procedures and requirements of the Exposure Draft or on those of *SFAS 96* if the Exposure Draft is not adopted.

Chapter 18, "Accounting for Leases"
* Accounting for lessor and lessee is covered in series rather than in parallel fashion; the lessee is considered first (emphasis on liabilities).
* Greater emphasis is placed on special issues including different interest rates, bargain renewal offers, and the use of guaranteed residual values to secure off-balance-sheet financing.
* An appendix covers real estate and leveraged leases.

Chapter 19, "Accounting for Pensions"
* The chapter is totally reorganized using a modularized approach to emphasize the basics and to ease into the complexities.
* New coverage of ERISA, PBGC and pension termination enhances the real-world flavor of the subject.
* Three new appendixes appear: postemployment benefits other than pensions; settlements, curtailments, and termination benefits; and accounting for the pension plan.

Chapter 20, "Corporations: Contributed Capital"
* Professional corporations and Subchapter S corporations are now discussed.
* Greater emphasis is placed on the issues underlying redeemable preferred shares.
* Examples of self-tender offers to acquire treasury stock and retirement of stock increase the comprehensive coverage of owners' equity accounting.

Chapter 21, "Corporations: Retained Earnings and Stock Options"
* Fractional share rights and stock appreciation rights receive greater emphasis.
* The discussion of quasi reorganizations is moved to an appendix.

Chapter 22, "Earnings per Share"
* EPS is given its own chapter to allow for more detailed discussion.
* Primary EPS is discussed before fully diluted EPS.
* Extensive examples are now provided.

Chapter 23, "Statement of Cash Flows"
* The spreadsheet is simplified to allow a simultaneous solution of the statement under both direct and indirect methods.
* The direct and indirect methods are discussed separately through the first complete statement example to emphasize their different characteristics; then both methods are discussed in the more complex examples because the reconciliation of net operating cash flow and net income are present in both.
* The approaches to preparing the statement are illustrated: format-free, spreadsheet, and the T-account.

Chapter 24, "Accounting Changes and Error Corrections"
* The issues affecting accounting changes and alternative views and motivations for changes are stressed.
* The direct and indirect effects of current accounting changes are now covered.
* Changing to LIFO is discussed.

Chapter 25, "Financial Statement Analysis and Changing Prices"
* The inclusion of both financial statement analysis and accounting for changing prices is a major organizational change aimed at streamlining the coverage of these two related topics now that firms no longer are required to report on changing prices.
* New ratios used in financial statement analysis are discussed.
* Discussed are four models for reporting the effects of price level changes, the advantages and disadvantages of each, and a brief example highlighting the nature of each model.

Chapter 26, "Special Topics: Segment Reporting, Interim Reporting, and Disclosures"
* The first section is an all new discussion of standards and information overload and the principle of full disclosure.
* A discussion of the conflict between the FASB and financial statement users highlights the political nature of the standard setting process.
* A more straight-forward presentation of interim and segmental disclosure is included in this chapter.

ANCILLARIES AND SUPPLEMENTARY MATERIALS
◆

FOR THE PROFESSOR:

INTERMEDIATE ACCOUNTING, Revised Edition, offers numerous teaching aids to assist the instructor.

Solutions Manual, Chapters 1–14 and 14–26—Done in two volumes, this comprehensive solutions manual provides complete solutions and explanations for all end-of-chapter questions, exercises, problems, and cases. The estimated completion time for each item is given in the assignment assistance schedule at the beginning of each chapter. Answers to the concept review questions are included at the end of the manual.

Test Bank, Chapters 1–14 and 14–26—Revised and expanded with this edition, the test bank offers approximately 4,000 questions and problems from which to choose in preparing examinations. This test bank contains true-false, short answer, problems and cases, and selected CPA examination questions. It was revised by Robert Su of California State University–Sacramento.

Solutions Transparencies—Acetate transparencies of solutions to all exercises and all problems are free to adopters. Now increased in clarity, these transparencies are especially useful when covering problems in large classroom settings.

Teaching Transparencies—Selected lecture transparencies based on text material are available for classroom use.

Instructor's Resource Manual—This manual includes overviews, learning objectives, lecture outlines, problem analysis by objective, summaries, key terms, review quizzes, and transparency masters. It was prepared by Dick D. Wasson of Central Washington University.

Computest 3—This advanced-feature test generator allows the adding and editing of questions; saves and reloads tests; creates up to 99 different versions of each test; attaches graphics to questions; imports and exports ASCII files; and permits the selection of questions based on type, level of difficulty, or keyword. Computest 3 provides password protection of saved tests and question databases and can run on a network. It is available in 5.25- and 3.5-inch versions.

Compugrade 3—More than a grading system on disk, Compugrade 3 is a complete classroom management system. This advanced software system tracks up to 100 scores per class—homework, project, bonus points, class participation, attendance, and more. A variety of reports can be printed depending on class needs, including student, class, and assignment summaries. Graphs of various statistics for individual students or the entire class may be viewed and printed.

Teletest—Through this service the instructor can create customized exams and receive masters and answer keys within 72 hours of contacting the publisher

The following item is intended for student use at the option of the instructors.

Spreadsheet Applications Template Software (SPATS)—Selected exercises and problems in each chapter, identified by a spreadsheet symbol in the margin, can be solved using SPATS. The software contains innovatively designed templates based on Lotus® 1-2-3® and includes a very effective Lotus® 1-2-3® tutorial. SPATS is available on 5.25- and 3.5-inch disks. Upon adoption, this package is available for classroom or laboratory use.

FOR THE STUDENT:

Several support materials have been designed especially for the student.

The Student Integrated Learning Systems, Chapters 1–14 (Volume I) and Chapters 14–26 (Volume II)—This option allows the student to purchase either Chapters 1–14 or Chapters 14–26 of the text with the related Study Guides and Working Papers in a three-ring binder. Students benefit by having all three course-related items in a single package at a significant cost savings.

Study Guides, Chapters 1–14 and Chapters 14–26—The study guides provide the student with a summarized look at each chapter's issues. Included are outlines, chapter overviews, key concepts, and review questions and exercises. The study guides were prepared by Rosita Chen and Sheng-Der Pan, both of California State University–Fresno.

Working Papers, Chapter 1–14 and Chapter 14–26—Two sets of working papers are available for completing assigned problems and exercises. In many instances, the working papers are partially filled in to reduce the "pencil pushing" required to solve the problems, yet not so complete as to reduce the learning impact.

Manual Practice Set—Video One, a manual practice set, can be assigned after Chapter 6 as a review of the accounting cycle.

Cases—Cases on Recognition and Measurement, prepared by Todd Johnson and Tim Lucas of the Financial Accounting Standards Board (FASB) staff contains 50 short cases that are based on the Accounting Education Change Commission (AECC) changes. The casebook includes an instructor's manual and is free to adopters of Intermediate Accounting.

Computer Supplement—Kellogg Business Systems by Leland Mansuetti and Keith Weidkamp, both of Sierra College, is a computerized simulation that can be used after Chapter 6. It is available on 5.25 and 3.5 disks.

Check Figures—A list of check figures for selected end-of-chapter material is available.

ACKNOWLEDGMENTS
◆

The text in its present form would not have been possible without the contributions of a great many people. We recognize and appreciate all of their efforts.

Our thanks and gratitude are extended to the outstanding faculty reviewers who provided criticism and constructive suggestions during the preparation of this revised edition. They spent a great deal of time with both the previous edition, letting us know of the areas needing modification, and with the first draft of the revised edition. Their comments and suggestions were instrumental in making this text more complete and understandable. They were also crucial to the text's accuracy and clarity. Each recommendation was considered, and many incorporated, to make this revised edition the most comprehensive and thorough edition to date. The reviewers were:

Myrtle Clark
University of Kentucky

Maurice Tassin
Louisiana Tech University

Joanne C. Duke
San Francisco State University

Douglas Cloud
Pepperdine University

Julie Sterner
*Southern Illinois University/
Carbondale*

Duane Baldwin
University of Nevada/Las Vegas

E. James Meddaugh
Ohio University

Mostafa M. Maksy
University of Illinois/Chicago

Abo Habib
Mankato State University

S. Thomas A. Cianciolo
Eastern Michigan University

David H. Sinason
University of North Florida

Dorian Olson
Moorehead University

Mary M. K. Fleming
California State University/Fullerton

James S. Worthington
Auburn University

Edward T. Ossman
California State University/Hayward

Gail B. Wright
University of Richmond

Charlene Abendroth
California State University/Hayward

Diane L. Adcox
University of North Florida

Joy S. Irwin
Louisiana State University

Kevin H. McBeth
Weber State College

Michael R. Lane
Bradley University

Paul H. Schwinghammer
Mankato State University

Nancy E. Smith
Western Illinois University

Walter I. Batchelder
University of Alabama

Louis F. Biagioni
Indiana University

Darrell W. David
University of Northern Iowa

Paul R. Graul
Eastern Washington University

Lola W. Dudley
Eastern Illinois University

Priscilla Slade
Florida A&M University

To the instructors who participated in our market survey go our special thanks. The information they provided was invaluable:

Lynn R. Thomas
Kansas State University

Ralph W. Newkirk, Jr.
Rutgers University

Daniel F. O'Mara
Quinnipiac College

Gary W. Heesacker
Central Washington University

Lorella J. Donlin
Black Hills State University

Kwangok Kim
University of Southern Indiana

Norman J. Gierlasinski
Central Washington University

Lynn M. Bailey
Furman University

Behrooz Amini
*California State University/
Stanislaus*

Joanne Edwards
Westbrook College

Kathleen Simons
Bryant College

Jan Gillespie
The University of Texas at Austin

Thomas Zaher
Bucks County Community College

Marilyn Young
Tulsa Junior College

Michael Trebesh
Alma College

Peter Theuri
Oakwood College

Linda H. Kistler
University of Lowell

Robert E. Hansen
Western Kentucky University

Jane B. Stockard
Georgia College

J. Richard Sealscott
Northwest Technical College

Henry Espenson
Rockford College

Barbara Parks Pooley
Mt. Mercy College

Gale Newell
Western Michigan University

Ken Macur
University of Wisconsin/Whitewater

Harold Joseph
Clayton State College

Elias E. Etinge
Paine College

G. Eddy Birrer
Gonzaga University

John E. Delaney
Southwestern University

Rebecca M. Floor
Greenville Technical College

Donald H. Minyard
Auburn University

Lloyd J. Buckwell, Jr.
Indiana University, Northwest

Ronald O. Huntsman
Texas Lutheran College

Larry A. Deppe
Brigham Young University

Richard G. Cummings
Benedictine College

LaVern E. Krueger
*University of Missouri/
Kansas City*

Christine P. Andrews
State College at Fredonia

Paul W. Parkinson
Ball State University

Donald F. Putnam
*California State Polytechnic
University/Pomona*

Barbara J. Shiarappa
Trenton State College

Glen Fackler
Northeastern Junior College

Joy Fair of the University of Washington, Ralph Robinson, Robert Donoho, and Donna Phoenix of Cornell University, and Robert Su of California State University, Sacramento, provided valuable assistance by checking the solutions to the end-of-chapter material. To numerous other colleagues and users whose constructive comments and suggestions have led to the improvements reflected in this latest edition, our thanks. We sincerely appreciate comments and suggestions from all sources. We also appreciate the permissions granted by several firms and organizations including the American Institute of Certified Public Accountants, Dow Jones & Company, The First Boston Corporation, and The Sherwin-Williams Company.

To our retired coauthor, Glenn A. Welsch, we are deeply indebted. His valuable contributions to the preceding editions of *Intermediate Accounting* established the foundation on which the present author team based its work. His tremendous energy and abilities are reflected in this and prior editions. None of us would have attempted this project without the basis of his prior efforts. We wish him well, as we do the other previous coauthors, D. Paul Newman, Thomas Harrison, and Charles T. Zlatkovich.

We are grateful to the people at Irwin for their never-ending support: Ron Regis, senior sponsoring editor; Cheryl Wilson, developmental editor; Margaret Haywood, project editor; Pat O'Hayer, copy editor; Laurie Entringer, designer; Anne Cassady, production manager; and Judy Besser, secretary—editorial. In particular, the level of involvement with Cheryl Wilson was extraordinary. She assisted in all phases of the project and kept us on track and working. She was our main source of day-to-day inspiration and we are deeply indebted to her for her work.

Finally, we wish to thank our families for giving us the encouragement and understanding needed to complete this text, and for being so patient in the process.

We welcome your ideas and comments as you use this text and look forward to hearing from you.

TO THE STUDENT

♦

Accounting has been described as the language of business. If this is so, your introductory course has given you an understanding of some fundamental building blocks: the nouns, verbs, adjectives, prepositions, and so forth. In accounting terms, these are the concepts of assets, liabilities, owner's equity, expenses, revenues, income, and so on. Intermediate acounting is designed to extend these concepts to form phrases, sentences, paragraphs, and chapters. Intermediate accounting allows us to tell the financial story of an organization. As such, intermediate accounting is essential to your education in accounting and, thereby, to your mastery of the language of business.

We believe accounting at this level is an exciting subject and have structured this text in a way that captures the excitement and realism. You will be learning about actual situations faced by companies and how accounting plays a role in the decisions. These examples are extracted from The *Wall Street Journal,* the *New York Times, Business Week,* and *Forbes,* as well as from our personal experiences. We feel they are important and illustrate the challenges that await you.

We expect that many of you will be considering a career in financial accounting either with a CPA firm or in business. Intermediate accounting is a key educational experience to have in preparing for that choice. Your instructor has selected this text from a number of alternatives because of the belief that this text will help you master the material needed in your career. Together, the instructor, the text, and your classmates provide the ingredients for a successful learning experience. Use each wisely.

We urge you to read the assigned material carefully. Sometimes two readings will be necessary. Learning is an active process. Keep paper and pencil handy. Work through each example, highlight important ideas. Actually write down answers to the concept review questions located at strategic points in the text. Work all assigned problems, particularly the comprehensive ones, and, if possible, check your answers. If the instructor permits, work with a classmate and share ideas. Remember, you are not finished until you not only have a satisfactory answer but you know why it is the best answer. Learn by doing.

It may be useful to think of an accounting issue or problem as a puzzle or mystery. Try asking what is going on and why. This will make your reading and learning more fun. In accounting, sometimes the answer depends on what is acceptable, what the rules are, or what is politically or operationally feasible.

If you find it difficult to master a chapter and to sort out what is important, try concentrating on the learning objectives given at the start of each chapter. Then, after reading the chapter, review the summary of key points and try solving the review problem located at the end of each chapter. In working the review problem, do not look at the answer until you have tried to solve the problem. When checking your answer, do not stop with noting what the authors did. Rather, ask why each step in the solution was made. Then work the problems, exercises, and cases assigned by your instructor. If you still have difficulties, talk to your instructor. The instructor wants to help you and can do so.

We think learning in general and accounting in particular can and should be both fun and exciting. We have worked many hours to achieve these goals in this text. When you finish your course, we sincerely hope you agree. We hope that you will have as much fun studying this text as we had in preparing it and the related materials, and that you find the study of accounting as interesting and challenging as we have. Our very best wishes to you in your studies and future career.

Thomas R. Dyckman
Roland E. Dukes
Charles J. Davis

CONTENTS IN BRIEF

◆

CONTENTS

◆

CHAPTER 19
Accounting for Pensions

Pension Plan Fundamentals
Current Pension Accounting
Measuring Pension Expense and Pension
Obligations
Prior Service Cost and Component 4 of Pension
Expense

Method of Amortizing PSC
Reconciliation of Funded Status

Unrecognized Gains and Losses and Component 5 of
Pension Expense

Amortization Methods

Unrecognized Transition Amount and Component 6 of
Pension Expense
Additional Minimum Pension Liability
Comprehensive Case and Pension Disclosure

Other Pension Disclosures
SFAS No. 87: A Compromise
Pension Terminations and Asset Reversions

Appendix 19A: Accounting for Postretirement
Benefits Other Than Pensions
Appendix 19B: Settlements and Curtailments of
Defined Benefit Pension Plans and Termination
Benefits
Appendix 19C: Financial Reporting by Pension
Plans

PART IV
OWNER'S EQUITY

CHAPTER 20
Corporations: Contributed Capital

Contributed Capital at Formation

Formation of a Corporation
Classification of Corporations
Advantages and Disadvantages of the Corporate
Form of Organization
Characteristics of Capital Stock
Concepts and Definitions Fundamental to
Corporate Equity Accounting

Different Kinds of Equity Securities

Par Value Stock
Nopar Value Stock
Legal Capital
Common Stock
Preferred Stock

Accounting for Various Equity Transactions

Accounting for the Issuance of Par Value Stock
Accounting for the Issuance of Nopar Stock
Capital Stock Sold on a Subscription Basis
Default on Subscriptions
Noncash Sale of Capital Stock
Special Sales of Capital Stock
Assessments on Capital Stock
Stock Issue Costs
Unrealized Capital

Changes in Contributed Capital after Formation

Treasury Stock
Recording and Reporting Treasury Stock
Transactions
Formal Retirement of Treasury Stock
Restriction of Retained Earnings for Treasury
Stock
Formal Retirement of Callable and Redeemable
Stock

Accounting for Changes in Equity

Conversion of Convertible Preferred Stock
Changing Par Value
Additional Contributed Capital

CHAPTER 21
Corporations: Retained Earnings and Stock Options

Characteristics of Retained Earnings
Nature of Dividends

Relevant Dividend Dates
Types of Dividends
Stock Dividends

Special Stock Dividends

Dividends and Treasury Stock
Fractional Shares Rights

Legality of Dividends
Stock Splits
Appropriations and Restrictions of Retained
Earnings
Reporting Retained Earnings
Stock Rights and Warrants
Accounting for Stock Rights
Stock Option Incentive Plans for Employees

Accounting for Noncompensatory Stock Option
Plans for Employees
Accounting for Compensatory Stock Option
Incentive Plans for Employees
Lapse of Stock Options

Stock Appreciation Rights
Additional Disclosures Required for Stock Option
Plans (Noncompensatory and Compensatory)
Appendix: Quasi Reorganizations

FOUNDATION AND REVIEW

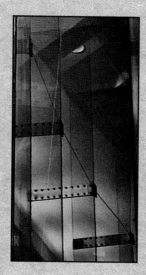

C H A P T E R

1

The Environment of Accounting

After you have studied this chapter, you will:

1. Recognize the value of the accounting function to external users of a company's financial statements.

2. Understand the difference between the internal and external uses of accounting information.

3. See that accounting can have an important impact on statement-users' decisions at all levels of the economy.

4. Understand the rule-making framework in which various organizations and environmental factors influence the setting of accounting standards.

5. Be acquainted with the major sources of the pronouncements that constitute GAAP (generally accepted accounting principles).

6. Be aware of the political nature of the standard-setting process and be cognizant of its impact on accounting standards, including the relevance of economic-consequence arguments.

7. Be acquainted with the important sections of the AICPA Code of Professional Conduct. (Refer to the appendix at the end of the chapter.)

♦

INTRODUCTION
♦

*F*inancial accounting principles, issues, methods, and techniques form the subject matter of this intermediate accounting textbook. Financial accounting is concerned with the manner and extent to which businesses communicate financial information about themselves to the outside public. The outside public, in this case, refers to the various categories of people who either invest in, lend money to, or do business with a company. To varying degrees, these people rely on a company's financial statements and other information reports as input for making investment and other financial decisions related to that company.

One of several specialized branches of accounting, financial accounting focuses on the information needs of people outside the company. Other specialized branches are primarily concerned with the internal needs of a company. *Management accounting,* in particular, addresses the needs of internal managers and the role accounting information plays in maintaining control over business operations and product lines, monitoring budgets and profit performance, and directing the company's future success.

Throughout the text, financial accounting practices and issues are discussed in the context of the corporate business world and publicly owned companies. This approach is taken to enhance the readability of the text and avoid terminology confusion that otherwise might occur if the full gamut of business structures were used for illustrative purposes. What applies to giant publicly owned corporations largely applies to smaller sole proprietorships as well, and to every type and size of business enterprise in between.

Financial accounting differs substantially from the other branches of accounting in several significant ways: First, the guiding principles of financial accounting are more open to interpretation and individual circumstances than is true of other specialized accounting fields. Tax accounting, by contrast, is an accounting field that tends to be dominated by exacting rules and regulations, leaving less room for interpretation. Second, the rule-making body that establishes the financial accounting principles—the **Financial Accounting Standards Board**—tends to be influenced more by issues that are not purely accounting in nature and by political pressure exerted by various business and special interest groups. Third, financial accounting is the one branch of accounting over which the Securities and Exchange Commission (SEC) exercises direct oversight authority. The SEC not only exerts influence over the financial accounting rule-making body, but can (and has) established certain accounting practice rules.

The rules and guiding principles of financial accounting often are complex, and some may seem somewhat contradictory. Even so, understanding the complex nature of financial accounting is vital. Moreover, many issues involved in the practice of public accounting are controversial, and differences of opinion and interpretations may have a substantive impact on the public's decision-making process. Only rarely is there a single, correct resolution or definitive answer to a financial accounting issue. And, when alternative resolutions and courses of action exist, the choice made may very well produce large differences in the accounting data being reported as well as the impression the figures leave with the public.

To gain an appreciation for the complexities involved in financial accounting and the role it can play in the corporate business world, consider the following account of what the business press described as "the deal of the century."

The takeover of RJR Nabisco: During the fall of 1988, F. Ross Johnson, chief executive officer (CEO) of RJR Nabisco, and Henry Kravis, senior partner with the limited-service investment banking firm of Kohlberg, Kravis, Roberts & Co., engaged in a bidding war for ownership of Johnson's company. By the end of November, Kravis had won. He took over RJR Nabisco for $25.1 billion. The following is a condensed account of the events and people involved.

The prize: RJR Nabisco, the combined grocery and tobacco products giant formed by the merger of Nabisco (National Biscuit Co.) and R. J. Reynolds Tobacco earlier in the 1980s was the takeover objective. With an array of well-known brand names ranging from Ritz crackers to Life Savers mints, plus cigarette brands such as Winston and Salem, the company was generating sales revenue of almost $16 billion and earnings of $1.2 billion annually.

The bidders: F. Ross Johnson was installed as CEO of RJR Nabisco after he engineered the merger of Nabisco with Reynolds Tobacco. Johnson was annoyed with the price performance of RJR Nabisco's stock; despite strong earnings, the price of the stock remained depressed. Analysts attributed the stock's poor performance to the fact that the company was still regarded largely as a tobacco products company in an era of antismoking sentiments, lawsuits, and declines in tobacco consumption. To remedy the situation, Johnson set about gaining absolute control over the company via a leveraged buyout.[1] For assistance in raising capital needed to finance the buyout, Johnson turned to his investment banking ally, Shearson Lehman Hutton.

Henry R. Kravis was the premier corporate dealmaker on Wall Street. His firm, Kohlberg, Kravis, Roberts & Co. (KKR), specialized in leveraged buyouts and other corporate takeover stratagems. For capital-raising purposes, Kravis had access to a $5 billion investment pool that was managed by KKR and formed specifically for the purpose of financing (and profiting handsomely from) corporate reorganizations. If additional financing was needed, Kravis, like Johnson, had relationships with many Wall Street investment banking firms.

The environment: Then and now, conventional wisdom holds that if a publicly owned corporation's stock price is undervalued and stagnating while the company itself is strong and growing—and especially if the company enjoys healthy cash flows—the company is ripe for a leveraged buyout. In effect, if the market value of the company itself is worth more than the market value of its stock, the shareholders stand to profit if the company itself can be sold to the highest bidder. But structuring the terms of a buyout is an extremely complex and often precarious operation. For a taste of the complexity involved, consider the following questions:

◆ How is the market value (breakup value) of an ongoing corporation determined?
◆ On a per-share basis, how is a fair buyout price determined?
◆ If a buyout offer includes both cash and securities (as many do), how is the value of the "buyout package" determined?
◆ Where will the capital needed to execute the buyout come from? How will it be repaid? And at what cost?
◆ After the buyout, will the reorganized company be able to support both the old debt capital structure and the new debt taken on in conjunction with the buyout?

In the RJR Nabisco case, a team of corporate finance experts from Shearson Lehman Hutton worked round the clock with RJR Nabisco's accounting and financial executives getting answers to the above questions. For weeks they scrutinized every aspect of the company's financial structure and evaluated each of the company's diverse business lines. With answers in place, F. Ross Johnson was ready to

---

[1] In a leveraged buyout, one or more individuals take over ownership of a publicly held corporation by buying all the equity stock outstanding. Most buyouts are led by the company's management team, but not always. Using large amounts of borrowed capital (leverage) and relatively small amounts of equity capital to finance the buyout transaction, the managers become sole owners and are free to do as they please with the company.

A leveraged buyout may be conducted quietly as a business transaction between the private buyers leading the takeover and the company's board of directors. If the board is not receptive, the buyers may resort to soliciting the shareholders directly, which is usually costly and noisy.

The financing capital needed comes from three major sources: (1) short-term loans from commercial banks, (2) high-yielding debentures (unsecured bonds known as *junk bonds*) issued by the buyers specifically to finance the buyout, and (3) direct-placement loans from limited partnerships and investment pools set up specifically as corporate takeover funding sources.

Much of the debt taken on in connection with a leveraged buyout is short-term and must be repaid quickly. To raise the needed cash, the new owners frequently sell off corporate assets such as separately managed operating companies or divisions. On the long-term debt front, the reorganized company is typically saddled with substantially larger debt service obligations spawned by the high-yielding junk bonds. To meet these interest and debt retirement obligations, large amounts of cash flow must normally be diverted from business operations. This typically means stern belt-tightening measures within the company and perhaps the sale or disposal of more assets.

take his leveraged buyout proposal to the RJR Nabisco board of directors for approval.

Key developments: On October 20, 1988, Johnson and Shearson jointly proposed a buyout of the company at $17.3 billion, or $75 for each of the 230 million shares outstanding. With the stock trading around $55 at the time, the shareholders were being offered a premium of $20 per share, which drove the market price of the stock to $77. The RJR Nabisco board approved Johnson's offer, but in keeping with its fiduciary responsibilities to the shareholders, it left open the opportunity for other interested parties to make an offer for the company in competition with Johnson and Shearson.

Four days later, Henry Kravis stepped forward with a competing proposal. Kravis's buyout featured cash and securities valued at $20.7 billion, equivalent to $90 per share. As a result, the price of the stock climbed to $85.

During November, Johnson and Kravis engaged in one-upmanship. Johnson increased the value of his buyout package to $92 per share, but Kravis bettered it at $94. Johnson came back with an offer valued at $100.

Before countering Johnson's $100 offer, Kravis petitioned the RJR Nabisco board for equal access to the internal accounting records and related documents that, up to that point, were available only to Johnson and his colleagues at Shearson. Kravis, as an outsider, was at a disadvantage. He and his staff of advisors were working from published financial statements and other public information sources on the company. Over Johnson's protest, the board granted Kravis's request. Kravis then restructured his proposal, initially to $106 per share, and finally at $25.1 billion, or $109 per share.

Midway through November, First Boston Corporation, another major investment banking firm, joined the bidding war. Representing a group of private investors, the firm at one point offered a package of cash and securities valued at over $27 billion. But after reexamining the situation, First Boston concluded that the company wasn't worth $27 billion, given the risks involved in incurring so much debt. The firm's offer was quickly withdrawn.

While leveraged buyouts typically offer windfall profit opportunities for a company's shareholders, for the company's bondholders they can be disastrous. Metropolitan Life Insurance Co. is a case in point. The insurance carrier owned millions of dollars worth of Reynolds Tobacco Company bonds issued before the merger with Nabisco and assumed by the new company, RJR Nabisco. The day Johnson announced his buyout proposal, the market value of these bonds plunged 20%. The reason: concern over the continued safety of the bonds in light of the enormous amount of new debt that would be piled on the company.

On November 30, 1988, RJR Nabisco's board made its decision, selling the company to Kravis for $25.1 billion, or $109 per share. Interestingly, Johnson's final bid came to $112 per share according to his calculations. But the board relied on the valuations made by their own advisers and downgraded the value of the bid to $109 per share, the same as Kravis's price. The board gave the edge to Kravis based on "better quality" and noneconomic reasons, which it said would be revealed in required disclosure documents filed with the SEC.

Accounting points to consider: The RJR Nabisco takeover story is usually regarded by the general public as a tale of corporate greed and power struggles, which indeed it was. But for accounting practitioners, academicians, and students alike, the RJR Nabisco case points up a number of issues of importance to financial accounting:

- Why did Henry Kravis feel that he was at a disadvantage in attempting to establish the total value of RJR Nabisco because he was working *only* from information reported in the company's financial statements? Is there any truth to one of the comments a Kravis staff member made, saying, in effect, that financial statements can be painted to depict any picture the management wants to paint?

- Can a company be worth substantially more than the net value of its assets? And, if so, why are assets allowed to be reported on a so-called undervalued basis on the balance sheet?

- What kinds of information does inside management possess that is not shared with outside investors, lenders, and other users of the company's financial statements? Why is this so?
- How is it that F. Ross Johnson's first bid for RJR Nabisco was only $75 per share, whereas his final price was $109, 45% higher? Did he not realize the value of the company at the outset? Or was he attempting to pick up a bargain of mammoth proportions?

Many things that contribute to an understanding of accounting information can be learned from financial statements, including how this information is used by external decision makers and the benefits these people derive. In fairness, however, we must also recognize the limitations of financial statements, understanding how some external decision makers might misinterpret the accounting information they contain.

It is therefore imperative to study just how financial statements are prepared. Knowing the rules and presentation procedures followed is essential to understanding the messages these reports convey. This is the objective.

The approach of this book is to explain how financial statements are prepared and to make certain the accounting rules and procedures followed in preparing them are understood. Once mastered, this knowledge can be applied throughout your business career—in the preparation and in the analysis of financial statements. As you begin this learning process, please note that we will not shy away from being critical of current accounting information preparation and reporting practices wherever such criticism is warranted.

◆

THE NATURE OF FINANCIAL ACCOUNTING

We can usefully treat **accounting as an information system**. As such, the purpose of accounting is to identify, collect, measure, and communicate information about economic units (corporations, partnerships, and sole proprietorships) to those with an interest in the financial affairs of the unit.

The RJR Nabisco buyout, discussed in the introduction to this chapter, is an example of the role an accounting information system can play (more examples are introduced later). But to provide a better understanding of what is covered in this book, let's expand on the purpose of an accounting information system. Because this book is concerned primarily with external users of accounting information, it is necessary to distinguish between information used for internal and external purposes. Then the objectives of reporting accounting information to external users and the basic reports used to communicate this information can be examined.

External versus Internal Accounting Information

The users of financial information can be classified as either external or internal decision makers.

External decision makers are people who lack direct access to the information generated by the internal operations of a company. Included in this category are present shareholders, potential investors, suppliers, creditors, rank-and-file employees, customers, competitors, financial analysts and advisors, brokers, underwriters, the stock exchanges, lawyers, economists, taxing and regulatory authorities, legislators, the financial press and reporting agencies, labor unions, trade associations, business researchers, teachers, students, and the public.[2] These external decision

---

[2] While those using accounting information for tax purposes are external users, it is worthwhile to identify this group of users separately. The tax law is designed to assist in the collection of monies for public purposes and, often, to support specific economic or political initiatives undertaken by government. Hence the tax reporting requirements are typically different from those followed for other accounting purposes.

makers use accounting information in deciding on matters such as whether to invest in the entity, extend it credit, or even do business with it.[3]

The process of developing and reporting accounting information to external decision makers is called *financial accounting*. Financial accounting theory and practices are the focus of this textbook. External users, because of their detachment from the entity, typically are not in a position to demand specific financial information from the entity; therefore, they must rely on general-purpose financial statements. To meet the information needs of external decision makers, the accounting profession has developed a network of accounting concepts, principles, and procedures intended to assure that external financial statements are relevant and reliable.[4] This body of concepts, principles, and procedures is better known as **generally accepted accounting principles (GAAP)**.

Internal decision makers are the managers of an entity. They are responsible for planning the future of the business, implementing those plans, controlling daily operations, and reporting information to other operating officers. Because of their close and direct relationship with the business, internal decision makers usually can obtain whatever financial data they need at dates of their choice. Much of this information is not intended to be relayed to outsiders. The process of developing and reporting financial information for internal users is called *management accounting*, and the related information reports being generated are called *internal management reports*. Because of the confidential nature of these reports and their primary focus on internal decision-making needs, there is no requirement (other than those specified by the management) that these reports conform to GAAP. Once again, the emphasis of this text is on external decision makers and financial statements, as opposed to internal decision makers and management reports.

Objective of Financial Reporting for External Decision Makers

The objective of external financial statements and their accompanying disclosure notes is to communicate information concerning the economic effects on the reporting entity of completed business transactions and other events. Although there are other ways to communicate external financial information—such as prospectuses (for security offerings), news releases, and management "letters"—the primary means of communication are a company's periodic financial statements. General-purpose financial statements report financial information of relevance to investment, credit, and public-policy decision makers. To accomplish the necessary reporting, two basic types of financial statements are used:

1. A statement of the company's financial position as of a specific point in time, the **balance sheet**, which reports the company's assets, liabilities, and owners' equity on a specified date. This statement is also called the *statement of financial position*.
2. Statements that relate to a specified period of time:
   a. **Income statement**, which reports the company's revenues, gains, expenses, losses, and net income. This statement is also called the *statement of income*.
   b. **Statement of retained earnings** (sometimes appended to the income statement), which reports changes in the company's accumulated earnings. This statement is also called the *retained earnings statement*.
   c. **Statement of cash flows**, which reports the company's cash flows from operating, investing, and financing activities.

---

[3] See Financial Accounting Standards Board (FASB), *Statement of Financial Accounting Concepts No. 1*, "Objectives of Financial Reporting by Business Enterprises" (Norwalk, Conn., November 1978), p. 11.

[4] FASB, *Statement of Financial Accounting Concepts No. 2*, "Qualitative Characteristics of Accounting Information" (Norwalk, Conn., May 1980), identifies relevance and reliability as the two primary qualitative characteristics that accounting information is designed to possess. These and other qualitative characteristics are discussed in chapter 2.

The purpose of external financial statements has been explained by the Financial Accounting Standards Board (FASB) in its *Statement of Financial Accounting Concepts No. 2 (SFAC No. 2, par. 22)* as follows:

> Financial reporting should provide information that is useful to present and potential investors and creditors and other users in making rational investment, credit, and similar decisions. The information should be comprehensible to those who have a reasonable understanding of business and economic activities and are willing to study the information with reasonable diligence.
>
> Financial reporting should provide information to help present and potential investors and creditors and other users in assessing the amounts, timing, and uncertainty of prospective cash receipts from dividends or interest and the proceeds from the sale, redemption, or maturity of securities or loans. The prospects for those cash receipts are affected by an enterprise's ability to generate enough cash to meet its obligations when due and its other cash operating needs, to reinvest in operations, and to pay cash dividends and may also be affected by perceptions of investors and creditors generally about that ability, which affect market prices of the enterprise's securities. Thus, financial reporting should provide information to help investors, creditors, and others assess the amounts, timing, and uncertainty of prospective net cash inflows to the related enterprise.
>
> Financial reporting should provide information about the economic resources of an enterprise, the claims to those resources (obligations of the enterprise to transfer resources to other entities and owners' equity), and the effects of transactions, events, and circumstances that change resources and claims to those resources.

The economic resources referred to are the company's assets, the claims to these assets are the company's liabilities, and the changes in resources and claims are reflected in changes to the owners' equity section of the balance sheet.

The overall purpose of financial reporting as stated in *SFAC No. 2* is to provide information that will be useful in making *decisions*. This objective influences the measurement rules and processes selected in preparing accounting information for financial-reporting purposes. If an alternative, less decision-oriented objective were to be adopted, the way accounting information is measured and reported would change dramatically. For example, if the objective in financial reporting simply became one of *stewardship*—focusing on information about managerial control, compliance, and custodial responsibilities—there would be little concern with predicting future cash flows. For example, in deciding whether to sell stock in a company, it is important to be able to estimate its future dividend payments. Keeping track of asset values initially entrusted to management, a stewardship approach, would be of little help in the sell-or-hold or other decisions requiring information on economic performance. The purpose of financial reporting and its influence on desirable characteristics or qualities of accounting information are discussed in more detail in Chapter 2.

Professional Accounting

The need to provide financial information to decision makers created a demand for people who could do the job. Further, these individuals needed to have credibility so that the data could be relied on by users. This has led to the development and acceptance of professional accountants.

Accounting dates back to at least 3600 B.C. The first published work on the double-entry system of accounting was authored by Luca Pacioli A.D. 1494 in Venice, Italy. Pacioli's work described double-entry accounting in much the same way as it is used today. Since that time, the need for financial accounting has grown as business has grown, starting with the industrial revolutions in Europe and the United States. This growth was accelerated by the emergence of the publicly owned corporation as a major form of business entity. Many other factors have affected accounting as well. Today, accountants have an important and unique role in society. The professional accountant in public or private practice is usually a certified public accountant (CPA), a certified management accountant (CMA), or certified internal auditor (CIA).

Large numbers of accountants are active in the three areas listed below.

Public Accounting   Independent accountants in public practice—most are CPAs—offer services such as auditing (the attest function),[5] tax planning and determination of the tax liability, and management consulting. Accountants in public practice have a unique relationship with their clients. These accountants act as independent and impartial auditors of the client's financial statements.[6] Although independent accountants are paid by the client, the courts, government regulators, and the public through the legislative process embodied in the Securities Act of 1933 have extended their responsibilities to third parties as well, such as the users of financial statements. The **American Institute of Certified Public Accountants (AICPA)** is the professional organization to which most CPAs belong. This organization establishes auditing standards and enforces a code of professional ethics on its members. Ethical behavior is critical to those who audit the financial statements that are an essential information source to the efficient functioning of our capital markets. Important sections of the AICPA's code of ethics are reproduced in the appendix at the end of this chapter.

Management Accounting   Large numbers of accountants (including CPAs and CMAs) are also employed by business firms as management accountants, internal auditors, income tax specialists, system experts, controllers, management advisory service consultants, financial vice presidents, and chief executives. Management accounting focuses on the planning and controlling functions in an enterprise with special emphasis on internal management reports and related analyses. These internal reports are prepared to meet the needs of internal management and are not intended to be distributed outside the enterprise. Accountants employed by a company are not considered independent accountants and cannot attest to the company's external financial statements.

Not-for-Profit Accounting   Accountants (including CPAs and CMAs) serve at all levels of government and other not-for-profit entities: local, state, national, and international. In these capacities, they also are not independent accountants. However, private-sector CPAs do act as independent accountants when auditing not-for-profit reports.

CONCEPT REVIEW

1. Are a firm's financial reports prepared primarily for internal or external users?
2. What are the two basic types of financial statements? Give an example of each.
3. What is the purpose of financial statement information?

THE INTERACTION OF FINANCIAL ACCOUNTING WITH ITS ENVIRONMENT

In the introduction to this chapter, a situation was recounted in which accounting information was relevant to an economic decision. In general, accounting measurements and financial reports have an impact on the distribution of scarce resources, including management talent, in the society. This allocation occurs as decision

---

[5] The auditor is required to express a written opinion on whether the firm's financial statements fairly present its financial position and operations. The auditor is said to attest to the statements.

[6] Professionals and legislators have debated extensively whether public accounting firms, which also perform consulting services for their audit clients, are fully independent.

makers assess opportunities for gains in relation to the inherent risks of devoting their monetary or human capital to a particular venture. Accounting helps decision makers evaluate opportunities by providing measurements such as net income, total assets and equities, and cash flow (along with associated footnotes). But caution against overreliance on accounting measures is advised. First, accounting measures have limitations, as we shall see. Second, many other sources of information may be more relevant and timely in any particular situation.

Accounting measures play an important role in numerous situations:
* Determining tax payments given statutory conditions.
* Establishing the attractiveness of a company as a takeover target.
* Evaluating the effectiveness of individual managers in using assets committed to their charge.
* Determining whether bond and other contract provisions are satisfied.
* Helping lenders evaluate the risk of a potential loan.
* Serving as one input to regulators making utility-rate decisions.

Many indirect effects, which are sometimes difficult to observe, are also involved. Thus, the financial reports may do the following:
* Influence the attractiveness of a company to its workers.
* Suggest bargaining strategies to unions or union organizers.
* Affect the willingness of suppliers to enter into long-term contracts with the company.
* Attract the attention of government units interested, perhaps, in unusual profit performance.
* Affect customers' willingness to purchase the company's products for either economic, environmental, or ethical reasons.[7]

Apart from the uses of accounting measures described above, accounting choices in compiling and reporting information can have a far-reaching impact on businesses themselves, and the economy as well. Consider the following situations:
* At one point, the alternative accounting treatments permited for oil and gas exploration costs were alleged to have directly altered the willingness of companies in this industry to develop new reserves at a time when the OPEC cartel was restricting oil supplies.
* In another case, arguments were advanced that U.S. business and industry would cut back on research and development (R&D) activities due to accounting treatments mandated by the FASB (the organization that sets accounting standards) that required expenditures for these activities to be expensed in full each year rather than capitalized as assets and amortized. To avoid the detrimental effects of having R&D expenditures treated as expense, which lowers reported net income, some companies, it was maintained, would set up separate R&D companies. R&D expenses could then be omitted from the parent company's income statement.
* The way the score is kept can have manifestations extending all the way to national policy and international trade relations. Some economists contend that because U.S. businesses are required to expense goodwill, which must be written off over time (thereby lowering net income), they are at a disadvantage relative to foreign companies that enjoy more-favorable accounting treatment in their home nations. The result is that U.S. companies must recognize higher expenses than their foreign counterparts. This, it is believed, leads business to increase the selling prices of U.S. goods, which in turn contributes to the U.S. trade deficit.

Concerns over the adequacy of financial accounting have been expressed by both the companies preparing financial statements and by external decision makers using these reports. For the most part, these concerns reflect back on the methods used in compiling accounting information and reporting results in financial statements. But accounting methods and procedures are often in use at the behest of the regulatory bodies that set financial reporting requirements. Thus, the Securities and Exchange

---

[7] G. Benston and M. Kreasney, "The Economic Consequences of Financial Accounting Statements," in *Economic Consequences of Financial Accounting Standards,* FASB Research Report (Norwalk, Conn.: FASB, 1978).

Commission (SEC) was sufficiently concerned that a particular reporting method for oil and gas exploration costs might cause energy companies to reduce the amount they would invest in such activities that it overruled the FASB on the accounting treatment for exploration expenses.

Other factors also influence accounting, information compilation, and reporting procedures:

* The U.S. legal system, which stresses verifiable facts as opposed to estimates and forecasts.
* The regulatory structure, such as public utility regulatory commissions, which among other decisions, decides what costs are capitalized into the asset base used to establish customer electric rates.
* The ethical climate, which strengthens (or weakens) the quality of the reported information.
* Concerns by financial statement preparers that disclosure will reduce the company's competitive advantage, for example, by providing information on the profitability of specific products.
* The demands for information by users, which influence whether certain data, such as leases, are reported on the balance sheet as a line-item with debt or in the footnotes or not at all.
* The costs and benefits of alternative reporting methods, which play a major role in whether the FASB adopts specific financial information reporting requirements (e.g., the FASB's requirement to report data adjusted for price level changes as supplemental information in financial statements and the subsequent repeal of this requirement).
* The importance of the quality of the information supplied, including trade-offs among different aspects of quality, for example, the timeliness versus the relevance of the information. The reporting of bad-debt expense—and the associated allowance for uncollectables—is an example where the need for timely information permits a forecast to be entered into the financial instruments.
* The development of new financial instruments.

In sum, accounting practice is influenced by legal, political, business, and social developments. As a result, accounting concepts, standards, and practices are constantly evolving. It is vitally important that accounting keep pace with and meet the changing needs and demands of society. At the same time, it must meet the cost-benefit test; that is, the benefits provided by accounting must exceed the costs.

Also, accounting must be consistent with the current legal and ethical standards of society. Pressures and influences must not be allowed to compromise the ethics of the accounting profession or to interfere with accounting measurements of economic events.

First and foremost, a professional accountant in public practice must be independent of the client whose report is to be certified. Often the reporting of unfavorable economic results can pose major problems for the reporting company, but the results must be fairly presented and reliably reported nonetheless. The public interest must predominate.

The Need for Financial Reporting Standards

Financial reporting standards are needed to ensure that the accounting information provided in financial statements is relevant to the types of decisions investors and other users must make. For example, short- and long-term creditors scrutinize this information in an effort to evaluate a company's ability to meet its future cash obligations. Information about the past is often useful to creditors in predicting future cash flows. Reported information about current liabilities, long-term debts, and stockholders' equity can be used to compute a company's ratio of debt to equity. This ratio indicates the portion of the company's assets that were provided by creditors.

Both investors and lenders find it useful to work with the reported cash flow from operating activities in evaluating a company's ability to make interest payments and repay debt. Prior to July 15, 1988, companies had a choice in reporting either cash flow or the change in working capital (current assets less current liabilities) from operating activities. However, studies showed that a cash flow report provides information more relevant to investor decisions and that cash flow data can be used as a better predictor of business failure than changes in working capital. As a result, accounting standards were changed to eliminate this choice, and the statement of cash flow is now required. (The cash flow statement is covered in Chapter 5.)

Researchers have found that investors are most concerned with a company's reported earnings. Earnings are one factor that drives the market price of the company's stock; share prices react to reported earnings as they become public information. The market is frequently able to anticipate a company's reported earnings before they are released to the media, in which case the stock's market price moves in advance of the earnings news release. Current market prices of publicly traded shares are reported daily in newspapers, accompanied by the ratio of share price to net income per share (price-earnings, or P/E, ratio). Security analysts use P/E ratios, financial statements, and other information sources to project future earnings. Furthermore, market prices tend to react to earnings forecasts made by a company's top executives or by a prominent securities analyst. Consequently, companies are understandably concerned about reported earnings because they wish to see the market value of their stock stay as high as possible.

Concerns about reported earnings have caused problems in financial reporting. Many corporations set goals for reported earnings in their planning process, often for a period of three to five years. The company has a strong desire to achieve these goals to increase share value. The chief executive officer may even announce an earnings goal or forecast to the financial press, which then exerts pressure on the company to reach the earnings goal. Unfortunately, however, there are documented cases where companies have been unable to attain their earnings goals through operations and have resorted to deceptive accounting, attempting to manufacture the desired result. Accounting standards have developed over time to remedy abuses and prevent blatant accounting trickery.

Earnings goals are commonly tailored to a smooth pattern of earnings growth each year or quarter. Companies thus have incentives to smooth out their earnings over time to avoid undesirable fluctuations. The smoothing may require a reduction or increase in earnings from the level otherwise reported. Thus, if earnings appear to be above goal, equipment write-offs may be taken now, whereas such write-offs may be delayed if earnings are inadequate. Deliveries of product may be accelerated late in the fiscal year if earnings are down, and the incurrence of expenses can be delayed if earnings are expected to be too low. Another ploy for manipulating earnings, which is now prohibited in the United States but still allowed in many countries, is to establish arbitrary reserves. If a company finds it advantageous to report lower net earnings, it might attempt to set up a reserve account for future losses due to lawsuits, asset obsolescence, a future catastrophe, uncollectible trade receivables, and so on. Or a company might want to artificially boost its earnings. In one documented case, a company followed a practice of selling just enough of the land it had bought in the past so that the gain on the land sales, when added to income for the year, produced a constant 30% growth in net income each year.[8]

Given the widespread use of financial statements by the public and the complex nature of the decision-making processes involved in their use, it is not surprising to find that the accounting profession has, over the years, developed a structure of accounting practice standards. The chief body of practice standards included in this

---

[8] Reported in *The Wall Street Journal*, April 27, 1971, p. 7.

structure is a set of generally accepted accounting principles (GAAP). GAAP is intended both to guide and to govern the preparation of financial statements, with the public's needs and interests held foremost in mind. The qualifier *generally accepted* denotes that each of the individual principles was either established by a designated rule-making body, such as the Financial Accounting Standards Board, or that through practice it has achieved general acceptance over time.

Prior to the 20th century, most businesses in the United States were small, and the accounting necessary was relatively simple. During the early part of this century, the development of more complex business organizations requiring large amounts of capital from diverse sources created a need to keep investors and creditors who were not in day-to-day contact with operations more fully informed. The creation of the income tax by the 16th Amendment to the U.S. Constitution, March 1, 1913, added to the pressures for outside accountability. Additionally, the stock market crash of 1929 paved the way for adoption of many new accounting rules. The severity of the Great Depression that followed was blamed in part on inadequate financial disclosure.

A direct result of the Great Depression was the Securities Act of 1933 and the Securities Exchange Act of 1934. The Securities and Exchange Commission was created as an independent regulatory agency of the government. Companies that issue publicly traded stock or stock listed on stock exchanges were thenceforth required to file annual audited reports with the SEC. In addition, the SEC was granted power to prescribe the accounting policies and practices to be followed by companies under its jurisdiction. Filings include a registration statement, Form S-1, when securities are initially issued; an annual report, Form 10K; and a report following the occurrence of a major event, Form 8K, such as changing the company's auditor.

During the years immediately following the Securities Acts, the SEC relied primarily on the American Institute of Certified Public Accountants to develop and enforce accounting standards. In response to the SEC and the growing need to report reliable financial information, the AICPA created the **Committee on Accounting Procedure (CAP)** in the 1930s. The CAP began the process of setting reporting requirements. In the late 1950s, CAP was replaced by the **Accounting Principles Board (APB)** and then by the Financial Accounting Standards Board (FASB) in the early 1970s. The FASB continues to set accounting standards today under the watchful eye of the Securities and Exchange Commission. Congress has the final authority in such matters, but it relies heavily on the SEC to oversee the standard-setting process. The SEC, in turn has ceded to the profession a major role in drafting accounting standards.

CONCEPT REVIEW

1. Give three specific decision situations in which accounting information may play an important role.
2. Do accounting reports include data that make assumptions about the future? If so, provide an example.
3. What major events led to the establishment of the accounting profession's framework under which generally accepted accounting principles are set?

Impact of Accounting-Related Organizations

Because of the importance of financial statements to users, there has always been widespread interest in how accounting standards are established. Interest in the accounting profession's public responsibility to establish accounting standards has recently increased. For example, accounting standards for banks influence the extent to which banks must write off distress loans to Third World countries. The write-offs lower the bank's assets and equity, dollar for dollar. In effect, the bank uses its own equity capital to pay off the bad loans. Too many write-offs will deplete the bank's equity, which poses solvency problems. Further, in the wake of one bank's problems with Third World countries, other banks may be unwilling to lend to these countries. The impact on these countries, shut off from financial assistance, can be ruinous. As foreign trade suffers, governments may topple, and the welfare of the citizens is placed in jeopardy. And the bad news gets worse. Back at the U.S. bank, diminished capital levels mean less money available for loans to long-standing, low-risk U.S. customers. Further, with loan money tight, the interest rates on loans increase.

On the other hand, if the loans are not written down sufficiently, investors are led to believe the bank is in better financial shape than is the case. The result can be a channeling of savings into unsound financial institutions to the detriment of the investor as well as the overall health of the banking community. To some extent the savings and loan crisis of the late 1980s and early 1990s reflects a similar problem with overvalued assets.

Among the factors that influence accounting is a group of organizations that expend considerable talents and resources to help develop financial accounting standards. The more influential organizations are described below.

American Institute of Certified Public Accountants. The AICPA is the national professional organization of certified public accountants. It responds primarily to the needs of CPAs in public practice. Therefore, its efforts and publications focus on the practice of public accounting. Its primary publications and standard-setting activities, which now are constrained to auditing issues, include the following:

1. *Journal of Accountancy*—a monthly magazine containing pronouncements, articles, and special sections of interest to independent CPAs.
2. *Accountants' Index*—an annual classified bibliography of the accounting literature published during the year.
3. *Accounting Trends & Techniques*—an annual publication containing a survey of the characteristics of the annual financial reports of 600 corporations.
4. *Accounting Research Studies*—a series of early studies that focused on specific accounting issues providing background information, alternative solutions, and in many cases, recommended practices.
5. *Statements of Auditing Standards*—audit standards promulgated by the Auditing Standards Board.
6. Statements covering specific accounting principles, standards, and procedures:
   a. *Accounting Research Bulletins (ARBs)*—Between 1938 and 1959, the AICPA's Committee on Accounting Procedure was responsible for "narrowing the areas of differences and inconsistencies" in accounting practice. To this end, CAP issued 51 *Accounting Research Bulletins* and 4 *Accounting Terminology Bulletins*; those not superseded are a part of GAAP. The first 42 of the 51 bulletins are collected in *ARB No. 43* and serve as the starting point for GAAP. More recent statements of the FASB often refer to and at times amend *ARB No. 43.*
   b. *Accounting Principles Board Opinions (Opinions)*—In 1959, the AICPA established the Accounting Principles Board (APB) to replace its Committee on Accounting Procedures. The APB designated its pronouncements as *Opinions*. During its existence from 1959 to 1973, the APB issued 31 *Opinions* and four *Statements*. In contrast to the *Opinions*, the *Statements* were couched as recommendations, rather than requirements, for improvement in financial accounting and reporting to external decision makers.[9]

---

[9] The contents of these *Bulletins, Opinions,* and *Statements* are listed inside the front and back covers. The ARBs and APBs are currently available from the FASB in Norwalk, Connecticut.

7. Auditing Standards Division, established in 1974, and its Accounting Standards Executive Committee (AcSEC) develop *Issue Papers* that identify, consider alternatives to, and present recommendations about current financial reporting issues.

Securities and Exchange Commission. A number of government regulatory agencies influence accounting and reporting by businesses. Among them is the Securities and Exchange Commission. The SEC holds the power delegated to it by Congress to establish and enforce accounting standards for those companies over which it has jurisdiction.

Under the Securities Act of 1933, before a company is allowed to sell an issue of securities interstate, it must file a prospectus with the SEC. The prospectus is a public document prepared for a new security issuance. The prospectus reports information about the company, its officers, and its financial affairs. The financial portion of the prospectus must be audited by an independent CPA. Once its securities have been sold to the public, the company must, under the Securities Act of 1933, file with the SEC, as a matter of public record, audited financial statements each subsequent year (10-K reports) and unaudited quarterly statements (10-Q reports). In most material respects, the annual 10-K reporting requirements are satisfied by the published financial statements.

The SEC filing and reporting requirements are as follows:

1. *Regulation S-X*—This is the original and comprehensive document issued by the Commission, as amended and supplemented. It prescribes the reporting requirements and forms to be filed with the SEC.
2. *Accounting Series Releases (ASRs)*—These releases are amendments, extensions, and additions to *Regulation S-X*.
3. *Special SEC Releases*—These relate to current issues as they arise.
4. *Accounting and Auditing Enforcement Releases (AAERs)*.
5. *Accounting Reporting Releases (ARRs)*.
6. *Staff Accounting Bulletins (SABs)*—These serve as interpretations of *Regulation S-X* and the *Accounting Series Releases (ASRs)*.

These publications continue in force as amended and superseded by the SEC.

Although the SEC has wide statutory authority to prescribe financial accounting and external reporting requirements for listed companies, the Commission has relied on the accounting profession to set and enforce accounting standards and to regulate the profession. The working relationship between the SEC and the accounting profession is positive, and accounting regulation has remained in the private sector. However, the SEC has occasionally forced the accounting profession to move forward in tackling critical problems, and once it rejected a standard (*Statements of Financial Accounting Standards No. 19*) issued by the FASB. These situations occur when the SEC concludes that the public interest is not being fully served. Also, at times when there has been disagreement within the accounting profession over significant issues, the SEC has exercised its influence to resolve matters.

Financial Accounting Standards Board

Of all of the accounting organizations, the FASB is the most influential. Its primary purpose is to promulgate financial accounting standards. It was created in 1973 to replace the Accounting Principles Board. Unlike the APB, the FASB is independent; its members have no affiliation with any other organization.

The AICPA's special committee, which suggested that the FASB replace the APB, recommended the FASB be part of the following structure, as amended:[10]

---

[10] AICPA, *Establishing Financial Accounting Standards*, Report of the Study on Establishment of Accounting Principles, (New York, American Institute of Certified Public Accountants, March 1972), p. 105 (chair of the Committee, F. Wheat). For an analysis of the mission and operations of the FASB, see P. Miller and R. Redding, *The FASB: The People, the Process, and the Politics* 2nd ed. (Homewood, Ill.: Richard D. Irwin, 1988).

1. *Financial Accounting Foundation (FAF)*—composed currently of sixteen trustees appointed by the board of directors of the AICPA. *Responsibilities:* to appoint members of the Financial Accounting Standards Board, to appoint a Financial Accounting Standards Advisory Council, to raise funds to support the organization's structure, and to periodically review and revise the FASB's basic structure.

2. *Financial Accounting Standards Board (FASB)*—composed of seven full-time members. *Responsibilities:* to establish financial accounting standards and to direct a research program structured to accomplish specific objectives to support the standard-setting process.[11]

3. *Financial Accounting Standards Advisory Council (FASAC)*—a group of senior-level individuals broadly selected from preparers, users, auditors, and CPA constituencies. The number of members has varied over time but is about 35. *Responsibilities:* to work closely with the FASB in an advisory capacity and to establish priorities, establish task forces, evaluate performance, and react to proposed standards.

Since its inception in 1973, the FASB has undergone several changes. Its current organization, primary activities, and other related organizational units are shown in Exhibit 1–1.

American Accounting Association (AAA)   The **American Accounting Association** is an organization primarily for accounting educators; however, its membership also includes accountants in public practice, industry, and not-for-profit organizations. Its objectives are to develop accounting theory, encourage and sponsor accounting research, and improve education in accounting. The statements of the AAA do not constitute GAAP. The Association operates through committees and publishes monographs, committee reports, research studies, and periodicals. The periodicals include *The Accounting Review, Accounting Horizons, Issues in Accounting Education,* and journals published by sections of the AAA. These periodicals contain articles and comments on a wide range of subjects pertaining to accounting research, concepts, and education.

The position papers relating to accounting theory and principles issued by the AAA are normative rather than descriptive. That is, they tend to express what accounting should be, rather than what accounting is, as reflected, for example, in GAAP. The AAA continues to have a significant impact on accounting standards through its responses to proposed statements of the FASB, and through the teaching, writing, and participating activities of its members.

Governmental Accounting Standards Board (GASB)   The **Governmental Accounting Standards Board** was created in 1984 to develop accounting standards for governmental units such as state and local entities. It operates under the oversight of the Financial Accounting Foundation (FAF) and the Governmental Advisory Council. This textbook focuses primarily on financial reports for businesses rather than on governmental accounting.

Financial Executives Institute (FEI) and the National Association of Accountants (NAA)   These organizations, composed primarily of business individuals, have influenced the content of accounting standards in recent years. The FEI publishes the *Financial Executive Magazine,* and the NAA publishes *Management Accounting.* The NAA also sponsors the CMA (Certified Management Accountant) exam.

All of these organizations, plus various business and industry representatives, lobby the FASB, making certain the Board is aware of their positions on current issues. Sometimes, these same groups do their lobbying indirectly through government committees, bureaus, and regulatory agencies.

---

[11] Research studies have been undertaken totally within the Board as well as contracted out to organizations and to academics.

EXHIBIT 1-1   Organizations that Have Primary Responsibilities for Setting Accounting Standards

Financial Accounting Foundation (FAF)
• Sixteen trustees appointed by the AICPA
• Appoints members of the FASB
• Raises funds to support standard setting
• Reviews and revises the basic structure

Financial Accounting Standards
Board (FASB)
• Seven members
• Establishes financial accounting
  concepts and standards
• Conducts a research program to
  support the standard-setting
  process

Governmental Accounting
Standards Board (GASB)
• Five members
• Establishes governmental
  accounting concepts and
  standards
• Conducts a research program
  to support the standard
  setting process

Financial Accounting Advisory
Council (FASAC)
• Consults with FASB on:
  -Accounting problems and
   issues
  -Project priorities
  -Organizing task forces
• Advises FASB on request

Governmental Accounting
Advisory Council (GASAC)
• Consults with GASB on:
  -Accounting problems and
   issues
  -Project priorities
  -Organizing task forces
• Advises GASB on request

The Current Standard-Setting Process

The initial development of accounting standards following the Great Depression was described earlier in this chapter. At this point, we examine how the FASB came to be the standard-setting organization, how it differs from its predecessors, and how it functions.

The first standards board, the Committee on Accounting Procedure, issued the *Accounting Research Bulletins (ARBs)* that set forth what the committee believed GAAP should be. However, the *ARBs* were recommendations only. They were not binding on the preparers and auditors because there was no requirement for adherence.

The committee made a substantive start in developing accounting standards. However, it was a part-time committee and could not devote sufficient time to formulating accounting standards. By the mid-1950s, the committee had become inactive. Therefore, in 1959, the Accounting Principles Board was set up by the AICPA. Its basic charge was to develop a statement of accounting concepts (i.e., a conceptual foundation of accounting) and issue pronouncements on current accounting problems. The APB designated its pronouncements as *Opinions* and 31 were issued.

At the outset, the force of the *Opinions*, as with the *ARBs*, depended on general acceptance. Acceptance was encouraged by *persuasion;* that is, by convincing preparers and independent CPAs that these recommendations were the best solutions to selected accounting problems. By 1964, many leaders of the profession were convinced that persuasion could not reduce the wide range of existing accounting and reporting differences and inconsistencies. In numerous cases, identical transactions could be accounted for by any of several different accounting methods. Net income could be manipulated by selecting a particular accounting approach from among several that were considered to be "generally accepted."

A significant event in the development of accounting practice occurred in October 1964. At that time, the Council (the governing body) of the AICPA adopted a requirement that was incorporated into the *rules of ethics* for independent CPAs.

> *Rule 203—Accounting principles.* A member shall not express an opinion that financial statements are presented in conformity with generally accepted accounting principles if such statements contain any departure from an accounting principle promulgated by the body designated by Council to establish such principles which has a material effect on the statements taken as a whole, unless the member can demonstrate that due to unusual circumstances the financial statements would otherwise have been misleading. In such cases his report must describe the departure, the approximate effects thereof, if practicable, and the reasons why compliance with the principle would result in a misleading statement.

This compliance requirement caused numerous organizations to focus greater attention on the *Opinions* and the *ARBs*. The APB continued the *Opinions* and *ARBs* in force because preparers and auditors were required to implement the prescribed accounting standards. Starting in the 1960s and continuing in the early 1970s, there were many complaints about the process used to develop accounting standards. These complaints, from industry, CPA firms, and government, criticized the lack of participation by organizations other than the AICPA, the quality of the *Opinions,* the failure of the APB to develop a statement of the objectives and principles underlying external financial reports, the insufficient output by the APB, and the APB's failure to act promptly to correct alleged abuses.

The difficulties experienced by the APB were dramatized in the mid-1960s by its attempt to resolve the question of accounting for the investment tax credit. The APB's initial decision, to require that the credit be considered a reduction in the asset's cost, met such strong resistance from business that the APB found it politically necessary in 1964 to rescind its earlier *Opinion (Opinion No. 2)* and permit the credit as a reduction in income tax expense (*Opinion No. 4*), hence increasing income.[12]

The early 1970s witnessed the creation of a Study Group on Establishment of Accounting Principles (the Wheat Committee) to ascertain whether improvements in the standard-setting process were possible. The leaders of the profession were frankly fearful of and wished to avoid government intervention into the standard-setting process. The Committee recommended a new and more independent standard-setting organization to replace the Accounting Principles Board. This recommendation, approved by the AICPA and effective July 1, 1973, established the Financial Accounting Standards Board.

The major differences between the FASB and its predecessors can be summarized under five broad categories:

1. *Reduced membership.* The FASB has 7 voting members, whereas the APB had 18.
2. *Financial independence.* Not only are the seven members paid a sufficient salary, but the FASB is also financed by a wide cross-section of organizations, none of which contributes a large percentage of its budget. Further, the Board produces substantial cash inflows through its publications. Currently, the Board has developed adequate cash balances that could see it through several years of activity. This is quite different from the APB, where members were paid directly by the organization from which they were appointed. The APB had no separate funding.
3. *Reporting autonomy.* Members resign from their prior organizations and are answerable only to the Financial Accounting Foundation. Members cannot retain investments in companies and hence may be more objective. Board members also serve for longer periods (currently, up to 10 years) than did members of the APB.

---

[12] In fact, Congress passed a law permitting the investment tax credit to be "flowed through" to income in the year taken for taxes. This situation illustrates the ultimate power of the Congress over accounting standard setting.

4. *Broad representation.* Membership does not require that members hold the CPA certificate. Lack of representation, particularly of business, on the APB was a major factor in the replacement of the APB with the FASB. The attempt to keep the Board membership diverse is a continuing problem due to two factors:
   a. The difficulty of getting individuals to serve who would represent the user viewpoint.
   b. Continued pressure by well-organized preparer groups to increase their proportional representation.
5. *Increased staff and advisory support.* The FASB has its own staff, research group, and a widely based advisory body (having overlapping appointments) available to advise the Board on its agenda and proposed releases. Further, it can create additional groups to help expedite its mission. This option has been exercised most prominently by the creation of the Emerging Issues Task Force (EITF) in 1984 to address issues that require technical guidance and are amenable to quick resolution but are of limited importance and scope.

Since July 1, 1973, the Financial Accounting Standards Board has been responsible for establishing the accounting standards that constitute generally accepted accounting principles. The organization quickly recognized the principles formulated by the two prior standard-setting groups established by the AICPA, the Committee on Accounting Procedure and the Accounting Principles Board. These principles consisted of CAP's *Accounting Research Bulletins* and the APB's *Opinions.*

The FASB has since added to this body of generally accepted accounting principles. To date, it has issued two primary categories of pronouncements:

1. *Statements of Financial Accounting Concepts (SFACs)*—The purpose of this series is to provide fundamental concepts on which financial accounting and reporting standards will be based. *SFACs* are not GAAP.
2. *Statements of Financial Accounting Standards (SFASs)*—The FASB calls its major pronouncements *statements of standards* rather than *Opinions*, the title used by the APB. These statements provide accounting principles and procedures on specific accounting issues. *SFASs* are GAAP.

The FASB currently follows a **due process** procedure in developing accounting standards. This process uses an open format that provides an opportunity for interested parties to express their views. The standard-setting process used by the FASB involves the following nine steps:

1. Select and prioritize issues for the Board's agenda.
2. Appoint a representative task force to identify and define the problems and alternatives related to each issue, and conduct research and analysis about the issue.
3. Prepare a *discussion memorandum* on the issue and distribute it to interested parties.
4. Invite public comment on the *discussion memorandum*.
5. Schedule a public hearing (usually within three months following the *discussion memorandum*). Analyze comments received about the issues.
6. Decide whether to issue a standard. If the decision is yes, prepare an *exposure draft* of the standard and distribute it to all interested parties.
7. Public comment period: Analyze comments received about the *exposure draft* and revise as necessary.
8. Public hearing.
9. Approve (or disapprove) the *exposure draft* as revised, by a vote of at least five of the seven Board members. If approved, distribute the new standard.[13]

---

[13] The five-to-two supermajority vote was reinstituted for statements issued after January 1, 1991. The Board was initially established with a supermajority voting rule, but this rule was changed to a simple majority in 1977. For an interesting discussion of the politics underlying the voting requirement changes, and one with which the authors agree, see D. Kirk, "Commentary on FASB Voting Requirements," *Accounting Horizons*, December 1990, pp. 108–13.

EXHIBIT 1-2   Nine Steps to Develop *SFAS No. 95*

Steps in the FASB Due Process	Approximate Chronology
1. Identify and study the problem	Dec. 1980–Dec. 1983
	1984—added to FASB agenda
2. Appoint a task force	1984
3. Issue Discussion Memorandum	2nd quarter 1984
4. Public comment period	1st quarter 1985
5. Public hearings	2nd quarter 1985
6. Issue Exposure Draft	July 31, 1986
7. Public comment period	Aug. 1986–Oct. 31, 1986
8. Public hearing	June 1987
9. Issue standard	Oct. 30, 1987

Typically the dates were often changed as unanticipated problems arose during the process.

For complex and controversial issues, some of these steps may be repeated. The process is typically lengthy and often consumes several years between the addition of an agenda item and a final statement. At times the process moves quickly. *SFAS No. 44,* "Accounting for Intangible Assets of Motor Carriers," was issued without either a *discussion memorandum* or a public hearing. The nine steps discussed above are illustrated in Exhibit 1–2 for *SFAS No. 95,* "Statement of Cash Flows" (issued October 30, 1987).

The form of due process is specified in the *FASB Rules of Procedure.* Due process is designed to ensure public input in the decisions of the FASB. Due process begins with the question of whether to add a topic to the Board's agenda. One member of the Board stated that "only things that are 'broke' get on the agenda, whether they are projects in new areas or reconsideration of old issues."

The average time from the date an issue is placed on the agenda (step 1) to the issuance of a standard (step 9) is two years.[14] A substantial part of this time is used to elicit and analyze written responses received in answer to invitations to comment, discussion memoranda, exposure drafts, and public hearings. The time needed for a particular statement is related to the complexity of its issues and how controversial they are.[15]

CONCEPT REVIEW

1. Which organization has the statutory authority to prescribe financial accounting standards?
2. Which organization currently formulates generally accepted accounting principles?
3. What is the essence of the FASB's due process procedure?

What Is GAAP?

The term *generally accepted accounting principles* (GAAP) has been used several times already in this chapter. But precisely what is GAAP?

Generally accepted accounting principles refers to the broad guidelines, conventions, rules, and procedures of accounting. GAAP comes from two main sources:

---

[14] Adapted from *FASB Viewpoints,* October 31, 1986. This is a periodic newsletter distributed by the FASB.

[15] The Board issues periodic status reports on potential standards under consideration.

1. Pronouncements by designated authoritative bodies that must be followed in all applicable cases. The primary designated bodies are the Financial Accounting Standards Board (*Statements* and *Interpretations*), Accounting Principles Board (*Opinions*), Committee on Accounting Procedures (selected pronouncements), and the Securities and Exchange Commission (regulations for listed companies). This part of GAAP is identified in the remaining chapters by references to the sources.
2. Accounting practices developed by respected bodies and industries or that have evolved over time. This part of GAAP sometimes is difficult to identify by source; the source may be "general acceptability." Therefore, considerable disagreement exists among accountants about GAAP from these sources. However, a considerable part of this kind of GAAP is formally expressed in such publications as *AICPA Statements of Position, Accounting and Auditing Guides,* and *FASB Technical Bulletins.* In some instances, specific topics not covered by these sources can be found in the accounting literature, including textbooks.

Official Accounting Pronouncements Related to GAAP

A list of official pronouncements currently in force and the addresses of organizations actively contributing to the pronouncement development process are given inside the front and back covers. For easy reference by pronouncement this list gives the (*a*) designated number, (*b*) date issued, and (*c*) title. The following pronouncements are listed:

1. *Accounting Research Bulletins (ARBs) Nos. 1–51;* issued by the AICPA, 1939 to 1959.
2. *Accounting Terminology Bulletins Nos. 1–4;* issued by the AICPA, 1953 to 1959.
3. *Accounting Principles Board (APB) Opinions;* issued by the AICPA, 1962 to 1973.
4. *Industry Audit Guides;* issued by the AICPA.
5. *Statements of Financial Accounting Concepts;* issued by the FASB, 1978 to 1985.
6. *Statements of Financial Accounting Standards;* issued by the FASB, 1973 to date.
7. *Interpretations;* issued by the FASB, 1974 to date.
8. *Technical Bulletins;* issued by the FASB, 1979 to date.
9. *Statements of Government Accounting Standards (SGASs);* issued by the GASB, 1984 to date.

Item 5, *Statements of Financial Accounting Concepts,* will be covered extensively in Chapter 2, with a discussion of the conceptual framework of accounting.

Attaining Consensus in a Political Environment

The development of generally accepted accounting principles began in the early 1930s. Throughout those efforts, the primary objective was to develop a conceptual framework and related implementation guidelines that would represent a *consensus* of the preparers, users, and independent auditors. This goal has not been wholly attained. The conceptual framework and implementation guidelines would serve the preparers, auditors, and users alike. That is, it was felt that each of these groups should benefit from financial statements that are based on a conceptual framework with consensus approval. The diverse goals, interests, and influence of each of these groups have, however, created many difficulties and conflicts. A *political process* is involved that must reconcile the general interest, the conceptual and technical characteristics of accounting itself, and the specific interests of all three groups—preparers, auditors, and users.

The cooperative approach of the preparers, auditors, and users to attain a consensus resulted in the establishment of the FASB (1973) as an independent, highly

EXHIBIT 1-3   Participation in Attaining a Consensus in Setting Accounting Standards

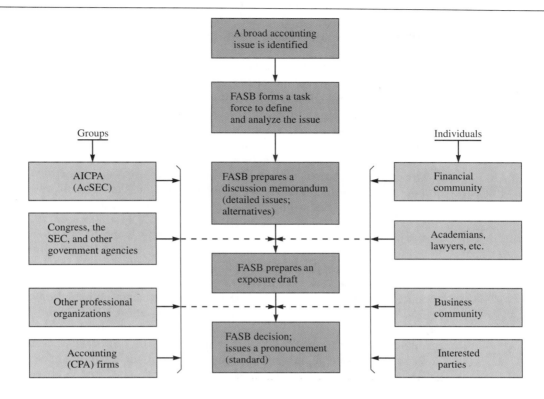

qualified, decision-making group. This approach also led to the development of a process for resolving accounting issues (see the nine steps summarized previously), and a requirement that the decisions of the FASB on accounting issues be followed. In the opinion of many people, the success of this process of formulating a consensus on accounting standards depends on the conceptual soundness, absence of bias, and appropriate cost-benefit trade-offs in the application of the decisions of the FASB. The consensus approach is illustrated in Exhibit 1-3.

A directly related issue is **compliance** with the prescribed accounting standards. The FASB has no authority or responsibility to enforce compliance. That responsibility rests with the preparers and the accounting profession primarily through the AICPA, SEC, state boards of accountancy, and the courts. Many observers believe that compliance is a weak link in the chain. This view is supported by recurring oversight actions of the SEC, increasing litigation in the courts, and the escalating cost of liability insurance premiums paid by auditing firms.

Throughout the evolution of the standard-setting activities and compliance, the issue persists of whether these activities should continue to be a responsibility of the private sector or should be taken over by the public sector; that is, by legislative action of the Congress and a federal agency. Many believe that these activities should reside with the private sector exclusively. These individuals maintain that governmental regulation would not be effective. They believe that the preparers, auditors, and users can provide adequate policing action to protect the public interest. They also think that legislative action and a federal agency would result in inflexibility in meeting new challenges, slow reaction time to problems, an ineffective public forum, stereotyped reporting, and a rule-bound environment. By contrast, others believe that legislative action and a responsible government agency are necessary to properly oversee the rule-making and enforcement activities. Still others feel that a cooperative effort by the private and public sectors would be more appropriate.

The concern reflects the increased interest evidenced by Congress in all professions recently. In particular, recent cases of corporate fraud, bankruptcies, and related issues have resulted in congressional inquiry into whether the current regulatory arrangement between the SEC and the FASB in accounting standard setting is working effectively.

A 1976 House of Representatives committee, chaired by Congressman John Moss, prepared a report that criticized the FASB for failing to remove alternative means of accounting for identical transactions. The Moss committee was followed in 1977 by a Senate committee chaired by Senator Lee Metcalf. This committee was even more critical of the standard-setting process. In particular, the committee deplored the delegation of standard setting to a privately constituted body, the FASB, which the committee believed acted in self-interest.

More recently, Congressman John Dingell's committee held hearings in 1988 on a number of accounting matters, including the timeliness and effectiveness of accounting standards. Congressional concerns arose due to extensive frauds and bankruptcies in the prior years, including the collapse of Drysdale Government Securities and Penn Square Bank. The profession's response was both substantive and timely. Because of this response and the testimony of the FASB's chairman before the Dingell committee, the Board apparently secured the support of this important senator for the current standard-setting process.[16]

Since its organization in 1973, the FASB alone has issued over 100 *Statements of Financial Accounting Standards* and 6 *Statements of Accounting Concepts*. Of these, approximately 10% have been on new issues, 10% deal with specific industry problems, and 80% revisit old issues. Statements on old issues tend to be the most controversial—one member of the board identified accounting for pensions and other postretirement benefits as the most controversial. The controversy basically concerns how much of the liability should be reported on the balance sheet. Some of the controversial issues have been around for more than 50 years. The following is a list of some recurring issues that are still controversial:[17]

1. Capitalization versus expensing.
   a. Research and development costs.
   b. Interest costs.
   c. Software development costs.
   d. Oil and gas accounting.
2. Off-balance-sheet financing.
   a. Leases.
   b. Pensions.
   c. Unconsolidated finance subsidiaries.
   d. Purchase commitments.
3. Income taxes.
   a. Deferred taxes.
   b. Investment tax credit.
4. Changing prices.
   a. Price-level adjustments.
   b. Current value.

The controversy in each case reflects the fact that these issues are complex, that they have more than one reasonable solution, and that the choice of treatment makes a substantial difference in the ultimate dollar amounts reported in the financial statements.

Influential groups and organizations use the due process procedures of the Board to plead their case for alternative solutions. The arguments include cost-benefit arguments, claims that the proposed accounting treatment is not theoretically sound, statements that the reporting will not be understandable by users, implementation issues, and concerns that the economic consequences of the proposed standard will be disastrous to the firm, the industry, or the country. Government agencies, preparer organizations such as the Business Roundtable, industry, and associations

---

[16] C. Loomis, "Will 'FASB' Pinch Your Bottom Line?" *Fortune,* December 19, 1988, p. 108.

[17] See Miller and Redding, *The FASB,* p. 84.

such as the Financial Executives Institute create substantial pressures on the board.[18] Unfortunately, users are not well represented in this political game. This lobbying, however, also has the positive result of informing Board members about issues they might otherwise overlook or underestimate.

Standard setting is carried out in a political environment that can't help but affect the process, whether we like it or not. The accounting for oil and gas exploration costs, noted earlier in the chapter, is illustrative. The substantive question is whether the motivation for a standard ought to be the impact of the standard on the distribution of wealth, the country's trade balance, the type of compensation packages offered employees, the level of research and development expenditures, and so on or, alternatively, whether it should be a neutral reporting of the financial events.

Some believe that if a standard has economic implications—and most, if not all, do—the Board should not ignore these implications. A few would go further and argue that standards *should* be a means of implementing economic policy. Others would argue this is not the province of the Board. The Board is not elected but rather appointed by private parties. Economic policy is appropriately left to the country's elected representatives. Further, they maintain, even were it appropriate for the Board to concern itself with economic consequences, its members are not wise enough to do so, given the complex and subtle nature of our economy.[19]

Regardless of the merits of the alternative positions, the important point for us is the Board's attitude toward the issue. The Board's position is articulated in its mission statement; in conducting its activities, the Board will "insure, insofar as possible, neutrality of information resulting from its standards. To be neutral, information must report economic activity as faithfully as possible without coloring the image it communicates for the purpose of influencing behavior in any particular direction." In *SFAC No. 2,* par. 102 the Board specifically rejects any attempt to influence government policy and argues, further, that any such response is inappropriate. "The Board concludes that it is not feasible to change financial accounting standards that accountants use every time government policy changes direction, even if it were desirable to do so. Moreover, only if accounting information is neutral can it safely by used to help guide those policies as well as measure their results."

This position is, however, not easily maintained. Not only does the Board concern itself with implementation costs, but it also tries subjectively to balance these against the financial reporting benefits, a tough task at best.[20] Moreover, although it may be difficult to document, it is likely that consideration of alleged consequences has influenced the Board's actions.

OTHER STANDARD-SETTING ORGANIZATIONS
◆

The Committee on Accounting Procedures and the Accounting Principles Board were both Committees of the AICPA. When the APB was replaced by the FASB, the AICPA set up the Accounting Standards Executive Committee (AcSEC), which was authorized to express the AICPA's position on matters involving financial reporting.

AcSEC quickly exercised its voice through the issuance of *Statements of Position (SOPs),* which addressed emerging problems not being considered by either the FASB or the SEC. By 1979, the FASB became concerned that AcSEC was becoming another standard-setting body. The issue was resolved by the FASB at its March

---

[18] A recent example is the extensive letter-writing campaign conducted by the utility industry prior to the issuance of *SFAS No. 90* dealing with abandonment and disallowance of plant costs in regulated enterprises.

[19] For a further discussion see S. Zeff, "The Rise and Fall of Economic Consequences," *Journal of Accountancy,* December 1978, pp. 56–63.

[20] Delays permitted in implementing new standards are, perhaps, the most visible sign of the Board's recognition of the implementation costs. The Board also commissions field tests to learn about implementation costs. An example was the study to determine the cost of implementing the reporting of the effects of changing prices before the issuance of *SFAS No. 33.*

22 and April 26, 1979, meetings when it "agreed to exercise responsibility for all specialized accounting and reporting practices in the existing AICPA *SOPs* and *Guides* by extracting those specialized principles and practices from the *SOPs* and *Guides* and issuing them as FASB Statements, after appropriate due process."[21] *SFAS No. 32* was then passed to allow the Board thereafter to exercise responsibility for amending and interpreting the *SOPs* and *Guides* on accounting and auditing matters until the relevant *SFASs* were issued. This action placed the standard-setting process more firmly under the FASB's control. The Board also initiated its Technical Bulletin Series at that time to respond to the AICPA's concern with timeliness. More recently, the creation of the Emerging Issues Task Force (EITF) in May 1984 further illustrates the Board's desire to deflect AICPA interest in becoming a standard setter. The EITF was created explicitly in response to a recommendation made by several accounting firms and proposed in the August 1982 report of the Financial Accounting Foundation Structure Committee. The Board remains open to AICPA concerns through communications from the AICPA in the form of issue papers that provide the Board with an early exposure to late-developing reporting problems, alternative approaches, and AICPA-recommended solutions.

In 1984, and after a good deal of often heated debate, the Financial Accounting Foundation established a separate body to develop standards for municipal and state units, hospitals, utility authorities, universities, and other not-for-profit organizations. The Governmental Accounting Standards Board (GASB) was established on a trial basis and operates similarly to the FASB. The trial period has now passed, and the GASB is continuing operations. Since some of the organizations covered under the standards set by GASB operate for profit and others do not (hospitals and universities, for example), jurisdictional problems with the FASB inevitably arise. An important task that will continue to face the FAF and the two Boards is finding a workable solution to the jurisdictional issue. Recently the FAF has adopted a solution that places primary responsibility for most of the jurisdictional issues with the FASB.

Still other organizations would like to play a role in this process by issuing statements on accounting practice. The insurance, real estate, savings and loan, and banking industries provide examples. In addition, the SEC has been known to reject a statement (e.g., regarding oil and gas accounting in *SFAS No. 19*). Several such actions by the SEC (which, given the close working relations between the SEC and FASB, seems highly unlikely) or intervention by government (e.g., the investment tax credit), could seriously weaken the current standard-setting structure. An alternative standard-setting model already exists in government agencies, which can establish reporting practices without regard for compliance with either *SFASs* or *SGASs*. The current extent of private standard setting should not be assumed to be inviolate. Continued vigilance and responsiveness is necessary if standard setting is to remain with an organization like the FASB.

CONCEPT REVIEW

1. What constitutes GAAP?
2. Would the FASB agree or disagree with the following statement? "Neutrality in standard setting means that the accounting should reflect the economic content of a transaction without regard to the ultimate social implications."
3. What is it about some accounting issues that makes them controversial and hence likely to appear on the FASB's agenda?

---

[21] *SFAS No. 32*, p. 1.

SUMMARY OF KEY POINTS

(L.O. 1, 2, 3) 1. Accounting is an information system whose purpose is to identify, collect, measure, and communicate information about economic units to those with an interest in the unit's financial affairs. This is accomplished through the periodic issuance of external financial statements.

(L.O. 2) 2. The objective of external financial statements is to disclose the economic effects of completed transactions and other events on the organization for use in decision making.

(L.O. 2) 3. The externally reported financial statements include the balance sheet, income statement, statement of retained earnings, and the statement of cash flows.

(L.O. 3) 4. The reporting of such information as the composition of assets and the changes in income allows decision makers to assess the opportunities for gain and the risks of loss inherent in the organization.

(L.O. 4, 5) 5. The rules and principles under which the external financial statements are constructed are known as *generally accepted accounting principles* (GAAP) and are currently established by the Financial Accounting Standards Board (FASB).

(L.O. 5, 6) 6. The FASB is an independently funded private organization operating under extensive due process procedures, broad participation, and authority delegated through Congress and the SEC to formulate accounting principles.

(L.O. 4, 6) 7. Setting external financial reporting standards is a complex process occurring within a political environment that influences both what reporting is required and when. Business, trade and consumer associations, courts, public accounting firms, individual users, and government at both state and federal levels can and do influence reporting practice.

(L.O. 3, 4, 6) 8. The FASB's mission statement indicates that the Board will adopt a neutral position toward the economic consequences of its standards. However, it has been difficult, and at times impossible, for the Board to ignore the impact of external financial statements on the allocation of economic resources and the distribution of wealth.

(L.O. 4) 9. Other organizations, including the Accounting Standards Executive Committee (AcSEC), the Governmental Accounting Standards Board (GASB), Congress, and the SEC, play a role in setting accounting standards.

REVIEW PROBLEM

Amendments to the Farm Credit Act permit crop losses to be spread over a 20-year period. Is this good accounting? Why do you suppose these amendments were formulated? Do you believe the FASB would support the passage of the amendments? Why or why not?

SOLUTION

It can be argued that this is not good accounting. Losses should be recognized when they occur. This includes losses from crop failures. The amendments were passed to ease the impact of large losses (probably inadequately covered by insurance) on farm income statements and balance sheets. Framers of the amendments probably believed it would be more difficult for these farms to qualify for new loans because the farms were more likely to be in default on existing loans if the losses were immediately recognized in full. Framers of the amendment apparently felt lenders would not restructure the current loans and would perhaps foreclose on existing mortgages if the new accounting rule were not adopted. The impact of "how the score is kept" on decisions is evident here. The question is not whether a loss has occurred but, instead, how and when that loss is recognized in the financial reports.

The political environment of standard setting is also evident. The FASB was not supportive of the amendments and so testified before Congress. Among other matters the Board was concerned about financial accounting and political precedents that might result. Nevertheless, Congress can pass such legislation, and government agencies may tend to favor expedient accounting when it serves policy objectives.

This is a major reason why the private sector overwhelmingly supports the formulation of financial reporting standards by an organization insulated, at least partly, from political pressure.

APPENDIX | *AICPA Code of Professional Conduct*

The Code of Professional Conduct is too lengthy to include in its entirety. We have elected to include the Preamble, Articles I through VI (without subsections), Applicability, Rules 101, 102, 201 to 203, 301, 302, 501 to 503, and 505. All rules are given without their related interpretations or rulings that existed before the adoption of the Code of Professional Conduct in January 1988. More extensive coverage can be found in *AICPA, Professional Standards,* Volume 2, published by the Commerce Clearing House, Inc., Chicago, Illinois, 1988.

Preamble

Membership in the American Institute of Certified Public Accountants is voluntary. By accepting membership, a certified public accountant assumes an obligation of self-discipline above and beyond the requirements of laws and regulations.

These Principles of the Code of Professional Conduct of the American Institute of Certified Public Accountants express the profession's recognition of its responsibilities to the public, to clients, and to colleagues. They guide members in the performance of their professional responsibilities and express the basic tenets of ethical and professional conduct. The Principles call for an unswerving commitment to honorable behavior, even at the sacrifice of personal advantage.

Article I—Responsibilities

In carrying out their responsibilities as professionals, members should exercise sensitive professional and moral judgments in all their activities.

Article II—The Public Interest

Members should accept the obligation to act in a way that will serve the public interest, honor the public trust, and demonstrate commitment to professionalism.

Article III—Integrity

To maintain and broaden public confidence, members should perform all professional responsibilities with the highest sense of integrity.

Article IV—Objectivity and Independence

A member should maintain objectivity and be free of conflicts of interest in discharging professional responsibilities. A member in public practice should be independent in fact and appearance when providing auditing and other attestation services.

Article V—Due Care

A member should observe the profession's technical and ethical standards, strive continually to improve competence and the quality of services, and discharge professional responsibility to the best of the member's ability.

Article VI—Scope and Nature of Services

A member in public practice should observe the Principles of the Code of Professional Conduct in determining the scope and nature of services to be provided.

Applicability

The bylaws of the American Institute of Certified Public Accountants require that members adhere to the Rules of the Code of Professional Conduct. Members must be prepared to justify departures from these Rules.

Rule 101—Independence

A member in public practice shall be independent in the performance of professional services as required by standards promulgated by bodies designated by Council.

Rule 102—Integrity and Objectivity

In the performance of any professional service, a member shall maintain objectivity and integrity, shall be free of conflicts of interest, and shall not knowingly misrepresent facts or subordinate his or her judgment to others.

Rule 201—General Standards

A member shall comply with the following standards and with any interpretations thereof by bodies designated by Council.

A. *Professional competence.* Undertake only those professional services that the member or the member's firm can reasonably expect to be completed with professional competence.

B. *Due professional care.* Exercise due professional care in the performance of professional services.

C. *Planning and supervision.* Adequately plan and supervise the performance of professional services.

D.. *Sufficient relevant data.* Obtain sufficient relevant data to afford a reasonable basis for conclusions or recommendations in relation to any professional services performed.

Rule 202—Compliance with Standards

A member who performs auditing, review, compilation, management advisory, tax, or other professional services shall comply with standards promulgated by bodies designated by Council.

Rule 203—Accounting Principles

A member shall not (1) express an opinion or state affirmatively that the financial statements or other financial data of any entity are presented in conformity with generally accepted accounting principles or (2) state that he or she is not aware of any material modifications that should be made to such statements or data in order for them to be in conformity with generally accepted accounting principles, if such statements or data contain any departure from an accounting principle promulgated by bodies designated by Council to establish such principles that has a material effect on the statements or data taken as a whole. If, however, the statements or data contain such a departure and the member can demonstrate that due to unusual circumstances the financial statements or data would otherwise have been misleading, the member can comply with the rule by describing the departure, its approximate effects, if practicable, and the reasons why compliance with the principle would result in a misleading statement.

Rule 301—Confidential Client Information

A member in public practice shall not disclose any confidential client information without the specific consent of the client.

This rule shall not be construed (1) to relieve a member of his or her professional obligations under rules 202 and 203, (2) to affect in any way the member's obligation to comply with a validly issued and enforceable subpoena or summons, (3) to prohibit review of a member's professional practice under AICPA or state CPA society authorization, or (4) to preclude a member from initiating a complaint with or responding to any inquiry made by a recognized investigative or disciplinary body.

Members of a recognized investigative or disciplinary body and professional practice reviewers shall not use to their own advantage or disclose any member's confidential client information that comes to their attention in carrying out their official responsibilities. However, this prohibition shall not restrict the exchange of information with a recognized investigative or disciplinary body or affect, in any way, compliance with a validly issued and enforceable subpoena or summons.

Rule 302—Contingent Fees

Professional services shall not be offered or rendered under an arrangement whereby no fee will be charged unless a specified finding or result is attained, or where the fee is otherwise contingent upon the findings or results of such services. However, a member's fees may vary depending, for example, on the complexity of services rendered.

Fees are not regarded as being contingent if fixed by courts or other public authorities, or, in tax matters, if determined based on the results of judicial proceedings or the findings of governmental agencies.

Rule 501—Acts Discreditable

A member shall not commit an act discreditable to the profession.

Rule 502—Advertising and Other Forms of Solicitation

A member in public practice shall not seek to obtain clients by advertising or other forms of solicitation in a manner that is false, misleading, or deceptive. Solicitation by the use of coercion, overreaching, or harassing conduct is prohibited.

Rule 503—Commissions

The acceptance by a member in public practice of a payment for the referral of products or services of others to a client is prohibited. Such action is considered to create a conflict of interest that results in a loss of objectivity and independence.

A member shall not make a payment to obtain a client. This rule shall not prohibit payments for the purchase of an accounting practice or retirement payments to individuals formerly engaged in the practice of public accounting or payments to their heirs or estates.

Rule 505—Form of Practice and Name

A member may practice public accounting only in the form of a proprietorship, a partnership, or a professional corporation whose characteristics conform to resolutions of Council.

A member shall not practice public accounting under a firm name that is misleading. Names of one or more past partners or shareholders may be included in the firm name of a successor partnership or corporation. Also, a partner or shareholder surviving the death or withdrawal of all other partners or shareholders may continue to practice under such name which includes the name of past partners or shareholders for up to two years after becoming a sole practitioner.

A firm may not designate itself as "Members of the American Institute of Certified Public Accountants" unless all of its partners or shareholders are members of the Institute.

KEY TERMS

Accounting as an information system (7)
Accounting Principles Board (APB) (14)
Accounting Principles Board Opinions (Opinions) (15)
Accounting Research Bulletins (ARBs) (15)
American Accounting Association (17)
American Institute of Certified Public Accountants (AICPA) (10)
Balance sheet (8)
Committee on Accounting Procedure (CAP) (14)
Compliance (23)
Due process (20)
Financial Accounting Standards Board (FASB) (4)

Generally accepted accounting principles (GAAP) (8)
Governmental Accounting Standards Board (GASB) (17)
Income statement (8)
Securities and Exchange Commission (SEC) (14)
Statement of cash flows (8)
Statement of retained earnings (8)
Statements of Financial Accounting Concepts (SFACs) (20)
Statements of Financial Accounting Standards (SFASs) (20)

QUESTIONS

1. How would you describe what accounting is?
2. Explain the distinction between financial and management accounting. Does this distinction mean that a company should have two accounting systems? Explain.
3. What is meant by general-purpose financial statements? What are their basic components?
4. What is the basic objective of external financial statements?
5. Why the emphasis in financial accounting on communication?
6. What are the primary areas of service provided by certified public accountants (CPAs)?
7. The independent CPA fulfills a unique professional role that involves the concept of independence. Why is that concept important to society in general?

8. The following statements relate to accounting principles, standards, and procedures. For each, explain its primary purpose and current status.
   a. *Accounting Research Bulletins.*
   b. *Opinions* of the APB.
   c. *FASB Statements of Financial Accounting Standards.*
   d. *FASB Interpretations.*
   e. *FASB Statements of Financial Accounting Concepts.*
9. What developments led to the establishment of the FASB?
10. Briefly explain the SEC's role in establishing accounting standards. What has been its relationship to the accounting profession in this role?
11. What is the AAA? What is its role in developing accounting theory and standards?
12. Why is there widespread interest in the development of accounting standards?
13. Briefly explain the due process system used by the FASB to develop an accounting standard.
14. Why is a consensus important with respect to accounting standards? How is a consensus attained at the present time?

EXERCISES

E 1-1
Chapter Overview
(L.O. 1, 2)

Indicate whether each statement is true or false.

T F 1. GAAP must be followed for all items in management accounting and financial accounting reports.
T F 2. Financial accounting focuses primarily on external users of financial statements.
T F 3. General-purpose financial statements are prepared primarily for internal users.
T F 4. Management accounting is directly concerned with stockholders and creditors.
T F 5. Management accounting reports usually are not subject to an independent audit.
T F 6. A CPA always serves in an independent role.
T F 7. CPAs in public accounting practice are not permitted to become involved in management services.
T F 8. The attest and audit functions are the same.
T F 9. Disclosure notes are considered an integral part of external financial statements.
T F 10. Management accounting reporting requires a balance sheet, an income statement, and a statement of cash flows.
T F 11. Internal reporting (i.e., management accounting) must follow GAAP in all respects.
T F 12. External financial reports are directed primarily to stockholders, creditors, and other similarly situated groups.

E 1-2
Distinguish between
Financial and
Management Accounting
(L.O. 2)

The two basic types of accounting and reporting are called *financial accounting* (F) and *management accounting* (M). Ten characteristics of accounting and reporting are listed below. Match the types with the characteristics by entering an F or M in each blank shown to the left. If not applicable, enter N.

Type	Characteristics of accounting and reporting
_____	1. GAAP must be followed in all respects.
_____	2. External users are of primary concern.
_____	3. Relates to planning and controlling the operations of an entity.
_____	4. Does not primarily use general-purpose financial statements.
_____	5. Information for both internal and external use.
_____	6. Of particular interest to investors and creditors.
_____	7. Does not have to conform to GAAP in all respects.
_____	8. Provides information that is useful to external users in predicting future cash flows.
_____	9. Internal users are of primary concern.
_____	10. Seldom, if ever, subject to independent audit.
_____	11. Does not relate primarily to internal planning and control.
_____	12. Information primarily for internal use.
_____	13. Usually not available to external users.
_____	14. Uses general-purpose financial statements.
_____	15. Users have direct access to the internal operations.

E 1–3
Identify Accounting
Organizations
(L.O. 4)

Organizations active in setting accounting standards and the designation of some of those standards are listed below. To the right are commonly used abbreviations. Match the designations with the abbreviations by entering the appropriate letters to the left.

Designation	Abbreviation
__A__ Sample: Certified Public Accountant.	A. CPA.
__H__ 1. Accounting Research Bulletin.	B. FASB.
__G__ 2. Accounting Principles Board.	C. GAAP.
__E__ 3. Committee on Accounting Procedures.	D. AICPA.
__J__ 4. Securities and Exchange Commission.	E. CAP.
__B__ 5. Financial Accounting Standards Board.	F. 10-Q report.
__K__ 6. SEC annual reports (required).	G. APB.
__D__ 7. American Institute of CPAs.	H. ARB.
__F__ 8. SEC quarterly report (required).	I. FAF
__L__ 9. Financial Executives Institute.	J. SEC.
__C__ 10. Generally accepted accounting principles.	K. 10-K report.
__I__ 11. Financial Accounting Foundation	L. FEI.
__M__ 12. Financial Accounting Advisory Committee.	M. FASAC.
__O__ 13. National Association of Accountants.	N. GASB.
__N__ 14. Governmental Accounting Standards Board	O. NAA.

E 1–4
Sources of GAAP
(L.O. 5)

The accounting profession has a long history of developing accounting concepts and their application that constitute generally accepted accounting principles (GAAP). Listed below are some representative documents. Identify each document with its source by entering the appropriate letters to the left.

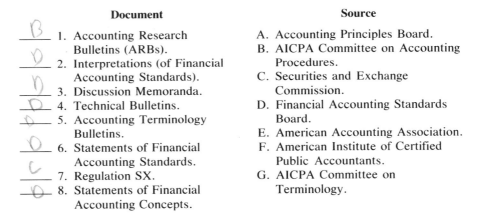

Document	Source
__B__ 1. Accounting Research Bulletins (ARBs).	A. Accounting Principles Board.
__D__ 2. Interpretations (of Financial Accounting Standards).	B. AICPA Committee on Accounting Procedures.
__D__ 3. Discussion Memoranda.	C. Securities and Exchange Commission.
__D__ 4. Technical Bulletins.	D. Financial Accounting Standards Board.
__D__ 5. Accounting Terminology Bulletins.	E. American Accounting Association.
__D__ 6. Statements of Financial Accounting Standards.	F. American Institute of Certified Public Accountants.
__C__ 7. Regulation SX.	G. AICPA Committee on Terminology.
__D__ 8. Statements of Financial Accounting Concepts.	

E 1–5
Consensus Groups in
Standard Setting
(L.O. 5)

The process of attaining a consensus in developing accounting standards involves three major groups, each of which is directly concerned with general-purpose financial statements. Each major group is composed of various subgroups.

The three major groups and some subgroups are listed below. Identify the subgroups with the major groups by entering appropriate letters to the left; provide comments when needed for clarification.

Subgroups	Major groups
_____ 1. American Institute of CPAs.	A. Preparers.
_____ 2. Current stockholder.	B. Auditors.
_____ 3. General Motors.	C. Users.
_____ 4. UAW (labor union)	D. None of the above
_____ 5. Financial Executives Institute	(explain).
_____ 6. Price Waterhouse (accounting firm).	
_____ 7. Lending institutions.	
_____ 8. Securities and Exchange Commission.	

———— 9. OK Bookkeeping Service.
———— 10. Financial analysts.
———— 11. Sole owner of a small business.
———— 12. American Accounting Association.
———— 13. State Board of Public Accountancy.
———— 14. Potential investors.
———— 15. Financial Analysts Federation.
———— 16. Employees of companies.
———— 17. Teachers and students.
———— 18. Taxing and regulatory authorities.
———— 19. Legislators.
———— 20. Two-member local CPA firm.

PROBLEMS

P 1-1
Accounting Principles
(L.O. 3, 4, 5)

At the completion of the annual audit of the financial statements of Alt Corporation, the president of the company asked about the meaning of the phrase *generally accepted accounting principles* that appears in the audit report on the management's financial statements. She observes that the meaning of the phrase must include more than what she considers to be "principles."

You have been asked to respond to the president's question. You have decided to respond in terms of the following:

a. The meaning of the term *accounting principles* as used in audit reports (excluding what "generally accepted" means).
b. How to determine whether an "accounting principle" is generally accepted. Consider sources of evidence to determine whether there is substantial authoritative support (do not merely list titles of documents).
c. Diversity in accounting practice will, and should, always exist among companies despite efforts to improve comparability. Discuss arguments that support this statement.

(AICPA adapted)

P 1-2
Sources of Accounting
Standards
(L.O. 5)

The four primary sources of specified accounting standards (GAAP) are the Committee on Accounting Procedures, Accounting Principles Board, Financial Accounting Standards Board, and the Securities and Exchange Commission. This problem involves consideration of these sources, their current status, their characteristics, and some assessments of the related successes and shortcomings.

Required:

1. Background—For each of the four sources of specified GAAP, identify the sponsoring or appointing organization and give the time period of activity.
2. Background continued—Give the designations of the pronouncements (or publications) issued and, in general, their current status.
3. Characterize each of the four sources of accounting standards as either a public- or private-sector organization. Assess the successes and weaknesses of each source.

P 1-3
Alternative Approaches to
Setting Accounting
Standards
(L.O. 6)

Explain and assess the following approaches to setting accounting standards.
a. Private sector exclusively.
b. Public sector exclusively.
c. Jointly. Include a consideration of the politics of a standard-setting approach.

CASES

C 1-1
Neutrality in Reporting
(L.O. 6)

Amendments to the Farm Credit Act permit crop losses to be spread over a 20-year future period (see the chapter review problem). Is this in accord with neutral reporting as articulated by the FASB?

C 1–2
Potential Accounting
Standard
(L.O. 4, 5, 6)

"We're just asking companies to 'fess up' to the cost of their promises" (*Forbes,* January 9, 1989, p. 322). The quote is attributed to Diana Scott, of the Financial Accounting Standards Board (FASB). What is Ms. Scott referring to? The issue is the extent of liabilities companies have for retiree health care programs currently not recorded on their financial books. Estimates of these liabilities run anywhere from $220 billion to $2 trillion, according to *Forbes.* If recognized, the amounts would drastically affect the debt levels of many firms. Christopher Steffen, vice president and controller of Chrysler, recently said he expects Chrysler's reported health costs to at least double to upwards of $1.2 billion under proposed reporting rules (*Fortune,* December 19, 1988, p. 108). "The liabilities exist and we have to recognize them," says Scott. Firms currently follow a pay-as-you-go philosophy. No liability is recognized. Is this practice good accounting from a conceptual point of view? Discuss.

C 1–3
Evaluating a New
Accounting Standard
(L.O. 3, 4)

In 1987, the FASB passed a new standard (*SFAS No. 94*) that requires companies to add together the results of all their subsidiary companies with the results of the parent regardless of the lines of business. In particular, this means that firms with finance subsidiaries, like General Motors (GM), would add their financing activities to their motor vehicle business results. For GM in 1987, revenues would have risen from $102 billion to $114 billion, and both assets and liabilities would have increased substantially. Does this change in reporting assist the decisions of those using financial statements? Does it influence GMs stock price? Should it?

The FASB's Conceptual Framework of Accounting

LEARNING OBJECTIVES
♦

After you have studied this chapter, you will:

1. Appreciate the need for and importance of the conceptual framework as it relates to financial reporting.

2. Be acquainted with who uses financial statements, why they use them, and what characteristics of accounting information are considered of critical importance.

3. Understand the recognition criterion and how it provides the conceptual basis of accrual accounting.

4. Be aware of the essential assumptions, implementation principles, and constraints underlying generally accepted accounting principles.

5. Know the elements of financial statements.

6. Be familiar with the history leading to the current conceptual framework and some potential future changes in the framework. (Refer to the appendix at the end of the chapter.)

◆

INTRODUCTION
◆

In a 1983 public offering of new securities, Sunshine Mining Company sold an issue of corporate bonds that set Wall Street brokers and investors abuzz. According to the prospectus filed with the SEC, Sunshine Mining, a major silver mining operator, proposed to redeem these bonds at maturity in a unique manner: each bondholder had the option of receiving either a flat $1,000 in cash, the bond's face value, or 50 ounces of silver—or the dollar equivalent of the silver.

Sunshine Mining's bonds were the first of a new breed of securities, later to be called *commodity-backed bonds*. The investing public was intrigued. If the market price for silver advanced to any point where 50 ounces of this semiprecious metal were worth more than $1,000, the bondholders stood to make a tidy profit, and the chance existed for a major killing if the price of silver went through the roof.

The unconventional nature of this bond offering raised a few eyebrows within the accounting profession as well. Sunshine Mining was setting a precedent that could become a trendsetter for other publicly owned corporations. What if General Motors used its products as an option for redeeming bond issues, offering to settle debt obligations in Oldsmobiles or Pontiacs as an alternative to cash? What if Procter & Gamble used its line of soaps and consumer products to do the same? Or McDonald's Corporation might join the parade offering to pay dividends to its shareholders in the form of burgers and fries.

As bizarre as these schemes might seem, none is completely unworkable. Given a particular prevailing investment mood and economic climate, almost anything is possible. In Sunshine Mining's case, it was a fairly desperate time, as it was for corporate capital raising in general. The early 1980s saw out-of-control inflation and interest rates. Even the so-called blue chip corporations couldn't sell new-issue securities to the public unless they offered investors some significant extra to sweeten the deal. Rated by investment analysts as a speculative-grade company, Sunshine Mining needed a sweetener in the worst way. Thus, the option to redeem the bonds for silver—the silver market was strong at the time—was dictated by the financial situation of the company and the current economic environment.

Accounting problems. On the accounting side of public offerings, the concern is for the issuing corporation's financial statements and the problems created when unconventional transactions, such as Sunshine Mining's bond offering, occur. What impact would this bond offering have on the company's balance sheet and, in turn, on the company's financial integrity? The answer depends in part on how the bonds are treated for accounting purposes.

Bonds are debt obligations, carried on the issuing corporation's books as liabilities. But in Sunshine Mining's case, at what dollar value should they be carried—at the face amount of the offering, $1,000 per bond, or at the current equivalent dollar value of the silver for which the bonds might be redeemed?

Depending on the accounting treatment elected—and in Sunshine Mining's case, depending on what happens in the silver market—a company might unwittingly misrepresent its financial position by either overstating or understating the dollar value of its debt obligations outstanding. External users could find it more difficult to evaluate the company. The stockholders and bondholders who rely on a corporation's financial statements for assurance that their investments are safe now and likely to remain so in the future might be misled. Bankers and other creditors that make loans and advance credit on the basis of financial strength as reported in the balance sheet might find it difficult to evaluate the company. Those that supply the company's material and service needs and that use the balance sheet to rate a corporate customer's creditworthiness might find it difficult to evaluate the company's ability to pay. Or the company's customers—especially in the industrial products markets—that also rely on financial statements for assurance of contract performance unimpeded by financial problems could face increased peformance uncertainty.

Accounting profession challenges. Chapter 2 discusses the accounting profession's responsibility to provide these external decision makers with financial statements they can use with reasonable levels of reliability and confidence. The challenge in carrying out the profession's responsibility, which extends to every accountant active in the practice, is twofold: (1) to determine the proper method of accounting and reporting and (2) to establish the amount, format, and principles underlying the information reported.

Corporate business and financial innovation. In the past, corporate America has never run short of creative ideas for conducting business and finding new ways to raise money and finance itself. There is no reason to suspect this high level of creativity and innovation to abate in the future. Each new form of business transaction typically means that new techniques are needed to account for it properly and report the results to external decision makers. The same is true for financing transactions—Sunshine Mining's commodity-backed bonds are a case in point. Each change in business practice and business financing brings with it the challenge of determining proper accounting and reporting.

The public's accounting information needs. No two individuals are exactly alike, nor do they have exactly the same information needs. This is especially true of external decision makers and their use of the accounting information presented in financial statements. Some people claim they need to know everything about a company, though the evidence suggests they actually use far less information than what is made available to them. At the other extreme are those who contend that they are bottom-line, cut-to-the-chase people who need only minimal information for their decision-making processes. The challenge for accountants is to determine how much accounting information to supply in *general purpose financial statements,* in what format, and under what assumptions, principles, and constraints.

Compounding the problem is the matter of corporate executives and CEOs who hold their own opinions on how much accounting information should be provided to external decision makers. Here, the spectrum of philosophies ranges from "Tell 'em only what they need to know" to "Tell 'em everything and let them figure it out."

Financial Accounting Standards Board. The information presented in this chapter focuses on the Financial Accounting Standards Board as the authoritative voice of the accounting profession. The FASB uses its rule-making authority and influence to keep the accounting profession and accounting practices in step with old and new business practices. The FASB also serves as the accounting profession's platform on matters concerning the manner and extent to which accounting information should be communicated. Explaining the role of the conceptual framework and how the Board uses it to help attain a consensus is an important focus of this chapter. Another focus is to become familiar with the accounting concepts and guidelines relied on by the Board as it considers the adoption or revision of accounting standards.

Sunshine Mining revisited. As this book is being prepared for printing, the price of silver is ranging between $5 and $6 per ounce. Sunshine's bonds mature in 1995. If you were asked to offer an opinion on how these bonds should be carried on Sunshine Mining's books, what would you say?

◆

THE FASB'S CONCEPTUAL FRAMEWORK
◆

Chapter 1 provides background information on a range of subjects related to the accounting profession's self-regulatory and rule-making composition. One of its main thrusts was to explain how the Financial Accounting Standards Board came into existence, how it functions, and how it serves the needs of the accounting profession.

The FASB's most important role is to keep the profession current and in general accord on topical accounting issues and interpretations of accounting principles. One of the FASB's goals is to keep accounting practice as standardized as possible. In that regard, the FASB is best known, both within the profession and without, for the various types of pronouncements it issues. These were detailed in Chapter 1. Among these pronouncements, the *Statement of Financial Accounting Standards (SFASs)* series is the Board's most recognized work. *SFASs* published by the Board since 1973 now constitute a major portion of the body of professional accounting principles and practice standards known as GAAP.

Chapter 2 continues the discussion of the Financial Accounting Standards Board. This time, however, the emphasis is on the Board's **conceptual framework** that is intended to serve as a constitution for the Board and the entire accounting profession. The conceptual framework provides a constitution that is used by the FASB to guide its deliberations and thereby the development of GAAP. It is the most recent attempt to develop a theoretical underpinning to support solutions to accounting reporting problems.

The development of this conceptual framework is an ongoing project. But its development need not be complete for the framework to have a major influence over the Board's policies and operations. And most important, the Board's conceptual framework is strongly reflected in the tone and motives imbedded in the *Statements of Financial Accounting Standards* the Board publishes, which are, in effect, the rules of accounting. Therefore, to understand the logic underlying any of the Board's *SFASs,* it is necessary to first understand the logic behind the Board's conceptual framework.

The Board, to date, has issued five *Statements of Financial Accounting Concepts. (SFAC No. 3* was superseded by *SFAC No. 6.)* Defining, approving, and publishing six *SFACs* was no small accomplishment given the nature of the task and the environment in which the Board operates. To better appreciate the complexities involved, consider what one prominent academician had to say on the subject.[1]

> Attempts to formulate a conceptual framework of accounting have been going on now for at least 50 years, and to get the board's project into perspective it is important to see it as only the latest in a series of attempts to formulate what W. A. Paton and A. C. Littleton in 1940 called "a coherent, coordinated, consistent body of doctrine." There have been many steps along the road from the American Accounting Association's 1936 *Tentative Statement of Accounting Principles Underlying Corporate Financial Statements* to Concepts Statement No. 5, with Accounting Principles Board Statement No. 4 (1970) and the American Institute of CPAs Trueblood report (1973) among the major landmarks.

Politics and Controversy

Politics and power plays are part of every business, government, social, or professional group. However, political factions and splinter groups within any professional association can make for healthy debate and act to safeguard the comprehensiveness and maximum suitability of its pronouncements.

It is unrealistic to expect the constituency of any professional association to immediately endorse and adopt all the pronouncements handed down by its authoritative body. In the FASB's case, differences of opinion and challenges from accounting practitioners are inevitable given the scope of matters upon which the Board comments and rules. Moreover, the issues brought to the Board are naturally difficult and possess no simple, readymade solutions. To better appreciate why controversy exists, consider the following explanations:

---

[1] D. Solomon, "The FASB's Conceptual Framework: An Evaluation," *Journal of Accountancy,* June 1986, pp. 114–24. A brief historical perspective on the conceptual framework is contained in the appendix at the end of the chapter.

EXHIBIT 2–1   Overview of the FASB Conceptual Framework and Implementation Guidelines for Accounting

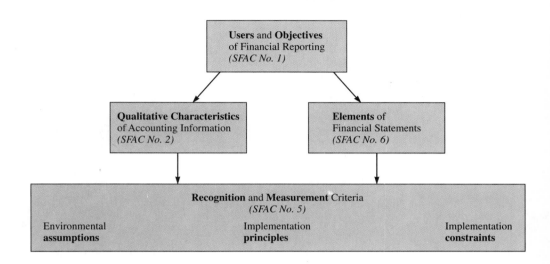

- ◆ Unlike biology, mathematics, and physics, accounting contains no principles or laws to be discovered. Accounting principles are formulated by individuals, which means that disagreements and challenges are inevitable.
- ◆ Accounting concepts are based upon reasoning, economic theory, experience, pragmatism, and general acceptability. Thus, accounting concepts change with the evolving social and economic environment within which the accounting process is applied.

CONCEPT REVIEW

1. Why did the FASB choose to develop a conceptual framework?
2. Do politics play a constructive role in the setting of accounting standards?
3. Do accounting concepts remain static?

Overview of the FASB's Conceptual Framework of Accounting

Exhibit 2–1 depicts the FASB's conceptual framework as a three-level hierarchy of priorities. These priorities guide the process the FASB uses in issuing standards and other pronouncements. Also, this hierarchy conforms with the content matter covered in the four *Statements of Financial Accounting Concepts* that are currently in effect for profit-oriented organizations. Each *SFAC* is discussed in this chapter.

The Board states the following as its rationale in support of the conceptual framework:

1. The accounting standards applicable to various accounting issues should be consistent with a conceptual framework developed by a prior consensus. This assures consistency among the guidelines and procedures used in accounting.
2. New and unique accounting problems, for which there are no current guidelines (no GAAP), can be more consistently resolved by preparers of financial statements in conformity with a conceptual framework.
3. Users of financial statements can benefit because of a better understanding of the accounting information that financial statements communicate.

Familiarity with the conceptual framework is necessary for several reasons:

EXHIBIT 2-2   FASB Conceptual Framework of Accounting

SFAC Number, Date, Title, Subject Matter*	Specific Content Covered
SFAC No. 1 (November 1978) "Objectives of Financial Reporting by Business Enterprises" Sets forth the purpose, aims, and goals of financial accounting	Identifies user target audience as investors and creditors (and those who advise these users) Lists the objectives of preparing financial statements to meet user needs Provides perspective on the entire conceptual framework of accounting, upon which work is in progress

SFAC No. 2 (May 1980)
 	
"Qualitative Characteristics of Accounting Information"
 	
Establishes a checklist system of accounting characteristics for evaluating information presented in financial statements
	Primary qualities
	  Relevance:
	    Timeliness
	    Predictive value
	    Feedback value
	  Reliability:
	    Representational faithfulness
	    Verifiability
	    Neutrality
	Secondary qualities
	  Comparability
	  Consistency

1. The pronouncements (statements) of the FASB are based on this framework and, what's more important, the application of each pronouncement requires an understanding of the Board's intentions as reflected in the framework.
2. These intentions are critical to many situations that do not meet the letter of a given statement and, hence, require judgment.
3. Since the environment of accounting is dynamic, predicting how the Board will resolve new issues is facilitated by understanding the conceptual framework.

For a preview of the content and intention of each of the four FASB concept statements relating to profit-oriented enterprises and to gain an overall perspective, refer to Exhibit 2-2.

SFAC NO. 1: OBJECTIVES OF FINANCIAL REPORTING BY BUSINESS ENTERPRISES

♦

Published by the FASB in November 1978, *SFAC No. 1* defines the main categories of external decision makers who use financial statements and sets forth the objectives that preparers of these documents should keep in mind when compiling and reporting accounting information. *SFAC No. 1* also provides an overall perspective on the conceptual framework of accounting that is comprehensive and goes beyond the scope of this first concept statement. In effect, *SFAC No. 1* serves as a preview of the Board's thinking on the entire conceptual framework subject.

Users of Financial Statements

Various users of financial statements (also known as external decision makers) employ accounting information in quite different ways. For example, many individual investors seldom look closely at the financial information contained in an annual report or the quarterly earnings statements that publicly owned companies must send to their shareholders. Being relatively unsophisticated in finance and investment matters, they may read the introductory text (normally written by public

EXHIBIT 2–2 (*concluded*)

SFAC Number, Date, Title, Subject Matter*	Specific Content Covered
SFAC No. 5 (December 1984)	

"Recognition and Measurement in Financial Statements of Business Enterprises"	Recognition criteria
	  Definitions
	  Measurability
	  Relevance
	  Reliability

Complements *SFAC No. 2* and sets forth criteria for determining when and under what circumstances to report accounting information in financial statements	Measurement criteria Cost basis

	Environmental assumptions
	  Separate entity
	  Continuity
	  Unit of measure
	  Time period

	Implementation principles
	  Cost
	  Revenue
	  Matching
	  Full disclosure

	Implementation constraints
	  Cost-benefit
	  Materiality
	  Industry peculiarities
	  Conservatism

	General-purpose financial statements
SFAC No. 6 (December 1985)	
"Elements of Financial Statements of Business Enterprises"	

Defines 10 elements of financial statements and lists criteria for classifying accounting information accordingly	Financial statement elements
	  Revenues
	  Expenses
	  Gains
	  Losses
	  Assets
	  Liabilities
	  Equity
	  Investments by owners
	  Distributions to owners
	  Comprehensive income

* *SFAC No. 3* was superseded by *SFAC No. 6. SFAC No. 4* addresses nonbusiness organization reporting issues and thus is beyond the scope of this text.

relations people, not accountants) and look at the glossy pictures. But the accounting information contained in the auditor's statement typically holds little interest for them, and most simply don't bother to read it, much less try to understand it.

On the other hand, securities analysts, lawyers, institutional investors, and corporate financial people pore over a company's financial statements, sometimes more intensely than the company's own management staff. The same intensity can be found inside banks and other lending institutions, especially if a multimillion dollar financing deal happens to be in the works.

Somewhere in the middle is the so-called prudent investor, a person who is reasonably sophisticated in business and finance matters, and who is said to make informed investment decisions. Informed investment decisions are based on factual matters and interpretation of facts—not on intuition and hearsay. Also in the middle ground is the prudent creditor, who is believed to make decisions concerning advancing loans or extending credit on factual matters, not simply on gut reaction.

In *SFAC No. 1* the Board recognizes the problem of diversity among users, knowing that the information needs of the full spectrum of users cannot all be satisfied at the same time. Thus, the Board aims at the middle-ground users, those investors and creditors most in need of accurate, reliable, and unbiased accounting information that they can apply in making investment and credit decisions. The people at the two opposite ends of the spectrum are not being ignored by the Board in its thinking, but they are not the target audience.

SFAC No. 1 identifies the target audience within the full range of financial statement users to be investors and creditors (and those who advise or represent them) who:

1. "Lack the authority to prescribe the information they want and must rely on information management communicates to them."
2. "Have a reasonable understanding of business and economic activities and are willing to study the information with reasonable diligence."

In truth, the professionals and institutional investors at one end of the spectrum have the power to get virtually whatever information they want from a corporation, whereas the people at the other end would be unlikely to change their behavior (through study with reasonable diligence) even if they had all the information they needed.

The FASB's conception of reasonably sophisticated investors and creditors (and those who represent or advise them) includes employees, managers and directors of the company, customers, lawyers, stock exchanges, taxing authorities, researchers, teachers, and students of business and accounting.

Financial Reporting Objectives

SFAC No. 1 states that the objective of financial reporting is to provide information that:

1. Is useful to both present and potential investors and creditors (and other users) in making rational investment, credit, and other related decisions.
2. Is helpful to current and potential investors and creditors (and other users) in assessing the amounts, timing, and uncertainty of future cash flows due them. These include dividends or interest payments, among other items. Also to be assessed is the degree of certainty of any future proceeds due them from the company. These include items such as the sale back, redemption, or maturity of securities or loans. An investor's incoming cash flow from an investment depends on the degree of certainty attached to the company's prospective net cash flows. The same is true for creditors of the company.
3. Is accurate in reporting the economic resources of the business, including any claims to those resources held by other entities (outstanding liabilities). Also, the effects of any pending transactions, events, and circumstances that will affect the company's resources and claims to those resources as presently reported must be made known.

SFAC No. 1 implicitly recognizes that there is a decision-making process that most investors and creditors use in evaluating various investment opportunities. This process helps investors in predicting, among other things, the future net cash receipts expected from the investment. Termed a *discounted cash flow analysis* (presented in detail in Chapter 6), this process is designed to render an economic justification for making, or not making, an investment based on the investment's current price. The process requires estimating[2]:

---

[2] The analytical process by which these estimates are incorporated into the decision process is discussed in Chapter 6.

1. The timing and amounts of all expected cash flows (dividend or interest payment dates and amounts due).
2. The risk that the company may not realize cash flows needed to make future dividend and/or interest payments.
3. An appropriate interest rate for discounting all expected cash flows (normally, interest rates prevailing at the time the investment is being contemplated are used).

Items 2 and 3 above are interrelated because the interest rate may attempt to reflect the risk.

Perspective of the Conceptual Framework

In issuing *SFAC No. 1,* the FASB informed the accounting profession that the directives contained in this first concept's statement were not a complete enumeration of the Board's thinking. In addition to defining users of financial statements and setting forth objectives for financial reporting, other components of the conceptual framework were yet to come. The Board alerted its constituency that criteria were needed for identifying and evaluating accounting information for quality, consistency, and conformity with GAAP. These criteria would offer increased assurance that accounting information was being prepared and reported in accordance with the objectives of financial statements communicated in this first concept's statement.

Also, accountants needed a more systematic approach to constructing financial statements and determining what information was reported and where, along with directives for recognizing and measuring various kinds of accounting information reported in financial statements. These additional matters are the subject of subsequent *SFACs* issued by the Board and are detailed next.

SFAC NO. 2: QUALITATIVE CHARACTERISTICS OF ACCOUNTING INFORMATION

SFAC No. 2 was published by the FASB in May of 1980, approximately two years after *SFAC No. 1* was published. *SFAC No. 2* identifies and defines a hierarchy of *characteristics of accounting information.* The purpose of the hierarchy—divided into primary and secondary tiers—is to provide preparers of financial statements and other interested parties with a checklist of quality standards for evaluating the usefulness of the accounting information being reported to external users. One reason the hierarchy places substantial weight on the qualitative characteristics of accounting data is that accounting numbers are estimates or statistical measures; they are typically not facts or truths. The value of an accounting measure is in its use as related to a specified objective. For a quick overview of *SFAC No. 2* and a complete list of its evaluation quality standards, refer to Exhibit 2–2.

Primary Qualities—Relevance and Reliability

In formulating *SFAC No. 2,* the FASB specified that the two most important attributes of accounting information in terms of usefulness to external decision makers were relevance and reliability. In arriving at this conclusion, the Board found itself in accord with similar conclusions reached in the Trueblood Report in 1973 (see the appendix at the end of the chapter).

Relevance Relevance refers to the capacity of accounting information to make a difference to the external decision makers who use financial reports. They use accounting information with either or both of two viewpoints in mind:

* Forecasting what the economic future is likely to hold.
* Confirming the accuracy of past forecasts (to improve future forecasting techniques).

Stated more technically, relevant accounting information helps users to make predictions about future events (predictive value), to confirm or correct prior expectations (feedback value), and to evaluate current conditions.

The degree to which accounting information is deemed to be relevant can be measured using three aspects of this quality:

1. **Timeliness:** Accounting information should be made available to external decision makers before it loses its capacity to influence decisions. Like the news of the world, stale financial information never carries the same impact fresh information carries. Lack of timeliness reduces relevance.
2. **Predictive value:** Accounting information should be helpful to external decision makers by increasing their ability to make predictions about the outcome of future events. Decision makers working from accounting information that has little or no predictive value are merely speculating intuitively.
3. **Feedback value:** Accounting information should also be helpful to external decision makers in confirming past predictions or in making updates, adjustments, or corrections to predictions currently outstanding.

Reliability   For accounting information to have **reliability** it must be free from error and bias, and it must faithfully represent what it purports to represent. External decision makers must feel confident that the information they rely on for making economic forecasts and confirming results is prepared by competent professionals who have no intention to mislead or deceive.

Like relevance, its twin evaluation characteristic, reliability must meet three quality aspects:

1. **Representational faithfulness:** Sometimes called *validity,* this attribute of accounting information applies to the whole of the text and numbers contained in a financial report and to what is being conveyed to the reader. Does the information give a faithful picture of the facts and circumstances involved? Accounting information must report in words and figures the economic substance of transactions, not just its form and surface appearance.
2. **Verifiability:** This quality standard is needed to ensure that a given piece of accounting information is what it purports to be. The concern here is that the source(s) from which the information is compiled may be in error or otherwise unreliable. Verifiability pertains to having audit trails back to information source documents that can be checked for accuracy. Verifiability also pertains to having alternative information sources as backup.
3. **Neutrality:** This standard is met if the accounting information is free from bias, and not subject to opinions that might influence the reader of financial statements. There should be no attempt on the part of the preparers of financial reports to induce a predetermined outcome or a particular mode of behavior (such as to induce investors to buy the company's stock). Accounting information should be unbiased regarding a particular viewpoint, predetermined result, or particular party.

External decision makers should be able to count on relevance and reliability in all accounting information communicated to them in financial statements. For example, a statement of cash flows has relevance for decision makers only if it provides information about current inflows and outflows of cash. Current data is essential for assessing and predicting future cash flows. Further, a statement of cash flows must present current data that is properly classified and understandable to decision makers.

Finally, a statement of cash flows, like all financial statements, must be reliable. It must report only what it purports to report, and the information should be both verifiable and free from bias.

Secondary Qualities—Comparability and Consistency

Certain types of accounting information hold little value for external decision makers unless the data can be compared with similar data from other companies, industry averages, or composite data on a group of like business enterprises. Similarly, specific information on a company covering one accounting period may be of no real significance unless the data can be compared to like information for other accounting periods.

Comparability **Comparability** is the quality of information that enables users to identify similarities and differences between two or more sets of economic phenomena. The ability to evaluate accounting information based on a comparison with similar data from other companies, industry averages, or internationally is possible only if the data are comparable. For example, an income statement should be designed so that revenue, expense, and net income information can be compared from one company to other companies in the same industry. The comparison is basically an across-firms notion.

Consistency Information is consistent if it conforms with procedures that remain unchanged from period to period. This quality pertains to comparing accounting information between accounting periods (fiscal year to fiscal year, current quarter to past quarters, etc.). Comparisons over time are difficult unless there is **consistency** in the way the accounting principles are applied. Otherwise, it's a situation of apples and oranges. The comparison here is across time.

The following example from the airline industry illustrates both consistency and comparability. Prior to 1988, Delta Air Lines depreciated its planes over 10 years; American Airlines used 14- and 16-year depreciation schedules for most of its aircraft. The difference in depreciation methods was a major factor behind Delta's reporting a loss of $3.06 per share in 1980 while American reported per-share earnings of $4.69 for the same period: a comparability problem.

In the airline industry, and in many other industries too, comparing financial information on two or more companies is not easy, even if the person making the comparisons is aware of differences in accounting principle applications. Thus, on July 1, 1986, Delta Air Lines increased the useful service life on its fleet of planes from 10 years to 15 years, with each aircraft expected to have a residual value of 10% upon retirement from service. Increasing the service life and thereby reducing depreciation expense added $69 million to Delta's net income and increased the carrier's 1987 per-share earnings by $1.54. Moreover, Delta switched from a 10-year to a 15-year service life, while Pan American was estimating 25 years of useful life for the same aircraft, with a 15% residual value. Not only was comparability affected, but the consistency with Delta's prior statements was reduced.

On a somewhat contradictory note, *APB Opinion No. 20,* "Accounting Changes," argues that "there is a presumption that an accounting principle once used should not be changed." However consistency carried too far can adversely affect relevance. Thus, a change to a preferred accounting principle is appropriate at times, even at the risk of impaired consistency. This apparent conflict can be resolved by the inclusion of supplemental note disclosures with the financial statements explaining the reason for the change and disclosing the effects of the change. The note disclosures act to restore consistency and comparability between financial statements for periods before and after the change in accounting principle application is in effect. Notes could be used to explain (and perhaps justify) the accounting choices made by Delta.

SFAC NO. 5: RECOGNITION AND MEASUREMENT IN FINANCIAL STATEMENTS OF BUSINESS ENTERPRISES

Published by the FASB in December 1984, *SFAC No. 5* provides a set of companion directives to those contained in *SFAC No. 2.* These two concept statements are similar in that both are aimed at promoting consistency, in how accounting principles are applied, and uniformity, in how accounting information is communicated to interested parties. As Exhibit 2-2 shows, *SFAC No. 5* addresses six specific topic areas:

1. Recognition criteria.
2. Measurement criteria.
3. Environmental assumptions.
4. Implementation principles.
5. Implementation constraints.
6. General-purpose financial statements.

Recognition Criteria

Recognition criteria and accrual basis accounting go hand in hand. Recognition pertains to the moment when business transactions are recorded on the books under the accounting system. *SFAC No. 5* broadly defines the term **recognition** as the process of recording and reporting an item as an asset, liability, revenue, expense, gain, loss, or change in owners' equity.

SFAC No. 5 states that recognition of an item is required when all four of the following criteria are met:

1. **Definition:** The item in question must meet the definition of an element of financial statements as defined in *SFAC No. 6.* (A list of financial statement elements is given in Exhibit 2-2 with *SFAC No. 6*).
2. **Measurability:** The item must have a relevant attribute (characteristic) that is reliably measurable. (See the primary qualitative accounting characteristics under *SFAC No. 2* in Exhibit 2-2.)
3. **Relevance:** The accounting information generated by the item must be significant, meaning capable of making a difference to external users in making decisions. (See the section above on *SFAC No. 2.* A list of relevance criteria is given with *SFAC No. 2* in Exhibit 2-2.)
4. **Reliability:** The accounting information generated by the item must be representationally faithful, verifiable (subject to audit confirmation or second-source collaboration), and neutral (bias free).

Measurement Criteria

SFAC No. 5 directs that all monetary measurements should be based on historical costs, unadjusted for inflation or deflation.

Environmental Assumptions

SFAC No. 5 addresses four basic environmental assumptions that significantly affect the recording, measuring, and reporting of accounting information:

1. Separate entity.
2. Continuity.
3. Unit of measure.
4. Time period.

These four environmental assumptions were not, however, newly formulated by the FASB. Rather, they were existing GAAP guidelines that the Board merely reiterated as directives and included in *SFAC No. 5*. This is also true of the Board's directives on implementation principles and constraints, presented later in this section on *SFAC No. 5*.

Separate Entity Assumption Accounting deals with specific, identifiable business entities, each considered an accounting unit separate and apart from its owners and from other entities. A corporation and its stockholders are separate entities for accounting purposes, even in the case of closely held, private corporations owned by family members. Also, partnerships and sole proprietorships are treated as separate from the owners, although this separation does not hold true in a legal sense.

Under the **separate entity assumption,** all accounting records and reports are developed from the viewpoint of a particular entity—whether it is the Jones proprietorship, SSN 997-00-5555, or Jones Corporation, tax ID 00-6897880. This assumption provides a basis for a clear-cut differentiation between an individual's transactions and those of the business the individual might own. For example, the personal residence of an individual business owner is not considered an asset of the business, even though the residence and the business are owned by the same person.[3]

Continuity Assumption Under the **continuity assumption,** also known as the **going-concern** assumption, the business entity in question is not expected to liquidate in the foreseeable future. The assumption does not imply that accounting assumes permanent continuance, but it does suggest that a company plans to stay in business for a period of time sufficient to carry out contemplated operations, contracts, and commitments. Thus, the overriding assumption is that business will continue on a nonliquidation basis. This nonliquidation basis in turn provides a conceptual basis for many of the classifications used in accounting. Assets and liabilities, for example, are classified as either current or long-term based on this assumption. If business continuity is not assumed, the distinction between current and long-term loses its significance; all assets and liabilities become current.

If a business entity expects to be liquidated in the near future, conventional accounting based on the continuity assumption is not appropriate. Such circumstances call instead for the use of liquidation accounting, in which case all assets and liabilities are accounted for at estimated net realizable amounts (liquidation values).

Unit-of-Measure Assumption The **unit-of-measure assumption** specifies that accounting should measure and report the results of a business's economic activities in terms of a monetary unit such as the U.S. dollar. The assumption recognizes that the use of a standard monetary unit throughout all financial statements is an effective means for

---

[3] The distinction does not always prevail in practice. *The Wall Street Journal* reported on November 27, 1978, p. 5, that the audit committees of several firms demanded that CEOs compensate their companies to the tune of $1 million for personal expenditures.

aggregating and communicating accounting information. Money amounts, thus, are the language of accounting—the common denominator and yardstick used to measure and evaluate business performance and financial results. Using money figures also allows for dissimilar items, such as the cost of a ton of coal and an account payable, to be aggregated into a single total.

Unfortunately, the use of a standard monetary unit for measurement purposes poses a dilemma. Unlike a yardstick, which is always the same length, the dollar, for example, experiences changes in value virtually all the time. During periods of inflation (or deflation) dollars of "different sizes" come into existence, are entered into a business's books, and commingled without regard to the fact that some have greater purchasing power than others.[4] Because it is standard practice to ignore changes in the purchasing power of a dollar (or any other currency denomination), accounting implicitly assumes that the magnitude of change in the value of the monetary unit is not material.

Time-Period Assumption   The operating results of any business enterprise cannot be known with certainty until the company has completed its life span and ceased doing business. But financial reports covering shorter time periods are needed because external decision makers require timely accounting information to satisfy their analytical needs. For this reason, the business community and the government have imposed a **time-period assumption** (or *calendar constraint*) on accounting, requiring that changes in a business's financial position be reported over a series of shorter time periods.

Although the reporting period varies, one year is common. Some companies adhere to the calendar year, and others use a fiscal year-end that coincides with the low point in business activity over a 12-month period. Thus, annual reports are sent to stockholders with a company's operating results reported on either a calendar year-end or a fiscal year-end basis. In addition, companies also report summarized financial information on an interim basis, usually quarterly.

A company may elect to use an alternative reporting period, either longer or shorter than the standard 12-month calendar or fiscal year, but only if doing so better fits the company's normal business cycle. An example industry in which longer reporting periods are used is shipbuilding, in which constructing a vessel and readying it for launch typically require more than one year's time.

The **time-period assumption** thus recognizes that decision makers need short-term financial information and also takes into account the importance of accruals and deferrals in reporting accurate information. Accrual and deferral items distinguish accrual-basis accounting from cash-basis accounting. If a demand for periodic reports did not exist during the life span of a business, accruals and deferrals would not be necessary. A company's financial statements are always dated to reflect either a precise point in time (balance sheet) or the particular time period covered (income statement and cash flow statement).

Implementation Principles

Implementation principles come into play when an accountant must determine whether, or to what extent, certain revenue, expense, gain, and loss items should be recognized for financial statement reporting purposes. Four separate implementation principles apply to the recognition process:

1. Cost.
2. Revenue.
3. Matching.
4. Full disclosure.

---

[4] Over time, the changing value of the monetary unit, coupled with the change in the nature of goods, makes comparability difficult at best.

Because income is defined as revenues plus gains minus expenses and losses, the cost, revenue, and matching principles described below are the fundamental building blocks of income recognition. In addition to coverage here, income recognition and the implementation principles aligned with it are covered in depth in Chapter 7.

Cost Principle Normally applied in conjunction with asset acquisitions, the **cost principle** specifies that the actual acquisition cost be used for *initial* accounting recognition purposes. The cash-equivalent cost of an asset is used if the asset is acquired via some means other than cash. The acquisition or cash-equivalent cost is then recorded in the appropriate ledger account and reported in financial statement totals. The cost principle applies to the initial recording of transactions and economic events in all cases, but not necessarily to subsequent revaluations that may be made.

The cost principle assumes that assets are being acquirred in an *arm's length* business transaction. An arm's length transaction is one that is conducted between buyer and seller at, or based on, fair market prices prevailing at the time of the transaction. Regarding noncash transactions conducted at arm's length, the cost principle assumes that the market value of the resources given up in a transaction provides reliable evidence for the valuation of the item acquired—meaning that in a swap of assets, the value of the assets being traded away is of equal value to those being acquired.

With noncash transactions, an appropriate cost basis is not easily established in many cases. For example, when an asset is received as a gift or in exchange for stock or in a swap of assets, determining a realistic cost basis can be quite difficult. In these situations, the cost principle requires that the cost basis be established based on the market value of the assets given up or the market value of the assets received, whichever value is more reliable.

In other instances, an asset may be acquired with a debt, such as a note payable, given in settlement for the purchase. The cost basis for the asset acquired in this instance is determined from the debt side of the transaction. The asset's cost basis is equal to the present value of the amount of the debt to be paid in the future.

Thé *cost* principle provides guidance primarily at the initial acquisition date. Once acquired, the original cost basis of some assets is then subject to depreciation, depletion, amortization, or write-down in conformity with the *matching* principle and the conservatism constraint, discussed later in this section. The following information, drawn from Merck & Co's 1989 balance sheet, illustrates the reporting:

Property, Plant, and Equipment, at Cost (in millions):

Land	$ 162.1
Buildings	1,129.1
Machinery, equipment, and office furnishings	2,417.2
Construction in progress	285.5
	$3,993.9
Less allowance for depreciation	1,701.4
	$2,292.5

Revenue Principle The **revenue principle** pertains to business revenues being recognized and reported in financial statements in accordance with *accrual basis* accounting principles. Applying this principle requires, first, that all four of the recognition criteria—definition, measurability, relevance, and reliability—be met.

Under the revenue principle, revenue from the sale of goods is recognized at the time of sale. The assumption is that goods are finished industrial products or ready-to-sell merchandise, which means that the earning process usually is completed at the time of sale. At that time, the relevant information about the asset inflows (normally either an increase in cash or a similar increase in accounts receivable) to the seller is reliably known. Sale must be accompanied by transfer of ownership or the performance of services. Two additional conditions must be met:

1. Reasonable assurance of collection.
2. Substantial completion of transaction.

The first condition—reasonable assurance of collection—provides the basis for the conclusion that the transaction results in a "probable future economic benefit." This means an increase in assets, normally interpreted as a profit on sales, for the seller. Without this first condition, the concept of revenue recognition would lack substantive economic content.

The second condition—substantial completion—assures that the seller has no major work to complete. Examples of incomplete sales include products or goods shipped by the seller (sometimes at the buyer's request) with components and substantial parts yet to be assembled. Or, if service contracts are involved, billing the client in full when certain services specified in the contract have yet to be performed is another example. The logic behind the second condition is that the buyer of goods or client for whom services are to be performed may elect to cancel the sale, citing the seller's failure to deliver or perform.

Revenue is defined by the FASB as inflows of cash or other enhancements of a business's assets, settlements of its liabilities, or a combination of both. The definition further states that such inflows must be derived from delivering or producing goods, rendering service, or performing other activities that constitute a company's ongoing business operations over a specific period of time. To quote from *SFAC No. 6* (which is fully discussed in the next section of this text): "revenues represent actual or expected cash inflows (or the equivalent) that have occurred or will eventually occur as a result of the enterprise's ongoing major or central operations during the period."

In general, "revenue is measured as the market value of the resources received or the product or service given, whichever is the more reliably determinable." This broader definition comes into play in conjunction with noncash transactions (swaps, trades, exchanges of goods and merchandise, or services performed).

For example, regarding sales discounts, the revenue principle requires that all discounts be viewed as adjustments of the amount of revenue earned. In determining the net cash exchange value of sales subject to discount, sales discounts should be subtracted from gross sales revenue in measuring the net amount of sales revenue.[5]

The revenue principle pertains to accrual basis accounting and is not relevant to cash basis accounting. Therefore, completed transactions for the sale of goods or services on credit usually are recognized as revenue for the period in which the sale or service occurred rather than in the period in which the cash is eventually collected.

Other types of revenue transactions that frequently pose recognition problems include installment sales, long-term construction contracts, sales of land with minimal down payments, and sales of franchises that require a certain level of performance on the part of the purchaser as a condition of sale. In these instances, and others, both the determination of when the earnings process is complete and the measurement of the revenue amount involved may be difficult tasks. A full discussion of revenue recognition as it applies in these special cases is presented in Chapter 7.

Matching Principle   Like the revenue principle, the **matching principle** is also predicated on accrual basis accounting, but in this instance, the concern is with the point when expenses are recognized for financial statement reporting purposes. Revenues for a given reporting period should be recognized in conformity with the revenue principle when the conditions for revenue recognition under the completed earnings process

---

[5] Discounts not taken represent a loss to the buyer who allowed the discount to lapse and a special revenue item to the seller. Since lost discounts reflect very high interest rates, good management seldom lets them lapse. The seller, on the other hand, should expect such discounts to be taken. Lapsed discounts represent interest revenue, not sales revenue.

are met. Meanwhile, expenses incurred in earning the revenue recognized should also be recognized during the same period. If revenue is carried over from a prior period or deferred for recognition to a future period, the related expenses should also be carried over or deferred.

In applying the matching principle, expenditures that otherwise would be expensed at the time cash is disbursed are typically carried on the books as asset accounts. The reason for this treatment is that the expenditures were made for materials, purchased services, and the like, that will help earn future revenue. Later, when the anticipated revenue is recognized, the asset accounts are expensed as the resources represented by these asset accounts are consumed. In this way recognized revenues and related expenses are matched during the same accounting period, which means they are reported in the financial statements for that period.

The pattern of expense recognition varies. Some expenses are linked with revenues by a direct *cause-and-effect* relationship, especially when the revenue and expense transactions occur simultaneously. Examples are packaging, sales commissions, and delivery expense. Other outlays are linked to revenues in a cause-and-effect relationship, but separated by time in terms of when the expense is incurred and when the matching revenue occurs. Examples include cost of goods sold, depreciation, and inspection expenses. In such cases cash is disbursed in one period, but the expense may often be recognized and matched with revenue in a different period.

Some expenses have no direct relationship to either a particular type of revenue-generating transaction or a particular accounting time period. These expenses are allocated to reporting periods on a somewhat subjective basis. Examples are expenditures for administration and promotional activities. In practice, these items are recognized as expenses in full during the period in which they are incurred.

To illustrate the matching principle, assume a home appliance is sold for cash with 100% warranty on parts and labor in effect for the first 12 months from date of sale. The revenue from the sale is recognized immediately, as are the directly related costs involved in manufacturing and assembling the unit and the shipping and direct selling expenses incurred. Furthermore, the expenses involved in honoring the warranty should also be recognized in the same period as the sales revenue, even though the actual warranty cost may not be known until the next year. At the end of the year in which the sale occurs, the warranty expense should be estimated, recorded on the books, and recognized for financial statement reporting purposes. In this way, the warranty expense is matched with the revenue to which it is related even though the cash may be expended at a later time.

The following table is helpful in determining the accounting disposition of costs and expenses in accordance with the matching principle:

Time Frame of Benefit	The Expenditure Should Be
Future economic benefits	Recorded as asset
Current economic benefits	Recorded as expense
No economic benefits	Recorded as a loss

Applying the matching principle and the revenue principle together determines the reporting of net income. Because of the wide diversity in types of expenses, the matching principle is one of the most pervasive principles in terms of the sheer number of accounting judgments based on its application.

The matching principle, which pertains only to accrual basis accounting, may require the use of adjusting entries at the end of the accounting period. Adjusting entries (discussed in Chapter 3) are needed to update expenses, thus recognizing correct expense amounts for financial statement reporting purposes in step with recognized sales revenue. Examples include wage expense earned but not paid, estimated warranty expense, and interest expense accrued but not paid. Adjusting entries are also used to update certain revenue accounts.

Full-Disclosure Principle   The **full-disclosure principle** requires that financial statements report all *relevant* information bearing on the economic affairs of a business enterprise. The aim of full disclosure is to provide external users with the accounting information they need to make intelligent, informed investment and credit decisions.

Full disclosure also requires that the major and special accounting policies used by the company be explained in the notes to the financial statements. Accounting information may be reported in the financial statements themselves, in disclosure notes to those statements, or in supplementary schedules and other presentation formats. For example, executory contracts often are disclosed in the footnotes. Even though the transaction has not occurred, existence of such contracts can have a material effect on a company's future financial position.

Additionally, the full-disclosure principle stipulates that the primary objective is to report the economic substance of a transaction rather than its form. This means that substance should not be made vague, blurred, or hidden by the way the mechanics, rules, and technical terminology are used.

CONCEPT REVIEW

1. Under what conditions can revenue be recognized?
2. If a company cannot be considered a going concern, how should it be valued?
3. Why isn't the calendar year always the appropriate time period for an income statement? Why might a longer period be appropriate?

Implementation Constraints

The FASB recognizes that its directives for instilling consistency in the application of accounting principles and promoting uniformity of practice within the profession may not be practical in all cases. Exceptions due to special situations will arise. Constraints exist that influence the reporting of accounting information.

SFAC No. 5 addresses four major constraints to be considered in implementing the Board's directives:

1. Cost-benefit.
2. Materiality.
3. Industry peculiarities.
4. Conservatism.

These constraints exert a modifying influence on financial accounting and reporting.

Cost-Benefit Constraint   Both *SFAC No. 2* and *SFAC No. 5* address the issue of **cost-benefit constraint**, focusing on how it affects the preparation and reporting of accounting information. The underlying concept is that the benefits derived by external users of financial statements should outweigh the costs incurred by the internal preparers of the information. Although the cost-benefit concept is important, it is difficult to quantify either the benefits or the costs. As part of its activities, the FASB often attempts to obtain information from preparers on the costs of implementing a new reporting requirement. It does not, however, try to estimate less direct costs such as the cost (or benefit) of an altered allocation of resources in the economy. The cost-benefit determination is essentially a judgment call by the Board.

Materiality Constraint   The **materiality constraint** is addressed in *SFAC No. 2*, where materiality is defined as "the magnitude of an omission or misstatement of accounting that, in the light of surrounding circumstances, makes it probable that the judgment of a reasonable person relying on the information would have been changed or influenced by the omission or misstatement." The message from the FASB is that the omission or inclusion of immaterial facts or inconsequential money amounts is not likely to change or influence the decision-making process of a rational external user. However, the materiality threshold does not mean that immaterial items and amounts do not have to be accounted for or reported. Rather materiality means that strict adherence to the related accounting standards is not required.

To illustrate one instance where strict conformity with GAAP is not necessary, consider sales discounts. If sales discounts are not taken, information need not be broken out and identified in a company's financial statements if the dollar amounts involved represent a small percentage of total sales. Similarly, a low-cost asset, such as a $9.95 pencil sharpener, can be recorded as an expense in full when purchased rather than as an asset subject to depreciation. The dollar amounts involved in these examples are simply too small for external users to worry about. In addition, in the case of the pencil sharpener, the dollar amount is such that it doesn't even warrant distinction as a separate expense account item. The amount is lumped instead into miscellaneous expenses.

Materiality judgments are situation specific, meaning that an amount considered material in one situation might be immaterial in another. It depends on the nature of the item, its dollar amount, and the relationship of the amount to the total amount of income, expenses, assets, or liabilities, as the case may be.[6] Because materiality matters tend to be case-by-case judgment calls, the FASB has not specified general materiality guidelines applicable to a wide range of situations. In practice, materiality guidelines such as "5% to 10% of net income or total assets" are typically used, even though the use of such arbitrary criteria may not be in keeping with the spirit of what materiality means.

This materiality constraint is also called a *threshold for recognition*.[7] Thus, an expenditure for the overhauling of a piece of equipment might represent a major cash layout for a small business concern and should be disclosed in its financial statements, but the same expenditure for a large corporation like IBM or AT&T is of no consequence, in terms of disclosure in financial statements.

Industry Peculiarities   One of the overriding concerns of accounting is the usefulness of information being presented in financial statements. The problem is that certain types of accounting information might be critical for decision-making purposes in one industry setting, but not in another. To illustrate, consider the differences between a public utility's business practices and those used in the banking industry or a railroad versus an investment company (mutual fund) or an insurance company versus a mining company.

Basically, each industry or economic sector tends to have its own way of doing things, its own business practice peculiarities. Thus, selective exceptions to generally accepted accounting principles and practice norms may be warranted. Under the **industry peculiarities constraint**, accounting for certain items is permitted, provided there is a clear precedent in the industry. Precedent is based on the uniqueness of the situation, the usefulness of the information involved, substance over form considerations, and whether representational faithfulness might be compromised.

Indeed, the FASB has often granted exceptions under the industry peculiarities constraint. A recent example is provided by *SFAS No. 102*, entitled "Statement of Cash Flows—Exemption of Certain Enterprises and Classification of Cash Flows from Certain Securities Acquired for Resale." In this pronouncement, which was

---

[6] The Foreign Corrupt Practices Act of 1977 established criminal penalties for making payments to foreign officials to obtain business. The Act requires business to keep accurate records and maintain a system of internal accounting controls to assure that transactions are proper. The legislation thereby specifically identifies transactions that accountants should treat as material where individual judgment was previously required.

[7] The courts have also not been consistent in setting a single benchmark value for materiality. See K. Jeffries, "Materiality as Defined by the Courts," *The CPA Journal*, October 1981, pp. 13–17.

aimed at the mutual fund industry, the Board concluded that for investment companies with highly liquid assets that do not finance their investment portfolios with debt, financial statements without a cash flow statement provide sufficient information for users' assessment of liquidity, financial flexibility, profitability, and risk.

Some differences in accounting also occur in response to legal requirements. This is especially so for companies that are subject to pervasive regulatory controls, for example, public utilities. Another exception permits the use of a principle or accounting procedure that is at variance with an official pronouncement if it can be shown that the procedure is more useful and is necessary to avoid misleading inferences. In such cases, departure from GAAP must be fully disclosed in the financial statements, including the reasons for the departure.

Conservatism   The **conservatism constraint** holds that where two alternative accounting methods are under consideration and both equally satisfy the conceptual and implementation principles set out by the FASB, the alternative having the *least favorable* effect on net income and/or total assets should be used.

- In recognizing assets where two alternative valuations are acceptable, the lower valuation would be used.
- In recognizing liabilities, the higher of two alternative liability amounts would be recorded.
- In recording revenues, expenses, gains, and losses where there is reasonable doubt as to the appropriateness of alternative amounts, the one having the least favorable effect on net income would be used.

Conservatism implies that when uncertainty exists as to a specific accounting treatment, the users of financial statements are better served by understatement than by overstatement of net income and assets. Practicing accountants must constantly use their judgment in making accounting decisions, selecting alternatives, making estimates, and applying accounting principles. The accountant's selections and judgments often have a major impact on how net income is reported, how assets are stated, and how owners' equity is presented in a company's financial statements. The practicing accountant must wrestle with the fact that there may not be a single, correct answer.

The concept of conservatism provides but one guideline for making choices between accounting alternatives. Prime examples of its application include valuing inventories and other assets at the lower of cost or current market value, and minimizing the estimated service life and residual value of depreciable assets. Since accountants and accounting standards should attempt to portray the financial affairs of a company as accurately as possible and with as little bias as possible, the use of overly conservative practices may also result in a biased portrayal of a company's financial condition. And there is no reason to believe that erring on the side of conservatism better serves the needs of external users.

General Purpose Financial Statements

The Board used *SFAC No. 5* to alert the accounting profession to the fact that at some future time it would address the problems caused by a lack of uniformity in the scope of accounting information included in financial statements and in the different types, titles, and sets of reporting documents in general use. The Board then outlined its present thinking on the subject of a *minimum set of financial statements*. At a minimum, a full set of financial statements for an accounting period should report the following:

1. Statement of financial position (balance sheet).
2. Earnings (income statement).
3. Comprehensive income (a new idea).
4. Cash flows (statement of cash flow).
5. Investments by and distribution to owners (statement of owners' equity).

The appendix at the end of this chapter contains a discussion of this development and provides some notion about how this prospective set of financial statements might evolve in the future.

A good deal of dissatisfaction exists within the FASB's constituency over *SFAC No. 5*. Critics argue that little, if any, guidance is supplied on measurement issues, implying that the Board, for the time being, is following in the footsteps of the CAP and the APB, preferring to deal with measurement issues case by case. The problem with a case-by-case approach in today's accounting environment is that it is likely to lead to inconsistency and ultimately to the unacceptability of any tightly defined measurement standards that might be promulgated by the FASB and published as GAAP in the future.

In other related matters, *SFAC No. 5* did resolve two issues. First, it made clear that information contained in disclosure notes to financial statements is supplemental to, *not a substitute for,* recognition of amounts included in financial totals displayed in the body of the statements.

Second, *SFAC No. 5* supported the concept of financial capital maintenance (rather than physical capital maintenance) as relevant to financial reporting. The term financial capital maintenance refers to situations where the dollar amount at which net assets are carried on the books at the end of a period exceeds the amount so carried at the start of the period, excluding transactions with owners (dividend payouts and capital contributions and withdrawals). If such an excess exists, a return on capital (earnings) results. In contrast, a return on physical capital results only if the physical productive capacity of the company increases over the period.

SFAC NO. 6: ELEMENTS OF FINANCIAL STATEMENTS OF BUSINESS ENTERPRISES

SFAC No. 6 was issued in December 1985 to replace *SFAC No. 3*, which carried the same title and covered the same basic accounting ground, and it covers that ground in an improved and more definitive fashion. *SFAC No. 6* defines 10 elements of financial statements. The Board felt these definitions were necessary to establish greater uniformity in how financial statements are prepared, which results in less confusion to external users.

Exhibit 2–3 offers thumbnail element definitions of each of the 10 financial statement elements, with criteria for determining which types of transactions are to be reported under each element. The first four elements (**revenues, expenses, gains,** and **losses**) relate directly to the income statement; the next three (**assets, liabilities,** and **equity**) pertain to a business's balance sheet.

The next two elements (**investments by owners** and **distributions to owners**) are related to a company's balance sheet, but they appear in the owner's equity section. The last element (comprehensive income) doesn't relate to the income statement that is in use today. **Comprehensive income** is a term devised by the Board for a new concept in income accounting. As a line item, comprehensive income does not appear on any income statement at the present time; however, in the future, comprehensive income could replace net income as the bottom-line item on American business's income statements—time will tell. The FASB's new comprehensive income concept is discussed further in the appendix under the title "Future Directions." An example of how it might appear in the future as a financial statement element is also included.

Accounting theoreticians and others were quick to note that *SFAC No. 6* broke new ground by its emphasis on assets and liabilities as fundamental accounting concepts, whereas revenues and expenses were repositioned as derived concepts—meaning they exist only as adjuncts to assets and liabilities. Taking a back seat as a derived concept, revenues represent either enhancements of assets or settlements of liabilities. In a similar position of reduced emphasis, expenses represent the use of an asset or the incurrence of a liability in conducting business operations.

EXHIBIT 2-3   Summary of Financial Statement Elements as Defined by *SFAC No. 6*

	Element Definition	Transaction Characteristics
Revenues	Defined as inflows of assets or settlement of liabilities (or a combination of both) during a particular accounting period, such inflows or settlements stem from the delivery or production of goods or rendering of services.	The two essential characteristics of a revenue transaction are: 1. It arises from the company's primary earning activity (mainstream business lines) and not from incidental or investment transactions (assuming the entity is a noninvestment company). 2. It is recurring and continuous.
Expenses	Defined as outflows of assets or the incurrence of liabilities (or both) during a particular accounting period, such outflows are necessary to delivery or production of goods or rendering of services.	The essential characteristic of an expense is that it must be incurred in conjunction with the company's revenue-generating process. Expenditures that do not qualify as expenses must be treated as either assets (future economic benefit to be derived) or losses (no economic benefit) or as distributions to owners.
Gains	Defined as increases to equity (net assets) resulting from peripheral or incidental transactions not associated with the company's major or central lines of business.	The transaction must not be one that meets the characteristics test of (1) a revenue-producing transaction (detailed above) or (2) a capital contribution transaction (detailed below).
Losses	Defined as decreases to equity (net assets) resulting from peripheral or incidental transactions not associated with the company's major or central lines of business.	The transaction must not be one that meets the characteristics test of (1) an expense transaction (detailed above) or (2) a capital distribution (investment by owner) transaction (detailed below).
Assets	Defined as business resources that have probable future economic benefits.	To qualify as assets, the resources involved must: 1. Have future economic benefits (capable of producing profits) 2. Be under management's control (can be freely deployed or disposed of). 3. Result from past transactions (meaning they are in place now, as opposed to being under contract for manufacture, creation, or delivery)
Liabilities	Defined as probable future sacrifices of economic benefits.	To qualify as liabilities, obligations must: 1. Transfer assets having future economic benefits. 2. Specify to whom the assets must be transferred (meaning that the terms, parties, and conditions under which asset transfers will take place must be specified). 3. Result from past transactions (meaning they are binding obligations now, as opposed to obligations that will exist once pending transactions are completed).
Equity	(*Owners' equity, stockholders' equity.*) Defined as the residual interest in the assets of a business entity. Also known as *net assets*.	The dollar amounts reported represent the residual interest in the assets after deducting the liabilities. In addition, the equity element is used to report capital transactions as described below.

For many years prior to the issuance of *SFAC No. 6,* the shoe was on the other foot: assets and liabilities were considered the derived concepts, while revenue and expense shared the driver's seat as fundamental accounting concepts. Assets, for example, were treated as costs awaiting recognition as expenses necessary to the generation of revenue.

Expenditures for research and development provide an example of this change in viewpoints. Previously these expenditures were considered assets (costs to be written off over time). Now research and development expenditures are treated as expenses, written off in the period incurred, the reasoning being that the related

EXHIBIT 2-3 (*concluded*)

	Element Definition	Transaction Characteristics
Investments by Owners	Defined as increases to equity (net assets) resulting from asset contributions (or liability decreases) by other entities (owners/stockholders).	Also known as *capital transactions*. Investments by owners are characterized as: 1. Cash or other assets exchanged for stock. 2. Service performance (sometimes called *sweat equity*) exchanged for stock. 3. Conversion of liabilities to equity ownership.
Distributions to Owners	Defined as decreases to equity (net assets) resulting from the distribution of assets (or liability increases) to other entities (owners/ stockholders).	Also known as *capital transactions*. Distributions to owners are characterized as: 1. Cash dividend payments or declarations. 2. Transfer of assets to owners. 3. Liquidating distributions (asset sale proceeds). 4. Conversion of equity ownership to liabilities.
Comprehensive Income	Defined as the change in equity (net assets) resulting from the aggregate of *all* transactions reported in a particular accounting period, *except* for investments by and distributions to owners.	The FASB's new comprehensive income incorporates certain gains and losses in its computation that are not currently included in net income. Capital transactions are still excluded. It would replace the retained earnings statement.

benefits gained from the expenditure cannot be identified with specific future revenues.

Another way to make this point is to say that *SFAC No. 6* emphasizes the balance sheet instead of the income statement. In the past, the income statement dominated the thinking of external users, who tended to focus on bottom-line net income and typically gave less attention to the balance sheet. Meanwhile, accountants, too, focused on the income statement first, thinking that one of their most important missions was to match expenses with revenues in an effort to report net income as accurately as possible. In some ways, the FASB's new emphasis on the balance sheet rather than on the income statement tends to diminish the centrality of the matching principle discipline.[8]

CONCEPT REVIEW

1. How is the materiality constraint implemented in practice?
2. What is the essence of the conservatism constraint and what is its effect on financial statements?
3. Which of the elements of financial statements have been most changed as to emphasis by the conceptual framework and what was the change?

SUMMARY OF KEY POINTS

♦

(L.O. 1)   1. The current conceptual framework provides a foundation to assist standard setters in developing a consistent approach to resolving financial reporting issues.

(L.O. 2)   2. Investors and creditors are the primary users of financial statement information.

---

[8] Even Professor William Paton, who is credited with conceiving the matching principle, along with Professor A. C. Litteton, once expressed second thoughts upon hearing the principle referred to as the *matching gospel*. See W. Paton, *Foundations of Accounting Theory*, ed. W. Stone (Gainsville, Fla.: University of Florida Press, 1971) p.x.

(L.O. 2)   3. The primary characteristics of accounting information are relevance and reliability.

(L.O. 2)   4. Emphasis in reporting is placed on the usefulness of the information for decisions. This means the information must be timely, assist in predicting the financial impact of present events, and help confirm or correct expectations.

(L.O. 3)   5. The recognition concept provides the conceptual basis for accrual accounting.

(L.O. 3)   6. Completion of the earning process requires that collection be reasonably assured and the seller's responsibilities be completed. When these conditions are satisfied, revenue can be recognized.

(L.O. 4)   7. The previously used assumptions in accounting (separate entity, going concern, periodic reporting), implementation principles (cost basis, accruals, matching, full disclosure), and constraints (cost-benefit, materiality, special industry reporting needs, conservatism) were retained by the conceptual framework, although sometimes given different emphasis.

(L.O. 4)   8. The matching principle requires that the expenses incurred in earning revenues should be recognized during the same period in which the revenues are recognized.

(L.O. 4)   9. Conservatism in accounting suggests that the least favorable alternative to the reporting firm be used when a choice exists and a more appropriate treatment of the item cannot be established.

(L.O. 5)   10. Assets and liabilities were given greater emphasis than the matching principle by the conceptual framework in determining the values that should appear on the balance sheet and income statement.

(L.O. 5)   11. Information that assists comparability across firms and consistency over time is particularly useful.

(L.O. 6)   12. The conceptual framework is not static. For example, a statement of comprehensive income has been suggested.

REVIEW PROBLEM
◆

Is revenue recognition appropriate in the following cases?

1. Allegheny Beverage Company (ABC) sold vending machines and soft drinks through a wholly owned subsidiary, Value Vend. Sales of vending machines by Value Vend were made on conditional sales contracts. Under these contracts, a purchaser was required to make a $50 down payment and to pay the balance in equal monthly installments over a 48-month period. The first payment was due 120 to 210 days after purchase. ABC recognized revenue when the sales contract was signed.

2. Metro-Goldwyn-Mayer (MGM) sold the Columbia Broadcasting Company (CBS) the rights to show the movie *Gone with the Wind* 20 times over 20 years. The sales price was $35 million. MGM reported essentially the entire amount as revenue in its first quarter's statement.

SOLUTION
◆

1. In the ABC case, given the payment terms in the sales contract, there was considerable uncertainty whether the collection was reasonably assured. ABC was required to delay recognizing revenue by its auditors, Alexander Grant. ABC changed auditors to a firm that permitted revenue to be recognized. Shortly thereafter, the company declared bankruptcy. Company officers and the new auditors were brought to court. The court declared the transactions were not sales.

2. The outcome in the MGM-CBS case was quite different. In this case, the accountants argued that the sale price was known, collection was reasonably assured, no further efforts were required by the seller (MGM), and the expenses of the sale were reliably determinable. Thus, revenue was recognized immediately, even though MGM argued to delay revenue recognition until each showing.

INTRODUCTION

It's May 4, 1977, and we are in Philadelphia for a conference on "The Conceptual Framework of Accounting," sponsored by the Wharton School, University of Pennsylvania, and supported by Peat, Marwick, Mitchell & Company, one of the larger accounting firms. The conceptual framework project has been on the FASB's agenda from its inception in 1973, and it was to be the Board's constitution, serving as a basis for its future pronouncements. Dr. Robert T. Sprouse, recently of Stanford University, and at the time one of the seven FASB board members, has just finished describing the Board's early work, which was published in a December 1976 discussion memorandum titled "Scope and Implications of the Conceptual Framework Project."

Near the end of his address, Dr. Sprouse comments: "For many of us, the conceptual framework project—and, more specifically, the conceptual framework discussion memorandum—is difficult to come to grips with because the subject matter is abstract, and we are accustomed to dealing with specific, concrete accounting problems."

Dr. Sprouse is followed to the dais by Dr. Robert Mautz, a partner with Ernst and Ernst, another of the larger accounting firms. He concludes his remarks on the FASB's conceptual framework project with the following evaluation:

> Then where are we? We have a failure of communication from the Board to its constituents. . . . We have objectives that ignore many of the interests in financial accounting. We have a choice of approaches . . . that will confuse many potential respondents. Now, I think that's a pretty weak reed on which to put our faith for maintaining the establishment of financial standards in the private sector.

The next speaker, Professor Nicholas Dopuch, a leading scholar then at the University of Chicago, ends his address, as have most of the speakers on the agenda, on a very negative note. Dopuch suggests the Board provide instead "an operational framework for itself, stating at the outset that the normative (an 'ought-to-be') theory cannot, in fact, be defined by an authoritative body."

It is perhaps a surprise that a conceptual framework could arise in such a diverse climate of views as those expressed by well-known individuals such as those quoted. While it may reflect Professor Dopuch's admonition that "it [the conceptual framework] may be universally relied upon in practice . . . simply because they [the FASB] have the power to impose it," it would seem that most of the conceptual framework has attained both a favorable response and acceptance from the constituency.

HISTORICAL PERSPECTIVE

As Professor Solomons noted (referenced early in this chapter), "Attempts to formulate a conceptual framework of accounting have been going on now for at least 50 years." Three major attempts were made under quite diverse organizations.[9] The

---

[9] The discussion in this section is drawn from R. Sprouse, "Developing a Conceptual Framework," *Accounting Horizons,* December 1988, pp. 121–27. Dr. Sprouse served on the FASB from its inception until 1986. This period saw the development of the FASB's conceptual framework. Other recent commentaries on the framework include D. Solomons, "The FASB's Conceptual Framework: An Evaluation," *Journal of Accountancy,* June 1986, pp. 114–24; D. Gerboth, "The Conceptual Framework: Not Definitions but Professional Values," *Accounting Horizons,* September 1987, pp. 1–8; L. Heath, "The Conceptual Framework as Literature," *Accounting Horizons,* June 1988 pp. 100–104; P. Miller and R. Redding, "The Conceptual Framework Project," in *The FASB: The People, the Process, and the Politics,* 2nd ed. (Homewood, Ill.: Richard D. Irwin, 1988), pp. 108–33.

first was begun by the AICPA's Committee on Accounting Procedure (CAP, 1936 to 1959), the second by the Accounting Principles Board (APB, 1959 to 1973), and the last by the Financial Accounting Standards Board (1973 to present).

The Committee on Accounting Procedures (1936–1959)

CAP initially considered the development of a comprehensive statement of accounting principles, but quickly turned away to tackle the pressing issues of the day. Progress on specific issues was viewed as necessary if CAP hoped to be accepted by the SEC in the role of formulating accounting principles. The committee produced a number of *Accounting Research Bulletins* that, although revised and organized by subject in *ARB No. 43,* continued to reflect separate, individual opinions rather than any comprehensive, underlying framework. The *ARBs* relied on general acceptance and were not formally part of GAAP.

The Accounting Principles Board (1959–1973)

In 1957, Alvin Jennings, president of the AICPA and senior partner of Lybrand, Ross Brothers & Montgomery (currently Coopers & Lybrand), appointed the Special Committee on Research Programs to examine the procedures by which accounting principles were determined and enforced. The committee's recommendations led to the replacement of the CAP with the APB and the formation of a research division, whose charge was to examine "the basic postulates underlying accounting principles generally, and a study of the broad principles of accounting." The research division quickly began studies of the basic postulates and principles, which were completed by 1962 and promptly rejected by the APB as "too radically different from present generally accepted accounting principles."

A subsequent APB project, undertaken by Paul Grady, a retired partner of Price Waterhouse, sought to inventory existing practices. Neither Grady's work, published as Accounting Research Study *(ARS) No. 7,* nor the work of the research division's initial two rejected studies had any documented effect on the establishment of an accounting framework. Moreover, the APB's *Statement No. 4,* titled "Basic Concepts and Accounting Principles Underlying Financial Statements of Business Enterprises," was similar in tone to Grady's work and equally limited in building the structure required. Future opinions of the APB in fact carried the caveat to the effect that "this Opinion amends *APB Statement No. 4.*"

During this period, the American Accounting Association, which had previously issued several statements on accounting principles, published *A Statement of Basic Accounting Theory.* This statement, issued in 1966, listed four attributes that accounting information should possess to be useful: relevance, verifiability, freedom from bias, and quantifiability. An additional attempt by the association to contribute to the process in 1978, *Statement of Accounting Theory and Theory Acceptance,* noted the difficulties to be faced in the quest for a single theoretical structure for accounting.

The Financial Accounting Standards Board (1973 to the present)

Dissatisfaction with the APB on several fronts[10] led the AICPA in 1971 to appoint one commission, the Wheat study group, to study the setting of accounting principles and a second commission, the Trueblood study group, to examine the objectives of financial statements. The Wheat study group's recommendations led to the establishment of the FASB in 1973.

---

[10] Among these concerns, one of the more important was the lack of representativeness of the APB: essentially, only members of the CPA firms were members.

The development of a conceptual framework was one of seven projects on the FASB's initial technical agenda. Energizing the Board was the report of the Trueblood committee (formally, the Study Group on Objectives of Financial Statements), published in October of 1973, which provided the basis for the Board's conceptual framework. The Trueblood study objectives were similar to those provided by *APB Statement No. 4*. While more tentative than the recommendations of the Wheat study group, the Trueblood objectives provided the basis for *SFAC No. 1*. The work was done in stages, and the committee recognized that some of the pieces, including the objectives of financial reporting and the definition of the elements of financial statements, would themselves prove useful as work continued on the additional aspects of the framework. Eventually the conceptual framework came to include the four major documents shown in Exhibit 2–2. Like the *ARB*s, the *SFAC*s are not formally GAAP.

The development of each concept statement proved both time-consuming and controversial. However, currently *SFAC No. 1, No. 2,* and *No. 6* appear to have wide acceptance. *SFAC No. 5,* on recognition and measurement, was and remains controversial due largely to the strong, diverse views held concerning the relevant and reliable attribute to measure and the circumstances responsible for recognizing changes in the measured attribute. For example, how should inventories be valued? Should original cost, replacement cost, disposal value, or some other concept be used?

Controversy implies that changes are to be expected in the future. The FASB suggests in *SFAC No. 5* a possible restructuring of future financial statements. A brief discussion of these possible reporting changes is given next.

FUTURE DIRECTIONS (NOT CURRENTLY GAAP)

Exhibit 2–3 lists the elements of financial statements that constitute the full set of interrelated statements envisioned for the future. *SFAC No. 5* does not illustrate the five individual statements, nor does it indicate an expected implementation time. This section discusses and briefly illustrates some ideas about how the restructured statements may evolve.

Balance Sheet

This statement would continue to report assets, liabilities, and owners' equity. The subclassifications will change and owners' equity will reflect a major restructuring because of the importance that will be given the change statements. For example, the restructured balance sheet may evolve with a new title to look like this:

Statement of Financial Position (summarized)
December 31, 1991
(in thousands)

Assets:		
(By new classifications not yet specified)		$611
Liabilities:		
(By new classifications not yet specified)		$150
Owners' equity:		
Accumulated equity contributed by owners $387*		
Accumulated comprehensive income . . . . 74†		
Total owners' equity		461
Total liabilities and owner's equity		$611

*From the statement of investments by and distributions to owners.

†From the statement of comprehensive income.

Income Statement

The statement of earnings (a change statement) described in *SFAC No. 5* corresponds to the traditional income statement now used *except* that it will be limited to continuing operations, unusual and infrequent items, and extraordinary items. It will exclude items that are extraneous to the current reporting period, such as the cumulative effect of a change in accounting principle (discussed in Chapter 4). The statement of earnings (or income statement) may look like this (also with a new title):

Statement of Earnings (summarized)
For the Year Ended December 31, 1991
(in thousands)

Revenues		$100
Expenses		(80)
Gain from unusual source		3
Income from continuing operations		23
Loss on discontinued operations:		
Income from operating discontinued segment	$ 10	
Loss on disposal of discontinued segment	(12)	(2)
Income before extraordinary items		21
Extraordinary loss		(6)
Earnings		15*

Earnings per share (to be specified):

*Carried to the statement of comprehensive income.

Statement of Comprehensive Income

This new statement would replace the traditional retained earnings statement. *Comprehensive income* is defined in *SFAC No. 5* (par. 30) as comprising *all recognized changes in equity (net assets) of the entity during the period from transactions and other events except those resulting from investments by owners and distributions to owners.* This new statement might appear something like this:

Statement of Comprehensive Income
For the Year Ended December 31, 1991
(in thousands)

Balance from prior period		$60
Earnings (from statement of earnings, given above)	$15	
Cumulative accounting adjustments:		
Cumulative effect of a change in accounting principle	(2)	
Other nonowner changes in owners' equity:		
Donated assets	1	
Comprehensive income		14
Ending balance, cumulative comprehensive income		$74*

*Carried to statement of financial position (the balance sheet).

Statement of Investments by and Distributions to Owners

This statement is briefly described in *SFAC No. 5*, pars. 55–57. It reports the "ways the equity increased or decreased from transactions with owners as owners during a period." *Investments by owners* establish or increase owners' equity and "may be received in the form of cash, goods or services, or satisfaction or conversion of the entity's liabilities." *Distributions to owners* decrease owners' equity by means of cash and property dividends when declared and "transactions such as reacquisitions of the entity's equity securities." This statement summarizes all capital changes. It starts with the beginning balance of each category of the capital stock accounts and ends with the balances at the end of the reporting period. The statement would be another change statement. The following statement continues the preceding examples:

Statement of Investments by and Distributions to Owners (summarized)
For the Year Ended December 31, 1991
(in thousands)

Items	Common Stock (Par $1)	Additional Contributed Capital	Treasury Stock	Dividends	Total Equity Contributed by Owners
Balance from prior period	$100	$200	$(10)		$290
Investments by owners:					
Stock issued	50	60			110
Treasury stock sold		2	5		7
Total investments	150	262	(5)		407
Distributions to owners:					
Cash dividend				$(20)	(20)
Stock dividend	30	36		(66)	–0–
Total distributions	30	36		(86)	(20)
Balance, December 31, 1991	$180	$298	$ (5)	$(86)	$387*

*Carried to statement of financial position (the balance sheet).

Statement of Cash Flows

This required statement reports the cash inflows and outflows classified by operating, investing, and financing activities during the reporting period. *SFAC No. 5* did not provide guidance about the details of this statement. However, it specified the basis for the statement of cash flows and discontinuance of the traditional statement of working capital flows. *SFAS No. 95* requires a statement of cash flows and provides detailed guidelines for its format, classifications, and terminology. The new statement of cash flow is discussed briefly in Chapter 5.

KEY TERMS

Assets (55)
Comparability (45)
Comprehensive income (55)
Conceptual framework (38)
Conservatism constraint (54)
Consistency (45)
Continuity assumption
  (going concern) (47)
Cost principle (48)
Cost-benefit constraint (52)
Definition (46)
Distributions to owners (55)
Equity (55)
Expenses (55)
Feedback value (44)
Full-disclosure principle (51)
Gains (55)
Industry peculiarities constraint (53)
Investments by owners (55)

Liabilities (55)
Losses (55)
Matching principle (50)
Materiality constraint (52)
Measurability (46)
Neutrality (44)
Predictive value (44)
Recognition (46)
Relevance (43)
Reliability (44)
Representational faithfulness (44)
Revenue principle (49)
Revenue (49)
Separate entity assumption (47)
Time-period assumption (48)
Timeliness (44)
Unit-of-measure assumption (47)
Verifiability (44)

QUESTIONS

1. What are the basic objectives of external financial reporting?
2. Identify and briefly explain the primary qualities of accounting information.
3. What is the secondary quality of accounting information? Briefly explain what this quality means.
4. Explain the difference between a revenue and a gain.
5. Explain the difference between an expense and a loss.
6. Explain the four basic environmental assumptions that underlie implementation of accounting.
7. What is the basic accounting problem created by the unit-of-measure assumption when there is significant inflation?
8. Explain why the time period assumption causes accruals and deferrals in accounting.
9. Relate the continuity assumption to periodicity of financial statements.
10. Which assumption or principle discussed in this chapter is most affected by the phenomenon of inflation? Give reasons for your choice.
11. Relate the continuity assumption to the use of accrual basis accounting.
12. Explain the cost principle. Why do you think cost is used in the basic financial statements instead of current value?
13. How is cost measured in noncash transactions?
14. Define the revenue principle and explain each of its three aspects: *(a)* definition, *(b)* measurement, and *(c)* realization.
15. How is revenue measured in transactions involving noncash items (exclude credit situations)?
16. Explain the matching principle. What is meant by "the expense should follow the revenue"?
17. Explain why the matching principle usually necessitates the use of adjusting entries. Use depreciation expense and unpaid wages as examples.
18. Relate the matching principle to the revenue and cost principles.
19. Briefly explain the continuity assumption.
20. Briefly explain the technical term *generally accepted accounting principles* (GAAP) as used by the accounting profession.
21. What accounting principle or assumption is manifested in each situation below?
    a. Prepayment for an annual license is allocated equally to expense over the next 12 months.
    b. Larry Williams owns a shoe repair shop, a restaurant, and a service station. Different and independent statements are prepared for each business.
    c. Inventories at King Store are valued at lower of cost or market (LCM).
    d. Although the inflation rate for the most recent fiscal year of Bill's Auto Dealership was 9%, no cognizance was taken of it in the year-end statements.
    e. While making a delivery, the driver for Bangs Appliance Store collided with another vehicle causing both property damage and personal injury. The party sued Bangs for damages that could exceed Bangs's insurance coverage. Existence of the suit was disclosed on Bangs's most recent financial statements.

EXERCISES

E 2–1
Topics of *FASB
Statements of Financial
Accounting Concepts*
(L.O. 1)

The *FASB Statements of Financial Accounting Concepts* discussd in this textbook are as follows:

No.	Title
1.	Objectives of Financial Reporting by Business Enterprises
2.	Qualitative Characteristics of Accounting Information
5.	Recognition and Measurement in Financial Statements of Business Enterprises
6.	Elements of Financial Statements of Business Enterprises

Listed below are primary topics of the above *Statements*. Match the topics with the *Statements* by entering the appropriate *Statement* numbers in the blanks to the left.

No.	Primary Topics	No.	Primary Topics
1	Example: Defines statement users.		*j.* Revenues and expenses (defined).
	a. Recognition criteria.		*k.* Comprehensive income (defined).
	b. Defines assets, liabilities, and owners' equity.		*l.* Cost-benefit.
	c. Threshold for recognition.		*m.* Primary qualities of accounting information.
	d. Quality constraint.		*n.* Guidance in applying recognition criteria.
	e. Reliability.		*o.* Accrual accounting.
	f. Objectives of financial statements.		*p.* Materiality.
	g. Consistency.		*q.* Gains and losses (defined).
	h. Comparability.		*r.* Secondary quality of accounting information.
	i. Balance sheet (described).		

E 2-2
FASB Qualitative Characteristics
(L.O. 2)

SFAC No. 2 identifies the following "levels of qualitative characteristics of accounting" (lettered for response purposes):

Hierarchy Levels

A. Purpose of the characteristics of accounting information.
B. Primary qualities.
C. Characteristics of the primary qualities.
D. Secondary qualities.

Listed below are the individual qualitative characteristics that relate to the levels. Match these characteristics with the levels by entering the appropriate letters in the blanks to the left. If one does not fit any of the hierarchy levels, use N for "None of the above is correct."

Qualitative Characteristics

1. Comparability.		9. Materiality.	
2. Relevance.		10. Representational faithfulness.	
3. Feedback value.		11. Reliability.	
4. Accrual basis accounting.		12. Predictive value.	
5. Timeliness.		13. Cost principle.	
6. Cost-benefit.		14. Neutrality.	
7. Includes consistency.		15. Decision usefulness.	
8. Verifiability.			

E 2-3
Definitions—Relevance and Reliability
(L.O. 2)

SFAC No. 2 sets forth relevance and reliability as the primary qualitative characteristics of accounting information. Each primary quality has three characteristics. This conceptual framework is listed below. Provide a brief definition of each hierarchy level listed using the following format.

Hierarchy Level	Brief Definition
A. Relevance.	
1. Timeliness.	
2. Predictive value.	
3. Feedback value.	
B. Reliability.	
1. Representational faithfulness.	
2. Verifiability.	
3. Neutrality.	

E 2-4
Elements of Financial Statements
(L.O. 3)

SFAC No. 6 defines the elements of financial statements listed on the left below. To the right, some important aspects of the definitions are listed. Match the aspects with the elements by entering appropriate letters in the blanks. More than one letter can be placed in a blank.

Elements of Financial Statements	Important Aspect of the Definition of the Element
A. Revenues.	_____ 1. Residual interest in the assets after deducting liabilities.
B. Expenses.	_____ 2. Decreases ownership claims.
C. Gains.	_____ 3. Constitute the entity's ongoing major or central operations.
D. Losses.	
E. Assets.	_____ 4. Probable future economic benefits obtained by an entity.
F. Liabilities.	_____ 5. Using up of assets or incurrence of liabilities.
G. Owners' equity.	_____ 6. Enhancement of assets or settlements of liabilities.
H. Investments by owners.	_____ 7. From peripheral or incidental transactions of the entity.
I. Distributions to owners.	_____ 8. Probable future sacrifices arising from present obligations.
J. None of the above.	_____ 9. Increases in equity from peripheral or incidental activities.
	_____ 10. Increases in net assets (e.g., through donation) for an ownership interest.
	_____ 11. Decreases in net assets by transferring assets to entity owners.

E 2-5
Questions on Concepts
(L.O. 2, 3, 5)

Indicate whether each statement is true or false.

_____ 1. The users of financial statements that are recognized in the *FASB Statements of Financial Accounting Concepts* are limited to owners and creditors.

_____ 2. Materiality is identified as the threshold for recognition.

_____ 3. Comparability (including consistency) is a primary quality of accounting information.

_____ 4. Neutrality in accounting means that the information reported is neither biased in favor of a particular party nor consistently too high or too low.

_____ 5. Comparability and consistency are defined in the same way (as qualitative characteristics of accounting information).

_____ 6. Relevance and reliability are necessary for recognition.

_____ 7. Both gains and losses relate to peripheral or incidental transactions of the entity.

_____ 8. All items (resulting from a transaction) must be recognized if they meet the definition of a financial statement element.

_____ 9. The matching principle is completely independent of the cost principle.

E 2-6
Concepts Violated?
(L.O. 2, 3, 4, 5)

The *FASB Statements of Financial Accounting Concepts* are intended to provide guidance in analyzing and recording certain transactions and events. Below are several such cases. Indicate the concept that applies to each case and state whether the concept was followed or violated.

Case A. Loran Company used FIFO in 1990; LIFO in 1993; and FIFO in 1994.

Case B. Loran acquired a tract of land on credit by signing a $55,000, one-year, noninterest-bearing note. The asset account was debited for $55,000. The going rate of interest was 10%.

Case C. Loran always issues its annual financial report nine months after the end of the annual reporting period.

Case D. Loran recognizes all sales revenues on the cash basis.

Case E. Loran records interest expense only on the payment dates.

Case F. Loran includes among its financial statement elements an apartment house owned and operated by the owner of the company.

Case G. Loran never uses notes or supplemental schedules as a part of its financial reports.

E 2-7
Cash versus Accrual
Basis
(L.O. 3, 4)

The following summarized data were taken from the records of Zenia Company at December 31, 1992, end of the accounting year:

a. Sales: 1992 cash sales, $150,000; and 1992 credit sales, $110,000.

b. Cash collections during 1992: on 1991 credit sales, $30,000; on 1992 credit sales, $80,000; and on 1993 sales (collected in advance), $20,000.

c. Expenses: 1992 cash expenses, $180,000; and 1992 credit expenses, $70,000.

d. Cash payments during 1992: for 1991 credit expenses, $10,000; for 1992 credit expenses, $40,000; and for 1993 expenses (paid in advance), $7,000.

Required:

1. Complete the following statements for 1992 as a basis for evaluating the difference between cash and accrual accounting.

	Cash Basis	Accrual Basis
Sales revenue	$_____	$_____
Expenses	_____	_____
Net income	_____	_____

2. Which basis is in conformity with GAAP? Explain the basis for your answer.

E 2–8
Recognition and Measurement
(L.O. 4)

Indicate the recognition or measurement problem associated with each of the following items:

a. Recording employee morale as an asset.
b. Recording a future liability for employees related to medical benefits to be paid after retirement.
c. Recording a liability (and expense) for cleaning up chemical dumps.
d. Recognizing the goodwill associated with increased market acceptance of a product brand name.
e. Recognizing an expense associated with the granting of a stock option to an employee at a price currently below the stock's current market price.

E 2–9
Examples of Assumptions, Principles, and Constraints
(L.O. 5)

Listed below are the implementation assumptions, principles, and constraints, lettered for response purposes.

Assumptions, Principles, and Constraints

A. Separate entity assumption.
B. Continuity assumption.
C. Unit-of-measure assumption.
D. Time period assumption.
E. Cost principle.
F. Revenue principle.
G. Matching principle.
H. Full-disclosure principle.
I. Cost-benefit constraint.
J. Materiality.
K. Industry peculiarities.
L. Conservatism.

Below is a list of key phrases directly related to the above list. Match these phrases with the above list by entering the appropriate letters to the left.

Key Phrase

_____ 1. Criteria—definition, measurability, relevance, and reliability must be met.
_____ 2. Least favorable effect on income and/or total assets.
_____ 3. Common denominator—the yardstick.
_____ 4. Expenses incurred in earning the period's revenues.
_____ 5. Preparation cost versus value of benefit to the user.
_____ 6. Separate and apart from its owners and other entities.
_____ 7. Report all relevant information.
_____ 8. Reporting periods—usually one year.
_____ 9. Cash-equivalent expenditures to acquire.
_____ 10. Going concern basis.
_____ 11. Relative amount of an item that would not have changed or influenced the judgment of a reasonable person.
_____ 12. Exception to accounting principles and practices because of uniqueness of the entity.

PROBLEMS

P 2–1
Qualitative Characteristics
(L.O. 2)

During an audit of L. R. Grant Company, the situations given below were found to exist.

Situation A. The company recorded a $27.50 wrench as expense when purchased, although it had a ten-year estimated life and no residual value.

Situation B. For inventory purposes, Grant switched from FIFO to LIFO to FIFO for the same items during a five-year period.

Situation C. The company recognizes earnings on long-term construction contracts at the end of each year of the construction period based on estimates, while its major competitors recognize earnings only at the date the contract is completed based on actual results.

Situation D. Grant follows a policy of depreciating plant and equipment on the straight-line basis over a period of time that is 50% longer than the most reliable useful-life estimate.

Situation E. As an accounting policy, interest is reported at the end of each reporting period as the amount of interest expense less interest revenue.

Required:

1. Identify and briefly explain the qualitative characteristic of accounting information that is directly involved in each situation.
2. Indicate what the company should do in the future by way of any change in accounting policy.

P 2–2

Application of Characteristics, Assumptions, Principles, and Constraints

(L.O. 2, 4, 5)

The list of statements given below poses conceptual issues.

a. The accounting entity is considered to be separate and apart from the owners.

b. A transaction involving a very small amount does not need to be recorded because of materiality.

c. The monetary unit is not stable over time.

d. GAAP always requires supplementary notes to the financial statements.

e. GAAP often requires that the lower-of-cost-or-market (LCM) method be used in valuing inventories.

f. The cost principle relates only to the income statement.

g. Revenue should be recognized only when the cash is received.

h. Accruals and deferrals are necessary because of the separate entity assumption.

i. Revenue should be recognized as early as possible and expenses as late as possible.

j. Relevance and reliability dominate all of the qualitative characteristics of accounting information.

Required:

1. Indicate whether each is correct or incorrect.
2. Identify the implementation assumption, principle, or constraint that is controlling.
3. Provide a brief discussion of its implications.

P 2–3

Accrual and Cash Basis Compared

(L.O. 3, 4)

The following summarized data were taken from the records of The SafeLock Corporation at the end of the annual accounting period, December 31, 1992:

Sales for cash	$311,000
Sales on account	84,000
Cash purchases of merchandise for resale	170,000
Credit purchases of merchandise for resale	40,000
Expenses paid in cash (includes any prepayments)	71,000
Accounts receivable:	
Balance in account on 1/1/1992	27,000
Balance in account on 12/31/1992	50,000
Accounts payable:	
Balance in account on 1/1/1992	14,000
Balance in account on 12/31/1992	16,000
Merchandise inventory:	
Beginning inventory, 1/1/1992	50,000
Ending inventory, 12/31/1992	62,000
Accrued (unpaid) wages at 12/31/1992 (none at 1/1/1992)	5,000
Prepaid expenses at 12/31/1992 (none at 1/1/1992)	3,000
Operational assets—equipment:	
Cost when acquired	100,000
Annual depreciation	9,000

Required:

1. Based on the above data, complete the following income statements for 1992 in order to evaluate the difference between cash and accrual basis (show computations):

	Accrual Basis	Cash Basis
Sales revenue	$_____	$_____
Less expenses:		
Cost of goods sold . . . . $_____	$_____	
Depreciation expense . . . . . _____	_____	
Remaining expenses . . . . . . _____	_____	
Total expenses	_____	_____
Pre-tax income	$_____	$_____

2. Which basis is in conformity with GAAP? Give support for your answer.

**P 2-4
Application of
Assumptions, Principles,
and Constraints
(L.O. 3, 5)**

An inspection of the annual financial statements and the accounting records revealed that the William F. Jones company had violated some implementation assumptions, principles, and constraints. The following transactions were involved:

a. Merchandise purchased for resale was recorded as a debit to inventory for the invoice price of $20,000 (accounts payable was credited for the same amount); terms were 2/10, n/30. Ten days later the account was paid (cash was credited for $19,600).

b. Accounts receivable of $95,000 was reported on the balance sheet; this amount included a $42,000 loan to the company president. The maturity date on the loan was not specified.

c. Usual and ordinary repairs on operational assets were recorded as follows: debit operational assets, $87,500; credit cash, $87,500.

d. W. F. Jones sustained a $47,000 storm damage loss during the current year (no insurance). The loss was recorded and reported as follows:

> Income statement: Extraordinary item—storm loss, $40,000
> Balance sheet (assets): Deferred charge, storm
>   loss, $7,000

e. Treasury stock (i.e., stock of the company that was sold and subsequently bought back from the stockholders) was debited to treasury stock and was reported on the balance sheet as an asset at the purchase cost, $72,000.

f. Depreciation expense of $227,000 was recorded as a debit to retained earnings and was deducted directly from retained earnings on the balance sheet.

g. Income tax expense of $15,000 was recorded as a debit to retained earnings and was deducted directly from retained earnings on the balance sheet.

Required:

1. For each transaction, identify the inappropriate treatment and the assumptions, principles, and constraints violated.
2. Give the entry that should have been made and the appropriate reporting.

P 2-5

COMPREHENSIVE PROBLEM
♦

**Implementation of
Principles
(L.O. 3, 4, 5)**

The transactions summarized below were recorded as indicated for The Rich Company during the current year.

a. The Rich company needed a small structure for temporary storage. A contractor quoted a price of $837,000. The company decided to build it itself. The cost was $643,000, and construction required three months. The following entry was made:

Buildings—warehouse	837,000	
Cash		643,000
Revenue—self-construction		194,000

b. Rich owns a plant located on a river that floods every few years. As a result, the company suffers a flood loss regularly. During the current year, the flood was severe, causing an uninsured loss of $157,000, which was the amount spent to repair the flood damage. The following entry was made:

Retained earnings, flood loss	157,000	
Cash		157,000

c. The company originally sold and issued 100,000 shares of $1 par value common stock. During the current year, 80,000 of these shares were outstanding and 20,000 were held by the company as treasury stock (they had been repurchased from the stockholders in prior years). Near the end of the current year, the board of directors declared and paid a cash dividend of $4 per share. The dividend was recorded as follows:

```
Retained earnings  . . . . . . . . . . . . . . . . . . . . . . . . 400,000
        Cash  . . . . . . . . . . . . . . . . . . . . . . . .          320,000
        Dividend income ($4 × 20,000) . . . . . . . . . . . . .         80,000
```

d. The Rich company purchased a machine that had a list price of $80,000. The company paid for the machine in full by issuing 8,000 shares of its common stock, par $10 (market price $15). The purchase was recorded as follows:

```
Machine . . . . . . . . . . . . . . . . . . . . . . . . . . . . 80,000
        Capital stock . . . . . . . . . . . . . . . . . . . . . . .        80,000
```

e. On December 28, the company collected $33,000 cash in advance for merchandise to be available and shipped during February of the next accounting year (the accounting period ends December 31). This transaction was recorded on December 28 as follows:

```
Cash  . . . . . . . . . . . . . . . . . . . . . . . . . . . . . 33,000
        Sales revenue  . . . . . . . . . . . . . . . . . . . . . .        33,000
```

Required:

1. For each transaction, determine what implementation accounting principle was violated (if any).
2. Explain the nature of the violation.
3. In each instance, indicate how the transaction should have been recorded.

CASES

C 2–1
Discuss: Any Conceptual
Violations?
(L.O. 1, 2, 3, 5)

Two independent cases given below violate some parts of the conceptual framework of accounting. For each case, explain *(a)* the nature of the incorrect accounting and reporting and *(b)* what parts of the conceptual framework are directly violated.

Case A. The financial statements of Raychem Corporation included the following note: "During the current year, plant assets were written down by $8,000,000. This write-down will reduce future expenses. Depreciation and other expenses in future years will be lower and, as a result this will benefit profits of future years."

Case B. During an audit of The Silvona Company, certain liabilities, such as taxes, appear to be overstated. Also some semiobsolete inventory items seem to be undervalued, and the tendency is to expense rather than to capitalize as many items as possible.

   Management states that "the company has always taken a very conservative view of the business and its future prospects." Management suggests that they do not wish to weaken the company by reporting any more earnings or paying any more dividends than are absolutely necessary, because they do not expect business to continue to be good. They point out that the lower valuations for assets, and so on, do not lose anything for the company but do create reserves for "hard times."

C 2–2
Full Disclosure
(L.O. 2)

Explain how each of the following items, as reported on General Tool Corporation's balance sheet violated (if it did) the full-disclosure principle.

a. There was no comment or explanation of the fact that the company changed its inventory method from FIFO to LIFO at the beginning of the current reporting period. A large changeover difference was involved.
b. Owners' equity reported only two amounts: capital stock, $200,000; and retained earnings, $130,000. The capital stock has a par value of $100,000 and originally sold for $200,000 cash.
c. Sales revenue was $950,000 and cost of goods sold, $600,000; the first line reported on the income statement was revenues, $350,000.
d. No earnings per share (EPS) amounts were reported.

e. Current assets amounted to $312,000 and current liabilities, $205,000; the balance sheet reported as a single amount, working capital, $107,000.

f. The income statement showed only the following classifications:
   (1) Gross revenues.
   (2) Costs.
   (3) Net profit.   (AICPA adapted)

C 2–3
Elements: Application
(L.O. 3)

For some time, new airlines have been offering frequent-flyer mileage credits to customers. Currently there exists a huge resource of potential trips the public could sign up for at the airlines' expense. Yet the airlines do not recognize a liability for these outstanding claims on their passenger-flying capacity.

Required:

1. Does an airline have a liability for unused frequent-flyer miles?
2. What argument might the airline make if it wished to avoid recognizing a liability?
3. If a liability is to be shown, how would the amount be established? What account would be debited when the liability was recognized?

C 2–4
Qualitative Characteristics
(L.O. 5)

The following quotation is from *Forbes* magazine, November 7, 1983, p. 106:

> Last summer followers of Rockwell International, the $7.4 billion conglomerate, probably noticed a *Wall Street Journal* article giving painful details of the company's computer-leasing fiasco with OPM Leasing Service. The story said that Rockwell has not revealed the amount of the losses, calling them "immaterial." But tucked away was the *Journal's* assertion that a member of the company's outside accounting firm, Deloitte, Haskins & Sells, told the paper that fraud-related losses that are less than 10% of the company's $2.2 billion in shareholder equity might properly be considered not material. Both Rockwell and Deloitte insist that the comment in question was taken out of context.

Required:

1. Explain the qualitative characteristic of accounting information that is at issue in this quotation.
2. Assess the situation as described in the quotation.
3. Suppose the controller is informed by the president that the amount is to be considered not material. What should the controller do?

C 2–5
Sherwin-Williams:
Analyzing Actual
Financial Statements
(L.O. 2)

This case relates to the 1990 financial statements of Sherwin-Williams which can be located in the appendix at the end of the book.

Required:

1. To become familiar with the 1990 financial statements respond to the following:
   a. Date the annual reporting period ends is _____. Is the firm a calendar-year reporting firm?
   b. Net sales for 1990 were $_____.
   c. Net increase (decrease) in cash and cash equivalents for 1990 was $_____.
   d. Total assets at the end of the 1990 reporting period were $_____.
   e. Note No. 1 to the consolidated financial statements was titled _____.
       How many notes were provided? _____.
   f. What is the name of the auditing firm?
2. The following questions related to the conceptual framework:
   a. What *FASB Standards* or *APB Opinions* are discussed? What does the reporting say, if anything, about their expected future impact on Sherwin-William's financial statements?
   b. Do the financial statements refer to GAAP at any point?
   c. How does the company apply the matching principle to:
       (1) Research and development costs?
       (2) Intangibles?
       (3) Depreciation?
       (4) Inventories?
       (5) Cost of health care and life insurance benefits?
       (6) Deferred compensation costs?

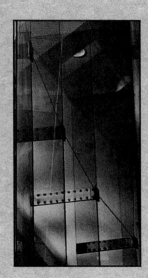

Review: The Accounting Information Processing System

After you have studied this chapter, you will:

1. Understand the purpose of an accounting information system.

2. Have a renewed understanding of the double-entry recording system and the relationships among financial statements.

3. Understand the relationships among accounting information system components: accounts, journals, ledgers, and financial statements.

4. Be able to perform the accounting cycle steps leading to the financial statements.

5. Recognize the difference between two methods of recording common operating transactions and understand the effects of each on adjusting and reversing entries.

6. Understand the role of the worksheet in the accounting cycle. (Refer to Appendix 3A.)

7. Be familiar with special journals and ledgers. (Refer to Appendix 3B.)

◆

INTRODUCTION
◆

Egghead Incorporated, the nation's largest personal-computer software vendor in 1989, reported a $12.1 million loss in that year. A portion of this loss was the result of misplaced paperwork and unrecorded transactions. It seems that the company's explosive growth "outpaced the systems and procedures that were in place" to handle the increased volume of transactions.[1]

S. E. Nichols, an East Coast retail chain, inadvertently underreported its 1988 ending balance in accounts payable by $2 million. The company hired Price Waterhouse, a large CPA firm, to help them determine the correct balance. The understatement resulted from improper accounting treatment.[2]

Phoenix Data Systems, a computer software company that went out of business in 1986, was another company with accounting system problems. "Lax procedures for recording sales often resulted in an inability to collect payment."[3] Phoenix was alerted by its auditors as early as 1983 about these problems.

The above examples illustrate the problems that can result from an ineffective **accounting information system (AIS).** They also illustrate internal control problems, which tend to go hand-in-glove with accounting system problems.[4] An AIS consists of physical components, including journals, ledgers, and computer software used to capture transaction data and process it into usable accounting information. Added to these physical components are company policies, procedures, and programs that administer data collection and processing for internal management needs and external financial reporting. The rather dire corporate situations illustrated above point up the importance of an AIS to survival and success.

Internally, an AIS provides data relevant to a large variety of questions faced by managers. For example:

+ What is our cash position? How is it expected to change?
+ When must inventory be purchased?
+ When should customers be billed?
+ How much is it costing to carry our accounts receivable?
+ Is a profit being made?
+ Are there more profitable products and services to market?
+ Where can costs be cut?

With a well-designed AIS, a business can determine whether its activities are adding value for its shareholders or, alternatively, consuming their investment.

State and federal laws require most large for-profit companies to maintain adequate records to support the information published in financial statements. For example, the Internal Revenue Service requires adequate evidence to substantiate tax returns. The Foreign Corrupt Practices Act, which amended the Securities Exchange Act of 1934, requires registrants to maintain reasonably accurate records in conformity with generally accepted accounting principles.

AIS costs are substantial for most firms. These costs increase with the expansion in the number and complexity of *FASB Statements* and other pronouncements, and as tax and regulatory reporting requirements grow. Many smaller businesses have difficulty coping with increased record-keeping and reporting requirements. One such company, AW Computer Systems, usually hired an accountant to do occasional bookkeeping work several times during the year. Then the company expanded its operations and sold capital stock to the public for the first time. The additional reporting requirements of going public caused annual AIS costs to increase $70,000.[5]

---

[1] "Egghead Inc. Posts Loss of $12.1 Million for Its Fiscal Year", *The Wall Street Journal,* June 30, 1989, p. B2.

[2] "S. E. Nichols Finds Balance-Sheet Error," *The Wall Street Journal,* December 14, 1988, p. C23.

[3] "Cracks in the Foundation," *Forbes,* November 16, 1987, p. 65.

[4] A firm's internal control system includes the policies and procedures designed to assure that the firm's goals are met. These policies and procedures are designed to safeguard assets, promote reliable accounting records, encourage compliance with firm policy, and evaluate efficiency.

[5] "The World Accounting to GAAP," *Forbes,* June 8, 1981, p. 148.

The primary objective of financial statements, an important output of the AIS, is *to provide investors and creditors with information useful for making decisions*.[6] These decisions involve assessments of the firm's profitability, its ability to generate cash flows, and the strengths and weaknesses of its financial position. This chapter reviews the fundamentals of the AIS cycle of steps leading to those financial statements.

◆

ACCOUNTS, TRANSACTION RECORDING, AND FINANCIAL STATEMENTS

◆

As noted earlier, the AIS serves both internal and external information needs. External information needs are the primary focus of financial accounting and this text.[7] In addition to the financial statements, companies release quarterly earnings reports and other financial disclosures. *The Wall Street Journal* and other business publications routinely report this information.

Financial accounting information is recorded in accounts that are the formal records of specific resources, obligations, and their changes. The seven major types of accounts are grouped into two fundamental classifications: permanent accounts (assets, liabilities, and owners' equity accounts) and temporary accounts (revenues, expenses, gains, and losses).[8] The permanent accounts appear in the balance sheet. The descriptive term *permanent* means that balances in these accounts are carried over to future accounting periods. The following *accounting identity* relates the balances of the permanent accounts:

$$Assets = Liabilities + Owners' Equity$$

This identity indicates the recorded value of assets, and their sources.

The temporary accounts report changes in permanent accounts related to income-generating activities. For example, when rent is paid and rent expense is recognized, the rent expense account describes the reason for the decrease in cash. Temporary accounts are closed at the end of the accounting period.

The recording of economic events is a central feature of an AIS. These recordings affect at least two accounts. This practice, called the double-entry system, records the change in a resource or obligation *and* the *reason* for, or source of, the change.[9] In the rent example above, if only the cash decrease is recorded, no record of the purpose of the transaction is maintained.

The double-entry system also ensures that the accounting identity remains in balance. For example, when a company acquires $10,000 worth of equipment by tendering a note to the seller for the full price, both assets and liabilities increase by $10,000. The accounting identity remains in balance.

In addition to the double-entry aspect of transaction recording, the debit-credit convention is a recording and balancing procedure common to all accounting systems. This convention divides accounts into two sides. The debit (dr.) side is always the left side, and the credit (cr.) side is always the right side. These terms carry no

---

[6]. *Statement of Financial Accounting Concepts No. 1*, "Objectives of Financial Reporting by Business Enterprises," (Norwalk, Conn.: FASB, 1978), par. 34.

[7] Internal accounting information needs are addressed in managerial accounting courses.

[8] Permanent accounts are also called *real* accounts, and temporary accounts are also called *nominal* accounts. Other temporary accounts are used, including the cash dividends declared account, income summary, and various "holding" accounts, which are accounts used for a specific purpose but are not disclosed in financial statements. The cash dividends declared account is debited when dividends are declared.

[9] The first published work describing the double-entry system was authored by Luca Pacioli in A.D. 1494 in Venice.

further meaning. Depending on the account type, a debit or credit records an increase or decrease, as illustrated in the T-accounts below. The **T-account** is a form of account used for demonstrating transactions; it takes the form of the letter **T**.

Permanent Accounts

Assets		=	Liabilities		+	Owners' Equity	
Debit entries *increase* assets	Credit entries *decrease* assets		Debit entries *decrease* liabilities	Credit entries *increase* liabilities		Debit entries *decrease* owners' equity	Credit entries *increase* owners' equity

Temporary Accounts

Expenses		Revenues	
Debit entries *increase* expenses	Credit entries *decrease* expenses	Debit entries *decrease* revenues	Credit entries *increase* revenues

Losses		Gains	
Debit entries *increase* losses	Credit entries *decrease* losses	Debit entries *decrease* gains	Credit entries *increase* gains

The increase and decrease sides of each account type are assigned to maintain the accounting identity and the equality of debits and credits. The debit-credit convention is a recording mechanism designed to achieve these two goals. For example, increases in assets (debits) are often associated with increases in liabilities (credits). Asset decreases are often associated with expenses. Salary payments are an example. The dollar amount of the salary expense debit (increase) equals the dollar amount of the cash credit (decrease).

Recording the previous $10,000 equipment purchase causes the following changes to the two affected accounts:

Equipment (asset)		Note Payable	
Dr. $10,000			Cr. $10,000

The debit change equal the credit change, and the accounting identity remains in balance.

The debit-credit convention is a convenient way to check for recording errors. When the sums of debits and credits are not equal, an error is evident.[10] Without the convention, only increases and decreases in accounts would be recorded. For example, the payment of an account payable would result in two decreases (from cash and accounts payable). Assuming no errors in recording, the dollar value of account increases would generally not equal the dollar value of account decreases. Therefore, inequality of total increases and total decreases cannot be used to signal errors.

At the end of a reporting period, after all transactions and events are recorded in the accounts, adjusting entries are recorded and financial statements are prepared.

---

[10] The reverse, however, is not true. Equality of total debits and total credits does not imply that no errors have been made.

The financial statements include the income statement, balance sheet, and the statement of cash flows. Two other statements, the retained earnings statement and the statement of stockholders' equity, also are commonly reported. The financial statements report account balances, changes in account balances, and aggregations of accounts such as net income.

Four of these statements are articulated in an interrelated series of equations:

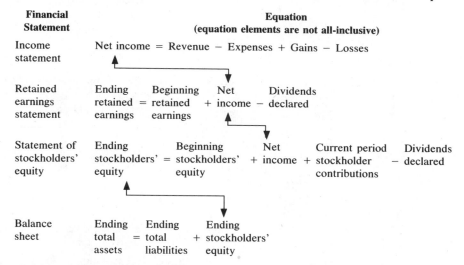

Financial Statement	Equation (equation elements are not all-inclusive)

Income statement

Net income = Revenue − Expenses + Gains − Losses

Retained earnings statement

Ending retained earnings = Beginning retained earnings + Net income − Dividends declared

Statement of stockholders' equity

Ending stockholders' equity = Beginning stockholders' equity + Net income + Current period stockholder contributions − Dividends declared

Balance sheet

Ending total assets = Ending total liabilities + Ending stockholders' equity

The income statement reports the portion of the change in net assets (owners' equity) described by income-producing activities. The retained earnings ending balance is a component of ending total owners' equity. The balance sheet reflects the accounting identity.

CONCEPT REVIEW

1. How does the double-entry system increase the effectiveness of an AIS?
2. Why is the debit-credit convention used, rather than merely recording increases and decreases in account balances?
3. Explain why an asset increase must be accompanied by an increase in liabilities or owners' equity, or both, or a decrease in another asset.

THE AIS AND THE ACCOUNTING CYCLE

An AIS is designed to accurately record and store financial data in a timely and chronological manner, facilitate retrieval of financial data in a form useful to management, and simplify periodic preparation of financial statements for external use. An AIS is fashioned to meet the company's information requirements. These requirements are affected by the firm's size, the nature of its operations, the volume of data, its organizational structure, and government regulation.

The **accounting cycle**, illustrated in Exhibit 3–1, is a series of sequential steps leading to the financial statements. This cycle is repeated each reporting period (normally a year).[11]

Depending on the information-processing technology used, certain accounting cycle steps are combined, or in some cases omitted. The fundamental nature of the

---

[11] Exhibit 3–1 applies to the preparation of all financial statements except the statement of cash flows, which requires additional input. The cash flow statement and its preparation are discussed in Chapter 5. Firms may combine some of these steps, or change their order, to suit their specific needs.

EXHIBIT 3-1   Steps in the Accounting Cycle and Their Objectives

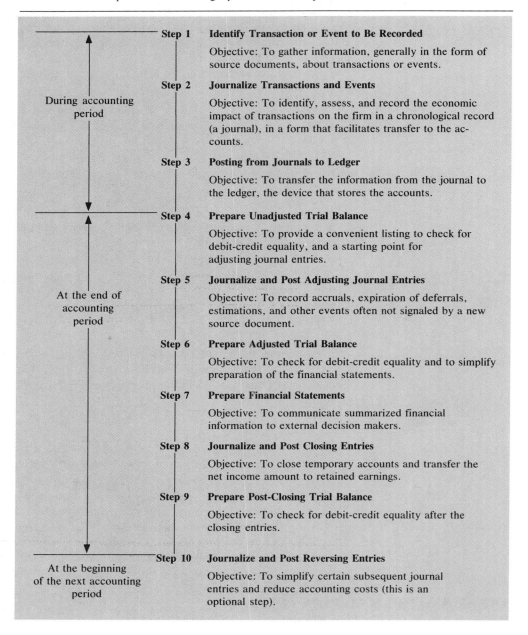

During accounting period

Step 1   Identify Transaction or Event to Be Recorded

Objective: To gather information, generally in the form of source documents, about transactions or events.

Step 2   Journalize Transactions and Events

Objective: To identify, assess, and record the economic impact of transactions on the firm in a chronological record (a journal), in a form that facilitates transfer to the accounts.

Step 3   Posting from Journals to Ledger

Objective: To transfer the information from the journal to the ledger, the device that stores the accounts.

At the end of accounting period

Step 4   Prepare Unadjusted Trial Balance

Objective: To provide a convenient listing to check for debit-credit equality, and a starting point for adjusting journal entries.

Step 5   Journalize and Post Adjusting Journal Entries

Objective: To record accruals, expiration of deferrals, estimations, and other events often not signaled by a new source document.

Step 6   Prepare Adjusted Trial Balance

Objective: To check for debit-credit equality and to simplify preparation of the financial statements.

Step 7   Prepare Financial Statements

Objective: To communicate summarized financial information to external decision makers.

Step 8   Journalize and Post Closing Entries

Objective: To close temporary accounts and transfer the net income amount to retained earnings.

Step 9   Prepare Post-Closing Trial Balance

Objective: To check for debit-credit equality after the closing entries.

At the beginning of the next accounting period

Step 10   Journalize and Post Reversing Entries

Objective: To simplify certain subsequent journal entries and reduce accounting costs (this is an optional step).

process, however, is independent of the technology used. Many systems are computerized to increase the speed and accuracy of the cycle. Worksheets often are used to perform several of these steps.[12] Worksheets are discussed in detail in Appendix 3A.

The first three steps in the accounting cycle require the largest amount of time and effort, and occur continuously throughout the period. The frequency of Step 3, posting, depends on the volume and nature of transactions. For example, firms with

---

[12] In manual systems, a worksheet is a sheet of acccounting paper used to plot adjusting entries and to develop a preliminary layout for the income statement, retained earnings statement, and the balance sheet. In automated systems, worksheets take the form of computer spreadsheets.

many daily cash transactions often post to the cash account daily. Steps 4 through 9 generally occur in the time period surrounding the fiscal year-end. Computerization can shorten the time required for these steps and improve the *relevance* of the reported information, without compromising the *reliability* of the information. The last step, reversing entries, is optional and occurs at the beginning of the next accounting period.

Step 1: Identify Transactions or Events to Be Recorded

The purposes of the first step are to *identify* those transactions and events that cause a change in the firm's resources or obligations and that require a journal entry, and to *collect* relevant economic data about those transactions.

Events that change a firm's resources or obligations are categorized into three types:

1. *Exchanges of resources and obligations between the reporting firm and outside parties.* These exchanges are **reciprocal transfers** or **nonreciprocal transfers**. In a reciprocal transfer the firm *(both)* transfers and receives resources (e.g., sale of goods). In a nonreciprocal transfer the firm *either* transfers *or* receives resources (e.g., payment of cash dividends or receipt of a donation) or nonresources (e.g., stock dividends). Exchanges generally require a journal entry.
2. *Internal events within the firm that affect its resources or obligations but that do not involve outside parties.* Examples include recognition of depreciation and amortization of long-lived assets and the use of inventory for production. These events also generally require a journal entry.
3. *Economic and environmental events beyond the control of the company.* Examples include changes in the market value of assets and liabilities, and casualty losses. Only some of these events require a journal entry.

Transactions[13] are often accompanied by a source document. Source documents generally are paper records that describe the transaction, the parties involved, the date, dollar amount, and other aspects of the event. Examples include sales invoices, freight bills, and cash register receipts. Certain events (e.g., the accrual of interest) are not signaled by a separate transaction or source document. Recording these transactions requires reference to the underlying contract or other source document supporting the original exchange of resources. Whether or not the AIS is computerized, source documents are essential for the initial recording of transactions (Step 2 in Exhibit 3–1). Source documents are also used for subsequent tracing and verification, for evidence in legal proceedings, and for audits of financial statements.

Step 2: Journalize Transactions and Events

The purpose of this step is to measure and record the economic impact of transactions in a form that simplifies transfer to the accounts. Accounting principles that guide measurement, recognition, and classification of accounts are applied at this step. Much of this text is concerned with the appropriate recording of economic events. The journal entry is an important means of illustrating the application of accounting principles, and it is used throughout this text.

Transactions are recorded in a journal, an organized medium for recording transactions in debit-credit format. A journal entry is a debit-credit recording of a transaction that includes the date, the accounts and amounts involved, and a description. A journal entry is a temporary recording; account balances are not changed until the information is transferred to the ledger accounts in Step 3.

---

[13] The term *transaction* in this text is applied to all changes requiring a journal entry.

EXHIBIT 3-2   General Journal Entry

	GENERAL JOURNAL			Page	J-16
Date 1991	**Accounts and Explanation**	**Post. Ref.**	**Amount**		
			Debit	**Credit**	
Jan. 2	Equipment	150	15,000		
	Cash	101		5,000	
	Notes payable	215		10,000	
	Purchased equipment for use in the business. Paid $5,000 cash and gave a $10,000, one-year note with 15% interest payable at maturity.				

Accounting systems usually have two types of journals: the general journal and several special journals. Nonrepetitive entries and entries involving infrequently used accounts are recorded in the general journal. Repetitive entries are recorded in special journals. If special journals are not employed, all transactions are recorded in the general journal. The following special journals are illustrated and discussed in Appendix 3B: sales journal, purchases journal, cash receipts journal, cash payments journal, and voucher systems. The general journal is used to illustrate most entries in this text.

Exhibit 3-2 illustrates a portion of a page from a general journal. The credited accounts are listed below and to the right of the debited accounts. This entry records equipment financed with cash and debt. The *historical cost* principle requires that the equipment be recorded at the value of the resources used to acquire it. The posting reference and page number reference are explained in Step 3.

The journal entry step is not absolutely essential; transaction data can be recorded directly into the accounts. However, the journal entry step has advantages. A journal is a place to record transactions when access to the ledger accounts is restricted. Also, the cost of immediately locating the ledger accounts involved in transactions is too expensive for many businesses. By using journals, review and analysis of transactions is much simpler, the accounts consume less storage space, and a chronological listing of transactions is provided. Transactions are difficult to reconstruct without a journal because the debits and credits are located in different accounts. Journals are part of the audit trail necessary for the audit of financial statements.

However, some companies use computerized systems to bypass the traditional journal entry step. Retailers, for example, can record all the relevant information about a transaction by using bar codes printed on many product packages. These codes contain machine-readable information, including sales price, cost, and quantity. Depending on the system, optical-scanning equipment reads the bar code and transmits the information to the computer, which records the proper amount directly in the affected ledger accounts at the point of sale. Accounting cost savings can be significant.

For example, before the use of bar codes at Tate Andale, a metal-fabricating firm in Baltimore, over 400 employee hours were required to record all inventory transactions each year. With bar code technology, that figure fell to 32 hours, and manual data entry was eliminated. The firm also experienced substantial increases in data accuracy.[14]

---

[14] "Wider Uses for Bar Codes," *Nation's Business,* March 1989, p. 34. The use of bar-code technology does not necessarily imply a bypass of the journal entry step, however.

CONCEPT REVIEW

1. Distinguish reciprocal and nonreciprocal transfers.
2. Does a journal entry immediately change account balances?
3. Explain why transactions usually are not recorded directly in the accounts as they occur.

Step 3: Post from Journals to Ledger

The process of transferring transaction data from the journal to individual accounts is called *posting*. Posting reclassifies the data from the chronological format in the journal to an account classification format in the ledger, the device for storing the formal accounts. Computerized systems store ledger data on tape or disc until needed for processing in conjunction with other steps in the accounting cycle.

Accounting systems usually have two types of ledgers: the general ledger and the subsidiary ledgers. The general ledger holds the individual accounts, grouped according to the seven account types previously discussed. Subsidiary ledgers support specific general ledger accounts that consist of many separate, individual accounts. For example, a firm with a substantial number of customer accounts receivable, one ledger account per customer, stores these separate accounts in an accounts receivable subsidiary ledger. The individual customer account is called the subsidiary account. The general ledger now needs only one account for accounts receivable, called the control account. The balance in accounts receivable control is the sum of all the individual customer account balances. In compiling financial statements, only the control accounts are considered.

To illustrate the relationship between control accounts and subsidiary ledgers, assume that a firm's accounts receivable consists of three individual accounts with a combined balance of $60,000. The firm's general and subsidiary ledgers show the following balances:

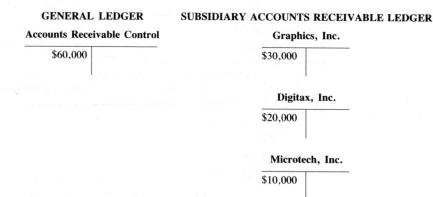

GENERAL LEDGER	SUBSIDIARY ACCOUNTS RECEIVABLE LEDGER
Accounts Receivable Control	**Graphics, Inc.**
$60,000	$30,000
	Digitax, Inc.
	$20,000
	Microtech, Inc.
	$10,000

Exhibit 3–3 illustrates a section of a general ledger. This ledger depicts the status of selected general ledger accounts after posting the January 2, 1991, journal entry shown in Exhibit 3–2. Posting references (or folio numbers) are used in both the journal and ledger to ensure that an audit trail exists. An audit trail provides answers to these questions: Where did this item in the account ledger come from? Where did this item in the journal go to? Posting references also serve to confirm that an entry was posted.

For example, when the $5,000 cash credit from the general journal entry in Exhibit 3–2 is posted to the cash ledger account, "101" is listed next to the amount in the journal to indicate the account number to which the credit is posted. Similarly, in the cash ledger account, "J-16" indicates the general journal page number from which this amount is posted. Cross-referencing is especially important for posting large

EXHIBIT 3-3   Portion of a General Ledger

<table>
<tr><td colspan="6" align="center">GENERAL LEDGER</td></tr>
<tr><td colspan="3" align="center">Cash</td><td colspan="3" align="right">Acct. 101</td></tr>
<tr><td>1991
Jan. 1</td><td>balance</td><td>18,700</td><td>1991
Jan. 2</td><td>J-16</td><td>5,000</td></tr>
<tr><td colspan="3" align="center">Equipment</td><td colspan="3" align="right">Acct. 150</td></tr>
<tr><td>1991
Jan. 1</td><td>balance</td><td>62,000</td><td></td><td></td><td></td></tr>
<tr><td>2</td><td>J-16</td><td>15,000</td><td></td><td></td><td></td></tr>
<tr><td colspan="3" align="center">Notes Payable</td><td colspan="3" align="right">Acct. 215</td></tr>
<tr><td></td><td></td><td></td><td>1991
Jan. 2</td><td>J-16</td><td>10,000</td></tr>
</table>

numbers of transactions, detecting and correcting errors, maintaining an audit trail, and in computerized systems in which original source documents are not filed in a manner convenient for retrieval.

Step 4: Prepare Unadjusted Trial Balance

An unadjusted trial balance is prepared at the end of the reporting period, after all transaction entries are recorded in the journals and posted to the ledger. The unadjusted trial balance is a list of general ledger accounts and their account balances, in the following order: assets, liabilities, owners' equity, and temporary accounts. Exhibit 3-4 illustrates an unadjusted trial balance for Sonora, Inc., a fictitious retailing company, at the end of the fiscal year. This trial balance reflects Sonora's transaction journal entries recorded during 1991 and is the basis for the remainder of the accounting cycle illustration.

The unadjusted trial balance is a convenient means for checking that the sum of debit account balances equals the sum of credit account balances. The unadjusted trial balance is the starting point for developing adjusting, closing, and reversing entries, and for the worksheet, if used. For accounts with subsidiary ledgers, only the control account balances are entered into the trial balance, after reconciliation with the subsidiary ledger.

If the sums of debit and credit balances are not equal, the error is identified and corrected. Equality of debits and credits does not, however, imply the accounts are error-free. An unposted journal entry, an incorrectly classified account, and an erroneous journal entry amount are examples of errors that do not cause inequality of total debits and credits.

Periodic and Perpetual Inventory Systems   As reported in Exhibit 3-4, Sonora uses a periodic inventory system. Under this system, merchandise on hand is counted and costed at the end of each accounting period. The resulting inventory amount updates the inventory account balance. During the period, however, the inventory account balance remains at the January 1 amount. The unadjusted trial balance for Sonora reflects the January 1, 1991, balance.

In contrast, when the perpetual system is used, the inventory account balance is constantly updated as merchandise is purchased and sold. Thus, under the perpetual

EXHIBIT 3–4 Unadjusted Trial Balance Illustrated

SONORA, INC.
Unadjusted Trial Balance
December 31, 1991

Account	Debit	Credit
Cash	$ 67,300	
Accounts receivable	45,000	
Allowance for doubtful accounts		$ 1,000
Notes receivable	8,000	
Inventory (periodic system)	75,000	
Prepaid insurance	600	
Land	8,000	
Building	160,000	
Accumulated depreciation, building		90,000
Equipment	91,000	
Accumulated depreciation, equipment		27,000
Accounts payable		29,000
Bonds payable, 6%		50,000
Common stock, par $10		150,000
Contributed capital in excess of par		20,000
Retained earnings		31,500
Sales revenue		325,200
Interest revenue		500
Rent revenue		1,800
Purchases	130,000	
Freight on purchases	4,000	
Purchase returns		2,000
Selling expenses*	104,000	
General and administrative expenses*	23,600	
Interest expense	2,500	
Extraordinary loss (pretax)	9,000	
Totals	$728,000	$728,000

Assets, *liabilities*, *owners' equity*, *temporary accounts* [handwritten annotations]

* These broad categories of expenses are used to conserve space.

system, the inventory account balance is correctly stated at the end of the accounting period, barring error.

As shown in Exhibit 3–4, Sonora's retained earnings account also reflects the January 1, 1991, balance since no transactions affected this account during 1991. Income tax expense is not listed in the unadjusted trial balance because the corporate income tax liability for the current year is not known until pretax income is computed.[15] The extraordinary loss does not yet reflect any tax effects.

CONCEPT REVIEW

1. Does the sum of the debit column in an unadjusted trial balance represent a meaningful total? If not, why is it computed?
2. Why might the retained earnings account balance in the unadjusted trial balance reflect the beginning-of-year balance?
3. Does equality of debits and credits in a trial balance assure the absence of errors in the accounts? Explain.

[15] Companies required to pay quarterly estimated income taxes would have a balance in this account at this point.

Step 5: Journalize and Post Adjusting Journal Entries

A firm's financial statements cannot be prepared until adjusting journal entries (AJEs) are recorded. AJEs are generally required when there is no source document to signal the need to recognize an event or transaction, or when a source document is not timely. Many economic changes take place continuously with the passage of time (e.g., depreciation, interest). Frequent recording of such economic events is costly and less efficient than recording AJEs at year-end.

AJEs also record changes in accounting estimates if new information is available, and are used to correct errors. AJEs generally record a resource or obligation change and usually involve both a permanent and a temporary account. Source documents from earlier transactions are the primary information sources for AJEs.

Accrual basis accounting requires these adjustments to reflect changes in resources and obligations under the *revenue, cost,* and *matching* principles, discussed in Chapter 2.[16] AJEs are recorded and dated *as of* the last day of the fiscal period. They are recorded in the general journal and posted to the ledger accounts.

Cash is generally not involved in AJEs because transactions affecting cash usually are accompanied by source documents. One exception is the entry required to adjust the cash balance upon receipt of a bank statement listing service charges and other items unknown until receipt of the statement.

Two Recording Methods   Many of the AJEs required in a particular situation depend on the method used for recording routine operational cash payments and receipts *that precede expense and revenue recognition*. One method, here called the **standard recording method**, records an asset on payment of cash before receiving a good or service, or a liability on receipt of cash before providing a good or service. For example, if two months' rent is prepaid on July 1, the standard method debits prepaid rent for the total amount. An adjustment is necessary later in the year to recognize rent expense and the expiration of prepaid rent.

The other method, here called the **expedient recording method**,[17] records an expense on payment of cash before receiving a good or service, or a revenue on receipt of cash before providing a good or service. In the rent example, the expedient method debits rent expense for two months' rent. This method is expedient because many such cash payments and receipts relate to expenses that apply only to the year in which the cash flow occurs. No adjustment is required for correct reporting of account balances at year-end. In the rent example, rent expense is correctly stated at year-end; no AJE is necessary.

However, if a portion of the expense or revenue applies to a future accounting period, an AJE is required for the expedient method. Our examples of AJEs include both reporting methods. AJEs are classified into three categories: deferrals, accruals, and other AJEs.

1. **Deferrals** (cash flows occur *before* expense and revenue recognition). These AJEs are used when cash is paid for expenses that apply to more than one accounting period, or when cash is received for revenue that applies to more than one accounting period. The portion of the expense or revenue that applies to future periods is deferred as a prepaid asset or unearned revenue (liability). In both cases, cash is paid or received before the asset is used or service is provided. Prepaid rent and revenue collected in advance are examples. The recording method used (standard or expedient) affects these AJEs.

[16] Cash basis accounting, which generally records a journal entry only upon an exchange of cash between firms, does not typically require many adjusting entries. For example, unpaid wages at the end of a fiscal year requires an adjusting entry under accrual accounting, but not under cash basis accounting. Cash basis accounting is not acceptable under GAAP but is used by some small companies.

[17] The terms *standard* and *expedient* are the authors' and are used to facilitate the discussion.

2. **Accruals** (cash flows occur *after* expense and revenue recognition). These AJEs are used when cash will be paid or received in a future accounting period, but all or a portion of the future cash flow applies to expenses or revenues of the current period. For example, unpaid wages accrued as wage expense at year-end represent wage cost matched against current-year revenues, but which will be paid next year. Uncollected interest accrued as interest revenue at year-end represents revenue earned in the current year, but which will be collected next year. In both cases, the expense or revenue is recognized before the cash flow occurs.

3. **Other Adjusting Entries** These AJEs do not fall into the previous two categories and include
   * Reclassifications of permanent accounts.
   * Estimations of expenses (bad-debt expense, for example).
   * Cost allocations (depreciation, for example).
   * Recognition of cost of goods sold and inventory losses.
   * Corrections of errors.

Examples of Adjusting Entries

Sonora's December 31, 1991, unadjusted trial balance (Exhibit 3–4) and additional information are used to illustrate AJEs. (A vertical line indicates a continuation of the Sonora Company example.)

Deferrals

prepaid expense

Deferred Expense   On November 1, 1991, Sonora paid a six-month insurance premium of $600 in advance. On that date, the $600 payment is recorded as a debit to prepaid insurance and a credit to cash (the standard method). On the unadjusted trial balance, the full $600 payment is reflected in prepaid insurance. But $200 worth of these insurance benefits (one third) are applicable to 1991. Therefore, under the matching principle, a $200 expense recognizing the partial expiration of the asset is recorded. Sonora records insurance expense and other similar expenses in the general and administrative expense account. AJE *a* adjusts prepaid insurance and recognizes the expense:

a. December 31, 1991:

General and administrative expense	200	
Prepaid insurance		200

The credit to prepaid insurance records the reduction in the asset that took place during the last two months of 1991 as insurance benefits were received. No source document or transaction signalled this entry although the underlying insurance document was probably consulted. The remaining $400 of prepaid insurance reflects insurance coverage for the first four months of 1992.

Unearned revenue

Deferred Revenue   Sonora leased a small office in its building to a client on January 1, 1991. The lease required $1,800 cash in advance for 18 months rent, which is recorded as a debit to cash and a credit to rent revenue (the expedient method). On December 31, 1991, the unadjusted trial balance reports $1,800 in rent revenue, which is overstated by the $600 (one third), relating to 1992. AJE *b* is required to reduce the revenue recognized in 1991 from $1,800 to $1,200, and to create a liability equal to the amount of rent relating to 1992 ($600).

b. December 31, 1991:

Rent revenue	600	
Rent revenue collected in advance		600

The expedient recording method is sometimes preferred because it reduces the number of AJEs required at year-end. Many similar assets and liabilities so recorded expire or are paid before year-end. If these expenditures or cash receipts are recorded initially as expenses or revenues, no AJE is required.

In the deferred-revenue example above, the ending account balances are the same under either recording method, assuming the correct AJEs are made. The end result in either case is a liability equal to the resources received for future services. These liabilities can be substantial. For example, the 1989 balance sheet of Time Warner, Inc. disclosed $449 million in current liabilities under the caption "Unearned portion of paid subscriptions." A footnote explained the liability:

> Revenues from paid magazine subscriptions are deferred until the magazines are delivered to subscribers. Upon each delivery, a proportionate share of the gross subscription price is included in revenues.

Accruals

Accrued Expense   Sonora previously issued, at face value, $50,000 of 6% bonds paying interest yearly each October 31. For the current accounting period, a two-month interest obligation developed, between October 31, 1991, and December 31, 1991. Under the matching principle, Sonora recognizes the appropriate amount of interest expense against the benefits obtained by using creditors' money. The amount for the two-month period is $500 ($50,000 $\times$ .06 $\times$ $\frac{2}{12}$). Therefore, on December 31, 1991, both the interest expense and associated payable are recognized in AJE *c:*

c. December 31, 1991:

Interest expense 500
     Interest payable   500

Accrued Revenue   Sonora's unadjusted trial balance lists $8,000 in notes receivable. The interest rate on these notes is 15% payable each November 30. As of December 31, 1991, the maker of the notes is obligated to Sonora for one month's interest of $100 ($8,000 $\times$ .15 $\times$ $\frac{1}{12}$). AJE *d* records the resulting receivable and revenue, and invokes the revenue recognition principle.

d. December 31, 1991:

Interest receivable 100
     Interest revenue   100

Other Adjusting Entries

Depreciation Expense   Property, plant, and equipment (plant assets) is the balance sheet category used to account for many productive assets with a useful life exceeding one year. The capital expenditures for these assets are matched against the revenues the assets help produce. Depreciation is a systematic and rational allocation of plant asset cost over a number of accounting periods.

The amount of depreciation expense recognized depends on a number of factors:
* The original expenditure and subsequent capitalized expenditures.
* The asset's useful life.
* The method chosen for depreciation recognition.
* The asset's residual value.

Depreciation is similar to the recognition of an expense on a deferred item such as prepaid insurance. In both cases, the cash flow occurs before the expense is recognized. The main differences are the longer life and greater uncertainty of expected benefits of plant assets.

AJE *e* illustrates depreciation recorded for Sonora at the end of 1991 under the straight-line method:[18]

| | | Residual | Useful | Proportionate Use by Function | |
| | | | | Selling | G & A* |
Asset	Cost	Value	Life—Years	Function	Function
Building	$160,000	$10,000	15	46%	54%
Equipment	91,000	1,000	10	40	60

*General and administrative.

The adjusting entry for these two assets is:

e. December 31, 1991:

Selling expense (depreciation)	8,200	
General and administrative expense (depreciation)	10,800	
Accumulated depreciation, building		10,000
Accumulated depreciation, equipment		9,000

Computation:

| | | | | General and |
		Total	Selling	Administrative
Building: [($160,000 − $10,000) ÷ 15 yrs.]	=	$10,000	× .46 = $4,600	× .54 = $ 5,400
Equipment: [$91,000 − $1,000) ÷ 10 Yrs.]	=	9,000	× .40 = 3,600	× .60 = 5,400
Totals		$19,000	$8,200	$10,800

AJE *e* also reduces the net carrying value of building and equipment accounts. Accumulated depreciation is a **contra account.** A contra account has a balance opposite that of the account to which it relates. Thus, accumulated depreciation is subtracted from the gross building and equipment accounts, leaving the net undepreciated account balances (net book value). Sonora's balance sheet (Exhibit 3–7) illustrates this offsetting. Contra accounts are useful when it is deemed advisable to report major assets at original cost.

Many methods of depreciation are permitted under GAAP. All entail a systematic and rational allocation of plant asset cost to accounting periods. However, depreciation expense recognized in a particular accounting period generally does not equal the portion of the asset's value that expired through use in that period. Depreciation expense recognition is not an asset valuation process. Furthermore, the undepreciated value of plant assets generally does not equal current value.

Depreciation expense is significant for companies with large investments in plant assets. For Rockwell International, in 1989, for example, depreciation expense was $496.5 million, or 68% of its net income.

Bad Debt Expense   A large percentage of goods and services are sold on credit. Typically, some accounts are never collected, resulting in bad debt expense. Uncollectible accounts receivable, which tend to rise with increased sales, represent a risk of doing business on credit terms. Accounts may become uncollectible one or more periods after the sale.

Based on past experience, most large firms are able to estimate the *probable* amount of uncollectible accounts. The bad debts estimate reduces income and accounts receivable in the period of sale. This practice avoids overstating both income and assets. Bad debt expense recognition is accomplished with an AJE

---

[18] Sonora debited two expense accounts because the company uses the building and equipment for selling and for general and administrative functions. Depreciation is commonly allocated to several functions, including manufacturing operations. Footnotes to the financial statements usually disclose the total amount of depreciation recognized.

debiting bad debt expense and crediting allowance for doubtful accounts, a contra-accounts receivable account.

Estimates of uncollectible accounts are based on credit sales for the period or the accounts receivable balance. To illustrate, assume that Sonora extends credit on $120,000 of sales during 1991. Prior experience indicates an expected 1% average bad debt rate on credit sales. Sonora treats bad debt expense as a component of selling expenses and records AJE *f*:

f. December 31, 1991:

Selling expense ($120,000 × .01)	1,200	
Allowance for doubtful accounts		1,200

The credit is made to the allowance account, rather than to accounts receivable, because the identities of the uncollectible accounts are not yet known. In addition, the use of the contra account maintains agreement between the balance in accounts receivable control and the total of account balances in the accounts receivable subsidiary ledger.

The $1,200 allowance is the portion of 1991 credit sales not expected to be collected. Net accounts receivable, the difference between the balance in accounts receivable and the allowance account, is an estimate of the cash ultimately expected to be received from sales on account. Bad debt expense is reported in the income statement although often not as a separate line-item.

Hughes Supply refers to bad debt expense as "provision for doubtful accounts," as illustrated in its 1988 income statement:

Provision for doubtful accounts $1,505,000

This provision (expense) relates to $432,366,000 of sales (less than 1%).

Of 600 surveyed companies, 47% used "allowance for doubtful accounts," and 84% used some type of contra account for the reduction in net accounts receivable associated with bad debt expense.[19]

For example, the 1989 balance sheet of USX Corporation disclosed the following:

	1989	1988
	(in millions)	
Receivables, less allowance for doubtful accounts of $13 and $17	$ 914	$1,536

Cost of Goods Sold   The determination of cost of goods sold, a retailer's largest expense, depends on whether a perpetual or periodic inventory system is used. In a perpetual system, an AJE is needed to recognize inventory losses due to theft and economic factors, or to correct errors. In a periodic system, cost of goods sold is determined either by an AJE or by closing entries, both of which update the inventory account and close inventory-related accounts.

A perpetual system maintains an inventory record for each item stocked. This record contains data on each purchase and each issue. An up-to-date balance is maintained in the inventory account. The cost of each item purchased is debited to the inventory account. To illustrate, assume an item that sells for $300 is carried in inventory at a cost of $180. A sale of this item requires two entries:

perpetual system

Cash or accounts receivable	300	
Sales revenue		300
Cost of goods sold	180	
Inventory		180

---

[19] *Accounting Trends and Techniques* (New York: American Institute of Public Accountants, 1990), p. 105.

Assuming no errors or inventory losses, the perpetual inventory ending balance equals the correct ending inventory amount. Under this assumption, cost of goods sold is also up-to-date, reflecting the recorded cost of all items sold during the period. Thus, no AJEs are needed unless the inventory account balance disagrees with the total of individual item costs determined by the annual physical count.

In contrast, a periodic system does not maintain a current balance in inventory or cost of goods sold. Instead, the physical inventory count at the end of the period is used to determine the ending balances of these two accounts. The purchases account, rather than the inventory account, is debited for all purchases during the period.

The unadjusted trial balance at the end of an accounting period reflects the beginning inventory in the periodic system, and cost of goods sold does not yet exist as an account. An AJE is therefore needed to set purchases, purchases returns, and other purchase-related accounts to zero (closed); to replace the beginning inventory amount with the ending inventory amount in the inventory account; and to recognize cost of goods sold for the period.

To illustrate, Sonora, which uses a periodic system, computes cost of goods sold and records AJE g as follows:

SONORA, INC.
Periodic Inventory Computation
December 31, 1991

Beginning inventory (carried over from the prior period)		$ 75,000
Add (from the current-year accounts):		
Purchases	$130,000	
Freight on purchases	4,000	
Purchase returns	(2,000)	
Net purchases		132,000
Total goods available for sale		$207,000
Less: Ending inventory (from physical count)		90,000
Cost of goods sold		$117,000

g. December 31, 1991:

Inventory (ending)	90,000	
Purchase returns	2,000	
Cost of goods sold (balancing amount)	117,000	
Inventory (beginning)		75,000
Purchases		130,000
Freight on purchases		4,000

Two sources of information contribute to entry g: the unadjusted trial balance from which several account balances are taken, and the physical inventory count indicating $90,000 of inventory on hand.[20]

Income Tax Expense   The recognition of income tax expense, an accrual item, is the final AJE. Most AJEs are recorded before determining pretax accounting income. Many firms pay estimated income taxes quarterly, which necessitates an AJE at the end of the accounting period to record fourth-quarter taxes due. For simplicity, assume that Sonora pays its income tax once each year after the end of the full accounting period.

A worksheet or partial adjusted trial balance (prior to income tax determination) simplifies the calculation of pretax income. For Sonora, this calculation follows. The

---

[20] Alternatively, the inventory-related accounts can be adjusted and *closed* in one step (see Footnote 23). The resulting reported income and financial position are not affected by the procedure chosen. The illustrated procedure may expedite the preparation of financial statements in some accounting systems. Recognition of shrinkage losses and other adjustments are discovered earlier, and cost of goods sold appears in the trial balance.

amounts in parentheses indicate the account balance in the unadjusted trial balance plus or minus the effects of AJEs, denoted by letter.

SONORA, INC.
Calculation of Pretax Income

Revenues:

Sales revenue	$325,200	
Interest revenue ($500 + $100 *d*)	600	
Rent revenue ($1,800 − $600 *b*)	1,200	$327,000

Expenses:

Cost of goods sold (*g*)	117,000	
Selling expenses	113,400	
($104,000 + $8,200 *e* + $1,200 *f*)		
General and administrative expenses	34,600	
($23,600 + $200 *a* + $10,800 *e*)		
Interest expense ($2,500 + $500 *c*)	3,000	
Extraordinary loss (pretax)	9,000	277,000
Total pretax income		$ 50,000

Assume that Sonora faces an average income tax rate of 40% and that the extraordinary loss is fully tax deductible. AJE *h* recognizes the resulting $20,000 ($50,000 × .40) income tax expense:

h. December 31, 1991:

Income tax expense 20,000		
Income tax payable		20,000

For simplicity, the entire income tax expense is recorded in one account. Sonora's income statement (Exhibit 3–6), however, separates the $3,600 income tax reduction associated with the extraordinary loss ($9,000 × .40) from income tax on income before extraordinary items. This practice, called *intraperiod tax allocation,* is discussed in Chapter 4.

Additional adjusting journal entries are illustrated in later chapters. In all cases, AJEs are posted to the appropriate ledger accounts.

CONCEPT REVIEW

1. Assuming the standard reporting method, prepare the AJE for the following situation: full payment of a $2,400, 2-year insurance policy on June 30, 1991, by a firm with a December 31 year-end.
2. Prepare the AJE for the situation in (1) assuming the expedient reporting method.
3. Why is the 1991 ending balance in prepaid insurance the same under either method?

Step 6: Prepare Adjusted Trial Balance

At this point in the cycle, the transaction journal entries and the AJEs are journalized and posted, and an **adjusted trial balance** is prepared. This trial balance lists all the account balances that will appear in the financial statements (with the exception of retained earnings, which does not yet reflect the current year's net income or dividends). The purpose of the adjusted trial balance is to confirm debit-credit equality, taking all AJEs into consideration. Exhibit 3–5 presents the adjusted trial balance for Sonora.

EXHIBIT 3-5   Adjusted Trial Balance Illustrated

SONORA INC.
Adjusted Trial Balance
December 31, 1991

Account	Dr.	Cr.
Cash	$ 67,300	
Accounts receivable	45,000	
Allowance for doubtful accounts		$ 2,200
Notes receivable	8,000	
Interest receivable	100	
Inventory	90,000	
Prepaid insurance	400	
Land	8,000	
Building	160,000	
Accumulated depreciation, building		100,000
Equipment	91,000	
Accumulated depreciation, equipment		36,000
Accounts payable		29,000
Interest payable		500
Rent revenue collected in advance		600
Income tax payable		20,000
Bonds payable, 6%		50,000
Common stock, $10 par		150,000
Contributed capital in excess of par		20,000
Retained earnings		31,500
Sales revenue		325,200
Interest revenue		600
Rent revenue		1,200
Cost of goods sold	117,000	
Selling expenses	113,400	
General and administrative expenses	34,600	
Interest expense	3,000	
Income tax expense	20,000	
Extraordinary loss (pretax)	9,000	
Total	$766,800	$766,800

The account balances in the adjusted trial balance reflect the effects of AJEs. For example, the $400 balance in prepaid insurance equals the $600 balance in the unadjusted trial balance less the reduction caused by AJE *a*. New accounts not appearing in the *unadjusted* trial balance emerge from the adjustment process. For Sonora, the following accounts are created as a result of an AJE: interest receivable, interest payable, rent revenue collected in advance, income tax payable, cost of goods sold, and income tax expense. AJE *g* has the opposite effect by closing purchases, freight on purchases, and purchase returns. The financial statements now can be prepared from the adjusted trial balance.

Step 7: Prepare Financial Statements

The primary objective of financial accounting is to provide information useful to decision makers. The financial statements are the culmination of the accounting cycle. Financial statements can be produced for a period of any duration. However, monthly, quarterly, and annual statements are the most common.

EXHIBIT 3-6   Income Statement Illustrated

SONORA INC.
Income Statement
For the Year Ended December 31, 1991

Revenues:		
Sales	$325,200	
Interest	600	
Rent	1,200	
Total revenues		$327,000
Expenses:		
Cost of goods sold	117,000	
Selling	113,400	
General and administrative	34,600	
Interest	3,000	
Total expenses before income tax		268,000
Income before extraordinary item and tax		59,000
Income taxes on income before extraordinary items ($59,000 × .40)		23,600
Income before extraordinary items		35,400
Extraordinary loss	9,000	
Less tax savings ($9,000 × .40)	3,600	5,400
Net income		$ 30,000

SONORA INC.
Retained Earnings Statement
For the Year Ended December 31, 1991

Retained earnings, January 1, 1991	$31,500
Net income	30,000
Retained earnings, December 31, 1991	$61,500

The income statement, retained earnings statement,[21] and balance sheet are prepared directly from the adjusted trial balance. The income statement is prepared first because net income must be known before the retained earnings statement can be completed.

The temporary account balances are transferred to the income statement, and the permanent account balances are transferred to the balance sheet. Exhibit 3–6 illustrates the 1991 income and retained earnings statements of Sonora.

As previously mentioned, total income tax expense ($20,000) in the income statement is allocated as follows: $23,600 on income before extraordinary items less $3,600 tax *savings* on the extraordinary items.

The retained earnings statement explains the change in retained earnings for the period. If Sonora declared dividends during 1991, they would be subtracted in the retained earnings statement.

Exhibit 3–7 illustrates the 1991 balance sheet. The ending retained earnings balance is taken from the retained earnings statement, not the adjusted trial balance.

---

[21] A retained earnings statement *or* a statement of stockholders' equity generally is included in the complete set of financial statements. However, neither is considered to be a basic financial statement. Sonora chose to report a retained earnings statement because no changes occurred in the contributed capital accounts during 1991.

EXHIBIT 3–7   Balance Sheet Illustrated

SONORA, INC.
Balance Sheet
At December 31, 1991

Assets			Liabilities		
Current assets:			**Current liabilities:**		
Cash		$ 67,300	Accounts payable		$ 29,000
Accounts receivable . . .	$45,000		Interest payable		500
Allowance for doubtful			Rent revenue collected in		
accounts	2,200	42,800	advance		600
Notes receivable		8,000	Income taxes payable		20,000
Interest receivable		100	Total current liabilities		50,100
Inventory		90,000	**Long-term liabilities:**		
Prepaid insurance		400	Bond payable, 6%		50,000
Total current assets . .		208,600	Total liabilities		100,100
Operational assets:			**Stockholders' Equity**		
Land		8,000	**Contributed capital:**		
Building	$160,000		Common stock, par $10,		
Accumulated			15,000 shares issued		
depreciation,			and outstanding	$150,000	
building	(100,000)	60,000	Contributed capital in		
Equipment	91,000		excess of par	20,000	
Accumulated			Retained earnings	61,500	
depreciation,			Total stockholders'		
equipment	(36,000)	55,000	equity		231,500
Total operational					
assets		123,000			
Total assets		$331,600	Total liabilities and stock-holders' equity		$331,600

Step 8: Journalize and Post Closing Entries

Closing entries reduce to zero (close) the balances of temporary accounts related to earnings measurement and dividends. Closing entries are recorded in the general journal at the end of the accounting period and are posted to the ledger accounts. Permanent accounts are not closed because they carry over to the next accounting period. The retained earnings account is the only permanent account involved in the closing process.

Income Statement Accounts   Because net income is measured for a specific interval of time, the balances of the income statement accounts are reduced to zero at the end of each accounting period. Otherwise, these accounts would contain information from previous periods.

Some firms use the *income summary account* to accumulate the balances of income statement accounts. Income summary is an example of a temporary clearing account, an account used on a temporary basis for a specific purpose. The balances in expenses and losses are reduced to zero and transferred to income summary by crediting each of those accounts and debiting income summary for the total. Revenues and gains are debited to close them, while the income summary account is credited.

This process leaves a net balance in the income summary account equal to net income (credit balance) or net loss (debit balance) for the period. The income summary account is then closed by transferring the net income amount to retained earnings.[22] The following three entries are made by Sonora to formally transfer 1991 net income to retained earnings:

December 31, 1991:

1. To close the revenue and gain accounts to income summary:

Sales revenue 325,200
Interest revenue   600
Rent revenue 1,200
    Income summary   327,000

2. To close the expense and loss accounts to income summary:

Income summary 297,000
    Cost of goods sold   117,000
    Selling expenses   113,400
    General and administrative expenses   34,600
    Interest expense   3,000
    Extraordinary loss   9,000
    Income tax expense   20,000

3. To close income summary (i.e., transfer net income to retained earnings):

Income summary 30,000
    Retained earnings   30,000

After the first two closing entries are recorded and posted, the balance in income summary equals net income ($30,000), as shown in the following T-account:

Income Summary

(2) $297,000	(1) $327,000
	$30,000

At this point, the temporary accounts have a zero balance and are ready to begin the next period's accounting cycle. The third entry closes the income summary account and transfers net income to retained earnings.[23]

Dividends   When cash dividends are declared, firms debit either retained earnings or cash dividends declared, a temporary account. Dividends payable is credited. If cash dividends declared is debited, another closing entry is required:

---

[22] Many accountants prefer to close temporary accounts directly to retained earnings, bypassing the income summary account entirely.

[23] As mentioned in footnote 20, inventory-related accounts can be adjusted and closed in the closing process, as an alternative to the AJE approach illustrated previously in AJE g. If the closing alternative is used, the following three closing entries replace AJE g. as well as the three closing entries illustrated above:

Income summary 389,000   Inventory (end) 90,000
    Inventory (beg.)   75,000   Sales revenue 325,200
    Purchases   130,000   Interest revenue   600
    Freight on purchases   4,000   Rent revenue   1,200
    Selling expense   113,400   Purchase returns   2,000
    G & A expenses   34,600   Income summary   419,000
    Interest expense   3,000   Income summary 30,000
    Extraordinary loss   9,000   Retained earnings   30,000
    Income tax expense   20,000

Using this approach, inventory-related accounts are included with expenses and revenues for closing entry purposes. The net impact on the income summary account and, in turn, retained earnings is identical under both approaches. However, this approach does not isolate cost of goods sold in a separate account.

EXHIBIT 3-8

SONORA INC.
Post-Closing Trial Balance
December 31, 1991

Account	Dr.	Cr.
Cash	$ 67,300	
Accounts receivable	45,000	
Allowance for doubtful accounts		$ 2,200
Notes receivable	8,000	
Interest receivable	100	
Inventory	90,000	
Prepaid insurance	400	
Land	8,000	
Building	160,000	
Accumulated depreciation, building		100,000
Equipment	91,000	
Accumulated depreciation, equipment		36,000
Accounts payable		29,000
Interest payable		500
Rent revenue collected in advance		600
Income tax payable		20,000
Bonds payable, 6%		50,000
Common stock, $10 par		150,000
Contributed capital in excess of par		20,000
Retained earnings		61,500
Total	$469,800	$469,800

Retained earnings . . . . (amount of dividends)
    Cash dividends declared   . . .   (amount of dividends)

In this case, the net result of closing entries is to transfer to retained earnings an amount equal to earnings less dividends declared for a period.

Step 9: Prepare Post-Closing Trial Balance

A post-closing trial balance lists only the balances of the permanent accounts after the closing process is finished (the temporary accounts have zero balances). This step is taken to check for debit-credit equality after the closing entries are posted. Firms with a large number of accounts find this a valuable checking procedure because the chance of error increases with the number of accounts and postings. The retained earnings account is now stated at the correct ending balance and is the only permanent account with a balance different from the one shown in the adjusted trial balance. Exhibit 3–8 illustrates the post-closing trial balance.

Step 10: Journalize and Post Reversing Journal Entries

After the adjusting and closing entries are journalized and posted to the general ledger, the accounts are ready for recording in the next period. Depending on the firm's accounting system and its accounting policy, the **reversing journal entry** (RJE) may be used to simplify certain journal entries in the next accounting period.

RJEs are *optional* entries that

• Are dated the first day of the next accounting period.
• Use the same accounts and amounts as an AJE but with the debits and credits reversed.
• Are posted to the ledger.

RJEs can reduce AIS costs. The following is an example of reversing an AJE:

December 31, 1991—Adjusting entry:

Interest expense 400
    Interest payable   400

January 1, 1992—Reversing entry:

Interest payable 400
    Interest expense   400

RJEs are appropriate only for AJEs that

1. Defer the recognition of revenue or expense items recorded under the expedient method, or
2. Accrue revenue or expense items during the current period rather than during future period when the associated cash flow occurs (e.g., wages expense).

In the following examples, assume a December 31 year-end.

Deferred Item—Expedient Method Assume that on November 1, 1991, $300 is paid in advance for three months' rent:

November 1, 1991—Originating entry:

Rent expense 300
    Cash   300

December 31, 1991—Adjusting entry:

Prepaid rent 100
    Rent expense   100

	With Reversing Entry	Without Reversing Entry
January 1, 1992 Reversing entry:	Rent expense . . . . . . 100 Prepaid rent 100	
1992 Subsequent entry:	None needed	Rent expense . . . . . . 100 Prepaid rent 100

With or without an RJE, rent expense recorded in 1992 is $100. However, the RJE saves the cost and effort required to review the relevant accounts and source documents to determine the subsequent year's entry. The RJE accomplishes the necessary adjustment to the accounts while the information used in making the AJE is available. The RJE is posted in 1992, the year it is recorded.

Under the standard method, the originating entry follows:

November 1, 1991—Originating entry:

Prepaid rent 300
    Cash   300

December 31, 1991—Adjusting entry:

Rent expense 200
    Prepaid rent   200

An RJE is not appropriate in this situation because a subsequent entry is required whether or not the AJE is reversed. No purpose is served by reinstating (debiting) prepaid rent $200 because that amount has expired.

Accrued Item Assume that the last payroll for 1991 is December 28. Wages earned through December 28 are included in this payroll. The next payroll period ends January 4, 1992, at which time $2,800 of wages will be paid. Wages earned for the

EXHIBIT 3–9   Summary Table: Reversing Entries and Recording Methods

Adjusting Entry Type*	Originating Entry Description	Adjusting Entry Description	Reversing Entry	Subsequent Entry
Deferrals, *standard recording*	Record an asset or liability	Recognize expense or revenue for current period, reduce the asset or liability	Not applicable	Recognize remaining expense or revenue, remove remaining asset or liability
Deferrals, *expedient recording*	Record an expense or revenue	Record asset or liability for portion of resource of obligation remaining, reduce the expense or revenue	If made	None
			If not made	Recognize remaining expense or revenue, remove remaining asset or liability
Accruals	None	Record an expense or revenue, and corresponding liability or asset	If made	Recognize expense or revenue equal to cash flow
			If not made	Recognize expense or revenue since start of fiscal year, remove the asset or liability

*The expedient recording method and RJEs are not appropriate for most "other" AJEs (such as depreciation).

three-day period ending December 31, 1991, are $1,500, which will be paid in 1992. The following AJE is necessary to accrue these wages:

December 31, 1991—Adjusting entry:

Wages expense 1,500
    Wages payable 1,500

	With Reversing Entry		**Without Reversing Entry**	
January 1, 1992 Reversing entry:	Wages payable 1,500			
	Wages expense	1,500		
January 4, 1992 Subsequent entry:	Wages expense 2,800		Wages expense 1,300	
	Cash	2,800	Wages payable 1,500	
			Cash	2,800

In this example, the RJE simplifies the subsequent payroll entry, which can now be recorded in a manner identical to all other payrolls. The use of RJEs eliminates the need to examine information about previous AJEs and can reduce accounting errors. With or without reversing entries, total 1992 wage expense recognized through January 4, 1992, is $1,300. Exhibit 3–9 is a summary of RJEs.

The following Sonora Company AJEs could be reversed:

b. Rent revenue (expedient method—deferred item).
c. Interest expense (accrual).
d. Interest revenue (accrual).
h. Income tax expense (accrual).

BEYOND THE PRIMARY FINANCIAL STATEMENTS

◆

The ending balances of some accounts reflect the choice from among several acceptable accounting methods. For example, several depreciation methods are in use. These choices can significantly affect the income and financial position of the reporting firm. Therefore, *APB Opinion No. 22* requires that major accounting principle choices be disclosed in footnotes to the financial statements. The following excerpts from the 1989 accounting policy disclosure footnote of The Washington Post Company illustrate this point:

Inventories. Inventories are valued at the lower of cost or market. Cost of newsprint is determined by the first-in, first-out method, and cost of magazine paper is determined by the specific-cost method.

Property, Plant, and Equipment. Property, plant, and equipment is recorded at cost and includes interest capitalized in connection with major long-term construction projects.

Deferred Program Rights. The broadcast subsidiaries are parties to agreements that entitle them to show motion pictures and syndicated programs on television. The unamortized cost of these rights and the liability for future payments under these agreements are reflected in the consolidated balance sheets.

Footnotes supplement the primary financial statements, providing information that is not normally recorded in accounts, but that can materially affect the decision-making process. Providing expanded information in this manner is an application of the *full-disclosure principle*. For example, information about pending lawsuits is often disclosed in footnotes. The footnotes to the 1989 financial statements of Tandy Corporation included the following:

An action alleging infringement of various patents relating to cellular telephones was filed against the Company by Motorola, Inc. in U.S. District Court in Chicago, Illinois, in April 1989, seeking damages in excess of $10,000,000 and an injunction against Tandy's importation of certain models of cellular telephones manufactured in Korea by its joint venture operation with Nokia Corporation.

One way that firms communicate with stockholders and other interested parties is by issuing annual reports. In addition to containing the primary financial statements and footnotes, an annual report typically includes a letter from the company president and descriptive information about the company, its location, products, and key executives. Also, a section entitled "Management Discussion and Analysis of Financial Condition and Results of Operations" (MD&A) is required of all SEC registrants.[24]

The MD&A section provides discussion about the firm's earnings and financial position for the reporting period, information about the effects of laws and other environmental aspects on the firm, discussion of the firm's liquidity position, and an evaluation of the effect of economic and business trends on the firm.

For example, the MD&A section of the 1989 annual report of Clark Equipment Company included the following discussion about its revenue increase from the year before:

The overall 1989 sales increase was principally from additional volumes resulting from improved market demand. Price increases also impacted sales while foreign currency fluctuations reduced sales levels. New products introduced in 1989 marginally contributed to total sales, with additional benefits expected in future years.

Prospective information about the firm must be disclosed in the MD&A section if certain conditions are met.[25] Most companies are reluctant to discuss future events. One reason is that positive expectations may not be fulfilled, and negative projections are viewed with concern by the investing community. Although the MD&A section is an ideal place for communicating information about the future, most respondents to a 1987 request for public comment on the issue indicated that disclosures about future events were inadequate.[26]

---

[24] An SEC registrant is a firm under the jurisdiction of the SEC. The 10-K report is the principal periodic report filed with the SEC. It contains information about the company and its business, as well as detailed financial statements.

[25] *Management's Discussion and Analysis of Financial Condition and Results of Operations,* SEC Financial Reporting Release No. 36, May 18, 1989.

[26] " 'What If' Accounting," *Forbes,* May 30, 1988, p. 112.

Firms must disclose information relating to future trends, commitments and events that are reasonably likely to affect materially a firm's operations or liquidity. Examples of areas requiring increased disclosure are holdings of junk bonds and off-balance-sheet commitments.

When preparing the MD&A section, firms should be prepared to answer the following questions:

> If I were an investor, what would I want to know about this company's liquidity, capital resources, and results of operations that the financial statements don't spell out clearly? What known trends, demands, commitments, events, or uncertainties would affect my judgment about the company?[27]

Clark Equipment disclosed the following prospective comments in its MD&A section:

> Barring any unforeseen change in the U.S. economic environment, demand in Clark's North American domestic markets is generally expected to remain strong. Overseas sales should continue at the current level. Some market uncertainty exists relating to the Company's Automotive business unit because of the upcoming government changeover in Brazil and the current softness in the U.S. medium-duty truck market. Additional cost reductions achieved from planned capital programs and product development are expected to contribute to 1990 profitability.

The SEC actively enforces the new guidelines. For example, Hiex Development USA, Inc., was cited for failing to refer to a major equipment purchase commitment and for failing to disclose how the firm planned to resolve its negative working capital problem.[28]

CONCEPT REVIEW

1. Why are temporary accounts closed and permanent accounts not closed?
2. What factors would cause a company to use the expedient recording method?
3. What is the purpose of the MD&A section of the annual report?

SUMMARY OF KEY POINTS

(L.O. 1)   1. The AIS provides information for daily management information needs and for preparation of financial statements.

(L.O. 2)   2. There are seven basic types of accounts. The balance sheet discloses the balances of the permanent accounts, which include assets, liabilities, and owners' equity accounts. The income statement discloses the pre-closing balances of the temporary accounts, which include revenues, gains, expenses, and losses. Debits to assets, expenses, and losses increase those accounts. Credits to liabilities, owners' equity, revenues and gains increase those accounts.

(L.O. 2)   3. The four financial statements: income statement, retained earnings statement, stockholders' equity statement, and balance sheet are interrelated.

(L.O. 3, 4)   4. The ten steps in the accounting cycle are
   a. Identify transaction to be recorded.
   b. Record journal entries.
   c. Post to ledger accounts.

---

[27] R. Dieter and K. Sandefur, "Spotlight on Management's Discussion and Analysis," *Journal of Accountancy*, December, 1989, p. 66.

[28] Ibid.

         d. Prepare unadjusted trial balance.

         e. Record AJEs.

         f. Prepare adjusted trial balance.

         g. Prepare financial statements.

         h. Record closing entries.

         i. Prepare post-closing trial balance.

         j. If appropriate, record RJEs.

(L.O. 3)   5. The application of accounting principles generally occurs at the journal entry step. Journal entries are the foundation for the financial statements.

(L.O. 5)   6. Companies use both the standard or the expedient method to record routine operating cash receipts and payments that precede revenue and expense recognition. The choice of methods affects some AJEs and the use of RJEs.

(L.O. 4, 5)   7. AJEs are required under accrual accounting to complete the measurement and recording of changes in resources and obligations.

(L.O. 5)   8. RJEs are optional entries, dated the beginning of the accounting period, that reverse certain AJEs from the previous period and that are used to facilitate subsequent journal entries.

(L.O. 6)   9. Worksheets facilitate the accounting cycle and are a tool for accumulating and organizing accounts data in conjunction with several accounting cycle steps.

(L.O. 7)   10. Control accounts, subsidiary ledgers, and special journals are used for similar, repetitive transactions. They reduce AIS costs by decreasing recording, retrieval, and posting time.

REVIEW PROBLEM

◆

Accounting cycle steps—Bucknell Company developed its unadjusted trial balance dated December 31, 1991, which appears below. Bucknell uses the expedient recording method whenever possible, adjusts its accounts once per year, records all appropriate RJEs, and adjusts its periodic inventory-related accounts in an AJE. Ignore income taxes.

BUCKNELL COMPANY
Unadjusted Trial Balance
December 31, 1991

	Dr.	Cr.
Cash	$ 40,000	
Accounts receivable	60,000	
Allowance for doubtful accounts		$ 6,000
Inventory	90,000	
Equipment	780,000	
Accumulated depreciation		100,000
Land	150,000	
Accounts payable		22,000
Notes payable, 8%, due April 1, 1996		200,000
Common stock, $5 par		300,000
Contributed capital in excess of par		100,000
Retained earnings		50,000
Sales revenue (all on account)		900,000
Subscription revenue		24,000
Purchases	250,000	
Rent expense	60,000	
Interest expense	12,000	
Selling expense	40,000	
Insurance expense	30,000	
Wage expense	110,000	
General and administrative expense	80,000	
Totals	$1,702,000	$1,702,000

Additional information:

a. Ending inventory by physical count is $70,000.
b. The equipment has a total estimated useful life of 14 years and an estimated residual value of $80,000. Bucknell uses straight-line depreciation and treats depreciation expense as a general and administrative expense.
c. Bad debt expense for 1991 is estimated to be 1% of sales.
d. The note payable requires interest to be paid semiannually, every October 1 and April 1.
e. $5,000 of wages were earned in December but not recorded.
f. The rent expense represents a payment made on January 2, 1991, for two years' rent (1991 and 1992).
g. The insurance expense represents payment made for a one-year policy, paid June 30, 1991. Coverage begins on that date.
h. The subscription revenue represents cash received from many university libraries for a one and one-half year subscription to a journal published by Bucknell. The subscription period begins July 1, 1991.

Required:

1. Record the required AJEs.
2. Prepare the adjusted trial balance.
3. Prepare the income statement and balance sheet for 1991.
4. Prepare closing entries.
5. Prepare RJEs.

SOLUTION

♦

1. Adjusting journal entries, dated December 31, 1991.

a. Inventory	70,000	
Cost of goods sold	270,000	
Purchases		250,000
Inventory		90,000
b. General and administrative expense ($780,000 − $80,000)/14	50,000	
Accumulated depreciation		50,000
c. Bad debt expense (.01 × $900,000)	9,000	
Allowance for doubtful accounts		9,000
d. Interest expense ($200,000 × .08 × ¼)	4,000	
Interest payable		4,000
e. Wage expense	5,000	
Wages payable		5,000
f. Prepaid rent ($60,000 × ½)	30,000	
Rent expense		30,000
g. Prepaid insurance ($30,000 × ½)	15,000	
Insurance expense		15,000
h. Subscription revenue ($24,000 × ⅔)	16,000	
Unearned subscription revenue		16,000

2. Adjusted trial balance.

BUCKNELL COMPANY
Adjusted Trial Balance
December 31, 1991

	Dr.	Cr.
Cash	$ 40,000	
Accounts receivable	60,000	
Allowance for doubtful accounts		$ 15,000
Prepaid rent	30,000	
Prepaid insurance	15,000	
Inventory	70,000	
Equipment	780,000	
Accumulated depreciation		150,000
Land	150,000	
Accounts payable		22,000
Interest payable		4,000
Wages payable		5,000
Unearned subscription revenue		16,000
Notes payable, 8%		200,000
Common stock, $5 par		300,000
Contributed capital in excess of par		100,000
Retained earnings		50,000
Sales revenue		900,000
Subscription revenue		8,000
Cost of goods sold	270,000	
Rent expense	30,000	
Interest expense	16,000	
Selling expense	40,000	
Insurance expense	15,000	
Wage expense	115,000	
Bad debt expense	9,000	
General and administrative expense	130,000	
Totals	$1,770,000	$1,770,000

3. Prepare the income statement and balance sheet for 1991.

BUCKNELL COMPANY
Income Statement
For the Year Ended December 31, 1991

Revenues:		
Sales	$900,000	
Subscription revenue	8,000	
Total revenue		$908,000
Expenses:		
Cost of goods sold	270,000	
Rent expense	30,000	
Interest expense	16,000	
Selling expense	40,000	
Insurance expense	15,000	
Wage expense	115,000	
Bad debt expense	9,000	
General and administrative expense	130,000	
Total expenses		625,000
Net income		$283,000

BUCKNELL COMPANY
Balance Sheet
December 31, 1991

Assets

Cash			$ 40,000
Accounts receivable	$ 60,000		
Allowance for doubtful accounts	(15,000)	45,000	
Prepaid rent		30,000	
Prepaid insurance		15,000	
Inventory		70,000	
Equipment	780,000		
Accumulated depreciation	(150,000)	630,000	
Land		150,000	
Total assets			$980,000

Liabilities

Accounts payable	$ 22,000	
Interest payable	4,000	
Wages payable	5,000	
Unearned subscription revenue	16,000	
Notes payable, 8%	200,000	
Total liabilities		247,000

Owners' Equity

Common stock, $5 par	300,000	
Contributed capital in excess of par	100,000	
Retained earnings	333,000*	
Total owners' equity		733,000
Total liabilities and owners' equity		$980,000

* $50,000 + $283,000

4. Prepare closing entries.

Sales revenue	900,000	
Subscription revenue	8,000	
Income summary		908,000
Income summary	625,000	
Cost of goods sold		270,000
Rent expense		30,000
Interest expense		16,000
Selling expense		40,000
Insurance expense		15,000
Wage expense		115,000
Bad debt expense		9,000
General and administrative expense		130,000
Income summary	283,000	
Retained earnings		283,000

5. Prepare RJEs.

Interest payable	4,000	
Interest expense		4,000
Wages payable	5,000	
Wage expense		5,000
Rent expense	30,000	
Prepaid rent		30,000
Insurance expense	15,000	
Prepaid insurance		15,000
Unearned subscription revenue	16,000	
Subscription revenue		16,000

The previous discussion on the accounting cycle is not specific to information technology. Many firms use a worksheet as a mechanical aid. A **worksheet** is a multicolumn workspace that provides an organized approach for performing several end-of-period accounting cycle steps, a format for preparing financial statements before posting AJEs, and evidence, for audit trail purposes, of an organized and structured accounting process that can be more easily reviewed than other methods of analysis.

In manual accounting systems, worksheet input is developed by hand-transferring account name and balance information from the general ledger to the worksheet. With most computerized systems, this task is accomplished automatically. Computer **spreadsheet** programs can be used to generate worksheets quickly and with relative ease. Spreadsheets also offer important labor and time savings in the planning and mechanical plotting of AJEs on the worksheet. This software is a powerful tool for accomplishing several steps in the accounting cycle.

Use of a worksheet is an optional procedure. The worksheet is not part of the basic accounting records. Worksheets assist with only a portion of the accounting cycle. Formal AJEs are recorded in addition to those entered on the worksheet. Exhibit 3A–1 compares the accounting cycle with and without a worksheet.

Illustration of the Worksheet Approach

Exhibit 3A–2 illustrates the multicolumn form used to prepare the worksheet for Sonora, Inc., the company used in the chapter to present the accounting cycle. The worksheet has debit and credit columns for the unadjusted trial balance, the AJEs, the adjusted trial balance, and the income statement, retained earnings statement, and balance sheet accounts.

The worksheet is prepared in four steps, corresponding to transparency overlay Exhibits 3A–3 through 3A–6. Exhibit 3A–7 presents the financial statements prepared from the worksheet.

First Step (Exhibit 3A–3): Enter the *unadjusted trial balance sheet* in the first two columns of the worksheet by inserting the year-end balances of all ledger accounts. The inventory and retained earnings balances are the beginning-of-year balances because no transactions have affected these accounts.

Confirm debit-credit equality of the totals. The cost of goods sold account (periodic system) does not yet exist. Cost of goods sold would appear in the unadjusted trial balance under the perpetual system.

Second step (Exhibit 3A–4): Enter the *adjusting entries,* including income tax. The lowercase letters refer to the same AJEs discussed in the chapter for Sonora, Inc.

The worksheet AJEs are facilitating entries only, and usually are not formally recorded in the general journal at this point. If a new account is created by an AJE, it is inserted in its normal position. Interest receivable (entry *d*) is one such example. Confirm debit-credit equality of the totals.

Determine income tax expense and payable. (Sonora's tax computation was illustrated earlier.) Enter the accounts, and amounts in the AJE columns. Income tax expense (entry *h*) is positioned below the totals of the AJE columns.

Third step (Exhibit 3A–5): Enter the *adjusted trial balance* by adding or subtracting across the unadjusted trial balance sheet columns and AJE columns, for each account. For example, the adjusted balance of the allowance for doubtful accounts is the sum of its unadjusted balance ($1,000), and the $1,200 increase from AJE *f*.

The inventory account now reflects the ending balance; purchases and related accounts no longer have balances; cost of goods sold is present. Confirm debit-credit equality of the totals.

Fourth step (Exhibit 3A–6): Extend adjusted trial balance amounts to the financial statements; complete the worksheet.

Each account in the adjusted trial balance is extended to *one* of the three sets of remaining debit-credit columns. Temporary accounts are sorted to the income statement columns (revenues to the credit column, expenses to the debit column). Real accounts are sorted to

EXHIBIT 3A-1   Accounting Cycle Steps

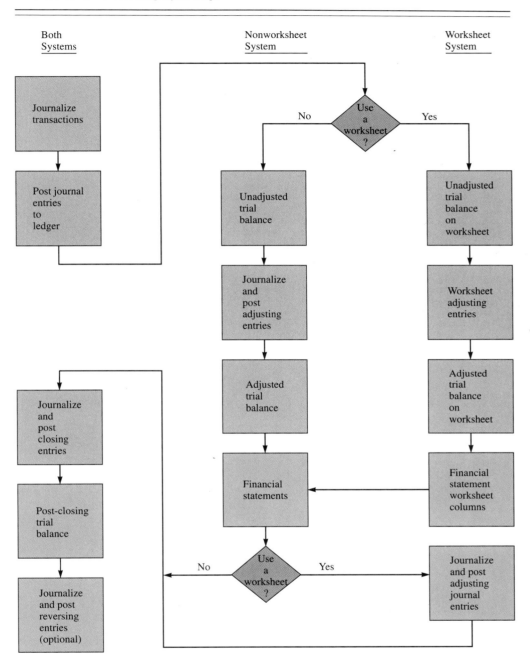

the balance sheet columns except for the beginning balance in retained earnings, which is extended to the retained earnings columns.

Total the income statement columns before income tax expense. Pre-tax income is the difference between the debit and credit column totals. A net credit represents income; a net debit represents a loss. For Sonora, pretax income is $50,000 ($327,000 − $277,000). Next, determine net income after taxes by extending the income tax expense amount ($20,000) into the debit column and again totaling the columns. Net income is the difference between the columns, equaling $30,000 for Sonora ($327,000 − $297,000).

SONORA, INC.
Worksheet for Year Ended December 31, 1991

	Unadjusted Trial Balance		Adjusting Entries		Adjusted Trial Balance		Income Statement		Retained Earnings Statement		Balance Sheet	
	Debit	Credit	Debit	Credit	Debit	Credit	Debit	Credit	Debit	Credit	Debit	Credit

The multicolumn worksheet is prepared manually or with a computer spreadsheet program.

The worksheet assists in the preparation of AJEs and financial statements.

SONORA INC.
Income Statement
For the Year Ended December 31, 1991

Revenues:

Sales	$325,200	
Interest	600	
Rent	1,200	
Total revenues		$327,000

Expenses:

Cost of goods sold	117,000	
Selling	113,400	
General and administrative	34,600	
Interest	3,000	
Total expenses before income tax		268,000
Income before extraordinary item and tax		59,000
Income taxes on income before extraordinary items ($59,000 × .40)		23,600
Income before extraordinary items		35,400
Extraordinary loss	9,000	
Less tax savings ($9,000 × .40)	3,600	5,400
Net income		$ 30,000

SONORA INC.
Retained Earnings Statement
For the Year Ended December 31, 1991

Retained earnings, January 1, 1991	$31,500
Net income	30,000
Retained earnings, December 31, 1991	$61,500

SONORA, INC.
Balance Sheet
At December 31, 1991

Assets

Current assets:

Cash		$ 67,300
Accounts receivable	$ 45,000	
Allowance for doubtful accounts	2,200	42,800
Notes receivable		8,000
Interest receivable		100
Inventory		90,000
Prepaid insurance		400
Total current assets		208,600

Operational assets:

Land			8,000
Building	$160,000		
Accumulated depreciation, building	(100,000)	60,000	
Equipment	91,000		
Accumulated depreciation, equipment	(36,000)	55,000	
Total operational assets			123,000
Total assets			$331,600

Liabilities

Current liabilities:

Accounts payable	$ 29,000
Interest payable	500
Rent revenue collected in advance	600
Income taxes payable	20,000
Total current liabilities	50,100

Long-term liabilities:

Bond payable, 6%	50,000
Total liabilities	100,100

Stockholders' Equity

Contributed capital:

Common stock, par $10, 15,000 shares issued and outstanding	$150,000	
Contributed capital in excess of par	20,000	
Retained earnings	61,500	
Total stockholders' equity		231,500
Total liabilities and stockholders' equity		$331,600

Next, add a line description (net income to retained earnings) and enter the $30,000 net income amount as a balancing value—positive net income is a debit balancing value, negative income is a credit. Then complete this entry by recording $30,000 in the credit column under the retained earnings column heading. (This time positive net income is a credit entry, and negative income a debit entry.)

Total the retained earnings columns and enter a balancing amount (the ending retained earnings balance) in the appropriate column to achieve debit-credit equality. For Sonora, the balancing amount is a $61,500 debit. Add a line description (retained earnings to balance sheet) and enter the balancing amount into the appropriate balance sheet column.

Total the balance sheet columns and confirm debit-credit equality.

The worksheet is now complete, and the financial statements are prepared directly from the last three sets of worksheet columns. The formal AJEs are then journalized and posted.

Worksheets and Interim Reports

Worksheets facilitate preparation of **interim reports**. The term *interim* is applied to quarterly reports filed with the SEC and to other financial statements for partial-year periods. Worksheet AJEs, rather than formal journal entries, are prepared for these reports. In addition, there is no need to close the temporary accounts to determine net income for an interim period when using a worksheet.

In general, when using a worksheet to prepare interim reports, the temporary account balances at the end of all preceding interim periods in the same fiscal year are subtracted from the balance at the end of the current interim period. This difference is the change in the account balance for the current interim period. This amount is used in an interim income statement for that period. This procedure is not necessary for permanent accounts because these balances are cumulative. However, the retained earnings statement pertains to each interim period and reflects the dividends and income for that period only.

To illustrate, assume that a firm's accounting year-end is December 31. Interim financial statements at the end of each of the first three months are prepared as follows:

January 31—enter the unadjusted trial balance (input from the general ledger) on a worksheet. Next, enter the AJEs and complete the worksheet, as discussed in the previous section. Prepare the January financial statements. Do not journalize or post adjusting or closing entries.

February 28—complete a worksheet as in January, but this time compile an unadjusted trial balance as of February 28, reflecting cumulative account balances for January and February. Then enter AJEs (also cumulative from the beginning of January). Then prepare an adjusted trial balance and complete the worksheet. This worksheet generates financial statements for January and February *combined*. Prepare the February income statement by subtracting the January income statement amounts from this combined income statement. The retained earnings statement reflects the February 1 balance, income and dividends for February, and the February 28 balance. The February balance sheet reports the combined amounts of all permanent accounts.

March 31—repeat the above process. This time the worksheet is used to generate *quarterly* financial statements. To determine the March income statement, subtract the combined January and February temporary account balances from the ending March 31 balances. The quarterly and March 31 statements of balance sheets are identical. The quarterly and March retained earnings statements reflect their respective income and dividends declared during the period.

The quality of information in quarterly reports issued to the public is sometimes questionable. The statements are not audited or reviewd by CPAs. Manufactured Homes, for example, reported $10.6 million of pretax earnings for the first three quarters of 1987. Then, in the fourth quarter, the company recognized an $8.5 million deficit sales adjustment. This adjustment almost completely wiped out the previous three quarters' earnings.[29]

---

[29] See "Nasty Surprises," *Forbes*, January 23, 1989, p. 72.

APPENDIX 3B   *Control Accounts, Subsidiary Ledgers, and Special Journals*

An accounting system often includes *control accounts, subsidiary ledgers,* and *special journals.* This appendix discusses these features.

The text discussed the use of control and subsidiary ledger accounts. The sum of all account balances in a subsidiary ledger must equal the related control account balance in the general ledger. To assure that this equality exists, frequent reconciliations are made. All posting must be complete, both to the control account and to the subsidiary ledger, before a reconciliation can be accomplished. To illustrate such a reconciliation, refer ahead to the accounts receivable subsidiary ledger in Exhibit 3B–5. Based on the information in Exhibit 3B–5, a reconciliation for *accounts receivable control* and the *accounts receivable subsidiary ledger* follows:

Reconciliation of
Accounts Receivable Subsidiary Ledger
(at January 31, 1991)

	Amount
Subsidiary ledger balances:	
112.13 Adams Co.	$ 980
112.42 Miller, J. B.	196
112.91 XY Manufacturing Co.	1,960
Total	$3,136
General ledger balance:	
Accounts receivable control	
($5,000 + $9,360 − $11,224)	$3,136

Both general and special journals are used in many accounting systems. Even when extensive use is made of special journals, a need exists for a general journal to record those transactions that do not apply to any of the special journals, and the adjusting, closing, reversing, and correcting entries. The chapter illustrated a general journal in Exhibit 3–2.

A *special journal* is designed to expedite the recording of similar transactions which occur frequently. Each special journal is constructed specifically to simplify the data processing tasks involved in journalizing and posting those particular types of transactions. Special journals can be custom-designed to meet the particular needs of the business. Commonly used special journals include these:

1. Sales journal for recording sales of merchandise on credit only.
2. Purchases journal for recording purchases of merchandise on credit only.
3. Cash receipts journal for recording cash receipts only, including cash sales.
4. Cash payments journal for recording cash payments only, including cash purchases.
5. Voucher system, designed to replace the purchases journal and cash payments journal, composed of:
   a. A voucher register for recording vouchers payable only. A voucher payable is prepared for each cash payment regardless of purpose.
   b. A check register for recording all checks written in payment of approved vouchers.

The special journals illustrated in this appendix carry page numbers preceded by letters indicating the journal name. The "S" in the page number of Exhibit 3B–1 denotes the sales journal, for example.

Sales Journal   This special journal is designed to record sales account, which otherwise would be recorded as follows in a general journal:

January 2, 1991:

Accounts receivable ($1,000 × .98) 980	
Sales revenue	980
Credit sale to Adams Company; invoice price, $1,000; terms 2/10, n/30.	

Terms 2/10, n/30 means that if the account is paid within 10 days after date of sale, a 2% cash discount is granted. The cash discount encourages early payment. If the bill is not paid

EXHIBIT 3B-1   Sales Journal

Date 1991	Sales Invoice No.	Accounts Receivable (name)	Terms	Post. Ref.	Receivable and Sale Amount	Dept. Sales	
						Dept. A	Dept. B
Jan. 2	93	Adams Co.	2/10, n/30	112.13	980		
3	94	Sayre Corp.	210, n/30	112.80	490		
11	95	Cope & Day Co.	net	112.27	5,734		
27	96	XY Mfg. Co.	2/10, n/30	112.91	1,960	(Not illustrated; the total of each column would also be posted to a sales subsidiary ledger.)	
30	97	Miller, J. B.	2/10, n/30	112.42	196		
31	—	Totals			9,360		
31	—	Posting			(112/500)		

SALES JOURNAL   Page S-23

within the 10-day discount period, the full amount is past due at the end of 30 days. The net method, which records the invoice price net of cash discount, is used here to record the sale. Chapter 8 discusses both the net and gross methods in detail.

Exhibit 3B–1 illustrates a typical sales journal for credit sales for a business with two sales departments. The above entry is shown as the first entry in 1991. The amount of the sale is recorded only once. Each entry in the sales journal records the same information found in the traditional debit-credit format.

The *posting* of amounts from the sales journal to the general and subsidiary ledgers is also simplified. The two phases in posting a sales journal are the following:

1. *Daily posting*—the amount of *each* credit sale is posted daily to the appropriate individual account in the *accounts receivable subsidiary ledger*. Posting is indicated by entering the account number in the posting reference column. For example, the number 112.13 entered in the posting reference column in Exhibit 3B–1 is the account number assigned to Adams Company and shows that $980 is posted as a debit to Adams Company in the subsidiary ledger. The number 112 is the general number used for accounts receivable (see Exhibit 3B–5).

2. *Monthly posting*—at the end of each month, the receivable and sale amount column is totaled. This total is posted to *two accounts* in the general ledger. In Exhibit 3B–1, the $9,360 total is posted as a debit to account No. 112 (accounts receivable control) and as a credit to account No. 500 (sales revenue control). The T-accounts shown in Exhibit 3B–5 illustrate how these postings are reflected in both the general ledger and the subsidiary ledger. The two ledgers show the journal page from which each amount is posted.

Purchases Journal   This special journal is designed to accommodate frequent purchases of merchandise on account, which otherwise would be recorded as follows in a general journal under the net method:[30]

January 3, 1991:

```
Purchases ($1,000 × .99) . . . . . . . . . . . . . . . . . . . . . . . . . . . 990
       Accounts payable (PT Mfg. Co.) . . . . . . . . . . . . . . . . . .        990
    (terms 1/20, n/30)
```

This entry is recorded as the first 1991 entry in the purchases journal illustrated in Exhibit 3B–2. The accounting simplifications found in the sales journal are present in the purchases

---

[30] The entry assumes a periodic inventory procedure. Under a perpetual inventory system, the debit would be to the inventory account.

EXHIBIT 3B-2 Purchases Journal

		PURCHASES JOURNAL				Page P-19
Date 1991	Purchase Order No.	Accounts Payable (name)	Terms	Posting Ref.	Purcnases and Payable Amount	
Jan. 3	41	PT Mfg. Co.	1/20, n/30	210.61	990	
7	42	Able Suppliers, Ltd.	net	210.12	150	
31	—	Totals	—	—	6,760	
31	—	Posting	—	—	(612/210)	

EXHIBIT 3B-3 Cash Receipts Journal

			CASH RECEIPTS JOURNAL				Page CR-19
				Credits			
Date 1991	Explanation	Debit Cash	Account Title	Post. Ref.	Accounts Receivable	Sales Revenue	Misc. Accounts
Jan. 4	Cash sales	11,200		—		11,200	
7	On acct.	4,490	Sayre Corp.	112.80	4,490		
8	Sale of land	10,000	Land	123			4,000
			Gain on sale of land	510			6,000
10	On acct.	1,000	Adams Co.	112.13	1,000		
19	Cash sales	43,600		—		43,600	
20	On acct.	5,734	Cope & Day Co.	112.27	5,734		
31	Totals	116,224		—	11,224	71,000	34,000
31	Posting	(101)		—	(112)	(500)	(NP)*

* NP—not posted as one total because the individual amounts are posted as indicated in the posting reference column.

journal as well. Each amount is posted daily as a credit to the account of an individual creditor in the *accounts payable subsidiary ledger*. At the end of the month, the total of the Purchases and Payable Amount column ($6,760 shown in Exhibit 3B-2), is posted to the general ledger as a debit to the purchases account (No. 612) and as a credit to the accounts payable control account (No. 210).

Cash Receipts Journal   A special cash receipts journal is used to accommodate a large volume of cash receipts transactions. Several different sources of cash are accommodated by including a *cash debit* column, *several* credit columns for recurring credits, and a miscellaneous accounts column for infrequent credits—all as shown in Exhibit 3B-3. Space is also provided for the names of particular accounts receivable.

EXHIBIT 3B-4   Cash Payments Journal

					Debits			
Date 1991	**Check No.**	**Explanation**	**Credits Cash**	**Account Name**	**Post. Ref.**	**Accounts Payable**	**Purchases**	**Misc. Accounts**
Jan. 2	141	Pur. mdse.	3,000				3,000	
10	142	On acct.	990	PT Mfg. Co.	210.61	990		
15	143	Jan. rent	660	Rent exp.	612			660
16	144	Pur. mdse.	1,810				1,810	
31	—	Totals	98,400		—	5,820	90,980	1,600
31	—	Posting	(101)		—	(210)	(612)	(NP)

CASH PAYMENTS JOURNAL — Page CP-31

EXHIBIT 3B-5   General Ledger and Subsidiary Ledger

GENERAL LEDGER (partial)

Cash   No. 101

1991				1991		
Jan. 1	balance	18,700		Jan. 31	CP-31	98,400
31	CR-19	116,224				

Accounts Receivable Control   No. 112

1991				1991		
Jan. 1	balance	5,000		Jan. 31	CR-19	11,224
31	S-23	9,360				

Equipment   No. 140

1991			
Jan. 2	J-14	9,000	

Notes Payable   No. 214

				1991		
				Jan. 2	J-14	9,000

Sales Revenue Control   No. 500

				1991		
				Jan. 31	S-23	9,360
				31	CR-19	71,000

During the month, each amount in the accounts receivable column is posted daily as a credit to an individual customer account in the *accounts receivable subsidiary ledger.* At the end of the month, the *individual* amounts in the miscellaneous account column are posted as credits to the appropriate general ledger accounts, and the totals (for the cash, accounts receivable, and sales revenue columns) are posted to the general ledger as indicated by the

EXHIBIT 3B-5 *(concluded)*

SUBSIDIARY LEDGER FOR ACCOUNTS RECEIVABLE (Accts. No. 112)					
Adams Company—Acct. No. 112.13					
Date	**Post. Ref.**	**Explanation**	**Debit**	**Credit**	**Balance**
1991 Jan. 1		balance			1,000
2	S–23		980		1,980
10	CR–19			1,000	980
Cope & Day Company—Acct. No. 112.27					
Jan. 11	S–23		5,734		5,734
20	CR–19			5,734	–0–
Miller, J. B.—Acct. No. 112.42					
Jan. 30	S–23		196		196
Sayre Corporation—Acct. No. 112.80					
Jan. 1		balance			4,000
3	S–23		490		4,490
7	CR–19			4,490	–0–
XY Manufacturing Company—Acct. No. 112.91					
Jan. 27	S–23		1,960		1,960

posting reference. The total of the miscellaneous accounts column is not posted because it consists of changes in different accounts. However, this column is totaled to ascertain overall debit-credit quality.

Cash Payments Journal Many companies use some form of a cash payments journal if there are many cash disbursements. This special journal has a column for cash credits, a number of columns for recurring debits, and a miscellaneous account debit column. Exhibit 3B–4 illustrates a typical cash payments journal. Journalizing and posting follow the same procedures explained for the cash receipts journal.

Voucher Systems Voucher systems are designed to enhance internal control over cash disbursements. In a voucher system, every transaction requiring payment by check begins with an invoice or other document that supplies information for completing a voucher. A voucher is a document that describes the liability and lists information about the creditor; a description of the good or service received; other details of the transaction, including invoice number, terms, amount due, and due date; and authorizing signatures.

Together, the voucher, purchase order, receiving report, and invoice form a packet of information that must be complete before a cash disbursement can be made. All authorizations must be indicated. Verification of amounts and calculations are part of the payment authoriza-

EXHIBIT 3B–6   Voucher Register

VOUCHER REGISTER						Page VR-1
Voucher		Payee	Date Paid	Check No.	Voucher Payable Credit	Account Debited
Date	Number					
1/1/91	1	Crowell Co.	1/2/91	141	$3,000	Purchases
1/3/91	2	PT Mfg. Co.	1/10/91	142	990	Purchases
1/9/91	3	Williams Co.	1/15/91	143	660	Rent Expense

EXHIBIT 3B–7   Check Register

CHECK REGISTER				Page CR-1
Date	Payee	Voucher Number	Check Number	Vouchers Payable Dr. and Cash Cr.
1/2/91	Crowell Co.	1	141	$3,000
1/10/91	PT Mfg. Co.	2	142	990
1/15/91	Williams Co.	3	143	660

tion process. Often several departments, including the internal audit and accounting departments, are required to authorize a large cash payment.

The completed voucher is the basis for an accounting entry in a special journal called the *voucher register*. The voucher register is not restricted to purchases. Before payment is made, the authorized voucher is recorded in the voucher register. Exhibit 3B–6 illustrates an abbreviated page from a voucher register.

A new account, vouchers payable, is used to record all routine liabilities. This new account replaces accounts payable and other payables used for routine payments. When a voucher is recorded, the Voucher Payable Credit column reflects the amount of the liability. The account debited reflects the good or service received. Unlike the voucher register shown in Exhibit 3B–6, most voucher registers have several debit columns for speedy recording of repetitive cash payments of the same type. The total of the vouchers payable column is posted to the vouchers payable control. The check number and date paid do not appear in the voucher register until a check is issued and payment is made to the payee. Although a voucher is prepared for each item, one check can be issued for the payment of several vouchers to the same creditor.

Unpaid vouchers are placed into a file pending payment and are typically filed by due date. It is important that payments be initiated within cash discount periods to obtain the lowest possible price for merchandise purchases. The unpaid voucher file is the subsidiary ledger in a voucher system.

When a voucher becomes due, it is sent by the accounting department to a person authorized to issue checks. After a review of the authorizations on the voucher is made, a check is prepared for the correct amount. The paid voucher is sent back to the accounting department, which enters the check number and payment into the voucher register. Information from the voucher is also entered in the *check register* illustrated in Exhibit 3B–7.

The total of the amount column in the check register is posted to the vouchers payable control account (dr.) and to the cash account (cr.). The paid voucher is retained to substantiate cash payments and for audit trail purposes. The voucher register and check register replace the purchases and cash payments journal.

The design and use of subsidiary ledgers, control accounts, and special journals depend on the characteristics of the business. They do not involve new accounting principles because they are only data processing tools. Their use simplifies journalizing, posting, and the subdivision of work.

KEY TERMS

Accounting cycle (77)
Accounting information system (AIS) (74)
Adjusted trial balance (90)
Contra account (87)
Control account (81)
Credit (75)
Debit (75)
Debit-credit convention (75)
Double-entry system (75)
Expedient recording method (84)

Interim report (106)
Nonreciprocal transfer (79)
Reciprocal transfer (79)
Reversing journal entry (95)
Spreadsheet (104)
Standard recording method (84)
Subsidiary account (81)
T-account (76)
Worksheet (104)

QUESTIONS

1. How are the income statement and balance sheet related (articulated)?
2. Explain the benefits of the double-entry system. What additional benefits does the debit-credit convention provide?
3. Number the following steps in the accounting information processing cycle to indicate their normal sequence of completion:
   _____ Journalize and post reversing entries.
   _____ Posting.
   _____ Identify transaction to be recorded.
   _____ Journalize and post adjusting entries.
   _____ Journalize and post closing entries.
   _____ Prepare financial statements.
   _____ Journalize current transactions.
   _____ Prepare post-closing trial balance.
   _____ Prepare adjusted trial balance.
   _____ Prepare unadjusted trial balance.
4. Why do some companies often record an expense or revenue upon routine payment or receipt of cash, prior to the expiration of cost or the earning of revenue (the expedient system)?
5. Give four examples of internal cost allocations that require adjusting entries.
6. Briefly explain the differences between perpetual and periodic inventory systems.
7. Explain the nature and purpose of closing entries.
8. Explain the purpose and nature of reversing entries. Why are they journalized and posted?
9. Xanthon Company owes a $4,000, three-year, 9% note payable. Interest is paid each November 30. Therefore, at the end of the accounting period, December 31, the following adjusting entry was made.

   Interest expense 30
       Interest payable 30

   Would you recommend using a reversing entry in this situation? Explain.
10. Explain which accounting cycle steps, and their order, are affected by using a worksheet.
11. What advantages do special journals, subsidiary ledgers, and control accounts bring to accounting systems?
12. How does a voucher system improve internal controls over cash disbursements?

EXERCISES

E 3–1
Account Classification
(L.O. 1, 2)

The following accounts were recorded in the 1991 adjusting entries of Jackson Corporation. Classify each account as an asset, liability, revenue, gain, expense, or loss, and explain the classification for each:

a. Prepaid insurance.
b. Property taxes payable.

c. Rent receivable.
d. Interest payable.
e. Rent revenue collected in advance.
f. Accumulated depreciation.
g. Allowance for doubtful accounts.

E 3–2
**Analyze and Record
Typical Transactions**
(L.O. 4)

The following selected transactions were completed during the current year by Blue Corporation:

a. Sold 60,000 shares of its own common stock, par $1 per share, for $70,000 cash.
b. Borrowed $20,000 cash on a six-month, 9% note payable (interest is payable at maturity date).
c. Purchased real estate for use in the business at a cash cost of $150,000. The real estate consisted of a small building ($90,000) and the lot on which it was located.
d. Purchased merchandise for resale at a cash cost of $30,000. Assume periodic inventory system; therefore, debit purchases.
e. Purchased merchandise for resale on credit, terms 3/10, n/30. If paid within 10 days, the cash payment would be $1,940; however, if paid after 10 days, the payment would be $2,000. Because the company takes all discounts, credit purchases are recorded at net of the discount.
f. Sold merchandise for $20,000; collected 60% in cash, and the balance is due in 30 days.
g. Paid the balance due on the purchase in (*e*) within the 10-day period.
h. Paid the note and interest in full for the loan in (*b*) on the due date.
i. Recorded income tax of $9,000 for the current year, which will be paid early next year.
j. Recorded straight-line depreciation for one year on the building in (*c*.); assume a 10-year useful life and an estimated residual value, $10,000.

Required:

1. Analyze each of the above transactions.
2. Enter each in a general journal.
3. Use the letter to the left to indicate the date.

E 3–3
**Review the Accounting
Information Processing
Cycle**
(L.O. 4)

The 10 steps that constitute the accounting information processing cycle are listed to the left in scrambled order. To the right is a brief statement of the objective of each step, also in scrambled order.

Required:

1. In the blanks to the left, number the phases in the usual sequence of completion.
2. In the blanks to the right, use the letters to match each phase with its objective.

Sequence (order)	Matching (with objective)	Phases	Objective
____	____	Journalizing.	*a*. Verification after closing entries.
____	____	Journalize and post reversing entries.	*b*. Communication to decision makers.
____	____	Identify transactions.	*c*. Verification before adjusting entries.
____	____	Prepare financial statements.	*d*. Transfer from journal to ledger.
____	____	Journalize and post closing entries.	*e*. Record resource changes not accompanied by new source documents.
____	____	Posting.	
____	____	Journalize and post adjusting entries.	*f*. An activity based on source documents.
____	____	Prepare adjusted trial balance.	
____	____	Prepare unadjusted trial balance.	*g*. An original input into the accounting system.
____	____	Prepare post-closing trial balance.	*h*. To facilitate subsequent entries.
			i. To obtain a zero balance in the revenue and expense accounts.
			j. Verification after adjusting entries.

E 3–4
**Journalize and Post
Typical Transactions**
(L.O. 3)

Darby Corporation completed the three transactions given below:

a. January 1, 1991—sold 10,000 shares of its own unissued common stock, par $1 per share, for $50,000 cash.
b. January 3, 1991—purchased a machine that cost $60,000. Payment was $20,000 cash plus a $30,000, one-year, 10% interest-bearing note payable and a $10,000, three year, 12% interest-bearing note payable. Interest on each note is payable every January 2.

c. February 1, 1991—sold two unneeded lots for $10,000. Received $4,000 cash down payment and a $6,000, 90-day, 9% interest-bearing note (interest payable at maturity date). The two lots had a total book value of $6,500.

Required:

1. Analyze each of the above transactions and enter each in the general journal.
2. Set up T-accounts and post the entries in (1) above. For posting purposes, set up a numbering system for both the journal pages and the ledger accounts. Use these numbers in your posting process.

E 3-5
Adjusting Journal Entries
(L.O. 4)

At the end of 1991, Baker Corporation had the following situations:

a. Prepaid insurance, $150; the policy was acquired on January 1, 1991, and expires on December 31, 1992.
b. Wages earned December 29–31, 1991, not yet recorded or paid, $2,400.
c. Rent collected for January 1992, $400, that was credited to rent revenue when collected.
d. Interest expense of $200 for November–December 1991 that will be paid April 30, 1992.
e. An asset that cost $10,000 (residual value, $1,000) is being depreciated over five years, straight-line (i.e., an equal amount each period).

Required:

1. Give the 1991 adjusting journal entry for each situation.
2. If none is needed, explain why.

E 3-6
Resolve Errors and
Correct a Trial Balance
(L.O. 3)

A clerk for Century Company prepared the following unadjusted trial balance, which the clerk was unable to balance:

Account	Debit	Credit
Cash	$ 35,563	
Accounts receivable	31,000	
Allowance for doubtful accounts	(2,000)	
Inventory		$ 18,000
Equipment	181,500	
Accumulated depreciation		12,000
Accounts payable	18,000	
Notes payable		25,000
Common stock, par $10		180,000
Retained earnings (correct)		14,000
Revenues		75,000
Expenses	60,000	
Total (out of balance by $63)	$324,063	$324,000

Assume you are examining the accounts and have found the following errors:

a. Equipment purchased for $7,500 at year-end was debited to expenses.
b. Sales on credit of $829 were debited to accounts receivable for $892 and credited to revenues for $829.
c. A $6,000 collection on accounts receivable was debited to cash and credited to revenues.
d. The inventory amount is understated by $2,000 (cost of goods sold is included in expenses).

Required:

1. Prepare a corrected trial balance.
2. Show computations.

E 3-7
Journalize Adjusting
Entries
(L.O. 4)

Rivers Corporation adjusts and closes its accounts each December 31. The following situations require adjusting entries at the current year-end. You are requested to prepare the adjusting entries in the general journal for each situation. If no entry is required for an item, explain why.

a. Machine A is to be depreciated for the full year. It cost $90,000, and the estimated useful life is five years, with an estimated residual value of $10,000. Use straight-line depreciation.
b. Credit sales for the current year amounted to $160,000. The estimated bad debt loss rate on credit sales is ½%.

    d. Property taxes for the current year have not been recorded or paid. A statement for the current year was received near the end of December for $4,000; if paid after February 1 in the next year, a 10% penalty is assessed.

    d. Office supplies that cost $800 were purchased during the year and debited to office supplies inventory. The inventories of these supplies on hand were as follows: $200 at the end of the prior year, and $300 at the end of the current year.

    e. Rivers rented an office in its building to a tenant for one year, starting on September 1. Rent for one year amounting to $6,000 was collected at that date. The total amount collected was credited to rent revenue.

    f. Rivers received a note receivable from a customer dated November 1 of the current year. It is a $12,000, 10% note, due in one year. At the maturity date, Rivers will collect the amount of the note plus interest for one year.

E 3–8
Compute Cost of Goods Sold
(L.O. 2)

The following data are available under a periodic inventory system: purchases, $70,000; sales, $150,000; returned sales, $5,000; returned purchases, $4,000; freight-in, $7,000; beginning inventory, $32,000; selling expenses, $18,000; and ending inventory, $29,000 (by count). Compute the cost of goods sold.

E 3–9
Relationships between Revenue and Cost of Goods Sold
(L.O. 2)

a. Analyze the relationships and amounts for each of the four cases and complete the following schedule to compute cost of goods sold:

	Case A	Case B	Case C	Case D
Sales revenue	$100,000	$136,000	$128,000	$110,000
Beginning inventory	20,000	25,000	?	26,000
Net income (loss)	10,000	25,000	16,000	(10,000)
Ending inventory	30,000	?	32,000	?
Total expenses	40,000	41,000	44,000	48,000
Purchases	?	60,000	70,000	73,000
Cost of goods sold	?	?	?	?

b. Give the adjusting entry for purchases, inventory, and cost of goods sold, assuming that a periodic inventory system is used in Case A.

E 3–10
Adjusting Entries
(L.O. 4)

a. On December 31, 1991, the maintenance supplies inventory account showed a balance on hand amounting to $350. During 1992, purchases of office supplies amounted to $1,000. An inventory of maintenance supplies on hand at December 31, 1992, reflected unused supplies amounting to $500. Give the adjusting journal entry that should be made on December 31, 1992, under the following conditions: Case A—the purchases were debited to the maintenance supplies inventory account, and Case B—the purchases were debited to maintenance supplies expense.

b. On December 31, 1991, the prepaid insurance account showed a debit balance of $900, which was for coverage for the three months, January–March. On April 1, 1992, the company obtained another policy covering a two-year period from that date. The two-year premium amounting to $9,600 was paid and debited to prepaid insurance. Give the adjusting journal entry that should be made on December 31, 1992, to adjust for the entire year.

E 3–11
Analysis; Adjusting Entries
(L.O. 4)

Voss Company adjusts and closes its accounts each December 31. Below are two typical situations involving adjusting entries.

a. During the current year, office supplies were purchased for cash, $750. The inventory of office supplies at the end of the prior year was $150. At the end of the current year, the inventory showed $240 unused supplies remaining on hand. Give the adjusting entry assuming the following at the time of the purchase: Case A—$750 was debited to office supplies expense, and Case B—$750 was debited to office supplies inventory.

b. On June 1, the company collected cash, $8,400, which was for rent collected in advance for the next 12 months. Give the adjusting journal entry assuming the following at the time of the collection: Case A—$8,400 was credited to rent revenue, and Case B—$8,400 was credited to rent revenue collected in advance.

E 3–12
Journalize Adjusting Entries
(L.O. 4)

Pacific Company adjusts and closes its books each December 31. It is now December 31, 1991, and the adjusting entries are to be made. You are requested to prepare, in general journal format, the adjusting entry that should be made for each of the following items:

a. Credit sales for the year amounted to $320,000. The estimated loss rate on bad debts is ⅜%.
b. Unpaid and unrecorded wages incurred at December 31 amounted to $4,800.
c. The company paid a two-year insurance premium in advance on April 1, 1991, amounting to $9,600, which was debited to prepaid insurance.
d. Machine A, which cost $80,000, is to be depreciated for the full year. The estimated useful life is 10 years, and the residual value, $4,000. Use straight-line depreciation.
e. The company rented a warehouse on June 1, 1991, for one year. They had to pay the full amount of rent one year in advance on June 1, amounting to $9,600, which was debited to rent expense.
f. The company received from a customer a 9% note with a face amount of $12,000. The note was dated September 1, 1991; the principal plus the interest is payable one year later. Notes receivable was debited, and sales revenue credited on September 1, 1991.
g. On December 30, 1991, the property tax bill was received in the amount of $5,000. This amount applied only to 1991 and had not been previously recorded or paid. The taxes are due, and will be paid, on January 15, 1992.
h. On April 1, 1991, the company signed a $60,000, 10% note payable. On that date, cash was debited and notes payable credited for $60,000. The note is payable on March 31, 1992, for the face amount plus interest for one year.
i. The company purchased a patent on January 1, 1991, at a cost of $11,900. On that date, patent was debited and cash credited for $11,900. The patent has an estimated useful life of 17 years and no residual value.
j. Pre-tax income has been computed to be $80,000 after all the above adjustments. Assume an average income tax rate of 30%.

E 3–13
Adjusting and Closing Entries
(L.O. 4)

At December 31, 1991 (end of the accounting period), Nicole Corporation reflected the following amounts on its worksheet:

Sales revenue	$190,000
Interest revenue	4,000
Beginning inventory (periodic inventory system)	30,000
Ending inventory	34,000
Freight-in (on purchases)	6,000
Purchases	108,000
Sales returns	8,000
Purchase returns	2,000
Operating expenses (including income tax)	52,000

Required:

1. Compute cost of goods sold.
2. Give the adjusting entry for purchases, inventory, and cost of goods sold. If none is required, explain why.
3. Give the closing entries for (a) revenues, (b) expenses, and (c) net income.

E 3–14
Adjusting and Closing Entries
(L.O. 4)

Seattle Company has completed its worksheet at December 31, 1991 (end of its accounting period). The following accounts and amounts were reflected on the worksheet:

Sales revenue	$110,000
Service revenue	2,000
Operating expenses	24,000
Income tax expense	5,000
Cost of goods sold	53,000
Interest expense	4,000
Ending inventory (perpetual inventory system)	11,000

Required:

1. Give the adjusting entry for inventory and cost of goods sold. If none is required, explain why.
2. Give the closing entires for (a) revenues, (b) expenses, and (c) net income.

**E 3–15
Reversing Entries
(L.O. 5)**

On December 31, 1991, Samuels Corporation made the following adjusting entries:

a. Wage expense 16,000
    Wages payable 16,000

b. Bad debt expense 1,000
    Allowance for doubtful accounts 1,000

c. Income tax expense 24,000
    Income tax payable 24,000

d. Depreciation expense 50,000
    Accumulated depreciation 50,000

Required:

1. Give the reversing entries that you think would be preferable on January 1, 1992.
2. For each adjusting entry, explain how you decided whether to reverse it.

**E 3–16
Reversing Entries
(L.O. 5)**

At the end of the annual accounting period, Rose Corporation made the following adjusting entries:

December 31, 1991:

a. Property tax expense 800
    Property taxes payable 800
    (These are paid once each year.)

b. Rent receivable 4,000
    Rent revenue 4,000
    (Rent revenue is collected at various dates each month.)

c. Patent amortization expense 2,000
    Patents 2,000

d. Warranty expense 600
    Estimated warranty liability 600

e. Wage expense 9,000
    Wages payable 9,000

Required:

1. Give the reversing entries that should be made on January 1, 1992.
2. Explain, for each adjusting entry, how you decided whether to reverse it.

**E 3–17
Appendix 3A,
Prepare a Monthly
Income Statement
(L.O. 2, 4)**

Tuffy Corporation prepares monthly interim financial statements for internal use. Its accounting period ends December 31. At the end of each month, the company accountant prepares a cumulative worksheet that uses (a) the unadjusted trial balance at the end of the month and (b) the adjusting entries based on cumulative amounts to the end of the month.

It is February 28 of the current year, 1991, and the worksheet has been completed. Therefore, the following data are available for preparing the income statement (summarized to simplify):

	Reported in January	Reflected on February 28 Worksheet
Sales revenue	$150,000	$365,000
Cost of goods sold	80,000	220,000
Operating expenses	30,000	63,000
Interest revenue	2,000	3,400
Interest expense	5,000	11,100
Gain (loss) on disposal of assets	7,000	(9,000)
Income tax expense	11,000	16,325

Required:

1. Prepare a summarized income statement for the month of February.
2. Show computations.

**E 3–18
Adjusting Entries,
Recording Methods
(L.O. 4, 5)**

a. Minnier Company sells magazine subscriptions for a one-year, two-year, or three-year period. Cash receipts from subscribers are credited to magazine subscriptions collected in advance, and this account had a balance of $1,700,000 at December 31, 1991. Information for the year ended December 31, 1992 is as follows:

Cash receipts from subscribers $2,100,000
Magazine subscriptions revenue credited
    at December 31, 1992   1,500,000

Required:

In its December 31, 1992, balance sheet, what amount should Minnier report as the balance for magazine subscriptions collected in advance?

b. Halo Company sublet a portion of its warehouse for five years at an annual rental of $18,000 beginning May 1, 1990. The tenant paid one year's rent in advance, which Halo recorded as a credit to unearned rental revenue. Halo reports on a calendar-year basis.

Required:

1. Record the adjusting entry on December 31, 1990.
2. Assume that Halo recorded the rental receipt as rent revenue. Record the adjusting entry on December 31, 1990.

(AICPA adapted)

E 3–19
Account Analysis
(L.O. 5)

a. Dane Company sells magazine subscriptions for one- and two-year periods. Cash receipts from subscribers are credited to magazine subscriptions collected in advance. This account had a balance of $2,100,000 at December 31, 1990, before the year-end adjustment. Outstanding subscriptions at December 31, 1990 expire as follows:

During 1991 . . . . $600,000
During 1992   900,000

Required:

In its December 31, 1990 balance sheet, what amount should Dane report as the balance in magazine subscriptions collected in advance?

b. Zinnie Company assigns some of its patents to other companies under a variety of licensing agreements. In some instances, advance royalties are received when the agreements are signed and, in others, royalties are remitted within 60 days after each license year-end. The following data are included in Zinnie's December 31 balance sheets:

	1990	1991
Royalties receivable	$90,000	$85,000
Unearned royalties	60,000	40,000

During 1991, Zinnie received royalty remittances of $200,000.

Required:

In its income statement for the year ended December 31, 1991, how much royalty revenue should Zinnie report?

(AICPA adapted)

E 3–20
Appendix 3B,
Special Journals
(L.O. 7)

Next to each transaction, place the number of the journal into which that transaction would be recorded. Assume that the company uses special journals whenever appropriate.

Journals	**Transactions**
1. General journal.	_____ *a.* Collect cash on account.
2. Sales journal.	_____ *b.* Purchase merchandise on account.
3. Purchases journal.	_____ *c.* Prepare adjusting entries.
4. Cash receipts journal.	_____ *d.* Pay the insurance bill.
5. Cash payments journal.	_____ *e.* Receive cash for services.
6. Voucher register.	_____ *f.* Prepare closing entries.
7. Check register.	_____ *g.* Record a completed but unpaid voucher.
	_____ *h.* Correct an erroneous journal entry.
	_____ *i.* Sell merchandise on credit.
	_____ *j.* Pay accounts payable.
	_____ *k.* Sell merchandise for cash.
	_____ *l.* Pay the voucher in *(g)*.

E 3–21
Appendixes 3A and 3B,
Multiple Choice
(L.O. 6, 7)

Choose the correct statement among the multiple choice alternatives for each question.

1. *a.* Worksheets are a mandatory part of an accounting information system.
   b. GAAP governs the use and format of worksheets.
   c. The order of accounting cycle steps is not affected by the use of a worksheet.
   d. Formal adjusting journal entries are not recorded in a worksheet.

2. *a.* Transactions are generally not recorded in a worksheet.
   b. Closing entries are often recorded in a worksheet.
   c. The financial statements are completed in a worksheet.
   d. Formal adjusting entries must be recorded and posted before financial statements can be prepared when a worksheet is used.

3. *a.* Reversing entries depend on the order of accounting steps in a worksheet.
   b. Worksheets, when used with computer software, can save processing time and costs.
   c. Spreadsheets and worksheets are the same.
   d. Worksheets must be used in a computerized environment.

4. *a.* Worksheet adjusting entries and formal adjusting entries produce different ending account balances.
   b. The retained earnings balance—in the worksheet, unadjusted trial balance—is generally equal to its ending balance.
   c. Net income is equal to the final difference between the debit and credit worksheet income statement columns.
   d. The total of the debit column of the unadjusted trial balance represents a meaningful total.

5. *a.* A cash receipts journal records more than one type of transaction.
   b. A voucher is the document that substantiates the existence of a liability.
   c. Authorizations are not required in a voucher system.
   d. Subsidiary ledgers are not used in a voucher system.

6. *a.* A subsidiary ledger would generally be used for retained earnings.
   b. Subsidiary ledgers completely replace the general ledger.
   c. A control account and the sum of its related subsidiary ledger account balances will generally not agree unless all transactions affecting the account have been posted.
   d. One special journal should be used for many different transactions involving many different accounts.

7. *a.* It is not possible to design an accounting information system that uses only a general ledger and no subsidiary ledgers.
   b. The sales journal generally records credit sales only.
   c. A voucher system replaces all other special journals.
   d. A voucher is paid before its recording in the voucher register.

8. *a.* A sales journal would normally have a cash debit column.
   b. Posting from the sales journal to the accounts receivable subsidiary ledger should occur frequently.
   c. Posting from the sales journal to the general ledger involves only one control account.
   d. The cash receipts journal would generally have only one credit column.

PROBLEMS

P 3–1
Journalize and Post;
Unadjusted Trial Balance
(L.O. 2, 4)

The following selected transactions were completed during 1991 by Rotan Corporation:

a. Sold 20,000 shares of its own common stock, par $1 per share, for $12 per share and received cash in full.

b. Borrowed $100,000 cash on a 9%, one-year note, interest payable at maturity on April 30, 1992.

c. Purchased equipment for use in operating the business at a net cash cost of $164,000; paid in full.

d. Purchased merchandise for resale at a cash cost of $140,000; paid cash. Assume a periodic inventory system; therefore, debit purchases.

e. Purchased merchandise for resale on credit terms 2/10, n/60. The merchandise will cost $9,800 if paid within 10 days; after 10 days, the payment will be $10,000. The company always takes the discount; therefore, such purchases are recorded at net of the discount.

f. Sold merchandise for $180,000; collected $165,000 cash, and the balance is due in one month.

g. Paid $40,000 cash for operating expenses.

h. Paid three fourths of the balance for the merchandise purchased in *(e)* within 10 days; the balance remains unpaid.

i. Collected 50% of the balance due on the sale in *(f);* the remaining balance is uncollected.

j. Paid cash for an insurance premium, $600; the premium was for two years' coverage (debit prepaid insurance).

k. Purchased a tract of land for a future building for company operations, $63,000 cash.

l. Paid damages to a customer who was injured on the company premises, $10,000 cash.

Required:

1. Enter each of the above transactions in a general journal; use *J*1 for the first journal page number. Use the letter to the left to indicate the date.
2. Set up appropriate T-accounts and post the journal entries. Use posting reference numbers in your posting. Assign each T-Account an appropriate title and number each account in balance sheet order, followed by the income statement accounts; start with Cash, No. 101.
3. Prepare an unadjusted trial balance.

P 3–2
Explain Some Adjusting and Closing Entries
(L.O. 4)

Below are some unrelated adjusting and closing (but no reversing) entries. Write a suitable explanation for each of the following end-of-period entries:

a. Salary expense	7,000	
Salaries payable		7,000
b. Rent revenue	800	
Unearned rent revenue		800
c. Ending inventory	10,000	
Cost of goods sold	72,000	
Purchases		70,000
Beginning inventory		12,000
d. Interest receivable	900	
Interest revenue		900
e. Supplies expense	400	
Supplies inventory		400
f. Income summary	79,000	
Operating expenses		21,000
Administrative expenses		16,000
Interest expense		2,000
Cost of goods sold		40,000
g. Interest expense	750	
Interest payable		750
h. Income summary	12,500	
Retained earnings		12,500
i. Investment revenue	600	
Unearned investment revenue		600
j. Warranty (guarantee) expense	500	
Estimated warranty liability		500
k. Income tax expense	3,700	
Income taxes payable		3,700
l. Property tax expense	360	
Property taxes payable		360
m. Sales revenue	90,000	
Rent revenue	2,000	
Interest revenue	1,000	
Sales returns		1,500
Income summary		91,500

P 3–3
Journalize Adjusting
Entries
(L.O. 4)

The following transactions and events for Susan Manfacturing Corporation are under consideration for adjusting entries at December 31, 1991 (end of the accounting period). Give the adjusting entry (or entries) that should be made on December 31, 1991, for each item. State any assumptions that you make. If an adjusting entry is not required, explain why.

a. Machine A used in the factory cost $450,000; it was purchased on July 1, 1988. It has an estimated useful life of 12 years and a residual value of $30,000. Straight-line depreciation is used.

b. Sales for 1991 amounted to $4,000,000, including $600,000 credit sales. It is estimated, based on experience of the company, that bad debt losses will be ¼% of credit sales.

c. At the beginning of 1991, office supplies inventory amounted to $600. During 1991, office supplies amounting to $8,800 were purchased; this amount was debited to office supplies expenses. An inventory of office supplies at the end of 1991 showed $400 on the shelves. The January 1 balance of $600 is still reflected in the office supplies inventory account.

d. On July 1, 1991, the company paid a three-year insurance premium amounting to $2,160; this amount was debited to prepaid insurance.

e. On October 1, 1991, the company paid rent on some leased office space. The payment of $7,200 cash was for the following six months. At the time of payment, rent expense was debited for the $7,200.

f. On August 1, 1991, the company borrowed $120,000 from Sharpstown Bank. The loan was for 12 months at 9% interest payable at maturity date.

g. Finished goods inventory on January 1, 1991, was $200,000; and on December 31, 1991, it was $260,000. The perpetual inventory record provided the cost of goods sold amount of $2,400,000.

h. The company owned some property (land) that was rented to B. R. Speir on April 1, 1991, for 12 months for $8,400. On April 1, the entire annual rental of $8,400 was credited to rent revenue collected in advance, and cash was debited.

i. On December 31, 1991, wages earned by employees but not yet paid (or recorded in the accounts) amounted to $18,000. Disregard payroll taxes.

j. On September 1, 1991, the company loaned $60,000 to an outside party. The loan was at 10% per annum and was due in six months; interest is payable at maturity. Cash was credited for $60,000, and notes receivable debited on September 1 for the same amount.

k. On January 1, 1991, factory supplies on hand amounted to $200. During 1991, factory supplies that cost $4,000 were purchased and debited to factory supplies inventory. At the end of 1991, a physical inventory count revealed that factory supplies on hand amounted to $800.

l. The company purchased a gravel pit on January 1, 1989, at a cost of $60,000; it was estimated that approximately 60,000 tons of gravel could be removed prior to exhaustion. It was also estimated that the company would take five years to exploit this natural resource. Tons of gravel removed and sold were: 1989—3,000; 1990—7,000; and 1991—5,000. Hint: amortize on output basis; no residual value.

m. At the end of 1991, it was found that postage stamps that cost $120 were on hand (in a "postage" box in the office). When the stamps were purchased, miscellaneous expense was debited, and cash was credited.

n. At the end of 1991, property taxes for 1991 amounting to $59,000 had been assessed on property owned by the company. The taxes are due no later than February 1, 1992. The taxes have not been recorded on the books because payment has not been made.

o. The company borrowed $120,000 from the bank on December 1, 1991. A 60-day note payable was signed at 9-½% interest payable on maturity date. On December 1, 1991, cash was debited and notes payable credited for $120,000.

p. On July 1, 1991, the company paid the city a $1,000 license fee for the next 12 months. On that date, cash was credited and license expense debited for $1,000.

q. On March 1, 1991, the company made a loan to the company president and received a $30,000 note receivable. The loan was due in one year and called for 6% annual interest payable at maturity date.

r. The company owns three company cars used by the executives. A six-month maintenance contract on them was signed on October 1, 1991, whereby a local garage agreed to do "all the required maintenance." The payment was made for the following six months in advance. On October 1, 1991, cash was credited and maintenance expense was debited for $9,600.

P 3-4
Adjusting Entries: Correct
Financial Statements
(L.O. 4)

Ace Service Corporation has been in operation since January 1, 1991. It is now December 31, 1992, the end of the annual accounting period. The company has never been audited by an independent CPA. The annual statements given below were prepared by the company book-keeper at December 31, 1992 (additional accounts needed in the solution are provided without amounts):

Income Statement

Revenues:
Service revenue	$250,000
Interest revenue	1,000
Total revenues	251,000

Expenses:
Salary expense	75,000
Wage expense	60,600
Depreciation expense	
Interest expense	2,400
Remaining expenses	50,000
Total operating expenses	188,000

Pretax income	63,000
Income tax expense	
Net income	$ 63,000
EPS	$3.50

Balance Sheet
Assets

Cash	$ 40,000
Note receivable (10%)	12,000
Interest receivable	
Inventory, office supplies	2,000
Prepaid insurance	1,500
Equipment	200,000
Accumulated depreciation	(22,500)
Remaining assets	85,500
Total assets	$318,500

Liabilities

Accounts payable	$ 18,000
Wages payable	
Unearned service revenue	
Interest payable	
Income taxes payable	
Notes payable (16%)	40,000
Total liabilities	58,000

Stockholders' Equity

Capital stock, par $10	180,000
Retained earnings	80,500
Total stockholders' equity	260,500
Total liabilities and stockholders' equity	$318,500

An outside accountant was engaged to adjust the statements for any items omitted. As a consequence, the following additional information was developed:

a. No depreciation has been recognized for 1992. The equipment has an eight-year life and residual value of $20,000.

b. Prepaid insurance at the end of 1992 was $500. Use remaining expenses account.

c. Wages unpaid and unrecorded at the end of 1992 amounted to $15,000.

d. Interest on the note receivable was collected on the last interest date, October 31, 1992.

e. The inventory count of office supplies at year-end showed $300. Use remaining expenses account.

f. On December 31, 1992, service revenues collected but unearned amounted to $8,000.

g. Interest on the note payable is paid each August 31.

h. Assume the income tax rate is 20 percent.

Required:

1. Prepare adjusting entries for the above items in general journal form at December 31, 1992.
2. Restate the above statements after taking into account your adjusting entries made in (1). Key each adjustment. You need not use additional subclassifications on the statements. Suggestion: use the following solution format:

| | | Changes from adjusting | |
Items	Reported amounts	entries (use + and −)	Correct amounts
(list the two statements here)			

P 3-5
Recording Systems,
Adjusting Entries,
Reversing Entries
(L.O. 5)

Ronald Company, a calendar year company, employs the expedient system and reversing entries whenever appropriate. For each of the following, provide (1) the December 31, 1991, adjusting entry; (2) the January 1, 1992, reversing entry (if a reversing entry is not appropriate, explain why); and (3) the entry for the associated transaction to occur in 1992 if one is expected.

a. One of Ronald Company's liabilities is a 12%, $40,000 long-term note payable, which requires interest to be paid each March and September 1.

b. Ronald Company owns a $20,000, 10% bond, which it purchased at face value and which pays interest each August and February 1.

c. Ronald Company performed and completed services for a customer in December for a $12,000 total fee. The customer was not billed and did not remit payment in the current year. The customer has a clean credit history.

d. Depreciation of $30,000 is to be recognized.

e. Wages totaling $15,000 were earned but not paid or recorded at year-end. Assume that the first payroll in 1991 will total $45,000.

f. Ronald Company receives the $36,000 annual rental fee on one of its real estate investments at the beginning of each contract year. The rental contract began on July 1, several years ago.

g. Estimated warranty expense on sales in the current year is $50,000. Products sold by Ronald Company carry a one-year warranty. $26,000 has been spent servicing warranty claims from last year's sales, and $34,000 on this year's sales. Costs of servicing claims are debited to estimated warranty liability. Assume that Ronald Company has been able to perfectly predict total warranty costs and will continue to do so.

P 3-6
Complete All Phases of
the Accounting Cycle
(L.O. 4)

The post-closing trial balance of the general ledger of Wilson Corporation at December 31, 1991, reflects the following:

Acct. No.	Account	Debit	Credit
101	Cash	$ 27,000	
102	Accounts receivable	21,000	
103	Allowance for doubtful accounts		$ 1,000
104	Inventory (perpetual inventory system)*	35,000	
105	Prepaid insurance (20 months remaining)	900	
200	Equipment (20-year estimated life, no residual value)	50,000	
201	Accumulated depreciation, equipment		22,500
300	Accounts payable		7,500
301	Wages payable		
302	Income taxes payable (for 1991)		4,000
400	Common stock, par $1		80,000
401	Retained earnings		18,900
500	Sales revenue		
600	Cost of goods sold		
601	Operating expenses		
602	Income tax expense		
700	Income summary		
		$133,900	$133,900

* Ending inventory, $45,000 (at 12/31/1992).

The following transactions occurred during 1992 in the order given (use the number at the left to indicate the date):

Date

1. Sales revenue of $30,000, of which $10,000 was on credit; cost, provided by perpetual inventory record, $19,500. Hint: when the perpetual system is used, make two entries to record a sale—first, debit cash and/or accounts receivable and credit sales revenue; second, debit cost of goods sold and credit inventory.
2. Collected $17,000 on accounts receivable.
3. Paid income taxes payable (1991), $4,000.
4. Purchased merchandise, $40,000, of which $8,000 was on credit.
5. Paid accounts payable, $6,000.
6. Sales revenue of $72,000 (in cash); cost, $46,800.
7. Paid operating expenses, $19,000.
8. On January 1, 1992, sold and issued 1,000 shares of common stock, par $1, for $1,000 cash.
9. Purchased merchandise, $100,000, of which $27,000 was on credit.
10. Sales revenue of $98,000, of which $30,000 was on credit; cost, $63,700.
11. Collected cash on accounts receivable, $26,000.
12. Paid cash on accounts payable, $28,000.
13. Paid various operating expenses in cash, $18,000.

Required:

1. Set up T-accounts in the general ledger for each of the accounts listed in the above trial balance and enter the December 31, 1991, balances.
2. Journalize each of the transactions listed above for 1992; use only a general journal.
3. Post the journal entries; use posting reference numbers.
4. Prepare an unadjusted trial balance.
5. Journalize the adjusting entries and post them to the ledger. Assume a bad debt rate of ½% of credit sales for the period and an average 40% income tax rate. Hint: income tax expense is $11,784. At December 31, 1992, accrued wages were $300. Use straight-line depreciation.
6. Prepare an adjusted trial balance.
7. Prepare the income statement and balance sheet (subclassifications are not required).
8. Journalize and post the closing entries.
9. Prepare a post-closing trial balance.

P 3-7

Appendix 3A, Worksheet, Adjusting and Closing Entries, Statements (L.O. 6)

Major Corporation adjusts and closes its books each December 31. At December 31, 1991, the following unadjusted trial balance has been developed from the general ledger.

	Balances (unadjusted)	
Account	Debit	Credit
Cash	$139,960	
Accounts receivable	34,000	
Allowance for doubtful accounts		$ 5,400
Inventory (periodic system)	62,000	
Prepaid insurance (15 months remaining as of 1/1/1991)	600	
Long-term note receivable (14%)	12,000	
Investment revenue receivable		
Land	27,000	
Building	240,000	
Accumulated depreciation, building		130,000
Equipment	90,000	
Accumulated depreciation, equipment		50,000
Accounts payable		23,000
Salaries payable		
Income taxes payable		
Interest payable		
Unearned rent revenue		
Note payable, 10%, long term		120,000
Common stock, par $10		200,000
Contributed capital in excess of par		10,000
Retained earnings		27,900
Sales revenue		300,000
Investment revenue		1,260
Rent revenue		6,000
Purchases	164,000	
Purchase returns		4,000
Cost of goods sold		
Selling expenses	51,000	
General and administrative expenses	35,000	
Interest expense	7,000	
Extraordinary loss (pretax)	15,000	
Income tax expense		
	$877,560	$877,560

Additional data for adjustments and other purposes:

a. Estimated bad debt loss rate is ½% of credit sales. Ten percent of 1991 sales were on credit. Classify as a selling expense.

b. The company uses the periodic inventory system—ending inventory (December 31, 1991), $70,000.

c. Interest on the long-term note receivable was last collected on September 30, 1991.

d. Estimated useful life on the building was 20 years; residual value, $40,000. Allocate 10% of depreciation expense to administrative expense and the balance to selling expenses. Assume straight-line depreciation (for proportionate usage).

e. Estimated useful life of the equipment was 10 years; residual value, zero. Allocate 10% of depreciation expense to administrative expense and the balance to selling expenses. Assume straight-line depreciation.

f. Unrecorded and unpaid sales salaries at December 31, 1991, were $7,500.

g. Interest on the note payable, long-term, was paid last on July 31, 1991.

h. On August 1, 1991, the company rented some space in its building to a tenant and collected $6,000 for 12 months rent in advance, which was credited to rent revenue.

i. Adjust for expired insurance. Classify as selling expense.

j. Assume an average 30% corporate income tax rate on all items including the extraordinary loss. Hint: income tax expense is $3,615.

Required:

1. Enter the above unadjusted trial balance on a worksheet.

2. Enter the adjusting entries (including the adjusting entry for inventory and cost of goods sold) on the worksheet and complete it.

3. Prepare a summary income statement and balance sheet (subclassifications are not required).
4. Journalize the closing entries.

P 3–8
Appendix 3A, Worksheet, Adjusting and Closing Entries, Statements (L.O. 6)

DAR Corporation currently is completing the end-of-the-period accounting process. At December 31, 1991, the following unadjusted trial balance was developed from the general ledger:

Account	Balances (unadjusted) Debit	Balances (unadjusted) Credit
Cash	$ 60,260	
Accounts receivable	38,000	
Allowance for doubtful accounts		$ 2,000
Inventory (perpetual inventory system)	105,000	
Sales supplies inventory	900	
Long-term note receivable, 14%	12,000	
Equipment	180,000	
Accumulated depreciation, building		64,000
Patent	8,400	
Interest receivable		
Accounts payable		23,000
Interest payable		
Income taxes payable		
Property taxes payable		
Unearned rent revenue		
Mortgage payable, 12%		60,000
Common stock, par $10		100,000
Contributed capital in excess of par		15,000
Retained earnings		32,440
Sales revenue		700,000
Investment revenue		1,120
Rent revenue		3,000
Cost of goods sold	380,000	
Selling expenses	164,400	
General and administrative expenses	55,000	
Interest expense	6,600	
Income tax expense		
Extraordinary gain (pre-tax)		10,000
	$1,010,560	$1,010,560

Additional data for adjustments and other purposes:

a. Estimated bad debt loss rate is ¼% of credit sales. Credit sales for the year amounted to $200,000; classify as a selling expense.

b. Interest on the long-term note receivable was last collected August 31, 1991.

c. Estimated useful life of the equipment is 10 years; residual value, $20,000. Allocate 10% of depreciation expense to general and administrative expense and the balance to selling expenses to reflect proportionate use. Use straight-line depreciation.

d. Estimated remaining economic life of the patent is 14 years (from January 1, 1991) and no residual value. Use straight-line amortization and classify as selling expense (used in sales promotion).

e. Interest on the mortgage payable was last paid on November 30, 1991.

f. On June 1, 1991, the company rented some office space to a tenant for one year and collected $3,000 rent in advance for the year; the entire amount was credited to rent revenue on this date.

g. On December 31, 1991, received a statement for calendar year 1991 property taxes amounting to $1,300. The payment is due February 15, 1992. Assume it will be paid on that date and classify it as a selling expense. The $1,300 has not been recorded during 1991.

h. Sales supplies on hand at December 31, 1991, amounted to $300; classify as a selling expense.

i. Assume an average 40% corporate income tax rate on all items including the extraordinary gain. Hint: income tax expense is $35,132.

Required:

1. Enter the above unadjusted trial balance on a worksheet.
2. Enter the adjusting entries and complete the worksheet.
3. Prepare the income statement and balance sheet (subclassifications are not required).
4. Journalize the closing entries.

P 3–9
Appendix 3B—A Cash Receipts Journal
(L.O. 7)

Hall Retailers uses special journals. A cash receipts journal with several selected transactions is given below.

		Debits		**Credits**			
Date	**Explanation**	**Cash**	**Account Title**	**Post. Ref.**	**Accounts Receivable**	**Sales Revenue**	**Misc. Accounts**
1991							
Jan. 1	Cash sales	30,000				30,000	
2	On account	4,200	Riley Corp.		4,200		
5	Cash sales	10,000				10,000	
6	On account	1,240	Brown, Inc.		1,240		
8	Sale of short-term investment	7,000	Short-term investments Gain on sale of investments				4,000 3,000
11	Cash sales	41,000				41,000	
12	Borrowed cash	10,000	Notes payable				10,000
15	On account	5,500	Watson Co.		5,500		
18	Collected interest	600	Internal revenue				600
31	Cash sales	52,000				52,000	

CASH RECEIPTS JOURNAL   Page CR–8

Required:

1. Sum the cash receipts journal and post it to the appropriate accounts in the general ledger. Set up the following T-accounts: Cash #101, Accounts Receivable Control #113 (beginning balance, $19,640), Short-term Investments #134, Notes Payable #326, Sales Revenue #500, Interest Revenue #509, and Gain on Sales of Investments #510. Also, set up a subsidiary ledger for accounts receivable (with systematic numbers starting with 113.03). Beginning customer balances were as follows: Brown, Inc., $1,240; Riley Corporation, $8,400; and Watson Company, $10,000.
2. Reconcile the subsidiary ledger with its control account.

P 3–10

COMPREHENSIVE PROBLEM
◆

Perform All Accounting Cycle Steps
(L.O. 1, 2, 3, 4)

Spectrum Enterprises began operations as a retailer in January 1991. You are to perform the 10 accounting cycle steps for Spectrum for 1991. Worksheets and special journals and ledgers are not required. Prepare journal entries in summary (for the year) form. Post to T-accounts. Spectrum uses the expedient recording system and records reversing entries whenever appropriate. Spectrum also uses a periodic inventory system and adjusts inventory in an adjusting entry.

Information about transactions in 1991:

a. Investors contributed $200,000 in exchange for 10,000 shares of $5 par common stock. On the advice of its investment banker, Spectrum offered the shares at $20.
b. Spectrum obtained a 10%, $100,000 bank loan on February 1. This loan is evidenced by a signed promissory note calling for interest payments every February 1. The note is due in full on January 31, 1995.
c. A rental contract for production and office facilities was signed February 1, which required $10,000 immediate payment covering the first month's rent and a deposit refundable in three years or upon termination of the contract, whichever occurs first. Monthly rent is $5,000. As an added incentive to pay rent in advance, Spectrum accepted an offer to maintain rent at $5,000 per month for the first three years if Spectrum paid the second through the thirteenth (March 1991 through February 1992) month's rent immediately. In all, Spectrum paid $70,000 for rent on February 1. Spectrum intends to occupy the facilities for at least three years.

d. Equipment costing $110,000 was purchased for cash in early February. It has an estimated residual value of $10,000 and a five-year useful life. Spectrum uses the straight-line method of depreciation and treats depreciation as a separate period expense.

e. Spectrum recognized various operating expenses for the year including the following:

Wage expense	$ 60,000
Utilities expense	40,000
Selling expenses	80,000
General and administrative expenses	100,000

f. Total merchandise purchases for the year amounted to $2,000,000. Ending inventory amounted to $200,000 at cost. Spectrum uses a periodic inventory system.

g. Total payables relating to merchandise purchases and other operating expenses is $40,000 at year-end.

h. All sales are made on credit and totalled $2,500,000 in 1991. $2,300,000 was collected on account during the year. Spectrum estimates that ½% of total sales will be uncollectible and has written off $3,000 of accounts.

i. Spectrum faces an average 40% income tax rate. Assume that all taxes for a fiscal year are payable in April of the following year.

j. Spectrum decided to declare a cash dividend equal to 60% of its income after taxes for 1991, payable in January 1992.

CASES

C 3–1
Analysis: Correcting
Financial Statements
(L.O. 2, 4)

Fannie Corporation started operations on January 1, 1991. It is now December 31, 1991, the end of the annual accounting period. A company clerk, who maintained the accounting records, has just prepared the following financial statements:

Profit and Loss Statement
December 31, 1991

Service income		$100,000
Costs:		
Salaries and wages	$30,000	
Repairs and maintenance	5,000	
Service	25,000	
Other miscellaneous	10,000	70,000
Profit		$ 30,000

Balance Sheet
December 31, 1991

Assets

Cash	$ 7,500
Note receivable, 16%	1,200
Inventory, supplies	6,000
Equipment	90,000
Other miscellaneous assets	7,300
Total	$112,000

Debts

Accounts payable	$ 8,000
Note payable (15%)	24,000
Total debts	32,000

Capital

Capital stock, par $10	50,000
Retained earnings	30,000
Total capital	80,000
Grand total	$112,000

The above statements (unaudited) were presented to a local bank, at the bank's request, to support a major loan. The bank requested that the statements be examined by an independent

CPA. You are the independent CPA, and among other accounting issues, you found that the following items were not considered by the company in preparing the income statement and balance sheet:

a. Service revenue amounting to $2,000 had been collected but not earned at December 31, 1991.
b. At December 31, 1991, wages earned by employees but not yet paid or recorded amounted to $9,000.
c. A count of the inventory of supplies at December 31, 1991, showed $4,000 supplies on hand.
d. Depreciation on the equipment acquired on January 3, 1991, was not recorded. The estimated residual value was $10,000, and the estimated useful life, 10 years.
e. The note receivable received from a customer was dated November 1, 1991; the principal plus interest is payable April 30, 1992.
f. The note payable to the local bank was dated June 1, 1991; the principal plus interest is payable May 31, 1992.
g. Assume an average income tax rate of 20% for Fannie Corporation and that no income tax has been recorded.
h. Although you did not do a complete audit of the accounting results, your judgment is that the daily recording of transactions was appropriate.

Required:

1. Recast the income statement, after giving effect to your findings. Use a format similar to the following to develop the statements:

Items	Reported Amount	Changes Due to Findings				Correct Amount
		Key	**+ or −**	**Amount**	**Comments**	
Income statement: (list the appropriate items here)						
Balance sheet: (list the appropriate items here)						

2. Write a brief narrative addressed to Fannie Corporation to explain the two corrected statements.
3. Give any recommendations that you would make to Fannie Corporation concerning its accounting function.

C 3–2
Ethical Considerations in
Transaction Recording
(L.O. 1)

a. Discuss a possible dilemma between the need for full disclosure and the potential harm to corporations arising from discussions of future events in the MD&A section of annual reports.
b. Adjusting journal entries are not signaled by new source documents or exchanges of resources between parties and may therefore be more easily omitted, altered, or forgotten. Considering the adjusting entries discussed in this chapter, describe intentional alterations of adjusting journal entries that would constitute unethical behavior on the part of the accountant or management.
c. Briefly discuss the responsibilities that the accounting staff and external auditors have toward the shareholders of a corporation, relative to transaction recording and financial reporting.

C H A P T E R

4

Review: The Income Statement and the Statement of Retained Earnings

LEARNING OBJECTIVES
♦

After you have studied this chapter, you will:

1. Be familiar with the nature of accounting income, including the all-inclusive and operating performance approaches to defining accounting income, and be able to relate accounting income to other definitions of income.

2. Understand the basic role of the income statement and the statement of retained earnings.

3. Know and understand the basic elements of the income statement.

4. Be able to describe and illustrate the single- and multiple-step forms of the income statement.

5. Understand and be able to illustrate special areas of reporting and disclosures on the income statement and the retained earnings statement governed by accounting pronouncements, in-cluding extraordinary items, unusual or infrequent items, discontinued operations, changes in accounting estimates and accounting principles, and prior period adjustments.

6. Understand the composition and purpose of the statement of retained earnings.

7. Be able to illustrate the computation and presentation of earnings per share on the income statement.

◆

INTRODUCTION
◆

Look at the statement of consolidated income for Armco, Inc., found in Exhibit 4–1. Scanning down the titles of the various lines, there are several purporting to be profit or income:

* Operating profit.
* Income before income taxes.
* Income of Armco and consolidated subsidiaries.
* Income from continuing operations.
* Income before extraordinary items and effects of changes in accounting principles.
* Net income.
* Earnings per share.

Which income item should a financial statement reader focus on first? Are some of these items more important than others? Would a prospective investor in Armco focus on one income item while a creditor focused on another? More directly, what does each of the various income figures tell us? What can be learned from this statement? What do the earnings per share figures mean? You may be tempted to ask, Will the real earnings figure please stand up and be recognized!

This chapter takes a close look at the statement of income.[1] Although the FASB recommends the use of this formal-sounding title, in practice the statement is commonly called the *income statement*. The more informal title, income statement, is used in this text.

Fundamentally, the income statement serves as a connecting link between a company's beginning and ending balance sheets for a given accounting period. The statement explains changes in financial position caused by operations (revenue and expense activities). The following diagram helps to illustrate this point:

Beginning balance sheet December 31, 1991		Income statement for 12 months ending December 31, 1992		Ending balance sheet December 31, 1992	
Assets	$1,000,000	Revenues	$900,000	Assets	$1,100,000
Liabilities	600,000	Expenses	700,000	Liabilities	500,000
Owners' equity	$ 400,000	Net income	$200,000	Owners' equity	$ 600,000

When there is no new investment by owners or disinvestment by the company during the period, the change in owners' equity from the beginning of the period to the end of the period is equal to the net income for the period. In the above illustration, the beginning owners' equity of $400,000 plus the net income for the period of $200,000, equals the end-of-period owners' equity of $600,000. The two owners' equity balances are linked, and sources or reasons for the changes can be found in the income statement.

From the standpoint of external decision makers, the income statement is a primary source of information on the company's current profit performance (or lack of it). Investors, lenders, investment analysts, and others use this information in predicting the amount, timing, and uncertainty (risks) of the firm's future performance and cash flows.

To illustrate how the income statement is used and to preview some of the major topics covered in this chapter, refer again to Exhibit 4–1. Armco's statement of consolidated income features comparative income statements for three consecutive years.[2] The Armco income statements are unusual in that they contain three special

---

[1] The term *income* is used most frequently in the title of the statement. The statement is also known by titles such as statement of earnings, profit and loss statement, statement of operations, and other descriptive captions. When two or more companies have been combined for the report because one owns a majority interest in the other(s), the statement is identified as a *consolidated* statement.

[2] It is desirable to present comparative financial statements for two or more reporting periods. In 1980, the Securities and Exchange Commission mandated that financial statements include a three-year comparison of income statements. This SEC requirement applies to all listed, publicly owned corporations.

EXHIBIT 4-1   Comparative Income Statements: ARMCO, Inc.

ARMCO, INC.
Statement of Consolidated Income
For the Years Ended December 31, 1989, 1988, and 1987
(Dollars in millions, except per share amounts)

	1989	1988	1987
Net sales	$2,422.7	$3,227.3	$2,927.2
Cost of products sold (Note 1)	(2,084.6)	(2,773.9)	(2,564.3)
Selling and administrative expenses	(179.0)	(196.1)	(205.4)
Special credits (charges) (Note 8)	80.7	(35.0)	(22.6)
Operating profit	**239.8**	**222.3**	**134.9**
Interest income	71.7	38.5	32.4
Interest expense	(66.5)	(82.1)	(91.1)
Sundry other—net (Notes 1, 9 and 13)	(41.7)	(29.1)	(28.6)
Income before income taxes	**203.3**	**149.6**	**47.6**
Credit (provision) for income taxes and in lieu of income taxes (Note 3)			
Current—United States	(3.0)	(6.1)	(20.3)
Foreign and state	(16.1)	(14.8)	(8.1)
Deferred	(5.8)	(3.3)	0.3
Tax credits/refunds	—	0.6	119.4
Total credit (provision) for income taxes	(24.9)	(23.6)	91.3
Income of Armco and consolidated subsidiaries	**178.4**	**126.0**	**138.9**
Equity in income of Armco Steel Company, L.P. (Note 15)	26.8	—	—
Equity in income of National-Oilwell (net of provision in lieu of income taxes of $1.8 for 1987) (Note 13)	4.8	4.1	1.6
Equity in income of AFSG companies to be sold (Note 2)	17.8	15.9	22.5
Income applied to AFSG advances (Note 2)	(17.8)	(15.9)	(22.5)
Income from continuing operations	**210.0**	**130.1**	**140.5**
Discontinued operations:			
Gain on sale of Aerospace and Strategic Materials (Note 14)	—	15.2	—
Loss of AFSG runoff companies (net of credit in lieu of income taxes of $19.9 for 1987) (Note 2)	(45.0)	(44.0)	(35.1)
Income before extraordinary items and cumulative effect of changes in accounting principles	**165.0**	**101.3**	**105.4**
Extraordinary items:			
Tax benefit of loss carryforwards (Note 3)	—	—	3.9
Gain on early retirement of debt (net of provision in lieu of income taxes of $0.8 for 1987) (Notes 4 and 6)	—	6.7	8.3
Cumulative effect of changes in accounting principles to December 31, 1987:			
Accounting for income taxes (Note 3)	—	(5.4)	—
Accounting for inventory costs (Note 1)	—	42.8	—
Net income	**$ 165.0**	**$ 145.4**	**$ 117.6**
Per share			
Earnings per share—primary (Note 1):			
Income from continuing operations	$ 2.28	$ 1.40	$ 1.67
Income before extraordinary items and cumulative effect of changes in accounting principles	1.78	1.07	1.23
Extraordinary items	—	.07	.15
Cumulative effect of changes in accounting principles	—	.43	—
Net income	1.78	1.57	1.38
Dividends:			
Common stock	.30	—	—
Preferred stock—Class A	2.10	2.10	2.10
Preferred stock—Class B	4.50	4.50	4.50

items that require explicit and special income statement disclosure: discontinued operations, extraordinary items, and cumulative effects of changes in accounting principles. Each is discussed later in this chapter.

Look at the net income line.[3] ARMCO's net income increased from $117.6 million in 1987 to $145.4 million in 1988 (a 24% increase), and to $165.0 million in 1989 (another 13% increase). Now, if you were an investor considering whether to buy stock in Armco, your interest most likely would be in estimating future earnings and cash flows.[4] You might ask whether these increases in net income are indicative of what to expect in future periods.

If you look for the subtotal above net income, you come to income before extraordinary items and cumulative effect of changes in accounting principles. Because the items found between these two income figures are not expected to be recurring, it is appropriate to discount or at least treat them differently when attempting to predict future earnings growth. Likewise, the data shown for discontinued operations should probably be excluded or treated differently in the prediction effort, as this is also a nonrecurring item.

Now move up one more subtotal to income from continuing operations. For this figure, the trend portrayed is much different than that of net income. Income from continuing operations declined 7% from 1987 to 1988 (from $140.5 million to $130.1 million), then increased a whopping 61% from 1988 (from $130.1 million to $210.0 million). An investor might also be concerned that a large portion of the income from continuing operations in 1987 was the result of a tax refund or credit, which is shown two lines above the figure for income of Armco and consolidated subsidiaries in the amount of $119.4 million.

Moreover, a careful study of the three years' statements reveals one or two additional items above the subtotal for income from continuing operations that might be considered as nonrecurring:

- Special credits (charges).
- Sundry other—net.

Consider the nature of each of the items discussed thus far: cumulative effects of changes in accounting principles, extraordinary items, discontinued operations, special credits, and tax credits/refunds. In the authors' opinion, none is indicative of Armco's mainstream business activity, that is, Armco's **continuing operations.** For Armco, the goal of continuing operations is the manufacture and marketing of steel products at prices sufficient to cover expenses and to net the company a profit. Continuing operations also includes income from such short-term investments as money market funds or equity securities and from long-term investments such as its investment in Armco Steel Company.

♦

WHAT THE INCOME STATEMENT REPRESENTS

♦

An important question from the point of view of a reader of the financial statements is, What earnings or income figure reported in the income statement best depicts a company's financial growth and offers the most assistance in predicting future

---

[3] Many firms would use the term *net earnings* instead of net income. In our opinion, these two terms are synonymous. Surveys of shareholders show that the average investor understands the term *earnings* more clearly than *income*, which many shareholders misconstrue to mean the income they are receiving from the corporation. Somewhat ironically, however, most corporations use the term *income* in the title of the statement (i.e., the income statement) rather than earnings.

[4] Earnings trends and trend lines are important analytical tools used by investment analysts and investors in forecasting a company's future earnings. Forecasts of future earnings are one factor often used in making investment decisions. Past trends and performance do not guarantee continuation of such trends and performance in the future, but they are often useful in prediction.

earnings? There is no simple, short answer to this question. It is important to realize that the income statement often contains several items related to income, and the nature of each must be understood in order to appropriately use the information portrayed.

In addition to differences of opinion on what items to include in the income statement, there are also differing viewpoints on when to recognize income. Part of the problem stems from the fact that income means different things to different people. To an economist, income represents a change in wealth. To illustrate, assume a firm owns a parcel of land for which it paid $10,000 several years ago. A new highway has just been built next to the property. Several individuals have offered to pay substantially more than $10,000 for the land, but the firm has not yet agreed to sell. The economist would say that an increase in wealth has occurred, which the economist would call *income*. This is called economic income. For the economist, a change in wealth, whether realized or not, is income.

An accountant would not recognize the increase in wealth described above as income. The accountant would first require *reliable verification* of the increase in value. If the land was sold at fair value to another party in an arm's-length transaction, this would provide the reliable verification the accountant seeks. Only at that point would the accountant recognize the increase in wealth as income.

Income recognition is a key concept in accounting. The issue is when and how revenues, gains, expenses, and losses are going to be recorded. Unfortunately the simplicity of the above example is not representative of the level of difficulty involved in income recognition. Chapter 2 pointed out that income has four elements (revenues, gains, expenses, and losses—net income is the algebraic sum of the four). These four elements are described in Exhibit 4–2. Questions about when and how a particular transaction or event should be classified are not easy matters to resolve. A significant portion of this text focuses on issues of revenue and expense recognition.

Limitations of Income Measurement

The accounting system has significant limitations as a method of measuring income. Financial statement users should not misinterpret net income as a measurement of the change in a company's value arising from operations. The discussion above of the Armco income statement suggests some of the reasons why this is not the case. The fundamental reason is that financial statements are prepared in accordance with generally accepted accounting principles, and GAAP is not designed to measure changes in value.

GAAP calls for accounting to be based on an analysis and recording of transactions. Income recognized and measured on this basis is called accounting income. It is based on the transaction approach to income measurement. Each transaction or event that potentially affects the company is analyzed to determine whether it is to be recorded in the accounting records. Questions about when to recognize income or its components—revenues, gains, expenses, and losses—are at the heart of the process. Indeed, a large part of the study of accounting addresses *measurement and recognition issues* as they apply to revenues, gains, expenses, and losses, as well as to assets and liabilities. When to recognize the elements of financial statements and in what amounts are the key questions considered.

There are two general problems with the transaction approach to reporting income. First, achieving reliable measurement requires agreement on the conditions that must be met before a transaction is recorded. Rules of measurement for each type of transaction are needed. These rules often represent a compromise between the two primary qualities of accounting information, discussed in Chapter 2: *relevance* and *reliability*. In the land example discussed earlier, knowing even the approximate increase in value may be relevant to the decision of the owner. However, only the actual sale of the land provides reliable information on the increase in value. Thus, if accounting measurement of income in this example were based on the estimated market value, relevant information would be included in the statements.

EXHIBIT 4-2   FASB Definitions of the Elements in the Income Statement

Revenues are inflows or other enhancements of assets of an enterprise or settlements of its liabilities (or a combination of both) during a period from delivering or producing goods, rendering services, or other activities that constitute the entity's ongoing major or central operations.

Gains are increases in equity (net assets) from peripheral or incidental transactions of an entity and from all other transactions and other events and circumstances affecting the entity during a period except those that result from revenues or investments by owners.

Expenses are outflows or other using up of assets or incurrences of liabilities (or a combination of both) during a period from delivering or producing goods, rendering services, or carrying out other activities that constitute the entity's ongoing major or central operations.

Losses are decreases in equity (net assets) from peripheral or incidental transactions of an entity and from all other transactions and other events and circumstances affecting the entity during a period except those that result from expenses or distributions to owners.

Source: FASB, *Statement of Financial Accounting Concepts No. 6*, "Elements of Financial Statements of Business Enterprises" (Norwalk, Conn., December 1985).

However, this information would be less reliable because it is only an estimate of what the change in value has been.

Second, often there are choices management can make regarding the accounting measurement method to be used. For example, management can choose to depreciate plant assets on an accelerated basis or on a straight-line basis. The choice affects the amount of net income reported for the period, and thus affects what is known as the **quality of earnings** for the firm. Earnings are generally considered to be of higher quality when management chooses accounting measurement rules that recognize revenues later, rather than sooner, and that recognize expenses earlier, rather than later. For example, accelerated depreciation is an accounting method choice that, many would argue, produces a higher quality earnings number than does straight-line depreciation. This is because greater amounts of depreciation are expensed in the early periods of the asset's life under accelerated depreciation. The choice reduces income in the earlier periods, and reduces the amount to be depreciated in future periods. Management must make many such choices in preparing a set of financial statements. The GAAP guidelines that govern the preparation of financial statements provide considerable flexibility in the computation of net income.

Although measurement and recognition issues are critical, this chapter focuses on how to display revenues, expenses, gains, and losses (given that they have been recognized). That is, the focus in this chapter is on *format issues* such as: Where on the income statement will interest income be shown? How should the gain on the sale of a division be reported? Is the settlement of an unusual lawsuit to be reported as an expense or as an extraordinary item? This chapter covers the general guidelines and acceptable formats for the income statement and the statement of retained earnings.

Because of their importance in assessing future earnings and cash flows, the disclosure and reporting of the following specific items are governed by accounting pronouncements:

- Extraordinary items.
- Unusual items.
- Discontinued operations.
- Effects of changes in accounting principles.

These are discussed later in this chapter. The next section considers aspects of the income statement formatting that can be selected by the preparer (firm management) and the aspects that are governed, and thus set, by specific accounting pronouncements.

> *CONCEPT REVIEW*
>
> 1. Briefly explain the difference between economic income and accounting income.
> 2. Briefly explain the difference between measurement and recognition issues and format issues.
> 3. Accounting income is the result of recording transactions in the accounting system when appropriate to do so according to the measurement rules selected by firm management. Identify two limitations of accounting income that result from this process.

ELEMENTS OF THE INCOME STATEMENT

Before addressing the specific issues of presentation, both covered and not covered explicitly by GAAP (those not covered are addressed first), the elements that make up an income statement and those aspects of income statement presentation where there is considerable freedom of choice by financial statement preparers are considered.

Statement of Financial Accounting Concepts No. 6 defines the **elements of the income statement.** The definitions, shown in Exhibit 4–2, are broad and must be made operational for the myriad of possible transactions that companies encounter. Operationalizing the *SFAC No. 6* definitions involves establishing specific measurement rules for classes of transactions. For example, revenue is broadly defined, but there is little guidance regarding when a specific revenue item is to be recognized by the accounting system. Hence, **revenue recognition** becomes a primary measurement issue in the computation of net income. Conceptually, revenue is recognized, and therefore recorded, when the earnings process is completed, and an exchange transaction involving the transfer of goods or services has occurred. Thus, revenue is generally recognized when there is:

1. A completed transaction to sell goods or services.
2. A transfer of ownership of goods from the seller to the buyer or the performance of specific services.
3. Collection of cash or a reasonable assurance that collection will occur.

Revenue and expense recognition are discussed in greater detail in Chapter 7.

The income statement reports all revenues, gains, expenses, and losses recognized for a specific period of time. The statement is titled with the name of the company and the type of statement and is dated to indicate the period covered (e.g., "For the Year Ended December 31, 1992"). The dating identifies the length and the ending date of the reporting period.

FORMAT ISSUES NOT GOVERNED BY ACCOUNTING PRONOUNCEMENTS

The manner in which accounting information is displayed in an income statement may well influence the reader's interpretation of the information. Depending on where an item is positioned in the income statement, it can be overlooked by the casual reader, or it can be so prominently displayed that it is unlikely to be overlooked. Positioning and other issues of display can either confuse or clarify. These questions are known as format issues.

Some aspects of income statement presentation are covered by GAAP, but others are not. In general, GAAP is concerned with how and where to present items not directly related to a business's continuing or primary operations and activities.

General Formats of the Income Statement

The elements discussed in Exhibit 4–2 constitute the primary components of the income statement. However, the accounting profession has not specified a standard *format* for organizing and presenting these elements on the income statement, although it has issued pronouncements guiding the presentation of certain items. Elements are organized in the income statement in two general ways: the single-step format and the multiple-step format.

Single-Step Format The single-step format uses only two broad classifications: (1) a revenues and gains section and (2) an expenses and losses section. It is a single-step statement because only one step is involved in arriving at the figure labeled "operating income" (or "income from continuing operations"). If the company had any items requiring separate reporting in the income statement, such as discontinued operations, extraordinary items, or cumulative effects of a change in accounting principle, the number of steps would increase because GAAP requires separate income statement disclosure of these items.

Exhibit 4–3 shows a single-step income statement for Graham Retail Company. It includes an extraordinary item, which adds a second subtotal to the format. Numerous variations to the single-step format exist in practice. For example, revenue items, such as interest income or investment income, are sometimes netted against related expenses. The key characteristic is that only two broad classifications are used in determining the earnings from continuing operations.

Multiple-Step Format The multiple-step format provides multiple classifications and intermediate subtotals. The multiple-step format typically distinguishes between the principal operations of the firm, any irregular activities, and financing activities. The Armco income statement in Exhibit 4–1 is a multiple-step format statement. There are computations of operating profit from the firm's basic operating activities, followed by a section for other expenses and revenues, a section for taxes, and a section for equity in earnings of unconsolidated subsidiary companies, all of which are included in the computation of income from continuing operations. Over time, an increasing number of firms are using a multiple-step format income statement.[5]

A typical multiple-step income statement would contain the following components:

I. *Operations section:* Includes the revenues and expenses of the company's primary operations.

  A. *Revenue (sales):* A subsection within the operations section presenting various specific revenue sources, possibly including information on discounts, allowances, returns, and other details to arrive at a net revenue amount.

  B. *Cost of goods sold or of service provided:* Presents the direct costs of goods sold or costs of services provided in generating the revenues. Details on how these figures were determined can be provided directly on the face of the statement or in notes to the financial statements.

The caption usually used for the difference between revenues and cost of goods sold is *gross margin on sales* or sometimes simply *gross margin* or *gross profit.* Armco does not compute a subtotal for gross margin. This intermediate figure is viewed as very important for retail and marketing firms, and somewhat less important for manufacturing companies.

---

[5] A recent survey of 600 major companies reported that 232 used essentially a single-step format while 368 used a multiple-step format. See AICPA, *Accounting Trends & Techniques, 1990* (New York, 1990).

EXHIBIT 4–3   Single-Step Format—Income Statement

GRAHAM RETAIL COMPANY
Income Statement
For the Year Ended December 31, 1991

Revenues and gains:

Sales (less returns and allowances of $20,000)		$670,000
Rent revenue		1,200
Interest and dividend revenue		4,800
Gain on sale of operational assets		6,000
Total revenues and gains		682,000

Expenses and losses:

Cost of goods sold*	$264,000	
Distribution expense*	153,500	
General and administrative expense*	73,500	
Depreciation expense	54,000	
Interest expense	6,000	
Loss on sale of investments	5,000	
Income tax expense ($126,000 × .30)†	37,800	
Total expenses and losses		593,800
Income before extraordinary items		88,200

Extraordinary item:

Loss due to earthquake	10,000	
Less: Income tax saving ($10,000 × .30)	3,000	7,000
Net income		$ 81,200

EPS of common stock (20,000 shares outstanding):

Income before extraordinary item ($88,200 ÷ 20,000)	$4.41
Extraordinary loss ($7,000 ÷ 20,000)	(.35)
Net income ($81,200 ÷ 20,000)	$4.06

*These expenses may be detailed in the statement or separately in the disclosure notes to the financial statements.

†Assumed average income tax rate, 30%. The income before income taxes (and before the extraordinary item) of $126,000 is determined as revenues ($682,000) less expenses to this part on the statement ($556,000).

C. *Selling expenses:* This subsection presents information on the expenses incurred by the company in its efforts to generate revenues. In addition to salaries and marketing expenses, this subsection also includes costs of delivering goods and overhead items allocated to the sales development process.

D. *General and administrative expenses:* This subsection presents information on the general administrative expenses of the company.

E. *Other operating expenses:* If a company has other operating expenses not included in the above classifications that management feels are important to identify on the face of the income statement, such expenses would be included here. Armco, for example, includes special credits (charges) at this point on its income statement.

When a subtotal is computed deducting all the above expenses from revenues, the caption found at this point in the statement is usually "income (or earnings) from operations before taxes" Armco uses the label "operating profit."

II. *Nonoperating section:* This subsection includes income and expense items that are routine and ordinary but not primary components of the company's operations. Examples are interest income or expense, or equity in the earnings of unconsolidated affiliated companies. This section often contains other revenues and gains and other expense and loss subsections that identify the specific items included. Also included, if such transactions occur, are any special gains or losses that are unusual or infrequent but not both.

Armco computes a subtotal at this point and labels it "income before income taxes."

III. *Income tax expenses:* This subsection presents the state and federal income tax expenses for the income recognized up to this part of the statement. Often even single-step format statements show income tax expense as a separate section of the statement, computing income before income taxes as an intermediate figure.

IV. *Other possible sections:* When a firm has investments in unconsolidated subsidiary companies that are generating earnings (or losses) for the company, they may be included at this point. This is partly because such earnings are taxed differently (compared to ordinary earnings) and because they arise from a source different from the primary operating activities of the company. (Such investments are considered in detail in Chapter 14.)

Armco has such investments, and thus includes equity in the earnings of its investees in a separate section. It labels the earnings computed before the inclusion of earnings of unconsolidated subsidiaries as "income of Armco and consolidated subsidiaries." The following section then presents Armco's equity in the earnings of its unconsolidated subsidiary companies.

The caption usually found on the subtotal computed at this point in the statement depends on whether there are any additional items below this line. If there are none, the caption is *net income* or *net earnings.* While most of the above sections are present in a typical multiple-step format statement, the form of presentation of this information is not specified in GAAP. Firms can alter the order of listing or grouping of the above items in a wide variety of ways.

If special items are to follow, the caption is *net income (earnings) before (discontinued operations, extraordinary items, or cumulative effect of accounting change),* depending on which items are present in the statement. These three items are not typical, and thus are not found in all income statements. However, if a company does have one or more of these items to report, the presentation is specifically governed by accounting pronouncements. The item(s) are reported as a separate component of the income statement, regardless of whether the company is reporting in a single- or multiple-step format.

V. *Discontinued operations* (if appropriate): This subsection presents gains or losses, *net of income taxes,* resulting from the disposition of a segment of the business. Accounting for discontinued operations is governed by *APB Opinion No. 30.*

VI. *Extraordinary items* (if appropriate): This subsection presents gains and losses, *net of income taxes,* resulting from unusual and infrequent items. The criteria and reporting requirements for extraordinary items are spelled out in *APB Opinion No. 30.*

VII. *Cumulative effect of a change in accounting principle* (if appropriate): This subsection presents the income effect, *net of income taxes,* of a change in accounting principle (for all but a specific set of accounting principle changes listed in *APB Opinion No. 20).*

The caption for the amount computed after all the above items is *net income* or *net earnings.*

VIII. *Earnings per share:* This item presents earnings per share information on the face of the income statement. It is required by *APB Opinion No. 15.* (Details of computing and presenting earnings per share information are covered in Chapter 22.)

A multiple-step income statement, using the data from Exhibit 4–3, is presented in Exhibit 4–4. In this example, the multiple-step statement presents two intermediate amounts that are not found on the single-step statement:

EXHIBIT 4–4   Multiple-Step Format—Income Statement

GRAHAM RETAIL COMPANY
Income Statement
For the Year Ended December 31, 1991

Sales revenue			$690,000
Less: Sales returns and allowances			20,000
Net sales			670,000
Cost of goods sold:			
Beginning inventory (periodic system)		$ 52,000	
Purchases of inventory	$268,000		
Freight-in	1,200		
Cost of purchases	269,200		
Less: Purchase returns and allowances	2,700	266,500	
Total goods available for sale		318,500	
Less: Ending inventory		54,500	
Cost of goods sold			264,000
Gross margin on sales			406,000
Operating expenses:			
Distribution expense*		153,500	
General and administrative expense*		73,500	
Depreciation expense		54,000	
Total operating expenses			281,000
Income from continuing (or primary) operations†			125,000
Other revenues and gains:			
Rent revenue		1,200	
Interest and dividend revenue		4,800	
Gain on sale of operational assets		6,000	12,000
Other expenses and losses:			
Interest expense		6,000	
Loss on sale of investments		5,000	11,000	1,000
Income before income tax and extraordinary items			126,000
Income tax expense ($126,000 × .30)‡			37,800
Income before extraordinary item			88,200
Extraordinary item:			
Loss due to earthquake		10,000	
Less: Income tax saving ($10,000 × .30)		3,000	7,000
Net income			$ 81,200
EPS of common stock (20,000 shares outstanding):			
Income before extraordinary item ($88,200 ÷ 20,000)			$4.41
Extraordinary loss ($7,000 ÷ 20,000)			(.35)
Net income ($81,200 ÷ 20,000)			$4.06

*These expenses may be detailed in the statement or separately in the *disclosure notes* to the financial statements.

†Also, variously labeled *income from primary operations* and *income from operations.*

‡Assumed average income tax rate, 30%.

1. Gross margin on sales (also called *gross profit*).
2. Income from (primary) operations.

Exhibits 4–1 and 4–4 contain typical classifications for a multiple-step format statement. Other formats can and should be used in operating environments where different but important relationships between revenues and expenses exist that should be disclosed. For example, a firm that produces and sells both goods and services might show two gross profit figures, one for activities involving the manufacturing and sale of goods, and one for the service activities.

The accounting literature provides little guidance on when it is appropriate to use a single-step format and when to use a multiple-step format. The single-step format has the advantage of simplicity and avoids the need to develop captions for intermediate classifications. No priority is suggested among the sources of income for the firm. The multiple-step format is potentially more informative to decision makers because it highlights important relationships in the reported items. Advocates of the multiple-step format believe important relationships exist in revenue and expense data, and the income statement is more useful when these relationships are explicitly shown. The number of firms using a multiple-step statement has been increasing in recent years.[6]

CONCEPT REVIEW

1. How might interest income be presented differently in a single-step format-versus a multiple-step format income statement?
2. How would an extraordinary gain be shown differently in a single-step format versus a multiple-step format income statement?
3. What characteristics of a firm should be considered in deciding whether to report using a single- or multiple-step format?

FORMAT ISSUES GOVERNED BY ACCOUNTING PRONOUNCEMENTS

Although management has considerable flexibility in presenting the regularly occurring revenue, expense, gain, and loss data in the income statement, specific accounting pronouncements govern the presentation of several income statement items:

1. Extraordinary gains and losses.
2. Unusual or infrequent gains and losses. *other revenues & expenses*
3. Discontinued operations.
4. Cumulative effects of changes in accounting principle.

These four items are reported separately on the income statement. All except item two are shown net of any related tax effect. *Net of related tax effect* means the tax consequences of the item have been determined and included in the amount reported for it. Determining this amount is the problem of **intraperiod tax allocation.** The *intra* prefix indicates the allocation is within the period, and thus the allocation is across items shown on the income statement for the period. **Interperiod tax allocation** is the process of allocating tax expense to reporting periods. Interperiod tax allocation is covered in a later chapter.

To briefly demonstrate intraperiod tax allocation before discussing the various items for which it is used, consider the following situation for Turtle Company. Sales for the year total $1 million and expenses before income taxes total $700,000. During the year, the company experiences an unusual loss of $200,000 when a foreign government turns hostile to the United States and expropriates Turtle's manufacturing facilities in that country.[7] Assume that the income tax rate is 40% and that the $200,000 expropriation loss is deductible for income tax purposes. Turtle Company's income statement with and without intraperiod tax allocation is as follows:

---

[6] Of the 600 firms surveyed in *Accounting Trends and Techniques,* the number using the multiple-step format increased from 304 in 1984 to 368 in 1989. Ibid.

[7] Expropriation is the action of a state or country in taking possession of or otherwise modifying the property rights of an entity. Firms that held property in Kuwait, for example, were at risk of having that property expropriated when Iraq took over Kuwait in August 1990.

TURTLE COMPANY
Income Statement
For the Year Ended December 31, 1991

	Without Intraperiod Tax Allocation	With Intraperiod Tax Allocation
Sales	$1,000,000	$1,000,000
Expenses	700,000	700,000
Income from continuing operations	300,000	300,000
Income tax expense:		
On operations ($300,000).40		120,000
On taxable income ($100,000).40	40,000	
Income before extraordinary loss	$ 260,000	$ 180,000
Loss from expropriation of ~~제조공장~~ manufacturing facilities by foreign government:		
Gross amount	(200,000)	
Net of tax effect ($200,000).60		(120,000)
Net income	$ 60,000	$ 60,000

In the left-hand column, the tax expense is shown at the actual net amount that will be paid, or 40% of the $100,000 net taxable income (revenues of $1 million less expenses of $700,000 and less the loss of $200,000). In the right-hand column, the tax effects of the two activities (operations and the loss from the expropriation) are shown separately. Thus, the income tax expense that would be paid if there were no loss from the expropriation would be 40% of $300,000, or $120,000. The tax effect of the expropriation loss reduces income tax for the period by 40% of the loss, or $80,000. The $80,000 tax savings resulting from the loss is subtracted from the gross loss of $200,000 to arrive at the net, after tax loss, of $120,000.

Many argue that the presentation as shown under the without-intraperiod-tax-allocation column is potentially misleading because the income tax is reported at $80,000 less than it would be if no loss had occurred. Also, the after-tax effects of the loss are overstated when presented at the gross amount (before tax). The with-intraperiod-tax-allocation column provides the reader with information on the consequences of both the company's operations and the expropriation loss on a net, after-tax basis. *APB Opinion No. 11* requires intraperiod tax allocation, as illustrated above, for extraordinary items and for all other items reported separately after income from continuing operations. In Exhibit 4–1, the following items for Armco are reported at their net of related tax effect amounts:

- Discontinued operations.
- Extraordinary items.
- Cumulative effect of changes in accounting principles.

The transactions or events that must be separately displayed on the face of the income statement are considered next. Also, classification and reporting of extraordinary items and discontinued operations are covered in detail. Since accounting changes are covered in more detail in a later chapter, this chapter covers only the requirements for disclosure on the income statement.

Reporting Extraordinary Items

For accounting purposes, an **extraordinary item** is a transaction or event that is both unusual in nature *and* infrequent. Extraordinary items are reported as a separate classification on the income statement to alert the reader of the special nature of these gains or losses. In effect, this prominent placement of an item provides a signal to users that this gain or loss is not expected to recur regularly. Knowing this, the readers might modify their predictions about future income and cash flows. Armco, Inc., reports extraordinary items for both 1987 and 1988 in the comparative income statements presented in Exhibit 4–1.

Extraordinary items can be controversial because sometimes it is difficult to define precisely what is extraordinary. Prior to *APB Opinion No. 30* (1973), some companies seemed to classify many gains and losses as ordinary or extraordinary depending on the motivations of management. Some managements appeared to be presenting income statements that were potentially misleading. They would include in continuing operations gains that were unusual and infrequent. For example, a company with an otherwise low net income might classify one or more large unusual and infrequent gains as ordinary. This would have the effect of increasing income from continuing operations. Alternatively, some firms might classify large losses as extraordinary in order to report a higher income from continuing operations. There was inconsistency across firms, and even over time for given firms, in the classification of items as ordinary or extraordinary.

As a result, the APB issued *Opinion No. 30* to define more precisely what could and should be classified as extraordinary. The *Opinion* had the effect of significantly reducing the number of items that could be classified as extraordinary. Extraordinary items are defined in *APB Opinion No. 30* as follows (emphasis added):

> Extraordinary items are events and transactions that are distinguished by their *unusual nature and by the infrequency of their occurrence.* Thus, both of the following criteria should be met to classify an event or transaction as an extraordinary item:
>
> *a. Unusual nature*—The underlying event or transaction should possess a high degree of abnormality and be of a type clearly unrelated to, or only incidentally related to, the ordinary and typical activities of the company, taking into account the environment in which the company operates.
>
> *b. Infrequency of occurrence*—The underlying event or transaction should be of a type that would not reasonably be expected to recur in the foreseeable future, taking into account the environment in which the company operates.[8]

Both criteria—unusual and infrequent—must be met before an item can be classified as extraordinary. You must consider the environment in which a company operates in applying these criteria and determining whether an underlying event or transaction is abnormally and significantly different from the ordinary and typical activities of the business. The environment in which a company operates includes factors such as these:

- Characteristics of the industry or industries in which it operates.
- Geographical location of its operations.
- Nature and extent of governmental regulations.

Similar events or transactions may be considered unusual for one company, but not for another, because of differences between each company's respective environment. For example, the two events described below are similar, but the first is treated as an extraordinary item, and the second is considered an ordinary event:

> *Extraordinary*—A tobacco grower's crops are destroyed by a hail storm. Severe damage from hail storms in the locality where the tobacco grower operates is rare.
>
> *Ordinary*—A citrus grower's crop is damaged by frost. The region has a long history of frost damage, which normally is experienced every three or four years.

Both events might be considered unusual, but the question becomes, Are these events unusual in this environment? The first situation is considered extraordinary because, given the environment in which the tobacco grower operates, hail storms are unusual and very infrequent. In the second situation, the criterion of infrequency of occurrence, taking into account the environment in which the company operates,

---

[8] AICPA, *APB Opinion No. 30*, "Reporting the Results of Operations," par. 20.

is not met. The history of losses by frost damage provides evidence that such damage may reasonably be expected to recur in the foreseeable future.[9]

APB Opinion No. 30 specifically identifies the following six events and transactions as items that should not be considered extraordinary because they can be expected during the customary and continuing business activities of a company:

1. Write-down or write-off of receivables, inventories, equipment leased to others, or other intangible assets. *Other* 貶低值
2. Gains or losses from exchange or translation of foreign currencies, including those related to major devaluations or revaluations.
3. Gains or losses on disposal of a segment of a business. *Discontinued operation*
4. Other gains or losses from sale or abandonment of property, plant, and equipment used in the business. *Discontinued*
5. Effects of a strike, including those against competitors and major suppliers.
6. Adjustments of accruals on long-term contracts.[10]

APB Opinion No. 30 also identifies three specific types of events that will give rise to gains or losses similar to (1) and (4) above that are to be classified as extraordinary:

1. *The direct result of a major casualty* (such as an earthquake).
2. An *expropriation.*
3. A *prohibition under a newly enacted law or regulation* that clearly meets both criteria.[11]

APB Opinion No. 30 greatly reduced the number of items that are recorded as extraordinary, but there is still considerable judgment involved in this classification. Management must decide, for example, what is a major casualty. The *Opinion* gives the example of an earthquake. What about a volcanic eruption, such as Mt. St. Helens in 1980, that destroys millions of board feet of lumber? How about the losses incurred when Pan Am's Boeing 747 was blownup by terrorists over Scotland in December 1988?

Each of the above might appear to be examples of extraordinary losses experienced as a direct result of a major casualty. The issue becomes whether the casualty was unusual and infrequent. It would seem that these two examples would likely be treated as extraordinary, but a case could be made for treating them as ordinary. Weyerhaeuser Company, a major producer of lumber and building materials, did record an extraordinary loss when the volcanic activity of Mt. St. Helens affected its timber operations in 1980. The Pan Am losses were not large enough, after insurance payments to warrant special reporting.

After the issuance of *APB Opinion No. 30,* the APB and FASB made specific exceptions to the above definition of *extraordinary.* Some specified items must be classified as extraordinary. One such specification is that gains and losses from the extinguishment of debt (discussed in Chapter 16) must be reported as extraordinary items.[12] The purpose of identifying these special items as extraordinary is to alert the financial statement reader to the unusual nature of the transaction. The FASB is likely to specify other items to be classified as extraordinary in future pronouncements.

As is illustrated above for the Turtle Company, extraordinary items are reported on the income statement under a separate classification *net of any income tax*

---

[9] AICPA, *Accounting Interpretation No. 1 of APB Opinion No. 30.*

[10] AICPA, *APB Opinion No. 30,* par. 23.

[11] Ibid.

[12] *SFAS No. 4* specifies that material debt extinguishment gains and losses are to be classified as extraordinary items. There have been other such specific classifications. For example, operating loss carryforward benefits were required to be treated as extraordinary gains until the issuance of *SFAS No. 96.* This *Statement* requires they be treated as a component of income tax expense rather than as extraordinary.

EXHIBIT 4-5   Excerpts from the Pacific Resources, Inc., Income Statement

(in thousands)	1987	1986	1985
Income before extraordinary item	$4,059	$27,783	$21,537
Extraordinary item (Note 4)	2,086	—	(3,375)
Net income	$6,145	$27,783	$18,162

Note 4. Extraordinary Item
As a result of the antitrust action discussed in Note 12, the Company recognized an extraordinary loss provision of $3,375,000 in 1985, net of $3,277,000 deferred income tax benefit. In 1987, as a result of a reversal of part of this antitrust judgment by the U. S. Court of Appeals, the Company reversed $2,086,000 of this extraordinary loss provision, net of $1,614,000 in deferred income taxes.

effect caused by their occurrence. If subject to income taxation, an extraordinary gain results in an increase in income tax, and an extraordinary loss creates a tax savings. In both situations, the tax effect is removed from the gain or loss in order to report a net-of-tax amount. Intraperiod income tax allocation, which is required for all items reported below income from continuing operations, is considered in more detail earlier in this chapter.

The amount of a gain or loss is not a factor in determining whether an item should be reported as an ordinary income component or as an extraordinary item. However, only *material* extraordinary gains and losses must be reported separately. Extraordinary gains and losses that are considered immaterial in amount could be reported as a component in continuing operations. Unfortunately, there is little guidance to help in determining what is material. Some companies show extraordinary gains or losses that are less than 1% of income before extraordinary items.

Exhibits 4–3 and 4–4 illustrate the reporting of extraordinary items, including their separate inclusion in EPS reporting. The earnings per share of extraordinary items are generally reported separately on the face of the income statement. Earnings per share reporting is discussed in a later chapter.

Finally, another interesting case is presented in Exhibit 4–5. This is an example of the recognition and subsequent reversal of an extraordinary item. Both the initial recognition in 1985 and the adjustment in 1987 are the result of regulatory action, which is defined by *APB Opinion No. 30* to be both unusual and infrequent. Exhibit 4–5 also represents an example of the typical note disclosure that explains an extraordinary item.

Reporting Unusual or Infrequent Gains and Losses

Some events or transactions are either unusual or infrequent but not both. Since they fail to meet both criteria, they do not qualify as extraordinary items. However, the prevailing view is that full disclosure should apply, and they should be clearly identified for the statement reader. *APB Opinion No. 30* required that effects of such events or transactions that are material be reported as follows (emphasis added):

A material event or transaction that is unusual in nature or occurs infrequently, but not both, and therefore does not meet both criteria for classification as an extraordinary item, should be *reported as a separate component of income from continuing operations*. Such item should *not* be reported . . . net of income taxes. [13]

---
[13] *APB Opinion No. 30*, par. 23.

A typical example of an unusual item, but one that occurs frequently, is the sale or disposition of assets. When such a transaction occurs and is material, the gain or loss from this transaction is usually reported as a separate line item on the income statement. The Times Mirror Company reported such items for all three years in its 1988 *Annual Report:*

Excerpts from the Times Mirror Company 1988 *Annual Report*

	1988 ($000)	1987 ($000)	1986 ($000)
Operating revenues	$3,259,372	$3,079,584	$2,920,310
Other income	73,256	62,761	27,826
Total revenues	3,332,628	3,142,345	2,948,136
Cost of sales	1,775,702	1,670,288	1,623,351
Selling, administrative, and general expenses	1,016,003	894,861	806,961
Interest expense	57,717	52,631	59,742
Income before gain (loss) on sale of assets and income taxes	483,206	524,565	458,082
Gain (loss) on sale of assets	**58,880**	**(29,225)**	**222,150**
Income Before Income Taxes	$ 542,086	$ 495,340	$ 680,232

The notes to the financial statements provide further information regarding the asset sales. For example, the note disclosure regarding the 1988 gain on sale of assets is:

> During 1988 the company sold certain assets of Times Mirror Press to GTE Directories Corporation for approximately $33,000,000 and also sold more than 171,000 acres of timberlands for approximately $85,511,000. These sales resulted in an aggregate gain of $58,880,000 before income taxes and $39,969,000 (31 cents per share) after applicable income taxes.

Another example of an item that occurs infrequently but is not unusual for any given company concerns expenses related to major corporate restructuring. Over the past several years, an increasing number of companies have reorganized major aspects of their operations, and significantly altered their capital structures in the process. These restructurings do not qualify as extraordinary items. Most accountants believe that these expenses should be fully disclosed and identified in financial reports. The SEC issued *Staff Accounting Bulletin No. 67 in 1986, requiring that restructuring charges be treated as a component of income for continuing operations.*[14] Exhibit 4–6 provides an example of such reporting from the Fuqua Industries financial statements for 1987.

Reporting Discontinued Operations (Disposal of a Segment of a Business)

Another item that requires separate and distinct reporting on the income statement is gains or losses resulting from **discontinued operations.** The disposal by a company of a segment of its business is likely to have a significant impact on future income and cash flow. Since information about the disposal is likely to affect predictions of future cash flows, it is an important accounting and reporting issue. *APB Opinion No. 30,* "Reporting the Results of Operations," provides reporting guidelines for discontinuance of a segment of a business that is sold, abandoned, spun off, or otherwise disposed of. The guidelines for discontinued operations require that any loss or gain on disposal, less the applicable income tax effect, be reported separately

---

[14] Securities and Exchange Commission, *Staff Accounting Bulletin No. 67.* In fact, the most frequently reported type of loss reported by 600 surveyed companies for 1985, 1986, and 1987 is a loss related to restructuring of operations.

EXHIBIT 4–6   Reporting an Unusual or Infrequent Item

FUQUA INDUSTRIES, INC.
Income Statement (excerpt)
For the Years Ended December 31, 1987, 1986, and 1985

(in thousands)	1987	1986	1985
Net Sales	$772,343	$701,194	$636,178
Equity in Pretax Income of Georgia Federal	44,827	29,503	—
	817,170	730,697	636,178
Costs and Expenses:			
Costs of products sold (includes materials, labor, plant overhead and depreciation, etc.)	520,253	469,092	427,645
Selling, general and administrative (costs of marketing, management and depreciation)	171,526	159,431	134,293
Provision for consolidation of manufacturing facilities	4,300	—	—
Total operating expenses	696,079	628,523	561,938
Operating Profit	$121,091	$102,174	$ 74,240

Notes to Consolidated Financial Statements

Consolidation of Manufacturing Facilities

During the first half of 1988, Fuqua intends to consolidate two of its home exercise equipment manufacturing facilities. Accordingly, a pre-tax provision of $4,300,000 ($2,580,000 net of tax benefit) was charged to income in 1987 to provide for the anticipated costs associated with the consolidation.

as a component of income before extraordinary items. For this purpose, the *Opinion* defines segment of business as a "component of an entity whose activities represent a separate major line of business or class of customer." A segment may be a subsidiary, division, department, or other part of the entity, provided that its assets, results of operations, and activities can be clearly distinguished physically and operationally, for financial reporting purposes, from the other operations of the company.

The disposal of a segment of a business must be distinguished from other disposals of assets that are incidental to the evolution of the business. Four examples of such incidental disposals for which the *Opinion* does not apply include:

1. The disposal of part of a line of business.
2. The shifting of production or marketing activities for a particular line of business from one location to another.
3. The phasing out of a product line or class of service.
4. Other changes resulting from technological improvements.

Three examples of transactions that should be classified as disposals of a segment of a business are:

1. Sale by a diversified company of a major division that represents the company's only activities in the electronics industry.
2. Sale by a retailing company of its 25% interest in a professional football team (all other company activities are in retailing).
3. Sale by a communications company of its radio stations, leaving only the television and publishing divisions.

On the other hand, the following three divestitures do not constitute disposals of a segment because the criteria are not met:

1. Sale of a major foreign subsidiary in silver mining by a mining company, leaving the company with silver mining operations in the United States and other foreign countries.
2. Discontinuation of design, manufacture and sale of children's wear in Italy by a manufacturer of children's wear.
3. Sale of all the assets used in the manufacture and sale of woolen suits, including the plant, by an apparel firm that plans to concentrate its activities in the manufacturing and marketing of suits made from synthetic materials.

Considerable judgment is required in deciding whether a disposal meets the criteria for separate reporting as required by *APB Opinion No. 30*. Firms generally tend to err on the side of identifying disposals as meeting the requirements of the *Opinion*. This seems reasonable, as it tends to provide more complete disclosure about the disposal.

To account for the discontinuance of a segment, two dates must be carefully identified: the measurement date and the disposal date.

The *measurement date* is the date on which the company formally commits itself to a plan to dispose of a specific segment. The plan of disposal must, at a minimum, include these six specifications:

1. Identification of the major assets to be disposed.
2. The exact method of disposal.
3. The period expected to be required for disposal.
4. An active program to find a buyer if disposal is to be a sale.
5. The estimated results of operations from the measurement date to the disposal date.
6. The estimated proceeds or salvage to be realized by disposal.

The *disposal date* is either the closing date of sale of the assets (when the business segment is transferred) or the date that operations cease, if the disposal is an abandonment. The measurement date and the disposal date may be the same. However, in most cases, the disposal date follows the measurement date. In situations where the two dates differ, the seller typically agrees to continue the usual operations of the segment being discontinued until the disposal date. Therefore, any gains or losses from segment operations during that period are considered to be those of the seller.

Determination of Gain or Loss on Disposal   At the measurement date, a determination is made of the gain or loss on disposal of the business segment. If there is a gain, it is recognized when realized, which is usually on the disposal date, assuming the disposal date is different from the measurement date. Losses, however, are to be recognized at the measurement date. The gain or loss includes two components:

1. The difference between the *net realizable value of the segment* after giving consideration to any estimated costs and expenses directly associated with the disposal, and the book value of the segment assets.
2. *Estimated income or loss from operations between the measurement date and the disposal date.* Income will be included only up to the amount of any loss from (1) above. Any remaining income will be recognized when realized.

In addition to the gain or loss on disposal, financial statements for accounting periods that include operating results attributable to the segment *prior* to the measurement date must separately disclose these results for those periods. As explained above, an estimate of the results of operations *subsequent* to the measurement date is included in the gain or loss on disposal.

Measurement and Disposal Dates the Same   If the measurement and disposal dates are the same, a single journal entry is made to record the full consideration received and to remove the carrying (i.e., book) values of all segment assets sold. The difference between these two amounts is the pretax "gain or loss on sale of segment," since there are no operations between the measurement date and the disposal date. When comparative statements include the year of disposal, the *gain or loss on disposal, net of tax,* must be reported on the income statement after income from continuing operations and before extraordinary items.

To illustrate the situation in which the measurement and disposal dates are the same, assume that on September 1, 1992, Acme Corporation sold and transferred its specialty products division for $200,000 cash. The carrying value of the segment's assets was $230,000. The accounting year ends December 31, and the applicable income tax rate was 30%. Assume income from continuing operations, after income taxes, is $262,000 in 1991, and $265,000 in 1992. Also assume the pretax income from the specialty products division is $15,000 in 1991, and totals $8,000 for the eight-month period ending September 1, 1992. The summary entry and appropriate reporting for Acme Corporation would be:

September 1, 1992 (measurement and disposal date):

```
Cash . . . . . . . . . . . . . . . . . . . . . . . . . . . . . . . . . . 200,000
Loss on disposal of segment (pretax) . . . . . . . . . . . . . .  30,000*
    Assets, Specialty Products Division . . . . . . . . . . . .           230,000
* Income tax saving $30,000 × .30 = 9,000 (reflected in income tax entry).
```

Comparative Income Statements

	1992	1991
Income from continuing operations (assumed)	$265,000	$262,000
Discontinued operations (Note 6):		
Income from discontinued operations, less income taxes of $2,400 in 1992 and $4,500 in 1991	5,600	10,500
Gain (loss) from disposal of discontinued operations, net of income tax ($9,000)	(21,000)	
	$249,600	$272,500

Note 6. Discontinued Operations

On September 1, 1992, the company sold its Specialty Products Division. This is the measurement date and the disposal date. The company received $200,000 cash for the sale of the division; a disposal loss of $30,000 (less an income tax savings of $9,000) was recognized. Pretax income from discontinued operations was $15,000 in 1991 and $8,000 in 1992.

Measurement and Disposal Dates Different—but in the Same Reporting Period   *When the measurement and disposal dates are different* and the selling entity continues the segment operations, the accounting and reporting are more complex. In this situation, the accounting and reporting are influenced by whether these two dates are in the *same* accounting period or *different* accounting periods. *When the measurement and disposal dates are different (the usual case) but both are in the same accounting period,* the accounting and reporting are demonstrated with the following changes to the above example:

Assume the same disposal transaction as above for Acme Corporation, except that the measurement date is September 1, 1992, and the disposal date is now December 31, 1992.

1. September 1, 1992—measurement date:
   The disposal entry may be made at this date. However, because the disposal date is also in this year, the entry usually is deferred to the later date within the current year to accommodate any subsequent changes agreed on by the parties.
2. September 1 to December 31, 1992—account for the operations of the discontinued segment separately.

3. December 31, 1992—end of accounting period and disposal date:
   a. Record disposal of the Specialty Products Division:

   Cash 200,000
   Loss on disposal of segment (pretax) 30,000*
       Assets, Specialty Products Division   230,000
   *Income tax saving, $30,000 × .30 = $9,000 (reflected in income tax entry).

   b. At December 31, 1992, the accounting records provided the following data for
      the Specialty Products Division: income (pretax), 1991, $15,000; January 1,
      1992, to August 31, 1992, $8,000; September 1, 1992, to December 31, 1992,
      $4,000. The $4,000 <u>income from segment operations during the *run-down*</u>
      <u>*period* from September 1, 1992, through December 31, 1992, and the $30,000</u>
      <u>loss on disposal of the segment are closed to income summary at year-end.</u>
      The income tax effect on each of these amounts is included in the 1992 income
      tax entry.

   Comparative Income Statements

	1992	1991
Income from operations, net of tax (assumed .30)	$265,000	$262,000
Discontinued operations (Note 6):		
Income from discontinued operations, net of tax:		
1991: ($15,000 × .70)		10,500
1992: From January 1, to August 31, 1992 *prior measurement date*		
($8,000 × .70)	5,600	
Gain (loss) on disposal of discontinued operations, net of tax:		
Income from operations of discontinued operations,		
September 1 to December 31, 1992 ($4,000 × .70) . . . . $ 2,800		
Loss on disposal of discontinued operations		
($30,000 × .70) . . . . (21,000)	(18,200)	
Net income	$252,400	$272,500

    Income between measurement date and disposal date

   Note 6. Discontinued Operations.
   In 1992, the company decided to sell its Specialty Products Division. The measurement date was September 1, 1992,
   and the disposal date was December 31, 1992. The company received $200,000 cash for the assets of the discontinued
   segment; a disposal loss of $30,000 (less an income tax saving of $9,000) was recognized. Incomes from the
   discontinued segment were: 1991, $15,000 (less income tax effect, $4,500), and 1992, $8,000 (less income tax saving,
   $2,400). Total loss on disposal recognized in 1992 was $26,000 (i.e., $30,000 − $4,000) less the income tax effect of
   $7,800 (i.e, $9,000 − $1,200), yielding an after-tax loss of $18,200.

Measurement and Disposal Dates Different—In Different Periods   *When the measurement and*
disposal dates are in different reporting periods, <u>the contract to sell a segment must</u>
<u>be recorded on the measurement date</u>. Because of the continuing operation of the
segment until the disposal date and the requirement that the contract for sale must be
recorded on the measurement date, <u>an *estimate* must be made of any expected loss</u>
<u>or gain</u> up to the amount of the loss on disposal from the segment's operations up to
the *disposal date*. <u>Additional gain is recognized only when it is earned.</u> An *estimated*
loss must be accrued on the measurement date.

   Returning to our example, suppose that on September 1, 1992, Acme Corporation
concluded an agreement to sell its Specialty Products Division for $200,000 cash,
payable on the disposal date, March 1, 1993. Acme Corporation will operate the
division between the measurement date, September 1, 1992, and disposal date,
March 1, 1993. The accounting period ends December 31. The carrying (or book)
value of the Division's net assets on the measurement date was $230,000; the income
tax rate is 30%. The incomes from discontinued operations were: 1991, $15,000 and
for 1992 (to August 31), $8,000.
   At the end of 1992, the accounting records reflected a $6,000 pretax loss from the
Specialty Division's operations for the period September 1, 1992, to December 31,
1992. An estimated pretax loss of $9,000 is expected for the period January 1, 1993,

to disposal date, March 1, 1993. However, on the latter date, the accounting records reflected an actual pretax loss from the division's operations of $12,000 for the period January 1, 1993 to March 1, 1993.

The accounting and reporting for this situation are as follows:

September 1, 1992—measurement date:

a. To record the loss on disposal:

Special receivable 200,000
Loss on disposal of segment (pretax) 30,000*
    Assets, Specialty Products Division   230,000

* Income tax saving, $30,000 × .30 = $9,000.

December 31, 1992—end of the accounting period:

b. To accrue the loss from operations of the segment from September 1 to December 31, 1992:

Loss on disposal of segment 6,000*
    Segment revenue and expense summary   6,000

* Income tax saving, $6,000 × .30 = $1,800.

c. To accrue the estimated loss from operations of the segment:

Estimated loss on segment operations (pretax) 9,000*
    Accrued loss on segment operations (a liability)   9,000

* Income tax saving, $9,000 × .30 = $2,700.

Note: This entry may be made on the measurement date; however, it often is not made until the end of the accounting period because a better estimate can be made at that time. The accrued loss on segment operations will be debited as losses are incurred in 1993.

Reporting at end of 1992:

Comparative Income Statements

	1992	1991
Income from continuing operations, after tax (assumed)	$265,000	$262,000
Discontinued operations (Note 6):		
Income (loss) from discontinued operations, net of tax:		
1991: ($15,000 × .70)		10,500[a]
1992: From January 1 to August 31, 1992 ($8,000 × .70)	5,600[a]	
Gain (loss) on disposal of segment, including estimated operating loss of $15,000 from September 1, 1992, to disposal date of		
March 1, 1993, net of tax ($45,000 × .70)	(31,500)[b]	
Net income	$239,100	$272,500

[a] Income (loss) prior to measurement date.

[b] Actual loss on sale of disposed segment of $30,000, plus operating loss of $6,000 in 1992 and estimated operating loss of $9,000 in 1993, all net of income tax savings of $13,500.

Note 6. Discontinued operations.
During 1992, the company decided to sell the Specialty Products Division for $200,000 cash. The measurement date was September 1, 1992, and the disposal date will be March 1, 1993, during which time the company has agreed to continue the normal operations of the Division. Loss from the discontinued segment operations from September 1, 1992, to the planned disposal date of March 1, 1993, is estimated at $15,000, less a $4,500 income tax saving; net loss, $10,500.

January 1, 1992, to March 1, 1993 Suppose that rather than the estimated $9,000 loss recorded in 1992, the accounting records reflect an actual loss of $12,000 from the discontinued segment. Of this amount, $9,000 is charged (debited) against the credit balance in the account accrued loss on segment operations (see December 31, 1992, entry (*c*) above), which reduces the accrued loss account balance to zero. Therefore, the accounting records pertaining to the discontinued segment reflect the following on March 1, 1993:

Loss on segment operations, pretax ($12,000 − $9,000) $3,000
Income tax saving (reflected in the income tax entry),
$3,000 × .30 900
Loss on 1993 segment operations, net of tax $2,100

March 1, 1993—entry on disposal date:

Accrued loss on segment operations 9,000
Loss on segment operations 3,000
    Segment revenue and expense summary 12,000
To record losses of segment during period of January 1
to March 1, 1993:
Cash 200,000
    Special receivable 200,000

Comparative Income Statements

	1993	1992
Income from continuing operations, after tax (assumed)	$279,000	$265,000
Discontinued operations (Note 6):		
Income (loss) from discontinued operations (net of income tax)	(2,100)	5,600
Gain (loss) on disposal of segment (net of income tax)		(31,500)
Net income	$276,900	$239,100

Note 6. Discontinued operations.
In 1992, the company decided to sell the Specialty Products Division for $200,000 cash, collectible on the disposal date, March 1, 1993. The company continued to operate the division until this disposal date. Loss from discontinued operations from January 1, 1993, to March 1, 1993, was $3,000 more than originally estimated, less a $900 income tax saving. A loss of $45,000 (less a $13,500 income tax saving) on the sale of the assets of the division was reported as of the measurement date, September 1, 1992.

Exhibit 4–7 is an example of the financial reporting of discontinued operations in 1987 by Lockheed Corporation. The company estimated the loss on the disposal at $9 million, net of tax effects. When the disposal was completed in 1988, any difference between the $9 million provision and the actual loss would be reported in the 1988 financial statements as a separate item under discontinued operations, similar to the $2,100 loss reported above for Acme.

Reporting Accounting Changes

Another event that requires separate disclosure on the income statement is a change in accounting principle. *APB Opinion No. 20* defines three types of accounting changes essentially as follows:[15]

1. *Changes in estimates*—The use of estimates (such as in determining depreciation expense or bad debt expense) is a natural consequence of the accounting process. However, experience and additional information may make it possible to later improve prior estimates. For example, the estimated useful life of an operational asset, after having been used (and depreciated) for 6 years, may be changed from the original 10-year estimated life to a 15-year estimated life. Changes of this type are referred to as *changes in estimates* and are easily distinguished from the next type of change—changes in accounting principle.
2. *Changes in accounting principle*—Because of a change in circumstances, or the development of a new accounting principle, a change in the recording and reporting approach for a particular transaction may be necessary. For example, a change in circumstances may make it desirable to change from straight-line

---

[15] Accounting changes *are not* due to accounting errors. They are approved accounting approaches for the three situations described. Correction of *accounting errors* are discussed in detail in a later chapter.

EXHIBIT 4-7   Excerpts from Lockheed Corporation Financial Statements Showing Reporting and Disclosure of Discontinued Operations

---

LOCKHEED CORPORATION
Income Statements (excerpt)
For Years Ending December 31, 1987, 1986, and 1985

(in millions)	1987	1986	1985
Earnings from continuing operations	$436	$410	$397
Discontinued operations, net of income tax			
Income (loss) from operations	(6)	(2)	4
Loss on discontinuance	(9)	—	—
Income (loss) from discontinued operations	(15)	(2)	4
Net earnings	$421	$408	$401

Notes to Consolidated Financial Statements

Note 5. Discontinued Operations

During the third quarter of 1987, the company decided to dispose of its shipbuilding operations. A provision of $9 million, net of income tax benefit of $6 million, has been made in connection with the discontinuance. Operating losses from shipbuilding operations are included in discontinued operations in the Consolidated Statement of Earnings.

Total assets of discontinued operations at December 27, 1987 were $74 million, consisting primarily of receivables and property, plant, and equipment. The net book value of the assets to be disposed of is presented separately in the Consolidated Balance Sheet.

Management anticipates that disposal of the shipbuilding operations will be completed during 1988.

Operating results of the shipbuilding operations were as follows:

(in millions)	1987	1986	1985
Sales	$49	$112	$149
Income (loss) before income tax	$(10)	$ (3)	$ 7
Income tax (provision) benefit	4	1	(3)
Income (loss) from operations	$ (6)	$ (2)	$ 4

---

depreciation to sum-of-the-years'-digits (SYD) depreciation. This would be a change in accounting principle, a *change from one acceptable principle to another acceptable principle.*

3. *Change in accounting entity*—A new entity or a first public reporting by an entity may give rise to special types of accounting changes.

Accounting changes are discussed in detail in a later chapter, "Accounting Changes and Error Corrections." Changes in estimates and changes in accounting principles are discussed prior to that chapter; therefore, these changes are reviewed here to provide background for the interim topics and homework.

Changes in Accounting Estimates   Revisions of accounting estimates, such as useful lives or the residual value of depreciable assets, the loss rate for bad debts, and warranty costs, are called *changes in accounting estimates.* As a company gains experience in such areas as depreciable assets, receivables, and warranties, it may have a sound basis for revising one or more of its prior accounting estimates. *APB Opinion No. 20* states that, in such instances, the *prior accounting results are not to be disturbed. Instead, the new estimate should be used during the current and remaining periods.* Thus, a change in estimate is made on a *prospective* (future-oriented) basis.

To illustrate the accounting for a change in estimate, assume a machine that cost $24,000 is being depreciated on a straight-line basis over a 10-year estimated useful life with no residual value. Early during the 7th year, on the basis of more experience with the machine, management determines that the total useful life should have been 14 years (and no residual value). Thus, the remaining life becomes 8 years from the start of the year in which the revised estimate was made (Year 7 in the example). This change in estimate does not require an entry to correct the prior depreciation already recorded (Years 1 to 6 in the example). Rather, new depreciation amounts will be recorded at the end of the current year (Year 7) and each year during the remaining useful life of the asset. The new depreciation amounts, starting with the year of change, are based upon the then *undepreciated* amount of the asset and the new *remaining* useful life of the asset.

To illustrate, the new depreciation amounts are computed and recorded as follows:

End of Years 7 to 14 (8 years' remaining life):

Depreciation expense		1,200
Accumulated depreciation, machinery		1,200
Computations (straight-line):		
Original cost		$24,000
Accumulated depreciation to date of change		
($24,000 × 6/10)		14,400
Difference—depreciated over eight years remaining life		$ 9,600
Annual depreciation over remaining life:		
($9,600 ÷ eight years)		$ 1,200

Changes in accounting estimates that have a material effect on the financial statements are disclosed in the notes. An example of such a disclosure from the 1987 Time, Inc., financial statement is as follows:

Notes to Financial Statements

Change in Estimate

In the first quarter of 1986 the Company changed the rate of amortization of its pay-TV programming costs to more closely reflect audience viewing patterns. The effect of this change was to reduce programming costs by $58 million and $57 million, resulting in increased net income of $35 million and $31 million, or $.58 per share and $.49 per share, during 1987 and 1986, respectively.

APB Opinion No. 20 requires disclosure of the effect of the change in estimate on income before extraordinary items, on net income, and on the related per share amounts.

Changes in Accounting Principle When there is a retroactive change from one generally accepted accounting principle to another, there generally is a gain or loss that must be accounted for. The gain or loss is often called a *catch up adjustment,* but it is more formally known as the **cumulative effect of a change in accounting principle.** *APB Opinion No. 20* requires that these gains or losses be separately reported in the income statement for the period in which the changes are made. These changes must be reported after income from continuing operations after taxes, and after extraordinary items. They also must be reported net of any applicable income taxes.

To illustrate the *reporting* of changes in accounting principle, consider the following example.[16] Assume that a company's management decides to change from accelerated to straight-line depreciation for its depreciable assets, and it is able to

---

[16] In this chapter, the methods used to compute and record the effects of the accounting principle are not considered. These methods are discussed in the chapter, "Accounting Changes and Error Corrections."

provide adequate justification for the change to its auditors.[17] The cumulative effect of the change is $60,000. This is the difference between the accumulated depreciation under the accelerated method previously used, and the depreciation that would have accumulated if the straight-line method had been used in all previous periods. That is, $60,000 more of depreciation expense has been taken using the accelerated method than would have been taken under straight-line. Assume an income tax rate of 30%. Thus the cumulative effect of the change in accounting principle, net of applicable income taxes, is $60,000 × .70, or $42,000. The catch-up adjustment, net of tax, is a credit (increase in earnings) of $42,000.

The reporting and positioning on the income statement of the above change in accordance with *APB Opinion No. 20 is:*

Income from continuing operations (assumed)	$100,000
Income taxes	30,000
Income from operations after taxes	$ 70,000
Cumulative effect of change in accounting principle, net of income taxes of $18,000	42,000
Net income	$112,000

Disclosure Guidelines for the Income Statement

An income statement must satisfy the *full disclosure* requirements discussed in Chapter 2, which are considered in greater detail in a later chapter, "Special Topics: Segment Reporting, Interim Reporting, and Disclosures." Briefly, companies are required to disclose all relevant information relating to the economic affairs of the firm in supporting notes and schedules. The typical income statement is supplemented with a number of disclosure notes to the financial statements. These notes contain schedules and written explanations to communicate more fully information about the amounts reported in the tabular portions of the statements. For example, Exhibit 4–8 presents a detailed expense schedule to supplement the income statement of Graham Retail Company, illustrated in Exhibit 4–4.

In Exhibit 4–1, there are many references to note disclosures expanding the information about the various line items on the report. For example, the line labeled "special credits (charges)" refers the reader to Note 8. Note 8 is a more detailed explanation of the special credits and charges and is presented in Exhibit 4–9. The note reveals that Armco has engaged in several restructurings of facilities and disposals/write-downs of assets, and has sold assets for a gain during the three years presented.

CONCEPT REVIEW

1. Name three items that require separate reporting on the income statement.
2. What is intraperiod tax allocation?
3. How is the gain or loss on disposal of a segment determined?

---

[17] *APB Opinion No. 20*, paragraphs 15 and 16, discuss the need to justify a change in accounting principle. The issuance of a standard by the FASB or other accounting standard-setting body that creates a new principle, or states a preference for an existing accounting principle, or that rejects a specific accounting principle are examples of sufficient support for a change in accounting principle. In practice, many reasons have been used successfully to justify a change in accounting principle.

EXHIBIT 4-8   Detailed Expense Schedule

GRAHAM RETAIL COMPANY
Schedule of Operating Expenses
For the Year Ended December 31, 1991

Operating expenses:
  Distribution expenses:
    Advertising $58,500
    Salaries 45,000
    Commissions 31,000
    Freight-out (on sales) 10,000
    Insurance on inventory 1,000
    Other selling expenses 8,000 $153,500

  Administrative expenses:
    Office expenses 24,800
    Office payroll 42,100
    Rent 3,600
    Bad debt expense 3,000   73,500

  Depreciation expense   54,000

  Total operating expense $281,000

EXHIBIT 4-9   Note Disclosure for Armco, Inc., Regarding Special Credits and Charges (taken from *1989 Armco Inc. Annual Report*)

Note 8: Special Credits (Charges)

The special credits (charges) recorded are:

	1989	1988	1987
Bar, Rod, and Wire Products:			
Restructuring of facilities:			
Disposal/write-down of assets	$ —	$ —	$(12.0)
Employee benefits other than pensions	(1.9)	—	(20.1)
Pensions	—	—	(28.5)
Other	(0.4)	—	(12.4)
Other Operations:			
Restructuring charges:			
Disposal write-off of assets	—	(35.0)	—
Employee benefits other than pensions	(1.0)	—	—
Carbon Flat-Rolled Steel:			
Disposal/write-off of assets	—	—	(6.2)
Gain on sale of business*	109.4	—	—
Other†	(25.4)	—	56.6
Total	$ 80.7	$(35.0)	$(22.6)

* In 1989, Armco sold certain assets and a portion of the Eastern Steel Division business to Kawasaki Steel Investments, Inc., for $350.0 million, resulting in a $109.4 gain.

† In the second quarter of 1989, Armco recorded a $40.4 charge associated with decision to further restructure Armco. This charge includes provisions for implementation and other costs related to reorganizing corporate services to become independent of the information and other support systems now provided by ASC. Also included are provisions to realign certain corporate functions. Also recorded was a $15.0 million credit for a favorable ruling on certain foreign export commitments. In December 1987, Armco sold its interests in Falconbridge Dominiciana C. Por A. to Falconbridge Limited for $34.9 million in cash and indemnification for any future funding requirements and for payment, if any, of Falcondo's outstanding debt guaranteed by Armco. In connection with the sale, Armco also reversed an accrual of $21.7 million previously provided for its obligation for such funding requirements.

CONCEPTUAL ISSUES IN THE DETERMINATION OF INCOME

Early in this chapter, several different line items on the Armco income statement were identified, all labeled as income of one kind or another (see Exhibit 4–1). The question of what to include in the determination of net income has long been an issue in financial reporting. *ARB No. 43* and *APB Opinion No. 9* were earlier attempts to provide guidance in this area. These guidelines proved insufficient, and the Accounting Principles Board issued *APB Opinion No. 30* in 1973 to provide further guidance. Indeed, many of the reporting requirements discussed in this chapter are from *APB Opinion No. 30*.

The conceptual issue is, What is income? At the more practical level the question becomes, Which items affecting shareholders' equity should be included in the computation of net income and thus be reported in the income statement? Which items, if any, should be recorded as a direct adjustment to equity and not included in the income computation? There are two extreme views or approaches to answering this question.

Current Operating Performance   At one extreme is the *current operating performance approach*, in which only items that are part of the ordinary, normal recurring operations of the firm during the period are included in the earnings computation. Other items related to extraordinary activities or to prior period transactions are recorded as direct adjustments to retained earnings. Advocates of the current operating performance approach believe users of financial statements attach a particular significance to the figure labeled "net income." They are concerned that some users may not be able to analyze the income statement and make adjustments for those extraordinary items and prior period adjustments (to be defined later in this chapter) that are unrelated to the company's current period operating performance.

All-Inclusive Approach   At the other extreme is the *all-inclusive approach,* in which all transactions affecting the net increase or decrease in equity during the period are included in the determination of net income, except contributions by or distributions to owners. Advocates of this approach believe that the extraordinary items and prior period adjustments are all part of the earnings history of the firm, and that the omission of such items from the income statement increases the possibility that these items will be overlooked in a review of the operating results for a period of years. They also point out the dangers of possible manipulation of the annual earnings figure if preparers of financial statements are permitted to omit certain items in determining net income. Advocates of the all-inclusive approach believe that full disclosure in the income statement of the nature of any extraordinary items and any prior period adjustments will enable income statement users to fully assess the importance of the items and their effect on operating results and cash flows.

Current GAAP is a compromise between these two approaches, but it tends to be closer to the all-inclusive approach. However, some items are closed directly to retained earnings, which is advocated under the current operating performance approach. Other concerns of advocates of the current operating performance approach are addressed in part by separately identifying and disclosing the various special nonoperating items on the face of the income statement. For example, income from continuing operations is determined and reported on the top portion of the statement, with the effects of nonoperating items (such as discontinued operations), extraordinary items, and accounting changes) separately identified and reported below income from continuing operations.

When it addressed the broad issue of developing a conceptual framework for financial reporting, the FASB took another look at the issue of what to include in the earnings computation. The FASB's conclusions on this topic are included in *SFAC No. 5* and presumably will be reflected in future accounting standards. The earnings computations presented in *SFAC No. 5* are not consistent with current GAAP.

However, *Statements of Financial Accounting Concepts* do not, themselves, establish generally accepted accounting principles.[18]

The following discussion of earnings and comprehensive income, both defined in *SFAC No. 5*, presents the FASB's position on this issue. Future pronouncements by the FASB will likely reflect this thinking. For the present, however, it is unlikely that the earnings and comprehensive income definitions as presented in *SFAC No. 5* will be used. They are not consistent with current GAAP.

Earnings and Comprehensive Income

In addressing the issue of what to include in the computation of income, *SFAC No. 5* discusses two conceptual measures of income, one labeled *earnings*, the other, *comprehensive income*.

Earnings as Defined by *SFAC No. 5*   **Earnings** is a measure of performance for a period, and to the extent feasible, it excludes items that are extraneous to the period—that is, items that belong to other periods.[19] Thus, the earnings measure focuses on what the firm has received or reasonably expects to receive for its output (revenues) and what it sacrifices to produce and distribute that output (expenses). Earnings also includes results of the company's incidental or peripheral transactions and some effects of other events and circumstances stemming from the environment (gains and losses).[20]

Comprehensive Income as Defined by *SFAC No. 5*   **Comprehensive income** is a broad measure of the effects of transactions and other events on a company. This definition of comprehensive income recognizes all changes in a company's equity (net assets) during a period from transactions and other events and circumstances, except those resulting from investment by owners and distributions to owners.[21] This definition is also found in *SFAC No. 6*, where comprehensive income is identified as one of the elements of financial statements.

In clarifying the difference between earnings and comprehensive income, *SFAC No. 5* lists two classes of gains and losses that would be included in comprehensive income but would be excluded from earnings:

1. Effects of certain accounting adjustments relating to earlier periods (such as the principal example in present practice—cumulative effects of changes in accounting principles) which under current GAAP are included in the determination of net income but would be excluded from earnings as defined in *SFAC No. 5*, and
2. Certain other changes in net assets (principally, certain holding gains and losses) that are recognized in the period, such as some changes in market values of investments in marketable securities classified as noncurrent assets, some changes in market values of investments in industries having specialized accounting practices for marketable securities, and foreign currency translation adjustments.[22]

---

[18] See the introduction to *SFAC No. 1* (1978). SFACs do not require a change in existing GAAP, nor do they amend, modify, or interpret existing standards. As the FASB examines existing standards, it will issue the standards it deems appropriate that are consistent with the concepts statements.

[19] *SFAC No. 5*, par. 34.

[20] Ibid., par. 38.

[21] Ibid., par. 39.

[22] Ibid. par. 42. The accounting standards that specify the appropriate accounting treatment for the various items discussed in these two paragraphs have not yet been addressed in this text. Briefly, a few items, generally holding gains and losses, are required to be recorded directly as adjustments to retained earnings without inclusion in the determination of net income. These items would be included in the determination of comprehensive income but not in the determination of earnings as defined by *SFAC No. 5*.

The relationship between earnings and comprehensive income can best be shown by comparing a statement of earnings and a statement of comprehensive income. These two statements in fact complement each other (all amounts are assumed):

Statement of Earnings

Revenues	$100,000,000
Expenses	75,000,000
	$ 25,000,000
Add: Gains	10,000,000
Less: Losses	(15,000,000)
Earnings (per *SFAC No. 5* definition)	$ 20,000,000

Statement of Comprehensive Income

Earnings (per *SFAC No. 5* definition)	$ 20,000,000
Cumulative effect of accounting adjustments	5,000,000
Other nonowner changes in equity*	(7,000,000)
Comprehensive income (as defined by *SFAC No. 5*)	$ 18,000,000

* For example, foreign currency translation adjustments.

The main difference between net earnings as defined under existing GAAP, and earnings as defined in *SFAC No. 5* is that *SFAC No. 5* earnings excludes the cumulative effect of certain accounting adjustments for earlier periods. These accounting adjustments are included in the determination of net earnings under GAAP (by *APB Opinion No. 30*).

The main difference between GAAP net income and *SFAC No. 5* comprehensive income is that the computation of net income under current GAAP excludes several nonowner changes in equity that are included in the determination of comprehensive income.

Future accounting pronouncements can be expected to modify the computations of net income so that there will be a computation of both earnings and comprehensive income. Reporting requirements for the cumulative effect of accounting principle changes are likely to be altered to comply with *SFAC No. 5*, and a new section of the income statement for nonowner changes in equity will probably arise. Such changes will most likely result in the required presentation of both a statement of earnings and a statement of comprehensive income.

Earnings per Share (EPS)

Earnings per share (EPS) is the value computed by dividing reported income available to the holders of common stock by the average number of common shares outstanding (during the year). EPS is not computed on preferred stock. To compute EPS on the common stock only, income must be reduced by any preferred stock dividend claim since such dividends are not available to common stock owners and have not been subtracted in computing income.

EPS is important to decision makers because it (1) relates the income of the company to a single share of stock, (2) helps investors to make relevant profit performance comparisons among companies with different numbers of common shares outstanding, and (3) makes possible comparisons of relative profitability of companies on the basis of a single share of stock. *APB Opinion No. 15* requires companies to report per share data on the income statement for both income before extraordinary items and net income.[23]

---

[23] AICPA, *APB Opinion No. 15*, "Earnings per Share," does not require reporting of EPS for extraordinary items. EPS for income before extraordinary items and net income are required. This textbook usually illustrates reporting EPS for all three amounts for completeness and because most companies follow this practice.

EXHIBIT 4-10   Calculation of Earnings per Share (EPS): Three Cases

Assumptions	Calculating and Reporting EPS
Case A: 30,000 common shares outstanding throughout the year; net income for the year, $106,000; dividends applicable to preferred stock, $10,000.	Net income applicable to common stock ($106,000 − $10,000) . . . . $96,000 Earnings per share ($96,000 ÷ 30,000 shares) . . . . . . $ 3.20

Case B:
30,000 common shares outstanding throughout the year; income applicable to common stock, before extraordinary item, $96,000; extraordinary loss less applicable tax saving, $21,000.
	Income before extraordinary item $96,000
	Extraordinary loss (less applicable
	tax saving) 21,000
	Net income $75,000
	Earnings per share:
	  Income before extraordinary item . . . . $ 3.20
	  Extraordinary loss . . . . (.70)
	  Net income . . . . $ 2.50
	    $96,000 ÷ 30,000 shares = $3.20
	    (21,000) ÷ 30,000 shares = (.70)
	    75,000 ÷ 30,000 shares = 2.50

Case C:
30,000 common shares outstanding from January 1 through April 1, on which date an additional 10,000 common shares were sold and issued; other data as in Case B.
	Income before extraordinary item $96,000
	Extraordinary loss (less applicable
	tax saving) 21,000
	Net income $75,000
	Earnings per share:
	  Income before extraordinary item . . . . $ 2.56
	  Extraordinary loss . . . . (.56)
	  Net income . . . . $ 2.00
	Calculation of weighted-average number of shares:

Calculation of weighted-average number of shares:

Dates	Months		Shares		Weighted Shares
Jan. 1–Apr. 1	3	×	30,000	=	90,000
Apr. 1–Dec. 31	9	×	40,000	=	360,000
	12				450,000

    Average: 450,000 ÷ 12 = 37,500.
  $96,000 ÷ 37,500 shares = $2.56
  (21,000) ÷ 37,500 shares = (.56)
  75,000 ÷ 37,500 shares = 2.00

Calculation of Earnings per Share   In this chapter, only the fundamentals of EPS for companies with *simple capital structures* are presented.[24]

To illustrate the calculation of EPS in simple situations, three separate cases are presented in Exhibit 4–10. These cases will provide sufficient background for the discussions and homework. The three cases are summarized as follows:

---

[24] Under certain conditions (i.e., complex capital structures), *APB Opinion 15* requires two presentations of EPS on the income statement: primary EPS and fully diluted EPS. Primary EPS relates income to the company's outstanding common stock and those securities that are most likely to become common stock. Fully diluted EPS relates income to the maximum number of shares of common stock that could conceivably become outstanding. Therefore, fully diluted EPS is an estimate of the company's minimum EPS under its existing capital structure.

Case A. This is the least complex case. It involves common and preferred stock with no changes in the number of common shares outstanding during the year and no extraordinary items on the income statement. In such a situation, calculation of EPS involves dividing net income applicable to common stock by the number of common shares outstanding.

Case B. A slight complexity occurs when there is an extraordinary gain or loss on the income statement. In this case, EPS amounts are calculated and reported for (1) income before extraordinary items, (2) extraordinary items, and (3) net income.

Case C. Another complexity occurs when there is a change during the period in the number of common shares outstanding because of the issuance of common stock or the purchase of treasury stock. This complexity requires calculation of the weighted-average number of shares outstanding during the year. New capital is included for the period the new stock is outstanding. The weighted average is divided into the income amounts.

Additional complexities occur when a company has outstanding preferred stock or bonds payable that are convertible into common stock. These complexities involve the concepts of common stock equivalents and fully diluted EPS. *SFAS No. 21,* "Suspension of Earnings per Share and Segment Information by Nonpublic Enterprises," exempts corporations that are not publicly held from the EPS disclosure requirement.

STATEMENT OF RETAINED EARNINGS

ARB No. 43 encourages firms to include a statement of retained earnings in comparative financial statements. A statement of retained earnings (also called a retained earnings statement) often is presented as a supplement to the income statement and the balance sheet. However, many companies present a *statement of owners' equity* instead, which shows all changes in owners' equity.

The purposes of the statement of retained earnings are to report all changes in retained earnings during the accounting period, to reconcile the beginning and ending balances of retained earnings, and to provide a connecting link between the income statement and the balance sheet. The ending balance of retained earnings is reported on the balance sheet as one element of owners' equity (see Chapter 5). In conformity with *APB Opinion 9 and SFAS No. 16,* the major components of a statement of retained earnings are as follows:

1. Prior period adjustments.
2. Net income or loss for the period.
3. Dividends.

Prior Period Adjustments   *Prior period adjustments must be reported on the statement of retained earnings.* Prior period adjustments *do not* flow through the income statement.

Current GAAP, as defined by *SFAS No. 16* and modified by *SFAS No. 96,* defines and prescribes the accounting for **prior period adjustments** in terms of only one item, as follows (emphasis added):

Items of gain and loss related to the following shall be accounted for and reported as prior period adjustments and excluded from the determination of net income for the current period:[25]
Correction of an error in the financial statements of a prior period.

---

[25] *SFAS No. 16* also required that a second item, "adjustments that result from realization of income tax benefits of preacquisition operating loss carryforward of purchased subsidiaries," be recorded as a prior period adjustment. *SFAS No. 96* subsequently changed this requirement, and this item is no longer a prior period adjustment. However, the FASB can be expected to require, from time to time, specific items to be recorded as prior period adjustments.

EXHIBIT 4-11   Retained Earnings Statement: Graham Retail Company

---

GRAHAM RETAIL COMPANY
Retained Earnings Statement
For the Year Ended December 31, 1991

Retained earnings, January 1, 1991 as previously reported (assumed)	$378,800
Prior period adjustment, correction of error	
(net of income tax of $2,100) (Note 6)	4,900
Retained earnings, January 1, 1991, after prior period adjustment	383,700
Net income (See Exhibit 4-3 or Exhibit 4-4)	81,200
Cash dividends declared and paid during 1991	(30,000)
Retained earnings, December 31, 1991 (Note 7)	$434,900

Notes to financial statements:

Note 6. Prior period adjustments—During the year, the company discovered that an expenditure made in 1988 was incorrectly expensed. This error caused net income of that period to be understated, and that of subsequent periods to be overstated. The prior period adjustment of $4,900 (a $7,000 credit less income tax of $2,100) corrects the error.

Note 7. Restrictions—Of the $434,900 ending balance in retained earnings, $280,000 is restricted from dividend availability under the terms of the bond indenture. When the bonds are retired, the restriction will be removed.

SFAS No. 16 requires that all other items of revenue, expense, gain, and loss recognized during the period be included in the determination of reported net income for that period.

To illustrate the recording of a prior period adjustment for an error correction, assume a machine that cost $10,000 (with a 10-year estimated useful life and no residual value) was purchased on January 1, 1988. Further, assume that the total cost was erroneously debited to an expense account in 1988. The error was discovered December 29, 1991. The following correcting entry would be required in 1991, assuming any income tax effects are recorded separately.

December 29, 1991:

Machinery	10,000	
Depreciation expense, straight-line (for 1991)	1,000	
Accumulated depreciation (1988 through 1991)		4,000
Prior period adjustment, error correction		7,000

The $7,000 prior period adjustment corrects the January 1, 1991, retained earnings balance on a before-tax basis. The balance is understated $7,000 before tax:

Understatement of 1988 income ($10,000—$1,000)	$9,000
Overstatement of 1989 and 1990 income ($1,000 × 2) . . .	(2,000)
Net pretax understatement	$7,000

Any income tax effect of the prior period adjustment could be included in the above entry or recorded separately. Assuming the same error was made on the income tax return, the entry to record the income tax effect of the prior period adjustment, assuming a 30% income tax rate, would be:

Prior period adjustment, error correction ($7,000 × .30)	2,100	
Income tax payable		2,100

The prior period adjustment, error correction account balance would be closed directly to retained earnings on December 31, 1991.

A prior period adjustment (net of its income tax effect) is reported on the statement of retained earnings as a *correction of the beginning balance* of retained earnings as illustrated in Exhibit 4-11.

Appropriations and Restrictions of Retained Earnings Appropriations of, and restrictions on, retained earnings limit the availability of retained earnings to support dividends.

Restrictions result from *legal requirements,* such as a state statute requirement that retained earnings be restricted for dividend purposes by the cost of any treasury stock held, or *contractual agreements,* such as a bond agreement (i.e., indenture) requiring that retained earnings of a specified amount be withheld from dividend purposes until the bonds are retired.

Appropriations of retained earnings result from formal decisions by the corporation to set aside, or appropriate, a specific amount of retained earnings (temporarily or permanently). The effect of an appropriation is to remove the specified amount of retained earnings from dividend availability. For example, corporations often set up appropriations such as "retained earnings appropriated for future plant expansion."

The primary purpose of restrictions and appropriations is to inform statement users that a portion of retained earnings is set aside for a specific purpose (usually long-term). This informs statement readers that these amounts are not available for dividend declarations.

Exhibit 4–11 illustrates a restriction of $280,000 on the retained earnings of Graham Retail Company. In this situation, the unrestricted balance of retained earnings is $154,900 (i.e., $434,900 − $280,000 = $154,900). Graham recorded the restriction, on the date it was imposed, as follows:

Retained earnings (unappropriated) 280,000
 Retained earnings appropriated (as required by
  the bond indenture) 280,000

When a restriction or appropriation is removed, the amount is returned to the retained earnings (unappropriated) account by reversing the above entry. Details regarding restrictions and appropriations usually are reported in a note (as illustrated in Exhibit 4–11). Retained earnings is discussed in the chapter titled "Retained Earnings."

Combined Statement of Income and Retained Earnings

The income statement and retained earnings statement may be presented together as a *combined statement.* The primary advantage of such a format is that it brings together related and relevant information for the statement user. A combined statement is employed by Texaco, Inc. and is shown in Exhibit 4–12. Note that Texaco uses a single step format income statement, but with a second step included to reflect the provision for income taxes.

SUMMARY OF KEY POINTS

(L.O. 1)   1. Accounting income is the result of applying the accrual basis accounting system which records transactions in accordance with established measurement rules. Because accounting income is generally based on historical cost, it is not always as relevant as might be desired, and because it is generally recorded only after a transaction has taken place, it is not always as timely as might be desired.

(L.O. 1)   2. Conceptually, economic income is the amount of resources a company could consume or use during a period and be as well off at the end of the period as it was at the beginning of the period. Because economic income often requires estimations, it is not always as reliable as might be desired.

(L.O. 1)   3. *SFAC No. 5* defines a concept of earnings that measures the performance for a period and excludes items that are extraneous to the period. The principle

EXHIBIT 4–12   Combined Income Statement and Retained Earnings Statement

TEXACO, INC.
Statements of Consolidated Income and Retained Earnings
For the Years Ended December 31, 1989, 1988, and 1987
(millions of dollars)

	1989	1988	1987
Revenues:			
Sales and services (includes transactions with significant nonsubsidiary companies of $3,431 million in 1989, $494 million in 1988, and $844 million in 1987)	$ 32,416	$ 33,544	$ 34,373
Equity in income of nonsubsidiary companies, income from dividends, interest, asset sales, and other (includes gains on asset sales related to restructuring of $2,112 million in 1989 and $530 million in 1988)	3,240	1,594	971
Total revenues	35,656	35,138	35,344
Deductions:			
Costs and operating expenses (includes transactions with significant nonsubsidiary companies of $2,174 million in 1989, $596 million in 1988 and $655 million in 1987)	26,944	25,600	26,933
Selling, general and administrative expenses	1,407	1,646	1,546
Restructuring and associated charges	378	185	2,880
Maintenance and repairs	573	771	724
Exploratory expenses	361	545	277
Depreciation, depletion and amortization	1,662	2,094	2,552
Interest expense	687	1,022	1,000
Pennzoil settlement	—	—	3,000
Taxes other than income taxes	558	801	822
Minority interest	2	85	69
Total deductions	32,572	32,749	39,803
Income (loss) before income taxes	3,084	2,389	(4,459)
Provision (benefit) for income taxes	671	1,085	(324)
Net income (loss)	$ 2,413	$ 1,304	$ (4,135)
Net income (loss) per common share (dollars):			
Primary	$ 9.12	$ 5.35	$ (17.03)
Fully diluted	$ 8.74	$ 5.19	$ (17.03)
Average number of common shares outstanding (thousands):			
Primary	257,722	243,642	242,764
Fully diluted	282,643	275,229	242,764
Retained Earnings:			
Balance at beginning of year	$ 7,172	$ 6,416	$ 10,732
Add: Net income (loss)	2,413	1,304	(4,135)
Deduct:			
Cash dividends on preferred stock:			
Series B ESOP Convertible Preferred Stock ($57 per share)	48	—	—
Series C Variable Rate Cumulative Preferred Stock ($1.123 per share)	6	—	—
Series E Variable Rate Cumulative Preferred Stock ($2,616.67 per share)	10	—	—
Dividends on common stock:			
Quarterly cash ($3.00 per share in 1989, $2.25 per share in 1988 and $.75 per share in 1987)	773	548	181
Special cash ($7.00 per share)	1,862	—	—
Special Series C Variable Rate Cumulative Preferred Stock issuance ($1.00) per share)	267	—	—
Preferred stock rights redemption	24	—	—
Balance at end of year	$ 6,595	$ 7,172	$ 6,416

example of an item currently included in the computation of income that would be excluded under *SFAC No. 5* is the cumulative effect of changes in accounting principle. The *SFAC No. 5* measure of earnings is currently not consistent with generally accepted accounting principles.

(L.O. 1)   4. *SFAC No. 5* defines a new conceptual measure of income called *comprehensive income*. Comprehensive income is a broad measure of the effects of all transactions and events on a company. The term takes into account all changes in equity during the period from transactions or other events and circumstances, except those resulting from investment by owners and distributions to owners. This measure is currently not consistent with generally accepted accounting principles.

(L.O. 2)   5. The quality of earnings can be affected by the choices management makes in choosing among acceptable alternative accounting measurement rules. The recognition of revenues later, rather than sooner, and of expenses earlier, rather than later, generally is viewed as resulting in a higher quality earnings figure.

(L.O. 2)   6. Full disclosure requires that all relevant information relating to the economic affairs of a company be reported in the financial statements, including the disclosure notes to the financial statements.

(L.O. 3)   7. Elements of the income statement, also called the earnings statement, are revenues, expenses, gains, and losses.

(L.O. 4)   8. Two general formats for presenting income statement information not specifically regulated by accounting pronouncements are the single-step and the multiple-step formats.

(L.O. 4)   9. The single-step format uses only two broad classifications in its presentation: a revenues and gains section, and an expenses and losses section. Total expenses and losses are deducted from total revenues and gains in a single computation to determine the net income (earnings) amount.

(L.O. 4)   10. The multiple-step format income statement presents intermediate components of income such as gross profit, income from continuing operations before financing activities, and income from continuing operations. The multiple-step format is designed to emphasize important relationships in the various revenue and expense categories.

(L.O. 5)   11. Extraordinary items result from transactions or events that are both unusual and infrequent. They are required to be reported, net of income tax effects, as a separate component of income, positioned after income from continuing operations.

Discontinued operations (L.O. 5)   12. The gains or losses resulting from the sale or abandonment of a component of a company whose activities represent a separate major line of business or class of customer must be reported, net of income tax effects, as a separate component of income, positioned after income from continuing operations and before extraordinary items.

(L.O. 5)   13. The cumulative effects of changes in accounting principles are to be reported on the income statement, net of income tax effects, as a separate component of income, positioned after extraordinary items.

(L.O. 5)   14. Intraperiod tax allocation is the process of allocating the total income tax expense for a period to income from continuing operations and other items that have income tax effects and are reported separately in the income statement or the statement of retained earnings.

(L.O. 6)   15. The statement of retained earnings reports all changes in retained earnings during the period, including prior adjustments, net income or loss, and dividends declared.

(L.O. 7)   16. Earnings per share amounts are required to be reported on the face of the income statement for (*a*) income from continuing operations, (*b*) cumulative effects of changes in accounting principles, if present, and (*c*) net income. Most companies also report per share amounts for any discontinued operations and extraordinary items.

The following pre-tax amounts are taken from the adjusted trial balance of Killian Company at December 31, 1992, the end of the annual accounting period.

Sales revenue	$1,000,000
Service revenue	200,000
Interest revenue	30,000
Gain on sale of operational asset	100,000
Cost of goods sold	600,000
Selling, general, and administrative expense	150,000
Depreciation expense	50,000
Interest expense	20,000
Income tax expense, tax rate 40% on all items	200,000
Loss on sale of long-term investment	10,000
Extraordinary item, loss on earthquake damage	200,000
Cumulative effect of change in accounting principle (gain)	50,000
Loss on disposal of business segment	60,000

Common shares outstanding, $1 par value, 100,000.
Assume simple capital structure of 100,000 shares of common stock.

Required:

1. Prepare a single-step income statement in good form.
2. Prepare a multiple-step income statement in good form.

1. Single-step income statement:

KILLIAN COMPANY
Income Statement
For the Year Ended December 31, 1992

Revenues and gains:		
Sales revenue		$1,000,000
Service revenue		200,000
Interest revenue		30,000
Gain on sale of operational asset		100,000
Total revenue and gains		$1,330,000
Expenses and losses:		
Cost of goods sold	$600,000	
Selling, general, and administrative	150,000	
Depreciation	50,000	
Interest expense	20,000	
Loss on sale of long-term investment	10,000	
Income tax expense (see computations below)	200,000	1,030,000
Income from continuing operations		$ 300,000
Discontinued operations:		
Loss on disposal of business segment, net of tax effects of $24,000		(36,000)
Income before extraordinary item and cumulative effect of change in accounting principle		$ 264,000
Extraordinary item:		
Loss from earthquake, net of tax effects of $80,000		(120,000)
Cumulative effect of change in accounting principle, net of tax effects of $20,000		30,000
Net income		$ 174,000
Per Share:		
Earnings per share:		
Income from continuing operations		$3.00
Discontinued operations		(.36)
Income before extraordinary item and cumulative effect of change in accounting principle		$2.64
Extraordinary item, loss due to earthquake damage		(1.20)
Cumulative effect of change in accounting principle		.30
Net income		$1.74

Computation of income tax expense:

Revenues		$1,330,000
Expenses before income taxes:		
Cost of goods sold	$600,000	
Selling, general, and administrative	150,000	
Depreciation	50,000	
Interest expense	20,000	
Loss on sale of long-term investment	10,000	830,000
Pretax Income		500,000
Tax rate		× .40
Income tax expense		$ 200,000

The discontinued operations, extraordinary item, and cumulative effect of change in accounting principle are reported net-of-tax, reflecting intraperiod tax allocation.

2. Multiple-step income statement format:

KILLIAN COMPANY
Income Statement
For the Year Ended December 31, 1992

Sales revenue		$1,000,000
Cost of goods sold		600,000
Gross margin on sales		$ 400,000
Operating expenses:		
Selling, general, and administrative expenses	150,000	
Depreciation expense	50,000	200,000
		$ 200,000
Other revenues and gains:		
Service revenue	$200,000	
Interest revenue	30,000	
Gain on sale of operational asset	100,000	
Total	330,000	
Other expenses and losses:		
Interest expense	20,000	
Loss on sale of long-term investment	10,000	
Total	30,000	300,000
Income from continuing operations before income tax		$ 500,000
Income tax expense		200,000
Income from continuing operations		$ 300,000
Discontinued operations:		
Loss on disposal of business segment, net of tax effects of $24,000		(36,000)
Income before extraordinary item and cumulative effect of change in accounting principle		$ 264,000
Extraordinary item:		
Loss from earthquake, net of tax effects of $80,000		(120,000)
Cumulative effect of change in accounting principle, net of tax effects of $20,000		30,000
Net income		$ 174,000
Per Share:		
Earnings per share:		
Income from continuing operations		$3.00
Discontinued operations		(.36)
Income before extraordinary item and cumulative effect of change in accounting principle		2.64
Extraordinary item, loss due to earthquake damage		(1.20)
Cumulative effect of change in accounting principle		.30
Net income		$1.74

Alternative arrangements of the information above the income from continuing operations line are allowed for both the single- and multiple-step formats. The presentation of the items below income from continuing operations, however, must be as shown. It is the same for both formats. Finally, the gains and losses for discontinued operations, extraordinary items, and cumulative effect of change in accounting principle are on a net-of-tax-effect basis.

KEY TERMS

Accounting income (135)
Changes in accounting estimates (154)
Comprehensive income (159)
Continuing operations (134)
Cumulative effect of the change in accounting principle (155)
Discontinued operations (147)
Earnings (per *SFAC No. 5*) (159)
Economic income (135)
Elements of income statement (137)

Extraordinary item (143)
Gross margin (138)
Interperiod tax allocation (142)
Intraperiod tax allocation (142)
Multiple-step format (138)
Prior Period Adjustments (162)
Quality of earnings (136)
Revenue recognition (137)
Single-step format (138)
Transaction approach (135)

QUESTIONS

1. Briefly explain how the income statement is a connecting link between the beginning and ending balance sheets.
2. Briefly explain the difference between economic income and accounting income.
3. Explain the basic difference between revenues and gains.
4. Explain the basic difference between expenses and losses.
5. Briefly explain the two formats used for income statements. Explain why actual income statements usually are a combination of these two formats.
6. Explain how gross margin is computed for a retail business. How would gross margin be computed for a service organization?
7. Explain how cost of goods sold is reported on a single-step income statement and on a multiple-step income statement.
8. List the four major income captions, in their order of appearance, on a typical multiple-step income statement.
9. What might be factors to take into consideration when choosing between the two alternative formats for the income statement?
10. Define an extraordinary item. How should extraordinary items be reported on (a) a single-step and (b) a multiple-step income statement?
11. How are items that are either unusual or infrequent, but not both, reported on the income statement?
12. Outline a situation when a large hurricane or tornado loss could (a) be an extraordinary item, and (b) not be an extraordinary item.
13. Does the amount of a gain determine whether it is an extraordinary item or not? Explain.
14. Briefly define a prior period adjustment. How is a prior period adjustment reported?
15. Briefly define intraperiod tax allocation.
16. TK Corporation computed total income tax expense for 1992 of $16,640. The following pretax amounts were used: (a) income before extraordinary loss, $60,000; (b) extraordinary loss, $12,000; and (c) prior period adjustment, $4,000 (a credit). The average income tax rate on all items was 32%. Compute the intraperiod income tax allocation amounts.
17. Define earnings per share (EPS). Why is it required as an integral part of the income statement?
18. Fluke Company reported the following amounts at the end of 1994:

Extraordinary gain $90,000
Net income 50,000
Average number of common shares outstanding, 25,000.

Prepare the EPS presentation. Which EPS amount is likely to be the most relevant? Explain.

19. What are three types of accounting changes discussed in *APB Opinion No. 20?* Explain what is meant by a change in estimate. Explain the basic approach used to account for and report a change in estimate.

20. VEE Company has a machine that cost $21,000 when acquired at the beginning of Year 1. It has been depreciated using straight-line, on the basis of a 10-year useful life and a $1,000 residual value. At the start of Year 5, the residual value was changed to $3,000. Compute the amount of depreciation expense per year that should be recorded for the remaining useful life of the machine.

21. What items are reported on a statement of retained earnings? Explain how it provides a link between the current income statement and balance sheet.

22. What is meant by appropriations and restrictions on retained earnings? How are such items usually reported?

EXERCISES

E 4–1
Market Value Basis
Income Statement
(L.O. 1)

Oro Corporation has been operating for five years. The 1995 detailed income statement, prepared in conformity with generally accepted accounting principles (i.e., the transactions approach on the accrual basis), reported income of $17,600. The principal owner, who is also the chief executive officer (CEO), believes that the company earned much more than that amount. To support this contention, the CEO developed the following schedule:

	Market Values	
	End 1994	End 1995
Total assets (70% plant and equipment)	$270,000	$360,000
Total liabilities	100,000	110,000
Contributions of owners during 1995		20,000
Dividends paid to owners		6,000

Required:

1. Prepare a 1995 income statement using the CEO's data.
2. How would you label this income amount?
3. What reservations would you have about this way of measuring income?

E 4–2
Classifications of Elements on the Income Statement
(L.O. 2)

Fifteen transactions are listed below (left) that may or may not affect the income statement. Income statement element classifications are listed by letters to the right. You are to match each transaction with the appropriate letter to indicate the usual classification that should be used. Provide comments when appropriate.

Answer	Selected Transactions	Income Statement Element Classifications
A	1. Sales of goods and services.	A. Revenues.
I	2. Prepaid insurance premium.	B. Expenses.
E	3. Loss on disposal of service trucks.	C. Gains (ordinary).
A	4. Cash dividends received on an investment in African diamond mine.	D. Gains (unusual or infrequent).
		E. Loss (ordinary).
		F. Loss (unusual or infrequent).
B+I	5. Wages accrued (unpaid and unrecorded).	G. Gain (extraordinary).
H	6. Cost of moving the only plant the company owns from Kansas to Idaho (a major expenditure).	H. Loss (extraordinary).
		I. None of the above.
B	7. Cost of goods sold.	
A	8. Services rendered.	
D	9. Gain (characterized as unusual or infrequent).	
I	10. Rent collected in advance.	
F	11. Fire loss (characterized as unusual).	
H	12. Loss due to a rare freeze which destroyed the citrus trees in the Rio Grande Valley.	
C	13. Gain on sale of short-term investments.	
I	14. Cash dividend declared and paid.	
H	15. Loss due to meteor which completely destroyed the factory.	

E 4–3
Formats of Income Statement, EO Item, and Periodic Inventory
(L.O. 3, 4)

The following items were taken from the adjusted trial balance of Kasper Manufacturing Corporation at December 31, 1992.

Sales revenue	$950,000
Cost of goods manufactured (including depreciation, $52,000)	580,000
Dividends received on investment in stocks	6,500
Finished goods inventory, 1/1/1992 (periodic inventory system)	48,000
Interest expense	4,200
Extraordinary item: fire loss (pretax)	48,000
Distribution expenses	135,300
Common stock, par $10	200,000
General and administrative expenses	113,000
Interest revenue	2,500
Finished goods inventory, 12/31/1992	53,000
Income tax, assume an average 30% tax rate	?

Required:
1. Prepare a single-step income statement (includes EPS). Set up cost of goods sold as a separate schedule to include the inventory amounts and cost of goods manufactured.
2. Prepare a multiple-step income statement. Include computation of cost of goods sold within the statement.

E 4–4
Formats of Income Statement, EO Item, and Periodic Inventory
(L.O. 3, 4)

Storm Company's records provided the following information at December 31, 1992 (end of the accounting period):

Sales revenue	$95,000
Service revenue	35,000
Gain on sale of short-term investments	11,000
Distribution expense	18,000
General and administrative expense	12,000
Depreciation expense	6,000
Interest expense	4,000
Income tax expense (30% rate on all items)	?
Rare tornado loss on building (infrequent and unsual)	15,000
Loss on sale of stone fixtures (infrequent but not unusual)	3,000
Beginning inventory (periodic inventory system)	20,000
Ending inventory	23,000
Purchases (including freight-in)	50,000
Purchase returns	2,000

Common stock shares outstanding, 10,000 shares.

Required:
1. Prepare a single-step income statement (show cost of goods sold computations in a separate supporting schedule).
2. Prepare a multiple-step income statement. Include computation of cost of goods sold within the statement.

E 4–5
Formats of the Income Statement, EO Item, and Perpetual Inventory
(L.O. 3, 4)

AAA Sales and Service Company's accounts provided the following information at December 31, 1993 (end of the accounting period):

Sales revene	$199,000
Service revenue	33,000
Sales returns and allowances	1,500
Interest revenue	2,500
Gain on sale of short-term investments	1,000
Distribution expenses	56,700
General and administrative expenses	32,500
Depreciation expense	18,500
Income tax expense (40% rate on all items)	?
Loss on disposal of service trucks (assume infrequent but not unusual)	4,000
Gain (assume both unusual and infrequent)	10,000
Cost of goods sold (perpetual inventory system)	54,000
Interest expense	4,300
Common stock, par $5	100,000

Required:

1. Prepare a single-step income statement.
2. Prepare a multiple-step income statement.

E 4–6

Formats of the Income Statement, EO Items, and Perpetual Inventory

(L.O. 3, 4)

The following items were taken from the adjusted trial balance of Big T Trading Corporation on December 31, 1992. Assume an average 30% income tax on all items (including the casualty loss). The accounting period ends December 31.

Sales revenue	$645,200
Rent revenue	2,400
Interest revenue	900
Gain on sale of operational assets (an ordinary item)	2,000
Distribution expenses	136,000
General and administrative expenses	110,000
Interest expense	1,500
Depreciation for the period	6,000
Extraordinary item: casualty loss (pretax)	22,000
Common stock (par $10)	100,000
Cost of goods sold (perpetual inventory system)	330,000

Required:

1. Prepare a single-step income statement.
2. Prepare a multiple-step income statement.

E 4–7

Income Statements and Retained Earnings Statements

(L.O. 3, 4, 5)

The following pretax amounts were taken from the adjusted trial balance of Como Corporation on December 31, 1992 (end of the annual accounting period):

Balance, retained earnings, 1/1/1992	$ 45,000
Sales revenue	300,000
Cost of goods sold (perpetual inventory system)	105,000
Distribution expenses	36,000
Administrative expenses	34,000
Extraordinary gain (pretax)	10,000
Prior period adjustment, correction of error from prior period, pretax (a debit)	20,000
Dividends declared and paid	16,000

Assume the income tax rate for all items is 30%. The average number of common shares outstanding during the year was 20,000.

Required:

1. Prepare a multiple-step income statement.
2. Prepare a statement of retained earnings.
3. Give the entry to record income taxes payable (assume not yet paid).

E 4–8

Income and Retained Earnings Statements

(L.O. 3, 4, 5)

The following pretax amounts were taken from the adjusted trial balance of Watson Corporation at December 31, 1993 (end of the annual accounting period):

Dividends declared and paid	$ 35,000
Sales revenue	300,000
Cost of goods sold (perpetual inventory system)	100,000
Operating expenses	60,000
Extraordinary loss (pretax)	22,000
Prior period adjustment, correction of error from prior period, pretax (a credit)	10,000
Common stock (par $5)	200,000
Beginning retained earnings 1/1/1993	60,000

Required:

1. Prepare a complete single-step income statement assuming the income tax rate is 30% on all items.
2. Prepare a statement of retained earnings.
3. Give the entry to record income taxes payable (assume not yet paid).

E 4–9

Income Statements, Retained Earnings Statements, and EPS

(L.O. 3, 4, 5, 6)

The following pretax amounts were taken from the adjusted trial balance of Olsen Corporation at December 31, 1991 (end of the annual accounting period):

Sales revenue	$260,000
Cost of goods sold (perpetual inventory system)	110,000
Operating expenses	80,000
Extraordinary gain (pretax)	20,000
Prior period adjustment, correction of error from prior period, pretax (a debit)	32,000
Retained earnings, balance 1/1/1991	30,000
Dividends declared and paid	25,000
Common stock (par $10)	
Outstanding shares, 1/1/1991	15,000
Sold and issued 4/1/1991	5,000
Sold and issued 10/1/1991	7,000
Outstanding 12/31/1991	27,000

Required:

1. Prepare a complete single-step income statement. Assume an average 30% tax rate on all items. Include EPS computations and disclosures.
2. Prepare a statement of retained earnings.

E 4–10

Income Statement, Unusual or Infrequent Items

(L.O. 3, 4)

The following pretax amounts were taken from the adjusted trial balance of Cortez Corporation at December 31, 1992 (end of the annual accounting period):

Sales revenue	$220,000
Service revenue	50,000
Cost of goods sold (perpetual inventory system)	130,000
Operating expenses	88,000
Unusual item, gain on sale of operational asset (pretax)	25,000
Extraordinary item, loss (pretax)	20,000
Prior period adjustment, correction of error from prior period, pretax (a debit)	5,000
Common stock (par $1), 10,000 shares outstanding.	

Assume an average 30% corporate tax rate on all items.

Required:

1. Prepare a single-step income statement.
2. Give the journal entry to record income tax (assume not yet paid).

E 4–11

Depreciation, Change in Estimate

(L.O. 4)

Knight Company purchased a machine that cost $40,000 on January 1, 1988. The estimated useful life was 12 years, and the estimated residual value was $4,000. Straight-line depreciation is used. On December 31, 1993, prior to the adjusting entry to record depreciation expense for the year, the company's chief accountant decided that the machine should be depreciated over a 15-year total useful life and that the estimated residual value at the end of the 15th year should be $1,000.

Required:

1. Give the adjusting entry at the end of 1993 depreciation expense. Show computations.
2. Give the correcting entry required at the end of 1993. If none is required, so state and give the reasons.

E 4–12

Change in Estimate, Error Correction

(L.O. 4)

It is December 31, 1993, and Owner Company is preparing adjusting entries at the end of the accounting year. The company owns two trucks of different types. The following situations confront the company accountant:

a. Truck No. 1 cost $7,700 on January 1, 1991. It is being depreciated on a straight-line basis over an estimated useful life of 10 years with a $700 residual value. At December 31, 1993, it has been determined that the total useful life should have been 6 years instead of 10, with a revised residual value of $900.

b. Truck No. 2 cost $4,550 on January 1, 1990. It is being depreciated on a straight-line basis over an estimated useful life of seven years with a $350 residual value. At December 31, 1993, it was discovered that no depreciation had been recorded on this truck for 1990 or 1991, but was recorded for 1992 and 1993.

Required:

1. For each truck, give the required adjusting entry for depreciation expense at December 31, 1993. Show computations.
2. For each truck, give the appropriate correcting entry and show computations. If no correcting entry is needed, give the reasons (ignore income tax effects).

E 4-13

Combined Income
Statements and Retained
Earnings Statements
(L.O. 3, 4, 5, 6)

The following pretax amounts were taken from the accounts of Scott Corporation at December 31, 1993 (end of the annual accounting period):

Sales revenue	$170,000
Cost of goods sold (perpetual inventory system)	85,000
Distribution and administrative expenses	45,000
Extraordinary gain (pretax)	15,000
Prior period adjustment, correction of error from prior period, pretax (a debit)	8,000
Interest expense	1,000
Cash dividends declared and paid	5,000
Retained earnings, 1/1/1993	51,400

Common stock (par $5), 10,000 shares outstanding.

Assume an average 30% tax rate on all items, including the extraordinary gain.

Required:

Prepare a combined single-step income and retained earnings statement, including intraperiod income tax allocation and EPS.

E 4-14

Discontinued Operations,
Recording and Reporting
(L.O. 4)

On August 1, 1991, Fischer Company decided to discontinue the operations of its Services Division, which qualifies as an indentifiable segment. An agreement was formalized to sell this segment for $156,000 cash. The book value of the assets of the Services Division was $180,000. The disposal date also was on August 1, 1991. The income tax rate is 35%, and the accounting period ends December 31. On December 31, 1991, the after-tax income from operations, including all operating losses and gains associated with the Services Division prior to August 1, 1991, was $400,000. The Services Division incurred a loss of $20,000 between January 1, 1991, and August 1, 1991.

Required:

1. Give the entry(s) to record the sale of the Services Division.
2. Complete the 1991 income statement, starting with income from continuing operations.

PROBLEMS

P 4-1

Formats of the Income
Statement, Extraordinary
Item, Periodic Inventory
(L.O. 3, 4)

The following pretax information was taken from the adjusted trial balance of Atra Corporation at December 31, 1991 (end of the accounting period):

Sales revenue	$957,000
Inventory, 12/31/1990	80,000
Inventory, 12/31/1991	92,000
Sales returns	7,000
Gain on sale of equipment (unusual but not infrequent)	8,000
Depreciation expense	25,000
Distribution expense	140,000
General and administrative expenses	92,300
Rent revenue	18,000
Investment revenue	7,000
Gain on sale of land (pretax)	6,000
Interest expense	9,000
Extraordinary gain (pretax)	80,000
Loss on sale of long-term investments, ordinary item (pretax)	10,000
Cost of goods sold	550,000
Loss due to leak in roof (infrequent but not unusual)	4,000
Extraordinary loss (pretax)	30,000

The company uses a periodic inventory system. Assume an average 35% income tax rate on all items. There are 40,000 shares of common stock outstanding.

Required:

1. Prepare a single-step income statement.
2. Prepare a multiple-step income statement.

P 4-2
Formats of the Income Statement, EO, Periodic Inventory
(L.O. 3, 4)

The following data were taken from the adjusted trial balance of Miami Retail Corporation at December 31, 1992 (end of the accounting period):

Merchandise inventory, 1/1/1992 (periodic inventory system) . . . . $ 71,000
Purchases 121,400
Sales revenue 405,000
Purchase returns 3,400
Sales returns 5,000
Common stock (par $10) 200,000
Depreciation expense (70% administrative expense, 30% distribution expense) 50,000
Rent revenue 4,000
Interest expense 6,000
Investment revenue 2,500
Distribution expenses (exclusive of depreciation) 105,500
General and administrative expenses (exclusive of depreciation) 46,000
Gain on sale of noncurrent asset (an ordinary gain) 6,000
Loss on sale of long-term investments (ordinary) 3,600
Income tax expense (not including the extraordinary item) . . . . ?
Extraordinary item: Flood loss (pretax) 10,000
Freight paid on purchases 1,000
Merchandise inventory, 12/31/1992 88,000

Assume an average 35% income tax rate on all items, including gains and losses on assets sold and extraordinary items.

Required:

1. Prepare a single-step income statement and a separate schedule of cost of goods sold to support it.
2. Prepare a multiple-step income statement (include cost of goods sold computation within the statement).

P 4-3
Financial Statement Classifications
(L.O. 2)

Listed below are the primary financial statement classifications coded with letters. Also, a list of 25 selected transactions and account titles is given.

For each transaction or account title, enter in the space provided a code letter to indicate the usual classification. Comment on doubtful items.

Financial Statement Classification

Code   **Income Statement**

A . . . . . . Revenue.
B . . . . . . Expense.
C . . . . . Unusual or infrequent (but not both) gain or loss.
D . . . . . . Extraordinary item.

Statement of Retained Earnings

E . . . . . . An addition or deduction.
F . . . . . . Addition to retained earnings.
G . . . . . Deduction from retained earnings.
H . . . . . . Note to the financial statements.

Balance Sheet

I . . . . . . Appropriately classified.

Response   **Transaction (summarized)**

1. _____ Estimated warranties payable.
2. _____ Allowance for doubtful accounts.
3. _____ Gain on sale of operational asset.
4. _____ Hurricane damages.
5. _____ Payment of $30,000 additional income tax assessment (on prior year's income).
6. _____ Earthquake damages.

Response	Transaction (summarized)
7. _____	Distribution expenses.
8. _____	Total amount of cash and credit sales for the period.
9. _____	Gain on disposal of long-term investments in stocks (nonrecurring).
10. _____	Net income for the period.
11. _____	Insurance gain on casualty (fire)—insurance proceeds exceed the book value of the assets destroyed.
12. _____	Cash dividends declared and paid.
13. _____	Rent collected on office space temporarily leased.
14. _____	Interest expense of the year paid plus interest accrued on liabilities.
15. _____	Dividends received on stocks held as an investment.
16. _____	Damages paid as a result of a lawsuit by an individual injured while shopping in the store; the litigation covered three years.
17. _____	Loss due to expropriation of a plant in a foreign country.
18. _____	A $10,000 bad debt is to be written off—the receivable had been outstanding for five years. The company estimates bad debts each year, and has an allowance for bad debts.
19. _____	Adjustment due to correction during current year of an error; the error was made two years earlier.
20. _____	On December 31 of the current year, paid rent expense in advance for the next year.
21. _____	Cost of goods sold.
22. _____	Interest collected on November 30 of the current year from a customer on a 90-day note receivable, dated September 1 of the current year.
23. _____	Year-end bonus of $50,000 paid to employees for performance during the year.
24. _____	Depreciation on a machine used in operations.
25. _____	A meteor destroys the plant ($5 million book value, no insurance).

P 4–4
Identify Reporting Deficiencies, Redraft Income Statement (L.O. 3)

Buffer Company prepared the following income statement at the end of its annual accounting period, December 31, 1993.

December 31, 1993
BUFFER COMPANY
Profit and Loss Report

Sales income		$98,000
Inventory	$12,000	
Merchandise	34,000	
Freight	1,000	
Inventory	(15,000)	
Cost of sales		32,000
Gross profit		66,000
Costs:		
Labor	15,000	
Depreciation	6,000	
Sales	21,000	
Overhead	8,000	
Interest	3,000	
Extraordinary	5,000	
Sale of used equipment	4,300	(61,400)
Other incomes:		
Service	3,600	
Interest	1,400	5,000
Taxable profit		9,600
Tax (25%)		2,400
Net profit		$ 7,200

EPS—$7,200 ÷ 5,000 shares = $1.40.

Required:

1. List all of the defects that you can identify on the above statement.
2. Recast the above statement in good format and terminology. Use the multiple-step format.

P 4–5

Relationships between Income Statements and Balance Sheets

(L.O. 1, 2)

Analyze the relationships and amounts for each case and complete the following schedule by entering the appropriate amount in the blank spaces:

a.

Case	Owners' Equity at Start of Period	Additional Investment by Owners	Withdrawals by Owners	Owners' Equity at End of Period	Net Income (loss)
A	$10,000	$2,000	$1,000	$17,400	$____
B	28,000	3,000	____	22,000	4,700
C	____	1,200	800	30,000	(2,200)
D	15,500	600	____	12,950	(2,000)
E	18,000	____	2,700	22,000	4,700

b.

Case	Sales Revenue	Beginning Inventory	Purchases	Ending Inventory	Cost of Goods Sold	Gross Margin	Total Remaining Expenses	Net Income
F	$____	$25,000	$60,000	$____	$67,000	$23,000	$____	$1,000
G	80,000	____	48,000	2,000	____	23,000	18,000	____
H	____	20,000	____	36,000	59,000	18,000	____	8,000

P 4–6

Combined Income and Retained Earnings Statements

(L.O. 3, 4, 5)

The following amounts were taken from the accounting records of Walker Corporation at December 31, 1992 (end of the annual accounting period):

Sales revenue	$340,000
Service revenue	64,000
Cost of goods sold (perpetual inventory system)	170,000
Distribution and administrative expenses	86,000
Investment revenue	6,000
Interest expense	4,000
Infrequent item: Loss on sale of long-term investment (pretax)	10,000
Extraordinary item: Earthquake loss (pretax)	14,000
Cash dividends declared and paid	8,000
Prior period adjustment, correction of error from prior period, pretax (a debit)	12,000
Balance, retained earnings, 1/1/1992	80,300

Common stock (par $5), 30,000 shares outstanding.
Restriction on retained earnings, $50,000 per bond payable indenture.

Assume an average 35% income tax rate on all items.

Required:

Prepare a combined single-step income and retained earnings statement, including tax allocation and EPS. Show computations.

P 4–7

Give Prior Period Adjustments, Correcting Entries

(L.O. 4)

Unitas Corporation is undergoing its annual audit by the independent CPA at December 31, 1991 (end of the annual accounting period). During the audit, the following situations were found that needed attention:

a. On December 29, 1989, an asset that cost $12,000 was debited in full to 1989 operating expenses. The asset has a six-year estimated life and no residual value. The company uses straight-line depreciation.

b. Late in 1991, the company constructed a small warehouse using their own employees at a total cost of $90,000. However, before the decision was made to self-construct it, Unitas obtained a $100,000 bid from a contractor. Upon completion of the warehouse, Unitas made the following entry in the accounts:

Warehouse (an operational asset)	100,000	
Cash		90,000
Other income (nonoperating)		10,000

c. Prior to recording 1991 depreciation expense, the management decided that a large machine that originally cost $128,000 should have been depreciated over a useful life of 14 years instead of 20 years. The machine was acquired January 2, 1986. Assume the residual value of $8,000 was not changed. Give the 1991 adjusting entry and any other entries incident to the change in useful life.

d. During December 1991, the company disposed of an old machine for $6,000 cash. Annual depreciation was $2,000. At the beginning of 1991, the accounts reflected the following:

Machine (cost) $18,000
Accumulated depreciation 13,000

At date of disposal, the following entry was made:

Cash 6,000
    Machine   6,000

No depreciation has been recorded for 1991.

e. A patent that originally cost $3,400 is being amortized over its legal life of 17 years at $200 per year. After the 1990 adjusting entry, it had been amortized down to a book value of $800. At the end of 1991, it was determined in view of a competitor's patent, that the patent will have no economic value to the company by the end of 1992. Straight-line amortization is used.

Required:

For each of the above situations, briefly explain the nature of each item and what should have been recorded in the accounts. If a journal entry is needed to correct the accounts, provide it along with supporting computations. Ignore income tax considerations.

P 4–8

COMPREHENSIVE PROBLEM
◆

Combined Income and Retained Earnings Statements, Intraperiod Income Tax Allocation (L.O. 3, 4, 5, 6)

The following pretax amounts were taken from the accounts of Jarvis Corporation at December 31, 1992, end of the annual accounting period:

Sales revenue $550,000
Cost of goods sold (perpetual inventory system) 280,000
Distribution expenses 100,000
Administrative expenses 70,000
Interest revenue 1,000
Interest expense 3,000
Unusual item: Gain from sale of noncurrent asset (pretax, an ordinary gain) 20,000
Extraordinary item: Casualty (pretax loss) 40,000
Balance, retained earnings, 1/1/1992 95,000
Cash dividends declared and paid 15,000
Prior period adjustment, correction of error from prior period, pretax (a debit) 8,000

Common stock (par $1), 40,000 shares outstanding.
Restriction on retained earnings amounting to $25,000 as required by the indenture agreement on bonds payable.

Assume an average 35% income tax rate on all items.

Required:

Prepare a combined multiple-step income and retained earnings statement, including intraperiod income tax allocation and EPS. Show computations.

P 4–9
Identify Statement
Deficiencies and Redraft
Statements
(L.O. 2, 3, 4)

The following income statement and retained earnings statement were prepared by the bookkeeper for Lax Corporation:

LAX CORPORATION
Statement of Profit
December 31, 1992

Sales income		$123,000
Service income		20,000
Total		143,000
Cost of sales (periodic inventory system):		
Inventory	$34,000	
Purchases (net)	71,000	
Inventory	(40,000)	65,000
Gross profit		78,000
Costs:		
Salaries, wages, etc.	35,000	
Depreciation and write-offs	7,000	
Rent	3,000	
Taxes, property	500	
Utilities	2,100	
Promotion	900	
Sales returns	2,000	
Sundry	6,700	(57,200)
Special items:		
Profit on asset sold		6,000
Inventory shortage		(2,800)
Pretax profit		24,000
Income tax		3,200
Net profit		$ 20,800

LAX CORPORATION
Earned Surplus
December 31, 1992

Balance, earned surplus		$27,000
Add:		
Profit		20,800
Correction of inventory error of 1991 (pretax)		5,000
Total		52,800
Deduct:		
Earthquake loss (pretax)	$13,000	
Dividends	10,000	
Earned surplus to capital	5,000	27,000
Balance		$ 25,800

Required:

1. List each item on the above statements that you believe should be changed and give your recommendations with respect to appropriate reporting, terminology, and format. The average income tax rate is 20%, and 10,000 shares of common stock are outstanding. Assume the earthquake loss is extraordinary.
2. Prepare a complete multiple-step income statement, and a complete statement of retained earnings.

P 4–10
Discontinued Segment
(L.O. 4)

Century Company, a diversified manufacturing company, had four separate operating divisions engaged in the manufacture of products in each of the following areas: food products, health aids, textiles, and office equipment.

Pretax data for the two years ended December 31, 1992, and 1991, are presented below:

	Net Sales		Cost of Goods Sold		Operating Expenses	
	1992	1991	1992	1991	1992	1991
Food products	$3,500,000	$3,000,000	$2,400,000	$1,800,000	$ 550,000	$ 275,000
Health aids	2,000,000	1,270,000	1,100,000	700,000	300,000	125,000
Textiles	1,580,000	1,400,000	500,000	900,000	200,000	150,000
Office equipment	920,000	1,330,000	800,000	1,000,000	650,000	750,000
	$8,000,000	$7,000,000	$4,800,000	$4,400,000	$1,700,000	$1,300,000

Additional pretax data:

a. On January 1, 1992, Century adopted a plan to sell the assets and product line of the office equipment division and expected to realize a gain on this disposal. On September 1, 1992, the division's assets and product line were sold for $2,100,000 (two-thirds cash collected on this date), resulting in a gain of $640,000 (exclusive of operations during the phaseout period). The office equipment division had operating losses of $420,000 in 1991 and $530,000 through September 1, 1992.

b. The company's textiles division had six manufacturing plants that produced a variety of textile products. In April 1992, the company sold one of these plants and realized a gain of $130,000 (carrying value, $200,000). After the sale, the operations at the plant that was sold were transferred to the remaining five textile plants that the company continued to operate.

c. In August 1992, the main warehouse of the food products division, located on the banks of the Bayer River, was flooded when the river overflowed. The resulting damage of $420,000 is not included in the financial data given above. Historical records indicate that the Bayer River normally overflows every four to five years causing flood damage to adjacent property; this loss was not covered by insurance.

d. For the two years ended December 31, 1992, and 1991, the company had interest revenue earned on investments of $70,000 and $40,000, respectively.

e. For the two years ended December 31, 1992, and 1991, the company's net income (after income tax) was $1,152,000 and $804,000, respectively.

f. Income tax expense for each of the two years should be computed at a rate of 40%.

Required:

1. Prepare in proper form a comparative income statement of Century Company for the two years ended December 31, 1992, and December 31, 1991.
2. Give or explain the entries related to the discontinued segment on *(a)* measurement date and *(b)* disposal date.

(AICPA adapted)

P 4–11
Discontinued Segment
(L.O. 4)

On April 1, 1991, Carter Company signed a contract to sell its Teck Products Division to Baker Company for $300,000 cash; one third on April 1, 1991, and the remainder on the disposal date, July 1, 1991. Carter will continue to operate the division until the disposal date. The book (i.e., carrying) value of the net assets of the Teck Division on June 30, 1991, is $280,000. The income tax rate is 40%, and the annual reporting period ends December 31. The estimated income (pretax) of the Teck Division, for the period January 1–June 30, 1991, was $13,000; however, the actual pretax income amount turned out to be $15,000.

At December 31, 1991, the accounting records provide the following data for Teck Products Division: Pretax income from operations: 1990, $16,500; 1991, $15,000. Carter's after-tax income from operations (excluding income from Teck Products Division) was $600,000 for 1990 and $630,000 for 1991.

Required:

1. Give the entries by Carter Company for 1991 related to the sale of the Teck Products Division, including explanations.
2. Prepare the comparative income statement dated December 31, 1991, including an appropriate disclosure note.

P 4–12

Discontinued Operations,
Changes in Accounting
Principle
(L.O. 3, 4)

The following trial balance of Garr Corporation at December 31, 1992, has been adjusted, except for income tax expense.

GARR CORPORATION
Trial Balance
December 31, 1992

	Dr.	Cr.
Cash	$ 675,000	
Accounts receivable (net)	1,695,000	
Inventory	2,185,000	
Property, plant, and equipment (net)	8,660,000	
Accounts payable and accrued liabilities		$ 1,895,000
Income tax payable		360,000
Deferred income tax		285,000
Common stock		2,300,000
Additional paid-in capital		3,675,000
Retained earnings, 1/1/92		3,350,000
Net sales, Regular		10,750,000
Net sales, Plastics Division		2,200,000
Cost of sales, Regular	5,920,000	
Cost of sales, Plastics Division	1,650,000	
Selling and administrative expenses, Regular	2,600,000	
Selling and administrative expense, Plastics Division	660,000	
Interest income, Regular		65,000
Gain on litigation settlement, Regular		200,000
Depreciation adjustment from accounting change, Regular	350,000	
Gain on disposal of Plastics Division		150,000
Income tax expense	835,000	
	$25,230,000	$25,230,000

Other financial data for the year ended December 31, 1992:

a. *Income tax expense:*

Estimated tax payments	$475,000	
Accrued	360,000	
Total charged to income tax expense (estimated)*	$835,000	
Tax rate on all types of income	40%	

The gain from litigation settlement is a taxable gain and is not considered infrequent.

* The $835,000 may not properly reflect income tax expense or intraperiod income tax allocation for financial statement purposes.

b. *Discontinued operations:* On October 31, 1992, Garr sold its Plastics Division for $2,950,000 when the carrying amount was $2,800,000. For financial statement reporting, this sale was considered a disposal of a segment of a business. Since there was no phaseout period, the measurement date and the disposal date were both October 31, 1992.

c. *Change in depreciation method:* On January 1, 1992, Garr changed to the 150% declining balance method from the straight-line method of depreciation for certain of its plant assets. The pretax cumulative effect of this accounting change was determined to be a charge of $350,000. There was no change in depreciation method for income tax purposes.

d. *Capital structure:* Common stock, $10 par, traded on a national exchange:

	Shares
Outstanding at 1/1/92	200,000
Issued on 7/1/92 at $11.50 per share	30,000
	230,000

Required:

Using the multiple-step format, prepare an income statement for Garr for the year ended December 31, 1992. All components of income tax expense should be appropriately shown.

(AICPA adapted)

CASES

C 4–1
Analytical: Discuss Statement Classifications
(L.O. 5)

During the 1994 audit, the independent CPA encountered the following situations that cause serious concern as to proper classification on the financial statements of selected clients. Assume all amounts are material.

a. A client was assessed additional income taxes of $100,000 plus $36,000 interest related to the past three years.
b. A client suffered a casualty loss (a fire) amounting to $500,000. The client occasionally experiences a fire, but this was significantly more than any such loss ever experienced by the client company.
c. A client company paid $175,000 damages assessed by the courts as a result of an injury to a customer on the company premises three years earlier.
d. A client sold a large operational asset and reported a gain of $70,000.
e. The major supplier of raw materials to a client company experienced a prolonged strike. As a result, the client company reported a loss of $150,000. This is the first such loss; however, the client has three major suppliers, and strikes are not unusual in those industries.
f. A client owns several large blocks of common stock of other corporations. The shares have been held for a number of years and are viewed as a long-term investment. During the past year, 20% of the stock was sold to meet an unusual cash demand. Additional sales of the stock are not anticipated.

Required:

1. Briefly define *(a)* income from ordinary business operations, *(b)* unusual or infrequent gains and losses, *(c)* extraordinary gains and losses, and *(d)* prior period adjustments. Explain how the effects of each should be reported.
2. For each transaction *a–f*, indicate how the financial effects should be classified; that is, classify as *(a)* income from ordinary business operations, *(b)* unusual or infrequent (but not both) gains and losses, *(c)* extraordinary, or *(d)* prior period adjustments. Explain the basis for your decision for each situation.

C 4–2
Analyze and Discuss Extraordinary Items
(L.O. 5)

The following information was taken from an article in the *Journal of Accountancy:*[26]

Case A: "XYZ Company's fruit crop was destroyed by a severe freeze. The loss was $40,000. A freeze in XYZ's location is very rare. . . . ABC Company's fruit crop was also destroyed by a severe freeze. The loss was $40,000. A severe freeze in ABC's locale occurs about every two years."

Case B: "Company A sold 100 shares of XYZ Company common stock for a gain of $5,000. This is the only stock that Company A owned or will ever own. . . . Company B also sold 100 shares of XYZ Company common stock for a gain of $5,000. Company B has several other investments in its common stock portfolio and is frequently involved in stock transactions."

Required:

1. Give the definition of an extraordinary item.
2. For Case A, explain how, and why, XYZ Company and ABC Company should report the $40,000 loss.
3. For Case B, explain how, and why, Company A and Company B should report the $5,000 gain.

C 4–3
Sherwin-Williams: Analysis of Actual Financial Statements
(L.O. 2, 3, 4, 5)

The appendix at the end of the book gives an actual set of financial statements for Sherwin-Williams. Examine them carefully and respond to the following questions (for 1990 only, unless otherwise specified):

a. Are the statements comparative? Why are comparative statements usually presented?
b. Are the statements consolidated? What do you understand this to mean?
c. Is this a retail, financial, or a manufacturing company? Explain.
d. How many different kinds of revenue were reported? How many different kinds of expenses were reported?

---

[26] B. Jarnigan, "Extraordinary Items: An Update," *Journal of Accountancy,* April 1984, pp. 42–44.

e. How were interest expense and interest revenue reported on the income statement?

f. Was the total amount of depreciation expense separately reported on the income statement?

g. Were any unusual or infrequently occurring (but not both) items reported on the income statement in 1989 or 1990?

h. Were any extraordinary items reported on the 1989 or 1990 income statement? What were they? Were they net of tax?

i. Was there any indication of an accounting change? If so, explain how it was reported and what type of change it was.

j. How many EPS amounts were reported?

k. What differences were reported on the income statement? Gross margin? Income from continuing operations? Income before extraordinary items? Net income? Others? Please list them.

l. What was the profit margin (net income dividend by revenue) for 1990?

m. What basis was used for valuing inventories?

n. What items are included in the income statement classification, other costs and expenses? Why might the company show the provision for disposition and termination of operations as a credit balance amount in 1990?

o. What was the primary depreciation method used for accounting purposes?

p. What was the amount of income tax expense for 1990?

q. In 1990, what was the total amount of cash dividends declared on (a) common stock and (b) preferred stock?

r. What were the total amounts of net sales and net income reported for the first quarter of 1990?

s. Did the auditor's report express any reservations about the financial statements? Explain.

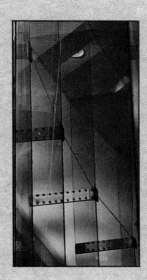

Review: The Balance Sheet and the Statement of Cash Flows

LEARNING OBJECTIVES

◆

After you have studied this chapter, you will:

1. Have gained additional knowledge of balance sheet formats and how each format reflects the basic accounting identity between assets and equities.

2. Know the different methods used to value assets, liabilities, and equities and understand why the use of market values is uncommon in balance sheets.

3. Understand the importance of terminology, comparative statements, reporting subsequent events, and footnote disclosure in communicating accounting information and the financial status of a company.

4. Understand the uses and limitations of the balance sheet.

5. Be familiar with two alternative formats for structuring a statement of cash flows.

6. Know the definitions of the major elements of the statement of cash flows.

7. Be familiar with the usefulness of the statement of cash flows.

♦

The following business news recaps illustrate how balance sheet information can be misleading:

> At one point during the mid-1980s, Corning Glass Works owned 2.9 million shares of Owens Corning Fiberglass. On the balance sheet of Corning Glass Works these shares were valued at $1 per share, or $2.9 million, which was the cost at which they were acquired many years earlier. Yet the value of these shares in the open market was $37 per share, or $107.3 million.

> In 1986, IBM and MCI Communications entered into an agreement in which Satellite Business Systems, one of IBM's subsidiaries, was sold to MCI. In lieu of cash, IBM accepted 47 million shares of MCI's stock, which was worth $528 million at the time of the sale, based on the stock's then-current market value. The agreement specified that IBM hold the MCI stock for a period of three years. In 1989, MCI repurchased the shares for $677 million, an amount $149 million above the figure of $528 million shown at the time on IBM's balance sheet.

Critics might charge that Corning Glass and IBM were deliberately undervaluing their assets. Defenders might answer that both companies were simply following generally accepted accounting principles.

> In 1988, Avon Products was forced to recognize substantial write-downs on certain of its assets. Avon was selling its health care businesses, which included assets that were being valued on Avon's balance sheet at $613 million more than anyone was willing to pay for them. Hence the write-downs.

Before the write-downs, some people described Avon's assets as being "puffed up" and seriously overvalued.

> In 1985, Clayton & Dubilier, an investment firm specializing in corporate takeovers (similar to Kohlberg, Kravis, Roberts & Co., discussed in the Introduction to Chapter 1), gained a controlling interest in Uniroyal and took the big tire company private. Having bought out the public shareholders, Clayton planned to strip the company and sell off Uniroyal's operating divisions at juicy profits. But Uniroyal's employees got in the way. They sued Clayton & Dubilier, charging that they were owed retirement benefits not shown as liabilities on Uniroyal's balance sheet. The employees won, costing Clayton & Dubilier $75 million and putting an end to the planned breakup. Uniroyal was later sold intact to a Japanese tire maker.

How could Clayton & Dubilier have ignored Uniroyal's pension and retirement benefit obligations? Companies insist that future pension funding obligations are not liabilities and, therefore, need not be recognized as such on the balance sheet. Management argues that these obligations cannot be quantified and concludes that it is better to wait and deal with pension obligations when they come due. Although the courts have consistently ruled that future pension and retirement benefits are legal contract obligations, the accounting profession now requires disclosure (and in many cases recognition) of these liabilities.[1] However, a substantial number of corporate executives would prefer to adopt a pay-as-you-go approach, which means these liabilities would not be reported on the books until they fall due for payment.

> Each spring, *Forbes* magazine publishes its annual list of the top 500 U.S. companies based on total assets. In 1989, Ford Motor Company moved up from 16th to 3rd place, the result of a 25% jump in reported assets.

Did Ford have a miracle year? No. The increase merely reflected Ford's compliance with *SFAS No. 94*, which requires corporations to consolidate all majority-owned subsidiaries for balance sheet reporting purposes.[2] In this case, Ford was now

---

[1] Although the FASB has moved toward full disclosure (as in *SFAS No. 87*), important assets and liabilities go undisclosed, or are not fully disclosed, under current GAAP.

[2] The move to consolidate majority-owned subsidiaries can be traced to a 1984 enforcement action by the SEC regarding Digilog, a computer company that buried operating losses in a minority-owned marketing subsidiary.

required to include the assets of its finance subsidiary, Ford Motor Acceptance Corporation, the consumer auto loan and dealer inventory financing arm of the company.

Prior to the consolidation, was Ford underreporting its assets? After consolidation, is Ford a financially stronger, more vibrant business entity? Probably not, but not everyone agrees. For one thing, compliance with *SFAS No. 94* required Ford to include the liabilities of the finance subsidiary along with those of the parent corporation. This raised Ford's debt-equity ratio from 25% to 61%. Is Ford that heavily leveraged? Probably yes, but some would argue that the debt (based on car-buyer loans) is of high quality and, thus, marketable. Although Ford's debt more than doubled, Ford's supporters would add that the company's exposure to the risks of heavy leverage did not double.

As this book is being written, the SEC, under its new chairman, Richard Breeden, is calling for reporting the financial investments of banks and other financial institutions at their market values rather than at cost. Since the market values are substantially below cost in many cases, write-downs would be necessary. Would such reporting improve the disclosure of these institutions' financial health? If some assets are adjusted to market values, should the same be done to other assets? Should market values be entered into the accounts only for assets traded in active markets? And should liabilities also be marked to market? These are important current issues to be addressed by those involved in setting reporting standards.

In this chapter, the balance sheet and the statement of cash flows are explored and analyzed. The emphasis is on the value of these statements to a company's investors and creditors, the way the statements are structured, how individual line items are organized and presented, and their limitations. How an item appears on a company's balance sheet can affect understanding the item, and what does not appear on the balance sheet can be as important as what does.

◆

THE BALANCE SHEET

◆

At the Louvre in Paris is a statue of a simple man dressed only with a pencil behind his ear, another pencil held in his right hand. He is an Egyptian scribe, circa 1000 B.C. He is keeping records of business matters for his master, such as cattle moving to market, corn and other crops being sold, and units of land being transferred. The scribe was responsible for keeping a running tally on what his master owed and what was owed him. Because coinage and standardized monetary systems were yet to be developed, he accounted for everything in physical terms—so many head of cattle, so many units of corn, so many measures of land.

The development of coinage and standard monetary units eased the scribe's accounting tasks and paved the way for trade expansion. Thanks to the standardization of monetary units, merchants could add up the values of their dissimilar assets, subtract what they owed to others, and determine the value of what remained (their net worth). At the same time, commerce expanded because various types of business ventures could be evaluated and measured in terms of the changes that participation in a business venture would have on an individual's assets, liabilities, and net worth. Also, interest could be calculated and charged based on the ability to convert the result from one currency to another.

Throughout much of recorded history, a listing of assets and liabilities made from time to time was the paramount measure of an individual's or business's financial position. This listing, which is now called the *balance sheet*, provides information on the resources, obligations, and equity of the business's owners.

During the half century starting about 1920, the balance sheet lost its preeminent position to the income statement. The balance sheet has only recently regained enhanced status with decision makers. Renewed interest in the balance sheet is due in part to the increase in concern for a firm's financial strength reflected in measures of liquidity and financial flexibility. **Liquidity** refers to the expected time before an asset is realized or converted into cash, or until a liability is to be paid. **Financial flexibility** reflects the ability of a company to manage its cash flows in order to respond to unexpected needs and opportunities.

Corporate merger and acquisition activities also require a thorough examination of every item and all aspects of a company's balance sheet. For example, in the 1970s, Penn Central abruptly backed away from the proposed acquisition of GK Technologies after the tragic MGM Grand Hotel fire. A subsidiary of GK Technologies had done most of the hotel's wiring, and Penn Central feared the uncertainty of the potential legal claims despite GK Technologies' insurance coverage. If Penn Central had acquired GK Technologies, under *SFAS No. 38*, the company would have been required to estimate the liabilities it was acquiring, a difficult task in itself, and report them on its financial statements.

An in-depth review of the balance sheet can often lead to questions, if not to immediate answers, concerning whether an organization can survive. The balance sheet provides information about a firms solvency. However, as the recent savings and loan crisis grew, all too frequently reports on ailing institutions failed to accurately portray their deteriorating financial condition. Donald Kirk, a professor at Columbia University and past chairman of the FASB, stated that "they [the S&Ls] created equity out of thin air."

The accounting profession has always been concerned with the question of how accurately the balance sheet provides a representation of a company's financial strengths and weaknesses. Beginning in the late 1930s, the Committee on Accounting Procedures attempted to codify generally accepted accounting principles with that specific issue in mind. Later, the Accounting Principles Board and the Financial Accounting Standards Board continued the effort, building on what had gone before. Along the way, the profession's rule makers also drew on early efforts made by the American Institute of Accountants and by the Federal Trade Commission.

But the primary event that sparked external decision makers into both scrutinizing a company's balance sheet and insisting that this statement be more informative did not come from the accounting rule makers; it came from the stock market. The market crash of 1929 put everyone on guard about the financial conditions of even the largest American corporations.

Format of the Balance Sheet

The balance sheet provides economic information about an entity's resources (**assets**), claims against those resources (**liabilities**), and the remaining claim accruing to the owners (**owners' equity**). **Statement of financial position** is the formal term for the balance sheet. It is also the term used by the FASB in its pronouncements. However, the more common term with statement preparers and statement users is *balance sheet*. One reason for this preference is that *balance sheet* reflects an important aspect of this report; namely, the statement balances in conformity with the basic accounting identity:

$$\text{Assets} = \text{Liabilities} + \text{Owners' equity}$$

$$A \quad = \quad L \quad + \quad OE$$

Report Form and Financing Form   The basic accounting identity can be rearranged to reflect the owners' viewpoint. Thus:

$$A - L = OE$$

The recorded value of the firm to the owners, called owners' equity, is what remains after the liabilities are subtracted from the assets. This amount is reported periodically to the owners. A balance sheet based on this form of the accounting identity is called the *report form*.

EXHIBIT 5-1   Alternative Representations of the Accounting Model*

	Report Form A − L = OE ($000)	Financing Form = Account form A = L + OE ($000)
Current assets:		
Cash and cash equivalents	$ 685.1	$ 685.1
Short-term investments	458.4	458.4
Accounts receivable	1,265.6	1,265.6
Inventories and prepayments	1,000.7	1,000.7
Total current assets	3,409.8	3,409.8
Property, plant, and equipment (PP&E):		
Land, building, equipment	1,291.2	1,291.2
Other	2,702.7	2,702.7
Accumulated depreciation	(1,701.4)	(1,701.4)
Total current assets and PP&E	5,702.3	5,702.3
Other assets	1,054.4	1,054.4
Total assets	$6,756.7	$6,756.7
Current liabilities	$1,907.3	$1,907.3
Long-term debt	117.8	117.8
Other liabilities	1,211.0	1,211.0
Total liabilities	3,236.1	3,236.1
Assets minus liabilities	$3,520.6	
Stockholders' equity:		
Common stock	152.4	152.4
Retained earnings	3,368.2	3,368.2
Total stockholders' equity	$3,520.6	
Total liabilities and stockholders' equity		$6,756.7

* Adapted from Merck's 1989 balance sheet

In its first form, the accounting identity can be viewed as expressing the means of financing the organization's assets. Funds must be raised from creditors (liabilities) or from owners (owners' equity), often by retaining the organization's earnings, to finance additional assets. This formulation accounts for the *financing* of the organization. A balance sheet based on this form of the accounting identity is called the *financing form*.[3] (This form is also referred to as the *account form*.) Exhibit 5-1 represents the two forms of the accounting identity.

Exhibit 5-2 provides an example of the less common financing form, for Merck Incorporated and its Subsidiaries, covering the 1989 calendar year. (Compare Exhibit 5-2 to 5-1, which uses data condensed from Merck's 1989 balance sheet to illustrate the two different report forms.) The notes referenced at the bottom of the statement are not included, despite their importance, because they are not needed at this point in the discussion.

Basic Definitions and Classifications

Assets, liabilities, and owners' equity are key concepts and, therefore, require precise definitions. *SFAC No. 6* provides these definitions.[4]

---

[3] *Accounting Trends and Techniques* (p. 101) for 1990 indicates that 67% of the companies surveyed used the report form and 33% used the financing form of presentation in 1989.

[4] In defining owners' equity, *SFAC No. 6* goes on to note: "In a business enterprise, the equity is the ownership interest. In a not-for-profit organization, which has no ownership interest in the same sense as a business enterprise, net assets is divided into three classes based on the presence or absence of donor imposed restrictions—permanently restricted, temporarily restricted, and unrestricted net assets."

EXHIBIT 5-2

MERCK & CO., INC., AND SUBSIDIARIES
Consolidated Balance Sheet
December 31, 1989 and 1988

($ in millions)	1989	1988
Assets		
Current assets:		
Cash and cash equivalents	$ 685.1	$ 854.0
Short-term investments	458.4	696.0
Accounts receivable	1,265.6	1,022.8
Inventories	779.7	657.7
Prepaid expenses and taxes	221.0	158.8
Total current assets	3,409.8	3,389.3
Property, plant, and equipment (PP&E), at cost:		
Land	162.1	130.5
Buildings	1,129.1	1,038.1
Machinery, equipment, and office furnishings	2,417.2	2,224.8
Construction in progress	285.5	197.1
Subtotal PP&E	3,993.9	3,590.5
Less allowance for depreciation	1,701.4	1,519.8
Total property, plant, and equipment	2,292.5	2,070.7
Investments	737.2	402.9
Other assets	317.2	264.6
Total assets	$6,756.7	$6,127.5
Liabilities and Stockholders' Equity		
Current liabilities:		
Accounts payable and accrued liabilities	$ 937.2	$ 832.9
Loans payable	327.3	458.8
Income taxes payable	464.8	470.5
Dividends payable	178.0	146.8
Total current liabilities	1,907.3	1,909.0
Long-term debt	117.8	142.8
Deferred income taxes and noncurrent liabilities	701.1	676.2
Minority interests	509.9	543.7
Stockholders' equity:		
Common stock:		
Authorized—900,000,000 shares		
Issued—455,524,308 shares	152.4	145.4
Retained earnings	5,394.2	4,580.3
Subtotal stockholders' equity	5,546.6	4,725.7
Less treasury stock, at cost:		
60,116,101 shares—1989		
58,784,163 shares—1988	2,026.0	1,869.9
Total stockholders' equity	3,520.6	2,855.8
Total liabilities and stockholders' equity	$6,756.7	$6,127.5

The accompanying notes are an integral part of this financial statement.

Assets: Probable future economic benefits obtained or controlled by a particular entity as a result of past transactions or events.

Liabilities: Probable future sacrifices of economic benefits arising from present obligations of a particular entity to transfer assets or provide services to other entities in the future as a result of past transactions or events.

Owners' Equity: The residual interest in the assets of an entity that remains after deducting its liabilities.

To make accounting information as understandable and usable by decision makers as possible, items reported in the balance sheet should be grouped and arranged according to the following guidelines:

* Assets should be classified and presented in decreasing order of liquidity (convertibility into cash). Those items nearest to cash—meaning readily convertible at any time without restriction—should be ranked first. Assets rated as having less liquidity (or as least likely to be converted to cash) should be listed last.
* Liabilities should be classified and presented based on time to maturity. Thus, obligations due today should be listed first, and those carrying the most distant maturity dates listed last. (Several exceptions are discussed later.)
* Owners' equity items should be classified and presented in order of permanence. Thus, paid-in capital contribution accounts, which typically change the least, should be listed first. Equity accounts used to report accumulated earnings and updated on an ongoing basis should be listed last.

Classifications of information reported in the balance sheet, and the array of items under each classification, are determined by GAAP.

However, the classifications used are strongly influenced by the unique characteristics of each industry and each business enterprise. The balance sheet of a financial institution, such as a bank, reflects classifications different from those of a manufacturing company. For example, financial institutions do not use current asset and liability designations.[5] Format and classifications should be designed for a particular enterprise and should comply with the *full disclosure* principle, which specifies that reporting be informative and sufficiently inclusive to avoid misleading inferences. Therefore, flexibility in format and classifications is desirable, although a reasonable degree of uniformity is still essential.

The following classification and presentation order are illustrative of current reporting practice and terminology.

A. Assets:
  1. Current assets
     a. Cash and short-term investments.
     b. Receivables.
     c. Inventories.
  2. Noncurrent assets.
     a. Investments and funds.
     b. Property, plant, and equipment.
     c. Intangible assets.
     d. Other assets.
     e. Deferred charges.
B. Liabilities:
  1. Current liabilities (including short-term deferred credits and the short-term portion of long-term liabilities).
  2. Long-term, or noncurrent, liabilities (including long-term deferred credits).
     a. Leases.
     b. Bonds.
C. Owners' equity:
  1. Contributed (or paid-in) capital.
     a. Capital stock at par, no par, or at stated value.

---

[5] Banking, insurance, railroads, and utilities are government-regulated industries. As such, they are required to furnish financial statement information in formats prescribed by the Federal Reserve Board, the Interstate Commerce Commission, and other regulatory bodies. In the case of banking, there is no need to distinguish between current and noncurrent assets because government regulators do not require it and because the nature of a bank's primary assets (marketable debt securities and loan portfolios) are such that they are all fairly liquid, at least in theory.

    b. Contributed (or paid-in) capital in excess of the par, or stated value of capital stock.

    c. Other contributed (or paid-in) capital.

2. Retained earnings.

Such classification provides a major caption for each balance sheet element—assets, liabilities, and owners' equity. Under each element's caption, further subdivisions, such as those listed, commonly are found. No one format or precise organizational approach is required, however. Merck's balance sheet, as shown in Exhibit 5–2, for example, differs in several respects.

Since it is a financial position statement, the balance sheet must be dated at a specific date, such as "December 31, 1991." In contrast, the income statement and the statement of cash flows are dated to cover a specific period of time, such as "For the Year Ended December 31, 1991." These coverage dates identify the end of the reporting period.

Assets

Current Assets[6]   *Current assets* include cash and other assets that are reasonably expected to be realized in cash, or to be sold or consumed during the *normal operating cycle* of the business or within one year from the balance sheet date, whichever is longer.[7]

The normal operating cycle of a business is the average period of time between the expenditure of cash (or creation of accounts payable) for goods and services and the date those goods and services are converted into cash. Thus, it is the average length of time from cash expenditure, to inventory, to sale, to accounts receivable, and back to cash.

Most companies use one year as the time period for classifying items as current or long-term because either the operating cycle usually is less than one year, or the length of the operating cycle may be difficult to measure reliably.

Current assets usually are presented on the balance sheet in order of decreasing liquidity. The major items included in current assets, in order of liquidity, are:

1. Cash.
2. Short-term investments.
3. Receivables.
4. Inventories.
5. Prepaid expenses.

Assets that are similar to, but not classified as, current assets are:

1. Cash and claims to cash that are restricted for uses other than current operations.
2. Receivables with an extended maturity date.
3. Long-term prepayments of expenses.

Current assets are relatively easy to define. However, problems may be encountered in implementing the definition. The phrases *normal operating cycle* and *reasonably expected to be realized in cash* involve judgments. When there is uncertainty, management may be inclined to classify certain items as current assets to produce a desired effect on working capital (current assets minus current lia-

---

[6] Any classification framework is arbitrary and, it could be argued, unnecessary. A listing of the assets in order of liquidity could be combined as desired by the user. See L. Heath, "Financial Reporting and the Evaluation of Solvency," *Accounting Research Monograph No. 3* (New York: AICPA, 1978), pp. 43–69.

[7] Until just after World War II, the term *current* was generally interpreted to mean within one year. *ARB No. 30,* issued in August 1947, opted for the operating cycle as a better measure, a position advocated by Anson Harrick, a CAP member at the time. See E. Becker, "The History of Accounting Research Bulletins," Working Paper No. 75, Nova University, June 1988, p. 3.

EXHIBIT 5-3   Inventory Note: Note 2 of Merck's 1989 Annual Report

2. INVENTORIES

Inventories at December 31 consisted of:

	1989	1988
Finished Goods	$372.3	$324.8
Raw materials and work in process	441.3	361.8
Supplies	48.3	42.1
Total (approximates current cost)	861.9	728.7
Reduction to LIFO cost	82.2	71.0
	$779.7	$657.7

bilities). For example, an *investment in marketable securities* may be classified as a current or noncurrent asset, depending on the stated intention of management regarding the planned holding period. An intention to hold the investment beyond the period specified for current assets would require its classification as a noncurrent asset. Thus, a change in the intention of management can be used to justify a change in the classification of the investment. Not knowing if the particular placement of an asset on a company's balance sheet is based on the actual intentions of management or, alternatively, on management's desire to show its accounts in a better light is a problem both for the auditors (whose professional reputations may be at stake) and for external decision makers (whose investment dollars may be at risk).

Prepaid expenses is another area for which classification varies. Prepaid expenses are cash outlays made in advance of receiving service, for example, rent paid May 31 for the month of June. A short-term prepayment should be classified as a current asset, whereas a long-term prepayment should be classified as a noncurrent asset. Prepaid expenses are current assets because an investment is made by paying cash in advance, thereby reducing cash outlays for the next reporting period. However, this argument could be used to justify many balance sheet items as current assets. Fortunately, many prepayments have no utility beyond one year. Also, prepaid items are relatively minor in amount, and their placement on the balance sheet as current assets normally creates no appreciable problems.

Some companies and industries do not use the current assets category. As discussed earlier in this chapter, financial institutions, such as banks and mutual funds, have no current assets caption because nearly all of their assets are readily marketable.

Accounts receivable should be reported net of any anticipated reduction due to uncollectible amounts. Receivables pledged (that is, committed to satisfy an obligation of the firm) or discounted should be indicated parenthetically or by footnote.

Short-term investments include investments in debt securities, such as U.S. Treasury securities, money market funds, and commercial paper. Short-term investments also include corporate equity securities. Significant amounts of short-term investments in debt or in equity securities should be separately listed among the current assets. (Investments in short-term securities are covered further in Chapter 14.) Short-term investments should be valued at the lower of their cost or current market value, that is, the lower-of-cost-or-market (LCM) basis should be reported.

Merchandise inventories also are usually reported at LCM. In addition, the valuation basis and, for a manufacturing firm, the completion stage should be indicated (raw materials, work in process, finished goods). Merck reports this information in a separate footnote, numbered Note 2, and shown in Exhibit 5-3.

A literal interpretation of current assets would also require the inclusion of any fixed assets expected to be used up in the next period. Under such an interpretation, items such as depreciation charges scheduled for the next accounting period would be considered a current asset. This conceptual alternative is not followed in practice by accountants, which thereby stresses the acceptance of convention and the need for judgment in account classification.

Investments and Funds   The investments and funds classification includes noncurrent investments and cash set aside in special-purpose funds for long-term use as needed. This classification often is reported immediately following the current assets section. The following long-term assets are reported under this caption:

1. Long-term investments in the capital stock of another company not intended for sale in the year despite their ready marketability.
2. Long-term investments in the bonds of another company; any unamortized premium is added to the investment, and any unamortized discount is subtracted (discussed in detail in Chapter 16).
3. Investments in subsidiaries, including long-term receivables from subsidiaries.
4. Funds set aside for long-term future use, such as bond sinking funds (to retire bonds payable), expansion funds, stock retirement funds, and long-term savings deposits.
5. Cash surrender value of life insurance policies carried by the company.
6. Long-term investments in tangible assets, such as land and buildings, that are not used in current operations (including operational assets that are only temporarily idle).

The important distinctions between *current* investments and funds and the above *long-term* assets are these:

1. The long-term items are not used in the central ongoing and major operations of the firm.
2. Management plans to retain the long-term items beyond one year from the balance sheet date or beyond the operating cycle if it is longer.

While long-term investments reported under this caption are usually shown at their original cost, some are not. Marketable securities, for example, are reported at the lower of cost or market.[8] Typically, the cost is given, and if the market value is less than cost, a valuation account (contra asset) is used to reduce the cost value to market.

Funds included under long-term investments are shown at the accumulated amount in the fund. The accumulated amount usually includes all contributions to the fund plus all interest earned to date.

fixed asset
tangible asset
operational asset

Property, Plant, and Equipment   Operational assets are long-term, noncurrent assets used in the continuing operations of a business; they are not held for resale. Thus, operational assets are different from inventories (that is, from raw materials, work in process, finished goods, and supplies). Historically, operational assets were called *fixed assets* because of their relative permanence or long-term nature. Fixed assets are also called tangible assets because they have physical substance. Examples include land, buildings, machinery, equipment, furniture, fixtures, and natural resources.

Tangible operational assets are reported in the balance sheet under various captions depending upon the business. These assets are aggregated rather than shown in detail. Additional detail is provided in the notes, particularly concerning major acquisitions and disinvestments. Thus, in Exhibit 5–4, Merck reports in

---

[8] An exception for some specialized firms is allowed, as discussed in Chapter 14.

EXHIBIT 5–4 Acquisition and Divestiture Note: Note 4 of Merck's 1989 *Annual Report*

---

4. ACQUISITIONS, DIVESTITURES, AND ALLIANCES

In 1989, the Company entered into an agreement with E. I. du Pont de Nemours and Company to form a long-term research and marketing collaboration. Also in 1989, the Company formed a joint venture with Johnson & Johnson to develop and market a broad range of nonprescription medicines for U.S. consumers. In January 1990, the joint venture acquired the U.S. over-the-counter medicines business of ICI Americas Inc., with ICI obtaining the U.S. rights to *Elavil*, one of the Company's products, along with other consideration.

In 1989, the Company sold its subsidiary in Lebanon. In 1988, the Company sold its subsidiaries in South Africa and Nigeria, and restructured its operations in Argentina, Brazil, and Venezuela. The sale of these subsidiaries and restructurings did not have a significant effect on net income. In addition, in 1988 the Company sold its 50.54% interest in Torii & Co., Ltd. The gain from this sale is included in Other (income) expense, net (see Note 6).

Note 4 to its 1989 statements that it sold its subsidiary in Lebanon as well as its South African and Nigerian subsidiaries. The note also indicates restructuring activities in Argentina, Brazil, and Venezuela, as well as a major agreement with E. I. du Pont de Nemours and activities involving a joint venture with Johnson and Johnson.

Manufacturing enterprises often use a caption such as "property, plant, and equipment." Other companies use "property and equipment," or simply "property."

Property, plant, and equipment includes items that are depreciable, such as buildings, machinery, and fixtures; items that are subject to depletion, including mineral deposits, timber stands, and agricultural land; and items that are not subject to depreciation, such as land. Land should be reported separately. The property, plant, and equipment account will also include certain leased property and plant when the lease arrangement is deemed to be a method of financing the permanent acquisition of the facilities.

APB Opinion No. 12 requires that the balance sheet, or the related notes, report the following items:

1. Balances of major classes of depreciable assets by nature or function.
2. Accumulated depreciation, either by major classes of depreciable assets or in total.
3. A description of the methods used in computing depreciation for the major classes of operational assets.

Tangible operational assets usually are shown on the balance sheet at their original cash equivalent cost, less any accumulated depreciation or depletion to date. Typically, depreciation and depletion are disclosed separately in the balance sheet, rather than giving only the asset's book value.

Intangible Assets Intangible assets are reported as a separate element in the balance sheet. Major items should be listed separately, and the accumulated amount of amortization also should be disclosed in the notes or elsewhere in the financial statements. By convention, the contra account, accumulated amortization, seldom is separately listed. This contrasts to the usual treatment given depreciation and depletion related to tangible operational assets.

Intangible assets can represent a major portion of a business's assets and yet may not appear or be disclosed separately in the firm's balance sheet. Merck shows no intangible assets at all on its balance sheet (Exhibit 5–2) although Note 3 (see Exhi-

EXHIBIT 5-5   Other Assets Note: Note 3 of Merck's 1989 Annual Report

3. OTHER ASSETS

Other assets at December 31 consisted of:

	1989	1988
Goodwill and other intangibles	$163.3	$135.4
Investment in licenses	64.0	66.7
Other	89.9	62.5
	$317.2	$264.6

bit 5–5) indicates that the caption "other assets" includes $163.3 million of goodwill and other intangibles for 1989.[9] Goodwill is the excess of the cost of an acquired company over the market value of the identifiable net assets.

Indeed, some important intangible assets are not valued at all in a company's balance sheets. United Airline's gate rights at O'Hare International Airport in Chicago are among the company's more valuable assets, but they are not reported on United's balance sheet. They were granted to the airline by the government. This reporting results because intangibles are capitalized only when purchased (such as with patents and copyrights) or obtained as part of the acquisition of another firm or when expenditures are made in regard to them such as legal fees. The legal fees protect their future use. The fees are capitalized and written off over the future period benefited, in accordance with the matching principle. Outlays made in the normal course of business to increase goodwill, say, through advertising a brand name, are not capitalized but instead written off as expenses. These expenses are not capitalized because the future benefits are much harder to determine. Conservatism prevails over matching.

Additionally, most research and development expenditures must also be expensed in the period made. The FASB reasoned in *SFAS No. 2* that the connection between research expenditures and a resulting valuable asset is too indirect to permit capitalization and subsequent amortization of the outlays. Yet the write-off of expenditures made in the expectation of future benefits, while being a conservative and practical approach, can substantially understate the intangible assets of the firm. Moreover, financial analysts may well ignore these values when calculating return on assets, thereby producing larger rates of return.

The practice of failing to report or underreporting intangibles stems from the lack of an arm's-length transaction for establishing a verifiable value. When intangibles are purchased, usually with other assets, and when a value can be established, intangibles are reported on the balance sheet at their original cash-equivalent cost, less accumulated amortization to date.

Other Assets   The other-assets classification is used for assets that are not easily included under alternative asset classifications. Examples include long-term receivables from company officers and employees and idle operational assets (such as a mothballed plant). An asset should be analyzed carefully before it is classified among "other assets" because there is often a logical basis for classifying it elsewhere. If a reported asset has no future economic benefit, it should be written off and reported in the income statement as a loss in the period in which the write-off occurs. Failure to consider assets carefully may lead to reporting assets that are no longer of value to the firm. This in turn distorts ratios that measure return on assets, for example.

---

[9] Most accountants agree that this is not good reporting, and it may be accepted only when the items are small. The value of intangibles involved in this instance is sufficiently large to justify reporting them separately.

Merck, in Note 3 to its financial statements (Exhibit 5–5), includes "investments in licenses" (which normally is classified as an intangible), and "other" in this category.

Deferred Charges   Deferred charges usually are the result of the prepayment of long-term expenses. These expenses have reliably determinable future economic benefits useful in earning future revenues. On this basis, they are viewed as assets until they are used. The only conceptual difference between a prepaid expense (classified as a current asset) and a deferred charge is the length of time over which the amount is amortized.

prepayment

The following accounts typify the "deferred charges" caption: machinery re-arrangement costs, pension costs paid in advance, and insurance prepayments (long-term prepayments not properly classified as current assets). Deferred charges sometimes are inappropriately reported as other assets. Organization costs, often found included in deferred charges, would be more appropriately included with intangible assets. As a general rule, the deferred charge classification should be avoided whenever possible in preparing the balance sheet because it is difficult to interpret, and a better reporting caption often exists.

Liabilities

Current Liabilities   *Current Liabilities* include those obligations expected to be liqui-dated using current assets or refinanced by other short-term liabilities. Liabilities usually are classified in the order in which they will be paid.

Current liabilities include:

1. Accounts payable for goods and services that enter into the operating cycle of the business (sometimes called *trade payables*).
2. Special short-term payables for nonoperating items and services.
3. Short-term notes payable.
4. Current maturities of long-term liabilities (including lease obligations).
5. Collections in advance of unearned revenue (such as rent revenue collected in advance).
6. Accrued expenses for payrolls, interest, and taxes (including unpaid income taxes and property taxes).
7. The current portion of deferred income taxes.

Liabilities that are similar to but are not classified as current liabilities include long-term notes, bonds, and obligations that will not be paid out of current assets. For example, even though a bond issue will come due during the next reporting period, it would not be classified as a current liability if the bond will be paid out of a fund reported in the noncurrent section of the balance sheet. Similarly, currently maturing bonds that are to be refunded by issuing a new bond usually would not be classified as a current liability. This reporting is specified in *SFAS No. 6*. In this case, a liability that at first appears to be a short-term liability is not; rather, it is noncurrent. There is no analogous situation with current assets.

类似的

Working Capital   The difference between total current assets (CA) and total current liabilities (CL) is called **working capital** (WC).[10]

$$\text{Working capital} = \text{Current assets} - \text{Current liabilities}$$

$$WC \qquad = \qquad CA \qquad - \qquad CL$$

In Exhibit 5–2, The Merck & Co. consolidated balance sheet, Merck's current assets for 1989 amount to $3,409.8 million, and current liabilities are $1,907.3 million

---

[10] This concept was formalized in *APB Opinion No. 30*.

for the same period. Merck's working capital is computed to be $1,502.5 million ($3,409.8 − $1,907.3). If a company's current assets were converted to cash at their reported value and its current liabilities paid at their reported value, working capital would be the amount of cash remaining. This is the case because valuations for these items are likely to be close to their cash equivalents.

Working capital ratio, commonly called the *current ratio,* is defined as current assets (CA) divided by current liabilities (CL):

$$\text{Working capital ratio} = \frac{CA}{CL}$$

A ratio of 1 or more implies that the company can discharge its current obligations with current assets over the operating cycle, usually one year. Merck's working capital ratio is $3,409.8 ÷ $1,907.3 = 1.79.

Although the concept of working capital is widely used in the business community, no one ever receives or pays working capital. In fact, a company may report an excellent working capital position and at the same time have a serious cash deficiency. For example, if all of Merck's cash and short-term investment were converted into inventories, the working capital position would be unaltered, but the company's ability to meet its trade payables would be seriously impaired. Merck would need to borrow funds to pay its suppliers.

The amount of working capital and the working capital (or current) ratio are viewed as measures of liquidity and are used to test a company's ability to meet its short-term obligations. For example, the working capital ratio computed for Merck shows that at book value the current assets were 1.79 times the current liabilities, meaning that for each $1 of current liabilities, there is $1.79 in current assets. Because of the widespread use of working capital as an index of liquidity, independent auditors sometimes encounter noncurrent assets reported as current and current liabilities reported as noncurrent. Such changes would make it possible for a company to show a better working capital position than actually exists.

Offsetting assets and liabilities in financial reporting is usually improper. Offsetting is a procedure by which a liability is subtracted from an asset or vice versa. Such a practice circumvents full disclosure and could permit a business to show a more favorable current ratio than actually exists. For example, if Merck were to offset its accounts payable of $937.2 against its accounts receivable, the current ratio would be computed as ($3,409.8 − 937.2) ÷ ($1,907.3 − $937.2) = 2.55 instead of the correct ratio of 1.79.

Offsetting is permissible only when a legal right to offset exists. For instance, it would be permissible to offset a $5,000 overdraft in one bank account against another account reflecting $8,000 on deposit in that same bank because the bank can legally offset the two deposit accounts.

Long-Term Liabilities   A *long-term liability* is an obligation that does not require the use of current assets for payment (or the incurrence of another current liability) during the next operating cycle or during the next reporting year, whichever is longer. Long-term liabilities are recorded at the exchange value of the assets or services received. Long-term liabilities involve interest that is recognized as an expense over time. A 10% note with a face value of $1,000 would result in $100 of interest expense and $100 in cash payments each year.

If the value received for a long-term promise to pay equals the stated maturity value, the promise (bond or note, for example) is said to be issued at face value. In this case, the rate of interest written into the contract (called the *nominal,* or stated, *rate*) is equal to the market rate (also called the *effective rate*) for promises of similar risk.

A bond liability issued at more than its maturity amount is issued at a *premium*. This occurs when the stated rate exceeds the effective rate. The premium causes the same contractual interest to be paid on a larger value, thereby reducing the effective rate. For example, if a 10% (the stated rate) bond with a maturity value of $1,000 is issued at 102, the bond is issued for $1,020 to the holder. The holder of the bond receives interest of 0.1($1,000), or $100, each year. Since the holder of the bond paid $1,020, the bond is issued at a premium of $20 and the effective rate at issue is $100 ÷ $1,020 or 9.8%. If the bond is issued for less than its maturity amount, it is issued at a discount. Unamortized debt premium is added to the debt obligation being reported. Unamortized debt discount is subtracted from the debt obligation being reported.

All liabilities not appropriately classified as current liabilities are reported as long-term. Typical long term liabilities are bonds payable, long-term notes payable, pensions, deferred long-term revenues (advances from customers), long-term capital lease obligations, and long-term deferred taxes.[11]

Deferred Credits   Some companys include the caption "deferred credits" between long-term liabilities and owners' equity. Deferred credits is a catch-all balance sheet classification of long-term accounts with credit balances that are difficult to classify elsewhere. Typical items included in deferred credits are long-term deferred income taxes, deferred revenues (revenues collected in advance), and deferred investment tax credits. Most accountants believe that this caption is an inappropriate classification for two reasons: it is difficult to interpret and more descriptive captions exist.

Owners' Equity

Owners' equity for a corporation is called *stockholders' equity*; for a partnership, *partners' equity*; and for a sole proprietorship, *proprietor's equity.* Owners' equity is the owners' residual interest in the firm. It is a residual interest since it's the amount left after the liabilities are subtracted from the firm's assets. Owners' equity includes contributed (or paid-in) capital and retained earnings.

Because of legal requirements, owners' equity is subclassified to reflect detailed sources. For corporations, the following sources are most commonly reported:
* Capital stock.
* Other contributed capital.
* Retained earnings.
* Treasury stock.

Capital Stock   This caption reports the sources of owners' equity that are represented by the stated or legal capital. The legal capital is the par value of the issued or outstanding preferred and common stock of the corporation and represents the amount that is not available for dividend declarations. Legal capital is specified by state law and the articles of incorporation (the charter) of the corporation. In some states, legal capital is based on issued shares; in other states, it is based on outstanding shares.

Each class of stock, common and preferred, should be reported at par, or, in the case of no-par stock, at either the stated value established by the state or the total paid-in amount. Actual specifications vary depending upon the law of the state of incorporation. Details of each class of capital stock should be reported separately. These details include the number of shares authorized, issued, outstanding, and subscribed; conversion features; callability; preferences; and any other special features.

---

[11] Merck also shows an account titled "minority interests" positioned between long-term liabilities and stockholders' equity. This account represents outside ownership interest in Merck's consolidated companies held by individuals and organizations other than Merck stockholders. Although not a legal obligation, minority interest is regarded as a liability on a consolidated balance sheet.

Contributed Capital in Excess of Par, or Stated, Value   This source sometimes is called *additional paid-in capital* or *premium on stock.* It too is considered legal capital in most instances. Contributed capital in excess of par (or stated value) reports the value of assets received by the corporation above the par (or stated value) of the capital stock given in exchange. These amounts usually arise when the corporation sells its stock above par (or the stated amount per share) or issues stock dividends.

Other Contributed Capital   This source of contributed capital arises from such transactions as the sale of treasury stock below acquisition cost, and capital arising from recapitalizations. For balance sheet presentation, there is generally at most one additional contributed capital account. The specific underlying subaccounts are maintained in a subsidiary ledger.

Retained Earnings   Retained earnings is essentially a corporation's accumulated net earnings, less dividend payouts, from the company's inception. Retained earnings may be divided between the amount available for dividends (unappropriated retained earnings) and any amounts restricted by management for other purposes (restricted retained earnings), such as for modernization of facilities or as in connection with a pending adverse legal judgment. In most corporations, retained earnings is the largest amount in the owners' equity section. Over a corporation's life, dividends are distributed to the stockholders in amounts that are usually less than the corporation's earnings. This policy establishes a continuing source of internally generated funds. Newer companies that are in their growth phase normally pay small or no dividends to their shareholders; instead, they retain all or most of their earnings for internal reinvestment and business expansion. More mature companies that are beyond their growth phase commonly pay out a higher percentage of their earnings in the form of shareholder dividends. Retained earnings represents additional indirect investments by the stockholders because they have forgone dividends equal to the cumulative balance of retained earnings. A negative balance in retained earnings is called a *deficit* and usually arises when a company experiences operating losses.

A portion of a company's retained earnings can be restricted or appropriated. This means that during the period of restriction or appropriation, the specified amount will be unavailable for dividends. After the restriction is removed, the restricted amount is again included in the total available for dividends.

A restriction on retained earnings may be contractual, as when a bond indenture restricts the amount of retained earnings available for dividend declaration. Alternatively, a restriction can result from a legal requirement, such as a restriction by state law equal to the cost of any treasury stock the company has reacquired. The purpose of such laws is to protect the creditors of the corporation. Also, a company's board of directors may exercise its discretion and appropriate a portion of retained earnings, for example, earmarking capital for future plant expansion. In such a case, the board is limiting the total amount of retained earnings that will be available for dividend payments to the shareholders.

Restrictions or appropriations of retained earnings can be reported in two ways. One way is to report restrictions or appropriations in the notes to the statements. Another approach is to make an entry in the accounts to reflect the restriction or appropriation. For example: the entry to record an appropriation of $120,000 in the accounts is:

Retained earnings	120,000	
Retained earnings restricted		
by bond indenture		120,000

Reporting on the balance sheet then would be:

Retained earnings:
Unappropriated	$4,000,000
Appropriated by bond indenture	120,000
Total retained earnings	$4,120,000

Treasury Stock Merck's 1989 consolidated balance sheet, Exhibit 5–2, illustrates several of the major subdivisions of stockholders' equity. Additionally, Merck reports that a total of 60.1 million shares of its common stock have been acquired (and not reissued) by the company at a total cost of $2,026 million, as of December 31, 1989. These shares, while issued, are no longer outstanding. The cost of the stock is deducted from subtotal stockholders' equity of $5,546.6 million to yield $3,520.6 million for total stockholders' equity.

Companies repurchase their own stock for several reasons:

1. To meet employee stock purchase or option plan needs.
2. To increase reported earnings per share.
3. To stabilize the stock's price.
4. To reduce the outstanding shares, perhaps to discourage a hostile takeover attempt.
5. To contract the firm's operations.

Such shares, if not retired, are called *treasury stock*. When a company buys its own stock, the company's capitalization is reduced. The company can neither vote the shares nor pay itself dividends on them. Treasury stock is not an asset but, rather, essentially identical to unissued shares.

CONCEPT REVIEW

1. Describe the difference between the report form and the financing form of the balance sheet.
2. What is the rule by which the items in the current assets section of the balance sheet are ordered? The current liabilities?
3. Should a firm offset a receivable against a payable? Why or why not?

ADDITIONAL REPORTING ISSUES

◆

Loss and Gain Contingencies

SFAS No. 5 requires companies to estimate any contingent loss that meets two basic requirements:

1. Information available prior to issuance of the financial statements indicates that it is probable that an asset has been impaired or that a liability has been incurred at the date of the financial statements.
2. The amount of the loss can be reasonably estimated.

Few situations meet both conditions, and, therefore, few contingent losses are recorded by journal entry. Even in cases (such as arise in lawsuits) where a loss can occur, *SFAS No. 5* does not require accrual unless the loss is *both probable and estimable*. If a loss is *probable or estimable*, but *not* both, or if there is at least a *reasonable possibility* that a liability may have been incurred, the nature of the contingency must be disclosed in a footnote, along with an estimate of the possible loss or the range of the possible loss if an estimate can be made. Most companies refrain from estimating the expected loss, arguing that no recognition is necessary because:

1. The situation does not meet the required reasonable probability level; or
2. It is not possible to estimate the loss.

Companies are particularly reluctant to disclose potential losses arising from litigation because such disclosure might provide the appearance of guilt.

An example of a contingent liability from Merck's 1989 annual report is reproduced in Exhibit 5–6.

EXHIBIT 5-6   Contingent Liabilities Note: Note 9 of Merck's 1989 Annual Report

9. CONTINGENT LIABILITIES

The Company is involved in various claims and legal proceedings of a nature considered normal to its business, including product liability cases brought against the Company and a number of other pharmaceutical companies, alleging injury from the use of certain synthetic estrogen drugs, including diethylstilbestrol (DES), manufactured by the defendant companies. While it is not feasible to predict or determine the outcome of any of these cases, it is the opinion of management that their outcome will have no material adverse effect on the financial position of the Company.

Despite most companies' reluctance to report such contingencies, they have appeared in special situations. A. H. Robins, after a long delay, began reporting a sizable liability related to one of its contraceptive products, the Dalkon Shield, which created extensive legal action against the company. In a similar situation, Johns Manville filed for bankruptcy, due in part to the reporting requirements of *SFAS No. 5.* Manville's management believed the company would be required to disclose contingent losses of as much as $2 billion, all stemming from the company's asbestos business.[12]

Warranties provide another example of a liability that would qualify for reporting as contingent. However, many other potential contingent losses—including guarantees of indebtedness, repurchase agreements wherein one company sells an asset to another company and agrees to repurchase it later, and other transactions—are unlikely to be reported. The desire not to release information that might be unfavorable to the company, coupled with the vagueness of such words as *reasonably possible,* used in *SFAS No. 5,* allows many contingencies to go unreported.

Although contingent gains are also possible, the accounting profession has adopted a conservative position of nonrecognition, as it has in countless other areas. Contingent gains may at most be disclosed in footnotes, and then only if there is a high probability of realization. Many instances of this take-the-loss-but-defer-the-gain approach are found throughout accounting. The conservative position is often advocated by those charged with setting accounting standards. These individuals believe that they should protect external decision makers, such as creditors and investors, who rely on the financial statements. When there is no logically preferable alternative, conservatism is appealed to in resolving the reporting issue. Critics, however, believe the lack of symmetry in the approach to be logically unjustifiable.

Valuations Reported in the Balance Sheet

When an asset is first acquired (or otherwise comes into existence), it is entered and initially carried on the books at its acquisition cost. In the case of noncash transactions, the prevailing market value of the asset acquired at the time of acquisition is normally used, if the asset is marketable. Once acquired, some assets continue to be reported at their acquisition cost. Inventories and land are examples.

Other assets do not continue to be reported at cost. For these assets, that portion of the cost treated as used up in the production of goods and services is subtracted from the cost, and the asset is reported at its amortized (book) value. Illustrations are property, plant, and equipment less accumulated depreciation, mineral deposits less depletion, and goodwill less amortization.

---

[12] Reported by the firm in an information advertisement in *The Wall Street Journal,* August 27, 1982.

Still other valuations are found, including net realizable values, present values, and market values. For example, receivables are usually valued at estimated net realizable amounts, equity securities at the lower of cost or market, and bonds at discounted present values. External decision makers using financial statements need to know which valuation methods are being used in order to properly assess the company's financial state.

A careful reading of the financial statements and notes will usually reveal the asset valuation methods in use. For example, one of the notes to Merck's 1989 statements states that "long-term investments, which are carried at cost, had a market value of $1,001.3 million and $650.0 million at December 31, 1989 and 1988, respectively." Indeed, *APB Opinion No. 22* requires disclosure of all significant accounting principles and methods. This disclosure is made generally (and primarily) in a paragraph entitled "Summary of Accounting Policies," which appears as Note 1 to each company's financial statements or just preceding the notes.

But why aren't current market values used at all times? They would seem to be the more relevant value for decision-making purposes.

Despite the relevance of market values, the balance sheet primarily reports historical cost valuations because they are considered to be both more reliable and more objective. The market value of most assets often can be known reliably only when they are bought or sold in a completed transaction. Such a transaction, called an *arm's-length transaction,* should involve parties that have different economic interests. For example, the seller wants a high price, and the purchaser wants a low price. At the balance sheet date, this situation usually does not exist; therefore, determination of market values generally is viewed as subjective and susceptible to manipulation, bias, and misrepresentation. In contrast, historical cost values are objective, measurable, and verifiable. It is important that decision makers understand what balance sheet valuations mean and equally important, what they do not mean.

It is instructive that even as this book is being written, the SEC and at least one major auditing firm appear to be stressing the decision relevance of market values over the reliability and objectivity of historical cost information for the investments of financial institutions.

Terminology

As is true of other professions, accounting has developed its own jargon. Frequently the same term or phrase is used to mean different things. In preparing financial statements, accountants should refrain from using jargon or vague terminology. Captions and titles should be selected carefully because the statements are read and used by a wide range of decision makers.

From time to time, the profession has recommended improved terminology.

An example of confusing terminology is the use of the term *reserve* in the following examples:

* a contra asset account, such as "reserve for doubtful accounts," instead of the more descriptive "allowance for doubtful accounts;"
* an estimated liability, such as "reserve for warranties," instead of "estimated warranty liability;" and
* an appropriation of retained earnings, such as "reserve for future expansion," instead of "retained earnings appropriated for future expansion."

Accounting Terminology Bulletin No. 1 recommended that *reserve* be restricted to retained earnings appropriations. Even in this context, some accountants do not believe that reserve is suitable to describe the nature of a restriction or appropriation of retained earnings. Reserve suggests that a fund of money is set aside somewhere, earmarked for a specific purpose. In fact, only an entry on paper is made to formally recognize a restriction the firm wishes to place on its retained earnings legally available for dividend declaration.

As early as October 1949, the Committee on Terminology recommended in *ARB No. 39* that the term *retained earnings* be used instead of *earned surplus* and *net income* be used instead of *net profit*. Differences in meanings of the terms *cost* and *expense* and *revenue* and *income* discussed in Chapter 4, provide additional examples of the importance of appropriate terminology. Still another problem is created by the introduction of new terminology. In *SFAC No. 6,* the FASB created the new term, *comprehensive income*. This term encompasses a wider range of revenues, expenses, gains, and losses than is contemplated by conventional net income. These two terms should not be used interchangeably because they connote quite different ideas. Terminology is important because the effective communication of accounting information and the lucid discussion of accounting concepts and their implementation depends largely upon the consistent use of precise and descriptive terminology.

Comparative Statements

To help decision makers assess or predict the future direction of a business, comparable financial information for several periods is of great value. For prediction purposes, trends are much more revealing than information for only one period. In recognition of this fact, *ARB No. 43* states:

> The presentation of comparative financial statements in annual and other reports enhances the usefulness of such reports and brings out more clearly the nature and trends of current changes affecting the enterprise. Such presentation emphasizes the fact that statements for a series of periods are far more significant than those for a single period and that the accounts for one period are but an installment of what is essentially a continuous history.[13]

Comparative financial statements for the current and prior reporting periods promote full disclosure. In 1980, the SEC began requiring three-year comparative statements, in lieu of the customary two-year statements, for listed companies. Hence, although comparative statements are not mandated under GAAP, practice makes them a virtual requirement.

In addition to comparative statements, many companies include in their annual reports special tabulations of selected financial items for time spans ranging from 5 to 10 years or more. Items often included are total revenues, income before extraordinary items, net income, depreciation expense, earnings per share, dividends, total assets, total owners' equity, and average number of shares of common stock outstanding. Long-term summaries of such data are particularly useful to those analyzing financial statements.

Subsequent Events

The term *subsequent events* refers to important events that occur after the balance sheet date but prior to the actual issuance of the financial statements, which ordinarily is one to four months later. To qualify for treatment as a subsequent event, the item must have a material effect on the financial statements. Subsequent events *must* be reported because they involve information that could influence the statement users' interpretation and evaluation of the future prospects of the business.

Auditing standards define these events and specify that they must be reported either in the tabular portion of the statements (balance sheet, income statement, etc.) or in the notes to the statements, depending on the nature of the events. The effects of subsequent events should be reported in the tabular portion of the statements if they provide additional evidence about conditions that existed at the balance sheet date or affect estimates inherent in the process of preparing the financial statements,

---

[13] AICPA, *Accounting Research Bulletin No. 43,* "Restatement and Revision of Accounting Research Bulletins" (New York, 1953), Chapter 2, Section A. In *ARB No. 6* (April 1940), the CAP recommended unanimously that comparative statements be used. Hatfield had previously recommended their use in his book, *Accounting: Its Principles and Problems* (New York: D. Appleton and Co., 1927).

and, therefore, require adjustments to the financial statements resulting from the estimates. For example, assume that as of the balance sheet date, a company is unaware that collection of one of its major accounts receivable is doubtful. During the interim period between the balance sheet's preparation and publication date, however, the company discovers that the account receivable in question belongs to a company that has declared bankruptcy; thus, collection in full is extremely doubtful. Presumably, the debtor's financial condition was deteriorating throughout the period, and therefore the expected loss should be recognized as of the balance sheet date (assuming an insufficient allowance for doubtful accounts).

Subsequent events should be disclosed in the notes to the statements rather than in the statements themselves if they result from conditions that did not exist at the balance sheet date, arose subsequent to that date, and do not merit adjustment to the current financial statements. Following are examples of such events taken from the Codification of Statements on Auditing Standards:

1. The sale of a bond or capital stock issue.
2. Litigation based on an event subsequent to the date of the balance sheet.
3. Inventory losses due to a casualty occurring after the balance-sheet date.
4. Losses caused by a condition that arose subsequent to the balance sheet date, such as fire or flood.

Many subsequent events do not require consideration in the preparation of the financial statements. These include matters such as changes in the market price of the company's stock, the advent of a strike, new product developments, management changes, or the recognition or decertification of a union.

Disclosure

Full disclosure requires complete reporting of all information relating to the economic affairs of a business to avoid the presentation of misleading financial statements. In addition to the information reported as line items with specific dollar amounts in the tabular portions of the financial statements, full disclosure requires additional information in the notes and schedules that supplement the financial statements.

Disclosure notes are narrative explanations relating to such items as accounting policies used by the company, pension plans, maturity dates on payables and receivables, restrictions relating to long-term debt, and the effects of subsequent events and contingencies (including pendings lawsuits). A note may refer to a single amount in the financial statements, to several amounts, or to a situation that is not directly reflected in any of the statements. Deciding between when a note is needed and when a note is not necessary, is largely a matter of judgment. For example, in Note 5 to its 1989 statements, Merck expands on its outstanding long-term debt, as shown in Exhibit 5–7.

A number of APB *Opinions* and FASB *Statements* require disclosures in the notes to the financial statements. For example, *APB Opinion No. 22,* Disclosure of Accounting Policies, requires that information about important accounting policies adopted by a company, including policy identification and description, be disclosed "in a separate Summary of Significant Accounting Policies preceding the notes to the financial statements or as the initial note." The summary should include policies that involve:

1. The choice of reporting method when several alternatives exist, such as the selection of LIFO to report inventories.
2. Principles and methods peculiar to the industry.
3. Unusual or innovative applications of GAAP.

Supporting schedules often are presented separately or are incorporated into the notes. Supporting schedules are typical for large and complex companies, and in

EXHIBIT 5-7   Loans Payable and Long-Term Debt Note: Note 5 of Merck's 1989 Annual Report

---

5. LOANS PAYABLE AND LONG-TERM DEBT

Loans payable at December 31, 1989, included $229.0 million of unsecured parent Company borrowings. The remainder of the 1989 balance was principally bank borrowings by foreign subsidiaries.

Long-term debt at December 31, 1989, of $117.8 million consisted of pollution control and industrial revenue financing and foreign debt at rates of 6.3% to 10.2%. Of this amount, $39.3 million is due in varying installments through 1994.

EXHIBIT 5-8   Treasury Stock Note: Note 10 of Merck's 1989 Annual Report: Shares in Thousands

---

10. TREASURY STOCK

	1989		1988		1987	
	Shares	Cost	Shares	Cost	Shares	Cost
Balance, January 1	58,784.2	$1,869.9	61,527.2	$1,954.7	46,322.4	$ 993.4
Purchases	2,973.5	208.2	—	—	17,110.2	1,000.0
Issued under stock option and executive incentive plans	(1,641.6)	(52.1)	(2,743.0)	(84.8)	(1,905.4)	(38.7)
Balance, December 31	60,116.1	$2,026.0	58,784.2	$1,869.9	61,527.2	$1,954.7

---

situations where a particular item involves a number of complex changes during the period. For example, Merck summarizes the changes in its treasury stock account for 1989 in Note 10 to its financial statements (partially reproduced in Exhibit 5–8).

Parenthetical notes are used in the financial statements to disclose information such as the method of inventory costing and valuation. For example:

Inventory (FIFO, applied on LCM basis)

Contra items, such as accumulated depreciation and allowance for doubtful accounts, are reported as separate line deductions, parenthetically or in footnotes. Merck relies on footnote disclosure.

The Auditors' Report

The auditors' report also is called the *accountants' report* or the *independent accountants' report.* It is typically the last item presented in the financial statements, although its presentation can, instead, precede the financial reports.

The independent auditors' primary function is to express the auditors' professional opinion on the financial statements. Although the auditors have sole responsibility for all opinions expressed in the auditors' report, company management has the primary responsibility for the financial statements themselves, including the supporting notes. Compilation and presentation of the accounting information and all

EXHIBIT 5-9 Merck's Independent Auditor Report

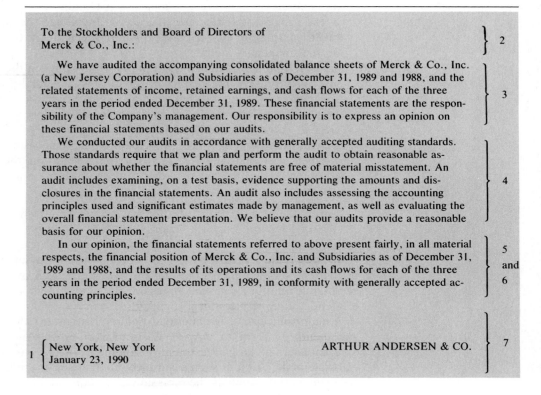

To the Stockholders and Board of Directors of
Merck & Co., Inc.:   } 2

We have audited the accompanying consolidated balance sheets of Merck & Co., Inc.
(a New Jersey Corporation) and Subsidiaries as of December 31, 1989 and 1988, and the
related statements of income, retained earnings, and cash flows for each of the three
years in the period ended December 31, 1989. These financial statements are the responsibility of the Company's management. Our responsibility is to express an opinion on
these financial statements based on our audits.   } 3

We conducted our audits in accordance with generally accepted auditing standards.
Those standards require that we plan and perform the audit to obtain reasonable assurance about whether the financial statements are free of material misstatement. An
audit includes examining, on a test basis, evidence supporting the amounts and disclosures in the financial statements. An audit also includes assessing the accounting
principles used and significant estimates made by management, as well as evaluating the
overall financial statement presentation. We believe that our audits provide a reasonable
basis for our opinion.   } 4

In our opinion, the financial statements referred to above present fairly, in all material
respects, the financial position of Merck & Co., Inc. and Subsidiaries as of December 31,
1989 and 1988, and the results of its operations and its cash flows for each of the three
years in the period ended December 31, 1989, in conformity with generally accepted accounting principles.   } 5 and 6

1 { New York, New York   ARTHUR ANDERSEN & CO.   } 7
    January 23, 1990

supporting text contained in a company's financial statements is company management's concern and responsibility; the auditors, in rendering their opinion, affirm or
disaffirm what management has compiled and presented.

The auditors' report is structured to include an introductory paragraph, a scope
paragraph, and an opinion paragraph.[14] The general look and standard format of an
auditors' report is illustrated in Exhibit 5-9.

Seven required elements in the auditors' report have special significance.

1. Date.
2. Salutation.
3. Identification of the statements examined.
4. Statement of scope of the examination.
5. Opinion introduction.
6. Reference to fair presentation in conformity with generally accepted accounting
   principles.
7. Signature of the CPAs.

Merck's auditor's report appears as Exhibit 5-9, with the seven elements indicated.

When an audit is finished, the auditors are required to draft an opinion paragraph
that best communicates their professional opinion about the company's financial
statements. One of the following four types of opinions is given:

1. *Unqualified opinion*—An unqualified opinion is given when the auditor has
   formed the opinion that the statements present fairly the results of operations,
   financial position, and cash flows in conformance with GAAP and provide reasonable assurance that the financial statements are free of material misstatement.

---

[14] AICPA, "Reports on Audited Financial Statements," *Statement on Auditing Standards No. 58* (New York: AICPA,
1988)

2. *Qualified opinion*—A qualified opinion is given when the requirements for an unqualified opinion are not met and the auditor has limited exceptions to the client's financial statements that do not invalidate the statements as a whole. A qualified opinion must clearly explain the reasons for the exception and its effect on the financial statements.

3. *Adverse opinion*—An adverse opinion is given when the financial statements do not fairly present the results of operations, financial position, and cash flows. Also, material exceptions require an adverse opinion on the statements. In such cases, the statements taken as a whole are not presented in accordance with GAAP. Adverse opinions are rare.

4. *Disclaimer of opinion*—When the auditors have not been able to obtain sufficient competent evidential matter, auditors must state that they are unable to express an opinion (i.e., they issue a disclaimer). Auditors must explain the reasons for not giving an opinion.

Merck's auditors' report, drafted by Arthur Andersen & Co. and dated January 23, 1990, is a standard form report that gives Merck an unqualified opinion. Most opinions are unqualified.

A comprehensive discussion of the responsibilities of independent auditors is beyond the scope of this book. The above summary is provided to describe the range of possible auditors' opinions regarding the extent to which the financial statements of a client company conform to GAAP.

A major purpose of the auditors' opinion is to assure the reader that the financial statements conform to GAAP. Assurance of GAAP conformity is important to external users making investment or lending decisions based on a company's financial statement. Without such assurance, an investor or creditor might be unaware of company actions such as the omission of certain liabilities, inclusion of nonexistent assets, or the misclassification of current and long-term items. The auditors' report should be viewed as a critical part of an annual financial report because it gives credibility to the report.

Usefulness of the Balance Sheet

The balance sheet complements the other financial statements, and in the process, it provides information concerning liquidity, the financial flexibility of an organization, and the basis used to calculate various financial ratios, such as rates of return.

Liquidity was discussed earlier in this chapter under the concept of working capital. Knowledge of a company's working capital provides insight on the organization's liquidity and its ability to pay short-term debts from its current assets.

Liquidity also refers to a company's ability to meet both short- and long-term obligations. Moreover, equity holders are interested in liquidity because it affects dividend payments. Unions examine liquidity to establish bargaining positions. Employees are concerned with the organization's long-run health and, hence, the company's continuing ability to pay wages. Municipalities may seek assurance of corporate liquidity before granting franchise rights, since it could affect area employment.

The balance sheet can also provide insights concerning the risk profile of the business and its flexibility to embark on new ventures. Has the company acquired new businesses? Has it disposed of any? If so, how do these acquisition or divestiture activities relate to the company's mainstream business? Are they doing what they know best? Or are they diversifying merely to reduce risk? Are the company's assets old and nearly fully depreciated or relatively new? Is the organization in a position to finance new activities with relative ease thanks to the fact that its debt level is low?

The lack of financial flexibility played a major role, for example, in the plight of the airlines following deregulation. Most carriers were in a poor position to respond to the new challenges faced. Debt levels from new aircraft purchases were high.

Increased fuel cost, high interest rates, and competitive price cutting reduced income and cash flows. Orders for new, more efficient aircraft were put on hold. Companies were forced to sell assets (for example, Pan American sold major real estate holdings in New York City). Unions accepted cost-cutting wage contracts. And two airlines, Braniff and Continental, declared bankruptcy. Recently Eastern, TWA, and Pan Am have also experienced extensive financial difficulties.

The balance sheet also provides data needed to calculate important financial ratios, including return on equity (ROE), return on assets (ROA), the ratio of total debt to equity (DE), and the number of times interest costs are covered by income before interest and taxes (IC). Merck reports net income of $1,495.4 million, taxes on income of $787.6 and interest costs (in Note 6, not reproduced here) of $53.2 million in 1989. Using this and additional data from Merck's 1989 consolidated balance sheet, provided earlier in Exhibit 5–2, the following ratios can be calculated:

$$ROE = \$1,495.4 \div \$3,520.6 = 0.425 \quad \textit{Net income} \div \textit{total stockholders' equity}$$
$$ROA = \$1,495.4 \div \$6,756.7 = 0.221 \quad \text{''} \qquad \div \textit{total assets}$$
$$DE = \$3,236.1 \div \$3,520.6 = 0.919 \quad \textit{Total liability} \div \textit{total stockholders' equity}$$
$$IC = (\$1,495.4 + \$787.6 + \$53.2) \div \$53.2 = 43.9$$
$$ \textit{net income} \quad \textit{taxes on income} \quad \textit{income cost}$$

A financial analyst would consider the above numbers as a reflection of Merck's strong financial condition.

Limitations of the Balance Sheet

As discussed earlier in this chapter, the values reported in the balance sheet are not all current values. Cash is current, but the amounts for items such as plant and equipment, or at least a major part of those amounts, are costs incurred years ago. Given even a modest level of inflation, combining these numbers into totals, such as total assets, is of questionable value. Ratios such as return on assets reflect a number in the numerator measured in current dollars and a number in the denominator measured in older, historical, dollars. Comparisons between companies can be misleading under such circumstances.

The typical balance sheet also contains many estimated amounts, such as the estimated loss from uncollectible receivables, and the estimate of any liability arising from warranties. Other estimates include: accumulated depreciation, depletion, amortization, income taxes, contingencies, and pension liabilities. Further, the values of certain other items commonly found on balance sheets may be of limited usefulness. Examples include intangible asset values and amounts recorded as deferred tax liabilities.

Finally, certain assets and liabilities are simply omitted entirely from the balance sheet. A brief listing of some of these assets might include the loyalty and morale of the work force, licenses (e.g., a liquor license), and the value of research and development activity. On the liability side, omitted items include certain leases, hazardous waste cleanups required by law, and corporate promises (such as frequent-flier miles). Difficulties in quantifying most of these items and the lack of

CONCEPT REVIEW

1. What requirements must be met before a loss contingency is shown in the balance sheet?
2. Identify an asset or liability valued on the balance sheet at:
   a. Historical cost.
   b. Market value.
   c. An estimate.
3. List several items of value to a firm that are unlikely to appear on the balance sheet. Explain why this is the case.

EXHIBIT 5-10   W. T. Grant Company Net Income, Working Capital, and Cash Flow from Operations for Fiscal Years Ending January 31, 1966 to 1975

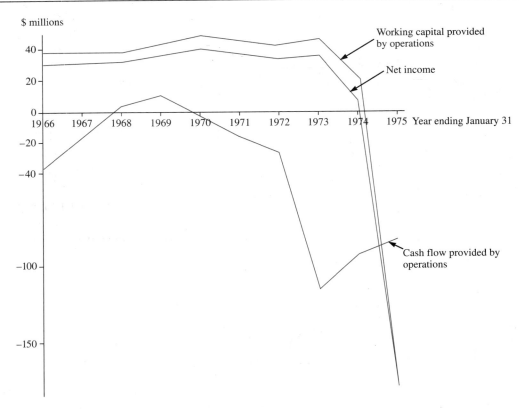

Source: J. Largay and C. Stickney, ''Cash Flow, Ratio Analysis and the W. T. Grant Company Bankruptcy,'' *Financial Analysts Journal,* July–August, 1980, p. 54.

authoritative accounting principles help explain their exclusion from the balance sheet.

THE STATEMENT OF CASH FLOWS

On the morning of October 2, 1975, W. T. Grant, the nation's largest specialty store chain at the time, filed for protection of the Court under Chapter 11 of the National Bankruptcy Act. Shortly before, in 1973, Grant's stock had sold at nearly 20 times earnings. ''But Grant's demise should not have come as a surprise. . . . A careful analysis of the company's cash flows would have revealed the impending problems as much as a decade before the collapse.''[15] Exhibit 5-10 dramatically illustrates the point. Although net income and working capital remained satisfactory through 1973 (as did ratios such as return on equity, turnover ratios, the current ratio, and debt to equity), cash flow from operations had been unhealthy since at least 1966—plunging to a disastrous $100 million deficit figure in 1973.

In addition to the income statement and the balance sheet, *SFAS No. 95* now requires companies to provide a **statement of cash flows (SCF).**[16] Such a statement was recommended earlier by the Financial Executives Institute and by the FASB in *SFAC No. 5.* The basic purpose of the SCF is to provide relevant information about

---

[15] J. Largay and C. Stickney, ''Cash Flow, Ratio Analysis and the W. T. Grant Company Bankruptcy,'' *Financial Analysts Journal,* July–August, 1980, p. 51.

[16] *SFAS No. 95* superseded *APB Opinion No. 19,* which required a statement of changes in financial position. Prior to *SFAS No. 95,* the statement of changes could be prepared on the basis of either working capital or cash. The new statement must be on a cash basis.

EXHIBIT 5-11   *Indirect*

MERCK & CO., INC., AND SUBSIDIARIES
Consolidated Statement of Cash Flows
For the Years Ended December 31, 1989, 1988, and 1987

($ in millions)	1989	1988	1987
Cash flows from operating activities:			
Net income	$1,495.4	$1,206.8	$ 906.4
Adjustments to reconcile net income to cash provided from operations:			
Depreciation and amortization	221.7	204.9	210.0
Deferred taxes	(65.9)	(140.4)	(66.6)
Other	4.3	(104.8)	(24.5)
Net changes in assets and liabilities:			
Accounts receivable	(304.3)	(106.0)	(63.1)
Inventories	(121.6)	(13.9)	(79.8)
Accounts payable and accrued liabilities	155.2	11.8	53.4
Income taxes payable	2.1	155.0	123.0
Noncurrent liabilities	53.2	147.1	80.6
Other	(59.4)	26.3	8.3
Net cash provided by operating activities	1,380.7	1,386.8	1,147.7
Cash flows from investing activities:			
Capital expenditures	(433.0)	(372.7)	(253.7)
Purchase of securities and subsidiaries	(8,848.2)	(2,420.6)	(5,004.3)
Proceeds from sale of securities and subsidiaries	8,659.3	2,677.7	4,938.5
Other	63.9	9.4	(15.1)
Net cash used by investing activities	(558.0)	(106.2)	(334.6)
Cash flows from financing activities:			
Proceeds from issuance of debt	961.1	1,996.8	3,027.6
Payments on debt	(1,115.0)	(2,383.5)	(2,562.9)
Purchase of treasury stock ✓	(208.2)	—	(1,000.0)
Dividends paid to stockholders	(650.3)	(504.7)	(334.9)
Proceeds from exercise of stock options	36.0	29.6	20.5
Other	21.0	31.5	8.4
Net cash used by financing activities	(955.4)	(830.3)	(841.3)
Effect of exchange rate changes on cash and cash equivalents	(36.2)	(4.3)	55.5
Net (decrease) increase in cash and cash equivalents	(168.9)	446.0	27.3
Cash and cash equivalents at beginning of year	854.0	408.0	380.7
Cash and cash equivalents at end of year	$ 685.1	$ 854.0	$ 408.0

a company's inflows and outflows of cash. Cash flow information is needed to help investors and creditors project the future net cash flows of the company being studied. In turn, these projections help a company's investors and creditors assess their own net cash flows from investments in, and loans to, a business. Exhibit 5–11 provides Merck's consolidated statement of cash flows. A later chapter is entirely devoted to the SFC. Only the highlights are given here.

Basic Definitions

A statement of cash flows reports cash flow data; it does not report accrual amounts. However, when the indirect method is used, accruals (such as depreciation) are reported and added to net income to obtain a cash flow figure. The reporting basis of the SEC is "cash plus cash equivalents." Cash equivalents are short-term highly liquid investments such as U.S. Treasury bills, money market funds, and commercial paper. Cash equivalents must be treated consistently over time by a company in its reports, and the reporting definitions should seldom be changed.

Six items specifically identified by *SFAS No. 95* should be reported on the SCF. These six items, or classifications, are listed below, along with their values, from Merck's 1989 consolidated statement of cash flows (Exhibit 5–11).

1. Cash flows from operating activities. $1,380.7
2. Cash flows from investing activities.   (558.0)
3. Cash flows from financing activities.   (955.4)
4. Effect of foreign exchange rate changes.   (36.2)
5. Net increase (or decrease) in cash during the period. (168.9)
6. Noncash investing and financing activities.   none reported

Information about investing and financing activities not involving cash can either be reported in narrative form or summarized in a schedule. (An example would be the acquisition of an asset by issuing stock.) Merck reports no such items for 1989.

The net increase (or decrease) in cash and cash equivalents during the period (Item 5) is the algebraic sum of the first four amounts. Adding this amount to the cash and cash equivalents account balance at the start of the year gives the year-end balance sheet value as of December 31, 1989. Refer to Merck's balance sheet (Exhibit 5–2) and find the ending cash and cash equivalent line entry for 1988 and 1989. The balance being reported as of year-end 1989 has decreased by $168.9 million (685.1 million ending balance for 1989 minus the $854.0 million ending balance for the previous year). Thus, in all cases, the increase (or decrease) in cash and cash equivalents as reported in the SCF can be determined in advance by inspecting the cash and cash equivalent line entry amounts reported in the balance sheet.

The classifications used in the SCF are defined in *SFAS No. 95:*

1. **Cash flows from operating/activities.** This caption includes all cash flows not defined as investing or operating activities. Reported under this classification are both the cash inflows and cash outflows that are related to net income. The usual cash flows under this classification are:

Inflows—cash received from:	Outflows—cash paid for:
• Customers.	• Purchase of goods for resale.
• Interest on receivables.	• Interest on liabilities.
• Dividends from investments.	• Income taxes, duties, and fines.
• Refunds from suppliers.	• Salaries and wages.

Each item should be shown if its value is material.

A gain (or loss) on an extraordinary item or a gain (or loss) from discontinued operations is removed from operating activities by subtracting the gain from (adding the loss to) net income. The full cash effect is included in investing or financing activities, whichever is the dominant source.

The difference between the above inflows and outflows is called the net cash inflow (outflow) from operating activities. Typically, the net amount will be an inflow because, over the long term, cash collections from operations should exceed cash outflows for a going concern.

2. **Cash flows from investing activities.** This major classification is used to report both cash inflows and cash outflows related to acquiring or disposing of operating facilities (plant, property, equipment) and other nonoperating (investment) assets. The *cash outflows* under this classification represent investments of cash by the entity to acquire its noncash assets. The *cash inflows* under this classification occur only when cash is received back from the sale or disposal of prior investments. The typical cash flows under the investing activities are:

Inflows—cash received from:	Outflows—cash paid for:
• Disposal/sale of property, plant, and equipment.	• Acquisition/purchase of property, plant, and equipment.

- ✦ Disposal/sale of investment securities.
- ✦ Collection of a loan (excluding interest, which is an operating activity).

- ✦ Investments in long-term debt and equity securities.
- ✦ Loans to other parties.

- ✦ Acquisition of other assets used in production, such as a patent (excluding inventories, which are included in operating activities).

The difference between the above cash inflows and outflows is called *net cash inflow (outflow) from investing activities.*

3. **Cash flows from financing activities.** This major classification on the statement of cash flows represents both cash inflows and outflows that are related to how cash was raised and deployed in financing the company's business. The cash inflows under this classification represent the financing activities used to obtain cash (long-term capital) for the business. The cash outflows occur only when cash is paid back to the owners and creditors for their earlier investments. The usual cash flows under this classification are:

Inflows—cash received from:

- ✦ Owners—issuing equity securities.
- ✦ Creditors—borrowing on notes, mortgages, and bonds.

Outflows—cash paid to:

- ✦ Owners for dividends and other distributions.
- ✦ Owners for treasury stock purchased.
- ✦ Repayment of principal amounts borrowed (excluding interest which is included in operating activities).

The difference between the above cash inflows and outflows is called *net cash inflows (outflows) from financing activities.*

4. **Effect of foreign exchange rate changes.** This classification applies only to companies that have foreign operations or foreign currency transactions and reports the effect of exchange rate changes on cash balances held in foreign currencies. These changes affect the amount of cash reported on the balance sheet.

5. **Reconciling balances.** *SFAS No. 95* requires the reporting of three related amounts: net increase (decrease) in cash, beginning cash balance, and ending cash balance.

6. **Noncash investing and financing activities.** This caption refers to investing and financing activities involving an exchange of value other than cash. There are two types: the transaction involves no cash (e.g., when settling a debt in full by issuing the company's capital stock to the creditor), and the transaction is partly in cash, (e.g., when a debt is settled with 30% cash and 70% capital stock). These noncash and part-cash activities may be reported either in a separate schedule or disclosed in the notes.

Statement of Cash Flows: Formats

Two formats are available for displaying cash flow information. The difference in formats pertains to the approach used in calculating *net cash flows from operating activities*. Computation and presentation of information pertaining to investing and financing activities are the same regardless of which format is used.

One format is called the **direct method.** Following this method, a company's net cash flow from operating activities is calculated by totaling the individual cash inflows (from customers, interest and dividends on investments, and refunds from suppliers) and deducting individual cash outflows (purchases of goods for resale, salaries and wages, interest on debt obligations, and income taxes. The direct method is favored by the FASB.

The other format is called the **indirect method**. This format starts with the net income and adds back expenses and charges that did not entail cash payments. The more important of these noncash expenses include depreciation, depletion, and amortization charges. Next, items that increase asset values or decrease liability values that have not resulted in corresponding increases or decreases in cash (and yet are involved in the determination of net income) are subtracted. Prime examples are increases in accounts receivable and decreases in accounts payable balances. Increases in accounts receivable from the sale of goods and services represent an increase in net income that is not reflected in cash. Since these sales are already included in net income, the increase in the receivables must be deducted from the net income figure. Increases in liabilities, on the other hand, conserve cash and hence are added to the net income figure.

Merck's SCF is an example of the indirect method. This format is preferred by preparers and analysts, even though the FASB's preference is for the more straightforward direct method format. If a company elects to use the direct method, the operating activity information which would have been reported under the indirect method must appear in a supplementary schedule.

Usefulness of the Statement of Cash Flows

There is general agreement that a statement of cash flows is useful in providing investors, creditors, and other interested parties feedback about cash inflows and outflows for each major activity—operating, investing, and financing. Information about the cash available from various sources for debt payments, dividends, investments by the entity, and the support of future growth is important to decision makers, be they investors or creditors. Moreover, decision makers are particularly interested in the amount of cash a company generates from its operating activities. The operating activities necessarily must be the primary cash source because operations must eventually pay for the company's debts, dividends, and provide for growth. Also, the SCF provides useful information about a company's borrowing patterns and subsequent repayments (its financing activities), new investments by owners, and dividends.

On a broader scale, the SCF also helps decision makers assess the financial strength of a business. In general, financial strength is evidenced by the relationship between the company's assets and liabilities and the company's credit standing with financial institutions and other lenders as reflected in the balance sheet. The SCF complements the information in the balance sheet by focusing on the inflows and outflows of cash.

Analysts think of the statement of cash flows as providing information on whether a company is generating sufficient cash to pay its bills, replace assets, take advantage of new opportunities, and pay the dividends it has declared.[17] In this sense, the SCF is an indispensable complement to the balance sheet.[18] However, it is dangerous to treat this statement in isolation. In any one year, unusual events can occur, which might be interpreted incorrectly or prompt inaccurate evaluations of the company's longer term financial position. A series of cash flow statements covering several years is essential. Further, there is no substitute for a careful analysis based on a complete set of financial statements, plus whatever else is known about a

---

[17] Cash available from operations (plus cash inflows from financing and investing activities) may not be sufficient to replace equipment even if it exceeds depreciation expense due to both inflation and changing technology.

[18] Numerous studies by accounting researchers document the usefulness of previous statements based on a working capital basis. The results of these studies are, in all probability, transferable to the statement of cash flow. Examples of these studies include W. Beaver, "Alternative Accounting Measures as Predictors of Failure," *The Accounting Review*, January 1968, pp. 113–122; and D. Hawkins and W. Campbell, "Equity Valuation: Models, Analysis and Implications," *Financial Executive Research Foundation* (New York: Financial Executives Research Institute, 1978).

particular company. Annual reports are but one source of financial information available to decision makers.

CONCEPT REVIEW

1. What are the major differences between the direct and indirect method for the SCF?
2. How can the net change in cash from the SCF be confirmed using the balance sheet?
3. What are the major headings in a SCF?

SUMMARY OF KEY POINTS

(L.O. 1)   1. The balance sheet reflects the basic accounting identity and the means of financing the organization's assets:

$$\text{Assets} = \text{Liabilities} + \text{Owners' equity.}$$

In the report format, the identity reflects the residual interests of the owners:

$$\text{Assets} - \text{Liabilities} = \text{Owners' equity.}$$

(L.O. 2)   2. The elements of the balance sheet are valued using different approaches, including historical costs, market values, net-realizable values and present values.

(L.O. 3)   3. The working capital of a firm is its current assets less its current liabilities. Together with the working capital ratio (current assets divided by current liabilities), working capital provides information on the financial strength and flexibility of the firm.

(L.O. 4)   4. The ability of a decision maker to use the balance sheet effectively is enhanced by the use of descriptive terminology, comparative statements, the reporting of subsequent events, and informative footnote disclosure.

(L.O. 5)   5. Although the balance sheet provides information on the financial strength and flexibility of a firm, many items either are estimated, omitted, or appear in the statement with amounts of limited usefulness. This situation makes aggregate figures particularly suspect.

(L.O. 6)   6. The direct method approach to the statement of cash flows provides the more logical means of disclosing cash flow information, although the indirect method is favored by many preparers and analysts.

(L.O. 7)   7. The statement of cash flows is designed to provide information on the cash generated (or used) by the operating, investing, and financing activities of a company.

(L.O. 8)   8. The statement of cash flow is particularly valuable in assessing a company's short-term financial strength, but other information is essential in estimating future cash flows including, for example, the trends suggested by several statements of cash flow combined with information such as expected advances in the technology used by the company.

REVIEW PROBLEM

Answer the following questions based on Merck's balance sheet (Exhibit 5–2) and statement of cash flows (Exhibit 5–11).

1. Are they comparative statements?
2. Do the statements include Merck's subsidiaries? Explain.
3. What is the date of the end of the fiscal or reporting year?
4. How many years' data are reported on the required financial statements?

5. What title is used on the SCF?
6. Is the statement that is referred to in (5) based on working capital or on cash?
7. What was the amount of cash and cash equivalents reported at the end of 1989?
8. What was the amount of working capital reported at the end of 1989?
9. What was the income tax obligation at the end of the current year?
10. What percentage of total assets was provided by *(a)* creditors and *(b)* owners?
11. How much did cash and cash equivalents increase (decrease) each year?
12. What item represented the largest use of cash in 1989?
13. What major change represented the largest source of cash in 1989?
14. What kind of opinion did the auditor give? Explain.
15. Who is responsible for the preparation and integrity of the company's financial statements?

SOLUTION
♦

Dollar amounts are in millions.

1. Merck reported comparative balance sheets for 1989 and 1988 and statements of cash flows that encompassed 1989, 1988, and 1987.
2. Yes, all of the financial statements are labeled to include subsidiaries.
3. The fiscal or reporting year ends on each December 31.
4. The statement of cash flows, three years; the balance sheet, two years.
5. Consolidated statement of cash flows.
6. Based on cash and cash equivalents.
7. $685.1 million.
8. Current assets, $3,409.8, minus current liabilities, $1907.3, equals working capital, $1502.5 at the end of 1989.
9. Income taxes payable, $464.8. Deferred income taxes (including noncurrent liabilities), $701.1 at the end of 1989.
10. *(a)* Total assets provided by creditors: total liabilities, ($1,907.3 + $117.8 + $701.2 + $509.9) ÷ total assets ($6,756.7) = 47.9%. *(b)* Total assets provided by owners: total owners' equity, ($5,546.6 − $2,026) ÷ total assets ($6,756.7) = 52.1%.
11. Cash and cash equivalents increased in 1987 by $27.3; and in 1988 by 446.0; and decreased in 1989 by $168.9. See the statement of cash flow.
12. The purchase of securities and subsidiaries, $8,848.2.
13. The sale of securities and subsidiaries.
14. The auditors gave an unqualified opinion because no qualifications were indicated.
15. The management.

KEY TERMS

Assets (188)	Statement of cash flows (210)
Direct method (213)	Statement of financial position (balance
Financial flexibility (188)	sheet) (188)
Indirect method (214)	Working capital (197)
Liabilities (188)	Working capital (or current) ratio (198)
Liquidity (188)	
Owners' equity (188)	

QUESTIONS

1. What is the basic purpose of a balance sheet?
2. What is a balance sheet? Why is it dated differently from the dating of the income statement and the statement of cash flows?
3. Basically, what valuations are reported on the balance sheet?
4. Define assets.
5. Define liabilities.
6. Explain the relationship between the balance sheet and full disclosure.

7. Define current assets and current liabilities and emphasize their interrelationship.
8. Define working capital. What is the working capital ratio?
9. Why aren't market values used exclusively in balance sheets?
10. Is it proper to offset current liabilities against current assets? Explain.
11. What would the "investments and funds" caption cover in a balance sheet?
12. What are operational assets? Distinguish between tangible and intangible operational assets.
13. Why is it sometimes necessary to use the caption "other assets"? Give two examples of items that might be reported under this classification.
14. Explain the term deferred charge.
15. Distinguish between current and noncurrent liabilities. Under what conditions would a noncurrent liability amount be reclassified as a current liability?
16. What is a deferred credit? Explain why this classification is a poor one to use.
17. What is owners' equity? What are the main components of owners' equity?
18. What is a restriction, or appropriation, of retained earnings? How are restrictions and appropriations reported?
19. What is the purpose of the statement of cash flows?
20. Explain the three major captions on the statement of cash flows.
21. What two items are included in cash on the statement of cash flows?
22. What is meant by "noncash investing and financing activities" on the statement of cash flows?
23. Explain the relationship between the balance in the cash account and the statement of cash flows.
24. Explain the position of the accounting profession with respect to use of the terms *reserves, surplus,* and *net profit.* Why is careful attention to terminology important in financial statements?
25. What are comparative financial statements? Why are they important?
26. What is meant by subsequent events? Why are they reported? How are they reported?
27. In general, why are notes to the financial statements important? How does the accountant determine when a note should be included?
28. What is the auditors' report? What are its basic components? Why is it especially important to the statement user?
29. Are the financial statements the representations of the management of the enterprise, the independent accountant, or both? Explain.

EXERCISES

E 5–1
Terminology
(L.O. 3)

Give the best answer for each of the following (explain any qualifications):

1. Which of the following is not a current asset?
   a. Office supplies inventory.
   b. Short-term investment.
   c. Petty cash (undeposited cash).
   d. Cash surrender value of life insurance policies.
2. The distinction between current and noncurrent assets and liabilities is based primarily upon which of the following?
   a. One year, no exceptions.
   b. One year or operating cycle, whichever is shorter.
   c. One year or operating cycle, whichever is longer.
   d. Operating cycle, no exceptions.
3. Under GAAP, what is unexpired insurance usually considered to be?
   a. Noncurrent asset.
   b. Deferred charge.
   c. Prepaid expense.
   d. Short-term investment.
4. What is the meaning of working capital?
   a. Current assets minus current liabilities.
   b. Total current assets.
   c. Capital contributed by stockholders.
   d. Capital contributed by stockholders plus retained earnings.
5. Which of the following is not a current liability?
   a. Accrued (unpaid) interest on notes payable.
   b. Accrued interest on bonds payable.

    c. Rent revenue collected in advance.

    d. Premium on long-term bonds payable, a credit (unamortized).

6. A deficit is synonymous with which item?

    a. A net loss for the current reporting period.

    b. A cash overdraft at the bank.

    c. Negative working capital at the end of the reporting period.

    d. A debit balance in retained earnings at the end of the reporting period.

7. The balance sheet is an expression of which model?

    a. Assets = Liabilities + Owners' equity.

    b. Assets = Liabilities − Owners' equity.

    c. Assets + Liabilities = Owners' equity.

    d. Working capital + Operational assets − Long-term liabilities = Contributed capital.

8. Acceptable usage of the term *reserve* is reflected by which description?

    a. Deduction from an asset to reflect accumulated depreciation.

    b. Description of a known liability for which the amount is estimated.

    c. Restriction or appropriation of retained earnings.

    d. Deduction on the income statement for an expected loss.

9. Which terminology essentially is synonymous with balance sheet?

    a. Operating statement.

    b. Statement of cash flows.

    c. Statement of financial value of the business.

    d. Statement of financial position.

10. The "operating cycle concept" does which of the following?

    a. Causes the distinction between current and noncurrent items to depend on whether they will affect cash within one year.

    b. Permits some assets to be classified as current even though they are more than one year removed from becoming cash.

    c. Is becoming obsolete.

    d. Affects the income statement but not the statement of cash flows.

E 5-2

Valuations on the Balance Sheet

(L.O. 2, 3)

Below left are some items from a typical balance sheet for a corporation. Below right are some brief statements of the valuations usually reported on the balance sheet for specific items.

Required:

Use the code letters given below to the right to indicate the usual valuation reported in the balance sheet. Comment on any doubtful items. Some code letters may be used more than once or not at all. The first item is completed for you as an example.

Balance Sheet Items

1. __C__ Land (held as investment).
2. __B__ Merchandise inventory, FIFO.
3. __D__ Short-term investments.
4. __H__ Accounts receivable (trade).
5. __I__ Long-term investment in bonds of another company (purchased at a discount; the discount is a credit balance).
6. __C__ Plant site (in use).
7. __J__ Plant and equipment (in use).
8. __E__ Patent (in use).
9. __A__ Accounts payable (trade).
10. __G__ Bonds payable (sold at a premium; the premium is a credit balance).
11. __F__ Common stock (par $10 per share) sold at par.
12. __L__ Contributed capital in excess of par.
13. __K__ Retained earnings.
14. __C__ Land (future plant site).
15. __N__ Idle plant (awaiting disposal).
16. __O__ Natural resource.

Valuations Usually Reported

A. Amount payable when due (usually no interest involved because short term).

B. Lower of cost or market.

C. Original cost when acquired.

D. Market value at date of the balance sheet, whether it is above or below cost.

E. Original cost less accumulated amortization over estimated economic life.

F. Par value of the issued shares.

G. Face amount of the obligation plus unamortized premium.

H. Realizable value expected.

I. Principal of the asset less unamortized discount.

J. Cost when acquired less accumulated depreciation.

K. Accumulated income less accumulated losses and dividends.

L. Excess of issue price over par or stated value of common stock.

M. No valuation reported (explain).

N. Expected net disposal proceeds, if below book value, otherwise net book value.

O. Cost less accumulated depletion.

P. None of the above (when this response is used, explain the valuation approach usually used).

E 5-3

Classifications on the Balance Sheet (L.O. 2, 3)

A typical balance sheet has the following subcaptions:

A. Current assets.
B. Investments and funds.
C. Operational assets (property, plant, and equipment).
D. Intangible assets.
E. Other assets.
F. Deferred charges.
G. Current liabilities.
H. Long-term liabilities.
 I. Capital stock (common or preferred).
J. Additional contributed capital.
K. Retained earnings.

Required:

Use the code letters above to indicate the usual classification for each balance sheet item listed below. If an item is a contra amount (i.e., a deduction) under a caption, place a minus sign before the lettered response. The first item is completed for you as an example.

1. __-C__ Accumulated depreciation.
2. __H__ Bonds payable (due in 10 years).
3. __G__ Accounts payable (trade).
4. __B__ Investment in stock of X Company (long-term)
5. __C__ Plant site (in use).
6. __K__ Restriction or appropriation of retained earnings.
7. __A__ Office supplies inventory.
8. __E__ Loan to company president (collection not expected for two years).
9. __K__ Accumulated income less accumulated dividends.
10. __-H__ Unamortized bond discount (on bonds payable; a debit balance).
11. __B__ Bond sinking fund (to retire long-term bonds).
12. __A__ Prepaid insurance.
13. __A__ Accounts receivable (trade).
14. __A__ Short-term investment.
15. __-A__ Allowance for doubtful accounts.
16. __C__ Building (in use).
17. __I__ Common stock (par $10).
18. __A__ Interest revenue earned but not collected.
19. __D__ Patent.
20. __B__ Land, held for investment.
21. __C__ Land, idle plant site held for sale.

E 5-4

Prepare a Classified Balance Sheet (L.O. 1, 2, 3)

The following data, in no particular order, were provided by the accounts of Regal Corporation, December 31, 1991, end of the current reporting year. All amounts are correct, all of the accounts have typical balances, and debits equal credits. The amounts are given in thousands.

Accounts payable (trade)	$ 8
Debt retirement fund (long-term)	10
Accounts receivable	16
Income taxes payable	4
Short-term investments, marketable securities (cost)	10
Bonds payable (long-term)	40
Accumulated depreciation, equipment and furniture	6
Common stock, par $1 (100,000 shares authorized)	70
Cash	20
Retained earnings, January 1, 1991	17
Allowance for doubtful accounts	1
Unearned rent revenue (or rent revenue collected in advance)	2
Cash dividends payable	5
Merchandise inventory (December 31, 1991)	30
Land held for future business site	18
Equipment and furniture	70
Net income for 1991	35
Dividends (cash) declared (a debit)	3
Prepaid expenses (short-term)	1
Unamortized bond premium (bonds payable, a credit)	1
Patent	4
Deferred rearrangement costs	2
Investment in capital stock of Tex Corporation (long-term)	10
Premium on common stock	5

Required:

1. Prepare a complete balance sheet (in thousands).
2. Show computation of the ending balance of retained earnings.

E 5-5
Prepare a Classified Balance Sheet and Compute Ratios
(L.O. 1, 2, 3)

The ledger of The Minnesota Manufacturing Company reflects obsolete terminology, but you find its accounts have been, on the whole, accurately kept. After closing the books at December 31, 1991, the following accounts were submitted to you for preparation of a balance sheet:

Accounts payable	$33,200
Accounts receivable	9,500
Accrued expenses (credit)	800
Bonds payable, 14%	25,000
Capital stock ($100 par)	70,000
Cash	10,000
Earned surplus (to be determined)	xx,xxx
Factory equipment	31,200
Finished goods	12,100
Investments	13,000
Office equipment	9,500
Raw materials	9,600
Reserve for bad debts	500
Reserve for depreciation	9,000
Rent expense paid in advance (a debit)	3,000
Sinking fund	7,000
Land held for future plant site	15,000
Note receivable	6,600
Work in process	23,300

Two thirds of the depreciation relates to factory equipment, one third to office equipment. Of the balance in the investments account, $4,000 will be converted to cash during the coming year; the remainder represents a long-term investment. Rent paid in advance is for the next year. The note receivable is a loan to the company president on October 1, 1991, and is due in 1993 when the principal amount ($6,600) plus 9% interest per annum will be paid to the company. The sinking fund is being accumulated to retire the bonds at maturity.

Required:

1. Prepare a balance sheet using preferred format, classifications, and terminology.
2. Compute (*a*) the amount of working capital and (*b*) the current (working capital) ratio.

E 5-6
Prepare a Classified Balance Sheet Using Preferred Terminology
(L.O. 1, 3)

The following trial balance was prepared by Vantage Corporation as of December 31, 1991. The adjusting entries for 1991 have been made, except for any specifically noted below.

Cash	$15,000	
Accounts receivable	15,000	
Inventories	17,000	
Equipment	22,400	
Land	6,400	
Building	7,600	
Deferred charges	1,100	
Accounts payable		$ 5,500
Note payable, 10%		8,000
Capital stock (par $10)		38,500
Earned surplus		32,500
	$84,500	$84,500

You find that certain errors and omissions are reflected in the above trial balance, including the following:

a. The $15,000 balance in accounts receivable represents the entire amount owed to the company; of this amount, $12,400 is from trade customers, and 5% of that amount is estimated to be uncollectible. The remaining amount owed to the company represents a long-term advance to its president.

b. Inventories include $1,000 of goods incorrectly valued at double their cost (i.e., reported at $2,000). No correction has been recorded. Office supplies on hand of $500 also are included in the balance of inventories.

c. When the equipment and building were purchased new on January 1, 1986 (i.e., 6 years earlier), they had estimated lives of, respectively, 10 and 25 years. They have been depreciated using the straight-line method on the assumption of zero residual values, and depreciation has been credited directly to the asset accounts. Depreciation has been recorded for 1991.

d. The balance in the land account includes a $1,000 payment made as a deposit of earnest money on the purchase of an adjoining tract. The option to buy it has not yet been exercised and probably will not be exercised during the coming year.

e. The interest-bearing note dated April 1, 1991, matures March 31, 1992. Interest on it has been ignored.

f. Common stock shares outstanding, 2,500.

Required:

Prepare a correct balance sheet with appropriate captions and subcaptions. Use preferred terminology and the A = L + OE format. Show the computation of the ending balance in retained earnings.

E 5-7

Prepare An Income Statement and a Balance Sheet

(L.O. 1, 3)

The following adjusted trial balance was prepared by the Denver Corporation at December 31, 1991:

Debits

Cost of goods sold	$230,000
Distribution and administrative expenses (including interest and rearrangement costs)	130,000
Income tax expense	51,500
Cash	44,000
Short-term investments	12,000
Accounts receivable	70,000
Merchandise inventory*	72,000
Office supplies inventory	2,000
Investment in bonds of Sigma Corp. (long-term), cost (market value, $35,000)	33,000
Land (plant site in use)	10,000
Plant and equipment	120,000
Franchise (less amortization)	8,000
Rearrangement costs†	15,000
Idle equipment held for disposal	7,500
Dividends declared and paid during 1991	40,000
	$845,000

Credits

Sales revenue	$490,000
Accumulated depreciation, plant and equipment	40,000
Accounts payable	50,000
Income taxes payable	11,000
Bonds payable	50,000
Allowance for doubtful accounts	3,000
Premium on bonds payable (unamortized)	1,000
Common stock, par $10 (authorized 50,000 shares)	150,000
Excess of issue price over par of common stock	18,000
Retained earnings, 1/1/1991	32,000
	$845,000

* Perpetual inventory system.

† Amortization period is three years; this is the unamortized balance on 12/31/1991.

Required:

1. Prepare a single-step income statement.
2. Prepare a balance sheet using appropriate captions and terminology.

E 5–8
Stockholders' Equity Classifications
(L.O. 2)

Based upon the following information, prepare the stockholders' equity section of the balance sheet for Raleigh Corporation at December 31, 1991.

Preferred stock, par $15, authorized 20,000 shares	$255,000
Cash received above par of preferred stock	15,000
Common stock, nopar, 60,000 shares issued (100,000 shares authorized)	200,000
Retained earnings:	
Unappropriated	80,000
Restricted by special contract	60,000

E 5–9
Analyzing Data and Reporting on the Balance Sheet
(L.O. 1, 3, 4)

Dawson Corporation is preparing its balance sheet at December 31, 1991. The following items are at issue:

a. Note payable, long term, $80,000. This note will be paid in installments. The first installment of $10,000 will be paid August 1, 1992.

b. Bonds payable, 12%, $200,000; at December 31, 1991, unamortized premium amounted to $6,000.

c. Bond sinking fund, $40,000; this fund is being accumulated to retire the bonds at maturity. There is a restriction on retained earnings required by the bond indenture equal to the balance in the bond sinking fund.

d. Rent revenue collected in advance for the first quarter of 1992, $6,000.

e. After the balance sheet date, but prior to issuance of the 1991 balance sheet, one third of the merchandise inventory was destroyed by flood (date, January 13, 1992); estimated loss, $150,000.

f. Ending balance of unappropriated retained earnings (December 31, 1991), $35,000.

Required:

Show by illustration, with appropriate captions, how each of these items should be reported on the December 31, 1991, balance sheet.

E 5–10
Terminology: "Reserves"
(L.O. 1, 3, 4)

The records of High Tech Corporation provided the following selected data on December 31, 1991:

Preferred stock, par $10, 100,000 shares authorized	$400,000
Common stock, no par, 200,000 shares authorized of which 100,000	
are outstanding	300,000
Premium on preferred stock	50,000
Earned surplus at end of 1991 (excluding all	
appropriations)	40,000
Reserves at end of 1991 for:	
Bad debts	11,000
Depreciation	90,000
Patent amortization	6,000
Warranty obligations	14,000
Income tax obligations	31,000
Future plant expansion (management decision plans are	
to remove this appropriation within five years after completion)	70,000
Retirement of bonds payable (required by the bond indenture;	
automatically ends when the bonds are paid)	60,000
Bond sinking fund	60,000

Required:

1. Use preferred terminology and format to prepare the stockholders' equity section of the balance sheet.

2. If any of the above items do not belong in the stockholders' equity section, explain how they should be reported.

E 5–11
Statement of Cash Flows Classification
(L.O. 5, 6)

The main parts of a statement of cash flows are shown below with letter identifications. Next, several transactions are given, preceded by a blank space. Match the transactions with the statement parts by entering a letter in each blank space.

Statement of Cash Flows

A. Cash inflows (outflows) from operating activities.
B. Cash inflows (outflows) from investing activities.
C. Cash inflows (outflows) from financing activities.
D. Not a cash flow.

Transactions

_____ 1. Acquisition of operational assets; paid cash.
_____ 2. Cash dividends declared but not paid.
_____ 3. Proceeds from note payable.
_____ 4. Sale of operational assets.
_____ 5. Loan on note receivable.
_____ 6. Purchase of a long-term security as an investment.
_____ 7. Collections on notes receivable (principal only).
_____ 8. Change in inventory.
_____ 9. Depreciation expense.
_____ 10. Payment of debt, 60% cash and 40% stock issued.
_____ 11. Issuance of the company's capital stock, for cash.
_____ 12. Sales revenue, cash.
_____ 13. Purchase of treasury stock, cash.
_____ 14. Payment on notes payable.
_____ 15. Paid cash dividend.

E 5–12
Prepare a Statement of Cash Flows
(L.O. 5, 6)

The records of Ranger Company provided the selected data given below for the reporting period ended December 31, 1991.

Balance sheet:

Paid cash dividend	$ 10,000
Established an external construction fund at 8% interest (building)	60,000
Increased inventory of merchandise	14,000
Borrowed on a long-term note	25,000
Acquired five acres of land for a future site for the company; paid in full by issuing 3,000 shares of Ranger capital stock, par $10, when the quoted market price per share was $15	—
Increase in prepaid expenses	3,000
Decrease in accounts receivable	7,000
Payment of bonds payable in full	97,000
Increase in accounts payable	5,000
Cash from disposal of old operational assets (sold at book value)	12,000
Decrease in rent receivable	2,000

Income statement:

Sales revenue	$400,000
Rent revenue	10,000
Cost of goods sold	(190,000)
Depreciation expense	(20,000)
Remaining expenses	(97,000)
Net income	$103,000

Required:

Prepare a statement of cash flows (in thousands). Use the direct method.

E 5–13
Recast a Deficient Statement of Cash Flows
(L.O. 5, 6, 7)

The following statement was incorrectly prepared by Vista Corporation.

VISTA CORPORATION
Cash Statement
December 31, 1991

Cash received:
  From operations:
    Net income $102,000
      Depreciation expense   40,000
      Amortization of patent   9,000
      Decrease in accounts receivable balance   5,000
      Increase in inventory balance . . . . (10,000)
      Increase in wages payable balance   4,000
    Machinery, old (sold at book value on credit)   7,000
    Long-term note given for land purchased   25,000
        Total funds received $182,000

Cash spent:
    Retirement of mortgage . . . . $ 60,000
    Cash dividends   20,000
    Machinery (new)   50,000
    Acquired land; issued capital stock in full payment
      (6,000 shares, par $5)*   36,000
    Invested in capital stock of Bittle Corporation   10,000
    Increase in cash balance   6,000
        Total funds spent $182,000

Income statement:
    Sales revenue $320,000
    Cost of goods sold . . . . (120,000)
    Depreciation expense . . . . (40,000)
    Amortization of patent . . . .   (9,000)
    Salaries and wages . . . . (11,000)
    Remaining expenses (all cash) . . . . (38,000)
        Net income $102,000

* Market price per share, $6.

Required:
Using the direct method, recast the above statement (in thousands.)

PROBLEMS

P 5-1
Classification on the
Balance Sheet
(L.O. 1)

Typical balance sheet classifications along with a code letter for each classification are as follows:

A. Current assets.
B. Investments and funds.
C. Operational assets, tangible (property, plant, and equipment).
D. Intangible assets.
E. Other assets.

F. Deferred charges.
G. Current liabilities.
H. Long-term liabilities.
I. Capital stock.
J. Additional contributed capital.
K. Retained earnings.

Typical balance sheet items are as follows:

1. __A__ Cash (*example*)
2. __B__ Cash set aside to meet long-term purchase commitment.
3. __C__ Land (used as plant site).

4. __G__ Accrued salaries.
5. __B__ Investment in the capital stock of another company (long-term; not a controlling interest).

6. __A__ Inventory of damaged goods.
7. __E__ Idle plant being held for disposal.
8. __B__ Investment in bonds of another company.
9. __B__ Cash surrender value of life insurance policy.
10. __O__ Goodwill.
11. __C__ Natural resource (timber tract).
12. __-A__ Allowance for doubtful accounts.
13. __E__ Stock subscriptions receivable (no plans to collect in near future).
14. __F__ Organization costs.
15. __-H__ Discount on bonds payable.
16. __G__ Service revenue collected in advance.
17. __G__ Accrued interest payable.
18. __-D__ Accumulated amortization on patent.
19. __A__ Prepaid rent expense.
20. __A__ Short-term investment (common stock).
21. __G__ Rent revenue collected but not earned.
22. __K__ Net of accumulated revenues, gains, expenses, losses, and dividends.

23. __G__ Trade accounts payable.
24. __G__ Current maturity of long-term debt.
25. __B__ Land (held for speculation).
26. __G__ Notes payable (short-term).
27. __B__ Special cash fund accumulated to build plant five years hence.
28. __H__ Bonds issued—to be paid within six months out of bond sinking fund.
29. __B__ Long-term investment in rental building.
30. __D__ Copyright.
31. __-C__ Accumulated depreciation.
32. __F__ Deferred plant rearrangement costs.
33. __D__ Franchise.
34. __A__ Revenue earned but not collected.
35. __H__ Premium on bonds payble (unamortized).
36. __I__ Common stock (at par value).
37. __A__ Petty cash fund.
38. __-K__ Deficit.
39. __J__ Contributed capital in excess of par.
40. __K__ Earnings retained in the business.

Required:

Enter the appropriate code letter for each item to indicate its usual classification on the balance sheet. When it is a contra item (i.e., a deduction), place a minus sign before the lettered response.

(AICPA adapted)

P 5-2
Redraft a Deficient
Balance Sheet: Reserves
(LO. 1, 2, 3)

The balance sheet given below, which was submitted for review, has been prepared for inclusion in the published annual report of the Font Company for the year ended December 31, 1991.

FONT COMPANY
Balance Sheet
December 31, 1991
(in thousands)

Assets

Current:			
Cash			$ 2,000
Accounts receivable		$4,050	
Less: Reserve for bad debts		50	4,000
Inventories—at the lower of cost (determined by the first-in, first-out method) or market			3,250
Total current			9,250
Investment in land			300
Fixed:			
Land—at cost		400	
Buildings, machinery and fixtures—at cost	$4,000		
Less: Reserves for depreciation	1,490	2,510	2,910
Deferred charges and other assets:			
Cash surrender value of life insurance		20	
Prepaid costs of major plant rearrangements		15	
Plant assets held for early resale		30	65
Total assets			$12,525

Liabilities

Current:

Notes payable to bank	$ 550
Current maturities of first-mortgage note	600
Accounts payable—trade	2,100
Reserve for income taxes for the year ended 12/31/1991	500
Accrued expenses	750
	$ 4,500

Funded debt:

9% first-mortgage bonds payable in annual installments of $600	$4,200	
Less: Current maturity	600	3,600

Reserves:

Reserve for various unexpected damages in the future on uninsured assets	50	
Reserve for possible future inventory losses	300	
Reserve for general contingencies	500	
Reserve for additional federal income taxes that may occur	100	950

Capital:

Common stock—authorized, issued and outstanding 100,000 shares of $10 par value	1,000	
Capital surplus paid in	300	
Earned surplus	2,175	3,475
Total liabilities		$12,525

Additional Information:

a. The reserve for damages was set up by a debit to 1991 expense and a credit to the reserve for damages possibly payable by the company as a defendant in a lawsuit in progress at the balance sheet date. The lawsuit was subsequently settled for $50,000 prior to issuance of the statement.

b. The reserve for possible future inventory losses was set up in prior years by the board of directors by debits to earned surplus and credits to the reserve. No change occurred in the account during the current fiscal year.

c. The reserve for contingencies was set up by debits to earned surplus and credits to the reserve over a period of several years by the board of directors to provide for a possible future recession in general business conditions.

d. The reserve for federal income taxes was set up in a prior year by a debit to earned surplus and a credit to the reserve. It relates to additional taxes the Internal Revenue Service contends the company owes. The company has evidence that suggests no payment will be required.

e. The capital surplus consists of the difference between the par value of $10 per share of capital stock and the price at which the stock was actually issued.

Required:

1. Redraft the above balance sheet using appropriate format, major captions, subcaptions, titles, and terminology. Use thousands of dollars. Report both appropriated and unappropriated retained earnings amounts.
2. What is (*a*) the amount of working capital and (*b*) the working capital ratio?
3. Explain when and how the four reserves will have a balance of zero.

(AICPA adapted)

P 5–3
Prepare Balance Sheet
Analytical Questions
(L.O. 1, 2, 3, 4)

The following data were provided by the accounts of Fuere Corporation, December 31, 1991, end of the current reporting year.

Cash	$ 16,000
Accounts receivable, trade	37,000
Short-term investment in marketable securities (cost $42,000)	40,000
Inventory of merchandise, FIFO	95,000
Prepaid expense (short-term)	1,000
Bond sinking fund (to pay bonds at maturity)	35,000
Advances to suppliers (short-term)	4,000
Dividends (cash) declared during 1992	10,000
Rent receivable	2,000
Investment in stock of Life Systems Corporation (long-term, at cost, which approximates market)	22,000
Unamortized discount on bonds payable	3,000
Loans to employees (company president; payment date uncertain)	25,000
Land (building site in use)	30,000
Building	450,000
Equipment	60,000
Franchise (used in operations)	12,000
Deferred equipment rearrangement cost (long-term)	4,000
Total debits	$846,000
Mortgage payable, long-term	$ 50,000
Accounts payable, trade	6,000
Dividends (cash) payable (payable March 1, 1992)	10,000
Deferred rent revenue	3,000
Interest payable	4,000
Accumulated depreciation, building	210,000
Accumulated depreciation, equipment	20,000
Allowance for doubtful accounts	2,000
Bonds payable (maturity 1999)	100,000
Common stock, nopar (50,000 shares outstanding)	200,000
Preferred stock, par $10	80,000
Premium on preferred stock	16,000
Retained earnings, January 1, 1991	17,000
Net income for 1991	88,000
Appropriation of retained earnings for plant expansion (set up prior to 1991)	40,000
Total credits	$846,000

Required:

1. Prepare a complete balance sheet. Assume all amounts are correct and round to the nearest thousand dollars. Use the account titles as given. Show computation of the ending balance in retained earnings and include any restrictions on retained earnings on the statement.
2. Interpretation—Refer to your response to (1) and respond to the following:
   a. Give the amount of working capital and the working capital ratio.
   b. Give the amount of total retained earnings.
   c. By what percent was the building depreciated?
   d. What were the per share issue prices of the preferred and common stock?
   e. Give the entry that was made to record the 1991 dividend declaration.
   f. Give the entry that was made for the appropriation of retained earnings.
   g. Give the entry that probably was made to record the issuance of the (1) preferred stock and (2) common stock. Assume cash transactions.
   h. Give the entry that was made for the advances to suppliers. Assume cash transactions.
   i. Give the adjusting entry that probably was made for rent revenue receivable.
   j. Give the adjusting entry that probably was made for deferred rent revenue.
   k. Give the probable closing entry for net income.

P 5–4
Income Statement and the Balance Sheet—Obsolete Terminology
(L.O. 1, 2, 3, 4)

The adjusted trial balance for Amana Corporation, and other related data, at December 31, 1991, are given below. Although the company uses obsolete terminology, the amounts are correct (but certain amounts may have to be reported separately). Assume that a perpetual inventory system is used.

AMANA CORPORATION
Adjusted Trial Balance
December 31, 1991

Debits

Cash	$ 38,600
Land (used for building site)	29,000
Cost of goods sold	125,500
Short-term securities (stock of Sanders Co.)	42,000
Goodwill (unamortized cost)	12,000
Merchandise inventory	29,000
Office supplies inventory	2,000
Patent	7,000
Operating expenses	55,000
Income tax expense	17,500
Bond discount (unamortized)	7,500
Prepaid insurance	900
Building (at cost)	150,000
Land (held for speculation)	31,000
Accrued interest receivable	300
Accounts receivable (trade)	22,700
Note receivable, 10% (long-term investment)	20,000
Cash surrender value of life insurance policy	9,000
Deferred store rearrangement costs (assume a deferred charge)	6,000
Dividends, paid cash during 1991	15,000
Prior period adjustment (correction of error from prior year—no income tax effect)	15,000
	$635,000

Credits

Reserve for bad debts	$ 1,100
Accounts payable (trade)	15,000
Revenues	245,000
Reserve for income taxes	7,500
Note payable (short-term)	12,000
Common stock, par $10, authorized 50,000 shares	100,000
Reserve for depreciation, building	90,000
Retained earnings, 1/1/1991	37,000
Accrued wages	2,100
Reserve for estimated damages (set up in 1990)	10,000
Premium on common stock	15,000
Reserve for patent amortization	4,000
Cash advance from customer	3,000
Accrued property taxes	800
Note payable (long-term)	16,000
Rent revenue collected in advance	1,500
Bonds payable, 11% ($25,000 due 6/1/92)	75,000
	$635,000

Additional information (no accounting errors are involved):

a. Market value of the short-term marketable securities, $44,000.
b. Merchandise inventory is based on FIFO, lower of cost or market (LCM).
c. Goodwill is being amortized (i.e., written off) over a 20-year period. The amortization for 1991 has already been recorded (as a direct credit to the goodwill account and a debit to expense). Amortization of other intangibles is recorded in this manner except for the patent (a contra account is used for it).
d. Reserve for income taxes represents the estimated income taxes payable at the end of 1991. Reserve for estimated damages was recorded as a credit to this reserve account and a debit to retained earnings during 1990. The $10,000 was the estimated amount of damages that would have to be paid as a result of a damage suit against the company. At December 31, 1991, the appeal was still pending. The $10,000 represents an appropriation, or restriction, placed on retained earnings by management.
e. Operating expenses as given include interest expense, and revenues include interest and investment revenues.

f. The cash advance from customer was for a special order that will not be completed and shipped until March 1992; the sales price has not been definitely established because it is to be based on cost (no revenue should be recognized for 1991).

Required:

1. Prepare a single-step income statement and a separate retained earnings statement.
2. Prepare a balance sheet including appropriate disclosures. Use preferred terminology, captions, subcaptions, and format.

P 5–5

COMPREHENSIVE PROBLEM
♦

Income Statement and
Balance Sheet—
Disclosure
(L.O. 1, 2, 3, 4)

*reported in separate
section after
Long-term liabilities:*
*- Deferred revenues
(collected in advance)*
*- long term deferred
income taxes*
*- deferred investment
tax credit*

The adjusted trial balance for Deck Manufacturing Corporation at December 31, 1991, is given below in no particular order. Debits and credits are not indicated; however, debits equal credits. All amounts are correct. Assume the usual type of balance in each account and a perpetual inventory system, FIFO, LCM.

Work in process inventory . . . *Inventory . . . current assets* . . .	$ 29,000
Accrued interest on notes payable . . . *current liab.* . . .	1,000
Accrued interest receivable . . . *" . . . asset* . . .	1,200
Accrued income on short-term investments . . . *" . . . " .*	1,000
Common stock, nopar, authorized 100,000 shares, issued 40,000 . . . *Retained Earn.*	150,000
Cash in bank . . .	30,000
Trademarks (unamortized cost) *Operational asset = Intangible*	1,400
Land held for speculation . . . *Investments & Funds*	27,000
Supplies inventory . . . *Inventory*	600
Goodwill (unamortized cost) . . . *Intangible*	18,000
Raw materials inventory . . . *Inventory*	13,000
Bond sinking fund . . . *Investments & Funds*	10,000
Accrued property taxes . . . *Current liab.*	1,400
Accounts receivable (trade) . . .	29,000
Accrued wages . . . *current liab.*	2,100
Mortgage payable (due in three years) . . . *long term . . . look*	10,000
Building . . . *P.P.&E*	130,000
Prepaid rent expense . . . *Current asset*	1,700
Organization expenses (unamortized cost—assume a deferred charge) . *Other asset*	7,800
Deposits (cash collected from customers on sales orders to be delivered next quarter; no revenue yet recognized) . . . *Unearned revenue - current liability*	1,000
Long-term investment in bonds of Kaline Corp. (at cost) *Investment & Funds*	50,000
Patents (unamortized cost) . . . *Intangible*	14,000
Reserve for bond sinking fund* . . . *+ Retained earnings*	10,000
Reserve for depreciation, office equipment *> contra account of PP&E*	1,600
Reserve for depreciation, building . . .	5,000
additional paid-in = Premium on preferred stock *+ owner's equity*	8,000
Cash on hand for change . . .	400
Preferred stock, par $100, authorized 5,000 shares, 10% noncumulative, nonconvertible	60,000
Precollected rent income . . . *unearned revenue - current liability*	900
Finished goods inventory . . . *Inventory*	43,000
Note receivable (short-term) . . . *current asset*	4,000
Bonds payable, 12% (due in 6 years) . . . *long-term liab.*	50,000
Accounts payable (trade) . . .	17,000
Reserve for bad debts . . . *Contra account of A/c*	1,400
Notes payable (short-term) . . .	7,000
Office equipment . . . *P.P.&E*	25,000
Land (used as building site) . . . *P.P.&E*	8,000
Short-term investments (at cost) . . .	15,500
Retained earnings, unappropriated (1/1/1991) . *beginning*	13,200
Cash dividends on preferred and common stock declared and paid during 1991 *minus from retained earning*	20,000
Revenues during 1991 . . . *I/S*	500,000
Cost of goods sold for 1991 . . . *I/S*	300,000
Expenses for 1991 (including income taxes) . . . *I/S*	100,000
Income taxes payable . . . *Current liab.*	40,000

* This is a restriction on retained earnings required by the bond indenture equal to the bond sinking fund that is being accumulated to retire the bonds.

Required:

1. Prepare a single-step income statement; use preferred terminology. To compute EPS, deduct $6,000 of net income as an allocation to nonconvertible preferred stock.

2. Prepare a complete balance sheet; use preferred terminology, format, captions and subcaptions.
3. Assume that between December 31, 1991, and issuance of the financial statements, a flood damaged the finished goods inventory in an amount estimated to be $20,000. This event has not been and should not have been recorded in 1991. However, disclosure in the 1991 statements is required. Prepare the necessary disclosure.

P 5–6
Prepare a Statement of Cash Flows Showing a Net Loss
(L.O. 5, 6)

At the end of the current reporting year, December 31, 1991, Felch Company's executives were very concerned about the ending cash balance of $4,000 (the beginning cash balance of $34,000 also had been considered serious at that time).

During 1991, management undertook numerous actions to attain a better cash position. In view of the decreasing cash balance, they asked the chief accountant to prepare a cash flow report (for the first time). The following information was developed from the accounting records:

a. Debt
   (1) Borrowing on long-term (LT) note, $10,000.
   (2) Payments on maturing long-term debt, $110,000.
   (3) Settled short-term debt of $50,000 by issuing Felch capital stock at par (which approximated market value).
   (4) Increase in accounts payable, $20,000.
b. Cash payments:
   (1) Regular cash dividends, $18,000.
   (2) Purchase of new operational assets, $22,000.
c. Cash received:
   (1) Sold and issued Felch capital stock, $11,000.
   (2) Sold old operational assets at their book value, $1,000.
   (3) Sold investment (long-term) in stock of Tech Corporation and made the following entry:

Cash	90,000	
Loss on sale of investment	30,000	
Investment in Tech Corporation stock		120,000

d. Relevant balance sheet accounts:
   (1) Decrease in income tax payable, $10,000.
   (2) Decrease in inventory, $38,000.
   (3) Increase in accounts receivable, $5,000.
e. Income statement data:

Sales	$ 160,000
Cost of goods sold	(150,000)
Depreciation expense	(58,000)
Amortization of patent	(2,000)
Income tax expense	(4,000)
Remaining expenses	(41,000)
Loss on sale of long-term investment	(30,000)
Net income (loss)	$(125,000)

Required:
Based on the above data, prepare a statement of cash flows (in thousands). Use the direct method.

P 5–7

COMPREHENSIVE PROBLEM
♦

Prepare Statement of Cash Flows—Analytical Questions
(L.O. 5, 6)

Joy Brown, the president of Xonic Corporation, has asked the company controller for a statement of cash flows for the reporting year just ended, December 31, 1991. The company has not previously prepared such a statement. The following balance sheet data has been obtained from the accounting records.

a. Cash account balances: January 1, 1991, $43,000; December 31, 1991, $18,000.
b. The balance in accounts receivable decreased by $10,000 during the year. Wages payable decreased by $5,000.
c. Inventory increased $9,000, and accounts payable increased $3,000 during the year.
d. Income tax payable increased $4,000 during the year.
e. During December 1991, the company settled a $10,000 note payable by issuing shares of its own capital stock with equivalent value.
f. Cash expenditures during 1991 were (1) payment of long-term debts, $64,000; (2) pur-

chase of new operational assets, $74,000; (3) payment of a cash dividend, $16,000; and (4) purchase of land as an investment, $25,000.

g. Sale and issuance of shares of Xonic capital stock for $20,000 cash.
h. Issuance of a long-term mortgage note, $30,000.
i. Sale of some old operational assets; the following entry was made:

Cash	5,000	
Accumulated depreciation	12,000	
Operational asset		15,000
Gain on sale of operational assets		2,000

Income statement data:

Sales revenue	$ 295,000
Cost of goods sold	(140,000)
Depreciation expense	(12,000)
Patent amortization	(1,000)
Income tax expense	(17,000)
Remaining expenses	(42,000)
Gain on sale of operational assets	2,000
Net income	$ 85,000

Required:

Prepare a statement of cash flows in thousands of dollars using the direct method.

CASES

C 5–1
Criticize a Deficient
Balance Sheet
(L.O. 1, 2, 4)

The president of Datra Manufacturing Company is a personal friend. She reports that the company has never had an audit and is contemplating having one principally because she suspects that the financial statements are not well prepared. As an example, the president hands you the following statement for review:

DATRA MANUFACTURING COMPANY
Balance Sheet
Year Ended December 31, 1991

Resources

Liquid assets:

Cash in banks	$ 8,500
Receivables from various sources net of reserve for bad debts ($200)	5,000
Inventories	10,000
Cash for daily use	500
Total	$24,000

Permanent assets:

Treasury stock, par	4,000
Fixed assets (net of depreciation)	26,000
Grand total	$54,000

Obligations and Net Worth

Short-term:

Trade payables	$ 3,500
Salaries accrued	500
Total	$ 4,000

Fixed:

Mortgage	8,000

Net worth:

Capital stock, par $10	$25,000
Earned surplus	17,000
Total	$42,000
Grand total	$54,000

Required:

1. List and explain your criticisms of the above statement.
2. Using the above data, prepare a balance sheet that meets your specifications in terms of format, terminology, and classification of data. If necessary, make realistic assumptions. *Hint:* Total assets are $50,000.

C 5-2
Criticize and Redraft a Deficient Balance Sheet
(L.O. 1, 2, 3, 4)

The most recent balance sheet of Blackstone Corporation appears below:

BLACKSTONE CORPORATION
Balance Sheet
For the Year Ended December 31, 1991

Assets

Current:

Cash	$ 23,000	
Marketable securities	10,000	
Accounts receivable	15,000	
Merchandise	31,000	
Supplies	5,000	
Stock of Co. Wilmont (not a controlling interest)	17,000	$101,000

Investments:

Cash surrender value of life insurance	$ 45,000	
Treasury stock (2,500 shares)	37,500	82,500

Tangible:

Building and land ($10,000)	$86,000		
Less: Reserve for depreciation	40,000	$ 46,000	
Equipment	$20,000		
Less: Reserve for depreciation	15,000	5,000	51,000

Deferred:

Prepaid expenses	$ 2,000	
Discount on bonds payable	3,000	5,000
Total		$239,500

Debt and Capital

Current:

Accounts payable	$ 16,000	
Reserve for income tax	17,000	
Customers' accounts with credit balance	100	$ 33,100

Fixed (interest paid at year-end):

Bonds payable (due at end of 1999), 10%	$ 45,000	
Mortgage, 11%	12,000	57,000
Reserve for bad debts		900

Capital:

Capital stock, authorized 10,000 shares, par $15	$117,000	
Earned surplus	22,500	
Capital surplus	9,000	148,500
Total		$239,500

Required:

1. List and explain your criticisms of the above statement.
2. Prepare a complete balance sheet; use appropriate format, captions, and teminology. Deduct treasury stock from stockholders' equity.

C 5-3
Sherwin-Williams: Analysis of Actual Financial Statements
(L.O. 2, 4, 6, 7)

The following questions deal with Sherwin-Williams's balance sheet and statement of cash flows (located at the end of the text).

a. Did Sherwin-Williams increase its dividend in 1990?
b. Does Sherwin-Williams use the direct or indirect method of presenting its statement of cash flows?
c. What was Sherwin-Williams's total debt-to-equity ratio as of December 31, 1990? What is a major limitation of this figure?
d. Why are depreciation and amortization added to net income to obtain cash flow from operations?
e. Depreciation and amortization for 1990 amounted to $44,507,000 in the statement of cash flows. However the allowance for depreciation on Sherwin-Williams's balance sheet (which includes amortization) increased by $26,635,000 ($314,508,000–$287,873,000). Why aren't the two figures the same?

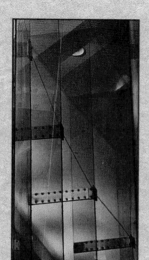

Interest: Concepts of Future and Present Value

After you have studied this chapter, you will:

1. Understand the time value of money, which underlies all interest calculations and a wide range of accounting issues.

2. Understand the difference between simple and compound interest.

3. Recognize the difference between future value and present value as these terms apply to both single payment amounts and annuities.

4. Understand the distinction between an ordinary annuity and an annuity due.

5. Be able to compute the following values, using future and present value tables:

   a. Future value of a single payment.
   b. Present value of a single payment.
   c. Future value of an annuity.
   d. Present value of an annuity.

6. Be able to solve complex time value problems that involve multiple elements by combining present and future value computations for both single payment and annuity amounts. (Refer to the appendix at the end of the chapter.)

◆
_____

INTRODUCTION
◆

D uring the second quarter of 1986, Standard Oil wrote off oil and gas reserves in the Gulf of Mexico worth $200 million. The company believed it would not recover all the costs it had invested in these balance sheet assets. In establishing the new and lower asset values, Standard Oil reduced the write-down by the total cash it expected to receive from marketing these reserves in the years ahead.

In the previous year, Diamond Shamrock Oil Company wrote down its oil and gas reserves in Sumatra, Indonesia, by $600 million. But rather than basing the write-down, as Standard Oil did, on the asset's initial cost as shown in the balance sheet less the total expected future cash flows, Diamond Shamrock discounted its future cash flows. Hence, if Diamond Shamrock expected to obtain $1 million in cash a year from now, the company concluded that, today, that amount should be valued at less than $1 million.[1]

The difference in treatment of essentially the same type of situation led to radically different valuation effects for each company's assets, as well as to income measures, that are not easily comparable between the two companies. This chapter suggests that discounting future cash flows, as Diamond Shamrock did, is the more logical procedure.

_____

◆

TIME VALUE OF MONEY
◆

In general business terms, **interest** is defined as the cost of using money over time. This definition is in close agreement with the definition used by economists, who prefer to say that interest represents the **time value of money**.

Thinking forward in time, $100 in hand today will be worth more in one year's time than a second $100 received one year from today. The assumption is that today's dollars can be put to work earning interest. Thus, today's money has a future value equal to its principal (face amount) plus whatever interest can be earned over a given period of time, one year in this case. If the interest rate on money invested for one year is 10%, then the **future value** of today's $100 principal at the end of 12 months is $110 ($100 principal + $10 interest). Numerically, $110 = $100 + $100(.10).

Now for that second $100, the amount coming in at the end of 12 months—this is "tomorrow"s money," that is, dollars scheduled to become available (or scheduled for payment) at some date in the future, whether next week, next year, or some time during the next century. Just as today's money has a future value, calculated by adding interest to principal, tomorrow's money has a **present value**, calculated by subtracting interest. For example, if the interest rate on money invested for one year is 10%, then the present value of $110 a year from now is the principal necessary to invest today to obtain $110 in a year. We already know this required principal is $100, since $100 + $100 (.10) yields $110 in one year. Suppose, instead, that $100 is to be received in one year. What is its present value? If the interest rate is again 10%, the present value is the principal needed today to yield $100 in one year at 10%. This principal amount is $91 because $91 plus 10% of $91 gives (approximately) $100 in one year ($91 principal + $9 interest). Numerically, $100 = $91 + $91(.10).

The purpose of this chapter is to provide the concepts necessary to facilitate measuring the time value of money and its impact on business. Accounting uses

_____

[1] Interest, particularly when compounded (interest on interest as well as on principal), has large and often underestimated effects. For example, consider the $24 paid to the Indians for the Island of Manhattan in 1626 by Peter Minuit of the Dutch West India Company. Historians tell us this was a real bargain. However, today that $24 invested at 10% compounded yearly yields a value of $2.5 quadrillion.

many applications of the concepts of present and future value. Several of the more prominent applications are covered in this book:

+ Receivables and payables.
+ Bonds.
+ Leasing.
+ Pensions.
+ Asset valuation.

In addition to its accounting applications, the time value of money is also a featured topic in other school disciplines, such as finance and economics.

BASIC INTEREST CONCEPTS

Concept of Interest

Interest is based on the *time value of money* in either borrowing or lending. It is the ''rent'' paid or collected for the use of money. Interest is measured by the excess of resources (usually cash) received or paid over the amount of resources loaned or borrowed at an earlier date. The amount loaned or borrowed is called the principal. The cost of the excess resources to the borrower for the use of the money is called interest expense. The benefit of the excess resources by the lender of the money is called interest revenue.

To illustrate the measurement of interest in a simple situation, assume the Debont Company borrowed $10,000 cash and promised to repay $11,200 one period later. The interest on this contract is:

Resources repaid at maturity	$11,200
Resources borrowed	10,000
Interest	$ 1,200

Analysis:	
Interest in dollars	$ 1,200
Interest rate for the one period ($1,200 ÷ $10,000)	12%

In addition to straightforward borrowing/lending situations, interest calculations and the time value of money are key considerations, for example, in negotiating business transactions with suppliers of goods and services that call for payment over one or more future time periods. Also, interest and time value considerations are part of the decision-making process in matters such as expenditures for business investments and the acquisition of operating assets; both types of expenditures are expected to produce returns over one or more future periods.

Consistent Interest Periods and Rates

Interest usually is expressed as a *rate per year,* such as 12%. However, contracts that require interest often specify interest payment periods of less than one year, such as monthly, quarterly, or semiannually.[2] Thus, a 12% annual interest rate may be specified as 1% per month, 3% quarterly, or 6% semiannually, assuming that interest is paid monthly, quarterly, or semiannually, respectively. However, if compound interest is specified, the compound interest rate must be clearly specified. If an interest rate is specified with no indication of an interest period of less than one year, annual compounding should be assumed.[3] The amount of interest in investing

---

[2] Throughout this textbook and in the problem materials, short-term periods are used to facilitate comprehension. Also, for instructional convenience, amounts usually are rounded to the nearest dollar.

[3] In recent years, the term *annual percentage rate (APR)* has come into common usage, especially in conjunction with consumer lending and consumer product financing. *Rate per year, annual rate,* and *annual percentage rate* are synonymous terms.

and financing transactions is determined by the principal amount, interest rate, and number of interest periods.

Simple versus Compound Interest

Business dealings and transactions subject to interest state whether simple or compound interest is to be calculated. **Simple interest** is computed using the three interest calculation elements referred to above, namely, principal amount, interest rate, and time period (one-year standard). However, the true significance of simple interest is best understood in conjunction either with long-term transactions extending beyond one year or with compound interest calculations involving interest periods shorter than one year. When applied to long-term transactions extending over multiple years, simple interest is based on the principal amount outstanding at the beginning of each year. The rate at which the interest is charged remains the same. Thus, a three-year loan at a rate of 10% simple interest produces the following numbers, assuming no installment payments are made on the principal:

Simple Interest Calculation,
3 Years @ 10%—No Installment Payments

Year	Principal Beginning Balance	Annual Interest @ 10%	Accumulated Interest	Simple Interest	
1992	$10,000	$1,000	$1,000	$10,000(.10)	$1,000
1993	10,000	1,000	2,000	$10,000(.10)	1,000
1994	10,000	1,000	3,000	$10,000(.10)	1,000
					$3,000

The equation for computing simple interest is:

$$\text{Interest amount} = (P)(i)(n)$$

where:

$$P = \text{Principal}$$
$$i = \text{Interest rate}$$
$$n = \text{Number of interest periods}$$
$$\text{For example: } \$100 = \$1,000(.10)(1)$$

Compound interest is based on the principal amount outstanding at the beginning of each interest period to which accumulated interest from previous periods has been added. In all compound interest problems, it is assumed that interest is allowed to accumulate rather than be paid (by the borrower) or withdrawn (by the lender). Thus, in addition to interest on principal, compound interest includes interest on interest. The following table illustrates compound interest calculations:

Compound Interest Calculation,
3 Years @ 10%—No Installment Payments

Year	Principal Beginning Balance	Annual Interest @ 10%	Accumulated Interest	Compound Interest	
1992	$10,000	$1,000	$1,000	$10,000(.10)	$1,000
1993	11,000	1,100	2,100	(10,000 + $1,000)(.10)	1,100
1994	12,100	1,210	3,310	(10,000 + $1,000 + $1,100)(.10)	1,210
					$3,310

In comparison, the compound interest calculation produces $310 more interest than the simple interest calculation over three years. This illustration uses three one-year interest periods in computing interest. However, compounding calculations frequently involve interest periods of less than one year. Semiannual (six months), quarterly (three months), monthly, weekly, and daily compounding are all in common use. Even continuous compounding is possible.

As stated earlier in this section, when interest periods of less than one year are used, the annual interest rate given must be converted to an equivalent rate for the time period specified for compounding purposes. The following example is a continuation of the $10,000 interest calculation example. However, this time interest at the annual of rate of 10% is computed based on quarterly compounding. Due to space considerations, the illustration covers only the first-year's interest calculations.

1992	Principal Beginning Balance	Quarterly Interest @ 10% Annual Rate	Accu-mulated Interest	Compound Interest 10% Annual Rate Equivalent to 2.5% Quarterly Rate	
1st	$10,000.00	$250.00	$ 250.00	$10,000.00(.025)	$ 250.00
2nd	10,250.00	256.25	506.25	($10,000.00 + $250.00)(.025)	256.25
3rd	10,506.25	262.66	768.91	($10,000.00 + $250.25 + $256.25)(.025) . . .	262.66
4th	10,768.91	269.22	1,038.13	($10,000.00 + $250.00 + $256.25 +	
				$262.66)(.025)	269.22
					$1,038.13

In the above example, quarterly compounding for the first year produces $38.13 more interest than annual compounding. Also the true annual interest rate is 10.38% ($1,038.13 ÷ $10,000).[4]

CONCEPT REVIEW

1. Is it more of a burden on a borrower to owe $50,000 to be paid back in one payment without interest (a) 1 year from now or (b) 10 years from now?
2. Which of the following two stipulations of an obligation places a larger financial burden on a borrower?
   a. The borrower of $10,000 agrees to repay the loan in equal installments. No interest rate is specified in the loan agreement.
   b. The borrower of $10,000 agrees to repay the loan in equal installments plus interest calculated at 10 percent per year.
3. Which of the following produces the larger value?
   a. $100,000 accumulated for 10 years at 10% simple interest.
   b. $100,000 accumulated for 10 years at 10% compound interest.

OVERVIEW OF FUTURE VALUE AND PRESENT VALUE CONCEPTS

Future value (FV) and present value (PV) concepts pertain to compound interest calculations.[5] Future value involves a current amount that is *increased* in the future as the result of compound interest accumulation. Present value, in contrast, involves a future amount that is decreased to the present as a result of compound interest discounting.

The fact that investments have starting points and ending points makes it easier to understand present and future values. Present value in general refers to dollar values at the starting point of an investment, and future value refers to end-point values. If the dollar amount to be invested at the start is known, the future value of that amount

---

[4] In an attempt to prevent fraud and consumer deception, certain federal and state laws have been enacted that require disclosure of the true annual rate of interest on loans quoted at rates other than at annual percentage rate. For example, a 1% loan rate quoted in advertising copy may seem enticing. But if the 1% rate is a monthly compounding rate, the true annual rate is 12.68%.

[5] Notations and abbreviations vary considerably; examples of alternative designations are *f* for future value and *p* for present value.

at the end point of the investment can be projected—provided the interest rate and number of interest compounding periods are also specified. Similarly, if the dollar amount available at the end of an investment period (future value) is known, the amount of money needed at the start of the investment period (present value) can be determined. To do so, the interest rate and number of interest compounding periods must again be specified.

Present value and future value concepts apply to interest calculations on both *single principal amounts* and *annuity amounts*.

Single Principal Amount

Also known as a *lump sum amount,* this interest calculation is based on one-time-only investment amounts earning compound interest from the start to the end of the investment time frame.

Applications	Example
Find the future value of a single current payment.	If $100,000 is available for investment today (present value date) and the current annual interest rate is 11% compounded semiannually, what total investment amount will result at the end of two years (future value date)?
Find the present value of a single future payment.	If it is known that $100,000 will be needed in two years (future value date) and the current annual interest rate is 11% compounded semiannually, what amount must be invested today (present value date) to produce $100,000 in two-years' time?

Annuity Amount

An **annuity** involves a series of uniform payments (also called *rents*) occurring at uniform intervals over a specified investment time frame, with all amounts earning compound interest at the same rate. The term *payments* is used because it accommodates the fact that annuity amounts may take the form of either cash payments into an annuity type of investment or cash withdrawals from an annuity type of investment.

Applications	Examples
Find the future value of a series of uniform periodic payments.	If $10,000 is invested on January 1 of each of the next five years at an annual interest rate of 11% compounded semiannually, what total amount will result at the end of the investment period (future value date)?
Find the present value of a series of uniform periodic payments.	If it is known that $10,000 will be received from an investment at the end of each of the next five years and the current annual interest rate is 11% compounded semiannually, what total amount today (present value date) must be invested now to yield these receipts?

The Ordinary Annuity and the Annuity Due

There are two distinct types of annuities: ordinary annuities and annuities due. The distinction is in the timing of the payments. With an **ordinary annuity**, the payments (or receipts) occur at the *end* of each interest compounding period. With an **annuity due,** payments (or receipts) occur at the *beginning* of each interest compounding period. The distinctions between an ordinary annuity (the more common type) and an annuity due are more fully discussed later in this chapter. As is noted in the summary of the tables in the next section, the value of any annuity due can be obtained from the value of an ordinary annuity by a single multiplication.

To illustrate the difference between an ordinary annuity and an annuity due, assume a $15,000, 10%, three-year note is issued on April 1, 1991. The debt is to be paid in three equal installments that include compound interest.

Case A: Assume payments of $6,032 are to be made each March 31 for the three annuity periods. The first payment is due March 31, 1992. This specification creates an *ordinary annuity* because the payments are to be made at the *end* of each annuity period.

Case B: Assume instead that payments of $5,483 are to be made April 1, 1991, 1992, and 1993. This specification creates an *annuity due* because the payments are to be made at the *beginning* of each annuity period (i.e., in advance). The difference in the periodic payments ($6,032 − $5,438 = $594) represents less interest under the annuity due. This occurs because each of the annual payments under the annuity due is paid one year earlier than under the ordinary annuity. The principal is paid off earlier, which means less interest is paid.

Future Value and Present Value Tables and Formulas

Because determining future and present values can involve complex calculations—especially with annuities—most accountants rely on published *future and present value tables*, which eliminate the need for tedious calculations by hand.[6] The appendix to this chapter, includes the following tables:

Table No.	Table Title (and use)	Math Formulas*
6A–1	Future value of 1 (FV1): Used to compute future value of single payments.	$FV1 = (1 + i)^n$ also expressed $(FV1, i, n)$
6A–2	Present value of 1 (PV1): Used to compute the present value of payments.	$PV1 = \dfrac{1}{(1 + i)^n}$ also expressed $(PV1, i, n)$
6A–3	Future value of ordinary annuity of 1 (FVA): Used to compute the end value of a series of payments made at the *end* of each interest compounding period.	$FVA = \dfrac{(1 + i)^n - 1}{i}$ also expressed (FVA, i, n)
6A–4	Present value of ordinary annuity of 1 (PVA): Used to compute the starting value of a series of payments made at the *end* of each interest compounding period.	$PVA = \dfrac{1 - \dfrac{1}{(1 + i)^n}}{i}$ also expressed (PVA, i, n)
6A–5	Future value of annuity due of 1 (FVAD): Used to compute the end value of a series of payments made at the *beginning* of each interest compounding period.	$FVAD = \left[\dfrac{(1 + i)^n - 1}{i}\right] \times (1 + i)$ also expressed $(FVAD, i, n) = (1 + i)(FVA, i, n)$
6A–6	Present value of annuity due of 1 (PVAD): Used to compute the starting value of a series of payments made at the *beginning* of each interest compounding period.	$PVAD = \left[\dfrac{1 - \dfrac{1}{(1 + i)^n}}{i}\right] \times (1 + i)$ also expressed $(PVAD, i, n) = (1 + i)(PVA, i, n)$

* In these equations, i refers to the compound interest rate, and n refers to the number of interest periods.

---

[6] Many hand-held calculators allow the user to solve complex math problems, like those involved with annuity calculations, without resorting to tables.

EXHIBIT 6-1   Excerpt from Table 6A-1 in the Appendix*

Periods (n)†	Selected Interest Rates (i)‡					
	6%	**7%**	**8%**	**9%**	**10%**	
1 . . . . . 1.06000		1.07000	1.08000	1.09000	1.10000	. . . .
2 . . . . . 1.12360		1.14490	1.16640	1.18810	1.21000	. . . .
3 . . . . . 1.19102		1.22504	1.25971	1.29503	1.33100	. . . .
4 . . . . . 1.26248		1.31080	1.36049	1.41158	1.46410	. . . .
5 . . . . . 1.33823		1.40255	1.46933	1.53862	1.61051	. . . .
6 . . . . . 1.41852		1.50073	1.58687	1.67710	1.77156	. . . .
7 . . . . . 1.50363		1.60578	1.71382	1.82804	1.94872	. . . .
8 . . . . . 1.59385		1.71819	1.85093	1.99256	2.14359	. . . .
9 . . . . . 1.68948		1.83846	1.99900	2.17189	2.35795	. . . .
10 . . . . . 1.79085		1.96715	2.15892	2.36736	2.59374	. . . .

* The table values are based on one unit of the relevant currency, for example, the dollar in the United States.

† Periods may be annual, semiannual, quarterly, monthly, or daily.

‡ Interest rates are compounded regardless of the length of the period. These notes hold for all the tables in the appendix to this chapter.

VALUES OF A SINGLE PAYMENT
♦

Future Value of 1 (FV1)

The symbol (FV1) refers to the future value of a single payment of 1 ($1) after a specified number of interest periods (n) when increased at a specified compound interest rate (i). For example, to find the future value of $1 left on deposit for six interest periods at an interest rate of 8%, (FV1, 8%, 6), use either the math formula for calculating the future value of 1 or the future value of 1 (FV1) table in the appendix. If the math formula is used, the following calculation results:

$$FV1 = (1 + i)^n \qquad \text{expressed as } (FV1, i, n)$$
$$FV1 = (1 + .08)^6$$
$$FV1 = 1.58687, \text{ or } \$1.59$$

The same result can be obtained by using Table 6A-1 in the appendix to this chapter. Exhibit 6-1 is an excerpt from Table 6A-1 and can be used to illustrate how the appropriate number, 1.58687, is located. When using the future value of 1 table, first locate the proper interest rate column horizontally, then read down the column to the intersecting line in agreement with the number of interest periods involved, found at the left-hand side of the table running vertically.

Once the correct future value of the factor is located, multiply it by the principal amount involved. For example, the future value of $5,000 at 8% for six interest periods is $7,934.35, or $5,000(1.58687).

Present Value of 1 (PV1)

The symbol (PV1) refers to the present value of a single payment of 1 ($1) for a specified number of interest periods (n) at a specific interest rate (i). For example, to find the present value of $1 to be received six interest periods from today at 8%, (PV1, 8%, 6), use either the math formula for present value of 1 calculations or the present value of 1 (PV1) table (Table 6A-2) found in the appendix. If the math formula is used, the following calculation results:

$$PV1 = \frac{1}{(1 + i)^n} \qquad \text{expressed as } (PV1, i, n)$$

EXHIBIT 6–2   Future Value and Present Value of a Single Payment of $1 Compared

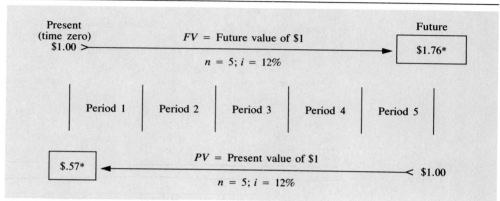

* Rounded. The reciprocal relationship is $1.00 ÷ $1.76 = $.57, rounded.

$$PV1 = \frac{1}{(1 + .08)^6}$$

$$PV1 = \frac{1}{1.58687}$$

$$PV1 = .63017, \text{ or } \$.63$$

If the present value of 1 table is used, the same answer is found. First locate the 8% interest rate column horizontally and then read down the column to the intersecting line in agreement with the *number of interest periods* involved, 6, found at the left-hand side of the table running vertically.

Once the correct present value of 1 factor is located, simply multiply by the principal amount involved. For example, the present value of $5,000 at 8% for six interest periods is $3,150.85, or $5,000(.63017).

Future and Present Value of 1 Compared and Computed

Future values and present values of 1 are the same in one respect—they both relate to a *single* payment. The future value looks *forward* from present dollars to future dollars. The present value looks *back* from future dollars to present dollars. This distinction is shown by "time lines" in Exhibit 6–2, which gives the present and future values of $1 for five periods at 12% at the bottom and top of the exhibit, respectively. The direction of the arrows in each instance acts as a visual aid to understanding the difference between present and future value computations.

Future Value   The future value of 1 (FV1) is the single payment plus all subsequent accumulated compound interest. For example, $1,000 deposited in a savings account on January 1, 1991, compounded each year at 12% interest, would amount to $1,762 at the end of the fifth year (December 31, 1995). The increase of $762 is the accumulated compound interest during the five years.

There are four ways to compute the future value of a single payment of $1: (1) make successive interest computations, (2) use a math formula, (3) use a present value table, or (4) use a calculator. Each of the four approaches requires that the *n* and *i* values be consistent for the interest periods and rates. For most calculation purposes, accountants use either method (3) or (4).

Method 1, successive interest computations, is illustrated in Exhibit 6–3 along with the simpler formula approach, method (2), for calculating (FV1, 12%, 5). It is, however, much easier to use the tables, method 3. Following the steps discussed in conjunction with Exhibit 6–1, Table 6A–1 gives the value of 1.76234 directly for (FV1, 12%, 5). Many calculators are also programmed to compute future and present

EXHIBIT 6-3   Computation of Future Value of $1 for $i = 12\%$ and $n = 5$

	Calculation			
	By Successive Interest Computations			By Formula
Period	Balance at Start of Period	× Multiplier (1 + i)	= Amount at End of Period	Alternative Computation: Amount at End: $(1 + i)^n$
1	$1	1.12	$1.12	$(1.12)^1 = \$1.12$
2	1.12	1.12	1.2544	$(1.12)^2 = 1.2544$
3	1.2544	1.12	1.40493	$(1.12)^3 = 1.40493$
4	1.40493	1.12	1.57352	$(1.12)^4 = 1.57352$
5	1.57352	1.12	1.76234	$(1.12)^5 = 1.76234$

values. Each calculator will have a handbook describing the steps by which the inputs *n, i* and the dollar amount are entered to obtain the desired result. The advantage of the calculator is that it is not restricted to just the values available in the table.

When making calculations, it is best to use all the decimal places given by the tabular value and round the figure to the desired number of decimal places only after all calculations have been completed.

Present Value   The concept of present value often is called *compound discounting*. The *present value* of a single payment is the future payment less all compound interest discounted to the present date at the specified interest rate. The present value is always less than the same amount discounted. For example, a single payment three years away of $10,000 discounted at 10% interest for three years is $10,000(.75131), or $7,513, using Table 6A–2.

Furthermore, present value of 1 amounts in Table 6A–2 and future value of 1 amounts in Table 6A–1, for a given *i* and *n*, are reciprocals of each other. That is:

$$PVI = \frac{1}{FVI} \text{ and } FVI = \frac{1}{PVI}$$

This reciprocal relationship can be illustrated as follows:

(1) The future value of $1 invested at 12% for five periods is $1.76 (rounded).
(2) The present value of $1 discounted at 12% for five periods is $.57 (rounded).

Reciprocal relationship:

$$\text{For (1): } 1 \div 1.76 = 0.57.$$
$$\text{For (2): } 1 \div 0.57 = 1.76.$$

Present value of 1 amounts can be computed in the same four ways discussed for future values. Again, for most accounting purposes, either tables (method 3) or a calculator (method 4) are typically used. The four approaches are identical to those discussed in conjunction with future values in the previous section and need not be repeated.

CONCEPT REVIEW

1. Which is larger at any positive interest rate?
    a. The present value of an annuity of $1,000 for 10 periods.
    b. The future value of an annuity of $1,000 for 10 periods.
2. Calculate the present value of $10,000 at 12% compounded semiannually for 5 periods.
3. Explain how an annuity due differs from an ordinary annuity.

ACCOUNTING APPLICATIONS OF A SINGLE PAYMENT
◆

Future Value of a Single Payment

Case A On January 1, 1991, Able Company deposited $100,000 in a special construction fund. The fund earns 10% interest compounded annually. Interest earned each period is added to the fund.

1. The amount that will be in the fund at the end of 1993 using Table 6A–1 is:

$$\$100,000(FV1, 10\%, 3) = \$100,000(1.33100) = \$133,100$$

2. The total amount of accumulated interest is:

$$\$133,100 - \$100,000 = \$33,100$$

3. The fund accumulation schedule is:

Fund Accumulation Schedule

Date	Interest Earned	Fund Balance
January 1, 1991		$100,000
December 31, 1991	$100,000 × 10% = $10,000	110,000
December 31, 1992	110,000 × 10% = 11,000	121,000
December 31, 1993	121,000 × 10% = 12,100	133,100

4. The journal entries related to the fund are:

January 1, 1991:

Special construction fund	100,000	
Cash		100,000

Each December 31:

	1991	1992	1993
Special construction fund	10,000	11,000	12,100
Investment revenue		10,000	11,000	12,100

Case B On January 1, 1991, Baker Company deposited $100,000 in a special savings account. The fund earns 10% interest compounded quarterly for three years. Interest earned is added to the fund. The three years encompass 12 interest periods, and the interest rate for each quarterly interest period is $10\% \div 4 = 2\frac{1}{2}\%$.

1. The amount that will be in the fund at the end of 1993 using Table 6A–1 is:

$$\$100,000(FV1, 2.5\%, 12) = \$100,000(1.34489) = \$134,489$$

2. The total amount of accumulated interest is:

$$\$134,489 - \$100,000 = \$34,489$$

The difference between the accumulated interest amounts in Case A versus Case B ($33,100 versus $34,489) is due to more frequent compounding in Case B.

Determination of an Unknown Interest Rate or Unknown Number of Periods

Situations are encountered when either the interest rate (i) or the number of periods (n) is not known, but sufficient data are available for their determination. For example, in Case A above, three values were provided: principal, $100,000; interest rate, 10%; and the number of periods, three. These three values were used to compute the future value, $133,100. Now consider two situations, where the unknown variable is not the future value.

Situation 1—The Interest Rate Is Unknown   A $100,000 investment will yield $146,933 in five periods. What is the implicit interest rate earned on the investment?

1. $146,933 ÷ $100,000 = 1.46933, which is the value in Table 6A–1 of $1 for five periods.
2. Use Table 6A–1 and read *across* for five interest periods to find this table value.
3. Table value 1.46933 is found under the 8% column.
4. The interest rate, therefore, is 8%.

If the exact value arrived at in computing (1) above is not found in the table, the interest rate can be approximated using interpolation techniques (described below). Business calculators can be used to determine the precise interest rate.

Situation 2—The Number of Interest Periods Is Unknown   A family can invest $150,000 today to provide for the college education of their child. The family believes $285,000 will be necessary for four years of college by the time the student matriculates. If the family can invest at 6%, how many years will it take to accumulate the required amount, $285,000?

1. $285,000 ÷ $150,000 = 1.90000, which is the table value of $1 at 6% interest.
2. Use Table 6A–1 and read *down* the 6% column to find this table value.
3. Table value 1.89830 is found on the line for 11 years and the value 2.01220 is found on the line for 12 years.
4. The implied number of interest periods required is just over 11 years.

Interpolation of Table Values   To determine an unknown interest rate or number of periods with greater accuracy requires interpolation. This is because the table values, computed in Situations 1 and 2 above, usually are between two interest rates or two periods. Assume, for example, that $5,000 is deposited in a savings account at compound interest, and a $15,000 balance is expected at the end of Year 10. Question: What is the implicit interest rate, assuming annual compounding?

Computation:
1. $15,000 = $5,000(FV1, i, 10). So (FV1, i, 10) = $15,000 ÷ $5,000 = 3.00000.
2. Refer to the excerpt from Table 6A–1 displayed below. Scanning the 10-period line for the 3.00000 value found in step 1 indicates that it falls somewhere between 2.83942 (which is for 11%) and 3.10585 (which is for 12%):

		i	
n		**11%**	**12%**
.	.	.	.
.	.	.	.
.	.	.	.
6	. . . . .	1.87041	1.97382
7	. . . . .	2.07616	2.21068
8	. . . . .	2.30454	2.47596
9	. . . . .	2.55804	2.77308
10	. . . . .	2.83942	3.10585
.	.	.	.
.	.	.	.
.	.	.	.

The interest rate that corresponds to the 3.00000 value being sought is closer to 3.10585 (12%) than it is to 2.83942 (11%)—approximately six tenths of the way from 11% to 12%.

3. For a close approximation, 11.6% could be used.[7]

Present Value of a Single Payment

Assume that on January 1, 1991, Cary Company purchased a machine. Cary immediately paid $25,000 cash and gave a $50,000 noninterest-bearing note, due on December 31, 1992. Assume interest rates for similar transactions carry interest at 10%.

1. The cost of the machine is:

```
Cash paid  . . . . . . . . . . . . . . . . . . . . . . . . . . $25,000
Note at present value, $50,000 (PV1, 10%, 2) =
    $50,000(.82645) . . . . . . . . . . . . . . . . . . . . .    41,323
Cost of the machine   . . . . . . . . . . . . . . . . . .   $66,323
```

If the note had specified interest at 10%, the cost of the machine would have been $75,000 ($25,000 cash plus the $50,000 note), and in addition, interest would be paid on $50,000. The initial noninterest-bearing note (also called a *discounted note*) involves implicit interest. The note's present value is equal to the face amount ($50,000) discounted at 10% for two years, which is $41,323. The $41,323 is the current amount that at 10% interest grows to $50,000 in two years.

2. The entry to record the acquisition of the machine is:

```
Machine . . . . . . . . . . . . . . . . . . . . . . . . . . . . . 66,323
    Cash  . . . . . . . . . . . . . . . . . . . . . . . . . .            25,000
    Note payable  . . . . . . . . . . . . . . . . . . . . . .            41,323*
```
* Alternately, this note could be recorded at $50,000 with an accompanying debit entry for $8,677 made to a "discounts on notes payable" account. Discounts on notes payable is a contra liability and the balance in this account (which represents interest) is deducted from the face value to arrive at net note payable ($50,000 − $8,677 = $41,323).

3. The debt payment schedule is:

| | | Liability (Note Payable) | |
| | Interest Expense Incurred | | |
Date	(Payable at Maturity)	Increase	Balance
January 1, 1991			$41,323
December 31, 1991	$41,323 × .10 = $4,132	$4,132	45,455
December 31, 1992	45,455 × .10 = 4,545	4,545	50,000

4. The remaining entries related to this case are:

	12/31/91		12/31/90	
Interest expense	4,132		4,545	
Note payable		4,132		4,545
Note payable			50,000	
Cash				50,000

Situations involving unknown interest rates or time periods are solved in the same way for present values as illustrated in the previous section on future values.

---

[7] If more precision is desired, linear interpolation can be used to derive 11.603%:

$$
\begin{array}{lll}
11\% = 2.83942 \\
\quad? \; = 3.00000 \quad \longrightarrow \Delta = .16058 \\
12\% = 3.10585
\end{array}
\quad\longrightarrow \Delta = .26643
$$

$$
11\% + \left[\left(\frac{.16058}{.26643} \right) \times (12\% - 11\%) \right] = 11.603\%
$$

A more precise answer can be obtained by using a calculator to solve $5,000 (1 + i)^{10} = \$15,000$ to obtain $i = 11.612\%$.

Selecting an Interest Rate

The results of future and present value computations are affected by the interest rate used. The effect can be substantial, particularly when the rates are high and the time period is long. For example, the future value of $100,000 for 20 periods at 10% per period is $672,750. If the interest rate is 8%, the future value is $466,096. When an interest rate is not specified, an appropriate rate must be selected.

Generally, an interest rate has three components: a pure no-risk component with inflation excluded; a credit risk component that varies depending on the borrower, security pledged, and types of loans; and an expected inflation component. The interest rate is the sum of these three components. However, this concept of interest assumes a competitive free market with fully informed borrowers. "What the traffic will bear" is thought by some people to be operative in most situations. Consequently, each of the three components is very difficult to determine in a given situation. The difficulty is illustrated currently by the high interest rates charged on bank credit cards.

In recognition of the difficulty in selecting a realistic interest rate and the possibility of management selecting an interest rate to produce desired FV and PV results for accounting purposes, *APB Opinion No. 21,* paragraphs 13 and 14, provides a general guideline. The guideline states that the rate selected should approximate "the rate which would have resulted if an independent borrower and an independent lender had negotiated a similar transaction under comparable terms and conditions with the option to pay the cash price upon purchase or to give a note for the amount of the purchase which bears the prevailing rate of interest to maturity." The rate described in this quotation usually is called the **going, prevailing,** or **market rate** for the transaction under consideration. This rate generally should be used for "GAAP applications" such as valuing notes that call for periodic payments but specify either no interest rate or an unrealistically low rate.

CONCEPT REVIEW

1. Calculate:
   a. The present value of $1,500 at 8% interest for five years compounded annually (PV1, 8%, 5).
   b. The future value of $1,800 at 4% for seven years compounded annually (FV1, 4%, 7).
2. What annual compound interest rate is implicit in a loan that provides a borrower with $8,264 today based on the promise to repay $10,000 two years from today?
3. Suppose $10,000 is invested today at 8% interest compounded quarterly. How long would it take (approximately) for this amount to grow to $20,000?

VALUES OF AN ANNUITY
◆

Future Value of an Ordinary Annuity (FVA)

The symbol (FVA) refers to the future value of a series of payments (or receipts) in equal dollar amounts being made over a specified number of equally spaced interest periods (n) at a specified interest rate (i). Unless otherwise stated, all annuities are assumed to be ordinary annuities, meaning that all payments occur at the end of interest periods. Determining the future value of an ordinary annuity can be accomplished using any of the four methods discussed in regard to the future value of 1. It is appropriate, however, to illustrate the calculation either by using the math formula shown below or by referring to the future value of an ordinary annuity of 1 table (Table 6A–3 in the appendix. For example, to find the future value of an annuity of $1 invested at 8% for six interest periods (FVA, 8%, 6), the following formula and calculation apply:

$$FVA = \frac{(1 + i)^n - 1}{i} \qquad \text{expressed as } (FVA, i, n)$$

$$FVA = \frac{(1 + .08)^6 - 1}{.08}$$

$$FVA = \frac{1.58687 - 1}{.08}$$

$$FVA = 7.33588, \text{ or } \$7.34$$

If the *future value of an ordinary annuity of 1 table* is used, the same answer is found. (The results differ slightly due to rounding.) Again, this table is used exactly as described for Table 6A–1 in Exhibit 6–1. When using the future value of an ordinary annuity of 1 table first locate the proper interest rate column horizontally, and then read down the column to the intersecting line in agreement with the *number of interest periods* involved, found at the left-hand side of the table running vertically.

Once the correct future value of ordinary annuity of 1 factor is located, simply multiply by the payment involved. For example, the future value of an ordinary annuity consisting of $5,000 rents at 8% for six interest periods is $36,679.65, or $5,000(7.33593).

Present Value of an Ordinary Annuity (PVA)

The symbol (PVA) refers to today's equivalent dollar amount of a series of payments (or receipts) made over a predetermined time frame. The assumption is that these payments are made at periodic intervals (at the end of each interest period in the case of an ordinary annuity) and at a constant, specific rate of interest. Determining the present value of an ordinary annuity can also be accomplished by using the math formula shown below or by referring to the present value of an ordinary annuity of 1 table, (Table 6A–4 in the appendix). For example, to find the present value of an ordinary annuity of $1 invested at 8% for six interest periods (PVA, 8%, 6), the following formula and calculation apply:

$$PVA = \frac{1 - \dfrac{1}{(1 + i)^n}}{i} \qquad \text{expressed as } (PVA, i, n)$$

$$PVA = \frac{1 - \dfrac{1}{(1 + .08)^6}}{.08}$$

$$PVA = \frac{1 - \dfrac{1}{1.58687}}{.08}$$

$$PVA = 4.62288, \text{ or } \$4.62$$

If the present value of an ordinary annuity of 1 table is used, the same answer is found. When using the present value of an ordinary annuity of 1 table, first locate the proper interest rate column horizontally, and then read down the column to the intersecting line in agreement with the *number of interest periods* involved, found at the left-hand side of the table running vertically.

Once the correct present value of an ordinary annuity of 1 factor is located, multiply it by the payment involved. For example, the present value of a series of $5,000 payments invested at 8% for six interest periods is $23,114.40, or $5,000 (4.62288).

EXHIBIT 6-4   Future Value of an Ordinary Annuity of 1 Compared to the Future Value of an
Annuity Due: (FVA, 10%, 3) vs. (FVAD, 10%, 3)

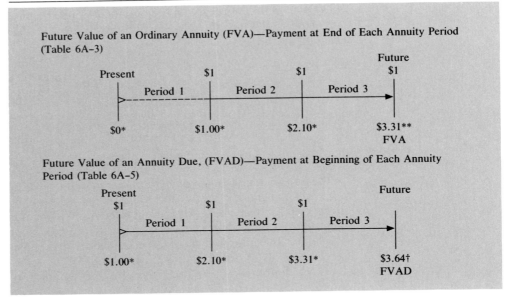

* Future values of the annuity on the date indicated.

** The first payment is compounded for two periods, the second payment for one period, and the third payment for
zero periods because the payments are at the *end* of each period.

† The first payment is compounded for three periods, the second payment for two periods, and the third payment for
one period because the payments are at the *beginning* of each period.

EXHIBIT 6-5   Future Value of an Ordinary Annuity and an Annuity Due Differentiated

	Type of Future Value Annuity	
Characteristic	FVA—Ordinary	FVAD—Due
1. Timing of each payment	End of each period	Beginning of each period
2. Number of payments (*n*)	Three $\}n = 3$	Three $\}n = 3$
3. Number of compounding periods (*j*)	Two $\}j = 2$	Three $\}j = 3$
4. Point in time of the future value	On date of last payment	End of compounding period following the last payment

Future Value of an Annuity Due (FVAD)

Exhibit 6–4 shows two time lines that compare the future value of an ordinary
annuity with the future value of an annuity due of $1 at 10% compound interest for
three annuity periods. The symbol FVA is used to designate the future value of an
ordinary annuity, and FVAD to designate an *annuity due.* Exhibit 6–5 identifies the
differences between FVA and FVAD.

Because of the difference in the timing of the periodic payments, the future value
of the ordinary annuity illustrated in Exhibit 6–4 involves three payments, but there
are only two interest periods. The annuity due involves three payments and three
interest periods. Therefore, for each of the three annuity values illustrated, FVA
$(1 + i)$ = FVAD. This relationship means that if an FVA value is known, it can be

EXHIBIT 6-6 Present Value of an Ordinary Annuity of 1 Compared to the Present Value of an Annuity Due: (PVA, 10%, 3) vs. (PVAD, 10%, 3)

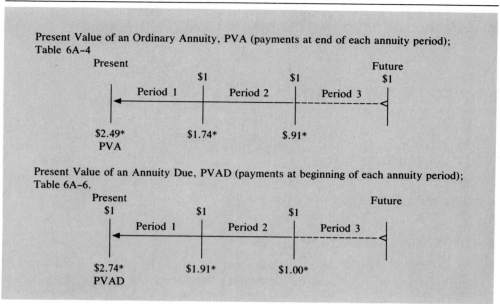

* Present values of the annuity on the date indicated.

multiplied by $(1 + i)$ to determine the FVAD value for the same i and n.[8] Tables 6A-5 and 6A-6 in the appendix to this chapter give annuity due values.

The future value of an *annuity due* can be determined most readily by multiplying the related FVA value (Table 6A-3) by $1 + i$, by using the annuity due table (Table 6A-5) or by using a programmed calculator. Using the example in Exhibit 6-4:

$$(FVAD, 10\%, 3) = 3.64 \text{ or } (FVA, 10\%, 3)(1 + .10) = 3.31000 (1.10) = 3.64$$

Present Value of an Annuity Due (PVAD)

Exhibit 6-6 shows two time lines and compares the present value of an ordinary annuity with an annuity due of $1 at 10%. The symbol PVA is used to designate the present value of an *ordinary annuity* and PVAD designates an *annuity due*. Exhibit 6-7 identifies the differences between PVA and PVAD annuities.

Because of the difference in the timing of the periodic payments, the value of the *ordinary annuity* illustrated in Exhibit 6-6 involves *three payments and three discounting periods*. In contrast, the *annuity due involves three payments but only two discounting periods*. The annuity due is discounted for one fewer period than the ordinary annuity, which means that the ordinary annuity amount is less than the comparable annuity due amount by $(1 + i)$; therefore, $PVA (1 + i) = PVAD$. This relationship means that if a PVA value is known, it can be multiplied by $(1 + i)$ to determine its comparable PVAD value. Table 6A-4 gives the present value amounts for an ordinary annuity, and Table 6A-6 gives the comparable annuity due amounts.

---

[8] Another procedure frequently used when the future value of an annuity due is needed, but when an annuity due table is not available, is to determine the future table value of an ordinary annuity for *one more* payment (i.e., $n + 1$) than the number of payments specified in the annuity problem, and then subtract 1.0 from that table value. The effect of this is to add one more period of compound interest while keeping the payments the same. This procedure frequently is expressed as: $(n + 1 \text{ payments}) - 1.0$. If the *present value of an annuity due* is needed, the relationships are essentially the opposite; thus, the procedure is: $(n - 1 \text{ payments}) + 1.0$. Calculators often are programmed to compute both ordinary annuity and annuity due values.

EXHIBIT 6-7   Present Value of an Ordinary Annuity and an Annuity Due Differentiated

	Type of Present Value Annuity	
Characteristic	PVA—Ordinary	PVAD—Due
1. Timing of each payment	End of each annuity period	Beginning of each annuity period
2. Number of payments (*n*)	Three $\rbrace$ *n = 3*	Three $\rbrace$ *n = 3*
3. Number of discounting periods (*j*)	*Three* $\rbrace$ *j = 3*	*Two* $\rbrace$ *j = 2*
4. Point in time of the first payment	End of first discounting period	Beginning of first discounting period

ACCOUNTING APPLICATIONS OF AN ANNUITY

◆

Future Value of an Annuity

In most situations, the amount of the equal payments, the number of payments (*n*), and the constant interest rate per period (*i*) are known. To determine the *future value,* the appropriate future value from Table 6A–3 or 6A–5 is multiplied by the amount of the periodic payment.

A typical accounting application of future value of an annuity is the accumulation of a fund by equal annual contributions. Funds are established to be used in the future for such purposes as expansion of a facility or payment of a debt on its maturity date.

To illustrate the accumulation of such a fund, two cases are presented. Case A is an ordinary annuity; Case B is an annuity due, which is the usual situation for a fund.

Case A   On April 1, 1991, Delta Company decided to accumulate a fund (an asset) to pay a debt that matures on March 31, 1994. The company decided to deposit $10,000 cash in this debt retirement fund each March 31, 1992, 1993, and 1994. The fund will earn 10% compound interest which is added to the fund balance on March 31, 1993, and 1994. The company's accounting period ends December 31. The debt matures on the date of the last deposit, which is when the annuity terminates. Delta's fiscal year ends March 31.

1. This is an ordinary annuity because the payments are deposited at the *end* of each of the three annuity periods. The *last payment is deposited on the last day that the annuity is in existence*—March 31, 1994.

The time line for this *ordinary annuity* is shown below:

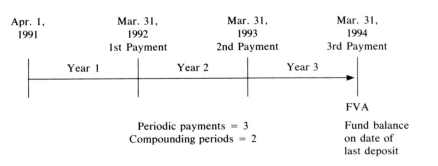

2. The amount in the fund at the end of the annuity's existence is found using Table 6A–3:

$$\$10,000 \ (FVA, \ 10\%, \ 3) \ = \ \$10,000(3.31000) \ = \ \$33,100$$

3. The fund accumulation schedule is:

Case A: Fund Accumulation Schedule—Ordinary Annuity

Month and Annuity Year	Cash Deposit	Interest Revenue	Fund Change	Balance
March 31, 1992	$10,000		+$10,000	$10,000
March 31, 1993	10,000	$10,000(.10) = $1,000	+ 11,000	21,000
March 31, 1994	10,000	21,000(.10) = 2,100	+ 12,100	33,100*
Totals	$30,000	$3,100	$33,100	

* Ordinary annuity balance, which is as of the date of the last deposit.

4. The journal entries required at each year-end, March 31, are:

	1992	1993	1994
Debt retirement fund	10,000	11,000	12,100
Cash	10,000	10,000	10,000
Interest revenue		1,000	2,100

5. The journal entry to record withdrawal of the fund balance on March 31, 1994 is:

Cash (or debt retired)	33,100	
Debt retirement fund		33,100

Case B Assume the same facts as in Case A, except that the annual deposits are made at the *beginning* of each interim annuity period on April 1, 1991, 1992, and 1993.

1. This is an annuity due because the payments are deposited at the *beginning* of each of the three annuity periods. The last payment is deposited one full interest or compounding period *prior* to the end of the annuity which is March 31, 1994. The time line for this *annuity due* is:

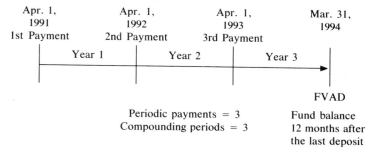

2. The amount in the fund at the end of the annuity using Table 6A–5 is:

$$\$10,000 \ (FVAD, \ 10\%, \ 3) \ = \ 10,000(3.64100) \ = \ \$36,410$$

3. The fund accumulation schedule is:

Case B: Fund Accumulation Schedule—Annuity Due

Month and Annuity Year	Cash Deposit	Interest Revenue	Fund Change	Balance
April 1, 1991	$10,000		+$10,000	$10,000
March 31, 1992		$10,000(.10) = $1,000	+ 1,000	11,000
April 1, 1992	10,000		+ 10,000	21,000
March 31, 1993		$21,000(.10) = $2,100	+ 2,100	23,100
April 1,1993	10,000		+ 10,000	33,100
March 31, 1994		$33,100(.10) = $3,310	+ 3,310	36,410*
Totals	$30,000	$6,410	$36,410	

* Annuity due balance, which is 12 months after the last deposit.

4. The journal entries required at each year-end, March 31, are:

March 31, 1991, 1992, 1993:

	1991	1992	1993	1994
Debt retirement fund . . .	10,000	11,000	12,000	3,310
Cash	10,000	10,000	10,000	
Interest revenue . . .		1,000	2,100	3,310

The journal entry to record withdrawal of the fund balance on March 31, 1994 (maturity date) is:

Cash (or debt retired)	36,410	
Debt retirement fund		36,410

Determination of Other Values Related to the Future Value of an Annuity

In the preceding example—Case A, ordinary annuity—*three* values were given: the periodic payment, (P), $10,000; the number of periodic payments (n), three; and periodic interest rate (i), 10%. A fourth value, the future value of an ordinary annuity, was unknown; however, it was obtained using Table 6A–3 as follows:

$$\$10,000 \text{ (FVA, 10\%, 3)} = \$10,000(3.31000) = \$33,100.$$

Situations may be encountered when either P, n, or i is unknown. If any three of the four variables are given, however, the fourth can be computed. Refer to the preceding example, Case A; determination of any value (other than the future value) can be computed.[9] For example, to compute the periodic payment, P, given the future value of ordinary annuity = $33,100, $n = 3$, $i = 10\%$ and using Table 6A–3:

$$P = \$33,100 \div \text{(FVA, 10\%, 3)} = \$33,100 \div 3.31000 = \$10,000$$

Compute the periodic interest rate (i), given the future value of ordinary annuity, $33,100; a periodic payment of $10,000; and $n = 3$.

$$\$33,100 \div \$10,000 = 3.31000$$ which is the value shown in Table 6A–3 for $n = 3$, $i = 10\%$.

Reference to the Table 6A–3 *line* for $n = 3$ indicates a periodic interest rate of 10%.

Compute the number of payments (n), given the future value of an ordinary annuity, $33,100; payment, $10,000; and $i = 10\%$.

$$\$33,100 \div \$10,000 = 3.31000$$

which is the Table 6A–3 value for $i = 10\%$.

Reference to the Table 6A–3 *column* for $i = 10\%$ indicates the number of payments to be three. If this example involved an *annuity due*, the annuity due amount given in Table 6A–5 would be used in the above computations.

Present Value of an Annuity

Tables of present value of an annuity of $1 are used to calculate the present value of a series of future payments at a specific compound discount rate. In most cases, the following variables are known: the amount of each equal payment, the number of payments, and the constant rate of interest per discounting period. To determine the

---

[9] The Case A data given above are used with one of the originally given values unknown in each instance to demonstrate the computational approaches and the correctness of the answers.

present value in a specific situation, the appropriate present value factor from Table 6A–4 or 6A–6 is multiplied by the amount of the periodic payment.

An accounting application of the present value of an annuity is the determination of the equal annual payment required in a debt contract. To illustrate, two cases are presented. Case C is an ordinary annuity, and Case D is an annuity due.

Case C On April 1, 1991, Echo Company owed a $15,000 liability (a present value amount). Because of Echo's cash flow problem, the creditor agreed to allow Echo Company to pay the debt in three equal installments at 10% compound interest. The payments of $6,032 are payable March 31, 1992, 1993, and 1994. Echo's fiscal year ends March 31.

1. This is an ordinary annuity because the three payments are due at the end of each year during the three-year extended credit period. The first payment is to be made 12 months after the debt payment was extended. The time line for this ordinary annuity is:

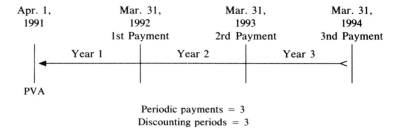

2. The present value of the three payments using Table 6A–4 is:

$$\$6,032 \ (PVA, 10\%, 3) = \$6,032(2.48685) = \$15,000$$

3. The amount of each equal annual payment is computed to be:

$$\$15,000 \div (PVA, 10\%, 3) = \$15,000 \div 2.48685 = \$6,032$$

4. The debt payment schedule is:

Case C: Debt Payment Schedule—Ordinary Annuity

Month and Annuity Year	Cash Payment	Interest Expense	Liability Change	Liability Balance
April 1, 1991				$15,000
March 31, 1992	$ 6,032	$15,000(.10) = $1,500	− $ 4,532	10,468
March 31, 1993	6,032	10,468(.10) = 1,047	− 4,985	5,483
March 31, 1994	6,032	5,483(.10) = 549*	− 5,483	-0-
Totals	$18,096	$3,096	$15,000	

* Rounded to come out even.

5. The entries required each March 31 are:

	1992	1993	1994
Interest expense	1,500	1,047	549
Liability	4,532	4,985	5,483
Cash	6,032	6,032	6,032

Case D Assume the same facts as in Case C, except that three equal annual payments of $5,483 are to be made on each April 1, 1991, 1992, and 1993.

1. This is an annuity due because the payments are due at the beginning of each year; the first payment is paid immediately. The time line for this annuity due is:

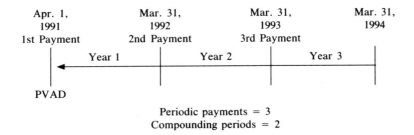

Periodic payments = 3
Compounding periods = 2

2. The present value of the three payments using Table 6A–6 is:

$$\$5,483 \times (PVAD, 10\%, 3) = \$5,483(2.73554) = \$15,000$$

3. The amount of each equal annual payment is computed to be:

$$\$15,000 \div (PVAD, 10\%, 3) = \$15,000 \div 2.73554 = \$5,483$$

4. The debt payment schedule is:

Case D: Debt Payment Schedule—Annuity Due

Date	Cash Payment	Interest Expense	Liability Change	Liability Balance
April 1, 1991				$15,000
April 1, 1991	$ 5,483		– $ 5,483	9,517
March 31, 1992		$9,517(.10) = $ 952	+ 952	10,469
April 1, 1992	5,483		– 5,483	4,986
March 31, 1993		4,986(.10) = 497*	+ 497	5,483
April 1, 1993	5,483		– 5,483	–0–
Totals	$16,449	$1,449	$15,000	

* Rounded to come out even.

5. The entries required on March 31 are:

March 31:	1991	1992	1993
Interest expense		952	497
Liability 5,483		4,531	4,986
Cash	5,483	5,483	5,483

Determination of Other Values Related to the Present Value of an Annuity

Determining an implicit interest rate for the present value of either an annuity due (or an ordinary annuity) involves the same procedure as illustrated previously for future values. To illustrate, for an annuity due this time, assume an overdue debt of $83,398 is paid in five equal installments of $20,000 each. The first payment is to be paid immediately; therefore, this involves the present value of an *annuity due*. The implicit compound interest rate is determined as follows:

$$\$83,398 \div \$20,000 = 4.1699 = (PVAD, i, 5).$$

Reference to Table 6A–6 for line $n = 5$ indicates a periodic interest rate of 10% (see also footnote 7). Proof:

$$\$20,000 (PVAD, 10\%, 5) = \$20,000 (4.16987) = \$83,398 \text{ (rounded)}$$

Using Multiple Present and Future Value Amounts

Situations occur that require the application of two or more future or present value amounts. Problems that use two or more of these values require a careful analysis of the situation and a precise knowledge of what each table value means.

Two cases are given below, to illustrate the application of multiple future and present values.

Case E—Deferred Annuity A *deferred annuity* occurs in two phases: (1) capital is invested over a given length of time in an effort to accumulate maximum interest compounding and principal growth, and (2) the principal is systematically paid out to the annuitant (investor or payee) in uniform amounts until the total accumulated principal is exhausted. Capital investments during the accumulation phase may be in the form of either periodic payments over a number of years or a lump sum payment at the front end. During the second phase, while withdrawals are being distributed to the annuitant, the remaining principal continues to earn interest.

To illustrate, assume that on January 1, 1991, Fox Company invests in a $100,000 deferred annuity for the benefit of one of its employees, George Golf, who was injured while at work. The terms of the deferred annuity call for Fox Company to make an immediate $100,000 lump sum payment, which will be invested at 11% interest for four years (the capital accumulation phase of the annuity). Then, beginning on January 1, 1995, when George Golf retires, the total amount of the annuity will be paid to him in five equal annual installment payments.

First, the fund grows at 11% for four years. At that time the fund will equal:

$$\$100,000(FV1, 11\%, 4) = \$100,000(1.51807) = \$151,807$$

Second, the fund is used in total to pay Mr. Golf a five-year annuity beginning January 1, 1995. The value of this annuity due is:

$$\text{Payment (PVAD, 11\%, 5)} = \text{Payment (4.10245)},$$

where the fund is assumed to continue to earn 11% until the last payment is made. Since what goes into the fund will be used up by the payments, the two amounts must be equal. Hence:

$$\text{Payment (4.10245)} = \$151,807$$

and the yearly payment to Mr. Golf is $37,004. The procedure is diagrammed as follows:

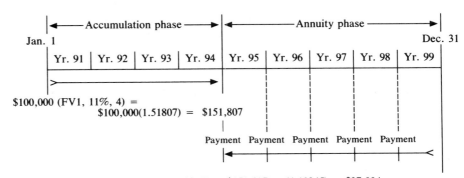

$$\text{Payment} = \$151,807 \div (\text{PVAD}, 11\%, 5) = \$151,807 \div (4.10245) = \underline{\$37,004.}$$

Fund Schedule

Date	Interest Revenue		Fund Change	Fund Balance
January 1, 1991	Single deposit		+ $100,000	$100,000
December 31, 1991	$100,000(.11) =	$11,000	+ 11,000	111,000
December 31, 1992	$111,000(.11) =	12,210	+ 12,210	123,210
December 31, 1993	$123,210(.11) =	13,553	+ 13,553	136,763
December 31, 1994	$136,763(.11) =	15,044	+ 15,044	151,807
January 1, 1995	Payment		− 37,004	114,803
December 31, 1995	$114,803(.11) =	12,628	+ 12,628	127,431
January 1, 1996	Payment		− 37,004	90,427
December 31, 1996	$ 90,427(.11) =	9,947	+ 9,947	100,374
January 1, 1997	Payment		− 37,004	63,370
December 31, 1997	$ 63,370(.11) =	6,971	+ 6,971	70,341
January 1, 1998	Payment		− 37,004	33,337
December 31, 1998	$ 33,337(.11) =	3,667	+ 3,667	37,004
January 1, 1999	Payment		− 37,004	–0–

Case F—Annuity and Salvage Explo Company is negotiating to purchase four acres of land containing a gravel deposit that is suitable for exploration. Explo Company and the seller are negotiating the price. Explo Company has completed an extensive study that provided reliable estimates as follows:

Expected net cash revenues over life of resource:
  End of 1991 . . . . $ 5,000
  End of 1992 to 1995 (per year) 30,000
  End of 1996 to 1999 (per year) 40,000
  End of 2000 (last year—resource exhausted) 10,000
Estimated sales value of four acres after exploitation and net
  of land-leveling costs (end of 2000) 2,000

Compute the maximum amount Explo Company could offer on Jan. 1, 1991 for the land, assuming it requires a 12% return on the investment. Assume all amounts are at year-end and that the above amounts are net of income taxes.

This case requires computation of the present value of the future expected cash inflows.

The amount that should be offered is the sum of the present values of the net cash inflows for the various years. The complexity in this situation arises because a variety of both single payment and annuities is involved.

For Explo Company the primary focus is on *present value* because estimated future cash inflows are provided, and the amount that the company should be willing to pay is the present value of those future expected cash inflows. Because equal future cash inflows are expected for Years 2 to 5 and 6 to 9, two annuities are involved. Because these two cash inflows are assumed to be at year-end, the annuities are ordinary.

This case is best solved in several steps. The steps involve separating the cash flows into either single payments or annuities and writing each of them in terms of their present value. This gives:[10]

---

[10] In Equation 2 of the calculation, the present value of the annuity at January 1, 1992, is established as $30,000 (PVA, 12%, 4). This value is then brought back to January 1, 1991, by the present value factor (PV1, 12%, 1). A similar calculation is made in Equation 3. In Equation 4 the salvage value is added to the final year's cash flow.

(1)	$5,000 (PV1, 12%, 1) = $5,000(.89286)	=	$ 4,464
(2)	[$30,000(PVA, 12%, 4)](PV1, 12%, 1) $30,000 (3.03735)(.89286)	=	81,358
(3)	[$40,000 (PVA, 12%, 4)](PV1, 12%, 5) $40,000(3.03735)(.56743)	=	68,939
(4)	$12,000(PV1, 12%, 10) = $12,000(.32197)	=	3,864
			$158,625

Explo should offer no more than $158,625 for the properties. These 4 steps are graphically depicted below.

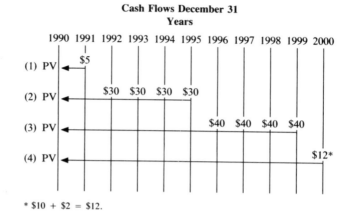

Cash Flows December 31
Years

* $10 + $2 = $12.

Exhibit 6–8 provides a summary of the interest concepts discussed in this chapter.

CONCEPT REVIEW

1. Calculate:
   a. The future value of an ordinary annuity of $1,000 for 10 years accumulated at an annual compound interest rate of 12%; (FVA, 12%, 10).
   b. The present value of an ordinary annuity of $15,000 for five years accumulated at an annual compound interest rate of 9% for seven years; (PVA, 9%, 7).
   c. Repeat (a) and (b) for an annuity due.
2. A company deposits $1,000 semiannually in the retirement annuity for an employee. How much will the retirement annuity amount to in 10 years at an annual compound interest rate of 4%? Payments at start of period.
3. A bond agreement promises to pay interest of $10,000 per year for 10 years and to return the principal amount of $100,000 at the end of the 10-year period. Payments at end of year.
   a. What is the implicit interest rate in this contract?
   b. What is the present value of this contract?
   c. If the bond did not offer annual interest payments, but the market interest rate did not change from part (a), what is the present value of the obligation?

EXHIBIT 6–8   Summary of Interest Concepts

Title (Symbol)	Basic Concept Summarized	Formula	Table	Illustrative Table Values	
				$n = 5; i = 10\%$	$n = 6; i = 10\%$
Simple Interest i	Interest on principal only, regardless of any prior accrued interest.	$P \times i \times n$	—	—	—
FV of 1 (FV1, i, n)	FV of a single payment increased by compound interest i for n periods.	$(1 + i)^n$	6A–1	1.61051 (always more than 1)	1.77156 (more by compound interest for one period)
PV of 1 (PV1, i, n)	PV of a single payment decreased by compound discount i for n periods.	$\dfrac{1}{(1 + i)^n}$	6A–2	.62092 (always less than 1)	.56447 (less by the discount for one period)
FV of Annuity of 1 Ordinary annuity (FVA, i, n)	FV of a series of n equal *end-of-period* payments at compound interest i.	$\dfrac{(1 + i)^n - 1}{i}$	6A–3	6.10510 (always more than sum of payments)	7.71561 (more by one payment, plus compound interest for one period)
Annuity due (FVAD, i, n)	FV of a series of n equal *beginning-of-period* payments at compound interest i.	$\dfrac{(1 + i)^n - 1}{i} \times (1 + i)$	6A–5	6.71561 or (6.10510 $\times$ 1.10)	8.48717 or (7.71561 $\times$ 1.10)
PV of annuity of 1 Ordinary annuity (PVA, i, n)	PV of a series of n equal *end-of-period* payments in the future decreased at compound discount i.	$\dfrac{1 - \dfrac{1}{(1 + i)^n}}{i}$	6A–4	3.79079 (always less than sum of payments)	4.35526 (more by one payment, less discount for one period)
Annuity due (PVAD, i, n)	PV of a series of n equal *beginning-of-period* payments in the future decreased at compound discount i.	$\dfrac{1 - \dfrac{1}{(1 + i)^n}}{i} \times (1 + i)$	6A–6	4.16987 or (3.79079 $\times$ 1.10)	4.79079 or (4.35526 $\times$ 1.10)

SUMMARY OF KEY POINTS

(L.O. 1) 1. Interest is the cost of using money over time. Interest occurs because there is a time value to money, meaning that a dollar today is worth more than a dollar one year from now.

(L.O. 2) 2. Simple interest requires interest to be computed on the same principal amount each period. Compound interest requires interest to be computed on the principal amount and, in addition, on all prior interest calculated and not paid or withdrawn.

(L.O. 3) 3. The future value (FV) of a current amount is the amount that will have accumulated at a specified date, given a specific interest rate. The present value (PV) of a future amount is the amount today that, with interest at a specific rate, will accumulate to a given sum at a specified future date.

(L.O. 3)   4. An annuity involves a stream of constant and regular periodic cash payments over a specified period of time.

(L.O. 4)   5. Ordinary annuities are annuities for which each regular payment occurs at the end of the period. An annuity due is an annuity for which the payments occur at the beginning of the period.

(L.O. 5)   6. The selection of the appropriate interest rate is not an easy task. The rate selected can have a significant effect on the calculation if the time period is long and if the appropriate rate is large. In general, the prevailing market rate for transactions of similar risk should be used. This is often easier said than done.

(L.O. 5)   7. The tables in the appendix to this chapter (6A–1 to 6A–6) can be used to solve PV and FV calculations. When tables are not available or if more precise results are required, the easiest procedure is to use a calculator programmed to solve present and future values.

(L.O. 6)   8. Complex interest problems can be solved by breaking them into separate pieces and then using one of the techniques introduced in this chapter on each part.

REVIEW PROBLEM
◆

Northern Airlines is negotiating to acquire four new Airbus planes. Three alternatives are available:

1. Purchase the aircraft for $35 million each. Payment due immediately.
2. Purchase the aircraft by paying $20 million immediately and $20 million each year for 11 more years.
3. Lease the aircraft for $21.5 million payable at the end of each year for 12 years.

The relevant market rate of interest (the discount rate) for ventures of this type is 10%. Assuming Northern has sufficient cash, which alternative is least expensive? Ignore tax considerations.

SOLUTION
◆

The value of each alternative is:

1. $35 million × 4 planes = $140 million.
2. $20 (PVAD, 10%, 12) = $20 (7.49506) = $150 million.
3. $21.5 (PVA, 10%, 12) = $21.5 (6.81369) = $146.5 million.

The least expensive option is to buy the aircraft for cash, alternative 1. If the discount rate is made sufficiently large, alternative 1 would no longer be the least expensive choice. A higher discount rate would reflect a lower burden to Northern for the future yearly $20 million payments: (PVAD, 20%, 12) = 5.32706. With a 20% discount rate, the burden of the 12 payments of $20 million, for example, is $20 (5.32706) = $106.5 million.

APPENDIX   *Present and Future Value Interest Tables*

TABLE 6A-1   Future Value of 1 (FV1): $FV1 = (1 + i)^n$ also expressed as $(FV1, i, n)$

This table shows the compound amount of $1 at various interest rates and for various time periods. It is used to compute the future value of single payments.

n Periods	2%	2½%	3%	4%	5%	6%	7%	8%	9%	10%
1	1.02000	1.02500	1.03000	1.04000	1.05000	1.06000	1.07000	1.08000	1.09000	1.10000
2	1.04040	1.05063	1.06090	1.08160	1.10250	1.12360	1.14490	1.16640	1.18810	1.21000
3	1.06121	1.07689	1.09273	1.12486	1.15763	1.19102	1.22504	1.25971	1.29503	1.33100
4	1.08243	1.10381	1.12551	1.16986	1.21551	1.26248	1.31080	1.36049	1.41158	1.46410
5	1.10408	1.13141	1.15927	1.21665	1.27628	1.33823	1.40255	1.46933	1.53862	1.61051
6	1.12616	1.15969	1.19405	1.26532	1.34010	1.41852	1.50073	1.58687	1.67710	1.77156
7	1.14869	1.18869	1.22987	1.31593	1.40710	1.50363	1.60578	1.71382	1.82804	1.94872
8	1.17166	1.21840	1.26677	1.36857	1.47746	1.59385	1.71819	1.85093	1.99256	2.14359
9	1.19509	1.24886	1.30477	1.42331	1.55133	1.68948	1.83846	1.99900	2.17189	2.35795
10	1.21899	1.28008	1.34392	1.48024	1.62889	1.79085	1.96715	2.15892	2.36736	2.59374
11	1.24337	1.31209	1.38423	1.53945	1.71034	1.89830	2.10485	2.33164	2.58043	2.85312
12	1.26824	1.34489	1.42576	1.60103	1.79586	2.01220	2.25219	2.51817	2.81266	3.13843
13	1.29361	1.37851	1.46853	1.66507	1.88565	2.13293	2.40985	2.71962	3.06580	3.45227
14	1.31948	1.41297	1.51259	1.73168	1.97993	2.26090	2.57853	2.93719	3.34173	3.79750
15	1.34587	1.44830	1.55797	1.80094	2.07893	2.39656	2.75903	3.17217	3.64248	4.17725
16	1.37279	1.48451	1.60471	1.87298	2.18287	2.54035	2.95216	3.42594	3.97031	4.59497
17	1.40024	1.52162	1.65285	1.94790	2.29202	2.69277	3.15882	3.70002	4.32763	5.05447
18	1.42825	1.55966	1.70243	2.02582	2.40662	2.85434	3.37993	3.99602	4.71712	5.55992
19	1.45681	1.59865	1.75351	2.10685	2.52695	3.02560	3.61653	4.31570	5.14166	6.11591
20	1.48595	1.63862	1.80611	2.19112	2.65330	3.20714	3.86968	4.66096	5.60441	6.72750
21	1.51567	1.67958	1.86029	2.27877	2.78596	3.39956	4.14056	5.03383	6.10881	7.40025
22	1.54598	1.72157	1.91610	2.36992	2.92526	3.60354	4.43040	5.43654	6.65860	8.14027
23	1.57690	1.76461	1.97359	2.48472	3.07152	3.81975	4.74053	5.87146	7.25787	8.95430
24	1.60844	1.80873	2.03279	2.56330	3.22510	4.04893	5.07237	6.34118	7.91108	9.84973
25	1.64061	1.85394	2.09378	2.66584	3.38635	4.29187	5.42743	6.84848	8.62308	10.83471

n	11%	12%	14%	15%	16%	18%	20%	22%	24%	25%
1	1.11000	1.12000	1.14000	1.15000	1.16000	1.18000	1.20000	1.22000	1.24000	1.25000
2	1.23210	1.25440	1.29960	1.32250	1.34560	1.39240	1.44000	1.48840	1.53760	1.56250
3	1.36763	1.40493	1.48154	1.52088	1.56090	1.64303	1.72800	1.81585	1.90662	1.95313
4	1.51807	1.57352	1.68896	1.74901	1.81064	1.93878	2.07360	2.21533	2.36421	2.44141
5	1.68506	1.76234	1.92541	2.01136	2.10034	2.28776	2.48832	2.70271	2.93163	3.05176
6	1.87041	1.97382	2.19497	2.31306	2.43640	2.69955	2.98598	3.29730	3.63522	3.81470
7	2.07616	2.21068	2.50227	2.66002	2.82622	3.18547	3.58318	4.02271	4.50767	4.76837
8	2.30454	2.47596	2.85259	3.05902	3.27841	3.75886	4.29982	4.90771	5.58951	5.96046
9	2.55804	2.77308	3.25195	3.51788	3.80296	4.43545	5.15978	5.98740	6.93099	7.45058
10	2.83942	3.10585	3.70722	4.04556	4.41144	5.23384	6.19174	7.30463	8.59443	9.31323
11	3.15176	3.47855	4.22623	4.65239	5.11726	6.17593	7.43008	8.91165	10.65709	11.64153
12	3.49845	3.89598	4.81790	5.35025	5.93603	7.28759	8.91610	10.87221	13.21479	14.55192
13	3.88328	4.36349	5.49241	6.15279	6.88579	8.59936	10.69932	13.26410	16.38634	18.18989
14	4.31044	4.88711	6.26135	7.07571	7.98752	10.14724	12.83918	16.18220	20.31906	22.73737
15	4.78459	5.47357	7.13794	8.13706	9.26552	11.97375	15.40702	19.74229	25.19563	28.42171
16	5.31089	6.13039	8.13725	9.35762	10.74800	14.12902	18.48843	24.08559	31.24259	35.52714
17	5.89509	6.86604	9.27646	10.76126	12.46768	16.67225	22.18611	29.38442	38.74081	44.40892
18	6.54355	7.68997	10.57517	12.37545	14.46251	19.67325	26.62333	35.84899	48.03860	55.51115
19	7.26334	8.61276	12.05569	14.23177	16.77652	23.21444	31.94800	43.73577	59.56786	69.38894
20	8.06231	9.64629	13.74349	16.36654	19.46076	27.39303	38.33760	53.35764	73.86415	86.73617
21	8.94917	10.80385	15.66758	18.82152	22.57448	32.32378	46.00512	65.09632	91.59155	108.42022
22	9.93357	12.10031	17.86104	21.64475	26.18640	38.14206	55.20614	79.41751	113.57352	135.52527
23	11.02627	13.55235	20.36158	24.89146	30.37622	45.00763	66.24737	96.88936	140.83116	169.40659
24	12.23916	15.17863	23.21221	28.62518	35.23642	53.10901	79.49685	118.20502	174.63064	211.75824
25	13.58546	17.00006	26.46192	32.91895	40.87424	62.66863	95.39622	144.21013	216.54199	264.69780

TABLE 6A-2 Present Value of 1 (PV1): $PVI = \dfrac{1}{(1 + i)^n}$ also expressed as (PVI, i, n)

This table shows the present value of $1 discounted at various rates of interest and for various time periods. It is used to compute the present value of single payments.

n Periods	2%	2½%	3%	4%	5%	6%	7%	8%	9%	10%
1	.98039	.97561	.97087	.96154	.95238	.94340	.93458	.92593	.91743	.90909
2	.96117	.95181	.94260	.92456	.90703	.89000	.87344	.85734	.84168	.82645
3	.94232	.92860	.91514	.88900	.86384	.83962	.81630	.79383	.77218	.75131
4	.92385	.90595	.88849	.85480	.82270	.79209	.76290	.73503	.70843	.68301
5	.90573	.88385	.86261	.82193	.78353	.74726	.71299	.68058	.64993	.62092
6	.88797	.86230	.83748	.79031	.74622	.70496	.66634	.63017	.59627	.56447
7	.87056	.84127	.81309	.75992	.71068	.66506	.62275	.58349	.54703	.51316
8	.85349	.82075	.78941	.73069	.67684	.62741	.58201	.54027	.50187	.46651
9	.83676	.80073	.76642	.70259	.64461	.59190	.54393	.50025	.46043	.42410
10	.82035	.78120	.74409	.67556	.61391	.55839	.50835	.46319	.42241	.38554
11	.80426	.76214	.72242	.64958	.58468	.52679	.47509	.42888	.38753	.35049
12	.78849	.74356	.70138	.62460	.55684	.49697	.44401	.39711	.35553	.31863
13	.77303	.72542	.68095	.60057	.53032	.46884	.41496	.36770	.32618	.28966
14	.75788	.70773	.66112	.57748	.50507	.44230	.38782	.34046	.29925	.26333
15	.74301	.69047	.64186	.55526	.48102	.41727	.36245	.31524	.27454	.23939
16	.72845	.67362	.62317	.53391	.45811	.39365	.33873	.29189	.25187	.21763
17	.71416	.65720	.60502	.51337	.43630	.37136	.31657	.27027	.23107	.19784
18	.70016	.64117	.58739	.49363	.41552	.35034	.29586	.25025	.21199	.17986
19	.68643	.62553	.57029	.47464	.39573	.33051	.27651	.23171	.19449	.16351
20	.67297	.61027	.55368	.45639	.37689	.31180	.25842	.21455	.17843	.14864
21	.65978	.59539	.53755	.43883	.35894	.29416	.24151	.19866	.16370	.13513
22	.64684	.58086	.52189	.42196	.34185	.27751	.22571	.18394	.15018	.12285
23	.63416	.56670	.50669	.40573	.32557	.26180	.21095	.17032	.13778	.11168
24	.62172	.55288	.49193	.39012	.31007	.24698	.19715	.15770	.12640	.10153
25	.60953	.53939	.47761	.37512	.29530	.23300	.18425	.14602	.11597	.09230

n Periods	11%	12%	14%	15%	16%	18%	20%	22%	24%	25%
1	.90090	.89286	.87719	.86957	.86207	.84746	.83333	.81967	.80645	.80000
2	.81162	.79719	.76947	.75614	.74316	.71818	.69444	.67186	.65036	.64000
3	.73119	.71178	.67497	.65752	.64066	.60863	.57870	.55071	.52449	.51200
4	.65873	.63552	.59208	.57175	.55229	.51579	.48225	.45140	.42297	.40960
5	.59345	.56743	.51937	.49718	.47611	.43711	.40188	.37000	.34111	.32768
6	.53464	.50663	.45559	.43233	.41044	.37043	.33490	.30328	.27509	.26214
7	.48166	.45235	.39964	.37594	.35383	.31393	.27908	.24859	.22184	.20972
8	.43393	.40388	.35056	.32690	.30503	.26604	.23257	.20376	.17891	.16777
9	.39092	.36061	.30751	.28426	.26295	.22546	.19381	.16702	.14428	.13422
10	.35218	.32197	.26974	.24718	.22668	.19106	.16151	.13690	.11635	.10737
11	.31728	.28748	.23662	.21494	.19542	.16192	.13459	.11221	.09383	.08590
12	.28584	.25668	.20756	.18691	.16846	.13722	.11216	.09198	.07567	.06872
13	.25751	.22917	.18207	.16253	.14523	.11629	.09346	.07539	.06103	.05498
14	.23199	.20462	.15971	.14133	.12520	.09855	.07789	.06180	.04921	.04398
15	.20900	.18270	.14010	.12289	.10793	.08352	.06491	.05065	.03969	.03518
16	.18829	.16312	.12289	.10686	.09304	.07078	.05409	.04152	.03201	.02815
17	.16963	.14564	.10780	.09293	.08021	.05998	.04507	.03403	.02581	.02252
18	.15282	.13004	.09456	.08081	.06914	.05983	.03756	.02789	.02082	.01801
19	.13768	.11611	.08295	.07027	.05961	.04308	.03130	.02286	.01679	.01441
20	.12403	.10367	.07276	.06110	.05139	.03651	.02608	.01874	.01354	.01153
21	.11174	.09256	.06383	.05313	.04430	.03094	.02174	.01536	.01092	.00922
22	.10067	.08264	.05599	.04620	.03819	.02622	.01811	.01259	.00880	.00738
23	.09069	.07379	.04911	.04017	.03292	.02222	.01509	.01032	.00710	.00590
24	.08170	.06588	.04308	.03493	.02838	.01883	.01258	.00846	.00573	.00472
25	.07361	.05882	.03779	.03038	.02447	.01596	.01048	.00693	.00462	.00378

TABLE 6A-3   Future Value of an Ordinary Annuity of n Payments of 1 Each (FVA): $FVA = \dfrac{(1 + i)^n - 1}{i}$ also expressed as (FVA, i, n)

This table shows the future value of an ordinary annuity of $1 at various rates of interest and for various time periods. It is used to compute the future value of a series of payments made at the *end* of each interest compounding period.

n Periods	2%	2½%	3%	4%	5%	6%	7%	8%	9%	10%
1	1.00000	1.00000	1.00000	1.00000	1.00000	1.00000	1.00000	1.00000	1.00000	1.00000
2	2.02000	2.02500	2.03000	2.04000	2.05000	2.06000	2.07000	2.08000	2.09000	2.10000
3	3.06040	3.07563	3.09090	3.12160	3.15250	3.18360	3.21490	3.24640	3.27810	3.31000
4	4.12161	4.15252	4.18363	4.24646	4.31013	4.37462	4.43994	4.50611	4.57313	4.64100
5	5.20404	5.25633	5.30914	5.41632	5.52563	5.63709	5.75074	5.86660	5.98471	6.10510
6	6.30812	6.38774	6.46841	6.63298	6.80191	6.97532	7.15329	7.33593	7.52333	7.71561
7	7.43428	7.54753	7.66246	7.89829	8.14201	8.39384	8.65402	8.92280	9.20043	9.48717
8	8.58297	8.73612	8.89234	9.21423	9.54911	9.89747	10.25980	10.63663	11.02847	11.43589
9	9.75463	9.95452	10.15911	10.58280	11.02656	11.49132	11.97799	12.48756	13.02104	13.57948
10	10.94972	11.20338	11.46388	12.00611	12.57789	13.18079	13.81645	14.48656	15.19293	15.93742
11	12.16872	12.48347	12.80780	13.48635	14.20679	14.97164	15.78360	16.64549	17.56029	18.53117
12	13.41209	13.79555	14.19203	15.02581	15.91713	16.86994	17.88845	18.97713	20.14072	21.38428
13	14.68033	15.14044	15.61779	16.62684	17.71298	18.88214	20.14064	21.49530	22.95338	24.52271
14	15.97394	16.51895	17.08632	18.29191	19.59863	21.01507	22.55049	24.21492	26.01919	27.97498
15	17.29342	17.93193	18.59891	20.02359	21.57856	23.27597	25.12902	27.15211	29.36092	31.77248
16	18.63929	19.38022	20.15688	21.82453	23.65749	25.67253	27.88805	30.32428	33.00340	35.94973
17	20.01207	20.86473	21.76159	23.69751	25.84037	28.21288	30.84022	33.75023	36.97370	40.54470
18	21.41231	22.38635	23.41444	25.64541	28.13238	30.90565	33.99903	37.45024	41.30134	45.59917
19	22.84056	23.94601	25.11687	27.67123	30.53900	33.75999	37.37896	41.44626	46.01846	51.15909
20	24.29737	25.54466	26.87037	29.77808	33.06595	36.78559	40.99549	45.76196	51.16012	57.27500
21	25.78332	27.18327	28.67649	31.96920	35.71925	39.99273	44.86518	50.42292	56.76453	64.00250
22	27.29898	28.86286	30.53678	34.24797	38.50521	43.39229	49.00574	55.45676	62.87334	71.40275
23	28.84496	30.58443	32.45288	36.61789	41.43048	46.99583	53.43614	60.89330	69.53194	79.54302
24	30.42186	32.34904	34.42647	39.08260	44.50200	50.81558	58.17667	66.76476	76.78981	88.49733
25	32.03030	34.15776	36.45926	41.64591	47.72710	54.86451	63.24904	73.10594	84.70090	98.34706

n	11%	12%	14%	15%	16%	18%	20%	22%	24%	25%
1	1.00000	1.00000	1.00000	1.00000	1.00000	1.00000	1.00000	1.00000	1.00000	1.00000
2	2.11000	2.12000	2.14000	2.15000	2.16000	2.18000	2.20000	2.22000	2.24000	2.25000
3	3.34210	3.37440	3.43960	3.47250	3.50560	3.57240	3.64000	3.70840	3.77760	3.81250
4	4.70973	4.77933	4.92114	4.99338	5.06650	5.21543	5.36800	5.52425	5.68422	5.76563
5	6.22780	6.35285	6.61010	6.74238	6.87714	7.15421	7.44160	7.73958	8.04844	8.20703
6	7.91286	8.11519	8.53552	8.75374	8.97748	9.44197	9.92992	10.44229	10.98006	11.25879
7	9.78327	10.08901	10.73049	11.06680	11.41387	12.14152	12.91590	13.73959	14.61528	15.07349
8	11.85943	12.29969	13.23276	13.72682	14.24009	15.32700	16.49908	17.76231	19.12294	19.84186
9	14.16397	14.77566	16.08535	16.78584	17.51851	19.08585	20.79890	22.67001	24.71245	25.80232
10	16.72201	17.54874	19.33730	20.30372	21.32147	23.52131	25.95868	28.65742	31.64344	33.25290
11	19.56143	20.65458	23.04452	24.34928	25.73290	28.75514	32.15042	35.96205	40.23787	42.56613
12	22.71319	24.13313	27.27075	29.00167	30.85017	34.93107	39.58050	44.87370	50.89495	54.20766
13	26.21164	28.02911	32.08865	34.35192	36.78620	42.21866	48.49660	55.74591	64.10974	68.75958
14	30.09492	32.39360	37.58107	40.50471	43.67199	50.81802	59.19592	69.01001	80.49608	86.94947
15	34.40536	37.27971	43.84241	47.58041	51.65951	60.96527	72.03511	85.19221	100.81514	109.68684
16	39.18995	42.75328	50.98035	55.71747	60.92503	72.93901	87.44213	104.93450	126.01077	138.10855
17	44.50084	48.88367	59.11760	65.07509	71.67303	87.06804	105.93056	129.02009	157.25336	173.63568
18	50.39594	55.74971	68.39407	75.83636	84.14072	103.74028	128.11667	158.40451	195.99416	218.04460
19	56.93949	63.43968	78.96923	88.21181	98.60323	123.41353	154.74000	194.25350	244.03276	273.55576
20	64.20283	72.05244	91.02493	102.44358	115.37975	146.62797	186.68800	237.98927	303.60062	342.94470
21	72.26514	81.69874	104.76842	118.81012	134.84051	174.02100	225.02560	291.34691	377.46477	429.68087
22	81.21431	92.50258	120.43600	137.63164	157.41499	206.34479	271.03072	356.44323	469.05632	538.10109
23	91.14788	104.60289	138.29704	159.27638	183.60138	244.48685	326.23686	435.86075	582.62984	673.62636
24	102.17415	118.15524	158.65862	184.16784	213.97761	289.49448	392.48424	532.75011	723.46100	843.03295
25	114.41331	133.33387	181.87083	212.79302	249.21402	342.60349	471.98108	650.95513	898.09164	1054.79118

TABLE 6A–4   Present Value of an Ordinary Annuity of n Payments of 1 Each (PVA): $PVA = \dfrac{1 - \dfrac{1}{(1 + i)^n}}{i}$ also expressed as (PVA, i, n)

This table shows the present value of an ordinary annuity of $1 at various interest rates and for various time periods. It is used to compute the present value of a series of payments made at the *end* of each interest compounding period.

n Periods	2%	2½%	3%	4%	5%	6%	7%	8%	9%	10%
1	.98039	.97561	.97087	.96154	.95238	.94340	.93458	.92593	.91743	.90909
2	1.94156	1.92742	1.91347	1.88609	1.85941	1.83339	1.80802	1.78326	1.75911	1.73554
3	2.88388	2.85602	2.82861	2.77509	2.72325	2.67301	2.62432	2.57710	2.53129	2.48685
4	3.80773	3.76197	3.71710	3.62990	3.54595	3.46511	3.38721	3.31213	3.23972	3.16987
5	4.71346	4.64583	4.57971	4.45182	4.32948	4.21236	4.10020	3.99271	3.88965	3.79079
6	5.60143	5.50813	5.41719	5.24214	5.07569	4.91732	4.76654	4.62288	4.48592	4.35526
7	6.47199	6.34939	6.23028	6.00205	5.78637	5.58238	5.38929	5.20637	5.03295	4.86842
8	7.32548	7.17014	7.01969	6.73274	6.46321	6.20979	5.97130	5.74664	5.53482	5.33493
9	8.16224	7.97087	7.78611	7.43533	7.10782	6.80169	6.51523	6.24689	5.99525	5.75902
10	8.98259	8.75206	8.53020	8.11090	7.72173	7.36009	7.02358	6.71008	6.41766	6.14457
11	9.78685	9.51421	9.25262	8.76048	8.30641	7.88687	7.49867	7.13896	6.80519	6.49506
12	10.57534	10.25776	9.95400	9.38507	8.86325	8.38384	7.94269	7.53608	7.16073	6.81369
13	11.34837	10.98318	10.63496	9.98565	9.39357	8.85268	8.35765	7.90378	7.48690	7.10336
14	12.10625	11.69091	11.29607	10.56312	9.89864	9.29498	8.74547	8.24424	7.78615	7.36669
15	12.84926	12.38138	11.93794	11.11839	10.37966	9.71225	9.10791	8.55948	8.06069	7.60608
16	13.57771	13.05500	12.56110	11.65230	10.83777	10.10590	9.44665	8.85137	8.31256	7.82371
17	14.29187	13.71220	13.16612	12.16567	11.27407	10.47726	9.76322	9.12164	8.54363	8.02155
18	14.99203	14.35336	13.75351	12.65930	11.68959	10.82760	10.05909	9.37189	8.75563	8.20141
19	15.67846	14.97889	14.32380	13.13394	12.08532	11.15812	10.33560	9.60360	8.95011	8.36492
20	16.35143	15.58916	14.87747	13.59033	12.46221	11.46992	10.59401	9.81815	9.12855	8.51356
21	17.01121	16.18455	15.41502	14.02916	12.82115	11.76408	10.83553	10.01680	9.29224	8.64869
22	17.65805	16.76541	15.93692	14.45112	13.16300	12.04158	11.06124	10.20074	9.44243	8.77154
23	18.29220	17.33211	16.44361	14.85684	13.48857	12.30338	11.27219	10.37106	9.58021	8.88322
24	18.91393	17.88499	16.93554	15.24696	13.79864	12.55036	11.46933	10.52876	9.70661	8.98474
25	19.52346	18.42438	17.41315	15.62208	14.09394	12.78336	11.65358	10.67478	9.82258	9.07704

n Periods	11%	12%	14%	15%	16%	18%	20%	22%	24%	25%
1	.90090	.89286	.87719	.86957	.86207	.84746	.83333	.81967	.80645	.80000
2	1.71252	1.69005	1.64666	1.62571	1.60523	1.56564	1.52778	1.49153	1.45682	1.44000
3	2.44371	2.40183	2.32163	2.28323	2.24589	2.17427	2.10648	2.04224	1.98130	1.95200
4	3.10245	3.03735	2.91371	2.85498	2.79818	2.69006	2.58873	2.49364	2.40428	2.36160
5	3.69590	3.60478	3.43308	3.35216	3.27429	3.12717	2.99061	2.86364	2.74538	2.68928
6	4.23054	4.11141	3.88867	3.78448	3.68474	3.49760	3.32551	3.16692	3.02047	2.95142
7	4.71220	4.56376	4.28830	4.16042	4.03857	3.81153	3.60459	3.41551	3.24232	3.16114
8	5.14612	4.96764	4.63886	4.48732	4.34359	4.07757	3.83716	3.61927	3.42122	3.32891
9	5.53705	5.32825	4.94637	4.77158	4.60654	4.30302	4.03097	3.78628	3.56550	3.46313
10	5.88923	5.65022	5.21612	5.01877	4.83323	4.49409	4.19247	3.92318	3.66186	3.57050
11	6.20652	5.93770	5.45273	5.23371	5.02864	4.65601	4.32706	4.03540	3.77569	3.65640
12	6.49236	6.19437	5.66029	5.42062	5.19711	4.79322	4.43922	4.12737	3.85136	3.72512
13	6.74987	6.42355	5.84236	5.58315	5.34233	4.90951	4.53268	4.20277	3.91239	3.78010
14	6.98187	6.62817	6.00207	5.72448	5.46753	5.00806	4.61057	4.26456	3.96160	3.82408
15	7.19087	6.81086	6.14217	5.84737	5.57546	5.09158	4.67547	4.31522	4.00129	3.85926
16	7.37916	6.97399	6.26506	5.95423	5.66850	5.16235	4.72956	4.35673	4.03330	3.88741
17	7.54879	7.11963	6.37286	6.04716	5.74870	5.22233	4.77463	4.39077	4.05911	3.90993
18	7.70162	7.24967	6.46742	6.12797	5.81785	5.27316	4.81219	4.41866	4.07993	3.92794
19	7.83929	7.36578	6.55037	6.19823	5.87746	5.31624	4.84350	4.44152	4.09672	3.94235
20	7.96333	7.46944	6.62313	6.25933	5.92884	5.35275	4.86958	4.46027	4.11026	3.95388
21	8.07507	7.56200	6.68696	6.31246	5.97314	5.38368	4.89132	4.47563	4.12117	3.96311
22	8.17574	7.64465	6.74295	6.35866	6.01133	5.40990	4.90943	4.48822	4.12998	3.97049
23	8.26643	7.71843	6.79206	6.39884	6.04425	5.43212	4.92453	4.49854	4.13708	3.97639
24	8.34814	7.78432	6.83514	6.43377	6.07263	5.45095	4.93710	4.50700	4.14281	3.98111
25	8.42174	7.84314	6.87293	6.46415	6.09709	5.46691	4.94759	4.51393	4.14742	3.98489

TABLE 6A-5　　Future Value of an Annuity Due of n Payments of 1 Each (FVAD): $FVAD = \left[\dfrac{(1 + i)^n - 1}{i}\right] \times (1 + i)$ also expressed as $(FVAD, i, n) = (1 + i)(FVA, i, n)$

This table shows the future value of an annuity due of $1 at various rates of interest and for various time periods. It is used to compute the future value of a series of payments made at the *beginning* of each interest compounding period.

n Periods	2%	2½%	3%	4%	5%	6%	7%	8%	9%	10%
1	1.02000	1.02500	1.03000	1.04000	1.05000	1.06000	1.07000	1.08000	1.09000	1.10000
2	2.06040	2.07563	2.09090	2.12160	2.15250	2.18360	2.21490	2.24640	2.27810	2.31000
3	3.12161	3.15252	3.18363	3.24646	3.31013	3.37462	3.43994	3.50611	3.57313	3.64100
4	4.20404	4.25633	4.30914	4.41632	4.52563	4.63709	4.75074	4.86660	4.98471	5.10510
5	5.30812	5.38774	5.46841	5.63298	5.80191	5.97532	6.15329	6.33593	6.52333	6.71561
6	6.43428	6.54743	6.66246	6.89829	7.14201	7.39384	7.65402	7.92280	8.20043	8.48717
7	7.58297	7.73612	7.89234	8.21423	8.54911	8.89747	9.25980	9.63663	10.02847	10.43589
8	8.75463	8.95452	9.15911	9.58280	10.02656	10.49132	10.97799	11.48756	12.02104	12.57948
9	9.94972	10.20338	10.46388	11.00611	11.57789	12.18079	12.81645	13.48656	14.19293	14.93742
10	11.16872	11.48347	11.80780	12.48635	13.20679	13.97164	14.78360	15.64549	16.56029	17.53117
11	12.41209	12.79555	13.19203	14.02581	14.91713	15.86994	16.88845	17.97713	19.14072	20.38428
12	13.68033	14.14044	14.61779	15.62684	16.71298	17.88214	19.14064	20.49530	21.95338	23.52271
13	14.97394	15.51895	16.08632	17.29191	18.59863	20.01507	21.55049	23.21492	25.01919	26.97498
14	16.29342	16.93193	17.59891	19.02359	20.57856	22.27597	24.12902	26.15211	28.36092	30.77248
15	17.63929	18.38022	19.15688	20.82453	22.65749	24.67253	26.88805	29.32428	32.00340	34.94973
16	19.01207	19.86473	20.76159	22.69751	24.84037	27.21288	29.84022	32.75023	35.97370	39.54470
17	20.41231	21.38635	22.41444	24.64541	27.13238	29.90565	32.99903	36.45024	40.30134	44.59917
18	21.84056	22.94601	24.11687	26.67123	29.53900	32.75999	36.37896	40.44626	45.01846	50.15909
19	23.29737	24.54466	25.87037	28.77808	32.06595	35.78559	39.99549	44.76196	50.16012	56.27500
20	24.78332	26.18327	27.67649	30.96920	34.71925	38.99273	43.86518	49.42292	55.76453	63.00250
21	26.29898	27.86286	29.53678	33.24797	37.50521	42.39229	48.00574	54.45676	61.87334	70.40275
22	27.84496	29.58443	31.45288	35.61789	40.43048	45.99583	52.43614	59.89330	68.53194	78.54302
23	29.42186	31.34904	33.42647	38.08260	43.50200	49.81558	57.17667	65.76476	75.78981	87.49733
24	31.03030	33.15776	35.45926	40.64591	46.72710	53.86451	62.24904	72.10594	83.70090	97.34706
25	32.67091	35.01171	37.55304	43.31175	50.11345	58.15638	67.67647	78.95442	92.32398	108.18177

	11%	12%	14%	15%	16%	18%	20%	22%	24%	25%
1	1.11000	1.12000	1.14000	1.15000	1.16000	1.18000	1.20000	1.22000	1.24000	1.25000
2	2.34210	2.37440	2.43960	2.47250	2.50560	2.57240	2.64000	2.70840	2.77760	2.81250
3	3.70973	3.77933	3.92114	3.99338	4.06650	4.21543	4.36800	4.52425	4.68422	4.76563
4	5.22780	5.35285	5.61010	5.74238	5.87714	6.15241	6.44160	6.73958	7.04844	7.20703
5	6.91286	7.11519	7.53552	7.75374	7.97748	8.44197	8.92992	9.44229	9.98006	10.25879
6	8.78327	9.08901	9.73049	10.06680	10.41387	11.14152	11.91590	12.73959	13.61528	14.07349
7	10.85943	11.29969	12.23276	12.72682	13.24009	14.32700	15.49908	12.76231	18.12294	18.84186
8	13.16397	13.77566	15.08535	15.78584	16.51851	18.08585	19.79890	21.67001	23.71245	24.80232
9	15.72201	16.54874	18.33730	19.30372	20.32147	22.52131	24.95868	27.65742	30.64344	32.25290
10	18.56143	19.65458	22.04452	23.34928	24.73290	27.75514	31.15042	34.96205	39.23787	41.56613
11	21.71319	23.13313	26.27075	28.00167	29.85017	33.93107	38.58050	43.87370	49.89495	53.20766
12	25.21164	27.02911	31.08865	33.35192	35.78620	41.21688	47.49660	54.74591	63.10974	67.75958
13	29.09492	31.39260	36.58107	39.50471	42.67199	49.81802	58.19592	68.01001	79.49608	85.94947
14	33.40536	37.27971	42.84241	46.58041	50.65951	59.96527	71.03511	84.19221	99.81514	108.68684
15	38.18995	41.75328	49.98035	5⁴ 71747	59.92503	71.93901	86.44213	103.93450	125.01077	137.10855
16	43.50084	47.88367	58.11760	6 07509	70.67303	86.06804	104.93056	128.02009	156.25336	172.63568
17	49.39594	54.74971	67.39407	74.83636	83.14072	102.74028	127.11667	157.40451	194.99416	217.04460
18	55.93949	62.43968	77.96923	87.21181	97.60323	122.41353	153.74000	193.25350	243.03276	272.55576
19	63.20283	71.05244	90.02493	101.44358	114.37975	145.62797	185.68800	236.98927	302.60062	341.94470
20	71.26514	80.69874	103.76842	117.81012	133.84051	173.02100	224.02560	290.34691	376.46447	428.68087
21	80.21431	91.50258	119.43600	136.63164	156.41499	205.34479	270.03072	355.44323	468.05632	537.10109
22	90.14788	103.60289	137.29704	158.27638	182.60138	243.48685	325.23686	434.86075	581.62984	672.62636
23	101.17415	117.15524	157.65862	183.16784	212.97761	288.49448	391.48424	531.75011	722.46100	842.03295
24	113.41331	132.33387	180.87083	211.79302	248.21402	341.60349	470.98108	649.95513	897.09164	1053.79118
25	126.99877	149.33393	207.33274	244.71197	289.08827	404.27211	566.37730	794.16526	1113.63363	1318.48898

TABLE 6A-6 Present Value of an Annuity Due of n Payments of 1 Each (PVAD): $PVAD = \left[\dfrac{1 - \dfrac{1}{(1 + i)^n}}{i}\right] \times (1 + i)$ also expressed as $(PVAD, i, n) = (1 + i)(PVA, i, n)$

This table shows the present value of an annuity due of $1 at various rates of interest and for various time periods. It is used to compute the present value of a series of payments made at the *beginning* of each interest compounding period.

n Periods	2%	2½%	3%	4%	5%	6%	7%	8%	9%	10%
1	1.00000	1.00000	1.00000	1.00000	1.00000	1.00000	1.00000	1.00000	1.00000	1.00000
2	1.98039	1.97561	1.97087	1.96154	1.95238	1.94340	1.93458	1.92593	1.91743	1.90909
3	2.94156	2.92742	2.91347	2.88609	2.85941	2.83339	2.80802	2.78326	2.75911	2.73554
4	3.88388	3.85602	3.82861	3.77509	3.72325	3.67301	3.62432	3.57710	3.53130	3.48685
5	4.80773	4.76197	4.71710	4.62990	4.54595	4.46511	4.38721	4.31213	4.23972	4.16987
6	5.71346	5.64583	5.57971	5.45182	5.32948	5.21236	5.10020	4.99271	4.88965	4.79079
7	6.60143	6.50813	6.41719	6.24214	6.07569	5.91732	5.76654	5.62788	5.48592	5.35526
8	7.47199	7.34939	7.23028	7.00205	6.78637	6.58238	6.38929	6.20637	6.03295	5.86842
9	8.32548	8.17014	8.01969	7.73274	7.46321	7.20979	6.97130	6.74664	6.53482	6.33493
10	9.16224	8.97087	8.78611	8.43533	8.10782	7.80169	7.51523	7.24689	6.99525	6.75902
11	9.98259	9.75206	9.53020	9.11090	8.72173	8.36009	8.02358	7.71008	7.41766	7.14457
12	10.78685	10.51421	10.25262	9.76048	9.30641	8.88687	8.49867	8.13896	7.80519	7.49506
13	11.57534	11.25776	10.95400	10.38507	9.86325	9.38384	8.94269	8.53608	8.16073	7.81369
14	12.34837	11.98319	11.63496	10.98565	10.39357	9.85268	9.35765	8.90378	8.48690	8.10336
15	13.10625	12.69091	12.29607	11.56312	10.89864	10.29498	9.74547	9.24424	8.78615	8.36669
16	13.84926	13.38139	12.93794	12.11839	11.37966	10.71225	10.10791	9.55948	9.06069	8.60608
17	14.57771	14.05500	13.56110	12.65230	11.83777	11.10590	10.44665	9.85137	9.31256	8.82371
18	15.29187	14.71220	14.16612	13.16567	12.27407	11.47726	10.76322	10.12164	9.54363	9.02155
19	15.99203	15.35336	14.75351	13.65930	12.68959	11.82760	11.05909	10.37189	9.75563	9.20141
20	16.67846	15.97889	15.32380	14.13394	13.08532	12.15812	11.33560	10.60360	9.95012	9.36492
21	17.35143	16.58916	15.87747	14.59033	13.46221	12.46992	11.59401	10.81815	10.12855	9.51356
22	18.01121	17.18455	16.41502	15.02916	13.82115	12.76408	11.83553	11.01680	10.29224	9.64869
23	18.65805	17.76541	16.93692	15.45112	14.16300	13.04158	12.06124	11.20074	10.44243	9.77154
24	19.29220	18.33211	17.44361	15.85684	14.48857	13.30338	12.27219	11.37106	10.58021	9.88322
25	19.91393	18.88499	17.93554	16.24696	14.79864	13.55036	12.46933	11.52876	10.70661	9.98474

n Periods	11%	12%	14%	15%	16%	18%	20%	22%	24%	25%
1	1.00000	1.00000	1.00000	1.00000	1.00000	1.00000	1.00000	1.00000	1.00000	1.00000
2	1.90090	1.89286	1.87719	1.86957	1.86207	1.84746	1.83333	1.81967	1.80645	1.80000
3	2.71252	2.69005	2.64666	2.62571	2.60523	2.56564	2.52778	2.49153	2.45682	2.44000
4	3.44371	3.40183	3.32163	3.28323	3.24589	3.17427	3.10648	3.04224	2.98130	2.95200
5	4.10245	4.03735	3.91371	3.85498	3.79818	3.69006	3.58873	3.49364	3.40428	3.36160
6	4.69590	4.60478	4.43308	4.35216	4.27429	4.12717	3.99061	3.86364	3.74538	3.68928
7	5.23054	5.11141	4.88867	4.78448	4.68474	4.49760	4.32551	4.16692	4.02047	3.95142
8	5.71220	5.56376	5.28830	5.16042	5.03857	4.81153	4.60459	4.41551	4.24232	4.16114
9	6.14612	5.96764	5.63886	5.48732	5.34359	5.07757	4.83716	4.61927	4.42122	4.32891
10	6.53705	6.32825	5.94637	5.77158	5.60654	5.30302	5.03097	4.78628	4.56550	4.46313
11	6.88923	6.65022	6.21612	6.01877	5.83323	5.49409	5.19247	4.92318	4.68186	4.57050
12	7.20652	6.93770	6.45273	6.23371	6.02864	5.65601	5.32706	5.03540	4.77569	4.65640
13	7.49236	7.19437	6.66029	6.42062	6.19711	5.79322	5.43922	5.12737	4.85136	4.72512
14	7.74987	7.42355	6.84236	6.58315	6.34322	5.90951	5.53268	5.20277	4.91239	4.78010
15	7.98187	7.62817	7.00207	6.72448	6.46753	6.00806	5.61057	5.26456	4.96160	4.82408
16	8.19087	7.81086	7.14217	6.84737	6.57546	6.09158	5.67547	5.31522	5.00129	4.85926
17	8.37916	7.97399	7.26506	6.95424	6.66850	6.16235	5.72956	5.35673	5.03330	4.88741
18	8.54879	8.11963	7.37286	7.04716	6.74870	6.22233	5.77463	5.39077	5.05911	4.90993
19	8.70162	8.24967	7.46742	7.12797	6.81785	6.27316	5.81219	5.41866	5.07993	4.92794
20	8.83929	8.36578	7.55037	7.19823	6.87746	6.31624	5.84350	5.44152	5.09672	4.94235
21	8.96333	8.46944	7.62313	7.25933	6.92884	6.35275	5.86958	5.46027	5.11026	4.95388
22	9.07507	8.56200	7.68696	7.31246	6.97314	6.38368	5.89132	5.47563	5.12117	4.96311
23	9.17574	8.64465	7.74294	7.35866	7.01133	6.40990	5.90943	5.48822	5.12998	4.97049
24	9.26643	8.71843	7.79206	7.39884	7.04425	6.43212	5.92453	5.49854	5.13708	4.97639
25	9.34814	8.78432	7.83514	7.43377	7.07263	6.45095	5.93710	5.50700	5.14281	4.98111

KEY TERMS

Annuity (238)
Annuity due (238)
Compound interest (236)
Future value (234)
Going, prevailing, or market rate of
  interest (246)
Interest (234)

Interest expense (235)
Interest revenue (235)
Ordinary annuity (238)
Present value (234)
Principal (235)
Simple interest (236)
Time value of money (234)

QUESTIONS

1. Explain what is meant by the time value of money.
2. Assuming the annual rate of interest is specified as 12%, what would simple interest rates be for the following periods: (a) semiannual, (b) quarterly, (c) monthly?
3. What is the fundamental difference between simple interest and compound interest?
4. Briefly explain each of the following:
   a. Future value of 1.
   b. Present value of 1.
   c. Future value of annuity of n payments of 1 each.
   d. Present value of annuity of n payments of 1 each.
5. Assume $10,000 is borrowed on a two-year, 10% note payable. Compute the total amount of interest that would be paid on this note assuming (a) simple interest and (b) compound interest.
6. Match columns 2 and 3 with column 1 by entering the appropriate letter from column 1:

Column 1	Column 2	Column 3
A. Future value of 1.	FV1 _____	$\dfrac{1}{(1 + i)^n}$ _____
B. Present value of 1.	PV1 _____	$(1 + i)^n$ _____
C. Future value of an ordinary annuity of 1.	PVA _____	$1 - \dfrac{\dfrac{1}{(1 + i)^n}}{i}$ _____
	FVA _____	
D. Present value of an ordinary annuity of 1.		$\dfrac{(1 + i)^n - 1}{i}$ _____

7. Match the following by entering the appropriate letter (n and i are the same for each value). (Hint: which number in column 2 is the most easily identified with the definition in column 1. Use it to find n and i.)

A. Future value of 1.	17.51851 _____
B. Present value of 1.	4.60654 _____
C. Future value of	.26295 _____
annuity of 1 (ordinary).	3.80296 _____
D. Present value of	20.32147 _____
annuity of 1 (ordinary).	5.34359 _____
E. Future value of	
annuity of 1 (due).	
F. Present value of	
annuity of 1 (due).	

8. Contrast a future value of 1 with a present value of 1.
9. The future value of 1 at 15% interest for 12 years is 5.35025: (a) What is the present value of 1 in this situation? (b) If the present value of 1 at 12% interest for 17 years is .14564, what is the future value of 1 at 12% for 17 years? Do not use tables.
10. (a) If the table value for a future value of 1 is known, how may it be converted to the table value for present value of 1? (b) Show the computations to convert the following future values of 1 to the equivalent present values of 1 as follows: 1.46933; 3.18547; and 216.54199.
11. If $15,000 is deposited in a savings account at 8% compound interest, what would be the balance in the savings account at the end of (a) 10 years? (b) 15 years? (c) 25 years?

12. Assume you have a legal contract that specifies that you will receive $200,000 cash in the future. Assuming a 9% interest rate, what would be the present value of that contract if the amount will be received (a) 10 years, (b) 15 years, or (c) 25 years from now?

13. Assume you deposited $20,000 in a savings account for a three-year period. How much cash would you receive at the end if 12% simple interest per annum is accumulated in the fund at the end of each quarter?

14. Assume you will receive $100,000 cash from a trust fund six years from now. What is the present value of the $100,000 assuming 12% interest on a quarterly basis?

15. What are the three characteristics of an annuity? Explain what would happen if any of these characteristics is changed.

16. Table 6A–3 gives a future value of an ordinary annuity of 1 of 3.09 (rounded) for $n = 3$, $i = 3\%$. Explain the meaning of this table value.

17. If $20,000 is deposited in a savings account at the end of each of n annual periods and will earn 9%, what would be the balance in the savings account at the date of the last deposit (i.e., an ordinary annuity), assuming $n = 10$ years, 15 years, and 25 years?

18. Explain the difference between (a) future value of an ordinary annuity and (b) future value of an annuity due.

19. Explain the difference between (a) present value of an ordinary annuity and (b) present value of an annuity due.

20. Compute the present value of an annuity of five payments of $9,000 each using a 12% interest rate, assuming (a) an ordinary annuity and (b) an annuity due. Explain why the two amounts are different.

21. Compute the future value of an annuity of six payments of $5,000 each using a 10% interest rate, assuming (a) an ordinary annuity and (b) an annuity due. Explain why the two amounts are different.

22. Ro Company will create a building fund by contributing $100,000 per year to it for 10 years; the fund will be increased each year at a 7% compound interest rate. Assume this is the current year: (a) Explain how you would determine whether this situation is an ordinary annuity or an annuity due. (b) In each instance, how many payments and compounding periods would be involved?

23. If an annuity value of 1 is computed by formula or read from an annuity table, explain the implicit dates for both a future value and present value, assuming (a) an ordinary annuity and (b) an annuity due.

24. J. Reed purchased a Mercedes with a cash "bargin" price of $40,000. Cash of $10,000 was paid at purchase date and the remainder was paid in eight quarterly payments (ordinary annuity) of $4,274 each. The going rate of annual interest used for this deal was 16%. How much did Reed pay for the auto? How much interest was paid? Was the interest implicit in the $4,274 payment greater or less than 16%?

EXERCISES

E 6–1 Compounding for Periods Less than One Year (L.O. 5)	Fox Company plans to deposit $60,000 today into a special building fund that will be needed at the end of 6 years. A financial institution will serve as the fund trustee and will pay 12% interest on the fund balance. *Required:* Compute the fund balance at the end of year 5, assuming: a. Annual compounding. b. Semiannual compounding. c. Quarterly compounding.
E 6–2 Compounding for Periods Less than One Year (L.O. 1, 5)	The two situations below are independent. a. Lace Company will need about $100,000 cash to renovate some old equipment four years from now. A local financial institution will increase the fund at 16% annual interest. Compute the amount of cash that would have to be deposited now to meet the future need, assuming (show computations): (1) Semiannual compounding. (2) Quarterly compounding. b. On January 1, TJ Company has a contract whereby the company is due to receive $70,000

cash in 6 years. The company is short of cash and desires to discount (sell) this claim. WT is willing to accept a 9% annual discount. Under these conditions, how much cash would TJ receive now?

E 6–3
Compounding for Periods Less than One Year
(L.O. 1, 5)

Each of the following situations is independent.

a. Suppose you invested $10,000 in a savings account at 8% compound interest. What balance would be in your savings account at the end of five years assuming:
  (1) Annual compounding?
  (2) Semiannual compounding?
  (3) Quarterly compounding?
     Explain why these amounts are different.

b. Suppose you wish to accumulate a fund of $40,000 at the end of six years by making a single deposit now. The fund will earn 8% compound interest. What amount must you deposit now to accumulate the $40,000 fund assuming:
  (1) Annual compounding?
  (2) Semiannual compounding?
  (3) Quarterly compounding?
     Explain why these amounts are different.

E 6–4
Present Value, Fund Accumulation, and Schedule
(L.O. 1, 5)

Each of the following situations is independent.

a. JAX Corporation plans a plant expansion that will require approximately $500,000 in three years. Because JAX has some idle cash on hand now, it desires to know how much it would have to invest as a lump sum now to accumulate the required amount, assuming 8% annual compound interest is added to the fund each December 31.

Required:
  1. Compute the amount that must be invested now.
  2. Prepare an accumulation schedule for the plant expansion fund.

b. On January 1, 1991, JAX Corportion signed a noninterest-bearing $400,000 note that is due on December 31, 1994 (the $400,000 includes both principal and interest). According to the agreement, JAX has the option to pay the $400,000 at maturity date or to pay the obligation in full on January 1, 1991, with a 10% compound interest discount. What would be the amount of cash required on January 1, 1991, to settle the debt in full under the early payment option?

E 6–5
Fund Accumulation, Schedule, and Entries
(L.O. 1, 5)

Frame Company has on hand $200,000 cash that will not be needed in the near future. However, the company will expand operations within the next three to five years. The company has decided to establish a savings account locally which will earn 10% interest compounded annually. The interest will be added to the fund each year. The deposit of $200,000 is made on January 1, 1992.

Required:
  1. Compute the balance in the fund at the end of 1994.
  2. Prepare a fund accumulation schedule.
  3. Give the journal entries for the fund for the first year. Assume Frame's reporting year ends December 31.

E 6–6
Fund Accumulation, Schedule, and Entries
(L.O. 1, 5)

R. Ball has a small child. Ball has decided to set up a fund to provide for the child's college education. A local financial institution will handle the fund and increase it each year on a 10% annual compound interest basis. Ball desires to make a single deposit on January 1, 1993, and specifies that the fund must have a $90,000 balance at the end of 2009.

Required:
  1. Compute the amount of cash that must be deposited on January 1, 1993.
  2. Prepare a fund accumulation schedule through 1995.
  3. Give the journal entries for the first year of the fund. Assume Ball's reporting year ends December 31.

E 6–7
PV, Acquisition of Equipment, Cost, Debt Schedule, and Entries
(L.O. 1, 5)

Act Company purchased some additional equipment that was needed because of a new contract. The equipment was purchased on January 1, 1992. Because the contract would require two years to complete and Act was short of cash, the vendor agreed to accept a down payment of $10,000 and a two-year, noninterest-bearing note for $45,000 (this amount includes the principal and all interest) due in 2 years. Assume the going rate of interest for this debt was 20% because of the extremely high risk.

Required:
1. Compute the cost of the equipment. Show computations.
2. Give the entry at date of acquisition of the equipment.
3. Prepare a debt payment schedule.
4. Give all additional entries related to the debt. Assume Act's reporting year ends December 31.

E 6–8
Savings Account, and Simple and Compound Interest Compared
(L.O. 2)

Assume you deposit $100,000 in a special savings account on January 1; the interest rate is 8%.

Required:
1. Compute the balance in the savings account at the end of five years assuming (a) simple interest and (b) compound interest.
2. Calculate and explain the cause of the difference.

E 6–9
Fund Accumulation, and Interest Rate or Time Unknown
(L.O. 1, 5)

The two following cases are independent.

a. Lot Company, at the present date, has $40,000 that will be deposited in a savings account until needed. It is anticipated that $111,000 will be needed at the end of 10 years to expand some manufacturing facilities. What approximate rate of interest would be required to accumulate the $111,000, assuming compounding on an annual basis? Show computations. Do not interpolate.
b. Lot Company is planning an addition to its office building as soon as adequate funds can be accumulated. The company has estimated that the addition will cost approximately $250,000. At the present time $90,600 cash is on hand that will not be needed in the near future. A local savings institution will pay 8% interest (compounded annually). How many periods would be required to accumulate the $250,000? Show computations. Do not interpolate.

E 6–10
Debt Retirement, Interest Rate Not Known
(L.O. 1, 5)

The two following cases are independent:

a. On September 1, Loft Company decided to deposit $200,000 in a debt retirement fund. The company needs $337,000 cash to pay a debt 10 years later. What rate of compound interest must the fund earn to meet the cash requirement to pay the debt? Do not interpolate.
b. Flare Company owes a $400,000 debt (this amount includes both principal and interest) that is payable eight years from now. Flare wants to pay the debt in full immediately. The creditor has agreed to settle the debt in full for $177,800 cash. What rate of compound discount is the creditor applying to the note? Do not interpolate.

E 6–11
Compounding with Increasing Interest Rate, Compute Expected Selling Price
(L.O. 1, 5)

The two cases that follow are independent.

a. Jason Fine has decided to invest $10,000 today in a mutual fund. He anticipates leaving this investment in the fund for 12 years. The fund will be increased each year-end by specified compound interest rates as follows: Years 1 to 4 inclusive, 8%; 5 to 8 inclusive, 9%; and 9 to 12 inclusive, 10%. Compute the balance that will be in the fund at the end of Year 12.
b. Bob Nixon owns a special kind of property that cost $6,000 five years ago. Now he wants to sell it for cash. Bob estimates reliably that this property will produce two net cash inflows as follows: End of Year 5 from now, $120,000; and end of Year 8 from now, $80,000. He deems it reasonable to use compound discount interest rates of 6% for the $120,000 cash inflow and 10% for the $80,000 cash inflow (it is riskier to the buyer). Given these estimates, compute the approximate selling price that Bob should expect.

E 6–12
Applications of Future and Present Value of 1
(L.O. 1, 3)

Each of the following cases is independent.

a. A compound interest table (or formula) value is .72198. Is this a future value of 1 or a present value of 1? Explain without consulting the tables.

b. What table value should be used to compute the balance in a fund at the end of Year 11 if $100,000 is deposited at the date the fund is established, assuming 6% annual compound interest, and semiannual compounding?

c. What table value should be used to compute the present value of $50,000, assuming 8% compound interest, quarterly compounding, and six years of discounting?

d. A fund is established by depositing $6,000 at compound interest; the fund will have a balance of $48,822 at the end of 15 years. What is the approximate annual rate of interest?

e. A discounted note payable of $40,000 (including both principal and interest) is due three years hence. Assuming 7% annual compound interest, at what amount should this debt be settled today (i.e., three years before maturity) on a cash basis?

E 6–13
Fund Balance with Changing Interest Rate
(L.O. 1, 5)

On January 1, Bill Zeff invested $10,000 cash in a special savings account. It will be increased by the compound interest each year-end. The fund will earn 8% for the first three years, 9% for the next three years, and 10% for the last four years.

Required:
Compute the balance in the fund at the end of year 10.

E 6–14
Ordinary and Annuity Due Compared
(L.O. 4)

United Company has decided to accumulate a fund by making equal periodic contributions. The fund will be increased each interest period by 8% compound interest. The current date is January 1.

Required:
1. Complete the following tabulation to compare an ordinary annuity with an annuity due:

   a. Ordinary annuity (end-of-period):

Compounding	Contribution	*n*	*i*	Table Value	Fund Balance
Annual	$5,000	5	___	_____	$___
Semiannual	2,500	___	___	_____	___
Quarterly	1,250	___	___	_____	___

   b. Annuity due (beginning of period):

Annual	$5,000	___	___	_____	___
Semiannual	2,500	___	___	_____	___
Quarterly	1,250	___	___	_____	___

2. Explain why the ordinary annuity and annuity due fund balances are different.
3. Give the journal entry at the end of the first compounding period for each of the six situations above (indicate dates and use simple interest because the differences are insignificant). Assume United's reporting year ends December 31.

E 6–15
Understanding Future and Present Value Concepts
(L.O. 3)

Complete the following table, assuming *n* = 9, and *i* = 18%.

Concept	Symbol	Formula	Table Value	Table (source)
1. Future value of 1.	___	___	___	___
2. Present value of 1.	___	___	___	___
3. Future value of ordinary annuity of *n* rents of 1 each.	___	___	___	___
4. Present value of ordinary annuity of *n* rents of 1 each.	___	___	___	___
5. Future value of annuity due of *n* rents of 1 each.	___	___	___	___
6. Present value of annuity due of *n* rents of 1 each.	___	___	___	___

E 6–16
Fund, Ordinary Annuity, Schedule, Entries
(L.O. 1, 4, 5)

Soltar Company has decided to accumulate a debt retirement fund by making three equal annual deposits of $11,000 beginning December 31, 1993. Assume the fund will accumulate annual compound interest at 7% per year which will be added to the fund balance.

Required:

1. What kind of annuity is this? Explain.
2. What will be the balance in the fund in three years (immediately after the last deposit)?
3. Prepare an accumulation schedule for this fund.
4. Prepare the journal entries for the three-year period. Assume Soltar's reporting year ends December 31.
5. What would be the balance in the fund at the end of three years if it were set up on an annuity due basis?

E 6–17
Debt Payment, Annuity Due, Schedule, Entries
(L.O. 1, 4, 5)

On September 1, 1992, Sault Company incurred a $60,000 debt. Arrangements have been made to pay this debt in three equal annual installments starting immediately at compound interest of 10%.

Required:

1. Is this an ordinary annuity or annuity due? Explain.
2. Compute the amount of the equal annual payments.
3. Prepare a debt payment schedule.
4. Give the journal entries related to the debt. Assume Sault's reporting year ends August 31.
5. Compute the annual payment if the debt payments were made annually beginning at the end of each year.

E 6–18
Debt Payment, Ordinary Annuity, Schedule, Entries
(L.O. 1, 4, 5)

On May 1, 1992 Job Company owes a $100,000 debt that will be paid in three equal annual payments. The first payment is to be made next April 30. The interest rate is 12%.

Required:

1. Is this an ordinary annuity or an annuity due? Explain.
2. Compute the amount of the equal annual payments.
3. Prepare a debt payment schedule.
4. Give the journal entries related to the fund. Assume Job's reporting year ends April 30.
5. Compute the annual payment if the debt payments were made annually beginning on May 1.

E 6–19
Debt, Annuity, Schedule, Entries
(L.O. 1, 4, 5)

Xeonics Company has decided to establish a debt retirement fund with three equal annual contributions of $15,000, starting on January 1, 1992. The fund will be increased at each year-end at 9% per annum. The $53,000 debt must be paid on December 31, 1994.

Required:

1. Is this an ordinary annuity or an annuity due? Explain.
2. What will be the balance of the fund at the end of 1994?
3. Prepare a fund accumulation schedule.
4. Give the journal entries related to the fund. Assume Xeonics reporting year ends December 31.
5. What balance would be in the fund if it had been set up on an ordinary annuity basis, with the first annual contribution on December 31, 1992.

E 6–20
Debt and Fund, Annuity, Interest Rate or Time Not Known
(L.O. 1, 5)

a. Oliver Company plans to establish a debt retirement fund, beginning December 31 of Year 1 to accumulate $90,120. End-of-period contributions of $20,000 will be made to a trustee each December 31, so that the desired amount will be available in four years, the date of the last payment. Compute the required interest rate that must be earned by the fund on an annual compound basis to satisfy these requirements. Show your computations to demonstrate that your answer is correct.

b. Polus Company has decided to create a plant expansion fund by making equal annual deposits of $30,000 on each January 1. Interest at 10% compounded annually will be added to the fund balance each year-end. The company wants to know how many deposits will be required to accumulate a fund of $313,077. Show your computations to demonstrate that your answer is correct.

E 6–21
Understanding Present and Future Value Cases
(L.O. 1, 3, 4, 5)

Each of the following cases is independent.

a. Bill Able has $25,000 in a fund that earns 10% annual compound interest. If he desires to withdraw it in five equal annual amounts, starting today (i.e., beginning of period) how much would he receive each year?

b. Bill will deposit $250 each semiannual period starting today (i.e, beginning of period); this savings account will earn 6% compounded each semiannual period. What will be the balance in Bill's savings account at the end of year 10?

c. Bill purchased a new automobile that cost $14,000. He received a $4,000 trade-in allowance for his old auto and signed an 16% note for $10,000. The note requires eight equal quarterly payments starting at the end of the first quarter from date of purchase. What is the amount of each payment?

d. Bill deposited $2,000 at the end of each year in a savings account for five years at compound interest. The fund had a balance of $12,456 at the date of the last deposit. What rate of interest did he earn?

e. On January 1, Bill owed a debt of $15,131.14. An agreement was reached that he would pay the debt plus compound interest in 24 monthly installments of $800, the first payment to be made at the end of January. What rate of annual interest is he paying?

E 6–22

Funds, Single Plus Periodic Deposits (L.O. 3, 5)

Straus Company established a construction fund on July 1, 1992, by making a single deposit of $250,000. Also, at the end of each year, the company will make $20,000 deposits in the fund. The fund will earn 14% compound interest each year, which will be added to the fund balance.

Required:

1. Compute the balance that will be in the fund June 30, 1996.
2. Give the journal entries that would be made for the first year. Assume Straus's reporting year ends December 31.

E 6–23

Compute the Price of a Used Machine (L.O. 1, 3, 5)

Rye Company is considering purchasing a used machine that is in excellent mechanical condition. The company plans to keep the machine for 10 years, at which time the residual value will be zero. An analysis of the capacity of the machine and the costs of operating it (including materials used in production) provided an estimate that the machine would increase after-tax net cash inflow by approximately $200,000 per year.

Required:

1. Compute the approximate amount that Rye should be willing to pay now for the machine assuming a target earnings rate of 20% per year. Assume also that the revenue is realized at each year-end. Show your computations.
2. What price should be paid assuming a $50,000 residual value at the end of the 10 years?

PROBLEMS

P 6–1

Future Values, Different Compounding Period (L.O. 5)

Avis Company deposited $100,000 in a special expansion fund on May 1, 1992, for future use as needed. The fund will accumulate 12% compounded interest per year.

Required:

1. Complete the following table by entering, into each cell, the balance that would be in the fund at the end of the intervals indicated:

Compounding Assumption	Periodic Interest Rate	Fund Balance at End of	
		Two Years	Four Years
Annual			
Semiannual			
Quarterly			

2. Prepare a fund accumulation schedule based on the first cell (annual, for two years).
3. Give journal entries for the fund based on the first cell (annual, for two years). Assume Avis' reporting year ends December 31.

P 6–2
How Much to Deposit to Build a Fund, Different Compounding Periods
(L.O. 1, 5)

Story Company anticipates that it will need $200,000 cash for an expansion in the next few years. Assume an annual compound interest rate of 8%. The company desires to make a single contribution January 1, 1993, so that the $200,000 will be available when needed.

Required:

1. Complete the following schedule by entering into each cell the appropiate values to meet the above specifications:

| | | Amount to Be Deposited Now | | | |
| | | Two Years | | Three Years | |
Compounding Assumption	Interest Rate	*n*	$	*n*	$
Annual	_____	_____	$_____	_____	$_____
Semiannual	_____	_____	$_____	_____	$_____

2. Prepare a fund accumulation schedule based on $n = 2; i = 8\%$.
3. Give journal entries for years 1 and 2 based on $n = 2$, $i = 8\%$. Assume Story's reporting year ends December 31.

P 6–3
Building a Fund, Three Cases, Unknown Time or Rate, Schedule
(L.O. 1, 5)

Case 1. On January 1, 1993, Smith deposited $8,000 in a savings account that would accumulate at 11% annual compound interest for four years.

Required:

1. Compute the balance that would be in the savings account at the end of the fourth year.
2. Prepare a fund accumulation schedule for this case.

Case 2. On March 1, 1993, Brown deposited $10,000 in a savings account that would accumulate to $12,597 at the end of three years, assuming annual compound interest. Do not interpolate.

Required:

1. Compute the interest rate that would be necessary. Show computations.
2. Prepare a fund accumulation schedule for this case.

Case 3. On September 1, 1993, Dan Jones deposited $7,000 in a savings account that would accumulate to $11,108, assuming 8% annual compound interest.

Required:

1. Compute the number of periods that would be necessary. Show computations.
2. Prepare a fund accumulation schedule for this case.

P 6–4
Fund, Compute Balances, Schedule, Entries
(L.O. 5)

Fox Company deposited $100,000 in a special expansion fund for use in the future as needed. The fund will accumulate at 10% annual compound interest. The fund was started on March 1, 1992 and the interest will be added to the fund balance on an annual compound interest basis.

Required:

1. Compute the balance that will be in the fund at the end of 3 years, 5 years, and 10 years, respectively.
2. Prepare a fund accumulation schedule for three years.
3. Give the journal entries for Fox Company for the first three years. Disregard adjusting and closing the entries. Assume Fox's reporting year ends February 28.
4. What adjusting entry would be made on December 31 of the first year assuming this is the end of the accounting period for Fox Company?

P 6–5
Funds, Time or Rate Unknown, Fund Balance
(L.O. 1, 5)

a. On September 1, 1991, Blare Johnson deposited $40,000 in a savings account that was expected to accumulate $43,600 at August 31, 1992.

Required:

1. Compute the implicit compound annual interest rate.
2. What would be the balance in the fund on August 31, 1996, 2001, and 2011?

b. On May 1, 1992, Jim Bolton deposited $100,000 in a savings account that would accumulate to $125,971 on April 30, 1995.

Required:

1. Compute the implicit compound annual interest rate.
2. Prepare the three-year fund accumulation schedule.

c. On October 1, 1992, Phil Hardy deposited $10,000 in a savings account and expects the fund to have a balance of $25,000 at the end of 10 years.

Required:

1. Compute the implicit interest rate. Show the interpolation that would be required to obtain the approximate interest rate to two decimal places.
2. What would be in the fund at the end of 20 years? (Hint: Use a programmed calculator, if available; otherwise round the answer in (1) to the nearest percent.)

P 6–6
Settle Old Debts with New Debt, Present and Future Value
(L.O. 1, 2, 5)

NIX Company is trying to clean up some of its debts. On January 1, 1991, the company has savings accounts as follows:

Date Established	Amount Deposited (Single Deposit for Each)	Annual Compound Interest Rate
1/1/80	$20,000	8%
1/1/86	30,000	10%

The outstanding debts on January 1, 1991, to be paid off are as follows:

Due Date	Type of Note	Face of Note*
12/31/94	Noninterest bearing	$ 60,000
12/31/01	Noninterest bearing	200,000

*These amounts include both principal and all interest thereon. The amount given for each note is the single sum to be paid at maturity date.

Required:

1. Compute the amount of cash that NIX can get from the two savings accounts on January 1, 1991.
2. Compute the amount for which the two debts can be settled on January 1, 1991, assuming a going rate of interest of 18%.
3. Assuming all cash is withdrawn from the savings accounts and all payments are made on the debts, would NIX have a cash shortage or an excess? How much?

P 6–7
Annuity: Ordinary and Due Compared, Schedules, Entries
(L.O. 1, 4, 5)

Strong Tools Company will establish a special debt retirement fund amounting to $100,000. A trustee has agreed to handle the fund and to increase it each year on a 20% annual compound interest basis. Strong Tools will make equal annual contributions to the fund during the next four years starting in 1993.

Required:

1. Compute the amount of the required annual deposit assuming that they are made on (*a*) December 31 and (*b*) January 1. If your answers are different, explain why.
2. Prepare a fund accumulation schedule for each starting date (*a*) and (*b*) above.
3. Give the journal entries related to each starting date for all four years. Date each entry. Use a tabulation similar to the following (assume Strong's reporting year ends December 31):

Date	Fund (Debit)	Cash (Credit)	Interest Revenue (Credit)

P 6–8
Special Fund, Annuity
Compute, Schedule,
Entries
(L.O. 1, 5)

Morse Company is contemplating the accumulation of a special fund to be used for expanding sales activities into the western part of the country. It is January 1, 1993, and the fund will be needed in three years, according to present plans. The fund will earn 6% interest compounded annually. Annual contributions will be $50,000. The management has not yet decided whether to start the deposits on January 1 or December 31 of 1993.

Required:

1. Compute the amount of the fund balance at the beginning of 1996, assuming three annual deposits are made on *(a)* January 1 and *(b)* December 31. If your answers are different, explain why.
2. Prepare a fund accumulation schedule for each starting date *(a)* and *(b)* above.
3. Give the journal entries related to each starting date for years 1993 through 1995. Date each entry. Use a tabulation similar to the following (assume Morse's reporting year ends December 31):

Date	Fund (Debit)	Cash (Credit)	Interest Revenue (Credit)

P 6–9
Annuity, Debt, Schedule,
Entries
(L.O. 1, 5)

It is January 1, 1992, and Delux Specialties Company owes a $100,000 past-due debt to City Bank. The bank has agreed to permit Delux to pay the debt in three equal installments, each payment to include principal and compound interest at 10%. One issue has not yet been settled. The bank desires that the first installment be paid immediately; however, because of a cash liquidity problem, Delux is asking to make the first payment at year-end, December 31.

Required:

1. Compute the amount of the three equal annual payments if *(a)* the first payment is on January 1 and *(b)* the first payment is on December 31. If the amounts are different, explain why.
2. Prepare a debt payment schedule for each payment.
3. Give the journal entries related to each payment date through the last payment. Use a tabulation similar to the following (assume Delux's reporting year ends December 31):

Date	Interest Expense (Debit)	Liability Debit	Liability Credit	Cash (Credit)

P 6–10
Annuity, Debt, Schedule,
Entries
(L.O. 1, 5)

Rapid Construction Company can purchase a used machine for $30,000. The machine will be needed on a new job that will continue for approximately three years. It is January 1, 1993 and the machine is needed immediately. Because of a shortage of cash, Rapid has asked the vendor for credit terms. The vendor charges 11% annual compound interest. The machine can be purchased under these terms by making three equal payments.

Required:

1. Compute the amount of the three equal payments assuming they are to be paid on *(a)* January 1 and *(b)* December 31. If your answers are different, explain why.
2. Prepare a debt payment schedule for *(a)* and *(b)* above.
3. Give the journal entries for *(a)* and *(b)* through Year 3. Date each entry. Use a tabulation similar to the following (assume Rapid's reporting year ends December 31):

Date	Interest Expense (Debit)	Liability Debit	Liability Credit	Cash (Credit)

4. What amount should be recorded as the cost of the machine in *(a)* and *(b)* above?

P 6–11
Annuity, Fund, Schedule
(L.O. 1, 5)

On January 1, Wick Company agreed with its president, J. Smith, to make a single deposit immediately, to establish a fund with a trustee that will pay Smith $80,000 per year for each of the three years following retirement. Smith will retire in 10 years on January 1, and the 3 equal annual payments are to be made by the trustee each December 31 starting in the 10th year. The trustee will add to the fund at 12% annual compound interest each year-end. The fund is to have a zero balance on December 31, immediately after the last payment to Smith.

Required:

1. Compute the single amount that Wick Company must deposit in the fund on January 1 to meet the specified payments to Smith.
2. Prepare a fund payout schedule to show the use of the fund during the payout period. Use captions similar to the following: date, cash payments to Smith, interest revenue earned on the fund, net fund decreases, and fund balance.
3. How much of the amount paid to Smith during the payout period was provided by interest earned during the payout period?

P 6–12
Debt, Compute Periodic Payments, Schedule
(L.O. 1, 3, 5)

Blair Richie is considering the purchase of a sailboat, which has a cash price of $6,726. Terms can be arranged for a $2,000 cash down payment and payment of the remaining $4,726, plus interest at 15% compound interest per annum, in three equal payments. Assume purchase on January 1, 1994, and payments on each December 31 thereafter.

Required:

1. Complete the amount of each annual payment.
2. What did Blair pay for the boat? What was the total amount of interest paid?
3. Prepare a debt payment schedule using the following format:

			Liability	
Date	Cash Payment	Interest Expense	Decrease	Balance

4. Upon graduation January 1, 1998. Blair sold the sailboat for three equal annual payments of $1,000 each; the first payment was paid on the date that the boat was transferred, assume January 1, 1998. Assume a 9% going rate of interest. What selling price did Blair get?

P 6–13
Annuities Compared, Ordinary and Due, Compute
(L.O. 4, 5)

For each of the independent cases given below, assume the interest rate is 12% and compounding is semiannual.

a. How much will accumulate by the end of eight years, if $3,000 is deposited each semi-annual interest period in a savings account *(a)* at the end of each period and *(b)* at the start of each period? Verify your answers, one with the other.
b. What will be the periodic payments each period on a $67,000 debt that is to be paid in semiannual installments over a six-year period, assuming compound interest, if payments are made *(a)* at the beginning of each period and *(b)* at the end of each period?
c. A special machine is purchased that had a list price of $45,000. Payment in full was cash, $9,000, and five equal semiannual payments of $6,000 each. The first payment will be made at the end of the first semiannual period from purchase date. How much should be recorded in the accounts as the cost of the machine?
d. A special investment is being contemplated. This investment will produce an estimated end-of-period cash income of $26,000 semiannually for five years. At the end of its productive life, the investment will have an estimated recovery value of $4,500. Determine a reasonable estimate of the value of the investment.

P 6–14
Annuity, Debt, Computation, Entry
(L.O. 1, 5)

a. On June 1, Road Rover Company owed an $80,000 overdue debt. The bank agreed to allow payment of it over the next three years at 12% compound interest; payments to be made each quarter. Compute the periodic payments assuming *(a)* the first payment is made August 31, and *(b)* the first payment is made June 1. If you get different answers, explain why they are different.
b. Sweringen Tool Company rents a warehouse from William Jones for $10,000 annual rent, payable in advance on each January 1. Sweringen Tool Company proposed to sign a three-year lease and to pay the three years' rent in advance. The owner agreed to the proposal with the stipulation that the $30,000 be paid immediately (i.e., on January 1). The Company has this proposal under consideration because it expected some discount in view of the fact that funds currently are earning above 8% per annum. Develop a counter proposal as to the amount the company should pay. Give the entry the company should make on January 1 to record your proposal, assuming it is accepted by Jones.

P 6–15
Annuity, Fund
Accumulation, Fund
Payout, Schedule
(L.O.1, 3, 6)

John Lane has a motivated daughter, Lois, who is 15 years old today. For her birthday, Lane invests $20,000 toward her college education. Lane stipulates that Lois may withdraw four equal annual amounts from the fund, the first withdrawal to be made on her 18th birthday. The savings and loan association in which Lane placed the investment will add to the fund annual compound interest at the rate of 12% at the end of each year.

Required:

1. Compute the amount of each of the four withdrawals by Lois which will completely deplete the fund on the date of the final withdrawal. Hint: Diagram the problem situation.
2. Prepare a schedule that reflects the *(a)* accumulation of the fund balance and *(b)* withdrawal period (i.e., from her 15th birthday through her 21st birthday). Use captions similar to the following:

Date	Cash	Interest Revenue	Fund	
			Changes	Balance

P 6–16

COMPREHENSIVE PROBLEM
◆

Overview of Future and
Present Value Application
(L.O. 1, 3, 4, 5)

Compute each of the following amounts (each one is independent of the others). Round to the nearest dollar or percent.

a. On January 1, Year 1, $30,000 is deposited in a fund at 16% compound interest. At the end of Year 5, what will the fund balance be, assuming the following:
(1) Annual compounding $_____
(2) Semiannual compounding $_____
(3) Quarterly compounding $_____

b. On January 1, Year 1, a machine is purchased at an invoice price of $20,000. The full purchase price is to be paid at the end of Year 5. Assuming 12% compound interest, what did the machine cost if compounding is as follows?
(1) Annual $_____
(2) Semiannual $_____
(3) Quarterly $_____

c. If $5,000 is deposited in a fund and it will increase to $13,598 by the end of Year 13, the implicit compound interest rate is _____ %.

d. If the present value of $15,000 is $5,864 at 11% compound annual discount, the number of periods is _____ .

e. On January 1, Year 1, a company decided to establish a fund by making 10 equal annual deposits of $6,000, starting on December 31. The fund will be increased by 9% compounded interest. What will be the fund balance at the end of Year 10 (i.e., immediately after the last deposit)?

f. On January 1, Year 1, a company decided to establish a fund by making 10 equal annual deposits of $8,000, starting on January 1. The fund will be increased by 7% compound interest. What will be the balance in the fund at the end of Year 10?

g. John Day is at retirement and has a large amount of ready cash. He wants to deposit enough cash in a fund to receive back $40,000 each December 31 for the next five years, starting on December 31 of this year. Assuming 10% compound interest, how much cash must Day deposit on January 1?

h. Ace Company is considering the purchase of a unique asset on January 1, Year 1. The asset will earn $8,000 net cash inflow each January 1 for five years, starting January 1, Year 1. At the end of Year 5, the asset will have no value. Assuming a 14% compound interest rate, what should Ace be willing to pay for this unique asset on January 1, Year 1?

i. In January of Year 1, Jobay Company decided to build a fund to equal $446,140 by the end of Year 7 by making seven equal annual deposits of $50,000, starting on December 31 of Year 1. What is the implicit compound interest rate for this fund?

j. The present value of several future equal annual cash payments at year-end of $30,000 each is $141,366; assuming 11% compound discount. What is the implicit number of cash payments?

k. M. Moe will retire 10 years from now and wants to establish a fund now that will pay him $30,000 cash at the end of each of the first five years after retirement. Specific dates are these: date of a single deposit by Moe, January 1, Year 1; date of first cash payment from the fund to Moe, December 31, Year 11. The fund will pay 10% compound interest. How much cash must Moe deposit on January 1, Year 1, to provide the five equal annual year-end cash payments from the fund?

CASES

C 6–1
Select Your Bonus
(L.O. 1)

Fred Reed is an executive of VIP Company and has earned a performance bonus. He has the option of taking the $25,000 bonus now, or to take $50,000 five years from now. Which option should he elect? Explain why. (Hint: Find the break-even interest rate.)

C 6–2
Compare the Cost of Two Alternatives
(L.O. 1, 5, 6)

Viable Corporation purchases large machines for use in its plant. Machine Type A is typical of these machines. Currently, Viable is considering the purchase of a new Type A machine. Two different brand names are being considered as follows:

	Brand A	Brand B
Cost (cash basis)	$100,000	$90,000
Operating expense to operate the machine (per year)	$ 7,000	$ 8,000
Estimated useful life (years)	8	8
Estimated residual value (% of cost)	20%	10%

Viable expects a 20% return on its investments.

Required:
1. Prepare an analysis to compare the relative cost of the two brands (assume all variables, other than the four listed above, are the same for both brands).
2. Which machine should Viable purchase? Why? Consider other factors along with your computations.

C 6–3
Compute an Implicit Interest Rate
(L.O. 1, 5)

Slick Real Estate Tax Shelters, Inc., advertised that its special tax-shelter partnerships "earn 21% interest for the investor each year." An independent analysis of the actual figures (obtained from a prior partner after considerable effort) showed that an individual who invested $100,000 would receive a projected return of $310,000 at the end of Year 10 (from investment date) (adapted from "How to Fool with Averages," *Forbes Magazine,* December 7, 1984, pp. 33–34).

Required:
1. Compute the actual interest rate implicit in the tax shelter (round to the nearest percent).
2. Was the advertised rate of return of 21% correct or was it misleading? Explain.

C 6–4
Mortgages
(L.O. 1, 5)

Ray Hughes buys a house for $150,000. He makes a down payment amounting to $20,000 and takes out a 12% mortgage for the balance. The bank requires that he pay off the mortgage in 25 equal annual installments, beginning one year from now.

Required:
1. Determine the amount of these installments.
2. What is the total amount paid by Hughes (over the 25 years) for the $150,000 house?
3. How much of this total represents interest charges?

C 6–5
Investment Alternatives
(L.O. 1, 5, 6)

Nancy Sly wishes to sell her business and receives the following three offers:

a. $284,000 cash (receivable immediately).
b. $100,000 cash right now plus an annual installment of $30,000 at the end of each year for 10 years, a total of $400,000.
c. An offer to manage the property for 10 years that would yield her $48,000 cash at the end of each of the 10 years. She would, however, have to make an initial investment of $10,000 cash right now. Total cash to be received = $470,000.

Which offer should be accepted if Sly has alternative opportunities that will yield a return of 10% per year?

C 6–6
Investment Evaluation
(L.O. 1, 4, 5, 6)

Glenview Grabbers Ball Club is contemplating the construction of a new stadium that is estimated to cost $5,000,000. Financing is expected to be accomplished by issuing 25-year bonds paying 10% interest annually.

Glenview Grabbers' management plans to have admission charges sufficiently large to break even—to cover interest on the bonds, annual operating costs of $300,000, and an annual deposit in a sinking fund to retire the bonds at maturity. The sinking fund is expected to earn 6% per year, and management expects to sell 80,000 $10 admission tickets annually.

Should the new stadium be constructed? Assume a tax rate of 40 percent. Can you determine the appropriate discount rate? Why or why not?

C 6–7
Decision to Overhaul or Replace
(L.O. 1, 3, 4, 5, 6)

A component is presently being manufactured on equipment that is fully depreciated. Although this old machine has a $20,000 cash value on the open market now, with suitable annual overhauls it can be used by the firm for the next three years. The cost of these overhauls is expected to be $40,000 per year (payable at the beginning of each year) and at the end of the third year the "overhauled" machine is expected to have a salvage value of $10,000.

On the other hand, a new machine with an expected life of three years and no expected salvage value at that time can be acquired at a cost of $134,350. The projected sales and cost of operations for each of the next three years are:

Data on Component	Old Machine	New Machine
Unit sales (transfer to other production departments) per year	20,000	20,000
Out-of-pocket operating costs per unit*	$8.00	$7.50

*These cash flows are assumed to occur at the end of each year.

Assume that time value of money for the firm is 10% per annum and ignore income taxes.

Required:

1. Should the old machine be overhauled or the new equipment acquired? Why?
2. If the component can be purchased at a cost of $10.30 per unit from outside suppliers, should it then be purchased or manufactured internally? Explain. Assume that payments to external suppliers are made at the end of each year.
3. At what level of output (unit sales per year) would management be indifferent *(a)* to buying the component from outside suppliers at $10.30 per unit and *(b)* to manufacturing it internally on the new equipment?

C 6–8
Sherwin-Williams:
Analysis of Actual
Financial Statements

Note 9 to Sherwin-Williams's 1990 annual report shows $50 million of outstanding 9.875% debentures due in 2016. Sinking fund payments of $5 million to repay the principal only, are scheduled to begin in the year 2007. Assume all payments are made on December 31.

Required:

1. What interest rate is Sherwin-Williams assuming it will earn on the sinking fund if nine payments are made?
2. If Sherwin-Williams could earn 10%, what do the sinking fund payments need to be?
3. If Sherwin-Williams wanted to make a single sinking fund payment December 31, 1991, to cover the debt, what would it be if the fund could be expected to earn 10%?

ASSET RECOGNITION AND MEASUREMENT

Revenue and Expense Recognition

After you have studied this chapter, you will:

1. Understand the theory and conceptual framework underlying revenue recognition practices.

2. Be familiar with the revenue and matching principles and their application to income determination in most routine sales transactions.

3. Be able to apply acceptable methods of accounting for revenue from long-term contracts and know under what circumstances each is appropriate.

4. Understand both the installment method and the cost recovery method of revenue recognition, and under what circumstances each is appropriate.

5. Know the process of revenue recognition when right of return exists.

6. Be familiar with the four different methods of revenue recognition for service sales: *(a)* specific performance, *(b)* proportional performance, *(c)* completed performance, and *(d)* collection.

7. Understand the theory and conceptual framework linking expense recognition to revenue recognition.

♦

INTRODUCTION
♦

On October 16, 1990, United Airlines and the Boeing Company announced a purchase agreement in which United placed a firm order for 64 Boeing aircraft, plus options to purchase 64 more. As reported in *The Wall Street Journal,* the order had a total potential value of $22 billion, the largest ever for an aircraft manufacturer. The order called for delivery of 30 Boeing 747s beginning in 1994 and extending through 2004. More important, the order also included 34 of the Boeing's newly developed 777, which are to be delivered between 1995 and 2000.[1]

Consider the interesting accounting ramifications attached to this huge contractual commitment between Boeing and United Airlines. Will Boeing recognize any revenue (or income) from this order before the first aircraft is delivered in 1994? Your prior accounting knowledge should lead you to answer no, which indeed is the case. On the other hand, is Boeing better off as a result of this order? The stock market certainly thought so. On the day of the announcement, Boeing's common stock jumped $1.50 (to $46), while the Dow Jones industrial average was unchanged. Did Boeing incur significant aircraft design and development costs essential to obtaining this order? This time the answer is a most assured yes. The Boeing 777 development effort took several years and hundreds of millions of dollars, all of which were incurred before a single airplane was ordered. One estimate of the development cost of the Boeing 777 puts it at $4 billion.[2]

The Boeing story as related here is one in which enormous effort was made to develop a competitive airplane, a firm order for the aircraft was placed, and the securities market made known its opinion that Boeing is better off. Yet Boeing's accounting system will not record one cent of revenue or any income from this transaction until 1994. In this situation, Boeing has *economic income* but not *accounting income.*[3] To understand how this treatment of income comes about, it is first necessary to gain an appreciation for the principles of revenue and expense recognition.

The measurement and reporting of income is one of the most important and controversial topics in financial accounting. A key aspect of income determination is timing the recognition of revenue and the related recognition of expense. The issue of revenue recognition is not easily resolved, especially in light of the many innovative marketing and selling methods used for products and services in today's economy. Consider the following examples, patterned after real-world situations.

Precious Metal Operations: In a recent year, a mining company produced 12,000 ounces of gold at a production cost of $1.2 million. Even though the precious metal could have been sold immediately upon completion of production at a quoted market price of $400 per ounce, management elected not to sell. They expect the price of gold to increase in the near future. In addition to their production costs, the company incurred administrative costs of $500,000 for the year. What will the company show as revenue for the period? And what will it report as income? What is your evaluation of the company's performance for the period? Is it better off or worse off at the end of the year, compared to the beginning of the year?[4]

Book Publishing: Sales transactions by publishing houses are another instance where revenue recognition problems are encountered. College textbooks, for example, are typically ordered and shipped to campus bookstores about eight weeks

---

[1] *The Wall Street Journal,* October 16, 1990, p. A3.

[2] *The Wall Street Journal,* October 16, 1990, p. A4.

[3] The conclusion that Boeing Company has economic income is arrived at indirectly by observing the increase in shareholder wealth. The owners of the company, the shareholders, see increases in value of the shares they own; thus, it is reasonable to conclude that value of the net assets of the company has increased.

[4] This example is in fact a simplification of the situation faced by the Alaska Gold Company. Alaska Gold mined gold for three straight years without selling any of its production. In its annual report to shareholders, Alaska Gold reported zero revenues from gold operations for these periods, and thus reported sizable losses each year. This is one of many interesting cases in G. Pfeiffer and R. Bowen, *Financial Accounting: A Casebook* (Englewood Cliffs, N.J.: Prentice Hall, 1985), pp. 24–29.

before the start of the new term. Textbook orders are based on anticipated enrollments in various classes. For the purposes of this example, assume an introductory marketing class instructor arranges to order 200 copies of the chosen marketing text for her class. Upon receipt of the order, the publisher ships the books in time for unpacking and stocking on the bookstore shelves before the term begins. The publisher's invoice accompanies this shipment, stating that payment is due in 30 days—with which the bookstore complies, paying the invoice amount in full. Three weeks into the term, the bookstore finds that 80 copies of the introductory marketing text remain unsold. Most textbook publishers provide retailers with the right to return unsold, damage-free books within 60 days or more from the original shipping date. Naturally, the bookstore exercises this right.[5] At what point or points during this sequence of events should the publisher record revenue and related expenses on the sale of textbooks to the campus bookstore?

Recreational Campsites: Thousand Trails, Inc., is a Bellevue, Washington, company that develops campgrounds and sells usage rights to consumers for a membership fee of several thousand dollars. Membership fees can be paid in full when the contractual arrangement is signed, but the more typical arrangement is for the consumer to pay a small percentage down and to remit the balance in periodic installments over a period of up to seven years. Membership allows the individual to use existing campgrounds and others planned for future development. One of the appeals of membership is the expanding list of interesting campgrounds the company claims will be developed in the future, although it has limited, if any, legal obligation to do so. Again the question is, when, in the above process, should revenue and related expenses be recognized?[6]

The above examples demonstrate how even minor departures from ordinary marketing and sales activities can complicate the problem of revenue and expense recognition. The objective of this chapter is to ensure that the conceptual guidelines for determining when revenue and expense should be recognized are understood, and that specific accounting applications that have been developed for use in resolving various types of revenue recognition problems are clear.

This chapter is focused on revenue recognition issues. Financial accounting relies on the *matching principle* to trigger expense recognition when revenue is recognized. In general, the matching principle will be used as the primary guideline for expense recognition in this chapter. More complex expense measurement and recognition issues are presented and discussed in later chapters.

♦

THE CONCEPT OF REVENUE
♦

Some of the material in this section serves as a review of key points covered in Chapter 2. However, the aim of this chapter is to gain a deeper understanding of the conceptual issues involved in the measurement of income. Since income is the difference between revenues and expenses (plus gains and less losses), it is necessary, first, to consider the nature of revenues, expenses, gains, and losses.

In Chapter 2, the elements of financial statements as defined in *SFAC No. 6* are presented as follows:

> *Revenues* are inflows or other enhancements of assets of an entity or settlements of its liabilities (or a combination of both) during a period from delivering or producing

---

[5] When right of return exists, revenue recognition decisions are complicated. The FASB has attempted to resolve this particular problem with the issuance of *SFAS No. 48*.

[6] Thousand Trails, Inc., is another case found in Pfeiffer and Bowen, *Financial Accounting*.

goods, rendering services, or other activities that constitute the entity's ongoing major or central operations.

Expenses are outflows or other using up of assets or incurrence of liabilities (or a combination of both) during a period from delivering or producing goods, rendering services, or carrying out other activities that constitute the entity's ongoing major or central operations.

Gains are increases in equity (net assets) from peripheral or incidental transactions of an entity and from all other transactions and other events and circumstances affecting the entity during a period except those that result from revenues or investment by owners.

Losses are decreases in equity (net assets) from peripheral or incidental transactions of an entity and from all other transactions and other events and circumstances affecting the entity during a period except those that result from revenues or investment by owners.

The definitions of revenues and expenses contain the terms *assets* and *liabilities;* the implication is that revenues and expenses are concepts derived from assets and liabilities. Therefore, clear knowledge of assets and liabilities is needed in order to understand revenues and expenses:[7]

Assets are probable future economic benefits obtained or controlled by a particular entity as a result of past transactions or events.

Liabilities are probable future sacrifices of economic benefits arising from present obligations of a particular entity to transfer assets or provide services to other entities in the future as a result of past transactions or events.

Although attention is focused on revenue and expense recognition and measurement issues in this chapter, remember that these issues are not separable from asset and liability recognition and measurement issues.

The Earnings Process   The earnings process for most companies is the composite result of many profit-directed activities, all taking place gradually and continuously. Included in the earnings process are business activities that give rise to revenue and expense, such as designing and engineering products and services; purchasing, tooling and assembling materials; rendering services; delivering goods; and so on. This process is related to the revenue and expense definitions articulated in *SFAC No. 6;* there is a continual "enhancement of assets . . . from delivery or producing goods, rendering services or other activities that constitute the ongoing major or central operations" (i.e., a revenue), and a continual "outflow of assets . . . from delivery or producing goods, rendering services or other activities that constitute the ongoing major or central operations" (i.e., an expense).

To illustrate, consider some of the ongoing major or central activities of Boeing. In the mid-1980s, the company began producing and selling a new generation of aircraft, the Boeing 757. A full detailing of all the activities Boeing undertook in delivering the first 757 to a customer would be lengthy and tedious; however, Exhibit 7–1 is a simplified description of at least some of the activities that constituted the earnings process for this project. The design and development of a new aircraft is a long and costly process. The time from initial research and design to assembly of the first aircraft is several years. The total costs incurred before the first aircraft is delivered are of such a magnitude that the sale of several hundred aircraft generally is required before the company breaks even. With production rates ranging from one to eight aircraft per month, it takes several years before a company like Boeing recovers the costs of its development effort.

---

[7] As was pointed out in Chapter 2, the conceptual framework adopted by the FASB in its *Statements of Financial Concepts* reveals the primacy the Board attributes to the balance sheet and, thus, to assets and liabilities.

EXHIBIT 7-1 An Idealized Summary of the Earnings Process for the Development, Production, and Sale of a New Commercial Airliner

1. Boeing economists and forecasters analyze the future of the air travel and air cargo traffic, translating this information into forecasts about aircraft characteristics that will be needed in the future.
2. Boeing engineers design an aircraft responsive to the needs outlined above. Cost analysts estimate the cost to build the aircraft, while Boeing's marketing unit analyzes potential demand for the aircraft.
3. If the project holds sufficient promise, Boeing commits more resources and proceeds further with preliminary development. This involves more detailed design and engineering efforts. Plans are made to provide a production facility, and production tooling begins to be acquired. Usually, millions of dollars have been spent on the project up to this point.
4. Boeing actively solicits orders for the new aircraft. Considerable effort is made to convey to airline companies the advantages and efficiencies of the new plane. Boeing establishes a minimum number of orders that must be committed before the company will proceed with development.
5. Once the minimum number of orders are received, Boeing begins production. Each aircraft Boeing builds is for a specific airline customer, except for prototypes (which can also eventually be sold). Boeing can ill afford to build airplanes on spec, nor can any aircraft manufacturer, due to the tremendous costs involved. The first few aircraft built are more costly than those assembled later. This is due to production efficiencies that are the result of learning from the experience of building the earlier planes. As more planes are built, Boeing advances along a learning curve, and production costs per unit decrease.
6. Once a plane is assembled, it is tested, custom-painted and outfitted, and prepared for delivery according to the specifications of the ordering airline.
7. The aircraft is formally delivered to the airline that ordered it. The purchasing airline's representative flies the airplane from the Boeing plant to the airline's home airport. This can be years after the airplane was initially developed and the order placed for it.
8. The purchasing airline makes payment for the new aircraft. Typically, the aircraft purchase contract requires that "progress payments" (discussed in this chapter) be made as the aircraft is being built. Boeing also frequently participates in the securing of financing sources for its airline customers.

Although Boeing's earnings process is longer than those more typically found in manufacturing companies, the components making up the process are common to most manufacturers. Each step in the manufacturing process contributes to the earnings process. In Boeing's case, the company incurs mounting costs as each phase of a new aircraft's introduction is completed, but, at the same time, the company is creating something that has value—the aircraft. The expectation is that over the production and marketing life cycle of the new product, the costs incurred will be less than the revenue realized. If this expectation comes to fruition, income (revenue minus expense) is being earned continuously as value is added to the product at each phase in the product's earnings process.

If the earnings process is continuous and revenues are being earned and expenses incurred continuously, why not record (i.e., recognize) revenues and expenses continuously? The answer to this question rests with the fact that certain accounting requirements for recognition must be met before an event or transaction may be recognized in the financial statements.

THE RECOGNITION PROCESS

◆

SFAC No. 5 defines *recognition* as the process of formally incorporating an item into the accounts and financial statements of an entity as either an asset, liability, revenue, expense, gain, or loss. Recognition includes depiction of an item in both words and numbers, with the amount included in the summarized figures reported in the financial statements.

SFAC No. 5 specifies *four fundamental criteria* that must be met before an item can be recognized:

1. *Definition.* The item or event in question must meet the definition of one of the six financial statement elements (asset, liability, revenue, expense, gain, or loss).
2. *Measurability.* The item or event must have a relevant *attribute* that is measurable with sufficient reliability. An attribute is a characteristic, trait, or aspect that can be quantified and measured. Examples of attributes are historical cost, current cost, market value, net realizable value, and net present value.[8]
3. *Relevance.* The information about the item or event is capable of making a difference in user decisions.
4. *Reliability.* The information about the item is representationally faithful, verifiable, and neutral.

Relevance and reliability are described in Chapter 2 as the two primary qualitative characteristics of accounting information. *SFAC No. 5* provides further guidance on the importance of these two criteria as interpreted below:[9] (Emphasis added.)

To be relevant information must have feedback value or predictive value (or both) for users, and must be *timely.* It must have the capability for making a difference in the decision-making process of investors, creditors, and others who use and rely on a company's financial statements for relevant, reliable information. The relevance of a particular piece of information cannot be determined in isolation. Rather, relevance should be evaluated in the context of the principal objective of financial reporting, which is to provide information that is useful in making informed investment, credit, and other related decisions.

To be reliable, information about an item or event must be representationally faithful, verifiable, and neutral. Reliability may affect the *timing of recognition.* For example, the first available information about a business transaction or event that could result in recording an asset or a liability (or change to an existing asset or liability) is sometimes too uncertain to be recognized. Based on the financial effects of a given business transaction or event, it may be too early to properly classify the matter and report it as one of the six financial statement elements. The financial outcome of the matter in question may not be easily measured for accounting purposes, at least not yet. Or it may be cost-prohibitive to investigate such matters to the extent needed to resolve the uncertainties that surround them. Indeed, situations may develop where a piece of accounting information is never recognized, simply because it cannot be categorized, or cannot be made measurable without incurring inordinate costs.

On the other hand, while the unavailability or unreliability of information may delay recognition of an item or event, waiting too long for more complete information to develop—or for the cost involved in gathering more complete information to justify itself—may result in the information losing its relevance. At some intermediate point, uncertainty may be reduced at a justifiable cost to a level tolerable in view of the peceived relevance of the information. If other criteria are met, this is the appropriate time for recognition. In short, *recognition may sometimes involve a trade-off between relevance and reliability.*

This *SFAC No. 5* interpretation points out the difficulty of establishing a point in time for recognition of revenue, especially in more complex situations. For example, Boeing investors and others at the time of the huge United Airlines order would have wanted to know what the income effects would be for Boeing. But the aircraft in question is new, and production costs are uncertain at this point. Any information immediately released on estimated expenses associated with the order would have

---

[8] FASB, *SFAC No. 1*, "Objectives of Financial Reporting by Business Enterprises" (Norwalk, Conn., 1978), par. 2.
[9] FASB, *SFAC No. 5*, "Recognition and Measurement in Financial Statements of Business Enterprises"(Norwalk, Conn., 1984), par. 73–77.

had relevance, but would have been of questionable reliability. In general, relevance indicates early recognition, while reliability suggests later recognition.

The four recognition criteria—definition, measurability, relevance, and reliability—apply to all items to be recognized in the financial statements. Since information about earnings and its components are primary measures of a company's financial performance, *SFAC No. 5* provides further guidance for recognizing the components of earnings.[10] This additional guidance is intended in part to provide more stringent requirements for recognizing components of earnings than is required for recognizing other changes in assets or liabilities.

THE REVENUE PRINCIPLE

The revenue principle, discussed in Chapter 2, provides implementation guidance for the recognition of revenues. *SFAC No. 5* is the latest official pronouncement focusing on revenue recognition.[11] The revenue principle applies to revenues from sale of products and services and to gains.

In addition to the four recognition criteria listed above, the revenue principle states that *revenue should be recognized* (hence recorded) (1) when *it is realized or is realizable,* and (2) when *it is earned.*

Realization occurs when products (goods or services) or other assets are sold for cash or noncash resources, or when claims to cash are received at the date of sale. *Realizability* occurs when the related noncash assets received or held are determined to be readily convertible to known amounts of cash in conformity with the sales terms.[12] Realizability is important because it provides information useful to assessing future cash flows.

Revenues are considered to be *earned* when the company has substantially accomplished what it must do to be entitled to receive the associated benefits. Finally, *SFAC No. 5* states that revenues are *measured* by the exchange values of the assets (goods and services) or liabilities involved.

The remainder of this chapter discusses the application of the revenue principle in a number of business situations. These situations can be broadly categorized according to the timing of the recognition of revenue relative to the delivery of the goods and services to the customer:

1. Revenue recognized at delivery (point of sale).
2. Revenue recognized after delivery.
3. Revenue recognized before delivery.

Exhibit 7–2 offers a quick overview of alternative timings of revenue recognition from slower to faster recognition. As a general rule, when revenue is recognized promptly, *relevance* is the overriding issue; reliability is either not an issue or is of less importance. Conversely, when revenue recognition is delayed, *reliability* is the overriding issue; relevance is either not an issue or is of less importance.

In addition to relative placement on the time line, Exhibit 7–2 separately identifies each method based on *realizability* and *earned* criteria. As noted at the bottom of Exhibit 7–2, revenue recognition methods listed above the time line tend to meet the

---

[10] *SFAC No. 5,* par 79.

[11] Prior to *SFAC No. 5,* a primary source of guidance was *APB Statement No. 4,* Basic Concepts and Accounting Principles Underlying Financial Statements of Business Enterprises'' (AICPA: New York, 1970). The guidance in *SFAC No. 5* is generally consistent with *APB Statement No. 4* and tends to provide more specific guidelines.

[12] *SFAC No. 5* (par. 83) states that readily convertible assets (1) have interchangeable (fungible) units and (2) have quoted prices in an active market that can easily absorb the quantity held without significantly affecting the current price.

EXHIBIT 7-2   Illustration of the Continuum of Revenue Recognition Methods

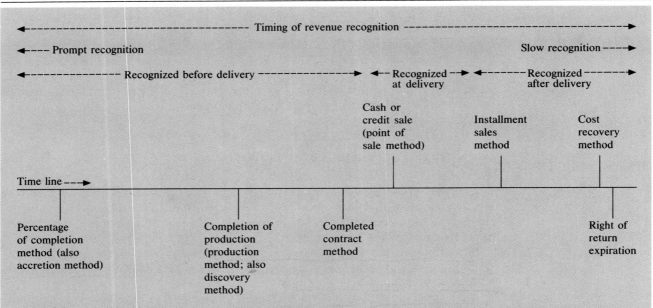

For those methods above the time line, *realizability* is generally the revenue recognition criterion met last, and thus revenue recognition is delayed to the point at which realizability is assured. For those methods below the time line, *realizability* is not generally a problem; thus, the *earned* criterion is met last, and revenue recognition is delayed until it is met. This is not a hard and fast distinction, but does suggest that the two criteria are met at different times for different methods.

Not all possible revenue recognition methods included on the above illustration are generally accepted methods. For example, the accretion method recognizes revenue as the value of a product increases through natural growth (e.g., recognizing revenue as trees grow to maturity) or through natural aging. The discovery basis or method for revenue recognition is a candidate for use in the extractive industries, where the values of discovered resources are recognized as revenues (and as assets) upon discovery, and changes in value are recognized over time as revenues (or losses). These methods result in the recognition of revenue on a timing basis similar to the percentage of completion method. These methods are not GAAP and are not discussed further in this chapter.

Finally, not all possible revenue recognition methods are included on this time-line illustration.

earned criterion first and then the *realizability* criterion. The opposite tends to be true for those methods listed below the time line; among those, the *realizability* criterion is met before the *earned* test for recognition is met. The criterion satisfied last is more weakly met because it is the more difficult criterion to meet.

CONCEPT REVIEW

1. What are the four fundamental criteria that must be met before a transaction or event can be formally recognized in financial statements?
2. In addition to the above four fundamental criteria, what are the additional requirements of the revenue principle?
3. Discuss the application of the revenue principle to the gold mining, textbook publishing, and recreational campsite example illustrations presented earlier in this chapter. In each case, determine the application of the revenue principle in terms of the *realizability* and *earned* criteria.

REVENUE RECOGNIZED AT DELIVERY (POINT OF SALE)

Most revenue-generating activities are easily dealt with using the above guidelines. The two conditions for revenue recognition—when realized or realizable and when earned—are usually met at the time goods or services are delivered. Thus, revenue from the sale of products is usually recognized at the *date of sale,* meaning the date the product is delivered to the customer. Revenue from services rendered is recognized when the services have been performed. This is the **point of sale method,** sometimes called the *sales method* or the *delivery method* of revenue recognition.

Some transactions do not qualify for point of sale revenue recognition because one of the two criteria is not met. For example, revenue from contractual arrangements allowing others to use company assets (as is the case with revenues such as rent, interest, lease payments, and royalties) is *recognized as time passes* or as the asset is used. Revenue is not earned until there is a passage of time; thus, it is recognized accordingly.[13]

When a product or service is sold with a guarantee or warranty, costs associated with servicing these products are likely to be incurred after delivery. When these costs can be reasonably estimated, revenue is recognized at the date of sale (point of sale method), and a provision is made for future warranty costs. In this case, revenue is both earned and realizable, provided the estimated future warranty costs are not so high as to make the earnings process substantially incomplete.

Deferred Revenue   When a company sells a magazine subscription or an airline sells a ticket for air travel sometime in the future, cash is received before the delivery of the product or service. The realizability criterion is met, but the earnings process is not complete until the product is delivered. In this case, cash inflow does not result in a revenue. Rather, the inflow generates an obligation to produce and deliver the product, and hence a liability is recorded. This liability is called **deferred revenue** or unearned revenue. It is not recognized as revenue until the product or service is delivered.

Gains and Losses   Finally, gains or losses resulting from the disposal of assets or other transactions that meet the definition of a gain or loss are generally recognized as soon as they are realized or become realizable.

In practice, there are situations where departures from recognizing revenue at the time of delivery of goods or services is both appropriate and necessary. This usually occurs because one of the two revenue recognition criteria is not met at delivery, or both criteria are met before the delivery of the goods or services. If one or both of the criteria are not met, revenue recognition is delayed until the criteria are met. For example, when a right of return exists, difficulty may occur in determining the ultimate amount of revenue that will be collected (realized), or in determining whether the earning process is in fact complete.

REVENUE RECOGNIZED AFTER DELIVERY

Revenue should be recognized and reported as soon as the revenue recognition criteria are met. Under some circumstances, the revenue recognition criteria are not met until after the delivery of the good or service to the customer. Among these situations are:

---

[13] If, however, the contract (lease) is essentially a noncancelable transfer of all the risks and rights of ownership for the asset, the transaction might qualify as a sale. Such transactions are called *capital leases.*

1. Situations where the substance of the transaction is different from the form, such as in product-financing arrangements.
2. Situations in which there is a right to return the product.
3. Situations in which the ultimate collectibility of the agreed-upon sales price is highly uncertain.

This is not an exhaustive listing, but it is representative and provides common examples of failure to meet the revenue recognition criteria at the point of sale. Each type of situation is considered in the following sections.

Product-Financing Arrangements

Product-financing arrangements include agreements in which a sponsoring company sells a product to another company, and in a related transaction, agrees to repurchase the product.[14] The sponsoring company bears all the business risk associated with the inventory even though it does not have legal title to the inventory. In essence, the second company is an extension of the sponsoring company in regard to this transaction. If revenue were to be recognized upon delivery of the goods to the second company, it would be recognized sooner than is appropriate because the realizability criterion is not met.[15]

The FASB has taken steps to prevent the recording of these kinds of product-financing agreements as sales. If a sponsoring company sells a product to another company and in a related transaction agrees to repurchase the product (or other processed goods of which the above product is a component), the sponsoring company must record a liability at the time the proceeds are received. The sponsoring company can neither record a sale nor remove the product from its inventory. Only when the product is sold to an outside party without a related repurchase agreement can the sponsoring company record a sale.[16]

Revenue Recognition When Right of Return Exists

In several industries, such as book publishing and equipment manufacturing, customers are given extensive rights to return goods under certain circumstances and over long periods of time. This gives rise to a possible problem at the time the product is delivered of determining precisely what amount will ultimately become realizable.

SFAS No. 48, "Revenue Recognition When Right of Return Exists" (par. 6 and 7), states the following (emphasis added):

If an enterprise sells its product but gives the buyer the right to return the product, revenue from the sales transaction shall be *recognized at time of sale only if all of the following conditions are met:*

a. The seller's price to the buyer is substantially fixed or determinable at the date of sale.
b. The buyer has paid the seller, or the buyer is obligated to pay the seller and the obligation is not contingent on resale of the product.

e.g. Consignment (buyer's obligation to pay the seller is contingent on resale of the product.

---

[14] Another form of this transaction would be for one firm (the sponsoring firm) to arrange for a second firm to purchase the product on its behalf, and in a related transaction agree to repurchase the product from the second firm at a later time. There may well be a legal transfer of title to the second firm, but the economic substance of the transaction is such that all the business risk is being borne by the sponsoring firm.

[15] Motivations for such transactions might be (1) for the sponsoring firm to share the business risks of the second firm in order to allow the sponsoring firm to market its product, or (2) as a means of financing its inventory without debt or inventory being shown in the financial statements of the sponsoring company (assuming the transaction is treated as a sale). In the latter case, the second firm borrows in order to "purchase" the inventory, using the inventory as collateral, and the proceeds from the borrowing are used to pay for the purchase. This latter case gives rise to describing the transaction as a *product-financing arrangement.*

[16] FASB, *SFAS No. 49,* "Accounting for Product Financing Arrangements" (Norwalk, Conn., June 1981), par. 8.

c. The buyer's obligation to the seller would not be changed in the event of theft or physical destruction or damage of the product.
d. The buyer acquiring the product for resale has economic substance apart from that provided by the seller.
e. The seller does not have significant obligations for future performance to directly bring about resale of the product by the buyer.
f. The amount of future returns can be reasonably estimated.

When all of the above conditions are met, the point-of-sale method is appropriate. If one or more of the conditions are not met, however, the uncertainty of realization is deemed high enough that this method should not be used. In this case, a variation of the point-of-sale method is used. With this variation, sales revenue, costs of goods sold, and therefore gross margin are deferred to the period in which either the return privilege expires or the six conditions listed above are met.

Illustration To illustrate the accounting for sales when the purchaser has extensive right of return and the sales method is not appropriate, consider the following example: On September 30, 1991, Boston Publishing sells 1,000 copies of a new textbook to bookstores at a unit price of $50. The textbooks have a unit cost to Boston of $30; Boston uses a perpetual inventory system. Because the new text's marketability is uncertain, Boston sells the text with terms of net 30 days, but gives the bookstores until March 31, 1992, to exercise their right to return any unsold textbooks for a cash refund. Boston Publishing does not have a reliable basis for estimating the quantity of returns. The accounting period ends December 31. On January 10, 1992, 100 texts are returned undamaged, and the appropriate bookstores are given credit for the returns. No other units are returned.

On September 30, 1991, Boston Publishing would record the sale of 1,000 textbooks, but would defer any recognition of sales revenue, cost of goods sold, and gross margin. **Gross margin,** also called gross profit, is sales less cost of sales. The accounting entries would be:

Accounts receivable	50,000	
Sales revenue (1,000 units × $50)		50,000
Cost of goods sold	30,000	
Inventory (1,000 units × $30)		30,000
Sales revenue	50,000	
Cost of goods sold		30,000
Deferred gross margin (1,000 × $20)*		20,000

*The deferred gross margin account would appear as a contra to the accounts receivable account on the balance sheet. The nature of this account is discussed further in the next section of this chapter.

Assume that as of October 30, 1991, $50,000 is collected on the account receivable. This collection of cash would not trigger the recognition of revenue because Boston Publishing would still be uncertain regarding the number of texts that might be returned. The gross margin is recognized only as it is realized when (1) the return privilege expires or (2) the six conditions of *SFAS No. 48* are met.

One hundred texts are returned on January 10, 1992. This results in the recognition of an inventory item, the reduction of gross margin, and the reduction of the accounts receivable (or in this case, the disbursement of cash to the bookstore returning the books because the bookstore has previously paid for the book purchase). The journal entry is:

Inventory (100 units × $30)	3,000	
Deferred gross margin	2,000	
Accounts receivable or cash (100 units × $50)		5,000

No revenue has previously been recognized on the returned books, and none is recognized now.

Finally, on March 31, 1992, when the right of return privilege expires, Boston Publishing will recognize net sales of 900 textbooks for revenue of $45,000 and with a cost of goods sold of $27,000. The deferred gross margin is reversed and recognized in this entry:

Cost of goods sold (900 units × $30)	27,000	
Deferred gross margin (900 units × $20)	18,000	
Sales revenue (900 units × $50)		45,000

The effect of the above entries is to cause Boston Publishing to recognize no sales revenue in 1991; instead, the net revenue of $45,000 was deferred until 1992. This was because condition *f* in *SFAS No. 48,* "The amount of future returns can be reasonably estimated," was not met until 1992.

Situations in which other conditions specified in *SFAS No. 48* are not being met come to mind. For example, consider condition *b,* which states that the buyer's obligation to pay the seller must not be contingent on the resale of the product. If it is contingent, this is essentially a consignment of the product. Consignment is a marketing arrangement whereby the consignor (the owner of the product) ships the product to another party, known as the consignee, who acts as a sales agent only. The consignee does not purchase the goods but assumes responsibility for their care and resale. Upon sale, the consignee remits the proceeds (less specified expenses and a commission) to the consignor. *Goods on consignment* are owned by the consignor until sold by the consignee. The goods are not a sale when they are shipped to the consignee; no revenue is recognized because condition *b* is not met.

Installment Sales Method of Revenue Recognition

In the situations presented above, the main issue was whether the earnings process was sufficiently completed to merit recognition of revenue. Now consider the problem of collectibility. When collection of the sales price is not reasonably assured, it becomes necessary to defer revenue recognition until the uncertainty is resolved. The installment sales method and the cost recovery method are alternatives used to defer the recognition of revenue and income until cash is received.[17]

Many consumer products are sold on an installment or deferred payment plan, but that does not mean they are accounted for using the installment sales method. With many large retailers, a large percentage of total sales are installment sales. Immediate revenue recognition is possible at the point of sale because the company has a reasonable basis for estimating an allowance for uncollectible accounts. Do not confuse a retail customer *installment sale* with the installment sales method of revenue recognition. An installment sale occurs when a contract is signed calling for the purchaser to make payments in accordance with a periodic payment plan. In contrast, the installment sales method is a method of revenue recognition employed only under very special circumstances for certain limited and specific types of installment sales.

In general, when the installment sales method is used, revenue is recognized when cash is collected rather than at the time of the sale. Under current GAAP, the

---

[17] The use of the installment sales method for revenue recognition is controversial, in part, because it lacks a firm conceptual basis. This method is discussed further later in this chapter. A full presentation of the controversial issues surrounding this installment sales method is found in R. A. Scott and R. K. Scott, "Installment Accounting: Is It Consistent?" *Journal of Accountancy,* November 1979, pp. 52–58.

installment sales method is used only when the point-of-sale method, or other GAAP revenue recognition method, is not appropriate. The installment sales method is a conservative method of revenue recognition, used only when there is uncertainty about whether the sales price will be collected and when an allowance for bad debts cannot be reasonably estimated. Thus, the installment sales method has very limited application under GAAP.[18] For instance, it is used to account for sales of real estate when the down payment is relatively low and ultimate collection of the sales price is not reasonably assured.[19]

Procedures for Deferring Gross Margin   Under the installment sales method, both sales and cost of sales are recognized in the period of sale, but the related gross margin is deferred to those periods when cash is collected. Deferring gross margin has the same effect on income as deferring both sales and cost of sales, but only one deferred account is needed. The procedures for deferring gross margin are:

1. Record sales and of cost of sales for installment sales in the usual way during the year, except that records on these items must be kept separately in order to compute a gross margin rate and to recognize gross margin correctly in the future.
2. Compute the gross margin rate for the installment sales as sales less cost of sales divided by sales.
3. At year-end, apply the gross margin rate to cash collections on the current year's installment sales. This determines the amount of gross margin realized on the current year's installment sales.
4. Gross margin not realized in the current year is deferred to future years when additional cash is collected.
5. For cash collected on installment sales made in prior years, apply the gross margin rate for the prior year to the amount of such cash collections. This determines the amount of gross margin to be recognized (realized) on that year's installment sales.

There are special recordkeeping requirements when the installment sales method is used. Separate accounts for installment sales must be maintained, as well as separate accounts for gross margin on installment sales for each year. The amounts collected on each year's installment sales must be known and separately recorded, and the amount of deferred gross margin related to each year's installment sales must be determined.

Illustration   To illustrate the accounting entries for the installment sales method, assume Tampa Company has the following transactions for 1991 and 1992 regarding sales and cost of goods sold to be accounted for using the installment sales method:

---

[18] The Accounting Principles Board greatly limited the situations in which the installment sales method may be used. *APB Opinion No. 10,* "Omnibus Opinion," par. 12, requires use of the point-of-sale method for installment sales except when "there are exceptional cases where receivables are collectible over an extended period of time and when, because of the terms of the transactions or other conditions, there is no reasonable basis for estimating the degree of collectibility." In the absence of these circumstances, the installment method is not acceptable.

[19] *SFAS No. 66,* "Accounting for Sales of Real Estate," par. 35. *SFAS No. 66* describes the accounting requirements for real estate sales. Paragraph 47 of *SFAS No. 66* explicitly requires use of the installment sales method when the sale of real estate does not meet the criteria for application of the point-of-sale method or the percentage-of-completion method (to be described in a later section).

	1991		1992	
Installment sales	$80,000	100%	$120,000	100%
Cost of goods sold	60,000	75%	80,000	67%
Gross margin on installment sales	$20,000	25%	$ 40,000	33%

Cash collections:	Applicable to 1991 Installment Sales	Applicable to 1992 Installment Sales
Customer payments in 1991	$10,000	
Customer payments in 1992	40,000	$ 45,000
Customer payments in 1993	30,000	55,000
Customer payments in 1994		20,000
Totals	$80,000	$120,000

The accounting entries to record the above installment sales and customer collections for 1991 and 1992 are illustrated and discussed below:

1991 Entries:

To record $80,000 of installment sales with a cost of goods sold of $60,000:

Installment accounts receivable, 1991	80,000	
Installment sales revenue		80,000
Cost of installment sales	60,000	
Inventory		60,000

To record the collection of $10,000 on the installment sale receivable:

Cash	10,000	
Installment accounts receivable, 1991		10,000

As of December 31, 1991, Tampa Company must establish an account for the deferred gross margin on installment sales for 1991. The amount to be credited to this account initially is $20,000, which is based on the gross margin percentage of 25% times the installment sales in 1991 of $80,000. The entry to record the deferred gross margin and to close the installment sales revenue and the cost of installment sales accounts for 1991 is:

Installment sales revenue	80,000	
Cost of installment sales		60,000
Deferred gross margin on installment sales, 1991		20,000

Also as of December 31, 1991, Tampa Company will record the recognition of gross margin based on the amount of cash collected and the gross margin percentage. Since $10,000 was collected and the gross margin percentage was 25%, $2,500 of gross margin is recognized:

Deferred gross margin on installment sales, 1991	2,500	
Realized gross margin on installment sales		2,500

The realized gross margin on installment sales is an income account and will be closed to the income summary.

1992 Entries:

Accounting entries for 1992 installment sales activities and cost of installment sales are handled in the same way as the above entries for 1991 installment sales:

Installment accounts receivable, 1992 120,000
    Installment sales revenue   120,000

Cost of installment sales 80,000
    Inventory   80,000

As of 1992, the gross margin percentage has increased to 33% (gross margin of $40,000 divided by installment sales of $120,000). The entry to record the deferral of gross margin on the installment sales and close the revenue and cost of sales accounts as of December 31, 1992, is:

Installment sales revenue 120,000
    Cost of installment sales   80,000
    Deferred gross margin on installment sales, 1992   40,000

During 1992, there are collections of $40,000 on the 1991 installment sales and $45,000 on the 1992 installment sales. The entry to record these collections is:

Cash 85,000
    Installment accounts receivable, 1991   40,000
    Installment accounts receivable, 1992   45,000

At December 31, 1992, Tampa Company recognizes gross margin from installment sales made in 1991 and 1992 for which cash is collected in 1992. The computation of these amounts and the entry to record them is as follows:

Computation of total realized gross margin in 1992 on installment sales:

Collections from installment receivable for 1991 . . . . . . $40,000
Times the gross margin rate for 1991 . . . .   × .25   _____
Realized gross margin from 1991 installment sales $10,000
Collection from installment receivable for 1992 . . . . $45,000
Times the gross margin rate for 1992 . . . .   × .33   _____
Realized gross margin from 1992 installment sales $15,000
    Total realized gross margin in 1992 . . . . $25,000

Entry to record realized gross margin:

Deferred gross margin on installment sales, 1991 10,000
Deferred gross margin on installment sales, 1992 15,000
    Realized gross margin on installment sales   25,000

The main characteristic of the installment sales method is that the gross margin is deferred until cash related to the sales is collected. Only the gross margin is deferred; the installment sales revenue and costs of sales are included in the income statement each year.

Financial statements under the installment sales method can be presented in several ways. If installment sales are a small part of a company's total revenue, it may be appropriate to include only the realized gross margin in the income statement as an item following gross margin on sales. Returning to the Tampa Company example, suppose that in addition to the installment sales presented above, there are other sales and cost of sales in 1992 of $500,000 and $450,000, respectively, for which the point-of-sale method is used for revenue recognition. Tampa's income statement would be:

TAMPA COMPANY
Income Statement
For the Year Ended December 31, 1992

Sales	$500,000
Cost of sales	450,000
Gross margin on sales	50,000
Realized gross margin on installment sales	25,000
Gross margin on sales and installment sales	$ 75,000

Alternatively, Tampa Company could provide more complete information by using a disclosure format such as the following:

TAMPA COMPANY
Income Statement
For the Year Ended December 31, 1992

	Installment Sales	Other Sales	Total Sales
Sales	$120,000	$500,000	$620,000
Cost of sales	80,000	450,000	530,000
Gross margin on sales	40,000	50,000	90,000
Less: Deferred gross margin on installment sales	(25,000)		(25,000)
Realized gross margin on current year sales	15,000	50,000	65,000
Add: Realized gross margin on installment sales of prior years	10,000		10,000
Total gross margin realized	$ 25,000	$ 50,000	$ 75,000

Yet another alternative is to prepare a separate schedule of installment sales with a final realized gross margin amount carried forward to the income statement.

Turning to the Tampa Company balance sheet at December 31, 1992, the remaining account balances relating to installment sales are these: installment accounts receivable, $105,000 ($30,000 for 1991 and $75,000 for 1992), and deferred gross margin on installment sales, $32,500 ($7,500 arising from 1991 installment sales and $25,000 from 1992 installment sales). This information should be disclosed within the current assets section of the balance sheet as follows:

Installment receivable	$105,000
Less: Deferred gross margin on installment sales	32,500
Net installment receivable	$ 72,500

The deferred gross margin on installment sales should be shown on the balance sheet as a contra account to installment accounts receivable. This treatment is consistent with *SFAC No. 6,* which states that "no matter how it is displayed in financial statements, deferred gross margin on installment sales is conceptually an asset valuation—that is, a reduction of an asset" (par. 234). In the past and continuing today, deferred gross margin frequently has been and is being reported as a current liability. This would be an appropriate treatment if the deferred gross margin were viewed as unearned revenue. But the earnings process is complete, and the revenue being deferred has been earned; the issue is whether it will be collected. Since collectibility is not assured, recording installment accounts receivable at the gross amount results in an overstatement of assets. This overstatement is corrected by classifying the deferred gross margin as a contra to this receivable. The net installment accounts receivable is the cost of the item sold. Although even this amount may overstate the value if the items are repossessed, it does correctly reflect the economics of the situation. Despite the logic of *SFAC No. 6*, however, many companies continue reporting deferred gross margin on installment sales as a current liability, and will continue to do so until the FASB resolves the matter.[20]

Interest Computations and the Installment Sales Method   When interest is charged on the unpaid balance of an installment sales method account receivable, the accounting procedures are conceptually the same as those outlined above, but a bit more complex. The accounting procedure used to account for interest on installment sales is illustrated below.

Illustration   Arizona Land Company sells a parcel of land for $60,000 on December 31, 1990. The buyer makes a $10,000 down payment and signs a note payable for the remaining $50,000, payable in equal annual installments over 10 years with interest at 15%. The original cost of the property to Arizona Land was $45,000. There is sufficient uncertainty about the realizability of receipt of the payments that the installment sales method is deemed appropriate. The entries to record the initial transaction are:

December 31, 1990—to record the installment sale, including the cash down payment:

Cash	10,000	
Installment receivable	50,000	
Installment sale		60,000

To record the cost of the land sold:

Cost of land sold	45,000	
Land inventory		45,000

At December 31, 1990, the gross margin on the above sale is deferred, with an appropriate amount realized because of the $10,000 down payment. The gross margin rate is 25%—(60,000 − 45,000)/60,000—thus, the amount of gross margin realized on the $10,000 down payment is $2,500:

Installment sales	60,000	
Cost of land sold		45,000
Deferred gross margin		15,000
Deferred gross margin	2,500	
Realized gross margin		2,500

At December 31, 1991, the net installment receivable is $50,000 less the deferred gross margin ($12,500), or $37,500. This is the unrecovered cost of the land sold in this transaction.

1991 Entries:

First the amount of the equal annual payments must be determined. To do so, the present value of the remaining balance ($50,000) is set equal to the 10-period annuity at a 15% rate of interest:

$$\$50,000 = \text{Annual payment} \times (PVA, 15\%, 10)$$

From Table 6A–4, the present value of an ordinary annuity of 1 for 10 periods at 15 percent is 5.01877. Solving for the annual payment (and rounding to whole dollars)

---

[20] *Statements of Financial Accounting Concepts* are not standards establishing GAAP; by themselves they do not alter existing generally accepted accounting principles. *SFACs* establish the objectives and concepts that the FASB intends to use in developing future financial reporting standards (i.e., future GAAP).

yields $9,963. The buyer will be making 10 payments of $9,963.[21] Each payment will consist of two components: interest income (earned on the unpaid receivable balance) and payment on the receivable balance, or principal. The payment received on the principal balance also has two components: return of cost and realized gross margin. The initial principal amount is the $50,000, the amount that would have been received had this been a cash sale. This is the amount upon which interest income is computed for the first period. Interest income in 1991 is thus $50,000 times 15%, or $7,500. Interest is deducted from the payment ($9,963) to determine the payment on principal. The amount of the principal payment must be divided into profit and cost in the same way as in the previous example. The specific computations and entries for the Arizona Land example, assuming payments are received as expected, are as follows.

1991 Payment Receipt:

At December 31, 1991, the first annual payment of $9,963 on the installment sale receivable is received. Interest on the unpaid installment receivable balance is $7,500 ($50,000 × .15); thus, payment on the receivable is the difference, $9,963 − $7,500, or $2,463. Of the $2,463 payment on the receivable, 25%, or $616, is the *realized* gross margin from this payment. The entries to record the payment and recognition of gross margin are as follows:

Cash		9,963
Interest income (.15 × $50,000)		7,500
Installment receivable		2,463
Deferred gross margin (.25 × $2,463)	616	
Realized gross margin		616

The components of the first $9,963 payment are diagrammed as follows:

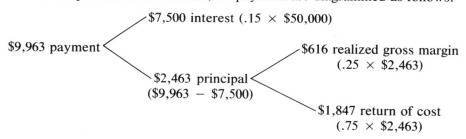

At December 31, 1991, the Arizona Land balance sheet would disclose the following:

(b)	Installment receivable ($50,000 − $2,463)	$47,537
(c)	Less: Deferred gross margin ($12,500 − $616)	(11,884)
(g)	Net installment sales accounts receivable	$35,653

The net installment receivable is the unrecovered cost of the parcel of land sold. This is easily verified:

Original cost of land sold		$45,000
Cost recovered to date from:		
Initial down payment ($10,000 × .75)	7,500	
First annual payment ($2,463 × .75)	1,847	9,347
(h) Unrecovered cost of land sold, 12/31/91		$35,653

---

[21] Some advocate recording as the sum of the payments the gross installment receivable; in this example, 10 times $9,963, or $99,630. A contra account called *unearned interest* is then established for the amount of interest to be collected in future periods ($49,630 in this example), and deducted from the gross receivable, leaving a net installment receivable that equals the deferred gross margin ($50,000 in this example). When payments are received, they are credited in full to the gross installment receivable. Separately, interest income is credited, and unearned interest is debited, with the appropriate amounts.

EXHIBIT 7-3 Schedule of Allocation of Annual Payments to Interest Income, Payment on the Installment Receivable, and to Realized Gross Margin for Arizona Land Company (in dollars)

(1) Date	(2) Annual Payment	(3) Interest Income (15% of beginning installment receivable)*	(4) Payment on Installment Receivable (col. 2 − col. 3)	(5) Realized Gross Margin (25% of col. 4)	(6) Installment Receivable (beginning balance less col. 4)	(7) Deferred Gross Margin (beginning balance less col. 5)
12/31/90	—	—	—	—	50,000	12,500
12/31/91	9,963	7,500	2,463	616	47,537	11,884
12/31/92	9,963	7,131	2,832	708	44,705	11,176
12/31/93	9,963	6,706	3,257	814	41,449	10,362
12/31/94	9,963	6,218	3,745	936	37,703	9,426
12/31/95	9,963	5,656	4,307	1,077	33,396	8,349
12/31/96	9,963	5,010	4,953	1,238	28,443	7,111
12/31/97	9,963	4,267	5,696	1,424	22,747	5,687
12/31/98	9,963	3,412	6,551	1,638	16,196	4,049
12/31/99	9,963	2,430	7,533	1,883	8,663	2,166
12/31/00	9,963	1,300	8,663	2,166	0	0

* Rounded

(6) − (7) = Net installment sales accounts receivable = Unrecovered cost of land sold

1992 Payment Receipt:

The entries to be made at December 31, 1992, to record the receipt of the second annual payment are:

```
Cash . . . . . . . . . . . . . . . . . . . . . . . . . . . . . . . . . . . . . 9,963
    Interest income (.15 × $47,537) . . . . . . . . . . . . . . . . . .        7,131
    Installment receivable . . . . . . . . . . . . . . . . . . . . . . .        2,832

Deferred gross margin (.25 × $2,832) . . . . . . . . . . . . . . . .   708
    Realized gross margin . . . . . . . . . . . . . . . . . . . . . . .          708
```

Similar entries will be made each year through the year 2000. Exhibit 7–3 is a schedule of the allocation of each payment to interest, payment on the principal balance, and realized gross margin for the 10-year period. The inclusion of interest in the computations delays the recognition of gross profit such that increasing amounts are recognized each period. This occurs because earlier payments include a larger component of interest income, as a larger amount of principal in the form of the installment receivable is outstanding in the earlier periods.

Repossessions under the Installment Method Repossessions are common under the installment sales method because this method is used only when there is substantial uncertainty of collection. When a repossession is made, it is necessary to ensure that all accounts related to the installment sale are current as of the date of repossession. The repossession entry records the asset recovered in an inventory account, reduces the related installment accounts receivable and deferred gross margin to zero balances, and records any gain or loss on repossession. The inventory amount is the estimated net realizable value of the item (to be discussed in Chapter 8). This inventory value is never more than the current market value of the item in its present condition.

Suppose for the Arizona Land example, the company repossesses the land in January 1993 because no payment is made in December 1992. The repossessed land is assumed to have a net realizable value of $30,000. Since the net installment receivable at December 31, 1991, was $35,653, and this represents unrecovered cost at that date, the loss on repossession is $35,653 less $30,000, or $5,653. The entry to record the repossession would be:

Land inventory 30,000
Deferred gross margin (balance as of December 31, 1991) . . . 11,884
Loss on repossession 5,653
    Installment receivable (balance as of December 31, 1991) .   47,537

The installment sales method has a significant conceptual flaw. The key reason for using the installment sales method is that the amount expected to be uncollectible cannot be estimated. However, the implicit assumption underlying a partial recognition of income with each dollar collected is that the *full* amount of the sale will be collected! If anything less than the full amount is collected, the amount recognized as income is overstated. Thus, only if there is certainty that the total sales price will be collected (which contradicts the premise for using the installment sales method) is it true that every dollar collected has a profit component equal to the gross margin rate.[22]

The Cost Recovery Method

The cost recovery method is sometimes called the *sunk cost method*. All of the related costs incurred (the sunk costs) must be recovered before any profit is recognized. The cost recovery method is used only for highly speculative transactions in which the ultimate realization of revenue or profit is unpredictable. For example, Lockheed Corporation used the cost recovery method in the early 1970s when it faced great uncertainty regarding the ultimate profitability of its TriStar Jet Transport program. Lockheed had invested in excess of $500 million in the initial planning, tooling, and production start-up costs of its widebody aircraft, the L-1011 TriStar. These costs were capitalized and were to be amortized over the production and sale of the first 300 planes. However, after Lockheed had incurred these production start-up costs and began to sell the airplane, considerable uncertainty developed concerning how many airplanes might ultimately be sold. Note 2 to Lockheed's 1973 *Annual Report* reported the company's decision to use the cost recovery method for revenue recognition for its TriStar program. The following is an abridged version of the Note (emphasis added):

> **Note 2:** All of the development costs and the normal production costs on the TriStar Jet Transport have been included in the inventory except for General and Administrative expenses which are charged to income in the year incurred. G & A expenses amounted to $70 million in 1973 and $81 million in 1972. Since the cumulative development costs to date have been substantial, it is estimated that 300 aircraft will have to be delivered to make the total program profitable. Since 56 aircraft have been delivered to date (all during 1972 and 1973), the Company does not expect a final determination of recoverability of Inventoried Cost can be made until a later date. *Zero gross profit was recorded on the $730 million of sales in 1973 and $302 million in sales in 1972 (for deliveries in those years) and no gross profit will be recorded on deliveries until uncertainties are reduced.*

On its income statement, Lockheed explicitly showed the effects of the cost recovery method for the TriStar program as follows:

---

[22] Many accountants, including your authors, believe the installment sales method should be discontinued for the reasons stated above. If collection uncertainty is so great that computation of an allowance for uncollectibles is not appropriate, it would seem that the best procedure to follow would be to view every dollar collected as recovery of product cost until that total is recovered in full. This describes the cost recovery method, which is discussed in the next section. However, *SFAS No. 66* prescribes the installment sales method in certain circumstances for retail land sales; thus, the method will continue to be used for the foreseeable future.

| | 1973 | | | 1972 | | |
(in millions)	TriStar	Other	Total	TriStar	Other	Total
Sales	$730	$2,027	$2,757	$302	$2,171	$2,473
Costs and expenses	800	1,875	2,675	383	2,021	2,404
Profit (loss)	$ (70)	$ 152	$ 82	$ (81)	$ 150	$ 69

Note: The losses for the TriStar program reflect the general and administrative expenses of $70 million in 1973 and $81 million in 1972 included in Cost and expenses.

The issue Lockheed had to face was whether the overall TriStar program would generate enough sales to recover the development costs. Since this was regarded as highly speculative—but still possible—Lockheed elected to use the cost recovery method until a better resolution of this issue emerged.[23]

The cost recovery method is also justified when an installment sale has been made, but there is uncertainty regarding its ultimate collectibility. _SFAS No. 66, par. 22,_ explicitly states that the cost recovery method is an acceptable alternative to the installment sales method when accounting for real estate sales: "The cost recovery method may be used to account for sales of real estate for which the installment sales method would be appropriate."

To demonstrate the cost recovery method, suppose Peninsula Land Sales Company sells undeveloped land to customers for their future retirement homes. During 1991, the company sells land with an original cost of $80,000 for a contract sales price of $140,000. During 1991, collections on these sales totaled $35,000. In 1992, an additional $55,000 is collected, and it is determined at year-end that an amount totaling $15,000 will be uncollectible. Property with an estimated net realizable value in the amount of $4,000 is recovered from the defaulted accounts.

To record land sales in 1991 and defer the gross margin the following entries would be made:

```
Land sales installment receivable ................. 140,000
    Land sales ...............................            140,000

Cost of land sold ........................... 80,000
    Inventory of land held for sale ...............           80,000

Land sales .................................. 140,000
    Deferred margin on land sales ................           60,000
    Cost of land sold .........................            80,000
```

The entry to record $35,000 in collections in 1991 is as follows:

```
Cash ....................................... 35,000
    Land Sales Installment Receivable ............           35,000
```

There is no recognition of realized gross margin in 1991 even though $35,000 in cash was collected. Under the cost recovery method, all cash collected from customers is first applied to the recovery of product costs. In Peninsula's case, the cost of the product (land) sold is $80,000. Applying this $35,000 against the $80,000 cost of sales figure leaves $45,000 still to be recovered. From a pure accounting entry viewpoint, the deferred gross margin on land sales (like the deferred gross margin on installment sales, discussed previously) is treated as a contra account to the land sales installment receivable account. After recording the $35,000 collection in 1991,

[23] In 1975, Lockheed reclassified the TriStar initial planning, tooling, and unrecovered production start-up costs as deferred charges and began amortizing them in the amount of approximately $50 million per year. This was done because of "increased uncertainties" regarding the number and timing of future TriStar deliveries. This write-off procedure was a means of spreading the loss over future years. A preferred alternative would be to write off the entire amount immediately.

the balance in the land sales installment receivable account is reduced from $140,000 to $105,000, which means that the net receivable is reduced by $35,000 as well:

Land sales installment receivable	$105,000
Less: Deferred margin on land sales	60,000
Net land sales installment receivable	$ 45,000

In 1992, the cash collection of $55,000 is recorded first as a recovery of the remaining $45,000 cost of land sold, with the $10,000 treated as realized gross margin. The entries to record the $55,000 in collections in 1992 and to record the $10,000 as realized gross margin are:

Cash	55,000	
Land sales installment receivable		55,000
Deferred gross margin on land sales	10,000	
Realized gross margin on land sales		10,000

At this point, the cost of the land sold has been fully recovered, and all additional cash collections are recorded entirely as realized gross margin.

Next consider $15,000 of the receivable that has been identified as uncollectible. The recognition of an amount as uncollectible does not by itself affect income. This amount must be removed from both the receivable and the deferred gross margin accounts:

Deferred gross margin on land sales	15,000	
Land sales installment receivable		15,000

Now assume that in conjunction with the above event, land having a net realizable value of $4,000 is recovered. Since the original cost of all land sold has already been recovered in our example, the value of the land recovered is recorded in the land inventory account, and the entire amount is treated as an increase in realized gross margin. The entry to record the recovery of the land is as follows:

Land inventory	4,000	
Realized gross margin on land sales		4,000

Also, any future collections in the above example will result in recognition of realized gross margin in the full amount of the collection.

Finally, the net balance of the installment receivable is equal to zero after the above entries:

Land sales installment account receivable, original balance . .			$140,000
Less: Cash collections 1991	$35,000		
Cash collections, 1992	55,000		
Uncollectible accounts recognized	15,000		105,000
Balance, December 31, 1992			$ 35,000
Deferred gross margin, original amount		$(60,000)	
Less: Realized gross margin in 1992	$10,000		
Uncollectible accounts written off in 1992	15,000	25,000	
Balance, December 31, 1992			$(35,000)
Net land sales installment account receivable			
balance, Dec. 31, 1992			–0–

Under the cost recovery method, revenues and cost of sales are reported on the income statement similar to the installment sales method except that no gross margin is realized until cash collections exceed the cost of sales. Income statement presentation for Peninsula Land Sales would be as follows:

PENINSULA LAND SALES COMPANY
Partial Income Statement

	1991	1992
Land sales	$140,000	$ -0-
Cost of land sold	80,000	-0-
Gross margin	60,000	-0-
Less: Deferred gross margin	(60,000)	-0-
Add: Realized gross margin	-0-	14,000
Total gross margin	-0-	$14,000

Reporting of the installment receivable on the balance sheet is analogous to the presentation under the installment sales method. The cost recovery method is a conservative method of revenue and expense recognition. There is no attempt made to match revenue and expense. The cost recovery method is justified only under extreme uncertainty associated with collecting the receivables or regarding the ultimate recovery of the capitalized production start-up costs, as in the Lockheed case.

CONCEPT REVIEW

1. What is the key difference between revenue recognition under the installment sales method and the cost recovery method?
2. Why is revenue recognition a problem when there are product financing arrangements?
3. When products are sold with extensive right of return privileges, at what point in the process is revenue to be recognized?

REVENUE RECOGNITION BEFORE DELIVERY
♦

In some instances, the earnings process extends over several accounting periods. Examples include the construction of large ships, bridges, office buildings, and the development of space exploration equipment. Often the contracts for these projects provide that the builder bill the buyer at various points in the construction process—called *progress billings*—as agreed-on milestones are reached. Delivery of the final completed project, however, may be years after the initiation of the construction effort. Most, if not all, of the progress billings will have been paid. If the builder (seller) waits until the construction is completed to recognize revenue, the information on revenue and expense included in the financial statements will be *reliable,* but it may not be *relevant* for decision-making purposes because it will not be timely. Faced with such a situation, it often is worthwhile to trade off reliability in order to provide timely, relevant earnings and cash flow information. This is the problem of accounting for revenues and expenses when a company engages in long-term construction contracts.

GAAP allows two methods of accounting for inventory and income on long-term contracts:

1. **Completed-Contract Method**—Revenues, expenses, and gross profit are recognized when the contract is completed. As construction costs are incurred they are accumulated in an inventory account (construction in process). Progress billings, if any, are not recorded as revenues, but rather are accumulated in a contra inventory account (billings on construction in process). At the completion of the

contract, all the accounts are closed to revenue and expense accounts, and the gross profit from the construction project is recognized.

2. **Percentage-of-Completion Method**—Revenues, expenses, and gross profit are recognized each accounting period based on an *estimate* of the percentage of completion of the construction project. Construction costs and *gross profit to date* are accumulated in the inventory account (construction in process). Any progress billings are accumulated in a contra inventory account (billings on construction in process).[24]

The percentage-of-completion method recognizes that the earnings process is continuous as work progresses on a contract, and that if timely information is to be provided to users, revenue must be recognized before the contract is completed.

Guidance on the Choice between the Two Methods

Management often has considerable freedom of choice in deciding between alternative accounting measurement rules. For example, there is considerable latitude in the choices available for depreciating assets or for valuing inventory. This is not the case in accounting for long-term construction contracts. For long-term contracts, the accounting profession has provided two sources of guidance: *ARB No. 45* and *SFAS No. 56. Accounting Research Bulletin No. 45 (ARB No. 45)* provides the initial guidance:

> When estimates of costs to complete and extent of progress toward completion of long-term contracts are reasonably dependable, the percentage-of-completion method is preferable. When lack of dependable estimates or inherent hazards cause forecasts to be doubtful, the completed-contract method is preferable.[25]

More recently, *SFAS No. 56* provides more specific guidance: "The percentage-of-completion and completed-contract methods are not intended to be free choice alternatives for the same circumstances" (par. 6). *SFAS No. 56* designates the specialized accounting principles and practices found in Statement of Position 81–1 (SOP 81–1), issued by the AICPA, as preferable in guiding the choice between the two methods. In addition to the criteria found in *ARB No. 45*, SOP 81–1 states that the percentage-of-completion method should be used if three additional conditions exist:

1. The contract specifies the enforceable rights of both the buyer and the seller, the amount of consideration to be exchanged, and the manner and terms of settlement.
2. The buyer can be expected to satisfy his or her obligations in the contract.
3. The contractor (seller) can be expected to perform according to the terms of the contract.

The criteria for determining whether to use the percentage-of-completion method focuses on the measurability of revenues and expenses. For contracts where the three SOP 81–1 criteria are met, there is generally little question that the seller has earned revenue and that collectibility is assured. The critical criteria are whether the construction company can estimate (1) the progress toward completion of the contractual obligation and (2) the costs to complete the project.

The completed-contract method should be used when the above conditions are not met. This includes situations in which the contractor is engaged primarily in

---

[24] *Accounting Trends & Techniques–1990* reports that in 1989, 133 of the 600 firms surveyed were engaged in long-term construction, and 125 of these used the percentage-of-completion method, or a modification of this method, to account for revenue from long-term contracts. AICPA, *Accounting Trends & Techniques* (New York, 1990), p. 285.

[25] AICPA, *Accounting Research Bulletin No. 45*, "Long-Term Construction-Type Contracts (New York, 1955), par. 15.

short-term contracts, and those in which the risks involved in completing the contract are beyond the normal, recurring risks of business. In this latter case, there may be considerable uncertainty regarding the ability of the contractor to complete the contractual obligations.

Measuring Progress toward Completion

Measuring progress toward completion of a long-term construction project can be accomplished in a number of ways. All such measurements, however, belong to one of two basic groups:

1. *Input measures*—these are measures of the effort devoted to a project to date compared to the total effort expected to be required in order to complete the project. Examples are costs incurred to date compared to total estimated costs for the project, or labor hours worked compared to expected total labor required to complete the project.
2. *Output measures*—these are measures of results to date compared with total results when the project is completed. Examples include number of stories of a building completed compared to total number of stories to be built, or miles of highway completed compared to total miles to be completed.

The objective in choosing among the alternative measures is to have a realistic measure of progress toward completion of the project. Neither type of measure is ideal in all circumstances. Input measures are misleading if a relatively constant relationship between the input measure and productivity does not exist. Suppose that in constructing a city skyscraper, a construction company must first excavate 100 feet deep into the ground. The first 50 feet proceed according to plan and cost estimates. But then unusually hard bedrock is encountered, and progress slips to less than half the expected rate. Costs per foot of excavation more than double. If the higher excavation cost is not included in the original cost estimates, using cost as the progress measure overstates progress toward completion. Also, cost incurred is misleading as a measure of progress when it includes expenditures at the start of a construction project for the purchase of large quantities of materials and supplies that are to be used over the entire construction period. Often a contractor purchases large quantities of materials at the start of a construction project in order to lock in current prices. But progress toward completion of the project is not made until the materials are actually used. It is important to distinguish between acquisition costs and costs actually contributing to progress.

Output measures can also be misleading. This is especially true when different output units actually require different amounts of input effort to complete. The first floor of a 10-story building may require considerably more input effort to complete (due to the foundation and subsurface support construction requirements) than the second floor. Using floors completed as a measure of progress toward completion is likely to understate the actual rate of progress. Also, later costs may be lower due to learning. As more units are produced, construction can become less costly because the contractor learns the most efficient procedures and methods of construction for the project. This is a typical problem in the production of aircraft. Thus, an aircraft manufacturer under contract with the government to design and produce 100 aircraft is likely to incur more costs in producing the first 10 aircraft than in producing the last 10 aircraft. Using the cost of producing the first ten aircraft as a measure of costs for all aircraft tends to overstate the actual cost of the progress being made.

In any given contractual situation, it is necessary to analyze carefully the circumstances to determine which type of measure—input or output—results in the most useful measures of revenue and expense. The most frequently used measures are input measures, and among input measures the most frequently used method is the *cost-to-cost method.* When the cost-to-cost method is used (as it will be in the examples included in the next section), it is the ratio of cost-incurred-to-date compared to the most recent estimate of the total costs for completion of the project. The formula for determining the percent complete on a project is:

$$\text{Percent complete} = \frac{\begin{array}{c}\text{Total costs incurred to the end}\\ \text{of the current accounting period}\end{array}}{\begin{array}{c}\text{Most recent estimate of}\\ \text{total costs of project}\end{array}}$$

Once the percent-complete computation has been made, the amount of revenue to recognize in the current period can be determined as follows:

$$\begin{array}{c}\text{Current}\\ \text{period}\\ \text{revenue}\end{array} = \left[\begin{array}{c}\text{Percent}\\ \text{complete}\end{array} \times \begin{array}{c}\text{Total revenue}\\ \text{from contract}\end{array}\right] - \begin{array}{c}\text{Total revenue}\\ \text{recognized in}\\ \text{prior periods}\end{array}$$

Illustration of Alternative Methods of Accounting for Long-Term Contracts

There are dramatic differences in the two measurement methods. Since the completed-contract method is the simplest and most straightforward, its application will be discussed first. The more complex percentage-of-completion method will be discussed second.

Illustration of the Completed-Contract Method   Assume the Ace Construction Company has contracted to erect a building for $1.5 million, starting construction on February 1, 1991, with a planned completion date of August 1, 1993. Management estimates total costs to complete the contract at $1.35 million. Thus, the estimated gross profit from the construction project is projected to be $150,000 ($1,500,000 in revenues less $1,350,000 in estimated expenses). Progress billings are to be made on a predetermined schedule and are payable within 10 days after billing.

Assume the following data pertain to the three-year construction period:

ACE CONSTRUCTION COMPANY
Construction Project Fact Sheet
Three Year Summary Schedule
Contract price: $1,500,000

	1991	1992	1993
1. Estimated completion costs (3 + 4)	$1,350,000	$1,360,000	$1,365,000
2. Costs incurred during year	350,000	550,000	465,000
3. Cumulated costs to date	350,000	900,000	1,365,000
4. Estimated costs to complete	1,000,000	460,000	–0–
5. Progress billings during year	300,000	575,000	625,000
6. Cumulative billings to date	300,000	875,000	1,500,000
7. Collections on billings during year	270,000	555,000	675,000
8. Cumulative collections to date	270,000	825,000	1,500,000

As shown in line 1 of the above schedule, the estimated completion costs increased by $10,000 in 1992 and increased by another $5,000 prior to completion in 1993. The total cost to complete the project turns out to be $1,365,000. As a result of this cost increase, the contract profit drops from $150,000 to $135,000.

Long-term contracts often provide for the contractor to bill the purchaser for progress payments (specified in the contract). When such billings are made, they are debited to accounts receivable and credited to billings on contracts. The latter is a contra account to construction-in-process inventory. If the net amount in the construction-in-process inventory (that is, construction-in-process inventory less billings on contracts) is a debit balance, it is reported as a current asset, inventory. This account balance represents the contractor's net ownership interest in the construction project; it is sometimes referred to as the *contractor's draw*. If the net between the construction-in-process inventory and the billings on contracts accounts is a credit balance, it represents the developer's (buyer's) interest in the project and is sometimes referred to as the *developer's draw*. Credit balances represent a liability for the contractor, and they must be reported as such in the contractor's financial statements.

The journal entries to record construction-in-process inventory, progress billings, and collections of progress billings each year for Ace Construction are:

| | ◄──────────── Year ────────────► |
	1991	**1992**	**1993**
Construction-in-process inventory (Cost incurred during year.) 350,000		550,000	465,000
Cash, payables, etc.	350,000	550,000	465,000
Accounts receivable 300,000		575,000	625,000
Billings on contracts	300,000	575,000	625,000
Cash 270,000		555,000	675,000
Accounts receivable	270,000	555,000	675,000

Under the completed-contract method, revenue, expense, and gross margin are not recognized until the contract is completed. At that point, income will be recognized as the difference between the accumulated credit balance in the billings on contracts account and the debit balance in the construction-in-process inventory account, assuming the total price of the contract has been billed. The accumulated amount of billings on contracts is recognized as sales revenue, and the accumulated amount of construction-in-process inventory on completion of the contract is recognized as cost of goods sold. The journal entries to recognize revenue and expense upon completion of the contract in August 1993 are:

Billings on contracts	1,500,000	
Revenue from long-term contracts		1,500,000
Costs of construction	1,365,000	
Construction-in-process inventory		1,365,000

During the construction period, the construction-in-process inventory is reported on the balance sheet as the total accumulated costs to date less the total progress billings to date. Exhibit 7–4 (which follows the next illustration) compares accounting and reporting for the contract for each of the three years under both the completed-contract method and the percentage-of-completion method.

Illustration of the Percentage-of-Completion Method   Accounting for a long-term construction contract under the percentage-of-completion method is similar to complete contract method except that a portion of revenue and expense (thus income) is recognized as it is earned in each accounting period. The amount of income that is recognized is added to the construction-in-process inventory. The *actual* income on the contract will not be known until completion; what is recognized each period is an estimate of income.

The cost-to-cost method is used to determine percent completed as follows:

Year	1991	1992	1993
Costs incurred to date	$ 350,000	$ 900,000	$1,365,000
Estimated total costs	1,350,000	1,360,000	1,365,000
Percent complete	25.926%	66.176%	100%

The percent complete is computed as costs-incurred-to-date divided by the estimated total costs. With the percent complete determined, the next step is to compute the total amount of revenue recognizable as of year-end. This is done by multiplying the total contract revenue ($1.5 million) by the percent complete for each year:

Total revenue recognizable:

Year	1991	1992	1993
1991 $1.5 million × .25926	$388,890	—	—
1992 $1.5 million × .66176	—	$992,640	—
1993 $1.5 million × 1.0000	—	—	$1,500,000

To determine revenue for each year, revenue recorded in prior years must be subtracted from the total revenue recognizable. Thus, revenue to be recognized in 1991 is $388,890, the amount shown as the total revenue to date. In 1992, the revenue to be recognized is the total revenue recognizable of $992,640, less the revenue recognized in 1991 of $388,890, or $603,750.

Once revenue for the period is determined, the amount of gross profit to be recognized is the difference between revenue and costs incurred in the period:

Year	1991	1992	1993	Totals
Revenue for the current period	$388,890	$603,750	$507,360	$1,500,000
Costs incurred in current period	350,000	550,000	465,000	1,365,000
Gross profit for the period	$ 38,890	$ 53,750	$ 42,360	$ 135,000

The journal entries to record the costs incurred on the construction, the progress billings, and the collections of progress billings are the same as under the completed-contract method (see page 309). In addition to these entries, an entry is needed to record the recognition of revenue and expense in each period as computed above. The gross profit is debited to the construction-in-process inventory:

	Year		
	1991	1992	1993
Construction in process inventory (gross profit for the period)	38,890	53,750	42,360
Costs of construction	350,000	550,000	465,000
Revenue from long-term contracts . .	388,890	603,750	507,360

Costs of construction is an account measuring expense of construction and is an income statement account. Construction-in-process inventory continues to accumulate even though a series of "sales" are being recorded each period. The construction-in-process inventory also includes the gross margin recognized to date. The construction-in-process inventory under the percentage-of-completion method is greater than under the completed-contract method by the amount of gross margin recognized to date.

When the contract is completed and turned over to the purchaser, a journal entry is needed to remove the costs of the contract and the progress billings from the accounts of Ace Construction:

Billings on contracts	1,500,000	
Construction-in-process inventory		1,500,000

Financial statement presentation of the completed-contract method and the percentage-of-completion method for this example are shown in Exhibit 7–4. Under the completed-contract method, inventory is carried at cost. Under the percentage-of-completion method, inventory is carried at cost plus recognized gross profit. The difference between the net inventory amounts under the two methods at each year-end is the accumulated gross margin recognized under the percentage-of-completion method but not under the completed-contract method. Finally, Exhibit 7–4 shows the dramatic differences the two methods have on gross profit on a year-to-year basis:

EXHIBIT 7-4 Financial Statement Presentation of Accounting for Long-Term Construction Contracts

Completed-Contract Method

		1991	1992	1993
Balance Sheet:				
Current assets:				
Accounts receivable		$30,000	$ 50,000	
Inventory:				
Construction in process	$350,000		$900,000	
Less: Billings on contracts	300,000		875,000	
Construction in process in excess of billings		$50,000	$ 25,000	
Income Statement:				
Revenue from long-term contracts		$ 0	$ 0	$1,500,000
Costs of construction		0	0	1,365,000
Gross profit		$ 0	$ 0	$ 135,000

Note 1: Summary of significant accounting policies.

Long-term construction contracts. Revenues and income from long-term construction contracts are recognized under the completed-contract method. Such contracts are generally for a duration in excess of one year. Construction costs and progress billings are accumulated during the periods of construction. Only when the project is completed are revenue, expense, and income recognized on the project.

Percentage-of-Completion Method

		1991	1992	1993
Balance Sheet:				
Current assets:				
Accounts receivable		$ 30,000	$ 50,000	
Inventory:				
Construction in process	$388,890		$992,640	
Less: Billings on contracts	300,000		875,000	
Construction in process in excess of billings		$ 88,890	$117,640	
Income Statement:				
Revenue from long-term contracts		$388,890	$603,750	$507,360
Costs of construction		350,000	550,000	465,000
Gross profit		$ 38,890	$ 53,750	$42,360

Note 1: Summary of significant accounting policies.

Long-term construction contracts. Revenue and income from long-term construction contracts are recognized under the percentage-of-completion method. Such contracts are generally for a duration in excess of one year. Construction costs and progress billings are accumulated during the periods of construction. The amounts of revenue recognized each year are based on the ratio of the costs incurred to the estimated total costs of completion of the construction contract.

Gross Profit Recognized Each Year

Year	Percentage-of-Completion	Completed-Contract
1991	$ 38,890	$ 0
1992	53,750	0
1993	42,360	135,000
Total	$135,000	$135,000

Accounting for Losses on Long-Term Contracts

A complication arises when the estimated costs to complete a contract increase to the point where losses occur. Two situations can arise:

1. Loss results in an unprofitable contract.
2. A current-year loss, but the total contract remains profitable.

Consider the first situation and continue with the Ace Construction Company example. Suppose that at the end of 1992, costs incurred are as shown ($350,000 in 1991 and $550,000 in 1992), but the estimate of the costs to complete the contract in 1993 increases to $625,000 from the original estimate of $465,000. Since costs incurred to date total $900,000, the total estimated cost of the contract is now $1,525,000. There is now an expected loss on the contract of $25,000.

For both methods, the projected loss is recognized in full in the period in which it is established. For the completed-contract method, the journal entry to record the loss in 1992 is:

```
Loss on construction contracts (an income statement account) . . 25,000
    Construction in process inventory . . . . . . . . . . . . . . .        25,000
```

The computations and entries are more complicated for the percentage-of-completion method. Since gross margin of $38,890 was recognized in 1991, this amount must be reversed and the overall loss of $25,000 must be recognized. The result is a net loss on construction contracts to be recognized in 1992 of $63,890. The amount of revenue recognized in 1992 is computed in the usual way:

```
Percent complete ($900,000 ÷ $1,525,000) . . . . . . . . . . .     59.016%
Revenue recognizable to date ($1,500,000 × .59016) . . . . .     $885,240
Less: Revenue recognized in prior periods . . . . . . . . . .      388,890
Revenue to be recognized in 1992 . . . . . . . . . . . . . .      $496,350
```

The conceptually correct method for computing the amount of cost of construction in 1992 is:

```
Estimated net loss (to be fully recognized in current period) .         $ 25,000
Remaining costs to be recognized . . . . . . . . . . . . . . $1,500,000
Times percent complete at 12/31/92 . . . . . . . . . . . . . .    × .59016
Portion of costs to be recognized by 12/31/92 . . . . . . . .          885,240
   Total . . . . . . . . . . . . . . . . . . . . . . . . . .          910,240
Less: Cost recognized in prior periods . . . . . . . . . . . .          350,000
Cost of construction to be recognized in 1992* . . . . . . .         $560,240
```

*The easiest way to compute the amount of cost of construction for 1992 is to add the amount of the loss to be recognized to the amount of revenue to be recognized:

```
        Loss to be recognized in 1992 . . . . . . . . . . . . . . . $ 63,890
        Revenue to be recognized in 1992 . . . . . . . . . . . .     496,350
        Costs of construction to be recognized in 1992 . . . . . . $560,240
```

With the above information, a journal entry can be made to reflect the recognition of revenue, costs of construction and the loss in 1992:

```
Costs of construction . . . . . . . . . . . . . . . . . . . . . . . 560,240
    Revenue from construction contracts . . . . . . . . . . . . .      496,350
    Construction in process inventory .(loss.) . . . . . . . . .       63,890
```

With the above entry, the full amount of the loss has been recognized. Actual costs of construction for 1992 were $550,000, but $560,240 are expensed. The difference of $10,240 is offset in 1993 when actual costs of construction are $625,000 but revenue and cost of construction expensed are $614,760:

Computation of 1993 revenue:

```
Total revenue to be recognized on contract . . . . . .     $1,500,000
Amount recognized in prior years:
   1991 revenue . . . . . . . . . . . . . . . . . . . . $388,890
   1992 revenue . . . . . . . . . . . . . . . . . . . .  496,350      885,240
Amount of revenue to be recognized in 1993 . . . . .       $  614,760
```

Computation of 1993 costs of construction:

Total costs to be recognized on contract		$1,525,000
Amount recognized in prior years:		
1991 costs of construction	$350,000	
1992 costs of construction	560,240	910,240
Costs of construction to be recognized in 1993		$ 614,760

Because the entire loss was recognized in 1992, the gross margin in 1993 is zero. Finally, note that before it is closed, the construction-in-process inventory account has an ending balance of $1,500,000:

Construction-in-Process Inventory

1991 construction costs	350,000		
1991 gross profit	38,890		
1992 construction costs	550,000	1992 loss recognition	63,890
1993 construction costs	625,000		
12/31/93 balance	1,500,000		

The balance in the construction-in-process account equals the amount of the progress billings. When the contract is completed, a journal entry is made to close the construction-in-process inventory and the progress billings accounts:

Progress billings	1,500,000	
Construction-in-process inventory		1,500,000

Current Period Loss on Profitable Contract Now consider a situation where there is a loss in the current accounting period, but the overall contract remains profitable. Continuing with the Ace Construction Company example, suppose costs incurred to the end of 1992 are as previously shown, but the estimate of costs to complete the contract have risen to $550,000. Costs totaling $900,000 have already been incurred; thus, the total estimated cost of completing the construction contract is $1,450,000. The overall contract still generates a gross profit of $50,000.

Under the completed-contract method, no entry is needed in 1992. At the completion of the contract, the usual revenue, costs of construction, and gross margin entries are made, but now the gross margin is reduced to $50,000.

An entry is needed, however, under the percentage-of-completion method to recognize revenue and expense in 1992. The computation of revenue for 1992 is:

Construction costs to 12/31/92	$ 900,000
Estimated costs to complete	550,000
Estimated total costs of contract	$1,450,000
Percent complete ($900,000 ÷ $1,450,000)	62.069%
Revenue recognizable as of 12/31/92 ($1,500,000 × .62069)	$ 931,035
Revenue recognized in prior periods	388,890
Revenue to be recognized in 1992	542,145
Costs of construction in 1992	550,000
Loss on construction contract in 1992	$ 7,855

These computations can be compared with those on page 310. The percent complete has decreased from 66.176% to 62.069% because of the increase in estimated future costs. When gross profit of $38,890 is recorded in 1991, it turns out that the rate of profit margin was overestimated. This prior period mis-estimate of margin is entirely absorbed in the current period, resulting in a loss for 1992.

The journal entry to record revenue, costs of construction, and loss for 1992 is:

Costs of construction 550,000		
Construction in process inventory (loss)		7,855
Revenue from construction contracts		542,145

In 1993, Ace Construction recognizes the remaining revenue of $568,965 ($1,500,000 less the $931,035 recognized in prior years) and costs of $550,000, yielding a gross profit of $18,965. The total gross profit over the three years of the contract totals $50,000 ($38,890 in 1991, a loss of $7,855 in 1992, and $18,965 in 1993). This is equal to the total revenue of $1,500,000 less the total costs of construction of $1,450,000 ($350,000 in 1991, $550,000 in 1992, and $550,000 in 1993).

In summary, when a loss on the contract is probable, the construction-in-process inventory is reported at estimated net realizable value under both the completed-contract method or percentage-of-completion method. When the contract is profitable, construction-in-process inventory is reported at cost plus recognized gross profit. Changes in projected profitability of the construction contracts are accounted for prospectively as a change in accounting estimate. Prior period gross profit amounts are not restated retroactively.

The completed-contract method is both more objective and more conservative than the percentage-of-completion method. Income is recognized only when all costs and revenues are known, and all revenue and income recognition is delayed until all income is earned. Yet many accountants view this method as deficient because income recognition does not reflect performance during each period of construction. Even though a considerable amount of income is earned and collectible before the completion of the project, the financial statements do not provide their readers with this information. The percentage-of-completion method is supported by these accountants because it recognizes income as it is earned over the life of the contract.

However, many accountants consider the percentage-of-completion method deficient because income is measured subjectively during the period of the contract: *Estimates* of work done (percentage of completion) and *estimated* total contract costs are used. Either of these two estimates can result in errors, and potentially misleading information. Even so, *SFAS No. 56* requires the percentage-of-completion method when the identified criteria (listed on page 306) are met. While it is still necessary to judge whether the criteria are met, company management no longer has a totally free choice between the two methods.

CONCEPT REVIEW

1. What are the conditions under which a company is required to use the percentage-of-completion method of accounting for long-term contracts?
2. If a loss is expected on a long-term contract after there have been one or more periods of recording a gross profit, what are the requirements for recording the loss if *(a)* the contract will still have an overall net gross profit, and *(b)* the loss is sufficiently large to cause the overall contract to have a net loss?
3. For a given contract, how will the construction-in-process inventory differ if the contract is accounted for using the percentage-of-completion method rather than the completed-contract method?

ALTERNATIVE METHODS OF REVENUE RECOGNITION BEFORE DELIVERY

◆

Three alternative additional methods for recognizing revenue before the delivery of the product are discussed in the accounting literature. They are (1) completion of production, (2) accretion basis, and (3) discovery basis. Each has theoretical merit, but each also has significant problems in implementation. The completion-of-production method is GAAP in certain circumstances. Neither the accretion basis nor the discovery basis methods are currently acceptable under GAAP.

Completion of Production

In certain special situations, revenue is, or at least reasonably can be, recognized at the completion of production. The key for using this method is that realizability is assured. More specifically, the product must be immediately marketable at quoted prices, and the prices cannot be influenced by the producer. This is the case in the production of some precious metals, agricultural products, and other commodities where there is a ready market for the product. Another characteristic of the product is that units are interchangeable and that no significant costs are involved in product distribution. The completion-of-production method can provide the producer with valuable information on the profit from production activities, with a separate recognition of any gains or losses that arise if the producer does not sell the product upon completion of production. Such gains or losses arise because the producer becomes a speculator in the commodity. Separation of the sources of profit (production or speculation) are potentially important for decision making.

Accretion Basis

Accretion is the increase in value resulting from natural causes such as the growing of a timberland or the aging of wines and liquors. As the value increases, revenue is being earned and some accountants believe that it should be recognized. The recognition may be important in situations where the natural process is very long and knowing the change in value is relevant information for decision making. On the other hand, there are difficulties of both determining future prices or value even if current prices are known, and of estimating future costs of activities such as harvesting or otherwise preparing the product for market. Accretion basis accounting is not currently acceptable, even though from an economic perspective it is logical.

Discovery Basis

The discovery method was suggested by the SEC in the early 1980s as a means of providing timely, relevant information to readers of financial statements of oil- and gas-producing companies. The SEC identified the proposed method as the "reserve recognition method." The notion is that upon discovery of a valuable mineral deposit such as oil and gas, the company has earned revenue. Many would agree that the firm is better off as a result of the discovery, and that it would be useful to reflect this information in the financial statements. The argument against such recognition is that there are still too many unknowns and uncertainties regarding costs and future prices to develop acceptably accurate measures of revenue and expense at the time of discovery. The discovery basis is not currently an acceptable method for revenue recognition in GAAP.

REVENUE RECOGNITION FOR SERVICE SALES
♦

To this point, the emphasis has been on accounting for transactions involving the sale of tangible products. There are, however, companies that provide services for which the revenue recognition issue is as complex as some of the situations described in the preceding sections. Indeed, there is considerable similarity in revenue recognition procedures between service transactions and tangible goods transactions. In this section four methods of revenue recognition for service sales are reviewed: (1) specific performance, (2) proportional performance, (3) completed performance, and (4) collection.

Specific Performance Method

The **specific performance method** is used to account for *service revenue* that is earned by performing a *single act*. For example, a real estate broker earns sales commission revenue on completion of a real estate transaction; a dentist earns revenue on completion of surgery to remove a tooth; a laundry earns revenue on completion of the cleaning process. *SFAS No. 45,* "Accounting for Franchise Fee Revenue," March 1981, deals with a particular type of service sales, use of franchises. The *Statement* prescribes the specific performance method to account for franchise fee revenue, which the franchisor earns by selling a franchise to the franchisee. For revenue recognition purposes, it is often difficult to determine the point at which the franchisor has "substantially performed" the service required to earn the franchise fee revenue. In this regard *SFAS No. 45* (par. 5) states (emphasis added):

Franchise fee revenue from an individual franchise sale ordinarily shall be recognized, with an appropriate provision for estimated uncollectible amounts, when *all material services or conditions relating to the sale have been substantially performed or satisfied by the franchisor.* Substantial performance for the franchisor means that *(a)* the franchisor has no remaining obligation or intent . . . to refund any cash received . . . *(b)* substantially all of the initial services[26] of the franchisor required by the franchise agreement have been performed, and *(c)* no other material conditions or obligations related to the determination of substantial performance exist. . . . The commencement of operations by the franchisee shall be presumed to be the earliest point at which substantial performance has occurred.

The following example illustrates the specific performance method applied to franchise fee revenue. Assume that on April 1, 1991, Chicago Pizza Corporation (franchisor) sold a franchise to Arthur Wilson (franchisee) for $20,000 cash and in addition received a note that required five annual payments of $8,739 beginning on March 31, 1992. The note is based on an interest rate of 14% and therefore has a present value of $30,000, or (PVA, 14%, 5) × $8,739 = 3.43308 × $8,739.

Case A   If no additional services are to be performed by the franchisor and collectibility is reasonably assured, Chicago Pizza should recognize the entire amount (the $20,000 cash payment and $30,000 note receivable) as revenue, using the following entry:

April 1, 1991, to record revenue:

Cash	20,000	
Note receivable	30,000	
Franchise fee revenue		50,000

Case B   If Chicago Pizza has additional services to perform for the francisee, such as preparing the new pizza restaurant's location, no franchise fee revenue would be recognized on April 1, 1991. Rather, the following entry would be made:

---

[26] *SFAS No. 45,* Appendix A, defines *initial service* as follows:

Common provisions of a franchise agreement in which the franchisor usually will agree to provide a variety of services and advice to the franchisee, such as the following:

a. Assistance in the selection of a site.
b. Assistance in obtaining facilities, including related financing and architectural and engineering services.
c. Assistance in advertising, either for the individual franchise or as part of a general program.
d. Training of the franchisee's personnel.
e. Preparation and distribution of manuals and similar material concerning operations, administration, and record keeping.
f. Bookkeeping and advisory services, including setting up the franchisee's records and advising the franchisee about income, real estate, and other taxes or about local regulations affecting the franchisee's business.
g. Inspection, testing, and other quality control programs.

April 1, 1991, to record the franchise sale and deferral of revenue pending performance of franchise services in full:

```
Cash  . . . . . . . . . . . . . . . . . . . . . . . . . . . . . . . .  20,000
Note receivable  . . . . . . . . . . . . . . . . . . . . . . . . .  30,000
    Deferred franchise fee revenue . . . . . . . . . . . . . . . . .          50,000
```

The deferred franchise fee revenue account will appear as a liability on Chicago Pizza's 1991 balance sheet. Although the franchisee has made cash payment and has executed the note which obligates payments in the future, this is not earned revenue because Chicago Pizza still has obligations it must complete. Assume that Chicago Pizza completes its obligations to the franchisee in 1992, expending $2,000 in the process. The entry to record this expenditure would be:

```
Prepaid expense, franchise services . . . . . . . . . . . . . . . .  2,000
    Cash . . . . . . . . . . . . . . . . . . . . . . . . . . . . . . .          2,000
```

The above $2,000 is treated as a prepaid asset account balance and will be charged off to expense only when the corresponding franchise fee is recognized as revenue.

On December 31, 1991, Chicago Pizza would make the following entry to accrue interest on the note receivable:

```
Interest receivable  . . . . . . . . . . . . . . . . . . . . . . . . .  3,150
    Interest revenue ($30,000 × .14 × 9/12) . . . . . . . . . . . .          3,150
```

On February 1, 1992, the entry to reflect the earned portion of the franchisor's fee revenue, assuming the franchise began operation on February 1, 1992, would be:

```
Deferred franchise fee revenue  . . . . . . . . . . . . . . . . . .  50,000
Franchise service expense . . . . . . . . . . . . . . . . . . . . .  2,000
    Franchise fee revenue . . . . . . . . . . . . . . . . . . . . . .          50,000
    Prepaid expense, franchise services . . . . . . . . . . . . . .          2,000
```

In conformity with the matching principle, the 1991 expenditures by the franchisor related to the franchise are deferred until the associated franchise fee revenue is recognized.

Proportional Performance Method

The **proportional performance method** is used to recognize service revenue that is earned by more than one performance act. The proportional peformance method is used only if performance of the service extends beyond one accounting period. Under this method, such revenue should be recognized based on the proportioinal performance of each act. The proportional performance method of accounting for service revenue is similar to the percentage-of-completion method (discussed previously). Proportional measurement of the service revenue is applied differently for different types of service transactions as described below:

1. *Similar performance acts*—Recognize an *equal* amount of service revenue for each such act. Example: processing of monthly mortgage payments by a mortgage banker.
2. *Dissimilar performance acts*—Recognize service revenue in proportion to the seller's direct costs to perform each act.[27] Example: providing lessons, examinations, and grading by a correspondence school.
3. *Similar acts with a fixed period for performance*—Recognize service revenue by the *straight-line method over the fixed period* unless another method is more

---

[27] If the direct cost of each act cannot be measured reliably, the total service sales revenue should be prorated to the various acts by the *relative sales value method*. If sales values cannot be identified with each act, the straight-line method to measure proportional performance should be used.

appropriate. Example: providing maintenance services on equipment for a fixed periodic fee.

Completed-Performance Method

The **completed-performance method** is used to recognize service revenue earned by performing a series of similar or dissimilar performance acts, the final act of which is so important in relation to the total service transaction that *service revenue can be considered earned only after the final act occurs*. For example, packing, loading, transporting, and delivery of freight by a trucking company earns service revenue only after delivery of the freight. The method is similar to the completed-contract method used for long-term contracts.

Collection Method

Under the **collection method**, revenue is recognized only when *cash is collected*. The collection method is used to account for service revenue when the uncertainty is so high or the estimates of expenses related to the revenues are so unreliable that the requirement of reliability is not satisfied. This method is similar to the cost recovery method used for product sales.

EXPENSE RECOGNITION
♦

SFAC No. 3 (par. 65) defines expenses as follows:

> Expenses are outflows or other using up of assets or incurrences of liabilities (or a combination of both) during a period from delivering or producing goods, rendering services, or carrying out other activities that constitute the entity's ongoing major or central operations.

After the revenue of the accounting period is measured and recognized in conformity with the *revenue principle,* the *matching principle* is applied to measure and recognize the expenses of that period. This is the second step in the process of income recognition.

Matching Principle

The matching principle requires that for any reporting period, consistent with the recognition criteria, revenues should be determined in conformity with the revenue principle; then expenses incurred in generating the revenue of the period should be recognized for that period.[28] The essence of the matching principle is that as revenues are earned, certain assets are consumed (such as supplies) or sold (such as inventory), and services are used (such as salaries). The cost of those assets and services used up should be recognized and reported as expense of the period during which the related revenue is recognized.

SFAC No. 5 (par. 86) categorizes expenses as follows:

1. *Direct expenses* are expenses, such as cost of goods sold, that are matched with revenues. These expenses are recognized based on recognition of revenues that result *directly* and *jointly* from the same transactions or other events as the expenses.

---

[28] Recognition of gains and losses is discussed in the next major section, titled "Recognition of Gains and Losses."

2. *Period expenses* are expenses such as selling and administrative salaries. These expenses are recognized *during the period* in which cash is spent or liabilities are incurred for goods and services that are used up either simultaneously with acquisition or soon after.
3. *Allocated expenses* are expenses such as depreciation and insurance. These expenses are *allocated* by systematic and rational procedures to the periods during which the related assets are expected to provide benefits.

Expenses Directly Related to Sales of Products or Services

Expenses Directly Related to the Sales of Products   Expenses *directly* related to the sales of products during the period usually include:

- Costs of materials and labor to manufacture, or the cost to purchase, inventory that is sold during the period (i.e., cost of goods sold).
- Selling expenses, such as sales commissions, salaries, rent, and shipping costs.
- Warranty expense on products sold.

Under the matching principle, expenses that are directly related to the sales of products should be recognized as expense during the reporting period in which the related sales revenue is recognized. For accounting purposes, certain expenses are difficult to classify in terms of the proximity of their relationship to sales revenue. For example, advertising and research and development (R&D) expenditures are made to enhance the marketability of a company's products. However, it is difficult to establish a direct causal link between those expenditures and specific revenues. Therefore, the allocation of such costs usually would be subjective. For this reason, GAAP requires that such costs be expensed as incurred.[29]

Expenses Directly Related to the Sales of Services   Expenses directly related to the sales of services can be classified as:

- *Initial direct costs* are costs that are directly associated with negotiating and consummating service transactions. These costs include commissions, legal fees, salespersons' compensation other than commissions, and nonsales employees' compensation that is applicable to negotiating and consummating service transactions.
- *Direct costs* are costs that have an identifiable causal effect on service sales. Examples include the cost of repair parts and service labor included as part of a service contract.

All *initial direct costs* and *direct costs* should be recognized as expense during the period in which the related service revenue is recognized under the *specific performance* and *completed-performance methods* to attain an appropriate matching of revenues and expenses. Thus, initial direct costs and direct costs that are incurred prior to the recognition of revenue from performance of the service should be *deferred* as prepayments and expensed when the related service revenue is recognized.

For service revenue recognized under the *proportional performance method,* initial direct costs should be expensed as the related service revenue is recognized. However, direct costs should be expensed as incurred because of the high correlation between the amount of direct costs incurred and the service revenue recognized under the proportional performance method.

For service revenue recognized under the *collection method,* all initial direct costs and direct costs should be expensed as incurred.

---

[29] *SFAS No. 2* specifically requires that most R&D costs be expensed as incurred.

Expenses Not Directly Related to Sales of Products or Services

Expenses not directly related to the sales of products or services include both *period* expenses and *allocated* expenses. Examples include certain types of advertising expense, compensation that is applicable to the time spent in negotiating product or service transactions that are *not* consummated, general administrative expenses, depreciation expense, and amortization expense. Because no objective basis exists for relating period expenses to product or service sales revenue of the period, these costs should be expensed as they are incurred. Similarly, allocated expenses must be assigned to periods on a systematic and rational basis.

RECOGNITION OF GAINS AND LOSSES

Gains and losses (defined in Chapter 2) result from peripheral or incidental transactions, events, and circumstances. Therefore, they are distinguished from revenues and expenses. Whether an item is a gain or loss or an ordinary revenue or expense depends on the reporting company's primary activities or businesses. For example, when a company primarily involved in manufacturing and marketing products sells some of its land or buildings, the transaction is a gain or loss because this is not the primary business of the company. However, when a real estate sales company engages in this type of transaction, it gives rise to revenues and expenses.

Most gains and losses are recognized when the related transaction is completed. Thus, gains and losses from disposal of operational assets, sale of investments, early extinguishment of debt, and restructure of troubled debt are recognized in the specific entry made to record the completed transaction. For example, an entry to record the disposal of a tract of land for cash would reflect a debit to cash, a credit to land (for its recorded cost), and a debit to loss (or credit to gain) on disposal.

Estimated losses, but *not gains,* are recognized prior to their ultimate realization. For example, *unrealized* losses on write-downs of short-term investments to market value below cost, disposal of a segment of the business, pending litigation, and expropriation of assets are recognized immediately if they are both probable and can be reasonably estimated (*SFAS No. 5,* "Accounting for Contingencies," par. 8). If both conditions are not met, the nature and estimated amount of the contingent loss must be disclosed in a note to the financial statements (This topic is also discussed in Chapter 15).

In contrast, gains are almost never recognized prior to the completion of a transaction that establishes the existence and amount of the gain.[30] For example, in the case of a "probable," but as yet unrealized gain on disposal of a segment of the business, *APB Opinion No. 30* (par. 15) states that "if a gain is expected, it should be recognized when realized, which ordinarily is the disposal date." In some cases, potential gains may be disclosed in notes to the financial statements, provided the notes are written carefully to "avoid misleading implications as to the likelihood of realization" (*SFAS No. 5, par. 17* [b]).

A gain or loss may result from purely internal events, such as a change in accounting principle. Such gains and losses are recognized in the period when the change occurs.

In sum, accounting for gains and losses reflects a conservative approach. This often causes losses to be recognized before their actual incurrence, but prevents the

---

[30] See *SFAS No. 5,* par. 17(*a*). Contingencies that might result in gains usually are not reflected in the accounts since to do so might be to recognize revenue prior to its realization.

recognition of gains before a completed transaction or event. *SFASC No. 5* (par. 81) states:

> In assessing the prospect that as yet uncompleted transactions will be concluded successfully, a degree of skepticism is often warranted. Moreover, as a reaction to uncertainty, more stringent requirements historically have been imposed for recognizing revenues and gains than for recognizing expenses and losses, and those conservative reactions influence the guidance for applying the recognition criteria to components of earnings.

Because companies usually can control when to engage in transactions or events that give rise to gains or losses (e.g., disposal of investment securities, disposal of an unprofitable division of the business, early extinguishment of its debt, or a change in accounting principle), companies exercise considerable latitude over the net income they report. This explains why GAAP contains relatively strict disclosure requirements for such gains and losses.

CONCEPT REVIEW

1. What distinguishing characteristics of a service would influence the choice of specific performance, proportional performance, or the completed-performance method of revenue recognition for service sales?
2. What are direct expenses? Period expenses? Allocated expenses? How are these different expenses accounted for under the different methods of revenue recognition for service sales?
3. Lucky Company fully expects to win a patent infringement suit against Unlucky Corp., which will result in a $100 million payment from Unlucky to Lucky. Unlucky fully expects to lose the suit, although final resolution will not occur until next fiscal year. How would you expect Lucky and Unlucky to report this event?

SUMMARY OF KEY POINTS

(L.O. 1) 1. For most companies, the earnings process is continuous. That is, the profit-directed activities of the company continuously generate inflows or enhancements of the assets of the company, and these activities result in outflows or the using up of assets.

(L.O. 2) 2. The four fundamental criteria that must be met before an item is recognized as an element in the financial statements are:
    a. It must meet the *definition* of an element.
    b. It must have a *measurable* relevant attribute.
    c. It must be *relevant* to users' decisions.
    d. It must possess the quality of *reliability*.

(L.O. 2) 3. Before the results of the earnings process are recognized in the accounting records an item must meet the four fundamental criteria mentioned in (2) above and the following two additional criteria:
    a. It is realized or realizable.
    b. It is earned.

(L.O. 2) 4. For most companies selling goods or rendering services, revenue is recognized when goods are delivered or the service is rendered. This is called the *point-of-sale method* (also the *sales method*) of revenue recognition.

(L.O. 2) 5. With product financing arrangements, *SFAS No. 49* requires that revenue not be recognized until there is a sale to a party with which there is no repurchase agreement.

(L.O. 2) 6. Most gains and losses are recognized when the related transaction is completed. Estimated losses but not estimated gains, are recognized when they are probable and can be reasonably estimated.

(L.O. 3) 7. Under the completed-contract method, revenues and expenses are recognized when the contract obligations are completed. Costs incurred in completing the contract are accrued in an inventory account, and if there are progress billings on the contract, such billings are accrued in a contra inventory account.

(L.O. 3) 8. Under the percentage-of-completion method, revenues and expenses are recognized each accounting period based on an estimate of the percentage of completion of the contract. Costs incurred in completing the contract and recognized gross profit are accrued in an inventory account. If there are progress billings, such billings are accrued in a contra inventory account.

(L.O. 3) 9. In choosing between the completed-contract and the percentage-of-completion methods of accounting for long-term contract, a company must use the percentage-of-completion method if estimates of cost to complete and of percentage of completion are reasonably dependable, and the following three conditions are met:

    a. The contract specifies the enforceable rights of both the buyer and the seller, the amount of consideration to be exchanged, and the manner and terms of settlement.

    b. The buyer can be expected to satisfy all obligations in the contract.

    c. The contractor (seller) can be expected to perform according to the terms of the contract.

(L.O. 3) 10. If estimated costs to complete a contract increase to the point where the contract is unprofitable, under the completed-contract or percentage-of-completion methods the projected loss is recognized in full in the period in which it is estimated.

(L.O. 4) 11. The installment sales method of revenue recognition delays recognition of gross profit until cash is collected, at which time gross profit is recognized at the gross profit rate for the original installment sale.

(L.O. 4) 12. The cost recovery method is a conservative method in which no profit is recognized until all costs associated with the sale item have been recovered in cash. All subsequent cash collections are profit. This method is a departure from the matching principle.

(L.O. 5) 13. When a product is sold with extensive right-of-return privileges given to the purchaser, *SFAS No. 48* identifies six conditions that must be met before revenue can be recognized:

    a. The seller's price to the buyer is substantially fixed or determinable at the date of sale.

    b. The buyer has paid the seller, or the buyer is obligated to pay the seller and the obligation is not contingent on resale of the product.

    c. The buyer's obligation to the seller would not be changed in the event of theft or physical destruction or damage of the product.

    d. The buyer acquiring the product for resale has economic substance apart from that provided by the seller.

    e. The seller does not have significant obligations for future performance to directly bring about resale of the product by the buyer.

    f. The amount of future returns can be reasonably estimated.

(L.O. 6) 14. There are four methods of revenue recognition for service sales:
   a. Specific performance—used when revenue is earned by performing a single act.
   b. Proportional performance—used when revenue is earned by the performance of several acts.
   c. Completed performance—used when the revenue can be considered earned only after the performance of the last act.
   d. The collection method—used when uncertainty is high or estimates of expenses are unreliable.

(L.O. 7) 15. The matching principle provides guidance for expense recognition. The matching principle states that for any reporting period, the expenses recognized in that period are to be those incurred in generating the revenues recognized in that period.

(L.O. 7) 16. Expenses directly related to the sale of products or rendering services are matched with the related sales. Expenses not directly related to the sale of products or to the rendering of services are one of the following:
   a. *Period expenses,* which are expensed in the period in which they are incurred.
   b. *Allocated expenses,* which are expensed by a systematic and rational allocation of the costs to the periods during which the related assets are expected to provide benefits.

REVIEW PROBLEM
♦

Precision Punctual Construction (PPC) has agreed to build a 76-story office building for the Mountain States Bank Corporation. The contract calls for a contract price of $15,000,000 for the building, with progress payments being made by Mountain States as the construction proceeds over the construction period. The period of construction is estimated to be 30 months. The contract is signed on February 1, 1995, and construction begins immediately. The building is completed and turned over to Mountain States Bank on December 1, 1997.

Data on costs incurred, estimated costs to complete, progress billings, and progress payments over the period of construction are as follows:

(in thousands)	◄------- Year ------►		
	1995	1996	1997
Costs incurred this period	$ 1,500	$ 7,875	$ 3,825
Costs incurred to date	1,500	9,375	13,200
Estimated costs to complete	10,500	3,125	-0-
Estimated total costs of project	12,000	12,500	13,200
Progress billings this period	1,200	6,000	7,800
Progress payments received this period	825	6,300	7,875

1. Show the entries to account for this project over the period of construction, assuming that Precision Punctual Construction uses the completed-contract method of recognizing revenue.
2. Show the entries to account for this project over the period of construction, assuming that Precision Punctual Construction uses the percentage-of-completion method of recognizing revenue.
3. Show the relevant balance sheet and income statement items for 1995, 1996, and 1997 for Precision Punctual Construction assuming the company uses:
   a. The completed-contract method of recognizing revenue.
   b. The percentage-of-completion method of recognizing revenue.

The entries to record the construction of the building for both the completed contract-method and the percentage-of-completion method, (1) and (2) above, are as follows (all amounts in thousands):

Entries to record 1995 transactions and events:

	Completed Contract		Percentage of Completion	
a. To record incurrence of construction costs:				
Construction-in-progress inventory	1,500		1,500	
Cash, payables, etc.		1,500		1,500
b. To record progress billings:				
Accounts receivable	1,200		1,200	
Billings on contract		1,200		1,200
c. To record billing collections:				
Cash	825		825	
Accounts receivable		825		825
d. To record revenue recognition for the percentage-of-completion method:				
Construction-in-progress inventory	—		375	
Cost of earned construction revenue	—		1,500	
Revenue from long-term contracts		—		1,875

*The percentage of completion is cost incurred to date divided by total estimated costs to complete, or $1,500 divided by $12,000, or 12.50%. The total amount revenue recognizable to this point is .1250 × $15,000, or $1,875.

Entries for 1996:

	Completed Contract		Percentage of Completion	
a. To record incurrence of construction costs:				
Construction-in-progress inventory	7,875		7,875	
Cash, payables, etc.		7,875		7,875
b. To record progress billings:				
Accounts receivable	6,000		6,000	
Billings on contract		6,000		6,000
c. To record billing collections:				
Cash	6,300		6,300	
Accounts receivable		6,300		6,300
d. To record revenue recognition for the percentage-of completion method:				
Construction-in-progress inventory	—		1,500	
Cost of earned construction revenue	—		7,875	
Revenue from long-term contracts		—		9,375

** The percentage of completion is cost incurred to date divided by total estimated costs to complete, or $9,375 divided by $12,500, which equals 75.00%. The total amount of revenue recognizable to this point is .75 × $15,000, or $11,250. Since $1,875 was recognized in 1995, the amount recognizable in 1996 is $11,250 − $1,875, or $9,375.

Entries for 1997:

		Completed Contract	Percentage of Completion

a. To record incurrence of construction costs:

	Completed Contract		Percentage of Completion	
Construction-in-progress inventory	3,825		3,825	
Cash, payables, etc.		3,825		3,825

b. To record progress billings:

Accounts receivable	7,800		7,800	
Billings on contract		7,800		7,800

c. To record billing collections:

Cash	7,875		7,875	
Accounts receivable		7,875		7,875

d. To record revenue recognition for the percentage-of completion method:

Cost of earned construction revenue	—		3,825	
Revenue from long-term contracts†		—		3,750
Construction-in-progress inventory		—		75

† The project is completed; thus, any remaining portion of the contract price not previously recognized as revenue should be recognized this period. In prior years, $1,875 plus $9,375 (totaling $11,250) has been recognized; thus, $3,750 is to be recognized in this year.

e. To record elimination of contact costs from inventory:

Billings on contract	—		15,000	
Construction-in-progress inventory		—		15,000

f. To record revenue recognition for the completed-contract method:

Billings on contract	15,000		
Cost of earned construction revenue	13,200		
Revenue from long-term contracts		15,000	
Construction-in-progress inventory		13,200	

3. The relevant financial statement presentations for both the completed-contract and the percentage-of-completed methods of revenue recognition, (3) above, are found in Exhibit 7–5.

EXHIBIT 7–5 Comparison of Completed-Contract and Percentage-of-Completion Financial Statement Presentations for Precision Punctual Construction

	December 31, 1995		December 31, 1996		December 31, 1997	
	Completed Contract	Percentage of Completion	Completed Contract	Percentage of Completion	Completed Contract	Percentage of Completion
Balance Sheet:						
Accounts receivable	$ 375	$ 375	$ 75	$ 75	–0–	–0–
Inventory						
Construction-in-progress	$1,500	$1,875	$9,375	$11,250	–0–	–0–
Less: Billings on contract	(1,200)	(1,200)	(7,200)	(7,200)	–0–	–0–
Construction in progress in excess of billings	$ 300	$ 675	$2,175	$ 4,050	–0–	–0–
Income Statement:						
Revenue from long-term contracts	—	$1,875	—	$ 9,375	$15,000	$3,750
Cost of construction	—	1,500	—	7,875	13,200	3,825
Gross profit	—	$ 375	—	$ 1,500	$ 1,800	($75)

KEY TERMS

Collection method (318)

Completed-contract method (305)

Completed-performance method (318)

Consignment (294)

Cost recovery method (302)

Deferred gross margin (295)

Deferred revenue (291)

Gross margin (293)

Installment sales method (294)

Installment sale (294)

Percentage of completion method (306)

Point of sale method (291)

Proportional performance (317)

Specific-performance method (316)

QUESTIONS

1. Explain the relationship between revenue recognition and the definitions of assets and liabilities.
2. State the six conditions that must be met for revenue to be recognized when a customer has the right to return purchased products. What accounting procedures are used until all six conditions are met?
3. Explain the cash basis and accrual basis of accounting. Explain why accounting uses the accrual basis.
4. What are the four fundamental criteria for recognition identified in *SFAC No. 5?* What are the constraints on recognition?
5. Why may the criterion of reliability affect the timing of recognition?
6. What do the terms *realization* and *earned* mean in the context of revenue recognition?
7. Give two typical examples of revenues for which recognition occurs on the basis of the passage of time.
8. When is sales revenue recognized under the sales method?
9. A three-year $360 subscription to a business periodical is paid, and delivery of the magazine starts immediately. When should the publishing company recognize this revenue?
10. Explain why accretion (i.e., a natural increase in value of a natural resource, such as growing of timber) is not accepted as a basis of recognizing revenue?
11. When is income first recognized, assuming the following:
    a. Completed-contract method?
    b. Cost recovery method?
    c. Percentage-of-completion method?
12. Explain the basic difference between the two acceptable methods of accounting for long-term construction contracts.
13. What are two different approaches to determining the extent of progress toward completion of a construction project? Identify some specific types of measurement for each.
14. Why is the ending inventory of construction in process different in amount when the percentage-of-completion method is used compared with the completed-contract method? How much different will the amount be?
15. When a loss is projected on a long-term construction contract, in what period(s) is the loss recognized under (a) percentage-of-completion and (b) completed-contract methods of accounting for long-term construction projects?
16. Describe the installment sales method of recognizing revenue.
17. Describe the cost recovery method of recognizing revenue. When is it appropriate?
18. What is a consignment? How is revenue recognized on a consignment transaction?
19. Distinguish between the specific performance method, the proportional performance method, the completed-performance method, and the collection method of recognizing revenue associated with service sales.
20. Identify the different types of costs for service types of transactions. What are the guidelines for expensing these costs?
21. Give a definition of expense. Provide three broad categories of expense.
22. What special characteristic distinguishes gains and losses from revenues and expenses?

EXERCISES

E 7-1

**Revenue Principle:
Special Applications
(L.O. 1)**

This exercise focuses on the revenue principle. Respond to each of the following:

a. Give a definition of revenue.
b. What should be the dollar amount of revenue recognized under the revenue principle in the case of (1) product sales and services for cash and (2) product sales and services rendered in exchange for noncash considerations?
c. How should revenue be recognized when there is a highly speculative transaction involving potential revenue that cannot be reliably estimated?
d. When should revenue be recognized in the case of long-term, low down-payment sales, for which collectibility is very uncertain?
e. When should revenue be recognized for long-term construction contracts?

E 7-2

**Review of Definitions of
Elements of Financial
Statements
(L.O. 1)**

Listed below are the seven elements of financial statements. Next are key phrases from each definition. Match the key phrases with the elements by entering one letter in each blank.

Elements: A—Revenues; B—Expenses; C—Gains; D—Losses; E—Assets; F—Liabilities; G—Equity.

Key Phrases

_____ 1. Residual interest.
__D__ 2. Decreases in net assets from peripheral or incidental transactions.
__A__ 3. Enhancement of assets from ongoing major or central operations.
__F__ 4. Future sacrifices of economic benefits, results from past transactions or events.
__C__ 5. Increases in net assets, peripheral or incidental transactions.
__B__ 6. Using assets, incurring debts, ongoing major or central operations.
__E__ 7. Future economic benefits, results from past transactions or events.

E 7-3

**Overview of Recognition
Criteria: *SFAC No. 5*
(L.O. 1)**

Listed below are the four recognition criteria given in *SFAC No. 5*. Next are key phrases from each definition. Match the key phrases with the criteria by entering one letter in each blank.

Criteria: A—Definitions; B—Measurability; C—Relevance; D—Reliability.

Key Phrases

_____ 1. Representationally faithful, neutral, verifiable.
_____ 2. Elements of financial statements.
_____ 3. Capable of making a difference in decisions.
_____ 4. Quantifiable, sufficiently reliable.

E 7-4

**Revenue Recognition:
Four Special Cases—
Amounts and Explanation
(L.O. 2, 4)**

York Company has been involved in several transactions that required careful interpretation of the revenue principle. For each of the following 1992 transactions, (1) specify the amount of revenue that should be recognized during 1992 and (2) explain the basis for your answer.

a. Regular credit sales amounted to $250,000, of which two thirds was collected by the end of 1992; the balance will be collected in 1993. *250,000 point of method.*
b. Regular services were rendered on credit amounting to $190,000, of which three fourths will be collected in 1993.
c. An item that had been repossessed from the first purchaser was sold again for $5,000. A $3,000 cash down payment was received in 1992. The balance is to be paid on a quarterly basis during 1993 and 1994. Repossession again would not be a surprise.
d. On January 1, 1991, the company purchased a $10,000 note as a speculative investment. Because the collectibility of the note was highly speculative, the company was able to acquire it for $1,000 cash. The note specifies 8% simple interest payable each year (disregard interest prior to 1991). The first collection on the note was $1,500 cash on December 31, 1992. Further collections are highly speculative.

E 7-5

**Revenue Recognition:
Three Cases—Entries and
Reporting
(L.O. 2)**

Three independent cases are given below for 1991. The accounting period ends December 31.

Case A On December 31, 1991, XT Sales Company sold a special machine (Serial No. 1713) for $100,000 and collected $40,000 cash. The remainder plus 10% interest is payable December 31, 1992. XT Company will deliver the machine on January 5, 1992. The buyer has an excellent credit rating.

Case B On November 15, 1991, VR Company sold a ton of its product for $500. The buyer will pay for the product with two units of its own merchandise. The buyer promised to deliver the merchandise around January 31, 1992.

Case C On January 2, 1991, RS Publishing Company collected $900 cash for a three-year subscription to a monthly *Investors Stock and Bond Advisory*. The March 1991, issue will be the first one mailed.

Required:

For each case give the following:
1. Any entry that should be made on the transaction date.
2. The revenue recognition method that should be used.
3. An explanation of the reasoning for your responses to (1) and (2).

E 7–6

Percentage Completion: Analysis of Criteria

(L.O. 3)

It has been argued that before the percentage-of-completion method can be used properly, the following criteria must be met:
a. There is a written contract executed by buyer and seller that clearly specifies what is to be provided and received, the consideration to be exchanged, and manner and terms of settlement.
b. The buyer can satisfy obligations under the contract.
c. The seller has the ability to perform the contractual obligations.
d. The seller can reliably estimate both the cost to complete and the percentage of completion of the contract.
e. The seller has a cost accounting system that adequately accumulates and allocates cost to final cost objectives in a manner consistent with the estimating process.

Required:

1. Are the foregoing criteria adequate? What, if anything, would you add or delete?
2. Is (d), concerning the ability to estimate cost to complete, consistent with the quality of reliability?

E 7–7

Completed Contract and Percentage Completion Compared—Entries

(L.O. 3)

Watson Construction Company contracted to build a plant for $500,000. Construction started in January 1991 and was completed in November 1992. Data relating to the contract are summarized below:

	1991	1992
Costs incurred during year	$290,000	$120,000
Estimated additional costs to complete	125,000	
Billings during year	270,000	230,000
Cash collections during year	250,000	250,000

Required:

Give the journal entries for Watson in parallel columns, assuming (a) the completed-contract method and (b) the percentage-of-completion method. Apportion on the basis of costs incurred to date to total estimated construction costs.

E 7–8

(Continuation of E 7–7) Financial Statements: Can Be Assigned Separately or Jointly

(L.O. 3)

Use the data given in E 7–7 to complete the following schedule:

	Completed-Contract Method	Percentage-of-Completion Method*
Income statement:		
Income:		
1991	$_____	$_____
1992	_____	_____
Balance sheet:		
Receivables:		
1991	_____	_____
1992	_____	_____
Inventory—construction in process, net of billings:		
1991	_____	_____
1992	_____	_____

* Apportion on basis of costs incurred to date compared to total estimated construction costs.

E 7–9

Percentage Completion and Completed Contract Compared: Analysis of Account Balances

(L.O. 3)

Mullen Construction Company contracted to build a municipal warehouse for the city of Dallas for $750,000. The contract specified that the city would pay Mullen each month the progress billings, less 10%, which was to be held as a reserve. At the end of the construction, the final payment would include the reserve. Each billing, less the 10% reserve, must be paid within 10 days after submission of a billing to the city.

Transactions relating to the contract are summarized below:

1991—Construction costs incurred during the year, $200,000; estimated costs to complete, $400,000; progress billing, $190,000; and collections per the contract.

1992—Construction costs incurred during the year, $350,000; estimated costs to complete, $115,000; progress billings, $280,000; and collections per the contract.

1993—Construction costs incurred during the year, $100,000. The remaining billings were submitted by October 1 and final collections completed on November 30.

Required:

1. Complete the following schedule:

Year	Method	Income Recognized	Receivable Ending Balance	Construction in Process Inventory Ending Balance	Costs in Excess of Billings Ending Balance
1991	Completed contract				
	Percentage of completion*				
1992	Completed contract				
	Percentage of completion*				
1993	Completed contract				
	Percentage of completion				

* Apportion on basis of costs incurred to date compared to total estimated construction costs.

2. Explain what causes the ending balance in construction in process to be different for the two methods.
3. Which method would you recommend for this contractor? Why?

E 7–10

Installment Sales Method: Entries

(L.O. 4)

Barr Corporation had credit sales of $55,000 in 1991 that required use of the installment method. Barr's cost of the mechandise sold was $44,000. Barr collected cash related to the installment sales of $25,000 in 1991 and $30,000 in 1992. The perpetual inventory system is used.

Required:

1. Give journal entries related to the installment sales for 1991 and 1992.
2. Give the ending 1991 balances (before the closing entries) in the following accounts: installment accounts receivable, installment sales revenue, cost of installment sales, deferred gross margin on installment sales, and realized gross margin.

E 7–11

Unconditional Right of Return: Entries

(L.O. 5)

McLaughlin Corporation developed a new product in 1991. To increase acceptance by retailers, McLaughlin sold the product to retailers with an unconditional right of return, which expires on February 1, 1992. McLaughlin has no basis for estimating returns on the new product. The following information is available regarding the product:

Sales—1991	$180,000
Cost of goods sold—1991	120,000
Returns—1991	12,000 (cost, $8,000)
Returns—January, 1992	15,000 (cost, $10,000)

All sales are on credit. Cash collections related to the sales were $40,000 in 1991 and $113,000 in 1992. McLaughlin uses the perpetual inventory system.

Required:

Give journal entries for sales, returns, and collections related to the new product. The closing or reversing entries are not required. How much sales revenue should McLaughlin recognize in 1991?

Handwritten annotations:

1992
Dr. Cost of goods sold
Dr. Deferred gross margin
   Cr. Sales revenue
      153,000
   (180,000 – 12,000
      – 15,000)

102,000 (120,000 – 8,000 – 10,000)
51,000 (180,000
      –120,000
      60,000
      – 4,000 → (12,000 – 8,000)
      – 5,000 → (15,000 – 8,000)

in 1991? zero , in 1992: $153,000

E 7–12
Cost Recovery Method
(L.O. 4)

Tony Company has an inventory of obsolete products that it formerly stocked for sale. Efforts to dispose of this inventory by selling the products at low prices have not been successful. At the end of the prior year (1991), the company reduced the value to a conservative estimate of net realizable value of $22,000. On March 1, 1992, Watson Trading Company purchased this entire inventory for $10,000 cash as a speculative investment. Watson hopes to be able to dispose of it in some foreign markets for approximately $30,000. However, prior to purchase, Watson concluded that there was no reliable way to estimate the probable profitability in the venture. Therefore, Watson decided to use the cost recovery method. Subsequent cash sales have been as follows: 1992, $4,000; 1993, $5,000; and 1994, $8,000. Approximately 12% of the inventory remains on hand at the start of 1995.

Required:
Give the 1992, 1993, and 1994 entries for Watson Trading Company.

PROBLEMS

P 7–1
LT Construction:
Percentage Completion—
Entries and Reporting
(L.O. 3)

Honaker Company contracted to construct a building for $975,000. The contract provided for progress payments. Honaker's accounting year ends December 31. Work began under the contract on July 1, 1991, and was completed on September 30, 1993. Construction activities are summarized below by year:

1991—Construction costs incurred during the year, $180,000; estimated costs to complete, $630,000; progress billings during the year, $153,000; and collections, $140,000.

1992—Construction costs incurred during the year, $450,000; estimated costs to complete, $190,000; progress billing during the year, $382,500; and collections, $380,000.

1993—Construction costs incurred during the year, $195,000. Because the contract was completed, the remaining balance was billed and later collected in full per the contract.

Required:
1. Give the contractor's entries assuming the percentage-of-completion method is used. Show computation of income apportionment on a cost basis. Assume that percentage of completion is measured by the ratio of costs incurred to date to total estimated construction costs.
2. Prepare income statement and balance sheet presentations for this contract by year; assume the percentage-of-completion method.
3. Prepare income statement and balance sheet presentations by year; assume the completed contract method. For each amount that is different from the corresponding amount in (2) above, explain the reason.
4. Which method would you recommend to this contractor? Why?

P 7–2
LT Construction:
Methods Compared—
Entries and Reporting
(L.O. 3)

Moody Corporation contracted to construct an office building for Mitchell Company for $1 million. Construction began on January 15, 1991, and was completed on December 1, 1992. Moody's accounting year ends December 31. Transactions by Moody relating to the contract are summarized below:

	1991	1992
Costs incurred to date	$400,000	$ 850,000
Estimated costs to complete	420,000	
Progress billings to date	410,000	1,000,000
Progress collections to date	375,000	1,000,000

Required:
1. In parallel columns, give the entries on the contractor's books; assume (*a*) the completed contract method and (*b*) the percentage-of-completion method. Assume percentage of completion is measured by the ratio of costs incurred to date to total estimated construction costs.
2. For each method, prepare the income statement and balance sheet presentations for this contract by year.
3. What is the nature of the item "costs in excess of billings" that would appear on the balance sheet?
4. Which method would you recommend the contractor use? Why?

P 7–3
Accounting for
Installment Sales: Entries
(L.O. 2, 4)

Mark Corporation made a number of sales in 1991 and 1992 that required use of the installment method. The following information regarding the sales is available:

	1991	1992	1993
Installment sales	$200,000	$150,000	$ –0–
Cost of installment sales	160,000	112,500	–0–
Collections on 1991 sales	40,000	50,000	60,000
Collections on 1992 sales		30,000	75,000

Mark uses a perpetual inventory system.

Required:

1. Give journal entries relating to installment sales for the years 1991 to 1993.
2. What is the year-end balance in installment accounts receivable (net of any deferred gross margin) for 1991, 1992, and 1993?
3. If the sales qualified for application of the sales method, what amounts of gross margin would Mark report in 1991, 1992, and 1993?

P 7–4
Installment Sales Method:
Entries and Reporting
(L.O. 4)

Ohio Retail Company sells goods for cash, on normal credit (20/10; n/30). However, on July 1, 1991, the company sold a used computer for $2,200; the perpetual inventory carrying value was $440. The company collected $200 cash and agreed to let the customer make payments on the $2,000 whenever possible during the next 12 months. The company management stated that it has no reliable basis for estimating the probability of default. The following additional data are available: (*a*) collections on the installment receivable during 1991, $300, and during 1992, $200, and (*b*) on December 1, 1992, repossessed the computer (estimated net realizable value, $700).

Required:

1. Give the required entries for 1991 and 1992; assume that the installment method is used.
2. Give the balances in the following accounts that would be reported on the 1991 and 1992 income statements and balance sheets: realized gross margin on installment sales, gain (loss) on repossession, installment accounts receivable, and inventory of used computers.

P 7–5
Accounting for a
Franchise: Entries
(L.O. 6)

On October 1, 1991, Baker Donut Shops, Inc. (a franchisor), sold a franchise to James Johnson. Under the terms of the sale, Johnson paid $20,000 in cash and issued a note payable in four equal annual installments of $10,000 beginning on October 1, 1992. The note payments were based on a 12% interest rate. In return, Baker agreed to locate a suitable site for the franchise and assist in training personnel for the donut shop.

A site was located on December 15, 1991, at a cost to Baker of $3,000. Training of Johnson's personnel cost Baker $5,000 and was completed on February 1, 1992. The franchise began operation on February 15, 1992.

Required:
Give journal entries for Baker associated with the franchise sale for 1991 and 1992.

P 7–6
Cost Recovery Method
(L.O. 4)

Saxon Department Store has accumulated a stock of obsolete merchandise that it formerly sold. Routine efforts have been made to dispose of it at a low, reasonable price. This merchandise originally cost $60,000 and was marked to sell for $132,000. The management decided to set up a special location in the basement to display, and it was hoped, to sell this stock starting in January 1992. All items will be marked to sell at a cash price that is 30% of the original marked selling price. On December 31, 1991, the company accountant transferred the purchase cost to a perpetual inventory account called, "inventory, obsolete merchandise," at 30% of its purchase cost, which approximates estimated net realizable value. The management knows that a reliable estimate of the probable sales cannot be made. Therefore, the cost recovery method will be used. Subsequent sales were these: 1992, $9,000; 1993, $7,000; and in 1994, the remaining merchandise was sold for $8,000.

Required:
Give the entries that Saxon should make for 1991 through 1994.

P 7–7

Revenue Recognition: Proportional Performance (L.O. 6, 7)

Jones and Wilson, a professional corporation, contracted to provide legal services for Brown Company. The contract specified a lump-sum payment of $60,000 on November 15, 1991. Assume that Jones and Wilson can reliably estimate future direct costs associated with the contract. The following services were performed based on the estimate by Jones and Wilson:

	Direct Costs	Date Completed
Research potential lawsuit	$ 5,000	December 15, 1991
Prepare and file documents	15,000	March 1, 1992
Serve as Brown's council during legal proceedings	15,000	October 15, 1992

Required:

1. What method of revenue recognition is appropriate for Jones and Wilson? Explain.
2. Give entries to recognize revenues related to this contract for Jones and Wilson.

P 7–8

Recognizing and Matching Expenses with Revenue (L.O. 1, 7)

The general ledger of Airtime, Inc., a corporation engaged in the development and production of television programs for commercial sponsorship, contains the following asset accounts before amortization and at the end of 1991:

Account	Balance
"Sealing Wax and Kings"	$75,000
"The Messenger"	36,000
"The Desperado"	19,000
"Shin Bone"	8,000
Studio rearrangement	7,000

An examination of contracts and records revealed the following information:

a. The first two accounts listed above represent the total cost of completed programs that were televised during 1991. Under the terms of an existing contract, "Sealing Wax and Kings" will be rerun during 1992 at a fee equal to 60% of the fee for the first televising of the program. The contract for the first run produced $300,000 of revenue. The contract with the sponsor of "The Messenger" provides that at the sponsor's option, the program can be rerun during the 1992 season at a fee of 75% of the fee for the first televising of the program. There are no present indications that it will be rerun.
b. The balance in "The Desperado" account is the cost of a new program that has just been completed and is being considered by several companies for commercial sponsorship.
c. The balance in the "Shin Bone" account represents the cost of a partially completed program for a projected series that has been abandoned.
d. The balance of the "Studio Rearrangement" account consists of payments made to a firm of engineers that prepared a report relative to the more efficient utilization of existing studio space and equipment.

Required:

1. State the general principle (or principles) of accounting that are applicable to recognizing revenue and expense for the first four accounts.
2. How would you report each of the first four accounts in the financial statements of Airtime? Explain.
3. In what way, if at all, does the studio rearrangement account differ from the first four? Explain.

(AICPA adapted)

P 7–9

Matching Expense with Revenue (L.O. 1, 6, 7)

Ogden Publishing Company prepares and publishes a monthly newsletter for an industry in which potential circulation is limited. Because information provided by the newsletter is available only on a piecemeal basis from other sources and because no advertising is carried, the subscription price for the newsletter is relatively high. Ogden recently engaged in a campaign to increase circulation that involved extensive use of person-to-person long-distance telephone calls to research directors of nonsubscriber companies in the industry. The telephone cost of the campaign was $38,000, and salary payments to persons who made the calls amounted to $51,000.

As a direct result of the campaign, new one-year subscriptions at $175 each generated revenue of $164,500. New three-year subscriptions at $450 each generated revenue of $324,000, and new five-year subscriptions at $625 generated $157,500. Cancellations are rare, but when they occur, refunds are made on a half-rate basis (e.g., if a subscriber has yet to receive $100 worth of newsletters, $50 is refunded).

Aside from the two direct costs of the campaign cited above, indirect costs, consisting of such items as allocated office space, fringe benefit costs for employees making telephone calls, and supervision amounted to $21,000.

Required:

1. Identify the specific accounting issues involved in recognizing revenue and expense for Ogden and give the accounting principles that are important in resolving each issue.
2. Assume the campaign was begun and concluded in May, new subscriptions begin with the July issue of the monthly newsletter, and the company's accounting year ends December 31. How should costs of the campaign be allocated among current and future accounting years? Show calculations.

CASES

C 7–1 Deferral of Revenue: Analysis (L.O. 1, 7)	Assume in 1989 the Federal Power Commission (FPC) issued a ruling raising the ceiling price on regulated (interstate) gas, but with a "vintaging" system. Gas suppliers could charge $1.42 per thousand cubic feet on "new gas" drilled after January 1, 1988, and $1.01 on gas drilled between January 1, 1986, and December 31, 1987. The old price had been 52 cents per thousand cubic feet and remained at this for all "old" gas (i.e., pre-1986 gas). The FPC soon reduced the $1.01 rate to 93 cents and retained the $1.42 rate. As a result of a lawsuit against the FPC seeking a rollback to the old 52-cent rate, a circuit court of appeals decided gas suppliers should go ahead and collect the higher prices provided they would agree to refund the money if the final decision went against the FPC.

Required:

1. If you were part of management of a gas supplier at the time of the circuit court decision, what position would you take with respect to recognition of the extra amounts of revenue from the sale of new gas? Give reasons for whatever position you take.
2. Disregard the answer you gave to (1) above. If the revenue is deferred, how would it be accounted for until a final court decision is rendered? How would the deferred revenue be recognized if the final court decision is delayed until a new accounting year and then is favorable?

C 7–2 Magazine Subscriptions Collected in Advance: Analysis (L.O. 1)	At a meeting of the board of directors of Vanguard Publishing Company, where you are the controller, a new director expressed surprise that the company's income statement reflects that an equal proportion of revenue is earned with the publication of each issue of the magazines the company publishes. This director believes that the most important event in the sale of magazines is the collection of cash on the subscriptions and expresses the view that the company's practice smooths its income and that its subscription revenue actually is earned as subscriptions are collected.

Required:

Discuss the propriety of timing the recognition of revenue on the basis of:

1. Cash collections on subscriptions.
2. Number of magazines delivered each month.
3. Both events, by recognizing part of the revenue with cash collections of subscriptions and part with delivery of the magazines to subscribers.

(AICPA adapted)

C 7–3 Liberalism versus Conservatism in Using Accounting Practices (L.O. 1, 2)	Two associates, Tom, an accountant, and Jerry, an engineer, are discussing the role of accounting in managing an enterprise and reporting on its operating results. Jerry argues, "When things are so-so or are going badly, the management uses current accounting practices to portray the picture reasonably accurately, but when things are going well, these practices are applied either liberally or conservatively to the extent that a company sometimes fails to tell the true story." You join their discussion.

Required:

1. Cite some specifics that support Jerry's general line of argument.
2. How can you and Tom respond to justify current accounting practices in good times as well as bad?

C H A P T E R

8

Cash and Receivables

After you have studied this chapter, you will:

1. Be familiar with the composition of cash and receivables accounts.

2. Have learned how to construct a bank reconciliation and understand other internal control procedures for cash.

3. Be familiar with the conditions under which receivables may be recorded.

4. Understand adjustments to accounts receivable, including uncollectible accounts, discounts, and returns and allowances.

5. Be able to determine when the transfer of a receivable is reported as a sale or a liability.

6. Understand and be able to apply appropriate valuation concepts to the reporting of notes receivable; in particular, how to establish their present value.

♦

INTRODUCTION
♦

In 1987, Citicorp Savings recorded a $3 billion loss on loans made to foreign countries. Did these loans suddenly become worthless in 1987? Between 1982 and 1987, Chase Manhattan Bank experienced a 60% increase, to $4.6 billion, in the face amount of its nonperforming loans. These loans were primarily to foreign countries.[1] From an accounting standpoint, should commercial banks who aggressively lend to less-developed nations be required to disclose the high-risk nature of these loans at the time they are extended?

In another matter concerning troubled receivables, Endo-Lase, a distributor of medical lasers, tripled its sales in 1984 over 1983. The company looked very strong—until its receivables were scrutinized: receivables jumped 625% over the same period! Much of the reported increase in revenue actually represented receivables from customers who later defaulted. The adjustment for overstated receivables decreased Endo-Lase's 1984 income by 90%. The company filed for bankruptcy in 1986.[2]

In the past, some companies have gone to great lengths to improve their reported receivables and income. Peabody International Corporation was particularly creative in this area. In 1979, Peabody was a $600 million energy systems and pollution control company. That year, 42% of its fourth-quarter profit resulted from anticipated victories in lawsuits against subcontractors: lawsuits receivable![3]

Common to these situations is the problem of turning receivables into cash. A *liquid* firm can meet current-period cash needs from its cash position and incoming cash flows during the same period. Liquidity is essential to the survival and adaptability of businesses. Inability to pay debts over an extended period often results in either reorganization or bankruptcy.

Cash management is increasingly important because of the greater complexity and global nature of financial markets. Competitiveness requires that a firm be able to obtain funds for innovation and growth. A firm's past record of liquidity and its future liquidity prospects are important to those contemplating investing in the business.

Correct disclosure and classification of cash and near-cash items are required for accurate assessments of a firm's liquidity. Which items are appropriately included in cash and cash equivalents, and how should receivables be measured?

The revenue principle, discussed in Chapter 7 provides help. This principle constrains recognition of revenue and receivables. Estimated *collectibility* is a key factor in recognizing receivables. Although receivables are initially *measured* at the value of the consideration given in exchange, collectibility fine-tunes that measurement. Estimated *net realizable value,* the appropriate valuation for short-term receivables, results from adjusting the initially recorded value for uncollectible accounts and other factors.

The measurement of long-term receivables presents still another challenge. These receivables represent claims to cash enforceable in the future, yet financial statement users periodically wish to know their value. What is the proper valuation of these receivables, and how is interest revenue on these items treated?

The sale of receivables to obtain immediate cash presents yet another important accounting issue. Should this transfer of receivables for cash be treated as a sale of assets or as a borrowing transaction? The answer depends on which party controls

---

[1] "Judgement? Or Foot-dragging?" *Forbes,* June 29, 1987, p. 88.

[2] "Now You See It . . . ," *Forbes,* February 9, 1987, p. 70

[3] "Slick Accounting Ploys Help Many Companies Improve Their Income," *The Wall Street Journal,* June 20, 1980, p. 1. Recording anticipated gains is not an accepted accounting procedure.

the receivables after the transfer. The financial statement implications are considerable because companies prefer to avoid increased debt.

◆

ACCOUNTING FOR CASH
◆

Characteristics of Cash and Cash Equivalents

The cash account includes only those items immediately available to pay obligations. Cash *includes* balances on deposit with financial institutions,[4] coins and currency, petty cash (discussed later), and certain negotiable instruments accepted by financial institutions for immediate deposit and withdrawal. These negotiable documents include ordinary checks, cashier's checks, certified checks, money orders, and money market funds with check-cashing privileges. The balance of the cash-control account reflects all items included in cash.

Cash equivalents are items similar to cash but not classified as such. They include Treasury bills,[5] commercial paper,[6] and certificates of deposit.[7] A delay or penalty may result upon conversion of cash equivalents to cash. Therefore, cash equivalents are *excluded* from the cash account. Often there is no intent to use these items immediately as a medium of exchange.[8] Cash equivalents are generally recorded in short-term investment accounts.

Cash also *excludes* postage stamps and travel advances to employees (prepaid expenses), as well as receivables from company employees, and cash advances either to employees or outside parties (receivables).

At the end of the accounting period, undelivered checks are not deducted from the balance in the cash account. Entries already made to record such checks are reversed before preparing the financial statements because no resources were exchanged. Some companies do not reduce the cash account balance until checks are presented for payment.

An **overdraft** is a negative bank-account balance and is reported as a current liability. Overdrafts occur when the dollar amount of checks honored by the bank exceeds the account balance. However, if a depositor overdraws an account but has positive balances in other accounts with that bank, it is appropriate to offset the negative and positive balances. In this case, the bank is both a creditor and debtor. Accounts with different financial institutions are not offset against each other.

A **compensating balance** is a minimum balance that must be maintained in a depositor's account as support for funds borrowed by the depositor. Compensating balances are not included in the cash account because they are not currently

---

[4] Checking accounts are considered cash. With normal savings accounts, the bank has the right to demand advance notification of a withdrawal, but rarely invokes this authority. Therefore, savings accounts also generally are included in cash.

[5] Treasury bills are noninterest-bearing obligations of the United States with a maturity of less than one year from issue date. They are sold at a discount and are redeemed at maturity. The difference between the maturity and issue amounts is interest revenue to the purchaser.

[6] *Commercial paper* refers to short-term notes issued by corporations as a means of financing short-term cash needs.

[7] Certificates of deposit, or bank time deposits, are not available on an immediate demand basis, although they can be redeemed subject to early withdrawal penalties.

[8] *Cash equivalents* has a more specific meaning for the statement of cash flows.

available for use. However, many companies choose to include these balances in cash and disclose the restrictions in notes to the financial statements. Either disclosure option avoids overstating the firm's liquidity position.[9]

Compensating balances increase the effective rate of interest on loans because the borrower can only use the net amount. For example, assume that a firm borrows $15,000 for one year at 10% but must maintain a $1,000 compensating balance in an account with the bank. The compensating balance increases the effective interest rate to 10.71% ($1,500 interest ÷ $14,000 loan). A compensating balance is an example of a *restricted* cash balance, an amount of cash held for a specific purpose which cannot be used, or is not intended for, general payment use.

Another common restricted cash balance is a *sinking fund,* an amount of cash set aside for debt retirement. Restricted cash balances are classified as short- or long-term investments, depending on the duration of the restriction. For example, the 1989 Addsco Industries, Inc. annual report disclosed the following footnote:

> The provisions of the U.S. Longshoremen and Harbor Workers Compensation Act require that the Company restrict certain assets for payments of workers' compensation claims. These restricted assets, all of which are on deposit with the Federal Reserve Bank of Atlanta, Georgia, are included in the Company's financial statements as restricted cash and investments with an aggregate cost of $838,620 and $663,958 on June 30, 1989 and 1988, respectively.

Items properly included in cash generally do not present valuation problems because they are recorded at nominal value. These items are worth their face value in terms of U.S. dollars. The U.S. dollar value of holdings in foreign currency, however, fluctuates with changes in the relevant exchange rate. Only foreign currencies convertible to U.S. dollars without restriction are included in cash. The valuation of foreign currency and other foreign currency accounting issues are considered in advanced accounting courses.

Although maintaining separate ledger accounts for cash and cash equivalents is normal practice, 60% of surveyed companies combine cash and cash equivalents for external reporting purposes.[10] For example, a portion of the 1989 Knape & Vogt Manufacturing Company annual report follows:

	1989	1988
Cash including cash equivalents of $417,750 and $247,230	$745,220	$748,356

Note 1 (in part): *Cash Equivalents*
All highly liquid debt instruments purchased with a maturity of three months or less are classified as cash equivalents.

Internal Controls for Cash

An internal control system is a set of policies and procedures designed to:
* protect assets,
* ensure compliance with laws and company policy,
* promote accurate accounting records, and
* evaluate performance.

---

[9] The SEC, in *Financial Reporting Release No. 1*, requires that *legally restricted deposits* held as compensating balances against short-term borrowing arrangements be reported as noncash current assets, and if they are held against long-term borrowing, they should be reported as noncurrent assets.

[10] AICPA, *Accounting Trends & Techniques*, (New York, 1990), p. 88. The trend toward combining cash with cash equivalents for reporting purposes is likely to further accelerate because *SFAS No. 95*, "Statement of Cash Flows," requires cash *and* cash equivalents as the basis for the statement of cash flows.

A strong system of internal control over cash and other liquid assets increases the likelihood that the reported values for cash and cash equivalents are accurate and may be relied upon by financial statement users.

The need to safeguard cash is critical in most businesses. Cash is easy to conceal and transport, carries no mark of ownership, and is universally valued. The risk of theft is directly related to the ability of individuals to access the accounting system and obtain custody of cash.

Internal controls over cash should accomplish the following:

- Separate custody and accounting for cash.
- Account for all cash transactions.
- Maintain only the minimum cash balance needed.
- Perform periodic test counts of cash balances.
- Reconcile ledger and bank cash account balances.
- Achieve an adequate return on idle cash balances.
- Physically control cash.

Control of Cash Receipts   Cash inflows have many sources, and cash control procedures vary across companies. However, the following procedures apply in most situations:

1. Separate the responsibilities for handling cash, recording cash transactions, and reconciling cash balances. This separation reduces the possibility of theft and of concealment through false recording.
2. Assign cash-handling and cash-recording responsibilities to different persons to ensure a continuous and uninterrupted flow of cash from initial receipt to deposit in an authorized bank account. This control requires immediate counting, immediate recording, and timely deposit of all cash received.
3. Maintain continuous and close supervision of all cash-handling and cash-recording functions. This control includes both routine and surprise cash counts, internal audits, and daily reports of cash receipts, payments, and balances.

Control of Cash Disbursements   Most firms disburse cash to a large number of different payees. Although cash disbusement control systems are tailored to each firm's specific needs, the following fundamentals apply in most cases.

1. Separate the responsibilities for cash disbursement documentation, check writing, check signing, check mailing, and record keeping.
2. Except for internal cash funds (petty cash), make all cash disbursements by check.
3. If petty cash funds are employed, develop tight controls and authorization procedures for their use.
4. Prepare and sign checks only when supported by adequate documentation and verification.
5. Supervise all cash disbursements and record-keeping functions.

The following discussion highlights two of the most common elements of cash control and management: petty cash funds and bank accounts.

Petty Cash Funds

A petty cash fund is a type of *imprest* fund, providing ready currency for routine disbursements.[11] The size of the fund can vary from $50 or less to $10,000 or more. A large organization may have several petty cash funds located throughout its offices

---

[11] Imprest funds are funds created for specific purposes, which periodically are replenished by reimbursement for amounts disbursed. Disbursements require authorization. A cash register drawer is another example of an imprest cash fund.

and production facilities. Although the amount in any one location is relatively minor, the total of all petty cash can be significant.

Petty cash funds are intended to handle many types of small payments including employee transportation costs, postage, office supplies, and delivery charges. Generally, control of cash in a petty cash system is less structured and somewhat informal. However, the dollar amounts are small, and the increased economy and convenience often justify the use of petty cash funds.

The following chronological steps illustrate a typical petty cash fund operation. The balance of the petty cash account is part of the total cash balance and changes only when the fund is established, changed in amount, or discontinued.

1. Assume a $3,000 fund is established at a specific location. This amount serves to minimize administrative costs and lost interest. The cash is placed in a secured location, usually a strongbox or safe. The journal entry to establish a fund for an assumed amount of $3,000 is:

Petty cash	3,000	
Cash		3,000

2. The custodian reviews authorization on vouchers for cash requests and dispenses the required cash. The vouchers are kept with the fund. The sum of cash and vouchers should equal $3,000. Journal entries are not made for disbursements.

3. At the end of the first month, $560 remained in the fund, indicating that $2,440 was disbursed during the month ($3,000 − $560). This also means that the custodian should have $2,440 in supporting payout vouchers. The following individual vouchers accompany the fund: postage, $900; office supplies $700; and taxi fares, $800 ($2,400 in total). Therefore, a $40 cash sortage ($2,440 − $2,400) occurred. Presumably, a voucher was lost, or a voucher understates the amount disbursed. The shortage is reflected in the following replenishment entry:

Postage expense	900	
Office supplies expense	700	
Transportation expense	800	
Cash short and over	40	
Cash		2,440

This entry is recorded by the accounting department, not the custodian. Replenishment of the petty cash fund occurs whenever the fund runs low and at the end of each fiscal period for proper reporting of expenses and cash balance.

Cash short and over is an expense (debit balance) or revenue account (credit balance). A shortage or overage is caused by recording or disbursing errors. If the shortage is larger than normal or if shortages occur regularly with the same fund, theft should be suspected. In certain situations where fraud or theft is suspected, a loss is recorded rather than cash short and over.

4. When a petty cash fund is increased, decreased, or closed, an entry is made affecting both the petty cash and cash accounts. For example, if the fund is increased to $5,000 because of increased office cash needs, the following entry is made:

Petty cash	2,000	
Cash		2,000

Petty cash systems foster internal control through the requirement that someone other than the recipient of cash must authorize the disbursement. Also, a record of each disbursement is made, the fund is created and replenished by check and reconciled, and the replenishment check is written by someone other than the custodian of the fund.

Control of Cash through Bank Accounts

The use of accounts with banks or other financial institutions is an important means of cash control. Bank accounts provide several advantages:

* Cash is physically protected off the company premises.
* A separate record of cash is maintained by the bank.
* Cash handling and theft risk are kept to a minimum.
* Customers may remit payments directly to the bank.
* Financial institutions provide cash management services such as checking privileges, investment advice, and interest revenue on accounts.

Large companies with widely dispersed activities often use multiple bank accounts in diverse locations to facilitate cash collection and to take advantage of float. *Float* consists of uncollected or undeposited checks in transit between companies. Firms attempt to maximize *payment* float to increase interest earned on the funds supporting checks written to other firms, and minimize *collection* float to reduce interest lost on checks received from other firms.

Lockbox systems can reduce collection float. Customers mail their payments to a local bank or post office box. A local bank is authorized (for a fee) to empty the box daily and deposit the funds to the company's account with the local bank.

Electronic funds transfer (EFT) is a means of transferring funds between banks and firms by telephone, wire, or computer and is also a means of reducing float. EFT provides online, real-time computer linkages for immediate posting of transactions to accounts. The advantages of EFT include reduced paperwork, fewer errors, and lower transaction costs. The chief disadvantages are the cost of new equipment and internal control systems required in the new EFT environment.[12]

Reconciliation of Bank and Book Cash Balances Banks send a monthly statement to each depositor, indicating the beginning and ending balances per the bank and transactions occurring during the month. These transactions include checks clearing the account, deposits received, and service charges. The ending cash balance on the bank statement and the firm's ending cash ledger account balance are generally different. Monthly reconciling of the bank balance with the depositor's cash account balance is an essential cash control procedure.

Generally, several items listed in the bank statement have not been recorded by the firm. These include interest credited to the account by the bank, notes collected by the bank, and service charges. *Debit* and *credit* memos inform the firm about changes in the cash account. In terms of the bank's accounting system, a firm's cash balance is a liability, the amount owed by the bank to the firm. Therefore, a debit memo describes the amount and nature of a decrease in the firm's cash account. A credit memo indicates an increase in the cash account.

At the end of a period, the balance per the bank also does not reflect all cash transactions. Outstanding checks (those that have not cleared the bank) and deposits reaching the bank after preparation of the bank statement are examples. A bank reconciliation explains why the book and bank balances are different.

Bank reconciliations are used to:

1. Determine whether the bank account and the company's cash balance are in agreement after taking into account unrecorded items.

---

[12] Westinghouse Corporation estimated that EFT would reduce routine transaction costs from $1.05 to $0.15 per item; $1.4 million would be saved on check collections alone. See R. Caruso, "Paying Bills the Electronic Way," *Management Accounting*, April 1984, pp. 25–27. Also, EFT reduced check-processing costs from $0.59 to $0.07 per check at the U.S. Treasury Department. See T. Hanley, C. D'Arista, and N. Mitchell, "Electronic Banking: Key to the Future—If Properly Planned and Integrated," *American Banker*, May 21, 1984, pp. 4–26.

EXHIBIT 8-1

WEST COMPANY
Information for
Bank Reconciliation
August 31, 1991

Bank Statement		Company's Cash Account	
August 1 balance	$32,000	August 1 balance	$30,000
Deposits recorded in August	77,300	August deposits	75,300
Checks cleared in August	(71,000)	August checks	(70,000)
Note collected (including		August 31 balance	$35,300
$100 interest)	1,100		
NSF check, J. Fox	(300)		
August service charges	(200)		
August 31 balance	$38,900		

Additional data, end of July: Deposits in-transit, $5,000, and checks outstanding, $8,000 (these two amounts were taken from the July bank reconciliation). End of August: Cash on hand (undeposited), $990. This amount will be deposited September 1.

2. Isolate recording errors and other problems in the bank records or company's recording system.
3. Establish the correct ending cash balance.
4. Supply information for adjusting entries.

Reconciliation Procedures   Three methods of reconciling bank account balances are illustrated: (1) bank balance and book balance to true cash balance, (2) bank balance to book balance, and (3) comprehensive bank reconciliation, or "proof of cash."

Bank and Book Balance to Correct Cash Balance Method   This method begins with the two cash balances, and lists the differences between those balances and the true ending cash balance.

One or more adjusting entries are recorded for each item reconciling the *book balance* because each represents a change in cash not recorded by the firm. Exhibit 8-1 gives the information for an example.

The bank statement reported an ending $38,900 balance, and the cash account disclosed an ending $35,300 cash balance. Exhibit 8-2 shows the completed reconciliation.

Each side of the reconciliation begins with one of the two balances, and ends with the correct cash balance, $35,890. The reconciliation has no effect on the bank's balance. The following steps describe the procedure.

I. Items are entered that reconcile the bank statement balance to the correct cash balance. These are amounts the bank could not have known at August 31. (Refer to Exhibit 8-2)

   A. *Cash on hand*—This is the cash held by the company but not deposited at August 31. This amount, usually representing undeposited checks, is added to the bank balance because it is not recorded in the bank's records.

   B. *Deposits in-transit*—These are deposits made too late to be reflected in the bank statement. This amount is determined by comparing the firms's record of deposits with the deposits listed in the bank statement or by using the following schedule:

EXHIBIT 8–2

WEST COMPANY
Bank Reconciliation: Bank and Book Balance to Correct Cash Balance Method
August 31, 1991

Bank Balance		Book Balance	
Ending bank balance, August 31 . . . . . $38,900		Ending book balance, August 31 . . . . . $35,300	
Additions:		Additions:	
Cash on hand (undeposited) 990		Note collected by bank:	
Deposits in transit, August 31		Principal 1,000	
($5,000 + $75,300 − $77,300) 3,000		Interest 100	
Deductions:		Deductions:	
Checks outstanding ($8,000 +		NSF check, J. Fox . . . . (300)	
$70,000 − $71,000) August 31 . . . . . (7,000)		Bank service charges . . . . (200)	
		Total $35,900	
		Cash shortage* . . . . (10)	
Correct cash balance $35,890		Correct cash balance $35,890	

*Discovered in making the reconciliation.

Deposits in-transit at end of prior period	$ 5,000
Deposits for the current period (per books)	75,300
Total amount that could have been deposited	80,300
Deposits shown in bank statement	(77,300)
Deposits in-transit at end of current period	$ 3,000

C. *Outstanding checks*—This amount is determined by comparing checks written with checks cleared or by using the following schedule:

Outstanding checks at end of prior period	$ 8,000
Checks written during the current period (per books)	70,000
Total checks that could have cleared	78,000
Checks cleared shown in bank statement	(71,000)
Outstanding checks at end of current period	$ 7,000

After entering the reconciling items, the resulting correct cash balance is $35,890.

II. Items are entered that reconcile the firm's cash ledger account to the correct cash balance. These are amounts the firm could not have known at August 31. The resulting August 31, 1991, adjusting entries are illustrated.

A. *Note collected by bank*—A note receivable with a face value of $1,000 plus $100 accrued interest, was collected by the bank but was not recorded by West.[13] Exhibit 8–2 reflects this addition of principal and interest to the book balance.

Cash	1,100	
Notes receivable		1,000
Interest revenue		100

---

[13] Credit advices, confirming collection and detailing the amounts involved, normally are transmitted to the company immediately upon completion. Therefore, the accounting entry to record the collected note could be prepared during the month.

B. NSF (nonsufficient funds—or "hot") check—A $300 check from customer J. Fox, which was not supported by sufficient funds in Fox's checking account, was returned to West by the bank.[14] West originally deposited the check, increased cash, and decreased accounts receivable. West's bank returned the check upon discovering it was not supported by funds and did not credit West's account. The $300 amount is included in the $75,300 deposits recorded in August.

Accounts receivable, J. Fox	300	
Cash		300

C. *Bank service charges*—The bank debited West's account for $200 of bank charges for August. This charge was for items such as check printing, checking account privileges, and collection of customer checks and notes. This amount was not recorded by West.

Miscellaneous expenses	200	
Cash		200

D. *Cash shortage*—this is the amount by which the recorded cash balance exceeds the correct cash balance. After the previous reconciling items are considered, the $35,900 subtotal on the right side of Exhibit 8–2 does not agree with the previously determined $35,890 correct cash balance. Expediency calls for writing off such amounts. However, if a shortage occurs regularly, if the difference were larger, or if West suspects theft, further investigation is warranted. In this case, expenses may be understated or revenues overstated. The write-off is accomplished with the following entry:

Miscellaneous expenses	10	
Cash		10

The shortage is subtracted from the book balance. Book and bank balances now are reconciled to the same value. The cash ledger balance is increased $590 ($1,100 − $300 − $200 − $10) as a result.

This example assumes only one bank account. When more than one account exists, each is reconciled separately with an individual subsidiary cash ledger account. In such cases, the sum of the correct ending subsidiary cash ledger balances equals the cash balance for reporting purposes.

Bank to Book Balance Method   The bank to book method is used frequently in practice and entails adding and subtracting items from the bank balance to derive the book balance. Exhibit 8–3 illustrates this method. Most reconciling items fall into four categories (West Company items are given as examples):

1. *Increases* in cash reflected only in the *bank* balance: these are *subtracted* from the bank balance because the bank added these amounts, but West has not (note collected by the bank).
2. *Increases* in cash reflected only in the *book* balance: these are *added* to the bank balance because the bank has not recorded them but West has (cash on hand, deposits in-transit).
3. *Decreases* in cash reflected only in the *bank* balance: these are *added* to the bank balance because the bank subtracted these amounts but West has not (service charges, NSF checks).
4. *Decreases* in cash reflected only in the *book* balance: these are *subtracted* from the bank balance because the bank has not recorded them but West has (outstanding checks).

---

[14] In practice, banks notify companies immediately that a check has been returned rather than wait to inform the company through the bank statement. In this case, the entry to record the NSF check could have been recorded earlier.

EXHIBIT 8-3

WEST COMPANY

Bank Reconciliation: Bank Balance to Book Balance Method
August 31, 1991

Ending bank balance, August 31		**$38,900**
Add:		
Cash on hand, August 31	990	
Deposits in transit	3,000	
Bank service charge	200	
NSF check	300	
Cash shortage	10	4,500
Subtract:		
Outstanding checks	7,000	
Note collected by bank	1,100	(8,100)
Ending book balance, August 31		**35,300**
Adjustment to cash account		590
Correct cash balance		**$35,890**

The unreconciled book balance ($35,300) is overstated by the $10 cash shortage. Therefore, to reconcile the bank balance to the book balance, the bank balance must also be increased $10. Reconciling the bank balance to the book balance does not determine the correct cash balance. The $590 net cash adjustment (see previous method), which reflects a $10 subtraction for the cash shortage, is added to the ending book balance to derive the correct cash balance.

The advantage of this second method is that it directly reconciles the unadjusted book balance to the bank balance. However, it does not present the necessary book adjustments as clearly as the first method.

Proof of Cash Method The proof of cash method results in a more comprehensive bank reconciliation often used by auditors as one test of the internal control system for cash. It is particularly appropriate when internal control is weak. This reconciliation is more comprehensive than the previous methods because it combines the previous and current month's reconciliation, and reconciles disbursements and receipts between the book and bank records, in one worksheet.

The West Company information for July appears below in reconciliation format:

WEST COMPANY
July 31

Items	Bank Balance	Book Balance
Ending balances, July 31	$32,000	$29,550
Deposits in transit, end of July	5,000	
Cash on hand (undeposited) end of July	1,000	
Checks outstanding, end of July	(8,000)	
Note collected for the company		600
Bank service charge for July		(150)
Correct cash balance, July 31	$30,000	$30,000

Exhibit 8–4 is the completed August proof of cash. Tracing the format of the proof of cash method, columns 1 and 4 are worksheet columns for reconciling the bank and book balances for July and August. Columns 2 and 3 are used to adjust receipts and payments, depending on the bank or book reconciliation entry. The four columns are divided vertically into bank and book sections.

EXHIBIT 8-4

WEST COMPANY
Comprehensive Bank Reconciliation (Proof of Cash)
August 31, 1991

Items	(1) Prior (July 31) Balances	(2) August Receipts	(3) August Payments	(4) August 31 Reconciled Balances
Bank:				
Per bank statement	$32,000	$78,400	$71,500	$38,900
Cash on hand:				
July 31	1,000	(1,000) *a*		
August 31		990 *b*		990
Deposits in transit:				
July 31	5,000	(5,000) *c*		
August 31		3,000 *d*		3,000
Checks outstanding:				
July 31	(8,000)		(8,000) *e*	
August 31			7,000 *f*	(7,000)
Correct cash balance or amount . . .	$30,000	$76,390	$70,500	$35,890
Books:				
Per cash account	$30,000	$75,300	$70,000	$35,300
Note collected by bank (August) . . .		1,100 *g*		1,100
NSF check, J. Doe			300 *h*	(300)
Bank service charge (August)			200 *i*	(200)
Cash shortage (August)		(10) *j*		(10)
Correct cash balance or amount . . .	$30,000	$76,390	$70,500	$35,890

Note: Letters denote explanation in text.

The following steps describe the procedure:

1. Prepare the reconciliation for the prior and current months in the first and fourth columns, using the bank and book balance to correct cash balance method. Items are not placed into the July 31 book to correct balance column because these items are already recorded as of August 1.
2. Enter the unreconciled bank and book receipts and disbursement totals for August at the head of columns 2 and 3 in the bank and book sections of the format.

    August receipts per the bank statement are $78,400, which equals deposits per the bank statement ($77,300) plus the note collected from customer ($1,100). August payments (or reductions in the cash balance) per the bank are $71,500, which equals checks clearing in August ($71,000) plus the NSF check ($300) and August service charges ($200).

    The August receipts and payments per the books are $75,300, and $70,000, respectively, as indicated in Exhibit 8-1.
3. Complete the worksheet by placing the reconciling items into the middle two columns. These items are denoted by letter and explained below:
    a. July 31 cash on hand (undeposited checks) is deposited in August but represents July receipts and is therefore subtracted from August receipts per the bank.
    b. August 31 cash on hand represents August receipts not deposited as of August 31 and is therefore added to the August receipts per the bank.
    c. July 31 deposits in transit are July receipts recorded as August receipts by the bank and are therefore subtracted from August receipts per the bank.

d. August 31 deposits in transit are August receipts not deposited as of August 31 and are therefore added to the August receipts per the bank.

e. July 31 outstanding checks are subtracted from August payments per the bank because they represent July payments.

f. August 31 outstanding checks are added to August payments per the bank because they represent August payments.

g. Note collected by the bank in August is an unrecorded August receipt and therefore is added to August receipts per the books.

h. NSF check in August is an unrecorded decrease in cash and is therefore added to August payments per the books.

i. August bank charge is an unrecorded cash payment and is therefore added to August payments per the books.

j. August cash shortage is the required reconciling amount in the receipts, suggesting that a receipt per the books is overstated.

After all items are entered, the reconciliation is totaled in two ways:

1. Vertically, each of the four column totals agrees for the bank and book amounts.
2. Horizontally, beginning balances plus receipts less payments equal ending balances for both the bank and book balances.

The proof of cash is an effective device for signaling discrepancies or errors requiring further investigation. For example, if bank and book disbursements do not agree after the reconciling adjustments are entered, then further investigation is warranted. Errors or deliberate alterations of the records are more difficult to conceal from this reconciliation.

Separation of duties is an important internal control attribute, regardless of the method used to reconcile the bank balance. For example, a person having responsibility for the bank reconciliation, cash disbursements, and accounting for cash could write and deliberately fail to record an unauthorized check. When the canceled check is returned, outstanding checks could be understated by the amount of the check, in turn overstating the correct cash balance by the amount of the check. The cash account would appear reconciled.

CONCEPT REVIEW

1. Why is a distinction made between those items qualifying for inclusion in the cash account and other items that are similar to cash, but that are not cash?
2. How does a bank reconciliation provide internal control for cash?
3. Why are adjusting entries made only for items reconciling the book balance to the correct cash balance?

ACCOUNTING FOR RECEIVABLES

♦

Receivables include claims for money, goods, services, and other noncash assets from other firms. Receivables are classified as current or noncurrent depending on the remaining time to maturity or expected collection date. Accounts receivable often are supported only by a sales invoice. Notes receivable usually are supported by formal promissory notes. Trade receivables are amounts owed the company for goods and services sold in the normal course of business. Nontrade receivables arise from many other sources.[15]

---

[15] Receivables from the following sources were disclosed by surveyed companies: tax refunds, contracts, investees, finance receivables, installment notes, sale of assets, and advances to employees (see AICPA, *Accounting Trends & Techniques* (New York, 1990), p. 95.

The earnings process is a crucial source of capital and a major source of receivables. For example, sales often are made on account. The receivable recorded in a sale is a claim on another party's assets. The main accounting issues pertaining to receivables are *recognition* and *valuation*. The collectibility of the receivable is the primary uncertainty affecting the measurement and reporting of receivables. Collectibility affects whether the receivable is recorded (the recognition issue) and at what amount (the valuation issue). Revenue, and the associated receivable, is recorded only if collection is *probable*.

Recognition and Measurement of Accounts Receivable

Accounts receivable are amounts owed by customers for goods and services sold in the firm's normal course of business. These receivables are supported by sales invoices or other documents rather than by formal written promises. These receivables include amounts expected to be collected either during the year following the balance sheet date or within the firm's operating cycle, whichever is longer. Generally a 30- to 60-day period is allowed for payment, beyond which the account is considered past due. Individual accounts receivable for customers with credit balances (from prepayments or overpayments) are reclassified and reported as liabilities. The credit balances are not netted against other accounts receivable.

Financial analysts are interested in the average number of days required for receivables to be collected (the average *age* of receivables). Ultimate Corporation, a fast-growing computer hardware wholesaler-dealer, was experiencing financial problems. The age of its receivables increased from 120 days (twice the industry average) to 158 days. The firm also was shipping computers to dealers before receiving orders. Because payment terms and return privileges were liberalized, the dealers did not protest. However, Ultimate recorded these shipments as sales. After a year or two, the company was forced to recognize large write-offs of receivables and a $1.2 million second quarter loss in 1988. This contrasted with $6.2 million of income for the same quarter of 1987.[16]

Accounts receivable are recognized only when the criteria for recognition are fulfilled. They are valued at the original exchange price between the firm and the outside party, less adjustments for uncollectible accounts, cash discounts, and sales returns and allowances. Subtracting these adjustments from the gross accounts receivable yields an approximation to *net realizable value,* the amount of cash expected to be collected. Interest is generally ignored because of the short period between sale and collection.

Cash Discounts   Companies frequently offer a **cash discount,** an amount subtracted from the *gross* invoice price if payment is received within the designated period. Cash discounts are used to increase sales and to encourage early payment by the customer. They also help to reduce uncollectible accounts.

Typical sales terms are 2/10, n/30; that is, 2% cash discount if paid within 10 days from sale; otherwise the amount, net of any returns and allowances, is due in 30 days. In this case, the *net* price is 98% of the original invoice price.

The buyer's incentive to pay within the discount period is generally significant. For example, assume South Company purchased merchandise with a $1,000 gross sales price on 2/10, n/30 terms. South decides to pay on the 30th day following the sale. Therefore, South pays $1,000 and does not take advantage of the $20 cash discount available. South's accounting system may not have signaled payment within the 10-day discount period, or South may have had alternative uses for the $20 discount amount.

---

[16] "No Question, It Looks Bad," *Forbes,* November 28, 1988, p. 62.

The decision cost South $20. However, the annualized interest rate paid by South for this decision is 37.2%! This amount is computed as follows:

$$37.2\% = \frac{.02(\$1,000)}{\$980} \times \frac{365}{20}$$

The total "interest" paid is $20, the amount of discount lost. This amount is slightly over 2% of the amount "borrowed," $980, the amount that would have satisfied the seller if paid within the discount period. However, this interest rate was paid for a period of only 20 days. The 365/20 factor represents the number of 20-day periods in one year; hence, the very large annualized rate. Few, if any, investments can offer this rate of return consistently. Hence, most buyers benefit by paying within the discount period. A well-designed accounting information system yields signals alerting the accounts payable staff to pay bills within the discount period.

Gross and Net Methods   When cash discounts are offered, the receivable and sale are recorded at either the gross or net amount. The key distinction between these methods is the treatment of sales discounts. The gross method records sales discounts only if the customer pays within the discount period. The net method recognizes sales discounts only if the customer *fails* to pay within the discount period. Both approaches are found in practice.[17]

To illustrate the accounting for the gross and net methods, assume that on August 1, 1991, North Company sold merchandise to South Company at a gross sales price of $1,000. Credit terms are 2/10, n/30. North's entries for selected events follow.

August 1, 1991—To record credit sale:

Net Method		**Gross Method**	
Accounts receivable 980*		Accounts receivable 1,000	
Sales revenue	980	Sales revenue	1,000
*$1,000(.98).			

North's offer of a cash discount supports the net valuation of sales and accounts receivable. North is satisfied with $980 if payment is made within 10 days of sale. This implies that the additional $20 is a finance charge.

Entry to record collection within the 10-day discount period:

Net method		**Gross Method**	
Cash 980		Cash 980	
Accounts receivable	980	Sales discounts 20	
		Accounts receivable	1,000

Sales discounts is a contra account to sales, and it reduces net sales by the amount of cash discounts taken by customers. The gross method specifically identifies *discounts taken* by customers.

Entry to record collection after the 10-day discount period:

Net Method		**Gross Method**	
Cash 1,000		Cash 1,000	
Accounts receivable	980	Accounts receivable	1,000
Sales discounts forfeited . .	20		

Sales discounts forfeited, a revenue account, is similar to interest revenue. The net method specifically identifies *discounts forfeited* by customers. Regardless of the payment date, the net method reports sales and receivables at the net amount, the amount acceptable to the seller for complete payment.

---

[17] Companies bill at the gross price, leaving the choice of whether to take the discount with the customer. Although billing and valuation of accounts are different functions, the gross method predominates in practice because companies find it expedient to use the gross price for both billing and accounting purposes.

The gross method reports *net* sales at invoice price less cash discount only if invoices are paid within the discount period ($1,000 − $20 sales discounts, in this example), and it reports sales at the gross amount if collection occurs after the end of the discount period. The date of payment affects the amount of recorded sales under this method.

Adjusting Entries   At year-end, under the *net* method, if the discount period on a material amount of accounts receivable has lapsed, an adjusting entry is required. This entry recognizes forfeited discounts and increases accounts receivable. For example, assume that at the end of 1991, North has $980,000 of accounts receivable recorded at net, on which the discount period has lapsed.

Assuming 2/10, n/30 terms, the following adjusting entry is made on December 31, 1991:

Net method
Accounts receivable (.02)($980,000 ÷ .98) 20,000
  Sales discounts forfeited . . . .   20,000[18]

Under the *gross* method, if a material amount of cash discounts is expected on outstanding accounts receivable at year-end, and if this amount can be estimated reliably, an adjusting entry is made for estimated sales discounts. This entry, required under the matching principle, decreases net sales and accounts receivable to the estimated amount collectible. To illustrate, assume that North has $2 million of accounts receivable recorded at gross at year-end, and expects 60% of these accounts to be collected within the discount period. North records the following adjusting entry on December 31, 1991:

Gross method
Sales discounts (.02)(.60)$2,000,000 24,000
  Allowance for sales discounts   24,000

This allowance account is a contra account to accounts receivable. During 1992, assuming the estimates were correct, the following summary entry represents the recording of receipts during the discount period on accounts receivable from 1991:

Gross method
Allowance for sales discounts   24,000
Cash 1,176,000
  Accounts receivable (.60)$2,000,000   1,200,000

A material discrepancy between estimated and actual discounts taken is treated as a change in accounting estimate and may affect future estimates of sales discounts.[19]

If proper adjusting entries are made, both the net and gross methods yield similar results. In practice, adjusting entries for sales discounts are not common because the relevant amounts from year to year are comparable.

Trade Discounts   **Trade discounts** are an efficient means of advertising prices for different quantities and to different customer groups, including wholesalers and retailers. Typically, a single invoice price is published in wholesaler catalogues. Then, several different discounts may apply, depending on customer type and quantity ordered. These trade discounts reduce the final sales price and are not affected by date of payment.

---

[18] However, *estimated* lapsed discounts on outstanding accounts receivable at year-end whose discount period has not ended are not recorded under the net method because a gain contingency would result. *SFAS No. 5*, "Accounting for Contingencies," does not recommend recording gain contingencies in the accounts.

[19] *APB Opinion No. 20*, "Accounting Changes," governs changes in estimate and other accounting changes. Changes in estimate are handled prospectively; prior periods are not affected.

For example, an item priced at $50 carries a trade discount of 40% for quantities over 1,000 units. The unit price for an order of 1,100 units is therefore $30 ($50 × .60). The percentage discount can be changed for different order quantities without changing the basic $50 price.[20]

For accounting purposes, the listed price *less* the trade discount is treated as the *gross* price to which cash discounts apply. Trade discounts are not entered into the accounting records, but rather help define the invoice price.

Sales Returns and Allowances Granting the privilege to return merchandise within a reasonable time period is part of a comprehensive marketing program and is required to maintain competitiveness in many industries. Returns often are made for defective or otherwise unacceptable merchandise. Sales allowances, in contrast, arise from dissatisfaction with a product attribute or from minor damage. To encourage the customer to keep the merchandise, the seller offers to reduce the amount owed by the customer.

Sales returns and allowances are material in various industries, including retailing and book publishing. For example, Regina Corporation, a New Jersey manufacturing company, experienced at 20% to 25% return rate in 1988 on sales of vacuum cleaners.[21]

Sales returns and allowances reduce both net accounts receivable and net sales. For example, assume that a company experiences $16,000 of returns and allowances in 1991, the first year of operations. The summary entry to record actual returns and allowances during the year is:

Summary journal entry for sales returns and allowances:

Sales returns and allowances	16,000	
Accounts receivable		16,000

Sales returns and allowances is a contra account to sales.

Chapter 7 discussed a related accounting issue, namely, whether a sale is recorded when a return privilege is extended. Sales are not recognized until six criteria are met or until the return privilege expires, whichever occurs first. If the six criteria are met, then at the end of the year, a firm records an adjusting entry for returns and allowances on outstanding accounts receivable for which the return privilege has not expired. These returns and allowances thus are recognized in the period of sale under the matching principle.

Returning to the previous example, assume that total estimated sales returns and allowances are 2% of the total $1 million sales for the year. The company then records the following adjusting entry at the end of 1991:

Adjusting journal entry for sales returns and allowances:

Sales returns and allowances (.02)$1,000,000 − $16,000	4,000	
Allowance for sales returns and allowances		4,000

The allowance account is a contra account to accounts receivable. The effect of the two entries in this example is to reduce 1991 net sales and net accounts receivable by $20,000, the total estimated returns and allowances on sales during 1991. In 1992, assuming the estimates were correct, the following entry records returns and allowances on 1991 sales:

Entry to record actual sales returns and allowances:

Allowance for sales returns and allowances	4,000	
Accounts receivable		4,000

---

[20] Several discounts (or *chain* discounts) may apply to the same item. The actual price paid for a $500 item subject to both a 15% and 20% trade discount is $340 [$500 (1 − .15) (1 − .20)]. An employee discount applied to already discounted merchandise is an example.

[21] "Cute Tricks on the Bottom Line," *Fortune,* April 24, 1989, p. 200.

A material discrepancy between estimated and actual returns and allowances is treated as a change in accounting estimate and may affect future estimates. If returns and allowances are either immaterial or relatively stable across periods, companies often do not estimate returns and allowances at year-end.

MEASURING UNCOLLECTIBLE ACCOUNTS RECEIVABLE

When credit is extended, some amount of uncollectible receivables generally is inevitable. Firms attempt to develop a credit policy neither too conservative (leading to excessive lost sales) nor too liberal (leading to excessive uncollectible accounts). Past records of payment, and the financial condition and income of customers are key inputs to the credit-granting decision.

If uncollectible receivables are both probable and estimable, estimated uncollectible accounts must be recorded in the accounts.[22] The matching principle requires that the loss from uncollectibles be recognized in the period of sale. Accounts receivable and income are reduced to reflect future uncollectibles from current-year sales. Estimated uncollectibles are recorded in *bad debt expense,* an operating expense usually classified as a selling expense.

If uncollectible accounts are not probable or estimable, no adjustment to income or accounts receivable is required; rather, accounts are written off when considered uncollectible. This approach is called the *direct write-off method.*

Events and Accounting Entries for Uncollectible Accounts

If uncollectible accounts are probable and estimable, an adjusting entry is needed at the end of an accounting period. For example, if a company estimates $9,000 of bad debts at year-end, the following adjusting entry is recorded:

Adjusting entry to recognize bad debt expense:

Bad debt expense	9,000	
Allowance for doubtful accounts		9,000

Allowance for doubtful accounts is a contra account to accounts receivable and is used because the identity of specific uncollectible accounts is unknown at the time of the above entry. *Net* accounts receivable (after subtracting the allowance account) is an estimate of the net realizable value of the receivables.

For example, USX Corporation reported the following in its 1989 balance sheet:

	1989	1988
	($ millions)	
Receivables, less allowance for doubtful accounts of $13 and $17	$914	$1,536

Other firms choose to report only the net amount of receivables in the balance sheet and report the allowance balance in a footnote.

Two other related events must be considered: (1) the write-off of a specific receivable and (2) collection of an account previously written off. The adjusting entry for bad debt expense creates the allowance for doubtful accounts for future uncollectible accounts. When specific accounts are determined to be uncollectible, that part of the allowance is no longer needed. The bad debt estimation entry previously recognized the estimated economic effect of future uncollectible accounts. Thus, write-offs of specific accounts do not reduce total assets further unless they exceed the estimate.

---

[22] *SFAS No. 5,* "Accounting for Contingencies," par. 4, 8.

For example, the following entry is recorded by a company deciding not to pursue collection of R. Knox's $1,000 account:

Entry to record write-off of a specific account receivable:

```
Allowance for doubtful accounts . . . . . . . . . . . . . . . . . . . . . 1,000
     Accounts receivable, R. Knox  . . . . . . . . . . . . . . . . . .        1,000
```

This entry affects neither income nor the net amount of accounts receivable outstanding. Instead, it is the culmination of the process that began with the adjusting entry to estimate bad debt expense. The write-off entry is recorded only when the likelihood of collection does not support further collection efforts.

When should an account be written off? In one collection expert's opinion,

> not more than three or four months after delivery of the product or service. The typical business won't resolve bad debts for nine or ten months. They're just unwilling to confront the fact they've lost. The time factor of money has to be factored in.[23]

Occasionally, amounts are received on account after a write-off. This might occur as the result of an improvement in the customer's financial condition. In this case, the write-off entry is reversed to reinstate the receivable, and cash collection is recorded. For example, assume that R. Knox is able to pay $600 on account some time after the previous write-off entry was recorded. The following entries are recorded:

Entries to reinstate and collect written-off receivable:

```
Accounts receivable, R. Knox . . . . . . . . . . . . . . . . . . . . . . 600
     Allowance for doubtful accounts . . . . . . . . . . . . . . . . .         600

Cash . . . . . . . . . . . . . . . . . . . . . . . . . . . . . . . . . . . . . 600
     Accounts receivable, R. Knox  . . . . . . . . . . . . . . . . . .         600
```

The debit and credit to accounts receivable record the partial reinstatement and collection of the account, for future reference.[24]

Estimating Bad Debt Expense

The two general methods of estimating bad debt expense are the *credit sales* method and the *accounts receivable* method. Both are acceptable under GAAP. The objective of the credit sales method is to measure accurately the expense caused by uncollectible accounts. The objective of the accounts receivable method is to measure accurately the net realizable value of accounts receivable. Some companies use both methods. Exhibit 8–5 presents background information for several examples in this section.

The current $500 debit balance in the allowance account does not necessarily indicate that past estimates of bad debt losses were too low. It is possible that some receivables originating in 1991 were written off. The debit balance does not yet reflect the estimate for bad debts based on 1991 sales.

Credit Sales Method   This method emphasizes the matching principle and income statement. Based on experience, the average percentage relationship between actual bad debt losses and net credit sales is estimated. This percentage then is applied to the actual net credit sales of the period to determine bad debt expense.

Assume that in the past, 1.2% of Rally's credit sales have not been collected. Barring changes in Rally's credit policies or major changes in the economy, Rally

---

[23] "Collecting Overdue Bills Involves Walking Delicate Line," *The Wall Street Journal*, October 10, 1990, p. B2.

[24] In some cases, the accounts receivable department records the second entry without immediate knowledge that it relates to a written off account. R. Knox's account would show a credit balance until the reinstatement entry is recorded.

EXHIBIT 8-5

RALLY COMPANY
Information for Bad Debt Estimation Examples

January 1, 1991, balances:

Accounts receivable (debit)	$101,300
Allowance for doubtful accounts (credit)	3,300

Transactions during 1991:

Credit sales	500,000
Cash sales	700,000
Collections on accounts receivable	420,000
Accounts written off as uncollectible during 1991	3,800

After posting sales, collections, and write-offs, accounts receivable and allowance for doubtful accounts appear as follows:

Accounts Receivable

1/1/91 balance	$101,300	Collections	$420,000
Credit sales	500,000	Write-offs	3,800
12/31/91 balance	$177,500		

Allowance for Doubtful Accounts

Write-offs	$3,800	1/1/91 balance	$3,300
12/31/91 balance before adjustment	$ 500		

---

expects this rate to continue. Under this method, the required 1991 adjusting entry is:

December 31, 1991—To recognize bad debt expense:

Bad debt expense $500,000(.012)	6,000	
Allowance for doubtful accounts		6,000

After posting this entry, the balance in the allowance account is $5,500 ($6,000 from the adjusting entry less the prior $500 debit balance). This method *directly* computes bad-debt expense *without regard* to the prior balance in the allowance account.[25] Rally would disclose $172,000 ($177,500 − $5,500) of net accounts receivable in the 1991 balance sheet as follows:

Accounts receivable	$177,500
Less: Allowance for doubtful accounts	5,500
Net accounts receivable	$172,000

The credit sales method emphasizes the income statement because its primary focus is on bad debt expense. The method only incidentally measures accounts receivable at net realizable value. The *matching principle* is the conceptual basis for this method because bad debt expense is based on sales. The method is simple and economical to implement. The percentage applied to credit sales should be updated periodically to approximate the rate of actual write-offs.

---

[25] One variation of this method applies a percentage to *total* net sales, rather than to credit sales. This percentage would be less than the percentage based on credit sales alone because cash sales are included in the base used for estimation. If the ratio of cash sales to credit sales is reasonably constant, this variation produces acceptable results.

Accounts Receivable Method   This method emphasizes balance sheet presentation of net accounts receivable and uses historical data to estimate the percentage of accounts receivable expected to become uncollectible. The primary focus is on estimating the net realizable value of accounts receivable—the amount of cash expected to be collected. The accounts receivable method results in a net accounts receivable balance that more closely fulfills the *SFAC No. 6* definition of an asset because it directly considers the collectibility of specific accounts receivable.

In contrast to the credit sales method, the accounts receivable method estimates the ending allowance account balance required to state net accounts receivable at estimated net realizable value. The current balance in the allowance account then is updated through the adjusting entry so that it equals this required balance. Bad debt expense is debited for the amount of this adjustment. Bad debt expense therefore is computed *indirectly*.

To estimate the required ending allowance balance, either a single composite rate based on total accounts receivable or a series of rates based on the age of individual accounts receivable (*aging of accounts receivable*) can be used.

Single Composite Rate   Assume that Rally Company (Exhibit 8–5) uses a single 3% composite rate based on experience. Therefore, the *required* ending allowance credit balance is $5,325 (.03 × $177,500). However, the allowance account reflects a $500 *debit* balance. Accordingly, the adjusting entry increases the allowance account $5,825 ($5,325 + $500), yielding the $5,325 ending balance:

December 31, 1991—To recognize bad debt expense:

Bad debt expense 5,825
    Allowance for doubtful accounts 5,825

Rally's 1991 current assets include the following:

Accounts receivable $177,500
Less: Allowance for doubtful accounts   5,325
Net accounts receivable $172,175

The estimated net realizable value of accounts receivable is $172,175 in this case. Previously discussed adjustments, including allowance for sales discounts and allowance for sales returns and allowances, would reduce this amount further.

Aging of Accounts Receivable   The aging approach categorizes the individual receivables according to age (the aging schedule) and applies a collection loss percentage to each age category to determine the required ending allowance balance. The collection loss percentages reflect past experience.

The age categories are based on the extent to which accounts are past due. An account is past due if it is not collected by the end of the period specified in the credit terms. For example, an account arising from a November 1 sale with terms 2/10, n/30, is due December 1. If the account remains unpaid at December 31, the aging analysis classifies the account as 30 days past due.

Exhibit 8–6 illustrates Rally's aging schedule and the application of the collection loss percentages. The $177,500 receivable balance (from Exhibit 8–5) is divided into four age classifications: current (not past due), 1 to 30 days past due, 31 to 60 days past due, and over 60 days past due. Each specific account receivable appears in one of these categories.

A collection loss percentage is applied to the total of the relevant age category. Rally's loss collection percentages increase with the age of the accounts. As accounts are collected and removed from each category, the proportion of uncollectible accounts increases.

Based on the computation in Exhibit 8–6, the *required* ending balance in the allowance account at December 31, 1991, is $5,690 (*cr.*). Because the allowance

EXHIBIT 8-6

RALLY COMPANY
Accounts Receivable Aging Schedule
and Application of Collection Loss Percentages
December 31, 1991

Aging Schedule

Customer	Receivable Balance Dec. 31, 1991	Current	Past due 1–30 days	Past due 31–60 days	Past due Over 60 Days
Denk	$ 500	$ 400	$ 100		
Evans	900	900			
Field	1,650		1,350	$ 300	
Harris	90			30	$ 60
King	800	700	60	40	
Zabot	250	250			
Total	$177,500	$110,000	$31,000	$29,500	$7,000

Application of Collection Loss Percentages to Age Categories:

Age Category	Total Balances	Uncollectible Experience Percentage	Amount Estimated to Be Uncollectible
Not past due (current)	$110,000	.2%	$ 220
1–30 days past due	31,000	1.0	310
31–60 days past due	29,500	8.0	2,360
Over 60 days past due	7,000	40.0	2,800
	$177,500		$5,690

balance is $500 *(dr.)* before adjustment, the allowance account is increased $6,190, yielding an ending $5,690 balance.

December 31, 1991—To record estimated bad debt expense:

Bad debt expense ($5,690 + $500) 6,190
    Allowance for doubtful accounts   6,190

In both the single composite rate and aging examples, had the allowance balance been a $500 *credit* before adjustment, bad debt expense would have been $4,825 and $5,190 respectively.

Which Method to Use?   Both the accounts receivable and credit sales estimation methods may be used together. Each is used to validate the other. For interim financial statements, many companies base monthly or quarterly adjusting entries on the credit sales method because of its low cost. At the end of the year, they age their accounts receivable to check the reasonableness of the allowance balance.

The popularity of the aging method is increasing because computer software has reduced implementation costs. Also, cash flow problems in recent years prompted companies to monitor more closely the age of their receivables to reduce losses.

The general condition of the economy, the economic health of specific customers, and the seller's credit policy and collection effort affect the rate of account write-offs. Over time, this rate changes, necessitating adjustment to the percentages applied to credit sales or receivables. For example, if the balance in allowance for doubtful accounts is found to increase each year, the estimate of uncollectibles is decreased to reflect actual experience. In this case, estimated uncollectibles consistently exceeded actual write-offs. Amounts reported in previous years are not corrected. This is an example of a change in accounting estimate.

Estimating uncollectible accounts receivable will never be an exact process. For example, FMC Corporation disclosed the following information in its 1987 annual report:

(*in thousands of dollars*)	1987	1986	1985
Beginning balance in allowance for doubtful accounts	$11,132	$11,182	$9,247
Provision for doubtful accounts	1,783	1,097	4,888
Receivables written off, net of recoveries	(2,127)	(1,147)	(2,953)

The label "provision for doubtful accounts" is another term for bad debt expense. The rate of net write-offs varied considerably from year to year.

Direct Write-Off of Uncollectible Accounts

Some companies are unable to reliably estimate uncollectible accounts. Companies in the first year of operations or in new lines of business may have no basis for forecasting uncollectibles. In these cases, and when uncollectible accounts are immaterial, GAAP allows receivables to be written off directly as they become uncollectible. The entry for the direct write-off of a $2,000 accounts receivable from M. Lynx is:

Bad debt expense	2,000	
Accounts receivable, M. Lynx		2,000

No adjusting entry is made at the end of an accounting period under the direct write-off method.

The inability to estimate uncollectible accounts creates several unavoidable problems. First, receivables are reported at more than their net realizable value, even though it is virtually certain that not all receivables are collectible. Second, the period of write-off is often after the period of sale. Therefore, reported amounts of bad debt expense are not in conformity with the matching principle. And third, direct write-off allows income manipulation by arbitrarily selecting the write-off period.

CONCEPT REVIEW

1. What are the advantages of the net method of recording cash discounts?
2. Explain the computation of the annual rate of interest for cash discounts lost.
3. What are the advantages and disadvantages of the two allowance methods of accounting for bad debt expense?

USE OF ACCOUNTS RECEIVABLE TO OBTAIN IMMEDIATE CASH

Companies frequently sell or use their accounts receivable as collateral to secure loans. The objective is to obtain more immediate access to cash, rather than wait for payment from the customer. Sales of accounts receivable (also called **factoring**,) **assignment**, and **pledging** are common forms of financing.[26] The original creditor, or

---

[26] Of companies surveyed in 1990, 19% reported entering into some form of financing arrangement involving receivables. See AICPA, *Accounting Trends & Techniques* (New York, 1990), p. 101.

holder of the accounts receivable, is called the *transferor* (in factoring), *assignor* (in assignment), and the *pledger* (in pledging). Similarly, the company providing the cash is called the *transferee, assignee,* and *pledgee,* and is usually a finance company or bank.

For example, McKesson Corporation reported the following footnote pertaining to receivable financing in its 1989 annual report:

> At March 31, 1989, the Company was contingently liable for $35.5 million of customer financing notes receivable. These notes were sold to a bank by the Company's finance subsidiary with recourse to the Company for certain uncollectible amounts.

Agreements to transfer or otherwise use accounts receivable for immediate cash are made on either a **notification** basis (customers are directed to remit to the new party holding the receivables) or a nonnotification basis (customers continue to remit to the original seller). Factoring arrangements are usually made on a notification basis.

Using receivables to obtain financing effectively shortens the operating cycle, hastens the return of cash to productive purposes, and alleviates short-run cash flow problems. The costs of these arrangements include initial fees and interest on loans collateralized by the receivables. Also, certain risks may be retained by the transferor, including bearing the cost of bad debts, cash discounts, and sales returns and allowances.

In *recourse* financing arrangements, the transferee can collect from the transferor if the original debtor (customer) fails to pay. If the arrangement is without recourse, the transferee assumes the collection losses. The fee is, therefore, higher under nonrecourse arrangements because more risk is transferred.

The key financial reporting issue in a receivable-financing arrangement is whether a *sale* or *loan* has occurred. In a *sale,* the transferor removes the receivables from the books and records a gain or loss. In a *loan,* the receivables remain on the transferor's books and a liability is recorded.[27]

How receivable transfers are treated for balance sheet reporting purposes is a matter of great concern for transferors of receivables. Generally, recording a sale is preferred, especially if a transferor's debt is already substantial. Also, recourse transfers leave the transferor with a contingent liability for the possible default on the receivables. This liability is disclosed in the footnotes under the full disclosure principle and the requirements of *SFAS No. 5.*

Factoring Accounts Receivable

Factoring transfers ownership of the receivables to the transferee (the **factor**). In some instances, the factor performs credit verification, receivables servicing, and collection agency services. In effect, the factor takes over a company's accounts receivable and credit operations. Other factoring arrangements are less inclusive. Factoring is common in the textile industry.

Factoring without Recourse   A nonrecourse factoring arrangement generally constitutes an ordinary sale of receivables because the factor has no recourse against the transferor for uncollectible accounts. Control over the receivables passes to the factor. The factor typically assumes legal title to the receivables, the cost of uncollectible accounts, and collection responsibilities. However, any adjustments or *defects* in the receivables (sales discounts, returns, and allowances) are borne by the transferor because these represent preexisting conditions.

---

[27] Receivables pledged for loans are sometimes reported as contra assets rather than as liabilities.

Factoring without recourse is treated as a sale of receivables because most of the risks and rewards are transferred. The receivables are removed from the transferor's books, cash is debited, and a financing fee is recognized immediately as a financing expense or loss on sale. Normally, the factor withholds an amount to cover probable sales adjustments (sales discounts, returns, and allowances). This amount is recorded as a receivable on the seller's books.

To illustrate factoring without recourse, consider the following case:

> Largo, Inc., factors without recourse $200,000 of accounts receivable on August 15, 1991, with a finance company on a notification basis. The factor charges a 12% financing fee and retains 10% of the accounts receivable for sales adjustments. Largo does not record bad debt expense on these receivables because, in nonrecourse transfers, the finance company must bear the cost of uncollectible accounts.

Entry 1—To record transfer of receivables:

Largo, Inc.
Cash $200,000 - (.12 + .10)$200,000	156,000	
Receivable from factor (.10)$200,000	20,000	
Loss on sale of receivables (.12)$200,000	24,000	
Accounts receivable		200,000

Finance company
Accounts receivable	200,000	
Payable to Largo		20,000
Financing revenue		24,000
Cash		156,000

Largo's loss equals the finance fee. This amount is also the book value of the receivables factored less the assets received from the finance company ($200,000 - $156,000 + $20,000). As customer sales adjustments occur, Largo records these deductions in the proper contra sales accounts and credits the receivable from factor. After all adjustments are recorded, any excess in the receivable is remitted to Largo. If adjustments exceed the amount withheld by the factor ($20,000 in this case), either the finance company or the seller absorbs this amount as a loss, or the two parties agree to allocate it in some other manner.

Assuming that the finance company estimates 1% of the receivables ($2,000) are uncollectible, the following entry is made:

Entry 2—To estimate uncollectible accounts:

Finance company
Bad debt expense	2,000	
Allowance for doubtful accounts		2,000

To complete the example, assume $4,000 of cash discounts, $12,000 of sales returns and allowances, and $2,000 of uncollectible accounts. Therefore, customers remitted $182,000 ($200,000 - $4,000 - $12,000 - $2,000) to the finance company.

Entry 2 for Largo reflects the sales adjustments, and Entry 3 records the return of the excess amount held back by the finance company.

Entry 2—To record returns, allowances, and discounts:

Largo, Inc.
Sales returns and allowances	12,000	
Sales discounts	4,000	
Receivable from factor		16,000

Entry 3—To record receipt of cash (settlement) from factor:

Largo, Inc.
Cash	4,000	
Receivable from factor ($20,000 - $4,000 - $12,000)		4,000

Entry 3 for the finance company records customer collections and reduces the payable to Largo by the amount of actual sales adjustments ($16,000). Entry 4 records actual write-offs, and Entry 5 settles the remaining payable to Largo.

Entry 3—To record remittances from customers:

Finance company
Cash 182,000
Payable to Largo 16,000
　　Accounts receivable 198,000

Entry 4—To record actual write-offs:

Finance company
Allowance for doubtful accounts 2,000
　　Accounts receivable 2,000

Entry 5—To record settlement of payable to Largo:

Finance company
Payable to Largo 4,000
　　Cash 4,000

The final entry for each firm is not recorded until all the receivables are either collected, written off, or otherwise reduced by sales adjustments. The sales adjustments are recorded on Largo's books because Largo recorded the original sale.

Exhibit 8–7 summarizes the income and cash flow effects of the financing arrangement for both parties.

Credit Card Operations　Although credit card companies such as VISA and MasterCard are not factors, they are sometimes considered in the same category for accounts receivable financing purposes. Two benefits accrue to the merchant who accepts credit cards. First, the merchant receives immediate cash on sales that otherwise would be made on credit (or not made at all). Second, unless the merchant prefers to maintain a proprietary credit card operation in addition to accepting national cards (which many department stores do), the merchant saves the cost of credit screening and accounts receivable servicing functions.

Normally, a merchant accumulates credit card sales in batches, depending on volume. The merchant's copies of the credit card vouchers are deposited with a local participating bank acting as an agent for the credit card company.[28] The total deposit is discounted by the credit card company. To illustrate, assume that a merchant accumulates $2,000 in credit card sales. The discount fee is 6%. The following entry is made at the time of deposit:

To deposit credit card vouchers:

Cash 1,880
Credit card fees expense (.06) ($2,000) 120
　　Sales 2,000

If sales are posted daily with deposits made less frequently, a receivable is debited, rather than cash.[29]

Factoring with Recourse　When receivables are factored with recourse, the transferor bears the risk and cost of sales adjustments and bad debts because the finance company has recourse against the transferor. Whether all the benefits of receivables are transferred in *recourse* arrangements is not as clear as in nonrecourse arrange-

---

[28] Virtually all major, full-service banks are depository agents for both bank-owned credit cards (VISA and MasterCard) and nonbank cards such as American Express and Diner's Club.

[29] Some banks and credit card companies sell their receivables to other parties. Banc One Corporation of Columbus Ohio is credited with starting the securitization of credit card accounts. In 1986, it sold $50 million of its credit card receivables as securities. See *The Wall Street Journal*, Centennial Issue, June 23, 1989, p. A2.

EXHIBIT 8-7   Summary of Nonrecourse Factoring Example

Largo:

Assumed gross margin percentage: 25%

Net cash received on $200,000 of financed receivables:

Original proceeds	$156,000
Settlement payment	4,000
Net cash received	$160,000

Increase in net income from sales and financing of receivables:

Gross sales	$200,000
Sales returns and allowances	(12,000)
Sales discounts	(4,000)
Net sales to Largo	184,000
Gross margin percentage	.25
Gross margin on net sales	46,000
Loss on sale of receivables	(24,000)
Increase in net income	$ 22,000

Finance Company:

Net cash received from financed receivables:

Collections on account	$182,000
Proceeds to Largo	(156,000)
Settlement payment	(4,000)
Net cash received	$ 22,000

Increase in net income from financing of receivables:

Financing revenue	$ 24,000
Bad debt expense	(2,000)
Increase in net income	$ 22,000*

Reconciliation of Cash and Factored Receivables Schedule:

Cash received by both parties:			Receivables sold to finance company:	
Largo	$160,000		Gross receivables	$200,000
Finance company	22,000		Sales discounts	(4,000)
			Sales returns and allowances	(12,000)
			Bad debt expense	(2,000)
Total cash received	$182,000		Net receivables collected	$182,000

*It is coincidental that net income for Largo and the finance company are equal.

ments. The transferor records a sale or a loan depending on which party controls the receivables and on whether the transferor can estimate future obligations to the transferee under the contract.

Although *SFAC No. 6,* "Elements of Financial Statements," is not recognized as GAAP, it defines an asset in terms of control (par. 183):

> Every asset is an asset of some entity; moreover, no asset can simultaneously be an asset of more than one entity. . . . To have an asset, an entity must control future economic benefit to the extent that it can benefit from the asset and generally can deny or regulate access to that benefit by others.

If control of the receivables passes to the transferee, then the transfer is reported as a sale.

SFAS No. 77, "Reporting by Transferors for Transfers of Receivables with Recourse," sets forth three criteria for determining whether a transfer with recourse is recorded as a sale or as a loan. These criteria are standards for judging whether control of the receivables passes to the transferee, and whether the transferor is obliged to repay the proceeds from the transfer.

If the following three criteria are met, a transfer of receivables with recourse is recognized as a sale by the transferor. If not, the transfer is recorded as a loan.

1. The transferor surrenders control of the future economic benefits of the receivables.
2. The transferor's obligation under the recourse provisions can be reasonably estimated.
3. The transferee cannot require the transferor to repurchase the receivables except under the recourse provisions.

If the transferor retains the option to repurchase the receivables, then control does not pass to the transferee, and the first criterion fails.

If the transferor cannot estimate the ultimate collectibility of the receivables, then criterion 2 fails. This situation is similar to sales made with a right-of-return, discussed in Chapter 7. If estimates of sales returns are not possible, a sale is not recognized until the right-of-return expires.

If the obligations of the transferor are limited to estimable payments under the recourse provisions (payments to the transferee for bad debt losses, cash discounts, returns and allowances), then there is no obligation to repay the proceeds from the transfer. In this case, a sale is properly reported, assuming the other criteria are met.

A recourse provision (criterion 3), requiring the transferor to repurchase receivables in the event of default by the original customer, does not imply the existence of a liability at date of transfer. However, if the factoring agreement allows the transferee to compel the transferor to repurchase the receivables at the transferee's option, criterion 3 fails.

Exhibit 8-8 repeats the relevant Largo, Inc. data previously given, and presents additional data to illustrate accounting for factoring with recourse.

The transferor's entries accounting for the transfer as a sale or a loan are given next. All entries shown are recorded by Largo because *SFAS No. 77* does not apply to accounting for transferees. The entries for the transferee are similar to the nonrecourse example described earlier.

Case 1: Factoring with Recourse Recorded as a Sale In a recourse factoring recorded as a sale, the transferor records the *probable* sales adjustments. The difference between the book value of receivables transferred and assets received from the factor is recognized immediately as a gain or loss on the sale.

Entry 1—Transfer of receivables:

Largo, Inc.

Cash $200,000 − (.06 + .10)$200,000	168,000	
Receivable from factor ($20,000 − $9,000 − $5,000 − $3,000)	3,000	
Bad debt expense	3,000	
Sales returns and allowances	9,000	
Sales discounts	5,000	
Loss on sale of receivables	12,000*	
Accounts receivable		200,000

*Book value of receivables less assets received = ($200,000 − $3,000 − $9,000 − $5,000) − ($168,000 + $3,000).

In general, the cash debit equals the gross accounts receivable factored less the finance fee and any amount held back by the factor. The receivable from factor represents the total amount held back less the estimated sales adjustments and uncollectibles. These adjustments are immediately recognized and matched against the previously recorded sales. The extra $3,000 held back by the transferee is a buffer for estimation errors.

The recognized loss also equals the product of the finance fee and gross accounts receivable (.06 × $200,000). The cost of uncollectibles is assumed by Largo, whereas in the nonrecourse agreement, the finance company assumed that cost.

EXHIBIT 8-8   Example: Largo, Inc. Information for Factoring with Recourse

Largo, Inc., factors with recourse $200,000 of accounts receivable on August 15, 1991, with a finance company on a notification basis. The factor retains 10% of the accounts receivable to protect against sales adjustments.

Additional information for sale example:

1. All three *SFAS No. 77* criteria are met, and the transfer is recorded as a sale.
2. The financing fee is 6% (less than in the nonrecourse example).
3. Largo estimates the following:
   a. Sales returns and allowances of $9,000 ($12,000 of returns and allowances are experienced, as in the previous illustration).
   b. Sales discounts of $5,000 ($4,000 actually occurred).
   c. Uncollectible accounts of $3,000 ($2,000 of accounts are actually written off)

Additional information for the loan example:

1. Largo is unable to estimate sales discounts and sales returns and allowances, and the transfer is recorded as a loan.
2. The financing fee is 6%.
3. Largo estimates $3,000 of uncollectible accounts ($2,000 of accounts are actually written off).

After all collections are received by the finance company, the final settlement is recorded in Entry 2.

Entry 2—Settlement:

Largo, Inc.
Cash 2,000
Sales expenses 1,000*
    Receivable from factor 3,000
*($12,000 + $4,000 + $2,000) − ($9,000 + $5,000 + $3,000)

The $1,000 difference between actual and estimated adjustments is expensed. The difference is the result of an estimation error and is therefore treated as a change in estimate.

Case 2: Factoring with Recourse Recorded as a Loan   In a recourse factoring recorded as a loan, the transferor recognizes the difference between the assets received from the factor and the book value of the receivables as interest over the term of the loan. This is in contrast to the sale example, in which the difference was immediately recognized as a loss. In this example, the transaction is treated as a loan because Largo is unable to estimate sales discounts and sales returns and allowances. Therefore, the transaction does not qualify as a sale under criterion 2. Entries 1 and 2 record the loan and estimated uncollectible accounts.

Entry 1—To record transfer of receivables:

Largo, Inc.:
Cash $200,000 − (.06 + .10)$200,000 168,000
Receivable from factor (.10)$200,000 20,000
Discount on payable to factor (.06)$200,000 12,000
    Payable to factor 200,000

Entry 2—To record estimated bad debt expense:

Largo, Inc.
Bad debt expense 3,000
    Allowance for doubtful accounts 3,000

The discount account is a contra account to the payable to factor account and represents the total interest to be paid by Largo. This contra account is amortized over the loan term.

Receivables are not removed from the transferor's books in a loan transaction.

Largo records the following entries as sales adjustments occur and customers remit cash to the factor.

Entry 3—To record sales adjustments:

Largo, Inc.
Sales discounts	4,000	
Sales returns and allowances	12,000	
Accounts receivable		16,000

Entry 4—At customer remittance, reduce payable:

Largo, Inc.
Payable to factor	182,000	
Accounts receivable ($200,000 − $12,000 − $4,000 − $2,000)		182,000

(Notification basis: customers remit to the finance company.)

Entry 5—To record write-offs:

Largo, Inc.
Allowance for doubtful accounts	2,000	
Accounts receivable		2,000

Entry 6—Settlement:

Largo, Inc.
Payable to factor	18,000	
Cash ($20,000 − $12,000 − $4,000 − $2,000)	2,000	
Receivable from factor		20,000

Assume Largo recognizes interest expense in proportion to collections on accounts receivable. That proportion is a measure of the expired portion of the loan term. Entry 7 records interest expense, assuming all collections were received by the end of the fiscal year.

Entry 7—To record interest expense on loan:

Largo, Inc.
Interest expense	12,000	
Discount on payable to factor		12,000

If accounts receivable are outstanding at the end of the year, a *pro rata* portion of the discount is not amortized. For example, if $20,000 of the accounts receivable (10% of the total factored) were outstanding at the end of 1991, only $10,800 of interest expense (.90 × $12,000) is recognized in Entry 7.

Assignment and Pledging of Accounts Receivable

Assignment and pledging entail the use of receivables as collateral for a loan. The important accounting issues in these arrangements include the measurement and disclosure of the borrower's net interest in the receivables and disclosure of the loan and interest expense.

In an assignment of accounts receivable, the assignor assigns the rights to *specific* receivables to the assignee. Frequently, the assignor and finance company enter into a long-term agreement whereby the assignor receives cash from the finance company as sales are made. The accounts are assigned with recourse: assignment gives the assignee the right to seek payment from the specific receivables.

The assignor usually retains title to the receivables, continues to receive payments from customers (nonnotification basis), bears collection costs, and agrees to use any cash collected from customers to pay the loan. A formal promissory note often provides the basis for the agreement between the parties, and allows the assignee (lender) to seek payment directly from the receivables if the loan is not paid when due.

The loan proceeds are typically less than the face value of receivables assigned to compensate for sales adjustments and to give the assignee a margin of protection. The risk of all sales adjustments and bad debts is retained by the assignor (borrower). The assignee charges a service fee and interest on the unpaid balance each month.

The receivables are reclassified as accounts receivable assigned, a separate category within accounts receivable used to disclose their status as collateral. The loan balance is disclosed as an amount that partially *offsets* the assigned receivables in the balance sheet. The difference between the assigned accounts receivable balance and the loan represents the assignor's equity, or residual ownership, in the assigned receivables. The subsidiary accounts are also reclassified to indicate their use as collateral, for internal accounting purposes.

This offsetting of receivables and loan is one of the rare instances of offsetting allowed in financial accounting, and it is justified by the direct nature of the assignee's claim to the collateral. Compared to a loan without collateral, the offsetting results in a lower proportion of debt to equity for the assignor (borrower).

> To illustrate assignment of accounts receivable, assume that on November 30, 1991, Franklin Corporation assigns $80,000 of its accounts receivable to a finance company on a nonnotification basis. Franklin agrees to remit customer collections as payment on the loan. Loan proceeds are 85% of the receivables less a $1,500 flat-fee finance charge. In addition, the finance company charges 12% interest on the unpaid loan balance. Interest is payable at the end of each month.

In Entries 1 and 2 below, accounts receivable assigned is a current asset listed under accounts receivable in the balance sheet. All entries are for Franklin.

Entry 1—To record receipt of loan proceeds:

Cash .85($80,000) − $1,500	66,500	
Finance expense	1,500	
Notes payable .85(80,000)		68,000

Entry 2—To classify accounts receivable as assigned:

Accounts receivable assigned	80,000	
Accounts receivable		80,000

By the end of December, assume that Franklin has collected $46,000 cash on $50,000 of the assigned accounts less $3,000 sales returns and $1,000 sales discounts, and remits the proceeds to the finance company.

Entry 3—To record sales adjustments:

Cash ($50,000 − $3,000 − $1,000)	46,000	
Sales discounts	1,000	
Sales returns and allowances	3,000	
Accounts receivable assigned		50,000

Entry 4—To remit collections to finance company:

Notes payable	45,320	
Interest expense $68,000(.12) (1/12)	680	
Cash		46,000

Franklin's December 31, 1991, balance sheet reflects the following accounts related to accounts receivable assigned:

Current assets:
Accounts receivable assigned ($80,000 − $50,000) $30,000
Less: Notes payable ($68,000 − $45,320) 22,680
Equity in accounts receivable assigned . . . . $ 7,320

The $7,320 equity in accounts receivable assigned represents Franklin's net ownership interest in these accounts. Although legal title to the receivables remains with Franklin, the finance company has an economic claim (enforceable by contract) on the remaining assigned receivables.

To complete the example, assume that in January 1992, $2,000 of the accounts are written off as uncollectible (the original $80,000 of receivables is included in the normal bad debt estimation process). Also, $25,000 is collected on account. The remaining entries complete the process assuming the loan is paid in full at the end of January.

Entry 5—To record collection and write-off in January:

Cash 25,000
Allowance for doubtful accounts 2,000
Accounts receivable assigned 27,000

Entry 6—January 31, 1992—Payment of remaining loan balance:

Notes payable 22,680
Interest expense $22,680(.12) (1/12) 227
Cash 22,907

Entry 7—To record reclassification of remaining accounts:

Accounts receivable ($80,000 − $50,000 − $27,000) 3,000
Accounts receivable assigned 3,000

Pledging of accounts receivable also uses receivables as collateral for loans but is less formal than assignment. The proceeds from the receivables must be used to pay the loan. However, accounts receivable are not reclassified. If the pledger (borrower) defaults on the loan, the pledgee (creditor) has the right to use the receivables for payment. The accounting for the receivables or loan is not affected by pledging. When the loan is extinguished, the pledge is voided.

Disclosure of Accounts Receivable Financing Arrangements

Footnotes supplement the income statement and balance sheet disclosure of receivable financing arrangements. Disclosures include information about revolving credit agreements, loan terms, and amounts of receivables used as collateral (and therefore not available to general creditors).

As an example, the 1989 annual report of Speizman Industries, Inc. included the following footnote information:

> The Company is a party to a Security Agreement with Colonial Acceptance Corporation ("Colonial") providing for advances by Colonial to the Company. The advances are collateralized by the Company's domestic accounts receivable and are limited to $600,000. Interest is paid monthly at prime plus 6%.

Disclosure of Credit Risk   Under *SFAS No. 105,* "Disclosure of Information about Financial Instruments with Off-Balance-Sheet Risk and Financial Instruments with Concentrations of Credit Risk," firms are required to disclose all significant concentrations of credit risk from receivables and other financial instruments. The amount of accounting loss due to credit risk the firm would incur if parties to the financial instruments fail to perform must be disclosed. Also, information on the firm's policy of requiring collateral to support receivables subject to credit risk, access to the collateral, and a brief description of the collateral should be disclosed.

CONCEPT REVIEW

1. Why does fulfilling the three criteria of *SFAS No. 77* imply a sale of receivables?
2. What role does a recourse provision have on reporting of transfers of receivables.
3. If a factored account (with recourse) becomes uncollectible, does this mean that the factoring must be recorded as a loan? Explain.

RECORDING AND MEASURING NOTES RECEIVABLE
♦

A note receivable is a written promise to pay specified amounts over a series of payment dates. The *maturity* date is the end of the note's term, at which time the final payment is due. Notes receivable are normally used for one or more of the following reasons:

• Extended payment terms.
• Stronger evidence of indebtedness than sales invoices and other commercial trade documents.
• A formal basis for charging interest.
• Negotiability.

Lending transactions are the primary source of notes receivable. Notes receivable also arise from normal sales, extension of the payment period of accounts receivable, exchanges of long-term assets, and advances to employees. In a loan transaction, the borrower is the *maker* of the note and the lender is the payee (note holder). When goods are transferred between a buyer and seller and a note receivable is involved, the buyer is the maker and the seller is the payee.

The interest rate stated in a note may not equal the market rate prevailing on obligations involving similar credit ratings or risks. Nevertheless, the stated rate is always used to determine the cash interest payments. If the stated and market rates are different, the market rate is used to value the note and to measure interest revenue. The market rate is the rate accepted by two parties with opposing interests engaged in an arm's-length transaction.

In some cases, it is difficult to estimate directly the market rate on a particular loan. If the value of the consideration given is known, the rate can be determined by equating the present value of the cash flows called for in the note to the market value of the consideration. The rate can be determined with a computer program or calculator that iteratively locates the correct rate.

For example, assume that on June 30, 1991, a firm sells equipment with a cash price of $10,000 and receives in exchange a note with the following payment schedule: $6,000 due on June 30, 1992, and on June 30, 1993. The note does not explicitly require interest, but $2,000 of interest is implicit in the note. The interest rate for accounting purposes is computed using the present value of an annuity as follows:

$$\$10,000 = \$6,000(PVA, i, 2)$$
$$\$10,000/\$6,000 = 1.66667 = (PVA, i, 2)$$

The value 1.66667 does not appear in the table for the present value of an ordinary annuity, but through a calculator equipped for present value, $i = 13.066\%$. Interpolation (see Chapter 6) could also be used.

In some cases, the value of the consideration given also may be difficult to determine, and an **imputed interest rate** must be estimated from other similar transactions in the market. This rate must be at least equal to the rate incurred by the debtor on similar financing.[30]

For accounting purposes, the *principal amount* of a note is measured by the fair market value or cash equivalent value of goods or services provided in exchange for the note, if this value is known, or the present (discounted) value of all cash payments required under the note using the market rate. The principal is also the amount initially subject to interest. The principal represents the sacrifice by the payee, and therefore the present value of the future payments, at the date of the transaction. Any amount paid in excess of the principal is interest.

The *face,* or *maturity,* value is the dollar amount stated in the note. The face value is the amount, excluding interest, payable at the end of the note term, unless the note requires that principal repayments be made according to an installment schedule. The principal value equals the maturity value if the stated interest rate equals the market interest rate. The total interest over the life of the note equals the total cash receipts less the principal amount.

Notes may be categorized into interest-bearing and noninterest-bearing notes. *Interest-bearing* notes specify the interest rate to be applied to the face amount in computing interest payments. *Noninterest-bearing* notes do not state an interest rate but command interest through face values that exceed the principal amount.

Interest-bearing notes in turn can be divided into two categories according to the type of cash payment required: (1) *notes whose* cash payments are interest only—except for final maturity payment—and (2) notes whose cash payments include both interest and principal.[31]

A 10%, $4,000, two-year note received by Seattle Sealines, which requires interest to be paid on its face value, is an example of the first type. The annual interest of $400 ($4,000 × .10) is payable at the end of each year of the note term. The $4,000 face amount is paid at the end of the second year. In total, $800 of interest is required over the term of the note. In notes of this type, the original principal is not decreased by the yearly payment.

Now assume that Seattle's note instead is a note of the second type, requiring two equal annual amounts payable at the end of each year. These payments each contain interest and principal in the amount necessary to discharge the debt at 10% in two payments. The payment is computed as follows:

$$\$4,000 = \text{Present value of an annuity} = \text{Payment}(PVA, 10\%, 2)$$
$$\$4,000 \div (PVA, 10\%, 2) = \text{Payment}$$
$$\$4,000 \div 1.73554 = \$2,304.76 = \text{Payment}$$

Payment	Interest Component	Principal Component
1	$400 ($4,000 × .10)	$1,904.76 ($2,304.76 − $400)
2	$209.52*	$2,095.24 ($2,304.76 − $209.52)
*($4,000 − $1,904.76)(.10)		$4,000.00

Total interest for the second type of note ($609.52) is less than for the first note because part of the first payment is a principal payment which reduces the principal on which interest is paid in the second period.[32]

---

[30] *AICPA, APB Opinion No. 21,* "Interest on Receivables and Payables" (New York, 1971), par. 13.

[31] These categorizations are made for expository purposes only. There are an unlimited number of principal and repayment options. Payment schedules are not limited to those used in the examples.

[32] Other types of notes also exist. For example, *negative amortization* is found in some mortgage notes. These notes allow the mortgagor to make payments early in the mortgage term that are less than the amount required to extinguish the debt over the mortgage. The difference between these payments and those required to pay off the mortgage is added to the principal and increases future amounts of interest.

Notes Receivable and Accounts Receivable Compared Some of the accounting issues affecting notes receivable and accounts receivable are similar. Recognition and valuation of notes receivable are affected by collectibility. If estimates of uncollectible notes can be made, procedures similar to those discussed for accounts receivable apply. If estimates cannot be made, the direct write-off method is employed.

Long-term notes involve two additional reporting issues not considered in accounts receivable: the time value of money and the recognition of interest revenue. According to *APB Opinion No. 21,* long-term notes are recorded at their *principal* value. Interest revenue is computed on the unpaid principal balance at the beginning of the period, using the market rate prevailing when the note was issued. This rate is not changed, for accounting purposes, over the life of the note.

Notes Receivable Accounting Illustrations

In the following examples, assume adjusting entries are not reversed.

Example 1: Short-Term Simple Interest Note On April 1, 1991, Weaver Company sold merchandise on credit and received a $3,000, one-year trade note with a 10% stated interest rate. The note pays interest at maturity. The stated and market rates are equal. The following journal entries are made by Weaver over the term of the note:

April 1, 1991:

Notes receivable, trade	3,000	
Sales revenue		3,000

December 31, 1991—Adjusting entry:

Interest receivable $3,000 (.10) (9/12)	225	
Interest revenue		225

March 31, 1992:

Cash	3,300	
Notes receivable, trade		3,000
Interest receivable		225
Interest revenue $3,000 (.10) (3/12)		75

The face value of this note ($3,000) equals its principal value because the market and stated interest rates are equal. As of April 1, 1991, the present value (principal) of the March 31, 1992, $3,300 cash flow is $3,000 ($3,300/1.10). The computation for interest assumes months of equal length.[33]

If the market rate were 15%, the present value is $2,869.57 ($3,300/1.15). Although *APB Opinion No. 21* does not require reporting short-term notes at present value, the note is best carried at present value under these circumstances.

Example 2: Long-Term Simple Interest Note On April 1, 1991, Lionel Company loaned $12,000 cash to Baylor Company and received a three-year, 10% note. Interest is payable each March 31, and the principal is payable at the end of the third year. The stated and market interest rates are equal. The entry to record the note is:

April 1, 1991:

Notes receivable	12,000	
Cash		12,000

---

[33] For very short-term notes such as a 30-day note, a convention often is followed for calculating interest: the day the note is issued is not counted in the 30 days. Rather, the first day of the note term is the day after the note is issued. A 10%, $1,000, 30-day note issued April 16 requires an April 30 adjusting entry to recognize $3.84 interest revenue (14/365 × $1,000 × .10).

The present value of the principal and interest payments on April 1, 1991, is $12,000 because the stated and market rates are equal. Cash interest received also equals interest revenue recognized over the terms of the note, as indicated in the remaining entries.

December 31, 1991, 1992, 1993—Adjusting entries:

Interest receivable $12,000(.10) (9/12)	900	
Interest revenue		900

March 31, 1992, 1993:

Cash	1,200	
Interest receivable		900
Interest revenue $12,000(.10) (3/12)		300

March 31, 1994:

Cash	13,200	
Notes receivable		12,000
Interest receivable		900
Interest revenue		300

Example 3: Long-Term Note, Different Market and Stated Rates Fox Company, which sells specialized machinery and equipment, sold equipment on January 1, 1991, and received a two-year, $10,000 note with a 3% stated interest rate. Interest is payable each December 31, and the entire principal is payable December 31, 1992.

The equipment does not have a ready market value. The market rate of interest appropriate for this note is 10%. The present value (and principal) of the note is computed as follows (amounts are rounded to the nearest dollar):

Present value of maturity amount

$$\$10,000 \ (PV1, \ 10\%, \ 2) = \$10,000(.82645) \qquad = \$8,265$$

Present value of the nominal interest payments
$$\$10,000(.03) \ (PVA, \ 10\%, \ 2) = \$300(1.73554) \quad = \quad \underline{521}$$
Present value of the note at 10% $\qquad\qquad\qquad \underline{\underline{\$8,786}}$

One of the effects of *APB Opinion No. 21* was to eliminate overstatement of notes receivable and sales. Before to this *Opinion*, there were no definitive guidelines to use when the stated and market rates were unequal. Some companies recorded notes at face value even though the market rate exceeded the stated rate, thus inflating notes receivable and sales. *APB Opinion No. 21* is an example of an accounting pronouncement requiring a recording of the substance of the transaction over its form.

Notes with low stated interest rates may be used by companies to increase sales. The Fox company note, for example, used a low nominal (stated) interest rate but used an increased face value to compensate. Many buyers of big-ticket items, including automobiles, home appliances, and even houses, are more concerned about the monthly payment than the final maturity payment—the balloon payment as it is called. A note with an $8,786 face value and a 10% stated rate achieves the same present value to Fox. A 3% interest payment on $10,000 ($300) may be more attractive than a 10% payment on $8,786 ($879). Under either structuring of the payments, Fox earns 10% over the two-year term.[34]

As the Fox Company example illustrates, when the stated and market interest rates are different, the face value and principal differ. Notes are recorded at gross

---

[34] Under the alternative structuring, Fox would receive two $879 payments plus $8,786, totaling $10,544, which is less than the total cash receipts under the original structuring ($10,600). Fox receives cash more quickly under the alternative arrangement.

(face) value plus a premium or minus a discount amount (the gross method), or at the net principal value (the net method). The two methods are illustrated for the Fox example:

January 1, 1991:

	Gross		Net
Notes receivable 10,000			8,786
Discount on notes receivable	1,214		
Sales	8,786		8,786

Under both methods, the net book value of the note is $8,786, the principal value. Discount on notes receivable is a contra account to notes receivable. The gross method discloses both the note's face value and the interest to be received over the remaining term. The entries at the end of the fiscal year are:

December 31, 1991:

	Gross		Net
Cash $10,000(.03) 300			300
Discount on note receivable 579			
Notes receivable			579
Interest revenue $8,786(.10)	879		879

The balance sheet dated December 31, 1991, discloses:

	Gross	Net
Notes receivable	$10,000	
Discount on notes receivable	635*	
Net notes receivable	$9,365	$9,365†

*$1,214 − $579.
†$8,786 + $579.

Both methods increase net notes receivable by $579. Under the gross method, the discount account is amortized, increasing net notes receivable. A substantial portion of the interest revenue is reflected in the increase in net notes receivable. The present value of the note on January 1, 1992, is the net note receivable, namely, $9,365. This value can be computed in either of two ways:

$$\$8,786 + \$579 = \$9,365$$

Or:

$$\$10,300 \text{ (PV1, 10\%, 1)} = \$10,300(.90909) = \$9,365 \text{ (rounded)}$$

This amount is the present value of the remaining cash flows on 1/1/92.

APB Opinion No. 21 requires that the market rate of interest be applied to the beginning balance in the net note receivable to compute interest revenue. This approach, called the *interest method,* results in a constant rate of interest throughout the life of the note. Another method, the *straight-line* method, which amortizes a constant amount of discount each period but which produces a varying rate of interest, is allowed only if the results are not materially different from the interest method. In this example, the straight-line method results in discount amortization of $607 ($1,214/2 years) and interest revenue of $907 ($607 + $300) in both years.

Continuing with the interest method, the entry at the end of 1992 is:

December 31, 1992:

	Gross		Net
Cash $10,000(.03)	300		300
Discount on note receivable	636		
Notes receivable			636
Interest revenue $9,365(.10)	936		936

After the December 31, 1992, entry, the net notes receivable balance is $10,000, the present value at that date. The discount account balance is now zero (rounded), and the note is collected at this time:

December 31, 1992:

	Gross	Net
Cash 10,000		10,000
Notes receivable	10,000	10,000

Example 4: Long-Term Note Issued for Noncash Consideration   Siever Company sold specialized equipment originally costing $20,000 with a net book value of $16,000 on January 1, 1991, to Bellow. The market value of the equipment was not readily determinable.

Siever received a $5,000 down payment and a $10,000, 4% note payable in four equal annual installments starting December 31, 1991. The current market rate on notes of a similar nature and risk is 10%. Because the stated rate is 4%, the payment (P) is determined as follows:

$$\$10,000 = P(PVA, 4\%, 4) = P(3.62990)$$
$$10,000/3.62990 = \$2,755 = P$$

Therefore, the note's principal equals the present value of four $2,755 payments at 10%:

$$\$2,755(PVA, 10\%, 4) = \$2,755(3.16987) = \$8,733$$

The present value of the consideration received is $13,733 ($5,000 + $8,733); which is, therefore, the agreed-upon value of the equipment.

The following entry records the sale (net method):

January 1, 1991:

Cash 5,000		
Notes receivable 8,733		
Accumulated depreciation ($20,000 − $16,000) 4,000		
Loss on sale of equipment 2,267		
Equipment	20,000	

The loss on sale equals the net book value of the equipment ($16,000) less the present value of consideration received ($13,733). The following entry is made at the end of the fiscal year:

December 31, 1991:

Cash 2,755		
Interest revenue (.10)$8,733	873	
Notes receivable	1,882	

The note's book value on January 1, 1992, is 6,851 ($8,733 − $1,882). Therefore, 1992 interest revenue is $685 (.10 × $6,851).

Discounting Notes Receivable

Rather than hold a note to maturity, payees often *discount* the note with a bank or financial institution. Notes can be discounted, or sold, by any third-party holder of a note, as well as the original payee. Discounting may occur at any time before the note's maturity date. The process has three steps, as indicated in Exhibit 8–9. In the first step, the maker receives goods, services, or cash from the payee in exchange for the note. In the second step, the payee discounts the note with a bank and receives the maturity value of the note less a discount (a fee) charged by the bank. In step three, the maker pays the bank at the maturity of the note.

Notes are discounted with or without recourse, and they are recorded as a borrowing or a sale. *SFAS No. 77* applies to discounting of notes with recourse. If the transaction fulfills the three criteria of *SFAS No. 77,* it is recorded as a sale of receivables. In most cases, notes are discounted with recourse and recorded as a sale. The payee records a gain or loss equal to the difference between the proceeds and book value of the note, including accrued interest, and has a contingent liability

EXHIBIT 8-9   Three Steps in Discounting a Note

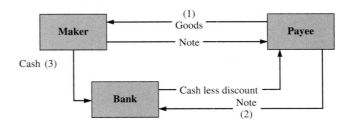

until the note is paid by the maker.[35] If the note is discounted without recourse, the payee has no contingent liability.

If a discounted note is recorded as a borrowing, a liability is recorded, and interest expense is recognized over the term of borrowing. The proceeds to the payee are not affected by the reporting alternatives and are based on the total of principal value plus interest to maturity, whether or not the note is interest-bearing. The bank charges its discount rate on this total amount for the period of time between date of discounting and maturity of the note. The sum of principal and interest is the amount at risk, from the bank's point of view.

Notes Receivable Discounting Recorded as a Sale

On April 1, 1991, Wyoming Company received a $3,000, 10%, one-year note in a sale of equipment to Nell Company. Interest on the note is due at maturity. Wyoming discounted the note on August 1, 1991, with recourse. Assume the discounting qualifies as a sale. The bank charges 15%. The proceeds to Wyoming are:

Principal value	$3,000
Interest to maturity $3,000(.10)	300
Total maturity value subject to discount	3,300
Interest charged by bank $3,300(.15)(8/12)	330
Proceeds to Wyoming[36]	$2,970

The bank charges interest on the maturity value a full eight months before that value is reached, which effectively raises the interest cost to Wyoming Company. Wyoming records the following entries to discount the note:

August 1, 1991:

Interest receivable $3,000(.10)(4/12)	100	
Interest revenue		100
Cash	2,970	
Loss on discounting of note	130	
Notes receivable		3,000
Interest receivable		100

The note is no longer an asset of Wyoming and is removed from the books. The loss equals the book value of the note plus accrued interest ($3,100) less the proceeds. Two factors contributed to the loss: the note was transferred relatively early in its term, and the bank charged a higher interest rate. If the note were held longer before

---

[35] This contingent liability is for the face value plus interest to maturity.

[36] In practice, banks charge interest on a daily basis.

discounting, the total interest charged by the bank is reduced, thus increasing the proceeds.

An alternative recording of the Nell note discounting is shown in the following entry:

August 1, 1991:

```
Cash . . . . . . . . . . . . . . . . . . . . . . . . . . . . . . . . . . . . . 2,970
Interest expense . . . . . . . . . . . . . . . . . . . . . . . . . . . . .     30
    Notes receivable . . . . . . . . . . . . . . . . . . . . . . . . . .          3,000
```

Interest expense represents the face value less the proceeds and is the net cost to Wyoming of this financing arrangement. The interest expense in this case is determined by offsetting the loss with the interest revenue. The first alternative recognizes the increase in the note's value through the date of discounting. *SFAC No. 6* supports recording a gain or loss on discounting the note, defining gains and losses as changes in owners' equity other than from revenues, expenses, and transactions with owners. In addition, Wyoming recognizes interest revenue for the period the note was held.

Regardless of the recording alternative chosen, a contingent liability exists and must be reported. Two ways of reporting that contingent liability are available.[37]

1. Wyoming reports in the footnotes to its financial statements that it is contingently liable on $3,300 of notes receivable and indicates that the contingency is a remote one.
2. Wyoming credits notes receivable discounted rather than notes receivable in the August 1, 1991, entry above. This $3,000 contra notes receivable account is subtracted from total notes receivable in the balance sheet. Total notes receivable *still includes* the note discounted. This alternative reduces net notes receivable by $3,000 and also discloses that $3,000 of total notes receivable is discounted. For example, assume $10,000 of notes receivable before discounting. After discounting, the notes are disclosed as follows:

```
Current assets:
    Notes receivable . . . . . . . . . . . $10,000
    Notes receivable discounted  . . . . .   3,000
        Net notes receivable  . . . . . . . $ 7,000
```

When the contingency is removed (upon payment of the note by maker), the following entry is made:

```
Notes receivable discounted . . . . . . . . . . . . . . . . . . . . . . . 3,000
    Notes receivable . . . . . . . . . . . . . . . . . . . . . . . . . . .        3,000
```

The advantages of footnote disclosure are that the maturity value including interest ($3,300) is disclosed, and a smaller number of accounts are affected. However, the notes receivable discounted account is more noticeable because it appears in the balance sheet. Either way, the contingency is removed when the maker pays the note. Generally, the bank or financial institution notifies the payee only upon *dishonor,* or default, by the maker. In the absence of notification by the bank, the contingency is removed a few days after the maturity date.

The Wyoming example illustrates accounting for a with-recourse note recorded as a sale. If the note is discounted without recourse, the entries are the same (although notes receivable discounted is not used), and no contingent liability exists.

Notes Receivable Discounting Recorded as a Borrowing   If the discounting does not qualify as a sale (for example, because the payee has the option to repurchase the note), Wyo-

---

[37] In most cases, defaults on notes are less than probable, and therefore no actual liability need be recorded. However, the *reporting* of a contingent liability is required by *SFAS No. 5.* (par. 12) for discounted notes.

ming makes the following entries on August 1, 1991:

August 1, 1991:

Interest receivable $3,000(.10)(4/12)	100	
Interest revenue		100
Cash	2,970	
Interest expense	130	
Liability on discounted notes receivable		3,000
Interest receivable		100

There is no loss because an asset was not sold. The note remains on the books of Wyoming. The net of interest expense and interest revenue is $30 interest expense. When the maker pays the note at maturity, the following entry is made:

After April 1, 1992:

Liability on discounted notes receivable	3,000	
Notes receivable		3,000

Dishonored Notes

When a note receivable is not renewed or collected at maturity, it is considered a **dishonored note,** and interest continues to accrue on the face value plus any previously accrued interest at the *legal* interest rate set by state law. The note is generally transferred to a special receivable account, and collection efforts ensue. For example, if the Nell note were held to maturity (i.e., not discounted), the default would be recorded as follows:

April 1, 1992:

Notes receivable past due	3,300	
Notes receivable		3,000
Interest receivable $3,000(.10)(9/12)		225
Interest revenue $3,000(.10)(3/12)		75

The accounting for *discounted* notes dishonored by the maker depends on the discounting transaction. Any contingent liability is removed. If the note was discounted without recourse and recorded as a sale, no entry is required and no contingent liability exists to be removed.

If the note was discounted with recourse (the more likely case) and recorded as a sale, the payee pays the maturity value, including interest, and any fee charged by the bank. A special receivable account is debited for the amount paid. For example, assume the note discounted by Wyoming and recorded as a sale is dishonored. The bank charges a $15 fee (called a *protest* fee) for the additional task of notifying Wyoming of the default. Assuming footnote disclosure of the continent liability, the entry to record the dishonor of the note (upon notification by the bank) is:

After April 1, 1992:

Notes receivable past due	3,315	
Cash		3,315

This amount is the maturity value plus bank fee. If the account method of disclosing the contingent liability were used, the entry is:

After April 1, 1992:

Notes receivable past due	3,315	
Notes receivable discounted	3,000	
Cash		3,315
Notes receivable		3,000

This entry removes the contingent liability and establishes the special receivable.

Finally, assume that the note Wyoming discounted is recorded as a liability and then is dishonored. The entry to record the default, with the $15 protest fee, is:

Notes receivable past due	3,315	
Liability on discounted notes receivable	3,000	
Cash		3,315
Notes receivable		3,000

Regardless of whether the note is discounted, if efforts to collect the past-due note fail, the accounting for the loss depends on whether notes are included in the bad debt estimation process. If they are included, the account is closed against the allowance for doubtful accounts at its carrying value. If they are not included in the bad debt estimation process, then the direct write-off method is used. The note is credited for the carrying value and a loss is debited.

Notes Exchanged for Cash and Other Privileges

APB Opinion No. 21 requires that long-term notes be recorded at their present value, using the appropriate interest rate. Companies may accept a note with a stated interest rate less than the market rate in exchange for cash or other consideration worth the face value of a note. To make this a reasonable transaction, other rights or privileges must, therefore, be received by the party accepting the note, beyond the cash payments required in the note.

Example   On January 1, 1991, Quail Corporation loaned River Corporation $10,000 and accepted a $10,000 note due December 31, 1992, with 5% interest paid annually each December 31, beginning 1991. The market interest rate is 12%. River also agreed to provide Quail with agricultural materials at a discount price over the note term. Two thirds of the supplies are to be furnished during the first year. The present value of the note itself is significantly less than $10,000:

$$\text{Principal value of note} = \$10,000(PV1, 12\%, 2) + \$10,000(.05)(PVA, 12\%, 2)$$
$$= \$10,000(.79719) + \$10,000(.05)(1.69005)$$
$$= \$8,817$$

In this example, Quail would lend $8,817 if only the note were received in exchange. The additional $1,183 ($10,000 − $8,817) loaned is a prepayment for discount pricing. Quail thus receives two payments of $500, one payment of $10,000, and discount pricing on purchases over the note term. *APB Opinion No. 21* requires that the value of the other privileges be recorded as an asset equal to the difference between the note's present and face values. The entries on Quail's books are (gross method):

January 1, 1991:

Notes receivable	10,000	
Prepaid purchases	1,183	
Discount on notes receivable		1,183
Cash		10,000

Two thirds of the prepaid purchases account is a current asset on January 1, 1991, and one third is a long-term asset.

December 31, 1991:

Cash	500	
Discount on notes receivable	558	
Interest revenue (.12)$8,817		1,058
Purchases (2/3 × $1,183)	789	
Prepaid purchases		789

The remaining prepaid purchases account is now a current asset for 1992. The entry on December 31, 1992, when the contract concludes is:

December 31, 1992:

Cash	500	
Discount on notes receivable	625	
Interest revenue (.12)($8,817 + $558)		1,125
Purchases (1/3)$1,183	394	
Prepaid purchases		394
Cash	10,000	
Notes receivable		10,000

CONCEPT REVIEW

1. Why are long-term notes receivable recorded at the present value of future cash receipts using the market rate of interest?
2. When is the principal amount of a long-term note not equal to its face value?
3. Under what conditions must an interest rate be imputed? How does imputation affect the valuation of a note?

SUMMARY OF KEY POINTS

(L.O. 1) 1. Cash includes only those items immediately available to pay obligations. Near-cash items are classified as short-term investments.

(L.O. 2)) 2. Bank reconciliations and petty cash funds are cash control and management tools. The reconciliation of book balance to correct balance provides the data for end-of-month adjusting entries for cash.

(L.O. 3) 3. Revenue recognition, valuation at estimated net realizable value, the use of present value for long-term notes, and the full-disclosure principle are the main principles affecting receivable accounting.

(L.O. 4) 4. Bad debt expense, cash discounts, and sales returns and allowances represent adjustments to the initial recorded value of sales and receivables. Subtracting these adjustments yields an estimate of net realizable value and the net recognizable sales for the period under the matching concept.

(L.O. 5) 5. Factoring, assignment, and pledging are methods of obtaining immediate cash from accounts receivable. The key accounting issue is whether the transfer is treated as a sale or loan. When control is transferred and the transferor's obligation can be estimated, the transfer is handled as a sale. Otherwise it is treated as a loan.

(L.O. 6) 6. Long-term notes are recorded at the present value of the consideration given, or the present value of all cash payments to be received using the appropriate market rate of interest, whichever is more clearly determinable. Interest revenue is based on that rate and the outstanding principal balance at the beginning of the period.

(L.O. 3, 5, 6) 7. Disclosure of contingent liabilities for transfers of receivables, including discounted notes receivable, is required under *SFAS No. 5*.

REVIEW PROBLEM

Three companies have asked you to record journal entries in three different areas associated with receivables, at the end of 1991. All reporting years end December 31.

A. Mandalay Company—Uncollectible accounts receivable: Mandalay Company requests that you record journal entries for its bad debt expense and uncollectible accounts receivable in 1991. Mandalay's January 1, 1991, balances relevant to accounts receivable are:

Accounts receivable	$400,000
Allowance for doubtful accounts	20,000

During 1991, $45,000 of accounts receivable is considered uncollectible, and no more effort to collect these accounts will be made. Total sales for 1991 are $1,200,000, of which $200,000 are cash sales. $900,000 was collected on account during 1991.

1. If Mandalay uses the credit sales method to estimate bad debt expense and uses 4% of credit sales as its estimate of bad debts, provide the journal entries to record write-offs and bad debt expense for 1991. Also, provide the December 31, 1991, balance sheet disclosure for net accounts receivable.
2. If Mandalay uses the accounts receivable method to estimate net accounts receivable, and uses 9% of accounts receivable as its estimate of uncollectibles, provide the journal entries to record write-offs and bad debt expense for 1991. Also, provide the December 31, 1991, balance sheet disclosure for net accounts receivable.

B. Berkshire Company—Assigning accounts receivable: Berkshire company requests that you record journal entries for the listed events related to accounts receivable it assigned in 1991.

1. On January 1, 1991, Berkshire borrows cash from a finance company and assigns $40,000 of accounts receivable (nonnotification) as collateral. A note is signed, and the finance company advances 75% of the receivables. The note requires that interest at the rate of 24% be paid on the outstanding note balance at the end of each month. No finance fee is charged because of the high rate of interest.
2. During January, $19,700 is collected on account and $800 of returns and allowances are granted to customers.
3. On January 31, Berkshire remits the cash collected on the receivables plus interest due.
4. During February, the remainder of the accounts receivable assigned is collected except for $200, which is written off as uncollectible. Berkshire uses the credit sales method to estimate bad debt expense.
5. On February 28, 1991, Berkshire remits the balance of the note and interest due the finance company.

C. White Mountain Company—Accounting for long-term notes: White Mountain Company requests that you record journal entries for a note it received in 1991. On April 1, 1991, White Mountain Company sold merchandise for $12,000 and received a $12,000, three-year, 10% note (10% is also the market rate). The note calls for three equal annual payments to be made beginning March 31, 1992. Provide the first three journal entries for this note.

SOLUTION

♦

A. Mandalay Company:

1. During 1991 (write-offs):

Allowance for doubtful accounts	45,000	
Accounts receivable (various)		45,000

December 31, 1991:

Bad debt expense (.04)$1,000,000	40,000	
Allowance for doubtful accounts		40,000

December 31, 1991, accounts receivable disclosure:

Accounts receivable $455,000*
Allowance for doubtful accounts . . . . . (15,000)†
Net accounts receivable $440,000

* $400,000 + $1,000,000 − $900,000 − $45,000.

† $20,000 − $45,000 + $40,000.

2. During 1991 (write-offs):

Allowance for doubtful accounts 45,000
    Accounts receivable (various)   45,000

December 31, 1991:

Bad debt expense 65,950
    Allowance for doubtful accounts   65,950

Ending gross accounts receivable from (1) $455,000

Desired allowance balance: $40,950*
Allowance balance before adjusting entry:
    January 1, 1991, balance $20,000
    1991 write-offs . . . . (45,000)   (25,000)
Required increase to allowance account $65,950

* .09($455,000)

December 31, 1991, accounts receivable disclosure:

Accounts receivable $455,000
Allowance for doubtful accounts . . . . . (40,950)
Net accounts receivable $414,050

B. Berkshire Company:

1. Accounts receivable assigned 40,000
       Accounts receivable   40,000

   Cash $40,000(.75) 30,000
       Note payable   30,000

2. Cash 19,700
   Sales returns and allowances   800
       Accounts receivable assigned   20,500

3. Interest expense $30,000(1/12)(.24)   600
   Note payable 19,700
       Cash   20,300

4. Cash   ($40,000 − $20,500 − $200) 19,300
   Allowance for doubtful accounts   200
       Accounts receivable assigned   19,500

5. Interest expense ($30,000 − $19,700)(1/12)(.24)   206
   Note payable 10,300
       Cash   10,506

C. White Mountain Company: The equal annual payment (P) is computed as follows:

$$\$12,000 = P(PVA,\ 10\%,\ 3) = P(2.48685)$$
$$\$12,000/2.48685 = P = \$4,825$$

1. April 1, 1991:

Note receivable 12,000
    Sales revenue   12,000

2. December 31, 1991:

Interest receivable $12,000(.10)(9/12)   900
    Interest revenue   900

3. March 31, 1992:

Cash   4,825
    Note receivable   3,625
    Interest receivable   900
    Interest revenue $12,000(.10)(3/12)   300

KEY TERMS

Assignment of accounts
  receivable (357)
Cash discount (348)
Cash equivalent (337)
Compensating balance (337)
Dishonored note (375)
Electronic funds transfer (341)
Factor (358)
Factoring of accounts
  receivable (357)

Imputed interest rate (368)
Notification (358)
Overdraft (337)
Petty cash (339)
Pledging of accounts receivable (357)
Proof of cash (345)
Trade discount (350)

QUESTIONS

1. Define *cash* as it is used for accounting purposes.
2. In what circumstances, if any, is it permissible to offset a bank overdraft against a positive balance in another bank account?
3. Define a compensating balance and explain the related reporting requirements.
4. Why is a petty cash fund replenished at the end of a reporting period?
5. Which of the following items should not be recorded in the cash account?
   - *a.* Money orders.
   - *b.* Postdated checks.
   - *c.* Ordinary checks.
   - *d.* Postage stamps.
   - *e.* Currency.
   - *f.* Cash deposited in savings accounts.
   - *g.* Certificates of deposit.
   - *h.* Deposits in checking accounts.
6. Where (if at all) do items in (*a*) through (*g*) belong in the following bank reconciliation?

Balance from bank statement, June 30 . . . . $x,xxx.xx
    Additions . . . . _____

    Deductions . . . . _____

June 30 correct cash balance . . . . $ 9,600.00

Balance from company cash account, June 30 . . . . . $x,xxx.xx
    Additions . . . . _____

    Deductions . . . . _____

June 30 correct cash balance . . . . $ 9,600.00

- *a.* Note collected by bank for the depositor on June 29; notification was received July 2 when the June 30 bank statement was received.
- *b.* Checks drawn in June that had not cleared the bank by June 30.
- *c.* Check of a depositor with a similar name that was returned with checks accompanying June 30 bank statement and was subtracted from the company's bank account.
- *d.* Bank service charge for which notification was received on receipt of bank statement.
- *e.* Deposit mailed June 30 that reached bank July 1 (not yet included in the bank statement).

f. Notification of charge for imprinting the company's name on blank checks was received with the June 30 bank statement.

g. Upon refooting the cash receipts journal, the company discovered that one receipt was omitted in arriving at the total that was posted to the cash account in the ledger.

7. Briefly explain the basic purposes of a bank reconciliation.

8. Define the following terms related to accounting for cash:
   a. Deposits in transit.
   b. Checks outstanding.
   c. NSF check.
   d. Correct cash balance.
   e. Cash short and cash over.

9. RS Company sold merchandise for $500; terms 2/10, n/30. Explain these terms and give the journal entry under the net approach and gross approach. Which approach is preferable? Why?

10. Briefly describe the different methods of estimating bad debt expense and the allowance for doubtful accounts for trade receivables. State which financial statement each method emphasizes. What is the conceptual basis for each emphasis?

11. It sometimes happens that a receivable that has been written off as uncollectible is subsequently collected. Describe the accounting procedures in such an event.

12. What is the difference between a cash discount and a trade discount?

13. How should customer accounts receivable with credit balances be reported in the financial statements?

14. Company X has a credit balance of $600 in its allowance for doubtful accounts. The amount of credit sales for the period is $80,000 and the balance in accounts receivable is $15,000. Assume the bad debt estimates are (a) related to accounts receivable, 9%, and (b) related to credit sales, 0.5%. Complete the following tabulation after the adjusting entry is made for bad debts.

Account	(a) Based on Accounts Receivable	(b) Based on Credit Sales
Bad debt expense	$_____	$_____
Allowance for doubtful accounts	$_____	$_____

15. Illustrate the differences between a one-year note received for a $5,000 credit sale and a going rate of interest of 12%, assuming (a) an interest-bearing note and (b) a noninterest-bearing note (interest included in face). Ignore adjusting entries but provide the entry for the date the note is received and the date it is collected.

16. T Company received from a customer a $1,000, 9% interest-bearing note that will mature in three months. After holding it two months, the note was sold by T to the bank to yield 12%. Compute T's proceeds. Give the required journal entry made by T at the time the note was sold.

17. RV Company sold accounts receivable of $10,000 (allowance for doubtful accounts, $300) for $9,000, with recourse. Estimated obligations due to the with-recourse provision amounted to $700 (uncollectible accounts, discounts, and sales returns). Give the required entry.

18. Under what circumstances should the direct write-off method for bad debts be used?

19. How does fulfilling the three criteria of *SFAS No. 77*, "Reporting by Transferors for Transfers of Receivables with Recourse," imply a *sale* of receivables?

20. The following disclosure appeared in a company's balance sheet:

Accounts receivable assigned $10,000
Less notes payable 3,000
Equity in accounts receivable assigned . . . . . $ 7,000

Explain the nature of the $7,000 net balance.

21. Why are long-term notes recorded at the present value of all future cash flows specified in the note, using the market interest rate?

22. Why did *APB Opinion No. 21* exempt short-term notes from valuation at present value?

EXERCISES

E 8-1
Cash Terminology
(L.O. 1)

Match the descriptions given below with the terms listed to the left by entering one capital letter in each blank space:

Term	Brief Description
_____ 1. Petty cash.	A. Cash inflows.
_____ 2. Checks outstanding.	B. Negotiable instruments that are accepted by a bank for immediate deposit and withdrawal.
_____ 3. Bank reconciliation.	C. Certificates of deposit.
_____ 4. Compensating balance.	D. A special cash fund used to make small payments.
_____ 5. Cash debits.	E. A negative balance in a bank account.
_____ 6. Cash equivalents.	F. Caused by theft, unintentional counting errors, and inappropriate accounting.
_____ 7. Deposits in transit.	G. Checks drawn and mailed but have not yet cleared the bank.
_____ 8. Lockbox system.	H. A loan constraint that requires a minimum balance at all times in a bank account.
_____ 9. NSF.	I. Cash outflows.
_____ 10. Overdraft in bank.	J. A deposit made but not included on the periodic bank statement.
_____ 11. Cash that is not reported as a current asset.	K. A system to reduce the mail time for delivery of collections from customers; uses a post office box number.
_____ 12. CDs.	L. Insufficient funds to support an account on which a check is written.
_____ 13. Cash credits.	M. A schedule that shows the correct cash balance for both the bank and the company.
_____ 14. Cash short and over.	N. A four-column bank reconciliation.
_____ 15. Comprehensive bank reconciliation.	O. A cash fund set aside to pay a long-term debt.

E 8-2
Petty Cash Entries
(L.O. 2)

Main Company decided to use a petty cash system for making small payments. The following transactions were completed during December 1991.

On December 1, 1991 the company treasurer prepared a $400 check payable to petty cash; the cash was given to the custodian.

Expenditures by the custodian (and signed receipts received) through December 20: postage, $80; office supplies, $70; newspapers, $36; office equipment repairs, $120; coffee room supplies, $30; and miscellaneous items, $24.

December 20, the treasurer fully replenished the fund.

Expenditures by the custodian through December 31: postage, $26; office supplies, $36; newspapers, $14; office equipment repairs, $42; coffee room supplies, $20; and miscellaneous items, $12. The fund was replenished on December 31.

Required:

1. Give all of the journal entries that should be made relating to the petty cash fund through December 31, 1991 (end of the annual accounting period), assuming petty cash expenditures were for administrative expenses.
2. Show how the petty cash fund should be reported on the balance sheet. The regular cash account showed an ending cash balance of $186,000.
3. How should the petty cash transactions affect the 1991 income statement?

E 8-3
Define Cash
(L.O. 1)

Carbine Company is preparing its December 31 Bank A reconciliation (end of the annual accounting period), and it must determine the proper balance sheet classification of the items listed below. You have been asked to complete the tabulation provided.

Item	Balance Sheet	
	Include in Cash Amount	Classification if Not Cash
1. Coins and currency, $1,000.		
2. Checks on hand received from customers, $12,000.		
3. Certificates of deposit (CDs), $16,000.		
4. Petty cash fund, $800.		
5. Postage stamps, $120.		
6. Bank A, checking account balance, $42,000.		
7. Postdated check, customer, $200.		
8. Money order, from customer, $300.		
9. Cash in savings account, $20,000.		
10. Bank draft from customer, $800.		
11. Cash advance received from customer, $160.		
12. Utility deposit to the gas company, refundable, $100.		
13. Certified check from customer, $2,000.		
14. NSF check, R. Roe, $400.		
15. Cash advance to company executive, collectible upon demand, $40,000.		
16. Bank B, checking account, overdraft, $4,000.		
17. IOUs from employees, $240.		

E 8-4
Define Cash
(L.O. 1)

Maze Company is preparing its 1991 financial statements; the accounting period ends December 31. The following items, related to cash, are under consideration. You have been asked to indicate how each item should be reported on the balance sheet and to explain the basis for your responses.

a. A $900 check received from a customer, dated February 1, 1992, is on hand.

b. A customer's check was included in the December 20 deposit. It was returned by the bank stamped NSF. No entry has yet been made by Maze to reflect the return.

c. A $20,000 CD on which $1,000 of interest accrued to December 31 has just been recorded by debiting interest receivable and crediting interest revenue. The chief accountant proposes to report the $20,000 as cash in bank.

d. Maze has a $200 petty cash fund. As of December 31, the fund cashier reported expense vouchers covering various expenses in the amount of $167 and cash of $32.

e. Postage stamps that cost $30 are in the cash drawer.

f. A cashier's check of $200 payable to Maze Company is in the cash drawer; it is dated December 29.

g. Three checks, dated December 31, 1991, totaling $465, payable to vendors who have sold merchandise to Maze Company on account, were not mailed by December 31, 1991. They have not been entered as payments in the check register and ledger.

h. Prior to December 30, Maze company left a note that matures December 31, 1991, with its bank for collection. The note is for $20,000 and bears interest at 9%, having been outstanding for three months. As yet, Maze has not heard from the bank about collection but is confident of a favorable outcome because of the high credit rating of the maker of the note. The company plans to include the $20,000 plus interest in its cash balance.

E 8-5
Petty Cash Entries
(L.O. 2)

As a part of their newly designed internal control system, DOT Corporation established a petty cash fund. Transactions for the first month were as follows:

a. Wrote a check for $500 on August 1 and gave the cash to the custodian.

b. Summary of the petty cash expenditures made by the custodian:

	August 1–15	August 16–31
Postage used	$ 40	$ 58
Supplies purchased and used	265	190
Delivery expense	98	178
Miscellaneous expenses	35	40
Totals	$438	$466

c. Fund replenished on August 16.

d. Fund replenished on August 31 and increased by $300.

Required:

Give all of the entries indicated through August 31.

E 8–6
Bank Reconciliation and Journal Entries
(L.O. 2)

Foster Company, as a matter of policy, deposits all cash receipts and makes all payments by check. The following were taken from the cash records of the company:

	May 31	June 30
Deposits in transit	$ 2,200	$ 3,900
Checks outstanding	1,400	800

June transactions:

	Bank	Books
Balance, June 1	$ 5,000	$ 5,800
June deposits	10,600	12,300
June checks	14,500	13,900
June note collected (including 10% interest)	2,200	—
June bank charges	10	—
Balance, June 30	3,290	4,200

Required:

1. Based on the above data only, show how to prove the deposits in transit and checks outstanding as of June 30.
2. Reconcile the bank account as of June 30, using the bank and book balance to correct cash format.
3. Give any journal entries that should be made based on the June bank reconciliation.

E 8–7
Bank Reconciliation, Hot Check, Journal Entries
(L.O. 2)

Reconciliation of Crabtree Company's bank account at May 31 was as follows:

Balance from bank statement	$10,500
Deposits in transit	1,500
Checks outstanding	(150)
Correct cash balance	$11,850
Balance from books	$11,864
Bank service charge	(14)
Correct cash balance, May 31	$11,850

June transactions:

	Bank	Books
Checks recorded	$11,500	$11,800
Deposits recorded	8,100	9,000
Service charges recorded	12	—
Collection by bank ($2,000 note plus interest)	2,100	—
NSF check returned with June 30 statement (will be redeposited; assumed to be good)	50	—
Balances, June 30	9,138	9,050

Required:

1. Compute deposits in transit and checks outstanding at June 30 by comparing bank and books for deposits and checks.
2. Prepare a bank reconciliation for June using the bank and book balance to correct cash balance format.
3. Give all journal entries that should be made based on the June bank reconciliation.

E 8–8
Bank Balance to Book Balance Reconciliation
(L.O. 2)

Required:

Using the information in E 8–7, provide the bank balance to book balance reconciliation.

E 8–9
Bank Reconciliation Based on Bank Statement and Cash Account
(L.O. 2)

a. First Commerce Bank, any location, address and phone, Customer Jones Company, address, June 30, 1991:

Statement summary:
Balance June 1, 1991 . . . . $23,000
Deposits and other credits 11,600
Checks and other debits . . . . (12,120)
Interest earned on this statement 100
Ending balance, June 30, 1991 . . . . $22,580

Account transactions:

Deposits			Checks			
6–1	$ 2,000	6–2 #61	$ 1,000	6–17 #65	$ 400	
6–8	3,000	6–7 #63	2,000	6–23 #60	1,100	
6–17	4,500	6–9 #66	3,000	6–27 #67	2,100	
6–22	2,100	6–14 #64	1,420	6–28 #59	1,100	
Total	$11,600				$12,120	

b.

Cash Account					
Balance June 1, 1991	23,900	Checks		13,220	
Deposits	12,300	60 $1,100	65 $ 400		
6–8 $3,000		61 1,000	66 3,000		
6–17 4,500		62 900	67 2,100		
6–22 2,100		63 2,000	68 1,300		
6–30 2,700		64 1,420			

c. Bank reconciliation at May 31, 1991:

Bank balance, $23,000, add deposit outstanding, $2,000, deduct check #59 outstanding, $1,100 book balance, $23,900.

Required:

Prepare the June bank reconciliation and give any entries required. Use the bank and book balance to correct cash balance format.

E 8–10
Correcting Ledger Accounts for Receivables
(L.O. 3)

During the annual audit of Coil Corporation, you encountered the following account entitled "receivables and payables":

Items	Debit	Credit
Due from customers	$156,000	
Payables to creditors for merchandise		$62,000
Note receivable, long term	80,000	
Expected cumulative losses on bad debts		4,000
Due from employees, current	2,200	
Cash dividends payable		24,000

Items	Debit	Credit
Special receivable, dishonored note*	22,000	
Accrued wages		2,400
Deferred rent revenue		1,600
Insurance premiums paid in advance	1,200	
Mortgage payable, long term		40,000

* Collection probable some time in the future.

Required:

1. Give the journal entry to eliminate the above account and to set up the appropriate accounts to replace it.
2. Show how the various items should be reported on a current balance sheet.

E 8–11

Accounting for Sale on Credit: Net versus Gross Methods

(L.O. 4)

On December 29, 1991, Sabre Company sold merchandise for $8,000 on credit terms, 3/10, n/60. The accounting period ends December 31.

Required:

1. Give the following entries under the net method and the gross method:
    a. To record the 1991 sale.
    b. To record collection of the account: Assumption A, on January 5, 1992; Assumption B, on April 1, 1992.
2. Show what should be reported on the 1991 and 1992 balance sheet and income statement under each approach and for each assumption for the above transactions only.

E 8–12

Recording Bad Debt Expense Based on Credit Sales

(L.O. 4)

At January 1, 1991, the credit balance in the allowance for doubtful accounts of the Master Company was $400,000. The provision (i.e., expense) for doubtful accounts is based on a percentage of net credit sales. Total sales revenue for 1991 amounted to $150 million, of which one third was on credit. Based on the latest available facts, the 1991 provision needed for doubtful accounts is estimated to be three fourths of 1% of net credit sales. During 1991, uncollectible receivables amounting to $440,000 were written off.

Required:

1. Prepare a schedule to compute the balance in Master's allowance for doubtful accounts at December 31, 1991. Show supporting computations.
2. Give all 1991 entries related to doubtful accounts.

(AICPA adapted)

E 8–13

Bad Debt Estimates Based on Credit Sales, Accounts Receivable, and Aging

(L.O. 4)

At December 31, 1991, end of the annual reporting period, the accounts of Bader Company showed the following:

a. Sales revenue for 1991, $360,000, of which one sixth was on credit.
b. Allowance for doubtful accounts, balance January 1, 1991, $1,800 credit.
c. Accounts receivable, balance December 31, 1991 (prior to any write-offs of uncollectible accounts during 1991), $36,100.
d. Uncollectible accounts to be written off, December 31, 1991, $2,100.
e. Aging schedule at December 31, 1991, showing the following:

Status	Amount
Not past due	$20,000
Past due 1–60 days	8,000
Past due over 60 days	6,000

Required:

1. Give the 1991 entry to write off the uncollectible accounts.
2. Give the 1991 adjusting entry to record bad debt expense for each of the following independent assumptions concerning bad debt loss rates:
    a. On credit sales, 1.5%.
    b. On total receivables at year-end, 2.5%.
    c. On aging schedule: not past due, 0.5%; past due 1–60 days, 1%; and past due over 60 days, 8%.
3. Show what would be reported on the 1991 balance sheet relating to accounts receivable for each assumption.

E 8–14

Note Receivable—Short Term, Interest-Bearing: Entries and Reporting

(L.O. 6)

On April 15, 1991 Welsch Company sold merchandise to Customer Rodriguez for $18,000; terms 2/10; n/EOM (i.e., end of month). Because of nonpayment by Rodriguez, Welsch received an $18,000, 15%, 12-month note dated May 1, 1991. The annual reporting period ends December 31. Customer Rodriguez paid the note in full on its maturity date.

Required:

1. Give all entries related to the above transactions.
2. Show what should be reported on the 1991 income statement and balance sheet.

E 8–15

Note Receivable— Short Term, Noninterest-bearing: Entries and Reporting

(L.O. 6)

On May 1, 1991, Darby Company sold merchandise to Customer Domo and received a $13,200 (face amount), one year, noninterest-bearing note. The going (i.e., market) rate of interest in this situation is 10%. The annual reporting period for Darby Company ends on December 31. Customer Domo paid the note in full on its maturity date.

Required:

1. Give all entries related to the above transactions.
2. Show what should be reported on the 1991 income statement and balance sheet.

E 8–16

Notes Receivable— Interest Bearing and Noninterest-bearing: Entries at Net and Gross and Reporting

(L.O. 6)

On November 1, 1991, Rouse Company sold merchandise on credit to Customer A for $14,000 and received a six-month, 12%, interest-bearing note. On this same date, Customer B purchased identical merchandise for the same price and credit terms except that the note received by Rouse was noninterest-bearing (the interest was included in the face of the note). The annual accounting period for Rouse ends December 31.

Required:

1. Give all required entries for each note from the date of sale of the merchandise through the maturity dates of the notes. For the noninterest-bearing note, give the entries for both the *net* and *gross* alternatives.
2. Show how the effects of these two notes should be reported on the 1991 income statement and balance sheet.

E 8–17

Discounting an Interest-Bearing Note: Entries

(L.O. 6)

On May 1, 1991, Mark Company sold merchandise to Customer K for $20,000, credit terms 2/10; n/EOM. At the end of May, Customer K could not make payment. Instead, a six-month, 12% note receivable of $20,000 was received by Mark (dated June 1, 1991). Mark Company's accounting period ends December 31. On August 1, 1991, Mark discounted (i.e., sold) this note, with recourse, to City Bank at 14% interest. On maturity date, Customer K paid the bank in full for the note.

Required:

Give all required entries for Mark Company on May 1, 1991, through the maturity date, November 30, 1991. Record sales at net.

E 8–18

Noninterest-bearing Note: Other Privileges

(L.O. 6)

On January 1, 1991, Jacobs Company provides a $40,000 loan to Andress Company by issuing a $40,000 noninterest-bearing note. Andress agrees (1) to repay the $40,000 proceeds on December 31, 1992, and (2) to sell a specified amount of construction materials to Jacobs at a 20% discount off the regular invoice price. The prevailing interest rate on similar notes, without the special purchase privilege, is 14%. Assume that Jacobs purchases material at an even rate throughout the note term.

Required:

Provide all entries for Jacobs over the note term.

E 8–19

Discounting an Interest-Bearing Note: Entries

(L.O. 6)

Aerobic Sports Company completed the following 1991 transactions related to a special note receivable:

a. February 1, 1991—Received a $200,000, 9%, interest-bearing, six-month note from Temple Company for a tract of land that had a carrying value of $60,000.
b. March 1, 1991—Discounted (sold with recourse) the note to Local Bank at a 12% interest rate.
c. July 31, 1991—Maturity date of the note:
  (1) *Case A*—Temple Company paid the bank for the note and all interest.

(2) *Case B*—Temple Company defaulted on the note. The bank charged a $1,000 protest fee.

Required:

Give all journal entries that Aerobic Sports Company should make for the term of the note, February 1, 1991, through July 31, 1991.

E 8–20

Sale of Accounts Receivable with and without Recourse: Entries (L.O. 5)

On April 1, 1991, DOS Company transferred $10,000 accounts receivable to SLK Finance Company to obtain immediate cash. The related allowance for doubtful accounts was $400.

Required:

1. The financial agreement specified a price of $8,000 on a without recourse, notification basis. Give the entry(s) that DOS Company should make. Explain the basis for your response.
2. The financial agreement specified a price of $8,500 on a with recourse, notification basis. DOS estimated $200 transfer obligations related to the with-recourse provision. Give the entry(s) that DOS should make. Explain the basis for your response.

E 8–21

Assignment of Accounts Receivable with Recourse: Entries (L.O. 5)

Fence, Inc., assigned $120,000 of its receivables to Miami Finance Company. A note payable was executed. The contract provided that Miami would advance 85% of the gross amount of the receivables. The contract specified recourse and nonnotification; therefore, Fence's debtors continue to remit directly to it; the cash (including finance charges) is then remitted to the finance company.

During the first month, customers owing $82,000 paid cash, less sales returns and allowances of $3,200. The finance charge at the end of the first month was $700.

During the second month, the remaining receivables were collected in full except for $800 written off as uncollectible. Final settlement was effected with the finance company, including payment of an additional finance charge of $300.

Required:

1. Give the entries for Fence to record (*a*) the assignment of the receivables and (*b*) the note payable.
2. Give the entries for Fence to record (*a*) the collections and (*b*) the payment to Miami for the first month.
3. Give the entries for Fence to record (*a*) the collections for the second month and (*b*) the final payment to Miami.

E 8–22

Accounting for an Account Receivable over a Six-Year Period (L.O. 4)

Given below is the history of a sale on credit by AB Company to J. Doe:

December 24, 1991—Sold merchandise to J. Doe, $2,000, terms 2/10, n/30.

January 2, 1992—Doe paid half of the receivable and was allowed the discount.

December 31, 1994—Because of the disappearance of Doe, AB Company wrote Doe's account off as uncollectible.

December 31, 1996—Doe reappeared and paid the debt in full, including 6% annual interest (not compounded, compute to the nearest month).

Required:

1. Give the entry(s) that AB Company should make at each of the above dates. Record at net.
2. Show how Doe's account should be reported each December 31 (end of AB Company's annual reporting period).

E 8–23

Long-Term Note: Interest-bearing versus Noninterest-bearing (L.O. 6)

Wilma Company sells large construction equipment. On January 1, 1991, the company sold Catner Company a machine at a quoted price of $60,000. Wilma collected $20,000 cash and received a $40,000, two-year, 10% note (simple interest payable each December 31).

Required:

1. Give Wilma's required entries for the two years assuming an interest-bearing note, face $40,000.
2. Give Wilma's required entries for the two years assuming a noninterest-bearing note, face $40,000.
3. Compare the interest revenue, sales revenue, and asset cost under each requirement.

E 8–24
Long-Term Note—
Interest-bearing: Entries
(L.O. 6)

Felix Company sold a pickup truck to RV Company on January 1, 1991, at a quoted price of $24,000. Felix collected $6,000 cash and received an $18,000 note. The note is payable in three equal (December 31) installments that include both principal and compound interest at 10%.

Required:
1. Compute the equal periodic collections.
2. Prepare a collection schedule and give the entries for Felix Company.

E 8–25
Note Receivable—Non-
Interest Bearing: Entries
(L.O. 6)

On January 1, 1991, EUD Company sold a special machine that had a list price of $39,995. The purchaser paid $9,995 cash and signed a $30,000 note. The note specified that it would be paid off in three equal annual payments of $13,798 each (starting on December 31, 1991).

Required:
1. Compute the implied rate of interest on the note.
2. Prepare a collection schedule for EUD.
3. Give all entries for EUD through 1993.

E 8–26
Note Receivable with
Unrealistic Interest Rate
(L.O. 6)

On July 1, 1991, SMX Company sold a large machine that had a list price of $18,000. The customer paid $3,000 cash and signed a three-year, $15,000 note that specified a stated interest rate of 3%. Annual interest on the full amount of the principal is payable each June 30. The principal is payable on June 30, 1994. The market (going) rate of interest for this transaction is 10%.

Required:
1. Compute the present value of this note.
2. Prepare a collection schedule for this note.
3. Give all entries required through maturity date.

PROBLEMS

P 8–1
Bank Reconciliation—
Errors: Journal Entries
(L.O. 2)

It is March 31, 1991, and Fry Company is ready to prepare its March bank reconciliation. The following information is available:

a.

Company Cash Account			
March 1 balance	14,175	Checks	26,500
Deposits	25,734		

b. Bank statement, March 31:

Balance, March 1	$15,400
Deposits	25,599
Checks cleared	(27,059)
NSF check (Customer X)	(50)
Note collected for depositor (including interest, $40)	840
Interest on bank balance	18
Bank service charge	(7)
Balance, March 31	$14,741

c. Additional information:
  (1) The company overstated one of its deposits by $10; the bank recorded it correctly.
  (2) The bank cleared an $89 check as $98; it has not been corrected by the bank.
  (3) End of February: deposits in transit, $775; checks outstanding, $2,000.

Required:
1. Based on the data given above, compute the March 31 deposits in transit and checks outstanding.
2. Prepare a bank reconciliation for March. (Hint: A check figure, $14,200.) Use bank and book balance to correct cash balance format.
3. Give all journal entries that should be made based on your bank reconciliation.

P 8–2
Reconciliation—
Collection, Deduction,
Transfer: Entries
(L.O. 2)

AB Company carries its checking account with Commerce Bank. The company is ready to prepare its December 31, 1991, bank reconciliation. The following data are available:

a. The November 30, 1991 bank reconciliation showed the following: (1) cash on hand (held back each day by AB Company for change), $400 (included in AB's Cash account); (2) deposit in transit, #51, $2,000; and (3) checks outstanding, #121, $1,000; #130, $2,000; and #142, $3,000.

b. AB Company Cash account for December, 1991:

Balance, December 1, 1991	$ 64,000
Deposits: #52–#55, $186,500 #56, $3,500	190,000
Checks: #143–#176, $191,000; #177, $2,500; #178, $3,000;	
and #179, $1,500	(198,000)
Balance, December 31, 1991 (includes $400 cash	
held each day for change)	$ 56,000

c. Bank statement, December 31, 1991:

Balance, December 1, 1991	$ 67,600
Deposits: #51–#55	188,500
Checks: #130, $2,000; #142, $3,000; #143–#176, $191,000	(196,000)
Note collected for AB Co. (including $720 interest)	6,720
Fund transfer received for foreign revenue	
(not yet recorded by AB Co.)	10,000
NSF check, Customer B	(200)
United Fund (per transfer authorization signed by AB Co.)	(50)
Bank service charges	(20)
Balance, December 31, 1991	$ 76,550

Required:

1. Identify by number and dollars the December 31, 1991, deposits in transit and checks outstanding.
2. Prepare the December 31, 1991, bank reconciliation. Use bank and book balance to correct cash balance format.
3. Give all journal entries that should be made at December 31, 1991, based on your bank reconciliation.

P 8–3
Four-Column
Reconciliation
(L.O. 2)

Rae Company is ready to reconcile its bank and book balances at March 31, 1991. The following information is available:

a. February bank reconciliation:

	Bank Balance	Book Balance
Ending balances, February 28	$49,550	$51,050
Additions:		
Deposits in transit	3,100	
Deductions:		
Checks outstanding	(1,650)	
Bank service charge		(50)
Correct cash balance, February 28	$51,000	$51,000

b. Company cash account for March:

Balance, March 1 (after February 28 entry)	$51,000
Deposits during March	52,800
Checks written during March	(54,150)
Balance, March 31	$49,650

c. Bank statement for March:

Balance, March 1	$49,550
Deposits recorded during March	53,850
Checks cleared during March	(53,800)
Note collected for Rae Co. (including interest, $200)	5,200
Service charge	(100)
Balance, March 31	$54,700

Required:

1. Compute the March 31 amounts for (a) deposits in transit and (b) checks outstanding.
2. Prepare a comprehensive bank reconciliation for March (proof of cash).
3. Give all journal entries that should be made on March 31 based on your bank reconciliation.

P 8-4
Four-Column
Reconciliation
(L.O. 2)

Springer Company has assembled the data needed to prepare the September 30, 1992, bank reconciliation. The following data are available (in thousands):

a. August 31, 1992, bank reconciliation:

	Bank	Book
Ending cash balance, August 31	$340	$291
Cash on hand	1	
Deposits in transit	10	
Checks outstanding	(7)	
Bank service charge		(2)
Note collected (including interest, $5)		55
Correct cash balance, August 31	$344	$344

b. Company cash account for September:

Balance, September 1, 1992 (before reconciliation)	$344
Deposits during September	400
Checks written during September	(413)
Balance, September 30	$331

c. Bank statement for September:

Balance, September 1, 1992	$340
Deposits recorded	375
Checks cleared	(390)
Bank service charge	(3)
NSF check (Person X)	(2)
Deduction for union dues	(1)
Balance, September 30	$319

d. Cash on hand, September 30, $1.

Required:

1. Prepare a comprehensive (four-column) bank reconciliation (proof of cash).
2. Give the entries required by the September bank reconciliation.

P 8-5
Classification of
Receivables
(L.O. 3)

When examining the accounts of Saad Company, you ascertain that balances relating to both receivables and payables are included in a single controlling account (called "receivables"), which has a $46,100 debit balance. An analysis of the details of this account revealed the following:

Items	Debit	Credit
Accounts receivable—customers	$80,000	
Accounts receivable—officers (current collection expected)	5,000	
Debit balances—creditors	900	
Expense advances to salespersons	2,000	
Capital stock subscriptions receivable	9,200	
Accounts payable for merchandise		$38,500
Unpaid salaries		6,600
Credit balances in customer accounts		4,000
Cash received in advance from customers for goods not yet shipped		900
Expected bad debts, cumulative		1,000

Required:

1. Give the journal entry to eliminate the above account and to set up the appropriate accounts to replace it.
2. How should the items be reported on Saad Company's balance sheet?

P 8–6
Interest Rate on Cash Discounts
(L.O. 4)

Maxfield Company sells $1,000 worth of merchandise on credit, terms 4/10, n/30. The buyer paid on the 15th day following the sale.

Required:

Using 365 days in a year, answer the following questions:

1. What is the effective annual interest rate paid by the buyer in this case?
2. How sensitive is the annual interest rate to (*a*) the number of days between the last day of the discount period and payment date, (*b*) gross purchase price, and (*c*) the cash discount percentage? And what implications does this have for buyers?

P 8–7
Returns and Allowances: Gross and Net Methods
(L.O. 3)

On August 12, 1991, Camel Company sells merchandise worth $20,000 (gross sales price) to Pyramid Company, terms 4/10, n/30. Camel grants cash discounts on amounts remitted within the discount period.

Required:

1. Record journal entries in general journal form for the following transactions under both the net and gross methods.
   a. The sale.
   b. Returns and allowances of $3,000 (gross) are granted Pyramid on August 17.
   c. Camel collects on $12,000 (gross) of the account on August 19.
   d. Returns and allowances of $2,400 (gross) are granted Pyramid on August 24 on items not yet paid for.
   e. The remaining account is collected on August 27.
   f. Returns and allowances of $1,000 (gross) are granted Pyramid on September 12 on merchandise paid for on August 19.
   g. Returns and allowances of $1,000 (gross) are granted Pyramid on September 14 on merchandise paid for on August 27.
2. Prepare a schedule showing the effect on Camel's net income of the above events under both methods (ignoring cost of goods sold), and compare that effect with the net cash inflow from these events.

P 8–8
Comparison of Four Ways to Estimate Bad Debt Expense
(L.O. 4)

The accounting records of GM Company provided the following data for 1991:

Cash sales	$1,200,000
Credit sales	900,000
Balance in accounts receivable, January 1, 1991	180,000
Balance in accounts receivable, December 31, 1991	200,000
Balance in allowance for doubtful accounts, January 1, 1991	3,000 (cr.)
Accounts already written off as uncollectible during 1991	5,000

Recently GM's management has become concerned about various estimates used in their accounting system, including those relating to receivables and bad debts. The company is considering various alternatives with a view to selecting the most appropriate approach and related estimates.

For analytical purposes, the following 1991 alternative estimates have been developed for consideration:

a. Bad debt expense approximates 0.6% of credit sales.
b. Bad debt expense approximates 0.25% of net sales (cash plus credit sales).
c. Two percent of the uncollected receivables at year-end will be uncollectible.
d. Aging of the accounts at the end of the period indicated that three fourths of them would incur a 1% loss while the other one fourth would incur a 6% loss.

The reporting period ends December 31.

Required:

1. For each of the four alternatives listed above, give the following: 1991 adjusting entry, ending 1991 balance in the allowance account, and an evaluation of the alternative.
2. Which alternative would you recommend for GM Company? Why?

P 8–9
Comparison and Evaluation of Three Ways to Estimate Bad Debt Expense
(L.O. 4)

The accounts of Long Company provided the following 1991 information at December 31, 1991, end of the annual period:

Accounts receivable balance, January 1, 1991	$ 51,000
Allowance for doubtful accounts balance, January 1, 1991	3,000
Total sales revenue during 1991 (⅙ on credit)	960,000
Uncollectible accounts to be written off during 1991 (ex-customer Slo)	1,000
Cash collected on accounts receivable during 1991	170,000

Estimates of bad debt losses based on:

a. Credit sales, 1%.
b. Ending balance of accounts receivable, 8%.
c. Aging schedule:

Age	Accounts Receivable	Probability of Noncollection
Less than 30 days	$28,000	2%
31–90 days	7,000	10
91–120 days	3,000	30
More than 120 days	2,000	60

Required:

1. Give the entry to write off customer Slo's long overdue account.
2. Give all entries related to accounts receivable and the allowance account for the following three cases:

   Case A—Bad debt expense is based on credit sales.
   Case B—Bad debt expense is based on the ending balance of accounts receivable.
   Case C—Bad debt expense is based on aging.

3. Show how the results of applying each case above should be reported on the 1991 income statement and balance sheet.
4. Briefly explain and evaluate each of the three methods used in Cases A, B, and C.
5. On August 1, 1992, customer Slo paid his long-overdue account in full. Give the required entry.

P 8–10
Establish an Allowance for Doubtful Accounts
(L.O. 4)

Pawn Company has been in business for five years but has never had an audit of its financial statements. Engaged to make an audit for 1991, you find that the company's balance sheet carries no allowance for doubtful accounts; instead, uncollectible accounts have been expensed as written off, and recoveries have been credited to income as collected. The company's policy is to write off, at December 31 of each year, those accounts on which no collections have been received for three months. The credit terms usually provide for equal monthly collections over two years from date of sale.

Upon your recommendation, the company agreed to revise its accounts for 1991 in order to account for bad debts on the allowance basis. The allowance is to be based on a percentage of credit sales that is derived from the experience of prior years.

Statistics for the past five years are as follows:

Year	Credit Sales	Accounts Written Off and Year of Sale			Recoveries and Year of Sale
1987	$100,000	(1987) $ 550			
1988	250,000	(1987) 1,500	(1988) $1,000		(1987) $300
1989	300,000	(1987) 500	(1988) 4,000	(1989) $1,300	(1988) 850
1990	325,000	(1988) 1,200	(1989) 4,500	(1990) 1,500	(1989) 500
1991	275,000	(1989) 2,700	(1990) 5,000	(1991) 1,400	(1990) 600

Accounts receivable at December 31, 1991, were as follows:

1990 sales	$ 15,000
1991 sales	135,000
	$150,000

Required:

Prepare the journal entry or entries, with appropriate explanations, to establish the allowance for doubtful accounts. Debit prior period adjustment because this is the correction of an accounting error. Support each item with computations; ignore income tax implications. The books have been adjusted but not closed at December 31, 1991.

(AICPA adapted)

P 8-11
Assignment of Accounts Receivable: Entries
(L.O. 5)

Verona Company finances some of its current operations by assigning accounts receivable to Adams Finance Company. On July 1, 1991, Verona Company assigned, with recourse, notification basis, accounts amounting to $100,000. The finance company advanced 80% of the accounts assigned (20% of the total to be withheld until the finance company has made full recovery), less a commission charge of 0.5% of the total accounts assigned.

On July 31, Verona Company received a statement from the finance company that it had collected $52,000 of these accounts, and in conformity with the contract, an additional charge of 0.5% of the total accounts outstanding as of July 31 was deducted.

On August 31, Verona Company received a second statement from the finance company, together with a check for the amount due. The statement indicated that the finance company had collected an additional $32,000 and had made a charge of 0.5% of the balance outstanding as of August 31.

Required:

1. Give Verona's entry to record (*a*) the assignment of the accounts and (*b*) the liability on July 1, 1991.
2. Give Verona's entry to record the data from the July 31 report from the finance company.
3. Reconstruct the report submitted to Verona by Adams Finance Company on August 31; show details to explain cash remitted and the uncollected accounts still held by the finance company.
4. Give Verona's entry to record the data in the report of August 31.
5. Explain how the items should be reported on the balance sheet of Verona Company at July 31 and August 31.
6. Give the entry to record the collection of the remaining assigned accounts receivable on September 15, 1991.

P 8-12
PV of a Note: Collection Schedule, Entries
(L.O. 6)

SAD Company sold a building and the land on which it is located on January 1, 1991, and received a $150,000 noninterest-bearing note receivable that matures December 31, 1993. The $150,000 is to be paid in full on maturity date. The sale was recorded as follows by SAD Company:

Note receivable 150,000		
Accumulated depreciation, building 100,000		
Building	150,000	
Land	60,000	
Gain on sale of assets	40,000	

It has been determined that 12% is a realistic interest rate for this particular note. The annual reporting period ends December 31. The accounts have not been adjusted or closed for 1991.

Required:

1. Compute the present value of the note. Use compound interest.
2. Prepare a correction and collection schedule as follows:

		Note Receivable	
Date	Explanation and Interest Revenue	Change	Balance
1–1–1991	Originally recorded		$150,000
12–31–1991	Corrections to present value	?	?

3. Give all entries through 1993.

P 8–13
Note Receivable with Equal Collections and Long-Term Note Receivable, with Unrealistic Interest Rate (L.O. 6)

During the annual reporting period (ends on December 31) Koke Company received two notes related to the sale of products (commercial autos). These notes are identified as Note A and Note B.

Note A: On August 1, 1991, Koke Company sold a special van with a price of $31,000. Koke received cash, $11,000, and a $20,000 six-month note that matures January 31, 1992. This note specifies equal monthly payments of $3,451, starting on August 31, 1991, which included principal and interest. The going, or market, rate of interest for this loan is 12%.

Required:

1. Prepare a schedule of collections that shows, by date, cash collections, interest revenue, and note receivable (reduction and balance).
2. Give all entries from August 1, 1991 through January 31, 1992.

Note B: On March 1, 1991, Koke Company sold a large vehicle equipped with a special crane mounted to it. The quoted price was $80,000. Koke Company received $20,000 cash and a $60,000, five-year note receivable. The note had a stated rate of 3%, although the imputed (going, or market) rate for this transaction was 9%. The interest concession was made to "beat a strong competitor." The note is payable in five equal annual payments starting on February 28, 1992.

Required:

1. Compute the annual cash collections and the present value of the note.
2. Prepare a schedule of collections to show, by date, cash collections, interest revenue and note receivable (reduction and balance).
3. Give all entries from March 1, 1991 through February 28, 1992.

P 8–14
Discounting Notes: Interest-Bearing and Noninterest-Bearing (L.O. 6)

On October 15, 1991, Farb Company sold identical merchandise for $12,000 on credit terms 2/10; n/30, to two different customers, designated as Customer X and Customer Y. Farb's annual reporting period ends December 31. These sales were recorded as follows:

	Customer X		Customer Y	
Accounts receivable 11,760			11,760	
Sales revenue	11,760			11,760

For each customer, the following events occurred:

Customer X:
11/1/1991   Could not pay the account; signed a note payable for $12,000, 10% interest-bearing, due in six months, on April 30, 1992.

12/1/1991   Sold (discounted) the "X" note to State Bank, with recourse, at 12% interest-per annum.

4/30/1992   Customer X defaulted and the bank charged a $20 protest fee.

7/31/1992   Collected in full on the defaulted note plus an additional interest charge of 10% per annnum.

Customer Y:

11/1/1991   Could not pay the account; signed a $12,600 noninterest-bearing note; maturity date, on April 30, 1992.

12/1/1991   Sold (discounted) the "Y" note to State Bank, with recourse, at 12% interest per annum.

4/30/1992   Customer Y paid the note in full on maturity date.

Required:

1. Give all of the entries related to the Customer X note from date initiated through July 31, 1992.
2. Give all of the entries related to the Customer Y note from date initiated through its final settlement, assuming (*a*) the net approach is used and (*b*) the gross approach is used. No need to recompute when the same as (1).
3. Show the effect of each note on the 1991 income statement and balance sheet of Farb Company. Set up the following column headings and side captions.

Items	Customer X Note	Customer Y Note Net Basis	Customer Y Note Gross Basis
Income Statement: (List items)			
Balance sheet: (List items)			

P 8–15

Overview of Notes: Four Different Notes

(L.O. 6)

REV Company had a critical cash problem related to collections from four customers—Smith, Johnson, Karnes, and Cates. The transactions, in order of date, are given below. You will notice discounting, defaults, and extensions. But finally, everyone paid in full. REV's annual accounting period ends December 31.

May   3   Received an $8,000, 90-day, 9% interest-bearing note from E. M. Smith, a customer, in settlement of an account receivable for that amount.

June 1   Received a $12,000, six-month, 9% interest-bearing note from M. Johnson, a customer, in settlement of an account receivable for that amount.

Aug. 1   Discounted (i.e., sold), with recourse, the Johnson note at the bank at 10%.

Aug. 1   Smith defaulted on the $8,000 note.

Sept. 1   Received a one-year, noninterest-bearing note from D. Karnes, a customer, in settlement of a $5,000 account receivable. The face of the note was $5,400, and the imputed going rate of interest was 8% (use the net method).

Oct. 1   Received a $20,000, 90-day note from R. M. Cates, a customer. The note was in payment for goods Cates purchased and was interest bearing at 15%.

Oct. 1   Collected the defaulted Smith note plus accrued interest to September 30 (10% per annum on the total amount due for two months).

Dec. 1   Johnson defaulted on the $12,000 note. REV Company paid the bank the total amount due plus a $25 protest fee.

Dec. 30   Collected Cates note in full.

Dec. 31   Collected Johnson note in full including additional interest on the full amount due at the legal rate of 10% since default date.

Dec. 31   Accrued interest on outstanding notes.

Required:

1. Give REV's entry to record each of the above transactions. Show computations.
2. Show how the outstanding notes at December 31, 1991, would be reported on the 1991 balance sheet.

P 8–16

Notes Receivable with Unrealistic Interest Rate

(L.O. 6)

Watt Service Company completed a major renovation contract and billed the customer $56,000 on January 1, 1991. Cash of $16,000 was collected, and a 5% note was received for the remaining $40,000, payable in three equal annual installments (including principal plus interest) each December 31. The going rate of interest for notes with comparable risk is 12%.

Required:
1. Compute the amount of the annual payments.
2. Compute the present value of the note.
3. Prepare a schedule of collections.
4. Give the entries on January 1, 1991, December 31, 1991, December 31, 1992, and December 31, 1993 (use the net method).

P 8–17
Note Interest Rate Using Calculator or Computer
(L.O. 6)

Falconcrest Company sold 20,000 cases of wine (cost: $160,000) to a large restaurant for an agreed-upon cash price of $600,000 and accepted $100,000 as a down payment. A note was signed for the remainder, which calls for two years of $27,000 monthly payments beginning one month after the sale.

Required:
Compute the implied monthly interest rate using a calculator equipped for interest calculations or a computer program you may have available. Compare that result with interpolation, using Table 6A–4.

P 8–18

COMPREHENSIVE PROBLEM
♦

Accounts Receivable Factoring
(L.O. 3, 4, 5)

Michael Company sells merchandise for $100,000 on credit and factors the receivables with a finance company. All events occur within the reporting year.

Required:
Make summary journal entries to account for all events of the following three independent situations:

1. The receivables are factored on a nonrecourse basis. The factor charges 8% as a financing fee and withholds 10% of the receivables for sales returns, allowances, and discounts. The factor absorbs sales adjustments beyond 10%. The factor estimates that 0.5% of the receivables are uncollectible. Actual adjustments are as follows: uncollectible accounts, $500; sales returns and allowances, $6,000; and sales discounts, $6,000. Record all entries for both Michael and the factor.
2. The receivables are factored on a recourse basis. The fee is 4%, and 15% is withheld. Michael estimates $5,000 each of sales returns and allowances, and sales discounts. Michael also expects $500 of uncollectibles. Michael bears the cost of all sales adjustments, including uncollectible accounts. The factor can neither compel nor allow Michael to repurchase the receivables. Assume the actual sales adjustments in (1). Record entries only for Michael.
3. Assume the facts in (2) except that the factor can compel Michael to repurchase uncollected receivables at any time. Record entries only for Michael.

CASES

C 8–1
Data from Two Well-Known Companies: Analyze Accounts Receivable and Any Related Contingencies
(L.O. 3)

The annual financial reports of two corporations included the following notes to the financial statements:[38]

a. Marathon sells certain of its accounts receivable to financial institutions. These accounts receivable sold are transferred subject to defined recourse provisions. Marathon collects the proceeds from the accounts receivable, and collection transfers are made in accordance with provisions of the agreements. As defined by the agreements, Marathon is required to calculate on a monthly basis the value of accounts receivable to be conveyed to the institutions. Accounts receivable sold as of December 31, 1983, and December 31, 1982, amounted to $260 million and $417 million, respectively, of which $173 million and $304 million, respectively, were subject to recourse.

b. Tonka Corporation: **Note C**—*Sale of accounts receivable:*
>   In December 1983, accounts receivable of approximately $14,558,000 were sold to a bank under an agreement without recourse that provided for replacement in certain circumstances. Net proceeds to the company were approximately $14,306,000.

---
[38] Source: AICPA, *Accounting Trends & Techniques* (New York, 1984), p. 119.

Required:

(Round amounts to the nearest million):

1. What were the amounts of accounts receivable sold by each company in 1982 and 1983?
2. What were the amounts of cash received from the sale of accounts receivable by each company in 1982 and 1983?
3. To whom were the accounts receivable sold?
4. Were the sales of accounts receivable on a notification or nonnotification basis? Explain.
5. Did each company incur a contingent liability as a result of the sale of accounts receivable? Explain.

C 8–2

Receivable Financing: Sale or Loan?

(L.O. 5)

The following situations involve transactions that should be classified either as a sale or a loan.

a. Sherman Company assigns $400,000 of accounts receivable as collateral for a loan, notification basis. Interest is charged on the monthly outstanding loan balance, and a 2% finance fee is charged immediately on the accounts assigned.

b. Hopper Company factors $50,000 of accounts receivable on a nonrecourse basis. The finance company charges an 8% fee and withholds 10% to cover sales adjustments. The finance company obtains title to the receivables and assumes collection responsibilities.

c. Pineapple Company factors $40,000 of accounts receivable on a recourse basis. Pineapple assumes the cost of all sales adjustments. The receivables are part of a much larger group of receivables. Pineapple's business is stable, and sales adjustments are readily estimable. Pineapple is compelled under the financing agreement to reimburse the finance company for any losses due to default by original customers.

d. Helms Company factors $80,000 of accounts receivable on a recourse basis. Helms assumes the cost of all sales adjustments. At the finance company's option, if it appears that the receivables are not collected as quickly as expected, Helms must repurchase the receivables.

e. Gilbert Company discounts on a nonrecourse basis a $20,000 note received in a sale.

f. Franklin Company discounts on a recourse basis a $10,000 note received in a sale. The only provision of the financing agreement is that Franklin must reimburse the bank in the event of default by the original maker of the note.

g. Puget Company discounts on a recourse basis a $30,000 note received in a sale. The bank allows repurchase of discounted notes at face value for a small fee.

h. Bellingham Company discounts on a recourse basis a $35,000 note received in a sale. The bank can compel Bellingham to repurchase the note if the maker's current ratio falls below 2.3 within five months of the note's due date.

i. Pobedy Company pledges all of its accounts receivable as collateral for a loan. Pobedy must use the proceeds from the accounts receivable to service the loan. Pobedy retains title to the receivables. In the event of default by Pobedy on the loan, the finance company has a claim against any of these receivables for payment of the loan.

Required:

For each of the preceding situations, refer to the three criteria of *SFAS No. 77,* "Reporting by Transferors for Transfers of Receivables with Recourse," and explain whether the financing of receivables should be recorded as a sale or a loan.

C 8–3

Ethical Considerations: Bank Reconciliation

(L.O. 2)

Blueridge Company recently hired you as a junior accountant. Blueridge is a closely held, medium-size retailing firm. One of your first assignments is to prepare the June bank reconciliation. You find the following information from the June 1991 bank statement and company records:

Deposits in transit	$ 7,200
Balance per bank statement	16,500
Bank service charges	30
Outstanding checks	9,750
NSF check returned	3,000
$3,300 deposit incorrectly recorded	
by the company as	3,030

Your immediate supervisor, the chief accountant for the company, who also has limited cash disbursement responsibilities, tells you that the unadjusted balance of cash per the ledger at the end of June is unavailable. However, he must have the reconciliation immediately for a report to the vice president of finance. Furthermore, he asks you to reduce the above outstanding check total by $2,600 "to adjust for certain errors before you were hired."

Accompanying the bank statement are the cancelled checks. Among them is a $2,600 check written to an individual not employed with the company, and signed by your superior.

Required:

1. Assuming the information in the above list is correct and complete, prepare the June bank reconciliation.
2. Comment on why the superior might have withheld information and made his unusual request for adjusting the bank reconciliation.
3. Discuss your options and responsibilities in this situation, including ethical considerations, and possible effects to yourself.

C 8-4
Sherwin-Williams:
Analysis of Actual
Financial Statements
(L.O. 1, 4)

Refer to the 1990 financial statements of Sherwin-Williams (see the appendix at the end of this book) and respond to the following questions. You may use more than one year's results in your answer.

a. Do the amounts in the balance sheet for the caption "Cash and cash equivalents" agree with those in the statement of cash flows? Explain.
b. Is there sufficient information to separate cash from cash equivalents? If so, determine the two separate amounts.
c. Are all investments which fulfill the definition of cash equivalents so classified by the firm?
d. Locate the information pertaining to bad debt expense and write-offs of accounts receivable. Is Sherwin-Williams experiencing an increasing or decreasing rate of uncollectible accounts receivable?

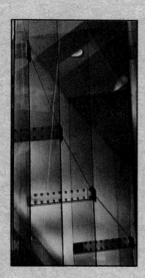

9

Inventory Measurement, Cost of Goods Sold, and DV LIFO

LEARNING OBJECTIVES

♦

After you have studied this chapter, you will:

1. Understand the characteristics of inventories.

2. Know the components of inventory cost.

3. Be able to apply the periodic and perpetual inventory methods.

4. Know the various alternative cost flow assumptions used to value inventory, including their effect on reported income, and the reasons for management's choice among the alternatives.

5. Be able to apply the dollar value last-in, first-out method (DV LIFO) and understand the reasons management might elect to use it.

6. Be familiar with three additional methods of inventory valuation that are used for internal purposes but are not GAAP. (Refer to the appendix at the end of this chapter.)

♦

Ralph E. Winter, writing in *The Wall Street Journal,* February 9, 1981, observed that "last-in, first-out inventory accounting, commonly known as LIFO, is an accounting technique designed to minimize the impact of inflation on inventory values, and thus avoid income taxes on phantom inventory profits."

In using the term *phantom inventory profits,* Mr. Winter was referring to the FIFO (first-in first-out) accounting cost flow method in which inventory items purchased some time ago at relatively cheaper prices than those prevailing today are charged to the cost of goods sold. The FIFO method contrasts with the LIFO cost flow method, in which current and more expensive inventory prices are charged to cost of goods sold. Thus, under FIFO, a major portion of a product's cost, unadjusted for inflation, is matched against sales revenues that, because they are in current dollars, are adjusted for inflation. This accounting results in overstated profit margins and net income from operations. Furthermore, in line with Winter's comment, the income tax expense is also higher.

During inflationary periods, the LIFO accounting method is believed by many accountants to keep costs and revenues better matched, which in turn keeps gross margins, net income, and the income tax liability better aligned.

Mr. Winter also informed his readers that the use of LIFO can be a two-edged sword. He cited the fact that Interlake Inc., a company that uses LIFO, reported an increase in earnings of $5.6 million in 1980 even though this was a period of rising prices. He also noted that Wallace Murray Company's fourth quarter profits for 1980 rose $1.2 million due to its use of LIFO. If you thought you might have misread these statements, you didn't. During inflationary periods (1980 was a year of double-digit inflation), FIFO, not LIFO, is supposed to increase gross margins and profits. LIFO is supposed to reduce profits by charging off higher costs. So what happened?

What happened was that another inventory management and accounting dynamic took hold within large segments of American business and industry, namely, inventory reductions. Sparked by record-high interest rates, which meant record-high costs for maintaining physical stockpiles of goods and materials, American business managers began to pare down their inventory levels. For example, rather than stockpile 10 months' worth of supplies, a company might not replenish its inventory with new purchases until the level fell to 8 months' or only 6 months' worth of production parts and supplies on hand. This change in inventory stock-level practices brought some cost savings through lower interest and handling outlays and thereby contributed to profits. Moreover, with declining inventory levels, firms were using up goods acquired in prior periods at lower costs. These goods were then reflected in the income statement at their lower, earlier costs. LIFO accounting under these circumstances led to higher gross margins and net income for both Interlake and Wallace Murray. These results were caused by the liquidation of LIFO layers, a topic discussed in detail later in this chapter.

LIFO can also lead to larger profits than FIFO accounting when the prices of the goods bought by the company decline. Falling prices in some markets occur even during an inflationary period. Thus, LIFO accounting can produce higher profits than FIFO when prices decline.

LIFO and FIFO are just two of many different inventory accounting methods. Each must be used with discrimination and full awareness of the part the method plays in the overall management of an inventory system—meaning the management of both the physical assets that constitute the company's inventories and the accounting system used to track, measure, and report on the use of these physical assets in the flow of business operations.

Inventory levels are important to companies in assuring production schedules and meeting customer requirements. At the same time, holding inventories is costly. We can understand, therefore, why firms wish to reduce inventory levels while assuring that adequate supplies are available to prevent production delays and satisfy customer requests. Japanese firms have made substantial gains in achieving lower inventory levels and higher profits by shortening set-up times, improving the quality of both incoming materials and finished goods, and attaining better working relationships with suppliers so that inventory is received just in time (JIT) for production. (U.S. inventory systems have been referred to as just-in-case systems; that is, keeping enough inventory to meet all possible requirements.)

Results of just-in-time systems have been impressive. American manufacturers currently carry an average of nine months' inventory, while Japanese firms carry less than two months'. Some of the difference is due to factors peculiar to the Japanese environment, including the geographical proximity of firms to each other, the existence of an effective rail system, and the lack of work disruptions.

Inventory accounting and management practices were once considered rather humdrum and not as exciting or important as some of the so-called glamorous aspects of accounting, such as corporate reorganizations, profit analysis, and earnings forecasts. At least that was the way it was before price volatility set in and relative economic instability became a way of life in the business world. Twenty-five years ago, Mr. Winter's article on inventory accounting techniques and their impact on net profit probably would not have been published in *The Wall Street Journal*—it just wouldn't have been considered newsworthy.

One reason for the increased interest is the fact that when prices are relatively stable from year to year—as they were 25 years ago—inventory accounting practices don't produce the kinds of dramatic changes in net profits alluded to in the Winter article. A second reason is that in the past, maintaining ample inventory levels was taken almost as an article of business faith. Stockpiling one or even two years' worth of production goods and materials was considered a surefire way to lock in prices.

In today's economic climate, with its ingrained volatility, inventory accounting methods and management practices are viewed by CEOs as profit-enhancing tools. Not only can better inventory systems increase a company's profitability, but poorly conceived systems can drain profits and put a business at a competitive disadvantage.

Chapters 9 and 10 cover a number of inventory accounting methods and techniques. In the process, several physical inventory management and operating systems outside of the direct province of accounting are introduced, systems that must be understood in order to understand and appreciate the value of the various accounting methods presented. Chapter 9 concerns manufacturing and how inventories interact with production lines and cost-of-goods-sold accounting systems. In Chapter 10, the content shifts to inventory valuation principles and practices, and retail inventory accounting methods are introduced.

◆

CHARACTERISTICS AND MEASUREMENT OF INVENTORIES

◆

Inventories are assets consisting of goods owned by a business and held either for use in the manufacture of products or as products awaiting sale. Perhaps the most widely known inventories are raw materials, work in process, finished goods, and merchandise inventories held by retailers. But depending on the nature of the company's business, inventory may consist of virtually any tangible good or material. An inventory might consist of hardware items, component pieces of equipment, bulk commodities such as wheat or milling flour, fuel oil held in storage awaiting use during the winter heating season, or the 3,600 airline seats available each day on

American Airlines between New York and Los Angeles. Machinery and equipment, for example, are treated as operational assets by the company that bought them, but before being purchased they were part of the inventory of the manufacturer who made them. Even a building, during its construction period, is an inventory item for the builder.

In many companies, inventories are a significant portion of current assets or even total assets. Inventories are being constantly used and replaced. Although many inventory items may appear to be relatively insignificant (e.g., hardware items such as nuts and bolts), in the aggregate they can have considerable value. Therefore, the problem of safeguarding inventories is similar to protecting cash. The need to stock adequate items for sale, coupled with the risk of loss and cost of overstocking, are critical management planning and control problems. Failure either to control physical inventories or to properly account for inventory costs can even lead to business failure.

Inventories are classified as follows:

1. **Merchandise inventory**—goods on hand purchased by a retailer or a trading company such as an importer or exporter for resale. Generally, goods acquired for resale are not physically altered by the retailer or trading company; the goods are in finished form when they leave the manufacturer's plant. In some instances, however, finished goods are acquired and then further assembled into other products. Computer components and electronics products are examples of this situation.
2. **Manufacturing inventory**—the combined inventories of a manufacturing entity consisting of:
    a. **Raw materials inventory**—tangible goods purchased or obtained in other ways (e.g., by mining) and on hand for direct use in the manufacture of goods for resale. Parts or subassemblies manufactured prior to use are sometimes classified as raw materials inventory or component parts inventory.
    b. **Work-in-process inventory**—goods requiring further processing before completion and sale. Work-in-process (also goods-in-process) inventory usually is valued at the sum of direct material, direct labor, and allocated manufacturing overhead costs incurred to date.[1]
    c. **Finished goods inventory**—manufactured items completed and held for sale. Finished goods inventory usually is valued at the sum of direct material, direct labor, and allocated manufacturing overhead costs related to its manufacture.
    d. **Manufacturing supplies inventory**—items on hand, such as lubrication oils for the machinery, cleaning materials, and other items, that make up an insignificant part of the finished product.
3. **Miscellaneous inventories**—items such as office supplies, janitorial supplies, and shipping supplies. Inventories of this type typically are used in the near future and usually are recorded as selling or general expense when purchased.

The major classifications of inventories depend on the operations of the business. A trading entity (i.e., wholesale or retail) acquires merchandise for resale. A manufacturing entity acquires raw materials and component parts, manufactures finished products, and then sells them. The flow of inventory costs through these different entities is shown in Exhibit 9–1 (assuming a perpetual inventory system in which inventory levels are kept up-to-date at all times).

The majority of inventory accounting problems stem from differences between the cost of goods sold as reported by the accounting records and what the physical inventory records confirm as the amount of materials used in producing these same

---

[1] The term *allocated overhead* refers to the allocation of nontraceable indirect expenses such as heat, light, and administrative salaries to the cost of goods manufactured.

EXHIBIT 9-1   Flow of Inventory Costs through a Typical Manufacturing Company's Accounting Records: Perpetual Inventory Method

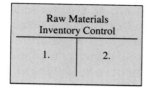

1. Purchases obtained on account or for cash are debited to the inventory control account and to individual inventory accounts in subsidiary ledgers. (If the periodic method is used, a purchases account would be used rather than direct entry to raw materials inventory). Credit accounts payable or cash and debit raw materials inventory control.

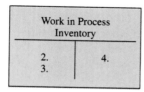

2. As raw materials are requisitioned to work in process, their cost is transferred to work in process. Credit raw materials inventory control and debit work in process inventory.

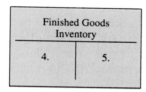

3. Recognize direct labor and overhead used in production. Credit accounts payable, cash, or other accounts and debit work in process.

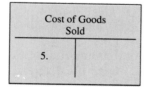

4. As products are assembled, costs per unit are transferred from work in process to finished goods inventory. Credit work in process inventory and debit finished goods inventory.

5. As products are sold and shipped to customers, costs per unit are transferred from finished goods inventory to cost of goods sold. Credit finished goods inventory and debit cost of goods sold.

goods. In a manufacturing setting, this means that the dollar amount of materials available for use during the production cycle (the opening inventory plus current period purchases) must be allocated between expense for the amount of materials used in production (cost of goods sold) and assets for the amount of materials that remain on hand (the closing inventory). This allocation involves two distinct phases:

1. *Phase 1:* Identification and measurement of the quantity of physical goods (items and quantities) that should be included in inventory at the end of the accounting period.
2. *Phase 2:* Assigning an accounting value to the physical amount of inventory at the end of the accounting period.

Items that Should Be Included in Inventory

To identify the items that should be included in inventory, accountants apply the general rule that all goods the company owns at the inventory date should be included, regardless of their location. At the end of an accounting period, a business may hold goods that it does not own or own goods that it does not hold. Therefore, care is necessary to identify the goods properly includable in inventory.

Goods purchased and in transit should be included in the inventory of the purchaser provided ownership to such goods has passed to the purchaser. Application of the passage-of-ownership rule usually is determined as follows: if the goods are shipped FOB (free on board) destination, ownership passes when the purchaser receives the goods from the common carrier; if the goods are shipped FOB shipping point, ownership passes when the seller delivers them to the common carrier, such as a railroad or independent trucker.

Goods out on consignment, those held by agents and those located at branches, should be included in inventory.[2] Goods *held* (but owned by someone else) for sale on commission or on consignment, and those received from a vendor but rejected and awaiting return to the vendor for credit, should be excluded from inventory.

Some companies engage in a practice that entails the sale and buyback of inventory items at prearranged prices as per the terms of a repurchase agreement. Sellers who engage in this practice achieve several advantages: The inventory sold to the buyer is, in effect, "parked" outside the company, which means the selling company avoids internal and external finance expenses that otherwise would be incurred if the inventory stayed in-house. This saving is possible because the buyer pays the seller all or most of the retail value of the inventory goods covered in the repurchase agreement. This condition remains in effect until the inventory goods are reacquired by the seller, again at a prearranged price.

In addition to the avoidance of inventory financing expenses, the selling company also avoids personal property taxes levied by many states. In such cases, the inventory is sold in advance of the tax assessment date and reacquired after the tax date. Still another motive in using repurchase agreements is to avoid the reporting of direct borrowing on the balance sheet. Avoidance is desirable to companies whose debt-to-equity ratios are already high, and the reporting of more debt would make matters worse. However, the FASB, in *SFAS No. 49,* requires that when a repurchase agreement exists at a set price, which covers all costs including holding (financing) costs, the inventory must remain on the seller's books. This ruling means that repurchase agreements normally must be treated as loans rather than sales, thus negating the use of these agreements to reduce reported debt.

From the buyer's standpoint, a repurchase agreement offers the opportunity to earn the equivalent of financing fees, derived from the predetermined price spread between the buy and sell back sides of these transactions. Another reason why some companies buy other companies' inventories is to avoid tax problems that can accrue with LIFO liquidations. A LIFO liquidation occurs when a company unintentionally allows its inventory levels to fall to the point where old, low-cost items must be assigned to the cost of goods sold for the current period. This decision results in inordinately high gross margins on sales and a correspondingly higher tax liability on income. In buying another company's inventory, in effect, the buying company is borrowing inventory to replenish its own depleted stocks temporarily. LIFO liquidation problems are discussed in detail later in this chapter.

To identify items that should be included in inventory when a question exists as to whether ownership has passed, judgment is required. While legal ownership is a useful starting point, a strict legal determination often is impractical. In such cases, the sales agreement, industry practices, and other evidence of intent should be considered.

---

[2] Consignment is a marketing arrangement whereby the consignor (the owner of the goods) ships merchandise to another party, known as a consignee,who acts as a sales agent only. The consignee does not purchase the goods but assumes responsibility for their care and sale. Upon sale, the consignee remits the proceeds (less specified expenses and a commission) to the consignor. Goods on consignment, because they are owned by the consignor until sold, should be excluded from the inventory of the consignee and included in the inventory of the consignor.

EXHIBIT 9-2   Comparison of the Periodic and the Perpetual Inventory Systems

Transaction or Event	Periodic Inventory System	Perpetual Inventory System
Routine purchases of various inventory items	All inventory items are debited to the purchases account regardless of the particular items acquired.	Similar to an accounts receivable subsidiary ledger operation, individual accounts are maintained for each type of inventory item, along with an inventory control account. This control account is debited for all purchases with supporting entries made to individual inventory accounts.
Items removed from inventory for use in production.	No accounting entries are made.	Individual credit entries are made to each inventory account (plus combined credit to the inventory control account) with an offsetting debit entry to the cost of goods sold account.
End-of-period accounting entries and related activities.	Physical count of the ending inventory is taken and dollar values are assigned. This activity is a prerequisite to computing the cost of goods sold for the period. Adjusting entries are made to compute the cost of goods sold based on the following formula: CGS = Beginning inventory + Purchases − Ending inventory	Physical count of inventory is not needed for calculation of cost of goods sold for the period, but such inventory counts are usually made just the same in order to verify the accuracy of the perpetual system and to identify inventory overages and shortages. Cost of goods sold is automatically determined from the sum of the daily postings to this account.

Inventory Recording Methods

The physical quantities in inventory may be measured by use of either a periodic inventory system or a perpetual inventory system. Exhibit 9–2 provides a simplified comparison of these two systems, presented in a manufacturing context. The essential difference between these two systems from an accounting point of view is the frequency with which the physical flows are assigned a value. Under the periodic system, the inventory value is determined only at important points in time such as at the end of a reporting period. This approach to valuation is used even though a perpetual record of physical flows is maintained. A good example is provided by supermarkets, which use automated scanners at checkout stations to keep track of physical inventory levels but which place accounting values on the physical flows only periodically.

Under a perpetual system of inventory valuation, the continuous physical flow is monitored, and the cost of the items is also maintained on a continuous basis.

Periodic Inventory System   When a periodic inventory system is used, an actual *physical count* of the goods on hand is taken at the end of each accounting period for which financial statements are prepared. The goods are counted, weighed, or otherwise measured, and then extended at unit costs to value the inventory. Under the periodic system, a continuous inventory record may, but need not, be kept of the units and amounts purchased, sold (or issued), and the balance on hand.[3] Under the periodic inventory system, purchases are debited to a purchases account and end-of-period entries are made to close the purchases account, close out the beginning inventory,

---

[3] If the physical flow is monitored continuously, the physical count serves only as an accuracy check. Statistical methods are commonly used by firms and by auditors to ease the task of verifying inventory levels.

and record the ending inventory as an asset (i.e., the ending inventory replaces the beginning inventory in the accounts).[4]

Under the periodic system, cost of goods sold (also commonly called *cost of sales*) is computed as a residual amount (beginning inventory plus purchases less ending inventory) and for all practical purposes cannot be verified independently of the inventory count. To illustrate, consider the following data for the Lea Company:

	Units	Unit Amount
Beginning inventory	500	$4.00
Purchases	1,000	4.00
Goods available for sale	1,500	
Sales	900	6.00
Ending inventory	600	

Based on this data, the computation of the cost of goods sold yields:

Beginning inventory (carried forward from the prior period)	$2,000
Merchandise purchases (accumulated in the purchases account)	4,000
Total goods available for sale during the period	6,000
Less: Ending inventory (quantity determined by a physical count)	2,400
Cost of goods sold (a residual amount)	$3,600

Perpetual Inventory System   When a perpetual inventory system is used, detailed perpetual inventory records, in addition to the usual ledger accounts, are maintained for each inventory item. An inventory control account is maintained in the general ledger on a current basis. The perpetual inventory record for each item must provide information for recording receipts, issues, and balances on hand, usually in both quantities (units) and dollar amounts. Thus, the physical quantity and valuation of goods on hand at any time are available from the accounting records. Therefore, a physical inventory count is unnecessary except to check on the accuracy of the perpetual inventory records. A physical count is usually made annually for auditing purposes to compare the inventory on hand with the perpetual record and to provide data for any adjusting entries needed (errors and losses, for example).

When a difference is found between the perpetual inventory records and the physical count, the perpetual inventory records are adjusted to the physical count. In such cases, the inventory account is debited or credited as necessary for the correction, and an inventory correction account such as inventory shortages (loss) or overages (gain) is debited or credited. The inventory correction account is closed to income summary at the end of the period. The balance in the inventory shortage account usually is reported separately on internal financial statements for control purposes. However, any balance is combined with the cost of goods sold amount on external statements.

For improved inventory control purposes, many companies choose to use a perpetual inventory system. This choice of systems is especially useful in situations in which the inventory consists of items that carry high unit values or where it is important to have ample inventory levels on hand to avoid running out of stock. Simultaneously the company does not want to overstock because this increases inventory carrying costs. Although perpetual inventory systems offer better accounting control over inventories and, for cost accounting purposes, are preferred over periodic inventory systems, problems remain. For example:

1. *Accounting information control versus physical property control.* Thanks to robotics and computer technology, today there are automated inventory systems that not only account for the inventory but actually manage the stocking and handling of inventory goods and materials. However, even with automated sys-

---

[4] The purchase returns and allowances account is also closed at this time.

tems (which are all outgrowths of perpetual inventory systems), certain aspects of physical inventory management and control tend to elude effective capture by computer. Inventory management concerns such as theft and pilferage, breakage and other forms of physical damage, misorders and misfills, and inadequate inventory supervision practices are matters that must be dealt with independently of the type of inventory accounting system (automated or manual, perpetual or periodic) being used.

2. *Higher costs associated with perpetual inventory systems.* Because of the level of detailed accounting work involved, perpetual inventory systems tend to be more costly to implement and maintain (at least initially) than are periodic systems, which tend to be far less complex. Here again, computers have helped make perpetual inventory systems more popular today than ever before.

Reporting Entries for Periodic and Perpetual Systems   The reporting entries for the periodic and perpetual inventory systems are illustrated next, step by step, from purchase through the reporting in the financial statements.

1. *Entries at date of purchase.* When the *periodic* inventory system is used, acquisitions of goods during the accounting period are entered in the company's accounts as shown below. In this example, three different kinds of inventory goods are purchased on three different dates during 1991.

Purchases		Accounts Payable (or Cash)	
1/15 Item A	200	1/15 Item A	200
1/18 Item B	100	1/18 Item B	100
1/20 Item C	300	1/20 Item C	300

When the *perpetual* inventory system is used, purchases are debited instead to an inventory control account and concurrently recorded in a subsidiary inventory ledger. Assume the balance reflects one unit of A, B, and C at $200, $100 and $300 respectively.

Inventory Control Account		Accounts Payable (or Cash)	
1/1 Balance	800	1/15 Item A	200
1/15 Item A	200	1/18 Item B	100
1/18 Item B	100	1/20 Item C	300
1/20 Item C	300		

In addition to the above entries, subsidiary inventory ledger accounts are posted:

Inventory Item A		Inventory Item B	
1/1 Balance 200		1/1 Balance 300	
1/15 Purchase 200		1/18 Purchase 100	

Inventory Item C	
1/1 Balance 300	
1/20 Purchase 300	

2. *Entries at the date of sale.* When the periodic inventory system is used, only one entry is made to record each sale as shown below. During the period, three sales are made:

Accounts Receivable		Sales Revenue	
1/25 Item A	225	1/25 Item A 225	
1/27 Item B	675	1/27 Item B 675	
1/29 Item C	900	1/29 Item C 900	

When the *perpetual* inventory system is used, two entries are required to record each sale—one to account for the sales revenue and another to account for the cost of goods sold. Only the *perpetual* inventory system provides a current accounting of goods sold as sales are made. Assuming a FIFO cost flow, under the perpetual system the entries are:

Accounts Receivable				Sales Revenue		
1/25 Item A	225				1/25 Item A	225
1/27 Item B	675				1/27 Item B	675
1/29 Item C	900				1/29 Item C	900

Cost of Goods Sold				Inventory Control Account				
1/25 Item A	200			1/1 Balance	800			
1/27 Item B	300			1/15 Item A	200	1/25 Item A	200	
1/29 Item C	300			1/18 Item B	100	1/27 Item B	300	
				1/20 Item C	300	1/29 Item C	300	

Inventory Item A					Inventory Item B			
1/1 Balance	200				1/1 Balance	300		
1/15 Purchase	200	1/25 Sale	200		1/18 Purchase	100	1/27 Sale	300

Inventory Item C			
1/1 Balance	300		
1/20 Purchase	300	1/29 Sale	300

3. *Inventory balances.* When the *periodic* inventory system is used, the beginning balance in the merchandise inventory account remains unchanged throughout the accounting period. The beginning inventory balance in this case is $800.

Merchandise Inventory		
1/1 Balance	800	

When the *perpetual* inventory system is used, all inventory purchase costs and individual cost of goods sold (CGS) per sale are accounted for in the merchandise inventory control account.

Inventory Control Account			
1/1 Balance	800		
1/15 Purchase A	200	1/25 Sale A	200
1/18 Purchase B	100	1/27 Sale B	300
1/20 Purchase C	300	1/29 Sale C	300

4. *Entries at the end of the accounting period.* When the *periodic* inventory system is used, the cost of goods sold during the period and the ending inventory must be computed. To do so, the beginning balance in the merchandise inventory account ($800) and the total in the purchases account ($600) are first closed to the cost of goods sold account. At the same time, a physical count of the remaining inventory is taken. The value of the remaining inventory is recorded as the ending inventory. This value is debited to the merchandise inventory account and credited to the cost of goods sold (CGS) account. The cost of goods sold is then closed to the income account.

Merchandise Inventory			
1/1 Balance	800	1/31 Close to CGS	800
1/31 Balance	600		

Purchases			
1/15 Item A	200	1/31 Close to CGS	600
1/18 Item B	100		
1/20 Item C	300		

Cost of Goods Sold			
1/1 Beginning Inv.	800	1/31 Ending Inv.	600
1/31 Purchases	600		
1/31 Balance	800		

When the *perpetual* inventory system is used, no end-of-period entries are needed to compute the cost of goods sold and ending inventory values (although adjustments due to shortages and possible breakage may be necessary). Both the merchandise inventory control and the cost of goods sold accounts carry their current balances. Cost of goods sold is again closed to the income account.

Merchandise Inventory Control			
1/1 Balance	800		
1/15 Purchase A	200	1/25 Sale A	200
1/18 Purchase B	100	1/27 Sale B	300
1/20 Purchase C	300	1/29 Sale C	300
1/31 Balance	600		

Cost of Goods Sold			
1/25 Sale A	200		
1/27 Sale B	300		
1/29 Sale C	300		
1/31 Balance	800		

Inventory Item A			
1/1 Balance	200		
1/15 Purchase	200	1/25 Sale	200
1/31 Balance	200		

Inventory Item B			
1/1 Balance	300		
1/18 Purchase	100	1/27 Sale	300
1/31 Balance	100		

Inventory Item C			
1/1 Balance	300		
1/20 Purchase	300	1/29 Sale	300
1/31 Balance	300		

5. *Closing entries to income summary account.* Regardless of which inventory system is used, the sales revenue account ($1,800) and the cost of goods sold account ($800) are closed to the income summary account. As a result of these entries, the income summary account will report a gross margin figure of $1,000($1,800 − $800). The next step would be to deduct expenses for the period (not covered in this illustration) to arrive at net income before taxes.

6. *Income statement reporting.* When the *periodic* inventory system is used, more detailed information is usually provided in the income statement.

Partial Income Statement
Periodic Inventory System

Sales revenue		$1,800
Less: Cost of goods sold		
Beginning inventory	$ 800	
Purchases	600	
Cost of goods available for sale	1,400	
Less: Ending inventory (by physical count)	600	
Cost of goods sold		800
Gross margin on sales		$1,000

When the perpetual inventory system is used, the cost of goods sold computation details normally are not provided in the income statement:

Partial Income Statement
Perpetual Inventory System

Sales revenue	$1,800
Less: Cost of goods sold	800
Gross margin on sales	$1,000

7. *Balance sheet reporting*. Regardless of which inventory system is used, the balance sheet reports only the ending balance in the merchandise inventory account.

Partial Balance Sheet
Periodic or Perpetual Inventory System

Current assets:	
Merchandise inventory	$600

Measurement of Inventory Values for Accounting Purposes

At date of acquisition, inventory items are recorded at their *cash equivalent cost* in conformity with the *cost principle*. Subsequently, when an item is sold, its cost is matched with the revenue from the sale in conformity with the *matching principle*. Inventory items remaining on hand at the end of an accounting period are assigned an accounting value. This value is based on the *cost principle* except when their value has declined below cost because of damage, obsolescence, a decrease in replacement cost, or similar factors. In this case, the items in inventory are typically assigned a lower value for accounting purposes in conformity with the *conservatism constraint*. For example, the item's net realizable value may be used.

The cost value assigned to merchandise and finished goods inventories results from an allocation of the total cost of goods available for sale between that portion sold (cost of goods sold) and that portion held as an asset for subsequent sale (ending inventory). The nature of this allocation is shown in Exhibit 9–3 based on the data given for the Lea Company.

A number of procedures used for measuring the accounting value of inventories satisfy the conceptual requirements. The variety of acceptable procedures reflects the wide variation in inventory characteristics and conditions caused by particular company situations and objectives.

Basically, the accounting values for inventories serve two different objectives. Each objective implies procedures that may not be fully compatible with the other objective. The first objective is to develop a monetary value for the inventory reported on the balance sheet. The second objective, focusing on the income statement, is to measure the value of the inventory sold in order to achieve a proper matching of cost of goods sold with the sales revenue of the period. Measurement of acceptable accounting values for inventory and cost of goods sold involves two distinct tasks:

1. *Inventory unit cost*—selection of an appropriate unit cost for valuation of the items in inventory. The principal inventory valuation methods are:
   a. The cost basis.
   b. Departures from the cost basis (discussed in Chapter 10):
      (1) Lower-of-cost-or market (LCM).
      (2) Net realizable value.
      (3) Replacement cost.
      (4) Current cost.
      (5) Selling price.

EXHIBIT 9-3 Allocation of Costs to Inventory and Cost of Goods Sold

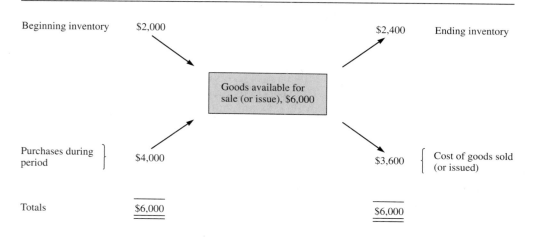

2. *Inventory cost flow*—selection of an inventory cost flow method; that is, selection of an *assumed flow* of inventory unit costs during the accounting period. The principal *inventory cost flow methods* discussed in this chapter are:
   a. Specific cost identification.
   b. Average cost.
   c. First-in, first-out (FIFO).
   d. Last-in, first-out (LIFO).

Content of Inventory Cost

The first objective of inventory accounting is to establish the unit cost of the inventory; that is, what costs should be included. Inventory cost is measured by the total cash equivalent outlay made to acquire the goods and to prepare them for sale.[5] These costs include the purchase cost and incidental costs incurred on the goods up to the time they are ready for use or for sale to the customer.

In conformity with the *cost-benefit constraint and materiality,* some incidental costs, although theoretically a cost of goods purchased, often are not included in inventory valuation but are reported as separate expenses. The cost of allocating these costs is not warranted by the related benefits. In such cases, *consistency* in application is particularly important. For example, insurance costs on goods in transit and material-handling expenses usually are not included in determining inventory costs because they are not directly related to the purchase or manufacture of goods for sale.

General and administrative (G&A) expenses are treated as *period* expenses because they relate more directly to accounting periods than to inventory. Selling and distribution costs are also considered period operating expenses and therefore are also not allocated to inventories. These expenses are recognized in the income statement in the period incurred.

---

[5] AICPA, *Accounting Research Bulletin No. 43*, "Restatement and Revision of Accounting Research Bulletins" (New York, 1961), Chapter 4, statement 3. The statement reads in part, "cost means in principle the sum of all the applicable expenditures and charges directly or indirectly incurred in bringing an article to its existing condition and location" and that (par. 4) "it should also be recognized that the exclusion of all overhead from inventory costs does not constitute an acceptable accounting procedure."

Freight-In (Freight on Purchases)   In conformity with the *cost principle,* freight charges and other incidental costs incurred in connection with the purchase of inventory are additions to unit cost. When these costs can be identified with specific goods, they should be added as part of the cost of such goods. However, in some cases, the necessary identification is impractical. Therefore, freight costs often are recorded in a special account such as freight-in, which is reported as an addition to cost of goods sold in the case of a retail company, and to cost of materials used in a manufacturing firm. This practical procedure may overstate cost of goods sold and understate inventory by the amount of costs that should be allocated to inventory (as opposed to including the full amount in cost of goods sold). When the amounts are material and it is practical, freight-in should be apportioned between cost of goods sold and the ending inventory.

Purchase Discounts (Cash Discounts on Credit Purchases)   Many companies offer cash discounts on purchases to encourage timely payment from buyers (which speeds up cash flow for the seller and oftentimes saves on borrowing costs). Most buyers make timely payments and take advantage of cash discounts because the savings are normally quite substantial. In fact, some companies find it to their advantage to borrow money in order to take advantage of these cash discounts. This tactic makes sense because the typical purchase discount terms of 2/10, n/30 (2% discount if paid within 10 days, full amount due not later than 30 days) is equivalent to an annualized interest rate of about 37%. Two methods are used to account for purchase and purchase discount amounts—the net method and the gross method. Both methods are acceptable under GAAP, although the net method is conceptually preferred.

Net Method   When the net method is used, purchase invoice amounts are recorded at the discounted (or net) invoice amount. A $1,000 face amount invoice with terms of 2/10, n/30, is thus recognized in the buying company's accounts at $980, or $1,000 − (.02 × $1,000). If the perpetual inventory system is used, the entry to record the purchase is:

Inventory	980	
Accounts payable		980

If the periodic inventory system is used, the debit side of this entry would be to the purchase account. Either way, the $980 in this example is considered to be the net cash equivalent amount of the materials or merchandise being acquired; it is the amount the seller is willing to accept as payment in full. This is the first reason the net method is preferable. If payment is made within the allotted cash discount period (10 days, normally) a check would be drawn for $980 and recorded as follows:

Accounts payable	980	
Cash		980

Under the net method, no further accounting entries are necessary if payment is made within the discount period. However, if for any reason payment is not made until after the expiration of the cash discount period, the gross invoice amount ($1,000) is due, which means that the $20 discount amount is lost to the buyer and must be recorded on the books. Some accountants use the interest expense account to record the expired purchase discount. Others use *purchase discounts lost,* an account similar to interest expense. Either way, the difference in invoice amounts is captured as interest expense, but use of a purchase discount lost account allows the company to track avoidable interest charges versus including them with other interest expense incurred in the normal course of doing business. Also, lost discounts do not qualify for interest deductions in computing taxes. If the purchase discount lost account is used, the required entry at the time of invoice payment is:

Accounts payable	980	
Purchase discounts lost	20	
Cash		1,000

If an invoice remains unpaid at the end of the accounting period and if the cash discount period has expired, an end-of-period adjusting entry is needed to record the amount of the discount:

Purchase discounts lost	20	
Accounts payable		20

Whether forfeited discounts are accounted for separately in a purchase discounts lost account or lumped in with general interest charges in an interest expense account, the amount should be reported as a period expense in the income statement and not added to the cost of the inventory.[6]

Gross Method When the gross method is used, purchase invoice amounts are entered in the books at their face amount whether or not the discount is taken. In the case of the $1,000 purchase invoice with terms of 2/10, n/30, the entry to record this invoice under the gross method is:

Inventory	1,000	
Accounts payable		1,000

Again, this entry assumes the use of a perpetual inventory system; if the periodic system is used, the debit side of the entry is to the purchases account. If invoice payment is made within the 10-day discount period, the amount of the discount is recorded in the purchase discounts account:

Accounts payable	1,000	
Purchase discounts		20
Cash		980

Purchase discounts is a contra account and carries a credit balance that is netted against the inventory account (or purchases account if the periodic inventory system is used). If the discount is not taken, payment of the invoice is recorded at the full amount:

Accounts payable	1,000	
Cash		1,000

If the invoice remains unpaid as of the end of the current accounting period, no adjusting entry is made, contrary to the case when the net method is used. Unfortunately in this case, the lost purchase discount is not separately disclosed; instead, it is left in the inventory account, implying that the inventory cost includes the lost discount. This is the second reason why the net method is preferable.

Key Points Regarding the Net and Gross Methods
* Although both gross and net methods are acceptable accounting practices, the net method is conceptually preferable.
* Under the gross method, if discounts are not taken, the cost of goods sold and ending inventory values are overstated by the amount of such forfeited discounts. Overstatement, in this context, is relative to the amounts that would be reported if the net method were used.
* Under the gross method, when discounts are taken, the cost of goods sold and ending inventory are not overstated. The purchase discounts contra account is credited for the amount of the discounts involved, which effectively lowers the net purchases balance (periodic system) or inventory account balance (perpetual system).
* Under the net method, if discounts are not taken, the cost of goods sold and ending inventory values are not overstated. Forfeited discounts are treated as period

---

[6] An exception to this rule is found in *SFAS No. 34,* "Capitalization of Interest Cost" (Norwalk, Conn., October 1979), par. 10., which states that capitalization of interest is required on one class of inventory as follows: assets intended for sale that are constructed or otherwise produced as discrete projects (e.g., ship building or real estate development).

expenses and reported in the income statement either separately identified in a purchase discounts lost account or commingled with other interest expense.

♦ Although the net method is conceptually preferable, the gross method is widely used for a number of practical reasons. For example, in some industries, purchase discounts are not commonly used. In other instances, discounts do not offer significant cash savings. In still other instances, management may choose to use the gross method simply to avoid disclosure of the company's failure to take discounts. Further, the gross amounts are more easily traced to source documents and are easily used for billing purposes.

♦ Because it can be used to isolate cash discounts forfeited, the net method is useful in internal control and cost reduction programs.

♦ Trade discounts (volume price reductions offered to wholesalers and dealers) are a separate matter, unrelated to purchase discounts. Trade discounts are not intended to induce timely payment from buyers. Instead, they are designed to induce volume sales and provide retailers and other sellers with price concessions.

CONCEPT REVIEW

1. Explain the essential differences in accounting for inventories under the periodic and perpetual inventory systems.
2. What are the two objectives of inventory accounting?
3. Why is the net approach to accounting for purchase discounts conceptually preferable to the gross approach?

INVENTORY COST FLOW METHODS

♦

Underlying Concepts of Cost Flow

The second objective of inventory accounting is to allocate the cost of goods available for sale between inventory sold during the period and inventory on hand at the end of the accounting period. This allocation process is common both to merchandise inventories stocked by retailers and wholesalers and to manufacturers' finished goods as well as to intermediate-step inventories. The purchase or manufacture costs of inventory are combined with the cost of inventory on hand at the beginning of the period. Together, these costs represent the cost of goods available for sale (or processing) during the accounting period. Assuming ongoing sales (or production) during the accounting period, some portion of the total cost of goods available for sale is converted to expense in the form of cost of goods sold; the remaining portion is assigned as the cost of inventory on hand at the end of the period.

An appropriate cost allocation procedure must be selected to allocate the total cost of goods available for sale during each period between the cost of goods sold and the cost of the ending inventory. If inventory unit acquisition costs are constant over time, the choice of an allocation process will not affect the result. However, inventory item costs—both acquisition and manufacturing costs—typically vary, trending up or down in response to prevailing conditions in the economy. For inventory accounting purposes, this price variability creates a need for management to select an explicit cost flow method (assumption) for use in allocating the total cost of goods available for sale between expense (cost of goods sold) and assets (ending inventory).

The physical movement of goods is nearly always on a first-in, first-out basis, especially if the product is perishable or subject to obsolescence. But the cost flow method used to account for the value of both the inventory used up during the period

EXHIBIT 9–4   Data on Inventories

Transaction Date	Units		
	Purchased	Sold	On Hand
January 1 Inventory @ $1.00			200
January 9 Purchases @ $1.10	300		500
January 10 Sales		400	100
January 15 Purchases @ $1.16	400		500
January 18 Sales		300	200
January 24 Purchases @ $1.26	100		300

The costs to be allocated are the total costs of the goods available for sale:

Beginning inventory		$200 \times \$1.00 = $	$ 200
Purchases	$300 \times \$1.10 = \$330$		
	$400 \times \$1.16 = 464$		
	$100 \times \$1.26 = \underline{126}$		920
Cost of goods available for sale*			$1,120

* The $1,120 is allocated between ending inventory and cost of goods sold, using one of the cost flow assumptions described in the next subsections.

and the inventory on hand at the end of the period can be quite different from the actual flow of goods. Inventory accounting concerns the flow of costs through the accounting system and not the flow of goods physically in and out of a stock room. On this issue, *ARB No. 43* states:

> Cost for inventory purposes may be determined under any one of several assumptions as to the flow of cost factors (such as first-in, first-out, average, and last-in, first-out); the major objective should be to choose the one which, under the circumstances, most clearly reflects periodic income.[7]

The phrase "most clearly reflects periodic income" is open to interpretation. The Committee on Accounting Procedure that issued the statement never made clear precisely what it meant by the phrase, although some accounting scholars believe the Committee meant the actual flow of goods. As a result, different accountants interpret the Committee's wording to mean different things, and some companies believe the phrase justifies using the accounting treatment that is most convenient or reasonable at the time financial statements are prepared.

The inventory cost flow methods discussed in this chapter conform to the *cost principle*. The central issue is the order in which the actual unit costs incurred are assigned to the ending inventory and cost of goods sold. The selection of an inventory flow method applies the *matching principle* to determine cost of goods sold, which is deducted from sales revenue for the period. The data given in Exhibit 9–4 are used to illustrate the allocation of costs to inventories and cost of goods sold.

Application of some of the inventory cost flow methods varies depending on whether a periodic or perpetual inventory system is used. The following discussion distinguishes between these systems because they affect the application of the inventory cost flow method.

Under a periodic inventory system, the quantity of the ending inventory is established at the end of the period. The unit costs are then applied to derive the ending inventory valuation by using one of the flow methods discussed next. Cost of

---

[7] AICPA, *Accounting Research Bulletin No. 43*, "Restatement and Revision of Accounting Research Bulletins" (New York, 1961), Chapter 4, statement 4.

goods sold (or used) is determined by subtracting the ending inventory valuation from the cost of goods available for sale amount.

Under a perpetual inventory system, each receipt and each issue of an inventory item is recorded in the inventory records to maintain an up-to-date perpetual inventory balance at all times. Thus, the perpetual inventory records provide the units and costs of ending inventory and cost of goods sold at any point in time. The unit costs applied to each issue or sale are determined by the cost flow method which is used.

Four inventory cost flow methods—specific cost identification, average cost, FIFO, and LIFO—are discussed in this chapter.

Reporting Inventories

In practice a company often uses several methods concurrently to report its inventories. *Accounting Trends & Techniques,* for example, reports that less than 25% of the 600 companies surveyed that use LIFO use it on all of their inventories. The choice is influenced by factors such as tax laws and other legislation specific to each country in which the firm operates. For example, companies that report on LIFO for tax reasons in the United States, typically use FIFO for inventories in their overseas operations where tax laws differ.

Information on which inventory costing method(s) a firm is using to value its inventories is provided in the notes to the financial statements. This information often appears in the initial note describing the accounting policies adopted by the firm. More detailed disclosure is often provided in additional notes. An example of inventory disclosure is provided in Exhibit 9–5 for the HARSCO Corporation.

Why So Many Methods?

Since nearly all organizations process physical inventories on a FIFO (first-in, first-out) physical flow, why are so many alternative cost flow assumptions used in practice to establish the values given to inventory and to cost of sales in the financial statements? The simplest method would seem to be one that used the cost of the specific item involved.

As business became more complex, specific identification of the cost of an item became increasingly burdensome. Using either an average cost or a flow assumption made little material difference in the financial results over time if the method chosen was used consistently, and it reduced much of the difficulty of recordkeeping. Average values were appealing where a mixing of inventories of different purchase values was necessary (e.g. liquids such as crude oil) or expedient (small interchangeable items such as bolts). The FIFO assumption represented a convenient and logical cost flow assumption for other items; thus, a tradition was created for these two approaches (average and FIFO). Specific identification continued to be used for high-cost distinguishable items, particularly when the item's cost was an important determinant of the final price charged. Specific identification also remained relevant where units were not physically interchangeable, for example, in car dealerships.

Use of a FIFO cost flow assumption is not only consistent with the physical flow of goods and, hence, with the matching concept, but it also provides a simpler system. Essentially, it's just easier to keep inventory records on a FIFO basis. Even companies that report on some other basis, such as last-in, first-out (LIFO), typically keep their internal records on a FIFO basis and convert the physical flow to a LIFO value only at the time financial reports are needed.

During the 1930s, the economy experienced increased inflation. Concurrently, the IRS required the same system for establishing a company's tax liability as the company used for financial reporting. Hence, most firms using FIFO found that the

EXHIBIT 9-5   Inventory Disclosure for the HARSCO Corporation

(in thousands)	1987	1986
Current assets:		
Cash and short-term investments	$ 32,381	$ 17,529
Notes and accounts receivable, less allowance		
for uncollectible accounts ($8,443 and $9,535) . .	183,586	182,094
Inventories	217,130	189,831
Deferred income tax benefits	16,165	21,953
Other	14,199	14,518
Total current assets	463,461	425,925

NOTES TO CONSOLIDATED FINANCIAL STATEMENTS
Note 1 [in part]. *Summary of Significant Accounting Policies: Inventory Valuation:*
Inventories are stated at the lower of cost or market, cost being determined using the last-in, first-out (LIFO), first-in, first-out (FIFO) and average cost methods.

Note 2. *Inventories:*
Inventories are summarized as follows:

(in thousands)	1987	1986
Classification:		
Long-term contract costs (including general and		
administrative costs of $10,257 and $8,343)	$153,826	$103,660
Less progress payments—U.S. Government	(54,396)	(21,831)
	99,430	81,829
Finished goods	29,480	31,865
Work in process	29,764	20,302
Raw materials and purchased parts	55,168	53,015
Stores and supplies	3,288	2,820
	$217,130	$189,831
Values at lower of cost or market:		
LIFO basis	$ 92,395	$ 93,732
FIFO basis	10,341	8,088
Average cost basis	114,394	88,011
	$217,130	$189,831

The Company has incurred costs that are assignable to units not yet produced. The aggregate amount incurred, which is included in long-term contract costs, was $34,914,000 and $1,854,000 as of December 31, 1987 and 1986, respectively. The significant increase is, for the most part, attributable to initial tooling and deferred start-up costs related to the five-ton tactical truck contract with the U.S. Government.

Inventories valued on the LIFO basis at December 31, 1987 and 1986, were approximately $33,721,000 and $34,541,000, respectively, less than the amounts of such inventories valued at current costs.

As a result of reducing certain inventory quantities valued on the LIFO basis, profits from liquidation of inventories were recorded, which increased net income by $1,490,000, $1,688,000, and $1,147,000 in 1987, 1986, and 1985, respectively. The fourth quarters of 1987, 1986, and 1985 reflect net income of $1,954,000, $1,963,000, and $2,923,000, respectively, representing final determination of price changes and liquidation of inventories which occurred during the year.

cost of the goods they sold—and, hence, their taxes—was based on older and lower prices, whereas replacement inventory required more current and higher prices. Firms believed that the funds necessary to replace higher cost inventory were being unfairly taxed away. They requested that the IRS let them charge their more recent costs, thereby reducing their tax liability and leaving more funds to replace inventories at their current prices. Ultimately the IRS agreed, but it did so only on the condition that firms using LIFO for establishing their tax liability also report on a LIFO basis in their published financial reports. Thus, firms wishing to save on taxes and faced with rising prices for the goods they bought had to prepare their external financial reports on a LIFO basis as well.

The impact of using LIFO or FIFO also falls on reported earnings. When prices are rising, using FIFO charges off older and, therefore, lower costs to cost of goods sold and, hence, to income. The result is higher earnings. If senior management compensation is based in part on the particular level of reported earnings, salary incentives may be considered in the choice of reporting method. The effects can be large. In its 1988 financial reports, Consolidated Paper indicated its inventories would have been 25% greater had it reported using FIFO. Consolidated's 1988 income is substantially smaller under LIFO reporting, as is its tax liability.

The concept of opportunity cost has also been used to support alternative inventory cost-flow approaches. The argument stresses the importance of matching the opportunity cost of the item sold with the revenue from the sale. The opportunity cost is created by the need to replace the item sold if business is to continue. The issue then remains how to establish the opportunity cost. A logical approach would be to use the cost of the item to be bought, a next-in, first-out (NIFO) concept. Because an unambiguous NIFO value is unavailable, accountants relying on the opportunity cost idea use instead the most recent costs actually incurred as the best measure available. Thus, the economists' opportunity cost concept becomes, in practice, an argument for using LIFO.

Specific Cost Identification Method

The **specific cost identification method** requires that each item stocked be specifically marked so that its unit cost can be identified at any time. When the items involved are large or expensive and small quantities are handled, it may be feasible to tag or number each item when purchased or manufactured. This method makes it possible to identify at date of sale the specific unit cost of each item sold and each item remaining in inventory. Thus, the specific cost identification method relates the cost flow with the specific flow of physical goods. It is the only method to do so.

Evaluation of Specific Cost Identification Method   The specific cost method requires careful identification of each item, which causes a practical limitation created by the detailed records that are required. However, computerized inventory systems can help alleviate this problem.

Another undesirable feature of the method is the opportunity to manipulate income by arbitrary selection of items at time of sale. Assume three identical stereo sets are for sale. Their costs are $800, $850, and $900. One is sold for $1,500. In this instance, reported cost of goods sold (and reported income) would depend on the unit arbitrarily selected for this particular sale. Thus the specific cost method can be applied selectively.

Nevertheless, this method is essential in cases where individual units have unique characteristics that, by their relative appeal to customers, determine which unit is sold.

Automobile dealers use the specific cost method for two reasons. First, the dealer's specific cost is an important determinant of the sales price. Second, this method is easily applied due to the existence of an identification number for each vehicle and a known invoice cost. In this case, the specific cost identification method has the advantage of establishing a definite gross margin on each item sold.

Average Cost Method

The **average cost method** is based on the view that the cost of inventory on hand at the end of a period and the cost of goods sold during a period should be representative of all costs incurred during the period. The average cost method is applied in two ways, depending on the inventory system used:
- *Periodic* inventory system—*weighted-average unit cost* for the entire accounting period.
- *Perpetual* inventory system—*moving-average unit cost*.

EXHIBIT 9–6   Weighted-Average Inventory Cost Method (Periodic Inventory System)

	Units	Unit Price	Total Cost
Goods available:			
January 1 Beginning inventory	200	$1.00	$ 200
9 Purchase	300	1.10	330
15 Purchase	400	1.16	464
24 Purchase	100	1.26	126
Total available	1,000	1.12*	1,120
Ending inventory at weighted-average cost:			
Jan. 31	300	1.12	336
Cost of goods sold at weighted-average cost:			
Sales during January	700†	1.12	$ 784

* Weighted-average unit cost ($1,120 ÷ 1,000 = $1.12).
† 400 units on January 10 plus 300 units on January 18.

Weighted-Average Cost (Periodic Inventory System)   The weighted-average cost method is used with the periodic inventory system because the average cost can be computed only at the end of the period. A weighted-average unit cost is computed by dividing the sum of the beginning inventory cost plus current purchase costs by the number of units in the beginning inventory plus units purchased during the period. A weighted-average unit cost can be computed using this formula:

$$\frac{\text{Beginning inventory} + \text{Current purchase cost}}{\text{Beginning inventory units} + \text{Current purchase units}} = \text{Weighted-average unit cost}$$

The weighted-average unit cost is then applied to the units in the ending inventory to compute the ending inventory balance, and to the units sold to compute cost of goods sold. Exhibit 9–6 illustrates application of the weighted-average method under a periodic system using the data given in Exhibit 9–4.

Evaluation of the Weighted-Average Cost Method   The weighted-average cost method is generally viewed as objective, consistent, not subject to easy manipulation, and easy to apply. The method is appropriate for *periodic* inventory systems because the inventory of physical units is not counted until the end of the period and the weighted-average unit cost can be determined only at the end of the period. Thus, the measurements needed to compute ending inventory and cost of goods sold are determined concurrently at the end of the accounting period.

Moving-Average Cost (Perpetual Inventory System)   When a perpetual inventory system is used, the weighted-average approach just described cannot be applied because a weighted-average unit cost cannot be calculated until the end of the period. To avoid this problem, a moving-average unit cost is used. The moving average provides a new unit cost after each purchase. When goods are sold or issued, the moving-average unit cost at the time is used. Application of the moving-average concept in a perpetual inventory system is shown in Exhibit 9–7. For example, on January 9, the $1.06 moving-average cost was derived by dividing the total cost ($530) by the total units (500). The January ending inventory of 300 units is costed at the latest moving-average unit cost of $1.18 (total $354). The cost of goods sold for the period is the sum of the sales, total cost column, $766 ($424 + $342).

Evaluation of Moving-Average Cost Method   The moving-average method is generally viewed as objective, consistent, and not subject to easy manipulation. It is appropri-

EXHIBIT 9-7   Moving-Average Inventory Cost (Perpetual Inventory System)

	Purchases			Sales (Issues)			Inventory Balance		
Date	Units	Unit Cost	Total Cost	Units	Unit Cost	Total Cost	Units	Unit Cost	Total Cost
Jan. 1							200*	$1.00	$200
9	300	$1.10	$330				500	1.06†	530
10				400	$1.06	$424	100	1.06	106
15	400	1.16	464				500	1.14‡	570
18				300	1.14	342	200	1.14	228
24	100	1.26	126				300	1.18§	354
Ending inventory									$354
Cost of goods sold						$766			

* Beginning inventory.
† $530 ÷ 500 = $1.06.
‡ $570 ÷ 500 = $1.14.
§ $354 ÷ 300 = $1.18.

ate for perpetual inventory systems because it provides a current average cost on a continuous basis.

Overall Evaluation of the Average Cost Methods   The average cost methods do not match the *latest* unit costs with current sales revenues. Rather, they match the average costs of the period against revenues and value the ending inventory at average cost. Therefore, when unit costs are steadily increasing or decreasing, they provide inventory and cost of goods sold amounts between the LIFO and FIFO extremes. The amounts reported in the balance sheet (ending inventory) and the income statement (cost of goods sold) are valued consistently because the same unit costs are used on both statements. Many accountants favor the average cost method (versus FIFO or LIFO) because unit values for inventory and cost of goods sold are consistent.

First-In, First-Out Cost Method

The first-in, first-out method is based on the assertion that the first goods purchased or manufactured should be the first units costed out on sale or issuance. Because the costs flow out in the same order they flowed in, goods sold (or issued) are valued at the oldest unit costs. The goods remaining in inventory are valued at the most recent unit cost amounts. Application of FIFO requires the identification of inventory layers for the different unit costs. FIFO can be used with either a periodic or a perpetual inventory system. No attempt is made under FIFO to match the specific cost incurred in purchasing or manufacturing specific inventory unit items with the revenue from the sale of the item. Most inventory items consist of either commodity goods or manufactured goods that are fungible (identical in appearance and interchangeable in use). When mixed together—which is normal practice—individual piece identification for inventory cost flow tracking and accounting purposes is extremely difficult and not usually worth the effort.

Periodic Inventory System   Using the data given in Exhibit 9–4 and assuming a physical inventory count at the end of the period, FIFO results are shown in Exhibit 9–8.

EXHIBIT 9–8 FIFO Inventory Costing (Periodic Inventory System)

Beginning inventory (200 units at $1)	$ 200
Add purchases during period (computed as in Exhibit 9–4	920
Cost of goods available for sale	$1,120
Deduct ending inventory (300 units per physical inventory count):	
100 units at $1.26 (most recent purchase—Jan. 24) $126	
200 units at $1.16 (next most recent purchase—Jan. 15) 232	
Total ending inventory cost	358
Cost of goods sold (or issued)	$ 762*

* Also 200 units on hand Jan. 1 at $1 plus 300 units purchased Jan. 9 at $1.10 plus 200 units purchased Jan. 15 at $1.16.

EXHIBIT 9–9 FIFO Inventory Costing (Perpetual Inventory System)

	Purchases			Sales (Issues)			Inventory Balance		
Date	Units	Unit Cost	Total Cost	Units	Unit Cost	Total Cost	Units	Unit Cost	Total Cost
Jan. 1							200*	$1.00	$200
9	300	$1.10	$330				200 300	1.00 1.10	200 330
10				200 200	$1.00 1.10	$200 220	100	1.10	110
15	400	1.16	464				100 400	1.10 1.16	110 464
18				100 200	1.10 1.16	110 232	200	1.16	232
24	100	1.26	126				200 100	1.16 1.26	232⎫ 126⎭
Ending inventory									$358
Cost of goods sold						$762			

* Beginning inventory.

Perpetual Inventory System Application of FIFO with a perpetual inventory system is illustrated in Exhibit 9–9. The maintenance of *inventory layers* by unit costs throughout the period is needed to assign the appropriate cost to each issue.

When FIFO is used with a *perpetual* inventory system, the issues on the inventory record may be costed out either currently throughout the period each time there is a withdrawal or entirely at the end of the period, with the same results. In Exhibit 9–9, issues from inventory on January 10 and 18 (FIFO basis) were costed out as they occurred. FIFO produces the same results regardless of whether a periodic or a perpetual system is used.

Evaluation of FIFO Cost Method FIFO is the most common method used for inventory costing purposes:
  ◆ It is easy to apply with either periodic or perpetual inventory systems.

* It produces an inventory value for the balance sheet that approximates current cost.
* The flow of costs *tends* to be consistent with the usual physical flow of goods.
* It is systematic and objective.
* It is not subject to manipulation.

Some accountants also believe that FIFO results in a proper profit measure under the historical cost approach, particularly when the cost flow assumption parallels the physical inventory flow. A criticism of FIFO is that it does not match the current cost of goods sold with current revenues; rather, the oldest unit costs are matched with current sales revenue. When costs are rising, reported income under FIFO is higher than under LIFO or average cost. This effect on income often is called an *inventory (or phantom) profit*. The inventory profit is the difference between the actual cost of goods sold at FIFO cost and the cost of goods sold measured at their current cost.

The income tax implications of FIFO are important. When inventory replacement costs are rising, companies that use FIFO report more income than those using LIFO or average cost, when all other factors are constant. Therefore, FIFO users pay more income taxes when prices are rising.[8]

Last-in, First-Out Cost Method

The **last-in, first-out method** of inventory costing is based on the view that the latest unit acquisition cost should be matched with current sales revenue. Therefore, under LIFO, the order of cost outflows recognized is the inverse of the order of cost inflows. The units remaining in the ending inventory are costed at the oldest unit costs available, and the units included in the cost of goods sold are costed at the newest unit costs available. Thus, the cost flow assumed under LIFO is the exact opposite of the FIFO cost assumption. Like FIFO, application of LIFO requires the use of inventory cost layers for different unit costs.

The LIFO inventory concept is applied in several ways, two of which are discussed next.

1. *Unit cost approach*—Units are multiplied by unit cost for each separate product.[9]
2. *Dollar value LIFO approach*—Large inventory pools (groups of similar products) and index prices are used to compute the LIFO inventory.

The unit cost approach is described first. Dollar value LIFO is the subject of the last major subdivision of the chapter (see page 433). Alternative approaches to straight LIFO are discussed in Chapter 10.

Unit Cost Approach for LIFO   To describe the application of LIFO using units and unit costs for each individual product, a situation involving a single product is used. LIFO may be applied with either a periodic or perpetual inventory system. However, the cost of goods sold amount and the ending inventory balance usually vary according to the inventory system used.

Periodic Inventory System Assuming a *periodic inventory system* and a physical inventory count of the units at the end of the period, LIFO results are determined as shown in Exhibit 9–10. The ending inventory is costed at the oldest unit costs. Cost

---

[8] The opposite is true during periods of declining prices.

[9] This application also is called the *quality, specific goods,* or *unit* LIFO method of applying the LIFO concept.

EXHIBIT 9-10   LIFO Inventory Costing (Periodic Inventory System)

Cost of goods available (see Exhibit 9-4)	$1,120
Deduct ending inventory (300 units per physical inventory count):	
200 units at $1 (oldest costs available, from January 1 inventory) $200	
100 units at $1.10 (next oldest costs available; from January 9 purchase) 110	
Ending inventory	310
Cost of goods sold	$ 810*

* Also 100 units at $1.26 plus 400 units at $1.16 plus 200 units at $1.10.

EXHIBIT 9-11   LIFO Inventory Costing (Perpetual Inventory System)

	Purchases			Sales (Issues)			Inventory Balance		
Date	Units	Unit Cost	Total Cost	Units	Unit Cost	Total Cost*	Units	Unit Cost	Total Cost
Jan. 1							200*	$1.00	$200
9	300	$1.10	$330				200	1.00	200
							300	1.10	330
10				300	$1.10	$330			
				100	1.00	100	100	1.00	100
15	400	1.16	464				100	1.00	100
							400	1.16	464
18				300	1.16	348	100	1.00	100
							100	1.16	116
24	100	1.26	126				100	1.00	100⎤
							100	1.16	116⎬
							100	1.26	126⎦
Ending inventory									$342
Cost of goods sold						$778			

* Beginning inventory.

of goods sold is determined by deducting ending inventory from the cost of goods available for sale. The *periodic LIFO system* permits the costs of purchases occurring after the last sale to be included in cost of sales. For example, the LIFO cost of the January 18th sale includes the cost of the January 24th purchase. The periodic system produces this seeming anomaly which cannot occur under LIFO using the perpetual system. The ending inventory consists of two layers, one at $1.00 and one at $1.10.

Perpetual Inventory System   When LIFO is applied with a perpetual inventory system, as shown in Exhibit 9-11, sales are costed currently throughout the accounting period as each sale occurs. In Exhibit 9-11, in both sales transactions (January 10 and January 18), sales were costed using the newest inventory items available.

Compare this with Exhibit 9–9, in which FIFO is illustrated and the same sales were costed using the oldest inventory items available. Under FIFO (Exhibit 9–9), the cost of goods sold for the January 10 sale is $420, but the same sale under LIFO (Exhibit 9–11) produces a cost of goods sold amount of $430, a $10 increase. Similar cost of goods sold amount differences are produced in connection with the January 18 sale. Also, the difference in the cost of the ending inventory with LIFO under a periodic inventory system (Exhibit 9–10) and LIFO when applied to a perpetual inventory system (Exhibit 9–11) is $32, ($342 − $310). The ending inventory consists of three distinct layers (at $1.00, $1.16, and $1.26 unit costs respectively).

In addition, Exhibits 9–9 and 9–11 illustrate the rather tedious nature of the perpetual inventory system under both the FIFO and LIFO. Thanks to computers, some degree of relief from the burdensome nature of this work has been made possible, but extensive recordkeeping is still required.

LIFO and Cash Flows   During periods of rising inventory costs, LIFO costed using a periodic system will provide a lower pretax income than LIFO using a perpetual system. A company wishing to minimize its tax payments would cost its inventory at the end of the period using a LIFO cost flow approach combined with a periodic system to ensure the very latest, and therefore highest, costs are expensed. Because of this result, if a perpetual LIFO system is used for internal purposes, the results usually are restated to the periodic system result for both income tax and external reporting purposes.

The lower income tax payments reduce cash outflow. The IRS has consistently taken a strong position to prevent what are called LIFO abuses. Specifically, the IRS specified an income tax **LIFO conformity rule** that states that a company can use LIFO for income tax purposes only if it also uses LIFO for financial reporting purposes. The IRS also specified strict rules that require LIFO companies to maintain detailed LIFO records to facilitate IRS income tax audits.

In response to the LIFO conformity rule, companies began giving supplemental data in disclosure notes about net income on a FIFO basis. This tactic raised IRS objections. Under pressure, the IRS relaxed the LIFO conformity rule somewhat. The basic requirement that LIFO could be used for tax purposes only if it is used for external reporting purposes was not changed, but supplemental disclosure about income under FIFO or average cost is now permitted, although not on the income statement. These rules do not apply to the other inventory methods.

An example of supplemental data disclosed in footnotes is provided by the inventory note for Courier Corporation's 1989 financial report:

> If the first-in first-out (FIFO) method of accounting had been used by the Company, reported net income would have been higher by $63,000 ($.03 per share) in fiscal 1988, $142,000 ($.08 per share) in fiscal 1987, and $13,000 ($.01 per share) in fiscal 1986. On a FIFO basis, reported year-end inventories would have increased by $5.4 million in 1988, $5.2 million in 1987 and $5.0 million in 1986.

Companies experiencing declining costs in their primary factor markets should not adopt LIFO if they wish to maximize cash flow. Also the cost of recordkeeping is higher under LIFO, and this fact should be considered, although computer technology has significantly reduced these costs. Finally, switching between LIFO and FIFO is not automatic with the IRS. The decision should be made with the advice of a knowledgeable tax specialist and the best available forecasts of future price movements. Moreover, for financial reporting purposes, changes, such as from LIFO to FIFO, are considered appropriate only if the company demonstrates that the newly adopted reporting method more clearly reflects income relative to the existing method. Substantial reliance is currently placed on management's judgment in assessing what constitutes better reporting.

> ### CONCEPT REVIEW
>
> 1. Using the following data, compute the inventory value using specific cost identification, average cost, FIFO, and LIFO under both the perpetual and periodic inventory approaches. Assume a zero beginning balance.
>
> June 1 . . . . . Bought one item @ $10
> June 2 . . . . . Bought one item @ $16
> June 3 . . . . . Sold one item @ $20*
> June 4 . . . . . Bought one item @ $18
> * The item sold was purchased on June 2.
>
> 2. Explain the reasons why a company might elect to use a FIFO cost flow approach.
> 3. Which inventory cost flow assumption permitted under GAAP is most compatible with the matching principle?

OTHER ASPECTS OF LIFO
♦

Adoption of Lifo

Income tax regulations permit taxpayers to use LIFO for all or part of the total inventory of goods (e.g., manufacturers use it for raw materials, work in process, finished goods; retailers and wholesalers use it for merchandise for sale). In the typical LIFO situation, the company has changed from some other method used in the past to LIFO for *tax* and *external reporting* purposes.

The switch to LIFO involves a *change in accounting principle* as described in *APB Opinion No. 20*, "Accounting Changes." Paragraph 20 of that *Opinion* requires that the cumulative effect of a change in accounting principle be reported between the captions "income before extraordinary items" and "net income." However, the *Opinion* does not require reporting of the cumulative effect when it is impossible to measure (par. 26). The specific example given in the *Opinion* is a change from FIFO to LIFO. Usually, it is virtually impossible to reconstruct the exact composition of old inventory cost layers that the company would have reported in prior periods if it had been using LIFO. The difficulty of computing the cumulative effect of a change to LIFO is due in part to the arbitrariness of deciding how far back in time to go to identify the base layer of LIFO inventory and, in part, due to the unavailability of past cost and price data. Ideally, the company would go all the way back to its origin, but in most cases that is not feasible. Therefore, when a company changes to LIFO, the base year is the year in which the change is made. The base year LIFO cost for the beginning inventory of the year of change, and for subsequent years, is the ending inventory for the prior year based on FIFO or whatever method was then used. Further, the base layer of LIFO inventory must be changed to cost regardless of the prior method used due to income tax regulations. This requirement means that write-downs of the prior year's ending inventory below cost (such as might occur under the lower-of-cost-or-market rule, see Chapter 10) must be eliminated.

Suppose, for example, that the Erie Valve Company uses a FIFO cost flow assumption and follows the practice of writing its inventory down to current market values when the market value at the end of the accounting period is below its original FIFO cost.[10] At the end of 1991, Erie shows an inventory value of $90,000, marked

---

[10] This inventory method is called the lower-of-cost-or-market and is abbreviated LCM. The LCM approach is used in combination with the cost flow assumptions such as FIFO. In the example, if LCM were not being used, Erie's inventory would already be valued on the books at $100,000, and no entry is required. LCM is discussed in Chapter 10.

down from its FIFO cost of $100,000. For 1992, Erie plans to switch to LIFO for tax reporting and, hence, is obligated to use LIFO also for financial reporting. The Erie Company would make the following entry to write the inventory back up to $100,000:

January 1, 1992:

```
Inventory* . . . . . . . . . . . . . . . . . . . . . . . . . . . . . . . 10,000
    Change in accounting principle FIFO to LIFO . . . . . . . . .        10,000
```

* This entry assumes the direct inventory method of recording LCM is used. If the allowance method is used, the debit would be made to the allowance to reduce inventory to LCM account (discussed in Chapter 10).

Recording FIFO/LIFO Differences in the Accounts

A **LIFO allowance** (often inappropriately called a reserve) is used by some companies to reflect the difference, on a cumulative basis, between the inventory costing method used in the accounts, such as FIFO, and the method used in the income tax return, such as LIFO. When LIFO is used in figuring the IRS income tax liability, LIFO must also be used in the firm's financial reports. If records are kept on a FIFO basis, an adjustment is required. The adjustment is the allowance.

Many companies that report inventory at LIFO cost do not use LIFO for internal accounting and control purposes. This is true in part because the system is costly to operate. For internal and control purposes, most companies use either FIFO, average, standard, or variable costing. At the end of the period, these results are converted to LIFO for income tax purposes and for external financial reporting. Usually this conversion is external to the accounts. However, in some cases the results of the conversion to LIFO are entered into the accounts as a single amount by using an inventory allowance account (allowance to reduce inventory to LIFO basis). This allowance is a contra account to the inventory account. The allowance-account procedure is used in either of two ways, assuming FIFO is recorded internally:

1. Report but do not record—the difference between FIFO used internally and LIFO used for external reporting is reported usually in parentheses with the inventory account on the balance sheet and called allowance to reduce inventories to LIFO cost. Under this procedure no formal entry is made in the accounts for the allowance.
2. Record and report—the difference is recorded in the accounts at the end of each year by revising the allowance balance so that the account reflects the current year-end balance. The other part of the entry is to cost of goods sold. Under this method an allowance account *is* used. For example, if the difference at the end of 1992 for Erie Company is $6,000, the following entry would be made:

```
Cost of goods sold . . . . . . . . . . . . . . . . . . . . . . . . . . . 6,000
    Allowance to reduce FIFO inventory to LIFO basis . . . . . . .        6,000
```

If the difference between FIFO and LIFO is $4,000 at the end of 1993, the entry would be:

```
Allowance to reduce FIFO inventory to LIFO basis . . . . . 2,000
    Cost of goods sold . . . . . . . . . . . . . . . . . . . . . .        2,000
Computation:
    Balance in the allowance account . . . . . . . . . . . . . . $6,000
    Balance needed in the allowance account . . . . . . . . . .   4,000
    Difference—reduction in the allowance account . . . . . $2,000
```

Note 2 to Merck's 1989 financial statements, given in Exhibit 5–3, illustrates the reporting of the allowance, called *reduction* by Merck.

LIFO Liquidation

A problem occurs under LIFO when a company fails to maintain the *base layer* of inventory (i.e., the *beginning* inventory of the period when LIFO was first adopted by the company).[11] To illustrate *LIFO inventory liquidation*, assume:

	Units	Unit Cost	Total Cost
Beginning inventory (assumed to be the base layer of LIFO inventory [year 1])	10,000	$1.00	$10,000
Purchases	40,000	1.50	60,000
Total available for sale	50,000		70,000
Sales (44,000 units, costed on LIFO basis) from:			
Purchases	40,000	1.50	60,000
Base inventory layer	4,000	1.00	4,000*
Cost of goods sold	44,000		64,000
Ending inventory	6,000	1.00	$ 6,000

* Base layer partially used.

In this example, the company did not maintain the base year inventory of 10,000 units. This situation could have been due to:

1. *Voluntary inventory liquidation*—management may have decided to reduce normal inventory quantity for some reason, such as a decline in demand, in anticipation of a decline in inventory replenishment costs, or in anticipation of improvement in the product.[12]
2. *Involuntary inventory liquidation*—an inventory reduction may have been forced by uncontrollable causes, such as shortages, strikes, delayed delivery dates, or unexpected customer demand.

As a result of the liquidation of part of the base inventory, cost of goods sold includes 4,000 units with an old cost ($1 per unit) matched against current revenue. This liquidation of part of the LIFO base layer distorts reported income relative to income under the normal LIFO relationship of cost and revenue. Assuming the inventory liquidation is temporary, should the 4,000 units be costed at $1 per unit or at some other cost? If the 4,000 units will be replaced in the next period at a higher cost (e.g., $1.60 per unit) should the restoration of the base inventory position be at $1 per unit or at $1.60 per unit? One approach that some companies use involves increasing cost of goods sold with the estimated replacement cost, decreasing inventory at LIFO cost, and crediting the difference to a holding account. Assuming a perpetual inventory system, the entry would be:

Cost of goods sold (40,000 × $1.50) + (4,000 × $1.60)	66,400	
Inventory (40,000 × $1.50) + (4,000 × $1)		64,000
Excess of replacement cost of LIFO inventory temporarily liquidated (4,000 × $.60)		2,400

When the base position is restored at $1.60 per unit, the following entry is made:

Inventory (4,000 × $1)	4,000	
Excess of replacement cost of LIFO inventory temporarily liquidated (4,000 × $.60)	2,400	
Accounts payable (4,000 × $1.60)		6,400

---

[11] The same problem occurs whenever a LIFO layer is not maintained.

[12] One criticism of LIFO is that it is subject to income manipulation. For example, a year-end purchasing policy can be used to reduce reported income by heavy buying if prices have increased, or increase reported income by permitting inventories to decline and old low prices to be included in cost of goods sold.

The credit balance, $2,400, in the excess of replacement cost of LIFO inventory temporarily liquidated account should be reported as a current liability. It represents an amount that will have to be spent to replace inventory.

If replacement occurs at a unit cost different from the estimate of $1.60 per unit, the difference is accounted for as a change in estimate. *APB Opinion No. 20,* "Accounting Changes," requires that changes in estimates be accounted for prospectively. Therefore, the difference between the actual replacement cost and the estimated replacement cost is treated as an increase or decrease in cost of goods sold for the period of replacement.

No official pronouncement specifies how LIFO inventory liquidation should be accounted for when it is due to uncontrollable causes. When LIFO liquidation occurs for reasons beyond the control of the company, some accountants believe that the procedure illustrated above is a reasonable accounting solution to the problem. In such cases, they argue that the approach is justified to protect the integrity of the LIFO concept. Other accountants disagree on the basis that it introduces subjective values into the accounts and financial statements. In addition, the argument that cost of goods sold should be reflected at inventory replacement cost could be applied to any liquidation of old layers, not just the base inventory layer. However, few companies use the replacement cost method described above when liquidating recently added layers only. As a practical matter, companies try to avoid liquidating old layers of LIFO inventory during periods of rising prices because it causes their income tax payments to increase.

The liquidation of LIFO layers is what caused the increased profits reported by Interlake, Inc., and Wallace Murray, discussed at the beginning of this chapter. The older costs in the LIFO layers of these companies produced larger profits. And because the companies had elected to use LIFO for tax reporting, they both paid higher taxes and showed higher income in their published financial reports to stockholders.

Comparison of LIFO with FIFO

Using LIFO versus FIFO can cause significant differences in the income statement and the balance sheet. The comparative effects *depend on* whether unit costs are increasing or decreasing. If unit costs remain constant, the two methods give the same results. With rising costs, FIFO matches low (older) costs with sales revenue. Also, FIFO provides an inventory valuation approximating higher current cost. In contrast, LIFO matches high (newer) costs with sales revenue and provides an inventory valuation on a low (older) cost basis.

Conversely, with declining costs, FIFO matches high (older) costs with sales revenue and provides an inventory valuation approximating lower current cost. By contrast, LIFO matches low (newer) costs with sales revenue and provides an inventory valuation on a high (older) cost basis.

With respect to the cash flow effects, when costs are rising and inventory quantities are not decreasing, LIFO results in lower pretax income and, consequently, less income tax; therefore, in terms of cash flows, LIFO provides an advantage over FIFO.

Consider the following data:

> Beginning cash balance . . . . $ 2,000
> Beginning inventory (5,000 units at $5)
> Purchases (5,000 units at $7)
> Sales (5,000 units at $18)
> Expenses (excluding income taxes) 35,000
> Income tax rate 40%

Based on this data a firm using LIFO shows a decline in income taxes payable of $4,000 and lower net income by $6,000. These effects can be seen in Exhibit 9–12.

EXHIBIT 9–12 LIFO Costing Compared with FIFO Costing

	Comparative Results						
	First-in, First-out			**Last-in, First-out**			**Increase (Decrease) from FIFO to LIFO**
	Units	**Per Unit**	**Amount**	**Units**	**Per Unit**	**Amount**	
Income statement:							
Sales revenue	5,000	$18	$90,000	5,000	$18	$90,000	$ –0–
Cost of goods sold	5,000	5	25,000	5,000	7	35,000	10,000
Gross margin			65,000			55,000	(10,000)
Expenses			35,000			35,000	–0–
Pretax income			30,000			20,000	(10,000)
Income taxes (at 40%)			12,000			8,000	(4,000)*
Net income			$18,000			$12,000	$ (6,000)*
Balance Sheet (limited to above transactions:							
Cash (assuming all transactions were cash)			$10,000†			$14,000†	$ 4,000 *
Inventory			35,000			25,000	(10,000)*
Net difference (same as difference in net income)							$ (6,000)

* Critical differences.
† Beginning cash balance + Sales − Purchases − Expenses − Income taxes = Ending cash balance.
$2,000 + $90,000 − $35,000 − $35,000 − $12,000 = $10,000 (FIFO).
$2,000 + $90,000 − $35,000 − $35,000 − $8,000 = $14,000 (LIFO).

The data given in that exhibit assume rising inventory costs. The expectation of increasing inflation explains why many firms changed to LIFO reporting in the mid-70s.[13]

Selection of LIFO versus FIFO by Management

An interesting paradox is evident in Exhibit 9–12. FIFO produces higher inventory and income amounts. However, LIFO results in a higher cash balance because it results in less income tax. If cash flows were the dominant factor, LIFO would be preferred by most companies during periods when inventory costs are expected to increase. If reported income were the dominant factor, most companies would prefer to use FIFO. The table below shows that both methods continue to find wide acceptance.

	Number of Disclosures*					
Methods	**1989**		**1988**		**1987**	
First-in, first-out (FIFO)	401	39.5%	396	38.2%	392	37.3%
Last-in, first-out (LIFO)	366	36.1	379	36.3	393	37.4
Average cost	200	20.7	213	20.6	216	20.6
Other	48	4.7	50	4.9	49	4.7
Total inventory method disclosures	1,015	100.0%	1,038	100.0%	1,050	100.0%

* Some companies use more than one method.
Source: Adapted from AICPA, *Accounting Trends & Techniques, 1990* (New York, 1990), Table 2–8, p. 105.

[13] See G. Biddle and R. Martin, "Inflation, Taxes, and Optimal Inventory Policies," *Journal of Accounting Research*, Spring 1985, pp. 57–83.

Several factors may account for a company's preference for reporting on a FIFO (or other inventory costing) basis rather than LIFO besides the previously mentioned simplicity of record keeping. One such factor is a contractual arrangement, such as a debt agreement, specifying that the borrower must either maintain a certain minimum current ratio (i.e., current assets ÷ current liabilities) or not exceed a certain *maximum* ratio of long-term debt to owners' equity. When inventory prices are rising, the use of FIFO (versus LIFO) increases inventory values, and this, in turn, produces more favorable current and debt-equity ratios.

A second possible factor in the selection of FIFO is that under some management compensation plans, executives receive a bonus based on reported income. Because FIFO (compared to LIFO) increases reported income, when prices are rising, FIFO may increase managers' compensation and, thus, motivate managers to use the FIFO method.[14]

A third possible factor in the selection of FIFO is management's desire to report higher income in the belief that this will lead to higher prices for the company's stock. However, in analyzing a company's reported earnings and earnings projections, investment professionals and experienced traders tend to recognize the use of accounting tactics intended to manipulate reported earnings. As a result, securities market prices today tend not to respond, to the extent that was common, to such company-initiated accounting maneuvers. Arguments suggesting that securities prices are influenced by the choice of cost flow assumption beyond the amount supported by the cost and tax effects is not supported by current research.[15]

A fourth possible factor influencing managers to select FIFO is the anticipation of future inventory declines or inventory liquidations. Because companies cannot easily change accounting methods each year based on current economic conditions, selection of LIFO may result in higher taxable income than FIFO in years in which either inventory costs decline or old, low-cost inventory layers are voluntarily or involuntarily liquidated.[16] Indeed, some industries have witnessed generally falling input prices over numerous periods. An example is the semiconductor industry.

Evaluation of LIFO Cost Method   Despite a continuing worldwide inflationary trend and the pervasiveness of income taxes, the number of companies using LIFO has not increased. In addition to the tax factors, arguments sometimes given for using LIFO are that it provides a matching of current costs with current revenue, and it reflects the usual pricing policy of an enterprise—raise selling prices when replacement cost increases even though goods are still on hand at the old lower cost.

The primary arguments cited *against LIFO* are the following:

* The inventory on the balance sheet is costed at old, out-of-date unit costs.
* It does not precisely match replacement cost with revenue, although LIFO comes closer than FIFO in this regard.
* It is subject to manipulation—profits can be affected by changing usual purchasing patterns (in a period of rapidly rising prices, a company can decrease its reported income by making large purchases at year-end or increase reported income by delaying purchases).

---

[14] However, in a study to test for this effect, the results suggested that "changes to LIFO did not have significant negative effects on executives' compensation." The author indicated that his results may reflect the fact that firms can easily modify their compensation agreements or may continue to use FIFO for computing bonus amounts. He also noted that he studied only firms switching to LIFO. See A. Rashad Abdel-khalik, "The Effects of LIFO-Switching and Firm Ownership on Executives' Pay," *Journal of Accounting Research,* Autumn 1985, pp. 427–48.

[15] See, for example, N. Dopuch and M. Pincus, "Evidence on the Choice of Inventory Accounting Methods: LIFO vs. FIFO, "*Journal of Accounting Research,* Spring 1988, pp. 28–59, and G. Biddle and W. Ricks, "Analysts Forecast Errors and Stock Price Behavior Near the Earnings Announcement Dates of LIFO Adopters," *Journal of Accounting Research,* Autumn 1988, pp. 169–94.

[16] Although the IRS enforces limitations on changing back and forth between LIFO and FIFO, there are a number of cases where multiple switches by a single company have been made.

⁙ It is subject to involuntary inventory liquidation, which can cause reported and taxable income to increase significantly.
⁙ Cost flows do not correspond to the physical flow of goods.
⁙ It is complex and costly to apply.

The tax advantage of LIFO is transitory when old layers of inventory are liquidated. Because LIFO (like FIFO and average cost methods) is based on cost, a company that uses LIFO has the same total pretax income over time as a company that uses FIFO or average cost if all inventory layers are ultimately liquidated. However, to the extent that old layers remain in ending inventory (i.e., are never liquidated), the tax advantage of LIFO remains intact. Therefore the tax advantage of LIFO involves the timing of the recognition of expense (i.e., cost of goods sold), and hence is often advantageous primarily because of the time value of money.

CONCEPT REVIEW

1. What are the arguments for and against the use of LIFO?
2. Under what conditions does LIFO lead to lower taxes?
3. What is a LIFO allowance? When and where would it be found?

DOLLAR VALUE LIFO METHOD

The unit cost approach to LIFO has five problems that affect its use in practice:

1. Liquidation of LIFO inventory layers.
2. The reluctance of companies to use it for internal planning and control purposes.
3. Complications when old products are dropped and new products are introduced.
4. The complexity involved in costing inventory and cost of goods sold differently for interim, year-end, and income tax purposes.
5. The costing of items on a separate (unit) basis is excessively expensive and time-consuming.

These problems have been the primary reasons for the development of an innovative, short-cut way to approximate LIFO results, called the **dollar value LIFO method (DV LIFO).** This method uses dollars and a price index to compute LIFO cost for inventory and cost of goods sold.[17]

Dollar Value LIFO Concepts

The dollar value (DV) LIFO method uses *price indexes* related to the inventory, instead of units and unit costs, and is applied to large groups of products, called *inventory pools*, rather than to each individual product stocked. These features of DV LIFO simplify the application of LIFO because most of the detailed computations of the unit cost LIFO method are avoided.

The purpose of this discussion is to present the basic application of DV LIFO, rather than the complexities that may arise from a wide variety of situations. DV LIFO is widely used in practice.

The term *dollar value* emphasizes that the LIFO inventory each period is determined for *pools of inventory dollars*. Both the units and the unit costs of individual products included in the inventory pool lose their identities.

---

[17] Nearly all companies using the LIFO cost flow assumption apply the method using either dollar value LIFO or the retail method using dollar value LIFO discussed in Chapter 10. See J. Reeve and K. Stanga, "The LIFO Pooling Decision," *Accounting Horizons*, June 1987, pp. 25–33.

Each pool represents a group of different, but related, inventory items that are considered a single entity for inventory accounting purposes. A bakery, for example, might group the following raw materials as one inventory pool:

Raw Material	Quantity	Price Per Pound	Total Cost
Flour	20,000 lb	$1.00	$20,000
Sugar	5,000 lb	.20	1,000
Yeast	1,000 lb	1.00	1,000
Margarine	4,000 lb	.50	2,000
	30,000 lb	$ .80*	$24,000

* Average cost/lb ($24,000 ÷ 30,000 lb)

The commonality among these raw materials is that they are all ingredients used to mix baking dough for bread products. Rather than maintaining four separate inventory accounts, the bakery's internal accounting records would contain but one inventory account, described as follows:

Inventory Pool Name	Quantity	Price Per Pound	Total Cost
Dough ingredients	30,000 lb	$.80	$24,000

For illustration purposes, assume that the above pool represents the bakery's beginning inventory and that the periodic inventory system is being used along with LIFO costing. During the accounting period (calendar year-end 1991), flour, sugar, yeast, and margarine are purchased for inventory at various points and requisitioned out of inventory on a daily basis for use in making bread products. In actual commercial bakery operations, baking ingredients tend to be purchased together and used together in the equivalent of packaged units—a packaged unit consisting of so many pounds of flour, so many pounds of sugar, and so on, in accordance with baking formulas and recipes. Thus, bakery ingredients are well-suited to pooled inventory accounting techniques. Also, the market prices of commercial baking ingredients normally trend up or down together, providing a further rationale for the use of inventory pools.

Based on this data, an accounting of the bakery's cost of goods available for use in making bread products (equivalent to cost of goods available for sale) is given in Exhibit 9–13. Each of the purchase transactions consisted of the same four baking ingredients (flour, sugar, yeast, margarine) that made up the beginning inventory, and in the same general proportions. The price per pound for each purchase is the melded average cost of the ingredients, computed in the same manner used in calculating the price per pound of the beginning inventory.

Assume that now it is the end of the accounting period. Because the periodic inventory system is being used, a physical count of the four baking ingredients is taken, which amounts to an aggregate of 40,000 lb. The next task is to assign a value to both the ending inventory pool (40,000 lb) and the cost of goods used during the period, based on 80,000 lb (120,000 lb − 40,000 lb) of ingredients used in the baking process. Drawing on the price data and assigned cost layers shown in Exhibit 9–13, and remembering that LIFO costing is being used, the cost assignments shown in Exhibit 9–14 can be made.

In summary, the use of inventory pools is first and foremost a labor-saving accounting technique. DV LIFO is used primarily, but not exclusively, by manufacturing companies that must stock large numbers of different inventory items. The Boeing Company, for example, stocks over 250,000 different kinds of inventory items used in the assembly of aircraft (and that doesn't include the jet engines, which are built by outside contractors such as General Electric and Rolls Royce). With

EXHIBIT 9-13   Cost of Goods Available (Bakery Example)

INVENTORY POOL—DOUGH INGREDIENTS
Schedule of
Cost of Ingredients Available for Use in Bread Making
(Cost layers identified for LIFO costing purposes)

Date	Inventory Acquisitions	Quantity	Price Per Pound	Total Cost	Cost Layer Assigned
1–1–91	Beginning inventory	30,000 lb	$.80	$ 24,000	1
2–1–91	Purchase	20,000 lb	.85	17,000	2
5–1–91	Purchase	30,000 lb	.90	27,000	3
9–1–91	Purchase	40,000 lb	.95	38,000	4
12–31–91	Total cost of goods available for use	120,000 lb		$106,000	

EXHIBIT 9-14   Cost of Goods Used and of Ending Inventory (Bakery Example)

Cost of Goods Used during Period (LIFO)

Date	Inventory Pool Element	Quantity	Price Per Pound	Total Cost	Cost Layer Assigned
9–1–91	Purchase	40,000 lb	$.95	$38,000	4
5–1–91	Purchase	30,000 lb	.90	27,000	3
2–1–91	Purchase	10,000 lb	.85	8,500	½ of 2
	Total Cost of goods used during period (LIFO)	80,000 lb	$.92	$73,500	

Costing of Ending Inventory Pool (LIFO)

Date	Inventory Pool Element	Quantity	Price Per Pound	Total Cost	Cost Layer Assigned
2–1–91	Purchase	10,000 lb	$.85	$ 8,500	½ of 2
1–1–91	Beginning inventory	30,000 lb	.80	24,000	1
	Total cost of ending inventory pool (LIFO)	40,000 lb	$.81	$32,500	

inventories of Boeing's size, pools are virtually mandatory as an accounting expedient, despite the widespread use of computer-based inventory systems that alleviate a good portion of the drudgery that comes with tracking, managing, and accounting for an industrial-sized inventory.

Also, inventory pools lessen the problem of LIFO liquidation. Under ideal conditions pooled inventory items are generally expected to be used (or sold; in the case of a wholesaler's or retailer's inventory) in a relative constant proportion to each other. For example, for every 10 units of pooled-item A used, 5 units of pooled-item B and 3 units of pooled-item C are expected to be used. But in practice, individual item usage rates and ratios vary somewhat, and changes in individual item usage can occur unexpectedly. If an unexpected jump in usage of a particular item occurs before the company's buyers have a chance to step-up replacement purchases, there is a risk that inventory stockpiles might be depleted to the point where old, low-cost inventory base layers are used to determine the cost of goods sold. If so, this can raise havoc with corporate profit- and tax-planning strategies being followed by top management.

By pooling inventory items, the risk of a LIFO liquidation in one or more particular items is somewhat reduced, cushioned by the fact that the average cost for the entire pool of items is used in computing the cost of goods sold and ending inventory values. Thus, if one or two items in the pool experience a surge in usage for some reason to the point where low-cost inventory base layers are encroached upon, if the pool is large enough, the average cost of the pool will not be affected as adversely as would be the case if a pool did not exist. However, this advantage is lost if a pool is too small to afford the protection of the average cost, or if the particular item experiencing liquidation constitutes a major portion of the pool.

Unfortunately, individual items in a pool may become outmoded or technologically obsolete, triggering the need for inventory replacements or merchandise upgrades. In the process of making inventory replacements, old items are allowed to run out of stock. From an inventory accounting standpoint, and if the firm is reporting using LIFO, this means that LIFO liquidations occur as requisitions from inventory are matched, of necessity, with low-cost base layers. Once again, pooled inventory techniques may soften the impact of LIFO liquidations, but only temporarily and never fully. Further, inventory replacements go into the pool costed at current market prices, which normally are higher than the cost basis at which the old inventory items are removed. The net impact is a rise in inventory values.

Application of the DV LIFO Method

The DV LIFO method groups a large number of products into each inventory pool, and then uses an inventory *price index* for each year to determine the DV LIFO inventory amount for the pool. LIFO inventory layers are identified by year with the price index for each year instead of in terms of units and unit costs for each separate product.

DV LIFO is not a distinctly different inventory method; rather, it is an approach to convert a FIFO or average inventory amount to LIFO cost. The conversion to LIFO is not recorded internally in the company's accounts. The DV LIFO approach determines the LIFO amounts of the ending inventory and, as a result, cost of goods sold for income tax and external reporting purposes. The company continues to implement and use either the FIFO or average cost results for internal purposes.

The annual price index used for each inventory pool can be derived in either of the two following ways:

1. *Internal index.* An internal index is computed using either the entire FIFO inventory pool or a statistical sample of the inventory pool. Both of these index computations are the same except for the number of products included. The statistical sample approach can be used when determination of detailed unit data for each item in the entire inventory pool is impractical because of technological changes, a wide variety of items, or extreme fluctuations in the variety of items. Statistical sampling uses a representative portion of the inventory pool. Under both approaches, the internal price index for each year is computed by costing the ending inventory in two ways: at current year FIFO cost and at base year FIFO cost. The current year's price index is derived from a ratio of these two costs.

$$\frac{\text{FIFO ending inventory at current year cost}}{\text{FIFO ending inventory at base year cost}} = \frac{\text{Current year inventory}}{\text{price index}}$$

2. *External index.* In situations where neither the entire ending inventory pool nor statistical sampling of the pool is feasible for computing an internal index, an appropriate external price index may be used. This situation often is difficult to justify to the IRS. The selection of an external price index avoids detailed index computations. The use of an external conversion price index in the DV LIFO

method sometimes is called *indexing*. External price indexes are prepared and published by the Bureau of Labor Statistics (BLS).

The *inventory pools* used in DV LIFO may be either:

1. *A single pool.* A single pool is used for the entire company when the company is a manufacturer or processor and overall operations constitute a so-called natural business unit. Thus, an automobile manufacturer may use a single pool that includes raw materials, component parts, work in process, and finished goods. The approach treats the pool as if it were composed of one inventory item.
2. *Multiple pools.* A separate inventory pool is formed for each natural business subunit of the company. Each pool includes a group of inventory items that are similar in respect to raw materials, manufacturing, and distribution. Income tax regulations specify that manufacturers may use either single pool or multiple pools; however, retailers, wholesalers, and jobbers must use multiple pools. For example, a large department store may use separate inventory pools for mens' clothing, ladies' clothing, home appliances, and so on.

A single pool usually is preferred to multiple pools when there is a choice because of simplicity and the lower probability of liquidating a LIFO layer.

Application of the DV LIFO method involves three sequential steps:

1. Identify the inventory pool and then obtain data about the FIFO, or average, cost for the beginning and ending inventories of the current period.
2. Compute a price index relevant to the inventory pool or select an index from an appropriate external source.
3. Restate the ending FIFO, or average cost, inventory (in dollars) to a LIFO basis by using the price index derived in (2) (units and unit cost data are not used).

For illustration, an inventory pool is used that includes only two inventory items. FIFO costing is assumed in the accounts. Two illustrations are provided: Exhibit 9–15, a simplified one-year case with an external price index, and Exhibits 9–16 and 9–17, an extended example with internally computed price indexes by year.

In Exhibit 9–15 the inventory pool already has been defined and the relevant FIFO data are given. The 1991 price index (1.10) was obtained from an external source.

Data for Exhibits 9–15, 9–16, and 9–17:

On January 1, 1991, Alean Corporation changed from FIFO to DV LIFO for income tax and external reporting purposes. The company continued using FIFO in the accounts for internal purposes. 1991 data from the company records were:

	Units	Unit Cost	Total Cost
FIFO inventory (non-LCM):			
January 1, 1991	10,000	$2.00	$20,000
December 31, 1991	10,200	2.20	22,440
Price index for 1990, 1.00, and			
for 1991, 1.10*			

* From an external source.

When the inventory method is changed from FIFO to DV LIFO, the beginning FIFO inventory amount for the year of change is used as the beginning *base year LIFO* inventory amount. It is called the base (or base year) inventory. This process starts on line 1 with the current (1991) ending FIFO inventory of $22,440, which is divided by the 1991 external price index (1.10) (or multiplied by 1.00 ÷ 1.10) to restate it in common base year dollars ($20,400). This restatement removes the 1991 price change (.10, or 10%) from the ending inventory to make it comparable with the 1991 beginning FIFO inventory amount ($20,000). Line 3 is the difference in common (base-year) dollars between the beginning and ending FIFO inventories. Finally, to

EXHIBIT 9-15   Conversion of a FIFO Inventory to a DV LIFO Inventory, Alean Corporation

The conversion of the FIFO ending inventory of $22,440 to a DV LIFO basis of $20,440 is made as follows:

	Inventory at Base Year Cost (in common dollars)*		Conversion Price Index		DV LIFO Cost (in current dollars)
(1) 1991 ending FIFO inventory ($22,440 ÷ 1.10)	$ 20,400				
(2) Base inventory layer (1/1/91)	(20,000)	×	1.00	=	$20,000
(3) 1991 inventory layer added	$ 400	×	1.10	=	440
(4) 1991 DV LIFO ending inventory					$20,440†

* Base year cost in this example is the cost of inventory in terms of prices at the beginning of the first year in which LIFO is used.

† Reported on the income tax return, balance sheet, and income statement.

EXHIBIT 9-16   Inventory Data, XONICS Corporation

	Product A			Product B			Total Amount
	Units	Cost	Total	Units	Cost	Total	
End of 1990 (base year):							
Ending inventory (FIFO)*							
Layer 1	1,000	$1.00	$1,000	2,000	$2.00	$ 4,000	
Layer 2				500	2.20	1,100	
	1,000	$1.00	$1,000	2,500	$2.04	$ 5,100	$6,100
Year 1991 (year of LIFO adoption):							
Purchases†	3,000	$1.20	$3,600	4,000	$2.50	$10,000	
Sales	(2,800)			(3,500)			
Ending inventory: FIFO (internal)	1,200	1.20	1,440	3,000	2.50	7,500	$8,940
Year 1992:							
Purchases†	3,300	1.30	4,290	4,200	2.60	10,920	
Sales	(3,200)			(4,200)			
Ending inventory: FIFO (internal)	1,300	1.30	1,690	3,000	2.60	7,800	$9,490

* Beginning inventory for the year of adoption of LIFO.

† Totals for the year; thus, the unit purchase costs are annual averages.

compute DV LIFO on line 4, line 3 must be multiplied by the current 1991 price index and then added to the base-year inventory to derive the 1991 DV LIFO ending inventory ($20,440) in 1991 dollars. This step is made to state the 1991 layer in terms of 1991 price levels. This ending LIFO inventory amount is reported in the 1991 balance sheet and may be reported in the income statement as a component of the cost of goods sold computation.

An Extended Illustration of DV LIFO

An extended case is given to show the linkage from year to year in both the internal price index computation and the DV LIFO conversion process. This case has an inventory pool that includes two products in a single department.

Consider the following example. On January 1, 1991, the XONICS Corporation

EXHIBIT 9-17 DV LIFO: Computation of Periodic Price Indexes and Conversion from FIFO to DV LIFO, XONICS Corporation

Computation of Price Indexes:

At end of base year 1990 <u>1.000</u>

	Product A	**Product B**	**Total**
End of Year 1991:			
FIFO inventory at current year cost*	1,200 × $1.20 = $1,440	3,000 × $2.50 = $7,500	$8,940
Inventory at base year cost	1,200 × 1.00 = 1,200	3,000 × 2.04 = 6,120	7,320
Price index, 1991; $8,940 ÷ $7,320 = <u>1.221</u>			
End of Year 1992:			
FIFO inventory at current year cost*	1,300 × $1.30 = $1,690	3,000 × $2.60 = $7,800	$9,490
Inventory at base year cost	1,300 × 1.00 = 1,300	3,000 × 2.04 = 6,120	7,420
Price index, 1992; $9,490 ÷ $7,420 = <u>1.279</u>			

* Taken from Exhibit 9–16.

Conversion of FIFO to DV LIFO Inventory:

Conversion schedule at end of 1991:

	Inventory at Base Year Cost	Conversion Price Index	DV LIFO Cost
1991 ending FIFO inventory ($8,940 ÷ 1.221)	$ 7,320		
Base inventory layer	(6,100) ×	1.000	= $6,100
Difference: 1991 additional layer	$ 1,220 ×	1.221	= 1,490
1991 DV LIFO ending inventory			$7,590

Conversion schedule at end of 1992:

	Inventory at Base Year Cost	Conversion Price Index	DV LIFO Cost
1992 ending FIFO inventory ($9,490 ÷ 1.279)	$ 7,420		
Base inventory layer	(6,100) ×	1.000	= $6,100
1991 inventory layer	(1,220) ×	1.221	= 1,490
Difference: 1992 additional layer	$ 100 ×	1.279	= 128
1992, DV LIFO ending inventory			$7,718

changed from FIFO to DV LIFO for income tax and external reporting purposes. XONICS Corporation will continue using FIFO in its accounts and for internal purposes. XONICS has one inventory pool comprising two products, A and B. The 1990, 1991, and 1992 FIFO inventory costs were taken directly from the FIFO inventory records shown in Exhibit 9–16.

An internal price index is computed each year based on the FIFO inventory data taken directly from the inventory records. This computation uses the formula given on page (436). For example, the computation in this case for year 1991 is:

$$\left\{ \begin{array}{l} \text{FIFO ending inventory} \\ \text{at } \textit{current year } \text{cost} \\ \text{from the inventory} \\ \text{records, \$8,940} \\ \text{(Exhibit 9–16)} \end{array} \right\} \div \left\{ \begin{array}{l} \text{FIFO ending inventory} \\ \text{at } \textit{base year } \text{cost,} \\ \text{\$7,320 (Exhibit 9–17)} \end{array} \right\} \begin{array}{l} \text{Current year} \\ = \text{price index,} \\ 1.221 \end{array}$$

This computation holds units constant, and the price is the variable. Therefore, it measures the ratio (or percentage) that prices increased. The conversion process then starts (Exhibit 9–17), with common or constant dollars to measure the inventory layers. Next, these common dollars, by inventory layer, are restated in current dollars by using the annual price index that corresponds to each layer.

Exhibit 9–17 shows the computation of the price indexes for 1991 and 1992. For convenience, the ending inventory for the year prior to the adoption of LIFO, which is also the beginning inventory for the year of adoption, usually is assigned an index of 1.000. Under the conversion price index column in Exhibit 9–17, the base year inventory is always related to 1.000. The computed internal indexes are used in exactly the same way in the conversion process as in Exhibit 9–15 for external price indexes. Exhibit 9–17 shows the conversion process for each year, 1991 and 1992.

In Exhibit 9–17, all prior inventory layers were retained in both 1991 and 1992. This was because the total inventory in base-year dollars increased each year— $6,100 to $7,320 in 1991, and to $7,420 in 1992. Also, notice that the price indexes for prior years are never changed.

When the total inventory decreases, some (or part) of the layers of prior years are used, and the LIFO assumption is that they are used in inverse order; that is, the last layer is used first, and so forth. To illustrate, assume that the total FIFO inventory for 1992 was $8,900 (instead of $9,490). That is, assume the FIFO inventory decreased from $8,940 to $8,900. Under this assumption, no 1992 layer was added; in fact, some of the 1991 layer was used. This assumption would result in a DV LIFO ending inventory for 1992 of $7,149.

Year 1992	Inventory at Base Year Cost	Conversion Price Index	DV LIFO Cost
1992 ending FIFO inventory ($8,900 ÷ 1.279)*	$ 6,959		
Base inventory layer	(6,100)	× 1.000	$6,100
1991 inventory layer ($6,959 − $6,100)	(859)	× 1.221	1,049
Difference: 1992 additional layer	$ –0–		–0–
1992 DV LIFO ending inventory			$7,149

* Assumes same composition of items as in original example.

No 1992 layer was added. A good portion of the 1991 layer was sold, and the base inventory layer remained the same. Since no 1992 layer was added, there will never be a 1992 layer in the future. A layer once reduced or eliminated, or not originally established in its current year, will never be restored or established. Also, any decrease in inventory is always taken out in LIFO order; that is, starting with the most recent layer and working backward in time. To reemphasize, the original price indexes used for prior years are never changed.

Exhibit 9–18 compares the FIFO and the DV LIFO inventory and cost of goods sold results for 1992 using Exhibits 9–16 and 9–17. The comparison reflects a lower 1992 ending inventory amount and a higher 1992 cost of goods sold amount for DV LIFO than for FIFO, as would be expected when inventory costs are rising. This difference causes lower pretax income and lower income tax under DV LIFO.

Advantages of DV LIFO

DV LIFO has three major advantages:

1. DV LIFO reduces the probability of liquidating an old LIFO layer of inventory for specific items. When LIFO ending inventory is less than beginning inventory, older costs from prior periods are reflected in cost of goods sold. When prices are rising, this inventory liquidation can cause a significant decrease in cost of goods sold and increase in reported income, relative to normal LIFO results, in the absence of liquidation. Because the tax consequences of LIFO liquidation can be severe, companies often apply LIFO costing to inventory pools to reduce the

EXHIBIT 9-18 FIFO and DV LIFO Results Compared, XONICS Corporation

| | Year 1992—Cost of Goods Sold Compared | |
	FIFO—for Internal Purposes	DV LIFO—for External Purposes
Beginning inventory	$ 8,940	$ 7,590
Purchases	15,210	15,210
Total	24,150	22,800
Ending inventory	(9,490)	(7,718)
Cost of goods sold	$14,660	$15,082

probability of liquidation. The logic of the pool concept is that the amounts of some items within an inventory pool may increase and the amounts of other items may decrease. If the size of the pool is stable or increasing, liquidation will not occur for the pool.

2. DV LIFO reduces the accounting cost of applying LIFO, despite the seeming complexity in these examples. The complexity of applying LIFO to individual units may not have been apparent in the illustrations in the introductory unit cost examples. When applied to many different types of items (each type of which can be represented by thousands of individual items), the accounting costs are significant and the chance for error large. In contrast, the application of LIFO to pools of similar items reduces accounting costs by reducing the level of detail.

3. FIFO or average cost can still be used for internal purposes.

Variations in Computing the Conversion Price Index   Two variations of the DV LIFO method are known as (1) the double-extension and (2) the link-chain approaches.[18] The presentations in this chapter are based on the double-extension approach.

The term *double-extension* is based on the fact that under DV LIFO, the ending inventory each period must be double costed (i.e., at base year costs and at current year costs).

Technological Changes in LIFO Inventories   The problem caused by technological changes in LIFO inventories can be viewed as a special case of inventory liquidation. As technology advances, older products and product lines are dropped, and new products are added. When LIFO is applied using the unit cost approach and liquidation of older LIFO layers occurs, the older costs are moved out of inventory to cost of goods sold. The effect of this liquidation is mitigated under DV LIFO because of the grouping of inventory into pools: newer units replace the older obsolete units.

CONCEPT REVIEW

1. What is the purpose of the DV LIFO method?
2. What is an inventory pool?
3. What are the advantages of a DV LIFO system?

---

[18] The link-chain method is designed for restrictive situations in which the double-extension method is not satisfactory, such as significant technological changes in the inventory. An example is the change in automobile technology that has taken place over time. The concept is the same and, hence, the method is not discussed here.

SUMMARY OF KEY POINTS

♦

(L.O. 1) 1. Inventories are assets consisting of goods owned by the business and held for future sale or for use in the manufacture of goods for sale.

(L.O. 2) 2. Cost at acquisition is used to value inventory and includes the costs to obtain the inventory such as insurance and freight.

(L.O. 2) 3. All goods owned at the inventory date, including those on consignment, should be counted and valued.

(L.O. 3) 4. Either a periodic or a perpetual inventory system may be used, but computer technology makes it easy and less costly to use a perpetual system, which provides up-to-date inventory records.

(L.O. 4) 5. Several cost flow assumptions are in current use, including specific identification, average cost, LIFO, and FIFO.

(L.O. 4) 6. Tax considerations and inflation expectations in a firm's factor markets are important in the choice among cost flow alternatives.

(L.O. 4) 7. LIFO has several disadvantages, including that of increased recordkeeping requirements, that cause many firms to use other cost flow assumptions.

(L.O. 4) 8. The liquidation of LIFO layers can lead to higher income and taxes because lower cost items are expensed. (Firms using LIFO for taxes must also prepare their financial reports using LIFO.)

(L.O. 5) 9. DV LIFO is the most common method of applying LIFO in practice because it reduces the recordkeeping costs dramatically, allows a firm to retain FIFO or average cost for internal purposes, and reduces the frequency of LIFO layer liquidations.

(L.O. 5) 10. DV LIFO groups large numbers of similar products into pools and then establishes the pool's value using an inventory price index.

(L.O. 5) 11. DV LIFO is used to convert an ending inventory value, based on either FIFO or average cost, to a LIFO cost value.

(L.O. 6) 12. The JIT, standard costing, and variable costing approaches to inventory valuation are not GAAP. They are used internally for control and decision making.

REVIEW PROBLEM

♦

Bay City Explosives bought and sold the following items in January for cash:

```
Cash: January 1 balance  . . . . . . . . . . . . . . . . . . . . . . . . . . . . . . . . . . $21
Bought: 1 barrel of powder, January 2  . . . . . . . . . . . . . . . . . . . . . . . . $15
Sold: 1 barrel of powder, January 30  . . . . . . . . . . . . . . . . . . . . . . . . . $20
Bought: 1 barrel of powder, January 31 . . . . . . . . . . . . . . . . . . . . . . . . $18
```

1. Using FIFO, LIFO, and the average cost method, determine Bay City's inventory value and income for January. Assume a periodic inventory system.
2. What profit did Bay City make in January?
3. What dividend could Bay City pay for January without contracting the size of the business?

SOLUTION

♦

1.

	FIFO	LIFO	Average Cost
Inventory value	$18	$15	$16.50
Income:			
Sales	$20	$20	$20.00
Cost of sales	15	18	16.50
Income	$ 5	$ 2	$ 3.50

2. Bay City's profits could be measured by any one of the three income measures calculated in (1) above. This result illustrates the difficulty of comparing the incomes of companies using different accounting methods.

3. Deciding what dividend would not cause Bay City to contract in size is more complex. One answer would be to pay out the income earned, which depends on the cost flow assumption used.

After purchasing the barrel of powder on January 31, the firm has $8 in cash remaining:

$$\$21 - \$15 + \$20 - \$18 = \$8$$

After paying out cash equal to its January earnings, Bay City would have cash under each alternative as follows:

FIFO	LIFO	Average Cost
$3	$6	$4.50

Bay City would also have one barrel of powder. If Bay City pays its $2 of LIFO earnings as a dividend, the firm would have cash of $6 left and one barrel of powder. This result is equivalent to having $21 in cash January 1, which was used at that time to buy one barrel of powder at the price of $15, leaving $6 in cash.

But if the firm is initially viewed as having $21 in value on January 1, and if the current barrel is valued at $18, its most recent cost, rather than the historical cost of $15, then $5 could be paid out, leaving $3 in cash and $18 in powder, a total of $21 in value ($3 + $18). This approach pays a dividend equal to the FIFO earnings.

Still another answer, based on an opportunity cost approach, would support Bay City paying a dividend of only $.80. The cost of a barrel of powder has risen from $15 to $18, an increase of 20% over the month. If the initial assets of the firm (cash of $21) must, therefore, also increase by 20% for the firm to be undiminished economically, Bay City's asset values must increase to 1.20 ($21) = $25.20 by the end of January. To do so requires cash of $7.20 to add to the barrel's value of $18. The firm has only $8 in cash on January 31. Therefore, the firm could pay a dividend of only $.80. If the barrel of powder is valued at its current selling price of $20, Bay City's assets are worth $8 + $20 = $28, permitting a dividend of $2.80 to be paid without contracting the company.

APPENDIX: *Additional Cost Flow Methods*

This appendix discusses three inventory cost methods used less often than average cost, FIFO, LIFO, and specific identification. The three methods discussed are JIT (just-in-time) costing, standard costing, and variable, (or direct) costing. These methods are not allowed under GAAP, but they are discussed in this supplement because they are used for internal accounting purposes.

Just-in-Time Inventory Systems

Just-in-time (JIT) inventory systems are a response to the high costs associated with stockpiling inventories of raw materials, parts, supplies, and finished goods. Rather than keep ample quantities on hand awaiting use, the idea is to reduce inventories to the lowest levels possible and thus save costs. As the name suggests, the ultimate goal is to see goods and materials arrive at the company's receiving dock *just in time* to be moved directly to the plant's production floor for immediate use in the manufacturing or assembly process. Then, taking the concept one step further, finished goods roll off the production floor and move directly to the shipping dock *just in time* for shipment to the customers. The net impact, zero inventory levels and zero inventory costs, in theory.

Physical Inventory Management   In practice, inventories are still maintained under JIT systems, but at substantially diminished levels. Minimum inventories are needed. If inventory levels are kept too lean, an unexpected surge in business can cause the company to run out of stock, thus causing production to stop and, perhaps, failure to meet an order. Or a bad batch of defective parts might be encountered, causing a work suspension.

Like other inventory systems, the success of a JIT system depends on how well it is conceived and implemented for a particular production setting (or selling situation—JIT techniques apply to merchandise inventories carried by retail outlets as well). Purely from a management standpoint, inventory problems shift from the cost of stockpiling production parts and materials needs—one week's expected needs or one month's or whatever—to coordinating and logistically marshalling the inventory to meet production needs. To illustrate using the extreme, under a JIT system some of the inventory may be in-house (today's needs), some of it may be in transit to the plant (tomorrow's needs), some of it may be in the process of being fabricated or otherwise finished by the supplier (the day after tomorrow's needs), and some of it may not have been ordered yet (next week's needs). Extremes aside, minimal inventory levels normally result in reduced need for storage space, materials moving and handling equipment, property and casualty insurance coverage, and materials obsolescence or deterioration.

JIT Inventory Accounting Practices   JIT systems tend to result in simplified inventory accounting procedures primarily because inventory levels are kept low, but also because raw materials and work-in process inventories are combined, in many cases. Hewlett Packard Corporation is an example. Raw materials are charged to a combined account and then transferred to finished goods upon completion of production.[19]

JIT systems also affect the way companies account for production costs. Conversion costs (labor and direct overhead costs) are charged directly to the cost of goods sold account as a matter of expediency. The working premise is that almost everything being produced is in response to orders from customers. Therefore, all conversion costs are charged to the cost of goods sold account and charge backs are made (finished items not sold or unfinished items still in production as of the end of the accounting period) to finished goods or work in process inventories, respectively. In effect, JIT systems work backwards in relationship to traditional inventory accounting systems. Under traditional systems, the cost of goods sold is derived from inventory balances. Under the JIT system, the cost of goods sold is the starting point for determining the inventory balances as of the end of the accounting period.

To illustrate the workings of a typical JIT inventory accounting system, assume the following facts about a particular manufacturing process and the resulting accounting entries:

Manufacturing Facts and Transactions

1. The company purchases 420 lb of raw materials @ $8/lb ($3,360) at the start of a production cycle. All or nearly all of these materials are expected to be used during the current production cycle (based on sales estimates) at the rate of 2 lb per finished unit.

2. Working from sales estimates of slightly more than 200 units, the plant manager authorizes a production run of 210 units. As of the end of the accounting period, labor charges (conversion costs) at the rate of $10/hr amounting to 103 hours ($1,030) are attributable to this production run.

3. As of the end of the accounting period, 200 units of the 210-unit production run are fully assembled and ready for shipment to customers.

Corresponding Accounting Entries

Work-in-process inventory 3,360
    Accounts payable   3,360
To record purchase of 420 lb of raw materials @ $8/lb for current production run needs.

Cost of goods sold 1,030
    Conversion costs   1,030
To close conversion costs (labor charges of 103 hr @ $10/hr) to cost of goods sold as of the end of current accounting period. (Conversion costs is a temporary holding account for labor and overhead.)

Finished goods inventory 3,200
    Work-in-process inventory   3,200
To transfer material costs on 200 units to finished goods at rate of 2 lb × $8/lb × 200 units.

---

[19] B. Newmann and P. Jaouen, "Kanban, Zips and Cost Accounting: A Case Study," *Journal of Accountancy,* August 1986, pp. 132–41.

Manufacturing Facts and Transactions

4. As of the end of the accounting period, 190 units of the 200 units in finished goods inventory have been sold.

5. As of the end of the accounting period, conversion costs (labor charges) applicable to production run units not sold and other runs still not complete are determined to be:
   —Finished goods inventory—5 hr @ $10/hr ($50).
   —Work in process inventory—3 hr @ $10/hr ($30).

Corresponding Accounting Entries

Cost of goods sold	3,040	
Finished goods inventory		3,040

To transfer material costs on 190 units to cost of goods sold at the rate of 2 lb × $8/lb × 190 units.

Finished goods inventory	50	
Work-in-process inventory	30	
Cost of goods sold		80

To transfer conversion (labor) costs from cost of goods sold to finished goods (5 hr @ $10/hr) and work in process (3 hr @ $10/hr).

The events just described can be shown using T-accounts:

Work-In-Process Inventory

1.	3,360	3.		3,200
5.	30			
Balance	190			

Accounts Payable

	1.	3,360

Finished Goods Inventory

3.	3,200	4.		3,040
5.	50			
Balance	210			

Conversion Costs

	2.	1,030

Cost of Goods Sold

2	1,030			
4.	3,040	5.		80
Balance	3,990			

The appeal of JIT and other systems based on keeping physical inventories at the lowest possible level appears to be growing as companies seek better ways to reduce investments in inventory assets and encourage production efficiencies and on-time product delivery to customers. 3M Corporation, for example, observed in a recent annual report that a JIT system installed in one of its plants increased total production capacity by 15%.

Standard Cost Method

In manufacturing entities using a standard cost system, the inventories are valued, recorded, and reported for internal purposes on the basis of a standard unit cost. The standard cost approximates an ideal or expected cost. Its use prevents the overstatement of inventory values because it excludes from inventory those losses and expenses due to inefficiency, waste, and abnormal conditions. Under this method, the differences between actual cost (which includes losses due to inefficiencies, etc.) and standard cost (which excludes losses due to inefficiencies, etc.) are recorded in separate variance accounts. These accounts are written off as a current period loss rather than capitalized in inventory. Standard costing may be applied to raw materials, work in process, and finished goods inventories. Standard costing is used more often in manufacturing situations because of its usefulness for cost control. To

EXHIBIT 9A-1   Standard cost method

Results for the period:

Purchases at actual cost:

10,000 units at $1.10	$11,000	
2,000 units at $.95	1,900	
Total		$12,900

Issues at standard cost:

8,000 units at $1	8,000	

Ending inventory at standard cost:

4,000 units at $1	4,000	12,000

Raw materials purchase price variance (debit—charged
against current income as a loss) ($1,000 − $100) . . . . $ 900

illustrate, assume a manufacturing company has just adopted standard cost procedures and that the beginning inventory is zero. During the current period, the company makes two purchases and one issuance and records them as follows:

1. To record the purchase of 10,000 units of raw material at $1.10 actual cost; standard cost has been established at $1:

Raw materials (10,000 units × $1)	10,000	
Raw materials purchase price variance (10,000 units × $.10) . .	1,000	
Accounts payable (10,000 units × $1.10)		11,000

2. To record issuance of 8,000 units of raw material to the factory for processing:

Material in process	8,000	
Raw materials (8,000 units × $1)		8,000

3. To record the purchase of 2,000 units of raw materials at 95 cents:

Raw materials (2,000 units × $1)	2,000	
Raw materials purchase price variance (2,000 units × $.05) .		100
Accounts payable (2,000 units × $.95)		1,900

Under the standard cost method procedures shown in Exhibit 9A-1 for raw material, there would be no need to consider inventory flow methods (such as LIFO, FIFO, and average) because only one cost—standard cost—appears in the records. In addition, perpetual inventory records could be maintained in units because all issues and inventory valuations are at the same standard cost. Because standard cost represents a departure from the cost principle it is *not* acceptable under GAAP.[20] Therefore, for external reporting, the standard cost inventory usually is restated by applying one of the generally accepted methods discussed in the chapter. Standard costs are widely used for internal management planning and control. A detailed discussion of standard cost procedures can be found in any cost accounting textbook.

Variable, or Direct, Cost Method

For internal management planning and control purposes, the concept of variable, or direct, costing often is used in manufacturing companies. Under this concept, fixed costs (those that relate to time, such as depreciation) and variable costs (those that vary with productive activities, such as direct material and direct labor) are segregated. This separation is useful for internal management planning and control. One important aspect of this concept is that the cost of goods manufactured is the sum of the variable costs only. These costs include direct materials, direct labor, and variable manufacturing overhead. All fixed costs, including fixed manufacturing overhead, are treated as period costs and are deducted when incurred from

---

[20] Standard cost figures may be used if the effect on inventory values is not material.

revenues of the period rather than being capitalized and carried forward in inventory. Hence, fixed costs are not reported as part of cost of inventory or cost of goods sold.

Valuation of inventories at only variable production costs, although useful for internal management purposes, is *not* GAAP for external financial reporting purposes. Also, it cannot be used for tax purposes except in special circumstances. Therefore, for external reporting and tax purposes, companies using variable costing internally convert the inventory and cost of goods sold to actual cost by using the other costing methods discussed in this chapter and including fixed overhead.

KEY TERMS

Average cost method (420)
Dollar value LIFO (433)
Finished goods inventory (404)
First-in, first-out method (421)
FOB (free on board) destination (406)
FOB shipping point (406)
Goods out on consignment (406)
Inventories (403)
Last-in, first-out method (423)
LIFO allowance (428)
LIFO conformity rule (424)

Manufacturing inventory (404)
Manufacturing supplies inventory (404)
Merchandise inventory (404)
Miscellaneous inventories (404)
Periodic inventory system (407)
Perpetual inventory system (407)
Raw materials inventory (404)
Specific cost identification method (419)
Work-in-process inventory (404)

QUESTIONS

1. In general, why should accountants and management be concerned with inventories?
2. List and briefly explain the usual inventory classifications for a trading entity and a manufacturing entity.
3. What general rule is applied by accountants in determining what goods should be included in inventory? How does the location of inventory affect this rule?
4. Complete the following:

	Include in Inventory	
	Yes	No
a. Goods held by our agents for us.	___	___
b. Goods held by us for sale on commission.	___	___
c. Goods held by us but awaiting return to vendor because of damaged condition.	___	___
d. Goods returned to us from buyer, reason unknown to date.	___	___
e. Goods out on consignment.	___	___
f. Goods held on consignment.	___	___
g. Merchandise at our branch for sale.	___	___
h. Merchandise at conventions for display purposes.	___	___

5. Assume you are in the process of adjusting and closing the books at the end of the accounting period (for the purchaser of inventory). For inventory purposes, how would you treat the following goods in transit?
   a. Invoice received for $10,000, shipped FOB shipping point.
   b. Invoice received for $18,000, shipped FOB destination.
   c. Invoice received for $6,000, shipped FOB shipping point and delivery refused on the last day of the period because of damaged condition.
6. Explain the principal features of a periodic inventory system.
7. Why is cost of goods sold sometimes characterized as a residual amount? In which inventory system is this characterization appropriate?
8. Which of the following items should be included in determining the unit cost for inventory purposes?
   a. Purchase returns.
   b. Cash discounts on credit purchases.
   c. Freight on goods purchased.
9. Should cash discounts on credit purchases be *(a)* deducted in part on the income statement and in part from inventory on the balance sheet or *(b)* deducted in total on the

income statement for the period in which the discounts arose? Assume that three fourths of the goods purchased were sold by year-end. Explain.

10. What is meant by the accounting value of inventory? What accounting principles predominate in measuring this value?

11. Assuming the LIFO method, what is meant by inventory liquidation? Why is it a serious problem for LIFO but not FIFO?

12. What are the primary purposes to be considered in selecting a particular inventory cost flow method? Why is the selection important?

13. Briefly explain the differences between periodic and perpetual inventory systems. Under what circumstances is each generally used?

14. Does the adoption of a perpetual inventory system eliminate the need for a physical count or measurement of inventories? Explain.

15. Explain the specific cost inventory method and explain when the method is not appropriate.

16. Distinguish between a weighted average and a moving average in determining inventory unit cost. When is each generally used? Explain.

17. Explain the essential features of first-in, first-out (FIFO). What are the primary advantages and disadvantages of FIFO? Explain the difference in the application of FIFO under periodic and perpetual inventory systems. In contrast with LIFO, how does FIFO affect cash flow?

18. Explain the essential features of last-in, first-out (LIFO). What are the primary advantages and disadvantages of LIFO? Explain the differences in application of LIFO under the periodic and perpetual inventory systems.

19. What is meant by inventory layers? Why are they significant with respect to the FIFO and LIFO methods?

20. Compare the balance sheet and income statement effects of FIFO versus LIFO when prices are rising and when prices are falling.

21. Explain why a company's management may be reluctant to use LIFO in a period of rising inventory costs even though such use would reduce the company's current income tax liability.

22. What is meant by the unit cost LIFO method? What type of entity would be most likely to use unit cost (versus dollar value) LIFO?

23. In describing a company's inventory position, the phrase *LIFO Reserve* is sometimes used. What is meant by LIFO Reserve? What alternative phrase is more appropriate?

24. Which accounting method leads to "inventory profits" in a rising-cost market? In a declining-cost market?

25. During the 1980s, which industry was more likely to use LIFO to achieve tax savings?
   a. Consumer electronics manufacturers.
   b. Real estate holding companies.

26. If the Bureau of Labor Statistics computes a price index of 1.15 for a merchandise pool with a base-year value of $200,000, why might XONICS Corporation record a DV LIFO amount of $250,000 for this merchandise pool?

EXERCISES

E 9–1
Items to Include in Inventory: Classification, Correction
(L.O. 2)

On December 31, 1991, Simpco computed an ending inventory valuation of $250,000 based on a periodic inventory system. The accounts for 1991 have been adjusted and closed. Subsequently, the independent auditor located several discrepancies in the 1991 ending inventory. These were discussed with the company accountant who then prepared the following schedule:

a. Merchandise in store (at 50% above cost) $250,000
b. Merchandise out on consignment at sales price
　　(including markup of 60% on selling price) 10,000
c. Goods held on consignment from Davis Electronics at sales price
　　(sales commission, 20% of sales price, included) 3,000
d. Goods purchased, in transit (shipped FOB shipping point,
　　estimated freight, not included, $600), invoice price 5,000
e. Goods out on approval, sales price, $1,500, cost, $1,000 1,500
　　Total inventory as corrected $269,500

Average income tax rate, 40%.

Required:

1. The auditor did not agree with the "corrected" inventory amount of $269,500. Compute the correct ending inventory amount (show computations) by modifying the corrected balance of $269,500.
2. List the items on the income statement and balance sheet for 1991 that should be corrected for the above errors; give the amount of the error in the balance of each item affected.
3. The accounts have been closed for 1991. Therefore, a correcting entry in January 1992 is needed. Give the required correcting entry.

E 9–2

Perpetual and Periodic Inventory: Income Statement, Closing Entries

(L.O. 1)

The records of Ferris Fashions reflected the following data for 1991: sales revenue, $200,000; purchases $140,000; net income as a percentage of sales revenue, 15%; beginning inventory, $25,000; and expenses including income tax, $45,000. The tax rate for 1991 is 25%.

Required:

1. Reconstruct the income statement. Assume a periodic inventory system.
2. Give the required journal entries at the end of the period for the inventories and the closing entries for revenues and expenses; assume in Case A a periodic inventory system, and in Case B a perpetual inventory system.

E 9–3

Periodic and Perpetual Inventory: Journal Entries

(L.O. 3)

The records for Cummings Company at December 31, 1991, reflected the following:

	Units	Unit Price
Sales during period (for cash)	10,000	$10 (sales price)
Inventory at beginning of period	2,000	6 (cost)
Merchandise purchased during period (for cash)	16,000	6 (cost)
Purchase returns during period (cash refund)	100	6 (cost)
Inventory at end of period	?	6 (cost)
Total expenses (excluding cost of goods sold), $30,000		

Required:

In parallel columns, give entries for the above transactions, including all entries at the end of the period, assume in Case A a periodic inventory system; and in Case B a perpetual inventory system. Use the following format:

Accounts	Case A	Case B

E 9–4

Credit Purchases Recorded Net versus Gross

(L.O. 2)

Belmonte Boot Company purchased merchandise on credit for $60,000; terms 2/10, n/30. Payment was made within the discount period. At the end of the reporting period, one fourth of this merchandise was unsold. Belmonte's tax rate is 40%.

Required:

Determine (1) the cost of goods sold that would be reported on the income statement and (2) the ending inventory valuation for this particular lot of merchandise assuming:

a. Purchases and accounts payable are recorded at gross, and cash discounts are deducted in total from purchases on the income statement.
b. Purchases and accounts payable both are recorded at net.
c. Purchases and accounts payable are recorded at gross, and cash discounts are reported on the income statement as other income.

Evaluate the three approaches. Which approach is preferable conceptually? Why?

E 9–5

Credit Purchases: Net versus Gross, Entries

(L.O. 2)

Largent Corporation purchased merchandise on credit for $50,000; terms 2/15, n/30. Payment for one half of the recorded liability was made during the discount period; the balance was paid after the discount period. The company uses a perpetual inventory system.

Required:

Give entries in parallel columns to record for purchase and payments on the liability assuming:
a. The net of discount approach is used for cash discounts.
b. The gross amount is used for cash discounts.

Which approach is preferable conceptually? Why?

E 9–6
Perpetual Inventory: Shortage, Entries
(L.O. 3)

Perforated Pipe Company uses a perpetual inventory system. The items on hand are inventoried on a rotation basis throughout the year so that all items are checked twice each year. At the end of the year, the following data relating to goods on hand are available:

Product	From Perpetual Inventory Units	Unit Cost	From Physical Count (Units)
A	450	$12	390
B	1,500	5	1,520
C	2,000	4	1,950
D	8,000	2	7,980
E	13,000	6	13,100

Required:

Determine the amount of the net inventory overage or shortage and give the adjustment to the perpetual inventory records. Give any entry needed to record the final disposition of any discrepancy. (Note: An inventory shortage is a loss.)

E 9–7
Inventory Cost with a Rebate
(L.O. 1)

Volume Stores, Inc., a dealer in radio and television sets, buys large quantities of a television model that costs $400. The contract reads that if 100 or more are purchased during the year, a rebate of $20 per set will be made. On December 15, the records showed that 150 sets had been purchased and that 50 more were ordered FOB destination. The sets were received on December 22, and a request for the rebate was made. The rebate check was received on January 20 after Volume's books were closed.

Required:

1. At what valuation should the inventory be shown on December 31? Why?
2. What entry should be made relative to the rebate on December 31? Why?
3. What entry would be made on January 20? Why?

E 9–8
Manufacturing Inventory Accounts
(L.O. 4)

Assume the following information for Murphy Manufacturing during 1991:

	1/1/91	12/31/91
Raw materials inventory	$10,400	$14,600
Work-in-process inventory	28,100	31,300
Finished goods inventory	15,700	12,500

In addition, direct labor and manufacturing overhead totalled $364,600, and cost of goods manufactured equaled $461,200 in 1991.

Required:

Calculate the correct amounts for raw materials purchased, raw materials used, and cost of goods sold for 1991.

E 9–9
Inventory and CGS; Five Cost Methods
(L.O. 2)

The inventory records of Acme Appliances showed the following data relative to a food processor item in inventory (assume the transactions occurred in the order given):

Transaction	Units	Unit Cost
1. Inventory	30	$19.00
2. Purchase	45	20.00
3. Sale	50	
4. Purchase	50	20.80
5. Sale	50	
6. Purchase	50	21.60

Required:

Compute the cost of goods sold for the period and the ending inventory assuming the following (round unit costs to nearest cent):
a. Weighted averaged (periodic inventory system).
b. Moving average (perpetual inventory system).

c. FIFO.
d. LIFO (unit basis, 30 units in base layer, periodic inventory system).
e. LIFO (unit basis, 30 units in base layer, perpetual inventory system).

E 9–10
Inventory and CGS: Four Cost Methods
(L.O. 4)

The inventory records of Gilman Company provided the following data for one item of merchandise for sale (assume the six transactions occurred in the order of the number given):

	Units	Unit Cost	Total Amount
Goods available for sale:			
Beginning inventory	500	$6.00	$ 3,000
(1) Purchases	600	6.10	3,660
(2) Sales	900		
(3) Purchases	600	6.20	3,720
(4) Sales	500		
(5) Purchases	400	6.30	2,520
(6) Sales	300		
Available for sale	2,100		$12,900

Required:

1. Complete the following schedule (round unit costs to nearest cent and total amounts to nearest dollar):

	Valuation	
Costing method	Ending Inventory	Cost Goods Sold
a. FIFO	$_____	$_____
b. LIFO (unit cost basis, periodic inventory system, assume base inventory is 500 units)	$_____	$_____
c. Weighted average	$_____	$_____
d. LIFO (same as [b] except perpetual inventory system)	$_____	$_____

2. Compute the amount of pretax income and rank the methods in order of the amount of pretax income (highest first) assuming FIFO pretax income is $50,000.
3. Which method is preferable in this instance? Explain your choice.

E 9–11
Inventory and CGS: Five Cost Methods
(L.O. 4)

The College Store inventory records showed the following data relative to a particular item sold regularly (assume transactions in the order given):

Transaction	Units	Unit Cost
1. Inventory	2,000	$5.00
2. Purchases	18,000	5.20
3. Sales (at $13 per unit)	7,000	
4. Purchases	6,000	5.50
5. Sales (at $13.50 per unit)	16,000	
6. Purchases	3,000	6.00

Required:

1. Complete the following schedule (round unit costs to nearest cent and total costs of inventory to the nearest $10):

	Ending Inventory	Cost of Goods Sold	Gross Margin
a. FIFO	____	____	____
b. Weighted average	____	____	____
c. LIFO (unit cost basis, periodic inventory system, 2,000 units in base layer)	____	____	____
d. LIFO (unit cost basis, perpetual inventory system, 2,000 units in base layer)	____	____	____
e. Moving average (show computations)	____	____	____

E 9–12
Ending Inventory: Three
Cost Methods
(L.O. 4)

Lorie Company was formed on December 1, 1991. The following information is available from the company's inventory records for hair blow dryers:

	Units	Unit Cost
January 1, 1992 (beginning inventory)	800	$ 9.00
Purchases:		
January 5, 1992	1,500	10.00
January 25, 1992	1,200	10.50
February 16, 1992	600	11.00
March 26, 1992	900	11.50

A physical inventory taken on March 31, 1992, showed 1,500 units on hand. Lorie uses a periodic inventory system.

Required:

Prepare schedules to compute the ending inventory at March 31, 1992, under each of the following inventory flow methods: FIFO, LIFO, and weighted average. Show supporting computations.

E 9–13
Inventory: Tax
Implications
(L.O. 4)

The owner of Valley Cyclery wants to maximize after-tax cash flows and is considering switching from FIFO. Assume the following data is available for the first quarter of 1992:

	Units	Unit Cost
January 1, 1992 (beginning inventory)	30	$200
Purchases:		
January 15, 1992	40	205
February 12, 1992	50	188
March 19, 1992	40	210

Sales for the quarter totaled 110 units. A physical inventory taken on March 31, 1992, showed 50 units on hand. Valley uses the periodic inventory method.

Required:

Which of the following inventory flow methods would you recommend Valley use to produce the greatest after-tax cash flows? Weighted average, FIFO, or LIFO. Show any supporting calculations.

E 9–14
LIFO Liquidation
(L.O. 4)

Chloride Chemical's lube oil storage facility was shut down due to a strike in December 1991, resulting in a drastic reduction in inventory. The firm had switched to LIFO effective January 1, 1991. Assume the following data:

	Units	Unit Cost
Beginning inventory (Base layer of LIFO—1/1/91)	20,000	$1.00
Lube oil purchases during 1991	450,000	1.25
Total available for sale	470,000	
Sales (costed on LIFO basis) from:		
Purchases	450,000	1.25
Base inventory layer	10,000	1.00
Total	460,000	
Ending inventory (12/31/91)	10,000	

Management believes that the base layer will be replaced at a cost of $1.40 per unit in January 1992. Chloride Chemical is on a calendar year reporting basis.

Required:

1. Assume management decides to increase cost of goods sold by the estimated replacement cost of the base layer of LIFO. What journal entries should be made in December 1991 and January 1992? The actual unit replacement cost is $1.35 per unit and management uses a perpetual inventory system.

2. Do you agree with management's decision? Justify your response.

E 9-15

Initial Adoption of LIFO
(L.O. 4)

On January 1, 1991, Harper Corporation decided to change from FIFO to LIFO for income tax purposes. However, the company will continue to use FIFO in its accounts for internal purposes. The following data are available:

Ending inventory 1990 (as shown in the accounts):
    FIFO at LCM (FIFO cost $75,000) $70,000
Ending inventory, 1991:
    FIFO at cost 80,000
    LIFO at cost 72,000
Ending inventory 1992:
    FIFO at cost 83,000
    LIFO at cost 76,000

Required:

Give the journal entries related to the change from FIFO (LCM) to LIFO on January 1, 1991, and the subsequent entries on December 31, 1991, and December 31, 1992.

E 9-16

DV LIFO: Conversion
from FIFO
(L.O. 5)

On January 1, 1989, Poole Company changed from FIFO to LIFO for income tax and external reporting purposes. At that date, the beginning FIFO inventory (the base inventory for LIFO purposes) was $140,000. The following information is available from Poole's records for the years 1989 through 1992.

Year	Ending Inventory on a FIFO Basis	LIFO Conversion Index
1989	$165,000	1.10
1990	174,000	1.20
1991	201,500	1.30
1992	200,000	1.25

Required:

Compute the ending inventory on a DV LIFO basis for each year, 1989 through 1992.

E 9-17

DV LIFO: Conversion,
External Index
(L.O. 5)

On January 1, 1992, Miller Company adopted LIFO for income tax and external reporting purposes. The ending inventory for 1991 (FIFO basis) amounted to $260,000. The physical inventory taken at the end of 1992, at 1992 costs, was valued at $400,000 (FIFO basis). The Bureau of Labor Statistics Price Index for this product was 1.2 for 1992.

Required:

1. Use the external index to compute the 1992 LIFO inventory amount assuming the DV LIFO approach.
2. Under what special conditions is the external index approach appropriate for converting a FIFO basis inventory to the DV LIFO basis?

E 9-18

DV LIFO: Conversion
from FIFO
(L.O. 3)

Brennan Bottlers uses LIFO for income tax and external reporting purposes. The LIFO base inventory (at end of 1991) for inventory pool No. 1 amounted to $170,000. The periodic inventory of pool No. 1 taken at the end of 1992, priced at 1992 costs on a FIFO basis, amounted to $220,000. Analysis of a statistical sample of the inventory and related computations showed a price index for 1991 of 100 and for 1992 of 110.

Required:

1. Use the internal indexes given above to compute the 1992 ending DV LIFO inventory.
2. Under what conditions is the statistical sample approach for DV LIFO appropriate?

E 9-19

FIFO and LIFO
Reporting
(L.O. 4)

At the end of the annual accounting period, the inventory records of Baird Company reflected the following:

	1992	1993
Ending inventory at FIFO	$50,000	$90,000
Ending inventory at LIFO	20,000	40,000

The company uses FIFO for internal purposes and LIFO for income tax and external reporting purposes.

Required:

1. Assume the inventory difference is recognized in the accounts. Give the appropriate journal entry for each year.
2. Show how the inventories should be shown on the 1992–1993 comparative balance sheet.

E 9–20
FIFO and LIFO:
Disclosure
(L.O. 4)

On January 1, 1992, Silva Company changed from FIFO to LIFO for income tax and external reporting purposes. The ending inventory for 1991 (FIFO basis) was $155,000 (this will be the base inventory amount for LIFO). At the end of 1992, the LIFO inventory amount, computed using the dollar value approach, was $180,000; had the company continued using FIFO, this amount would have been $204,000. The average income tax rate is 40%.

Required:

1. Compute the difference in net income for 1992 attributable to the change from FIFO to LIFO. Show computations.
2. Prepare an appropriate note to the financial statements for 1992.

PROBLEMS

P 9–1
Recording Credit
Purchases: Gross and Net
(L.O. 2)

Nevada Company purchased merchandise during 1992 on credit for $52,000 (includes $2,000 freight charges paid in cash), terms 2/10, n/30. All of the purchase liability, except $20,000, was paid within the discount period; the remainder was paid within the 30-day term. At the end of the annual accounting period, December 31, 1992, 80% of the merchandise had been sold and 20% remained in inventory. The company uses a perpetual system.

Required:

1. Give entries in parallel columns for the purchase and the two payments on the liability assuming (a) purchases and accounts payable are recorded at gross and (b) purchases and accounts payable are recorded at net.
2. What amounts would be reported for the ending inventory and cost of goods sold under (a) and (b) in (1) above? Assume cash discounts under the gross method are reported as a deduction from cost of goods sold. Explain in general terms why the amounts are different between the two methods.
3. Which method is preferable? Why?

P 9–2
Perpetual and Periodic
Inventory Systems
Compared: Entries
(L.O. 3)

Carlisle Company completed the following selected transactions during 1992 for men's slacks:

	Units	Unit Price
Beginning inventory	6,000	$18 (cost)
Purchases	20,000	18 (cost)
Purchase returns	1,000	18 (cost)
Sales (gross)	18,000	25 (selling price)
Sales returns	100	25 (selling price)
Damaged merchandise (unsaleable)	100	18 (cost)
Ending inventory or physical count	6,900	
Inventory shortage	?	

Expenses (excluding damaged goods, cost of goods sold, and income taxes), $47,800.

Required:

1. In parallel columns, give entries for the above transactions, including entries at the end of the accounting period, December 31, 1992, for the following cases (assume a 40% income tax rate and cash transactions):

   Case A—periodic inventory system.
   Case B—perpetual inventory system.

2. Prepare a multiple-step income statement assuming a periodic inventory system and 10,000 shares of common stock outstanding.
3. What amounts, if any, would be different on the income statement if a perpetual inventory system is used? Explain.

P 9–3

Inventory, CGS, Gross Margin—Five Inventory Methods

(L.O. 4)

The records of Barnett Company showed the following transactions, in the order given, relating to the major inventory item:

	Units	Unit Cost
1. Inventory	3,000	$6.90
2. Purchase	6,000	7.20
3. Sales (at $15)	4,000	
4. Purchase	5,000	7.50
5. Sales (at $15)	9,000	
6. Purchase	11,000	7.66
7. Sales (at $18)	9,000	
8. Purchase	6,000	7.81

Required:

Complete the following schedule for each independent assumption (round unit costs to the nearest cent for inventory; show computations):

	Units and Amounts		
Independent Assumptions	**Ending Inventory**	**Goods Sold**	**Gross Margin**
a. FIFO.			
b. LIFO, periodic inventory system (base inventory, 1,000 units).			
c. LIFO, perpetual inventory system (base inventory, 1,000 units).			
d. Weighted average, periodic inventory system.			
e. Moving average, perpetual inventory system.			

P 9–4

Inventory Cost Flow Issues: Four Methods, Two Inventory Systems

(L.O. 4)

The records of Johnson Brothers showed the following data about one raw material used in the manufacturing process. Assume the transactions occurred in the order given.

	Units	Unit Cost
1. Inventory	4,000	7.00
2. Purchase No. 1	3,000	7.70
3. Issue No. 1	5,000	
4. Purchase No. 2	8,000	8.00
5. Issue No. 2	7,000	
6. Purchase No. 3	3,000	8.40

Required:

1. Compute cost of materials issued (to work in process) and the valuation of raw materials ending inventory for each of the following independent assumptions (round unit costs to the nearest cent for inventory; show computations):
   a. FIFO.
   b. LIFO, periodic inventory system (base inventory, 4,000 units).
   c. Weighted average, periodic inventory system.
   d. Moving average, perpetual inventory system.
2. In parallel columns, give all entries indicated for FIFO assuming a count of the raw material on hand at the end of the period showed 6,000 units.

   Case A—periodic inventory system.
   Case B—perpetual inventory system.

P 9–5

Inventory, CGS, Gross Margin—Three Inventory Methods

(L.O. 4)

The records of Betsworth Company showed the following data relative to one of the major items being sold. Assume the transactions occurred in the order given.

	Units	Unit Cost
Beginning inventory	8,000	$4.00
Purchase No. 1	6,000	4.20
Sale No. 1 (at $12)	9,000	
Purchase No. 2	8,000	4.50
Sale No. 2 (at $13)	4,000	

Required:

1. Complete the following schedule under each independent assumption given (round unit costs to nearest cent):

	Units and Amount		
Independent Assumptions	Ending Inventory	Cost of Goods Sold	Gross Margin
a. Weighted-average cost, periodic inventory system.			
b. FIFO, perpetual inventory system.			
c. LIFO, periodic inventory system (base inventory, 7,000 units).			

2. Give all transaction entries indicated by the above data assuming FIFO and a perpetual inventory system, (*b* above).

P 9–6

Ending Inventory, CGS, Five Methods—Two Inventory Systems (L.O. 4)

Kim Corporation's records showed the following transactions, in order of occurrence, relative to inventory Item A:

	Units	Unit Cost
1. Inventory	400	$5.00
2. Purchase	600	5.50
3. Sale	700	
4. Purchase	900	5.70
5. Sale	800	
6. Purchase	200	5.75

Required:

Compute the cost of goods sold and ending inventory in each of the following independent situations (round unit costs to the nearest cent for inventory; show computations):

	Units and Amount	
Assumption	Ending Inventory	Cost of Goods Sold
a. Weighted average.		
b. Moving average.		
c. FIFO.		
d. LIFO, perpetual inventory system.		
e. LIFO, periodic inventory system.		

P 9–7

Ending Inventory, CGS, Income—Three Cost Methods (L.O. 4)

Patterson Corporation maintains a periodic inventory system. The following transactions occurred during 1992 for its major inventory item (in order of occurrence):

	Units	Unit Cost
1. Beginning inventory	1,000	$50
2. Purchase	900	40
3. Sale (at $100)	800	
4. Purchase	800	51
5. Sale (at $100)	200	

Other expenses (excluding income taxes) during 1992 were $20,000. Patterson's tax rate is 40%.

Required:

1. Complete the following schedule for each of the independent assumptions given (show supporting computations):

Independent Assumptions	Ending Inventory	Cost of Goods Sold	Net Income
a. Weighted average			
b. FIFO			
c. LIFO			

2. Which method results in the highest tax liability? Explain why this occurred.

P 9–8
FIFO to LIFO: Reporting the Change
(L.O. 4)

Simpson and Sons decided at the beginning of 1992 to change from FIFO to LIFO. The records of the company showed the following data for 1992 relative to one major inventory item distributed:

	Units	Unit Cost
Beginning inventory (LIFO base inventory) 1/1/92	10,000	$3.10
Purchases and sales (in order given):		
1. Purchase	8,000	3.20
2. Sold (at $8)	9,000	
3. Sold (at $8.25)	5,000	
4. Purchase	7,000	3.20
5. Purchase	6,000	3.40
6. Sold (at $8.75)	8,000	
7. Purchase	3,000	3.50
Expenses (excluding income taxes), $40,000.		
Average income tax rate, 40%.		

Required:

1. Prepare an income statement for 1992, unit cost LIFO basis, periodic inventory system. Assume 10,000 shares of common stock outstanding.
2. Prepare an appropriate footnote, and any other required supporting data, for the change in 1992 from FIFO to LIFO.
3. What would be disclosed in 1993 relative to the change? Why?

P 9–9
A Hypothetical Inventory Riddle to Solve!
(L.O. 4)

Stigler Corporation sells two main products. The records of the company showed the following information relating to one of the products:

	Units	Unit Cost
Beginning inventory	500	$3.00
Purchases and sales (in order given):		
Purchase No. 1	400	3.10
Purchase No. 2	600	3.15
Sale No. 1	1,000	
Purchase No. 3	800	3.25
Sale No. 2	700	
Sale No. 3	500	
Purchase No. 4	700	3.30

In considering a change in inventory policy, the following summary was prepared:

	Illustration			
	(1)	(2)	(3)	(4)
Sales	$16,000	$16,000	$16,000	$16,000
Cost of goods sold	7,110	6,996	6,905	6,930
Gross margin	$ 8,890	$ 9,004	$ 9,095	$ 9,070

Required:

Identify the inventory flow method used for each illustration assuming only the ending inventory was affected. Show computations.

(AICPA adapted)

P 9-10
An Overview of Perpetual
Inventory: Entries, Partial
Income Statement
(L.O. 3)

Walsh Company maintains perpetual inventory records on an FIFO basis for the three main products distributed by the company. A physical inventory is taken at the end of each year in order to check the perpetual inventory records.

The following information relating to one of the products, blenders, for the year 1992, was taken from the records of the company:

	Units	Unit Cost
Beginning inventory	9,000	$8.10
Purchases and sales (in order given):		
Purchase No. 1	5,000	8.15
Sale No. 1	10,000	
Purchase No. 2	16,000	8.20
Sale No. 2	11,000	
Purchase No. 3	4,000	8.40
Purchase No. 4	7,000	8.25
Sale No. 3	14,000	
Purchase No. 5	5,000	8.10
Ending inventory (per count)	10,500	
Replacement cost (per unit), $8.10.		

Required:

1. Reconstruct the perpetual inventory record for blenders.
2. Give all entries indicated by the above data assuming selling price is $22 per unit.
3. Prepare the income statement through gross margin for this product.

P 9-11
LIFO Liquidation
(L.O. 4)

Rathman Company switched from FIFO to LIFO for tax and reporting purposes in 1979 to gain cash savings from its real estate holding and renovation business. This strategy was extremely successful, saving the company several million dollars in tax payments during the 1980s as California real estate prices escalated. However, market prices began to level off in the early 1990s. Rathman's records revealed the following information as of December 15, 1992:

	Units	Unit Cost	Unit Sales Price
Beginning Inventory:			
LIFO base inventory	10	$ 88,000	
Additional LIFO layers	24	216,000	
Purchase and sales:			
1/15/92 Purchased	8	240,000	
2/29/92 Sold	16		$320,000
8/01/92 Sold	18		300,000
11/10/92 Purchased	12	224,000	
12/01/92 Sold	11		298,000
Expenses (excluding income taxes): $1,668,000			
Average income tax rate: 40%			

Required:

1. Assume no other transactions take place during 1992. Prepare an income statement for 1992 on a unit cost LIFO basis, assuming a periodic inventory system. Compute earnings per share if 10,000 shares of stock are outstanding.
2. Assume now that Rathman Company is faced with two new options on December 15, 1992. The first involves selling five units for $300,000 each. The second option is to purchase five units for $320,000 each. An independent appraiser claims that units in both options are priced fairly. What would you recommend? Support your decision. Rathman uses LIFO for tax reporting.

P 9-12 Appendix:
Standard Costs—
Perpetual versus Periodic
(L.O. 6)

Walton Woodstompers specializes in snowshoe manufacturing. Three raw materials (fine ash, leather hides, and laminated wax) are used in the production process. The company carries all manufacturing inventory accounts at standard cost. The following data applies to the first quarter of 1992, just ended:

	Ash		Leather		Wax	
	Units	Cost	Units	Cost	Units	Cost
Beginning Inventory	75	$7.60	170	$5.60	20	$4.80
Purchases:						
1/7/92	50	$7.70	110	$5.60	10	$4.60
2/10/92	100	$7.50	145	$6.20	40	$4.50
3/24/92	55	$7.80	120	$5.40	10	$4.80
Issues:						
1/5/92	60		120		15	
2/17/92	100		200		25	
3/28/92	50		100		10	
Ending Inventory:						
Physical count (3/31/92) . . .	70		120		30	
Standard cost		$7.60		$5.60		$4.80

Required:

1. Determine ending inventories and provide journal entries for the three raw material accounts during the period (assume periodic inventory system).
2. Redo your answer to (1) using a perpetual inventory system.

P 9–13
Manufacturing Firm:
Periodic versus Perpetual
(L.O. 4)

Cofer Manufacturing produces sporting goods. The following data pertains to its wooden baseball bat inventory accounts for January:

		Units
1/1	Beginning balance:	
	Raw materials (@ $3.50)	100
	Work in process (@ $8.40)	300
	Finished goods (@ $12.80)	220
1/4	Purchased wood (@ $3.75)	100
1/11	Sold bats at retail (@ $16.50)	120
1/15	Issued to work in process	100
1/17	Completed production	300
1/25	Sold bats at retail (@ $16.75)	240
1/28	Purchased wood (@ $3.60)	200
1/30	Issued work in process	180

Required:

1. Prepare journal entries for each of the above transactions using a FIFO perpetual flow. Assume it takes $10.00 in labor and overhead to complete one finished item (this figure is constant throughout the month) and that beginning work in process is 50% complete.
2. What is the dollar value of the three ending inventory accounts at January 31? Assume work in process is 40% complete at this time.

P 9–14
DV LIFO: Conversion
from FIFO
(L.O. 5)

Robinson Corporation has been using FIFO for all internal and external reporting purposes. At the start of 1992, the company adopted DV LIFO for external financial statement and income tax purposes. The FIFO inventory records reported the following for one inventory pool:

	FIFO Basis
1991 ending inventory	$250,000
1992 ending inventory	291,500
1993 ending inventory	356,500
1994 ending inventory	360,000

Internal price index derived: 1991, 1.00; 1992, 1.10; 1993, 1.15; and 1994, 1.20.

Required:

Convert the ending FIFO inventory amounts to an LIFO basis for 1992, 1993, and 1994, assuming the DV LIFO method, using the internal price index values given above.

P 9–15
DV LIFO: Conversion
from FIFO
(L.O. 3)

Ohio Corporation maintains its internal inventory records on a FIFO basis. On January 1, 1992, Ohio changed to DV LIFO for external reporting and income tax purposes. The following data are available regarding Ohio's inventory:

	1992	1993	1994
Ending inventory at current year cost	$140,000	$160,000	$175,000
LIFO conversion index*	1.20	1.30	1.45

*Computed internally.

Ohio's base inventory is $100,000.

Required:

1. Compute the ending inventory on a DV LIFO basis for the year 1992, 1993, and 1994.
2. Assume the 1995 ending inventory on a DV LIFO basis is $144,195, and the 1995 LIFO conversion index is 1.50. What is the ending inventory on a current cost basis?

P 9–16
DV LIFO: Conversion
from FIFO—Calculate
Price Index
(L.O. 5)

Young Brothers has been using FIFO since its organization for internal management reports and control, external reporting to shareholders, and income tax purposes. On January 1, 1992, management decided to change from FIFO to DV LIFO for external reporting and income tax purposes. FIFO will continue in use for internal purposes.

The company has a number of LIFO inventory pools; however, this problem deals with only one of them. The company will apply the dollar value approach for converting the FIFO results to a LIFO basis and will use an internal conversion index computed each year.

The FIFO results for a three-year period, taken directly from the accounts and internal reports for inventory pool No. 1 (composed of five similar items in a so-called natural business unit) are shown below.

	Year 1991			Year 1992			Year 1993		
	Units	Unit Cost	Total	Units	Unit Cost	Total	Units	Unit Cost	Total
Sales revenue			$18,200			$24,280			$23,300
Cost of goods sold (FIFO):									
Beginning inventory	800	$2.40	$ 2,000	600	$3.00	$ 1,800	700	$3.30	$ 2,310
Purchases	2,000	3.00	6,000	2,500	3.30	8,250	2,400	3.45	8,280
Ending inventory	(600)	3.00	(1,800)*	(700)	3.30	(2,310)	(900)	3.45	(3,105)
Cost of goods sold	2,200		$ 6,200	2,400		$ 7,740	2,200		$ 7,485

*Base inventory.

Required:

1. Compute the conversion price indexes needed for the DV LIFO application in 1992 and 1993. Show computations and round conversion ratios to two decimal places.
2. Convert the FIFO results to a LIFO basis for 1992 and 1993 using the DV approach. Show computations.
3. Assuming $8,000 operating expenses, a 30% average tax rate, and 4,000 shares of common stock outstanding, prepare income statements for 1992 and 1993 with two headings for each year: *(a)* for internal reports (FIFO basis) and *(b)* for external reports and tax returns (LIFO basis). *Suggestion:* Use one set of side captions and four money columns.

P 9–17
DV LIFO: Conversion
from FIFO,
Disclosure, Calculate
Price Index
(L.O. 5)

Montana and Company sells two main products. FIFO, with a perpetual inventory system, is used for internal cost accounting and management purposes. On January 1, 1992, the company adopted DV LIFO for external reporting and income tax purposes; FIFO will continue to be used for internal purposes. The FIFO inventory records are shown below.

Perpetual Inventory Record

Inv ending

	Purchases			Issues			FIFO Balance		
	Units	Cost	Total	Units	Cost	Total	Units	Cost	Total
Product X:									
December 31, 1991							200	$100	$20,000
1992: Purchases	400	$120	$48,000						
Sales				200	$100	$20,000			
				200	120	24,000	200	120	24,000
1993: Purchases	500	126	63,000						
Sales				200	120	24,000	500	126	63,000
1994: Purchases	300	130	39,000						
Sales				500	126	63,000	300	130	39,000
Product Y:									
December 31, 1991							300	$ 80	$24,000
1992: Purchases	400	$ 83	$33,200						
Sales				300	$ 80	$24,000	400	83	33,200
1993: Purchases	100	95	9,500						
Sales				400	83	33,200	100	95	9,500
1994: Purchases	400	104	41,600						
Sales				100	95	9,500			
				100	104	10,400	300	104	31,200

Required:

Assume the two products form one pool for inventory purposes. Convert the ending inventory at FIFO to a DV LIFO basis for 1992, 1993, and 1994. Round conversion indexes to two places.

P 9–18

COMPREHENSIVE PROBLEM
♦

DV LIFO: Conversion from FIFO, Disclosure Reporting
(L.O. 3, 4, 5)

Westshore Corporation sells three main products regularly. The products form one pool for inventory purposes. The company used FIFO through 1990 for all purposes. After 1990, FIFO was continued for internal management and accounting purposes; however, at the start of 1991, DV LIFO was adopted for income tax and external reporting purposes. The following data (for the three products combined) were taken from the records for the three years following the adoption of LIFO:

	FIFO Basis per Accounts		
	Units	Cost	Total
1990:			
Ending inventory	2,000	$3.00	$ 6,000
1991:			
Purchases	7,000	3.30	23,100
Sales	6,000		
Ending inventory	3,000	3.30	9,900
1992:			
Purchases	10,000	3.45	34,500
Sales	7,000		
Ending inventory	6,000	3.45	20,700
1993:			
Purchases	5,000	3.90	19,500
Sales	9,000		
Ending inventory	4,000	3.90	15,600

Required:

1. Convert the ending inventory at FIFO to a DV LIFO basis for 1991, 1992, and 1993. Round conversion indexes to two decimal places.
2. Prepare a schedule (which includes inventory, tax, and income) that compares the results of the methods, FIFO and LIFO. For analytical purposes, assume an average tax rate of

40% and a pretax income amount of $5,000 each year under FIFO. Which method should be used? Why?

3. Prepare an appropriate footnote to the financial statements for 1991 assuming LIFO is used for external reporting and tax purposes.

P 9–19
Appendix:
Standard Costs
(L.O. 6)

Wood Manufacturing Company manufactures one main product. Two raw materials are used in the manufacture of this product. The company uses standard costs in the accounts and carries the raw material, work in process, and finished goods inventories at standard. The record of the company showed the following:

	Material A	Material B
Beginning inventory (units)	8,000	5,000
Standard cost per unit	$2.00	$7.00
Purchases during period:		
No. 1	10,000 at $2.00	7,000 at $7.00
No. 2	20,000 at 1.90	8,000 at 7.20
Issues during period (units)	28,000	16,000
Ending inventory per physical count (units)	10,000	3,900

Required:

1. Give all entries indicated relative to raw materials assuming standard costs (assume a perpetual system).
2. Determine the value of the ending inventory and cost of issues for each raw material.
3. Accumulate the amount of the variations from standard for each raw material. Explain or illustrate the reporting and accounting disposition of these amounts.

CASES

C 9–1
Inventories
(L.O. 1, 2)

Gould, Inc., is an electronics company that manufactures and markets a wide range of products. The company switched to the LIFO method for substantially all domestic inventories at the beginning of 1978. Gould's income statement ("Consolidated Statements of Earnings") for 1978 and 1979 and the asset section of the 1978 and 1979 balance sheet ("Consolidated Statements of Financial Position") are presented.

The notes to Gould's Consolidated Financial Statements stated that the company would have reported primary earnings per share of $4.63 if it had used the FIFO method in 1979.

Required:

What was the amount of the LIFO reserve at December 31, 1979?

GOULD INC. AND CONSOLIDATED SUBSIDIARIES

Consolidated Statements of Earnings
For the years ended December 1979 and 1978
(Amounts in thousands except per share amounts)

	1979	1978
Revenues:		
Net sales	$2,023,885	$1,869,944
Equity earnings	5,333	8,605
Royalty income	5,123	2,958
Interest income	10,871	2,406
Gain on involuntary conversion	9,038	—
Total revenues	2,054,250	1,883,913
Cost and expenses:		
Cost of products sold	1,445,638	1,304,596
Selling, administrative and general expenses (includes internal research and development expenditures: 1979–$68,184; 1978–$72,593)	396,026	367,804
Interest expense	50,081	33,895
Other (income)	(2,943)	2,430
Total costs and expenses	1,888,802	1,708,725
Pretax earnings	165,448	175,188
Federal, state and foreign income taxes	59,561	74,155
Net earnings	$ 105,887	$ 101,033
Earnings per share:		
Earnings per share	$3.78	$3.77
Earnings per share assuming full dilution	$3.71	$3.56

GOULD INC. AND CONSOLIDATED SUBSIDIARIES

Consolidated Statements of Financial Position
At December 31, 1979 and 1978
(All amounts are in thousands)

Assets	1979	1978
Current assets:		
Cash	$ 18,105	$ 32,440
Marketable securities—at cost, which approximates market	906	1,908
Accounts receivable, less allowances (1979, $7,732; 1978, $6,148)	324,593	284,355
Inventories, less LIFO reserve (1979– 1978, $21,178)	429,203	388,810
Other current assets	73,558	50,870
Total Current Assets	846,365	758,383
Investments and other assets:		
Unconsolidated financial subsidiary	24,722	19,559
Unconsolidated real estate subsidiary	18,296	5,659
Unconsolidated joint venture	37,498	—
Affiliated companies and other investments	48,914	45,327
Other assets	45,992	58,595
Total investments and other assets	175,422	129,140
Property, plant, and equipment:		
Land	26,669	23,215
Buildings	226,546	209,013
Machinery and equipment	448,137	389,503
Construction in process	68,932	66,225
	770,284	687,956
Less allowances for depreciation and amortization	255,701	231,684
Total property, plant, and equipment	514,583	456,272
Cost of acquired businesses in excess of net assets at acquisition dates—net of amortization	76,693	77,168
Total assets	$1,613,063	$1,420,963

C 9–2

Ethics, LIFO, Profit
Manipulation
(L.O. 4)

Butte Company uses a periodic inventory system and LIFO, unit basis, to cost the ending inventory for income tax and external reporting purposes. Near the end of 1991, the records and related estimates provided the following annual data for one item sold regularly:

	Units	Unit Cost
Beginning inventory (LIFO basis):		
Base inventory (normal minimum level)	8,000	$20
Increment No. 1	5,000	25
Purchases (actual)	60,000	35
Sales* (at $50 per unit)	65,000	
Expenses* (excluding income taxes), $700,000.		
Average income tax rate, 30%.		

*Including estimates for remainder of 1991.

On December 26, 1991, the company has an opportunity to purchase not less than 30,000 units of the above item at $30 (a special price) with 10-day credit terms. Delivery is immediate, and the offer will expire January 3, 1992. The question has been posed whether the purchase (and delivery) should be consummated in 1991 or 1992; the management has tentatively decided to make the purchase in 1991.

Required:
1. What purchase date do your recommend? Support your recommendation with reasons and pro forma (as if) income statement and balance sheet data. Include computations. Assume 50,000 shares of common stock are outstanding.
2. Explain and illustrate why EPS would be changed if the purchase is made in 1991.
3. Would you suspect profit manipulation in this situation if Butte elected to make the purchase in 1991? Does this create an ethical problem? Explain.

C 9–3

Ethics, LIFO, Profit
Manipulation
(L.O. 4)

R. Babinski, S. Chasnoff, and T. Doland formed a partnership to import furniture. Their initial partnership agreement provided for equal investments, equal sharing of responsibilities, equal work, equal salaries, and equal shares of the partnership income. After a few years of operation, sales took off and the business prospered. On January 1, 1990, they incorporated as BCD, Inc., with each of the former partners owning 33⅓% of the stock of the corporation. The board of directors of BCD comprised of Babinski, Chasnoff, and Doland. The board elected Chasnoff as chairman of the board of directors, Babinski as president of the corporation in charge of operations, and Doland as vice president and controller (Doland was a CPA). Annual compensation of the three officers was set as follows:

Chasnoff	. . . . . $130,000	plus bonus equal to 2% of annual net income
Babinski	 135,000	plus bonus equal to 1% of annual net income
Doland	 140,000	plus 5% of annual decrease in income tax payments

The compensation plan was intended as an incentive device as well as to reflect the relative contributions of the three officers to corporate success. In particular, the bonus plan was intended to motivate Chasnoff and Babinski (who represented the corporation in the business community) to increase sales and to encourage Doland (the accountant) to decrease income tax payments. During 1991, 1992, and 1993, sales and income increased steadily. In the year ended December 31, 1993, net income of the corporation was $500,000, which put the annual earnings of all three officers at $140,000 (this amount cannot be verified). Income tax payments for 1993 were $150,000. During 1994, net income, computed on the basis of the FIFO inventory method, which BCD used, increased to $750,000. This increase in corporate income was destined to put Chasnoff's annual earnings at $145,000 and Babinski's at $142,500, but to leave Doland's at $140,000 (neither Babinski nor Chasnoff were aware of this). A major reason for the increase in corporation income was Doland's skill at controlling costs; however, the compensation plan did not adequately reflect this factor. Doland tried to persuade Chasnoff and Babinski to renegotiate his salary, but they refused because they knew very little about finance and accounting, and, therefore, were unable to appreciate Doland's effectiveness at controlling expenses. They were convinced the reason for the success of BCD was their superlative sales and management skills.

The cost to BCD of its imported furniture was rising rapidly near the end of 1994, and, due to increased competition, the outlook for the company's sales was not bright for 1995. Without notifying Chasnoff or Babinski, Doland changed inventory methods from FIFO to LIFO, effective January 1, 1994. Also, near year-end 1994, Doland, who controlled all purchases of inventory, stocked up on inventory in response to a pending 20% cost increase announced by BCD's suppliers; the price increase was to become effective in January 1995. Because of the change to LIFO, income tax payments for 1994 decreased to $70,000.

Required:
1. What was the likely effect of the change in inventory method on reported income of BCD for 1994. On the annual bonuses of Babinski and Chasnoff?
2. What was the likely effect of stocking up of inventory on reported income of 1994? On the annual earnings of Babinski and Chasnoff?
3. What was the effect of Doland's actions on his annual bonus? Does this raise any ethical issues?
4. What conclusions can you draw from this situation about accounting income?

C 9–4
Sherwin-Williams:
Analyzing Actual
Financial Statements
(L.O. 4)

Using the Sherwin-Williams annual report given in the back of this book, answer the following questions:
1. How does Sherwin-Williams value its inventories?
2. What would Sherwin-Williams have reported as net income if the company had used FIFO instead of LIFO for the year 1990?
3. What does the value $81,205 in Note 5 to the firm's annual report tell us?

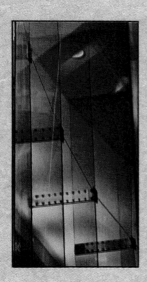

Alternative Inventory Valuation Methods

After you have studied this chapter, you will:

1. Be able to establish inventory values based on the lower-of-cost-or-market (LCM) approach.

2. Understand under what conditions the gross margin method of estimating inventories is used and how it is applied.

3. Learn how to use the retail inventory method to value inventory and what types of businesses use it.

4. Know how the retail inventory method is combined with dollar value LIFO to estimate inventory values.

5. Be familiar with several special inventory problems, including the valuation of inventories using other methods, losses on purchase commitments, and the effects of errors in valuing inventories.

◆

◆

INTRODUCTION
◆

Imagine for the moment that you have been assigned to a team of accountants given responsibility for constructing the balance sheet and income statement for Sears, Roebuck & Co. One of your first tasks is to get a handle on the carrying value of the thousands of items Sears stocks in its stores, catalogue operations, and distribution centers across the country. The task is to compile information and compute the value of inventory as of the end of the company's fiscal year—with sales taking place up to the last minute, the firm's buyers making purchases throughout the period, and sales returns occurring on each day Sears is open for business.

Fortunately, hand-held price scanners and other forms of automation are being used by sales personnel throughout Sears catalogue stores and retailing outlets. From a quick pass over the bar code affixed to each item of merchandise, the scanner automatically records the current retail sales price, which typically may have been marked up and marked down several times during the product's inventory shelf life. Even more important, the bar code, which the scanner electronically registers in a network of main frame computers, includes the product's inventory identification number. This number controls a host of critical inventory accounting details, most of which are discussed in this chapter.

Even though scanners and other types of automated equipment have taken much of the drudgery out of inventory accounting work, inventory accounting remains one of the most significant areas of accounting, in terms of both its importance to the integrity of a company's financial statements and the efforts that must be made in gathering, processing, and reporting the required accounting information.

In any business operation of size—for example, Sears, K mart, or A&P on the retailing side or Procter & Gamble or RJR Nabisco on the product supply side—inventory valuation methods provide only a basic estimate of inventory values. The case of Sears is somewhat akin to the problems with taking a U.S. population census: to actually count each member of the group (let alone assign a value to each piece of merchandise) simply is not feasible. Although counting the physical inventory is still a necessary part of the inventory control process (even when perpetual inventory record systems are in use), valuing the inventory is equally important and substantially more difficult.

Over the years, accountants have developed a number of estimation methods for valuing inventories that serve the needs of most companies and that are within acceptable error-tolerance levels. One such inventory estimation method—dollar value (DV) LIFO—was presented in Chapter 9. Chapter 10 continues this discussion by presenting two additional widely used methods for estimating inventory values: the gross margin method and the retail inventory method. First, however, the lower-of-cost-or-market (LCM) method is presented. The LCM method is an inventory valuation approach that is used with other valuation methods to obtain an alternative value often required for reporting purposes.

◆

LCM INVENTORY VALUATION METHOD
◆

Under GAAP, inventories must be valued either at cost or at current market value, whichever is less. This is something of a departure from the historical cost principle that applies in most other asset valuation practices. Using the approach known as the **lower of cost or market (LCM)** means that during inflationary economic periods (when prices are rising), inventories should be carried on the books and reported in financial statements at their original acquisition cost, even though the inventory's replacement value may be substantially higher according to current market prices. Under deflationary conditions (when prices are trending down), inventories must be carried and reported at their current replacement market value (subject to certain floor and ceiling price levels discussed below). The rationale for the LCM rule, which is defined in *ARB No. 43,* is conservatism. When prices are rising, conservative accounting practices ignore paper gains resulting from higher current market values; instead, such gains are recognized only if the inventory is sold or otherwise disposed of at this higher market value.[1]

However, when prices are declining, paper losses may result if current market prices decline below the inventory's original cost. When this occurs, the paper losses are recognized and inventories are reported at the lower replacement market value (again, subject to floor and ceiling limits). This treatment is in keeping with the same conservative approach to inventory accounting, this time predicated on the fact that the inventory now has less utility value to the company.

The phrase *less utility value* means that the goods constituting the inventory have reduced revenue-generating power. With finished goods inventories (or retail merchandise inventories), reduced revenue-generating power simply means a lower selling price, which may or may not cover the cost to produce the inventory (or acquire the merchandise, in the case of a retailer). With raw materials and work in progress inventories, less utility value refers to the future sales revenue expected to be generated after such inventories are converted to finished goods in the normal flow of production and inventory costs.

Whenever an inventory valuation loss occurs due to a decline in current market prices below original cost, such a loss must be recognized in the period during which the market price decline (and loss) occurs. However, the cost of a component of a larger unit can decline without affecting the unit's sales value. In this case, the component's cost is not written down to LCM. In general, for a loss to be recognized under the LCM method, both a decline in replacement cost and in the final sales value must have occurred.

To illustrate the basic operation of the LCM inventory valuation method, assume that a retailer has an inventory consisting of a single line of office electronics products, all purchased during 1991 at a cost of $165 per unit, the going wholesale price at the time the merchandise was acquired. Late in the year, due to stiff competition in the electronics and office products market, wholesale prices for the retailer's products in inventory drop substantially, with retail prices following suit. As of the end of the year, manufacturers are quoting wholesale prices of only $125 per unit. Assume that none of the retailer's inventory has been sold. The retailer's ending inventory for 1991 should be valued and reported at $125 per unit, which represents a $40 loss per unit based on the $165 original purchase cost. This $40-per-unit loss must be reported in the retailer's 1991 financial statements, the period during which the market price decline took place. The value of the inventory itself is reported at $125 per unit, which is the market replacement value.

In the following year (1992), assume that the retailer's inventory is sold. For each unit sold, the cost of goods sold is now $125, not $165. Assuming that retail selling prices dropped commensurate with last year's decline in wholesale prices, the lower cost of goods sold figure provides the retailer with approximately the same gross margin on sales as would have been available in 1991, when both wholesale and retail prices were higher. The net effect of the LCM application in this instance was to shift the $40-per-unit loss from the period when the inventory was sold to the period in which the replacement cost decreased.

In addition to conservatism, the LCM rule is supported by the matching principle, which suggests that a decline in the utility value of goods on hand, as evidenced by a decrease in the final sales value, be recognized and reported in the income statement as a loss for the period when the decline took place.

---

[1] Gains in market value are recognized in volatile market situations where market prices have declined (and were previously reported as losses) and have now recovered. Gain recognition in such instances is limited to the amount of the previously established loss, which means market value recoveries up to the amount of the original inventory cost. Any gains above original cost are disregarded in keeping with the LCM rule.

Net Realizable Value and Net Realizable Value less a Normal Profit Margin

In applying the LCM inventory valuation method, certain constraints were recognized by the AICPA Committee on Accounting Procedures, the ruling body responsible for the creation of the LCM rule. While *market* usually may be interpreted to mean the current replacement cost of the inventory (first-level definition), the following constraints apply to this definition (thereby establishing a second-level definition):

1. Market should not exceed the **net realizable value** of the inventory, which is defined as the estimated selling price of the goods in the ordinary course of business less reasonably predictable costs of completion and disposal.
2. Market should not be less than the net realizable value reduced by an allowance equal to the approximate **normal profit margin**.[2] A normal profit margin is that profit margin, expressed as a percentage achieved on the item or similar items in normal circumstances.

Net realizable value and net realizable value less normal profit are illustrated in Exhibit 10–1. For reading and understanding ease, one unit of an inventory, Item A, is used in this illustration.

The following explanations apply to Exhibit 10–1 assuming a manufacturing company:

Line *a:* Inventory Item A is currently being valued at $70, which includes raw materials, direct labor, and allocated overhead expenses incurred to date in bringing Item A to its present condition. (If this were a retail merchandise item, the $70 would represent the item's original purchase price.)

Line *b:* For a variety of reasons, inventory Item A, which originally sold for $122, has declined in sales value, perhaps due to the fact that another manufacturer has attempted to capture a greater share of the market by lowering the selling price dramatically, forcing all other manufacturers to lower their prices in order to compete. Thus, the current selling price of Item A is down to $100. (If this were a retailing example, the same price-cutting practice by a competitor could force the other retailers to cut their prices as well.)

Line *c:* At the present time inventory Item A is not quite ready to be transferred to finished goods inventory. The company estimates that $5 additional direct labor and overhead are needed to complete the conversion and $35 in selling expenses are expected to be incurred to transfer the fully assembled Item A to the retailer's selling floor. Thus, $40 is estimated as the completion and selling costs for Item A. (If this were a retailing inventory situation, the merchandise would have been completed at the time of purchase by the retailer.)

Line *d:* The net realizable value of inventory Item A is $60 ($100 selling price less $40 in completion and selling costs), which represents Item A's maximum utility value to the manufacturer. (In retailing situation, the same maximum utility value to the seller applies.)

Line *e:* The normal profit margin for items similar to Item A is on average 10% of selling price, or in this case $10.

Line *f:* The net realizable value less normal profit is the lowest cost recovery amount expected by the manufacturer based on a selling price of $100. Thus, the minimum utility value of inventory Item A is $50 ($100 selling price less $40 in completion and selling costs and $10 in profit).

---

[2] AICPA, *Accounting Research Bulletin No. 43*, "Restatement and Revisions of *Accounting Research Bulletins Nos. 1–42*," New York, 1953, chapter 4, statement 6.

EXHIBIT 10–1   Net Realizable Value and Net Realizable Value Less a Normal Profit Margin

a. Inventory Item A, at original cost	$ 70
b. Inventory Item A, at estimated current selling price in present condition	$100
c. Less: Estimated costs to complete and sell*	40
d. **Net realizable value**	$ 60
e. Less: Allowance for normal profit (10% of sales price)	10
f. **Net realizable value less normal profit**	$ 50

*For goods already completed, as in a retail company, this amount would be the cost to repair and sell.

Establishing Inventory Valuations Under LCM

When the current replacement cost exceeds original cost, the original cost is used to value the inventory. When the current replacement cost is below the original cost, the net realizable value, *(d)* in Exhibit 10–1, represents the ceiling price for inventory valuation purposes, and the net realizable value less normal profit margin, *(f)* in Exhibit 10–1, represents the floor price. If the current replacement cost of the inventory is higher than the ceiling price (net realizable value), the ceiling price is used for valuing the inventory; if the current replacement cost is below the floor price (net realizable value less normal profit margin), the floor price is used for valuing the inventory. If the current replacement cost falls between the floor and ceiling prices, the current replacement cost figure is used.[3] In short, *market* as used in LCM is the middle value of the ceiling value, the floor value, and replacement cost.

These floor and ceiling constraints were adopted by the AICPA and incorporated into the LCM rule to prevent abuses and unethical manipulation of reported inventory values. The floor price constraint, for example, is designed to prevent the recognition of large inventory losses in one year only to be followed by large profit margins in later years when products are sold out of inventory at profit margins based on current selling prices. In such cases, the profit margins may be quite generous because the cost of goods sold, which is derived from the inventory carrying value, is unreasonably low.

For similar reasons, the ceiling price exists to prevent a company from overstating its inventory and not recognizing the full extent of the inventory loss for the current year. Failure to recognize the current loss also overstates the cost of goods sold in future years, which in turn understates gross margins on sales in future years.

Applications of the LCM Rule

Exhibit 10–2 on page 472 shows how the LCM rule is applied in five different cases. Exhibit 10–2 is based on the data given immediately below Exhibit 10–2, which assumes, for convenience, a single unit of inventory. The same procedures apply to an entire inventory, provided it consists of homogeneous goods or materials.

---

[3] Use of LCM is a conservative approach to inventory accounting. When LIFO is used to obtain the cost value used in LCM, the accounting approach takes on an even stronger conservative posture since LIFO usually produces lower inventory values. Precisely because of the conservative nature of LCM, the floor constraint to LCM (net realizable value less a normal profit margin) is often not needed when LIFO is used to establish cost because the LIFO cost is already very low.

EXHIBIT 10-2   Determination of Lower of Cost or Market (LCM) Illustrated

Computations	Case				
	I	**II**	**III**	**IV**	**V**
a. Cost (per unit)	$1.00	$1.00	$1.00	$.45	.$40
b. Current replacement cost (per unit)	.55	.65	.45	.40	.45
c. Ceiling (net realizable value, i.e., estimated sales price less predictable costs of completion and sale)	.60	.60	.60	.60	.58
d. Floor (net realizable value less a normal profit margin)	.51	.51	.52	.52	.51
e. Market, selected from (b), (c), and (d) values	.55	.60	.52	.52	—
f. Inventory valuation under LCM rule, selected from (a) and (e)	.55	.60	.52	.45	.40

LCM

→ If current replacement cost is above ceiling, use ceiling for market.

→ If current replacement cost is between ceiling and floor, use current replacement cost for market.

→ If current replacement cost is below floor, use floor for market.

Information for Five Cases	Case				
	I	**II**	**III**	**IV**	**V**
Estimated selling price (later period)	$ .85	$ .90	$ .80	$ .75	$ .70
Less: Estimated cost to complete and sell	.25	.30	.20	.15	.12
Net realizable value (ceiling)	$ .60	$ .60	$ .60	$ .60	$ .58
Less: Estimated normal profit*	.09	.09	.08	.08	.07
Net realizable value less profit (floor)	$ .51	$ .51	$ .52	$ .52	$ .51
Original cost	$1.00	$1.00	$1.00	$ .45	$ .40
Current replacement cost	.55	.65	.45	.40	.45

*10% of selling price rounded for instructional convenience.

For Case V, the current replacement cost is higher than the original cost. Case V, therefore, is disposed of under the LCM rule simply by keeping the original cost of the inventory ($.40) for end-of-period valuation purposes. In the other four cases given by the data, it is necessary to determine which amount to use as market under the LCM rule since the current replacement cost is below original cost. The analysis is done in Exhibit 10–2.

In Case I, the $.55 current replacement cost is used as market because it falls between the floor and ceiling prices; thus, $.55 is used to value the inventory. In Case II, the ceiling price ($.60) applies because the current replacement cost ($.65) exceeds this ceiling. In Case III, the floor price ($.52) applies because the current replacement cost ($.45) is below this floor price. In Case IV, the original cost ($.45)

EXHIBIT 10–3   Application of LCM to Inventory Categories

Inventory	Cost	Market	Individual Items	Classifications	Total
			LCM Applied To		
Classification A:					
Item 1	$10,000	$ 9,500	$ 9,500		
Item 2	8,000	9,000	8,000		
	18,000	18,500		$18,000	
Classification B:					
Item 3	21,000	22,000	21,000		
Item 4	32,000	29,000	29,000		
	53,000	51,000		51,000	
Total	$71,000	$69,500			$69,500
Inventory valuation			$67,500	$69,000	$69,500

takes precedence as it is lower than market ($.52) in which current replacement cost is subject to the floor constraints. Case V, once again, was disposed of immediately because the original cost was lower than the current replacement cost.

Accounting Problems in Applying LCM

In applying LCM, the following accounting problems arise:

1. How should LCM be applied to determine the overall inventory valuation?
2. How should the resulting inventory valuation be recorded in the accounts and reported on the financial statements?

Determination of Overall Inventory Valuation   In applying LCM to determine the overall inventory valuation, three approaches are available:[4]
• Comparison of cost and market separately for each item of inventory.
• Comparison of cost and market separately for each classification of inventory.
• Comparison of total cost with total market for the inventory.
Exhibit 10–3 shows the application of each approach. Consistency in application over time is essential. The individual unit basis produces the most conservative inventory value because units whose market value exceeds cost are not allowed to offset items whose market value is less than cost. This offsetting occurs to some extent in the other approaches.

A problem arises when different unit costs of a particular commodity must be compared with a single unit market price. This case frequently occurs when the first-in first-out cost flow assumption is used. In such cases, the aggregate cost for the commodity should be compared with the aggregate market as shown under Total in Exhibit 10–3. *Market* here means market as defined under LCM.

Recording and Reporting Lower of Cost or Market (LCM)   Purchases are recorded at cost; therefore, the introduction of LCM valuation of the inventory each period raises the question of how the difference between actual cost and LCM should be recorded and

[4] *ARB No. 43*, chapter 4, statement 7.

reported. This difference arises only because inventory items on hand can now be replaced for less than their original cost. This difference is called an *inventory holding loss*. The basic issue is whether the inventory holding loss should be separately recorded in the accounts and separately reported on the financial statements or merged into cost of goods sold. The following two methods of recording and reporting the effects of the application of LCM are used in practice.

1. **Direct inventory reduction method.** Under this method, the inventory holding loss is not separately recorded and reported. The LCM amount, if it is less than the original cost of the inventory, is recorded and reported each period. Under this procedure, the inventory holding loss is automatically included in cost of goods sold and ending inventory is reported at LCM.

2. **Inventory allowance method.** Under this method, the inventory holding loss is separately recorded and reported each period. This separation is recorded by using a *contra inventory* account, allowance to reduce inventory to LCM. Using this procedure, the inventory and cost of goods sold amounts are recorded and reported at original cost, while any inventory holding loss is recognized separately. The entry for a loss of $1,000 would be:

Holding loss on inventory 1,000
Allowance to reduce inventory to LCM   1,000

Both of the above methods yield exactly the same income and total asset amounts. The two methods differ only with respect to the detail in the entries and disclosures on the income statement and balance sheet. Both methods are shown in Exhibit 10–4 based on the data for three consecutive years given below. Exhibit 10–4 illustrates the related accounting entries under both methods (assuming a periodic inventory system). Exhibit 10–5 on page 476 presents the related balance sheet and income statement amounts.

Case Data (in thousands of dollars)

	1991		1992		1993	
	Beginning	Ending	Beginning	Ending	Beginning	Ending
a. Cost	–0–	$10	$10	$20	$20	$30
b. Market	–0–	11	11	17	17	26
c. LCM, lower of (a), (b)	–0–	10	10	17	17	26

Under the *direct inventory reduction method,* the LCM amount of the ending inventory, rather than the inventory's original cost, is recorded directly in the accounts and reported on the financial statements. The amount of ending inventory at LCM is carried forward to the next period as the beginning inventory. Thus, both the beginning and ending inventory amounts are reflected at LCM. These characteristics are evident in Exhibits 10–4 and 10–5 under the heading Direct Inventory Reduction Method.

In contrast, under the *inventory allowance method,* the entries and financial statements retain the actual costs for inventory and cost of goods sold. The entries also record and report the holding loss each period in a contra inventory account, allowance to reduce inventory to LCM. The net holding loss (which is the net effect of the holding losses in the beginning and ending inventories) is reported separately on the income statement. These characteristics are evident in Exhibits 10–4 and 10–5 under the heading Inventory Allowance Method.

The LCM method shifts a portion of the inventory cost as an expense or loss to the year of the write down. In the year of the sale, the remaining portion of the original purchase cost is expensed. Ultimately, the entire historical cost of the inventory is expensed. However, this shifting affects earnings in both years. Fur-

EXHIBIT 10–4 Recording and Reporting LCM (Periodic Inventory System)

End-of-Period Inventory Entries	Direct Inventory Reduction Method		Inventory Allowance Method	
1991 (no holding loss):*				
a. Beginning inventory—none				
b. Ending inventory:				
Inventory (ending)	(cost) 10		(cost) 10	
Income summary (cost of goods sold)		10		10
1992 (holding loss, $3):				
a. To close beginning inventory:				
Income summary (cost of goods sold)	(cost) 10		(cost) 10	
Inventory (beginning)		10		10
b. To record ending inventory:				
Inventory (ending)	(LCM) 17		(cost) 20	
Income summary (cost of goods sold)		17		20
c. To record holding loss in ending inventory:				
Holding loss on inventory ($20 − $17)			3	
Allowance to reduce inventory to LCM . .				3
1993 (holding loss, $1):				
a. To close beginning inventory:				
Income summary (cost of goods sold)	(LCM) 17		(cost) 20	
Inventory (beginning)		17		20
b. To record ending inventory:				
Inventory (ending)	(LCM) 26		(cost) 30	
Income summary (cost of goods sold)		26		30
c. To record holding loss on ending inventory:				
Holding loss on inventory			1	
Allowance to reduce inventory to LCM† . .				1

*There is no entry for holding loss in 1991 because market is above cost.
†1993 balance required in allowance account, ($30 − $26), less 1992 balance in allowance account, $3, = $1.

thermore, to determine the effect of applying LCM to earnings of a particular year, both the beginning and ending effects on inventory must be considered.

For example, the $3 write-down of the 1992 ending inventory also reduces the 1993 beginning inventory by $3, thereby increasing 1993 earnings by $3. The $4 write-down of 1993 ending inventory reduces 1993 earnings by $4. The net effect of LCM on 1993 earnings is, therefore, only a $1 decrease. The inventory allowance method captures the net earnings effect in any year.

A net gain from holding inventory is also possible if market declines below cost in one period and partly or completely recovers in a subsequent period. For example, if the market value of the 1993 ending inventory described in Exhibit 10–4 were $32 rather than the $26 figure shown, a holding gain of $3 would be recognized under the allowance method. The market value of the inventory would have shown a positive gain of $5 from the beginning of the year when the market value of the inventory was $17 ($3 below the inventory's $20 cost and thus a loss) to the end of the year when the market value of the inventory is $32 ($2 above the inventory's $30 cost and thus a gain). Using the direct method, the $3 write-down for 1993 beginning inventory increases 1993 income by $3, agreeing with the allowance method. However, only the amount of the previously recognized loss ($3) can be recovered in the form of holding gains, effectively offsetting these losses. Gains beyond the amount of the holding loss are ignored, in keeping with the LCM rule. Inventory is never written up to a higher amount.

EXHIBIT 10-5   Financial Statement—Reporting LCM for Inventory: Direct Inventory Reduction and Inventory Allowance Methods Compared

Reporting LCM—Direct Inventory Reduction Method
(Inventory Holding Loss Merged with Inventory and Cost of Goods Sold)

	Year 1991	Year 1992	Year 1993
Balance sheet:			
Current assets:			
Merchandise inventory	$10	$17	$26
Income Statement:			
Sales revenue (assumed)	$50	$65	$81
Cost of goods sold:			
Beginning inventory (at LCM)	$ 0	$10	$17
Purchases (assumed)	40	47	61
Total goods available for sale	40	57	78
Ending inventory (at LCM)	(10)	(17)	(26)
Cost of goods sold	30	40*	52*
Gross margin	20	25	29
Expenses (assumed)	(10)	(13)	(16)
Income (pretax)	$10	$12	$13

Reporting LCM—Inventory Allowance Method
(Holding Losses Reported Separately from Inventory and Cost of Goods Sold)

	Year 1991		Year 1992		Year 1993	
Balance sheet:						
Current assets:						
Merchandise inventory (at cost)	$10		$20		$30	
Less: Allowance to reduce						
inventory to LCM	(0)	$10	(3)	$17	(4)	$26
Income Statement:						
Sales revenue (assumed)		$50		$65		$81
Cost of goods sold:						
Beginning inventory (at cost)	$ 0		$10		$20	
Purchases (assumed)	40		47		61	
Total goods available for sale	40		57		81	
Ending inventory (at cost)	(10)		(20)		(30)	
Cost of goods sold (at cost)		30		37		51
Gross margin		20		28		30
Expenses (assumed)		(10)		(13)		(16)
Deduct net holding loss effect:						
1991		–0–				
1992				(3)		
1993						(1)
Income (pretax)		$10		$12		$13

*The holding loss merged with these amounts is: 1992, $3; and 1993, $1. For 1992; $40 = $37 + $3 and for 1993, $52 = $51 + $1.

The *direct inventory reduction method* is widely used because it is less complex than the allowance method when the periodic inventory system is used, the inventory holding loss amount for the period often is not material or unusual, and disclosure notes can be used to report the holding loss information. In contrast, some companies prefer the inventory allowance method because it provides full disclosure of the effects of LCM on inventories (the direct inventory reduction method does not), is required under certain conditions,[5] is less complex than the direct inventory reduction method when the perpetual inventory system is used (perpetual records usually are maintained at cost, not LCM), and provides insight into the interperiod effects of using LCM.

The Use of LCM for Tax Reporting

Chapter 9 pointed out that if a company uses the LIFO inventory method in reporting its tax liability to the IRS, it must use the same method in reporting inventory values in its financial statements. In addition, for tax reporting purposes, the IRS prohibits the use of LIFO when computing inventory values under LCM; instead, FIFO or average cost must be used. However, LIFO can be used in reporting inventory values under LCM in financial statements.

Companies often write down inventory values of goods that are not selling well. In such cases, if the company is computing inventory values under LCM for tax reporting purposes, the IRS allows deductions for such write-downs. The deduction must be taken in the same year in which the price decline (or obsolescence) occurs. Further, these write-downs must be computed on an item-by-item basis rather than as a nonspecific write-down of the entire inventory. For financial statement reporting purposes, write-downs should be recognized when it becomes clear that the inventory items in question will not recover their lost value.

CONCEPT REVIEW

1. What does *market* mean in LCM terms?
2. Why is a floor and a ceiling placed on the determination of market under LCM?
3. What is the difference in reporting holding losses under the direct inventory reduction method and the inventory allowance method?

GROSS MARGIN METHOD AND INVENTORY ESTIMATION
♦

At the start of this chapter, the problems associated with establishing the inventory values for Sears were considered. Imagine how many individuals would be required to maintain a physical count of all the different items in Sears' inventory. Fortunately, there are simpler approaches that can be used to estimate inventory values. One such approach is called the *gross margin method*. Although the gross margin method is generally unacceptable for use in external financial statements, it is used by many companies in estimating the cost of an inventory. **The gross margin method** (also known as the *gross profit method*), is a method of estimating inventory based on the assumption that a constant gross margin estimated on recent sales can be used to estimate inventory values from current sales. The gross margin method provides a test check on the accuracy of the results of other inventory methods. The method assumes that the gross margin rate (gross margin divided by sales), based on recent

---

[5] Ibid., chapter 7, statement 7, par. 14, states: "When substantial and unusual losses result from the application of this rule (LCM), it will frequently be desirable to disclose the amount of the loss in the income statement as a charge separately identified from . . . *cost of goods sold*" (emphasis supplied). The inventory allowance method provides for separate reporting of the holding loss. The direct inventory reduction method merges the holding loss with cost of goods sold automatically; therefore, to some accountants it does not appear compatible with this quotation from *ARB No. 43* when the difference is substantial in amount and unusual.

EXHIBIT 10-6 Gross Margin Method Applied

	Known Data	Computations*	Computation (Step)†
Net sales revenue (base amount)	$10,000	100%	
Cost of goods sold:			
Beginning inventory . . . . $ 5,000			
Add: Purchases 8,000			
Goods available for sale . 13,000			2
Less Ending inventory . . ?		$13,000 − $6,000 = $7,000	5
Cost of goods sold . . .	?	$10,000 − $4,000 = $6,000	4
Gross margin rate (estimated as percent of sales) 40%	?	40% × $10,000 = $4,000	3

*These computations can be arranged in numerous ways. The most abbreviated one is $13,000 − $10,000 × (1.00 − .40) = $7,000, ending inventory.

†Step one has been made already and the result was 40% (See discussion in text below.)

past performance, is reasonably constant in the short run. The gross margin method has two basic characteristics: it requires the development of an estimated gross margin rate, and then applies the rate to groups of items (such as all items sold in a Sears sporting goods department).

Estimating the ending inventory by the gross margin method requires five steps:

1. Estimate the gross margin rate: (sales − cost of goods sold) ÷ sales.
2. Compute total cost of goods available for sale in the usual manner (beginning inventory plus purchases), based on actual data provided by the accounts.
3. Compute the estimated gross margin by multiplying sales by the estimated gross margin rate.
4. Compute cost of goods sold by subtracting the computed gross margin from sales.
5. Compute ending inventory by subtracting the computed cost of goods sold from the cost of goods available for sale.

Application of the gross margin method is illustrated in Exhibit 10–6 based on the following data:

1. Net sales revenue during the period, $10,000.
2. Beginning inventory, $5,000. } Provided by the accounting records.
3. Purchases during the period, $8,000.
4. Estimated gross margin rate, computed as a percentage of sales, 40% (based on recent past performance). This is step 1.

The gross margin method has two significant limitations. First, the estimated gross margin rate, based on data from past period(s), may not appropriately reflect markup changes relating to the current or future periods. Second, the average gross margin rate may include widely varying markup rates on different types of inventory. Most companies, like Sears, carry a number of different lines of merchandise, each having a different markup rate. A change during the period in the markup rate on one or more lines, or a shift in the relative quantities of each line sold (shifts in sales mix), changes the average gross margin rate. This change affects the reliability of the results derived by the method.

When the gross margin method is applied in a situation that involves broad aggregations of inventory items with significantly different markup rates, the computations should be developed for each separate class. Then the estimate of the total inventory can be determined by summing the estimates for the separate classes.

The gross margin method can be used with different inventory cost flow assumptions (FIFO, LIFO, average cost) because the computed gross margin rate is based implicitly on the cost method used by the company. The cost of goods sold used to determine the gross margin rate reflects the cost-flow assumption used.

Sometimes the gross margin method uses a cost percentage (cost of goods sold divided by sales) rather than the gross margin percentage (gross margin divided by sales). If either percentage is known, the other can be determined because the two percentages must sum to 100 percent. In the example used for Exhibit 10–6, the gross margin rate is 40% of sales; therefore, the cost percentage is 60% (100% − 40%) of sales.

Also, the gross margin rate, or markup, may be available as a percentage of selling price, total sales, cost, or cost of goods sold. In Exhibit 10–6, for example, the markup is given as a percentage of selling price. If necessary, the markup on sales can be converted to a markup on cost based on the relationship:

$$\text{Selling price \%} \quad - \quad \text{Cost of goods sold \%} \quad = \quad \text{Gross margin \%}$$

or:

$$\text{Selling price \%} \quad - \quad \text{Gross margin \%} \quad = \quad \text{Cost of goods sold \%}.$$

For the situation described in Exhibit 10–6, a 40% gross margin on sales implies that the cost of goods sold is 60% of the selling price:

$$\begin{array}{ccccc} \text{Selling price} & - & \text{Gross margin} & = & \text{Cost of goods sold} \\ 100\% & - & 40\% & = & 60\% \end{array}$$

Thus, the markup on cost is $(100\% - 60\%) \div 60\% = 40\% \div 60\% = 66.67\%$. Similarly, given a 66.67% margin on cost, the markup on selling price is:

$$\begin{array}{ccccc} \text{Cost of goods sold} & + & \text{Gross margin} & = & \text{Selling price} \\ 100\% & + & 66.67\% & = & 166.67\% \end{array}$$

Hence, the markup on selling price is $(166.67\% - 100\%) \div 166.67\% = 66.67\% \div 166.67\% = 40\%$. Traditionally markups are quoted on sales price because of the marketing function's importance in establishing prices. Occasionally, however, markups are quoted on cost because they are based on cost.

Applications of the Gross Margin Method

The gross margin method is used in the following situations:

1. To test the reasonableness of an inventory valuation provided by some other person or determined by some other means, such as a physical inventory count or from perpetual inventory records. For example, assume the company in Exhibit 10–6 submitted to an auditor an ending inventory valuation of $10,000. The gross margin method provides an approximation of $7,000, which suggests that the inventory should be examined because it appears to be overvalued.
2. To estimate the ending inventory for interim financial reports prepared during the year when it is impractical to physically count the inventory and a perpetual inventory system is not used.
3. To estimate the cost of inventory destroyed by a casualty, such as fire or storm. This application is limited to cases in which the accounting records are not destroyed because certain data from the accounts are essential. Valuation of inventory lost through casualty is necessary to account for the casualty and to establish a basis for related insurance claims and income tax computation. This is an example of a case where it would be helpful to know the markup on cost since cost is needed for the insurance claim and to establish the tax deductible loss.

4. To develop budget estimates of cost of goods sold, gross margin, and inventory consistent with a sales revenue budget.

THE RETAIL INVENTORY METHOD AND INVENTORY ESTIMATION

The **retail inventory method** often is used by retail stores, particularly department stores that sell a wide variety of items. In such situations, perpetual inventory procedures may be impractical, and it is unusual to take a complete physical inventory count more often than annually. The retail inventory method also can be used for accounting and income tax purposes. Two major advantages of the retail inventory method are its ease of use and the reduced detail in recordkeeping required.

The retail inventory method is appropriate when items sold within a department have essentially the same markup rate, and articles purchased for resale are priced immediately.

The retail inventory method is based only on dollar amounts. The retail inventory method uses both retail value and actual cost data provided by the accounts to compute a ratio of cost to retail (referred to as the *cost ratio*), calculates the ending inventory at retail value, and converts that retail value to a cost value by applying the computed cost ratio to the ending retail value.

Application of the retail inventory method requires that internal records be kept to provide the following data:

* Sales revenue.
* Beginning inventory valued at both cost and retail.
* Purchases during the period valued at both cost and retail.
* Adjustments to the original retail price, such as additional markups, markup cancellations, markdowns, markdown cancellations, and employee discounts.
* Data relating to other adjustments, such as interdepartmental transfers, returns, breakage, and damaged goods.

The retail inventory method is similar to the gross margin method in that the inventory valuation is based on the ratio of cost to selling price. The gross margin method uses an estimate of the gross margin rate for the current period based upon historical cost. The retail inventory method, however, uses a computed cost ratio based on the actual relationship between cost and retail for the current period. The computed cost ratio is an average across several different kinds of goods sold. Thus, the computed inventory amount is an estimate but, nevertheless, one acceptable for external financial reporting.

The retail inventory method is illustrated in Exhibit 10–7 using the following data (from the accounting records):

1. Beginning inventory (January 1, 1992):
   a. At cost, $15,000.
   b. At retail, $25,000.
2. Purchases during January 1992:
   a. At cost $195,000.
   b. At retail, $275,000.
3. Sales revenue, $260,000.

The objective of the retail inventory method is to find the ending inventory value at cost. To do this, the following information is needed:

* The total cost of goods available for sale at both cost and retail.
* Sales for the current period at retail.

Based on the case data presented above:

1. The total cost of goods available for sale during January 1992 was determined to be $210,000 at cost and $300,000 at retail, as shown in Exhibit 10–7.

EXHIBIT 10–7   Retail Inventory Method Illustrated, Average Cost

	At Cost	At Retail
Goods available for sale:		
Beginning inventory (January 1, 1992)	$ 15,000	$ 25,000
Purchases during January 1992	195,000	275,000
Total goods available for sale	$210,000	300,000
Cost ratio:		
$210,000 ÷ $300,000 = .70 (average, January 1992)		
Deduct January sales at retail		260,000
Ending inventory (January 31, 1992):		
At retail		$ 40,000
At cost ($40,000 × .70)	$ 28,000	

2. Next, the cost ratio (ratio of cost to sales) is computed. This is done by dividing the total cost of goods available for sale at cost ($210,000) by the same items at retail ($300,000). In this instance, the cost ratio is ($210,000/$300,000) = .70, or 70%, as shown in Exhibit 10–7. This is an average cost application of the retail method, because both beginning inventory and purchases are included in determining the cost ratio.
3. The next step in the operation is to subtract January sales ($260,000) from the total cost of goods available for sale at retail ($300,000), which results in the value of the ending inventory at retail ($40,000), again as shown in Exhibit 10–7.
4. The last step is to compute the ending inventory at cost. This is done by applying the cost ratio (.70), derived in (2), to the ending inventory at retail ($40,000), derived in (4). The result is an ending inventory of $28,000 at cost ($40,000 × .70).

In Exhibit 10–7, accounting data were used to derive ending inventory. For financial reporting, the count or actual total ending inventory at retail is used. For example, assume that the count of retail items on hand January 31, 1992, is $35,000. In this case, the ending inventory at cost would be $24,500, (.70 × $35,000). Shrinkage, therefore, is estimated to be $3,500, ($28,000 − $24,500).

Markups and Markdowns   The data used for Exhibit 10–7 assumed no changes in the sales price of the merchandise as originally set. Frequently, the original sales price on some merchandise is raised or lowered, particularly at the end of the selling season or when replacement costs are changing. The retail inventory method requires that a careful record be kept of all changes to the original sales price because these changes affect the inventory cost computation. To apply the retail inventory method, it is important to distinguish among the following terms:

- **Original sales price**—sale price first marked on the merchandise.
- **Markup**—the original or initial amount that the merchandise is marked up above cost. It is the difference between the purchase cost and the original sales price, and may be expressed either as a dollar amount or a percent of either cost or sale price. Sometimes this markup is called initial markup or markon.
- **Additional markup**—any increase in the sales price above the original sales price. The original sales price is the base from which additional markup is measured.
- **Additional markup cancellations**—cancellation of all, or some, of an additional markup. Additional markup less additional markup cancellations usually is called net additional markup.
- **Markdown**—a reduction in the original sales price.

EXHIBIT 10-8   Computation of Final Sales Price

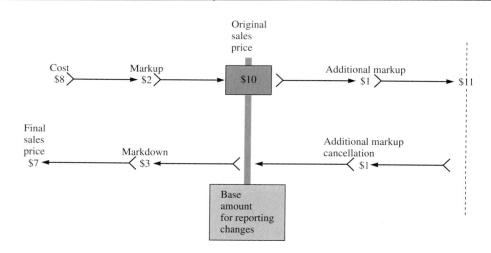

* **Markdown cancellation**—after a reduction in the original sales price (i.e., after a markdown), an increase in the sales price that does not exceed the original sales price (if it exceeds the original sales price, the excess is an additional markup).

   The definitions are illustrated in Exhibit 10–8 by assuming an item that cost $8 is originally marked to sell at $10. This item is subsequently marked up $1 to sell at $11, then marked down to $10, and finally reduced to sell at $7.

Application of the Retail Inventory Method

The retail inventory method can be applied in different ways to estimate the cost of ending inventory under alternative inventory cost flow assumptions, such as: FIFO with LCM, average cost with LCM, and LIFO. Since LCM is a required valuation process under GAAP, it will be used with FIFO and average cost for illustration.

   To illustrate the FIFO and average cost bases, the information given in Exhibit 10–9 is used. Assume this information was provided by the accounting records of the Sandia Company at the end of the accounting period. Units are not used, only dollars.

FIFO Basis   To estimate the FIFO cost of ending inventory, the cost and retail amounts of the beginning inventory are excluded from the computation of the cost ratio because under FIFO the cost of the ending inventory is assumed to come from the purchases made during the current period, not from the beginning inventory. Thus, the cost ratio affects the relationship of cost to retail values for current period purchases only. In instances where the ending inventory exceeds the amount of purchases for the accounting period, the cost ratio no longer represents the current period relationship only. The ending inventory, in this case, includes a portion of the previous period's ending inventory.

Average Cost Basis   To estimate the cost of ending inventory on an average cost basis, the cost ratio is computed on total goods available for sale (i.e., the sum of beginning inventory plus purchases) because the cost of the ending inventory is assumed to represent the total goods available for sale during the period. Thus, this cost ratio reflects the relationship of cost to retail values for all inventory items available for sale, including the beginning inventory. (See Exhibit 10–7.)

EXHIBIT 10-9 Data Used to Illustrate the Retail Inventory Method, Sandia Company

	At Cost	At Retail
Inventory at beginning of period	$ 550	$ 900
Purchases during period	6,290	8,900
Additional markups during period		225
Additional markup cancellations during period		25
Markdowns during period		600
Markdown cancellations during period		100
Sales revenue for the period		8,500

LCM Basis (The Conventional Method) To estimate the LCM of ending inventory, the cost ratio *excludes net markdowns*. The reason is that exclusion of net markdowns from the computation of the retail value of goods available (markups and markdowns do not affect cost) causes the retail value of goods available (the denominator of the cost ratio) to be higher than if net markdowns were subtracted from goods available for sale. In turn, this decreases the cost ratio and, thus, produces a conservative estimate of the value of ending inventory. Although the resulting cost value would only coincidentally be equal to the actual LCM value based on replacement cost, the result is an acceptable approximation.

As indicated in Exhibit 10-10 on page 484, LCM is applied to FIFO and average cost. The LCM method is not applied to LIFO under the retail method. This is in part because the *conventional retail method* is designed to approximate the lower of average cost or market, and also because even though the IRS allows the LCM-retail method for tax reporting, it does not allow the use of LIFO with it. The LIFO-retail method is discussed later in this chapter.

Retail Method, FIFO with LCM Illustrated

When FIFO is used, the ending inventory is costed at the current period's unit costs; therefore, the costs in the beginning inventory are included in cost of goods sold rather than in the ending inventory. To accomplish this result with the retail method, the beginning inventory is excluded from the computation of the cost ratio. The result will approximate the FIFO cost of the ending inventory. Then to approximate LCM, net markdowns are excluded from the cost ratio. (It is assumed that all markups and markdowns relate to purchases and not to beginning inventory.) The LCM computations on the FIFO basis are shown for the Sandia Company in Exhibit 10-10. When any version of the retail inventory method is used, cost of goods sold is computed in the usual manner: goods available for sale minus ending inventory at cost.

Retail Method, Average Cost with LCM Illustrated

Under the *retail method,* using the average cost basis, the cost ratio is derived by dividing total goods available for sale at cost by total goods available for sale at retail. Both totals include the beginning inventory. Therefore, if the cost ratio is calculated on the basis of totals, including the beginning inventory, the retail method approximates average cost. To approximate LCM, net markdowns are excluded from the cost ratio. The LCM computation using the average cost basis, is also shown for The Sandia Company in Exhibit 10-10.

The retail inventory method of estimating the LCM of inventory, shown in Exhibit 10-10, assumes markdowns occur because the utility of the merchandise has declined. That is, the current purchase price of identical new goods decreased, or,

EXHIBIT 10-10   Retail Inventory Method Illustrated: Sandia Company (FIFO with LCM and Average Cost with LCM)

		At Cost		At Retail
Goods available for sale:				
Beginning inventory		$ 550		$ 900
Purchases during period		6,290		8,900
Additional markups during period	$225			
Less: Additional markup cancellations	(25)			
Net additional markups				200
Markdowns	(600)			
Less: Markdown cancellations	100			
Net markdowns				(500)
Total goods available for sale		$6,840		9,500
Deduct:				
Sales				(8,500)
Ending inventory:				
At retail				$1,000
At approximate FIFO cost with LCM ($1,000 × .691[a])		$ 691		
At approximate average cost with LCM ($1,000 × .684[b])		$ 684		

Note: Computation of cost ratios:

a. FIFO with LCM cost ratio:

$$\frac{\$6,290}{\$8,900 + \$225 - \$25} = .691$$

Based on current period costs and retail values; beginning inventory excluded from numerator and denominator; net markdowns excluded from denominator in computation of cost ratio.

b. Average with LCM cost ratio:

$$\frac{\$550 + \$6,290}{\$900 + \$8,900 + \$225 - \$25} = .684$$

Based on average costs and retail values; beginning inventory included in numerator and denominator; net markdowns excluded from denominator in computation of cost ratio.

stated differently, the goods had a replacement cost that is lower than historical cost. The decrease in replacement cost could result from such factors as obsolescence, spoilage, or excess supply. Therefore, to value the inventory at LCM, the net markdowns are omitted from computation of the cost ratio.

For example, assume two items are purchased for $4 and first marked up to sell at $12 each. Later markdowns amounted to $8 in total. Using the conventional retail method (LCM), which does not recognize markdowns, the cost ratio is 2($4) ÷ 2($12) = .33. If markdowns are considered, the ratio is 2($4) ÷ [2($12) − $8] = .500. When applied to the ending retail value of $16, the LCM value is obtained by applying the .33 ratio to obtain $5.33 for ending inventory at cost. If the .50 cost ratio were applied, the resulting inventory at cost is $8 per unit, which is historical cost. However markdowns, by definition, represent a decline in the inventory's utility. Therefore the conventional retail method produces results which are more reflective of that decline.

Special Items Related to the Retail Inventory Method

Several items may complicate computation of the ending inventory using the retail inventory method. In resolving these issues it is essential to protect the integrity of the computed cost ratio and the amount of ending inventory at retail. Six complicating items, and the way each usually is treated are discussed next and illustrated in Exhibit 10–11 on page 486.

1. **Freight-in.** The expenditure for freight adds to the cost of merchandise; therefore, it is added to goods available for sale (or directly to purchases) at cost (but not at retail).

2. **Purchase returns.** Because purchase returns, as distinguished from allowances, reduce the amount of goods available for sale, they are deducted from goods available for sale at both cost and retail.

3. **Abnormal casualty losses** and missing merchandise arising from unusual or infrequent events (such as a fire or theft) are deducted from goods available for sale at both cost and retail because they will not be sold; removal from both cost and retail eliminates their effect on the cost ratio as if they had not been purchased in the first place. The damaged merchandise is set up in a special inventory account at its net realizable value.

4. **Sales returns and allowances.** Because this is a contra account to the sales revenue account, sales returns and allowances are deducted from gross sales. If the returned merchandise is placed back into inventory for resale, no change in the "at cost" column in Exhibit 10–10 is needed because its cost is already properly included in the purchases amount. However, if the merchandise is not returned to inventory (because of damage, for example), then its cost should be deducted in the "at cost" column on the sales line after the cost ratio. (Because net sales has been reduced, the cost also should be reduced.)

5. **Discounts to employees and favored customers.** These discounts result from selling merchandise below the normal sales price and are not caused by market value decreases. Therefore, they are different from markdowns. Such discounts are deducted below the cost ratio, which means they reduce ending inventory at retail but not the total cost of goods available for sale. Net sales includes sales made to employees at discount prices and therefore, understates the retail value of goods sold. Hence they are, in effect, added back to net sales to determine ending inventory at retail. (See Exhibit 10–11.) Employee discounts of $200 are an additional deduction used to derive ending inventory at retail.

6. **Normal spoilage** including shrinkage and breakage. This is the retail value of the units lost. This amount is deducted below the cost ratio, along with sales, because the expected cost of normal spoilage implicitly is included in determining the selling price and does not reflect market value changes. Normal spoilage, then, is not included in the cost-to-retail ratio calculation. Deduction of normal spoilage in arriving at the cost ratio would overstate the cost ratio and the estimated cost of the ending inventory. Abnormal spoilage and theft is not deducted from the total cost of goods available for sale since it is not included in determining selling prices. Instead, abnormal spoilage is deducted in establishing the cost ratio. Failure to deduct abnormal spoilage in arriving at the cost ratio would understate the cost ratio and the estimated cost of ending inventory.

The preceding discussion of the retail inventory method assumed that the goods included in a single set of computations are similar in terms of their markup percentage and relative proportion of the total inventory of the company. In individual departments this usually is the case. However, on a storewide basis it often is not. For example, three fourths of the total inventory may have a markup of 80%, and one fourth of the inventory may have a markup of 50%. Therefore, the essential data should be accumulated for each sales department. The retail inventory computations then should be made on a departmental basis. The departmental inventories are summed to derive the total ending inventory.

EXHIBIT 10-11   Retail Inventory Method (Average Cost, LCM), with Special Items Illustrated: Data Assumed*

	At Cost	At Retail
Goods available for sale:		
Beginning inventory	$ 6,050	$ 11,000
Purchases	57,120	102,000
Freight-in (1)	1,020	
Purchase returns (2)	(560)	(1,000)
Net additional markups		600
Casualty loss:† (3)		
At cost	(3,630)	
At retail		(6,600)
Total	$60,000	106,000
Cost ratio: $60,000 ÷ $106,000 = .566		
Deduct:		
Gross sales	$71,200	
Sales returns (merchandise returned to stock) (4)	(1,200)	
Net sales		(70,000)
Discounts to employees (5)		(200)
Normal spoilage (6)		(1,300)
Net markdowns		(4,500)
Ending inventory:		
At retail		$ 30,000
At average cost, LCM ($30,000 × .566)	$16,980	

* The numbers in parentheses refer to the factors discussed in the text.

† The casualty loss could have been recorded as follows per the assumed situation:
Cash (from insurance company: assumed)	2,000	
Casualty loss (fire damage)	1,630	
Purchases (or cost of goods sold)		3,630

CONCEPT REVIEW

1. When is the gross margin method used? Explain, using a major grocery chain as an example.
2. How is the retail method related to the gross margin method of estimating inventories? Why are markdowns excluded from the cost ratio in applications of the retail method?
3. Explain how to compute the cost ratios for the inventory methods discussed in this section.

USING THE RETAIL INVENTORY METHOD WITH DV LIFO
◆

This section discusses the application of LIFO by companies that also use the retail inventory method to estimate their inventory costs. The dollar value LIFO method is acceptable for interim financial reports, external financial reports, and for income tax purposes (subject to specific constraints in the tax regulations).

The dollar value LIFO retail method (abbreviated, DV LIFO retail method) requires that the FIFO retail method (not LCM) be used. The results then are converted to a LIFO basis by applying the DV LIFO conversion process discussed in Chapter 9. *The DV LIFO retail method is the only acceptable way to convert the retail data to a LIFO basis.* This method requires that a distinction be maintained between the base year inventory and subsequent incremental layers, and that the subsequent layers be costed by applying two different ratios: (1) a conversion price index and (2) a cost ratio for the year the layer was added.

Treasury regulations specify that variety stores using the DV LIFO retail method for income tax purposes must use an internally computed price index. On the other hand, retailers that qualify as department stores (as defined for tax purposes) may use a published (external) price index. In the discussions and illustrations that follow, a published price index is used for conversion purposes.

The DV LIFO retail method is similar to DV LIFO (discussed in Chapter 9) in that it uses dollars only (not units and unit costs) and an inventory price index. The DV LIFO retail method can be outlined as follows:

I. Computation of Ending Inventory at FIFO cost:

    a. List the DV LIFO inventory layers carried over from the prior year in base year retail dollars.

    b. For each period, apply the FIFO retail method without considering LCM to compute that period's cost ratio. Thus, net markdowns must be included in the computation of the FIFO cost ratio, thereby ignoring the adjustment for LCM. The FIFO method, which excludes the beginning inventory from the cost ratio, must be used. (The average cost method, which includes the amounts of the beginning inventory, cannot be used.) The cost ratio is applied to the ending inventory at retail to obtain the FIFO cost.

    The beginning base year inventory for the year of change to LIFO used in this calculation is the ending FIFO (not LCM) inventory carried over from the year prior to the change.

II. Conversion to LIFO Cost:

    c. Compute an internal conversion price index (for variety stores) for the current period, or select an external price index for conversion purposes (for department stores). This step was illustrated in Chapter 9. (In the example to follow, an external price index is used.)

    d. Convert the ending inventory amount, at retail, to a LIFO cost basis by using the conversion price index related to each layer of inventory and the FIFO cost ratio of the period. The LIFO effect is attained by assuming the last layers of inventory purchased are the first layers sold. Thus the DV LIFO retail method is a LIFO method between years when inventory layers are liquidated. When layers are added, they are costed at FIFO for the current period.

Step *d* starts with the ending inventory, valued at retail, stated in the current year's dollars. This retail amount then is *restated* to retail in the base year's dollars by dividing it by the current year conversion price index. The result is the total ending inventory for the current year valued at retail but stated in base year dollars. This base year retail value then is identified in terms of the base layer and any additional layers added in years subsequent to the year of the base layer. Each layer then is converted to LIFO cost by multiplying the base year retail amount by, first, its conversion price index to convert base year retail dollar values into dollars of the year the layer was added and, second, its FIFO cost ratio to restate those retail dollar values to cost amounts. The sum of the costs of the various layers, as converted, provides the ending inventory at LIFO cost. This amount is reported on the balance sheet and used on the income statement to compute cost of goods sold.

The application of the DV LIFO retail method is illustrated for the Chicago Corporation for each of the three years given in Exhibit 10–12.[6] The computations are shown separately for each year in Exhibits 10–13, 10–14, and 10–15.

---

[6] Three years are shown to illustrate initial adoption of LIFO, the buildup of additional layers, and subsequent liquidation of parts of layers.

EXHIBIT 10-12   Data from Inventory Records to Illustrate DV LIFO Retail Computations, Chicago Corporation

1. The company has been using the retail inventory method (FIFO, not LCM) for (1) internal reporting and control purposes, (2) external reporting to shareholders, and (3) income tax purposes. Starting on January 1, 1992, the company decided to use the DV LIFO retail method for the latter two purposes.

2. The ending inventory at December 31, 1991, using the retail inventory method, FIFO basis (not LCM), was:
   At retail, $30,000
   At cost ($30,000 × cost ratio, .58), $17,400

3. Detailed data subsequent to December 31, 1991 (date of the change):

	1992		1993		1994	
	At Cost	At Retail	At Cost	At Retail	At Cost	At Retail
Purchases	$90,480	$147,000	$101,500	$169,000	$115,800	$186,800
Net additional markups		8,800		9,000		7,000
Net markdowns		5,000		6,000		4,000
Sales		140,000		162,800		197,800

4. Selected external price
   index (1991 = 100)   102   106   110

Based on the LIFO costs (beginning inventory of $17,400 and ending inventory of $23,520, see Exhibit 10–13), Chicago Corporation would make the following entries at the end of 1992 (assuming a periodic inventory system):

1. To close out beginning inventory:

   Cost of goods sold (or income summary) 17,400
       Inventory   17,400

2. To establish the 1992 ending inventory:

   Inventory 23,520
       Cost of goods sold (or income summary)   23,520

The end-of-year entries for 1993 and 1994 are identical to those for 1992 except the amounts are $23,520 and $28,004 respectively for 1993 and $28,004 and $22,407 for 1994. (See Exhibits 10–14 and 10–15, respectively.)

Evaluation of the Retail Inventory Method

The retail inventory method has been sponsored by the National Retail Merchants Association and approved by the Internal Revenue Service. Therefore, it has become an important method of inventory determination. Like the gross margin method, the retail inventory method is an approach for estimating the amount of the ending inventory and cost of goods sold. The retail inventory method can be used for both financial accounting and income tax purposes.

Because the retail inventory method provides only an estimate of the ending inventory, a physical inventory count should be taken at least annually as a check on the accuracy of the estimated inventory amounts. Differences between the inventory valuations based on the physical inventory count and retail inventory estimate should be analyzed because a difference may indicate:
* Inventory losses due to breakage, loss, or theft.
* Incorrect application of the retail method.

EXHIBIT 10-13   Application of DV LIFO Retail, Chicago Corporation, 1992

I. Computation of Ending Inventory at FIFO Cost:

   a. Base layer (carried over from 1991): Retail $30,000 × .58 = Cost $17,400.
   b. Computation of 1992 ending FIFO inventory (not LCM):

	At FIFO Cost	At Retail	Cost Ratio
Goods available for sale:			
Inventory, 1/1/1992 (Exhibit 10–12)	$ 17,400	$ 30,000	
Purchases (Exhibit 10–12)	90,480	147,000	
Net additional markups (Exhibit 10–12)		8,800	
Net markdowns (Exhibit 10–12)		(5,000)	
Subtotal (excluding beginning inventory due to FIFO)	90,480 ÷	150,800 =	.60
Total goods available for sale	$107,880	180,800	
Deduct: Sales		140,000	
Ending 1992 inventory: At retail		$ 40,800	
At FIFO cost ($40,800 × .60) . . .	$ 24,480		

II. Conversion to LIFO Cost:

   c. Conversion:
      Use external price index for 1992 = 1.02
   d. Conversion of ending inventory at retail ($40,800) to LIFO cost:

	At Base Year Retail	Conversion Price Index	Cost Ratio	DV LIFO Cost
Ending inventory at retail converted to base year retail, $40,800 ÷ 1.02	$40,000			
Composed of: Base inventory layer	$30,000	× 1.00	× .58	= $17,400
1992 additional inventory layer	10,000	× 1.02	× .60	= 6,120*
Ending 1992 inventory at LIFO cost				$23,520

---

* Multiplication of this retail amount by the current year conversion price index restates it to current year prices ($10,000 × 1.02 = $10,200); multiplication of that result by the current year cost ratio restates this 1992 layer to 1992 cost ($10,200 × .60 = $6,120).

- Failure of departmental managers to correctly report markdowns, additional markups, or cancellations.
- Errors in the inventory records.
- Errors in the physical inventory.
- Inventory manipulation.

The inventory accounts must be changed to the actual count by using a correcting entry.

Uses of the Retail Inventory Method   The primary uses of the retail inventory method are:
- To provide estimates of inventory cost for interim periods (e.g., monthly or quarterly) when it is not practical physically to count the inventory and a perpetual inventory system is not used. The method provides estimated inventory valuations needed for interim statements, analyses, and purchasing policy considerations.
- To provide a means for converting inventory amounts determined by a physical count of inventory, priced at retail, to a cost basis. To eliminate the necessity of marking the cost on the merchandise, or referring to invoices, some retail estab-

EXHIBIT 10-14   Application of DV LIFO Retail, Chicago Corporation, 1993.

I. Computation of Ending Inventory at FIFO Cost:

a. Beginning DV LIFO inventory carried over from end of 1992 (from Exhibit 10–13):

	At Base Year Retail	Conversion Price Index	Cost Ratio	DV LIFO Cost
Base inventory layer	$30,000	× 1.00	× .58 =	$17,400
1992 additional layer	10,000	× 1.02	× .60 =	6,120
Total	$40,000			$23,520

b. Computation of 1993 ending FIFO inventory (not LCM):

	At FIFO Cost	At Retail	Cost Ratio
Goods available for sale:			
Inventory, 1/1/1993 (Exhibit 10–13)	$ 24,480	$ 40,800	
Purchases (Exhibit 10–12)	101,500	169,000	
Net additional markups (Exhibit 10–12)		9,000	
Net markdowns (Exhibit 10–12)		(6,000)	
Subtotal (excluding beginning inventory)	101,500 ÷	172,000 =	.59
Total goods available for sale	$125,980	212,800	
Deduct: Sales		162,800	
Ending 1993 inventory: At retail		$ 50,000	
At FIFO cost ($50,000 × .59)	$ 29,500		

II. Conversion to LIFO Cost:

c. Conversion price index for 1993 = 1.06

d. Conversion of ending inventory at retail ($50,000) to LIFO cost:

	At Base Year Retail	Conversion Price Index	Cost Ratio	DV LIFO Cost
Ending inventory at retail converted to base year retail, $50,000 ÷ 1.06	$47,170			
Composed of: Base inventory layer	$30,000	× 1.00	× .58 =	$17,400
1992 inventory layer	10,000	× 1.02	× .60 =	6,120
1993 additional inventory layer	$ 7,170	× 1.06	× .59 =	4,484
Ending 1993 inventory at LIFO cost				$28,004

lishments, after physically counting the inventory, extend the inventory sheets at retail. The retail value then is converted to cost by applying the retail inventory method without reference to the costs of individual items.

* To provide a basis for control of inventory, purchases, theft, markdowns, and additional markups when neither a traditional periodic nor a perpetual inventory system is used for these interim purposes.
* To provide inventory cost data for external financial reports.
* To provide inventory cost data for income tax purposes.
* To provide a test of the overall reasonableness of a physical inventory costed in the normal manner.

EXHIBIT 10-15 Application of DV LIFO, Retail Chicago Corporation, 1994.

I. Computation of Ending Inventory at FIFO Cost:

a. Beginning DV LIFO inventory carried over from end of 1993 (see Exhibit 10–14):

	At Base Year Retail	Conversion Price Index	Cost Ratio	DV LIFO Cost
Base inventory layer	$30,000	× 1.00	× .58 =	$17,400
1992 additional layer	10,000	× 1.02	× .60 =	6,120
1993 additional layer	7,170	× 1.06	× .59 =	4,484
Total	$47,170			$28,004

b. Computation of 1994 ending FIFO inventory (not LCM):

	At FIFO Cost	At Retail	Cost Ratio
Goods available for sale:			
Inventory, 1/1/1994 (Exhibit 10–14)	$ 29,500	$ 50,000	
Purchases (Exhibit 10–12)	115,800	186,800	
Net additional markups (Exhibit 10–12)		7,000	
Net markdowns (Exhibit 10–12)		(4,000)	
Subtotal (excluding beginning inventory)	115,800 ÷	189,800 =	.61
Total goods available for sale	$145,300	239,800	
Deduct: Sales		197,800	
Ending 1994 inventory: At retail		$ 42,000	
At FIFO cost ($42,000 × .61) . .	$ 25,620		

II. Conversion to LIFO Cost:

c. Conversion price index for 1994 = 1.10

d. Conversion of ending inventory at retail ($42,000) to LIFO cost:

	At Base Year Retail	Conversion Price Index	Cost Ratio	DV LIFO Cost
Ending inventory at retail converted to base year retail, $42,000 ÷ 1.10	$38,182			
Composed of: Base inventory layer . . .	$30,000	× 1.00	× .58 =	$17,400
1992 inventory layer remaining	8,182*	× 1.02	× .60 =	5,007
Ending 1994 inventory at LIFO cost . .				$22,407

* After subtracting the base layer of $30,000, $8,182 remained. Therefore, all of the 1993 layer was liquidated, and $8,182 of the 1992 layer remained. Layers are liquidated in LIFO order and both the conversion price index and the cost ratio are *always* identified with the layer created at those ratios. A layer once liquidated is never restored.

ADDITIONAL INVENTORY ISSUES

♦

This section concludes the discussion of inventories with four topics:

1. Inventory valuation at current replacement cost, net realizable value, and selling price.
2. Relative sales value method.
3. Losses on purchase commitments.
4. Effects of inventory errors.

Methods of Inventory Valuation

Inventories Valued at Current Replacement Cost and Net Realizable Value   Special inventory categories often contain items that are not in new condition for resale because they are damaged, shopworn, obsolete, defective, trade-ins, or repossessions. These inventory items must be assigned a cost related to their current condition. In such cases, for inventory valuation purposes, *current replacement cost* is used as a substitute if it can be determined reliably in an established market for the items in their current condition.

Current replacement cost is defined for used inventory valuation purposes as the price for which the items can be purchased in their present condition. To illustrate a typical situation in which the currrent replacement cost can be determined reliably, assume Apple Appliance Company has on hand a repossessed TV set that had an original cost of $650 when new. The set was originally sold for $995 and was repossessed when $500 was owed by the customer. Also, assume that similar used TV sets can be purchased in the wholesale market for $240. The repossessed item should be recorded as:

Inventory, repossessed merchandise	240	
Loss on repossession*	260	
Account receivable		500

* In some situations this may be a gain. If losses, such as the one above, are included in bad debt estimates, the allowance for doubtful accounts is debited.

Assume further that during the following year the repossessed TV set was sold for $270 cash. The entry to record the sale would be recorded as follows (assuming a perpetual inventory system):

Cash	270	
Sales revenue, repossessed merchandise		270
Cost of goods sold	240	
Inventory, repossessed merchandise		240

When the replacement cost cannot be determined reliably, such items should be valued for inventory purposes at their estimated *net realizable value* (NRV). NRV is defined for inventory valuation purposes as the estimated sale price less all costs expected to be incurred in preparing the item for sale. Replacement cost takes precedence over NRV because replacement cost is typically a more objective value, established by existing market forces rather than by managerial estimates. To illustrate accounting for inventory at NRV when replacement cost cannot be determined reliably, assume Apple suffered fire damage to 100 units of its regular inventory. The item, which originally cost $10 per unit (as reflected in the perpetual inventory records), was marked to sell before the fire for $18 per unit. The replacement cost of each item in its present condition cannot be determined reliably because no established used market exists. Therefore, the company should value the item for inventory purposes at its NRV. Apple estimated that after cleaning the items and making repairs, they would sell for $7 per unit; the estimated cost of the repairs for all the units is $150, and estimating selling cost is 20% of the new selling price. Based on these data, the total inventory valuation for the items is:

Estimated sale price (100 × $7)		$700
Less:		
Estimated cost to repair	$150	
Estimated selling costs ($700 × 20%)	140	(290)
NRV for inventory		$410

Assuming no insurance indemnity, the casualty loss and the inventory would be recorded as follows (assuming a perpetual inventory system):

```
Inventory, damaged merchandise (NRV) . . . . . . . . . . . . . . . . .  410
Casualty loss, fire damage  . . . . . . . . . . . . . . . . . . . . . . . . .  590
        Inventory (regular merchandise) (100 × $10) . . . . . . . . . . . .      1,000
```

Inventories Valued at Selling Price   Under unusual circumstances, an inventory item may be valued at selling price. *ARB 43* states[7]:

> Only in exceptional cases may inventories be stated above cost. For example, precious metals having a fixed monetary value with no substantial cost of marketing may be stated at such monetary value; any other exceptions must be justifiable by inability to determine appropriate approximate costs, immediate marketability at quoted market price, and the characteristic of unit interchangeability. [Stating inventories above cost is not uncommon for inventories representing agricultural, mineral, and other products, units of which are interchangeable and have an immediate marketability at quoted prices and for which appropriate costs may be difficult to obtain. Where such inventories are stated at sales prices, they should be reduced by expenditures to be incurred in disposal.] Where goods are stated above cost, this fact should be fully disclosed.

Under the selling price method, when a decrease in selling price occurs, a holding loss is reported; when an increase in selling price occurs, a *holding gain* is reported. Thus, income includes the gross margin and the holding gain or loss for the period. Assume the following simplified data:

Year	Sales	Purchases at Cost	Ending Inventory at Selling Price	Expenses
1991	$ -0-	$1,000	$1,750	$300
1992	1,700	-0-	-0-	300

The financial statements with inventory valued at selling price would appear as shown below; the cost basis statement data are shown for comparison.

	Cost Basis		Selling Price Basis	
	1991	**1992**	**1991**	**1992**
Balance Sheet				
Inventory	$1,000	-0-	$1,750	-0-
Income Statement:				
Sales revenue	$ -0-	$1,700	$ -0-	$1,700
Cost of goods sold	-0-	(1,000)	-0-	(1,750)
Expenses	(300)	(300)	(300)	(300)
Holding gain	-0-	-0-	750*	-0-
Net income (loss)	$ (300)	$ 400	$ 450	$ (350)

* $1,750 − $1,000 = $750.

Relative Sales Value Method

Two or more different kinds of inventory items may be purchased for a lump sum. A separate cost for each kind is required for accounting purposes. Thus, the total joint cost must be apportioned to individual kinds of items. The apportionment of the total cost should be related to the economic utility of each kind or group of items. If the sales value of a particular item is a reasonable indication of its relative utility,

---

[7] *ARB No. 43*, chapter 4, statement 9; the inserted language is from par. 16.

EXHIBIT 10–16   Relative Sales Value Method Applied

Grade	Quantity (Bushels)	Unit Sales Price	Total Sales Value	Fraction of Total Sales Value	Apportioned Cost
A	200	$5.00	$1,000	$1,000/$3,450	$ 600*
B	300	4.00	1,200	1,200/ 3,450	720
C	500	2.50	1,250	1,250/ 3,450	750
	1,000		$3,450		$2,070

Entry indicated (assuming a perpetual inventory system):
Inventory—Grade A apples, 200 units 600
Inventory—Grade B apples, 300 units 720
Inventory—Grade C apples, 500 units 750
  Cash   2,070

* ($1,000 ÷ $3,450) × $2,070 = $600. Or alternatively, $2,070 ÷ $3,450 = 60%; $1,000 × 60% = $600; $1,200 × 60% = $720; and $1,250 × 60% = $750.

apportionment of the joint cost of such "basket purchases" is made on the basis of the relative sales value of the several items. Also, additional joint costs incurred subsequent to purchase may be allocated on the basis of relative sales value.

Assume, for illustration, that a packing plant purchased 1,000 bushels of apples (ungraded) for $2,070. After purchase, the apples were sorted into three grades at a cost of $70, with the following results: Grade A, 200 bushels; Grade B, 300 bushels; and Grade C, 500 bushels. The sorted apples were selling at the following retail prices per bushel: Grade A, $5; Grade B, $4; and Grade C, $2.50. The cost apportionment is made as shown in Exhibit 10–16.

In joint cost allocations, quantities lost due to shrinkage or spoilage should be assigned no cost, thus increasing the unit cost for the remaining units. In the case of real estate developments, improvements such as streets and parks are apportioned to the cost of the salable areas as joint costs.

Losses on Purchase Commitments

To lock in specific prices for needed items of inventory and assure sufficient quantities, companies often contract with a supplier to purchase a specified quantity of materials during a future period at an agreed unit cost. Some purchase commitments (contracts) are subject to revision or cancellation before the end of the contract period, whereas others are not. Each case requires different accounting and reporting procedures.

In the case of purchase contracts subject to revision or cancellation where a future loss is possible and the amount of the commitment can be reasonably estimated and is material in amount, the full-disclosure principle requires note disclosure of the contingency. To illustrate, assume the Bayshore Company entered into a purchase contract during October 1991 that stated: "During 1992, 50,000 tanks of compressed chlorine will be purchased at $5 each. On 60 days' notice, this contract is subject to revision or cancellation by either party." If the current cost of the inventory under contract for purchase at the end of 1991 is $240,000, a disclosure note similar to the following should be included in the financial statements for 1991:

Note: At the end of 1991, a contract was in effect that will require the Company to pay $250,000 for materials during 1992. The purchase contract can be revised or canceled upon 60 days' notice by either party. At the end of 1991, the materials under contract had a current replacement cost of $240,000.

This note should give the relevant aspects of the contingency. No entry is required for the $10,000 (i.e., $250,000 − $240,000) contingent loss; the loss is not probable because the contract can be revised or cancelled.

When purchase contracts are not subject to revision or cancellation, and when a loss is probable and the loss amount can be reasonably estimated and is material in amount, the loss and related liability should be recorded in the accounts and reported in the financial statements. In the above example, assume the $240,000 current replacement cost is measured reliably and the $10,000 loss is probable. In this case, the loss on the purchase commitment should be recorded as follows:

Estimated loss on purchase commitment ($250,000 − $240,000)	10,000	
Estimated liability on noncancellable purchase commitment		10,000

The estimated loss is reported on the 1991 income statement, and the liability is reported on the balance sheet.[8] When the goods are acquired in 1992, merchandise inventory (or purchases) is debited at the current replacement cost, and the estimated liability account is debited. Assume the above materials have a replacement cost at date of delivery of $235,000. The purchase entry would be:

Materials inventory (or purchases)	235,000	
Estimated liability on noncancellable purchase commitment	10,000	
Loss on purchase contract	5,000	
Cash		250,000

This treatment records the loss in the period when it became probable and is consistent with the provisions of *ARB No. 43*, chapter 4, statement 10, and *SFAS No. 5,* "Accounting for Contingencies."

On the other hand, if there were a full or partial recovery of the purchase price, the recovery would be recognized (as a gain) in the period during which the recovery took place. Thus, if in 1992 the materials had a replacement cost at date of delivery of $255,000, the purchase entry would be:

Materials inventory (or purchases)	250,000	
Estimated liability on noncancelable purchase commitments	10,000	
Recovery of loss on purchase commitment		10,000
Cash		250,000

No recognition is given to the increase above the contract price of $250,000 because Bayshore has a noncancelable contract to buy at that price. Gains are not recognized until the earnings process is complete. The $5,000 gain ($255,000 − $250,000) will be realized through higher selling prices for Bayshore's products.

The accounting for commitments, including purchase commitments, is controversial among accountants. Some accountants believe these contracts should be given formal recognition in the accounts when binding agreements have been signed. Others prefer recognition at the date of delivery. The authors of this text have a preference for recognition of the date of the contract and support disclosure of such commitments regardless of the decision concerning formal recognition.

Effects of Inventory Errors

Errors in measuring inventory quantities or values occur because of the size of the inventory, the number of different kinds of items, their physical characteristics, and their means of storage. This section discusses the effect of inventory errors on the financial statements. A periodic inventory system is assumed.

---

[8] Even if no loss is probable, *SFAS No. 47*, "Disclosure of Long-Term Obligations," requires disclosure, either in a note or by way of entries in the accounts, as appropriate, of the nature and term of the obligation, the fixed amount of the obligation, and any amounts purchased to date under the obligation.

EXHIBIT 10-17   Effects of Inventory Errors Illustrated—Periodic Inventory System
(in $ Thousands)

| | Income Statement | | | | | | | Balance Sheet |
| | Cost of Goods Sold | | | | | | | Asset |
Sales − (BI	+ PUR	− EI	= CGS)	= GM	− EXP	= NI		EI
Case. Correct ⟶ 10	3	12	8	7	3	1	2	8
Error								
A. EI, 1* 10	3	12	9*	6†	4*	1	3*	9*
B. EI and PUR, 1* 10	3	13*	9*	7	3	1	2	9*
C. EI, 1† 10	3	12	7†	8*	2†	1	1†	7†
D. EI and PUR, 1† 10	3	11†	7†	7	3	1	2	7†
E. BI, 1* 10	4*	12	8	8*	2†	1	1†	8
F. BI, 1† 10	2†	12	8	6†	4*	1	3*	8

Abbreviations: BI = beginning inventory, PUR = purchases, EI = ending inventory, CGS = cost of goods sold, GM = gross margin, EXP = expenses, NI = pretax net income.

* Overstated.

† Understated.

Overstatement of the ending inventory understates cost of goods sold and therefore overstates pretax income by the same amount. Understatement of the ending inventory understates pretax income by the same amount. Conversely, an overstatement of the beginning inventory understates pretax income, and an understatement of the beginning inventory overstates pretax income. Overstatement of purchases (with correct measurement of beginning and ending inventories) overstates cost of goods sold and understates pretax income by the same amount.

Inventory overstatement or understatement will cause errors in the income statement and balance sheet. Often the inventory amount can be inconsistent with the amounts recorded in accounts payable. The inventory and purchases errors discussed below are common.[9] Exhibit 10–17, using the periodic inventory system, shows the pretax effects of several errors. Exhibit 10–17 is based on these relationships:

1. Cost of goods sold = Beginning inventory + Purchases − Ending inventory
2. Gross margin = Sales − Cost of goods sold
3. Income = Gross margin − Operating expenses

In Cases A through F assume the *correct* figures are:

Sales $10
Beginning inventory   3
Purchases   12
Ending inventory   8
Expenses   1

Then the correct cost of goods sold is:

$$\$3 + \$12 - \$8 = \$7$$

The gross margin is:

$$\$10 - \$7 = \$3$$

---

[9] Some of the effects of these errors will differ depending upon the cost flow method (FIFO, LIFO, etc.) used.

And net income is:

$$\$3 - \$1 = \$2$$

The correct ending inventory for the balance sheet is $8, as given. In Exhibit 10–17 several values are given. CGS, GM, and NI are established based on the values given.

Situation 1:   Ending inventory *overstated,* beginning inventory *correct.*

Case A.   Ending inventory is overstated by $1, but the purchases amount is correct. This error causes cost of goods sold to be understated and both gross margin and income to be overstated by the same amount.

$$\text{Cost of goods sold} = \$3 + \$12 - \$9 = \$6 \text{ (understated by \$1)}$$
$$\text{Gross margin} = \$10 - \$6 = \$4 \text{ (overstated by \$1)}$$
$$\text{Net income} = \$4 - \$1 = \$3 \text{ (overstated by \$1)}$$

Case B.   Ending inventory and purchases are both overstated by the same amount, $1. These two errors go in the opposite direction; therefore, gross margin and income are correct. However, on the balance sheet, both inventory and accounts payable are overstated by the same amount.

$$\text{Cost of goods sold} = \$3 + \$13 - \$9 = \$7 \text{ (correct)}$$
$$\text{Gross margin} = \$10 - \$7 = \$3 \text{ (correct)}$$
$$\text{Net income} = \$3 - \$1 = \$2 \text{ (correct)}$$

Situation 2:   Ending inventory *understated,* beginning inventory *correct:*

Case C.   Ending inventory is understated by $1, but the purchases amount is correct. This error causes cost of goods sold to be overstated and both gross margin and income to be understated by the same amount.

$$\text{Cost of goods sold} = \$3 + \$12 - \$7 = \$8 \text{ (overstated by \$1)}$$
$$\text{Gross margin} = \$10 - \$8 = \$2 \text{ (understated by \$1)}$$
$$\text{Net income} = \$2 - \$1 = \$1 \text{ (understated by \$1)}$$

Case D.   Ending inventory and purchases are both understated by the same amount, $1. These two errors have opposite effects; therefore, gross margin and income are correct. However, on the balance sheet, both inventory and accounts payable are understated by the same amount, $1.

$$\text{Cost of goods sold} = \$3 + \$11 - \$7 = \$7 \text{ (correct)}$$
$$\text{Gross margin} = \$10 - \$7 = \$3 \text{ (correct)}$$
$$\text{Net income} = \$3 - \$1 = \$2 \text{ (correct)}$$

Situation 3:   Beginning inventory *overstated,* ending inventory *correct:*

Case E.   Beginning inventory is overstated by $1, but the purchases amount is correct. This error causes cost of goods sold to be overstated, while gross margin and net income are understated by the same amount, $1.

$$\text{Cost of goods sold} = \$4 + \$12 - \$8 = \$8 \text{ (overstated by \$1)}$$
$$\text{Gross margin} = \$10 - \$8 = \$2 \text{ (understated by \$1)}$$
$$\text{Net income} = \$2 - \$1 = \$1 \text{ (understated by \$1)}$$

Situation 4:   Beginning inventory *understated,* ending inventory *correct:*

Case F.   Beginning inventory is understated by $1, but the purchases amount is correct. This error causes cost of goods sold to be understated, while gross margin and net income are overstated by the same amount, $1.

$$\text{Cost of goods sold} = \$2 + \$12 - \$8 = \$6 \text{ (understated by \$1)}$$
$$\text{Gross margin} = \$10 - \$6 = \$4 \text{ (overstated by \$1)}$$
$$\text{Net income} = \$4 - \$1 = \$3 \text{ (overstated by \$1)}$$

Errors similar to those illustrated above not only cause the financial statements for the current period to be in error but also frequently cause future amounts to be wrong. That is, an error in the ending inventory, if not corrected, will cause a counterbalancing error in the next period because the ending and beginning inventories have opposite effects on the income amounts of the two consecutive periods.

For example, assume Case A in Exhibit 10–17 refers to 1991. Then net income is overstated by $1 in 1991. Thus beginning inventory is overstated by $1 in 1992 causing income to be understated by $1 in 1992 (Case E). Assuming no new errors in 1992, inventories would be reported at the correct amount. The 1991 and 1992 errors counterbalance each other.

The inventory figure carries over. The ending inventory for one year becomes the beginning inventory for the next year. If ending inventory is overstated in one year, then beginning inventory is overstated by the same amount for the next year, if no correction is made. So, if net income for 1991 is overstated by $2,000 because 1991 ending inventory is overstated by $2,000, net income for 1992 will be understated by $2,000, but the combined income for the two-year time span will be correct. However, cost of goods sold and net income for each year are incorrect by the same amount. A later chapter, "Accounting Changes and Error Corrections," considers the reporting guidelines for errors and error corrections.

An issue related to inventory errors is the effect of errors made in determining sales revenue. There are two types of errors (that carry over to the next accounting period) in sales revenue—sales price and sales quantity mistakes. An error in sales price only (one not involving units sold) has an equal effect on pretax income. In contrast, an error that involves units sold (one not involving unit sales prices) affects cost of goods sold by one amount and income by another amount.

CONCEPT REVIEW

1. Describe the steps necessary to convert inventory figures based on retail values to the DV LIFO basis.
2. What are the major uses of the retail inventory method?
3. Suppose there is an error in the beginning inventory that results in an understatement of $1. If no further errors are made, what accounts are affected for the period?

SUMMARY OF KEY POINTS

(L.O. 1) 1. The lower-of-cost-or-market (LCM) method of estimating inventory recognizes declines in market value (but not gains) in the period of decline. The inventory value obtained is conservative.

(L.O. 1) 2. The lower-of-cost-or-market method values inventories at market if market is below cost. Market is interpreted to be replacement cost but not more than net realizable value or less than net realizable value less a normal profit margin.

(L.O. 1) 3. The lower-of-cost-or-market method can be used with any cost flow (FIFO, LIFO, etc.) for statement purposes but not with LIFO to establish the IRS tax liability.

(L.O. 2) 4. The gross margin method is used to estimate inventory values when it is difficult or impractical to take a physical count of the goods. Items are grouped in broad categories, and different cost flow assumptions can be accommodated.

(L.O. 2) 5. The gross margin method is generally unacceptable for external financial reporting.

(L.O. 3) 6. The retail method of estimating inventory, used extensively by department stores, applies the ratio of actual cost to sales value to the ending inventory's sales value in order to estimate the inventory's cost.

(L.O. 3) 7. The retail inventory method can be used for both external and tax reporting.

(L.O. 4) 8. The retail inventory method is often used with dollar value LIFO for tax purposes. In this case, a specified price index method is required to convert each layer of inventory from its FIFO cost.

(L.O. 5) 9. Items not in new condition are valued at replacement cost or net realizable value.

(L.O. 5) 10. Items for which guaranteed markets exist can be valued at current selling prices, and changes in current selling prices are recognized in the accounts for the period in which the change occurs.

(L.O. 5) 11. The relative sales value method can be used to allocate the cost of different items purchased together when sales is the best indicator of their relative values.

(L.O. 5) 12. Losses on firm purchase commitments, when they can be reasonably estimated and are material, are recognized in the accounts if the loss is probable and can be estimated. But they need only be disclosed in the notes if the loss is just possible.

(L.O. 5) 13. Errors in establishing inventory values should be corrected since they produce both current and future mistakes in the accounts and financial statements.

REVIEW PROBLEM
◆

Jensen Hardware experienced substantial damage to its inventory of 100 snow shovels carried over from the prior winter season. These shovels had originally cost Jensen $10 each when new, and Jensen sells them for $15 each. Jensen estimates it will take $400 to put the shovels in salable condition and another $200 to advertise them for special sale. Jensen believes the repaired shovels will sell for $12 each. Similarly damaged shovels from Jensen's current supplier of new shovels could be obtained for $5 each.

1. Assuming the lower-of-cost-or-market rule can be used:
   a. Establish a net realizable value for the shovels.
   b. Determine a value for net realizable value less a normal profit margin.
   c. What value should be assigned to the repaired shovels using the lower-of-cost-or-market rule?

2. If these items were valued as damaged or distressed merchandise, what value should be used?

3. Should Jensen repair and sell the items?

SOLUTION
◆

1. a. The net realizable value is:

$$\$12 - (\$4 + \$2) = \$6$$

   b. The only information available on normal profit margins is based on the new shovels, where the margin is $5 on a selling price of $15, or 33%. Assuming it is reasonable to apply the same margin to the repaired shovels, the net realizable value less a normal profit margin is:

$$\$6 - .33(\$12) = \$2$$

   c. Since replacement cost, $5, is between net realizable value, $6, and net realizable value less a normal profit margin, $2, the inventory would be valued at $5 a shovel, or a total of $500.

2. If the shovels were valued as damaged or distressed merchandise, Jensen would probably use the net realizable value of $6 a shovel, or $600 in total, because the shovels cannot be purchased in their present condition.

3. Jensen should repair and market the shovels since it can obtain $6 each for them. If Jensen does so, the firm will obtain a net of $600. This is likely to exceed their junk value. The $600 also exceeds the wholesale value of damaged shovels, estimated here at $5 each. Jensen should attempt to repair and market the shovels even though the company would need to write the current inventory down and recognize a loss of either $500 ($1,000 − $500, using LCM) or $400 ($1,000 − $600, using NRV).

KEY TERMS

Direct inventory reduction method (474)   Net realizable value (NRV) (470)
Gross margin method (477)   Normal profit margin (470)
Inventory allowance method (474)   Retail inventory method (480)
Lower of cost or market (LCM) (468)

QUESTIONS

1. Why is the LCM rule applied to inventory valuation?
2. Why are the ceiling and floor values used in determining market in the application of the LCM concept?
3. What is the holding loss (gain) recognized using the LCM, inventory allowance method, for each of the following years:

	Cost	Market
1990 Beginning inventory	$ -0-	$ -0-
Ending inventory	12,000	14,000
1991 Ending inventory	15,000	13,000
1992 Ending inventory	18,000	17,000
1993 Ending inventory	20,000	16,000
1994 Ending inventory	22,000	23,000

4. What basic assumption is implicit in the gross margin method?
5. Approximate the valuation of the ending inventory assuming the following data are available:

Cost of goods available for sale	$170,000
Sales	150,000
Gross margin rate (on sales)	25%

6. Assume the gross margin rate in question 5 is based on cost of goods sold. Approximate the valuation of the ending inventory.
7. Distinguish between (a) gross margin rate on sales, (b) gross margin percentage on cost of goods sold, (c) cost percentage, (d) markup on cost, and (e) markup on sales.
8. List four uses of the gross margin method.
9. Why is it frequently desirable to apply the gross margin method by classes of merchandise?
10. Explain the basic approach of the retail method of estimating inventories (FIFO and average). What data must be accumulated in order to apply the retail method?
11. The ending inventory estimated by the retail inventory method was $90,000. A physical inventory of the merchandise on hand extended at retail showed $75,000. Suggest possible reasons for the discrepancy.
12. What are the primary uses of the retail method of estimating inventories?
13. When are markdowns and markdown cancellations excluded in computing the cost ratio in the retail inventory method?
14. Explain the difference between the FIFO with LCM, and the average cost with LCM, methods under the retail method of estimating inventories.
15. What are the primary differences between the retail inventory method under FIFO and average cost versus the DV LIFO retail method?
16. Explain why the FIFO (not LCM) retail cost ratio must be used in combination with DV LIFO retail to attain LIFO retail results.
17. When dollar value LIFO retail is adopted, why must the ending inventory of the period prior to the base year often be recomputed?
18. How should damaged or obsolete merchandise on hand at the end of the period be valued for inventory purposes?
19. What types of inventory does GAAP allow to be measured at selling price in excess of cost?
20. What are the basic assumptions underlying the relative sales value method when used in allocating costs for inventory purposes?
21. Briefly outline the accounting and reporting of losses on purchase commitments when

(a) the purchase contract is subject to revision or cancellation and (b) it is noncancelable and a loss is probable.

22. Explain the effect of each of the following errors in the ending inventory of a retail business (ignore income taxes):

   a. Incorrectly excluded 300 units of Commodity C, valued at $3 per unit, from the ending inventory; the purchase was recorded.

   b. Incorrectly excluded 400 units of Commodity D, valued at $4 per unit, from the ending inventory; the purchase was not recorded.

   c. Incorrectly included 100 units of Commodity A, valued at $5 per unit, in the ending inventory; the purchase was recorded.

   d. Incorrectly included 200 units of Commodity B, valued at $3 per unit, in the ending inventory; the purchase was not recorded.

23. Assume that inventory, cost, $1,000, was sold on credit for $1,200 and held pending pickup by the customer. The goods were incorrectly included in the ending inventory. What is the pretax effect of this error if (a) the sale was not recorded? (b) the sale was correctly recorded? Assume that a periodic inventory system is used.

EXERCISES

E 10–1
LCM: Maximum and Minimum
(L.O. 1)

Clark Company had 1,000 units of analog microchips in inventory at the end of the accounting period. The unit cost was $60; estimated distribution costs, $3 per unit; and the normal profit is $5 per unit. Compute the unit valuation of the inventory based on LCM under each separate case listed below.

Case	Anticipated Sales Price	Current Replacement Cost
a	$61	$53
b	66	57
c	68	61
d	50	44
e	59	57
f	56	50
g	73	59
h	65	61
i	70	62
j	60	58

E 10–2
LCM: Maximum and Minimum
(L.O. 1)

The management of Tarry Hardware Company has taken the position that under the LCM procedure the two items listed below should be reported in the ending inventory at $16,600 (total). Do you agree? If not, indicate the correct inventory valuation by item. Show computations.

Handyman edgers: 300 on hand; cost, $22 each; replacement cost, $16; estimated sale price, $30; estimated distribution cost, $3 each; and normal profit, 10% of the sales price.

Handyman hedge clippers: 200 on hand; cost $50 each; replacement cost, $36 each; estimated sales price, $90; estimated distribution cost, $28; and normal profit, 20% of the sales price.

E 10–3
LCM: Compute the Holding Gain or Loss
(L.O. 1)

The records of Volatility Company showed the following inventory data:

		Cost	Market
1989	Beginning inventory	$ 4,000	$ 4,000
1989	Ending inventory	5,000	6,000
1990	Ending inventory	8,000	7,500
1991	Ending inventory	4,000	3,000
1992	Ending inventory	12,000	10,000
1993	Ending inventory	8,000	7,500
1994	Ending inventory	10,000	11,000

Required:

Compute the holding gain or loss recognized by Volatility in each year due to the use of LCM.

E 10-4
LCM: Direct and
Allowance Compared
(L.O. 1)

The inventories for the years 1991 and 1992 are shown below for Colbert Corporation.

Inventory Date	Original Cost	LCM	Difference	Purchases
1/1/91	$6,000	$6,000	–0–	—
12/31/91	7,000	6,800	$400	$50,000
12/31/92	9,000	9,000	–0–	56,000

Required:

1. Give the journal entries to apply the LCM procedure to the inventories for 1991 and 1992 assuming the company uses the inventory allowance method and periodic inventory procedures.
2. Give the journal entries to apply the LCM procedure to the inventories for 1991 and 1992 assuming the company uses the direct inventory reduction method and periodic inventory procedures.
3. What are the primary advantages and disadvantages of each method?

E 10-5
Gross Margin Method:
Estimate the Ending
Inventory
(L.O. 2)

You are auditing the records of Coolidge Corporation. A physical inventory has been taken by the company under your observation. However, the valuation extensions have not been completed. The records of the company provide the following data: sales, $315,000 (gross); return sales, $5,000 (returned to stock); purchases (gross), $155,000; beginning inventory, $50,000; freight-in, $5,000; and purchase returns and allowances, $2,000. The gross margin last period was 35% of net sales; you anticipate that it will be 40% for the year under audit.

Required:

Estimate the cost of the ending inventory using the gross margin method. Show computations.

E 10-6
Gross Margin Method:
Results Evaluated
(L.O. 2)

The records of Carson Company provided the following data for January for two products sold:

	Product A	Product B
Beginning inventory, January 1	$ 50,000	$ 60,000
Purchases during January	147,000	180,000
Freight-in on purchases	3,000	4,000
Sales revenue during January	300,000	400,000

Gross margin rates on sales for the prior year were as follows: company overall, 45%; Product A, 42%; and Product B, 47%.

Required:

1. Estimate the cost of the ending inventory separately, by products, and in the aggregate.
2. Under what conditions would one of your responses to (1) above be suspect?

E 10-7
Gross Margin Method:
Estimate a Fire Loss
(L.O. 2)

On November 15, 1991, a fire destroyed Young Corporation's warehouse where croquet mallets were stored. It is estimated that $10,000 can be realized from sale of usable damaged inventory. The accounting records concerning croquet mallets reveal:

Inventory at 11/1/91	$120,000
Purchases from 11/1/91 to 11/15/91	140,000
Net sales from 11/1/91 to 11/15/91	220,000

Based on recent history the gross margin has averaged 35% of net sales.

Required:

Prepare a schedule to calculate the estimated loss of inventory based on the gross margin method. Show supporting computations.

(AICPA adapted)

E 10-8
Gross Margin Method:
Markup on Sales and Cost
Compared
(L.O. 2)

Assume the following data for Cressy Company for the year 1992:

Sales revenue	$120,000
Beginning inventory	16,000
Purchases	80,000

Required:

For each of the separate situations below, estimate the ending inventory (round all ratios to three decimal places):
1. Markup is 50% on cost.
2. Markup is 60% on sales.
3. Markup is 25% on cost.
4. Markup is 40% on sales.
5. Markup is 60% on cost.

E 10–9
Gross Margin Method:
Estimate Inventory Loss,
Markup on Sales versus
Costs
(L.O. 2)

The books of Leigh Company provided the following information:

Inventory, January 1	$ 10,000
Purchases to July 19	100,000
Net sales to July 19	85,000

Before opening for business on July 20, the assets of the company were totally destroyed by flood. The insurance company adjuster found that the average rate of gross margin for the past few years had been 45%.

Required:

What was the approximate value of the inventory destroyed assuming the gross margin percentage given was based on *(a)* sale and *(b)* cost of goods sold? Round all ratios to two decimal places.

E 10–10
Retail Inventory Method:
Average LCM
(L.O. 3)

Dan's Clothing Store values its inventory using the retail inventory method at the lower of average cost or market. The following data are available for the month of June 1991:

	Cost	Selling Price
Inventory, June 1	$ 53,800	$ 80,000
Markdowns		21,000
Markups		29,000
Markdown cancellations		10,000
Markup cancellations		9,000
Purchases	173,200	223,600
Sales		250,000
Purchase returns and allowances	3,000	3,600
Sales returns and allowances		10,000

Required:

Prepare a schedule to compute the estimated inventory at June 30, 1991, at the lower of average cost or market using the retail inventory method. Round the cost ratio to three decimals.

(AICPA adapted)

E 10–11
Retail Inventory Method:
FIFO and Average
(L.O. 3)

Chic Department Store uses the retail method of inventory. At the end of June, the records of the company provided the following information:

Purchases during June: at cost, $240,000; at retail, $400,000.

Sales during June: $350,000.

Inventory, June 1: at cost, $40,000; at retail, $75,000.

Required:

Estimate the ending inventory and cost of goods sold for June assuming *(a)* FIFO cost basis and *(b)* average cost basis. Show all computations (round cost ratios to two decimals).

E 10–12
Retail Inventory Method:
FIFO and Average
(L.O. 3)

The records of Rainey Retailers showed the following data for January: beginning inventory at cost, $20,000, and $26,000 at selling price; purchase at cost, $150,000, and $300,000 at selling price; gross sales, $310,000; return sales, $5,000 (returned to stock); purchase returns at cost, $3,000, and $6,000 at selling price; and freight-in, $9,000.

Required:

Determine the approximate valuation of the ending inventory using the retail inventory method (*a*) at average cost and (*b*) at FIFO. Show all computations. Round all cost ratios to two decimal places. Which is lower? What may have accounted for the result? Was LCM applied implicitly by Rainey? If yes, explain.

E 10–13
Retail Inventory Method:
FIFO and Average, LCM
(L.O. 1, 3)

Use the retail inventory method to estimate the ending inventory (*a*) at average cost with LCM and (*b*) FIFO with LCM for Post Corporation based on the following data (round all cost ratios to three decimal places):

	At Cost	At Retail
Beginning inventory	$101,000	$150,000
Purchases	323,000	563,000
Purcases returned	6,000	10,000
Freight-in	8,000	
Additional markups		12,000
Additional markup cancellations		5,000
Markdowns		9,000
Markdown cancellations		2,000
Sales		540,000
Sales returned (and restored to inventory)		6,000

How is LCM introduced into the computations? Explain the logic of this procedure. Will LCM always produce a lower inventory cost estimate under the retail method than FIFO or average without LCM?

E 10–14
Retail Inventory Method:
Average LCM,
Discrepancy
(L.O. 1, 3)

Franklin Retail Company has just completed the annual physical inventory, which involved counting the goods on hand and then pricing them at selling prices. The inventory valuation derived in this manner amounted to $106,000. The records of the company provided the following data: beginning inventory, $80,000 at retail and $50,000 at cost; purchases (including freight-in and returns), $750,000 at retail and $500,000 at cost; additional markups, $20,000; additional markup cancellations, $8,000; gross sales, $733,000; return sales (restored to inventory), $13,000; and markdowns, $10,000.

Required:

Round all costs ratios to three decimal places.
1. Estimate the cost of the ending inventory assuming average cost with LCM.
2. Note any discrepancies and give possible reasons for them.

E 10–15
Retail Inventory Method:
LCM with Shrinkage
(L.O. 1, 3)

Dover Department Store uses the retail inventory method. Information relating to the computation of inventory for 1992 is as follows:

	At Cost	At Retail
Beginning inventory	$ 40,000	$ 80,000
Sales		600,000
Purchases	300,000	590,000
Freight-in	8,000	
Markups		60,000
Markup cancellations		20,000
Markdowns		25,000
Markdown cancellations		5,000
Estimated normal shrinkage is 1% of sales.		

Required:

Calculate the estimated ending inventory for 1992 at the lower of average cost or market. Show supporting calculations. Round all cost ratios to three decimal places.

(AICPA adapted)

E 10–16
DV LIFO Retail: Entry
to Restate FIFO
(L.O. 4)

Anderson Company used the retail inventory method for a number of years. On January 1, 1992, the company changed to DV LIFO retail for external reporting and income tax purposes. The following data were provided by the inventory records for the accounting year ended December 31, 1991:

	At Cost	At Retail
January 1, 1991, inventory	$48,000	$ 95,000
Purchases	80,000	170,000
Net additional markups		4,000
Net markdowns		8,000
Sales revenue		190,000

Required:

Round all cost ratios to three decimal places.

1. Compute the December 31, 1991, retail inventory results assuming (a) average cost with LCM; (b) FIFO with LCM; and (c) FIFO.
2. Give the adjusting entry to restate the inventory to FIFO (not LCM) to be used as the base inventory for the DV LIFO retail method assuming Anderson has been using (a) average with LCM; (b) FIFO with LCM.

E 10–17
DV LIFO Retail: Conversion from FIFO (L.O. 4)

Riley Retail Store used the retail inventory method, determined on the average cost, LCM basis, for a number of years for all purposes. On January 1, 1993, the company changed to DV LIFO retail for external reporting and income tax purposes, but retained average cost with LCM, for internal purposes.

At the end of 1992 and 1993 the retail inventory computations (average with LCM) for internal purposes were as shown below.

	Year 1992		Year 1993	
	At Cost	At Retail	At Cost	At Retail
Beginning inventory, January 1 . .	$ 17,000	$ 30,000	$ 28,000	$ 50,000
Purchases	151,000	268,000	179,200	325,000
Net additional markups		2,000		3,000
Total	$168,000	300,000	$207,700	378,000
Cost ratio		.56*		.55*
Sales		(245,000)		(305,000)
Net markdowns		(5,000)		(9,000)
Inventory, December 31:				
At retail		$ 50,000		$ 64,000
At cost (average cost with LCM)	$ 28,000		$ 35,200	

Conversion price indexes: 12/31/92, 125; and 12/31/93, 140.
* ($168,000 ÷ $300,000 = .56) and ($207,700 ÷ $378,000 = .55)

Required:

Round all cost ratios to two decimal places.

1. Compute the inventory values (at cost and at retail) that should be used as the base inventory and the ending inventory for 1993 for conversion purposes. Why are the above inventory values not appropriate for this purpose?
2. Convert the FIFO retail inventory results, computed in (1) to the DV LIFO retail basis for the external reports and income tax use at the end of 1993.
3. Complete the following tabulation for 1993:

	Year 1993		
	Average, LCM	FIFO	DV LIFO
Sales revenue	$_____	$_____	$_____
Cost of goods sold:			
Beginning inventory	_____	_____	_____
Purchases	_____	_____	_____
Total	_____	_____	_____
Ending inventory	_____	_____	_____
Cost of goods sold	_____	_____	_____
Gross margin	_____	_____	_____

E 10-18
Net Realizable Value of Damaged Goods: Entries
(L.O. 5)

A fire damaged some of the merchandise held for sale by AAA Appliance Company. Seven television sets and six stereo sets were damaged. They were not covered by insurance. The sets will be repaired and sold as used sets. Data are as follows:

	Per Set	
	Television	**Stereo**
Inventory (at cost)	$400	$250
Estimated cost to repair	50	30
Estimated cost to sell	20	20
Estimated sales price	200	110

Required:

1. Compute the appropriate inventory net realizable value for each set.
2. Give the separate entries to record the damaged merchandise inventory for the television and stereo sets. Assume a perpetual inventory system.
3. Give the entries to record the subsequent repair of the television sets and the stereo sets (credit cash).
4. Give the entry to record sale for cash of two television sets and one stereo set; credit distribution costs in the entry to record the sale (it will be necessary to record payment of the distribution costs in a separate entry). Assume the actual sales prices equaled the estimated sales prices.

E 10-19
Relative Sales Value Method
(L.O. 5)

Chewy Nut, Inc., purchased 1,200 bags of pecans that cost $4,200. In addition, the company incurred $300 for transportation and grading. The pecans graded out as follows:

Grade	Quantity	Current Market Price per Bag
A	400	$6.75
B	600	6.00
C	100	4.50
Waste	100	

Required:

The relative sales value method is used to apportion the joint costs; give:

1. The entry for purchase assuming a perpetual inventory system (show computations).
2. Valuation of ending inventory assuming the following quantities are on hand: grade A, 100 bags; grade B, 80 bags; and grade C, 40 bags.
3. The entry for sale of 20 bags of the grade A pecans at the above market price for cash.

E 10-20
Relative Sales Value Method: Entries
(L.O. 5)

Arizona Land Developers purchased and subdivided a tract of land that cost $900,000. The subdivision was divided on the following basis:

10% used for streets, alleys, and parks.
50% divided into 100 lots to sell for $4,000 each.
30% divided into 200 lots to sell for $3,000 each.
10% divided into 100 lots to sell for $2,000 each.

Required:

1. Give the entry for the purchase of the lots. Use the relative sales value method to apportion the total cost of $900,000 to the three categories of lots. Assume a perpetual inventory system.
2. During the final month of the year, the paving was completed (included in the $900,000 cost), and sales were made. At the end of the first year, 20, $4,000 lots, 50, $3,000 lots, and 10, $2,000 lots are on hand. Compute the valuation of the inventory at year-end, and record the sales and cost of goods sold amounts for each category of lots. Assume cash sales only.

E 10-21
Relative Sales Value Method: Land, Entries
(L.O. 5)

Florida Development Company purchased a tract of land for development purposes. The tract was subdivided as follows: 30 lots to sell at $6,000 per lot and 80 lots to sell at $9,000 per lot. The tract cost $335,000, and an additional $25,000 was spent in general development costs, including streets and alleys.

Required:

Assuming cost apportionment is based on the relative sales value method, give entries for (*a*) purchase of the tract and payment of the development costs, (*b*) sale of one $6,000 lot, and (*c*) sale of one $9,000 lot. Florida uses a perpetual inventory system. Assume cash transactions.

E 10–22

Relative Sales Value Method: Entry (L.O. 5)

Quick Company purchased 2,630 bushels of ungraded apricots at $2 per bushel. The apricots were sorted as follows: grade 1, 1,000 bushels; grade 2, 700 bushels; grade 3, 900 bushels; and spoilage, 10 bushels. Handling and sorting costs amounted to $140. The current market prices for graded apricots were: grade 1, $5 per bushel; grade 2, $3 per bushel; and grade 3, $1 per bushel. The company uses a perpetual inventory system.

Required:

What entry should be made to record the purchase? Show computations of total costs for each grade assuming the relative sales value method of cost apportionment is used.

E 10–23

Loss on Purchase Commitment (L.O. 5)

During 1991, Delta Company signed a contract with Alpha Corporation to "purchase 15,000 subassemblies at $30 each during 1992."

Required:

1. On December 31, 1991, end of the annual accounting period, the financial statements are to be prepared. Under what additional contractual and economic conditions should disclosure of the contract terms be made only by means of a note in the financial statements? Prepare an appropriate note. Assume the cost of the subassemblies is dropping and the estimated current replacement cost is $400,000.
2. What contractual and economic conditions would require accrual of a loss? Give the accrual entry.
3. Assume the subassemblies are received in 1992 when their cost was at the estimate given in (1) above. The contract was paid in full. Give the required entry.

E 10–24

Loss on Purchase Commitments (L.O. 5)

On November 1, 1991, Xit Corporation entered into a purchase contract (not subject to revision or cancellation) to purchase 10,000 units of Material X at $7 per unit (to be used in manufacturing). The contract period extends through February 1992. Xit's accounting period ends December 31. On December 31, 1991, Material X was being sold at a firm price of $5 per unit. On January 25, Xit purchased the 10,000 units; however, the market price per unit of Material X on this date was $4.75. The company uses a perpetual inventory system.

Required:

Give all relevant entries or disclosure notes on November 1, 1991, December 31, 1991, and January 25, 1992. Explain the basis for each entry.

E 10–25

Correct Four Inventory Errors on the Income Statement (L.O. 5)

The records of Varga Company reflected the following:

Sales revenue		$205,000
Cost of goods sold:		
Beginning inventory	$ 10,000	
Purchases	105,000	
Goods available for sale	115,000	
Ending inventory	25,000	90,000
Gross margin		115,000
Expenses		60,000
Income (pretax)		$ 55,000

The following errors were found that had not been corrected:

a. Revenues collected in advance amounting to $5,000 are included in the same revenue amount.
b. Accrued expenses not recognized, $6,000.
c. Goods costing $10,000 were incorrectly included in the ending inventory (they were being held on consignment from Carter Company). No purchase was recorded.

d. Goods costing $5,000 were correctly included in the ending inventory; however, no purchase was recorded (assume a credit purchase).

Required:

1. Prepare the income statement on a correct basis.
2. What amounts would be incorrect on the balance sheet if the errors are not corrected?

PROBLEMS

P 10–1
LCM: Three Ways to Apply
(L.O. 1)

The information shown below relating to the ending inventory was taken from the records of Quick Print Company.

Inventory Classification	Quantity	Per Unit	
		Cost	Market
Paper:			
Stock X	200	$300	$330
Stock Y	60	250	230
Ink:			
Stock D	20	70	65
Stock E	10	60	62
Toner fluid:			
Stock A	8	75	70
Stock B	4	90	80
Stock C	7	100	110

Required:

1. Determine the valuation of the above inventory at cost and at LCM assuming application by (*a*) individual items, (*b*) classifications, and (*c*) total inventory. The unit costs of the three categories are significantly different; however, within each category the unit costs are similar.
2. Give the entry to record the ending inventory for each approach assuming periodic inventory and the allowance method.
3. Of the three applications described in (1) above, which one appears preferable in this situation? Explain.

P 10–2
LCM, Allowance Method: Recording and Reporting
(L.O. 1)

The records of Cool Aire Company provide the following data relating to inventories for the years 1992 and 1993.

Inventory Date	Original Cost	At LCM
1/1/92	$40,000	$40,000
12/31/92	50,000	46,000
12/31/93	46,000	45,000

Other data available are as follows:

	1992	1993
Sales	$240,000	$260,000
Purchases	135,000	150,000
Administrative and selling expenses	49,000	61,000

The company values inventories on the basis of LCM and uses the periodic inventory system. For problem purposes, ignore income taxes.

Required:

1. In parallel columns, give the entries to apply the LCM procedure under the allowance method for 1992 and 1993.
2. Prepare an income statement for 1992 and 1993, and show the inventory amounts for the balance sheet.

P 10–3

LCM: Allowance and Direct Methods Compared

(L.O. 1)

Ninja Frogs Corporation uses a perpetual inventory system. The following data are available from company records:

	1991	1992
Sales revenue	$80,000	$120,000
Cost of goods sold	40,000	60,000
Remaining expenses	20,000	35,000

The cost of goods sold is based on inventories valued at cost. Additional information regarding inventories are:

	Cost	Market
January 1, 1991	$ 6,000	$7,000
December 31, 1991	10,000	8,000
December 31, 1992	12,000	9,000

Required:

1. In parallel columns, give the entries to apply the LCM procedure under the allowance method for 1991 and 1992. Prepare an income statement for 1991 and 1992. Ignore income taxes.
2. In parallel columns, give the entries to apply the LCM procedure under the direct inventory reduction method for 1991 and 1992. Prepare an income statement for 1991 and 1992. Ignore income taxes.

P 10–4

LCM: Allowance and Direct Methods Compared

(L.O. 1)

York Corporation's summarized income statements for 1991 and 1992 are shown below. The inventories given below were valued at cost.

	1991	1992
Sales	$107,000	$97,000
Cost of goods sold:		
Beginning inventory	25,000	20,000
Purchases	75,000	73,000
Total	100,000	93,000
Ending inventory	20,000	15,000
Cost of goods sold	80,000	78,000
Gross margin	27,000	19,000
Less: Operating expenses	14,000	12,000
Pretax income	$ 13,000	$ 7,000

The inventories valued at LCM would have been as follows: at the beginning of 1991, $25,000 (the same as cost); end of 1991, $18,000; and end of 1992, $12,000.

Required:

1. Restate the 1991 and 1992 income statements applying the LCM rule for each of the following procedures. Disregard income taxes.
   a. Direct inventory reduction method, where the inventory holding loss is not reported separately.
   b. Allowance method.
2. Which procedure is preferable? Why?

P 10–5

Gross Margin Method: Inventory Fire Loss, Evaluation

(L.O. 2)

The records of Carolina Company provided the following information on September 1, 1991:

Inventory, 1/1/91	$ 50,000
Purchases, January 1 to September 1	300,000
Sales, January 1 to September 1	400,000
Purchase returns and allowances	3,000
Sales returns (goods returned to stock)	5,000
Freight-in	4,000

A fire completely destroyed the inventory on September 1, 1991, except for goods marked to sell at $6,000, which had an estimated residual value of $4,000, and for goods in transit to which Carolina had ownership; the purchase had been recorded. Invoices recorded on the latter show merchandise cost, $2,000, and freight-in, $100. The average rate of gross margin on sales in recent years has been 40%.

Required:
1. Compute the inventory fire loss.
2. Under what conditions would your response to (1) above be questionable?

P 10–6
Gross Margin Method:
Use in Profit Planning
(L.O. 2)

Neiman Company is developing a profit plan. The following data were estimated for 1992 and 1993.
a. January 1, 1992, estimated inventory, $80,000.
b. Estimated average rate of gross margin on sales, 40%.

Required:
Complete the following profit plan:

	Profit Plan Estimates	
	1992	1993
Sales planned	$160,000	$190,000
Cost of goods sold:		
Beginning inventory	?	?
Purchases budget	120,000	130,000
Total goods available	?	?
Less: Ending inventory	?	?
Cost of goods sold	?	?
Gross margin planned	?	?

P 10-7
Gross Margin Method:
Inventory Burned,
Indemnity
(L.O. 2)

Wood Wholesaler Company's warehouse burned on April 1, 1992. The following information (up to the date of the fire) was taken from the records of the company: inventory, January 1, $30,000; gross sales, $160,000; purchases, $90,000; sales returns (restored to stock), $5,000; purchase returns and allowances, $2,000; and freight-in, $8,000. The cost of goods sold and gross margin for the past three years were as follows:

Year	Cost of Coods Sold	Gross Margin
1989	$500,000	$125,000
1990	460,000	120,000
1991	500,000	120,000

Required:
1. Estimate the cost of the inventory destroyed in the fire.
2. Under what conditions would your response to (1) above be questionable?
3. The insurance company pays indemnity on market value at date of the fire. What amount would you recommend that Wood submit as an insurance claim? Explain.

P 10–8
Gross Margin Method:
Inventory Records
Destroyed, Income
Statement
(L.O. 2)

In the past, SWT Corporation valued inventories at cost. At the end of the current period, the inventory was valued at 40% of selling price as a matter of convenience. However, the cost ratio is not 40%. The current financial statements have been prepared, and the inventory sheets inadvertently destroyed; consequently, you find it impossible to reconstruct the ending inventory at actual cost per the physical count. Fortunately, the following data are available.

Sales	$300,000
Ending inventory (at 40% of selling price)	25,000
Purchases (at cost)	190,000
Pretax income	40,000
Beginning inventory (at cost)	27,500

Required:

Prepare a corrected (and detailed) income statement. Show computations and round the cost ratio to four decimal places.

P 10–9

Retail Inventory Method: Average, FIFO, and LCM

(L.O. 3)

The records of Diskount Department Store provided the following data for 1990:

Sales (gross)	$800,000
Return sales (restored to inventory)	2,000
Additional markups	9,000
Additional markup cancellations	5,000
Markdowns	7,000
Purchases:	
At retail	850,000
At cost	459,500
Purchase returns:	
At retail	4,000
At cost	2,200
Freight on purchases	7,000
Beginning inventory:	
At cost	45,000
At retail	80,000
Markdown cancellations	3,000

Required:

Estimate the valuation of the ending inventory and cost of goods sold assuming the following cases. Show computations, carry cost ratios to four decimal places, and round inventory to the nearest dollar.

Case A—average cost (for illustrative purposes only).

Case B—average cost with LCM.

Case C—FIFO cost (for illustrative purposes only).

Case D—FIFO cost with LCM.

P 10–10

Retail Inventory Method: an Audit Test

(L.O. 3)

Auditors are examining the accounts of Detroit Retail Corporation. They were present when Detroit's personnel physically counted the Detroit inventory; however, the auditors made their own tests. Detroit's records provided the following data for the current year:

	At Retail	At Cost
Inventory, January 1	$ 300,000	$180,500
Net purchases	1,453,000	955,000
Freight-in		15,000
Additional markups	31,000	
Additional markup cancellations	14,000	
Markdowns	8,000	
Employee discounts	2,000	
Sales	1,300,000	
Inventory, December 31 (per physical count valued at retail)	475,000	

Required:

1. Compute the ending inventory at average cost and LCM as an audit test of the overall reasonableness of the physical inventory count. Round the cost ratio to three decimals.
2. Note any discrepancies indicated. What factors should the auditors consider in reconciling any difference in results from the analysis?
3. What accounting treatment (if any) should be accorded the discrepancy?

P 10–11

Inventory Concepts, Recording, Adjusting, Closing, Reporting

(L.O. 1, 5)

Fame Company completed the following selected (and summarized) transactions during 1991:

a. Merchandise inventory on hand January 1, 1991, $105,000 (at cost, which was the same as LCM).

b. During the year, purchased merchandise for resale at quoted price of $200,000 on credit, terms 2/10, n/30. Immediately paid 85% of the cash cost.

c. Paid freight on merchandise purchased, $9,000 cash.

d. Paid 40% of the accounts payable within the discount period. The remaining payables were unpaid at the end of 1991 and were still within the discount period.

e. Merchandise that had a quoted price of $3,000 (terms 2/10, n/30) was returned to a supplier. A cash refund of $2,940 was received because the items were unsatisfactory.

f. During the year, sold merchandise for $370,000, of which 10% was on credit, terms 2/10, n/30.

g. A television set caught fire and was damaged internally; it was returned by the customer because it was guaranteed. The set was originally sold for $600, of which $400 cash was refunded. The set cost the company $420. Estimates are that the set, when repaired, can be sold for $240. Estimated repair costs are $50, and selling costs are estimated to be $10.

h. Operating expenses (administrative and distribution) paid in cash, $115,000; includes the $10 in (*g*).

i. Excluded from the purchase given in (*b*) and from the ending inventory was a shipment for $7,000 (net of discount). This shipment was in transit, FOB shipping point at December 31, 1991. The invoice was on hand.

j. Paid $50 cash to repair the damaged television set; see (*g*) above.

k. Sold the damaged television set for $245; selling costs allocated, $10.

l. The ending inventory (as counted) was $110,000 at cost, and $107,000 at market. Assume an average income tax rate of 40%.

Accounting policies followed by the company are (1) the annual accounting period ends December 31, (2) a periodic inventory system is used, (3) purchases and accounts payable are recorded net of cash discounts, (4) freight charges are allocated to merchandise when purchased, (5) all cash discounts are taken, (6) used and damaged merchandise is carried in a separate inventory account, and (7) inventories are reported at LCM and the allowance method is used.

Required:

1. Give the entries for transactions (*b*) through (*k*).
2. Give the end-of-period entries (adjusting and closing).
3. Prepare a multiple-step income statement (1991). Assume 20,000 shares of common stock outstanding.
4. Show how the ending inventory should be reported on the balance sheet at December 31, 1991.

P 10–12
DV LIFO Retail:
Price Indexes Given,
Conversion, Three Years
(L.O. 4)

Casey Retailers has used the FIFO retail method with LCM basis of inventory for all purposes. On January 1, 1989, the company decided to use the DV LIFO retail method to convert the inventory to the LIFO basis. The results will be used for external reporting and for income tax purposes. The base inventory at the start of 1989 was as follows: 1/1/89, base inventory (carried over from 12/31/88), at cost, $31,000; at retail, $50,000.

Data from the inventory records for 1989 to 1991 are given below.

	1989		1990		1991	
	At Cost	At Retail	At Cost	At Retail	At Cost	At Retail
Sales (net)		$120,000		$140,000		$145,000
Purchases (net)	$100,800	143,000	$112,000	164,000	$117,000	175,000
Net additional markups		7,000		11,000		5,000
Applicable price index (1988 = 100)		104		107		111
Administrative and selling expenses	25,000		27,000		36,000	

Required:

1. Compute the inventory values (at cost and at retail) that should be used for 1989, 1990, and 1991 to determine cost ratios.
2. Convert the inventory results for each year, computed in (1) above, to DV LIFO retail for use in developing the external financial statements and the income tax return (round all cost ratios to three decimal places).

3. Complete the following tabulation for 1991:

	Year 1991	
	FIFO Basis	**DV LIFO Basis**
Sales revenue	$_____	$_____
Less expenses:		
Cost of goods sold:		
Beginning inventory	_____	_____
Purchases	_____	_____
Total	_____	_____
Ending inventory	_____	_____
Cost of goods sold	_____	_____
Administrative and selling expenses	_____	_____
Total expenses	_____	_____
Pretax income	_____	_____
Income taxes (assume a 35% rate)	_____	_____
Net income	_____	_____
Reduction in cash outflows by using DV LIFO	$_____	

P 10–13

DV LIFO Retail Conversion: Price Indexes Given (L.O. 4)

Richard's Retailers keeps its internal inventory records on a FIFO (not LCM) basis. At interim reporting dates, Richard's accountants convert the book balances to a LIFO basis for reporting purposes by using the DV LIFO retail method. The following data for the quarter ended March 31, 1992, are available:

	Quarter Ended 3/31/92	
	At Cost	**At Retail**
Base layer from 1990 (when LIFO was adopted); index = 100	$ 19,750	$ 38,500
Additional LIFO layer added in 1991; index = 104; cost ratio = .60	30,900	51,500
Beginning inventory, 1992 index = 110	49,500	90,000
Purchases (net)	231,000	400,000
Net additional markups		30,000
Net markdowns		10,000
Return sales		6,000
Sales (gross)		396,000
Price index at end of March 1992 = 120.		

Required:

Compute the ending inventory at March 31, 1992, at DV LIFO cost using the retail inventory method. Show all computations in order and round all cost ratios and price index ratios to the nearest three decimal places.

P 10–14

DV LIFO Retail: Price Indexes Given, Conversion (L.O. 4)

White Company changed to the DV LIFO retail method for external reporting and income tax purposes on January 1, 1989. The following data are available from White's records for the year ended December 31, 1990:

	At Cost	At Retail
Purchases	$70,000	$100,000
Net additional markups		4,000
Net markdowns		4,000
Sales		80,000

The December 31, 1989, ending inventory was $88,000 at retail and $51,450 at DV LIFO cost. Relevant external price indexes are: 1988 (base year), 110; 1989, 121; and 1990, 132.

Required:

Compute the December 31, 1990, ending inventory using the DV LIFO retail method. Round all cost ratios to three decimal places.

P 10–15
DF LIFO Retail:
Overview Three Years,
Price Indexes Given
(L.O. 4)

Miller Department Store has been using the retail inventory method (average cost with LCM) for a number of years. After extensive consideration, the company decided to change to DV LIFO retail for all purposes. Thus, after the change, instituted on January 1, 1991, FIFO retail cost basis will be computed each period, then these results will be converted to DV LIFO retail for external reporting and income tax purposes.

The inventory records for the year 1990 showed the following computations (i.e., for the year prior to the change):

	At Cost	At Retail
Inventory, 1/1/1990	$ 55,000	$ 74,000
Purchases	540,000	724,000
Net additional markups		6,000
Total	$595,000	804,000
Cost ratio: $595,000 ÷ $804,000 = .740		
Sales		(700,000)
Net markdowns		(10,000)
Inventory, 12/31/1990:		
At retail		$ 70,000
At average cost, LCM ($70,000 × .740)	$ 51,800	

Data for the three years 1991–1993 are as shown in the following schedule:

	1991		1992		1993	
	At Cost	At Retail	At Cost	At Retail	At Cost	At Retail
Purchases	$500,000	$618,000	$580,000	$700,000	$600,000	$750,000
Net additional markups		16,000		10,000		10,000
Net markdowns		9,000		11,000		7,000
Sales		600,000		650,000		725,000
Applicable price index (1990 = 120)	132		144		150	
Administrative and selling expenses	45,000		48,000		50,000	

Required:

Round all cost ratios to three decimal places.
1. Compute the inventory value that should be used as the base inventory on January 1, 1991.
2. Compute the inventory values (at cost and at retail) that should be used as the ending inventories for 1991, 1992, and 1993 for conversion purposes (and for internal use).
3. In view of the change from average cost with LCM, the company decided to adjust the inventory account to the FIFO cost basis for internal purposes. Give the entry to effect this change at the start of 1991.
4. Convert the FIFO inventory results for each year, computed in (2) above, to DV LIFO retail for use in developing the external financial statements and the income tax return.
5. Complete the schedule for 1993 shown below:

	Year 1993	
	FIFO Basis	DV LIFO Basis
Sales revenue	$_____	$_____
Less expenses:		
Cost of goods sold:		
Beginning inventory	_____	_____
Purchases	_____	_____
Total	_____	_____
Ending inventory	_____	_____
Cost of goods sold	_____	_____
Administrative and selling expenses	_____	_____
Total expenses	_____	_____

	Year 1993	
	FIFO Basis	**DV LIFO Basis**
Pretax income	_____	_____
Income taxes (assume a 34% rate)	_____	_____
Net income	_____	_____
Reduction in cash outflows by using DV LIFO	$_____	

P 10–16
Relative Sales Value
Method
(L.O. 5)

Valley Grocers Co-op purchased a large quantity of mixed grapefruit for $41,000, which was graded at a cost of $1,000, as indicated below. Sales (at the sales prices indicated) and losses (frozen, rotten, etc.) are also listed.

Grade	Baskets Bought	Sales Price per Basket	Baskets Sold	Baskets Spoiled
A	5,000	$4.00	2,000	50
B	4,000	3.00	3,000	60
C	10,000	2.00	8,000	40
Culls	1,000	.50	900	
Loss	100			

Required:

1. Give the entry for the purchase assuming a perpetual inventory system. Show computations.
2. Give entries to record the sales and cost of goods sold.
3. Give the entry for the losses assuming the losses are recorded separately from cost of goods sold.
4. Determine the valuation of the ending inventory.
5. Compute the direct contribution to pretax income for each grade of grapefruit. (Disregard operating, administrative, and selling expenses.)

P 10–17
Relative Sales Value
Method: Land
(L.O. 5)

On January 1, 1990, Rob and Will each invested $100,000 cash in a partnership for the purpose of purchasing and subdividing a tract of land for residential building purposes.

On June 1, they purchased a 30-acre subdivision at $5,000 per acre, paying $50,000 in cash and giving a one-year, 15% interest-bearing note (with mortgage) for the balance. Development costs amounted to an additional $110,000 (paid in cash).

The property was subdivided into 300 lots, 200 of which were to sell at $4,000 each and the balance at $5,000 each.

During July through December 1990, the following sales were made for half cash and half interest-bearing notes receivable due in six months from date of sale.

	Lots
Group A (sold at $4,000 each)	50
Group B (sold at $5,000 each)	60

Cash collections on the notes receivable up to December 31, 1990, amounted to $49,000 principal plus $1,000 interest. Accrued interest recorded at December 31, 1990, amounted to $1,000.

Operating and selling expenses amounted to $125,000 by the end of December 1990. No payment was made on the note payable.

Required:

1. Give the entries for all of the above transactions. Disregard income taxes.
2. Prepare an income statement for 1990.
3. Compute the valuation of the inventory of unsold lots on December 31, 1990.

P 10–18
Correcting Errors on an
Income Statement
(L.O. 5)

Bass Company has completed the income statement and balance sheet (summarized and uncorrected, shown below) at December 31, 1991. Subsequently, during an audit, the following items were discovered.

a. Expenses amounting to $5,000 were not accrued.

b. A conditional sale on credit for $12,000 was recorded on December 31, 1991. The goods, which cost $8,000, were included in the ending inventory; they had not been shipped because the customer's address was not known and the credit had not been approved. Ownership had not passed.

c. Merchandise purchased on December 31, 1991, on credit for $9,000 was included in the ending inventory because the goods were on hand. A purchase was not recorded because the accounting department had not received the invoice from the vendor.

d. The ending inventory was overstated by $15,000 due to an addition error on the inventory sheet.

e. A sale return (on account) on December 31, 1991, was not recorded: sales amount, $15,000, and cost, $8,000. The ending inventory did not include the goods returned.

Required:

Set up a schedule similar to the one below; make the corrections and derive the corrected amounts. Indicate increases and decreases for each transaction. Explain any assumptions made with respect to doubtful items. Disregard income taxes.

	Uncorrected Amounts	Items for Correction					Corrected Amounts
		(a)	(b)	(c)	(d)	(e)	
Income statement:							
Sales revenue	$90,000						
Cost of goods sold	50,000						
Gross margin	40,000						
Expenses	30,000						
Pretax income	$10,000						
Balance sheet:							
Accounts receivable	$42,000						
Inventory	20,000						
Remaining assets	30,000						
Accounts payable	11,000						
Remaining liabilities	6,000						
Common stock	60,000						
Retained earnings	15,000						

P 10–19
Correcting Inventory Errors
(L.O. 5)

On January 3, 1992, Jonah Corporation engaged an independent CPA to perform an audit for the year ended December 31, 1991. The company used a periodic inventory system. The CPA did not observe the inventory count on December 31, 1991; as a result, a special examination was made of the inventory records.

The financial statements prepared by the company (uncorrected) showed the following: ending inventory, $72,000; accounts receivable, $60,000; accounts payable, $30,000; sales, $400,000; net purchases, $160,000; and pretax income, $51,000.

The following data were found during the audit:

a. Merchandise received on January 2, 1992, costing $800 was recorded on December 31, 1991. An invoice on hand showed the shipment was made FOB supplier's warehouse on December 31, 1991. Because the merchandise was not on hand at December 31, 1991, it was not included in the inventory.

b. Merchandise that cost $18,000 was excluded from the inventory, and the related sale for $23,000 was recorded. The goods had been segregated in the warehouse for shipment; there was no contract for sale but a "tentative order by phone."

c. Merchandise that cost $10,000 was out on consignment to Bar Distributing Company and was excluded from the ending inventory. The merchandise was recorded as a sale of $25,000 when shipped to Bar on December 2, 1991.

d. A sealed packing case containing a product costing $900 was in Jonah's shipping room when the physical inventory was taken. It was included in the inventory because it was marked Hold for Customer's Shipping Instructions. Investigation revealed that the customer signed a purchase contract dated December 18, 1991, but that the case was shipped and the customer billed on January 10, 1992. A sale was recorded on December 18, 1991.

e. A special item, fabricated to order for a customer, was finished and in the shipping room on December 31, 1991. The customer had inspected it and was satisfied. The customer was billed in full on that date. The item was included in inventory at cost, $1,000, because it was shipped on January 4, 1992.

f. Merchandise costing $1,500 was received on December 28, 1991. The goods were excluded from inventory, and a purchase was not recorded. The auditor located the related papers in the hands of the purchasing agent; they indicated, "On consignment from Baker Company."

g. Merchandise costing $2,000 was received on January 8, 1992, and the related purchase invoice recorded January 9. The invoice showed the shipment was made on December 29, 1991, FOB destination. The merchandise was excluded from the inventory.

h. Merchandise that cost $11,000 and which was sold on December 31, 1991 for $16,000, was included in the ending inventory. The sale was recorded. The goods were in transit; however, a clerk failed to note that the goods were shipped FOB shipping point.

i. Merchandise that cost $6,000 was excluded from the ending inventory and not recorded as a sale for $7,500 on December 31, 1991. The goods had been specifically segregated. According to the terms of the contract of sale, ownership will not pass until actual delivery.

j. Merchandise that cost $15,000 was included in the ending inventory. The related purchase has not been recorded. The goods had been shipped by the vendor FOB destination; and the invoice, but not the goods, was received on December 30, 1991.

k. Merchandise in transit that cost $7,000 was excluded from inventory because it was not on hand. The shipment from the vendor was FOB shipping point. The purchase was recorded on December 29, 1991, when the invoice was received.

l. Merchandise in transit that cost $13,000 was excluded from inventory because it had not arrived. Although the invoice had arrived, the related purchase was not recorded by December 31, 1991. The merchandise was shipped by the vendor FOB shipping point.

m. Merchandise that cost $8,000 was included in the ending inventory because it was on hand. The merchandise had been rejected because of incorrect specifications and was being held for return to the vendor. The merchandise was recorded as a purchase on December 26, 1991.

Required:

1. Prepare a schedule with one column for each of the six financial statement items given in the problem introduction (starting with the uncorrected balances), plus a column for explanations. Show the specific corrections to each balance and the corrected balances. Explain the basis for your decision on all items.
2. Give the entry to correct the accounts assuming the accounts for 1991 have been closed.

(AICPA adapted)

CASES

C 10–1
Estimate the Inventory of Books
(L.O. 2)

The manager of Seton Book Company, a book retailer, requires an estimate of the inventory cost for a quarterly financial report to the owner on March 31, 1993. In the past, the gross margin method was used due to the difficulty and expense of taking a physical inventory at interim dates. The company sells both fiction and nonfiction books. Due to their lower turnover rate, nonfiction books are typically marked up at a 60% rate on cost. Fiction, on the other hand, has a 40% markup rate on cost. The manager has used an average markup of 50% to estimate interim inventories.

You have been asked by the manager to estimate the book inventory cost as of March 31, 1993. The following data is available from Seton's accounting records:

	Fiction	Nonfiction	Total
Inventory, 1/1/93	$100,000	$ 40,000	$140,000
Purchases	600,000	200,000	800,000
Freight	5,000	2,000	7,000
Sales	590,000	160,000	750,000

Required:

Round gross margin ratios to three decimal places.

1. Using an estimated markup on cost of 50%, compute the estimate of inventory as of March 31, 1993 based on the gross margin method applied to combined fiction and nonfiction books.
2. Compute the estimate of ending inventory as of March 31, 1993, based on the gross margin method applied separately to fiction and nonfiction books.
3. Which method is preferable in this situation? Explain.

C 10–2
Repurchase Commitment:
Probable Loss
(L.O. 5)

Stauffer Chemical Company is a major agricultural chemical supplier. The following excerpts are from an article in *The Wall Street Journal* (August 14, 1984, p. 2):

> Stauffer, which relies on agricultural chemicals for more than half its profits, has been hammered in the past three years by bad weather, depressed farm prices, and lowered farm output caused by a federal price-support program. In the summer of 1982, "aware that agricultural chemical sales for its 1982–83 season would probably fall off sharply," Stauffer undertook a plan to accelerate sales of certain products to dealers during fiscal 1982, according to the SEC.
>
> The commission charged that the plan was "tantamount to consignment sales which shouldn't have been recognized in 1982," and that Stauffer's annual report to shareholders for that year failed to reflect this fact.
>
> Stauffer, the SEC charged, offered its dealers incentives to take products during the fourth quarter of 1982. As a result, the company reported $72 million of revenue that ordinarily wouldn't have been booked until early 1983. By March 1983, according to the commission, Stauffer realized that it would have to "offer its distributors relief" from the oversupply of unsalable products. Stauffer offered dealers refunds for as much as 100% of unsold products taken in 1982, compared with 32% the previous year.
>
> Stauffer ended up refunding nearly 40% of its 1982 agricultural chemical sales, but failed disclose the "substantial uncertainties" surrounding the sales in the annual report filed with the SEC in April 1983. The omission was "materially false and misleading," according to the SEC.
>
> "Their business was down and they wanted to accelerate sales," said a government official familiar with the year-long SEC investigation.
>
> H. Barclay Morley, Stauffer's chief executive officer, conceded that fears about the fading popularity of the company's best-selling farm products had prompted some of the accounting policies questioned by the SEC. "Our theory was that if the distributor had title on the product he would have more incentive to move it," Mr. Morley said. But he declined to comment on the SEC charge that the company was aware of severe problems with a substantial portion of its agricultural chemical sales when it filed its annual report.

Required:

Discuss the appropriate accounting treatment and disclosures by Stauffer for its agricultural chemical inventories and sales in 1982.

C 10–3
Sherwin-Williams:
Analyzing Financial
Statement
(L.O.1)

Note 5 to the Sherwin-Williams 1990 annual report reproduced at the end of the text indicates that the company's "inventories are stated at the lower of cost or market. Cost is determined principally on the last-in, first-out (LIFO) method."

Required:

Is this reporting permitted under GAAP and is it allowed for IRS income tax reporting? Explain.

C H A P T E R
11

Operational Assets: Acquisition, Disposal, and Exchange

◆

INTRODUCTION

◆

General Motors Corporation reported $60.8 billion in gross property, plant, and equipment in its 1988 balance sheet. The net book value of these assets equalled $28 billion after deducting $32.8 billion of accumulated depreciation. Were these assets worth $28 billion to GM? Would they be worth that much on the open market? If not, of what use are these disclosures?

Power Corporation, a real estate development company, purchased the Polo Ralph Lauren building in New York City in 1989 for $43 million, paying a record $1,600 per square foot. The building was built in 1894 at a cost of $500,000, or less than $19 per square foot.[1] Can the retention of older book values in published balance sheets be justified?

International Paper Company increased the recorded value of its plant assets by $11 million in 1989 by capitalizing interest during the construction of plant assets. Does interest incurred during the construction of plant assets increase the value of those assets? The firm's pretax income also increased by $11 million as a result of interest capitalization. Does International Paper have $11 million more spendable pretax income?

The Times Mirror Company recorded a $58.9 million gain on the sale of equipment, timberland, and other plant assets in 1988. This gain added $.31 to the firm's earnings per share. Yet, is Times Mirror better off economically as a result of this transaction?

These situations and the accounting issues they raise relate to the main issue of this chapter: the valuation of property, plant, and equipment. The accounting issues are important since operating assets often constitute the largest single asset category for corporations. Further, the recorded value of plant assets is the basis for subsequent depreciation. This chapter discusses the valuation of plant assets when acquired using debt, equity securities, or other assets; the valuation of self-constructed assets; accounting for the disposal and exchange of nonmonetary assets; and accounting for post-acquisition costs.

◆

VALUATION OF PLANT ASSETS AT ACQUISITION

◆

This chapter extends the discussion of accounting for assets that began with Chapter 8. The focus of this chapter and the next two is on a broad category of assets often described as *operational assets* because they are used in the operations of a business and are not held for resale.

Classifying Operational Assets

For accounting purposes, operational assets usually are classified into tangible and intangible assets.

Tangible operational assets are defined as those that:

◆ Are actively used in operations rather than held as an investment or for resale.
◆ Are expected to provide benefits beyond the current accounting period.
◆ Have physical substance.

Tangible operational assets are typically reported in the balance sheet using captions such as *property, plant, and equipment*, or *plant assets*, or *tangible fixed assets*.

Tangible operational assets are, in turn, further divided and grouped into three subclassifications:

---

[1] "Power Corp. Buys New York Building for $1,600 a Foot," *The Wall Street Journal*, July 31, 1989, p. A5A.

* Those subject to depreciation, such as buildings, equipment, furniture, and fixtures.
* Those subject to depletion, such as mineral deposits and timber tracts.
* Land, which is not subject to depreciation or depletion.

By contrast, *intangible* operational assets are defined as those that:

* Are actively used in operations rather than held as an investment or for resale.
* Are expected to provide future benefits beyond the current accounting period.
* Do not have their value tied to physical substance.

The value of intangible assets is represented solely by grants or business rights that produce an operating, financial, or income-producing benefit. Examples include goodwill, patents, copyrights, and trademarks. The cost of an intangible asset is periodically amortized to expense over the asset's useful life. Intangible assets are discussed in Chapter 13.

Expenditures related to the acquisition and use of operational assets are accounted for and classified as either capital expenditures or revenue expenditures. **Capital expenditures** are those expenditures expected to yield benefits beyond the current accounting period. Therefore, such expenditures are *capitalized,* meaning they are treated as asset acquisitions and debited to an appropriate asset account. The cost of an asset acquired through a capital expenditure is recognized as expense in current and future periods through depreciation, amortization, or depletion.

Revenue expenditures are those expected to yield benefits only in the current accounting period. Therefore, they are recorded in expense accounts and matched against the revenue of the period as part of the process of determining income.

It is important to classify expenditures correctly. An incorrect classification affects reported income for the entire life of an asset. For example, if costs are misclassified as capital expenditures and carried as asset accounts, then current income is overstated and future income is understated by depreciation on those costs. In contrast, if the capital expenditure is relatively small, if the expected future benefit is insignificant, or if the estimation of future benefit is not reliable, materiality and conservatism support immediate expensing.

General Principles for the Valuation of Plant Assets

SFAS No. 34, "Capitalization of Interest Cost," states (par. 6): *"The historical cost of acquiring an asset includes the costs necessarily incurred to bring it to the condition and location necessary for its intended use."* Historical cost is used because it is the result of arm's-length transactions between unrelated parties, and is therefore considered objective and reliable.

The *matching* principle requires that costs be deferred or held in asset accounts until revenues are generated. As plant assets are placed into service and contribute to the revenue-generating process, the acquisition cost is matched against revenues through depreciation.

Historical acquisition cost is the cash outlay, or equivalent, made to acquire an asset and prepare it for use. This amount is also the fair market value of the asset at time of acquisition. When plant assets are acquired for noncash consideration, the assets are recorded at either the market value of the consideration transferred or the market value of the acquired asset, whichever amount is more objective. Accounting for asset exchanges includes an exception to this principle and is discussed later in this chapter.

The list (sticker) price of a plant asset is not necessarily the asset's value. List prices are often merely a starting point for negotiations between buyer and seller, with each party using experience and knowledge to bargain for a favorable price.

Valuation bases other than historical cost exist, although they are not in common use. These bases include replacement cost (a measure of entry value), net realizable value (a measure of exit value), and price-level adjusted values (a measure of current value). Although reliable and verifiable, historical cost is often criticized as irrelevant when prices of specific assets change.

Many kinds of costs are incurred to acquire plant assets, in addition to the invoice price (less available discounts). These expenditures include sales tax, insurance during transit, freight, back property taxes assumed by the buyer, title insurance premiums, import duties, ownership registration, installation, commissions, interest during construction, and break-in costs. Break-in costs include practice runs with machinery and the initial set-up before the first production run. These expenditures are necessary to make the asset ready for use and are required to obtain benefits from the asset. Therefore, all these expenditures are capitalized.

Subsequent to acquisition, and in conformity with the matching principle, plant assets are carried in the accounts at their historical acquisition cost less accumulated depreciation. Depreciation is not recognized until the asset is placed into use, at which time the asset begins to produce benefits.

Costs Not Capitalized   Not all expenditures associated with acquiring plant assets are capitalized. For example, if a discount is offered by the seller, it is deducted from the invoice price whether taken or not, for purposes of valuing the asset. Discounts not taken are recorded as a financing expense because they do not increase the value of the asset. Instead, they represent a financing cost, as was the case with inventories discussed in Chapter 9.

Interest on debt incurred to purchase plant assets is not capitalized because the asset is already in its intended condition for use. Prepaid interest, called **points,** and loan origination fees charged by lending institutions are also period expenses.

The costs of training employees to use plant assets are not capitalized. Training costs enhance the value of employees, not the assets.[2] Annual property taxes and insurance costs also are not capitalized. These costs only maintain or protect the asset over the period. In addition, the costs of dismantling and disposing of an old asset are not added to the cost of the new asset. Rather, such costs are treated as adjustments to any gain or loss on disposal of the old asset.

Make-Ready Costs   Subsequent to acquisition, but prior to the use of a plant asset, all expenditures incurred to ready the asset for use are included in the cost of the asset. For example, a secondhand asset might require substantial outlays for repairs, reconditioning, remodeling, and installation. Each of these is capitalized. Machinery reinstallation and rearrangement costs, rearrangement of building partitions, renovation and structural changes made to buildings, and similar outlays directly related to plant assets purchased new or in used condition are capitalized as part of the original asset's cost.

During a period of renovation, overhead expenditures, including insurance, taxes, supervisory salaries, and similar incidental expenditures directly related to refurbishing a used asset, also are capitalized. These expenditures increase the value of the asset and generate long-term benefits to the firm. Similar costs that would have been incurred independent of the refurbishing work are not capitalized. In general, costs that do not enhance the expected utility of the asset are not capitalized. For example, an expenditure to repair damage resulting from improper installation is not capitalized.

Classification within Property, Plant, and Equipment   For classification purposes, plant assets are subdivided into the following categories:
* Buildings.
* Machinery, furniture, and fixtures.

---

[2] An argument based on the matching principle can be made for capitalizing training costs. However, the lack of an assured connection to specific revenues causes accountants to be conservative and expense them.

+ Land.
+ Land improvements.
+ Natural resources.

Subsidiary ledgers are maintained for individual assets in each of these categories to ensure accurate records and to serve as a basis for internal control of fixed assets. The first four categories are discussed in this chapter. Natural resources, which raise accounting issues not pertinent to other plant assets, are discussed in Chapter 13.

APB Opinion No. 12 (par. 5) requires that the balances of all major classes of depreciable assets be disclosed. Correct classification is important for subsequent depreciation calculations. Different depreciation methods and useful lives are applied to the various account classifications within plant assets. Also, for internal accounting purposes, a detailed list of costs that constitute the individual accounts is important for complying with income tax laws, determining the gain or loss on disposal or exchange, assisting external audits, and evaluating capital budgeting decisions.

Buildings   The cost of buildings includes architectural fees, construction costs, cost of permits, and the cost of excavating foundations. Excavations vary according to the specifications of the building and are a necessary cost of construction.

Machinery, Furniture, and Fixtures   This category includes special platforms, foundations, and other required installation costs. The costs of building modifications necessary for specific equipment are also debited to equipment. However, the costs of broad rearrangements of plant facilities to accommodate major changes in the production process are capitalized to the building account.

Land   Land is not depreciated because its value is neither expected to diminish over time nor be exhausted by production activities. In certain instances, discussed in Chapter 12, land is written down to reflect a permanent decline in value. Expenditures are capitalized to the land account only for properties currently in service as a building site or in other productive use. General land preparation costs, including grading, filling, draining, and surveying, are capitalized to land. In contrast to excavation costs which are capitalized to buildings, these activities are required for general land use and add permanent value to the land.

Land held by real estate development companies and land sales organizations is classified as inventory rather than as land. In general, idle land constitutes an investment and is not included in the land account. For example, National Technical Systems, Inc. included the following footnote in its 1990 annual report:

> The Company owns a parcel of land in San Diego County, California, which was placed for sale in the fourth quarter of fiscal 1988. The property was originally acquired for approximately $544,000. The Company anticipates that sales proceeds will exceed the net book value of the property.

If land is acquired for redevelopment or use as a building site, the cost of removing existing structures and other obstructions is capitalized to land. Such razing costs are necessary for many land uses. Proceeds from salvaged materials reduce the costs capitalized. However, if the land is already owned by the firm and existing structures are razed to make way for new construction, razing costs are not capitalized to the land account. Instead, they increase any loss or reduce any gain on the disposal of the old structure.

Special assessments for local government-maintained structures, including streets, sidewalks, sewers, and street lights, are also capitalized to land. The rationale for this accounting treatment is that the assessed company has no responsibility to maintain or replace these structures, and the benefits derived from these municipal improvements are perpetual.

Certain types of landscaping and other property enhancements are included in land if they are permanent. Examples include artificial lakes and terracing. Treatment of these enhancements contrasts with land improvements discussed in the following section.

Property taxes, insurance, and other holding costs are incurred on land not in current productive use. Treatment of these costs is controversial. Some accountants contend that capitalization is proper because the land is not currently producing benefits. On the other hand, although these costs are necessary to maintain the property on the tax rolls and protect the company from legal liability, they do not increase the value of the land. In most cases, these costs are expensed on grounds of expedience and conservatism.

If idle land is held for investment or lease, *SFAS No. 67,* ''Accounting for Costs and Initial Rental Operations of Real Estate Projects,'' specifies that property taxes and insurance are capitalized only during periods in which the property is prepared for sale or lease. Unfortunately, the statement did not resolve the issue for land held by a firm for its own use.

Land Improvements   Land improvements are depreciable site enhancements, including driveways, parking lots, fencing, and landscaping, that are not permanent. Although a parking lot appears permanent and not subject to depreciation, gradually the elements cause damage requiring maintenance and eventual replacement. The cost of land improvements is not added to the land account. Instead, these expenditures are capitalized to the land improvements account and depreciated.

Examples of Plant Asset Classification   A footnote to the 1988 financial statements of Dow Chemical Company gives an example of the variety of account classifications found in property, plant, and equipment.

Dow Chemical Company
Plant properties (in millions)

	1988	1987
Land	$ 268	$ 260
Land and waterway improvements	455	410
Buildings	1,402	1,268
Machinery and equipment	11,001	10,187
Wells and brine systems	107	211
Office furniture and equipment	396	320
Mineral reserves	691	19
Other	140	150
Construction in progress	900	677
Total	$15,360	$13,502

To reinforce the concepts of plant asset valuation and classification, the costs incurred by Martex Company, a hypothetical company, are given as an example. Exhibit 11-1 provides information related to the acquisition of plant assets and the construction of a building. Exhibit 11-2 shows the resulting ending balances of the plant assets accounts.

Lump-Sum Purchase of Several Assets   Occasionally, several assets are acquired for a single lump-sum price. The aggregate price often is lower than the sum of the asset prices if purchased individually, to induce the large purchase. In other cases, the assets are attached, as in the case of a land and building. This type of acquisition, called a *basket, group,* or *lump-sum purchase,* poses the problem of allocating a portion of the single lump-sum price to each asset acquired.

EXHIBIT 11-1 Costs Associated with Acquisition of Plant Assets, Martex Company

Item	Description	Amount
1.	Invoice price of equipment (Available cash discount if invoice paid in 15 days, 3%. Martex paid for the equipment on the 30th day after purchase)	$ 50,000
2.	Sales tax of 4% applies to the equipment purchase	2,000
3.	Insurance and freight costs in transit incurred by Martex for the equipment	600
4.	Sales commissions and title insurance premium cost incurred by Martex to acquire the land	7,000
5.	Price of land parcel	100,000
6.	Costs to set up equipment and perform extensive practice runs	2,000
7.	Costs to train employees to run equipment	500
8.	Interest incurred on debt used to acquire the equipment	1,200
9.	Costs to remove old structure from land	30,000
10.	Proceeds on materials salvaged from old structure	2,000
11.	Cost of foundation excavation	3,500
12.	Cost to survey and grade land	12,000
13.	Cost of concrete and labor for foundation	26,000
14.	Several months after acquiring the land, Martex paid its first installment of property tax	550
15.	Asphalt for a parking lot	11,000
16.	Fencing for the property	6,000

EXHIBIT 11-2 Ending Plant Asset Account Balances, Martex Company

Equipment Account:
1.	Invoice price	$ 50,000
1.	Less available cash discount	(1,500)
2.	Sales tax (.04)$50,000	2,000
3.	Insurance and freight in transit	600
6.	Set-up and practice runs	2,000
	Equipment account balance	$ 53,100

Land Account:
4.	Sales commission and title insurance	$ 7,000
5.	Land price	100,000
9.	Cost to remove old structure	30,000
10.	Proceeds from salvage materials	(2,000)
12.	Surveying and grading	12,000
	Land account balance	$147,000

Building under Construction Account:
11.	Cost to excavate foundation	$ 3,500
13.	Foundation costs	26,000
	Building account balance	$ 29,500

Land Improvements Accounts:
15.	Parking lot	$ 11,000
16.	Fencing	6,000
	Land improvements account balance	$ 17,000

Current Period Expenses:
1. $1,500 cash discount lost is a finance charge.
7. $500 employee training is wages and salary expense.
8. $1,200 interest on debt incurred to acquire equipment is interest expense.
14. $550 property tax is a period expense.

The portions of the lump-sum price directly attributable to particular assets in the group are assigned in full to those assets. Land appraisal costs are assigned only to the land account, for example.

An allocation of the remaining lump-sum price (after directly attributable costs) to each asset in the group is necessary in order to record each asset in an individual account. This recorded amount for each individual asset is the basis for subsequent depreciation. Each asset in the group is subject to different estimates of useful life and residual value, and possibly a different depreciation method. Under the historical cost principle, the sum of the individual asset account balances at acquisition is limited to the lump-sum price.

The allocation of the purchase price is based on the best available indicator of the relative values of the several assets involved. Possibilities include market prices for similar assets, current appraised value, assessed value for property tax purposes, relative expected manufacturing cost savings, and the present value of estimated future net cash flows. The seller's book values generally do not reflect the relative current value of the assets in the group.

If market value is used, each asset in the group receives a valuation based on the proportion of its market value to the total market value of the group; this procedure is called the *proportional* method. If the market value of only the first of two assets in a group is determinable, that amount is used to value the first asset. The second asset is valued with the remaining cost to be allocated. This procedure is called the *incremental* method.

To illustrate the proportional method, assume that $90,000 is the negotiated acquisition price paid for land, a building, and machinery. These assets are appraised (the best available indication of value) individually as follows: land, $30,000; building, $50,000; and machinery, $20,000. The cost apportionment of the single lump-sum price and the entry to record the transaction are shown below:

Asset	Appraised Value	Apportionment of Cost	Apportioned Cost
Land	$ 30,000	.3*($90,000)	$27,000
Building	50,000	.5(90,000)	45,000
Machinery	20,000	.2(90,000)	18,000
Total	$100,000		$90,000

* .3 = $30,000/$100,000.

To record lump-sum purchase:

Land	27,000	
Building	45,000	
Machinery	18,000	
Cash		90,000

CONCEPT REVIEW

1. Why are costs such as freight and insurance in transit capitalized to plant assets?
2. Why are annual property taxes on land not capitalized to land?
3. Why is the cost of excavating a building foundation debited to the building when the excavation is performed on the land site?

ACCOUNTING FOR NONCASH ACQUISITIONS OF PLANT ASSETS

The general principles for valuation of plant assets are independent of the type of consideration or method used to acquire plant assets. Plant assets are acquired in several nonmutually exclusive ways:

- With cash.
- On credit.
- In exchange for equity securities of the acquiring company.
- Through donation from another entity.
- Through construction.
- In exchange for nonmonetary assets.[3]

The next several sections of this chapter consider noncash acquisition of plant assets.

Plant Assets Purchased on Credit

In conformity with the historical cost principle, the recorded cost of an asset purchased on credit is based on one of the following, whichever is more objective and reliable *(APB Opinion No. 21)*:

1. Its cash equivalent price (market value).
2. The present value of the future cash payments required by the debt instrument discounted at the prevailing (market) interest rate for that type of debt instrument.

If the debt instrument does not bear interest and the current cash price of the asset is determinable, the excess to be paid over the cash price is treated as interest expense and apportioned over the term of the debt. If the cash price is not determinable, the prevailing interest rate is used to determine total interest cost and to compute the asset's present value for recording purposes *(APB Opinion No. 21)*. The valuation of assets acquired in exchange for debt securities is similar to the valuation of long-term notes receivable, discussed in Chapter 8.

To illustrate the purchase of a plant asset on credit, assume that Cobb Corporation purchased equipment on January 1, 1991, with a $600 cash down payment and a 12%, $1,000, one-year note with interest payable on December 31, 1991. The stated interest rate is equal to the current market rate. Its present value equals its face value.

The asset is recorded at the sum of the cash down payment plus the present value of the note because the cash equivalent price of the asset is not available. The recorded amount is:

$$\text{Equipment valuation} = \text{Cash down payment} + \text{Present value of note}$$
$$= \$600 + \$1,000 = \$1,600$$

Cobb records the following entry:

January 1, 1991:

Equipment	1,600	
Cash		600
Note payable		1,000

Cobb will pay and recognize as expense $120 in interest ($1,000 × .12) for the year ended December 31, 1991.

The valuation of notes receivable is discussed in Chapter 8. The same principles apply for notes issued to acquire plant assets. The example that follows illustrates some of the complexities discussed in Chapter 8.

Assume that Feller Company acquired a machine on January 1, 1991, with a note that required $8,615 to be paid on December 31, 1991, 1992, and 1993. The note has no stated rate, but the prevailing interest rate is 14% on liabilities of this risk and duration. The face amount of the note is $25,845 ($8,615 × 3). The cash equivalent

---

[3] Nonmonetary assets are not readily convertible into fixed amounts of cash. Their value fluctuates as the demand and supply for them change. All plant assets are nonmonetary. Cash is an example of a monetary asset.

cost of the machine is unknown; therefore, the asset is recorded at the present value of the three payments discounted at 14%:

$$\text{Recorded cost} = \$8,615(PVA, 14\%, 3)$$
$$= \$8,615(2.32163)$$
$$= \$20,000 \text{ (rounded)}$$

Feller journalizes the following entries to record the asset and recognize interest expense on the note. The gross method is illustrated.

January 1, 1991:

Equipment	20,000	
Discount on note payable	5,845	
Note payable ($8,615 × 3)		25,845

Discount on note payable is a contra note payable account. It reduces the net note payable balance to the present value of the future cash flows ($20,000). The following entries record the debt payments, each composed of principal and interest.

December 31:

	1991		1992		1993	
Interest expense	2,800*		1,986†		1,059‡	
Note payable	8,615		8,615		8,615	
Discount on note payable		2,800		1,986		1,059
Cash		8,615		8,615		8,615

* $2,800 = $20,000(.14).
† $1,986 = ($20,000 − principal reduction in 1991) (.14)
  = [$20,000 − ($8,615 − $2,800)] (.14)
  = $14,185(.14).
‡ $1,059 = [$14,185 − ($8,615 − $1,986)] (.14) (rounded)

Plant Assets Acquired in Exchange for Equity Securities

When equity securities are issued to acquire plant assets, the assets are recorded at either the fair market value of the asset or the fair market value of the securities issued, whichever is more objective and reliable.

The market value of the securities issued is reliable if the securities are publicly traded and if the number of shares involved in the exchange is considerably lower than the market volume used to establish the stock price on a daily basis.

For example, assume that Medford Corporation purchased used equipment in 1991. The equipment is in reasonable condition but is not normally sold before the end of its useful life. Thus, it has no reliable market value. In payment for this equipment, Medford issued 2,000 shares of its common stock. Medford's common stock is actively traded on the American Stock Exchange and currently trades at $10 per share. Medford has 10 million common shares outstanding. Therefore, the proper valuation for the equipment is $20,000 (2,000 × $10) because the volume of stock used in the acquisition is likely to be far lower than the daily trading volume. This amount also is assigned to the appropriate owners' equity accounts.

Several factors can complicate the situation, however. For example, the effect of a substantial stock issuance on the market price of the stock often is not known until after issuance. In addition, the stock of many companies is not traded with sufficient frequency to establish a daily market price. In other cases, organizers of a newly formed corporation are willing to exchange a substantial number of shares for plant assets, in the absence of a clear value for the shares or the assets. The uncertainty in the stock's value is increased for unexplored or unproven mineral deposits, manufacturing rights, patents, chemical formulas, and mining claims.

If the market value of the securities (in the volume exchanged) cannot be determined reliably, the market value of the assets acquired is used if it can be determined reliably. In the absence of a recent cash basis sale of the assets involved, an independent appraisal can be used to value the assets.

If a reliable market value for neither the securities issued nor the assets acquired can be determined, the board of directors of the corporation establishes a reasonable valuation. Unfortunately, the directors have considerable discretion in establishing values in this situation. Some firms experiencing financial difficulty are tempted to overstate the value of these assets, which in turn overstates owners' equity as well. A disincentive to overvaluation, however, is the increased depreciation expense in future years.

Donated Assets

Assets occasionally are donated to a company by municipalities or nonprofit organizations as an inducement to locate a plant in the area. By so doing, local governments hope to improve the local tax base and employment. Some donations are conditional upon specific performance by the company, such as the employment of a certain number of individuals by a specified date. Donations also are made occasionally by shareholders to assist the company during difficult financial times.

Only the nominal cost to process the donation would be recorded in the donated asset account under strict adherence to the historical cost principle. However, the full market value of contributed assets should be recognized upon receipt.

The FASB, in its 1990 *Exposure Draft* "Accounting for Contributions Received and Contributions Made and Capitalization of Works of Art, Historical Treasures, and Similar Assets," defines a contribution as:

> a transfer of cash or other assets to an entity or a settlement or cancellation of its liability from a voluntary *nonreciprocal transfer* by another entity acting other than as an owner. (par. 5)[4]

Contributions are restricted if the donor limits the use of the asset by the donee. For example, if land donated by a municipality to a firm must be used as the site of a specific type of production facility, the contribution is restricted.

Firms also receive pledges, which are promises by other organizations or individuals to make future contributions. An unconditional pledge depends only on the passage of time or demand by the pledgee for performance. A conditional pledge depends on the occurrence of a specific future event which binds the pledger.

The *Draft* specifies that both restricted and unrestricted contributions received be recognized as revenues at the fair value of items received, in the period received.[5] An asset, or liability if extinguished, is debited. Depreciable assets received by donation are depreciated in the normal manner on the basis of the fair market value recorded in the accounts.

Receipt of contributed services is recognized as both an expense and a revenue if the services create or enhance assets, are supplied by entities that normally provide such services for compensation, or are substantially the same as those normally purchased by the recipient. Contributions of works of art and historical treasures are recognized as revenue at fair value only if the items are intended to be sold, or could be sold. A contribution need not be recognized if the value of items received is not determinable or if the item is to be held only for a future scientific or educational purpose and has no alternative use. Unconditional pledges received are recognized as receivables and revenues at fair value. Conditional pledges are recognized when the conditions are met (when they become unconditional).

The *Draft* changes accounting for contributions to profit-oriented organizations in one significant respect. Rather than credit a contributed capital account for the

---

[4] The authors assume that the anticipated *Statement of Financial Accounting Standards* will follow the *Draft* in substance. The end-of-chapter material reflects the principles as discussed in the *Draft*.

[5] They can also be recognized as gains. The FASB (footnote 3 of the *Draft*) decided not to make a distinction between revenues and gains in this instance.

amount of the contribution, the income of the donee is increased by recognizing a revenue or gain. This is consistent with the concept of comprehensive income, as defined by *SFAC No. 6* (par. 70):

> Comprehensive income is the change in equity of a business enterprise during a period from transactions and other events and circumstances from nonowner sources. It includes all changes in equity during a period except those resulting from investments by owners and distributions to owners.

To illustrate accounting by a donee, assume that a building (fair market value $400,000) and the land (fair market value $100,000) on which it is located are given by a city to Stanford Corporation on May 1, 1991, as an inducement to establish a plant in that locale. A $5,000 legal and deed transfer cost is borne by Stanford, which records the donation as follows:

May 1, 1991:

Plant building (market value)	400,000	
Plant land (market value)	100,000	
Cash		5,000
Revenue from contributed plant assets		495,000

Self-Constructed Assets

Companies sometimes construct plant assets for their own use. For example, a utility employs its personnel to extend transmission lines and construct pipelines. All costs directly associated with construction projects are capitalized to the constructed asset. These costs include incremental material, labor, and overhead costs. Overhead, in turn, includes general costs not directly related to production, such as utility costs, maintenance on equipment, and supervision.

Under certain conditions, some of the general overhead, as well as interest expense, incurred during construction is included in the cost of these assets. Determining the amount of general overhead cost that should be allocated to a construction project is controversial and undecided. The accounting issues are whether and how to allocate overhead costs to self-constructed assets.

One view is that self-constructed assets should be assigned only the incremental overhead costs directly traceable to the project. Another view is that self-constructed assets should bear the incremental overhead cost and the portion of general overhead cost that would be assigned to any regular production displaced by the special project. According to this view, if general overhead is allocated on the basis of labor hours and 8% of labor hours are associated with self-construction, then 8% of total general overhead during construction should be included as a cost of the self-constructed asset. Many accountants contend that failure to allocate some portion of the general overhead to self-construction projects results in an undervaluation of self-constructed assets and an overstatement of inventory and cost of goods sold on regular production. Furthermore, had the asset been purchased, the acquisition price undoubtedly would have reflected a portion of the seller's overhead costs.

The actual cost of a self-constructed asset does not necessarily equal fair market value. Consistent with the valuation of other assets, the maximum valuation allowed by GAAP for self-constructed assets is fair market value. If total construction cost (including overhead and interest during construction) exceeds the market value of a similar asset of equal capacity and quality, the excess is recognized as a loss. Failure to do so carries forward cost elements that have no future benefit, causes overstated depreciation in future years, and violates the *conservatism constraint*.

In contrast, when the cost of a self-constructed asset is less than its external acquisition or replacement cost, the asset is recorded at total construction cost. Using the higher market value would imply a gain on construction. The *conservatism* constraint applies in this situation and requires waiting for more objective evidence, including lower operating costs or increased revenues, to support increased income.

The lower cost ultimately will be reflected in higher net income due to lower depreciation expense.

Accumulated construction costs generally are recorded in an account such as asset under construction, and classified as an investment or "other asset" in the balance sheet until completion of the project. Prior to completion, the asset is not classified as a plant asset because it is not in service. Upon completion and placement into service, the account is reclassified as a plant asset, and is subject to depreciation.

To illustrate the accounting for a self-constructed asset, assume that Kelvin Corporation completed the construction of equipment on November 10, 1991. The following list itemizes total construction costs:

Material	$200,000
Labor	500,000
Incremental overhead	60,000
Applied general overhead	40,000
Capitalized interest	100,000
Total	$900,000

Kelvin recorded all construction costs in the equipment under construction account. If the asset's market value at completion equals or exceeds $900,000, the following entry is made:

November 10, 1991:

Equipment	900,000	
Equipment under construction		900,000

If the asset's market value is only $880,000, the following entry is made:

November 10, 1991:

Equipment	880,000	
Loss on construction of equipment	20,000	
Equipment under construction		900,000

CONCEPT REVIEW

1. At what amount would you record a plant asset purchased on credit, if the asset does not have a ready market value?
2. If a large publicly held corporation whose shares are actively traded issued a small number of shares in exchange for a plant asset, what value would most likely be used to record the asset?
3. What is the argument for including some overhead as part of the cost of self-constructed assets?

CAPITALIZATION OF INTEREST DURING CONSTRUCTION
◆

Interest incurred during construction of plant assets is capitalized in certain cases. **Interest capitalization** is a controversial and complex issue. Recall that interest incurred on debt used to *purchase* an asset is not capitalized because the asset is already in its intended condition. Such interest is a financing cost and does not increase the utility of the asset purchased. Furthermore, purchased assets are generally placed into service immediately, providing revenues against which the interest on funds borrowed for purchase is matched.

In contrast, interest cost incurred *during construction* of assets is considered by many a cost necessary to place the asset into its intended condition. Under this view, the asset cannot generate revenue until it is completed; therefore, the interest incurred through the completion of the asset should be capitalized. The capitalized interest is expensed subsequently as part of the periodic depreciation. This is the present GAAP position on the issue.

When interest is capitalized, interest expense is reduced and plant assets are increased. For example, assume that $2,000,000 of previously recorded interest expense is capitalized to equipment under construction. The following entry is made to record capitalized interest:

To record interest capitalization:

Equipment under construction	2,000,000	
Interest expense		2,000,000

Both total assets and current pretax income are increased by the amount of capitalized interest.[6]

The period required for construction of plant assets can be lengthy. There is general agreement that time-related costs, including taxes and insurance during construction, should be capitalized to the asset under construction. Consistent logic supports capitalization of interest during the construction period. Moreover, had the company chosen to apply the funds used in construction to retire debt, a certain amount of interest cost would have been avoided. In addition, had the asset been purchased rather than self-constructed, the purchase price normally would have included a cost component to cover the seller's financing expenses. Also, many firms would be unable to construct assets without debt financing.

A contrasting view is that interest incurred during construction does not increase the value of constructed assets, but rather is a finance cost, as is the case with purchased assets. Proponents of this view maintain that the method of financing is independent of the asset's value (although it can have some effect on the total funds otherwise invested in the asset). A debt-free company using its own funds to construct an asset does so without interest cost. Another company with debt would construct the identical asset at a cost including capitalized interest. This anomaly is caused by the different capital structures and resource positions of the two firms. According to this view, the capital structure of a firm should have no bearing on the recorded value of a constructed asset.

Independent of the debate about capitalization of *actual* interest cost, an opportunity cost arises from the use of funds for self-construction. If those funds are derived from owners' equity rather than debt, some accountants argue that an **imputed interest** rate, an estimated rather than an actual rate, should be used to assign the cost of funds to a project. All financing, they argue, has an implicit cost. Furthermore, many firms have continuing credit agreements with financial institutions that make it impossible to relate a specific self-construction project to a specific source of debt financing. Capitalizing imputed interest would solve the problem of associating a project with a specific source of financing.

Public utilities traditionally have capitalized interest during construction. If construction-related interest were recognized as a current expense, current customers would then pay increased utility rates to cover the added expense. In effect, current customers would finance facilities of benefit to future customers. By including the interest (both actual and imputed) in the cost of the constructed assets (thereby raising future depreciation amounts), future customers who benefit from the assets pay for the interest incurred in creating the assets and the related utility service.

Before 1970, capitalization of interest during construction by nonutility companies was limited. During the 1970s, a growing number of companies began capitalizing interest, thereby increasing both their current income and total assets. The lack of

---

[6] This example assumes that interest is capitalized as an adjustment to interest expense already recorded. In practice, some companies capitalize interest charges directly to the equipment under construction account as they are incurred.

uniformity in accounting for interest during construction, and the resulting SEC moratorium[7] on interest capitalization by nonutility registrants led the FASB to issue *SFAS No. 34* in 1979. This standard governs the capitalization of interest.

The FASB's four to three vote on this *Statement* reflects the controversial nature of the subject. *SFAS No. 34* requires capitalization of actual interest cost only. Inputed interest is not capitalized. The SEC lifted its ban on interest capitalization in 1979, following the issuance of *SFAS No. 34*. The FASB therefore chose a middle ground among three possible accounting alternatives:

• Capitalize no interest.
• Capitalize only actual interest.
• Capitalize both actual interest and imputed interest on equity capital.[8]

Both the income statements and balance sheets of many companies immediately benefitted from *SFAS No. 34*. For example, in 1979, Avon's earnings per share increased 9 cents, Borden's 11 cents, Northwest Industries' 16 cents, and Phelps Dodge's 65 cents.[9] AT&T capitalized $109 million in interest charges in 1986, an amount which equaled 15% of the firm's total interest cost for the year and 82% of operating income. Although interest capitalization increases future depreciation expense and reduces future income, many companies were pleased with the financial statement effects of *SFAS No. 34*.

Not everyone agrees with the FASB's position. For example, John C. Burton, former chief accountant of the SEC and controller for the city of New York, said that the calculation of capitalized interest yields "nothing other than an arbitrary allocation. It is futile."[10] Many accountants and financial statement users contend that the earnings of many companies are artificially increased by interest capitalization while the quality of earnings is diminished. Capitalized interest does not increase liquidity, for example, yet it increases net income.

Provisions of *SFAS No. 34*

The essence of interest capitalization is that interest could have been avoided had the expenditures on constructed assets been applied instead to retire debt. The amount of interest to capitalize in any period is that amount of **avoidable interest**. The maximum avoidable interest is the actual interest expense during the period. Avoidable interest is the interest on debt that could have been retired using the cash otherwise invested in a construction project during the period.

The **average accumulated expenditures** (AAE) on a constructed asset for a given accounting period is the *average* cash investment in the project *during* that period. For example, assume Wharton Corporation began constructing a building for its own use on January 1, 1991, with a $1,000,000 cash expenditure. Wharton later made a $2,400,000 cash expenditure on November 1, 1991. The 1991 AAE is computed as follows:

$$AAE = \$1,000,000(12/12) + \$2,400,000(2/12) = \$1,400,000$$

The $2.4 million payment is invested in the project for only two months and therefore contributes only $400,000 to the average cash investment for 1991. Although the total project cost at December 31, 1991, is $3.4 million, the company's *average* cash investment in the project is only $1.4 million for the entire year. Assuming at least

---

[7] SEC, *ASR No. 163*, "Capitalization of Interest by Companies Other than Public Utilities," 1974.

[8] The FASB decided that allowing imputed interest to be capitalized would require basic changes in the measurement of income and recognition of assets (*SFAS No. 34*, par. 28). Actual interest expense is an objective resource outflow, whereas imputed interest requires estimation and linkage to a past contributed capital transaction, the price of which may no longer represent the true cost of capital.

[9] "Minor Matters," *Forbes*, March 31, 1980, p. 108.

[10] Ibid.

$1.4 million of debt outstanding the entire year, the company could have retired that much debt instead of embarking on the construction project. Consequently, the interest on $1.4 million of debt *could have been avoided* in that period.[11]

To determine whether interest is capitalized, and the amount, *SFAS No. 34* provides guidelines on qualifying assets, qualifying expenditures to be capitalized, the conditions under which interest is capitalized, and the calculation of capitalized interest. Immaterial amounts of interest need not be capitalized.[12]

Qualifying Assets   Interest is capitalized on assets constructed for a company's own use, whether or not constructed by the company, and on assets constructed as *discrete* projects for sale or lease. Examples of the second category include ships and real estate developments. Qualifying assets are those constructed assets not routinely produced and that require significant construction time. Firms incur a significant opportunity cost (the interest expense that otherwise could have been avoided) during the construction of qualifying assets.[13] Inventories routinely manufactured or otherwise produced in large quantities, even if they require an extended maturation period such as whiskey and tobacco, do not qualify for interest capitalization.

Assets in use or ready for use do not qualify for capitalization because construction is complete. There is no further opportunity cost because the asset presumably is contributing to the company's revenue. For example, only certain assets of an oil and gas company qualify for interest capitalization. These include unproved projects under development and not currently being depleted, and properties in cost centers with no production.[14]

Land deserves special mention. When land is developed for sale, interest is capitalized and added to the land cost based on expenditures made for its development. If land is to be used as a building site, the amount of interest capitalized on the land expenditures becomes part of the building cost. Idle land is not a qualifying asset.

Qualifying Expenditures   A qualifying expenditure is included in the AAE (average accumulated expenditures) and creates an opportunity cost for the firm. These expenditures include cash payments for construction, the transfer of other assets, and incurrence of interest-bearing liabilities. Interest-bearing liabilities are similar to cash expenditures in that they create an opportunity cost. In contrast, short-term noninterest-bearing liabilities do not qualify because they cause no interest expense. Qualifying expenditures include all the elements of self-constructed assets discussed before: material, labor, overhead, and previously capitalized interest on the asset.

Conditions for Capitalizing Interest   These conditions define the accounting periods during which interest is capitalized. Each of the following three conditions must be met for interest to be capitalized for a period:

1. Qualifying expenditures were made.
2. Construction and related activities occurred for substantially the entire period.
3. Interest cost was incurred.

---

[11] The same average investment results from a single $1.4 million expenditure on January 1, 1991. To bring the ending total cost to $3.4 million, an additional $2 million expenditure on December 31 is required. There is no avoidable interest on this second payment for 1991 because it occurred at the end of the year.

[12] Paragraphs 7 and 10 of *SFAS No. 42*, "Determining Materiality for Capitalization of Interest Cost," require that the usual tests for materiality be applied to interest capitalization.

[13] Interest is not capitalized on assets constructed with funds from gifts or grants restricted by donor or grantor, because the funds do not carry a financing cost. Consequently there is no opportunity cost in the usual sense (*SFAS No. 62*, par. 5).

[14] *FASB Interpretation No. 33*, "Applying *FASB Statement No. 34* to Oil and Gas Producing Operations Accounted for by the Full Cost Method." This interpretation applies only to those firms using the full cost method (capitalization of all exploration costs to the depletion base). Chapter 13 discusses this method in detail.

Interest capitalization ceases when any one of the three conditions is not met or when the asset is substantially complete.

If the first condition is not met, no opportunity cost is incurred and the conceptual basis for interest capitalization is absent. If the second condition is not met, construction activities are not the cause of the opportunity cost. If the third condition is not met, there is no interest to capitalize. *SFAS No. 34* limits interest capitalized to the actual interest *expense* recognized in the period. Interest expense does not necessarily equal interest paid.[15]

Brief construction interruptions, both externally imposed and unavoidable, as well as interruptions inherent in normal construction work, do not stop the capitalization process for materiality reasons. These interruptions are part of the normal construction process. However, intentional delays stop the interest capitalization process. Stopping construction of a building for a substantial period to allow the customer to choose fixtures is an example. Interest during these periods is a financing, rather than an acquisition, cost.

Calculating Capitalized Interest   The amount of **interest potentially capitalizable** (IPC) for a given period is determined by applying the appropriate interest rate to the AAE amount. This result is capitalized if it is less than or equal to actual interest expense for the period.[16] A set of four general steps along with a simple example designed to illustrate the calculation of capitalized interest is presented below.

Assume that Harvard Company hired Superior Builders on January 2, 1991, to construct a warehouse on land Harvard Company acquired several years earlier. The following information relates to Harvard's debt and construction payments:

> *Debt:*
> 10%, $2 million construction loan obtained January 3, 1991
> 12%, $5 million mortgage loan obtained January 2, 1980 (unrelated to the contruction project)
>
> *Construction payments:*
> $1 million paid January 3, 1991
> $4 million paid evenly throughout 1991
>
> *Warehouse completion:*
> December 29, 1991

Step 1 *Compute actual interest expense for the period.* This is the maximum capitalizable amount. All interest-bearing debt is considered, and Harvard's actual interest expense for 1991 is:

$$\text{Interest expense for 1991} = \$2,000,000(.10) + \$5,000,000(.12)$$
$$= \$800,000$$

Step 2 *Compute AAE for the period.* Harvard need not analyze each payment to the contractor if they were made on a reasonably even basis throughout the year. In the Wharton Corporation example discussed previously, only two payments were made. In that case, each payment was weighted for the fraction of the period invested in the project. In contrast, AAE for Harvard is:

$$AAE = \$1,000,000 + \$4,000,000(.5) = \$3,000,000$$

The $1 million payment is invested in the project for the entire year and therefore receives a weight of 1 (or 12/12). The $4 million is spread evenly throughout 1991 and

---

[15] For example, unpaid accrued interest and amortization of discount on bonds payable are included in interest expense, but are not included in interest paid for the current period.

[16] If the IPC exceeds the actual interest expense, then the actual interest expense is capitalized.

has the same effect as \$2 million invested at the beginning of the year. Therefore, a weight of .5 (or 6/12) is applied to it. This result also is achieved by computing one half of the beginning (\$1 million) and ending (\$5 million) cash investment balance:

$$AAE = (\$1,000,000 + \$5,000,000)/2 = \$3,000,000.$$

The alternative calculation should not be used with unequal payments or unevenly spaced payments, as is the case with the Wharton example.

Step 3 *Compute the interest potentially capitalizable (IPC).* Harvard's 1991 AAE (\$3 million) exceeds the principal balance of the specific construction loan (\$2 million). Therefore, the interest rate on the mortgage is applied to the excess of AAE over the specific debt (\$3 million − \$2 million), and IPC is computed as follows:

$$IPC = \$2,000,000(.10) + (\$3,000,000 - \$2,000,000).12$$

(interest on   (interest on excess of AAE
construction loan)   over construction loan)

$$= \$320,000$$

The IPC represents the interest that could have been avoided had the funds used in the construction project been applied to retire debt. Some accountants contend that only interest on the specific debt (construction loans) should be capitalized because only that interest is directly associated with the project. The mortgage interest for Harvard continues independently of the construction project.

Step 4 *Capitalize the lesser of actual interest and IPC.* In Harvard's case:

Capitalized interest in 1991 = lesser of IPC and actual interest
= lesser of \$320,000 and \$800,000
= \$320,000

Assuming Harvard has already recorded interest expense for 1991 and has recorded the construction payments in building under construction, the following adjusting entry is made:

December 31, 1991:

Building under construction 320,000
Interest expense   320,000

Interest expense recognized for 1991 is therefore \$480,000 (\$800,000 − \$320,000). The building under construction account has a \$5,320,000 ending balance (\$1,000,000 + \$4,000,000 + \$320,000). The capitalized interest is matched against revenues during the asset's service period, in the form of increased depreciation.

SFAS No. 34 allows for flexibility in calculating capitalized interest. If a project is financed with specific construction debt, the rate on that debt can be applied first to AAE. If AAE exceeds the principal amount of that specific debt, the weighted-average interest rate on all other interest-bearing debt is applied to the excess. The authors call this procedure the *specific* method. This method is used in the Harvard example above.

In other cases, it is difficult to associate borrowings and projects. Cash derived from debt is fungible, and companies often have continuing lines of credit with financial institutions, allowing them to borrow up to the credit limit in amounts unrelated to specific projects. In these cases, it is easier to apply the weighted-average interest rate on *all* interest-bearing debt to AAE in order to determine IPC. The authors call this procedure the *weighted-average* method.

Only Steps 3 and 4 are affected by the choice of method, and the two methods can yield the same amount of capitalized interest. The weighted-average method is applied to Step 3 of the Harvard example below:[17]

$$\text{Weighted-average interest rate on all debt} = \frac{\text{Total actual interest}}{\text{Total interest-bearing debt}}$$
$$= \$800,000/\$7,000,000 = .1143$$
$$IPC = \$3,000,000(.1143) = \$342,900$$

In this instance, IPC is different because a higher overall interest rate is applied to AAE under the weighted-average method. IPC is again less than actual interest; thus, $342,900 is capitalized (Step 4).

Firms are free to adopt either method. Firms wishing to maximize income would choose the specific method when interest rates on specific construction loans exceed rates on other debt. The specific method first exhausts the interest on the higher interest rate construction loans before applying the lower interest rate. The result is higher capitalized interest, greater income, and greater net assets.

The authors of this text prefer the specific method because it more logically relates debt to construction projects. The difference between the two methods is not material unless interest rates have changed significantly, and AAE exceeds specific construction debt by a considerable amount.

The capitalization of interest calculation is affected by two additional factors. First, it can be performed monthly, quarterly, or over interim periods of any length. Monthly calculations easily accommodate significant changes in debt structure during the year. Public companies publish quarterly earnings reports and, therefore, capitalize interest on a quarterly basis. The annual capitalized interest, however, is limited to annual recognized interest expense. The procedure for partial-year periods is illustrated in the example to follow.

Second, not all interest-bearing debt need be considered. The objective is to achieve a reasonable measure of the financing cost involved in construction. If interest rates on older debt are significantly different from present interest rates, that debt can be ignored for interest capitalization purposes. In the examples in this text, all interest-bearing debt is included when calculating IPC.

Examples Illustrating the Calculation of Capitalized Interest   These examples are presented to illustrate more complex cases and other details of the capitalized interest calculation.

1. More than One Nonspecific Debt, Noninterest-Bearing Construction Payables, Interim Period   Assume that the Gunnard Corporation calculates capitalized interest on a monthly basis and has the following debt outstanding during July, 1991:

Debt Outstanding During July, 1991		Monthly Interest
$ 800,000	12% Construction loan	$ 8,000
1,000,000	15% Note payable	12,500
600,000	8% Mortgage	4,000
150,000	16% Bond payable	2,000
$2,550,000		$26,500

Each of the obligations requires payment of interest at the end of the month. Total interest (Step 1) for July is $26,500. Gunnard has been constructing a building for several months. Assume that expenditures are applied evenly to the project during July. The following table presents the data leading to AAE (Step 2) for July:

---

[17] If debt is not outstanding the entire year, an adjustment to this procedure is required. This adjustment is discussed at the end of example 1 (Gunnard Corporation).

Total expenditures incurred to July 1 . . . . $2,000,000
Less construction-related payables, July 1 . . . . . . (200,000)

Cash expenduitures incurred to July 1 . . . . $1,800,000

Total expenditures incurred through July 31 2,500,000
Less construction-related payables, July 31 . . . . . . (300,000)

Cash expenditures incurred through July 31 . . . . . $2,200,000

$$AAE = (1,800,000 + 2,200,000)/2 \text{ or}$$
$$= 1,800,000 + (2,200,000 - 1,800,000)/2$$
$$= \$2,000,000.$$

The construction-related payables are removed from total expenditures because only cash and other resource transfers that create an opportunity cost for the firm are included in AAE. The payables represent unpaid resources received by Harvard. They are not qualifying expenditures even though they represent the cost of resources included in the building. The total expenditures include previously capitalized interest.

Using the specific method, IPC (Step 3) is calculated as follows:

$$\frac{\text{Weighted-average interest}}{\text{rate on nonspecific debt}} = \frac{\$12,500 + \$4,000 + \$2,000}{\$1,000,000 + \$600,000 + \$150,000}$$
$$= .0106 \text{ (for July)}$$

$$IPC = \$800,000(.12) (1/12) + (\$2,000,000 - \$800,000) (.0106)$$
$$\quad\quad\quad \text{(interest on} \quad\quad\quad \text{(interest on excess of AAE}$$
$$\quad\quad\quad \text{construction loan)} \quad\quad \text{over construction loan)}$$
$$= \$20,720.$$

Interest of $20,720 is capitalized (Step 4) in July because IPC is less than the $26,500 actual interest. This amount is added to the July ending cash expenditures for interest capitalization in August. For periods of less than a year, the interest rates reflect the length of the period. The weighted-average rate on nonspecific debt reflects only one month of interest in the numerator. Interest of $5,780 ($26,500 − $20,720) is recognized as expense.

If the construction loan principal were $2 million or more, only the construction loan would be considered in computing IPC under the specific method. For example, if the construction loan were for $2.5 million, IPC and capitalized interest would have been:

$$\$2,000,000(.12) (1/12) = \$20,000$$

Under the weighted-average method, and assuming the original data, IPC is computed as follows:

$$\begin{array}{ll} \text{Weighted average interest} & \\ \quad \text{rate on all debt} & = \$26,500/\$2,550,000 = .0104 \\ IPC = \$2,000,000(.0104) & = \$20,800 \end{array}$$

Therefore, $20,800 of interest is capitalized in July under this method, and $5,700 of interest is recognized as expense ($26,500 − $20,800).

Interim period computations are treated in the same manner as annual computations except that interest rates are adjusted for the relevant fraction of a year. If new interest-bearing debt is incurred during an interim period, the average interest rate for that period reflects the interest for the partial period. For example, if $100,000 of 12% debt is incurred on May 1, $2,000 of interest is recognized during the second calendar quarter ($100,000 × 12% × 2/12). Assuming quarterly calculations, the $2,000 interest is included in the numerator of any weighted-average rate needed for the second quarter of the year, and the $100,000 is included in the denominator.

Expenditures are not adjusted for partial-year periods, but instead are weighted by the percentage of the interim period they are outstanding. For example, if the interim period is three months, an expenditure occurring at the beginning of the second month receives a weight of two thirds (2 of 3 months in the quarter).

2. Second Interim Period, Interest Compounding, Project Completion To complete this illustration of interest capitalization, the Gunnard Corporation example is used again with the following assumptions:

Assumptions for the final example: Gunnard Corporation

1. Employs the specific method.
2. Incurred additional debt in the form of a 14%, $600,000 note payable not related to the construction on August 1.
3. Settled the July 31 construction payables on August 1.
4. Made the last two payments to the contractor ($500,000 on August 15 and $500,000 on August 31).
5. Completed the building on August 31.

The new debt increased total interest expense (Step 1) for August, computed as follows:

$$\text{August interest} = \$26,500 + \$600,000(.14)\,(1/12)$$
$$= \$26,500 + \$7,000 = \$33,500$$

Gunnard made only three construction-related expenditures in August. Therefore, each is weighted by the appropriate fraction of the month. AAE (Step 2) is computed as follows:

Cash Expenditure	Amount	Portion of Month	Weighted Expenditure
Cash expenditures through July 31	$2,220,720*	100%	$2,220,720
Settle July 31 payables	300,000	100%	300,000
August 15 contractor payment	500,000	50%	250,000
August 31 contractor payment	500,000	0%	0
AAE			$2,770,720

*$2,200,000 cash construction expenditures at July 31 plus $20,720 capitalized interest in July.

The July 31 cash expenditures include July's $20,720 capitalized interest under the specific method because interest is part of the asset's acquisition cost and interest was paid at the end of July. Capitalized interest contributes to the AAE base upon which future capitalized interest is computed and is therefore *compounded*. The August 31 payment to the contractor does not contribute to AAE because it does not create an opportunity cost.

The new weighted-average interest rate on nonspecific debt and IPC (Step 3) is:

Weighted-average interest rate on nonspecific debt

$$= \frac{\$12,500 + \$4,000 + \$2,000 + \$7,000}{\$1,000,000 + \$600,000 + \$150,000 + \$600,000}$$
$$= .01085 \text{ (for August)}$$
$$IPC = \$800,000(.12)(1/12) + (\$2,770,720 - \$800,000)(.01085)$$
$$= \$29,382$$

Gunnard capitalizes $29,382 (Step 4) in August, the lesser of IPC and actual interest cost for August ($33,500). The following summary entries are made by Gunnard to record the events related to construction in August:

To record interest expense:

Interest expense	33,500	
Cash		33,500

To record construction-related payments:

Building under construction	1,000,000	
Construction-related payables	300,000	
Cash		1,300,000

To record interest capitalization:

Building under construction	29,382	
Interest expense		29,382

To reclassify building under construction:

Buildings	3,550,102*	
Building under construction		3,550,102

*Balance in building under construction, July 31	$2,500,000
July capitalized interest	20,720
August contractor payments	1,000,000
August capitalized interest	29,382
Total building cost	$3,550,102

The July 31 construction-related payables ($300,000) are included in the July 31 balance in building under construction. They represent unpaid but incurred building costs at July 31.

Exhibit 11–3 is a flowchart which summarizes the calculations leading to capitalized interest.

Losses on Self-Constructed Assets and Interest Capitalization

Self-constructed assets are not capitalized above market value. Interest is capitalized on self-constructed assets independently of whether a loss is recognized upon completion. The loss is recognized in the normal manner. Capitalized interest increases the asset's cost and therefore the loss. When total cost exceeds market value.

For example, assume that Arundel Corporation completed the construction of equipment at a total cost of $2.3 million, which includes $300,000 of capitalized interest. However, the market value of the equipment at completion is only $2.1 million. Therefore, the asset is recorded at $2.1 million, and a $200,000 loss is recognized. The loss would not have occurred without interest capitalization, or any other cost causing the total construction cost to exceed market value.

Interest Revenue on Idle Funds Borrowed

Interest revenue earned on borrowed funds not yet incorporated into the construction project cannot offset the interest expense on that debt (SFAS No. 62). Interest earned on temporarily idle funds does not affect the avoidable interest cost. In these cases, the firm enjoys two increases to income: the interest capitalized and the interest revenue earned.

However, interest earned on idle funds received from tax-exempt borrowings that restrict the use of borrowed funds to specific assets is offset against interest expense on that debt. In this case, the idle funds are directly related to the project. It usually is expected that interest will be earned on these funds prior to their complete incorporation into the project. This expectation is often a factor in deciding whether to acquire the asset or to use the specific financing. The FASB considered the net

EXHIBIT 11-3   Interest Capitalization Computation Summary Flowchart

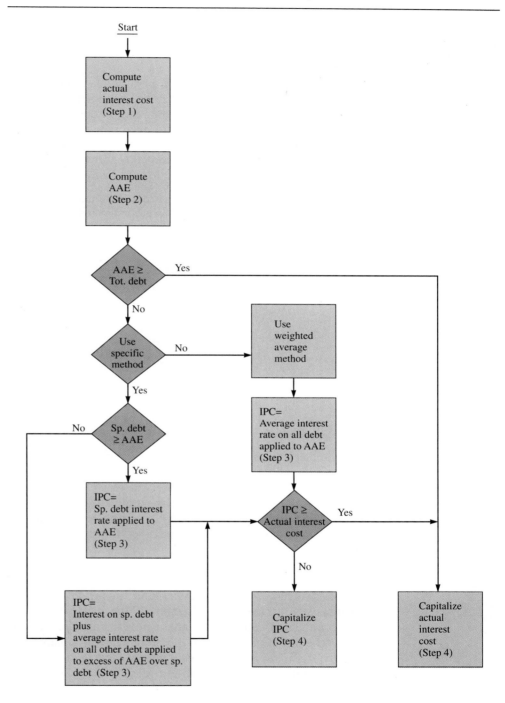

Notes:
Steps 1–4 refer to text discussion.
AAE = Average accumulated expenditures.
IPC = Interest potentially capitalizable.
Sp. debt = specific construction debt.
Tot. debt = total interest-bearing debt.

interest cost a more appropriate measure of the interest cost involved. Lower recorded values of constructed assets result from this offsetting, particularly early in the construction period, because less interest expense is available for capitalization.

Financial Statement Disclosure of Interest

SFAS No. 34 requires that, in periods of no interest capitalization, the amount of interest expense be disclosed in the financial statements or footnotes. In periods of interest capitalization, both the total interest cost incurred and the amount capitalized are disclosed. The difference between these two values is interest expense for the period.

A footnote from the 1990 annual report of International Paper Corporation illustrates disclosures related to capitalized interest:

> Interest costs for the construction of certain long-term assets are capitalized and amortized over the related asset's estimated useful life. The Company capitalized net interest costs of $11 million in 1989, $6 million in 1988, and $4 million in 1987.

CONCEPT REVIEW

1. What are the major arguments for and against interest capitalization?
2. What is the justification for capitalizing interest on debt not related to construction of plant assets?
3. What does the average accumulated expenditures amount for a period represent?

ACCOUNTING FOR DISPOSALS OF PLANT ASSETS

The disposal of plant assets is either voluntary, as a result of a sale, exchange, or abandonment, or involuntary, as a result of a casualty such as a fire or storm.[18] Involuntary conversions are asset disposals beyond the control of the company and can result, for example, from a government's exercise of its right of eminent domain.

An exchange of plant assets is both an acquisition and a disposal of plant assets. Accounting for disposals is discussed first to facilitate coverage of exchanges in the succeeding section.

If the asset to be disposed of is subject to depreciation, it is depreciated up to the date of disposal in order to update the recorded book value. Applicable property taxes, insurance premium cost, and similar costs also are accrued up to the date of disposal. At the date of disposal, the original cost of the asset and its related accumulated depreciation are removed from the accounts.

The difference between the book value of a plant asset and the price received on disposal is recorded as a gain or loss. The gain or loss ideally should be segregated from ordinary income, and is reported in the income statement as part of income from continuing operations unless extraordinary. If the gain or loss is deemed unusual and infrequent as defined in *APB Opinion No. 30,* it is classified with extraordinary items. This treatment is often applied to involuntary conversions.

According to *FASB Interpretation No. 30,* the use of the proceeds from disposal of an asset does not affect the recognition of the gain or loss on disposal. The interpretation relies on the *historical cost principle* and reiterates the notion that a transaction with an outside party substantiates the value of the asset relinquished.

---

[18] Uninsured casualties in which an asset is rendered unfit for future use are treated as normal asset disposals. Uninsured partial casualty losses are discussed in Chapter 12 in the section "Impairment of Value of Operating Assets," and insured casualty losses are covered in Appendix 12B.

To illustrate the disposal of a plant asset, assume that on February 1, 1987, Brown Company purchased for $32,000 office equipment with an estimated service life of five years and an estimated residual value of $2,000. Brown uses straight-line depreciation and decides to sell the asset on July 1, 1991, for $8,000. The entries for Brown, a calendar-year company, at date of disposal are:

Depreciation expense	3,000*	
Accumulated depreciation—equipment		3,000

* ($32,000 − $2,000) (1/5) 6/12

Cash	8,000	
Accumulated depreciation—equipment	26,500*	
Equipment		32,000
Gain from disposal of equipment		2,500

* ($32,000 − $2,000) (53 months used)/60 months total useful life

The $26,500 accumulated depreciation balance includes the $3,000 depreciation recognized on July 1. The gain from disposal is the difference between the $8,000 cash received and the $5,500 book value of the asset at disposal ($32,000 − $26,500).

However, the economic value of Brown Company is unaffected by the disposal. Brown received an asset worth $8,000 (cash) for an asset worth $8,000. Why is a gain recognized? Brown depreciated the equipment faster than it declined in value. The book value ($5,500) is less than market value ($8,000) at date of disposal. If depreciation reflected market value changes, there would be no gain or loss from disposal. The accounting gain in this example is a correction for excessive depreciation charges recognized before disposal. In effect, the gain is a "change in estimate." Additional problems arising from historical cost depreciation are discussed in Chapter 12.

The disposal of an asset with no market value is handled in the same manner as the Brown Company example except without disposal proceeds. The loss recognized equals the book value of the asset at disposal. If the Brown Company asset had no market value, the loss recognized is $5,500. Involuntary conversions (e.g., uninsured casualty losses) are handled in a similar fashion. No cash is received, and the loss recognized equals book value.

The costs of dismantling, removing, and disposing of plant assets are treated as reductions of any proceeds obtained from disposal. Therefore, the resulting gain is reduced, or the resulting loss is increased by these costs. If Brown Company had incurred $500 in disposal costs, the net cash debit is $7,500 ($8,000 − $500), reducing the gain to $2,000.

When the decision to abandon plant assets is made near the end of a fiscal year, an estimated loss from disposal is recognized in that year if the loss is estimable according to SFAS No. 5, "Accounting For Contingencies." Expected costs of disposal increase the estimated loss and cause an estimated liability to be recorded for those costs. Some companies include the estimated loss in depreciation. For example, Sun Company, Inc., disclosed the following footnote to its 1987 financial statements:

> *Dismantlement, Restoration, and Abandonment Costs* . . . Estimated costs of future dismantlement, restoration, and abandonment are accrued as part of depreciation, depletion, and amortization expense; actual costs are charged to the accrual.

Gains are not recognized before disposal, however.

Because of the rapid rise in real estate values that occurred in many parts of the United States in the 1980s, many companies own land and buildings with market values greatly exceeding book value. These companies stand to record large gains if the properties are sold. The difference between market and book value is so great in certain cases that some stock analysts have recommended purchasing the common stock of these companies on the basis of undervalued real estate holdings alone. For example, in 1989, Bassett Furniture Industries owned a square mile of land in Virginia, which it carried on its books at $4.5 million, but whose market value was estimated at $130 million.[19]

Companies have long included gains from disposal of assets in operating income. This practice is criticized by accountants who believe that disposal gains should be segregated from operating income to prevent misleading income reporting. A firm wishing to increase earnings, for example, might sell an asset at a large gain at the end of the reporting period. They argue that gains from disposal of assets cannot be expected to continue. Both gains and losses on plant asset disposals are substantial in many cases.

For example, Cineplex Odeon Company, the second largest cinema chain in North America, reported $55 million of gains from sales of equipment and real estate in 1988. Without these disposal gains, Cineplex would have lost $14.5 million before tax.[20] In contrast, Oryx Energy Company reduced its estimate of fourth-quarter 1989 earnings by 53% based on an expected sale of interests in oil and gas properties at a $19 million loss.[21]

Disposal by Donation   Assets occasionally are donated by corporations to other organizations. Computer manufacturers frequently donate computing equipment to universities, for example. The donor recognizes an expense equal to the market value of the donated asset.[22] Market value equals the economic sacrifice of the donor rather than the book value of the donated asset. A gain or loss equal to the difference between book value and market value is recorded on donation. An expense and a payable are recognized when an unconditional pledge to make a contribution is made.

In the Brown Company disposal example, if the asset is donated rather than sold, the two entries are the same except that donation expense is debited instead of cash, and the gain refers to the donation.

Reclassification of Plant Assets Removed from Service   A plant asset removed from service before its usefulness expires also is removed from the plant asset accounts. Depreciation is recorded up to the date of reclassification, and the accumulated depreciation and asset accounts are closed to a new account labeled "other assets." In addition, if the market value of the asset is less than book value, a loss is recorded, and other assets is debited for the market value. In contrast, if the market value exceeds book value, other assets is debited for the book value but a gain is not recorded.

In the Brown Company disposal example, if the equipment is removed from service, other assets is debited for $5,500 because the book value is less than the market value ($8,000). A gain is not recognized because the reclassification is internal. An arm's-length transaction with an outside entity is generally required to support increased asset values. The conservatism constraint justifies the recognition of a loss.

SEC: Gains on Disposal when Seller Makes Guarantee   During the late 1980s, leveraged buy-outs became popular as a method of acquiring a company. In a typical leveraged buy-out, the purchase price of the target company is financed largely through high-interest debt. Segments of companies were also acquired in this manner with the

---

[19] "Hidden Value of Real Estate Assets May Be One Clue to Stocks with a Strong Potential," *The Wall Street Journal,* June 23, 1989, p. C2.

[20] "Every Trick in the Books," *Forbes,* May 29, 1989, p. 46.

[21] "Oryx Slashes Estimate of 4th-Quarter Profit by More than 53%," *The Wall Street Journal,* January 4, 1990, p. B3.

[22] FASB, *Exposure Draft,* "Accounting for Contributions Received and Contributions Made and Capitalization of Works of Art, Historical Treasures, and Similar Assets, 1990.

seller normally recognizing a gain on the increased value of the segment. However, when the seller guarantees the performance of the segment to the buyer or guarantees all or part of the debt incurred by the buyer to finance the purchase of the segment, the SEC (in *Staff Accounting Bulletin No. 81*) requires deferral of the gain on the disposal of the segment until the contingencies are removed.

The logic behind this ruling is that the selling company has no gain until the contingencies are removed. If the segment does not perform for the buying firm, the seller must discharge the guarantees, often at substantial cost.

In 1987, Hospital Corporation of America sold 104 hospitals to Health-Trust, Inc., a newly formed company, and received $1.6 billion in borrowed cash and $460 million in preferred stock and other equity securities. Hospital Corporation guaranteed $240 million of the debt incurred by Health-Trust to purchase the hospitals and agreed to repurchase $40 million of the preferred stock if Health-Trust's cash flow fell below certain levels. Hospital Corporation was forced to comply with the SEC ruling and deferred a $300 million gain.[23]

CONCEPT REVIEW

1. Why would a company dispose of an plant asset at a loss? Is the company in a worse position economically after doing so?
2. How would you interpret the gain on the disposal of a plant asset?
3. How might income be manipulated by plant asset disposals?

ACCOUNTING FOR EXCHANGES OF NONMONETARY ASSETS

◆

Plant assets and other nonmonetary assets often are exchanged for other plant assets. Accounting for exchanges involves both acquisition and disposal principles. Exchanges of nonmonetary assets can also involve cash **boot.**[24] The book value and market value of nonmonetary assets are normally not equal because market value fluctuates with supply and demand. The valuation of the acquired asset is the substantive accounting issue in nonmonetary asset exchanges. This valuation determines whether a gain or loss is recognized.

In general, the recorded cost of a nonmonetary asset acquired in exchange for another nonmonetary asset is the market value of the asset transferred, plus any cash paid or less any cash received, unless the market value of the asset acquired is more readily determinable. In the latter case, the market value of the acquired asset is used for recording purposes. This is the same valuation principle applicable to all other plant asset acquisitions discussed in previous sections of this chapter, and to long-term notes receivable (Chapter 8). This general valuation principle, as applied to nonmonetary assets acquired in exchange for other nonmonetary assets, is summarized in Exhibit 11–4.

For example, if Bull Company exchanged a nonmonetary asset worth $4,000 for another nonmonetary asset and received $1,000 on the exchange, the recorded value of the acquired asset is $3,000 according to the general valuation principle. This principle makes sense because Bull Company's net sacrifice for the acquired asset is $3,000.

APB Opinion No. 29, which governs the accounting for nonmonetary exchanges, includes a major exception to the general valuation principle for nonmonetary asset

---

[23] "Hassling the Dealmakers," *Forbes,* May 15, 1989.

[24] From the Middle English, profit or advantage. In the context of nonmonetary exchanges, boot refers to cash paid or received to even the exchange.

EXHIBIT 11-4   General Valuation Principle for Acquired Nonmonetary Asset Received in Exchange for a Nonmonetary Asset*

Market Value of Asset *Transferred* Is Known

If:	*Then the Recorded Value of the Acquired Nonmonetary Asset Equals:*
Cash is paid	Market value of transferred asset + cash paid
Cash is received	Market value of transferred asset − cash received

Market Value of Asset *Acquired* (Only) Is Known

If:	*Then the Recorded Value of the Acquired Nonmonetary Asset Equals:*
Cash is paid or received	Market value of acquired asset

* The exceptions to this valuation involve gains on exchanges of similar nonmonetary assets.

exchanges. The accounting for exchanges of nonmonetary assets depends on whether the earnings process is considered completed.[25] An earnings process is not completed when the nonmonetary assets exchanged are *similar*. Nonmonetary assets are similar if they are held for resale in the same line of business or if they are productive assets used for comparable purposes. An exchange of land parcels is an exchange of similar nonmonetary assets, and an exchange of equipment for a building is an exchange of dissimilar nonmonetary assets.

Exchanges of similar assets do not complete an earnings process because the operations of the business are not altered substantively by the exchange. Replacement of an assembly line with another assembly line does not change how the firm uses assembly lines. In contrast, the exchange of a fleet of rental cars for an office building concludes the rental car business and its earnings.

If the assets are *dissimilar* (the earnings process is considered completed), the exchange is treated as a monetary transaction. The recorded value of the acquired asset conforms to Exhibit 11-4. *Both* gains and losses are recognized in full regardless of cash boot received or paid. Determination and disclosure of gains and losses on exchange is similar to plant asset disposals. The gain or loss is the difference between the book value and the market value of the asset transferred and is disclosed as a nonrecurring item in the income statement. When book value exceeds market value, a loss results; when market value exceeds book value, a gain results. Gains and losses do not represent increases (gains) or decreases (losses) in the value of the firm but rather are adjustments to previously recognized depreciation.

Losses also are recognized in full on exchanges of similar assets, and the valuation of the acquired asset conforms to Exhibit 11-4 whether or not cash boot is received or paid. If the assets are similar, *gains* are recognized *only* to the extent of cash boot received. The earnings process is not completed for the portion of the exchange involving only the nonmonetary assets, as the acquired asset merely replaces the asset exchanged. The future earnings of the firm will reflect any increase in productivity inherent in the acquired asset. Rather than recognize a gain on the exchange of similar nonmonetary assets immediately, the accounting profession chose to postpone recognition of the gain until the increase in income is verified through use or sale of the asset. This is the exception to the general valuation principle presented in Exhibit 11-4.

---

[25] In the earlier discussion of disposals of plant assets for cash (a monetary asset), the earnings process is completed. Therefore, a gain or loss is recognized. The value of the disposed asset is established by the arm's-length transaction.

If application of the general valuation principle in Exhibit 11–4 would result in a gain on the exchange of similar assets when cash is paid, the acquired asset is recorded at the sum of the book values of assets transferred, including cash paid, and the gain is not recognized. However, losses are recognized in full, and the valuation of the acquired asset conforms to Exhibit 11–4.

If application of the general valuation principle in Exhibit 11–4 results in a gain on the exchange of similar assets when cash is received, a gain is recognized in the proportion of cash received to the total market value of items received. This case is illustrated in the examples to follow along with the general application of the *APB Opinion No. 29* guidelines.

In general, the accounting for exchanges of nonmonetary assets does not imply that if one party recognizes a gain, then the other party recognizes a loss. The gain or loss recognized on exchange depends on the relationship between market and book value.

Examples of Nonmonetary Asset Exchanges

The following information for Tacoma Corporation is used in the examples which follow:[26]

Asset transferred: crane
    Original cost $50,000
    Accumulated depreciation at date of exchange $40,000

1. *Exchange does not involve cash.*
    a. Gain on exchange for dissimilar asset. Tacoma exchanges its crane, valued at $12,000, for a used truck. Using the general valuation rule in Exhibit 11–4 (with no cash paid or received), the truck is valued at $12,000, the value of the crane transferred. The book value of the crane is $10,000; therefore, a $2,000 gain is recognized on exchange:

To record exchange of plant assets:

Machinery (truck) 12,000
Accumulated depreciation—crane 40,000
    Machinery (crane)   50,000
    Gain on exchange   2,000

The gain equals the difference between market value ($12,000) and book value ($10,000) of the crane, but does not represent an increase in the value of the firm.
b. Gain not recognized on exchange for similar asset. It is helpful to construct a tentative (not recorded) worksheet entry which records the new asset according to the general valuation principle. *Then,* if the assets are similar *and* a gain results from this tentative entry, adjust the tentative entry by removing the gain and record the acquired asset at the book value of the transferred asset in the entry actually recorded.[27] This practice emphasizes an almost universal valuation principle and requires adjustment only for gains on exchanges of similar assets. In addition, without this worksheet entry, it is not known whether a gain or loss would have occurred under the general valuation principle.

Assume the facts in the above example except that Tacoma exchanges its crane for another crane. The *tentative* entry using the general valuation principle for the acquired crane is the entry recorded in (1*a*) resulting in a $2,000 gain. However, without cash boot received, gains on exchanges of similar nonmonetary assets

---

[26] Although depreciation is recognized (updated) on the asset transferred up to the date of exchange, for simplicity this entry is omitted. The balance of the accumulated depreciation account at the date of exchange reflects this depreciation update.

[27] The required adjustments for cash paid and received are illustrated in later examples.

are not allowed under *APB Opinion No. 29*. Therefore, the acquired crane is recorded at the book value of the crane transferred ($10,000) in the entry actually recorded:

To record exchange of plant assets:

Machinery (crane)	10,000	
Accumulated depreciation—crane	40,000	
Machinery (crane)		50,000

The nonrecognition of the gain in this example understates the valuation of the acquired asset by $2,000, relative to market value.[28] In a series of similar asset exchanges in which the market value of the asset transferred exceeds the book value, the "error" builds, and each successive valuation for the acquired asset increases the understatement, relative to market value. In subsequent periods, depreciation on the acquired assets is understated and income is overstated, compared to cash purchases of the same string of assets. The cycle is broken when a loss on exchange of assets occurs, in which case the new asset is recorded at its market value.

c. *Loss on exchange for dissimilar or similar asset.* Assume the facts in (1a) except that the market value of the crane is only $7,000. In this case, the book value of the crane exceeds market value by $3,000; therefore a loss in that amount is recognized. Losses are recognized in full for both similar and dissimilar asset exchanges. The exchange of the crane for either the truck (dissimilar) *or* the crane (similar) is recorded as follows:

To record exchange of plant assets:

Machinery (crane or truck)	7,000	
Accumulated depreciation—crane	40,000	
Loss on exchange	3,000	
Machinery (crane)		50,000

2. *Cash paid on exchange.* The payment of cash on exchange alters neither the general valuation principle nor the recognition of gains and losses. Losses are recognized in full on exchanges of both similar and dissimilar assets, and gains are recognized only on exchanges of dissimilar assets.

a. *Gain on exchange for dissimilar asset.* Now assume that Tacoma exchanges its crane and $15,000 cash for a new truck with a $30,000 list price. The market value of the crane is not determinable. The truck dealer had offered a cash price of $27,000 without the exchange. List prices often exceed the cash price acceptable to an equipment dealer and therefore ordinarily are not used as the market value of the acquired asset. The cash price is a more reliable value to use for market value because it is acceptable to an outside party. Using the valuation principle outlined in Exhibit 11–4, the truck is recorded at $27,000 because the market value of only the acquired asset is known. The following entry records the exchange:

To record exchange of plant assets:

Machinery (truck)	27,000	
Accumulated depreciation—crane	40,000	
Machinery (crane)		50,000
Cash		15,000
Gain on exchange		2,000

---

[28] The income tax laws produce similar results. No gain or loss is recognized in a noncash exchange of assets if they qualify as "like-kind" property.

The implied market value of the crane is $12,000, the difference between the market value of the truck, and the cash paid. The truck dealer accepted the crane in place of $12,000 cash. The gain on exchange represents the difference between the crane's implied market value and its book value ($10,000). The $15,000 **trade-in allowance**, the difference between list price and cash paid, is not used as the market value of the crane because that would imply the market value of the truck equals its list price.

b. Gain not recognized on exchange for similar asset. Assume that Tacoma exchanges its crane and $15,000 cash for a new crane with a list price of $30,000. Again the dealer indicated acceptance of a $27,000 cash price without trade-in ($15,000 cash plus a crane worth $12,000). Applying the general valuation principle again results in a $27,000 valuation for the new crane (in a tentative entry), and the same $2,000 gain. However, no gain is recognized on similar asset exchanges when cash is paid. Therefore, the new crane is valued at $25,000, the sum of the book values of assets transferred: crane ($10,000) and cash ($15,000). The following entry records the exchange:

To record exchange of plant assets:

Machinery (crane)	25,000	
Accumulated depreciation—crane	40,000	
Machinery (crane)		50,000
Cash		15,000

3. *Cash received on exchange.* Cash is received on an exchange of nonmonetary assets when the market value of the transferred asset exceeds that of the acquired asset. This occurs, for example, when a company decides to reduce its overall investment in the type of asset transferred. The boot received compensates for the difference in market value between the two assets.

a. Loss on exchange for dissimilar or similar asset. Assume that Tacoma exchanges its crane (market value $8,000) for other equipment and receives $5,000 on the exchange. The implied market value and valuation of the acquired equipment under the general valuation principle is $3,000 ($8,000 − $5,000). The book value of the transferred asset ($10,000) exceeds its market value; thus, a loss of $2,000 is recognized, whether or not the two assets are dissimilar. The following entry records the exchange:

To record exchange of plant assets:

Machinery (similar or dissimilar)	3,000	
Accumulated depreciation—crane	40,000	
Cash	5,000	
Loss on exchange	2,000	
Machinery (crane)		50,000

b. Gain on exchange for dissimilar asset. Assume the same facts as in (3a) except that the market value of the crane is $12,000. Tacoma trades its crane for a used truck and receives $5,000 on the exchange. Application of the general valuation principle results in a $7,000 valuation for the acquired asset ($12,000 − $5,000). The assets are dissimilar; therefore, the $2,000 gain ($12,000 crane market value − $10,000 crane book value) is recognized in full. The following entry records the exchange:

To record exchange of plant assets:

Machinery (truck)	7,000	
Accumulated depreciation—crane	40,000	
Cash	5,000	
Machinery (crane)		50,000
Gain on exchange		2,000

c. Gain on exchange for similar asset. Now assume, in this final example, that Tacoma exchanges its crane worth $12,000 for another crane and receives $5,000 boot. This is the 3*b* situation except that the assets exchanged are similar. Using the general valuation principle, the same $2,000 gain is *tentatively* computed. However, in this case, *APB Opinion No. 29* views this transaction as a partial disposal of the crane and a partial exchange. Therefore, a portion, but not all, of the $2,000 gain is allowed.

Part of the old crane effectively is sold for cash, thus removing the prohibition on the recognition of gains for similar asset exchanges. The cash portion is treated as a disposal of a plant asset for cash. The fraction of the transferred asset "sold" for cash is the fraction of the gain that can be recognized. The following formula determines the allowable gain:

$$\begin{array}{c} \text{Gain allowed on exchange} \\ \text{of similar assets} \\ \text{when boot is received} \end{array} = \left[\frac{\text{Boot received}}{\begin{array}{c}\text{Market value of}\\\text{asset exchanged}\end{array}} \right] \left[\begin{array}{c}\text{Gain resulting from}\\\text{applying general}\\\text{valuation principle}\end{array} \right]$$

The denominator of the fraction in the above equation is also equal to the sum of boot received ($5,000) and the market value of the asset acquired ($7,000). Tacoma therefore recognizes the following gain on exchange:

$$(\$5,000/\$12,000)\$2,000 = \$833$$

As a result, Tacoma records the following entry for the exchange:

To record exchange of plant assets:

Machinery (crane)	5,833	
Accumulated depreciation—crane	40,000	
Cash	5,000	
Machinery (crane)		50,000
Gain on exchange		833

In effect, Tacoma sold 5/12 of its crane and therefore is allowed to recognize 5/12 of the gain that would have been recorded had the assets been dissimilar. $1,167 of the gain remains unrecognized. The resulting valuation of the acquired asset ($5,833) is the market value of the acquired asset ($7,000) less the portion of the gain not recognized ($1,167).

Fair Market Value Determination

Generally, a quoted cash price is a reliable measure of market value. In the absence of a price quote, a company can invite bids for the asset to be exchanged. The highest bid for the asset, subsequently exchanged, is used as the market value. A less defensible but commonly used alternative is published information on the average price of specific used assets, such as the *Kelley Blue Book Auto Market Report* for automobiles. These references consider the condition and age of similar assets.

Knowledge of the market value of the asset exchanged is sufficient to determine the valuation of the acquired asset. In the absence of a reasonably determinable market value for either asset, the valuation of the acquired asset is based on the book value of the asset(s) transferred, and is one of the following:

1. If cash is paid, record the acquired asset at the sum of the book values of the assets transferred, including cash.
2. If cash is received, record the acquired asset at the difference between book value of the asset transferred and cash received.

Thus, when market values cannot be determined reliably, gains and losses are not recognized. The book value of assets transferred determines the recorded value of the acquired asset. For example, if a plant asset ($10,000 book value) and $4,000 cash

EXHIBIT 11-5   Summary: Nonmonetary Asset Exchanges with Market Value Determinable

Dissimilar Assets

Acquired asset is valued under the general valuation principle, Exhibit 11–4. Gains and losses are recognized in full.

Similar Assets

Apply the general valuation principle (Exhibit 11–4) to the acquired asset:

1. Recognize a loss in full and use the general valuation principle.
2. If a gain occurs and cash is paid (or not involved), do not recognize the gain. Record the acquired asset at the sum of cash paid and book value of transferred asset.
3. If a gain occurs and cash is received, recognize the gain in the proportion:
   Boot/Market value of asset exchanged
   Record acquired asset at market value less the portion of the gain not recognized.

are exchanged for another plant asset, the asset acquired is recorded at $14,000, assuming the market value of neither plant asset is determinable.

Required Disclosures and Summary

APB Opinion No. 29 (par. 28) requires disclosure of the nature of exchange transactions during a reporting period, the basis for recording assets transferred, and the gains and losses on exchanges of nonmonetary assets. Accounting for exchanges of dissimilar and similar assets is summarized in Exhibit 11–5.

Evaluation of *APB Opinion No. 29*—Nonmonetary Exchanges

Allowing losses but disallowing gains on similar assets is an example of asymmetry in GAAP. The approach is justified on the basis of the conservatism constraint and the absence of realization in monetary asset terms. For example, if Trader Company exchanges a truck with a $5,000 book value and $8,000 market value for another truck in a pure trade, Trader is, according to *APB Opinion No. 29*, in the same position as it was before the trade. Thus the $3,000 gain is not recognized and the acquired asset is recorded at $5,000.

Most agree with the assessment that the company is no better off after the trade. However, GAAP allows full recognition of gains and losses on disposal of nonmonetary assets for cash (an exchange of a nonmonetary asset for a monetary one), yet the company is again no better or worse off after the disposal in those cases.

Had the market value been $4,000 in the Trader Company example, the same conclusion is true, but a loss is recognized under GAAP and the acquired asset is recorded at $4,000 (market value). Not all accountants agree with present GAAP regarding exchanges of similar nonmonetary assets. They argue that the value of assets is not contingent on realization in cash terms and that the value of all nonmonetary assets acquired should reflect market value.

CONCEPT REVIEW

1. What is the general valuation principle for plant assets received through exchange of nonmonetary assets when cash is also paid on the exchange?
2. Why is an exception to the general valuation principle made for gains on exchanges of similar nonmonetary assets.
3. Why does GAAP allow partial recognition of gains on exchanges of similar nonmonetary assets when boot is received on exchange?

POST-ACQUISITION EXPENDITURES

◆

After acquisition, many costs related to plant assets are incurred. Examples include repairs, maintenance, betterments, and replacements. The accounting disposition of these expenditures affects balance sheet classification and subsequent depreciation calculations.

General Accounting Principles

Expenditures that increase the original useful life or productivity (the quantity or quality of service) above the *original* level estimated at acquisition are capitalized. A capitalized post-acquisition expenditure is depreciated over the number of periods benefited, which can be less than the remaining useful life of the original asset.

The service potential of assets and their estimated useful life at acquisition assume a certain minimum level of maintenance and repair. These expenditures, which do not increase useful life or utility beyond the original levels obtained at acquisition, are revenue expenditures, and are expensed in the period incurred. In addition, companies often establish a policy of expensing all post-acquisition expenditures less than a certain dollar amount (for example, $500). This policy is acceptable under the *materiality constraint*. The policy also is applied to material expenditures if the expenditures are relatively stable over time.

Expenditures that result from accidents, neglect, intentional abuse, and theft are recognized as losses. For example, if a computer work station is dropped during installation, the repair cost is recognized as a loss. After repair, the asset is no more valuable than it was before the mishap. In addition, outlays made to restore uninsured assets damaged through casualty are recorded as losses. These restorations do not enhance the utility of the asset beyond the value before the casualty. When such a loss is both unusual and infrequent as defined in *APB Opinion No. 30,* it is treated as an extraordinary loss.

If the asset's useful life or utility is increased upon restoration, the costs are capitalized to the extent of the improvement.

Significant post-acquisition expenditures fall into four major categories:

1. Maintenance and ordinary repairs.
2. Improvements (betterments), replacements, and extraordinary repairs.
3. Additions.
4. Rearrangements and other adjustments.

Maintenance and Ordinary Repairs

Maintenance expenditures include lubrication, cleaning, adjustments, and painting, incurred on a continuous basis to keep plant assets in usable condition. Ordinary repair costs include outlays for parts, labor, and related supplies that are necessary to keep assets in operating condition but that neither add materially to the use value of assets nor prolong their useful life significantly. Ordinary repairs are recurring and usually involve relatively small expenditures.

Ordinary repair and maintenance expenses are revenue expenditures. Two approaches are used to account for them.

1. *Incurred approach.* This approach records actual maintenance and repair expenditures as expenses as they occur and presumes an even distribution of expenditures over time. In many cases, however, annual expenditures for repairs and maintenance are not evenly distributed. The interim periods in which these expenditures occur would bear a disproportionate amount of maintenance cost under this approach. When a refinement of the matching process is desirable for interim reporting purposes, the second approach is appropriate.

2. *Allocation approach.* This approach is based on estimated repair and maintenance amounts. It is particularly useful when repairs are seasonal in nature and material in amount. This approach estimates the total cost of repairs and maintenance expected for the current year and allocates the estimate on the basis of time or production, depending on the situation. If based on time, an equal amount of repair and maintenance expense is recognized each interim period, and a contra plant asset account is credited for the estimated amount. Actual expenditures for ordinary repairs and maintenance are charged against this contra account.

To illustrate the allocation approach, assume that $18,000 of ordinary repairs and maintenance are estimated for a year. This amount is allocated equally to each month. Suppose the total repairs and maintenance cost incurred for the first month is $1,100. The entry to record the estimated expense and the related contra plant asset account for the month are:

To record estimated repair expense:

Repair and maintenance expense ($18,000/12 months)	1,500	
Allowance for repairs and maintenance		1,500

The entry to record actual outlays in the first month for ordinary repairs and maintenance is:

To record actual repair costs:

Allowance for repairs and maintenance	1,100	
Cash or payables		1,100

The income statement reports $1,500 of repair and maintenance expense each month. The $400 credit balance in the allowance account is reported in the interim balance sheet as a reduction from the appropriate assets. The allowance account carries a credit balance whenever the expense recognized to date exceeds actual expenditures. At the end of the year, any remaining credit balance in the allowance account is closed to repair and maintenance expense, reducing the expense to the actual level. The allocation yields a better matching of interim expense and revenue assuming that the benefits of annual maintenance and repair programs are received evenly throughout the year.

Improvements (Betterments), Replacements, Extraordinary Repairs (Renewals)

An *improvement* (or betterment) involves substituting a major component of a plant asset with a significantly improved component. Examples include the replacement of an old shingle roof with a modern fireproof tile roof, installation of a more powerful engine in a ship, and significant improvement of the electrical system in a building.

A *replacement* involves substituting a major component of a plant asset with one of comparable quality. Replacement of a truck engine with a similar engine is an example.

Extraordinary repairs or renewals involve large expenditures, are not recurring in nature, and usually increase the utility or the service life of the asset beyond the original estimate. Major overhauls of equipment and strengthening of a building foundation are examples.

Each of these categories of expenditures increases the useful life or productivity of the original asset. Three different approaches have evolved to account for these expenditures, all of which cause the book value of the original asset to increase.

1. *Substitution.* This approach removes the cost of the old component and related accumulated depreciation, recognizes a loss equal to the remaining book value, and increases the original asset account in the amount of the expenditure. To illustrate, assume that a shingle roof with an original cost of $20,000, and 80% depreciated, is

replaced by a fireproof tile roof costing $60,000. The two entries to record the betterment are:

To remove old component accounts:

Accumulated depreciation (old roof, $20,000 × .80)	16,000	
Loss on asset improvement	4,000	
Building (old roof)		20,000

To record cost of new component:

Building (new roof)	60,000	
Cash		60,000

The loss represents the undepreciated portion of the original roof cost. This approach is conceptually sound but is applied only when the cost of the old subunit and the related accumulated depreciation amount are known. This approach is not used for extraordinary repairs that do not involve replacement of components.

2. *Increase asset account.* This approach is used when the old costs and related accumulated depreciation amounts are not known, and when the primary effect is to increase efficiency rather than the economic life of the basic asset. The cost of the betterment is debited to the original asset account under the historical cost principle. The cost and accumulated depreciation of the unit replaced are not removed from the accounts because they cannot be determined reliably. One result of this treatment is an overstatement of the basic asset's book value, and subsequent depreciation. Normally, the remaining book value of the old unit is relatively minor at time of replacement. This approach is appropriate for extraordinary repairs.

3. *Reduce accumulated depreciation.* This is the traditional approach used when the primary effect is to lengthen the remaining life of the related asset. (This approach is not required under GAAP, however.) The expenditure is debited to the related accumulated depreciation account as a recovery of previously recognized depreciation, on the grounds that some of the useful life is restored. The cost of the unit replaced is not removed from the accounts. Often the depreciation rate must be revised. This approach is also appropriate for extraordinary repairs.

In certain situations, replacements are required by law to preserve public safety or to meet environmental standards. For example, many localities require removal of asbestos insulation for health reasons. Is asbestos removal and replacement capitalizable or should it be expensed? A case can be made for either disposition. The useful life of the building is likely to remain unchanged as is the overall productivity of the building. In contrast, employee safety is increased, and the firm has less exposure to health-related lawsuits. The tax law also is not clear. Firms have argued that asbestos removal and replacement are ordinary and necessary current expenses that do not increase the value of the building, but rather maintain its operating condition.[29] Many firms would prefer capitalization for financial statement purposes while receiving the tax deduction in the year of the removal.

Additions

Additions are extensions, enlargements, or expansions made to an existing asset. An extra wing or room added to a building is an example. An addition is a capital expenditure and is recorded in the plant asset accounts at cost. Work done on the existing structure, such as shoring up the foundation for the addition or cutting an entranceway through an existing wall, is a part of the cost of the addition and is capitalized. If the addition is an integral part of the older asset, its cost, less any

---

[29] "Tax Report," *The Wall Street Journal,* October 26, 1988, p. A1.

estimated residual value, normally is depreciated over the shorter of its own service life or the remaining life of the original asset. If the addition is not an integral part, it is depreciated over its own useful life.

Many firms retrofit production facilities with pollution control equipment to comply with laws and court orders. In some cases, the cost of antipollution devices are significant and can exceed the cost of the polluting assets. In this case, the devices are separately capitalized and depreciated as plant additions.

Rearrangements and Other Adjustments

The costs of *reinstallation, rerouting, or rearrangement* of factory machinery to increase efficiency are capital expenditures if the benefits of the rearrangement extend beyond the current accounting period. Such costs are capitalized as an other asset, a deferred charge, or a specific plant asset if the association can be made. These costs are amortized over the ensuing periods benefiting from the rearrangement.

Companies often disclose the accounting treatment of post-acquisition expenditures in the footnotes to financial statements. For example, Texaco, Inc. indicated the following in a footnote to its 1989 annual report:

> Periodic maintenance and repairs applicable to marine vessels and manufacturing facilities are accounted for on the accrual basis. Normal maintenance and repairs of all other properties, plant, and equipment are charged to expense as incurred. Renewals, betterments, and major repairs that materially extend the life of properties are capitalized and the assets replaced, if any, are retired.

CONCEPT REVIEW

1. Why are ordinary maintenance and repair costs expensed if they prolong the useful life of a plant asset?
2. What is a limitation of the accepted accounting for the replacement of a major asset component when the cost of the original component is unknown?
3. What is the general rule for capitalizing post-acquisition expenditures?

SUMMARY OF KEY POINTS

(L.O. 1) 1. The original cost of a plant asset equals the cash paid plus the market value of all other consideration transferred, or the value of the asset received, whichever is more reliably determinable.

(L.O. 1, 2) 2. To be capitalized as a plant asset, an expenditure must contribute to placing the asset into its intended condition and location. Other costs are expensed.

(L.O. 3) 3. If debt is incurred for the acquisition of plant assets, the present value of the debt is used to value the asset. If equity securities are issued, the market value of the securities or the market value of the asset acquired, whichever is more objective, is used to value the asset.

(L.O. 4) 4. The general rule for capitalizing expenditures as plant assets and the matching principle support interest capitalization during construction.

(L.O. 4) 5. Interest incurred during a plant asset's construction period is not capitalized unless three criteria are met. The interest that could have been avoided had the construction expenditures been applied to debt retirement constitutes the interest to be capitalized. The debt need not have been incurred specifically for construction.

(L.O. 5)   6. The gain or loss recognized on disposal of plant assets equals the difference between the market value of the consideration received and the book value of the asset at date of disposal.

(L.O. 6)   7. A plant asset acquired by exchanging a nonmonetary asset is valued at its market value or the market value of assets exchanged, whichever is more objective. If a gain would result from applying this principle to a similar asset exchange, the gain is recognized only to the extent of cash received on the exchange.

(L.O. 7)   8. Expenditures made on plant assets after their acquisition are classified as capital expenditures and debited to an asset account or accumulated depreciation if either the useful life or productivity of the asset is enhanced. Otherwise, the expenditures are classified as expenses.

REVIEW PROBLEM
◆

The following five short cases are independent.

1. *Plant asset cost classification*. Maldive Company completes the construction of a building. The following independent items are the costs and other aspects relevant to the purchase of the lot and construction:

Cash payments to contractor	$100,000
Total sales tax on materials used in construction in addition to payments made to contractor	3,000
Cost of land (building site)	50,000
Gross cost to raze old building on land	20,000
Proceeds from old building salvage	5,000
Power bill for electricity used in construction	2,000
Interest on purchase of materials	1,000
Capitalized interest on construction	3,000

What is the final recorded value of the land and building, respectively?

2. *Accounting for debt incurred on acquisition*. The Round Wheel Barn Company purchases a tractor by making a down payment of $10,000. In addition, Round Wheel Barn signs a note requiring monthly payments of $2,000, starting one month after purchase and continuing for a total of 20 months. The contract calls for no interest, yet the prevailing interest rate is 24% on similar debts. What is the correct recorded value of the asset at purchase? What is the interest expense recognized one month after purchase?

3. *Interest capitalization*. Whitehouse Company spent a total of $300,000 cash on a construction project during 1989 and 1990. During 1991, Whitehouse spends an additional $200,000 evenly during the year on the project and completes it at the end of 1991. Debt outstanding during 1991 is:

Accounts payable average balance	$ 50,000
10% bonds payable	700,000
12% construction loan	200,000

   a. What is average accumulated expenditures for 1991?
   b. Assume average accumulated expenditures for 1991 is $600,000, without prejudice to your answer in (a). Using the specific method of capitalization of interest, compute the amount of interest capitalized in 1991.
   c. Again assume average accumulated expenditures for 1991 is $600,000. Using the weighted average method of capitalization of interest, compute the interest capitalized in 1991.

4. *Accounting for exchange of plant asset*. Ocular Company trades an electron microscope with an original cost of $200,000 and accumulated depreciation of $80,000 for new optical equipment (a similar asset). The old equipment has a fair market value of $160,000 at trade-in time, and Ocular receives $30,000 on the trade-in. Give the entry to record the exchange.

5. *Post-acquisition costs*. After one fourth of the useful life had expired on equipment with an original cost of $100,000 and no salvage value, a major component of

the equipment is unexpectedly replaced. The old component was expected to last as long as the equipment itself, and the company records on the component indicates it originally cost $20,000 and had no expected salvage value. The replacement component cost $30,000 and has no usefulness beyond that of the equipment. Give the entry(ies) to record the component replacement. Assume straight-line depreciation.

SOLUTION
◆

1.

Land		Building	
Land cost	$50,000	Cash payments—contractor	$100,000
Razing cost	20,000	Sales tax on materials	3,000
Salvage proceeds	(5,000)	Power bill	2,000
		Capitalized interest	3,000
Total land cost	$65,000	Total building cost	$108,000

2. Recorded value of tractor $= \$10,000 + \$2,000(PVA,2\%,20)$
$$= \$10,000 + \$2,000(16.35143)$$
$$= \$42,703$$

Interest expense after one month $= (\$42,703 - \$10,000)(1/12).24$
$$= \$654$$

3. *a.* $AAE = \$300,000 + \$200,000/2 = \$400,000$
   b. Actual interest $= .10(\$700,000) + .12(\$200,000) = \$94,000$
   IPC $= .12(\$200,000) + .10(\$600,000 - \$200,000) = \$64,000$
   Therefore: ~specific~ borrowing   ~AAE~   ~specific borrowing~ → 700,000 × 10%

$$\text{Capitalized interest} = \$64,000 \qquad 700,000$$

   c. Weighted-average interest rate on all interest bearing debit $= \dfrac{\$94,000}{\$900,000} = .10444$

$$IPC = .10444(\$600,000) = \$62,667$$

Therefore:

$$\text{Capitalized interest} = \$62,667$$

4. Tentative worksheet entry (to determine initial gain) not entered into the accounts:

Equipment	130,000*	
Accumulated depreciation	80,000	
Cash	30,000	
Equipment		200,000
Gain		40,000

* $160,000 - $30,000 = $130,000, the implied market value of the new equipment.

Because cash boot is received, the amount of the initial gain (above) that is recognized is:

$$(\$30,000/\$160,000)\$40,000 = \$7,500$$

Therefore, the entry actually recorded is:

Equipment	97,500*	
Accumulated depreciation	80,000	
Cash	30,000	
Equipment		200,000
Gain		7,500

* $130,000 - ($40,000 - $7,500)

5.

Loss	15,000	
Accumulated depreciation $20,000/4	5,000	
Equipment		20,000
Equipment	30,000	
Cash		30,000

KEY TERMS

Average accumulated expenditures (533)	Interest capitalization (531)
Avoidable interest (533)	Interest potentially capitalizable (535)
Boot (545)	Points (522)
Capital expenditure (521)	Revenue expenditure (521)
Imputed interest (532)	Trade-in allowance (549)

QUESTIONS

1. Operational assets are classified as tangible or intangible; distinguish between the two, and give examples. Under what balance sheet caption are tangible operational assets reported? Give at least one synonym for whatever title you specify.

2. How does the historical cost principle apply to the acquisition of operational assets? What implications does the matching principle have for operational asset accounting?

3. Distinguish between capital and revenue expenditures. What accounting implications are involved?

4. To determine the cost of an operational asset, how should the following items be treated: (a) invoice price, (b) freight-in, (c) discounts, (d) title verification costs, (e) installation costs, (f) break-in costs, and (g) cost of major overhaul before operational use?

5. A machine was purchased on the following terms: cash, $100,000, plus five annual payments of $5,000 each. How should the acquisition cost of the machine be determined? Explain.

6. How is an asset's acquisition cost determined when the consideration given consists of equity securities?

7. Basically, how are assets recorded when they are acquired by exchanging another asset?

8. When does the "culmination (completion) of an earnings process" occur upon exchange of assets?

9. When dissimilar assets are exchanged, what value is used as the cost of the asset acquired?

10. When several operational assets are purchased for a single lump-sum consideration, cost apportionment is usually employed. Explain the procedure. Why is apportionment necessary?

11. Should donated assets be recorded in the accounts? If so, how should they be recorded and at what value?

12. Under what conditions should general overhead be allocated to a self-constructed asset?

13. Some businesses construct plant assets for their own use. What costs should be capitalized for these assets? Explain what to do about (a) general company overhead and any incremental costs incurred and (b) costs of construction in excess of the purchase price from an outsider.

14. Basically, what amount of interest should be capitalized as a part of the cost of an asset?

15. For what types of assets requiring a substantial completion or processing time is interest capitalization inappropriate?

16. If interest can be capitalized on an asset requiring a substantial completion period, when must interest capitalization begin and cease?

17. XYZ Company borrowed $2 million at 10% to finance construction of a new loading pier, which turned out to cost $3 million aside from capitalized interest. XYZ has other debt. To what extent, if any, can interest in excess of $200,000 be capitalized in any full year the pier is under construction? As to the other debt, how is the interest rate determined for capitalization purposes?

18. XY Corporation added a new wing at a cost of $300,000 plus $10,000 spent in making passageways through the walls of the old structure. The plant was 10 years old and was being depreciated by an equal amount each year over a 30-year life. Over what period should the new wing be depreciated?

19. When are post-acquisition costs capitalized rather than expensed?

20. What is the nature of a gain or loss on disposal of an operational asset when cash is received?

21. Outline the accounting steps related to the disposition of an operational asset, assuming it is not traded in on another asset.

22. If interest is capitalized in 1991, what is the effect on income in 1991? What is the effect of interest capitalized in 1991 on income in future years?
23. Briefly explain how to compute the amount of gain to be recognized in an exchange of similar operational assets when cash boot is received.
24. Under what conditions are gains on disposal of assets disallowed by the SEC?
25. What value is assigned to an operational asset received in exchange for a dissimilar asset when cash is also received and the market value of the asset transferred is known.

EXERCISES

E 11–1

Acquisition of Land: Noncash Considerations

(L.O. 1)

Under the cost principle, what cost should be used for recording the land acquired in each of the following independent cases? Give reasons in support of your answer.

a. At the middle of the current year, a check was given for $40,000 for the land and, in addition, the buyer assumed the liability for unpaid taxes in arrears at the end of last year, $1,000, and those assessed for current year, $900.

b. A company issued 14,000 shares (par $1) of capital stock with a market value of $6 per share (based upon a recent sale of 10 shares) for the land. The land was recently appraised at $80,000 by independent and competent appraisers.

c. A company rejected an offer to purchase the land for $8,000 cash two years ago. Instead, the company issued 1,000 shares of capital stock for the land (market value of the stock, $7.80 per share based on several recent large transactions and normal weekly stock trading volume).

d. A company issued 1,000 shares of capital stock, par $40, for the land. The market value (stock sells daily with an average daily volume of 5,000 shares) was $60 per share at time of purchase of the land. The vendor earlier offered to sell the land for $59,000 cash. Competent appraisers valued the land at $61,000.

E 11–2

Asset Acquisition: Note Payable

(L.O. 3)

Vee Corporation acquired equipment on credit. Terms were $14,000 cash down payment plus payments of $10,000 at the end of each of the next two years. The seller's implicit interest rate was 14%. The list price of the equipment was $34,000.

Required:

Round to the nearest dollar.
1. Give the entry to record the purchase.
2. Give the entry to record the last $10,000 payment.

E 11–3

Assets Acquired: Note Payable, Discount

(L.O. 2)

The following situations are independent:

a. Delivery equipment with a list price of $60,000 was purchased; terms were 2/10, n/30. Payment was made within the discount period.

b. Delivery equipment with a list price of $40,000 was purchased; terms were 2/10, n/30. Payment was made after the discount period.

c. Delivery equipment listed at $18,000 was purchased and invoiced at 2/10, n/30. In order to take advantage of the discount, the company borrowed $16,000 of the purchase price by issuing a 60-day, 15% note, which was paid with interest at maturity date.

Required:

Give entries in each separate situation for costs, borrowing, and any expenses involved.

E 11–4

Acquisition of Multiple Assets for a Single Price

(L.O. 1)

Freeman Company purchased a tract of land on which were located a warehouse and an office building. The cash purchase price was $140,000 plus $10,000 in fees connected with the purchase. The following data were collected concerning the property:

	Tax Assessment	Vendor's Book Value	Original Cost
Land	$20,000	$10,000	$10,000
Warehouse	40,000	20,000	60,000
Office building	60,000	50,000	80,000

Required:

Give the entry to record the purchase; show computations.

E 11–5

Asset Acquisition: Time Payment Plan

(L.O. 3)

Wolf Company bought a machine on a time payment plan. The cash purchase price was $25,615. Terms were $7,000 cash down payment plus four equal annual payments at year-end of $6,000, which include interest on the unpaid balance at 11% per annum.

Required:

1. Give the entry to record the purchase. Show computations (round to nearest dollar).
2. Prepare a schedule to reflect the accounting entries for each of the four installment payments. Round amounts in the schedule to the nearest dollar.

E 11–6

Similar and Dissimilar Assets Exchanged

(L.O. 5)

Bloem Corporation has some old equipment that cost $140,000; accumulated depreciation is $80,000. This equipment was traded in on a new machine that had a list price of $160,000; however, the new machine could be purchased without a trade-in for $150,000 cash. The difference between the market value of the new asset and the market value of the old asset will be paid in cash.

Required:

Give the entry to record the acquisition of the new machine under each of the following independent cases:

1. The new machine was purchased for cash with no trade-in.
2. The equipment and the machine are dissimilar. The old equipment is traded in, and $100,000 cash is paid.
3. Same as (2) except that the equipment and the machine are similar.

E 11–7

Assets Exchanged: Five Different Cases

(L.O. 5)

On January 1, 1991, Seismographics Corporation exchanged old equipment that cost $10,000 (accumulated depreciation, $4,500) for new equipment. The market value of the new equipment was $8,000. The market value of the old equipment could not be reliably estimated.

Required:

Give the entry to record the acquisition of the new equipment under each of the following independent cases:

1. The assets are dissimilar. No cash was involved.
2. The assets are dissimilar. Cash of $3,000 was paid by Seismographics.
3. The assets are similar. No cash was involved.
4. The assets are similar. Cash of $1,000 was paid by Seismographics.
5. The assets are similar. Cash of $2,000 was received by Seismographics.

E 11–8

Acquisition of Multiple Assets for a Single Price

(L.O. 1)

Brushy Machine Shop purchased the following used equipment at a special auction sale for $80,000 cash: drill press, lathe, and a heavy-duty air compressor. The equipment was in excellent condition except for the electric motor on the lathe, which will cost $1,800 to replace with a new motor. Brushy has determined that the selling prices for the used items in local outlets are approximately as follows: drill press, $16,800; lathe, with a good motor, $48,000, and air compressor, $21,000.

Required:

Give the entry to record (a) acquisition of the operational assets and (b) to replace the motor.

E 11–9

Donated Assets

(L.O. 3)

The city of Akron gave New Company a building, including the land on which it is located, as an inducement to start a high-technology operation in the city. The property was reliably appraised at a value of $160,000 (one fourth related to the land). The company paid transfer costs of $4,000. The building has an estimated remaining life of 25 years (no residual value).

Required:

Give the entries to record the (a) transfer and (b) depreciation expense at the end of the first year. Assume a full year of depreciation and the straight-line method.

E 11–10
Self-Constructed Asset: Rationale for Accounting Treatment
(L.O. 3)

Amethyst Company constructed a building and incurred the following costs directly associated with construction:

Materials	$50,000
Labor	80,000
Incremental overhead	30,000
Interest on the construction loan incurred before completion	5,000
Interest on the construction loan incurred after completion	2,000
Total	$167,000

The building was worth $155,000 (market value) upon completion.

Required:

1. Provide summary journal entries to record construction and completion of the building. Assume that all qualifying interest during the current year is to be capitalized to the building.
2. Discuss the rationale for the limitation on the valuation of Amethyst's building in terms of the historical cost principle.

E 11–11
Capitalization of Interest: Specific Method
(L.O. 4)

Weld Corporation is constructing a plant for its own use. Weld capitalizes interest on an annual basis. The following expenditures were made during 1991: January 1, $30,000; July 1, $290,000; September 1, $800,000; and December 31, $2,110,000. The following debts were outstanding throughout the year:

Construction note, 12%	$100,000
Short-term note payable, 15%	400,000
Accounts payable (noninterest-bearing)	400,000

Weld capitalizes interest first using the interest rate on debt directly associated with the construction and then using the weighted-average rate of all other debt (i.e., the specific method).

Required:

1. Compute the amount of interest to be capitalized and the amount of interest to be expensed.
2. Give the entry to record the construction expenditures and interest.

E 11–12
Capitalization of Interest: Weighted-Average Method
(L.O. 4)

Required:
Using the information in E 11–11, compute the amount of interest to be capitalized under the weighted-average method.

E 11–13
Capitalization of Interest: Weighted-Average Method
(L.O. 4)

Bullock Company is constructing a building for its own use and has been capitalizing interest based on average expenditures on a quarterly basis since the project began. The following expenditures were made during the first quarter: January 1, $2,800,000; February 1, $2,550,000; and March 31, $3,650,000.

Bullock had the following debts outstanding during the quarter:

Note payable, 10%, incurred specifically to finance the construction	$1,600,000
Short-term note payable, 15%	2,500,000
Mortgage note payable, 8%	1,200,000
Capitalized lease (on which the first quarter's interest amounted to $3,000)	250,000

Required:

1. Compute interest to be capitalized and interest to be expensed for the first quarter. Use the weighted-average method. *130,500*
2. Give the entry to record the expenditures and the interest.
3. Explain what effect, if any, the costs of land on which the building is being erected would have on the amount of interest properly capitalizable.

E 11-14
Capitalization of Interest:
Specific Method
(L.O. 4)

Required:

Using the information in E 11-13, compute the amount of interest to be capitalized under the specific method.

E 11-15
Ordinary Repairs:
Incurred Approach versus
Allocation Approach
(L.O. 7)

Jenkins Company operates two separate plants. In Plant A, the accounting policy is to expense all ordinary (minor) repairs as incurred. In contrast, in Plant B, the accounting policy is to use the allocation approach that debits repair and maintenance expense equally each period. Jenkins Company has little seasonality in its production. Selected data for 1991 are as follows:

	Plant A	Plant B
Estimated repair costs budgeted for year	$5,000	$5,000
Actual repair costs incurred and paid:		
First quarter	1,200	400
Second quarter	800	1,500
Third quarter	1,000	1,100
Fourth quarter	2,100	2,200

Required:

1. Give the entries in parallel columns for each plant for each of the four quarters.
2. Would you recommend any changes in the accounting policies? Explain and justify your response.

E 11-16
Repairs, Replacements,
Betterments, and
Renovations
(L.O. 7)

The plant building of Xon Corporation is old (estimated remaining useful life, 12 years) and needs continuous maintenance and repairs. The company's accounts show that the building originally cost $600,000; accumulated depreciation was $400,000 at the beginning of the current year. During the current year, the following expenditures relating to the plant building were made:

a. Continuing, frequent, and low-cost repairs . . . . $ 34,000
b. Added a new storage shed attached to the building, estimated useful life, eight years . . . 72,000
c. Removed original roof; original cost, $80,000; replaced it with guaranteed, modern roof . . 100,000
d. Unusual and infrequent repairs due to damage from flood in desert; repairs did not
increase the use value or the economic life of the asset 12,000
e. Complete overhaul of the plumbing system (old costs not known) 25,000

Required:

Give the journal entry to record each of the above items. Explain the basis for your treatment of each item.

E 11-17
Disposal of Operational
Assets: Interpretation of
Resulting Gain or Loss
(L.O. 5)

Renny Company sells a machine on June 1, 1991, for $139,000. Renny incurred $800 of removal and selling costs on disposal. The machine originally cost $250,000 when it was purchased on January 2, 1988. Its estimated residual value and useful life were $40,000 and 10 years, respectively. Renny uses straight-line depreciation and records annual depreciation on December 31.

Required:

1. Provide the journal entries needed to record the disposal.
2. How would the gain or loss in (1) be affected if the machine were abandoned (zero market value)?
3. Provide an interpretation of the gain or loss in (1) for someone with little or no background in accounting.

E 11-18
Disposal of Asset
(L.O. 5)

On April 1, 1992, one of the two large production machines used by Unlucky Company stripped a gear, causing major internal damages. On April 10, 1992, the company decided to purchase a new machine (cost, $182,500) so that production could continue. On January 1, 1992, the accounts showed the following for the old machine: original cost, $90,000; accumulated depreciation, $63,000 (20-year life; no residual value). The company would not accept a trade-in offer of $13,500. Instead, the old machine was sold on May 1, 1992, to an out-of-state company for $24,000. Unlucky spent $3,000 cleaning and moving the machine prior to shipping, which cost another $1,000. Insurance premiums (prepaid) for 1992 on the old machine was $45; the unused portion of the premium will be applied to the new machine. The insurance was paid on January 1, 1992; and covered the period January 1, 1992, through December 31, 1992.

Required:

Give all entries, by date, that Unlucky Company should make from April 1 through May 1, 1992.

E 11–19
Asset Cost—Seven Cases
(L.O. 1, 2)

Select the best answer for each of the following. Briefly justify your choice for each item.

1. May Company purchased certain plant assets on credit. May agreed to pay $10,000 per year for five years. The plant assets should be valued at:
   a. $50,000.
   b. $50,000 plus a charge for the market rate of interest.
   c. Present value of a $10,000 annuity for five years at the market interest rate.
   d. Present value of a $10,000 annuity for five years discounted at the bank prime interest rate.

2. The debit for a sales tax properly levied and paid on the purchase of machinery preferably would be to:
   a. A separate deferred charge account.
   b. Miscellaneous tax expense (which includes all taxes other than those on income).
   c. Accumulated depreciation, machinery
   d. The machinery account.

3. When a closely held corporation issues preferred stock for land, the land should be recorded at the:
   a. Total par value of the stock issued.
   b. Total book value of the stock issued.
   c. Appraised value of the land.
   d. Total liquidating value of the stock issued.

4. An improvement made to a machine increased its market value and its production capacity by 25% without extending the machine's useful life. The cost of the improvement should be:
   a. Expensed.
   b. Debited to accumulated depreciation.
   c. Capitalized in the machine account.
   d. Allocated between accumulated depreciation and the machine account.

   Items 5, 6, and 7 are based on the following information.
   Two independent companies, Ball and Brown, are in the home building business. Each owns a tract of land held for development, but each company would prefer to build on the other's land. Accordingly, they agree to exchange their land. An appraiser was hired, and from the report and the companies' records, the following information was obtained:

	Ball Co.'s Land	Brown Co.'s Land
Cost (same as book value)	$ 80,000	$50,000
Market value based upon appraisal	100,000	90,000

   The exchange of land was made, and based on the difference in appraised values, Brown paid $10,000 cash to Ball.

5. For financial reporting purposes, Ball would recognize a pretax gain on this exchange in the amount of:
   a. $2,000.
   b. $6,000.
   c. $10,000.
   d. $20,000.

6. For financial reporting purposes, Brown would recognize a pretax gain on this exchange in the amount of:
   a. $-0-.
   b. $10,000.
   c. $30,000.
   d. $40,000.

7. After the exchange, Ball would record its newly acquired land at:
   a. $70,000.
   b. $72,000.
   c. $80,000.
   d. $92,000.

(AICPA adapted)

PROBLEMS

P 11–1
Asset Acquired: Installment Payments
(L.O. 3)

Acme Cement Company contracted to buy equipment, agreeing to make an equal annual payment of $10,832 at the end of each of the next four years. The equipment has a list price of $32,900 (which is also the cash price), an estimated service life of five years, and estimated residual value of $2,000.

Required:
Round to nearest dollar.

1. Determine the approximate interest rate implicit in the contract and prepare a debt amortization schedule for the four-year period. Record the purchase of the equipment in conformity with GAAP.
2. Assuming Acme's fiscal year coincides with the payment dates, record (a) the first payment and (b) the depreciation at the end of the first year (use straight-line depreciation).
3. Give similar entries at the end of the fourth year.

P 11–2
Asset Acquisition: Noncash Consideration
(L.O. 3)

Machinery with a market value of $15,000 is acquired in a noncash exchange. Below are six independent assumptions (a to f) as to the consideration given in the noncash exchange:

a. Bonds held as a long-term investment, which originally cost $28,000 and had been written down 50% because of a perceived permanent loss of their value.
b. Common stock held as a short-term investment, which originally cost $14,300, included in the short-term portfolio of similar investments. The stock had a market value of $15,000 on the latest balance sheet date.
c. Inventory carried at $9,500 on the most recent balance sheet as part of a perpetual inventory carried at LCM. When originally acquired, the goods had cost $9,900.
d. Similar used machinery with a book value of $6,000 and a market value of $6,700 plus cash of $8,300. When new, the used machinery cost $8,800.
e. Land with a book value of $7,500 and a market value of $15,000.
f. A noninterest-bearing note for $17,250 maturing in one year. Similar risk notes required 15% interest at the date of the exchange.

Required:
Give the journal entry required for each of the above independent assumptions.

P 11–3
Acquisition Cost: Five Cost Changes
(L.O. 1, 2, 7)

An examination of the property, plant, and equipment accounts of James Company on December 31, 1992, disclosed the following transactions:

a. On January 1, 1991, purchased a new machine having a list price of $30,000. The company did not take advantage of a 1% cash discount available upon full payment of the invoice within 10 days. Shipping cost paid by the vendor was $100. Installation cost was $400, including $100 that represented 10% of the monthly salary of the factory superintendent (installation period, two days). A wall was moved two feet at a cost of $800 to make room for the machine.
b. During January 1991, the first month of operations, the newly purchased machine became inoperative due to a defect in manufacture. The vendor repaired the machine at no cost;

however, the specially trained operator was idle during the two weeks the machine was inoperative. The operator was paid regular wages ($650) during the period, although the only work peformed was to observe the repair by the factory representative.

c. On January 1, 1991, bought fixtures with a list price of $4,500; paid cash $1,500 and gave a one-year, noninterest-bearing note payable for the balance. The current interest rate for this type of note was 15%.

d. On July 1, 1991, contracted for a building for $400,000. The contractor was paid by transferring $400,000 face value, 20-year, 8% company bonds payable, at which time financial consultants advised that the bonds would sell at 96 (i.e., $384,000).

e. During January 1992, exchanged the electric motor on a machine for a heavier motor and paid $400 cash. The market value of the new motor was $1,250. The parts list showed a $900 cost for the original motor (estimated life, 10 years).

f. On January 1, 1991, purchased an automatic counter to be attached to a machine in use, cost $700. The estimated useful life of the counter was 7 years, and the estimated life of the machine was 10 years.

Required:

1. Prepare the journal entries to record each of the above transactions. Explain and justify your decisions on questionable items. James Company uses straight-line depreciation.
2. Record depreciation at the end of 1991. None of the assets is expected to have a residual value except the fixtures (residual value is $500). Estimated useful lives: fixtures, 5 years; machinery, 10 years; and building, 40 years. Give a separate entry for each asset.

P 11–4

Multiple Choice: Asset Acquisition and Post-Acquisition Costs

(L.O. 1, 7)

Choose the correct answer for each of the following questions.

1. Discounts available for early payment of liabilities incurred for the purchase of operational assets should be:
   a. Recorded and reported as a contra account to the related liability account.
   b. Given no recognition until taken or until the discount period has expired; if not taken, the discounts should be added to the cost of the asset.
   c. Deducted from the invoice price whether taken or not.
   d. Capitalized as a part of the cost of the asset, whether taken or not, and subsequently included in depreciation expense.
2. Able Corporation purchased an old building and the land on which it is located. The old building will be demolished at a net cost of $10,000. A new building will be built on the site. The net demolition cost (after salvage proceeds) should be:
   a. Depreciated over the remaining life of the new building.
   b. Written off as an extraordinary loss in year of demolition.
   c. Capitalized as part of the cost of the land.
   d. Written off as an expense.
3. Shwee Corporation purchased land by signing a note with the seller calling for $10,000 down, $12,000 one year from purchase, and $8,000 three years from purchase. The note is not interest-bearing, but the going rate for similar land purchase notes is 10%. What value should be recorded in the land account?
   a. $25,019.
   b. 26,920.
   c. 27,000.
   d. 30,000.
4. The cost to train employees to run new robotic technology used in manufacturing should be debited to:
   a. Machinery.
   b. Deferred charge.
   c. Manufacturing expense.
   d. Office salaries.
5. At great cost, a special plastic film was applied to all the south- and west-facing windows of a 12 story office building. This film reduces the radiant energy entering the building and is expected to pay for itself in saved air-conditioning costs in five years. The useful life of the windows is not affected. The cost of this film should be debited to:
   a. Maintenance and repair expense.
   b. Building.

   c. Leasehold improvement.

   d. Other expense.

6. A music system was added to the office building and elevators to create a more pleasant environment. The system consists of new wiring, speakers, and state-of-the-art amplification equipment. The cost of the system should be debited to:

   a. Entertainment expense.

   b. Furniture.

   c. Building.

   d. Employee expenses.

7. The cost of repaving a parking lot with a new, longer life asphalt should be debited to which of the following accounts? The company owns the land and the lot. The new asphalt will increase the life of the present lot significantly over the original expected useful life.

   a. Land improvements.

   b. Land.

   c. An expense account.

   d. Deferred charge.

P 11–5

Asset Acquisition

(L.O. 1, 2, 3)

At December 31, 1991, certain accounts included in the property, plant, and equipment section of Hine Corporation's balance sheet had the following balances:

> Land . . . . $ 600,000
> Buildings 1,300,000
> Leasehold improvements   800,000
> Machinery and equipment 1,600,000

During 1992, the following transactions occurred:

a. Land site number 101 was acquired for $3 million. Additionally, to acquire the land, Hine paid a $180,000 commission to a real estate agent. Costs of $30,000 were incurred to clear the land. During the course of clearing the land, timber and gravel were recovered and sold for $16,000.

b. A second tract of land (site number 102) with a building was acquired for $600,000. The closing statement indicated that the land value was $400,000 and the building value was $200,000. Shortly after acquisition, the building was demolished at a cost of $40,000. A new building was constructed for $300,000 plus the following costs:

> Excavation fees $12,000
> Architectural design fees   16,000
> Building permit fee   4,000

The building was completed and occupied on September 30, 1992.

c. A third tract of land (site number 103) was acquired for $1,500,000 and was put on the market for resale.

d. Extensive work was done to a building occupied by Hine under a lease agreement that expires on December 31, 2001. The total cost of the work was $250,000, as follows:

Item	Cost	Estimated Useful Life (Years)
Painting of ceilings	$ 10,000	1
Electrical work	90,000	10
Construction of extension to current working area	150,000	25
	$250,000	

The lessor paid half the costs incurred for the extension to the current working area.

e. During December 1992, $120,000 was spent to improve leased office space. The related lease will terminate on December 31, 1995 and is not expected to be renewed.

f. A group of new machines was purchased under a royalty agreement, which provides for payment of royalties based on units of production for the machines. The invoice price of the machines was $270,000, freight costs were $2,000, unloading costs were $3,000, and royalty payments for 1992 were $44,000.

Required:

Disregard the related accumulated depreciation accounts.

1. Prepare a detailed analysis of the changes in each of the following balance sheet accounts for 1992. (Hint: set up a separate analysis for land, buildings, leasehold improvements, and machinery and equipment.)
   a. Land.
   b. Buildings.
   c. Leasehold improvements.
   d. Machinery and equipment.
2. List the items in the fact situation which were not used to determine the answer to (1) above, and indicate where, or if, these items should be included in Hine's financial statements.

(AICPA adapted)

P 11-6
Operational Asset Acquisition through Debt: Gross and Net Methods of Recording
(L.O. 3)

Lien Company purchased machinery on January 1, 1991, and gave a two-year, 6%, $1,000 note that pays interest each December 31. The market interest rate is 12% on such notes.

Required:

Record the purchase of the asset, the two interest payments, and note extinguishment under the following two methods:
1. Gross method.
2. Net method.

P 11-7
Assets Exchanged; Similar and Dissimilar Compared
(L.O. 6)

Trader Joe, Inc., has a policy of trading in equipment after one year's use. The following information is available from Trader Joe's records:

January 1, 1991—Acquired Asset A for $12,000 cash.
January 1, 1992—Exchanged Asset A for Asset B. Asset B had a market value of $14,000. Paid $3,000 in cash in the exchange.
January 1, 1993—Exchanged Asset B for Asset C. Asset C had a market value of $16,000. Paid $4,000 in cash in the exchange.
January 1, 1994—Exchanged Asset C for Asset D. Asset D had a market value of $11,000. Received $2,000 in cash in the exchange.

Assume a five-year estimated useful life and no residual value for all assets. Straight-line depreciation is used by Trader Joe.

Required:

1. Assume the assets are all similar. Give the journal entries required for each exchange.
2. Assume the assets are all dissimilar. Give the journal entries required for each exchange.

P 11-8
Assets Exchanged: Similar and Dissimilar, No Cash versus Cash Paid
(L.O. 6)

This problem presents two independent cases—Case A, similar assets, and Case B, dissimilar assets.

a. *Case A.* Two similar operational assets were exchanged when the accounts of the two companies involved reflected the following:

Account	Company M (Designate as Asset M)	Company N (Designate as Asset N)
Operational asset	$8,000	$8,200
Accumulated depreciation	5,500	4,800

The market value of Asset M was reliably determined to be $2,800; no reliable estimate could be made of Asset N.

Required:

Round amounts to nearest dollar.

1. Give the exchange entry for each company assuming no cash difference is involved.

2. Give the exchange entry for each company assuming a cash difference of $800 was paid by Company M to Company N.

   b. *Case B.* Two dissimilar operational assets were exchanged when the accounts of the two companies involved reflected the following:

Account	Company A (Designate as Asset A)	Company B (Designate as Asset B)
Operational asset	$10,000	$14,000
Accumulated depreciation	7,000	10,500

The market value of asset A was reliably determined to be $4,500; no reliable estimate of market value could be made for asset B.

Required:

1. Give the exchange entry for each company assuming no cash difference was involved.
2. Give the exchange entry for each company assuming a cash difference of $1,200 was paid by Company A to Company B.

P 11–9
Assets Exchanged, Entries for Both Parties: Five Transactions
(L.O. 6)

In this problem, all items of property refer to operational assets, not inventory, unless specified to the contrary. List prices are not necessarily market values.

Required:

Give journal entries where specified to record the following transactions:

1. Land carried on the books of Company A at $18,000 is exchanged for a computer carried on the books of Corporation B at $25,000 (cost, $35,000; accumulated depreciation, $10,000). Market value of both assets is $30,000. Give the journal entry for both A and B. The land and the computer are used in different lines of business.
2. A truck, which cost Company A $6,000 ($3,000 accumulated depreciation) has a market value of $3,400. It is traded to a dealer, plus a $5,600 cash payment, for a new truck which has a $12,400 list price. Give the journal entry for Company A.
3. A truck that cost Company A $6,000, on which $5,000 depreciation has been accumulated, is traded to a dealer along with $6,300 cash. The new truck would have cost $7,000 if only cash had been paid; its list price is $7,500. Give the journal entry for Company A.
4. Land carried on the books of Company A at $90,000 is exchanged for land carried on the books of Corporation B at $78,000. Market value of each tract is $100,000. Give the journal entry for Corporation B.
5. Fixtures that cost Company A $15,000 ($9,000 accumulated depreciation) and are worth $8,000 are traded to Corporation B along with $500 cash. In exchange, A received fixtures from B carried by B at cost of $13,000 less $6,000 accumulated depreciation. Give the journal entries for both Companies A and B; if necessary, round amounts to the nearest dollar.

P 11–10
Donated Assets
(L.O. 3)

Iowa City gave Hermanson Company a vacant building located on city property. The building was no longer needed by the city, and it was given to the company as an inducement to relocate. Hermanson has relocated to Iowa City. The building has a 20-year estimated useful life (no residual value), which was recognized in the donation agreement at the time that the company was guaranteed occupancy. Transfer costs of $12,000 were paid by the company. The building originally cost $300,000 10 years earlier. The building was recently appraised at $160,000 market value by the city's tax assessor. Anticipating occupancy within the next 10 days, the company spent $36,000 for repairs and internal rearrangements (good for 10 years). There are no unresolved contingencies about the building and Hermanson's permanent occupancy.

Required:

Give all entries for Hermanson Company related to the (*a*) donation, (*b*) renovation, and (*c*) any depreciation or amortization at the end of the first year of occupancy, assuming Hermanson uses straight-line depreciation and assets have no residual value.

P 11-11
Asset Cost: Numerous
Related Expenditures
(L.O. 1, 2)

The following transactions relate to operational assets:

a. Purchased land and buildings for $157,800 cash. The purchaser agreed to pay $1,800 for taxes already assessed. The purchaser borrowed $100,000 at 15% interest (principal and interest due in one year) from the bank to help make the cash payment. The property was appraised for taxes as follows: land, $50,000; and building, $100,000.

b. Prior to use of the property purchased in (*a*) above, the following expenditures were made:

Repair and renovation of building	$16,000
Installation of 220-volt electrical wiring	4,000
Removal of separate shed of no use (sold scrap lumber for $100)	600
Construction of new driveway	3,000
Repair of existing driveways	1,200
Deposits with utilities for connections	100
Painting company name on two sides of building	1,800
Installation of wire fence around property	5,000

c. Purchased a tract of land for $64,000; assumed taxes already assessed amounting to $360. Paid title fees, $100, and attorney fees of $600 in connection with the purchase. Payments were in cash.

d. The land purchased in (*c*) above was leveled, and two retaining walls were built to stop erosion that had created two rather large gulleys across the property. Total cash cost of the work was $6,000. The property is being held as a future plant site.

e. Purchased a used machine at a cash cost of $17,000. Subsequent to purchase, the following expenditures were made:

General overhaul prior to use	$2,400
Installation of machine	600
Cost of moving machine	300
Cost of removing two small machines to make way for larger machine purchased	200
Cost of reinforcing floor prior to installation	800
Testing costs prior to operation	120
Cost of tool kit (new) essential to adjustment of machine for various types of work	440

Required:

Prepare journal entries to record the above transactions. Give special attention to the cost of each asset. Justify your position on doubtful items.

P 11-12
Self-Constructed Assets:
Factory Case
(L.O. 3)

Shear Corporation used its own facilities to construct a small addition to its office building. Construction began on February 1 and was completed on June 30 of the same year. Prior to the decision to construct the asset with its own facilities, Shear accepted bids from outside contractors; the lowest bid was $240,000. Costs accumulated during the constuction period are summarized as follows:

Materials used (including $120,000 for normal production)	$180,000
Direct labor (including $300,000 for normal production)	450,000
General supplies used on construction	6,000
Rent paid on construction machinery	5,000
Insurance premiums on construction	2,000
Supervisory salary on construction	7,000
Total general overhead for year	115,000
Total factory overhead for year:	
Fixed ($10,000 due to construction)	100,000
Variable	60,000
Direct labor-hours (including 100,000 hours for normal production)	120,000

Shear allocates factory overhead to normal production on the basis of direct labor hours.

Required:

Compute the amounts that might be capitalized:

1. Assuming the plant capacity to be 120,000 direct labor-hours and that the construction displaced production for sale to be the extent indicated.
2. Assuming the plant capacity to be 200,000 direct labor-hours and that idle capacity was used for the construction. This company allocates general overhead to self-constructed assets.

Hint: Use separate fixed and variable overhead rates for factory overhead (i.e., cost ÷ direct labor-hours).

P 11–13
Asset Cost: Allocation, Entries
(L.O. 1, 2)

Feltham Company was incorporated on January 2, 1991, but was unable to begin manufacturing activities until July 1, 1991, because new factory facilities were not completed until that date.

The Land and Building account at December 31, 1991, was as follows:

Date	Item	Amount
1991		
Jan. 31	Land and building	$107,000
Feb. 28	Cost of removal of building	6,000
May 1	Partial payment of new construction	40,000
1	Legal fees paid	2,000
1	Insurance premium	1,800
June 1	Second payment on new construction	45,000
1	Special tax assessment	2,500
30	General expenses	18,000
July 1	Final payment on new construction	50,000
Dec. 31	Asset write-up	18,000
		290,300
31	Depreciation—1991 at 1%	2,903
	Account balance	$287,397

The following additional information is to be considered:

a. To acquire land and building, the company paid $50,000 cash and issued 500 shares of its 5% cumulative preferred stock, par value $100 per share; market value, $57,000.
b. Cost of removal of old building amounted to $6,000, with the demolition company retaining all materials of the building.
c. Legal fees covered the following:

Cost of organization	$ 500
Examination of title covering purchase of land	1,000
Legal work in connection with construction work	500
	$2,000

d. The insurance premium covers three-year term beginning May 1, 1991.
e. The special tax assessment covered street improvements.
f. General expenses were incurred for the following from January 2, 1991, to June 30, 1991.

President's salary	$10,000
Plant superintendent covering supervision on new building	7,000
Office salaries	1,000
	$18,000

g. Because of a general increase in construction costs after entering into the building contract, the board of directors increased the value of the building $18,000, believing such an increase was justified to reflect market value at the time the building was completed. Retained earnings was credited for this amount.
h. Estimated life of building—50 years. Write-off for 1991 for one half year—1% of asset value.

Required:

1. Prepare entries to reflect correct land, building, and accumulated depreciation accounts at December 31, 1991. Assume the 1991 books have not yet been closed.

2. Show the proper presentation of land, building, and accumulated depreciation on the balance sheet at December 31, 1991.

(AICPA adapted)

P 11–14

Multiple Choice: Interest Capitalization

(L.O. 4)

Choose the correct answer for each of the following questions.

1. The interest capitalization period for a self-constructed asset begins when certain conditions are met. Which of the following is not one of those conditions?
   a. Qualifying expenditures for the asset have actually been made.
   b. Interest cost has actually been incurred.
   c. Liabilities, such as trade payables or accruals, are incurred in connection with the asset.
   d. Activities necessary to get the asset ready for its intended use actually are in progress.
2. Capitalization of construction period interest is based primarily upon the:
   a. Full disclosure principle.
   b. Revenue principle.
   c. Matching concept.
   d. The *SFAC No. 6* definition of an asset.
3. Choose the correct statement regarding interest capitalization:
   a. If average accumulated expenditures are greater than the amount of the specific construction loan and the specific method is used, only interest on the specific loan is capitalized.
   b. If the weighted-average method is used, all interest-bearing debt is considered in the interest capitalization calculations.
   c. A corporation can assume expenditures were incurred evenly throughout the year even though there are material variations in the pattern of expenditures during the year.
   d. If interest potentially capitalizable exceeds actual interest, a corporation records a gain equal to the difference.
4. A company made the following cash expenditures this year on a self-constructed building begun January 2 of the current year:

January 2	$20,000
September 1	30,000
December 1	60,000

   The building is still under construction at year-end. What is average accumulated expenditures for the purpose of capitalizing interest?
   a. $55,000.
   b. 110,000.
   c. 30,000.
   d. 35,000.

5. The following is information on a self-constructed asset.

	January 1	December 31
Incurred costs to date	$300,000	$600,000
Balance of related construction payables	100,000	200,000

   The building is still under construction at year-end. Determine average accumulated expenditures.
   a. $300,000.
   b. 450,000.
   c. 600,000.
   d. 900,000.

6. Average accumulated expenditures were $200,000 on a project for which work steadily proceeded during the entire year, and the following debt was outstanding the entire year:

   construction loan: $100,000 at 10%.
   note payable: $500,000 at 8%.
   mortgage payable: $150,000 at 12%.

   What is the capitalized interest according to the specific method?
   a. $32,000.
   b. 18,923.

c.   18,133.

d.   22,467.

7. Assume the same facts as in (6) but using the weighted-average method, what is the capitalized interest?

    a. $32,000.

    b.   18,923.

    c.   18,133.

    d.   22,467.

P 11–15

Capitalization of Interest: Weighted-Average Method

(L.O. 4)

Rose Company began construction of a small building on January 1, 1991. The company's only debt during the first quarter was an unrelated long-term $300,000 note bearing interest at 11% per annum, maturity date, December 31, 1993. On May 1, 1991, the company borrowed $100,000 on a 9% construction note (interest bearing); the note matures on April 30, 1992. The company capitalizes interest on the building on the basis of average quarterly cumulative expenditures. As of the end of each quarter of the six-month construction period, construction expenditures (not including interest) are as shown below. Rose's reporting year ends on December 31. Interest is paid quarterly.

The construction expenditures were as follows:

Date, 1991		Expenditure	Date, 1991		Expenditure
Jan. 1	Land	$ 20,000	April 30	Construction	$200,000
Jan. 31	Construction	70,000	May 31	Construction	170,000
Feb. 28	Construction	100,000	June 30	Construction	80,000
March 31	Construction	180,000			

Required:

1. Compute the amount of interest cost to be capitalized and expensed each quarter. Use the weighted-average method.

2. Give all journal entries related to construction and interest cost.

P 11–16

Capitalization of Interest: Weighted-Average Method

(L.O. 4)

Dobie Industries began construction of a new plant for its own use on January 1, 1991. During 1991, Dobie had the following debt outstanding:

Accounts payable (noninterest-bearing)	$ 80,000
Short-term note payable (14%)	500,000
Bonds payable (12%, issued at par)	1,300,000

On April 1, 1991, Dobie borrowed an additional $500,000 on a 14%, one-year construction note to finance the plant construction. Interest on all debt is paid at the end of each quarter. The average accumulated expenditures on construction for each quarter of 1991 have already been computed. Assume these amounts include the correct amounts of previously capitalized interest. The payments and average accumulated expenditures are as follows:

Quarter	Payments to Contractors	Average Accumulated Expenditures
First	$150,000	$150,000
Second	450,000	300,000
Third	750,000	675,000
Fourth	950,000	850,000

Required:

Dobie capitalizes interest using the weighted-average method (based on a weighted-average interest rate on all debt). Compute the amounts of interest to be capitalized and expensed for each quarter in 1991. Also, give the required entry in each quarter.

P 11–17

Capitalization of Interest: Specific Method

(L.O. 4)

The problem facts to use are exactly the same as those given in P 11–16.

Required:

Assume Dobie capitalizes interest using the specific method (first applying the interest rate on loans identified with self-construction, and then applying a weighted-average interest rate based on all other debt). Compute the amounts of interest to be capitalized and expensed for each quarter in 1991 and give the entry in each quarter.

P 11–18
Extraordinary and
Ordinary Repairs: Entries
(L.O. 7)

The plant asset records of Reston Company reflected the following at the beginning of 1991:

Plant building (residual value, $30,000; estimated
   useful life, 20 years) $150,000
Accumulated depreciation, plant building   90,000
Machinery (residual value, $35,000; estimated useful
   life, 10 years) 180,000
Accumulated depreciation, machinery   90,000

During the year ending December 31, 1991, the following transactions (summarized) relating to the above accounts were completed:

Extraordinary repairs   *a.* Expenditures for nonrecurring, relatively large repairs that tend to increase economic utility but not economic lives of assets:

    Plant building $45,000
    Machinery 15,000
b. Replacement of original electrical wiring system of plant building (original cost, $18,000) . . 29,000
c. Additions:
    Plant building—added small wing to plant building to accommodate new equipment
    acquired; wing has useful life of 18 years and no residual value 54,000
    Machinery—added special protection devices to 10 machines; devices are attached
    to the machines and will have to be replaced every five years (no residual value) 10,000

Revenue   *d.* Outlays for maintenance parts, labor, etc., to keep assets in normal working condition:
expenditure

Quarter	Plant Building	Machinery
1	$1,600	$ 1,900
2	1,800	6,100
3	1,600	1,000
4	2,000	10,000

Required:

1. Give appropriate entries to record transactions *(a)* through *(c)*. Explain the basis underlying your decisions.
2. In parallel columns, give the appropriate entries by quarter for the transactions in *(d)* under each of the following assumptions: (1) the accounting policy is to record all ordinary repairs as expense when incurred, and (2) the accounting policy requires use of the allocation approach. The annual budgeted amounts for repair and maintenance expense were plant building, $7,200, and machinery, $17,000.
3. Which approach used in (2) above do you prefer? Explain.

P 11–19
Disposal of Asset:
Addition, Depreciation,
Reporting
(L.O. 5)

Equipment that cost $18,000 on January 1, 1991, was sold for $10,000 on June 30, 1996. It had been depreciated over a 10-year life by the straight-line method, assuming its residual value would be $1,500.

A warehouse that cost $150,000, residual value $15,000, was being depreciated over 20 years by the straight-line method. When the structure was 15 years old, an additional wing was constructed at a cost of $90,000. The estimated life of the wing considered separately was 15 years, and its residual value is $10,000. The accounting period ends December 31.

Required:

1. Give all required entries to record:
  a. Sale of the equipment.
  b. The addition; cash was paid.
  c. Depreciation on the warehouse and its addition after the latter has been in use for one year.
2. Show how the building and attached wing would be reported on a balance sheet prepared immediately after entry (1c) was recorded.

P 11–20
Multiple Choice:
Exchanges of Operational
Assets
(L.O. 6)

Choose the correct answer for each of the following questions.

1. Silo Corporation owns an asset originally costing $75,000, with accumulated depreciation of $38,000. Its current market value is $38,000. Silo traded in this old asset and paid $4,500 for a similar asset. The new asset should be recorded at:
   a. $54,000.
   b. 41,500.
   c. 42,500.
   d. 40,500.

2. WNZ traded in its old textbook building (cost $350,000, accumulated depreciation $100,000) for a new building, whose market value is $180,000, and received $80,000 on the trade. The new building should be recorded at which of the following values, on WNZ's books?
   a. $173,077.
   b. 180,000.
   c. 100,000.
   d. 167,021.

3. Choose the correct statement concerning operational asset exchanges.
   a. Gains are not allowed on exchanges of similar assets for the corporation receiving cash since the value of the new asset is not objectively determinable.
   b. When boot is received on the exchange of a dissimilar asset, the full gain derived from debiting the new asset with its fair market value is recognized.
   c. Gains are allowed on all operational asset exchanges.
   d. Losses are not allowed on noncash exchanges of similar assets.

The following information relates to questions 4, 5, and 6, which are independent.

Original cost of an operational asset . . . . . . $10,000.
Accumulated depreciation on the asset . . . . .   6,000.
XOR Corporation is the owner of the asset.

4. The old asset is traded for a dissimilar new asset with a $12,000 fair market value. XOR paid $7,000 on the exchange. The new asset's recorded value is:
   a. $12,000.
   b. 11,000.
   c. 10,000.
   d. 13,000.

5. The old asset is traded for a similar new asset with a $12,000 fair market value. XOR paid $7,000 on the exchange. The new asset's recorded value is:
   a. $12,000.
   b. 11,000.
   c. 10,000.
   d. 13,000.

6. The old asset is traded for a new similar asset. XOR received $4,000 on the exchange. The fair market values of the assets are indeterminate but the new asset has a list price of $14,000. The new asset's recorded value is:
   a. $14,000.
   b. –0–.
   c. 3,111.
   d. 12,111.

P 11–21
Measuring Asset Cost:
Overview
(L.O. 1, 2, 7)

The accounts of Pall Corporation had never been audited prior to 1994. In auditing the books for the year ended December 31, 1994, the auditor found the following account for the plant:

Plant and Equipment

1991:		1991:	
Plant purchased	$90,000	Sale of scrap	$ 300
Repairs	5,300	Depreciation (6%)	6,000
Legal	600	1992:	
Title fees	50	Depreciation (6%)	8,040
Insurance	3,000	1993:	
Taxes	1,200	Cash proceeds from	
1992:		old machine	1,150
Addition to plant	15,000	Depreciation (6%)	8,160
Write-up	20,000	1994:	
Interest cost related		Depreciation (6.4%)	8,520
to the plant addition	1,500		
Repairs	500		
Machinery for new addition	2,000		
1993:			
New machine	3,000		
Installation	600		
1994:			
Machinery overhaul	1,350		
Replaced roof	900		
Fence	2,000		

(Balance, $114,830)

Additional data relating to plant and equipment developed during the audit are as follows:

a. The plant was purchased during January 1991. At that time, the tax assessment listed the plant as follows: plant site, $10,000; building, $20,000; and machinery therein, $30,000. The estimated life of the plant and machinery was 20 years.

b. During the first six months of 1991, the company expended the amounts listed in the account for the year to get the plant ready for operation; operations began July 1. The repairs relate to both the building and machinery; no detail was available. The legal fees related to the plant purchase and to all aspects of it. The $3,000 insurance premium was for a one-year policy on the plant and equipment, dated January 1, 1991 ($1,000 of the premium applied to the machinery). The property tax rate for the year was 2%. The scrap was accumulated during the repair period.

c. In 1992, a plant addition was completed for $15,000, at which time the company was paying 10% on some borrowed funds. The addition, which was not self-constructed, was under construction for four months. During the year, $1,500 was spent for ordinary repairs, of which one third was capitalized. Machinery that cost $2,000 was purchased. The asset account was written up by $20,000 to bring it in line with the bank's security allowance on loans (contributed capital was credited).

d. During 1993, a new machine was purchased (July 1) for $3,000 plus installation costs of $600. An old machine that cost $2,100 was sold for $1,150. The old machine was acquired when the plant was acquired.

e. During 1994, several items of equipment were completely reconditioned at a cost of $1,350. Minor repairs were debited to expense during the year. The roof was replaced on one wing of the plant. A fence was constructed around the plant to keep unauthorized personnel out; it is estimated that the fence will have 10 years of remaining life.

Required:

1. Set up a spreadsheet to compute the correct balances for the following accounts (suggested columnar captions): land, buildings, machinery, and land improvements. (The company follows a policy of recording 6% straight-line depreciation on ending balances except for land improvements. Assume residual values are zero for all depreciable assets, and round amounts to nearest dollar.) Use a separate schedule to compute the balances for accumulated depreciation. Justify any assumptions that you make.

2. Give one compound entry to correct the accounts assuming the accounts have already been closed for 1994. Ignore income tax effects.

P 11-22

COMPREHENSIVE PROBLEM
◆

Self-Constructed Asset
and Interest Capitalization
(L.O. 1, 2, 3, 4)

Mannheim Company begins construction of a factory facility on January 4, 1991. Mannheim uses its own employees and subcontractors to complete the facility. The following list provides information relevant to the construction. The facility is completed December 27, 1991.

a. At the beginning of January, Mannheim obtains construction financing: a 10%, $12,000,000 loan with principal payable at the end of construction provides significant financing for the project. Interest on the loan is payable semiannually. Mannheim pays the interest and principal when due.

b. Mannheim also has (1) $40,000,000 of 12% bonds payable issued at face value in 1983, which pay interest every June 30 and December 31, and (2) an 11%, $20,000,000 note paying interest every December 31, outstanding the entire year.

c. Mannheim owns the land site (cost, $4,000,000). In January, a subcontractor is employed to raze the old building (cost, $800,000; accumulated depreciation, $600,000) on the site for $80,000. Mannheim received $10,000 from salvaged materials.

d. Also in January, subcontractors survey, grade, and prepare the land for construction at a cost of $200,000 and excavate the foundation of the new facility for $1,000,000.

e. In January, a subcontractor poured and finished the foundation for $1,500,000. This is financed separately through a one-year, 9% loan. Mannheim secured the financing at the beginning of January. The principal and interest were paid on December 30.

f. The total material cost for construction excluding other items in this list is $8,000,000.

g. Payments to subcontractors excluding others in this list amount to $2,000,000.

h. Payments to Mannheim employees for work on construction are $16,000,000.

i. In October, a subcontractor constructed a parking lot and fences for $300,000.

j. Incidental fees and other costs associated with facility construction were $150,000.

k. The market value of the building upon completion is $25,000,000.

l. For purposes of interest capitalization, Mannheim assumes an even distribution of cash payments for all construction costs throughout the year and capitalizes interest once per year as an adjusting entry. The specific method is used. Construction costs are accumulated in Mannheim's facility under construction account.

Required:

Provide general journal entries to account for all aspects of construction and related events during 1991. Your entries should lead to the correct total cost to record for the building. You may record the events in any order you feel is easiest for you.

CASES

C 11-1
Acquisition Cost:
Expenditures Subsequent
to Acquisition
(L.O. 1, 2, 7)

Assume that the market value of equipment acquired in a noncash transaction is not determinable by reference to a cash purchase.

Required:

1. Explain how the acquiring company should determine the capitalizable cost of equipment obtained through each of the following exchanges:
   a. Bonds that have an established market price.
   b. Common stock that does not have an established market price.
   c. Similar equipment that has a determinable market price.
2. Assume that the equipment was acquired and had been used by the acquiring company for three years. Expenditures related to the equipment must be made. Identify the various types of expenditures that might be involved and explain the appropriate accounting for each.

(AICPA adapted.)

C 11-2
Court Settlement:
Capitalize versus Expense
(L.O. 1)

Consolidated Smelting Company, which operates in the Southwest, agreed in a court settlement to:

a. Install pollution control equipment on its smelters at an estimated cost of $18 million.

b. Pay specified medical expenses for children livng near its facilities who were suffering from lead poisoning; tentatively estimated cost of $2 million to be paid as families incur expenses.

c. Pay the city and state a civil penalty of $200,000 over a four-year term in equal $50,000 installments.

Required:
1. For each item above, discuss the propriety of capitalizing versus expensing the cost.
2. What amount should be attributed to each item immediately after the settlement (before any payments are made)?

C 11–3
Asset Cost: Related Incidental Costs
(L.O. 1)

The invoice price of a machine is $20,000. Various other costs relating to the acquisition and installation of the machine amount to $5,000 and include such things as transportation, electrical wiring, special base, and so forth. The machine has an estimated life of 10 years and no residual value.

The owner of the business suggests that the incidental costs of $5,000 be debited to expense immediately for three reasons: (1) if the machine should be sold, these costs could not be recovered in the sales price; (2) the inclusion of the $5,000 in the machinery account will not necessarily result in a closer approximation of the market price of this asset over the years because of the possibility of changing price levels; and (3) debiting the $5,000 to expense immediately will reduce federal income taxes.

Required:
Discuss each of the points raised by the owner of the business.

(AICPA adapted)

C 11–4
Asset Cost: After Acquisition but before Use
(L.O. 1)

One of your clients, a savings bank with several local branches, recently acquired ownership of a lot and building located in a historical part of the city. The building was in a dilapidated condition, unsuitable for human habitation. The bank thought at the time that it was acquiring a site for a new branch. Although a firm of architects recommended demolition, the city council, in whose discretion such activity rests, refused consent to demolish the building in view of its historical and architectural value.

In order to comply with safety requirements and to make the building suitable for use as a branch location, the bank spent $250,000 restoring and altering the old building. It had paid $90,000 for the building and lot and had contemplated spending $200,000 on a new building after demolishing the old structure. Somewhat similar old buildings in less run-down condition could have been bought in the same area for about the same $90,000 price. It is possible, even likely, that some of these that were not so old could have been demolished without governmental intervention, and the bank could have carried out its original plan.

Now that the restoration has been completed and the bank is making final plans to open its newest branch in the restored building, the bank has been informed by the State Historical Commission that the building qualifies for and will receive a plaque designating it as a historical site. The designation will be of some value in attracting traffic to the site, probably will result in the building being pointed out when tours of the city visit the area, and so on. Under present laws, receipt of the designation may well mean that the bank can never demolish the structure and is obligated to preserve it, even if the property is later vacated.

Required:
1. Discuss the pros and cons of capitalizing the entire $250,000 spent on restoration of the building.
2. How should the $90,000 original expenditure be treated? What would have been the cost of the land if the bank had been able to carry out its original plans?
3. Sooner or later, your client is likely to seek advice as to proper accounting for subsequent costs—repairs, depreciation, possible improvements, and so on. What advice would you give?

C 11–5
Interest Capitalization: Rationale and Discussion
(L.O. 4)

Two competing publicly held firms in the same city, Infosystems Company and Data Capability Company, built very similar buildings in the same year. Both buildings were built at a hard-dollar cost of approximately $30,000,000. This amount included material, labor, and other incremental input costs. The common stock (voting ownership shares) of both companies is traded on the same stock exchange.

Infosystems, which has been in business several decades has very little debt. Consequently, according to *SFAS No. 34*, it capitalized only $2,000,000 of interest, bringing the total cost of its building to $32,000,000. Data Capability, a relatively new company, is highly leveraged and was required to capitalize $12,000,000 of interest, bringing its building cost up to $42,000,000.

Required:

Discuss the rationale for interest capitalization in the context of these two companies. Include in your discussion reasons for and against interest capitalization, the matching principle, and the *SFAC No. 6* definition of an asset.

C 11–6
Ethical Considerations
(L.O. 1, 4, 5, 7)

Robert Baker, accountant for Miller Motor Company, is aware that the rules for interest capitalization are relatively flexible. He understands that either the specific or weighted-average method may be used to compute interest potentially capitalizable (IPC). He also understands that either a continuous expenditure assumption (construction payments are assumed to be evenly distributed throughout the construction period) or a discrete assumption (each payment receives a weight based on the time it is invested in the project) may be used.

Bob was recently congratulated on his choice of accounting methods at the annual holiday dinner held for management and top level staff. Among his choices were FIFO for inventories, straight-line depreciation, and long useful lives for operational assets. Bob, without informing management, also consistently employs the IPC calculation method which capitalizes the greatest amount of interest. When current interest rates are high and specific construction debt balances are high, he chooses the specific method. When interest rates moderate, particularly after a period of relatively high general interest rates, he goes back to the weighted average method.

He also times payments to contractors, through his influence over the accounts payable department, so that significant payments are made near the end of the year. He then uses the continuous expenditure assumption to measure average accumulated expenditures.

Required:

Discuss the propriety of Bob's accounting methods. Why might they have been chosen? Do you think that any ethical considerations are relevant to the case?

C 11–7
Sherwin-Williams:
Analysis of Actual
Financial Statements
(L.O. 1, 2)

Refer to the 1990 financial statements of Sherwin-Williams (included at the end of the book) and respond to the following questions. You may use more than one year's results in your answer.

1. Has there been a significant change in the composition of total property, plant and equipment from 1988 through 1990? Consider the percentage of gross component cost to total gross property, plant, and equipment.
2. Has Sherwin-Williams increased or decreased its capital expenditures (expenditures on property, plant, and equipment) from 1988 through 1990?
3. Were capital expenditures paid completely in cash for the years 1988 through 1990?
4. Explain the change, net of accumulated depreciation, in property, plant, and equipment from 1989 to 1990.

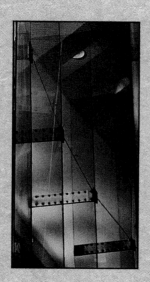

Operational Assets: Depreciation and Impairment

After you have studied this chapter, you will:

1. Understand the nature of and factors affecting depreciation.

2. Be able to apply several depreciation methods and understand the incentives for choosing among them.

3. Appreciate the relationship between depreciation, taxes, cash flows, and dividends.

4. Know how to calculate and account for fractional year depreciation and depreciation of post-acquisition costs.

5. Be familiar with the basic principles of accounting for changes in depreciation estimates and methods, and for depreciation errors.

6. Recognize the circumstances under which special depreciation systems are used and how to apply them.

7. Be aware of the current lack of guidelines for reporting asset impairments and the implications for financial statements.

8. Be familiar with tax regulations as they relate to depreciation. (Refer to Appendix 12A.)

9. Acquire a basic understanding of accounting for casualty losses. (Refer to Appendix 12B.)

◆

INTRODUCTION
◆

American Telephone & Telegraph Company (AT&T) reported $3.69 billion in depreciation expense in 1988, a year in which the company sustained a loss of $1.67 billion. Despite this loss, AT&T's net cash flow from operations was $4.75 billion. How is it possible for a company to report a net loss, yet enjoy a healthy cash flow? Depreciation comes to mind first as an explanation. What is the nature of this expense? Is it the portion of plant assets consumed during each accounting period? Or does it have another meaning?

AT&T uses several different methods of depreciation. General Motors Corporation primarily employs accelerated methods that recognize decreasing depreciation amounts as assets age. Why are different methods allowed? And how can readers of financial statements compare income figures across companies?

In a matter akin to depreciation, General Motors announced a $2.1 billion special charge against 1990 earnings to cover plant closings and other losses. Although some plant closings were not planned until 1992, GM recognized the huge loss in 1990 "to clear the way for greater profits in the future."[1] What portion of this loss resulted from events occurring before 1990? Was the loss caused by discrete events or by a gradual deterioration of asset values? Were depreciation estimates insufficient in the past?

These issues and situations serve as a preview of the major topics covered in this chapter. Chapter 11 described the characteristics of plant assets and their valuation and disposition, focusing on accounting events that *increase* plant asset carrying values. In contrast, Chapter 12 focuses on depreciation and asset impairments that *decrease* plant asset carrying values.

◆

DEPRECIATION CONCEPTS
◆

Terminology

The attribute common to all operational assets is their revenue-producing potential through use rather than through resale. Operational assets can be viewed as quantities of economic service potential to be consumed over time in the earning of revenues. The costs of the three types of operational assets (plant assets, natural resources, and intangibles) are matched against revenue over their useful lives. The accounting terminology for the three related expenses is:

1. *Depreciation*—the accounting process of allocating the periodic expiration of the cost of *plant assets* against the periodic revenue earned.
2. *Depletion*—the accounting process of allocating the periodic expiration of the cost of *natural resources,* (such as mineral deposits and timber) against the periodic revenue earned (discussed in Chapter 13).
3. *Amortization*—the accounting process of allocating the periodic expiration of *intangible assets,* (represented by special rights or benefits, including patents, copyrights, and goodwill) against the periodic revenue earned (discussed in Chapter 13). Amortization is a general term often applied to accounts in other areas, including discounts and premiums on bonds.

These three terms refer to the same process of cost allocation, but they apply to different asset categories. The process of recognizing depreciation transfers a por-

---

[1] "Huge GM Write-Off Positions Auto Maker To Show New Growth," *The Wall Street Journal,* November 1, 1990, p. A1.

tion of the acquisition cost and capitalized post-acquisition cost of plant assets to an expense account—*depreciation expense*.[2] The following journal entry recognizes $12,000 of depreciation cost and expense for a nonmanufacturing firm:

To record depreciation expense:

Depreciation expense	12,000	
Accumulated depreciation		12,000

Depreciation expense is generally recorded in an adjusting entry at the end of interim and annual reporting periods. Depreciation expense for a nonmanufacturing company is classified as a selling or administrative expense, depending on the asset's function.

The accumulated depreciation account is a contra plant asset account that reduces gross plant assets to net undepreciated plant assets (book value). This account appears in the balance sheet parenthetically or as a line item deduction from gross property, plant, and equipment. Occasionally the value is disclosed in a footnote. Mattel, Inc., disclosed accumulated depreciation as a line item in its 1989 balance sheet:

	1989 ($000)
Property, plant, and equipment:	
Land	$ 5,812
Buildings	46,490
Machinery and equipment	72,513
Capitalized leases	39,425
Leasehold improvements	19,068
Less *accumulated depreciation*	(55,496)
	127,812
Tools, dies, and molds, less amortization	37,053
Property, plant, and equipment, net	$164,865

Rather than directly reducing the related asset account, the contra plant asset account is used to separate the asset's original cost and the amount of depreciation to date. One reason for maintaining separate asset and related accumulated depreciation accounts is to preserve the historical cost of the asset, especially if the asset's life expectancy changes or if changes in depreciation method are made. Another reason is to support internal control procedures for plant assets. Accumulated depreciation records often are maintained in a subsidiary ledger for each major asset owned, but only aggregate amounts are reported in the balance sheet.

Accumulated depreciation does not represent cash set aside for the replacement of plant assets, nor does depreciation recognition imply the creation of reserves for asset replacement. Most firms do not specifically reserve cash for replacement of plant assets.

The *book value* (carrying value) of an asset is its original cost plus any capitalized post-acquisition cost less accumulated depreciation to date. **Depreciable cost** is the total amount of depreciation recognized over the useful life of the asset and equals original cost plus capitalized post-acquisition cost less estimated residual value (salvage value). The estimated residual value is the amount expected to be realized on disposal at the end of the asset's useful life. Several methods are discussed in this chapter which apply a depreciation rate to depreciable cost to determine periodic depreciation expense.

---

[2] Companies that manufacture goods include depreciation on plant assets used in manufacturing in the cost of goods produced. When the goods are sold, the depreciation becomes part of cost of goods sold. Managerial accounting courses discuss issues in depreciation accounting for manufacturing firms.

Nature of Depreciation

For many businesses, depreciation is one of the largest expenses and frequently exceeds net income. For example, General Motors Corporation earned $4.86 billion in 1988 and reported over $5 billion of depreciation. Few areas of accounting offer greater variety of practice and choice of specific accounting treatment. The sheer size of the expense for most companies increases the implications of this flexibility.

A new automobile is said to depreciate by several thousand dollars once it leaves the dealer's premises. However, the meaning of the term *depreciation* as used in accounting is different from this common usage of the term. The accounting profession defines depreciation accounting for financial reporting purposes as

> a system of accounting which aims to distribute the cost or other basic value of tangible capital assets, less salvage value (if any), over the estimated useful life of the unit (which may be a group of assets) in a *systematic and rational* manner. *It is a process of allocation, not of valuation. (ARB No. 43,* Chapter 9C, par. 5; emphasis added)

The term *systematic and rational* implies that depreciation methods should be both precisely specified, rather than haphazard or arbitrary, and defensible on the grounds that the result follows logically from the asset's use.

For financial reporting purposes, the cost of property, plant, and equipment can be thought of as a long-term prepayment of an expense. The cost is recorded as an asset because the physical unit represents a quantity of future economic service potential. A portion of the cost is assumed to benefit each period of use. Although the actual amount of the cost relating to any specific period cannot be known with certainty, depreciation expense is the systematically determined amount recognized for this purpose.

The depreciation process does not revalue the asset at the end of a reporting period. Gradual market value changes are not recorded in the plant asset accounts, and the book value of a plant asset typically does not equal its market value. Depreciation is not a valuation process. To understand this concept better, refer to Grange Company's 1991 balance sheet in Exhibit 12–1.

Although the two accounts portrayed in Grange's partial balance sheet yield identical book values, they have quite different interpretations. The net accounts receivable is an estimate of net realizable value, the cash reasonably expected to be collected from Grange's receivables. The net book value of the building account, however, represents only the undepreciated acquisition cost at the end of 1991. The realizable value or replacement cost of the building is most likely some other amount.

Periodic market value changes are not a sufficiently reliable or objective basis for depreciation accounting, and they are not supported by arm's-length transactions. The *historical cost* principle supports the objective original cost as the depreciation base. Furthermore, the *conservatism* constraint prohibits recording a market value increase in the absence of a transaction supporting the increased value.

Causes of Depreciation   The decline in usefulness or useful life of plant assets is caused by physical factors (including wear and tear from operations, action of time and the elements, and deterioration and decay) and obsolescence. Obsolescence normally comes about as the result of new technology making older assets less efficient and therefore more expensive to operate. Obsolescence also occurs when facility expansion renders certain assets unusable under new operating conditions, or when demand for the product or service supplied by the asset declines. Assets rendered obsolete are typically in good condition and still capable of supplying the service originally expected of it. Depreciation accounting considers all predictable factors that limit the usefulness and useful life of plant assets.

Technological change does not automatically render older equipment obsolete, however. If the older equipment fills the present needs of the company, obsoles-

EXHIBIT 12-1

GRANGE COMPANY
Partial Balance Sheet Information
December 31, 1991

Assets:

Accounts receivable	$200,000	
Less allowance for doubtful accounts	(20,000)	
Net accounts receivable		$180,000
Buildings	$200,000	
Less accumulated depreciation	(20,000)	
Net buildings, at book value		$180,000

cence is not necessarily a factor. For example, in the microcomputer industry, new computer chips are frequently developed that substantially increase computer speeds and capabilities. The development of the 386 chip eclipsed the 286 chip, for example. However, PCs built around the 286 chip continued to be in widespread use, fully supported by software and maintenance agreements. For many companies, changing to more expensive 386 chip-based computers was not immediately cost-effective.[3]

The useful life of plant assets also is influenced by the repair and maintenance policies of the company. Inadequate maintenance is a short-run cost saving strategy that can result in higher future cost and can contribute to a premature revision of useful life.

Assets under construction or otherwise not yet placed into service are not depreciated. Such assets are not generating benefits; therefore, their acquisition cost is not matched against current revenue.

When facilities are temporarily idle or held pending future use, the recognition of depreciation continues because the physical and functional causes, which tend to reduce the ultimate economic usefulness of the asset to the company, continue. Plant assets taken out of service are reduced to their estimated net realizable value in anticipation of disposal. This write-down is recorded as a loss rather than as part of depreciation expense.

Depreciation expense is not recognized for sudden and unexpected factors such as damage from natural phenomena, sudden changes in demand, or radical misuse of assets that impair their revenue-generating ability. For example, a loss is recognized to account for fire damage to a building. The asset is written down by the amount of the loss immediately rather than gradually depreciated. Asset impairments are not recorded as depreciation expense.

Factors in Determining Depreciation Expense

The following four factors are used in determining depreciation expense for a period:

1. Acquisition cost and capitalized post-acquisition costs (defined in Chapter 11).
2. Estimated residual value.
3. Estimated useful life.
4. Method of depreciation.

Generally, *acquisition cost* is the most definite of the four factors. However, as discussed in Chapter 11, complete agreement is lacking on certain inclusions to plant

---

[3] *Tax and Business Adviser,* Grant, Thornton, vol. 1, no. 9, September 1989, p. 5.

assets. For example, landscaping is included in land or land improvements, depending on the permanence of the landscaping and the firm's capitalization policy. Also, flexibility exists with respect to interest capitalization. Furthermore, there are different approaches to the treatment of post-acquisition costs, which affect the depreciation base.

The *residual value* is the estimated net recoverable amount from disposal or trade-in of the asset. Residual value is not derived from using an asset but, rather, is the portion of an asset's acquisition cost not consumed through use. Therefore, residual value is not matched against revenues through depreciation.

To estimate residual value, allowance is made for the costs of dismantling, restoring, and disposing of the retired asset. For example, if the estimated realizable value upon retirement of an asset is $2,500 and estimated dismantling and selling costs are $500, the residual value is $2,000. Net residual value is negative if disposal costs exceed the expected proceeds from sale of the asset. Using the same example, if estimated dismantling and selling costs are $3,000, residual value is −$500. When negative, residual value increases the asset's depreciable cost.

In practice, residual values often are ignored. This is acceptable when the recovery proceeds and disposal costs are expected to offset, or when the amounts involved are immaterial. Moreover, because residual value is estimated years in advance, its present value is often immaterial. However, if a firm expects to retire an asset relatively early in its useful life, a substantial residual value can be involved.[4]

The *useful life* (economic life) generally has a greater impact on depreciation than estimated residual value. The useful life of an asset must be finite to justify depreciation recognition. Land is not depreciated, for example, because its useful life is considered indefinite. Estimates of useful life require assumptions about potential obsolescence, severity of use, and maintenance.

Useful life is measured in terms of definite time periods such as total months or years, total units of output, or total hours of operating time. Where possible, the measurement standard depends on the nature of the asset involved and the primary causes of its depreciation. For example, assume a delivery truck has an estimated useful life of five years or 200,000 miles. Depreciation based on miles driven might more accurately reflect the truck's use and yield a more accurate matching of expense and revenue than would depreciation based on useful life in years.

In certain regulated industries, companies must maintain equipment in superior condition for public safety reasons. There are no definite guidelines for useful life in the airline industry, for example, because airline firms must maintain their planes as long as they are used. Economic considerations govern the choice of useful life, and lead to different decisions by the firms in this industry.[5]

Useful life can affect earnings significantly. Longer useful lives lower the annual depreciation charges and result in higher net income. In the past, General Motors used more conservative practices for depreciating manufacturing equipment than its major competitors. As a rule, GM's useful lives were one half those of Ford's, and one third Chrysler's.[6] In 1987, GM increased the useful lives of plant assets to be more consistent with its competitors, thus increasing earnings. GM Chairman Roger Smith remarked: "All GM is trying to do is get to the middle of accounting practices."[7]

---

[4] Residual value can affect a taxpayer's depreciation deduction. For example, a musician attempted to depreciate a 1736 Stradivarius violin over 12 years for tax purposes. The taxpayer was denied the deduction because the value of the instrument was expected to rise rather than fall. See "Tax Report," *The Wall Street Journal*, July 13, 1988, p. A1.

[5] "The Wild Blue Yonder," *Forbes*, November 9, 1981, p. 94.

[6] Therefore, GM would depreciate plant assets more rapidly. This was a more conservative practice because it produced lower earnings than would otherwise be the case.

[7] "Fiddling with Figures While Sales Drop," *Forbes*, August 24, 1987, p. 32.

Among the four factors affecting depreciation computations, the *method of depreciation* chosen usually has the greatest effect on periodic depreciation expense. Several methods are allowed. Under the matching principle, periodic depreciation expense reflects an allocation of the depreciable cost of the asset proportional to the periodic benefits received from the asset.

However, depreciation expense is typically not equal to the decline in market value of the asset for the period, nor is it equal to the portion of original cost (or asset utility) consumed in the period. Depreciation is usually some other value because of these considerations:

* Market value changes are ignored in the depreciation process.
* The portion of original cost consumed in a period is not observable and cannot be directly measured.
* GAAP does not strictly require that the choice of depreciation method be based on the pattern of benefits derived from the asset, the pattern of its use, or its decline in usefulness or value.
* The amount of revenue or cash produced by a plant asset's use is usually impossible to determine unequivocally.[8]

The systematic and rational requirement, as stated in *ARB No. 43*, does not place many constraints on depreciation policy. The selection from among the various depreciation methods is a free choice. Depreciation, as measured and reported in practice, is related only incidentally to aging or deterioration. As such, depreciation expense is not really an estimate of any particular value or measure.

Depreciation for Tax Purposes   Businesses must report depreciation for both financial accounting and tax purposes. The methods used and results obtained for these two systems of reporting are generally not the same. Although this chapter is primarily concerned with financial reporting, the tax law requirements regarding depreciation can affect depreciation policy for financial accounting. The tax law specifies the amount of depreciation deductible for tax purposes.[9] This amount is often different from depreciation expense recognized for income statement purposes.

GAAP and the tax law have different objectives. GAAP is concerned with expense recognition and reporting, while the tax law is concerned with the depreciation deduction allowance.[10] The theoretical objective guiding GAAP in the depreciation area is to achieve the best matching of depreciation expense and the benefits (revenues) the asset helped to produce.

In contrast, the tax law is not concerned with matching expenses and revenues. The tax law offers an incentive for firms to replace and expand plant asset holdings by allowing **accelerated depreciation.** Under accelerated depreciation methods, a firm is allowed to deduct greater amounts of depreciation from taxable revenues in early years, and less in later years. This is a tax advantage because the firm obtains greater tax savings, and therefore has use of more after-tax dollars earlier in the asset's life. The present value of these tax savings exceeds those generated under a constant amount of annual depreciation. Some of the basic guidelines for depreciation accounting under the tax law are discussed in Appendix 12A.

---

[8] A. Thomas, in "The FASB and the Allocation Fallacy," *Journal of Accountancy,* November 1975, p. 66, argues that all allocations of the costs of assets that interact are inherently arbitrary. Revenues are not generated by assets used in isolation. Rather, they are produced by a number of assets and people working together. Therefore, it is impossible to associate specific revenues (benefits) to specific assets, making it impossible to allocate the cost of most operational assets on the basis of benefits or revenues produced.

[9] A deductible amount reduces taxable income, the amount upon which the tax rate is applied to determine the tax liability. Deductions are analogous to expenses in financial accounting in that both reduce income in their respective reporting systems.

[10] The tax law's primary objective is to raise revenue for governmental expenditures. It is also used to encourage economic activity deemed important. For example, a special deduction is allowed many businesses engaged in oil exploration.

CONCEPT REVIEW

1. What are the main causes of the decline in value or usefulness of plant assets over time?
2. Why is depreciation expense not necessarily an accurate measure of the decline in value of plant assets?
3. What is the conceptual difference between the amounts reported as accumulated depreciation for plant assets and the allowance for doubtful accounts?

DEPRECIATION METHODS

◆

Depreciation measurement procedures are classified as depreciation methods and depreciation systems. Depreciation methods typically are applied individually to assets, while depreciation systems are applied to classes of assets. Fixed asset software packages streamline the process of calculating, recording, and posting depreciation in the accounts for both methods and systems. The aggregate nature of depreciation systems serves to lower accounting information system costs in certain instances. The individually applied depreciation methods and related concepts are discussed before proceeding to depreciation systems. Exhibit 12–2 lists the methods discussed in this chapter.

Assets are not depreciated below residual value under any method. Therefore, the minimum book value is residual value. However, declining balance methods do not employ residual value in calculating periodic depreciation expense. For this reason a determination is made at the end of each accounting period to ensure that book value is at least equal to residual value.

Exhibit 12–3 presents information for a hypothetical plant asset used to illustrate five of the depreciation methods applied on an individual basis.

Straight-Line Method

The straight-line (SL) method is based on the assumption that a plant asset declines in usefulness at a constant rate over time. The SL method relates depreciation directly to the passage of time rather than to the asset's use, resulting in a constant amount of depreciation recognized per time period. The formula for computing periodic SL depreciation, with its application to the asset in Exhibit 12–3, is:

$$\text{Annual SL depreciation} = \frac{\text{Acquisition cost} - \text{Residual value}}{\text{Estimated useful life in years}}$$

$$= (\$6{,}600 - \$600)/5 = \$1{,}200 \text{ per year}$$

SL depreciation frequently is expressed in terms of a percentage rate. The annual SL rate is the ratio of annual depreciation expense to depreciable cost. This rate is constant over the life of the asset and represents the percentage of depreciable cost recognized as depreciation per period. The Exhibit 12–3 asset has a 20% SL rate ($1,200/$6,000). Each year, 20% of depreciable cost is recognized as depreciation. This rate also equals the reciprocal of useful life, or 1/5 (20%). Once the rate is known, it can be applied to the depreciable cost to determine the $1,200 annual SL depreciation (.20 × $6,000). Exhibit 12–4 illustrates the SL method over the useful life of the asset described in Exhibit 12–3.

The use of the SL method allows financial statement readers to estimate the proportion of original service life of plant assets remaining at a balance sheet date. For example, the asset in Exhibit 12–4 has a book value of $4,200 at December 31, 1992. The ratio $4,200/6,600 (64%) is an estimate of the portion of useful life

EXHIBIT 12-2 Classification of Depreciation Methods and Systems

I. Depreciation Methods.
    A. Based on equal allocation to each time period—the straight-line (SL) method.
    B. Based on inputs and outputs.
        1. Service hours method (SH).
        2. Productive output (PO), or units-of-production, method.
    C. Accelerated methods.
        1. Sum-of-the-years'-digits (SYD) method.
        2. Declining-balance methods (DB).
    D. Present value-based methods.

II. Depreciation systems.
    A. Inventory appraisal system.
    B. Group and composite systems.
    C. Retirement and replacement systems.

EXHIBIT 12-3 Data Used to Illustrate Depreciation Methods

Item	Illustrative Amount
Acquisition cost, January 1, 1991	$ 6,600
Residual value	600
Estimated useful life:	
Years	5
Service hours	20,000
Productive output in units	10,000

EXHIBIT 12-4 Depreciation Schedule—Straight-Line Method

Year	Depreciation Expense (Debit)	Accumulated Depreciation (Credit)	Balance, Accumulated Depreciation	Undepreciated Asset Balance (Book Value)
January 1, 1991				$6,600
December 31, 1991	$1,200	$1,200	$1,200	5,400
December 31, 1992	1,200	1,200	2,400	4,200
December 31, 1993	1,200	1,200	3,600	3,000
December 31, 1994	1,200	1,200	4,800	1,800
December 31, 1995	1,200	1,200	6,000	600 (residual value)
Total	$6,000	$6,000		

remaining at that date. The actual portion of useful life remaining is 60% (3 years/ 5 years); the difference is caused by the residual value.

Evaluation The SL method is logically appealing as well as systematic and rational. It is particularly appropriate when the decline in service potential of the asset is approximately the same each period, the use of the asset is essentially the same each period, and repairs and maintenance expenditures are constant over the useful life. The method is not conceptually appropriate for assets whose decline in service potential or benefits produced does not relate to the passage of time, but rather to other variables such as units produced or hours in service. The SL method also is inappropriate when obsolescence is the primary factor in depreciation.

The SL method is the most popular method in use (see Exhibit 12–9). Of 600 firms surveyed by the AICPA in 1990, 562 used this method (although the SL method is not the only method used by some of these firms). Expedience and relative low cost partially explain the method's popularity. In addition, SL depreciation results in the highest long-run earnings levels among the methods for growth firms. This income effect is attractive to managers whose compensation packages and promotions are tied to the firm's earnings performance.

Methods Based on Inputs and Outputs

Service Hours Method   The service hours method (SH) assumes that the decrease in useful life of a plant asset is directly related to the amount of time the asset is used. The useful life of the asset in terms of total service or working hours is estimated. The depreciation rate per service hour is the ratio of depreciable cost to total estimated working hours. Periodic depreciation expense is then found by multiplying the hours used during the period by the depreciation rate. This method generally results in a varying amount of depreciation expense per period, depending on the extent of asset use.

The formula for computing the depreciation rate and amount under the SH method is:

$$\frac{\text{Depreciation rate}}{\text{per service hour}} = \frac{\text{Acquisition cost } - \text{ Residual value}}{\text{Estimated service life in hours}}$$

$$= \frac{\$6,600 - \$600}{20,000} = \$.30 \text{ per service hour}$$

$$\frac{\text{Annual service hours}}{\text{method depreciation}} = \frac{\text{Depreciation rate}}{\text{per service hour}} \times \frac{\text{Service hours}}{\text{used during year}}$$

$$1991 \text{ depreciation amount} = \$.30(3,800) = \$1,140$$

(Calculation assumes 3,800 actual hours of running time in 1991.)

Exhibit 12–5 illustrates the service hours method over the life of the asset described in Exhibit 12–3, assuming an estimated and actual life of 20,000 hours.

Evaluation   The SH method is systematic and rational. The SH method also produces a logical matching of expense and revenue if the asset's service potential can be measured reliably in terms of service time. One conceptual problem with this method is that running time is not necessarily associated with productive output or benefits to the firm. For example, the increasingly heavy traffic in urban areas such as the Los Angeles basin causes vehicles to run many more hours per week without any increase in their productive output (miles driven).

The SH method usually is inappropriate if obsolescence is the primary factor in depreciation. Furthermore, for many assets such as buildings, furniture, and office equipment, applying the SH method is impracticable, if not impossible. These assets do not have a definite total running time, and service hours are difficult to estimate. In contrast, the SH method is appropriate for assets such as railroad rolling stock, delivery vehicles, and oil-drilling equipment.

Productive Output Method   The productive output (PO) and SH methods are the same except for the underlying variable used to measure asset use. The PO output method assumes that the decrease in useful life of a plant asset is determined primarily by the number of units of output produced rather than by service time. A constant amount

EXHIBIT 12-5 Depreciation Schedule—Service Hours Method

Year	Service Hours Worked	Depreciation Expense (Debit)	Accumulated Depreciation (Credit)	Balance, Accumulated Depreciation	Undepreciated Asset Balance (Book Value)
January 1, 1991					$6,600
December 31, 1991	3,800	(3,800 × $.30) = $1,140	$1,140	$1,140	5,460
December 31, 1992	4,000	(4,000 × $.30) = 1,200	1,200	2,340	4,260
December 31, 1993	4,500	(4,500 × $.30) = 1,350	1,350	3,690	2,910
December 31, 1994	4,200	(4,200 × $.30) = 1,260	1,260	4,950	1,650
December 31, 1995	3,500	(3,500 × $.30) = 1,050	1,050	6,000	600 (residual
Total	20,000	$6,000	$6,000		value)

of depreciable cost is allocated to each unit of output as a cost of production. Consequently, depreciation amounts fluctuate with changes in the volume of output.

The formula for computing the depreciation rate and amount under the PO method is:

$$\text{Depreciation rate per unit of output} = \frac{\text{Acquisition cost} - \text{Residual value}}{\text{Estimated productive output in units}}$$

$$= \frac{\$6,600 - \$600}{10,000} = \$.60 \text{ per unit of output}$$

$$\text{Annual productive output method depreciation} = \frac{\text{Depreciation rate}}{\text{per unit of output}} \times \frac{\text{units produced}}{\text{during year}}$$

$$\text{1991 depreciation amount} = \$.60(1,800) = \$1,080$$

(Calculation assumes 1,800 units produced in 1991.)

Exhibit 12–6 illustrates the productive output method over the life of the asset described in Exhibit 12–3, assuming an estimated and actual productive output of 10,000 units.

Evaluation The PO method is particularly appealing when actual output can be measured reliably, the useful life in units of output can be estimated reliably, obsolescence is not a major factor, and the useful life of the asset is directly related to production in units. When these conditions are met, the PO method achieves a logical matching of acquisition cost to benefits (production) obtained. Mining, oil-drilling, and steel-making equipment often are depreciated under the PO method. International Paper Company reported using the PO method in a footnote to its 1989 financial statements:

> For financial statement purposes, the Company uses the unit-of-production method for depreciating its major pulp and paper mills and certain wood products facilities.

Of 600 firms surveyed by the AICPA in 1990, 50 used this method (see Exhibit 12–9).

When the SH and PO methods are used, the depreciation charge varies each year according to asset usage. In addition, the two methods can produce different results, depending on the ratio of machine hours to units produced. For the asset under study, 2.11 machine hours were required to produce one unit in 1991 (3,800/1,800), while in 1992 that figure was reduced to 2.00 (4,000/2,000), indicating a greater efficiency (see Exhibits 12–5 and 12–6). The SH method, therefore, yielded slightly higher depreciation per unit of output in 1991 than in 1992.

EXHIBIT 12-6   Depreciation Schedule—Productive Output Method

Year	Units of Output	Depreciation Expense (Debit)	Accumulated Depreciation (Credit)	Balance, Accumulated Depreciation	Undepreciated Asset Balance (Book Value)
January 1, 1991					$6,600
December 31, 1991	1,800	(1,800 × $.60) = $1,080	$1,080	$1,080	5,520
December 31, 1992	2,000	(2,000 × $.60) = 1,200	1,200	2,280	4,320
December 31, 1993	2,400	(2,400 × $.60) = 1,440	1,440	3,720	2,880
December 31, 1994	1,800	(1,800 × $.60) = 1,080	1,080	4,800	1,800
December 31, 1995	2,000	(2,000 × $.60) = 1,200	1,200	6,000	600 (residual value)
Total	10,000	$6,000	$6,000		

Benefits derived from the use of certain assets are more appropriately measured in units of output than in hours of service. When both SH and PO methods are appropriate, the latter method is conceptually preferable.

Accelerated Depreciation Methods

The depreciation methods discussed thus far recognize depreciation at a constant rate per time period, hour of service, or unit of output. The next group of methods—the accelerated depreciation methods—are designed to recognize greater amounts of depreciation early in the useful life of plant assets and lesser amounts later. Thus, they *accelerate* the recognition of depreciation.

Accelerated methods assume that assets, when newer, produce more benefits per period because they are more productive and require less maintenance and repair. Therefore, accelerated methods match more of the acquisition cost against revenue in these earlier periods when greater benefits are obtained. A smoother pattern of total annual operating expense often is the result, with the sum of depreciation and maintenance expense closer to a constant amount each reporting period than is obtained with SL depreciation.

The principal accelerated methods in use today are the sum-of-the-years' digits (SYD) method and the declining balance methods. The use of accelerated methods in the United States originated with the 1954 *Internal Revenue Code*. Firms adopting these methods for tax purposes found it expedient to employ the same methods for financial statement purposes as well. *ARB No. 43* specifically allows accelerated methods for financial statement purposes because they are systematic and rational.[11]

Sum-of-the-Years'-Digits (SYD) Method   Under SYD, annual depreciation is computed by multiplying an asset's depreciable cost by a fraction made up as follows:

Numerator: the number of years remaining in the useful life at the *beginning* of the period. The numerator declines with each year of asset use. For the asset in Exhibit 12–3, the numerator for 1993 is 3, for example, because at the beginning of 1993, three years of useful life remain.

Denominator: the sum of digits counting from 1 to the useful life (the sum-of-the-

---

[11] *ARB No. 43*, as amended by *SFAS No. 96*, effectively maintained the option to use accelerated methods for financial statement purposes. The tax law concerning depreciation frequently changes. The use of accelerated methods for financial reporting purposes, however, need not follow the changes in the tax law.

EXHIBIT 12-7   Depreciation Schedule—SYD Method

Year	Depreciation Expense (Debit)	Accumulated Depreciation (Credit)	Balance, Accumulated Depreciation	Undepreciated Asset Balance (Book Value)
January 1, 1991				$6,600
December 31, 1991	(5/15 × $6,000) = $2,000	$2,000	$2,000	4,600
December 31, 1992	(4/15 × $6,000) = 1,600	1,600	3,600	3,000
December 31, 1993	(3/15 × $6,000) = 1,200	1,200	4,800	1,800
December 31, 1994	(2/15 × $6,000) = 800	800	5,600	1,000
December 31, 1995	(1/15 × $6,000) = 400	400	6,000	600 (residual value)
Total	$6,000	$6,000		

years'-digits). For an asset with a useful life of five years, the denominator equals 15 $(1 + 2 + 3 + 4 + 5)$.[12]

Depreciation expense in 1991 for the Exhibit 12–3 asset is:

$$1991 \text{ SYD depreciation} = (\$6,600 - \$600)(5/15) = \$2,000$$

SYD is an accelerated method because it recognizes the largest amount of depreciation in the first year of the asset's life and then lesser amounts in each successive year. Exhibit 12–7 illustrates the SYD method over the life of the Exhibit 12–3 asset.

Evaluation   The SYD method is systematic and rational and is particularly appropriate for assets supplying proportionately greater benefits early in their useful life. Computers and other high-technology equipment often provide more benefits early in their life, and then they gradually or suddenly become obsolete as technology changes.

Accelerated methods are particularly applicable when obsolescence is an important factor in the estimate of useful life. For example, an asset with a three-year useful life is 50% depreciated at the end of its first year under the SYD method: $3/(3 + 2 + 1) = 3/6$, or 50%. If the asset becomes obsolete in its second year, most of the asset is already depreciated. Of 600 firms surveyed by the AICPA in 1990, 16 used this method (see Exhibit 12–9).

The Raytheon Company disclosed its use of SYD in a footnote in its 1988 annual report:

> Provisions for depreciation are computed generally on the sum-of-the-years'-digits method, except for certain operations which use the straight-line or declining-balance method.

Declining-Balance (DB) Methods   Unlike the previously discussed methods, DB methods do not base depreciation on depreciable cost. Rather, depreciation expense for a period in this class of methods is the product of three values:

1. The book value at the beginning of the period (for the first period, book value equals acquisition cost; residual value is not subtracted).

---

[12] For extended useful lives, the SYD can be computed with the following formula: $SYD = n(n + 1)/2$, where n is the useful life. With a 25-year useful life, $SYD = 25(25 + 1)/2 = 325$.

EXHIBIT 12-8   Depreciation Schedule—Double-Declining-Balance Method

Year	Annual Rate	Depreciation Expense (Debit)	Accumulated Depreciation (Credit)	Balance, Accumulated Depreciation	Undepreciated Asset Balance (Book Value)
January 1, 1991					$6,600
December 31, 1991	40%	(40% × $6,600) = $2,640	$2,640	$2,640	3,960
December 31, 1992	40%	(40% × $3,960) = 1,584	1,584	4,224	2,376
December 31, 1993	40%	(40% × $2,376) = 950	950	5,174	1,426
December 31, 1994	40%	(40% × $1,426) = 570	570	5,744	856
December 31, 1995	40%	256*	256	6,000	600
Total		$6,000	$6,000		

* Depreciation expense stops when accumulated depreciation equals the $6,000 depreciable cost, leaving the $600 residual value intact. Thus, the maximum depreciation for 1995 is $256 ($6,000 − $5,744) rather than $342 (40% of $856).

2. The straight-line rate (1/useful life).
3. An acceleration percentage, which varies from 100% to 200%. This percentage depends on the asset. When the acceleration percentage is 200% (the most popular), the method is called *double-declining balance* (DDB) and depreciation is recognized at twice the straight-line rate.

For example, using double-declining balance, depreciation expense for 1991 and 1992 on the Exhibit 12–3 asset is:

$$1991 \text{ depreciation} = \$6,600(1/5)(200\%) = \$2,640$$
$$1992 \text{ depreciation} = (\$6,600 - \$2,640)(1/5)(200\%) = \$1,584$$

Annual depreciation expense declines along with the declining book value under these methods. The book value at the beginning of any year is reduced by the depreciation in all previous years.

For convenience, an alternative way to compute depreciation is to first calculate the rate of depreciation, and then multiply the rate by the beginning book value. The declining balance rate equals the product of the straight-line rate and the acceleration percentage. For example, the double-declining-balance depreciation rate is 200%/ useful life, or $2/n$ where n is the useful life. A 150% acceleration percentage yields a $1.5/n$ depreciation rate.

For the asset under study, the DDB depreciation rate is 2/5, or 40%. 1991 double-declining-balance depreciation expense is therefore alternatively calculated as $6,600(.40) = $2,640. Exhibit 12–8 carries out the calculations for the full five-year expected useful life of the Exhibit 12–3 asset.[13]

Evaluation   Declining-balance methods are significantly different from the previously discussed methods in three ways:
* Residual value is not subtracted from cost when calculating depreciation.
* The depreciation rate is applied to a declining balance rather than to the constant depreciable cost.
* Special care must be taken to ensure that assets are not depreciated below their residual value, the minimum book value for a plant asset.

---

[13] A way to directly compute double-declining-balance depreciation for any year is:

Depreciation in year t of the asset's life = (Acquisition cost)(2/Useful life)$(1 - 2/\text{Useful life})^{t-1}$

For example: 1993 (Year 3) depreciation = $\$6,600(2/5)(1 - 2/5)^{3-1} = \$950$

EXHIBIT 12-9   Depreciation Methods Used by 600 Firms in 1989 (Surveyed by the AICPA)

Method	Number of Firms Using Method	Percentage of 600 Firms Using Method
Straight-line	562	94%
Declining-balance	40	7%
Sum-of-the-years'-digits	16	3%
Other accelerated, not specified	69	12%
Productive output	50	8%
Other	8	1%

Note: Total responses exceed 600 and percentages add to more than 100% because some firms use more than one method.

Source: AICPA, *Accounting Trends & Techniques* (New York, 1990), p. 261.

Declining-balance methods eventually reach a point beyond which continued application of the constant rate yields a book value less than residual value. In these situations, firms can change to the SL method in the year in which depreciation under the declining balance method is equal to or less than SL depreciation. Alternatively, a firm can change to the SL method the year the declining-balance method otherwise would reduce the book value below residual value (the approach taken in Exhibit 12-8 for 1995—the last year of useful life).

The declining-balance and SYD methods are applicable under the same conditions. Both methods are acceptable under GAAP, yield similar results, and recognize depreciation on an accelerated basis. Of 600 firms surveyed by the AICPA in 1990, 40 used a declining balance method (see Exhibit 12-9).

Motorola indicated its use of declining balance depreciation in the footnotes to its 1989 financial statements:

> The cost of buildings, machinery and equipment is depreciated, generally by the declining-balance method over the estimated useful lives of such assets, as follows: buildings and building equipment, 5–50 years; machinery and equipment, 2–12 years.

Present Value–Based Depreciation

Although present value depreciation methods are not in common use and are not acceptable under GAAP, the FASB has requested comment from interested parties on these methods.[14] Under the present value, or interest method of depreciation, the cost of a plant asset is equated to the present value of the stream of cash receipts generated by the asset. Each receipt consists of interest (return on investment) and principal (depreciation expense).

For example, assume a firm purchases an asset with a two-year useful life on January 1, 1991, for $10,000. The firm anticipates a 6% return on its investment in the asset, equivalent to a net cash flow of $5,454 per year, computed as follows:

$$\$10,000 = (PVA, 6\%, 2)(\text{Annual net cash inflow})$$
$$\$10,000/1.83339 = \text{Annual net cash inflow} = \$5,454$$

---

[14] FASB, *Discussion Memorandum,* "Present Value–Based Measurements in Accounting," December 1990. The DM also considers the application of present value techniques to other accounting issues.

The following schedule illustrates the interest method of depreciation:

Date	Estimated Net Cash Inflow	Return on Investment	Depreciation Expense	Asset Book Value
1/1/91				$10,000
12/31/91	$ 5,454	$600*	$ 4,854†	5,146‡
12/31/92	5,454	308§	5,146**	
	$10,908	$908	$10,000	

* $10,000(.06).
† $5,454 − $600.
‡ $10,000 − $4,854.
§ $5,146(.06).
** $5,454 − $308.

The interest method treats a plant asset as a monetary asset, such as a note receivable with payments that include both principal and interest. Before a return *on* investment is recognized, the firm must be reimbursed for its investment. The excess of cash flow over the return *of* capital or reimbursement (depreciation expense) is income to the firm. Depreciation expense increases in later years because a greater portion of the net cash inflow represents a return of capital.

CONCEPT REVIEW

1. List the features that distinguish declining-balance methods from the other depreciation methods discussed in the chapter.
2. What is the conceptual basis for choosing an accelerated depreciation methods?
3. What is the straight-line rate of depreciation and how is it calculated?

DEPRECIATION POLICY
♦

Firms have considerable latitude in choosing a depreciation method. The systematic and rational requirement does not limit the field to only one method. Exhibit 12–9 gives current information about the depreciation methods used by companies. As the exhibit points out, straight-line depreciation is predominant in the firms surveyed.

Many accountants maintain that the method resulting in the best matching of expense and revenue should be required. However, the choice of method hinges on a variety of factors. Accounting information system costs are an important factor, the "computer revolution" notwithstanding. Detailed information about acquisition costs, post-acquisition costs, useful life, residual value, and accumulated depreciation must be maintained. The system must facilitate retrieval of this information for depreciation calculations. In addition, complexity influences the choice of method.

As previously discussed, expected obsolescence can affect the choice of method. Accelerated methods are particularly appropriate in this instance. The income tax law also affects the choice of methods. The use of accelerated methods was initiated by the tax law and was sanctioned by the profession shortly thereafter. Many firms employ SL depreciation for financial accounting and acclerated depreciation for tax reporting. Typically this results in higher earnings reported to shareholders and lower tax liabilities. Tradition is another factor. Some firms continue to use the same method each year mainly because it satisfies their reporting needs, but also to avoid the cost of changing methods.

Other factors affecting depreciation policy are the belief that depreciation methods that maximize net income have a positive effect on share price, and management's desire to maximize their own financial well-being through employment contracts linking compensation to reported earnings. Both factors many contribute to the dominance of the straight-line method. However, research findings suggest that stock prices are not directly affected by the choice of depreciation method for financial accounting purposes.

The great variety in depreciation methods and in estimates of useful life and residual value is at odds with uniformity and consistency in financial reporting across firms. Add the large dollar amount of depreciation expense reported by many firms and the inherently approximate nature of depreciation, and the result is a potentially difficult comparison problem for financial statement users.

For example, in 1989, Delta Air Lines depreciated its planes over 15 years using a residual value equal to 10% of original cost. In contrast, Pan Am used 25 years and a 15% residual value.[15] Many firms also use more than one depreciation method, further complicating the problem of comparing income across firms.

Depreciation, Cash Flow, and Dividend Policy

Depreciation is the systematic allocation of historical depreciable cost to periods of asset use. The cash outflow used to acquire plant assets occurs before the process of recognizing depreciation begins.[16] Depreciation, depletion, and amortization are expenses that reduce both net income and tax liabilities, but they *are not cash outflows*.

Depreciation reduces reported income and hence retained earnings. Depreciation over the life of a depreciable asset reduces retained earnings by the depreciable cost less the tax savings associated with depreciation. Dividends generally are limited by law to the amount of earnings retained in the business. Therefore, in certain cases, depreciation reduces the amount of dividends that can otherwise be paid. To illustrate this effect, Exhibit 12–10 compares the earnings generated by a depreciable asset with that of a nondepreciable asset.

Relative to Option 1, depreciation on the equipment in Option 2 reduced income and retained earnings by $4,200 ($18,200 − $14,000). This difference equals the after-tax income effect of depreciation:

Depreciation for two years	$6,000
Less tax savings (.30) $6,000	1,800
Net effect of depreciation on income and retained earnings for 2 years	$4,200

Next assume that Stable's policy is to pay out 100% of retained earnings in dividends to its shareholders. In this example, Stable pays $18,200 under Option 1 and $14,000 under Option 2. Option 2 (depreciable asset) thus conserves a total of $6,000 cash, relative to Option 1 (nondepreciable asset), computed as follows:

Dividends saved ($18,200 − $14,000)	$4,200
Tax savings (.30)$6,000	1,800
Total assumed cash savings	$6,000

The Stable Company example illustrates that depreciation can indirectly conserve resources in an amount equal to the acquisition cost of depreciable assets, depending on the dividend payout and tax depreciation policies of the firm. The is the **capital maintenance** characteristic of depreciation. The tax savings occur regardless of dividend policy.

Depreciation, however, does not guarantee that sufficient capital will be available for asset replacement. The replacement cost of most plant assets normally exceeds the original cost, especially during periods of inflation. Even if the cash conserved is

---

[15] "Earnings Helper," *Forbes*, June 12, 1989, p. 150.

[16] Depreciation accounting is independent of the method of acquiring operational assets. For example, assets financed with debt are subject to the same depreciation calculations as they would be if financed with cash.

EXHIBIT 12-10

STABLE COMPANY

Effect of Depreciation on Amount of
Retained Earnings Available for Dividends
Two-Year Period Ending December 31, 1992

Information for example:
  Start of Stable Company's operations: January, 1991
  Assets under consideration for purchase:
   land (Option 1) or equipment (Option 2)
  Cost: $6,000 each (only one asset is purchased)
  Useful life of equipment: 2 years
  Residual value of equipment: $0
  Annual sales revenues: $20,000 regardless of the asset acquired
  Tax rate: 30%
  Annual cash expenses: $7,000 regardless of the asset acquired
  Method of depreciation: SL for accounting and tax purposes

Combined Results for 1991 and 1992	Option 1 Purchase Land	Option 2 Purchase Equipment
Sales revenue	$40,000	$40,000
Cash expenses	(14,000)	(14,000)
Depreciation expense		(6,000)
Pretax income	26,000	20,000
Income tax expense (30%)	(7,800)	(6,000)
Net income for two-year period, and December 31, 1992 retained earnings balance	$18,200	$14,000

invested, the chances are that the earnings generated combined with the principal will not fully cover asset replacement costs. Further, few firms pay the maximum dividend allowed by law. Therefore, in general, depreciation does not conserve resources in the amount of depreciation recognized as expense.

A related misconception is that depreciation generates cash inflows equal to the amount of depreciation expense recognized in a period. The financial press frequently refers to "cash provided by depreciation." These references stem from interpretations of published cash flow statements. Occidental Petroleum's 1989 statement of cash flows, shown below is an example.

OCCIDENTAL PETROLEUM CORPORATION

Partial Consolidated Statement of Cash Flows
For the Year Ended December 31, 1989
(Dollars in Millions)

Operating Activities:
Net income . . . . $ 285
  Adjustments to reconcile income to net
  cash provided by continuing operations
    Depreciation, depletion, and amortization **1,031**
    All other adjustments, net[17] . . . . __293__
Net cash provided by operating activities $1,609

Readers of this statement might erroneously interpret the $1,031 million adjustment (64% of total cash provided by operating activities) as the contribution that depreciation, depletion, and amortization made to net operating cash inflow. Actually, these expenses are added back because they did not cause a cash outflow but

---

[17] The data in the original statement are aggregated here.

were deducted from revenues. Tax savings are the only definite contribution made by depreciation to cash inflows. The tax savings are determined by the method used for tax reporting, which may not be the same as the method used for book reporting, and the applicable tax rate.

Depreciation and Price Level Changes

Both GAAP and the tax law limit total depreciation on plant assets to historical depreciable cost. This dollar limitation ignores increases in the replacement cost of plant assets.[18] Furthermore, advances in technology and changing market demands often require replacement of plant assets with more expensive ones.

Many accountants and others interested in improving financial reporting contend that depreciation based on the historical cost of plant assets significantly understates the cost on a going-concern basis. If so, reported income is then significantly overstated and is a poor predictor of future income. Moreover, many companies disinvest permanent capital by maintaining dividends based on overstated earnings.

For example, in 1979, the Ford Motor Company reported historical earnings per share of $9.75, and earnings per share based on the current cost of plant facilities of only $1.78! Ford paid dividends of $3.90 per share that year. Assuming eventual replacement of facilities, many contend that Ford divested itself of $2.12 per share— $3.90 − $1.78, an amount representing $225 million that Ford should have retained for replacement. This phenomenon is not an isolated problem. Most capital-intensive firms fell victim to overstated earnings due to inflation in the 1970s and early 1980s.

The understatement of depreciation and ensuing overstatement of income also results in the overstatement of various rates of return that relate earnings to investment, total assets, and owners' equity.[19] These ratios are commonly used for evaluating performance.

Other accountants point out that selling prices of products can be expected to keep pace with inflation and that net income will rise to a level sufficient to replace existing capacity at higher prices when the need arises. However, regardless of the outcome of this debate, financial statement users should be aware of the potential distortion inherent in historical cost depreciation and its effect on performance measures.

Furthermore, although all GAAP depreciation methods reflect the bias due to inflation, accelerated depreciation methods produce results closer to depreciation adjusted for price level changes.[20] The higher depreciation amounts recognized early in the useful life of plant assets under accelerated depreciation more closely approximate depreciation based on price-level adjusted cost.

ADDITIONAL DEPRECIATION ISSUES

The following additional issues related to depreciation are discussed in this section of the text: fractional year depreciation, depreciation of post-acquisition costs, depreciation changes, and depreciation systems.

---

[18] For example, the consumer price index for all Urban Consumers (CPI-U), published by the U.S. Department of Labor in its *Monthly Labor Review*, and used as a primary measure of inflation, increased 71% between 1979 and 1989. A new plant asset costing $100,000 in 1979 would cost $171,000 in 1989 if replacement cost kept pace with inflation.

[19] Both the numerator and the denominator of these ratios are changed in a way that increases the ratio. The numerator is overstated since it is an income measure. The denominators are understated because book values of operational assets understate their true market value during times of inflation. The numerator and denominator effects combine to cause historical rates of return for some firms to exceed those based on current-cost values by hundreds of percent.

[20] Tax depreciation (see Appendix 12A) alleviates many of the problems due to underestimation of reported depreciation, according to R. Mohr and S. Dilley, "Current Cost and ACRS Depreciation Expense: A Comparison,"*The Accounting Review* (October 1984), p. 690–701.

Fractional Year Depreciation

Most plant assets are not placed in service at the beginning of a reporting period, nor are disposals typically made on an asset's service-entry anniversary date. Therefore, some adjustment is needed to account for depreciation during the resulting fractional year periods. Firms approach this problem in two different ways. Some compute the exact amount of depreciation for each fractional period, and others apply an accounting policy convention. To illustrate fractional year depreciation, the following information is used for each example:

Asset used for fractional depreciation examples: An asset costing $20,000 with a residual value of $2,000 and useful life of four years is placed into service on April 1, 1991. The firm has a calendar year reporting cycle.

Exact Calculation Approach   This approach computes the precise amount of depreciation for each fractional period. The asset in question is used only 9/12 of a year in 1991. Under SL depreciation, the asset's fractional service period is applied to the annual depreciation amount, as illustrated:

$$\text{Depreciation expense, 1991} = (\$20,000 - \$2,000)(1/4)(9/12) = \$3,375$$
$$\text{Depreciation expense, 1992–1994} = (\$20,000 - \$2,000)(1/4) = \$4,500$$
$$\text{Depreciation expense, 1995} = (\$20,000 - \$2,000)(1/4)(3/12) = \$1,125$$

The use of the service hours or productive output methods is unaffected by the fractional year depreciation problem. Under these methods, the number of hours used or units produced in the partial-year period is applied to the depreciation rate in the normal manner.

To determine the exact depreciation for a fraction of a fiscal year under accelerated depreciation methods, first compute depreciation for each *whole year* of the asset's useful life (without regard to the fiscal year). Then apply the relevant fraction of the fiscal year to the appropriate whole year depreciation amount. This process applied to the asset for the double-declining-balance method (the double-declining-balance rate is 2/4 years = 50%) yields:

Whole Year	Double-Declining-Balance Depreciation for Whole Year	
1. April 1, 1991 to March 31, 1992	.50($20,000)	= $10,000
2. April 1, 1992 to March 31, 1993	.50($20,000 − $10,000)	= $ 5,000
3. April 1, 1993 to March 31, 1994	.50($20,000 − $15,000)	= $ 2,500
4. April 1, 1994 to March 31, 1995	.50($20,000 − $17,500)	= $ 1,250*

*Using this amount causes total depreciation to exceed depreciable cost. The switch to straight-line is explained in the text discussion.

Recognized Depreciation

1991 depreciation = $10,000(9/12)	= $ 7,500
1992 depreciation = $10,000(3/12) + $5,000(9/12)	= $ 6,250
1993 depreciation = $5,000(3/12) + $2,500(9/12)	= $ 3,125
Depreciation through December 31, 1993	$16,875

Depreciation for 1991 includes only the *first* 9/12 of the first whole year depreciation amount because the asset is in service only 9/12 of 1991. Fiscal year 1992 contains the last 3/12 of whole Year 1 and the first 9/12 of whole Year 2.[21]

---

[21] Accelerated depreciation methods are accelerated only in terms of whole years. Within each whole year, a constant rate of depreciation applies.

Applying the fractional calculation to 1994 yields $1,562.5 depreciation ($2,500 × 3/12 + $1,250 × 9/12). Total depreciation through December 31, 1994, then amounts to $18,437.50 ($16,875 + $1,562.50), which *exceeds* depreciable cost ($18,000). Therefore, assume that the firm switches to straight-line depreciation beginning January 1, 1994. The remaining depreciation is computed as follows:

Remaining depreciable cost, January 1, 1994 = $20,000 − $2,000 − $16,875
$$= \$1,125$$
Remaining months in useful life at January 1, 1994 = 15 months
1994 depreciation = $1,125(12/15) = $900
1995 depreciation = $1,125(3/15) = $225

Total depreciation from 1991 through 1995 equals $18,000 (depreciable cost).[22] The whole-year method illustrated above also is applicable to the sum-of-the-years'-digits method.

The schedule below shows depreciation for each year under the sum-of-the-years'-digits method for the asset:

Sum of the years' digits = 1 + 2 + 3 + 4 = 10

Whole Year	Sum-of-the-Years'-Digits Depreciation for Whole Year
1. April 1, 1991 to March 31, 1992	$18,000(4/10) = $ 7,200
2. April 1, 1992 to March 31, 1993	$18,000(3/10) = 5,400
3. April 1, 1993 to March 31, 1994	$18,000(2/10) = 3,600
4. April 1, 1994 to March 31, 1995	$18,000(1/10) = 1,800
	Total $18,000

Recognized Depreciation

1991 depreciation = $7,200(9/12)	= $5,400
1992 depreciation = $7,200(3/12) + $5,400(9/12) =	5,850
1993 depreciation = $5,400(3/12) + $3,600(9/12) =	4,050
1994 depreciation = $3,600(3/12) + $1,800(9/12) =	2,250
1995 depreciation = $1,800(3/12)	= 450
	Total $18,000

Accounting Policy Convention To avoid the complexities of fractional year depreciation, many firms adopt a policy convention to expedite depreciation recognition and to ensure consistent financial reporting.[23] Several conventions are in current use. Depreciation in 1991 for the asset used in the previous fractional-year depreciation examples is given for each of the following conventions under the straight-line method:

Accounting policy conventions for depreciation:

1. Compute annual depreciation based solely on the balance in the plant asset accounts at the beginning of the period. Assets disposed of during a period are

---

[22] A faster approach to computing exact depreciation under the declining-balance methods is to multiply the asset's book value at the beginning of each period by the appropriate declining balance rate. This approach, applied to the asset for the first three years, yields:

1991 depreciation = .50($20,000) (9/12) = $7,500
1992 depreciation = .50($20,000 − $7,500) = $6,250
1993 depreciation = .50($20,000 − $7,500 − $6,250) = $3,125

The depreciation recognized in the disposal year, however, generally is not equal under the two approaches. The gain or loss on disposal also differs. The differences generally are not material.

[23] To address the fractional-year depreciation problem for tax purposes, a half-year convention is used. Under this convention, assets are assumed to be placed into service in the middle of their first year of use (see Appendix 12A).

depreciated a full period, and assets purchased during a period are not depreciated that period. (No depreciation is recognized in 1991 on the asset.)

2. Compute annual depreciation based solely on the balance in the asset account at the end of the period. Assets purchased during a period are depreciated a full period, and assets disposed of during a period are not depreciated that period. ($4,500 of depreciation is recognized in 1991 on the asset ($18,000/4).

3. Compute a full year's depreciation on assets placed into service before mid-year, and none on assets placed into service after mid-year. Assets retired before mid-year are not depreciated that year; those retired after mid-year are depreciated a full year. ($4,500 of depreciation is recognized in 1991 on the asset.)

4. Compute a full month's depreciation on assets placed into service on or before the 15th of the month, and none on assets placed into service after the 15th. Assets retired on or before the 15th of the month are not depreciated that month; those retired after the 15th are depreciated a full month. ($3,375 of depreciation is recognized in 1991 on the asset, the same amount as under the exact computation.)[24]

These conventions satisfy GAAP if the results are not materially different from the exact-calculation approach. However, the same policy must be used consistently to achieve similar results from period to period.[25]

Depreciation of Post-Acquisition Costs

This chapter so far has illustrated depreciation of the original acquisition cost of plant assets. However, capitalized post-acquisition costs also must be depreciated. The example to follow applies the straight-line method to illustrate the ideas, but the general concept is the same regardless of method: depreciate the new expenditure over its economic useful life.

How this is accomplished depends on the account capitalized with the amount of the post-acquisition cost: the original asset, accumulated depreciation, or a separate new asset. The useful life of the post-acquisition item relative to that of the original asset must also be considered. Depreciation on the original asset is recognized to the date of the post-acquisition expenditure. Depreciation on the new balance begins as of the date the new item is placed into service.

Subsequent Cost Combined with Original Asset   If the new item is an integral part of the original asset, is expected to be retired with the original asset, or only extends the life of the original asset, the expenditure need not be classified and depreciated as a separate plant asset. While accumulated depreciation is often debited for the cost of an extraordinary repair, other types of post acquisition expenditures are debited to the original asset account. Either way, depreciation from the date of the post-acquisition expenditure is based on the increased book value of the original asset.

---

[24] However, if the asset were purchased on April 9, the exact calculation would depreciate the asset for the period April 9 through December 31, resulting in a different amount of expense. The amount under the fourth convention would remain $3,375.

[25] The exact approach to fractional year depreciation should be used only if the information advantages justify the added cost.

For example, assume the following information for Macro Corporation:

Original asset: office building purchased January 1, 1985.
Useful life: 20 years.
Original cost: $800,000.
Straight-line depreciation is used.
Post-acquisition cost: wall partitions placed into the third floor executive office suite to increase the number of private offices (an addition). The partitions do not extend the life of the building and have no separate utility apart from the building. The partitions were installed July 1, 1991, at a cost of $150,000.

Macro debits the building account for the cost of the partitions.

Book value of building on July 1, 1991:

Original cost	$800,000	
Depreciation through Jan. 1, 1991 ($300,000/20)(6 years)	(240,000)	
1991 depreciation through June 30, 1991 ($800,000/20)1/2	(20,000)	$20,000
Post-acquisition cost—partitions	150,000	
Building book value July 1, 1991	$690,000	

Remaining useful life of building at July 1, 1991:
20 years original life − 6.5 years in use = 13.5 years

1991 depreciation on building, July 1 through December 31 ($690,000/13.5)(1/2)		25,556
Total 1991 depreciation		$45,556

Subsequent Cost Not Combined with Original Asset If the new item is not an integral part of the original asset and has separate utility or is not expected to be retired with the original asset, it should be depreciated separately.

For example, assume that removable refrigeration units with a useful life of 10 years are added to railroad boxcars with a remaining useful life of 5 years (an addition). Because the refrigeration units can be used in other rolling stock, the units should be depreciated independently over their respective useful lives. In this case, the subsequent expenditure has no effect on the depreciation of the original asset.

Depreciation Changes

Consistent application of useful life and residual value estimates and of depreciation methods fosters readers' confidence in financial statements and enhances comparability across reporting periods. However, significant changes in economic conditions and new information about operating assets may require either a revision of the estimates used in depreciation or a change in method. For example, unanticipated obsolescence can necessitate a significant reduction in useful life and, hence, the need to write off the remaining book value over the new and shorter life. Alternatively, a prolonged economic recession can reduce the demand for the firm's product, which could prompt a switch from an accelerated depreciation method.

Three accounting adjustments can affect depreciation recognition: change in an estimate, change in the depreciation method, and correction of an error. *APB Opinion No. 20,* "Accounting Changes" and *SFAS No. 16,* "Prior Period Adjustments," are the governing pronouncements for these effects. This section briefly outlines these accounting adjustments as they relate to depreciation.

In all cases, if a journal entry is required to effect the change, it is made as of the first day of the fiscal year in which the change is made, even though the decision to make a change typically is made late in the fiscal year when the adjustments and other year-end procedures are performed.

Change in Estimate   The estimated useful life and residual value are based on information available at time of acquisition. As experience is obtained, these estimates are modified to reflect more recent information. New information does not invalidate estimates previously made in good faith. Therefore, a change in estimate is made on a current and prospective basis. No retroactive adjustment is made because the new information was not available in earlier periods.

When a change is made to the estimated useful life or residual value, the asset's remaining book value at the beginning of the year is allocated to the revised remaining useful life, using the new residual value. Ideally, estimates should be reviewed at the end of each reporting period for significant changes. This review is not always accomplished in practice, however. For example, it is common for assets to be fully depreciated before their usefulness ends.

The following example for Ames Company illustrates a change in estimate:

Equipment purchased: January 1, 1988.
Cost: $10,000.
Residual value: $2,000.
Useful life: six years.
Depreciation method: SYD.
Estimate change: In September 1991 the total useful life is reestimated to be seven years, and the residual value is revised downward to $1,000.

$$\text{Sum-of-the-years'-digits} = 6 + 5 + 4 + 3 + 2 + 1 = 21$$
$$\text{Depreciation recognized through Dec. 31, 1990} = (\$10,000 - \$2,000)(6 + 5 + 4)/21 = \$5,714.$$
$$\text{Remaining book value, Jan. 1, 1991} = \$10,000 - \$5,714 = \$4,286$$
$$\text{Remaining useful life, Jan. 1, 1991} = 7 \text{ years} - 3 \text{ years} = 4 \text{ years}$$
$$\text{New sum-of-the-years'-digits} = 4 + 3 + 2 + 1 = 10$$
$$\text{1991 depreciation} = (\$4,286 - \$1,000) (4/10) = \$1,314$$

Changes in estimates for depreciation can affect reported income significantly. Blockbuster Entertainment, a major videotape rental store chain, changed the useful life of its videotapes (classified as property, plant, and equipment) from 9 months to 36 months in 1988, increasing the company's reported net income by nearly 20%.[26]

Changes in Accounting Principle   According to GAAP, changes in accounting principle should be made only to improve financial statement measurement and disclosure. Changes for the sole purpose of enhancing reported net income are not appropriate. Consistency in application of accounting methods is required unless conditions warrant a change. A change from the straight-line method to the double-declining-balance method is an example of a change in accounting principle. This change is justified if assets are deteriorating faster than expected. Firms often justify depreciation changes on the basis of a better matching of expenses and revenues, or by arguing that it makes their reports more comparable to other firms in their industry.

Most accounting changes, including changes in depreciation method, are treated on a current and prospective basis. A change in depreciation method requires recalculating depreciation using the new method for all prior years affected by the change. The difference between reported depreciation and depreciation under the new method for all prior years affected is reported by recognizing cumulative effect of the accounting principle change. This account is disclosed net of tax after income from continuing operations and before net income. The new method is used in the period of change and in subsequent periods; no retroactive changes are made. Using the cumulative effect account avoids the need to make retroactive changes to the company's books or to issue amended financial statements for past periods.

---

[26] "Analyst's Bashing Rocks Blockbuster Entertainment," *The Wall Street Journal,* May 10, 1989, p. C1.

The information for the Ames Company is used to illustrate a change in depreciation method (ignore taxes):

The depreciation method is changed from SYD to straight-line in 1991.

Reported depreciation under SYD, 1988–1990
(from estimate change example) $5,714
Depreciation using the straight-line method, 1988–1990:
(3 years) ($10,000 − $2,000)/6 4,000
Cumulative effect of change from SYD to SL $1,714

To record accounting change, January 1, 1991:

Accumulated depreciation 1,714
    Cumulative effect of accounting principle change 1,714

To record depreciation, December 31, 1991:

Depreciation expense ($10,000 − $2,000)/6 1,333
    Accumulated depreciation 1,333

The cumulative effect increases 1991 income because $1,714 less depreciation would have been recognized under the SL method in the years 1988 to 1990.

Depreciation Errors Depreciation errors are caused by arithmetic mistakes, use of the wrong information, or omission of assets from depreciation calculations. Material errors are corrected. The entry to correct a depreciation error affecting prior periods involves making a prior period adjustment. A prior period adjustment is a correction to retained earnings for the effect of the error on the net income of all prior years affected. This is a retroactive change and does not affect current earnings. The FASB reasoned (in *SFAS No. 16*) that the error is made in a prior year and does not involve current income. If prior years' financial statements are reported in the current annual report for comparison purposes, any accounts affected by the past errors are restated.

To illustrate the correction of a depreciation error, assume that a machine costing $10,000 with an estimated useful life of five years and no residual value is incorrectly debited to an expense account on acquisition at the beginning of 1989. The error is discovered in January 1992, during the closing process for 1991. Two entries are required: to correct retained earnings as of the beginning of 1991 and to record the correct amount of depreciation for 1991 (ignore taxes):

Correcting entry, as of January 1, 1991:

Machine 10,000
    Accumulated depreciation ($10,000 × 2/5) 4,000
    Prior period adjustment (retained earnings) 6,000

Adjusting entry, December 31, 1991:

Depreciation expense ($10,000/5) 2,000
    Accumulated depreciation 2,000

Ignoring taxes, the expensing of the machine in 1989 reduced income by $10,000. The company should have capitalized the asset and recognized a total of $4,000 of depreciation in the years before 1991. Therefore, retained earnings at January 1, 1991, is understated by $6,000. The prior period adjustment account is closed to retained earnings, restating retained earnings to the correct balance. Accumulated depreciation is now correctly stated as of December 31, 1991.

If a depreciation error affects only the current period, a prior period adjustment is not required; only current accounts are corrected.

Depreciation Systems

Unique features of certain depreciable assets, as well as practical considerations, cause firms to modify the depreciation methods already discussed. The most commonly used adaptations are referred to as depreciation *systems:*

1. Inventory appraisal system.
2. Group and composite systems.
3. Retirement and replacement systems.

These systems compute depreciation typically on an aggregate, rather than individual, asset basis and are used, in part, because they reduce the costs of computing and recording. Depreciation systems require less information to be maintained on individual assets, and they often attain acceptable levels of reliability, especially when materiality is considered.

Inventory Appraisal System   Under the **inventory appraisal system,** at the end of each accounting period, plant assets are appraised in their present condition. This appraisal is the result of applying a deterioration percentage to the cost of the assets remaining at the end of the reporting period. Firms can also obtain an outside assessment of replacement cost for this purpose. This system is particularly suitable for firms with numerous low-cost plant assets.

The decline in the total appraisal value during the period is recorded as depreciation expense. Depreciation is recorded directly in the plant asset account. Cash received on disposal is recorded as a credit to depreciation expense—an adjustment to depreciation expense for the residual value. Under this system, the book value (appraisal value) of the assets at the end of the period is an estimate of the current acquisition cost, taking into account current condition and usefulness. In no case are assets revalued upwards.

To illustrate how this system works, assume the following facts regarding the hand tools plant asset account of Miller Company, which began operations in 1991:

Purchases of hand tools in 1991: $1,900.
Appraisal value of tools at end of 1991: $1,080.
Proceeds from disposal of tools in 1991: $70.

The entries for 1991 are:

During 1991:

Hand tools	1,900	
Cash		1,900
Cash	70	
Depreciation expense		70

December 31, 1991:

Depreciation expense	820	
Hand tools ($1,900 − $1,080)		820

Reported depreciation expense in 1991 for hand tools equals $750 ($820 − $70), the net decrease in the value of hand tools experienced in 1991, and the net change in the depreciation expense account. The value of tools on hand decreased $820, but the $70 received on disposal offsets that decline.

Accounting cost savings are evident from the elimination of individual subsidiary asset and accumulated depreciation accounts. Depreciation is not recorded for individual assets; instead, the value of the group of assets is maintained in one account. Disposals do not require retrieval of accumulated depreciation information, and no gain or loss is recorded. Furthermore, the appraisal value can be made on the entire group rather than on each individual asset.

Evaluation The inventory appraisal system appears at first to be a departure from the historical cost principle. However, assets are not written up in value, and the resulting depreciation expense must be reasonably similar to results obtained with other depreciation methods based on historical cost. Moreover, total depreciation is limited to original cost. The method is, however, criticized because appraisals can be quite subjective.

Group and Composite Systems Plant assets are sometimes grouped together for depreciation purposes. For example, all small trucks can be grouped together, or an entire operating assembly consisting of different types of assets is depreciated as a single unit. In these cases, an average depreciation rate is applied to the group. This rate reflects the characteristics of all the assets in the group. **Group depreciation** is the name given to this system when applied to relatively homogeneous assets, and **composite depreciation** is the term used for heterogeneous assets. Otherwise, these systems are identical with respect to calculation and journal entries.[27]

These systems record all the assets of the group in one asset control account, and one accumulated depreciation account is established for the entire group. Group book value is the difference between these two accounts. Subsequent additions to the group are debited to the group asset control account. Individual accumulated depreciation accounts are not maintained, thus saving accounting costs. The original cost of each group member, however, must be maintained for use on disposal.

As with the inventory appraisal method, gains and losses are not recognized on disposal, and there is no need to retrieve accumulated depreciation records on individual assets to record the disposal. Rather, the group control account is credited for the original cost of the item, and the accumulated depreciation account is debited with the difference between the cash received and original cost of the asset. The debit to accumulated depreciation is therefore a balancing amount and is not directly computed. This system acknowledges the inherent difficulties in estimating depreciation and recognizes no catch-up gain or loss on disposal.

Under the group and composite systems, annual depreciation expense is the product of an average depreciation rate multiplied by the balance in the asset control account (the original cost of assets in the group). Alternatively, a rate can be applied to cost less residual value.

The example to follow uses heterogeneous assets for a more comprehensive discussion of the system. The depreciation rate is based on cost. Homogeneous assets involve similar calculations. Exhibit 12–11 presents the case information and certain calculations for the example.

The composite depreciation rate is the ratio of the total annual straight-line depreciation on all assets in the group to the total acquisition cost.[28] It is the percentage of total cost depreciated each year. Residual value is taken into account because the numerator used in determining the composite rate reflects the straight-line method. The advantage of using total acquisition cost as the denominator is that future depreciation can then be computed by applying the composite rate to the remaining balance in the asset control account, avoiding the need to compute depreciable cost.

---

[27] For a full discussion of depreciation of multiple asset accounts, see J. Coughlan and W. Strand, *Depreciation: Accounting, Taxes and Business Decisions* (New York: Ronald Press, 1969), Chapter 5.

[28] The double-declining-balance method can also be used in composite and group systems. In the example, twice the straight-line rate (.1794) would be used for depreciation purposes. Other declining-balance methods are also appropriate. The sum-of-year's-digits method, however, cannot be applied because the assets have different useful lives; therefore, the numerator and denominator of the fractional rates used each year cannot be computed.

EXHIBIT 12-11 Case Data for Composite Depreciation Example: Components of Operating Assembly Acquired Early 1991

Component	Quantity	Unit Original Cost	Unit Residual Value	Unit Useful Life	Unit Annual SL Depreciation
A	10	$50,000	$5,000	15 years	$3,000
B	4	20,000	4,000	10 years	1,600
C	6	7,000	600	8 years	800
D	20	3,000	0	3 years	1,000

Total annual depreciation:
10($3,000) + 4($1,600) + 6($800) + 20($1,000) = $61,200.

Total asset acquisition cost:
10($50,000) + 4($20,000) + 6($7,000) + 20($3,000) = $682,000.

Total depreciable cost:
$682,000 − 10 ($5,000) − 4($4,000) − 6($600) = $612,400.

Composite annual depreciation rate = $61,200/$682,000 = .0897.

Composite group useful life = $612,400/$61,200 = 10 years.

Annual depreciation expense for the group of assets from Exhibit 12–11 is:

$$\text{Annual group depreciation expense} = \text{Composite rate} \times \text{Total group acquisition cost}$$

$$\$61,200 = (.0897)\$682,000 \quad \text{(rounded)}$$

Depreciation expense is recorded in the normal manner:

December 31, 1991:

```
Depreciation expense . . . . . . . . . . . . . . . . . . . . . . . . . . . 61,200
    Accumulated depreciation—operating assembly . . . . . . . .      61,200
```

The composite useful life of the group of asssets is also the ratio of two values, namely, total depreciable cost and annual depreciation. The ratio yields the number of years over which depreciation is taken (in this case, 10 years, from Exhibit 12–11). In 10 years, the group is fully depreciated and has a net book value equal to total group residual value. The composite life is not the simple average useful life of the group, but rather depends on the relative contribution each type of asset makes to the total depreciable cost of the group. For example, Component A contributes $450,000 of depreciable cost to the group, and each Component A has a useful life of 15 years. In contrast, Component D contributes only $60,000 to depreciable cost, and each unit has a useful life of 3 years. The composite life is, therefore, closer to the useful life of Component A.

If no changes occur in the makeup of the group during the entire composite life, annual depreciation does not change. Technically, either addition of assets to the group or disposal of assets before the end of their useful life necessitates a revision of the depreciation rate. However, maintaining the original depreciation rate is justified for changes not significant to the overall depreciable cost and useful life composition of the group. Particularly with homogeneous assets, the original composite rate can be maintained. Depreciation then is computed with the old rate and the new balance in the group asset control account, which reflects the addition or deletion of assets. Changes in the makeup of composite groups, however, are more likely to involve changes in depreciation rates because these assets are heterogeneous.

The following entry is made to dispose of one Component B sold for $18,000 in 1992:

During 1992:

Cash 18,000
Accumulated depreciation—operating assembly (to balance) . . . 2,000
    Operating assembly   20,000

No gain or loss is recognized on disposal because accumulated depreciation records are not maintained on individual assets. This disposal alters the composition of the group and changes the depreciation rate. However, if this disposal is not a significant change in the group, 1992 depreciation is recorded as follows:

December 31, 1991:

Depreciation expense 59,381*
    Accumulated depreciation—operating assembly   59,381
*$59,381 = ($682,000 − $20,000).0897

Evaluation The variance in the useful life and depreciable cost among group assets is the basis for criticisms about this system. The group of assets in the example is depreciated for 10 years. Before the end of the first 10 years, Components C and D have probably been retired. After the group is fully depreciated, Component A remains in service. Critics charge that, compared to depreciation methods individually applied, there is a significant compromise in the degree to which acquisition costs are matched against periods of use.

Group and composite systems are used by many companies and include a portion of those reporting the use of the straight-line method. Georgia-Pacific Corporation disclosed its use of the composite method in its 1988 financial statements:

> Depreciation expense is computed using the straight-line method with composite rates based upon estimated service lives. The ranges of composite rates for the principal classes are: land improvements—5% to 7%; buildings—3% to 5%; and machinery and equipment—5% to 20%.
>
> Under the composite method of depreciation, no gain or loss is recognized on normal property dispositions because the property cost is credited to the property accounts and charged to the accumulated depreciation accounts and any proceeds are credited to the accumulated depreciation accounts.

Retirement and Replacement Systems These depreciation systems are used by public utilities and railroads as a means of reducing the recordkeeping costs associated with depreciation calculations. These companies typically own large numbers of items dispersed over extensive geographic areas. Operating assets include rolling stock, track, wire, utility poles, and microwave telephone equipment. The cost to depreciate these items individually is prohibitive.

Under both the **retirement** and **replacement systems,** depreciation is not recorded for individual assets, no gain or loss is recognized on disposal, and the accumulated depreciation account is not used. The total original cost of acquisitions is maintained although often not on an individual asset basis. Residual value is treated as a reduction from depreciation expense in the disposal period. Depreciation expense under both systems is based on assets retired during the period. The distinction between the two systems concerns which side of the retirement/replacement transaction is used for recording depreciation.

The key difference between the two systems is the assumed cost of the retired assets. This difference can be substantial. Depreciation under the retirement system equals the original cost of the item retired less residual value. Alternatively, if the cost of acquisitions cannot be associated with physical units, the oldest remaining cost of the type of asset retired less residual value is used for depreciation purposes. This is essentially a FIFO system.

In contrast, depreciation under the replacement system equals the cost of the most recent acquisition of the type of item retired less residual value. This is essentially a LIFO system and is called the replacement system because the most recent acquisition is considered the replacement for the item retired. However, acquisitions and retirements are treated as separate events, rather than combined as replacements, for generality. Not all acquisitions and retirements are associated with replacements.

To illustrate these systems, assume the following events for Western Power Utility:

1. In 1980, its first 100 miles of power lines are installed for a total cost of $300,000 at an average cost of $3,000 per mile.
2. In 1988, 12.5 miles of additional lines are installed for $50,000 at an average cost of $4,000 per mile.
3. In 1991, 16 miles of new lines are installed for $80,000 at an average cost of $5,000 per mile. Also in 1991, 20 miles of line installed in 1980 at an original cost of $60,000 are retired. $5,000 is received on the disposal.

The following entries are made under both systems to record the acquisitions which total $430,000:

To record acquisitions:

Retirement and Replacement Systems

	1980	1988	1991
Transmission lines	300,000	50,000	80,000
Cash	300,000	50,000	80,000

The retirement system recognizes the cost of the asset retired ($60,000) less the $5,000 residual as depreciation in 1991.[29] The replacement system uses the *latest* acquisition cost for calculating depreciation. Therefore, depreciation under the replacement system is computed as follows:

All 1991 lines installed: 16 miles @ $5,000/mile	$80,000
Part of 1988 installation: 4 miles @ $4,000/mile	16,000
1991 replacement system depreciation before residual	96,000
Proceeds on disposal	5,000
1991 replacement system depreciation	$91,000

The following entries record 1991 depreciation under the two systems:

	Retirement System	Replacement System
Depreciation expense	55,000	91,000
Cash	5,000	5,000
Transmission lines	60,000	96,000

The ending balances in the transmission line account are $370,000 ($430,000 − $60,000) for the retirement system and $334,000 ($430,000 − $96,000) for the replacement systems.

When assets of a particular type are phased out and not replaced, the retirement system recognizes as depreciation the cost of the latest acquisition(s) less residual value as depreciation expense because the earlier costs have been removed in previous periods. In contrast, the replacement system recognizes the cost of the very first acquisition(s) less residual value as depreciation expense because only these remain to be expensed. To illustrate, assume the following information:

---

[29] Assets need not be sold immediately to recognize a reduction from depreciation expense; rather, if held in salvage inventory they are recorded at estimated residual value. The effect on depreciation is recognized at the point of removal from service.

Purchases and retirements of a type of rolling stock of Chicago & Southern Railroad:

Year	Purchases	Retirements
1960	200 @ $30,000	—
1970	100 @ $40,000	100
1980	200 @ $50,000	200
1990	—	200

After 1990, Chicago & Southern Railroad no longer expects to purchase this type of rolling stock.

Ignoring residual value, depreciation in 1990 under the retirement system equals $10 million (200 × $50,000) because 200 units are retired. The earlier purchases were expensed in previous years under this system. In contrast, the replacement system recognizes $6 million (200 × $30,000) depreciation expense. The 1960 purchase, the very first of its kind for this type of car, was not used for previous depreciation expense because the later acquisitions were used first. This is equivalent to liquidating layers when LIFO is used for inventory accounting.

Evaluation   Retirement and replacement systems can result in depreciation amounts that bear no relationship to those of individually applied methods. For example, some deterioration of Western Power Utility assets very likely occurred between 1980 and 1991, but no depreciation is recognized during that period. The replacement system yields a current value for depreciation expense, but only in years when assets are retired. Furthermore, the balance in the asset account under the replacement system can be distorted to the point of meaninglessness. Some firms, for example, reported assets at values that include 19th century costs under the replacement system![30] The results of the retirement system are opposite those of the replacement system: relatively more current reported values for assets, and less current reported values for depreciation expense.

Neither system fulfills the systematic and rational requirement because a preset orderly procedure is not followed. Rather, the results are heavily influenced by retirement of assets. In addition, these systems are not designed to match depreciable cost to periods of use. Depreciation recognition is not a gradual process under either of these systems. Severe distortion of profitability and economic position occurs in early years when few assets are retired. However, if the firm reaches a period of stable growth and replaces assets on an even basis, depreciation results approximate those of one of the more traditional methods.

CONCEPT REVIEW

1. What is the difference between the retirement and replacement depreciation systems?
2. How is annual depreciation expense computed under the inventory appraisal system?
3. What are the main criticisms of the group and composite systems?

IMPAIRMENT OF VALUE—PLANT ASSETS

Plant assets that lose a significant portion of utility or value suffer an **impairment of value**. Asset impairments are caused by casualty, obsolescence, lack of demand for a company's products, negligence, or mismanagement. Other reasons for writing down assets include decisions to close a plant or sell a product line, edicts by

---

[30] In 1983, railroads reporting to the Interstate Commerce Commission were required to compute depreciation under more traditional methods. Many railroads also switched to these methods for financial statement purposes.

regulators that a product must be taken off the market, and expropriation of assets by a foreign government.[31] Asset impairments lead to a write-down of assets to net realizable value.

A general acceleration of asset write-downs began in the early 1980s.[32] Between 1986 and the middle of 1988, the firms constituting the Dow Jones industrials recognized $10 billion in write-downs.[33] Losses from discontinued operations had been relatively common, but now firms were writing down assets that they were keeping. Changes in technology and a high level of merger activity contributed to this phenomenon.

Asset write-downs often result from a corporate restructuring. A restructuring is a partial or complete overhauling of the organization that changes employee composition, corporate policy, product, operating location, and other strategic attributes of the company. The management of a reorganized firm often prefers to publish financial statements reflecting new starting values for major classes of plant assets. Corporate restructurings also are common when companies face difficult times. Entire groupings of plant assets are considered to be overvalued and written down in the restructuring process.

For example, in the 4th quarter of 1989, intensified competition in the U.S. computer industry led International Business Machines Corporation (IBM) to develop a restructuring plan. IBM planned to reduce the number of its employees by 10,000, purchase $4 billion of its stock, and consolidate many of its manufacturing operations. In so doing, IBM expected to recognize a $2.3 billion ($2.25 per share) restructuring charge, or loss. This loss included the write-down of software investments and assets used in manufacturing.[34]

Land, although not depreciated, also is subject to impairment loss. Land can be written down to market value when one or more of the following occur:
* Permanent erosion.
* Natural and man-made pollutants making land unusable.
* Excessive depletion of underground aquifers causing sinkholes.
* Encroachment from competing businesses.
* Impairment caused by changing demographics and competition.

General Guidelines for Loss Recognition

As a general guideline, the book value of a plant asset cannot exceed its economic value in use (the present value of net future cash inflows from use in operations—usually estimated by the cost to replace the asset in its present condition) or net realizable value if not in use. When a permanent impairment occurs, the asset is written down to one of these two values, and a loss is recognized. Otherwise, the asset's book value exceeds its future benefit.[35]

To record the impairment, a nonrecurring loss is debited for the decline in value, and accumulated depreciation usually is credited. The loss typically is not extraordinary because it is neither unusual or infrequent. Asset write-ups are not allowed because stronger evidence (a transaction) is needed to substantiate increases in asset values.

---

[31] Squibb, for example, took a $68 million write-down of its pharmaceuticals operations in South America and Asia fearing unfavorable political and economic conditions, although it continued to operate there. See "You Know It When You See It," *Forbes*, July 25, 1988, p. 84.

[32] The dollar amount and frequency of write-offs increased during the years 1980–85. In "Impairments and Writeoffs of Long-Lived Assets," *Management Accounting*, August 1989, D. Fried, M. Schiff, and A. Sondhi found, for 702 companies during that period, that the average pretax write-off increased from $28.3 million (38 write-offs) to $117.5 million (207 write-offs).

[33] "You Know It When You See It," *Forbes*, July 25, 1988, p. 84.

[34] "IBM Announces Big Write-Off, Restructuring," *The Wall Street Journal*, December 6, 1989, p. A3.

[35] The *SFAC No. 6* (par. 25) definition of an asset is based on economic benefits: "Assets are probable future economic benefits obtained or controlled by a particular entity as a result of past transactions or events."

For example, assume that Ithaca Corporation owns $2,000,000 (cost) of specialized equipment used in the production of video display terminals (VDTs). The equipment was purchased and installed in January 1981 and has an expected useful life of 20 years and a residual value of $200,000. Ithaca uses straight-line depreciation. In January 1991, one of Ithaca's competitors completed the development of a reduced-radiation VDT. The demand for Ithaca's older model VDTs immediately fell considerably. Ithaca estimates that 90% of the demand for its older VDTs is permanently lost.[36] As a result, the manufacturing equipment, which can be used only to produce the older model VDT, is estimated to be worth only $400,000 in use, has no residual value, and will be used only during the estimated five remaining years that the older model VDTs are manufactured. The following entries recognize the impairment loss and depreciation for 1991.

January 1991:

Impairment loss	700,000*	
Accumulated depreciation		700,000

*Original cost of equipment	$2,000,000
Depreciation 1981–1990:	
(10/20) ($2,000,000 − $200,000)	900,000
Book value, January 1991	$1,100,000
Market value, January 1991	400,000
Impairment loss	$ 700,000

December 31, 1991:

Depreciation expense ($400,000/5)	80,000	
Accumulated depreciation		80,000

If the equipment has no further value in use, it is written down to residual value and reclassified as an other asset or investment pending disposal. No further depreciation is recognized.

Need for Specific Accounting Principles

The recognition of an impairment loss is a departure from the historical cost principle. The conditions supporting the asset's value at the time of acquisition no longer apply. Although asset write-downs are commonplace, no specific accounting principles guide their timing, recognition, or measurement. The FASB added this topic to its agenda in 1990 in response to inconsistencies in practice and the lack of authoritative guidance.[37] Several questions must be resolved before a final statement is released:

* Which attribute should be used for measuring value (current cost, current market value, net realizable value, present value of future cash flows, or sum of future cash flows)?
* Which assets, when used jointly in production, should be subject to write-down?
* Should impairments be recognized periodically, or only when circumstances indicate?[38]
* Which criterion should be used for recognition (decline in value, permanent decline in value, or likelihood of decline in value)?[39]

---

[36] This example was suggested by an actual development in the computer industry: IBM planned to lower the electromagnetic fields generated by its VDTs in 1989. See "IBM's Plan to Reduce VDT Radiation Fails to Impress Most Computer Makers," *The Wall Street Journal*, November 24, 1989, p. B3.

[37] FASB, *Discussion Memorandum*, "Accounting for the Impairment of Long-Lived Assets and Identifiable Intangibles" (New York, December 1990).

[38] Examples of events that might give rise to an asset impairment include the reduction in use of an asset, a change in the way an asset is used, a decline in market value, or a change in a law or the environment.

[39] For example, an asset can be temporarily or permanently impaired, or a probable impairment might occur. Which is the most appropriate event triggering recognition? The Financial Executives Institute, *Survey of Unusual Charges, September 26, 1986*, p. 4, found that 60% of firms used a probabilistic criterion.

* Upon recovery of asset value, should restoration of book value be recognized?
* Which should be required—recognition in the accounts or footnote disclosure?

In a study of accounting for asset impairments in nine foreign countries, the FASB found variation across these issues in practice. For example, the accounting principles in eight countries required recognition of asset write-downs, those of seven require a loss to be permanent for recognition, and those of seven allowed restoration of book value when market value increased.[40]

Although many asset write-downs are legitimate and are recorded properly, the absence of specific guidelines governing the timing and measurement of impairment losses creates an opportunity to manage reported income. Firms may take the write-downs as part of a "big bath" in which one or more losses are recognized in a year of poor peformance.[41] The reported performance of future years is thereby relieved of these losses, and individual losses lose some of their negative effect.

There are other reasons to recognize asset impairments. Asset write-downs create tax deductions. Future depreciation expense is decreased by the loss, reducing the burden on future income. Financial ratios involving net income and total assets are improved in future years. Furthermore, write-downs serve to smooth income in years of unexpectedly high income.

Large write-downs also give the capital markets a message that perhaps management or company policy have changed, and that better times are ahead. The reporting firm can argue that the write-down signals to readers that the firm is strong, can afford to recognize impairment losses, and is interested in the quality of its earnings.

These incentives can be attractive. For example, AT&T recognized a $6.72 billion write-off of obsolete telephone network equipment in 1988. The loss also reflected job reductions caused by the replacement of old technology with newer, more automated equipment. The decision to take the write-down "indicates that the telephone giant finally may have put its many troubles behind it. 'I am smiling today because of our financial results,' said . . . a senior vice president."[42]

Managers understand the benefits of asset write-downs. Only 38% of surveyed firms indicated that additional accounting guidelines would be useful.[43] Many firms apparently wish to maintain flexibility in this area.

Financial statement users often express concern about the size and the abrupt nature of asset write-downs. Many contend that the disclosures are unnecessarily delayed, and that the sudden and seemingly arbitrary timing of write-downs erodes confidence in financial statements. Interyear income comparisons become less meaningful with large write-downs.

Until the FASB rules on this issue, it is reasonable to expect continued variation in accounting for asset write-downs. Although write-downs are part of corporate restructurings, objectivity should govern their amounts and timing. Furthermore, the new values assigned to assets also must be acceptable to outside auditors.

CONCEPT REVIEW

1. Although land is not subject to depreciation, under what conditions is it written down?
2. How is an asset impairment loss presently computed?
3. What incentives exist for recognizing impairment losses?

---

[40] FASB, *Discussion Memorandum,* "Accounting for Impairment," p. 55.

[41] For example, M. Pearson and L. Okubara, "Restructurings and Impairment of Value: A Growing Controversy," *Accounting Horizons,* March 1987, found that 85% of a sample of companies reporting write-downs reported the loss in the last half of the fiscal year.

[42] "AT&T Reports Loss for Quarter and All of 1988,"*The Wall Street Journal,* January 27, 1989, p. C20.

[43] Financial Executives Institute, *Survey of Unusual Charges,* p. 8.

EXHIBIT 12-12

Quaker State Corporation: *Summary of Significant Accounting Policies* [in part]

Property, plant, and equipment, at cost: Costs of buildings and equipment, other than petroleum producing properties, are charged against income over their estimated useful lives, using the straight-line method of depreciation. Repairs and maintenance, which are not considered betterments and do not extend the useful life of property, are charged to expense as incurred. When property, plant, and equipment are retired or otherwise disposed of, the asset and accumulated depreciation are removed from the accounts, and the resulting profit or loss is reflected in income.

Estimated costs of future dismantlement, restoration, reclamation, and abandonment of petroleum producing and mining properties are accrued through a charge to operations on a unit of production basis.

The company capitalizes interest as part of constructing major facilities. Interest cost capitalized in 1989, 1988, and 1987 was not material.

Major classes of property, including land and construction work in progress of $50,754,000 in 1989 and $49,378,000 in 1988 are:

(*in thousands*)	1989	1988
Petroleum properties and equipment:		
Production—producing assets	$177,821	$180,840
Production—other	29,697	29,619
Refining	162,079	161,795
Fast lube	115,101	105,153
Marketing	45,405	42,198
Transportation	10,566	10,282
Coal mining properties and equipment	147,253	144,054
Other	53,319	49,175
	741,241	723,116
Less accumulated depreciation and	406,935	386,348
depletion	$334,306	$336,768

PLANT ASSET AND DEPRECIATION DISCLOSURES

APB Opinion No. 12 (par. 5) requires that the following disclosures related to depreciation and depreciable assets be made for each reporting period:

1. Depreciation expense.
2. The balances of major classes of depreciable assets, by nature or function.
3. Accumulated depreciation by asset or in total.
4. A general description of the depreciation methods used with respect to major classes of assets.

These disclosure requirements are augmented by *APB Opinion No. 22,* which cites depreciation methods as examples of required disclosures. Annual reports should also disclose information regarding post-acquisition costs and idle plant assets. Significant liens on assets should be disclosed in the liability section rather than offset against assets. Information about the depreciation methods employed helps financial statement users interpret the meaning and impact of depreciation on income and financial position.

An excerpt from the footnotes to the 1989 financial statements of Quaker State Corporation (shown in Exhibit 12–12) illustrates disclosure of depreciation and operating assets.

SUMMARY OF KEY POINTS

(L.O. 1)   1. Depreciation is a systematic and rational process of allocating depreciable cost (acquisition cost less residual value) to the periods in which plant assets are used. Depreciation expense for a period does not represent the change in market value of assets, nor does it necessarily equal the portion of the asset's utility consumed in the period. Depreciation is justified on the basis of physical deterioration, reduction in utility, and obsolescence.

(L.O. 1)   2. Four factors contribute to the determination of periodic depreciation expense: original acquisition cost and any capitalized post-acquisition costs, estimated residual value, estimated useful life or productivity measured either in service hours or units of output, and the depreciation method chosen.

(L.O. 2)   3. Several methods of depreciation are acceptable under GAAP; these include straight-line, service hours and productive output, and accelerated methods. For all methods, the estimated residual value is the minimum book value. Except for the declining-balance methods, depreciable cost is multiplied by a rate to determine periodic depreciation.

(L.O. 3)   4. In some cases, depreciation reduces the amount of dividends which would otherwise be paid. Tax depreciation reduces the tax liability and thereby reduces the outflow of cash.

(L.O. 4)   5. Fractional year depreciation problems arise when plant asset acquisitions and disposals do not coincide with the fiscal year. Depreciation is computed on a whole-year basis, with the appropriate fraction of a period applied to the depreciation for the relevant whole year of the asset's life.

(L.O. 4)   6. Depreciation of any capitalized post-acquisition cost is affected by the remaining useful life of the original asset relative to that of the subsequent cost, and whether or not the subsequent cost is combined with the original asset for accounting purposes.

(L.O. 5)   7. GAAP allows changes in accounting for depreciation to reflect new information and new methods. Changes in estimates of useful life and residual value affect current and future depreciation expense. For changes in depreciation method, the impact on after-tax income for all previous years affected by the change is recognized in income item in the year of the change. Errors in prior years' depreciation require that retroactive changes be made to the affected accounts.

(L.O. 6)   8. Three depreciation systems (appraisal, composite, and replacement/retirement) are alternatives to depreciation methods applied individually to assets. These systems save accounting costs and are justified under the cost-benefit and materiality constraints.

(L.O. 7)   9. An impairment loss is recorded when it is probable that the value of a plant asset has materially declined below its book value.

(L.O. 8)   10. Current tax laws allow accelerated depreciation schedules based on the type of plant asset. A schedule of declining percentages is applied to asset cost to determine the applicable tax deduction.

(L.O. 9)   11. The recognized gain or loss from an insured casualty is the difference between the insurance proceeds and book value of the asset involved. Coinsurance clauses effectively require insured companies to carry substantial insurance, based on the market value of assets, to guarantee a full recovery.

REVIEW PROBLEM

The following short cases are independent.

1. *Partial-year depreciation*—Whitney Company purchases equipment on July 1, 1989, for $34,000. This equipment has a useful life of five years, and a residual value of $4,000. What is depreciation for 1990 under the double-declining-balance method?

2. *Change in estimate of useful life*—Whitney Company purchases equipment on January 1, 1989, for $34,000. This equipment has a useful life of five years, and a residual value of $4,000. Then, sometime in 1991, Whitney revised the total useful

life of the equipment to eight years. What is depreciation for 1991 under the sum-of-the-years'-digits method?

3. *Composite depreciation*—Baja Company uses the composite method of depreciation and has a composite rate of 25%. During 1991, it sells assets with an original cost of $100,000 (residual value of $20,000) for $80,000 and acquires $60,000 worth of new assets (residual value $10,000). The original group of assets has the following characteristics:

> Total cost $250,000
> Total residual value   30,000

Assuming the new assets conform to the group and the company does not revise the depreciation rate, what is depreciation in 1991?

4. *Retirement and replacement depreciation systems*—Rolling Company at the end of 1990 has $250,000 in its plant asset account. During 1991, it acquires $100,000 of new property and sells property with an original cost of $50,000, receiving only 10% of the original cost on disposal.

a. Under the retirement system of depreciation, what is depreciation expense for 1991, and what is the December 31, 1991, balance in the property account?
b. Under the replacement system of depreciation, what is depreciation expense for 1991, and what is the December 31, 1991, balance in the property account?

SOLUTION
◆

1.

$$\text{Depreciation (1989)} = .50(2/5)(\$34,000) = \$6,800$$
$$\text{Depreciation (1990)} = (2/5)(\$34,000 - \$6,800) = \$10,880$$

2.

$$\text{Accumulated depreciation, 12/31/90} = (\$34,000 - \$4,000)(5 + 4)/15$$
$$= \$18,000$$

New useful life $= 8 - 2 = 6$
New SYD $= 6 + 5 + 4 + 3 + 2 + 1 = 21$
Book value (1/1/91) $= \$34,000 - \$18,000 = \$16,000$
Depreciation (1991) $= (\$16,000 - \$4,000)(6/21) = \$3,429$

3.

$$\text{Depreciation (1991)} = (\$250,000 - \$100,000 + \$60,000).25$$
$$= \$52,500$$

4*a.*

$$\text{Depreciation (1991)} = \$50,000 - (.10 \times \$50,000) = \$45,000$$

Balance in property account (12/31/91) =
$$\$250,000 - \$50,000 + \$100,000 = \$300,000$$

4*b.*

$$\text{Depreciation (1991)} = \$100,000 - (.10 \times \$50,000) = \$95,000$$

Balance in property account (12/31/91) =
$$\$250,000 + \$100,000 - \$100,000 = \$250,000$$

APPENDIX 12A: *Depreciation under the Income Tax Law*

Depreciation under GAAP rules and depreciation under the current tax code are different matters. Under both authorities, depreciation acts to reduce income before tax, and total depreciation over the life of an asset is limited to original cost. But there the similarity ends. Under GAAP, depreciation guidelines are intended to allocate an asset's historical cost to the accounting periods in which the asset is used, in accordance with the matching principle.

In contrast, tax depreciation is geared to the revenue needs of the federal government, which change in response to economic conditions and the fiscal policies of the elected administration. For example, tax depreciation currently provides an incentive for replacement, modernization, and expansion of industrial facilities through accelerated depreciation schedules.

Before the Economic Recovery Tax Act of 1981 (as amended by the Deficit Reduction Act of 1984), companies chose a depreciation method for tax purposes from among the methods discussed in this chapter, including straight-line, sum-of-the-years'-digits, declining-balance, as well as methods based on production or input use. For some older assets, these methods remain applicable for tax purposes.

Accelerated Cost Recovery System

The 1981 Act established a new accelerated depreciation system for income tax purposes. This change in the tax law created the **accelerated cost recovery system** (ACRS). ACRS modifies the use of estimated useful life and residual value in determining the depreciation deduction. The Act specifies "cost recovery periods" for various classes of assets. As a form of accelerated depreciation, ACRS allows greater depreciation deductions, compared to straight-line depreciation, early in the asset's life; thus, taxable income is lower, compared to using straight-line depreciation, during these periods. Under ACRS, a company has an option to use either the accelerated cost recovery method or the straight-line method. Residual value is disregarded under either option.

The estimated useful life of assets is not used in the ACRS depreciation calculation. Instead, assets are assigned to a class with a specified life over which depreciation deductions are taken. ACRS requires that personal property[44] be assigned to one of the following classes:

3-year property—primarily automobiles and light trucks, machinery, and equipment used in connection with research experimentation.

5-year property—primarily property that does not fit into any other class of property. This includes most other personal property such as furniture and fixtures.

10-year property—public utility property with useful lives of more than 18 but not more than 25 years, amusement park structures, manufactured homes (including mobile homes), railroad tank cars, and coal utilization property. In addition, real property with a life of no more than 12.5 years is included.

The annual ACRS deduction is determined by multiplying the cost of the asset by a statutory recovery percentage pertinent to the asset's class. The percentages for personal property placed in service between 1981 and 1986 are given in Exhibit 12A–1.

To illustrate the ACRS deduction, assume that equipment in the three-year class is purchased for $10,000. The firm reports on a calendar year basis and uses SL for book purposes. The equipment has a three-year useful life and residual value of $1,000. Depreciation of the equipment for tax purposes and financial reporting purposes is:

	Tax (ACRS) Depreciation	Financial Reporting (SL) Depreciation
Year 1 . . . . . $10,000(.25) =	$ 2,500	$3,000*
Year 2 . . . . . $10,000(.38) =	3,800	3,000
Year 3 . . . . . $10,000(.37) =	3,700	3,000
	$10,000	$9,000

*($10,000 − $1,000)/3

Half-Year Convention The accelerated nature of ACRS depreciation is not readily apparent from the schedule of percentages by class of asset. This is due to the half-year convention built into the first year percentage for each property class. Under the half-year convention, an asset is assumed to begin service in the middle of the year of purchase, reflecting, on average, a midyear acquisition date.

---

[44] Real property (real estate) is assigned to another class.

EXHIBIT 12A-1   ACRS Rates: Personal Property Placed in Service between 1981 and 1986

Recovery Year	Class 3-Year	5-Year	10-Year
1	25%*	15%*	8%*
2	38	22	14
3	37	21	12
4		21	10
5		21	10
6			10
7			9
8			9
9			9
10			9
Total	100%	100%	100%

*Half-year convention rate, explained in text.

If the taxpayer chooses not to use accelerated depreciation as illustrated above, straight-line depreciation can be adopted. For each class of property, three alternative optional recovery periods can be used with the straight-line method:

Property Class	Optional Recovery Periods (years)
Personal property:	
3-year	3, 5, or 12
5-year	5, 12, or 25
10-year	10, 25, or 35
Real property (real estate):	
15-year	35 or 45
18-year	18, 15, or 45
19-year	19, 35, or 45

If the taxpayer elects the optional straight-line method, only one-half year's depreciation (based on the recovery period selected) is allowed in the first year. Residual values are ignored. To illustrate, assume that a company acquired the $10,000 asset described earlier and elected to use the optional straight-line method with a three-year recovery period. Annual tax depreciation is:

Year	Tax Depreciation		
1	$10,000(1/3) (1/2) =	$	1,667
2	10,000(1/3) =		3,333
3	10,000(1/3) =		3,333
4	10,000(1/3) (1/2) =		1,667
Total			$10,000

Modified Accelerated Cost Recovery System

The **modified accelerated cost recovery system (MACRS)** was enacted by the Tax Reform Act of 1986. It applies to most depreciable property placed in service after 1986. MACRS generally increases the number of recovery years under ACRS by one.

MACRS defines the following classes of personal property:

3-year property—primarily horses, special tools, and assets used in research and development activities.

5-year property—primarily all machinery and equipment not included in other categories, and automobiles and light trucks (property with a life of more than 4 years and less than 10).

7-year property—office furniture and fixtures, agriculture equipment, equipment used in oil exploration and development, railroad track, and certain manufacturing equipment (property with a life of 10 or more years and less than 16).

EXHIBIT 12A–2   MACRS Rates by Class of Personal Property

Recovery Year	3-Year	5-Year	7-Year	10-Year	15-Year	20-Year
1	33.33%	20.00%	14.29%	10.00%	5.00%	3.750%
2	44.45	32.00	24.49	18.00	9.50	7.219
3	14.81*	19.20	17.49	14.40	8.55	6.677
4	7.41	11.52*	12.49	11.52	7.70	6.177
5		11.52	8.93*	9.22	6.93	5.713
6		5.76	8.92	7.37	6.23	5.285
7			8.93	6.55*	5.90*	4.888
8			4.46	6.55	5.90	4.522
9				6.56	5.91	4.462*
10				6.55	5.90	4.461
11				3.28	5.91	4.462
12					5.90	4.461
13					5.91	4.462
14					5.90	4.461
15					5.91	4.462
16					2.95	4.461
17						4.462
18						4.461
19						4.462
20						4.461
21						2.231
Total	100%	100%	100%	100%	100%	100%

* Denotes year in which MACRS depreciation is less than or equal to straight-line depreciation; the schedule switches to straight-line depreciation in this year.

10-year property—certain public utility property, real estate, railroad tank cars, manufactured homes, and coal conversion boilers and equipment (property with a life of 16 or more years and less than 20).

15-year property—public utility property and certain low-income housing (property with a life of at least 20 years and less than 25).

20-year property—property not depreciated using the 15-year property class (property with a life of more than 25 years).

For brevity, Exhibit 12A–2 lists the depreciation percentages for personal property only, and applies to assets placed into service after 1986.

MACRS shifts to the SL method once SL yields an equal or higher deduction. For example, for five-year property, the remaining tax basis (book value for tax purposes) beginning with Year 4 is depreciated on the straight-line basis, with the final year subject to half-year convention. For this class of property, 28.8% (1 − 20% − 32% − 19.2%) of the basis remains to depreciate over two and a half years, yielding 11.52% (28.8%/2.5) of the asset to be depreciated in the remaining two full years and half that amount in the final year.

Before the switch to the SL method, the MACRS pecentages yield results identical to the double-declining-balance method, after considering the half-year convention for the first year. For example, the fractions of the cost of a five-year-class asset deductible under MACRS, and recognized under the double-declining-balance method in the first three years are:

Year	MACRS*	Double Declining Balance	
1	20%	20%	= (.40†) (.50‡)
2	32%	32%	= (1 − .20) (.40)
3	19.2%	19.2%	= (1 − .20 − .32) (.40)

* From Exhibit 12A–2.
† Twice the straight line = 2(1/5) = .40.
‡ Half-year convention.

As with ACRS, firms have the option to use the straight-line method for the entire tax-life of the asset. A half-year convention also applies. The following table illustrates the percentage of cost taken as the depreciation deduction for a five-year asset under this option:

Year	Percent of Cost Allowed for Depreciation
1	10
2	20
3	20
4	20
5	20
6	10

ACRS and MACRS allocate the cost of a plant asset without considering its estimated useful life or residual value. Therefore, the tax depreciation deduction for a given year equals the GAAP depreciation expense only by coincidence.

APPENDIX 12B: *Accounting for Insured Casualty Losses and Gains*

Losses due to abandonment or casualty are discussed in Chapter 11 (disposals) and under asset impairments in this chapter. In this appendix, accounting for insured casualty losses and the **coinsurance** characteristic of casualty insurance are considered. Coinsurance refers to the fact that if a company is intent on underinsuring its assets to reduce insurance premiums, the insurance carrier reserves the right not to accept full responsibility for certain casualty losses.

A casualty insurance policy is a contract between an insurance company and the company desiring insurance coverage for losses from disasters such as fires and storms. In exchange for an insurance premium, the insurance company assumes an obligation to reimburse the policy holder for a casualty loss. Many casualty insurance policies carry a **coinsurance clause** requiring that if property is insured for less than the coinsurance percentage (often 80%) of its replacement cost at time of loss, the owner becomes a coinsurer of the property and must absorb some of the loss.

Casualty Insurance Policy Settlement

The amount of reimbursement for a casualty loss from a policy with an 80% coinsurance clause is the lowest of the following three potential settlement amounts:"[45]

1. Face value of the policy.
2. Replacement cost of the property lost:

$$\text{Replacement cost of property at date of casualty} - \text{Replacement cost of property after the casualty}$$

3. **Indemnity formula:**

$$\left[\frac{\text{Face value of policy}}{.80 \, (\text{Replacement cost of property at date of casualty})} \right] \left[\begin{array}{c} \text{Replacement cost of} \\ \text{the property lost} \end{array} \right]$$

The second value above is the economic loss from the casualty before insurance proceeds are collected. This value is not likely to equal the amount recorded as a loss for financial accounting purposes because the variables used to determine insurance settlement are measured in terms of market value. The accounting gain or loss, which can be classified as extraordinary for reporting purposes, is the difference between insurance proceeds and the portion of the book value lost.

---

[45] For an insurance policy with no coinsurance clause, the recoverable amount is the lower of the first two potential reimbursement amounts.

Example

To illustrate coinsurance and the accounting for a casualty, assume Hazard Company experienced a fire that destroyed equipment insured under a casualty insurance policy:

1. Equipment originally costing $140,000 has a $20,000 accumulated depreciation balance on January 1, 1991. It is depreciated $20,000 per year.
2. The equipment has a replacement cost of $90,000 on June 30, 1991, just prior to a fire on that date that caused major damage to the equipment. The equipment is worth $40,000 after the fire. The replacement cost of equipment lost is therefore $50,000 ($90,000 − $40,000). Thus 55.56% of the equipment's replacement value is lost ($50,000/$90,000).
3. The equipment is insured under a $70,000 casualty insurance policy with an 80% coinsurance clause. The annual $1,600 premium is paid on January 1, 1991, and prepaid insurance is debited. The policy apportions the premium on face value; face value is reduced by insurance proceeds in the event of a casualty.

The three potential settlement amounts for Hazard are:
1. Face value: $70,000.
2. Replacement cost of property lost:

$$\$90,000 - \$40,000 = \$50,000$$

3. Indemnity formula value:

$$\frac{\$70,000}{.80(\$90,000)} \times \$50,000 = \$48,611$$

Hazard receives $48,611 from the insurance company (the lowest of the three values), which is less than full recovery of the economic loss.

The following entries, dated June 30, 1991, are recorded by Hazard.

Depreciation for 1/2 year:

Depreciation expense	10,000	
Accumulated depreciation		10,000

Insurance expense for 1/2 year:

Insurance expense	800	
Prepaid insurance		800

Recognition of casualty loss:

Cash	48,611	
Accumulated depreciation	16,668*	
Casualty loss	13,061	
Prepaid insurance		556†
Equipment		77,784‡

* ($20,000 + $10,000) (.5556).
† ($48,611/$70,000) ($800).
‡ $140,000(.5556).

The casualty loss represents the net asset reduction resulting from the fire, considering insurance proceeds, and is measured in terms of the book value of assets involved. The percentage of replacement cost lost (55.56%) is applied to the book value of the equipment. The face value of the insurance policy is reduced by the proceeds. Therefore, $556 of the premium is absorbed in the fire loss. The remaining $244 ($800 − $556) of prepaid insurance relates to the $21,389 face value remaining in the policy ($70,000 − $48,611) for the remainder of 1991.

Firms desiring full settlement for a casualty loss must guarantee that the economic loss (second potential settlement amount) is the minimum, or at least tied for the minimum, of the three potential settlement amounts. The lowest of the three potential settlement amounts determines the insurance proceeds.

To achieve this guarantee a policy with an 80% coinsurance clause must have a face value equalling or exceeding the greater of (a) the economic loss itself or (b) 80% of the replacement cost of property at date of casualty (the coinsurance requirement). If face value equals or exceeds the economic loss, then the face value is eliminated as a candidate for the settlement amount.

If the face value of the policy also equals or exceeds 80% of the replacement cost at date of casualty, then the indemnity formula value equals or exceeds the economic loss, thus eliminating the indemnity value from contention.[46] The economic loss is therefore the lowest of the three potential settlement amounts, and is fully reimbursed.

In the Hazard example, a policy with a face value equaling or exceeding the greater of (a) $50,000, and (b) $72,000 (.80 × $90,000), is required for full recovery. In this case, a $72,000 face value results in an indemnity value of $50,000, which is equal to the economic loss. Therefore Hazard would receive $50,000, a full recovery.

Perhaps surprisingly, a face value exceeding the economic loss is no guarantee of full recovery. If the face value were $60,000, (exceeding the loss by $10,000), the lowest of the three potential settlement amounts is the indemnity value:

$$\frac{\$60,000}{.80(\$90,000)} \times \$50,000 = \$41,667$$

which is less than a full recovery.[47]

Hazard's economic loss is less than 80% of the property's value at date of casualty. If the loss exceeded $72,000, the face value of the policy must equal or exceed the economic loss to guarantee full recovery (in this case, the economic loss exceeds 80% of the replacement cost at date of casualty). This means that, for large losses, full recovery does not occur even though the coinsurance requirement is met (face value equaling or exceeding 80% of replacement cost). In the event of a total loss, the face value must at least equal the replacement cost of the property at date of casualty to achieve a complete recovery.

These examples illustrate the role of the coinsurance clause in transferring part of the risk from insurance company to the insured. The clause effectively requires the policy holder to carry insurance well beyond the expected loss to guarantee full recovery. Most casualty losses are not total losses. Without this clause in the policy, companies would insure property for considerably less than 80% of value, thus lowering their insurance costs. Insurance firms would be responsible for 100% of small percentage losses even though the property is insured for much less than 100% of value.

Multiple Insurance Policies

Companies often purchase more than one policy to insure an asset against casualty. Assuming more than one policy, the recoverable cash amount from Policy A (with an 80% coinsurance clause) is determined from the following formula:

$$\left[\frac{\text{Face value of Policy A}}{\substack{\text{Greater of: 80\% of replacement cost} \\ \text{of property at date of casualty} \\ \text{or} \\ \text{Sum of face values of all} \\ \text{policies on asset.}}}\right] \left(\substack{\text{Replacement} \\ \text{cost of} \\ \text{property lost}}\right)$$

This formula is similar to the indemnity value for single policies. Firms cannot expect to insure property with a number of small face value policies and reap full recovery if a casualty occurs. The coinsurance clause produces a large denominator (due to the coinsurance requirement), resulting in a smaller fraction and lower ultimate cash recovery. The policy holder again is a coinsurer.

Using the Hazard example again, assume two policies with 80% coinsurance clauses are maintained on the equipment. The face value of the two policies are: Policy A, $10,000, and Policy B, $40,000. The sum of the face values is $50,000, and 80% of the replacement cost of the property at date of casualty is $72,000. The amounts recoverable from each policy are therefore:

---

[46] This result occurs because the denominator of the fraction in the indemnity formula (80% of the replacement cost of property at date of casualty) is equal to or less than the face value, making the fraction equal to or greater than 1. The indemnity value is therefore equal to or greater than the replacement cost of the property lost—the economic loss itself.

[47] An 80% coinsurance clause does not imply that the insurance company pays only 80% of the loss, nor does it mean that the insured need pay only 80% of the policy premium to maintain coverage.

$$
\begin{array}{lrr}
\text{Policy A: (\$10,000/\$72,000)\$50,000} & = & \$\ 6,944 \\
\text{Policy B: (\$40,000/\$72,000)\$50,000} & = & \underline{27,778} \\
\text{Total amount recovered} & & \underline{\$34,722} \\
\end{array}
$$

Hazard did not insure the property for at least 80% of its $90,000 replacement value and thus bears 31% of the loss (1 − $34,722/$50,000). If the sum of the face values of the policies were $72,000 (the total 80% coinsurance requirement), full recovery would be achieved.

Companies generally insure assets at market value. Therefore, casualty insurance proceeds can exceed the book value of the damaged asset, causing large gains. For example, Delta Air Lines recognized a $5.5 million gain on the crash of one of its 727 aircraft in Dallas in 1988. The plane was insured for $6.5 million, but only had a book value of approximately $1 million.[48]

KEY TERMS

Accelerated cost recovery system (ACRS) (616)
Accelerated depreciation (585)
Capital maintenance (595)
Coinsurance (619)
Coinsurance clause (619)
Composite depreciation (605)
Depreciable cost (581)

Group depreciation (605)
Impairment of value (609)
Indemnity formula (619)
Inventory appraisal system (604)
Modified accelerated cost recovery system (617)
Replacement depreciation system (607)
Retirement depreciation system (607)

QUESTIONS

1. Explain and compare amortization, depletion, and depreciation.
2. A company reported $2 million of depreciation expense in its income statement. Explain what this means to a friend who has little or no background in accounting. Also explain what it does not imply.
3. List several factors a firm would consider in choosing a depreciation method.
4. Explain the difference in meaning between the balances in the following two accounts: (a) accumulated depreciation and (b) allowance to reduce inventory to LCM.
5. What are the primary causes of depreciation? What effect do changes in the market value of the asset being depreciated have on the depreciation estimates?
6. Explain the three factors (other than depreciation method) that must be considered in allocating the cost of an operational asset.
7. Explain the effects of depreciation on (a) the income statement and (b) the balance sheet.
8. In estimating the service life of an operational asset, obsolescence should be considered. Explain this factor.
9. Explain the relationship of depreciation to (a) cash flow and (b) tangible operational assets.
10. Explain the relationship between depreciation and replacement of the assets being depreciated.
11. Compare the effect of straight-line and productive output methods of depreciation on the per unit cost of output for a manufacturing company.
12. What is meant by accelerated methods of depreciation? Under what circumstances would these methods generally be appropriate?
13. Which method, SYD or DDB, will always produce the larger amount of depreciation in the first year of an asset's useful life? Show why by example and in general.
14. Explain the basic accounting policy problems that arise with respect to depreciation when a firm's reporting year and the asset year do not coincide. Consider the case of a company that closes its books on June 30 and has purchased a depreciable asset on January 1.
15. Explain the inventory appraisal system of depreciation. Under what circumstances is such a system appropriate?
16. Compare retirement and replacement depreciation systems. Explain when each of these systems would be appropriate.
17. When would the replacement method of depreciation result in lower depreciation expense than the retirement system?

---

[48] "Crash Accounting," *Forbes*, October 17, 1988, p. 13.

18. How are the composite and group depreciation systems similar?
19. Explain the difficulties that may arise when using group depreciation.
20. What are some of the advantages of using depreciation systems?
21. There are three types of depreciation "changes." Briefly explain each and outline the accounting involved as specified in *APB Opinion No. 20* and *SFAS No. 16*.
22. Explain what is meant by ACRS depreciation. Explain why ACRS may not conform to GAAP.
23. In computing a corporation's tax liability, is tax or GAAP depreciation used?
24. What are the three values leading to determination of the settlement from an insurance company for a casualty loss covered by a casualty insurance policy with an 80% coinsurance clause?
25. What does an 80% coinsurance clause mean to the insured company?

EXERCISES

E 12–1
Depreciation Schedules
(L.O. 2)

Stoner Company acquired an operational asset at a cost of $10,000 that is estimated to have a useful life of five years and residual value of $2,500.

Required:

1. Prepare a depreciation schedule for the entire life of the asset using the following methods (show computations and round to the nearest dollar):
   a. Straight-line method.
   b. SYD method.
   c. DB (200% rate) method.
2. What criteria should be considered in selecting a method?

E 12–2
Several Methods of
Depreciation Computation
(L.O. 2)

To demonstrate the computations involved in several methods of depreciating an operational asset, the following data are used:

Acquisition cost	$12,500
Residual value	$ 500
Estimated service life:	
Years	5
Service hours	10,000
Productive output (units)	24,000

Required:

Give the formula and compute the annual depreciation amount using each of the following methods (show computations and round to the nearest dollar):

1. Straight-line depreciation; compute the depreciation rate and amount for each year.
2. Service hours method; compute the depreciation rate and amount for the first year assuming 2,200 service hours of actual operation.
3. Productive output method of depreciation; compute the depreciation rate and amount for the first year assuming 4,000 units of output. Is all of the depreciation amount (computed in your answer) expensed during the current period?
4. SYD method; compute the depreciation amount for each year.
5. DB (200% acceleration rate) method; compute the depreciation amount for each year.

E 12–3
Depreciation Computation
(L.O. 1, 2)

Mace Company acquired equipment that cost $36,000, which will be depreciated on the assumption that it will last six years and have a $2,400 residual value. Several possible methods of depreciation are under consideration.

Required:

1. Prepare a schedule that shows annual depreciation expense, accumulated depreciation, and book value for the first two years assuming (show computations and round to nearest dollar):
   a. SYD method.
   b. Productive output method. Estimated output is a total of 105,000 units, of which 12,000 will be produced the first year; 18,000 for each of the next two years; 15,000 the fourth year; and 21,000 the fifth and sixth years.
2. What criteria would you consider important in selecting a method?

E 12–4

Identify Depreciation
Methods: Depreciation
Schedules
(L.O. 2)

Veto Company bought equipment on January 1, 1991, for $45,000. The expected life is 10 years, and the residual value is $5,000. Based on three acceptable depreciation methods, the annual depreciation expense and cumulative balance of accumulated depreciation at the end of 1991 and 1992 are shown below.

	Case A		Case B		Case C	
Year	Annual Expense	Accumulated Amount	Annual Expense	Accumulated Amount	Annual Expense	Accumulated Amount
1991	$9,000	$ 9,000	$4,000	$4,000	$7,273	$7,273
1992	7,200	16,200	4,000	8,000	6,545	13,818

Required:

1. Identify the depreciation method used in each case.
2. Based on your answer to (1), prepare a depreciation schedule for each case for 1991 through 1994.

E 12–5

Identify Three
Depreciation Methods
(L.O. 2)

On January 1, 1991, Gopher Company acquired a machine for $15,000. The estimated residual value of the machine is $1,000, and the estimated useful life is five years. Gopher's year-end is December 31.

Required:

Identify the method of depreciation used by Gopher if 1992 depreciation expense is (*a*) $3,600, (*b*) $2,800, (*c*) $3,733.

E 12–6

Application of the
Inventory Appraisal
System
(L.O. 6)

Mite Engineering Company acquired a large number of small tools at the beginning of operations on January 1, 1991, for $2,000. During 1991 and 1992, Mite disposed of several used tools, receiving cash salvage value of $200 in 1991 and $250 in 1992. During 1992, Mite acquired additional tools at a cost of $800. Inventories of tools on hand, valued at current acquisition cost adjusted for the present condition of the tools, indicated a value of $1,400 on December 31, 1991, and $1,800 on December 31, 1992. Mite uses the inventory appraisal system of depreciation for small tools.

Required:

Give the entries for the inventory appraisal system to record the above transactions. Include adjusting entries for depreciation and the related closing entries.

E 12–7

Depreciation:
Multiple Choice
(L.O. 1, 2, 3)

Select the best answer for each of the following.

1. As generally used in accounting, what is depreciation?
   (*a*) It is a process of asset valuation for balance sheet purposes.
   (*b*) It applies only to long-lived intangible assets.
   (*c*) It is used to indicate a decline in market value of a long-lived asset.
   (*d*) It is an accounting process that allocates long-lived asset cost to accounting periods.
2. Property, plant, and equipment should be reported at cost less accumulated depreciation on a balance sheet dated December 31, 1991, unless:
   (*a*) Some obsolescence is known to have occurred.
   (*b*) An appraisal made during 1991 disclosed a higher value.
   (*c*) The amount of insurance carried on the property is well in excess of its book value.
   (*d*) Some of the property still on hand was written down in 1989 due to permanent impairment of its use value.
3. Upon purchase of certain depreciable assets used in its production process, a company expects to be able to replace these assets by adopting a policy of never declaring dividends in amounts larger than net income (after deducting depreciation). If a net income is earned each year, recording depreciation will coincidentally result in sufficient assets being retained within the enterprise, which, if in liquid form, could be used to replace those fully depreciated assets if:
   (*a*) Prices remain reasonably constant during the life of the property.
   (*b*) Prices rise throughout the life of the property.
   (*c*) The retirement depreciation system is used.
   (*d*) Obsolescence was an unexpected factor in bringing about retirement of the assets replaced.

4. Which of the following statements is the assumption on which straight-line depreciation is based?
   (*a*) The operating efficiency of the asset decreases in later years.
   (*b*) Service value declines as a function of time rather than use.
   (*c*) Service value declines as a function of obsolescence rather than time.
   (*d*) Physical wear and tear are more important than economic obsolescence.

(AICPA adapted)

E 12–8
Depreciation: Multiple Choice
(L.O. 1, 2, 4)

Choose the correct answer for each of the following questions, and assume a calendar year reporting period. Accounting conventions are not used for fractional period depreciation.

1. Accumulated depreciation, as used in accounting, represents:
   (*a*) Funds set aside to replace assets.
   (*b*) The portion of asset cost written off as an expense since the acquisition date.
   (*c*) Earnings retained in the business that will be used to purchase another operational asset when the related asset becomes fully depreciated.
   (*d*). An expense on the income statement.
2. Corporations A and B purchased identical equipment having an estimated service life of 10 years. Corporation A uses straight-line depreciation and B uses SYD. Assuming the companies are identical in all other respects, choose the correct statement below.
   (*a*) B will record more depreciation on this asset over the entire 10 years than will A.
   (*b*) At the end of the third year, the book value of the asset will be lower for A than for B.
   (*c*) Net income will be lower for A in the ninth year than for B.
   (*d*) Depreciation expense will be higher the first year for A than for B.
3. Depreciation:
   (*a*) Is an allocation of property, plant, and equipment cost to the time period of usefulness, in a systematic and rational manner.
   (*b*) Is a process of recognizing the decreasing value of an asset over time.
   (*c*) Is a cash expense.
   (*d*) Expense of $2,000 reflects a $2,000 increase in liquid funds.
4. Group or composite depreciation:
   (*a*) Is not based on historical cost.
   (*b*) Requires changing the composite rate each year.
   (*c*) Does not provide effective results if the group members' useful lives are widely different.
   (*d*) Usually records a gain or loss on retirement of assets.
5. What is 1991 depreciation using the SYD method on an asset purchased October 1, 1990, costing $10,000, with a residual value of $2,000 and a three-year useful life?
   (*a*) $4,000.   (*c*) $4,583.
   (*b*) $2,667.   (*d*) $3,667.
6. Pepple Company purchased a computer on June 30, 1991, for $21,000. The computer had a salvage value of $6,000 and useful life of six years. Using double-declining-balance depreciation, determine depreciation expense for 1992.
   (*a*) $4,167.   (*c*) $5,833.
   (*b*) $4,667.   (*d*) $4,863.

E 12–9
Depreciation of Post-Acquisition Costs
(L.O. 4)

Fender Company purchased a mainframe computer on January 2, 1991, for $1,200,000. The system has a useful life of six years, considering obsolescence. Its residual value is $20,000. Fender uses the straight-line method. The following events took place in 1992:

a. March 1: peripheral equipment costing $30,000 was added to the mainframe. This equipment has a useful life of seven years, and residual value of $2,000. This equipment can be used with several different mainframes. Fender may replace the mainframe before the disposing of this equipment.
b. September 1: an additional memory device was added to the mainframe, costing $250,000. This device has no utility apart from the mainframe but will increase the total residual of the mainframe to $40,000.

Required:
Provide the general journal entry to record depreciation expense for 1992 on the mainframe and related equipment.

E 12–10

Group Depreciation:
Asset Torn Down, Entries
(L.O. 6)

Ohio Company owned 10 warehouses of a similar type except for varying size. The group system of depreciation is applied to the 10 warehouses, and the rate is 6% each year on cost. At the end of 1991, the asset account warehouses showed a balance of $5,300,000 (residual value $300,000), and the accumulated depreciation account showed a balance of $2,400,000. Shortly after the end of 1991, Warehouse No. 8, costing $400,000, was torn down. Materials salvaged from the demolition were sold for $53,000, and $15,000 was spent on demolition.

Required:

Give entries to record (*a*) depreciation for 1991, (*b*) disposal of the warehouse, and (*c*) depreciation for 1992.

E 12–11

Composite Depreciation
System Applied
(L.O. 6)

Wilson Company owned the following machines, all acquired on January 1, 1991:

Machine	Original Cost	Estimated Residual Value	Estimated Life (Years)
A	$14,000	None	4
B	20,000	$2,400	8
C	36,000	4,000	10
D	38,000	2,000	12

Required:

1. Prepare a schedule based on straight-line depreciation that shows for each machine the following: cost, residual value, depreciable cost, life in years, and annual depreciation.
2. Compute the composite depreciation rate (based on cost) and the composite life if the machines are depreciated using the composite system.
3. Give the entry to record 1991 composite depreciation.

E 12–12

Composite Depreciation
System Applied
(L.O. 6)

California Utilities owned a power plant that consisted of the following, all acquired on January 1, 1991:

	Cost	Estimated Residual Value	Estimated Life (Years)
Building	$500,000	$50,000	30
Machinery, etc.	250,000	10,000	10
Other equipment	100,000	10,000	5

Required:

Carry decimals to the nearest two places.

1. Compute the total straight-line depreciation for 1992 on all items combined.
2. Compute the composite depreciation rate (based on cost) and the composite life on the plant.
3. Give the entry to record 1991 composite depreciation.

E 12–13

Replacement and
Retirement Systems
Compared
(L.O. 6)

Lincoln Utility Company purchased 600 poles at $220 per pole, debiting the poles inventory account. Subsequent to the purchase, 100 of the new poles were used to replace an equal number of old poles, which were carried in the tangible operational asset account, poles. The old poles originally cost $140 each and had an estimated residual value of $20 per pole.

Required:

1. Give all indicated entries (*a*) assuming the replacement system is employed and (*b*) assuming the retirement system is used.
2. Compare the effect of these two systems on depreciation expense and the related asset accounts.

E 12–14

Fractional-Year
Depreciation: SL and
SYD Compared
(L.O. 4)

Jackson Company's records show the following property acquisitions and disposals during the first two years of operations:

			Disposals	
Year	Acquisition Cost of Property	Estimated Useful Life (Years)	Year of Acquisition	Amount
1991	$50,000	10	—	—
1992	20,000	10	1991	$7,000

Property is depreciated for one half year in the year of acquisition. Property disposed is depreciated for one half year in its year of disposal. Assume no residual values. There are no sale proceeds upon retirement.

Required:

1. Compute depreciation expense for 1991 and for 1992 and the balances of the property and related accumulated depreciation accounts at the end of each year under the following depreciation methods. Show computations and round to the nearest dollar. (Hint: set up separate schedules for "property" and for "accumulated depreciation.")
   a. Straight-line method.
   b. SYD method.
2. Give entries for the acquisition, periodic depreciation, and retirement of the property assuming:
   a. Straight-line method.
   b. SYD method.

(AICPA adapted)

(Hint: set up parallel columns for 1991 and 1992)

E 12–15
Impairment of Value: Operational Assets
(L.O. 7)

Down Manufacturing Company has a small facility, called Plant XT, that has not been used for several years due to low product demand. The company does not expect to use the facility in the foreseeable future. Efforts are being made to sell the plant for $35,000, but a realistic recovery amount is $20,000 (net of disposal costs). The accounting records show cost, $145,000; accumulated depreciation, $80,000.

Required:

Give the entry that Down should make to record the permanent impairment of use-value.

E 12–16
Appendix 12A: MACRS Depreciation Calculations
(L.O. 8)

Delton Company purchased equipment in 1991 for $200,000, which qualifies as a three-year class asset for tax depreciation purposes. The equipment has a useful life of six years. Delton chooses to use the MACRS tax depreciation tables to compute its depreciation deduction.

Required:

1. Compute Delton's depreciation tax deduction for each year using the MACRS tables.
2. Compute Delton's depreciation tax deduction for each year using the DDB method using a 3-year useful life (remember the half-year convention).
3. Compute the present value of tax benefits from depreciating this asset for tax purposes, assuming (*a*) an applicable 14% after-tax minimum rate of return for Delton, (*b*) Delton has sufficient income to obtain the tax benefits of depreciation in each year, (*c*) tax payments for a tax year are made at year-end, and (*d*) the applicable tax rate is 30%. What is the effect of this amount on the total economic cost of the asset?

E 12–17
Appendix 12B: Multiple Choice: Casualty Losses
(L.O. 9)

Choose the correct answer for each of the following questions.

1. A company carries casualty insurance on one of its buildings. The policy features an 80% coinsurance clause.
   (*a*) If the company carries insurance equal to or exceeding 80% of the fair value of the building prior to a casualty, it is guaranteed a full recovery.
   (*b*) The company must bear 20% of any casualty loss.
   (*c*) The company will receive full recovery on any loss that is less than or equal to 80% of the fair value of the building prior to a casualty.
   (*d*) The company has less of a chance of a full recovery than if it had a 65% coinsurance clause.
   (*e*) If face value exceeds a loss, a full recovery is guaranteed.
2. Mabel Corp. suffered fire damage to one of its buildings. The building was insured by a casualty insurance policy that had a face value of $100,000 and a 65% coinsurance clause. The fair market value of the building before and after the fire were $155,000 and $65,000 respectively. Mabel will receive which of the following amounts from the insurance company?
   (*a*) $100,000.   (*c*) $90,000.
   (*b*) $65,000.   (*d*) $89,330.

3. A casualty insurance policy was written on a building with a fair market value of $350,000. If a fire caused $150,000 damage and there was an 80% coinsurance requirement, what is the minimum face value of the policy required to guarantee a full settlement of this loss?

(*a*) $280,000.   (*c*) $350,000.
(*b*) $150,000.   (*d*) $200,000.

4. The market and book value of a building partially destroyed by fire are $100,000 prior to the fire and $70,000 after the fire. The casualty insurance policy covering the property carried an 80% coinsurance clause. What is the net loss for accounting purposes if face value of the policy is $60,000.

(*a*) $30,000.   (*c*) $12,000.
(*b*) $7,500.   (*d*) There was no loss.

E 12–18
Appendix 12B: Fire Loss, Coinsurance
(L.O. 9)

Grife Company operates retail branches in various cities. Branches in four cities are served out of Warehouse No. 16, which sustained fire damage to part of the inventory on April 10.

Between January 1 and April 10, shipments from Warehouse No. 16 to its four stores were recorded as follows: Branch W, $80,500; X, $92,000; Y, $69,000; and Z, $23,000.

Shipments to branches are marked up 15% above cost, and sales prices are reflected in the foregoing amounts. The January 1 inventory at Warehouse No. 16 was $48,100; purchases between January 1 and April 10 totaled $224,600; freight-in was $2,300; and purchase returns totaled $9,200.

To arrive at the total replacement cost of the April 10 inventory for insurance settlement purposes, it was agreed to deduct 10% for goods shopworn and damaged prior to the fire.

A compromise agreement between the insurance adjuster and Grife Company management set the current replacement cost of inventory lost in the fire at $21,480.

Required:

1. Estimate the total replacement cost of total inventory in the warehouse at April 10.
2. Determine the indemnity claim if the warehouse contents were insured by a single $20,000 policy having a 65% coinsurance clause. Calculate to the nearest dollar.

E 12–19
Appendix 12B: Fire Loss, Coinsurance
(L.O. 9)

On January 1, Carson's Store had a fire insurance policy with a face amount of $15,000 and an 80% coinsurance clause. At that date, the company had $360 recorded in its records for unexpired insurance for one year. On January 1, the inventory was $20,000; Carson uses a perpetual inventory system. January purchases were $44,000, and January sales were $60,000. A fire on February 1 destroyed the entire stock on hand. At that time the historical cost of the inventory represented replacement cost as well.

Required:

Give journal entries to record the estimated inventory and the fire loss assuming a 30% gross margin rate on sales.

PROBLEMS

P 12–1
Depreciation Schedule
(L.O. 2)

Quick Producers acquired factory equipment on January 1, 1991, costing $78,000. In view of pending technological developments, it is estimated that the machine will have a resale value upon disposal in four years of $16,000 and that disposal cost will be $1,000.

Data relating to the equipment follow:

Estimated service life:
Years   4
Service hours 20,000

Actual operations:

Calendar year	Service Hours
1991	5,700
1992	5,000
1993	4,800
1994	4,400

Required:

Round to the nearest dollar and show computations.

1. Prepare a depreciation schedule for the service hours method assuming the accounts are closed each December 31.
2. Compute depreciation expense for the first and second years assuming (*a*) straight-line, (*b*) SYD, and (*c*) DB (200% rate).

P 12–2
Discussion: Overview of Depreciation
(L.O. 1, 3)

Depreciation continues to be one of the more important problem areas in accounting.

Required:

1. Explain the factors that should be considered when applying the conventional concept of depreciation to determine how the value of a newly acquired computer system should be assigned to expense for financial reporting purposes. (Ignore income tax considerations.)
2. What depreciation methods might be used for the computer system in (1)?
3. Explain the conventional accounting concept of depreciation accounting.
4. Discuss the conceptual merit of depreciation accounting with respect to (*a*) the value of the asset, (*b*) periodic amounts of expense, and (*c*) the discretion of management in selecting the method.

(AICPA adapted)

P 12–3
Depreciation Schedules
(L.O. 2)

Constar Company purchased a machine that cost $145,000. The firm estimated that the machine would have a net resale value at the end of its useful life of $8,000. Data relating to the machine over its service life were as follows: estimated service life in years, 5; output (units), 8,000. Actual operations in units of output were: 1991, 1,600; 1992, 1,900; 1993, 1,000; 1994, 1,800; and 1995, 1,700.

Required:

Prepare a depreciation schedule for the asset over the useful life for each of the following methods: (*a*) straight line, (*b*) output, (*c*) SYD, and (*d*) DB (200% rate). Show computations and round to the nearest dollar.

P 12–4
Analysis of Four Depreciation Methods: Maximize Income, Minimize Tax
(L.O. 2, 8)

On January 1, 1991, Vello Company, a tool manufacturer, acquired new industrial equipment for $2 million. The new equipment had a useful life of four years, and the residual value was estimated to be $200,000. Vello estimates that the new equipment can produce 14,000 tools in its first year. Production is then estimated to decline by 1,000 units per year over the remaining useful life of the equipment.

The following depreciation methods are under consideration: (*a*) DB (200% rate), (*b*) straight-line, (*c*) SYD, and (*d*) units of output.

Required:

1. Which depreciation method would result in maximum income for financial statement reporting for the three-year period ending December 31, 1993? Prepare a schedule showing the amount of accumulated depreciation at December 31, 1993, under the method selected. Show supporting computations in good form. Ignore present value, income tax, and deferred income tax considerations in your answer.
2. Which depreciation method would result in minimum income for tax reporting for the three-year period ending December 31, 1993? (Assume for problem purposes that all four methods are allowable for tax purposes.) Prepare a schedule showing the amount of accumulated depreciation at December 31, 1993, under the method selected. Show supporting computations in good form. Ignore present value considerations in your answer.

(AICPA adapted)

P 12–5
Analyze Cash Flows: Depreciation
(L.O. 2, 3, 8)

Bryan Company acquired equipment on January 1, 1991, for $80,000. It is estimated that the equipment has a four-year life and a residual value of $5,000. Bryan uses the same method of depreciation for financial reporting and tax purposes and is taxed at a 30% rate. For purposes of this problem, ignore ACRS and MACRS.

Required:

1. Calculate the cash flow effect of depreciation on income taxes for each year of the equipment's useful life assuming:
   a. Straight-line.
   b. DB (200% acceleration rate).
   c, SYD.
2. Assume Bryan can invest any idle cash to yield an annual return of 12%. Which depreciation method is preferable from a tax perspective? Show computations to support your answer.

P 12–6

Match Four Depreciation Methods with Depreciation Expense
(L.O. 2)

Equipment was acquired for $80,000 that has a six-year estimated life and a residual value of $8,000. The equipment will be depreciated by various amounts in this third full year depending on the depreciation method used.

Third-year depreciation expense under the four methods listed below (but not in the same order) amounted to (1) $12,000; (2) $11,852; (3) $13,714; and (4) $19,800. The depreciation methods used were (*a*) DB (200% rate), (*b*) productive output, (*c*) straight line, and (*d*) SYD.

The productive output method assumed 800,000 units could be produced; in the first three years, actual output was: 200,000 units; 180,000 units; and 220,000 units, respectively.

Required:

Analyze the above data. Based on this analysis, alongside each letter (*a*) through (*d*), which identifies the four methods, write the number (1) through (4), associated with the amount of third-year depreciation for that method. Support each answer with calculations.

P 12–7

Analyze Asset and Accumulated Accounts
(L.O. 1, 2)

Selected accounts included under the property, plant, and equipment caption of Abel Company's balance sheet at December 31, 1991, had the following balances (at original cost):

Land	$220,000
Land improvements	75,000
Buildings	600,000
Machinery and equipment (acquired 1/1/84)	650,000

During 1992, the following transactions occurred:

a. A plant facility consisting of land and building was acquired from Club Company in exchange for 10,000 shares of Abel's common stock. On the acquisition date, Abel's stock had a closing market price of $39 per share on a national stock exchange. The plant facility was carried on Club's accounts at $95,000 for land and $130,000 for the building at the exchange date. Current appraised values for the land and building, respectively, are $120,000 and $240,000.

b. A tract of land was acquired for $85,000 as a potential future building site.

c. Machinery was purchased at a total cost of $250,000. Additional costs were incurred as follows:

Freight and unloading	$ 5,000
Sales and use taxes	10,000
Installation	25,000

d. Expenditures totaling $90,000 were made for new parking lots, streets, and sidewalks at the corporation's various plant locations. These improvements had an estimated useful life of 15 years.

e. A machine that cost $50,000 on January 1, 1984, was scrapped on June 30, 1992. DB (200% rate) depreciation has been recorded on the basis of a 10-year life.

f. A machine was sold for $25,000 on July 1, 1992. Original cost of the machine was $37,000 at January 1, 1989, and it was depreciated on the straight-line basis over an estimated useful life of eight years and a residual value of $1,000.

Required:

1. Prepare a detailed analysis of the changes in each of the following balance sheet accounts for 1992 (disregard accumulated depreciation): (*a*) land, (*b*) land improvements, (*c*) buildings, and (*d*) machinery and equipment. Hint: analyze each asset separately.
2. List the items in the fact situation which were *not* used to determine the answer to (1) above, showing the relevant amounts and supporting computations for each item. In

addition, indicate where, or if, these items should be included in Abel's financial statements. (Hint: set up three schedules: (*a*) loss or gain on scrapping the machine, (*b*) accumulated depreciation, DB method, and (*c*) loss or gain on sale of machine.)

P 12–8
Depreciation Schedules and Depreciation Changes
(L.O. 2, 5)

On January 1, 1991, Medarts Corporation acquired an operational asset at a cost of $80,000 that is to be depreciated over five years to a residual value of $5,000. You have been asked to develop alternative depreciation schedules based on various depreciation methods and assumptions as to usage given below. Medarts has a calendar reporting year.

Assumptions

a. The straight-line method will be used. After recording depreciation three years in accordance with the original assumptions, the residual value is changed to $10,000.
b. The SYD method will be used (no revision in life or residual value).
c. The productive output method will be used. Scheduled production using the asset will be: 1991, 153,000 units; 1992, 160,000 units; 1993, 140,000 units; 1994, 100,000 units; and 1995, 72,000 units.
d. The productive output method will be used as in (*c*); through the first two years, the total expected and planned production are the same. However, at the start of 1993, the total production estimate over the service life of the asset is revised to 729,000 units, and scheduled production in 1993, 1994, and 1995 will be 200,000 units, 90,000 units, and 126,000 units, respectively.

Required:

Prepare a depreciation schedule for each of the assumptions given above that shows depreciation expense, accumulated depreciation, and book value.

P 12–9
Multiple Choice: Depreciation Changes
(L.O. 5)

Choose the correct answer for each of the following situations.

1. Choose the correct statement concerning changes in accounting for depreciation:
   (*a*) A change in the estimated useful life of a building should cause a correction to prior years' retained earnings.
   (*b*) A change in the method of accounting for depreciation should cause an adjustment to the current year's depreciation expense and a cumulative effect for the effect of the change on prior years' earnings.
   (*c*) An error affecting prior years' depreciation is treated as a change in estimate.
   (*d*) A cumulative effect account is a prior period adjustment.
2. A change in the estimated useful life of a building:
   (*a*) Is not allowed under GAAP.
   (*b*) Affects depreciation on the building beginning with the year of the change.
   (*c*) Must be handled as a retroactive adjustment to all accounts affected, back to the year of building acquisition.
   (*d*) Creates a new account to be recognized on the income statement and reflects the depreciation difference up to the beginning of the year of change.
3. A change in depreciation method:
   (*a*) Is not allowed under GAAP.
   (*b*) Affects depreciation on the building beginning with the year of the change.
   (*c*) Must be handled as a retroactive adjustment to all accounts affected, back to the year of building acquisition.
   (*d*) Creates a new account to be recognized on the income statement and reflects the depreciation difference up to the beginning of the year of change.
4. Swallow Corporation decided, on March 1, 1994, to change the total useful life on an asset from five years to eight years, and to change the residual value from $500 to $2,000. The asset was purchased on January 1, 1991, for $8,500. What is depreciation expense, using the straight-line method, in 1994.
   (*a*) $740.   (*c*) $240.
   (*b*) $212.50.   (*d*) $340.
5. Answer (4) assuming the SYD method is used:
   (*a*) $20.   (*c*) $33.
   (*b*) $15.   (*d*) $140.
6. Intelco Corporation decided to change its method of depreciation on December 31, 1991, from SYD to DDB for financial reporting. The affected years and depreciation amounts follow:

	SYD	DDB
1991	$3,000	$2,800
1990	4,000	4,100
1989	4,800	5,200

The cumulative effect of an accounting change account will be recorded at which of the following amounts, ignoring taxes.

(a) $500 cr.   (c) $200 dr.

(b) $500 dr.   (d) $180 dr.

7. Carlisle Company discovered in 1991 that depreciation expense in 1987 and 1988 was overstated $10,000 each year. Ignoring taxes, choose the correct accounting response to this situation:

(a) Accumulated depreciation is debited $20,000.

(b) Retained earnings is debited $20,000.

(c) 1991 depreciation expense is credited $20,000.

(d) Accumulated depreciation is credited $20,000.

(e) Cumulative effect of an accounting change is credited $20,000.

P 12–10

Multiple Choice: Depreciation Systems (L.O. 6)

Choose the correct answer for each of the following questions.

1. Information relevant to the assets designated "small equipment" for a corporation follows:

Beginning balance $16,000

Acquisitions this year 3,000

Cash from disposals 100

Inventory at appraisal value 14,500

Assuming the inventory appraisal system is used, depreciation expense for this year for small equipment equals:

(a) $4,500.   (c) $3,000.

(b) $4,400.   (d) $1,500.

The following information is used for questions 2 and 3:

Mills Corporation began 1991 with 100 railroad cars each with a $4,000 unit book value. During 1991, Mills purchased 50 cars for $6,000 each and retired 60 cars. Mills received $60,000 in total from the disposal of the railroad cars. What is the balance in the ledger account for railroad cars on January 1, 1992 using the:

2. Retirement system?

(a) $360,000.   (c) $180,000.

(b) $460,000.   (d) $280,000.

3. Replacement system?

(a) $360,000.   (c) $180,000.

(b) $460,000.   (d) $280,000.

4. Endo Corporation uses the retirement system of depreciation. At the beginning of 1991, Endo had 200 trucks (cost $8,000 each) in use. During 1991 Endo sold 50 trucks and received $1,000 each, and purchased 80 more at $10,000 each. What is depreciation expense for 1991?

(a) $400,000.   (c) $800,000.

(b) $350,000.   (d) $750,000.

5. Answer question 4 assuming the replacement system.

(a) $500,000.   (c) $450,000.

(b) $800,000.   (d) $750,000.

6. Manara Corporation purchased the following assets January 1, 1991:

Quantity	Type	Unit Cost	Estimated Unit Salvage Value	Unit Useful Life
10	Truck	$ 6,000	$1,000	5 years
5	Bus	12,000	2,000	8 years

Using the composite system of depreciation, what is the composite rate based on cost?

(a) 13.54%.   (c) 1.88%.

(b) 16.25%.   (d) 6.15%.

7. Without prejudice to your answer in question 6, assume that the composite rate is 20% and that in 1992, Manara sold two trucks for $4,000 salvage each and replaced them with trucks costing $8,000 each, with $2,000 estimated salvage value each. The new vehicles are considered representative of the group. What is depreciation in 1992?

(a) $16,250.   (c) $24,800.

(b) $24,000.   (d) $20,000.

P 12–11
Application of the Composite Depreciation System
(L.O. 6)

Operational assets acquired on January 1, 1991, by Sculley Company are to be depreciated using the composite system. Details regarding each asset are given in the schedule below:

Component	Cost	Estimated Residual Value	Estimated Life (Years)
A	$90,000	$10,000	10
B	30,000	–0–	6
C	76,000	16,000	15
D	12,400	400	8

Required:

1. Calculate the composite life and annual composite depreciation rate (based on cost) for the asset components listed above. Give the entry to record depreciation after one full year of use. Round the depreciation rate to the nearest two decimal places.
2. During 1992, it was necessary to replace component B, which was sold for $16,000. The replacement component cost $36,000 and has an estimated residual value of $3,000 at the end of its estimated six-year useful life. Record the disposal and substitution, which was a cash acquisition.
3. Record depreciation at the end of 1992.

P 12–12
Operational Asset and Depreciation Schedule
(L.O. 1, 2, 4)

General Corporation, a manufacturer of steel products, began operations on October 1, 1991. The accounting department of General has started the operational asset and depreciation schedule accompanying this problem. You have been asked to assist in completing this schedule. In addition to ascertaining that the data already on the schedule are correct, you have obtained the following information from the company's records and personnel:

a. Depreciation is computed from the first of the month of acquisition to the first of the month of disposition.
b. Land A was acquired on October 2, 1991, in exchange for 3,000 newly issued shares of General's common stock. At the date of acquisition, the stock had a par value of $5 per share and a market value of $45 per share. During October 1991, General paid $26,000 to demolish an existing building on this land so that it could construct a new building.
c. Construction of Building A on the newly acquired land began on October 1, 1992. By September 30, 1993, General had paid $250,000 of the estimated total construction costs of $300,000. Estimated completion and occupancy date is July 1994.
d. Land B and Building B were acquired from a predecessor corporation. General paid $890,000 for the land and building together. At the time of acquisition, the land had an appraised value of $72,000 and the building had an appraised value of $828,000.
e. Certain equipment was donated to the corporation on October 1, 1991, by a local university. An independent appraisal of the equipment when donated placed the market value at $34,000 and the residual value at $2,000.
f. Machinery A's total cost of $110,000 includes installation expense of $550 and normal repairs and maintenance of $11,000. Residual value is estimated at $5,500. Machinery A was sold on February 1, 1993.
g. On October 1, 1992, Machinery B was acquired with a down payment of $4,000 and the remaining payments to be made in 10 annual installments of $4,000 each beginning October 1, 1993. The prevailing interest rate was 18% on debts with risk characteristics similar to this debt.

GENERAL CORPORATION
Operational Asset and Depreciation Schedule
For Fiscal Years Ended September 30, 1992, and September 30, 1993

Assets	Acquisition Date	Cost	Residual Value	Depreciation Method	Estimated Life in Years	Depreciation Expense Year Ended September 30	
						1992	1993
Land A	10/2/1991	$ (1)	n.a.	n.a.	n.a.	n.a.	n.a.
Building A	Under construction	250,000 (to date)	—	Straight-line	30	—	$ (2)
Land B	10/1/1991	(3)	n.a.	n.a.	n.a.	n.a.	n.a.
Building B	10/1/1991	(4)	$20,000	Straight-line	(5)	$19,970	(6)
Donated equipment	10/1/1991	(7)	2,000	DB (150% rate)	10	(8)	(9)
Machinery A	12/2/1991	(10)	5,500	SYD	10	(11)	(12)
Machinery B	10/1/1992	(13)	—	Striaght-line	10	—	(14)

Note: n.a.—Not applicable.

Required:

There are the 14 numbers in parenthesis in the above schedule. You are to respond about each one. Number your answer sheet from (1) to (14). For each numbered item on the schedule accompanying this problem, supply the correct amount next to the corresponding number on your answer sheet. Round each answer to the nearest dollar. Do not recopy the schedule. Show supporting computations in good form.

(AICPA adapted)

P 12–13
Retirement and Replacement Systems Compared
(L.O. 6)

Alton Company uses a large number of identical small tools in operations. On January 1, 1991, the first year of operations, 1,200 of these tools were purchased at a cost of $3 each. On December 31, 1991, 150 of the tools were sold or scrapped for $100 and were replaced at a cost of $4.20 each. On December 31, 1992, 300 of the tools were sold or scrapped for $120; they were replaced at a cost of $4.50 each. On December 31, 1993, 160 of the tools were sold or scrapped for $55, each being replaced at a cost of $3.60.

Required:

1. Give the entries to record all indicated transactions, assuming the company employed (*a*) the retirement system and (*b*) the replacement system.
2. Compare the results under the two systems by showing periodic depreciation for each year and the balance in the tools account at each December 31, 1991 to 1993.

P 12–14
Depreciation Schedule and Correcting Entry
(L.O. 2, 5)

As of December 31, 1996, the machinery account of Barger Company was as below:

Machinery			
1/1/91 Purchase	$50,000	12/31/91 Depreciation	$5,000
7/1/92 Purchase	10,000	9/1/92 Machinery sold	1,000
11/1/93 Purchase	36,000	12/31/93 Depreciation	6,300
		12/31/94 Depreciation	7,800
		7/1/95 Machinery sold	1,000
		12/31/95 Depreciation	7,800
		12/31/96 Depreciation	9,300

Machinery sold September 1, 1992, cost $3,600 on January 1, 1991; machinery sold July 1, 1995, cost $2,500 on January 1, 1991. Machinery costing $2,000, which was purchased on July 1, 1992, was destroyed on July 1, 1996, and was a total loss. Assume the debits in the machinery account are correct.

Required:

1. Prepare a depreciation schedule that shows the annual depreciation and account balances. Assume a 10-year life on all items, straight-line depreciation, and no residual value.

Suggested captions: date acquired, machinery (debit-credit), correct depreciation by year (six columns), and accumulated depreciation (debit-credit).
2. Prepare the journal entry or entries to correct the accounts on December 31, 1996, assuming the accounts are not closed for 1996 (ignore income taxes).

P 12–15
Depreciation Methods and Change in Estimate
(L.O. 2, 5)

Machinery purchased January 1, 1991, and costing Dutton Corporation $19,000 is expected to last 10 years and have a $1,000 residual value. Several depreciation methods in common use were applied to these data. The results in terms of annual depreciation amounts covering 1992 and 1993 are set out below:

Year	Method A	Method B	Method C
1991	?	?	?
1992	$2,945	$1,800	$3,040
1993	2,618	1,800	2,432

Required:
Round to the nearest dollar.
1. Identify each method used. What is the book value of the asset at the end of 1993 for each of the three methods used to compute 1992 and 1993 depreciation given in the table above?
2. In connection with Methods A and B, suppose that after the completion of 1993, it is determined that the total remaining life of the machinery is five years instead of seven years. Determine the annual depreciation amount and the balance of accumulated depreciation at the end of 1994 and 1995.

P 12–16
Impairment of Asset Value
(L.O. 7)

Hilltop Mining Company has several mining operations in New Mexico. Plant HM-40 has property, plant, and equipment that has been idle for the past three years. Because of continuing weak prices and low demand for the output, the auditor has advised the company that, in view of the probability that the plant will not be opened in the foreseeable future, it should be written down to expected net realizable value. The property, plant, and equipment is shown in the accounts as original cost, $800,000; accumulated depreciation, $300,000. The estimated net realizable value is $50,000. The assessed property tax for the current year of $6,000 has not been recorded.

Required:
1. Give the entries that Hilltop should make to record the decline in use value.
2. Write an appropriate full-disclosure note.

P 12–17
Mathematical Aspects of Depreciation Methods
(L.O. 2)

Several depreciation methods discussed in this chapter can be described algebraically and have certain interesting properties. This problem requires that you explore some of these methods and introduces a depreciation method not discussed in class and not widely used in practice.

Required:
Show in general why each of the following statements to be proved is true. You may wish to begin by using examples, but finish with a purely algebraic set of assertions leading to each statement. The useful life in years is denoted by n.

1. The SL rate of depreciation is often referred to as a percentage. This percentage is the ratio of annual depreciation to depreciable cost. For example, an asset with a useful life of five years has a 20% depreciation rate. Prove that the double-declining-balance rate, being twice the straight-line rate (based on depreciable cost), is always $2/n$.
2. Prove that in the first year of an asset's useful life, DDB depreciation always exceeds SYD.
3. Prove that an alternative way to determine DDB depreciation for a particular year t is:

$$(2/n) \times (1 - 2/n)^{t-1} \times \text{Cost}$$

4. A depreciation method occasionally discussed by accountants is the fixed rate of declining balance method. This method uses a rate R and applies it to the declining balance of the asset at the beginning of each year to determine depreciation expense. The rate is between

$1/n$ and $2/n$ in magnitude. It therefore produces results between those of the straight-line method and DDB. R is defined as:

$$1 - (\text{residual value}/\text{cost})^{(1/n)}$$

Depreciation in Years 1 and 2, $D(1)$ and $D(2)$ below are computed as follows:

$$D(1) = R \times Cost$$
$$D(2) = R \times [Cost - D(1)]$$

One of the more interesting features of this method is that an asset's book value at the end of its useful life equals its residual value. This is the statement you are to prove.

P 12–18
Appendix 12B: Casualty Losses
(L.O. 9)

Smithson Company suffered a casualty loss to equipment that cost $300,000 and that had been depreciated $40,000 before the casualty. The market value of the asset just before the misfortune was $320,000. Smithson insured the asset for casualty. The policy has a 90% coinsurance clause.

Required:

1. If the market value of the asset after the casualty is $50,000, what is the minimum policy face value that guarantees full recovery to Smithson? Explain your answer.
2. Answer (1) except that the market value is only $20,000 after the casualty.
3. Explain the difference in your answers to (1) and (2).

P 12–19
Appendix 12B: Fire Loss
(L.O. 9)

South Company operates in a leased building and closes the books each December 31. On April 30, a fire seriously damaged its inventory and fixtures. Inventory was totally destroyed; fixtures were two-thirds destroyed. Different insurance policies cover the assets, but both have a common feature under which they are canceled for future or remaining coverage to whatever extent a portion of the total potential indemnity is collected by the insured.

The company uses a periodic inventory system, and the accounting records were saved; these reveal that in the past three years gross margin has averaged 38% of sales price. The January 1 inventory was $73,280. Between January 1 and April 30, purchases were $116,320 and sales were $206,500. Inventory was insured by a $65,000 policy with no coinsurance clause. The latest premium payment covering a one-year period from September 1 of last year amounted to $720 on this policy.

When the books were closed last December 31, the fixtures were two and one-half years old. Accounts related to the fixtures and their insurance policy are set forth below.

Fixtures		Accumulated Depreciated		Prepaid Insurance (on fixtures only)	
Balance $20,000		Year 1 $900	Policy A $42		
		Year 2 1,800	Policy B 480		
		Year 3 1,800			

Policy A on the fixtures expired February 28 of the current year. Policy B was immediately put in force to replace the expired policy on the fixtures; a two-year premium was paid on it. Policy B is for $10,000 maximum coverage, provides for indemnity on the basis of replacement cost of any loss, and has an 80% coinsurance clause. It is determined that the replacement cost of the fixtures when the fire occurred was $15,000 and that the damage amounted to a loss of two-thirds of their replacement cost.

Required:
Round amounts to nearest dollar.
1. Adjust the books to April 30 and reflect the inventory as of that date.
2. Open a casualty loss account; set up the indemnities collectible as a receivable due from the insurance company.
3. Transfer the net balance in casualty loss to income summary.

P 12–20

COMPREHENSIVE PROBLEM
♦

Depreciation Calculations
(L.O. 2, 4, 5, 7)

In 1991, Spencer Company purchased an operational asset that experienced several events requiring modification to its ledger account. Spencer is a calendar–fiscal year company. The events follow:

a. On June 30, 1991, equipment is purchased for $240,000. The equipment has a $40,000 residual value and an expected useful life of five years.
b. A new component is added to the equipment on June 30, 1992, costing $150,000. As a result, the residual value of the original equipment is raised to $60,000. The useful life of the equipment is unchanged and the component has no useful life separate from the equipment.
c. The remaining useful life of the equipment is changed to two years as of January 1, 1993. Residual value is unaffected.
d. The equipment becomes totally impaired as a result of a casualty on September 1, 1994. The equipment functions normally through that date. Because the equipment is uninsured, Spencer charges the remaining book value to a loss account.

Required:

For the following depreciation methods, (a) provide journal entries to completely account for this equipment from acquisition to write-off, and (b) prepare a schedule proving that total charges sum to the total cost of the equipment.
1. SL.
2. SYD.
3. DDB (assume the switch to the SL method occurs on January 1, 1993—this is not a change in accounting method but rather a normal event in the DDB method).

CASES

C 12–1
Depreciable Tangible
Assets Fully Depreciated
but Still in Use
(L.O. 1, 3)

a. Baker Corporation has certain fully depreciated tangible operational assets that are still used in the business.
(1) Discuss the possible reasons why this could happen.
(2) Comment on the significance of the continued use of these fully depreciated assets.
b. In the past, these fully depreciated assets and their accumulated depreciation have been merged with other operational assets and related depreciation on the balance sheet. Discuss the propriety of this accounting treatment, including a consideration of other possible treatments and the circumstances in which they would be appropriate.

(AICPA adapted)

C 12–2
Depreciation and Gain or
Loss on Disposal
(L.O. 1)

Some of the major car rental companies account for the gain or loss on disposal of their used cars as an adjustment to depreciation expense in the period of disposal rather than reporting gains or losses on disposal.

Required:

On what grounds, if any, can such a procedure be justified? Would your answer be different if the procedure were used by relatively few (versus most) companies in the industry?

C 12–3
Depreciation: Single Asset
Unit or Separate Subunits
(L.O. 6)

In situations where depreciable properties are treated as units rather than as part of a group of assets depreciated on a composite or group basis, the question sometimes arises as to what constitutes an appropriate property unit for accounting purposes. For example, a building as a single entity may be designated as the basic property unit. Alternatively, the elevators, escalators, heating and air-conditioning system, other mechanical equipment, plumbing, electrical system, and the basic building structure could be accounted for as separate property units.

Required:

1. What accounting problems arise if an item that could be accounted for as a single property unit is instead accounted for as a number of separate asset units?
2. Identify and explain some advantages of accounting separately for smaller property units as opposed to aggregation as a single property unit.

C 12–4
Ethical Considerations
(L.O. 1, 4, 5)

Discuss ethical factors relevant to each of the following examples of financial reporting and disclosure. Comment on the propriety of the accounting chosen, GAAP flexibility, and the degree to which underlying economic effects are disclosed.

a. The manager of a large division of a major corporation has significant input to accounting policy for the division and has authority over all line decisions, including purchasing, maintenance, and capital expenditures. The manager has occupied the position for three years; the average time for promotion to the corporate staff level is five years.

The manager has successfully endorsed capitalizing all post-acquisition costs, including improvements and general maintenance and repair. His justification is that all maintenance increases the useful life or productivity of assets relative to lower levels of such costs. In addition, he has recommended postponing many routine repairs on equipment used in manufacturing the division's product. Furthermore, he has resisted requests from lower managers to upgrade and expand facilities in several important areas. Divisions are evaluated on rate-of-return on investment (ROI), the ratio of divisional income to divisional investment.

b. "Earnings Helper," *Forbes*, June 12, 1989, p. 150, discussed the cases of two firms that chose somewhat unusual accounting practices for depreciating and amortizing assets. Cineplex Odeon amortizes its movie theater seats, carpets, and related equipment over 27 years. Blockbuster Entertainment changed the period of amortization of the videotapes it rents from 9 months to 36 months. In Blockbuster's case, a *Wall Street Journal* article critical of its accounting practices was followed by significant declines in the price of its common stock. In both cases, these firms have adopted accounting practices that are unrepresentative of those chosen by most firms in their respective industries. One effect of these policies is increased income.

C 12–5
Sherwin-Williams:
Analysis of Actual
Financial Statements
(L.O. 1, 3)

Refer to the 1990 financial statements of Sherwin-Williams (see the appendix at the end of the book) and respond to the following questions. You may use more than one year's results in your answer.

1. What method of depreciation is used by Sherwin-Williams?
2. Assuming the midpoint of the range of straight-line rates disclosed for buildings is the average straight-line rate, what is the average estimated useful life for depreciation purposes of buildings owned by Sherwin-Williams?
3. At December 31, 1990, what percentage of the useful life of buildings remains, on average?
4. What is the book value of machinery and equipment retired in 1990?
5. In 1990, what percentage was total depreciation and amortization of property, plant, and equipment of (a) total expenses, and (b) pretax earnings?
6. Does it appear that depreciation caused the amount of dividends declared in 1990 to be reduced? Comment on the degree to which depreciation provided funds for Sherwin-Williams in 1990.

C H A P T E R
13

Intangible Assets and Natural Resources

After you have studied this chapter, you will:

1. Understand the concept and characteristics of intangible assets.

2. Be familiar with the general accounting treatment for intangibles.

3. Be familiar with the accounting for other categories of intangible assets, including deferred charges, leaseholds, organization costs, and licensing agreements.

4. Know how goodwill arises and how it is measured, recorded, and amortized.

5. Know the accounting treatment required for research and development costs.

6. Understand the accounting for the cost of computer software.

7. Understand the accounting issues and reporting for natural resources.

8. Understand the major (and controversial) issue in accounting for oil and gas exploration costs. (Refer to the appendix at the end of the chapter.)

♦

T he 1987 annual report of Gannett Company includes assets labeled "intangible and other assets: excess of acquisition cost over the value of assets acquired." This asset's value is recorded as $1.4 billion, which is greater than the $1.2 billion the company reports as net property. What is this so-called intangible asset? And why is it recorded on Gannett's financial statements?

In its June 30, 1988, balance sheet, Microsoft Corporation reports an asset in the amount of $7.9 million labeled "intellectual property rights—net." What are these property rights and how did they arise?

A review of Dun & Bradstreet's balance sheet reveals the following "other assets":

    Other assets:
        Deferred charges . . . . . . $ 44,508,000
        Computer software 110,941,000
        Other intangibles 170,757,000
        Goodwill 365,445,000

What are these assets? And what led Dun & Bradstreet to include them on its balance sheet?

All of these assets are examples of intangible assets, although not all the possibilities are illustrated by these examples. Intangible assets have rather special characteristics and, as such, are accounted for separately, and sometimes differently, from tangible assets. Accounting for the cost of natural resources, including the exploration costs incurred to find oil and gas, gives rise to yet another form of intangible asset. Accounting for natural resources is also covered in this chapter.

How can tangible and intangible assets be distinguished from each other? Typically, the term *tangible* refers to an asset's stable physical characteristics, while the term *intangible* implies a lack of stable physical characteristics. For accounting purposes, however, this distinction, while necessary, is not sufficient. This chapter discusses the key accounting distinctions relating to intangible assets, and how to account for this special group of assets.

♦   ◉

INTANGIBLE ASSETS
♦

For accounting purposes, **intangible assets** have four important characteristics:

1. They lack physical substance.
2. They possess future economic benefits (ownership rights) that can be difficult to measure.
3. Their useful life is often difficult to determine.
4. Generally they are acquired for operational use.

The first characteristic distinguishes tangible assets from intangible assets, while the last three characteristics are common to both tangible and intangible assets. However, the difficulties encountered under the second and third characteristics in measuring and determining future benefits and useful life are generally greater for intangible assets. Thus, although there is considerable similarity in the problems of accounting for tangible and intangible assets, it generally is more difficult to identify, measure, and estimate the periods of economic benefit for intangibles.

APB Opinion No. 17 addresses the issues and difficulties in accounting for intangibles:

Accounting for an intangible asset involves the same kinds of problems as accounting for other long-lived assets, namely, determining an initial carrying amount, accounting for that amount after acquisition under normal business conditions (amortization), and accounting for that amount if the value declines substantially and permanently. Solving the problems is complicated by the characteristics of an intangible asset: its lack of physical qualities makes evidence elusive, its value is often difficult to estimate, and its useful life may be indeterminable.[1]

Classification of Intangible Assets

Intangibles are listed on the balance sheet under a number of different labels, such as intangible assets, intangible operational assets, intangible fixed assets, and other assets. The more common specific intangible assets are patents, copyrights, franchises, trademarks, organizational costs, defended charges, and goodwill.[2]

Intangible assets can be classified according to four attribute dimensions:

1. *Manner of acquisition.* Intangible assets can be acquired externally by purchase from another entity. Examples include a franchise or a patent that was developed and registered by another firm. Alternatively, intangible assets can be developed internally in the course of operations; patents and trademarks are examples.

2. *Identifiability.* Some intangible assets can be separately identified from the other assets of the firm. Examples include patents, trademarks, and franchises. Other intangible assets, however, cannot be separately identified but instead derive their value from their association with the assets of the firm. One example of the latter is the goodwill of a business, which is based on the loyalty of its customers or the quality of its products or employees.

3. *Exchangeability.* Separately identifiable intangible assets that can be sold or purchased are exchangeable. Examples include patents, franchises, and trademarks. Other intangible assets, however, while separately identifiable, are not exchangeable independently of selling the firm. Organization costs provide an example. No one would be willing to separately purchase the organization costs of another firm. Goodwill is an example of an intangible asset that is neither separately identifiable nor separately exchangeable. Goodwill has value only in combination with the other assets of the firm, and cannot be acquired without simultaneously acquiring the other assets.

4. *Period of expected benefit.* Some intangible assets, such as organizational costs, have an indefinite period of expected benefit to the firm. The expected period of benefit of other intangibles is limited either by economic factors or by legal or contractual restrictions. Patents, for example, have a legal life of 17 years, and a leasehold's period of benefit is specified in the lease.

These four types of attributes or characteristics influence the accounting treatment required for the various categories of intangible assets. Before discussing the special accounting issues associated with intangibles, however, it is useful to review the basic accounting principles that apply to all assets.

Basic Principles of Accounting for Intangible Assets

Accounting for intangible assets involves the same accounting principles and procedures that apply to tangible assets such as property, plant, and equipment. Briefly, these principles are:

---

[1] AICPA, *APB Opinion No. 17,* "Intangible Assets" (New York: 1970), par 2.

[2] The discussion in this chapter is in conformity with the requirements of *APB Opinion No. 17* and applies to intangible assets acquired after October 31, 1970. Intangible assets acquired before this date are to be accounted for in accordance with *Accounting Research Bulletin No. 43,* Chapter 5. Briefly, *ARB No. 43* is more flexible than *APB No. 17* in that it requires intangible assets be either (1) accounted for as an asset and not amortized if the asset has no evident limited life, or (2) amortized by systematic charges in the income statement over the period benefited if the asset does have a limited life. *APB No. 17* requires amortization, whereas *ARB 43* does not.

1. At acquisition, application of the *cost principle*.
2. During the period of use, application of the *matching principle,* which requires that the expenses incurred and the revenues generated from those expenses should be recognized at the same time.
3. At disposition, application of the *revenue principle,* under which a gain or loss is recognized on disposal equal to the difference between the consideration received and the book value of the asset sacrificed.

Prior to *APB Opinion No. 17,* intangible assets were accounted for on the basis of life expectancy. Intangible assets with limited lives were amortized over their estimated period of future use. Intangible assets with indeterminable lives were not amortized until a realistic determination of their useful life could be made. Often this determination was never made; thus, the cost of such intangibles was never amortized. *APB Opinion No. 17* changed this practice for assets acquired after October 1970. The *Opinion* provides the following logic and guidance:

> The value of intangible assets at any one date eventually disappears and . . . the recorded costs of intangible assets should be amortized by systematic charges to income over the period estimated to be benefited. . . . The cost of each type of intangible should be amortized on the basis of the estimated life of that specific asset. . . . The period of amortization should not, however, exceed 40 years.[3]

The discussion in this chapter is based on the requirements of *APB Opinion No. 17.*

Exhibit 13–1 broadly summarizes accounting treatments for various types of intangible assets. All but one of the intangible assets discussed are identifiable. The only unidentifiable intangible asset covered in this chapter is goodwill.

Recording the Cost of Intangible Assets

In conformity with the cost principle, intangible assets should be recorded at acquisition at their current cash equivalent cost. Cost includes all expenditures made to acquire the asset, including purchase price, transfer and legal fees, and any other expenditures related to acquisition. The acquisition cost is the current market value of all considerations given, or of the asset received, whichever is more reliably determinable. When an intangible asset is acquired for noncash considerations, in whole or in part, its cost is any cash paid plus the current market value of the noncash consideration given. If that value cannot be determined reliably, then the market value of the right acquired is used.[4] For example, if a patent is acquired by a corporation by issuing its own capital stock as the consideration, the cost of the patent should be measured as the current market value of the shares of stock issued. If the shares issued do not have an established market value consistent with the number of shares issued for the patent, evidence of the market value of the patent itself should be used as the measure of cost of the transaction.

Amortizing the Cost of Intangible Assets

The cost of an intangible asset must be allocated to expense in a *rational and systematic manner* over the legal life or the estimated useful life of the asset, whichever is shorter, in conformity with the *matching principle.* This allocation process is called *amortization.* Estimating the economic useful life of an intangible asset is often difficult. Therefore, the APB suggested that the following factors should be considered in estimating the life of an intangible asset.[5]

---

[3] *APB Opinion No. 17,* par. 27, 28, and 29.

[4] If neither the market value of the consideration given nor the intangible asset acquired can be determined with sufficient reliability, the company may have to assign a value to the intangible asset.

[5] *APB Opinion No. 17,* par. 27.

EXHIBIT 13-1 Summary of Accounting Treatments for Various Types of Intangibles Assets

Type	Manner of Acquisition	
	Purchased	**Internally Generated**
Identifiable intangible asset.	1. Capitalized.	1. Expensed or capitalized depending on the specific intangible.
	2. Amortize over the legal life or the estimated useful life, whichever is shorter, with a maximum of 40 years.	2. If capitalized, amortize as for purchased intangibles.
Unidentifiable intangible asset.	1. Capitalized	1. Expense as incurred.
	2. Amortize over the legal life or the estimated useful life, whichever is shorter, with a maximum of 40 years.	2. There is no option to capitalize, thus there is no amortization.

1. Legal, regulatory, or contractual provisions that may limit the maximum useful life.
2. Provisions for renewal or extension that may alter a specified limit on useful life.
3. Effects of obsolescence, demand, and other economic factors that may reduce useful life.
4. Useful life that may parallel the service life expectancies of individuals or groups of employees.
5. Expected actions of competitors and others that may restrict present competitive advantages.
6. An apparently unlimited useful life that may in fact be indefinite, and benefits that cannot be reasonably projected.
7. An intangible asset that may be a composite of many individual factors with varying effective useful lives.

Because of their characteristics, intangible assets seldom have a residual value. The cost of an intangible asset that does not have a determinable useful life or an indefinite legal life must, nevertheless, be amortized on the basis of a reasonable estimate of useful life. *APB Opinion No. 17* requires that, in all instances, the period of amortization should not exceed 40 years. Although this rule is arbitrary, it prevents potential abuses of the *matching principle* to manipulate reported income.

Because of the inherent difficulty in estimating the economic useful life of an intangible asset, periodic evaluations should be made to determine whether the estimate needs revision. A change in estimated useful life is a *change in accounting estimate*. When estimates are changed, the unamortized cost should be amortized over the revised useful life that remains. However, under no circumstances may the amortization period exceed 40 years from acquisition date.

APB Opinion No. 17 states that "the straight-line method of amortization—equal annual amounts—should be applied unless a company demonstrates that another systematic method is more appropriate." For example, a patent of a high-technology company might be expected to generate most of its benefits in the early periods of its existence, suggesting an accelerated form of amortization. *SFAS No. 86* specifically requires the consideration of an accelerated form of amortization for one intangible asset, computer software costs.

Amortization of an intangible asset usually involves a year-end adjusting entry. The amount to be amortized is recorded as a debit to amortization expense and as a credit either directly to the asset account (because of accounting precedent) or to an accumulated amortization expense account (contra to the asset account).

CONCEPT REVIEW

1. Define an intangible asset.
2. How is an intangible asset different from a tangible asset?
3. How can intangible assets be categorized and how does this categorization influence the accounting?

EXCHANGEABLE INTANGIBLE ASSETS

Exchangeable intangible assets are intangible assets that can be separately identified apart from the other assets of the firm, and that can be sold separately. Examples include patents, copyrights, franchises, and trademarks (but not organization costs). They may be either acquired externally by purchase or developed internally. In either case, they are initially recorded at cost, in conformity with the *cost principle*. As the economic service value of the asset declines, its cost is amortized and expensed in conformity with the *matching principle*.

Because there is a wide variety of intangible assets, application of the above principles and guidelines varies. Several exchangeable intangible assets commonly encountered in business are discussed next.

Patents

A **patent** is an exclusive right recognized by law and registered with the U.S. Patent Office. A patent right enables the holder to use, manufacture, sell, and control the item, process, or activity covered by the patent without interference or infringement by others. In reality, the registration of the patent with the Patent Office is not a guarantee of protection. A patent does not become established until it has been successfully defended in court. For this reason, there is general agreement that the cost of successful court defense should be capitalized as part of the cost of the patent. If the suit is lost, the legal cost, as well as the unamortized cost of the patent, is written off. The carrying amount of the patent is reduced to its impaired value, which could be zero. An impairment loss should be debited for the amount of any write-down. The cost of a patent acquired externally by purchase is determined in conformity with the cost principle.

Internally developed patents resulting from a company's own research and development (R&D) activities must be accounted for as specified by *SFAS No. 2*, which is discussed later in the chapter under the heading, "Research and Development (R&D) Costs." This *Standard* specifies that laboratory costs leading to the development of the patent must be *expensed as incurred*. The only costs of an internally developed patent that can be capitalized are legal fees and other costs associated with registration of the patent, such as models and drawings required for the registration.

Patents have a legal life of 17 years. The useful life of many patents is shorter because technological progress, substitute products, and other improvements cause the products or processes covered by the patents to lose their competitive advantages in fewer than 17 years. The cost of a patent should be amortized over the estimated useful life or legal life, whichever is shorter. Because the legal life of a patent is 17 years, that usually is the upper limit. Sometimes an old patent is improved or modified so that a new patent is registered. If the new patent causes the old patent to have no value, a case can be made for adding the unamortized cost of the old patent to the cost of the new patent for the new 17-year amortization period. However, most companies rely on the *conservatism constraint* and immediately write off the unamortized cost of the old patent.

To illustrate the accounting for a typical patent situation, assume that early in January 1991, Alto Company purchased a patent that cost $27,200. The patent had a 17-year legal life. However, it was purchased one year later than the registration date. During Year 2 (1992), Alto Company won a patent infringement suit. The cost for legal fees and court costs was $4,750. The entries are:

Beginning of 1991—Purchase of patent:

Patent	27,200	
Cash		27,200

End of 1991—Amortization:

Patent amortization expense	1,700	
Patent [or accumulated patent amortization]		1,700

$27,200 ÷ 16 = $1,700.

During 1992—Patent infringement suit:

Patent	4,750	
Cash		4,750

End of 1992—Amortization:

Patent amortization expense	2,017	
Patent [or accumulated patent amortization]		2,017

($27,200 − $1,700 + $4,750 = $30,250) ÷ 15 = $2,017

Patent owners often enter into a contractual agreement with another party to let that party use the patent for a stipulated amount of periodic royalties. In such cases, the amounts earned should be recognized as revenue in conformity with the *revenue principle*.

Copyrights

A **copyright** is a form of protection given by law to the authors of literary, musical, artistic, and similar works (such as the musical score for the play *West Side Story*). Owners of copyrights are granted certain exclusive rights, including the right to print, reprint, and copy the work; to sell or distribute copies; and to perform and record the work.

Under the provisions of the 1978 copyright law, a copyright is protected for the life of the author plus 50 years. Copyrights can be sold or contractually assigned to other persons.

As expected, the cost of a copyright is measured in conformity with the *cost principle*. A copyright often does not have economic value for its entire legal life. The cost of a copyright should be amortized over the period the copyrighted item is expected to produce revenue. However, in no case should a copyright be amortized over a period in excess of its legal life (life of the author plus 50 more years), or in excess of the 40-year maximum specified in *APB Opinion No. 17*, whichever is shorter.

For example, suppose a company acquires a copyright from another company after the author has been dead for 20 years. The copyright protection exists for an additional 30 years, which would be the maximum period of amortization. On the other hand, if a company acquired a copyright from a living author, the maximum period of amortization would be 40 years (as specified by *APB Opinion No. 17*) even though the legal life of the copyright is longer. The accounting entries for a copyright are similar to those for a patent.

Trademarks and Trade Names

Trademarks (such as McDonald's Golden Arches) and **trade names** (such as Coca-Cola) are names, symbols, or other distinctive identities given to companies, products, and services. They can be registered with the U.S. Patent Office to help substantiate ownership. Registered trademarks and tradenames can be renewed for 20-year periods, thus extending their lives indefinitely. Thus, names, symbols, or any other distinctive identity for a product are given legal protection.

The cash equivalent amount paid for the purchase of a trademark is capitalized. Amounts directly incurred in the development, protection, expansion, registration, or defense of a trademark should be capitalized. Such capitalized amounts should be amortized over the useful life of the trademark or 40 years, whichever is shorter.

Franchises

Franchises (such as for a cable television company) often are granted by governmental units for the right to use public properties or to furnish public utility services (such as electricity, in the case of New York Electric and Gas), and by business entities for the right to use a particular designation and specified services (such as U-Haul Trailers and Holiday Inn). Each franchise contract specifies a period of time for which the franchise is valid and the rights and obligations of the franchisor and franchisee. Accounting for franchise revenue earned by the franchisor is covered in the chapter on revenue and expense recognition.

The cost of obtaining a franchise often is high and usually requires an initial franchise fee be paid by the franchisee to the franchisor. The initial cost of a franchise should be capitalized and then amortized as an expense. If the franchise is for a limited period of time, its cost should be amortized over the period in a rational and systematic manner. If the time is indefinite, amortization should be based on a reliably estimated life, with periodic evaluations. These evaluations determine whether the prior estimate needs revision; however, the total amortization period may not exceed 40 years.

Annual and current payments by the franchisee to the franchisor for services, such as assistance with promotional campaigns, accounting, and organizational matters, should be expensed by the franchisee as incurred because they do not create a measurable future benefit for the franchise. If a franchise becomes worthless or is voided by law, the unamortized amount should be written off immediately as an impairment of asset value.

Leaseholds

A **lease** is a right granted to one party by a second party to use property, plant, or equipment. Often a business leases property from a second party under an operating lease and makes lease or rental prepayments.[6] Lease prepayments, such as a "lease bonus" payment, cover the entire term of the lease. Such a prepayment initially should be debited to an account often entitled "leasehold" or "prepaid rent expense." The cost of this asset should be amortized over the period benefited (which is usually the lease term) by periodically debiting rent expense and crediting the asset account. Detailed coverage of accounting for leases appears in the chapter on lease accounting.

The cost of leasehold improvements (under an operating lease), such as modifications of the leased property, should be debited to a leasehold improvement account. Leasehold improvements usually are classified as intangible assets because the leased property does not belong to the lessee. Leasehold improvements should be

---

[6] An operating lease does not convey ownership; that is, it does not effectively transfer most of the rewards and risks of ownership to the lessee. A lease that transfers such rewards and risks of ownership is referred to as a *capital lease*.

amortized as expense over the remaining term of the lease or the life of the improvements, whichever is shorter.

IDENTIFIABLE BUT NOT EXCHANGEABLE INTANGIBLE ASSETS
◆

Balance sheets often report captions such as intangibles, deferred charges and other assets. In most cases these are catchall classifications. Such captions should not be used; however, the accounting profession has not provided any definitive guidance in this area. Some of these intangibles have two special characteristics: they are long-term prepayments of expenses, and they do not confer any rights to the owner that could be sold to a second party. These intangible assets can be separately identified but are not exchangeable.

Deferred Charges

A **deferred charge,** as it is commonly called in accounting, is an expenditure for a service that will contribute to the generation of future revenues; it is reported as a *long-term prepaid expense* on the balance sheet. Deferred charges are classified as noncurrent assets because their effect on revenues extends beyond the period for current assets. Deferred charges have no physical substance and can rarely be realized through sale.[7] Examples of deferred charges include machinery rearrangement costs, long-term prepaid insurance premiums, and prepaid leasehold costs. Research and development costs and organization costs do not fall under the purview of *APB Opinion No. 17.* However, when they are capitalized, they usually are classified as deferred charges.[8]

Deferred charges are amortized over the future periods during which they will contribute to the generation of revenues. The 40-year maximum useful life for amortization of intangible assets specified in APB Opinion No. 17 also applies to deferred charges. However, deferred charges seldom have 40-year life spans.

Startup Costs

A **development stage company,** that is, a newly organized company, often incurs a wide range of *startup* costs before it has significant revenues against which such costs can be matched. These companies often capitalize such costs as intangibles and in later years amortize them when they earn revenue. Development stage companies are permitted to capitalize certain costs as intangible assets when these costs would otherwise have been expensed as incurred.

Because of the lack of guidelines and the wide variety of accounting practices, the FASB issued *SFAS No. 7,* "Accounting and Reporting by Development Stage Enterprises." The *Standard* (par. 8) defines development stage enterprises (emphasis added):

An enterprise shall be considered to be in the development stage if it is devoting substantially all of its efforts to establishing a *new business* and either of the following conditions exists: (*a*) planned principal operations have *not* commenced or (*b*) planned principal operations have commenced but there has been *no* significant revenue therefrom. A development stage enterprise will typically be devoting most of its

---

[7] Some deferred charges are reported as current assets where appropriate. The current portion of a deferred tax asset provides one example.

[8] *APB Opinion No. 17* (par. 6) states: "The provisions of this *Opinion* apply to costs of developing intangible assets that a company defers and records as assets. Certain costs, for example, research and development costs and preoperating costs, present problems which need to be studied separately." Specific mention in the *Opinion* of research and development (R&D) costs and preoperating (i.e., organization) costs, both of which usually are classified as deferred charges, implies that the *Opinion* applies to deferred charges except those two, which were specifically singled out for separate treatment.

efforts to activities such as financial planning; raising capital; exploring for natural resources; developing natural resources; research and development; establishing sources of supply; acquiring property, plant, or other operating assets, such as mineral rights; recruiting and training personnel; developing markets; and starting up production.

SFAS No. 7 requires development stage enterprises to present financial statements prepared on the same basis as other businesses; that is, they cannot use special reporting formats. Capitalization of costs is subject to the same assessment of future benefit and recoverability applicable to established businesses. Thus, the *Standard* specifies that a development stage enterprise is required to present a balance sheet showing the "deficit accumulated (from operations) during development stage," an income statement, a statement of cash flows, and a statement of stockholders' equity. The current statements must show information for each period covered by the past and present statements and the cumulative amounts. Also, the statements must be specifically identified as those of a development stage company. Reporting by a development stage company organized January 1, 1991, is shown in Exhibit 13–2.

Organization Costs

Organization costs are expenditures incurred in organizing a business. Costs directly related to the organizing activities, such as expenditures for legal, accounting, promotional, and clerical activities, may be properly capitalized as organization costs. Organization costs are not initially included in full in the "deficit accumulated during development stage," illustrated in Exhibit 13–2. The accumulated deficit account relates only to operating losses. The rationale for capitalizing organization costs is that such costs benefit the operations of future years. To expense the total amount in the first year of operation would result in a mismatching of expense with revenue.

Because the life of a business usually is considered indefinite, the length of the period receiving the benefits of these costs usually is indeterminate. For this reason, and because the recognition of organization costs as an asset depends upon intangible values presumably attached to the particular business, organization costs usually are amortized over an arbitrarily chosen relatively short period of time. This conservative practice is encouraged by the tax rules, which permit a business to amortize most organization costs ratably over any period not less than five years. Organization costs generally are not amortized up to the maximum 40-year rule because of their indeterminate characteristics.

Stock Issuance Costs

Expenditures associated with the issuance of capital stock are called **stock issuance costs.** Such costs include printing stock certificates and related items, professional fees, commissions paid for selling capital stock, and the costs of filing with state agencies and the SEC. Stock issuance costs, as opposed to organizational costs, are accounted for either as an offset to the issuance price of the capital stock to which they relate or as a deferred charge, which is amortized to expense in conformity with the matching principle (usually on a conservative basis). Stock issuance costs are excluded from the 40-year rule of *APB Opinion No. 17.*

Impairment of the Value of Intangible Assets

During the period an intangible asset or a deferred charge is used, a periodic assessment of the value of future benefits associated with the asset may show that its current book value exceeds its economic utility (i.e., use value) to the enterprise. In

EXHIBIT 13-2   Reporting by a Development Stage Company (new company)

New company was organized January 1, 1991.
Balance Sheet—December 31, 1993:

Assets (detailed)	$130,000
Liabilities (detailed)	$ 75,000
Capital stock, nopar (Note 4)	95,000
Deficit accumulated during development stage	(40,000)*
Total liabilities and stockholders' equity	$130,000

* Debit balance in retained earnings.

Note 4:

	Shares Issues		Resources Received	
Date	**No. Shares**	**Total**	**Cash: Amt/per Share**	**Noncash: Amt/per Share**
1991	15,000	$75,000	$65,000/$4.33	$10,000/$.67
1992	5,000	20,000	20,000/ 4.00	–0–
1993	None	–0–	–0–	–0–
	20,000	$95,000	$85,000	$10,000

Income statement—years ended December 31:

	1991	1992	1993	Cumulative
Revenues (detailed)	$110,000	$145,000	$175,000	$430,000
Expenses (detailed)	(145,000)	(160,000)	(165,000)	(470,000)
Net income	$(35,000)	$(15,000)	$ 10,000	$(40,000)
EPS	$ (2.33)	$ (.75)	$ .50	$ (2.00)

Statement of cash flows and stockholders' equity (not illustrated) use the standard side captions and the same column captions shown above for the statements.

such cases, the unamortized cost should be written down, and a loss recognized. This reflects impairment of value. The revised value should be amortized over the estimated remaining useful life, not to exceed 40 years from date of acquisition (*APB Opinion No. 17,* par. 31). When a write-down occurs due to an impairment of value, disclosure is required in notes to the financial statements (*APB Opinion No. 17,* par. 31).

DISPOSAL OF INTANGIBLE ASSETS

♦

When an intangible asset is sold, exchanged, or otherwise disposed of, its unamortized cost (or cost net of accumulated amortization, if separately recorded) must be removed from the accounts and a gain or loss on disposal recorded.

Because financial analysts often view intangibles as having highly uncertain value and because of a desire to be conservative on the part of many accountants, accounting practice in the past encouraged an arbitrary write-down of intangibles to a nominal amount (such as $100) either by a lump sum in one period or over an unrealistically short estimated life. Current accounting principles do not permit this practice because it misstates income and financial position. On this point, *APB Opinion No. 17* (par. 28) states that intangible assets "should not be written off in the period of acquisition," and "analysis of all factors should result in a reasonable estimate of the useful life."

EXHIBIT 13-3   Example of Intangible Asset Reporting, Fruehauf Corporation

	1988	1987
Amounts in thousands		
Total property, plant and equipment	$735,827	$790,509
Intangible assets less accumulated amortization of $6,648 and $3,324 at December 31, 1988 and 1987, respectively (Note 3)	120,318	123,643

NOTES TO CONSOLIDATED FINANCIAL STATEMENTS

Note 1 [in part]: Organization and Summary of Accounting Principles

Intangible Assets

Intangible assets are amortized on a straight-line basis over the estimated lives of the assets as follows:

	Years
Trade names	40
Manufacturing technology	40
Sales and service network	20
License agreements	20

Note 3: Intangible Assets

The intangible assets, net of amortization at December 31, 1988, and December 31, 1987, recorded in connection with the acquisition are as follows (dollars in thousands):

	December 31 1988	1987
Trade names	$ 60,491	$ 62,197
Manufacturing technology	50,109	51,428
Sales and service network	9,097	9,375
License agreements	621	643
Total	$120,318	$123,643

REPORTING INTANGIBLES

◆

Noncurrent assets classified as intangibles are reported under such balance sheet headings as intangibles, deferred charges, and *other assets*. Although precise definitions are desirable, distinctions often are not made in practice for these three captions. There is variation in the manner in which companies report intangibles on their balance sheet. Often each major intangible asset reported on the balance sheet is described in detail in the financial statement notes.

An abridged example of the reporting of intangible assets is shown in Exhibit 13-3.

CONCEPT REVIEW

1. List five different types of exchangeable intangible assets.
2. What is the maximum period over which an intangible asset may be amortized?
3. What are organization costs? Why are they capitalized on the balance sheet rather than being expensed when incurred?

GOODWILL—AN UNIDENTIFIABLE INTANGIBLE ASSET
♦

In 1988, Philip Morris acquired Kraft Inc. for a purchase price of approximately $12.9 billion. The fair market value of Kraft's net assets that were acquired totaled only $1.3 billion. The difference, a staggering $11.6 billion, cannot be identified with any separable tangible or intangible asset. What does this amount represent? Philip Morris recorded it as an asset and called it "goodwill."

Goodwill is the most common and important unidentifiable intangible asset. It represents the value arising from the favorable characteristics of a firm that give rise to earnings beyond (in excess of) those expected from identifiable assets of the firm. Exhibit 13–4 shows the total intangible assets reported on the 1988 balance sheets for several major firms. For most of these firms, the entire intangible asset amount shown is goodwill. Since the mid and late 1980s, goodwill has become a major asset of many firms. The increase in reported goodwill is due in large part to the extensive merger and acquisition activity of that period.

In the Philip Morris example, goodwill was recorded when one firm acquired another. This is not an accident; goodwill is recorded *only* when there is an acquisition of one firm by another. Goodwill can *exist* without an acquisition; however, it is *recorded* only when one company is acquired by, or merged with, another. The discussion of goodwill begins by considering the nature of goodwill, in particular, what gives rise to goodwill, and then addresses problems of measuring, recording, amortization, and reporting goodwill.

Conceptual Nature of Goodwill

Essentially, goodwill represents the expected value of a firm's future above-normal financial performance. This expectation arises because there are intangible, favorable characteristics or factors relating to the firm or its operating environment that make it likely that the firm will produce higher than average earnings. The following are examples of such favorable factors:

♦ A superior management team.
♦ An outstanding sales organization.
♦ Weakness in the management of one or more major competitors.
♦ Especially effective advertising.
♦ A secret manufacturing process.
♦ Exceptionally good labor relations.
♦ An outstanding credit rating.
♦ A top-flight training program for employees.
♦ An unusually good reputation in its industry for total quality.
♦ Unfavorable developments in the operations of a competitor.
♦ A particularly favorable association with a supplier.
♦ A highly advantageous strategic location.
♦ Discovery of previously unknown resources or employee skills.
♦ Favorable tax conditions.
♦ Favorable government regulations.[9]

Each of these factors, and possibly others not included in this list of examples, gives rise to increasing the earning power of the firm over what it would be in the absence of that factor. By increasing earnings, these factors give rise to an increase in value of the firm above that of the value of the individual assets. The increase in value is often reflected in the price of the firm's stock.

---

[9] See G. Catlett and N. Olson, "Accounting for Goodwill," *Accounting Research Study No. 10* (New York: AICPA, 1968), pp. 17–18.

EXHIBIT 13-4   Amounts of Goodwill on Balance Sheets of Several Major Companies and Their Percentage of Total Stockholders' Equity.

How Goodwill Weighs on the Balance Sheets

When one company buys another, the difference between the purchase price and the fair value of the physical assets is goodwill. Most companies put it under the heading of intangible assets.

| Company | Intangible Assets | |
	Millions of Dollars	Percentage of Total Stockholders' Equity
Viacom	$2,468	721%
Fruit of the Loom	908	352
Tele-Communications	3,143	261
Philip Morris	15,071	196
Coca-Cola Enterprises	2,935	188
Baxter International	2,705	87
Gannett	1,526	85
Dow Jones	964	83
Pepsico	2,582	82
Shearson Lehman Hutton	1,758	76
Capital Cities/ABC	2,217	73
Eastman Kodak	4,610	68
McGraw-Hill	507	55
General Electric	8,552	46
Waste Management	838	38
Chrysler	2,688	35
American Home Products	643	22
Xerox	1,089	20
General Motors	5,392	15
IBM	717	2

Data: Standard & Poor's Compustat Services, Inc.

Source: *Business Week,* July 31, 1989, p. 73.

A characteristic of the factors that give rise to goodwill is that they derive value from their association with the other assets of the firm. They are not independent of the firm of which they are part and, furthermore, cannot be sold separately. This dependence, in turn, gives rise to a serious measurement problem: since a firm's goodwill cannot be separated from the firm or bought or sold independently, it can be measured objectively only when the firm is sold. Goodwill can be generated by a firm as it carries out its business plans, but there is no market or arm's-length transaction with which to measure the cost of the goodwill. In sum, goodwill is recorded by a firm only when it acquires a second firm at a cost greater than the current market value of the identifiable net assets obtained.

For accounting purposes goodwill can be thought of as the difference between the actual purchase price of an acquired firm and the estimated fair market value of the

EXHIBIT 13-5 Cafe Corp. Balance Sheet as of December 31, 1994, as Reported and Fair Market Values

	As Reported	Fair Market Value	Difference
Assets:			
Cash	$ 30,000	$ 30,000	
Receivables	90,000	85,000	(5,000)
Inventory	60,000	60,000	
Other current assets	33,000	30,000	(3,000)
Plant and equipment (net)	220,000	235,000	15,000
Other assets	85,000	90,000	5,000
Total assets	$518,000	$530,000	
Liabilities:			
Short-term notes payable	$ 85,000	$ 85,000	
Account payable	45,000	45,000	
Other current liabilities	30,000	30,000	
Long-term debt	250,000	240,000	(10,000)
Stockholders' equity	108,000	130,000	22,000
Total equities	$518,000	$530,000	

identifiable net assets acquired. *APB Opinion No. 16,* par. 87, states that "the excess of the cost of the acquired company [i.e., the purchase price] over the sum of the amount assigned to identifiable assets acquired less liabilities assumed should be recorded as goodwill." An acquisition by purchase is the only objective means of measuring the cost of goodwill such that it conforms to the cost principle.

The next section considers the problem of measuring goodwill. Measuring goodwill requires valuing a firm that is being considered for acquisition. The discussion returns to further consideration of the issues in accounting for goodwill in the following section.

Measuring Goodwill after Purchase Price Is Determined

The value of goodwill cannot be directly computed because it is not separable or identifiable. Any method used will be indirect. Generally the total value of a firm is first estimated. Then the value of the various identifiable assets, both tangible and intangible, and the current value of the liabilities of the firm are determined. The difference between the two is considered the value of the goodwill.

Example Assume Hotel Company is considering the acquisition of Cafe Corp. Hotel Company obtains financial statements and other financial data on Cafe and estimates the fair market value of Cafe's identifiable assets at $530,000. (See Exhibit 13-5.)

Several assets are estimated to have a fair market value different from that reported in the published financial statements of Cafe Corp. Indeed, there is no particular reason why amounts shown in the balance sheet should equal fair market values. Accounting is based on recorded historical costs rather than current market values. In this situation, the management of Hotel Company has determined that Cafe's receivables are overstated by $5,000 and its other current assets are overstated by $3,000; an appraisal of plant and equipment and of other assets results in estimated market values $20,000 greater than the reported amounts. Finally, the long-term debt of Cafe has an estimated market value that is less than its carrying amount. This situation could happen if, subsequent to issue, the interest rate for debt of similar risk increased. Hence, to achieve the same risk-adjusted return, the market price of the debt dropped.

The total value of the firm's net assets is determined to be $130,000, shown as stockholders' equity under the fair market value column. This value is established by estimating, not the value of Cafe as a firm, but rather the aggregate value resulting from summing up the values of individual assets and liabilities. This value is similar to the concept of liquidation value. If the firm were broken up and sold as individual assets, and the liabilities were paid off at current market prices, the resulting net cash to be distributed to the owners would be approximately $130,000. Management of Hotel Company, however, must determine the value of Cafe as a going concern. Assume they are not planning to liquidate Cafe. For now, assume that Hotel negotiates a purchase price with the owners to acquire Cafe as of December 31, 1994, for $202,000. There may be many reasons, such as those listed on page 651, why Hotel might be willing to pay more than $130,000 for Cafe. (The logic and computation of the $202,000 figure is provided later in this section. However, the specific reason why Hotel Company agreed to pay a premium over the current market value of the net identifiable assets is not a matter of concern here.)

The amount of goodwill in this acquisition can now be computed. The purchase price is $202,000, and the current market value of the identifiable net assets totals $130,000; thus, goodwill is the difference, or $72,000. When Hotel absorbs Cafe, the various assets and liabilities of Cafe will be recorded at their current market values on Hotel Company's books, and goodwill of $72,000 will also be recorded. The entry Hotel Company would make to reflect the acquisition of Cafe is:

Cash	30,000	
Receivables	85,000	
Inventory	60,000	
Other current assets	30,000	
Plant and equipment	235,000	
Other assets	90,000	
Goodwill	72,000	
Short-term note payable		85,000
Accounts payable		45,000
Other current liabilities		30,000
Long-term debt		240,000
Cash		202,000

The various assets and liabilities are recorded at current market values in Hotel's financial records. This recording reflects the costs Hotel incurred for these items. These costs will be used in subsequent accounting by Hotel.

Estimating Goodwill

How is the purchase price determined in a corporate acquisition? The purchase price is important since it is one of the two determinants (the other being current market value of net identifiable assets) that the accountant uses in measuring goodwill.[10]

The purchase price reflects the results of the negotiations between the seller and the buyer. It may be greatly influenced by the negotiating skills of the parties at the bargaining table. Both parties must estimate a value for the firm. Several approaches are available by which the value of a firm can be estimated. However, only one method is presented here: the excess earnings approach.[11]

Excess earnings approach   One important method of estimating the value of a firm is to evaluate its earning power. Often called the **excess earnings approach**, the method requires five steps:

---

[10] *APB Opinion No. 16*, par. 88, provides guidance on assigning amounts of purchase price as the cost of individual assets acquired and liabilities assumed. This topic is covered in more detail in advanced accounting textbooks.

[11] Other methods can be found in texts on advanced accounting.

1. Estimate future earnings.
2. Determine a normal rate of return.
3. Determine normal earnings.
4. Determine excess earnings.
5. Computation of goodwill.

Step 1. Estimate Future Earnings Estimates of a firm's future earnings usually begin with an analysis of the firm's past earnings. Past earnings are a useful point of departure because they reflect neither optimistic nor pessimistic thinking about the future. Forecasters will have to justify why they expect earnings to differ from the historical trend.

Suppose Cafe Corp. has the following five-year earnings history:

Year	Earnings
1990	$26,000
1991	25,000
1992	30,000
1993	32,000
1994	37,000
Five year total	$150,000

What should be used as the assessment of the future earnings of the firm? If a simple five-year average is used, the estimate of future earnings is $30,000 ($150,000/5 years). However, a five-year average may be too long. Perhaps because of changes in the business the most recent three years is more appropriate. If that were the case, the estimate of future earnings would be $33,000 (($30,000 + $32,000 + $37,000)/3). Arguments could be advanced in support of other estimates as well. The purpose is to select a realistic and reasonable time frame to use in estimating a value for goodwill. For exposition, assume an annual earnings estimate of $30,000.[12]

Step 2. Determine a Normal Rate of Return The rate of return on net assets varies across firms, although it is usually reasonably constant within industries. If an industry estimate of a normal rate of return can be obtained, this rate can be used in the analysis. Industry averages are available through various financial services, or they can be determined by an analysis of annual reports and other financial data. One problem is that estimates of normal rates of return are typically computed from historical cost–balance sheet data, rather than from data on fair market value. This approach tends to bias the estimate of the normal rate of return upwards because fair market values are generally higher than historical cost. For the current example, assume the industry rate of return for Cafe is 12%.

Step 3. Determine Normal Earnings Once the normal rate of return for the industry and the fair value of the net assets acquired are known, the expected, normal earnings for the firm can be established:

Normal earnings = (Rate of return) (Fair value of net assets)
Normal earnings = (0.12) ($130,000)
Normal earnings = $15,600

Step 4. Determine Excess Earnings The difference between the computed normal earnings for the firm and the estimate or forecast of future earnings represents the excess earnings of the firm. These are earnings not related specifically or individ-

---

[12] Adjustments to earnings may be necessary before they are used to forecast future earnings. For example, if the above earnings for Cafe include an extraordinary gain of $5,000 in 1994, the 1994 earnings should be adjusted to $32,000 for purposes of forecasting future earnings. Also, if the acquired firm uses accounting methods different from the acquiring firm's and these methods will be changed after the acquisition, forecast earnings should be computed using the new accounting methods. For more on valuing closely held businesses, see W. Rissin and R. Zulli, "Valuation of a Closely Held Business," *The Journal of Accountancy*, June 1988, pp. 38–44.

ually to the net identifiable assets. They are considered the earnings resulting from the goodwill of the firm. In this case the excess earnings are:

$$\text{Excess earnings} = \text{Estimated future earnings} - \text{Normal earnings}$$
$$= \$30,000 - \$15,600$$
$$= \$14,400$$

Considerable estimation goes into the determinatioin of excess earnings. The estimate depends on estimating the firm's future earnings, assigning an amount as the fair value of the net identifiable assets, and establishing the appropriate rate of return to apply to the fair value of the assets. Rather than proceed with a single figure as the estimate of excess earnings, a range of excess earnings could be used and then a range of values of goodwill values computed. Despite the appeal of a range of values, only a single value is used in the current example.

Step 5. Computation of Goodwill A number of values for goodwill could result depending on what discount rate is used to value the excess earnings stream and on how many periods the excess earnings are assumed to continue in the future. Several examples follow:

a. Excess earnings are expected to continue indefinitely (in perpetuity). If the appropriate discount rate is 12%, then the computed present value of the excess earnings stream is:[13]

$$\text{Value of goodwill} = \frac{\text{Excess earnings}}{\text{Discount rate}} = \frac{\$14,400}{0.12} = \$120,000$$

b. If the risk associated with the excess earnings is regarded as greater than that of the identifiable assets, a higher discount rate, say 20%, is appropriate for determining the value of the goodwill. In this case the value of the goodwill is:

$$\text{Value of goodwill} = \frac{\text{Excess earnings}}{\text{Discount rate}} = \frac{\$14,400}{0.20} = \$72,000$$

The higher the assumed risk, the higher the discount rate and the lower the value of goodwill. Selecting the appropriate discount rate is difficult and can greatly influence the final result. Accountants generally agree that excess earnings are more risky than normal earnings and, hence, a higher discount rate is appropriate. If the value of goodwill is assumed to be $72,000, the purchaser would be willing to pay up to this amount plus the fair market value of the net assets ($130,000), or a total of up to $202,000 to acquire the firm. (This is the value assumed earlier in the Cafe example.)

Excess earnings may not be expected to continue indefinitely. In this situation, determining the periods during which excess earnings might reasonably be expected presents another difficult problem. If a period of 10 years for Cafe Corporation's excess earnings is assumed, present value annuity tables can be used to determine the value of goodwill. Assuming a discount rate of 12% is appropriate:

$$\text{Value of goodwill} = (PVA, 12\%, 10) (\text{Excess earnings})$$
$$= (5.65022) (\$14,400)$$
$$= \$81,363$$

The value of goodwill would increase (decrease) if the number of periods the excess earnings are expected to continue is increased (decreased). Analogous to the computation in Step (5b) above, if the discount rate is increased, the value of goodwill is reduced.

---

[13] The present value of an ordinary annuity given in Table 6A–4 is $\left[1 - \frac{1}{(1 + i)^n}\right] \div i$. As n gets larger without limit, $1 \div (1 + i)^n$ approaches zero and the present value (discount) factor approaches $1 \div i$.

In the above analysis, several alternative computations of the value for goodwill in the acquisition of Cafe by Hotel Company have been considered. The results range from a low $72,000 to a high of $120,000. A different range of values would result if different assumptions had been made. In each case, however, the value for goodwill was determined by discounting excess earnings. Other methods for estimating the value of goodwill that might be used can be more or less complex. These methods are beyond the scope of this text. While the determination of the value of goodwill is a difficult and highly uncertain task, the most important concerns from an accounting point of view are: that goodwill is determined for recording purposes after the acquisition purchase price has been set, and that the value of the goodwill equals the purchase price less the fair value of the net identifiable assets acquired.

In summary, when a firm is purchased, the purchaser records the acquisition by debiting each identifiable asset and, where appropriate, goodwill, and by crediting each liability assumed in conformity with the cost principle. The cost principle provides that all items be recorded at their fair market value as measured in the purchase transaction. Subsequent to the acquisition date, depreciation, depletion, and amortization of each asset, including goodwill, must be recognized. Before the issue of amortizing goodwill is considered, the question of what to do if the purchase price is less than the fair value of the net identifiable assets acquired is addressed.

Negative Goodwill

When the fair value of the net assets acquired is greater than the purchase price of the firm, the acquiring firm has made what might be called a bargain purchase. The amount of goodwill, again computed as the difference between the purchase price and fair value of assets acquired, is negative. This amount is often identified as badwill, or **negative goodwill**. A transaction in which there is negative goodwill would appear not to be rational for the seller, as it seems the seller could benefit from selling the assets individually rather than selling the firm as a whole. Such situations do occasionally occur, however, especially when the seller does not have the time or resources to take on the risks associated with the alternative of selling the assets separately. If such a situation occurred, the recorded goodwill (actually, negative goodwill) would have a credit balance.

APB Opinion No. 16, par. 91, however, requires that any negative goodwill must first be allocated proportionally to reduce the values assigned to the noncurrent assets (except long-term investments in marketable securities) of the acquired firm. If this allocation reduces the fair values of these assets to zero, any remaining negative goodwill should be classified as a "deferred credit" and be systematically amortized to income over the period estimated to be benefited, but not in excess of 40 years. The method and period of amortization should be disclosed in the notes.

Recording negative goodwill occurs infrequently. A survey of 600 annual reports in 1989 revealed two instances of firms reporting a deferred credit as "excess of acquired net assets over cost."[14]

Returning to the example of Hotel Company purchasing Cafe Corporation, assume the purchase price is $97,500. The purchase price is $32,500 less than the fair value of the net assets acquired. In this situation there would be negative goodwill of $32,500. The $32,500 would be allocated proportionally to reduce the recorded values for plant, equipment, and other assets. Two entries are required. The first records all the assets and liabilities of Cafe at their fair values and sets up a goodwill account with a credit balance of $32,500. The second entry writes down the plant and equipment and the other asset accounts proportionally.

---

[14] AICPA, *Accounting Trends & Techniques* (New York, 1990), p. 195.

Under these revised conditions the entry to reflect the combination of Hotel and Cafe is:

Cash	30,000	
Receivables	85,000	
Inventory	60,000	
Other current assets	30,000	
Plant and equipment	235,000	
Other assets	90,000	
Goodwill		32,500
Short-term note payable		85,000
Accounts payable		45,000
Other current liabilities		30,000
Long-term debt		240,000
Cash		97,500

The computation of the proportional reductions of the two long-term asset accounts is:

$$\text{Writedown of plant and equipment} = \frac{\$235,000}{\$235,000 + \$90,000} (\$32,500) = \$23,500$$

$$\text{Writedown of other assets} = \frac{\$90,000}{(\$235,000 + \$90,000)} (\$32,500) = \$9,000$$

The entry to write down these accounts proportionally is:

Goodwill	32,500	
Plant and equipment		23,500
Other assets		9,000

Amortizing Goodwill

After goodwill has been recognized, the next issue is what should be done with it. There are three alternatives, each of which has been advocated by at least some accountants at one time or another:

1. Write off the goodwill immediately to stockholders' equity, Since internally generated goodwill is expensed immediately, some accountants believe that consistent treatment requires the immediate write-off of purchased goodwill. Moreover, because it is difficult to establish how long goodwill will last, some accountants argue an immediate write-off is justified.
2. Retain the goodwill indefinitely (do not amortize) unless a reduction in value occurs. Some accountants contend that goodwill has an indefinite life and should be maintained as an asset until a definite decline in value occurs. Their view is that without evidence that a decline in value has occurred, writing off goodwill over any period is arbitrary. Unfortunately, often it is not clear when a decline in the value of goodwill has occurred, or how to measure any decline. One approach would be to estimate the number of years remaining in the beneficial life of the goodwill when there is reason to believe the life is no longer indefinite, and to amortize the goodwill over this period.
3. Amortize the goodwill over its useful life. Still other accountants argue that goodwill is gradually eroded or used up and that it should be amortized to expense over the periods benefited. These accountants believe amortization results in a better matching of revenues and costs.

APB Opinion No. 17 requires that goodwill be written off over its estimated useful life (alternative three above), but in no case should the period of amortization exceed 40 years. An example is provided by the savings and loan industry. When one S&L firm acquires a second, goodwill often results from valuing the loans at market value. In this case, the average loan period provides a reasonable life over which to amortize goodwill.

Unfortunately, estimating the useful life of goodwill is usually difficult. Moreover, a company amortizing purchased goodwill at the same time that its investment in internally generated goodwill is being expensed will cause a difference in the measurement of income relative to a competitor that has no purchased goodwill requiring amortization.

Example of Goodwill Disclosure Nortek, Inc., provides the following information regarding goodwill on the balance sheet:

	Year	
(Dollars in thousands)	**1988**	**1987**
Other assets:		
Goodwill less accumulated amortization of $11,543,000 and $7,693,000	$135,487	$142,432

In the Notes to Consolidated Financial Statements Nortek discloses:

> **Note 1** [in part]: *Summary of Significant Accounting Policies and Goodwill (Cost of Purchased Business in Excess of Net Assets Acquired)*
> The Company has classified as goodwill the cost in excess of fair value of the net assets (including tax attributes) of companies acquired in purchase transactions. Purchase price allocations are subject to refinement until all pertinent information regarding the acquisitions is obtained. Goodwill is being amortized on a straight-line method over 40 years. Amortization charged to continuing operations amounted to $3,834,000, $2,993,000, and $2,341,000 for 1988, 1987, and 1986, respectively.

CONCEPT REVIEW

1. What is goodwill and how does it arise?
2. How is goodwill measured for accounting purposes?
3. Once goodwill has been recognized, how is treated for accounting purposes?

RESEARCH AND DEVELOPMENT (R&D) COSTS

Research and development (R&D) costs are among the more important expenditures made by many companies. In 1988, Microsoft Corporation spent approximately $70 million on R&D, which amounted to 11.9% of every sales dollar. In the same year, Boeing spent $751 million on R&D, equal to 4.4% of its sales. Some industries, such as pharmaceuticals, regularly spend upwards of 10% of each sales dollar on R&D.

Prior to the implementation of *SFAS No. 2,* the reporting and accounting treatment of R&D costs varied greatly among firms. Unamortized R&D costs were often a significant balance sheet asset reported as a deferred charge and included in intangible assets. Other firms expensed all R&D costs as they were incurred. There was a perception that the variations in reporting and the potential to amortize R&D expenditures in various ways were being used to manipulate income. This was one reason R&D expenditures were one of the first topics the FASB chose to address. After due deliberation and analysis, the FASB issued *SFAS No. 2,* "Accounting for Research and Development Costs," in 1974. The *Standard* provides definitions of research and of development:

Research is planned search or critical investigation aimed at discovery of new knowledge with the hope that the new knowledge will be useful in developing a new product or service or a new process or technique or in bringing about a significant improvement in an existing product.

Development is the translation of research findings or other knowledge into a plan or design for a new product or a signficant improvement to an existing product or process whether intended for sale or use. It includes the conceptual formulation, design and testing of product alternatives, construction of prototypes, and operation of pilot plants. It does not include routine or periodic alterations to existing products, production lines, manufacturing processes, and other ongoing operations. Development also does not include market research or market testing activities.

SFAS No. 2 delineates five cost elements of R&D activities:

1. Materials, equipment, and facilities.
2. Personnel.
3. Intangibles purchased from others.
5. Contract services.
5. Allocated indirect costs related to R&D activities.

The *Standard* specifies that equipment and facilities acquired or constructed for R&D activities should be capitalized. Depreciation on these acquired or constructed assets constitutes R&D expense for the period in which these assets are used for R&D purposes.

The objective being pursued in many firm activities is similar to R&D: to provide future benefit to the firm. Examples include relocation costs of facilities, start-up costs of a new product or facility, training costs of personnel, and promotion costs for products or services. To help distinguish between what is and what is not R&D, the *SFAS No. 2* provides examples of each. Exhibit 13–6 lists examples of activities that typically would be included in research and development, and of activities that would not be included as R&D.

The *Standard* specifies accounting for R&D as follows:

1. All R&D costs covered by the *Standard* are to be expensed when incurred except those incurred on projects being completed under contract for outside entities.
2. R&D costs incurred when projects are completed under contract for outside entities do not need to be immediately expensed. There are also exceptions for certain government-regulated entities. In these cases, any R&D costs incurred because they are required by contract are capitalized as part of work-in process-inventory. Upon completion of the contract, or specified parts of the contract, the capitalized costs, along with all of the other project costs, are removed from inventory and reported as an expense similar to cost of goods sold.[15]
3. The financial statements must disclose the total R&D costs included in expense in each period for which an income statement is presented.

SFAS No. 2 provides a practical solution to what had been a serious problem. It has resulted in consistent, uniform practice across firms. Because R&D is undertaken with the expectation that it will benefit the firm in the future, some accountants believe R&D expenditures should be capitalized rather than expensed. While not every R&D project that a firm initiates will generate benefits, on average, the expectation is that some will, thus resulting in assets for the firm.

Accountants who argue in support of expensing R&D costs see the requirement as having little effect on the income statement. For these accountants, the immediate expensing will result in approximately the same level of expense in each accounting period as capitalizing the R&D costs and amortizing them over time. Those accountants supporting capitalization of R&D, on the other hand, point to the effect expensing has on the balance sheet. In some cases, they observe, the firm's most valuable asset would not be reported as an asset at all. Nevertheless, the difficulties associated with measuring the asset and the potential for abuses are such that the

---

[15] FASB, *Statement of Financial Accounting Standards No. 68,* "Research and Development Arrangements" (Norwalk, Conn., 1982), provides accounting guidelines on contract research.

EXHIBIT 13-6   Example of Activities Included and Excluded from the Definition of R&D Costs

Activities included in R&D costs:
* Laboratory research aimed at discovery of new knowledge.
* Searching for applications of new research findings.
* Conceptual formulation and design of possible products or process alternatives.
* Testing in search for or evaluation of product or process alternatives.
* Modification of the formulation or design of a product or process.
* Design, construction, and testing of preproduction prototypes and models.
* Design of tools, jigs, molds, and dies involving new technology.
* Design, construction, and operation of a pilot plant that is not at a scale economically feasible for commercial production.
* Engineering activity required to advance the design of a product to the point that it meets specific functional and economic requirements and is ready for manufacture.

Activities excluded from R&D costs:
* Engineering follow-through in an early phase of commercial production.
* Quality control during commercial production, including routine testing of products.
* Trouble-shooting in connection with breakdowns during commercial production.
* Routine, on-going efforts to refine, enrich, or otherwise improve upon the qualities of an existing product.
* Adaptation of an existing capability to a particular requirement or customer's need as part of a continuing commercial activity.
* Seasonal or other periodic design changes to existing products.
* Routine design of tools, jigs, molds, and dies.
* Activity, including design and construction engineering, related to the construction, relocation, rearrangement, or start-up of facilities or equipment other than (a) pilot plants and (b) facilities whose sole use is for a particular research and development project.
* Legal work in connection with patent applications or litigation and the sale or licensing of patents.

Source: FASB, *SFAS No. 2*, "Accounting for Research and Development Costs" (Norwalk, Conn., 1974), pars. 9 and 10.

FASB decided the most appropriate solution was to require the expensing of R&D costs. This *Standard* represents an example of the trade-offs that often must be made between relevance, reliability, and other cost-benefit considerations in providing guidance for accounting of complex transactions.[16]

CONCEPT REVIEW

1. What are the arguments that would support the capitalizing of R&D costs?
2. What are the arguments that would support the immediate expensing of R&D costs?
3. A solid waste management equipment manufacturer is building a pilot plant to investigate a new technique for extracting energy from solid waste. The plant will be scrapped once the tests of the feasibility of the new process are completed. How should the costs of building the plant be treated? Suppose, alternatively, there is a reasonable probability that the plant will be sold to the local city for use in solid waste management activities. Now how should the costs of the plant be treated?

[16] For a more thorough discussion of the conceptual issues and arguments for capitalizing R&D under certain conditions, see H. Bierman Jr. and R. Dukes, "Accounting for Research and Development Costs," *The Journal of Accountancy*, April 1975, pp. 48–55.

ACCOUNTING FOR COMPUTER SOFTWARE COSTS

SFAS No. 2 resolved the problems of accounting for R&D costs. A decade after the resolution of this issue, however, a new industry emerged, namely, computer software firms. The FASB found it necessary to address the specific problem of how to account for the rather special costs involved in developing computer software.

One of the fastest growing sectors of the economy is in the area of information technology, especially computers of all sizes and the associated software programs these computers use. Thousands of companies are engaged in the development and sale of computer software, spending around $10 billion annually to develop new software products. Accounting for the costs of developing computer software has become increasingly important as the industry has grown and as a wide diversity of accounting procedures developed in practice. Since the major asset of many computer software companies is their investment in software and software development, narrowing the range of accounting alternatives became a controversial issue.

Capitalization of Computer Software Costs   The development of computer software to sell or lease to external parties involves significant costs. The basic accounting issue is what costs incurred in developing software packages should be expensed and what costs should be capitalized. This issue became a major reporting concern in the early 1980s. The Securities and Exchange Commission and the American Institute of Certified Public Accountants requested the FASB to resolve this issue. In August 1985, the FASB issued *SFAS No. 86,* ''Accounting for the Costs of Computer Software to Be Sold, Leased, or Otherwise Marketed.'' The basic provisions of the *Standard* are these:

- All costs incurred to establish the *technological feasibility* of a computer software product to be marketed or leased are R&D costs and should be expensed when incurred.
- Costs of producing *product masters* incurred subsequent to establishing technological feasibility shall be capitalized. These costs include coding and testing subsequent to establishing technological feasibility.

Thus, an engineering study to establish whether a proposed software package could be produced is expensed, while the costs of constructing the masters to be used in actual production of the product should be capitalized.

The key point at which development costs can begin to be capitalized is the point where technological feasibility is established. Technological feasibility is established when all planning, designing, coding, and testing activities necessary to establish that the product can be produced to meet its design specifications are completed. That is, technological feasibility is established when a detailed program design is completed. However, if the software development effort does not include such a design, then a working model of the product must be completed.

Costs of production of the software from the masters and of the documentation and training materials, and the costs of physically packaging the materials for distribution are all production costs. These costs are inventoriable and are transferred (debited) to cost of sales when sales revenue is recognized.

Amortization of Capitalized Software Costs   The *Standard* is specific regarding the amortization of capitalized computer software costs. The annual amortization amount is computed on a product-by-product basis and must be the greater of:

- The ratio of current period gross revenues from the product to total current and anticipated gross revenues from the product over its remaining estimated economic life times the remaining amount to be amortized.
- The amount determined by the straight-line method of amortization over the remaining estimated economic life of the product.

For example, assume Supersoft Company has capitalized software costs of $1 million for its newly developed word processing program. The package is expected to be on the market for the next four years yielding revenues of $1.2 million in the first year and a total of $4.8 million in subsequent years for a total anticipated revenue of $6.0 million. To determine the amortization for the first year, compute first the amortization under both methods given above:

1. Ratio of revenue method:

$$\text{Amortization} = \left(\frac{\text{Current period revenue}}{\text{Total anticipated revenue}}\right) \text{(Capitalized amount)}$$

$$\text{Amortization} = \left(\frac{\$1,200,000}{\$6,000,000}\right) (\$1,000,000)$$

$$\text{Amortization} = \$200,000$$

2. Straight-line method:

$$\text{Amortization} = \$1,000,000/\text{four years} = \$250,000$$

The greater amortization is given by the straight-line method; thus, this is the amount that would be taken in the first year. If the firm expects a sufficiently large portion of the total anticipated revenues to be earned in the first year the product is sold, the revenue ratio method of computing amortization would give the greater amortization amount. For example, assume first year revenues are $3 million, and all other aspects of the situation are unchanged. Now the revenue ratio amortization amount is ($3 million/$6 million) ($1 million) = $500,000. The straight-line amortization amount is unchanged; thus, the firm would be required to use the revenue ratio amortization amount of $500,000. This approach attempts to provide a reasonable application of the *matching principle*. FASB *Standards* are seldom this specific in setting the accounting method to be used.

The calculations illustrated above must be repeated each year. Hence, if in Year 2, the facts are:

Remaining life: 3 years, at the start of Year 2.

Total current and expected revenues remaining at the start of Year 2: $4.8 million.

Revenues in Year 2: $2.4 million.

Then the ratio method yields:

$$(\$2.4 \div \$4.8) (\$1.0 - \$0.250) = \$0.375 \text{ million}$$

The straight-line method yields:

$$(\$1.0 - \$0.250) \div 3 = \$0.250 \text{ million}.$$

Thus, for the second year, amortization is calculated to be $375,000 now under the ratio method. The entry for each year is (in thousands):

	Year 1	Year 2
Amortization expense 250		375
Accumulated amortization—		
computer software	250	375

At each balance sheet date, the inventory of computer software must be written down to net realizable value if that value is below cost. Once it is written down to net realizable value it cannot be subsequently written back up to cost.

Disclosures of Computer Software Costs   *SFAS No. 86* requires the following disclosures:
- Unamortized computer software costs included in each balance sheet presented.
- The total amount charged to expense for amortization of capitalized computer software costs in each income statement presented.
- The amounts charged to expense for writing down the software costs to net realizable value in each income statement presented.

SFAS No. 86 deals only with computer software developed for sale or lease or otherwise for marketing to external parties. There is currently no specific guidance from the FASB on accounting for software developed for internal uses. Because the costs of most software developed for internal purposes is expensed as incurred, the FASB did not see the need for a standard in this area.

CONCEPT REVIEW

1. When is it appropriate to capitalize the development costs for developing computer software?
2. What is the requirement for amortizing capitalized computer software costs?
3. What disclosures are required for computer software costs?

ACCOUNTING FOR NATURAL RESOURCES

Natural resources are also called **wasting assets** to denote that they are consumed physically in production. Examples of wasting assets include timberland, oil and gas, and various types of mineral deposits such as gold, silver, copper, and coal. These properties present unique accounting problems. The two most important of these problems are:

1. Determining the cost of such properties when they are developed (as opposed to when they are purchased).
2. Writing off (amortizing) the cost to the income statement.

The determination of the cost of the properties requires a decision regarding exactly which costs should be capitalized in the intangible asset that represent the cost of the natural resource. The second problem concerns the rate at which the intangible asset is expensed. The amount of cost of a natural resource that is expensed each period is called **depletion**. Depletion describes what is happening. The term signifies that the resource is being used up.

Depletion Base

The **depletion base** is the amount capitalized as an intangible asset that will be expensed over the period of extraction of the natural resource. It is the amount of capitalized cost that is not expected to be recovered at the end of the period during which the natural resource is used. The residual value affects the determination of the asset's depletion base. The residual value can be positive or negative. A positive residual value is deducted from the capitalized costs in determining the depletion base of the wasting asset. In addition, any costs expected to be incurred in preparing the wasting asset for disposal are added to the depletion base. For example, the anticipated cost of restoring the ground surface of a strip mining operation would be added to the depletion base. If the cost of restoring the asset is expected to exceed the asset's residual value, the depletion base will exceed the asset's capitalizable cost.

SFAS No. 19 describes five categories of cost that are applicable to natural resources.[17]

---

[17] See FASB, *Statement of Financial Accounting Standards No. 19*, "Financial Accounting and Reporting by Oil and Gas Producing Companies" (Norwalk, Conn., 1977), par. 15–26. *SFAS No. 19* describes these costs specifically regarding oil and gas, but they are applicable to other forms of natural resources as well.

1. **Acquisition costs**—costs incurred to purchase, lease, or otherwise acquire the rights to property for purposes of exploring and, if found, producing a natural resource. Acquisition costs are capitalized as part of the depletion base.
2. **Exploration costs**—costs incurred to identify areas that may warrant testing or to actually examine and test specific areas for the presence of the natural resource. When the exploration effort results in the discovery of the natural resource in sufficient quantities to be economically extracted, these costs are capitalized as part of the depletion base. The determination of the appropriate exploration costs to capitalize is a controversial topic that is covered in more detail in the Appendix.
3. **Development costs**—when a natural resource is discovered in sufficient quantities to make extraction economically feasible, development costs are incurred to provide facilities for extracting, treating, gathering, and storing the resource. Development costs are also capitalized as part of the depletion base.
4. **Production costs**—costs incurred to physically extract the natural resource. Production costs are capitalized as part of the cost of the product as they are incurred.
5. **Support equipment and facilities costs**—the cost of tangible assets used in the exploration, development, and production of the natural resource. These costs are included in the plant and equipment accounts of the firm and are accounted for the same as other equipment. (See Chapters 11 and 12.)

Methods of Depletion for Financial Reporting

The amortization of a wasting asset is called *depletion*. Depletion then is the periodic allocation of the depletion base of a natural resource (a wasting asset) against revenue as the resource is exploited and sold. The depletion base is allocated over the estimated total production in conformity with the matching principle.

The most common method of calculating depletion is the *units-of-production method*. Knowing an estimate of the amount of recoverable or extractable units of the natural resource and the depletion base, the **unit depletion rate** is calculated as:

$$\text{Unit depletion rate} = \frac{\text{Depletion base}}{\text{Estimated recoverable units}}$$

The depletion amount for any period is equal to the number of units produced multiplied by the unit depletion rate. This amount may be initially debited to expense or to the inventory account of the natural resource and credited to the related wasting-asset account. If an inventory account is used, then as the inventory is sold, the inventory's cost, including the depletion, is expensed as a cost of the goods sold. At the end of the accounting peiod a portion of the depletion amount will be included in the inventory account to the extent that units have been produced but not sold during the period.

Example Burlington Southern Resources, Inc., leases and operates a large copper strip mining activity. The firm incurred costs of $4 million to lease, explore, and develop the mine. The company estimates the property will yield 2 million tons of copper ore. In 1991, the firm produced and sold 300,000 tons of copper ore.

The depletion base is the total capitalized cost less any residual value and plus any costs to return the strip mine to saleable condition. Since the property reverts back to its owners after the mining activity is completed in this case, the residual value of the property is zero. Therefore the unit depletion rate per ton of production is:

$$\text{Unit depletion ratio per ton} = \frac{\text{Depletion base}}{\text{Estimated recoverable tons of ore}}$$

$$\text{Unit depletion rate per ton} = \frac{\$4,000,000}{2,000,000 \text{ tons}}$$

$$= \$2 \text{ per ton}$$

The depletion amount for 1991 during which 300,000 tons are extracted is:

$$\text{Depletion amount} = (\$2 \text{ per ton}) (300{,}000 \text{ tons})$$
$$= \$600{,}000$$

The entry to recognize the depletion for the period, skipping the inventory account, is:

Depletion expense	600,000	
Mine property		600,000

Accountants typically credit the capitalized property account as shown in the above entry, rather than an accumulated depletion account, which would be the normal procedure for a plant and equipment asset. Crediting a contra asset account called "accumulated depletion" is an acceptable, if not common, practice.

Depletion is a portion of the product cost. As such, depletion is a portion of the cost of goods sold when the product is sold. If the product is not sold during the period, the depletion cost is included in the inventory cost, along with other costs of production.

Example In the original Burlington Southern example, assume the firm sold only 250,000 of the 300,000 tons of copper ore produced in 1991. The journal entry to reflect both the depletion expenses and the depletion cost remaining in the inventory account is:

Depletion expense	500,000	
Copper inventory	100,000	
Mining property		600,000

The depletion expense would be included as an item in cost of goods sold. To the extent in future years that sales are made from inventory, there would be a credit to the copper inventory account using a cost flow assumption such as average cost.

Example Suppose, however, that the terms of the lease call for restoration of the land back to its original state after the mining is completed. Suppose further that at the completion of the mining operation, the firm expects to spend $1 million to restore the property, at which time it will revert to the owners. In this case, the depletive asset's residual value is a negative $1 million since this is the cost that will be incurred to restore the property. The revised depletion base is $4 million plus $1 million or $5 million. The revised depletion rate per ton is:

$$\text{Unit depletion rate per ton} = \frac{\$5{,}000{,}000}{2{,}000{,}000 \text{ tons}}$$
$$= \$2.50 \text{ per ton}$$

The depletion for 1991 when 300,000 tons are extracted and sold is now:

$$\text{Depletion} = (\$2.50 \text{ per ton}) \times (300{,}000 \text{ tons})$$
$$= \$750{,}000$$

Assuming no remaining unsold inventory of copper, the entry to record the depletion expense for the period would now be:

Depletion expense	750,000	
Mine property		600,000
Accrued mine restoration costs		150,000

The entry to record the depletion includes a portion that is an accrued liability because the expenditure to restore the property has not yet been made. When the restoration expense is made, the liability is satisfied. The entry at that time, assuming $1 million is ultimately required, is a debit to the liability ($1 million by that time) and a credit to cash of $1 million. Another way to compute the amount of the accrual is to compute a restoration expense per ton of production, that is, ($1,000,000 ÷ 2 million tons estimated recoverable), or $0.50 per ton. Since 300,000 tons were produced, the cost of restoration associated with this production is, again, ($0.50) (300,000), or $150,000.

Depletion and Income Taxes

The depletion procedures discussed above are used for financial reporting. For federal income tax purposes, other depletion methods may be used in conformity with the Internal Revenue Code. For example, the Code allows taxpayers to use **statutory depletion** (also called **percentage depletion**). The taxpayer is allowed to compute both the cost-based depletion amount and a statutory depletion amount, and then claim the higher amount as the depletion deduction for tax purposes. Under the IRS statutory depletion rules, a stated percentage of the gross income derived from the sale of the natural resource may be taken as the depletion deduction on the tax return. The percentage varies from 5% on some natural resources to 22% on others. Some of the more common statutory depletion percentages in the current tax laws are:

	Percent
Sulfur and uranium if from deposits in the United States	22.0
Asbestos, lead, zinc, nickel, and certain other ores	22.0
Oil and Gas	15.0
Gold, silver, copper, iron ore, and oil shale if from U.S. deposits	15.0
Coal sodium chloride	10.0
Clay and shale for certain purposes	7.5
Gravel, sand, and other items	5.0
Certain other minerals and metallic ores	14.0

Under the Code, the sum of the statutory depletion deductions may exceed the original cost of the resources. The use of cost-based depletion for financial reporting purposes and statutory depletion for tax purposes can cause timing and possibly permanent differences in the deductions for tax and financial reporting.

Depletion and Liquidating Dividends   Cash dividends are sometimes paid by small natural resource companies in an amount equal to income plus the amount of depletion. State laws often permit such dividends. This practice is common when the company has no plans to replace the natural resource in kind and operations are to cease when the natural resource has been exhausted. In such cases, the stockholders should be informed (for tax purposes and because this is a liquidating dividend) of the portion of each dividend that represents a return of capital; that is, they should be told the amount of the depletion. For example, assume that Tex Oil Company has the following summarized balance sheet at December 31, 1991:

Assets	$1,000,000
Accumulated depreciation	(200,000)
Accumulated depletion	(100,000)
Total assets	$ 700,000
Liabilities	$ 150,000
Capital stock	500,000
Retained earnings	50,000
Total liabilities and equity	$ 700,000

If the board of directors declared and paid a cash dividend of $150,000 and if $100,000 of this amount represented a return of capital in an amount equal to accumulated depletion, the entry to record the dividend would be as follows:

Retained Earnings   50,000
Capital stock (return of capital to owners)   100,000
Cash   150,000

The return of capital to stockholders ($100,000) would be shown as a reduction in the owners' equity section of the balance sheet.

Change in Estimate

With nearly all natural resources, there is considerable uncertainty regarding the amount of the resource that will be produced or recovered. Frequent updates are made to the estimate of the recoverable amount. When a new estimate is made, the accountant must recompute the depletion rate. The new rate is computed prospectively, based on the amount of cost remaining in the depletion base and on the newly estimated number of units to be recovered. There is no revision in the prior depletion charges or to prior year's income. For example, suppose that in 1992, Burlington Southern revised its estimate of recoverable tons of copper ore for the mine to only 1 million tons (instead of the 1.7 million that would be expected based on the original estimate). The depletion rate for 1992 and thereafter would be the remaining depletion base, or $3.4 million, divided by the remaining estimated recoverable units, or 1 million tons, resulting in a depletion rate of $3.40 per ton.

CONCEPT REVIEW

1. How is the depletion base calculated?
2. How is depletion expense determined?
3. Under what conditions will exploration costs be capitalized as part of the depletion base?

SUMMARY OF KEY POINTS

(L.O. 1)   1. Accounting issues associated with intangible assets are similar to those for other long-lived assets:
   * Determining the initial carrying amount of the asset.
   * Amortizing the initial carrying amount.
   * Accounting for the asset when there is a permanent impairment of value.

(L.O. 1)   2. Intangible assets are long-lived assets with these attributes:
   * They lack physical substance, which distinguishes them from tangible assets.
   * They have future economic benefits that are difficult to measure.
   * They have a useful life that is difficult to determine.
   * They usually are acquired for operational use.

(L.O. 1)   3. Intangible assets can be categorized according to their:
   * Manner of acquisition.
   * Identifiability.
   * Exchangeability.
   * Period of expected benefit.

(L.O. 2)   4. The conceptual guidelines for accounting for intangible assets are the same as for tangible assets:
   * The cost principle is used to determine the initial carrying amount.
   * The matching principle is used to determine periodic amortization.

* The revenue principle is used to guide the recording of revenues, gains and loses upon sale or impairment of value.

(L.O. 3)   5. *APB No. 17* requires that the cost of an intangible asset be allocated to expense in a rational and systematic manner over the estimated useful life of the intangible asset. In no case can the period over which the allocation takes place exceed 40 years. This process is called *amortization.*

(L.O. 3)   6. The cost of patents, including costs of successfully defending them in court, is capitalized and amortized over a period of their estimated useful life. Since the legal life of a patent is 17 years, in no case should the period of amortization of a patent exceed 17 years.

(L.O. 3)   7. Copyrights provide protection to the author of literary, musical, artistic, and similar works. Although a copyright provides protection for the life of the author plus an additional 50 years, *APB No. 17* requires amortization over the lesser of the estimated useful life or 40 years.

(L.O. 3)   8. Organization costs are incurred in organizing a business and include costs such as legal, accounting, promotional, and clerical activities. Organization costs should be capitalized and amortized. While the maximum period allowed is 40 years, most firms amortize organization costs over a much shorter period.

(L.O. 4)   9. *SFAS No. 7* requires development stage companies to use the same assessment of future benefit and recoverability as those used by established companies in determining what costs can be capitalized.

(L.O. 4)   10. Goodwill is the most common unidentifiable intangible asset and is recognized in the financial statements only when there is an acquisition. Goodwill is recorded in an amount equal to the excess of the cost of the acquired company over the sum of values assigned to the net identifiable assets. Goodwill is amortized over its estimated useful life, but in no case should the period exceed 40 years.

(L.O. 4)   11. Negative goodwill (badwill) is allocated proportionally to reduce the values assigned to the noncurrent assets of the acquired firm except long-term investments in marketable securities. If the allocation reduces the values assigned to the noncurrent assets to zero, any remaining negative goodwill is recognized in the financial statements as a deferred credit and is amortized over a period not to exceed 40 years.

(L.O. 5)   12. *SFAS No. 2* requires that research and development costs be expensed as incurred. Firms engaged in R&D activities are required to disclose the amount of R&D expense for each period reported.

(L.O. 6)   13. *SFAS No. 86* specifies that the costs incurred in the development of computer software to be sold or leased should be capitalized as an intangible asset. All computer software costs are expensed until the technical and economic feasibility of the software has been established.

(L.O. 7)   14. Natural resources are wasting assets that are consumed during production. The major accounting problems for natural resources are determining the depletion base and the depletion rate.

(L.O. 8)   15. Oil and gas companies may use either the successful efforts or the full-cost methods for accounting for exploration costs (see chapter appendix). Under the successful efforts method, only the exploration costs of successful exploration are capitalized as the cost of finding the resource. Under the full-cost method, all costs of exploration are capitalized as long as this amount is less than the estimated value of the resources discovered.

REVIEW PROBLEM

◆

Munn, Inc., reported other noncurrent asset account balances on December 31, 1993, as follows:

Patent	$192,000
Accumulated amortization	(24,000)
Net patent	$168,000

Transactions during 1994 and other information relating to Munn's other noncurrent assets included the following:

1. The patent was purchased from Grey Company on January 2, 1992, at which date the remaining legal life was 16 years. On January 2, 1994, Munn determined that the remaining useful life of the patent was only eight years from the date of its acquisition.
2. On January 3, 1994, in connection with the purchase of a trademark from Cody Corp., the parties entered into a noncompetition agreement. Munn paid Cody $800,000, of which three quarters related to the trademark, and one quarter reflected Cody's agreement not to compete for a period of five years in the line of business covered by the trademark. Munn considers the life of the trademark to be indefinite.
3. On January 3, 1994, Munn acquired all the noncash assets and assumed all liabilities of Amboy Company at a cash purchase price of $1,200,000. Munn determined that the fair value of the net assets acquired in the transaction is $800,000.

Required:

1. Prepare a schedule of expenses for 1994 relating to Munn's other noncurrent assets at December 31, 1993, and of its transactions during 1994.
2. Prepare the other noncurrent assets section of the balance sheet for Munn on December 31, 1994.

SOLUTION

◆

1. Schedule of expenses relating to other noncurrent assets for the year ended December 31, 1994:

Amortization of intangibles:	
Patent	$28,000
Trademark	15,000
Noncompetition agreement	40,000
Goodwill	10,000
Total amortization expense	$93,000

2. Other noncurrent asset section of balance sheet, December 31, 1994:

Patent, net of accumulated amortization of $52,000	$140,000
Trademark, net of accumulated amortization of $15,000	585,000
Noncompetition agreement, net of accumulated amortization of $40,000	160,000
Goodwill, net of accumulated amortization of $10,000	390,000

Computations for review solution

1. *Patent.* On January 3, 1994, Munn determined that the patent has a shorter useful life than originally used in establishing an amortization schedule. This is a *change in estimate* and is accounted for prospectively. The remaining amortized balance is written off over the new estimate of useful life:

Net patent balance at 1/2/94: ($192,000 − $24,000)*	$168,000
Remaining life of patent (divide by)	÷ 6
Amortization for 1994	$ 28,000

* The accumulated amortization at 1/2/94 is computed as ($192,000 ÷ 16 years) × 2 years = $24,000.

2. *Trademark.* The cost of the trademark is three quarters of $800,000, or $600,000. Munn considers the trademark to have an indefinite life, but the maximum period

over which intangibles can be amortized is 40 years. The trademark need not be amortized over 20 years even though this is the legal life of a trademark. Trademarks are renewable; hence, in reality they have an indefinite legal life. To determine the amortizaton for 1994, divide the cost of the trademark, $600,000 by the maximum period allowed, 40 years. The amortization for 1994 is $600,000 divided by 40 years, or $15,000.

3. *Noncompetition agreement.* The cost of the noncompetition agreement is one quarter of $800,000, or $200,000. The agreement has a useful life of five years; thus, the amortization for 1994 is $200,000 divided by five years, or $40,000.

4. *Goodwill.* First compute the amount of goodwill.

Purchase price of acquired firm	$1,200,000
Less: Fair value of net assets acquired	800,000
Excess of cost over net assets acquired	$ 400,000

The goodwill is $400,000. No mention is made of the period over which the goodwill is expected to yield excess earnings. Munn could select a shorter period, but in this solution, the maximum of 40 years is assumed. The amortization for 1994 is $400,000 divided by 40 years, or $10,000.

Computations of account balances at December 31, 1994

	Patent	Trademark	Noncompet. agreement	Goodwill
Balance, 12/31/93	$168,000			
Balance, 1/3/94		$600,000	$200,000	$400,000
Deduct 1994 amort	(28,000)	(15,000)	(40,000)	(10,000)
Balance, 1/3/94	$140,000	$585,000	$160,000	$390,000

APPENDIX   *Accounting for Exploration Costs—The Case of the Oil and Gas Companies*

Accounting for the extraction of natural resources in the oil and gas industry is a difficult area that has led to establishing special accounting measurement rules. The major issue focuses on the appropriate accounting measurement and treatment of exploration costs.

Oil and gas companies incur large costs in the process of exploring for oil and gas deposits. Individual firm exploration activities are the result of management's decision that there is a reasonable expectation the firm will earn an acceptable rate of return on its overall exploration program. There is risk, however, since at the time the exploration efforts are made, the firm does not know which exploration efforts will be successful and which will be unsuccessful. The situation faced by the company is similar to the issue faced by a firm electing to engage in R&D activities. For the same reasons, the accounting issues are similar to those in accounting for R&D costs.

There have been two quite different methods of accounting for exploration costs. The choice results in a different flow of costs through the financial statements. The most frequently used method results in the capitalization of only those exploration costs that are associated with successful exploration, and the immedite expensing of all exploration costs associated with unsuccessful efforts. This approach is called the **successful-efforts method** and is used most frequently by the larger oil companies. The second method, called the **full-cost method,** capitalizes all exploration costs so long as the value of the estimated recoverable units from producing wells is expected to exceed the total capitalized costs. To illustrate the differences between these two approaches, consider the following example.

Illustration of Successful-Efforts and Full-Cost Accounting for Exploration Costs

Wildcat Exploration incurs costs of $2 million each in exploring 20 different sites for oil and gas. Nineteen of the exploration efforts are unsuccessful, but one effort results in a successful well with an estimated value of $80 million.

Successful Efforts   If the firm uses the successful-efforts method, the entry to record the above facts would be:

> Oil reserves (an asset) 2,000,000
> Exploration expenses 38,000,000
>   Cash (or accrued liabilities)   40,000,000

An asset in the amount of $2 million would be recorded on the balance sheet. The estimated value of this asset is $80 million. The $2 million would be amortized as depletion expense over the period of productivity of the oil well.

Full Cost   If the firm uses the full-cost method, it would capitalize all of the exploration cost of the period since the estimated value of the successful well is greater than the total of the exploration costs:

> Oil reserves 40,000,000
>   Cash (or accrued liabilities)   40,000,000

Using the full-cost method, the asset is recorded at $40 million, or $38 million more than under the successful efforts method. Expenses for the period (ignoring the depletion expense for the period) are $38 million less than under the successful efforts method. The depletion rate for the full-cost method will be substantially greater than under the successful-effort method.

Suppose, to continue this example for a second year, Wildcat has no further exploration costs and calculates depletion cost based on an estimate of 10 million barrels of recoverable oil. Assume, further, that one million barrels are pumped and sold. The year's entry to recognize expenses under the two methods are:

Successful efforts:

> Depletion expense 200,000*
>   Oil reserves   200,000
> * ($2.0 million ÷ 10 million barrels) × 1.0 million barrels

Full cost:

> Depletion expense 4,000,000**
>   Oil reserves   4,000,000
> ** ($40.0 million ÷ 10 million barrels) × 1.0 million barrels

If there had been exploration costs (but no additional pumping activity) at the same amount and with same results as in the first year, the depletion and exploration expense total for the successful-efforts method would be $38 million plus $.2 million, or $38.2 million. There would be no change under the full-cost method assuming only 1 million barrels are produced and sold.

Substantively different financial statements can result from using these two different accounting methods on the same facts. The difference is most noticeable in the balance sheet, where the full-cost method produces a much larger asset base than the successful efforts method. If and when exploration activity becomes relatively constant from one year to the next, the differences on the income statement may not be as large because the larger periodic depletion expense recorded under the full-cost method will eventually be approximately equal to the exploration expense being recorded under the successful-efforts method.

Accountants advocating full costing as the desired accounting treatment argue the cost of finding the one successful well includes not only the direct costs of that well but also all the costs of exploring, including for all the unsuccessful wells. The concept is that the firm engaged in a large number of exploration projects with the expectation that some will be sufficiently successful (i.e., result in oil and gas reserves of sufficient value) that the costs of the entire portfolio of exploration efforts would be recovered, in addition to earning an acceptable return on the entire investment. Thus, they maintain, matching requires capitalizing all the exploration costs and matching them against future revenues from the successful wells. To do otherwise, they believe, results in understating income in the period of the exploration while overstating income in future periods.

Accountants advocating successful-efforts accounting, on the other hand, argue that only those exploration efforts that result in future benefits are properly capitalized. Since exploration costs associated with an unsuccessful well do not provide future benefits, these costs should be expensed as they are incurred. They hold that to capitalize these costs gives the misleading impression that future cash flows are expected from the unsuccessful wells. This, they also believe, results in an overstatement of current period income under the full-cost method.

The resolution of this controversy is one of the more interesting to examine and demonstrates the difficulty in establishing accounting standards. The FASB studied the accounting for exploration costs carefully in the early and mid 1970s. In 1977 the Board issued *SFAS No. 19,* which required that all companies use the successful efforts method.[18]

Many small exploration companies strenuously opposed this ruling. These firms lobbied extensively with the FASB, the SEC, and with various divisions of the federal government.[19] The SEC, which normally quickly accepts a *Standard* promulgated by the FASB, procrastinated on the acceptance of *SFAS No. 19.* In doing so, the SEC may have been influenced by the claims made by the small exploration companies that exploration efforts would be curtailed by their inability to raise capital if successful-efforts accounting were required.

During this period, Congress considered a bill that specifically permitted firms the option to use either method. Further, the SEC in 1978 issued *Accounting Series Release No. 253,* which essentially allowed firms to use either the full-cost or the successful-efforts methods of accounting for exploration costs.[20] In February 1979, the FASB issued *SFAS No. 25,* which canceled the requirement for successful efforts reporting by suspending the effective date of the *Standard.* Currently both the successful-efforts and full-cost methods are acceptable.

In November 1982, as a result of a request from the SEC, the FASB issued *SFAS No. 69,* in which disclosure requirements for all publicly traded firms with significant oil and gas activities are specified. It requires the following:
* Proved estimates of oil and gas reserve quantities.
* Capitalized costs relating to oil- and gas-producing activities.
* Capitalized costs incurred in oil and gas property acquisition, exploration, and development activities.
* Reporting of results of operations for oil- and gas-producing activities.
* Providing a standardized measure of the discounted future net cash flows relating to proved oil and gas reserve quantities.

The above discussion presents a significant accounting issue that was not settled by the FASB alone because of the strongly held and differing positions of several parties. Further, those concerned about the standard had the ability to influence the standard-setting process. The situation illustrates emphatically the difficulty in establishing accounting standards when powerful interest groups, politicians, and regulatory agencies do not agree. When disagreement exists, the conceptual framework may not lead all the parties involved to the same conclusion. Nevertheless, the conceptual framework should still facilitate the inevitable political process of developing acceptable accounting approaches in the face of difficult issues such as this one.

---

[18] In addition, disclosures were required of the net quantities of a company's interests in proved reserves and proved developed reserves of crude oil (in barrels) and natural gas (in cubic feet). Discovery and current value measures of these reserves were rejected because the uncertainties in estimation cause the results to be subjective and relatively unreliable. Disclosure of any changes in these net reserves for any of several reasons were mandated. The reporting of all capitalized costs, including depreciation, depletion, and amortization, was also required, including separate reporting for any of these costs relating to reserves in foreign countries.

[19] The lobbying took place during a severe oil crisis. During this time, Congress was very sensitive to any action that might decrease U.S. firms' exploration activity.

[20] *ASR No. 253* proposed a third method of accounting for all petroleum companies, called *reserve recognition accounting* (RRA). This method would have required each company to estimate the quantity of its underground reserves, place an estimated value on the estimated reserves, and estimate how much the company would produce each year in the future. The SEC received considerable criticism of RRA because it contained so many estimates, and in 1981 the SEC backed away from its experiment with RRA. Instead, the SEC directed the FASB not to take up the successful efforts versus full-cost accounting issue (both would continue to be acceptable methods of reporting), but did direct the FASB to develop disclosure guidelines for oil and gas companies.

KEY TERMS

Copyrights (645)

Deferred charges (647)

Depletion (664)

Depletion base (664)

Development (660)

Development stage company (647)

Excess earnings approach (654)

Franchises (646)

Full-cost method (671)

Goodwill (651)

Intangible asset (640)

Lease (646)

Negative goodwill (657)

Organization costs (648)

Patents (644)

Research (659)

Statutory or percentage depletion (667)

Stock issuance costs (648)

Successful-efforts method (671)

Trademarks and trade names (646)

Unit depletion rate (665)

Wasting assets (664)

QUESTIONS

1. What distinguishes intangible assets from tangible assets? How are intangible assets reported on the balance sheet?
2. What outlays are properly considered part of the cost of an intangible asset?
3. Cite the factors that should determine whether or not an intangible asset is amortized and, if so, over what period of time.
4. What is an identifiable intangible asset? Give some examples of such assets.
5. What is a franchise? A trademark?
6. Explain goodwill and the basis on which goodwill is amortized.
7. What is the role of the accountant in valuation of goodwill?
8. What is negative goodwill? How does it arise? How is it treated for accounting purposes?
9. What is the maximum number of years over which a patent should be amortized? What determines this maximum? Under what circumstances, if any, should a shorter amortization period be used?
10. Define a deferred charge. Is it an intangible? Explain. How are deferred charges distinguished from prepaid expenses? Give two examples of each.
11. What items are properly debited to organization costs? Should organization costs be amortized? Explain.
12. What are the basic guidelines for accounting for research and development (R&D) costs?
13. Distinguish between trademarks and copyrights.
14. Give examples of situations in which the accounting carrying value of an intangible asset can increase. Does the accounting value of an intangible necessarily bear a close relationship to its economic value?
15. What are the primary characteristics of goodwill?
16. Under what circumstances is goodwill capitalized?
17. What is the general formula for computing goodwill?
18. Explain impairment of value of an intangible asset. Assume a patent that originally cost $50,000 (accumulated patent amortization, $35,000) that probably will not be used further by the company. Its estimated current value is $1,000. Give any indicated entry; if none, explain why.
19. Carter Company owns a trademark that it purchased originally for $40,000; it has been amortized to date in the amount of $26,000. The trademark has just been sold for $10,000 cash. Give any indicated entry; if none is needed, explain why.
20. What are the differences between natural resources and depreciable assets?
21. Describe the types of costs incurred by firms in connection with natural resources. Generally, how is each treated for accounting purposes when incurred?
22. How do firms determine the amount of depletion to be charged as an expense each accounting period?
23. What is statutory or percentage depletion?
24. There are similarities between expenditures for research and development and expenditures for exploration of oil and gas. Describe the similarities.
25. Describe the successful efforts method and the full-cost method of accounting for exploration costs. What method is required for financial reporting?

EXERCISES

**E 13-1
Overview: Characteristics
of Intangible Assets
(L.O. 1)**

For each of the following independent events, indicate by placing a check mark (✔) in the appropriate cells (a) whether the asset involved is identifiable or unindentifiable, (b) its manner of acquisition, and (c) whether it should be capitalized.

Independent Event	Identifiability		Manner of Acquisition		Whether Capitalized	
	Identifiable	Unidentifiable	External	Internal	Yes	No
a. Purchased a patent.						
b. Purchased a trademark.						
c. After 10 years of operation, a company's goodwill had increased considerably.						
d. Trademark developed by the company.						
e. Patent developed by the company's research program.						
f. Copyright developed by the company over a five-year period.						
g. Prepaid insurance (five-year premium).						
h. Leasehold improvements (operating lease).						
i. Purchased a company (including $1 million goodwill).						
j. Purchased a copyright.						
k. Franchise received by a public utility company.						

**E 13-2
Sale and Purchase of a
Patent: No Cash
(L.O. 2)**

On January 1, 1991, Vox Company sold a patent to Baker Company; the patent had a net carrying value on Vox's books of $20,000. As payment, Baker gave Vox an $80,000 note, which was payable in five equal annual installments of $16,000, with the first payment payable on December 31, 1991. There was no established exchange price for the patent, and the note had no ready market value. The prevailing rate of interest for a note of this type at January 1, 1991, was 12%. Disregard income taxes.

Required:

1. Give the entry on January 1, 1991, that Vox Company should make. Also, give any related entries that Vox should make on December 31, 1991.
2. Give the entry that Baker Company should make on January 1, 1991.
3. Give the entries for payment of the first annual installment on the note and for patent amortization that Baker Company should make December 31, 1991 (end of the annual reporting period). At January 1, 1991, 5 years of the patent's legal life of 17 years had already expired.

E 13-3
Reporting Intangible
Assets
(L.O. 2)

The adjusted trial balance of Jackson Corporation showed the following selected account balances (all debits) at December 31, 1992, end of the annual reporting period:

Cash	$ 44,000
Patent (unamortized balance)	14,000
Accounts receivable (net of allowance)	90,000
Prepaid rent expense	1,000
Marketable equity securities, short-term	50,000
Leasehold (rental prepayment)	7,000
Franchise (unamortized balance)	18,000
Rent revenue receivable (current)	3,000
Organization costs (unamortized)	9,000
Goodwill (unamortized)	70,000
Trademark (unamortized)	19,000
Prepaid insurance (two thirds is long-term)	6,000
Copyright (unamortized)	12,000
Equipment (net of accumulated depreciation)	300,000
Notes receivable, trade (short-term)	10,000
Cash in closed bank (percent expected to recover, 40%)	30,000
R&D costs (not capitalizable)	39,000

Required:

Prepare the asset section of Jackson's balance sheet at December 31, 1992. Include the proper balance sheet classifications with separate captions for intangible operating assets, deferred charges, and other assets. Assume all needed amortization entries have been made.

E 13-4

Accounting for Intangible
Assets
(L.O. 2, 3, 4, 5)

Select the best answer to each of the following. Briefly justify your choice.

1. Which of the following cost items would be matched with current revenues on a basis other than association of cause and effect?
   (*a*) Goodwill.   (*c*) Cost of goods sold.
   (*b*) Sales commissions.   (*d*) Purchases on account.
2. How should R&D costs be accounted for according to *SFAS No. 2?*
   (*a*) They must be capitalized when incurred and then amortized over their estimated useful lives.
   (*b*) They must be expensed in the period incurred in all but a few instances.
   (*c*) They may be either capitalized or expensed when incurred, depending upon the judgment of management.
   (*d*) They must be expensed in the period incurred unless it can be demonstrated that the expenditure will have some future benefits.
3. The accounting for a development stage company:
   (*a*) May be different from that of other companies in numerous ways with regard to expenditures during the development stage.
   (*b*) Must be exactly the same as other companies in respect to accounting, reporting, and disclosure.
   (*c*) Allows certain development stage companies to capitalize costs that other companies are not permitted to capitalize.
   (*d*) Requires presentation of financial statements on the same basis as other companies and disclosure of certain cumulative amounts, along with the fact that the company is a development stage company.
4. Hilary Company's R&D records contained the following information for 1993:

Materials used in R&D projects	$ 400,000
Equipment acquired that will have significant alternate future uses including future R&D projects	2,000,000
Depreciation expense for 1993 on above equipment	500,000
Personnel costs involved in R&D projects	1,000,000
Consulting fees paid to outsiders for R&D projects	100,000
Indirect costs reasonably allocable to R&D projects	200,000

The amount of R&D costs debited to expense and reported on Hilary's 1993 income statement should be:

(a) $1,500,000.   (c) $2,200,000.
(b) $1,700,000.   (d) $3,500,000.

5. Peter Company has invested $40,000 in a royalty-producing copyright. Peter's expected rate of return from the three-year project is 20%. The cash flow, net of income taxes, was $15,000 for the first year and $18,000 for the second year. Assuming the rate of return is exactly 20%, what would be the cash flow, net of income taxes, for the third year?

(a) $8,681.   (c) $11,497.
(b) $11,000.   (d) $25,920.

(AICPA adapted)

E 13-5
Accounting for Intangible Assets
(L.O. 1, 2, 3, 4)

Select the best answer to each of the following. Briefly justify your choice.

1. A copyright granted to a composer in 1988 has a legal life of:
   (a) 17 years.
   (b) 28 years.
   (c) The life of the composer plus 50 years.
   (d) 40 years.
2. Which of the following is not properly classified as an intangible asset:
   (a) A copyright acquired by purchase.
   (b) Goodwill.
   (c) A patent acquired by purchase.
   (d) Losses incurred by a development stage company.
3. Pan Corporation acquired Company Able in 1969 and Company Baker in 1989. In both instances the acquired companies were dissolved, and their assets and operations merged with other assets and activities of Pan. In both instances Pan paid more than the current market value of the identifiable net assets for its acquisitions, and most of the difference was attributable to goodwill. In accounting for the goodwill:
   (a) Pan must amortize the goodwill related to each company.
   (b) Pan need not amortize the goodwill of either company.
   (c) Pan need not amortize the goodwill associated with Able but must amortize the goodwill associated with Baker.
   (d) Pan need not amortize the goodwill associated with Baker but must amortize the goodwill associated with Able.
4. Patents and copyrights have definite legal lives and should be amortized over:
   (a) Their legal lives, but not more than 40 years.
   (b) Their useful lives, but not more than 40 years.
   (c) Their legal or useful life, whichever is shorter, but never in excess of 40 years.
   (d) A period of 40 years.
5. X company incurred $50,000 of costs in R&D activities. These costs need not be expensed if:
   (a) They give promise of a successful outcome.
   (b) The projects are completed and have culminated in a profitable patent for X.
   (c) X is doing contract research for another company, and the costs relate to the contract that is still in progress.
   (d) The projects were begun before the issuance of SFAS No. 2.
6. Organizational costs:
   (a) Are not covered by APB Opinion No. 17 and need not be amortized.
   (b) Must be amortized over a period not to exceed 40 years.
   (c) Should be reported as a contra item under owners' equity.
   (d) Should be expensed as soon as they are incurred.
7. Some intangibles are characterized as specifically identifiable, while another classification is unidentifiable. An example of the latter is:
   (a) A trademark.   (c) A franchise for a limited term.
   (b) A perpetual franchise.   (d) Goodwill.

8. The legal life of a patent currently is:
   (*a*) 28 years.   (*c*) The life of the holder of the patent.
   (*b*) 17 years.   (*d*) 40 years.

E 13-6
Amortization of
Intangibles
(L.O. 2, 3, 5)

Select the best answer to each of the following. Briefly justify your choices.

1. If a company constructs a laboratory building to be used as an R&D facility, the cost of the building is matched against earnings as:
   (*a*) R&D expense during the period(s) of construction.
   (*b*) Depreciation deducted as part of R&D costs.
   (*c*) Depreciation or immediate write-off, depending on company policy.
   (*d*) An expense at such time as productive research and development has been obtained from the facility.

2. Why are certain costs of doing business capitalized when incurred and then depreciated or amortized over subsequent accounting cycles?
   (*a*) To reduce the federal income tax liability.
   (*b*) To aid management in the decision-making process.
   (*c*) To match operating costs with revenues as earned.
   (*d*) To adhere to the accounting concept of conservatism.

3. In January 1992, Idea Company purchased a patent for a new consumer product for $170,000. At the time of purchase the patent was valid for 17 years. Due to the competitive nature of the market, the patent was estimated to have a useful life of 10 years. During 1996, the product was removed from the market in response to a government order because of a potential health hazard present in the product. What amount should Idea debit to expense during 1996, assuming amortization is recorded at the end of each reporting year?
   (*a*) $10,000.   (*c*) $102,000.
   (*b*) $17,000.   (*d*) $130,000.

4. In conformity with GAAP, which of the following methods of amortization is almost always used for intangible assets?
   (a) Sum-of-the-years'-digits (SYD).   (*c*) Units of production.
   (*b*) Straight line.   (*d*) Declining balance (DB).

5. On January 1 of the current year, Melvin Corporation sold a patent. Melvin Corporation originally paid $50,000 for the patent, which now has a book value of $9,000. The terms of sale included cash payments as follows:

   $5,000 down payment.

   $5,000 per year, payable on December 31 of each of the next two years.

   The sale agreement did not specify any interest; however, 10% would be a reasonable rate for this type of transaction. Melvin Corporation should report a gain on disposal of:
   (*a*) $4,678.   (*c*) $6,000.
   (*b*) $5,000.   (*d*) $5,678.

(AICPA adapted)

E 13-7
Goodwill: Negotiating
Price and Valuation
(L.O. 4)

Dow Corporation is negotiating with Fox Company to purchase all of Fox's assets and assume its liabilities. You have been asked to help develop a tentative offering price in the negotiations and to evaluate "goodwill on the basis of the latest concepts." Accordingly, you decide to use the present value approach. The following data have been assembled on Fox Company.

	Estimated Current Market Value	Fox Book Value
Total identifiable assets (exclusive of goodwill)	$2,500,000	$2,400,000
Liabilities	1,000,000	1,000,000
Average annual net cash earnings expected (next five years)	520,000	

Dow expects a 16% earnings rate on this investment.

Required:

1. Compute (*a*) the tentative offering price and (*b*) the amount of goodwill included in that price.
2. Assume the deal is consummated on January 1, 1991, at a $1.6 million actual cash price.
   a. Give the acquisition entry for Dow Corporation.
   b. Give the December 31, 1991, adjusting entry for goodwill. Assume a 20-year estimated useful life.

E 13–8
Goodwill: Negotiating Price and Valuation
(L.O. 4)

Big Company is considering the purchase of Small Company for cash. The following data concerning Small Company has been collected:

	Small Company Book Values	Estimated Current Market Values
Total identifiable assets	$380,000	$400,000
Total liabilities	280,000	280,000
Owners' equity	$100,000	—

Cumulative total net cash earnings for the past five years, $255,000, which includes extraordinary cash gains of $45,000 and nonrecurring cash losses of $30,000.

Big Company expects a 20% earnings rate on the investment.

Required:

1. Compute (*a*) an offering price based on the information given above that Big should be willing to pay and (*b*) the amount of goodwill included in that price.
2. Compute the amount of goodwill, assuming the negotiations resulted in an actual purchase price of $140,000 cash.
3. Give the acquisition entry for Big Company, assuming the actual purchase price given in (2).

E 13–9
Compute Goodwill: Entries
(L.O. 4)

On January 1, 1992, the balance sheet of Nance Company (a sole proprietorship) was as follows:

Assets:		
Accounts receivable (net of allowance)		$ 60,000
Inventory		90,000
Plant and equipment (net of depreciation)		200,000
Land		30,000
Total		$380,000

Liabilities:		
Current	$38,000	
Noncurrent	80,000	$118,000
Owners' equity		262,000
Total		$380,000

On January 1, 1992, Major Corporation purchased all of the assets, and assumed all of the liabilities, listed on the above balance sheet for $290,000 cash. The assets, on date of purchase, were valued by Major as follows: accounts receivable (net), $50,000; inventory, $85,000; plant and equipment (net), $200,000; and land, $45,000. The liabilities were valued at their carrying amounts.

Required:

1. Compute the amount of goodwill included in the purchase price paid by Major Corporation.
2. Give the entry that Major Corporation should make to record the purchase of Nance Company.
3. What is the minimum amount of goodwill that Major Corporation can amortize at the end of 1992. Give the amortization entry.

E 13-10
Compute Goodwill:
Entries
(L.O. 4)

After considerable analysis, the following projections relating to Bite Company were derived as a basis for estimating the potential value of goodwill in anticipation of negotiations for the purchase of Bite Company by High Company:

Average annual net cash earnings projected	$ 84,000
Market value of total identifiable assets of Bite	340,000
Total liabilities	100,000

Rate of return expected on investments by prospective purchaser, 18%. Expected recovery period for the investment, five years, starting in Year 1.

Required:

1. Compute (*a*) the tentative offering price by High Company and (*b*) the amount of goodwill included in that price.
2. Give the Year 1 entries for High Company, assuming negotiations resulted in an actual cash purchase price of $235,000. Any goodwill will be amortized over 20 years.

E 13-11

Recording a Franchise
Contract
(L.O. 3)

On January 1, 1991, Shopping Center Cleaners (SCC) signed a contract with Super-Cleaners, Incorporated. The agreement provided for the payment of a franchise fee by SCC, and subsequent periodic franchise royalties based on sales. In return for these royalties, Super-Cleaners will provide specified services in the future (e.g., promotional suggestions). The franchise fee was $50,000, payable as $10,000 in cash and the remaining balance payable in three equal annual installments including interest and principal, starting on December 31, 1991. The market rate of interest for such loans is 10%.

Required:

Give the entries that SCC should make on January 1, 1991, and December 31, 1991.

E 13-12

Depletion of Gravel Pit:
Expense and Reporting
the Asset
(L.O. 7)

Miller Company's investment in a gravel quarry was $6,000,000, of which $400,000 represented land value after removal of the gravel. Geologists who were engaged to estimate the removable gravel reported originally that 5 million cubic yards (units) could be extracted. In the first year, 880,000 units were extracted, and 820,000 units were sold. In the second year, 830,000 units were extracted, and sales were 850,000 units.

At the start of the third year, management of Miller had the quarry examined again, at which time it was determined that the remaining removable gravel was 2 million units. Production and sales for the third year amounted to 400,000 units. In the fourth year, production was 750,000 units, while sales amounted to 600,000 units.

Required:

1. Calculate the depletion expense that should be reported on Miller's income statement for each of the four years. Assume a FIFO basis and show supporting computations.
2. Show how the gravel inventory and the gravel deposit should be reported on Miller's balance sheet at the end of the fourth year. Assume an accumulated depletion account is used.

E 13-13

Depletion: Expense,
Reporting, Entries
(L.O. 7)

Arizona Mining Company acquired property with processed ore estimated at 2 million pounds for $1,800,000. The property has an estimated value of $100,000 after the ore has been extracted. Before any ore could be removed, it was necessary to incur $500,000 of developmental costs. In the first year, 200,000 pounds were removed and 160,000 pounds of ore were sold; in the second year, 400,000 pounds were removed and 410,000 pounds were sold. In the course of the second year's production, discoveries were made that indicated that if an added $1,460,000 is spent on developmental costs during the third year, future removable ore will total 2.5 million pounds. After incurring these added costs, production for the third year amounted to 460,000 pounds with sales of 450,000 pounds.

Required:

1. Calculate the depletion expense that Arizona should report on its income statement for each of the three years. Show supporting computations and round unit costs to the nearest three decimal places (assume FIFO).
2. Show how the resource and the inventory should be reported by Arizona on its balance sheet at the end of the third year (FIFO basis). Assume an accumulated depletion account is used.
3. Give the journal entry to record depletion expense at the end of each of the three years.

E 13–14
Analyze the Accounting for Depreciation and Depletion
(L.O. 7)

The accounting treatments of depreciation and depletion have both similarities and differences.

Required:

1. List (*a*) the similarities and (*b*) the differences in accounting treatments of depreciation and cost depletion.
2. Describe cost depletion and statutory depletion. Under what conditions, if any, is statutory depletion permitted?

(AICPA adapted)

E 13–15
Amortization of Computer Software Costs
(L.O. 6)

During 1992, the Elephant Software Company capitalizes computer software costs in the amount of $2,000,000 in accordance with the requirements of *SFAS No. 86.* During 1993, the first year the product is released to sell, sales total $1,000,000. Estimated future sales for the remaining three-year life (through 1996) of the product are $7,000,000.

Required:

1. Describe the method that Elephant must use to determine the amount to amortize of the capitalized computer software costs.
2. Compute the amount of amortization of capitalized computer software costs for 1993.

E 13–16
Capitalization and Amortization of Computer Software Costs
(L.O. 6)

During 1993, PC Software, Inc., developed a new personal computer data base management software package. Total expenditure on the project was $3,000,000, of which 40% was after the technological feasibility of the product was established. The product was completed and offered for sale to third parties as of January 1, 1994. During 1994, revenues from sales of the product totaled $2,400,000. The package is expected to be successfully marketable for five years, and the total revenues over the life of the product will be $10,000,000.

Required:

1. Prepare the journal entries to account for the development of this product in 1993.
2. Prepare the journal entries to record the amortization of capitalized computer software development costs as of December 31, 1994.
3. What disclosures are required in the December 31, 1994, financial statements regarding computer software costs.
4. Suppose this product were developed for internal use. How would your answers to (1), (2), and (3) change?

PROBLEMS

P 13–1
Organization, Franchise and Trademark Costs and Goodwill
(L.O. 2, 3, 4)

Transactions during 1991, the first year of the newly organized Astor Corporation, included the following:

Jan. 2 Paid $6,000 attorney's fees and other related costs for assistance in securing the corporate charter, drafting bylaws, and advising on operating in other states (which the company intends). Amortize over five years.

31 Paid $2,000 for television commercials advertising the grand opening. In addition, during the grand opening the company gave away samples of its products, which were taken from inventory; cost $8,000 (perpetual inventory system).

Feb. 1 Paid an invoice received from the financial institution that underwrote and sold the company's $400,000 par value stock at a 10% premium. Under the contract, the underwriter charged 1% of the gross proceeds from the stock sale. The stock issuance has already been recorded.

Mar. 1 Paid $30,000 to a franchisor for the right to open a Tastee Food lunch counter on the company's premises. The initial franchise runs 10 years from March 1 and can be renewed upon payment of a second amount to be computed later on the basis of sales under the initial franchise.

May 1 Acquired for $10,200 a newly issued patent, which will be held as a long-term investment to produce royalty revenue.

July   1   Paid consultants $6,400 for services in securing a trademark enabling the company to market under the now-protected name Astor's Recipe.

Oct.   1   Obtained a license from the city to conduct operations in a newly opened department. The license, which cost $600, runs for one year and is renewable.

Nov.   1   Acquired another business and paid (among other amounts) $12,000 for its goodwill. Expected useful life, five years.

Dec. 31   Apportioned the costs of those assets subject to amortization over their indicated lives. Where no life is indicated, amortized over the longest term possible. Amortization is calculated to the nearest monthly basis; in other words, acquisition of an intangible in July would call for amortization for half of the year.

Required:

1. Give the journal entry that Astor should make for each of the above transactions. December 31 is the end of the annual accounting period; six adjusting entries are required on this date. Ignore closing entries.
2. Classify each of the intangible assets (and their amounts) for balance sheet reporting at the end of 1991. Set deferred charges and any other appropriate items out separately from the other intangibles.

P 13–2
Accounting for Intangibles
(L.O. 1, 2, 3, 4, 5)

Select the best answer for each of the following and indicate the basis for your choice.

1. An intangible asset (excluding R&D costs) should be:
   (*a*) Expensed as incurred.
   (*b*) Capitalized and not amortized until it clearly has no value.
   (*c*) Capitalized and amortized over the estimated period benefited.
   (*d*) Capitalized and amortized over the estimated period benefited but not exceeding 40 years.
2. Most R&D costs incurred after *SFAS No. 2* was issued should be:
   (*a*) Capitalized on a selective basis and not amortized.
   (*b*) Capitalized, then amortized over 40 years.
   (*c*) Expensed in the year in which they are incurred.
   (*d*) Debited directly to retained earnings.
3. Goodwill is amortized over:
   (*a*) Its useful life if it was acquired externally.
   (*b*) A 40-year period if it was acquired externally.
   (*c*) Its useful life, but not to exceed 40 years, if it was acquired externally.
   (*d*) Its useful life, but not to exceed 40 years, if it was developed internally.
4. On January 15, 1991, a corporation was granted a patent. On January 2, 2000, to protect its patent, the corporation purchased another patent that originally was issued on January 10, 1996. Because of its unique plant, the corporation does not believe the competing patent can be used in producing a product. The cost of the competing patent should be:
   (*a*) Amortized over a maximum period of 17 years.
   (*b*) Amortized over a maximum period of 13 years.
   (*c*) Amortized over a maximum period of 8 years.
   (*d*) Expensed in 2000.
5. Goodwill should be written off:
   (*a*) As soon as possible against retained earnings.
   (*b*) As soon as possible as an extraordinary item.
   (*c*) By systematic debits against retained earnings over the period benefited, but not more than 40 years.
   (*d*) By systematic debits to expense over the period benefited, but not more than 40 years.
6. A large, publicly held company registered a trademark during 1991. How should the cost of registering the trademark be accounted for?
   (*a*) Debited to an asset account with no amortization to follow.
   (*b*) Expensed as incurred.
   (*c*) Amortized over 25 years if in accordance with management's evaluation.
   (*d*) Amortized over its useful life or 17 years, whichever is shorter.

7. Unidentifiable assets incude:
   (a) Patents, copyrights, franchises, etc.   (c) Deferred charges and goodwill.
   (b) Deferred charges only.   (d) Goodwill only.
8. Which of the following is not properly reported as a deferred charge?
   (a) Stock issue costs.   (c) Organization costs.
   (b) Discount on bonds payable.   (d) Deferred income taxes.
9. Prepaid expenses and deferred charges are alike in that they are both:
   (a) Reported as current assets on a classified balance sheet.
   (b) Destined to be debited to expense in some subsequent period in harmony with the matching principle.
   (c) Reported as other assets.
   (d) Applicable to the fiscal period immediately following the balance sheet on which they appear.
10. Inger Company bought a patent in January 1991 for $6,800. For the first four years, it was amortized on the assumption that the total useful life would be eight years. At the start of the fifth year, management determined that six years would be the probable total life. Amortization at the end of the fifth year should be:
   (a) $1,133.   (c) $850.
   (b) $1,700.   (d) None of the foregoing.
11. Chance Company has a lease on a site that does not expire for 25 years. With the landowner's permission, Chance erected on the site a building that will last 50 years. Chance should recognize expense in connection with the building's cost:
   (a) One fortieth each year.   (c) In totality as soon as it is completed.
   (b) One twenty-fifth each year.   (d) One fiftieth each year.

(AICPA adapted)

P 13–3
Reporting: Patent, Franchise, R&D
(L.O. 3, 5)

Able Company provided information on its intangible assets as follows:

a. A patent was purchased from XT Company for $1,500,000 on January 1, 1991. Able estimated the remaining useful life of the patent to be 10 years.
b. On January 1, 1992, a franchise was purchased from the YW Company for $500,000. In addition, 5% of revenue from the franchise must be paid to YW. Revenue from the franchise for 1992 was $1,200,000. Able Company estimates the useful life of the franchise to be 10 years and records a full year's amortization (straight-line) in the year of purchase.
c. Able incurred R&D costs in 1992 as follows:

Materials and equipment	$120,000
Personnel	140,000
Indirect costs	60,000
	$320,000

Able estimates that these costs will be recouped by December 31, 1995.

d. On January 1, 1992, Able, based on new events that have occurred in the field, estimates that the remaining life of the patent purchased on January 1, 1991, is only five years from January 1, 1992.

Required:

1. Prepare a schedule showing the intangible assets that should be reported on Able Company's balance sheet at December 31, 1992.
2. Prepare an income statement for the year ended December 31, 1992, as a result of the above facts. Assume a 35% average income tax rate.

(AICPA adapted)

P 13–4
Accounting for Intangibles:
(L.O. 3, 4)

Brannen Corporation was incorporated on January 3, 1991. The corporation's financial statements for its first year's operations were not examined by a CPA. You have been engaged to examine the financial statements for the year ended December 31, 1992, and your examination is substantially completed. The corporation's adjusted trial balance appears as follows:

BRANNEN CORPORATION

Adjusted Trial Balance

December 31, 1992

	Debit	Credit
Cash . . . . $	11,000	
Accounts receivable	68,500	
Allowance for doubtful accounts		$ 500
Inventories	38,500	
Machinery	75,000	
Equipment	29,000	
Accumulated depreciation		10,000
Patents	102,000	
Prepaid expenses	10,500	
Organization costs	29,000	
Goodwill	24,000	
Licensing agreement No. 1	50,000	
Licensing agreement No. 2	49,000	
Accounts payable		147,500
Unearned revenue		12,500
Capital stock		317,000
Retained earnings, 1/1/1992	27,000	
Sales revenue		668,500
Cost of goods sold	454,000	
Selling and general expenses	173,000	
Interest expense	3,500	
Extraordinary loss	12,000	
Totals	$1,156,000	$1,156,000

The following information relates to accounts that may still require adjustment:

a. Patents for Brannen's manufacturing process were acquired January 2, 1992 for $68,000. An additional $34,000 was spent in December 1992 to improve machinery covered by the patents and was debited to the patents account. Depreciation on operational assets has been properly recorded for 1992 in accordance with Brannen's practice, which provides a full year's depreciation for property on hand June 30 and no depreciation otherwise. Brannen uses the straight-line method for all depreciation and amortization.

b. The balance in the organization costs account properly includes costs incurred during the organization period. Brannen has exercised its option to amortize organization costs over a five-year period beginning January 1, 1991, for federal income tax purposes and will amortize these costs for accounting purposes in the same manner. No amortization has yet been recorded.

c. On January 3, 1991, Brannen purchased licensing agreement No. 1 which was believed to have an unlimited useful life. The balance in the licensing agreement No. 1 account includes its purchase price of $48,000 and costs of $2,000 related to the acquisition. On January 1, 1992, Brannen bought licensing agreement No. 2, which has a life expectancy of 10 years. The balance in the licensing agreement No. 2 account includes the $48,000 purchase price and $2,000 in acquisition costs, but it has been reduced by a credit of $1,000 for the advance collection of 1993 revenue from the agreement. No amortization on the No. 2 agreement has been recorded.

In early 1992, an explosion caused a permanent 60% reduction in the expected revenue-producing value of licensing agreement No. 1. No entries have been made during 1991 for amortization nor for the explosion in 1992.

d. The balance in the goodwill account includes (1) $8,000 paid December 30, 1991, for an advertising program that management believes will assist in increasing Brannen's sales over a period of three to five years following the disbursement and (2) legal expenses of $16,000 incurred for Brannen's incorporation on January 3, 1991. No amortization has ever been recorded on the goodwill.

Required:

Prepare journal entries as of December 31, 1992, as required by the information given above, in conformity with the provisions of *APB Opinion No. 17*. If the estimated life is not given, use the maximum.

(AICPA adapted)

P 13–5
Goodwill, Negotiation:
Entries
(L.O. 4)

During 1991, Baker Corporation has been negotiating to purchase all of Charlie Company's noncash assets and to assume all of its liabilities for a single cash price. The target closing date is January 1, 1992. Baker requested, and was provided, considerable data, including the following mid-year balance sheet (summarized for problem purposes):

CHARLIE COMPANY
Balance Sheet
At June 30, 1991

Assets:

Cash	$ 19,000
Accounts receivable *	60,000
Inventory (LIFO)	140,000
Property, plant, and equipment	300,000
Land	11,000
Franchise (unamortized balance)	20,000
Total	$550,000

Liabilities:

Current liabilities	$ 40,000
Bonds payable	200,000
Stockholders' equity	310,000
Total	$550,000

* Net of the allowance for doubtful accounts and accumulated depreciation, respectively.

Based on appraisals, price lists, and specific price level indexes, Baker Corporation developed the following estimates of fair market values: cash, not to be purchased; accounts receivable, $60,000 (the allowance account is adequate); inventory (converted to FIFO), $70,000; propety, plant, and equipment, $280,000; land, $40,000; and franchise, $22,000. The liabilities are appropriately valued at book value.

Based on an analysis of the income statements and other data (and excluding all nonrecurring and extraordinary gains and losses), Baker Corporation's executives projected an average year-end annual net cash inflow from operations (i.e., from the income statement) of $72,000 for each of the next seven years.

Required:

1. Compute the following: (*a*) a tentative offering price and (*b*) the amount of goodwill therein, for negotiating purposes. Assume Baker expects a 20% rate of return on this investment. Round to the nearest $1,000.

Negotiations continued throughout the remainder of 1991. During December 1991, a final purchase price of $265,000 was agreed on "to be adjusted upward (for a decrease) or downward (for an increase) for any change from the June 30, 1991, cash account balance (i.e., from $19,000)."

The December 31, 1991 balance sheet prepared by Charlie Company is shown below in column *a* and the revised market values added later by Baker Corporation are shown in column *b*.

CHARLIE COMPANY
Balance Sheet
At December 31, 1991

	(*a*) Book Values of Charlie Co.	(*b*) Market Values Developed by Baker Corp.
Assets:		
Cash	$ 20,000	$ —
Accounts receivable (net)	58,000	58,000
Inventory (LIFO)	160,000	90,000
Property, plant, and equipment (net)	309,000	285,000
Land	11,000	40,000
Franchise (unamortized balance)	19,000	21,000
Total	$577,000	

Liabilities:		
Current liabilities	$ 37,000	37,000
Bonds payable	200,000	200,000
Stockholders' equity	340,000	—
Total	$577,000	

Required:

2. Compute the amount of goodwill purchased by Baker Corporation.
3. Give the entry for Baker Corporation to record the purchase of Charlie Company.
4. Give the entry at the end of 1992 to record the minimum amount of goodwill that can be amortized.

P 13–6

COMPREHENSIVE PROBLEM
♦

Accounting for Intangibles
(L.O. 2, 3, 4, 5)

Your new client, Laser Company, is being audited for the first time on December 31, 1993, the end of the accounting period. In the course of your examination, you encounter in the ledger an asset account titled "intangibles" (balance, $85,224), which is presented below:

Intangibles

6/30/1991 Goodwill	9,000	12/31/1992 Amortization, 5%	2,890 *
12/31/1991 R&D	10,700	12/31/1993 Amortization, 5%	4,486 *
4/1/1992 Goodwill	14,600		
6/30/1992 Patent	9,600		
12/31/1992 R&D	13,900		
6/1/1993 Goodwill	12,900		
7/1/1993 Bond discount	4,800		
12/31/1993 R&D	17,100		

* Offsetting debit was to Amortization expense each year.

By tracing entries to the journal and other supporting documents, you ascertain the following facts:

a. The June 30, 1991, entry was made when the first six months' operations were profitable, although a small loss had been anticipated. At the direction of the company president, and with the approval of the board of directors, an entry was made debiting intangibles and crediting retained earnings for $9,000.

b. All debit entries dated December 31 pertaining to R&D arise from the fact that the company has continuously engaged in an extensive R&D program to keep its products competitive and to develop new products. The debits represent half of the costs of the R&D program for each year and were transferred at year-end from the R&D expense account.

c. The April 1, 1992, entry was made after an extensive advertising campaign had seeemingly proved particularly successful. Sales rose 8% after the campaign and never dropped again to less than a 4% increase over their former level. The debit represents the expenditures for the campaign.

d. The $9,600 debit on June 30, 1992, represents the purchase price of a patent bought because the company feared that if it fell into other hands, it would damage the company's products competitively. See (*g*) for amortization information.

e. The debit for June 1, 1993, was made after Laser acquired another company, which will continue to operate as a 100%-owned subsidiary. The price represented an excess payment of $12,900 over the market values of identifiable net assets acquired (which were properly recorded) and was based on an expectation of continued high profitability. See (*g*) for amortization information.

f. The July 1, 1993, debit for $4,800 represents discount on a 10-year, $100,000 bond issue marketed by the company on that date. The amount is not material; therefore, straight-line amortization is appropriate.

g. The two credits to the intangibles account represent 5% of the ending balance in the intangibles account at the end of 1992 and 1993, respectively; the offsetting debit was to amortizaton expense. The patent and goodwill costs are to be amortized over 10 years, computed to the nearest month.

Required:

1. Give journal entries to clear out the old intangibles account. The accounts at the end of 1993 have been adjusted, but not closed. Key your entries with the letters that identify the items in the problem. Explain each entry and give the resulting account balances.

2. Give the 1993 adjusting entries based on your results in (1). Give the final account balances immediately prior to the 1993 closing entries.

P 13-7
Capitalizing and Amortizing Intangible Assets
(L.O. 3, 4)

Select the best answer to each of the following questions:

1. Bye Corporation was organized during 1991 and started opeations in 1992. Expenditures during 1991 and early 1992: professional fees, $25,000; meetings and promotional activities incidental to organization, $11,000; filing and related fees, $2,000; and initial capital stock issuance costs, $3,000. If organization costs are to be amortized over a 10-year period starting in 1992, the amount of organization costs amortized in 1992 would be:
   (a) $2,500.   (d) $4,100.
   (b) $3,600.   (e) None of the above; explain.
   (c) $3,800.

2. During 1991, Starnes Corporation developed a patent. Expenditures related to the patent: legal fees for patent registration, $7,000; tests to perfect the use of the patent for production processes, $6,000; research costs in the research laboratory, $21,000; and depreciation on equipment (that has alternative future uses) used in developing the patent, $4,000. Assuming amortization of the patent costs over the legal life of the patent, the annual patent amortization amount would be:
   (a) $2,000.   (d) $1,000.
   (b) $1,882.   (e) None of the above; explain.
   (c) $1,824.

3. On April 1, 1993, Penn Corporaton purchased all of the assets and assumed all of the liabilities of Suber Company for $140,000 cash. Suber's total identifiable asset values: Suber's book value, $200,000; estimated market value, $230,000. Suber's total liabilities were $105,000. The amount of goodwill purchased by Penn Corporation was:
   (a) $75,000.   (d) $15,000.
   (b) $45,000.   (e) None of the above; explain.
   (c) $30,000.

4. On January 1, 1991, Kiker Company purchased a new patent for $10,200 and started amortizing it over the legal life of 17 years. At the start of 1994, Kiker estimated that the total useful life of the patent (from acquisition date) was 12 years. Kiker should record amortization on the patent at the end of 1994 in the amount of:
   (a) $700.   (d) $850.
   (b) $933.   (e) None of the above; explain.
   (c) $600.

5. On January 1, 1991, Thin Company purchased a patent from the inventor, who was asking $110,000 for it. Thin paid for the patent as follows: cash, $40,000; issued 1,000 shares of its own common stock, par $10 (market value, $20 per share); and a note payable due at the end of three years, face amount, $50,000, noninterest-bearing. The current interest rate for this type of financing is 12%. Thin Company should record the cost of the patent at:
   (a) $85,589.   (d) $110,000.
   (b) $95,589.   (e) None of the above; explain.
   (c) $98,800.

P 13-8
Depreciation and Depletion: Schedule, Entries
(L.O. 7)

Colorado Mining Corporation bought mineral-bearing land for $150,000 that engineers say will yield 200,000 pounds of economically removable ore; the land will have a value of $30,000 after the ore is removed.

To work the property, Colorado built structures and sheds on the site that cost $40,000; these will last 10 years, and because their use is confined to mining and it would be expensive to dismantle and move them, they will have no residual value. Machinery that cost $29,000 was installed at the mine, and the added cost for installation was $7,000. This machinery should last 15 years; like the structures, usefulness of the machinery is confined to these mining operations. Dismantling and removal costs when the property has been fully worked will approximately equal the value of the machinery at that time; therefore, Colorado does not plan to use the structures or the machinery after the minerals have been removed.

In the first year, Colorado removed only 15,000 pounds of ore; however, production was doubled in the second year. It is expected that all of the removable ore will be extracted within eight years from the start of operations.

Required:

1. Prepare a schedule showing unit and total depletion and depreciation and book value of the operational assets for the first and second year of operation. Use the units of production method of depreciation.
2. Assuming that in the first year 80% of production was sold, and in the second year, the inventory carried over from the first year plus 80% of the second year's production was sold, give the entries to record accumulated depreciation and depletion. To show the effect of these costs, make the offsetting debits to cost of goods sold and inventory. Use accounts labeled "accumulated depreciation" and "accumulated depletion."

P 13–9
Depletion and
Depreciation Expense
(L.O. 7)

On July 1, 1991, Miller Mining, a calendar-year corporation, purchased the rights to a copper mine. Of the total purchase price, $2.8 million was allocable to the copper. Estimated reserves were 800,000 tons of copper. Miller expects to extract and sell 10,000 tons of copper each month. Production began immediately. The selling price is $25 per ton. Miller uses percentage depletion (15%) for tax purposes. To aid production, Miller also purchased some new equipment on July 1, 1991. The equipment cost $76,000 and had an estimated useful life of eight years. However, after all the copper is removed from this mine, the equipment will be of no use to Miller and will be sold for an estimated $4,000.

Required:

1. If sales and production conform to expectations, what is Miller's depletion expense on this mine for financial accounting purposes for the calendar year 1991?
2. If sales and production conform to expectations, what is Miller's depreciation expense on the new equipment for financial accounting purposes for the calendar year 1991? Assume straight-line depreciation.
3. Repeat question 2, except assume units of production depreciation.

P 13–10
Computer Software Costs
(L.O. 6)

Fox is a new computer software company. In 1993, the firm incurred the following costs in the process of designing, developing, and producing its first new software package, which it expects to begin marketing in 1994:

Designing and planning costs	$150,000
Production of product masters	400,000
Cost of developing code	240,000
Testing	60,000
Production of final product	500,000

The costs of designing and planning, code development, and testing were all incurred before the technological feasibility of the product had been established. Fox estimates total revenues over the four-year life of the product will be $2,000,000, with $800,000 in revenues expected in 1994.

Required:

1. Prepare the entries to account for the costs incurred in 1993.
2. Assuming 1994 revenues are as estimated, prepare the entry to record the amortization of computer software costs for 1994.
3. Assume the net realizable value of the product is estimated at December 31, 1994, to be $500,000. What entry, if any, is required? What disclosures are required?

CASES

C 13–1
NBC Settles a Logo
Problem
(L.O. 2, 4)

The National Broadcasting Company (NBC) incurred costs of $750,000 in the development of its N logo shown at intervals in its TV broadcasts. Shortly after the N was announced and first used by NBC, it was discovered that an educational TV network in Nebraska had already been using a similar logo. To obtain exclusive rights to its already costly N, NBC agreed, in an out-of-court settlement, to pay $55,000 cash to Nebraska Network and to furnish it with various new and used color TV equipment without cost (NBC book value, $350,000). The equipment to be transferred was conservatively valued at $500,000 by independent appraisers. A spokesman for the Nebraska Network said the equipment to be provided by NBC would have cost $750,000 if bought new and that, for the two years preceding the settlement, efforts to get a $750,000 appropriation from the Nebraska legislature to buy such equipment had been unsuccessful. Terms of the settlement provided that $2,500 of the cash settlement was to be paid to William Korbus, who had designed the Nebraska Network's N at a cost of $100. Delivery of the equipment to the Nebraska Network was to begin approximately three months after the announced settlement and was to occur over a four-month interval.

Required:

1. How should NBC account for its original costs of $750,000 related to the logo? How should it account for the settlement with the Nebraska Network and Korbus?
2. Assuming that accounting principles for not-for-profit organizations such as the Nebraska Network were similar to those for a commercial entity, how should the Nebraska Network account for the settlement?

C 13–2
Depletion: What Does It Mean in Financial Statements?
(L.O. 2, 7)

A friend of yours recently inherited capital stock in Megamining Corporation. The friend has just received the first annual financial report from the company since the inheritance. One aspect of the report in particular troubles your friend; consequently, you have been asked for an explanation of what the company seems to be saying. The excerpt reads:

Depletion of mines is computed on the basis of an overall unit rate applied to the pounds of principal products sold from mine production. The corporation makes no representation that the annual amount represents the depletion actually sustained or the decline, if any, in mine values attributable to the year's operations, or that it represents anything other than a general provision for the amortization of the remaining book value of mines.

Specifically, your friend asks: (1) Is the depletion amount reported on the income statement meaningless? (2) Are the company's mines becoming more or less valuable? (3) What is the significance of the book value of the company's mines?

Required:

Respond to your friend's questions. Identify each element of your response with the three questions your friend has asked.

C 13–3
The Directors Want to Increase Goodwill
(L.O. 2, 4)

Blass Corporation, a retail farm implements dealer, has increased its annual sales volume to a level 10 times greater than the annual sales of the dealership when purchased 28 years ago. At that time, a material amount of goodwill was recorded. The goodwill has never been amortized because it predated *APB Opinion No. 17*.

The board of directors of Blass Corporation recently received an offer to negotiate the sale of Blass Corporation to a larger competitor. As a result, the majority of the board members want to increase the current amount of goodwill on the balance sheet because of the larger sales volume developed through intensive promotion and the current market prices of the company's products. However, a few of the company's board members would prefer to eliminate goodwill altogether from the balance sheet in order to prevent "possible misinterpretations." Goodwill was properly recorded when the business was acquired 28 years ago.

Required:

1. *a.* Discuss the meaning of the term *goodwill*. Do not discuss goodwill arising from consolidated statements or the conditions under which goodwill is recorded.
   b. What technique is commonly used to estimate the value of goodwill in negotiations to purchase a going concern?
2. Why are the book and market values of the goodwill of Blass Corporation different?
3. Discuss the propriety of:
   a. Increasing the stated value of goodwill prior to the negotiations.
   b. Eliminating goodwill completely from the balance sheet prior to negotiations.
4. From an ethical point of view, do you believe the goodwill should be written down or left alone? Explain.

(AICPA adapted)

CHAPTER

14

Investments: Temporary and Long Term

LEARNING OBJECTIVES

◆

After you have studied this chapter, you will:

1. Appreciate why firms invest in debt and equity securities.

2. Understand classification criteria and the initial recording of investment securities at the date of acquisition.

3. Understand the conceptual basis for the accounting for various types of investments.

4. Be able to account for investments in short-term equity securities.

5. Be able to account for investments in short-term debt securities.

6. Understand and be able to use (*a*) the cost method, (*b*) the lower of cost or market method, (*c*) the equity method, and (*d*) the market value method in

accounting for long-term investments in equity securities.

7. Be familiar with the disclosure requirements for all types of investment securities.

8. Understand how to account for stock dividends, stock splits, and stock warrants received by the investor.

9. Be familiar with the procedures for preparing consolidated financial statements. (Refer to Appendix 14A.)

10. Understand how to account for the cash surrender value of life insurance and other special purpose funds. (Refer to Appendix 14B.)

◆

INTRODUCTION

◆

In its 1988 financial statements, Spectrum Control Inc. shows investments in marketable equity securities in the amount of $2.3 million and other investments in the amount of $.5 million, both as current assets. These total to more than 15% of current assets. There were no such investments in 1987. The note on "Investments in Marketable Equity Securities" explains that this investment was noncurrent in 1987, and management reclassified it to current in 1988 to "reflect Management's decision to make funds available for current operations." The note also explains that the marketable equity securities are carried at the lower of aggregate cost or market value, and that the other investments are carried at cost. It goes on to provide disclosures regarding "aggregate market values, gross unrealized losses, gross unrealized gains, and the recognition of a realized loss as a result of the reclassification of the marketable equity securities from noncurrent to current."

Several questions arise from the above description of Spectrum Control's financial reporting:

- How are investments in marketable equity securities different from investments in other securities? Why are they accounted for differently?
- Why is a loss recorded when an investment is reclassified from noncurrent to current? What are unrealized gains and losses? And why are they reported?
- Why do firms invest in the securities of other firms in the first place?
- In general, what types of items are included under the investments caption? How are they recorded, and how is income from investments measured?

After you have studied this chapter, you will know the answers to these questions and more. The primary objective of this chapter is developing an understanding of how to account for the investments a firm makes in the financial instruments of other firms and organizations. Investments can include many different types of financial instruments: equity securities, debt securities, stock options and warrants, municipal and state bonds and notes, U.S. Treasury bills and bonds, money market funds, commercial paper, and, in general, any contract that obligates a party to convey financial resources to the investing firm. The accounting procedures and disclosures differ according to the type of investment and whether the investments are classified as short- or long-term. Before getting into the details of accounting for each type and classification, consider first why a firm might invest in the financial instruments of another organization, and how these financial instruments are recorded at their acquisition.

◆

WHY FIRMS INVEST IN SECURITIES

◆

Sound financial management dictates that a firm maximize the profit-generating capacity of all its assets, and this includes cash. One profit-generating use of cash is to invest it in the financial instruments of other firms.[1]

More generally, firms invest in the securities of other firms for two basic reasons:

1. To earn a return on otherwise idle cash.
2. To acquire the voting stock of another firm in order to gain influence, control, or some other business advantage.

---

[1] The FASB has begun using the term *financial instrument* to describe all forms of contracts that convey ownership in firms or obligations to convey financial resources from one party to another. All the securities and other investments discussed in this chapter are financial instruments. A more detailed definition of financial instruments is found later in the chapter.

Investments made to earn a return on otherwise idle cash might be short-term (temporary), or they might be longer term. For example, a higher than necessary cash balance can arise due to seasonality of a business: the highly seasonal sales patterns generally result in greater cash needs immediately preceding the peak sales period when production and inventories are increasing. Higher cash inflows then occur at and after the peak in sales. Sound financial management requires the investment of idle funds from the peak inflow periods until they are needed during the peak outflow periods. Typically, government short-term securities and bank certificates of deposit are used for this purpose. As an example of a longer term but still profit-driven investment, a firm might accumulate the cash that will be needed within the next few years to pay off a long-term debt obligation and invest it in marketable securities prior to the maturity date of the debt. The investing firm has a long-term investment, usually in a diversified holding of government obligations or several other firms' shares, with a relatively small number of shares of each. The purpose of the investment is to earn a return.

The second reason involves establishing some form of beneficial business relationship with a second firm, generally of a long-term nature. Corning Glass Works, for example, joined with Owens-Illinois, Inc., many years ago to establish a new company, Owens Corning Fiberglas (OCF), for the purpose of entering a new market with a new product, fiberglass. Corning held its investment in OCF for nearly 50 years. A firm might invest in the securities of another corporation simply to create a desirable relationship with a supplier or customer. The 1989 annual report of IBM, for example, reports a significant ownership interest in MCI Communications Corporation. It is likely that this investment is in part to enhance the relationship between the two firms.

In this chapter, the basic topic is accounting for investments in the securities of other corporations. There are two basic classifications of securities: *equity securities* and *debt securities*. Each can be further classified according to whether management views the investment in that particular security as *short-term* (temporary), or *long-term*. Different accounting treatments are required for each type of investment, and for short- and long-term classifications. Finally, those investments which are marketable have a different accounting treatment than those that are not.

With regard to investments in debt securities, only those classified as short-term will be covered in this chapter. Accounting for long-term investments in debt securities is covered in detail in Chapter 16. Because there are important similarities in the recording of debt by the issuer and by the investor, it is useful to study the accounting for both parties at the same time.

Preliminary to the specific coverage on accounting for investments, the general characteristics of investment securities and the recording of investment securities at their acquisition are considered. Then accounting for equity securities is covered, with short-term securities considered before long-term securities. Following long-term equity securities the accounting for short-term debt securities is discussed. The chapter concludes with a discussion of some other types of investments that are not characterized as either equity or debt.

CHARACTERISTICS AND CLASSIFICATION OF INVESTMENT SECURITIES

The two broad types of investment securities are debt securities and equity securities. *Equity securities* are ownership claims on the investee firm. *Debt securities* are creditor claims, with a fixed obligation and usually some interest obligation. The distinction between ownership and debt securities is discussed in Chapter 5. Investments in either type of security can be classified as short-term or long-term.

For accounting purposes, short-term investments must satisfy the definitional requirements of a current asset. Current assets are assets that are readily marketable and are expected to be consumed or converted to cash within one year of the balance sheet date or during the normal operating cycle of the firm, if it is longer. Short-term investments must be readily marketable.[2] A security is readily marketable if it is listed on one of the stock exchanges. If an investment is not readily marketable, it does not meet the definition of a current asset and is classified as a long-term investment.

In the case of investment securities that are readily marketable, the investor's intention determines the classification as short- or long-term. Thus, short-term investments are those that meet the other criteria of current assets, and that managers of the investing firm classify as short-term. The accounting literature does not provide further guidance.

Short-term investments in equity securities often include common stock, preferred stock, warrants, options, and stock rights. Short-term debt securities include corporate and other entity bonds and notes, and other investments such as certificates of deposit, U.S. Treasury bills, commercial paper, and other types of financial instruments that have a ready market.

Long-term investments include all securities that do not meet the requirements for short-term investments. The following are examples of investments to be classified as long-term:

1. Long-term investments in the capital stock of another company. This category can include investments in common stock, preferred stock, options, warrants, and, in general, any security that represents an ownership claim on the firm.
2. Long-term investments in the bonds of another company.
3. Investments in subsidiaries, including long-term receivables from subsidiaries.
4. Funds set aside for long-term future use, such as bond sinking funds (to retire bonds payable), expansion funds, stock retirement funds, and long-term savings deposits.
5. Cash surrender value of life insurance policies carried by the company.
6. Long-term investments in tangible assets, such as land and buildings, that are not used in current operations (long-term includes operational assets that are only temporarily idle).

ACQUISITION OF INVESTMENT SECURITIES

Investment securities may be purchased directly from the issuing company, from individual investors, or indirectly from stockbrokers and dealers on the stock exchanges and the over-the-counter market. At the date of acquisition of an investment security, an appropriately designated investment account is debited for the cost of the investment in conformity with the *cost principle*. Cost includes:

1. The basic purchase price of the security.
2. Any brokerage fees and/or excise taxes.
3. Other transfer costs incurred by the purchaser.

Investments in equity securities may be by purchased for cash, on margin, or for noncash consideration. When stock is purchased on margin, only part of the purchase price is paid initially. The balance is borrowed (usually through a brokerage firm). The stock investment should be recorded at its cost, including the portion financed with borrowed funds.

When noncash consideration (property or services) is given for an investment, the cost assigned to the securities should be measured by (1) the market value of the consideration given or (2) the market values of the securities received, whichever can be more reliably determined. Inability to reliably determine either one of these market values—for example, an exchange of unlisted or closely held securities for

---

[2] *FASB Interpretation No. 16*, "Clarification of Definitions and Accounting for Marketable Securities that Become Nonmarketable" (Norwalk, Conn., February 1977), provides detailed rules pertaining to determining marketability.

property for which no established market values exists—will require the use of appraisals or estimates.

Securities frequently are purchased between regular interest or dividend dates. For such purchases, accrued interest is recorded on debt securities because interest is a legal obligation. Dividends are not accrued on equity securities because dividends are a legal liability only when declared.

The following examples illustrate applications of the preceding discussion to purchases of equity investments.

Example On October 1, 1993, Blue Corporation purchased 5,000 shares of the common stock of Clear Inc. at $20 per share. Commissions incurred by Blue were $500. The investment is recorded as follows:

```
Long-term (or short-term) investment, common shares, Clear Inc.
  [(5,000 shares × $20) + $500] . . . . . . . . . . . . . . . . . 100,500
  Cash  . . . . . . . . . . . . . . . . . . . . . . . . . . . .            100,500
```

Example Assume the same facts as in Example 1 above, except Blue transferred a tract of vacant land (carried in Blue's accounts at $35,000) plus $5,500 cash as payment in full for the common stock. The common stock of Clear is currently selling at $20 per share. The disposal of the land and the purchase of the stock are recorded as follows:

```
Long-term (or short-term) investment, common shares, Clear Inc.
  [(5,000 shares × $20) + $500]  . . . . . . . . . . . . . . . . 100,500
  Land . . . . . . . . . . . . . . . . . . . . . . . . . . . .             35,000
  Gain on disposal of land . . . . . . . . . . . . . . . . . .             60,000
  Cash  . . . . . . . . . . . . . . . . . . . . . . . . . . .              5,500
```

Since the market value of the securities acquired is known, it is the basis for recording the investment. The gain on the disposal of the land is the difference between the market value of securities ($110,500) and the book value of the assets transferred ($40,500).

A purchase of two or more classes of securities for a single lump sum (called a *lump sum*, or *basket, purchase*) requires the allocation of portions of the total cost to each class of securities based upon available market value information. When the market value of each class is available, the *proportional method* is used to allocate the lump-sum price based on relative market values. Alternatively, if the market price(s) of all but one class of securities is known, the *incremental method* is applied. The incremental method allocates total cost first to the class(es) of securities with the known market value(s), and then assigns the remainder of the lump-sum price to the class of stock that does not have a market price.

Example On October 3, 1993, Blue purchased 5,000 shares of common stock of Clear and 10,000 shares of preferred stock of CX Corp. for a lump sum of $170,000, and paid a commission of $1,000. At the date of the purchase, the market prices of the acquired shares were: Clear, $20 per share; CX Corp., $8 per share.

The total market value of the acquired shares is $180,000, of which 10/18 ($100,000 ÷ $180,000) is Clear, Inc. and 8/18 ($80,000 ÷ $180,000) is CX Corp. Therefore, 10/18 of the $171,000 purchase price is allocated as the cost of the investment in Clear, Inc., and 8/18 as the cost of the investment in CX Corp.:

Stock	Shares Acquired	Market Price Per Share	Market Value	Proportion of Market Value	Allocation of Purchase Price
Clear, Inc.	5,000	$20	$100,000	10/18	95,000
CX Corp.	10,000	$ 8	80,000	8/18	76,000
Totals			$180,000	18/18	171,000

The entry to record the purchase is:

Long-term (or short-term) investment, common shares, Clear, Inc. 95,000
Long-term (or short-term) investment, preferred shares, CX Corp. 76,000
  Cash 171,000

Cost Flow Assumptions in Multiple Acquisitions and Disposals of Investment Securities   Accounting for investments is facilitated if a consistent system of security cost identification is used. A record of each individual security should be maintained. This record documents units purchased (by certificate number), dates, and unit cost. These details are important when a security is sold because its cost should be determined on a systematic basis. Otherwise, errors and possible distortions of gains and losses may occur.

Identification of securities sold is usually not difficult. However, identification can be difficult when the number of transactions is large, when blocks of securities have been transferred through an estate, or when the issuer has exchanged substitute securities for those originally purchased. When specific identification cannot be made, income tax law requires the use of the first-in, first-out method. Use of specific identification, FIFO, or average (but not LIFO) cost procedures is acceptable for financial accounting purposes. Most firms, however, use the same method for financial accounting and tax reporting purposes.

The choice of a particular cost flow assumption method may affect the gain or loss reported. To illustrate, assume 10 shares of Red Company were purchased at $150 per share, and later an additional 30 shares were purchased at $200 per share. There is a subsequent sale of 5 shares at $180 per share. If the 5 shares can be identified by certificate number as a part of the first purchase, a gain of $30 per share is recognized. Alternatively, if they are identified with the second purchase, a loss of $20 per share is recognized. The averaging procedure would report a loss of $7.50 per share computed as follows:

First purchase	10 shares × $150	$1,500
Second purchase	30 shares × $200	6,000
Total	40	$7,500
Average cost per share ($7,500/40)		$187.50
Sale price per share		180.00
Loss per share		$ 7.50

CONCEPT REVIEW

1. State two reasons why a firm might invest in securities.
2. What principle is used to determine the amount to be recorded for the acquisition of an investment security? What items are included in the recording of an investment security?
3. What methods are used to allocate the purchase cost of a group of securities for a lump sum?

ACCOUNTING FOR SHORT-TERM INVESTMENTS IN MARKETABLE EQUITY SECURITIES

Prior to the issuance of *SFAS No. 12*, accounting for short-term investments in marketable securities was characterized by a wide diversity of practice, both in initial recording and in subsequent reporting. Part of the problem was that short-term debt and equity securities have different characteristics. Because of the numerous ways that were being used to measure, record, and report investments in marketable securities, the FASB issued *SFAS No. 12*, "Accounting for Certain Marketable

Securities," in December 1975. This *Standard* improved the accounting for *equity* securities by specifying measurement and reporting rules, but did not resolve the accounting for *debt* securities. Accounting for debt securities continues to be guided by *ARB No. 43*, Chapter 3A, par. 9.

SFAS No. 12 requires that both short-term and long-term investments in marketable equity securities be valued at each balance sheet date using the **lower of aggregate cost or market (LCM) method** *(italics added):*

> The carrying amount of a marketable securities portfolio shall be the lower of its *aggregate* cost or market value, determined at the balance sheet date. The amount by which aggregate cost of the *portfolio* exceeds market value shall be accounted for as the *valuation allowance*.
>
> Marketable equity securities owned by an entity shall . . . be grouped into separate portfolios according the current or noncurrent classification of the securities for the purpose of comparing aggregate cost and market value to determine carrying amount.[3]

The LCM method of valuing the investment on the balance sheet has applicability to both short-term and long-term equity investments. In both instances, a valuation allowance is created when aggregate cost is greater than aggregate market value. The valuation allowance is a credit balance account that is contra to the investment account. The treatment of the debit side of the entry, which is the unrealized loss on the investment, differs depending on whether the investment is classified as *short-term* or *long-term*.

Aggregate versus Individual-Security Level LCM   The key concept is determining aggregate market value of the total portfolio of equity securities and comparing it to the aggregate cost. An alternative that might be used is to compare the market value and cost of individual securities, and thus to have a security-by-security LCM. *SFAS No. 12* requires the portfolio approach; it does not allow individual-security level LCM for equity securities.[4]

The rationale for the portfolio level comparisons is that when management makes a decision to invest in more than one equity security, it is the overall investment that must be evaluated. To write down only those securities that declined in value while not allowing for the gains of those that increased in value would be an extremely conservative asymmetric rule. The portfolio requirement allows unrealized gains to offset unrealized losses. In addition, firms are required to disclose aggregate amounts of unrealized gains and unrealized losses. Disclosure requirements are covered in a later section. Since GAAP does not require the use of security-by-security LCM, it is not discussed further.

The following example shows the application of the LCM method to short-term equity investments. The procedure for computing the valuation allowance is also used for long-term equity investments, which are discussed in a later section.

Example of Lower of Cost or Market   Assume the following transactions relate to investments by Tree Corporation:

> January 2, 1991—Tree Corporation acquires 10 shares of Pear Company common stock at a market price of $15 per share, and 20 shares of Apple Inc. common stock for $11 per share. Assume there are no brokerage fees and that these investments are classified as short-term.

---

[3] *SFAS No. 12*, par. 8 and 9. This *Statement* specifically relates only to equity securities (not to debt securities). However, it does make one exception as follows: The term *equity securities* "does not encompass preferred stock that by its terms either must be redeemed by the issuing enterprise or is redeemable at the option of the investor, nor does it include treasury stock or convertible bonds." The exception recognizes that the specified redemption requirement makes such preferred stock essentially a debt security. Also, *SFAS No. 12* is not applicable to mutual life insurance companies because of specified practices.

[4] Firms may use security-by-security level LCM for marketable debt securities. It is not expressly prohibited.

The entry to record the investment in the accounts of Tree Corporation is:

Investment in short-term marketable equity securities 370
    Cash   370

December 31, 1991—The two firms in which Tree has invested report the following results:

	Pear Company	Apple Inc.
Earnings per share for 1991	$ 2.00	$1.50
Dividends per share paid December 31	.50	.75
Market value per share at 12/31/91	$17/share	$9.50/share

The initial cost of the investment is:

Pear Company	10 shares × $ 15/share	$150
Apple Inc.	20 shares × $ 11/share	220
Total investment		$370

Investment revenue for Tree is the dividends received from the investment securities. In this example, Tree Corporation would have investment income of $20 (dividends of 50 cents per share times the 10 Pear shares owned, plus dividends of 75 cents per share times the 20 Apple shares owned).

The entry to record investment revenue is:

Cash (or dividends receivable) 20
    Investment revenue (or dividend income)   20

At the end of the year it is necessary to determine whether there is a need to write down the aggregate investment. The aggregate cost was $370. The aggregate market value at December 31 is:

Company	Market Value Computation	Market	Cost	Difference
Pear Company	10 shares × $17/share	$170	$150	+ $20
Apple Inc.	20 shares × $9.50/share	190	220	− 30
Total		$360	$370	− 10

The aggregate market value has fallen to $360, or $10 less than the aggregate original cost. The LCM method requires the investment be written down to $360 (a write-down of $10). The entry to record the write-down would be as follows:

Unrealized loss on short-term investments 10
    Allowance to reduce short-term investments to market   10

For short-term investments in equity securities, the unrealized loss on short-term investments account is an income statement account. Generally, it is netted against investment revenue. The allowance to reduce short-term investments to market account becomes a contra account to the short-term investments account on the balance sheet. These accounts are discussed in greater detail in the following section.

If the above analysis were on an individual security-by-security basis, the write-down would be $30, which is the decline in value of the investment in Apple Inc. The end-of-period market value of Pear Company is greater than its original cost ($170 market value versus $150 cost). Since market value is greater than cost for Pear, an individual-security–based LCM would not require any adjustment to the carrying amount for Pear. Apple Inc., however, has a market value of $190 and an original cost of $220—a $30 decline or loss. Individual-security–based LCM would record this decline in value of $30. This distinction between portfolio or aggregate value/cost and individual security value or cost is important. *SFAS No. 12* requires the use of portfolio level comparisons of costs and market values for marketable equity securities. As this example illustrates, the portfolio approach may result in less conservative reporting.

Realized and Unrealized Gains and Losses

SFAS No. 12 makes a careful distinction between realized and unrealized gains and losses in specifying accounting for both short- and long-term investments in equity securities. Realized gains and losses usually relate to the sale of the securities. Unrealized gains and losses relate to the application of the LCM rule to the aggregate investment portfolio (of equity securities) at the end of each annual accounting period. *SFAS No. 12* also distinguishes between an unrealized gain and an unrealized loss recovery. The following definitions are applied in accounting for investments in equity securities:

1. **Realized gain.** If at the date of sale the net amount received is more than the original cost (i.e., purchase cost) on an individual equity security basis, there is a realized gain of the amount of the difference.

2. **Realized loss.** A realized loss is recognized when:
   a. At the date of sale, there is an excess of original cost of an individual security over the net proceeds received by the investor.
   b. An individual equity security is transferred between the long- and short-term portfolios, and its market value at the date of transfer is below its original cost.
   c. An individual security is written down due to a permanent decline or impairment in its market value below its original cost.

3. **Unrealized loss.** An unrealized loss occurs when the end-of-period market value of a portfolio of investments in equity securities is less than the carrying value of the portfolio. An unrealized loss is recognized only at the end of the accounting period. If the portfolio of securities is a short-term investment, the unrealized loss is reported on the income statement. However, if the portfolio is a long-term investment, the unrealized loss is reported as a negative element of stockholders' equity (to be discussed later). In either case, the year-end adjustment is to debit an unrealized loss account (e.g., unrealized loss on equity investments) and credit an allowance account (e.g., allowance to reduce short-term equity investments to LCM). If the equity investment is classified as short term, the unrealized loss reduces current period income. The allowance account is reported on the balance sheet as a contra to the related investment account.

4. **Unrealized gain.** There is an unrealized gain when the current market value of the portfolio of investments in equity securities is above the total portfolio valued at LCM at the end of the accounting period. Unrealized gains can be recorded only to the extent that there have been previously recorded unrealized losses. The carrying value of the portfolio in the financial statements cannot exceed the original cost of the total portfolio. Thus, the only unrealized gains that are recorded are actually recoveries of previously recorded unrealized losses. In order to be clear on this point, the term *unrealized loss recovery* is used to identify an unrealized gain that is recorded because it is a recovery of a previously recorded unrealized loss. Unrealized gains in excess of the original cost cannot be recorded until they are realized.

An unrealized loss recovery requires an adjusting entry at the end of the accounting period. The debit is to the allowance account which reduces short-term equity investments to LCM. The account credited depends on whether the investment in equity securities has been carried as a short-term or long-term investment. For short-term investments the unrealized loss recovery is credited to an income statement account such as "loss recovery on short-term equity security investments." This account increases income for the period. If the equity investment is classified as long-term, the unrealized loss recovery is credited to the account established in the stockholders' equity section of the balance sheet in which the unrealized loss had previously been debited.

In sum, application of the LCM method as required by *SFAS No. 12* for marketable equity securities, is at the portfolio level, not the individual-security level. It requires the write-down of unrealized losses, and the writing back up of unrealized loss recoveries. In no case can the write-up be above the original cost of the portfolio. The sale of a short-term equity investment is recorded as a debit for the resources received, a credit to the investment account for the original cost of the equity investment, and the difference is recorded as a *realized* gain or loss.

Example of LCM for Short-Term Equity Securities   Suppose Tree Corporation's investments totaling $370 in Pear and Apple described in the previous example were short-term investments, and the market value of the portfolio at December 31, 1991, is $360 as shown in the example.

The difference between the portfolio cost ($370) and the portfolio market value ($360) is an unrealized loss of $10 as was shown before. The unrealized loss will appear as an item on the 1991 income statement (along with the investment revenue of $20), and the allowance account will be a contra to the investment in equity securities account. The balance sheet would appear as follows:

```
Current assets:
    Investment in equity securities, short-term  . . . . . $370
    Less: Allowance to reduce to market  . . . . . . . .    10    $360
```

When a short-term equity security is sold, amounts in the allowance account are ignored. This account is adjusted only at each year-end. To illustrate, assume Tree Corporation sold all of its short-term investments on January 30, 1992, for cash as follows: Pear common, $25 per share, and Apple common, $4 per share. The transaction would be recorded on January 30, 1992, as follows:

```
Cash (10 shares × $25 + 20 shares × $4) . . . . . . . . . . . . . . . . . 330
Loss on sale of investments  . . . . . . . . . . . . . . . . . . . . . . . . . . 40
    Investments in short-term equity securities . . . . . . . . . . . . .          370
```

Continuing the example, assume that on June 6, 1992, Tree purchases another short-term equity security—AB Corporation, 10 shares at $7 per share. The entry to record this transaction is:

```
Investment in short-term equity securities . . . . . . . . . . . . . . . . 70
    Cash . . . . . . . . . . . . . . . . . . . . . . . . . . . . . . . . . . . . . . . .          70
```

At the end of 1992, assume AB Corporation common stock is selling at $6.50. The allowance account had a credit balance of $10 at the end of 1991. At the end of 1992, the portfolio of short-term equity securities held by Tree contains only the AB Corporation stock. The portfolio cost is $70 and the portfolio market value is $65 (10 shares × $6.50). The market value is lower than cost, but the allowance account is too large at $10. It must be reduced to a balance of $5. The entry to reduce the balance at December 31, 1992 is:

```
Allowance to reduce short-term investments to market . . . . . . . . . . 5
    Unrealized loss recovery on short-term investments . . . . . . . .          5
```

As a result of the above 1992 transactions, Tree Corporation would report the following in its 1992 financial statements:

Income statement:
Loss on sale of short-term investments $40
Unrealized loss recovery on short-term investments . . . . . (5)

Net loss on short-term investments $35

Balance sheet:
Current assets:
Investment in equity securities, short-term at cost $70
Less: Allowance to reduce to market . . . . (5)
Investment (at market) $65

The effect of recording the LCM unrealized loss of $10 in 1991 was to reduce income by that amount in 1991, and to reduce the investment carrying value to its market value. In the following year (1992), when the securities are sold, the unrealized loss recorded in 1991 has the effect of reducing the amount of loss in the current period. In this example, the net impact on income in 1992 is not the total realized loss of $40, but rather the portion that occurred in 1992, $35 ($40 less the $10 that was recorded in 1991 plus the $5 that occurred on the new investment). The effect is to recognize unrealized losses in the year when they occur. This results in better compliance with the matching principle.

Disclosures Required for Investments in Short-Term Equity Investments Because all investments included in the short-term classification must be marketable, they are highly liquid. As such they are usually listed immediately after cash in the current assets section of the balance sheet. *SFAS No. 12* specifies the required disclosures for all marketable equity securities, regardless of whether they are classified as short- or long-term. The requirements listed here also apply to long-term investments in marketable equity securities.

As of each balance sheet date presented, the aggregate cost and the aggregate market value of marketable equity securities for the portfolios of short-term and of long-term investments must be disclosed, either in the body of the financial statements or in the notes. For the latest balance sheet presented, disclosures are required of (1) gross unrealized gains, and (2) gross unrealized losses.

For Tree Corporation the December 31, 1991, financial statement would include disclosures of gross unrealized gains of $20 (the unrealized gain on the Pear common) and of gross unrealized losses of $30 (the unrealized loss on the Apple common).

For each income statement presented, disclosures of (1) the net realized gain or loss included in net income, (2) the basis on which cost was determined in computing gain or loss included in net income, and (3) the change in the amount of the valuation allowance included in net income.

Examples of disclosures in accordance with *SFAS No. 12* are found in Exhibit 14–1, which presents notes to the financial statements of CSP Inc., regarding its short-term investments in addition to those in equity securities. For all the investment securities except the equity securities, cost is either less than current market value or cost approximates market value. The disclosures for these investments is simply their source and cost. CSP Inc. exceeds the disclosure requirements by disclosing gross unrealized gains and losses for both the latest balance sheet and the prior year balance sheet.

The next section covers accounting for investments in equity securities that are classified as long-term. Such investments may or may not be readily marketable. When they are readily marketable, *SFAS No. 12* applies, and the accounting is similar to the accounting for short-term equity investments. When they are not marketable, alternative accounting procedures are used.

EXHIBIT 14-1   Note disclosures by CSP Inc. of Investments in Short-Term Marketable Securities

From the Balance Sheet:	1988	1987
($ *in thousands*)		
Current assets:		
Cash	$2,306	$5,298
Marketable securities (Note 2)	9,047	7,952
Accounts receivable, net	2,237	2,486
Inventories	2,370	1,911
Deferred income taxes	88	153
Refundable income taxes	45	—
Prepaid expenses	76	84
Total current assets	$16,169	$17,884

Notes to Consolidated Financial Statements

Note 1. (In Part) Summary of Significant Accounting Policies: Marketable Securities:

Marketable equity securities are carried at the lower of cost or market value. Interest income is accrued as earned. Dividend income is recorded as income on the date the stock traded "ex-dividend." The cost of marketable securities sold is determined on the specific identification method and realized gains or losses are reflected in income.

Note 2. Marketable Securities:

At August 31, 1988 and 1987, marketable securities consisted of the following:

	1988	1987
($ *in thousands*)		
Marketable equity securities, at cost	$1,000	$1,000
Less: valuation allowance	127	137
Marketable equity securities, at market	873	863
Bonds and municipal revenue notes, at cost	2,327	2,232
Money market funds and commercial paper	3,359	4,664
Bankers' acceptance	—	193
U.S. treasury bills	2,488	—
Total	$9,047	$7,952

Net realized gains on the sale of securities included in the determination of income before taxes amounted to $13,000, and $67,000 for fiscal 1987 and 1986, respectively.

At August 31, 1988 and 1987, gross unrealized gains (losses) pertaining to marketable equity securities were as follows:

	1988	1987
($ *in thousands*)		
Gross unrealized loss	$ 147	$ 160
Gross unrealized gain	20	23
Net unrealized losses	$ 127	$ 137

CONCEPT REVIEW

1. How are unrealized losses computed under the LCM method? How are they treated for accounting purposes for short-term equity investments?
2. Explain the accounting entry that is made when a short-term equity investment is sold for more than its original cost. What effect will this transaction (by itself) have on any amounts in the allowance to reduce to market account when there is an unrealized loss for the portfolio recorded?
3. What entry is made when at year-end there is an increase in the aggregate market value to an amount greater than the original cost for a short-term investment portfolio that has a valuation allowance recorded?

ACCOUNTING FOR LONG-TERM INVESTMENTS IN EQUITY SECURITIES

♦

Five different methods are used to account for long-term investments, depending on the characteristics of the investment:

1. The lower of cost or market (LCM) method.
2. The cost method.
3. The equity method.
4. The market value method.
5. Consolidation.

The investor firm is not given a free choice in selecting which of these methods to apply. Based on specified conditions, only one method is appropriate for each individual investment.

For long-term investments that do not represent a *controlling interest* (to be defined), guidance on accounting procedures is found in *SFAS No. 12* and in *APB Opinion No. 18*. *APB Opinion No. 18* defines two important factors related to the investor firm's ability to control or influence the decision of the investee.

1. *Significant influence*. A firm has significant influence if it has the ability to affect, to an important degree, the operating and financial policies of another company through ownership of a sufficient portion of its voting stock. The ability to exercise significant influence also may be shown in several other ways. These include representation on the board of directors, interchange of managerial pesonnel, material intercompany transactions, and technological dependency. To attain a reasonable degree of uniformity, the APB provided an operational rule. This rule states that an investment of *20% or more* of the outstanding voting stock leads to the presumption that, in the absence of evidence to the contrary, an investor has the ability to exercise significant influence over the company.[5]

2. *Controlling interest*. A controlling interest exists when the investor company owns enough of the voting stock of the investee company to determine its operating and financing policies. Ownership of over 50% of the outstanding voting stock usually would assure control; however, in some cases, this percentage may not be sufficient. In still other cases, ownership of less than 50% of the outstanding voting stock may create a controlling interest. Factors such as the number of stockholders and the extent of stockholder participation in voting have some bearing on the point at which a controlling interest is attained. Operationally, the APB presumption is that a controlling interest is represented by over 50% of the voting stock, absent other compelling factors.

When a company owns a controlling interest in a second company, the controlling company must prepare *consolidated financial statements*. Appendix 14A is a summary discussion of preparing consolidated financial statements; the topic is covered in depth in advanced financial accounting courses. Coverage of the basic principles of consolidation is included here because a recent *Standard* issued by the FASB has increased the number of consolidated statements that are required to be prepared.

---

[5] An investor may not be able to exercise significant influence over the investee's policies, even though the investor owns more than a 20% interest, when:

Opposition by the investee, such as litigation or complaints to governmental regulatory authorities, challenges the investor's ability to exercise significant influence.

The investor and the investee sign an agreement under which the investor surrenders signficant rights as a stockholder.

Majority ownership of the investee is concentrated among a small group of stockholders who operate the company without regard to the views of the investor.

The investor tries and fails to obtain representation on the investee's board of directors.

The above list, from *FASB Interpretation No. 35*, "Criteria for Applying the Equity Method of Accounting for Investments in Common Stock" (Norwalk, Conn., May 1981), is intended to be illustrative and not all-inclusive.

Specifically, *SFAS No. 94* requires the consolidation of all majority-owned subsidiaries, including finance and other nonrelated business subsidiaries that generally were not consolidated prior to the issuance of *SFAS No. 94*.[6] *SFAS No. 94* requires that majority-owned subsidiaries not be consolidated (1) if control is likely to be temporary, or (2) if control does not rest with with the majority owner. In these situations, the cost method is used to account for the investments.

The next section of this chapter considers long-term equity investments when the investor does not have a controlling interest. In general, when the investor does not have significant influence, the LCM method is used for *marketable* equity securities. When the securities are not marketable, the cost method is used. If, however, the investor firm has significant influence, the equity method is used. Finally, the market value method is used in certain industries. The application of the LCM method is covered first.

LCM Method of Accounting for Long-Term Investments in Equity Securities

The LCM method of accounting used for short-term equity investments is, in specified conditions, also used for long-term investments in equity securities. In conformity with *SFAS No. 12*, the LCM method must be used for long-term investments in marketable equity securities except when the investor has stock holdings that confer significant influence or control. Investments in which the investor company has significant influence are accounted for by the equity method (to be discussed shortly) in compliance with *APB No. 18*. These investments are not covered by *SFAS No. 12*. *Thus, the LCM method is used when the following conditions exist:*

+ A market value for the equity securities can be determined.
+ The number of voting shares held is relatively small—defined in *APB No. 18* as less than a 20% ownership of voting stock absent other evidence that significant influence exists.

If the shares held are nonvoting, the investor does not have any control with such shares, and the LCM method is appropriate no matter what the percentage of ownership is.

The LCM method is applied to long-term investments in equity securities in the same way as for short-term investments in equity securities except for one important difference—how the unrealized loss and unrealized loss recovery are reported. In short-term investments, the unrealized loss is reported on the income statement as a current loss. In contrast, when the investment is long-term, the unrealized loss is debited to a stockholders' equity account. This account is a contra (i.e., negative) stockholders' account.

The credit to the allowance account (allowance to reduce long-term equity investments to LCM) is essentially the same as for short-term investments. This account is reported, as with short-term investments, on the balance sheet as a contra account to the related investment account.

To illustrate, consider again the Tree Corporation example presented earlier, in which the accounting for short-term equity investments was illustrated.

The entries made to account for these investments when they are classified as long-term are as follows:

To record the initial cost of the investment:

Investment in long-term equity securities	370	
Cash		370

To record investment revenue (receipt of dividends):

Cash	20	
Investment revenue		20

---

[6] See *FASB No. 94*, par. 13 and 15.

At December 31, 1991—To record unrealized loss:

Unrealized loss on long-term investments 10
    Allowance to reduce long-term investments to market 10

The unrealized loss on long-term investments account is now treated as a contra account in the stockholders' equity section. It is often labeled ''Investment valuation allowance'' or ''Net unrealized loss on long-term marketable securities.''

Continuing the example, suppose that on April 14, 1992, the market value of Apple common stock decreased to $7 per share, and that this decrease is determined to be permanent.[7] Tree must record a loss related to this permanent decline (impairment) in the value of Apple common stock:

Loss in market value of long-term investment [20 × ($11 − $7)] 80
    Long-term investments in equity securities 80

The loss decreases income by $80 for the period. The credit entry is made directly to the investment account (not to the allowance account). Since the decline in value for Apple was deemed to be permanent, the new cost basis for this investment is 20 shares × $7 per share, or $140. Even if the market value of the stock should increase above $7 per share in the future, Tree Corporation will not record the increase.

Continuing the example, suppose that in August 1992, Tree Corporation unexpectedly sells 5 shares of Pear for $24 per share cash. Since the original cost of this investment was $15 per share, Alex will record a realized gain on the transaction of $45:

Cash (5 × $24) 120
    Long-term investments in equity securities (5 × $15) 75
    Gain on sale of equity securities [5 × ($24 − $15)] 45

Finally, suppose that at December 31, 1992, the market value per share for the two investments is as follows:

Pear common stock . . . . $22 per share
Apple common stock . . . . $5 per share

Again the aggregate cost and aggregate market value of the long-term investment portfolio must be computed. The original cost was $370, but there was a permanent reduction in the value of Apple common stock of $140. Also, Tree sold 5 shares of Pear common, which had an original cost of $15 per share. These transactions have reduced the cost of the portfolio to $215:

Original aggregate cost of portfolio $370
Less: Permanent impairment writedown . . . . . (80)
Less: Cost of securities sold . . . . (75)
Remaining aggregate cost of portfolio $215

The aggregate market value is determined as follows:

Pear common stock   5 × $22 = $110
Apple common stock   20 × $5 = 100
      Total $210

The allowance needed to reduce the recorded cost to market for the portfolio is $215 less the market value of $210, or a total allowance of $5. Since the allowance

---

[7] Normal market fluctuations in security prices would not be considered a permanent impairment. There is little guidance in the literature in defining a permanent impairment of value. In general it must result from a significant economic event that permanently affects (decreases) the value of the investee.

was established at $10 in 1991, Tree must now reverse $5 of the allowance ($10 less the correct amount of $5) to establish the correct allowance balance:

Allowance to reduce long-term investments
in equity securities to market 5
        Unrealized loss on long-term
        investments in equity securities   5

With this entry, a portion of the write-down that was made in 1991 is reversed. However, neither the original write-down nor the reversal has any effect on net income since neither entry affects any income statement account. The unrealized loss account for these long-term investments is a contra account to stockholders' equity.

Very few equity-decreasing and equity-increasing items are recorded directly to the stockholders' equity section rather than flowing through the income statement. Unrealized losses (and unrealized loss recoveries) on long-term marketable equity securities are one type of item that is treated this way.

The presentation of the Tree Corporation financial statements would be as follows:

	1991	1992
Income statement:		
Investment revenue:	$ 20	0
Loss in market value of long-term investments	0	($80)
Gain on sale of long-term investments	0	45

Balance sheet—December 31:	1991	1992
Investments of equity securities, at cost	$370	$215
Less: Allowance to reduce equity		
securities to market	(10)	(5)
Investment portfolio at LCM	$360	$210
Stockholders' equity:		
Unrealized capital loss:		
Unrealized loss on long-term		
investments in equity securities	(10)	(5)

The 1988 annual report of Hecla Mining Company given in Exhibit 14–2 is an example of the disclosure that is made when there is a write-down for a long-term equity investment.

Change in Classification between Short-Term and Long-Term for Marketable Equity Securities

It is possible for management to change the classification of an investment from current to noncurrent, or visa-versa. When this happens, the security involved must be reclassified on the balance sheet. *SFAS No. 12,* par. 10, specifies that the security be transferred between the two portfolios at the lower of cost or market value at the date of transfer. If market is lower than cost, the new cost basis for the security will be the market value. The difference is accounted for as if it were a *realized loss* and included in the determination of net income.

Example Suppose Tree Corporation in the example decides as of January 30, 1993, to reclassify its holdings of 20 shares of Apple, Inc. from long-term to short-term. Recall that Apple was originally acquired at $11 per share, but during 1992 there was a permanent impairment of value, and a loss was recognized to reduce the cost basis of the holdings to $7 per share. Assume the market price at January 30, 1993, is $6 per share.

Tree would make the following entry to record the change in classification:

Investments in short-term equity securities (20 × $6) 120
Realized loss on reclassification of equity securities 20
        Investments in long-term equity securities (20 × $7)   140

EXHIBIT 14-2   Write-Down of Long-Term Equity Investment, Hecla Mining Company

($ in thousands)	1988	1987
Total current assets	$ 29,984	$ 31,459
Investments (Note 3)	15,915	13,025
Properties, plants and equipment, net	135,707	122,492
Other noncurrent assets	7,246	3,740
Total assets	$188,852	$170,716

Note 3 (In Part): Investments
Investments consist of the following components (*in thousands*):

	Carrying Value	Cost	Market Value
December 31, 1988			
Marketable equity securities	$ 6,613	$17,300	$6,613
Other investments	9,302	9,302	
Total	$15,915	$26,602	
December 31, 1987			
Marketable equity securities	$ 7,155	$15,630	$7,155
Other investments	5,870	5,870	
Total	$13,025	$21,500	

At December 31, 1988, the portfolio of marketable equity securities includes gross unrealized gains of approximately $3,000 and gross unrealized losses of approximately $10,690,000 (of which approximately $9,625,000 is attributable to the Company's ownership of Sunshine Mining Company common stock). The other investments are principally large blocks of common and preferred stock in several mining companies, and investments in various mining ventures. These securities are generally restricted as to trading or marketability, although some of the shares are frequently traded on the over-the-counter market in Spokane, Washington, and certain Canadian exchanges. At December 31, 1988 and 1987, the shares of some of these companies that were traded on these markets were quoted at values approximating or exceeding the Company's cost basis.

($ in thousands)	1988	1987
Shareholders' Equity:		
Preferred stock, 25¢ par value, authorized 5,000,000 shares none issued		
Common stock, 25¢ par value, authorized 50,000,000 shares, issued 1988— 27,044,812, and 1987—27,040,832	$ 6,761	$ 6,760
Additional paid-in capital	53,326	53,286
Earnings retained in the business	94,071	80,292
Net unrealized loss on marketable equity securities (Note 3)	(10,687)	(8,475)
Less common stock required, at cost; 1988—40,999 shares, 1987—38,539 shares	(611)	(571)
Total shareholders' equity	$142,860	$131,292

No adjustment is needed to the allowance account or to the contra account in stockholders' equity relating to the long-term investment portfolio, as the appropriate adjustments will be made when the LCM method is applied to the long-term investment at year-end.

The Cost Method of Accounting for Nonmarketable, Long-Term Equity Securities

At this point it is appropriate to briefly describe how an equity security is accounted for when it is not readily marketable, and the investor does not have significant influence. When a market value is not determinable, the LCM method cannot be applied. Securities that are not readily marketable and that do not qualify for the equity method are accounted for using the cost method. Under the cost method, the investment is carried at the original investment amount, and investment revenue is the dividends received from the investee. Gains and losses on the investment are recorded when realized, which is when the investment is sold. There are no market values to compare with cost; thus, there are no determinations or any entries for recording unrealized losses. This is the difference between the cost method and the LCM method.

Prior to the issuance of *SFAS No. 12*, nearly all short-term equity investments and those long-term investments not qualifying for the equity method were accounted for using the cost method.

CONCEPT REVIEW

1. How are unrealized losses computed under the LCM method when a portfolio of investments is classified as long-term? How are they treated for accounting purposes for short-term equity investments?
2. Explain the accounting entries that are made when a short-term equity investment is reclassified as long-term and its current market value is less than its cost. What effect will this transaction (by itself) have on any amounts in the allowance account?
3. What is an unrealized loss recovery? How is it treated for accounting purposes when it is related to a short-term marketable equity investment? to a long-term marketable equity investment?

EQUITY METHOD FOR LONG-TERM EQUITY INVESTMENTS

The **equity method** of accounting for long-term investments is not appropriate for the investments discussed above because the investor did not own enough voting shares to be able to exercise significant influence or control. *APB No. 18* specifies that the equity method is used when the investor has significant influence or control.

Conceptual Basis of the Equity Method

For the investor, the LCM method and the equity method are different because they are based on different concepts of investment revenue and investment valuation. The conceptual difference is that under the LCM method the investor and the investee are viewed as two separate companies. In contrast, the equity method views the investor and the investee as a special type of single entity. *APB No. 18* gives the accounting guidelines for the equity method.[8]

The *single entity* concept underlying the equity method requires that the investor's investment and investment revenue be measured as follows:

1. End-of-period investment account balance equals:
    a. Beginning of period investment account balance.
    b. *Plus* proportionate share of investee's income for the period.
    c. *Minus* proportionate share of investee's dividends paid during the period.
    d. *Minus* adjustments of investee's reported income for the period.
2. Investment revenue for the period equals:
    a. Proportionate share of investee's income for the period.
    b. *Minus* adjustments of investee's reported income for the period.

It is important to distinguish between *voting* and *nonvoting* shares of equity stocks. With voting shares an investor can exercise some influence over the financial policies of the investee corporation. The proportion of voting shares owned deter-

---

[8] *APB No. 18* states that income and owners' equity amounts should be the same whether a subsidiary is consolidated or accounted for by the equity method. A discussion of the principles of consolidation is found in Appendix 14A.

mines the extent or degree of influence or control. For example, if the investor owns more than 50% of the outstanding voting shares, the investor can exercise control over the investee. With less than 50% but still a "large ownership" interest, the investor is deemed to be able to exercise "significant influence."

APB No. 18 also sets forth procedures for reporting under the equity method. The procedures include:

* The investment in common stock is shown in the balance sheet of the investor as a single amount, and the investor's share of the investee's earnings or losses is shown in the income statement of the investor as a single amount except for the items reported below income from continuing operations.
* The investor's share of the investee's extraordinary items and prior period adjustments are reported by the investor in conformity with *APB No. 30* and *SFAS No. 16.* Specifically, the investor classifies such items in a manner similar to its own items reported below income from continuing operations and prior period adjustments.
* Gains and losses on sale of the investee's stock are accounted for as the difference between the selling price and the carrying amount of the stock sold.
* Intercompany profits and losses are eliminated.
* Any difference between the cost of an investment and the market value of the underlying net assets of an investee (i.e., goodwill) is amortized according to the requirements of *APB Opinion No. 17.*

Equity Method Illustrated

The application of the procedures described above can best be demonstrated with an example. On January 2, 1992, Giant Company purchased 3,600 shares of the 18,000 outstanding common shares of Small Corporation for $300,000 cash. Two Giant senior executives were voted on to the Small Corporation board of directors. Giant is deemed to be able to exercise significant influence over Small's operating and financial policies. The equity method of accounting for the investment is appropriate.

At the acquisition of the 20% interest in Small, Giant would record its investment as follows:

Investment in Small, at equity 300,000
Cash   300,000

Suppose the balance sheet for Small at January 2, 1992, and estimated the market values of its assets and liabilities were as follows:

	Book Value	Market Value	Difference
Cash and receivables	$ 100,000	$ 100,000	$ 0
Inventory (FIFO basis)	400,000	405,000	5,000
Plant and equipment (10-year life)	500,000	700,000	200,000
Land	150,000	165,000	15,000
Total assets	$1,150,000	$1,370,000	$220,000
Liabilities	$ 150,000	$ 150,000	$ 0
Stockholders' equity	1,000,000	1,220,000	220,000
Total liabilities & equity	$1,150,000	$1,370,000	$220,000

The net book value of the claim Giant has on Small is 20% times Small's stockholders' equity ($1,000,000), or $200,000. Since Giant paid $300,000 for its interest in Small, what was acquired to justify the purchase price being $100,000 greater than book value? If items can be identified whose market value is greater than their net book value, the $100,000 premium over book value will be allocated to these items in accordance with the equity method.

The market value information presented above shows several specific assets where the market value exceeds book value. Giant acquired a portion (20%) of each of these items, including the amount by which market value exceeds book value:

	Book Value	Market Value	Difference	20% of Difference
Inventory	$400,000	$405,000	$ 5,000	$ 1,000
Plant and equipment (10-year remaining life)	500,000	700,000	200,000	40,000
Land	150,000	165,000	15,000	3,000
Excess value of assets acquired by Giant				$44,000

Thus, $44,000 of the $100,000 purchase price premium over book value that was paid by Giant is identified with the above specific assets. The remaining difference, $56,000, cannot be specifically identified with any asset. It will be termed goodwill. Recall from Chapter 13 that goodwill is the excess of the amount invested in acquiring all or a portion of another firm over the fair value of the net identifiable assets acquired. The direct computation of goodwill is as follows:

Computation of Goodwill Purchased by Giant Company

Purchase price (of 20% interest)		$300,000
Market value of identifiable assets	$1,370,000	
Less: Liabilities of Small	(150,000)	
Total market value of identifiable net assets acquired	$1,220,000	
Market value of 20% of identifiable net assets acquired:		
($1,220,000 × .20)		$244,000
Purchased goodwill		$ 56,000

To summarize, Giant has acquired a 20% interest in Small at a cost of $300,000. The items acquired can be represented as follows:

20% of book value of Small	$200,000
20% of excess of market value over book value for:	
Inventory (20% × 5,000)	1,000
Plant and equipment (20% × 200,000)	40,000
Land (20% × 15,000)	3,000
Purchased goodwill	56,000
Total	$300,000

The equity method requires that Giant account for the $300,000 investment in Small as is detailed above. Thus, when Small disposes of any of the above items, either in the normal course of business or by asset sales, Giant must record the appropriate adjustments to its investment account. For example, since Small uses the FIFO method of costing its inventory, the beginning inventory will be sold during the coming year. Likewise, the plant and equipment of Small will be used and depreciated during the coming year. Since the valuation of these items from Giant's perspective is different from that recorded by Small, Giant will need to record adjustments to reflect the using up of the difference between the market value and the book value of these assets.

Thus, assuming all of Small's beginning inventory is sold during 1992, cost of goods sold for 1992 is understated by Small by $1,000 from the single entity (Giant) perspective. Also, depreciation is understated. If the plant and equipment has a remaining useful life of 10 years and Small uses straight-line depreciation, Giant will need to increase the depreciation expense for Small by $40,000 divided by 10 years, or $4,000 each year for the next 10 years. Finally, the goodwill must be amortized, as was discussed in Chapter 13, over a period of 40 years or less. Assuming Giant amortizes goodwill over the maximum period, the annual charge for goodwill amortization will be $56,000 divided by 40, or $1,400 each year for the next 40 years. These are the types of adjustments referred to by items 1 (*d*) and 2 (*b*) on page 708.

No adjustments need be made for the excess of market value over book value for the land. Only if Small disposes of the land would an adjustment need to be made, showing that the cost of 20% of the land from the Giant perspective is understated by $3,000. Giant's proportionate share of any gain (loss) on disposal of the land would be decreased (increased) by $3,000.

When Giant records investment revenue from its investment in Small, it makes adjusting entries to reflect the above analysis.

Suppose that for the fiscal year ending December 31, 1992, Small reports the following:

Income before extraordinary items	$ 80,000
Extraordinary item	30,000
Net income	$110,000
Cash dividends paid on December 31	$ 50,000

At December 31, Giant would make the following entries to reflect its interest in the earnings of Small:

1. To recognize investment revenue based on Giant's proportionate share of income reported by Small:

Investment in Small, at equity (110,000 × .20)	22,000	
Investment revenue (80,000 × .20)		16,000
Extraordinary gain (30,000 × .20)		6,000

2. To record additional costs of goods sold associated with the excess of market value over book value of inventory at the acquisition of Small:

Investment revenue	1,000	
Investment in Small, at equity		1,000

3. To record depreciation on the $40,000 of depreciable assets implicit in the purchase price paid for Small:

Investment revenue ($40,000 ÷ 10 years)	4,000	
Investment in Small, at equity		4,000

4. To record periodic amortization of goodwill:

Investment revenue ($56,000 ÷ 40 years)	1,400	
Investment in Small, at equity		1,400

5. To record the receipt of cash dividends paid by Small:

Cash ($50,000 × .20)	10,000	
Investment in Small, at equity		10,000

After these entries are posted, the balance in the investment in Small account would be $305,600:

Beginning balance (acquisition price)	$300,000
Proportionate share of Small's net income	22,000
Additional cost of goods sold adjustment	(1,000)
Additional depreciation adjustment	(4,000)
Amortization of goodwill	(1,400)
Dividends received	(10,000)
Investment account balance, Dec. 31	$305,600

The investment revenue for 1992, after all the adjustments, is $9,600 of ordinary income plus an extraordinary item of $6,000:

Investment revenue (ordinary):
Proportionate share of Small net income	$16,000
Additional cost of goods adjustment	(1,000)
Additional depreciation adjustment	(4,000)
Amortization of goodwill	(1,400)
	$ 9,600

Extraordinary gain:
Extraordinry gain (as recorded by Small)	6,000
Total investment revenue (ordinary and extraordinary)	$15,600

The total investment income Giant reports from its investment in Small is $15,600. Since Giant received $10,000 of this in the form of cash dividends, the net increase of its investment is $5,600. This increase is shown in the investment account from the beginning to the end of the year.

Summary of the Equity Method   Equity basis accounting for investments in equity securities can become complex because the investor firm must maintain records outside its own accounting records on transactions of the investee firm, and make the appropriate adjusting entries at the appropriate time. In general, six types of entries are involved in accounting for an investment under the equity method.

1. Record the proportionate share of the investee's reported income. This is a debit to the investment account, and a credit to investment revenue (also often labeled "equity in the earnings of equity-based companies"). If the investee firm reports extraordinary items, the investor firm must separately report these items. The concept being applied is that the investee and the investor firms are a single entity, at least with respect to the portion of the investee firm owned by the investor firm.

2. Record any dividends paid by the investee firm as a debit to cash and a credit to the investment account. The dividends are not income, but rather are a conversion of a portion of the investment to cash. Dividends represent a liquidation of the investment.

3. Record the proportionate share of additional expense items related to the investor's cost of the investment over the proportionate share of the book value of the investee firm. In the above example, these included the cost of goods sold and the depreciation adjustments. These entries are made to adjust the investment account and the investment revenue. These entries can be complex and are covered in considerable detail in most advanced accounting textbooks.[9]

4. Record the amortization of any purchased goodwill. Since the goodwill is associated with the investment, it is recorded as a debit to the investment revenue account and a credit to the investment account. There is no goodwill separately identified on the books of the investor firm; the purchased goodwill is included in the investment acount.

5. Record any gain or loss on the sale of portions of the investment. The gain or loss is the difference between the sale proceeds from disposing of the shares and the carrying amount of the investment. The gain or loss on disposal is separately identified in the income statement accounts of the investor firm.

6. Eliminate any intercompany gains or losses arising from transactions between the investor and investee firms. This topic is covered in more detail in Appendix 14A,

---

[9] For example, consider the complications that would arise in the example had Small been using LIFO rather than FIFO for inventory costing. In this instance, the additional cost would have been assigned to various layers of the inventory and would have been an expense adjustment only when those layers were sold.

and in more detail in advanced accounting textbooks. The basic concept being applied is the perspective that (*a*) the investor and investee are a single entity and (*b*) an entity should not earn profits in transactions with itself. Thus, when the investor firm sells an asset to the investee firm (or vice versa) at a profit, the item is carried on the books of the investee at its cost. Its cost, however, is the original cost of the item as was recorded on the books of the selling firm plus the profit that the selling firm records. The profit recorded by the selling firm (in this example, the investor) must be eliminated.

Consider a simple example. Suppose Giant sells land to Small. The land had originally cost Giant $10,000, and the sales price to Small is $15,000. Giant makes the following entry to record the disposal of land:

Cash (or Accounts receivable) 15,000		
Land	10,000	
Gain on disposal	5,000	

The land will be recorded by Small at a cost of 15,000, but for the single entity of Giant and Small combined, the land had an original cost of $10,000. To adjust and remove the profit recorded by Giant, the following entry is made at closing (in the year the land is sold):

Gain on disposal 5,000	
Investment in Small	5,000

With this entry, the profit that would otherwise have been reported by Giant is eliminated. The credit is to the investment account because Small has paid $5,000 more to Giant than the original cost of the land. This additional payment is analogous to a dividend, and dividends paid by the investee to the investor are credited to the investment account.

The equity basis method is a modified cost basis method. The investment account is carried at original cost plus the investor's equity in the undistributed earnings of the investee. While the notion of lower of cost or market does not appear to be applicable, nonetheless, some firms do indicate that their equity basis investments are carried at the lower of cost or market.

CONCEPT REVIEW

1. Conceptually, what are the components of the carrying amount recorded in an investments account under the equity method?
2. What are the components of investment revenue under the equity method?
3. How are dividends received by the investor firm from the investee firm recorded under the cost method? Under the equity method?

Changing between the LCM Method and the Equity Method

The ownership level or level of influence an investor company has in or over an investee company can change over time. For example, an investor company using the LCM method might acquire more shares of the investee, thereby gaining sufficient shares to have significant influence. The investor firm would then be required to account for its investment using the equity method. Alternatively, an investor accounting for an investee using the equity method might sell some of its holdings, or the investee might issue shares to parties other than the investor. The result in either case could be that the investor no longer meets the requirements of the equity method. In this case, the accounting would change from the equity method to the LCM method. In this section the accounting for changes between the LCM method and the equity method are considered.

Changing *from* the Equity Method to the LCM Method   When the ownership level or the level of influence an investor has over an investee currently accounted for on the equity basis falls below what is deemed necessary to continue this method, a change must be made to the LCM method. In making the change, the currently recorded carrying amount for the investment becomes the cost basis of the investment. That is, any previously recorded equity in earnings (or losses) included in the balance in the investment account remains a part of the cost of the investment when the change is made to the LCM method.

Example   Suppose Raven Corp. acquired 25% of Owl Inc. on January 2, 1991, paying $1,000,000. At the time, the net book value of the interest Raven acquired in the net assets of Owl was $800,000, and the excess of cost over book value of net assets acquired ($200,000) is accounted for as goodwill. Raven amortizes goodwill over 20 years, therefore the amortization will be $10,000 per year. Owl has earnings of $600,000 and $800,000 in 1991 and 1992, respectively, and pays no dividends. The entries Raven would make to record the investment and to record recognition of its interest in the earnings of Owl in 1991 and 1992 would be as follows:

To record the initial investment:

Investment in Owl Corp.	1,000,000	
Cash		1,000,000

To record investment revenue in 1991:

Investment in Owl Corp.	150,000	
Equity in earnings of Owl Corp. (.25 × $600,000)		150,000

To record amortization of goodwill:

Equity in earnings of Owl Corp.	10,000	
Investment in Owl Corp.		10,000

To record investment revenue in 1992:

Investment in Owl Corp.	200,000	
Equity in earnings of Owl Corp. (.25 × $800,000)		200,000

To record amortization of goodwill:

Equity in earnings of Owl Corp.	10,000	
Investment in Owl Corp.		10,000

As of January 2, 1993, the investment in Owl Corp. account has a balance of $1.33 million ($1 million initial investment, plus equity in earnings of Owl Corp. for 1991 of $150,000 and for 1992 of $200,000, less two years of amortization totaling $20,000). Assume that on January 2, 1993, Owl Corp. issues additional shares of common stock and that after the issuance, Raven Company has an ownership interest of 15%. Assuming there is no evidence to the contrary, Raven no longer is deemed to have a significant influence over Owl, and would begin accounting for its investment in Owl using the LCM method. Any dividends received from Owl would be accounted for as investment revenue. If the aggregate market value of the portfolio of long-term equity investments were less than the aggregate cost, Raven would record the unrealized loss as a reduction in the carrying amount of the investments and a reduction from stockholders' equity. The cost of Owl Corp. used for computing the aggregate cost of the portfolio would be $1.33 million. As with any LCM investment, any dividends received in subsequent periods that exceed the amount of the investor's cumulative interest in the investee's earnings is accounted for as a reduction of the carrying amount of the investment account.

Changing *to* the Equity Method from the LCM Method At the time an investment qualifies for use of the equity method (after having been accounted for by the LCM method for one or more periods), *APB Opinion No. 18* (par. 19) requires that the investor firm adopt the equity method retroactively. That is, the investor must adjust the carrying amount, the results of operations for the current and other prior periods presented in the financial statements, and the retained earnings as if the equity method had been in effect for all previous periods.

Example On January 2, 1991, Right Corp. purchased 10% of the outstanding common shares of Wrong Company for $1 million. On that date, the net assets acquired of Wrong Company have a net book value of $700,000. The excess of the cost of the investment over the net book value of assets acquired ($300,000) is attributed to goodwill. Right amortizes goodwill over a 10 year period. On January 3, 1993, Right Corp. purchases an additional 15% of Wrong Company's common stock for $2 million. At that date the net book value of Wrong assets acquired is $1.35 million. With a total of a 25% interest in Wrong, Right must adopt the equity method of accounting for its investment in Wrong.

The net earnings and dividends paid by Wrong during the period 1991 through 1993 are as follows:

Year	Earnings	Dividends
1991	$ 800,000	$ 300,000
1992	2,000,000	500,000
1993	2,400,000	1,000,000

During 1991 and 1992, Right accounts for its investment in Wrong using LCM method. The carrying amount of the investment is maintained at the original investment of $1 million, and investment revenue of $30,000 and $50,000 (i.e., 10% of the dividends paid by Wrong each year) is recorded as investment revenue in 1991 and 1992, respectively. To restate the investment account as of January 2, 1993, on an equity basis, a schedule of how the account would have been affected for each prior year is computed:

	1991	1992	Total
Right Corp. equity in earnings of Wrong (10% of Wrong earnings)	$80,000	$200,000	$280,000
Less: Annual goodwill amortization	(30,000)	(30,000)	(60,000)
Equity in earnings after amortization	$50,000	$170,000	$220,000
Less: Dividends received	(30,000)	(50,000)	(80,000)
Adjustment to investment account	$20,000	$120,000	$140,000

To adjust the investment account to the equity basis at January 3, 1993, the total adjustment computed above is debited to the investment account, with the credit recorded as an adjustment to retained earnings:

Investment in Wrong Corp.	140,000	
Retained earnings		140,000

With the additional investment of $2 million on January 3, 1993, reflecting the purchase of an additional 15% of Wrong, the investment account becomes $3.14 million:

Original investment	$1,000,000
Adjustment to equity basis	140,000
Additional investment	2,000,000
Total at January 3, 1993	$3,140,000

During 1993, Right receives dividends from Wrong totaling $250,000 (25% of the total dividends of $1 million). These are recorded as a reduction in the carrying amount of the investment:

Cash	250,000	
Investment in Wrong Co.		250,000

At year-end, Right must determine the amount to record as its equity in the earnings of Wrong, including the appropriate amounts of amortization for the two acquisitions:

Right Corp. equity in earnings of Wrong Co.	
before amortizations ($2,400,000 × .25)	$600,000
Less: Amortization of goodwill resulting from 1991 acquisition	(30,000)
Less: Amortization of goodwill resulting from 1992 acquisition	
[($2,000,000 − $1,350,000)/10 years)]	(65,000)
Equity in earnings of Wrong Co.	$505,000

The entry to record equity in the earnings of Wrong for 1993 is:

Investment in Wrong Co.	505,000	
Equity in earnings of Wrong Co.		505,000

If Right Corp. includes an income statement for 1992 in its 1993 financial statements, the investment revenue it would show for its investment in Wrong would not be the $50,000 in dividends as previously reported, but rather 10% of Wrong Company earnings ($200,000) less amortization of $30,000, or $170,000. All financial statements presented by Right are restated to show the investment in Wrong on the equity basis.

Disclosures Required for Long-Term Investments in Equity Securities

SFAS No. 12 specifies the disclosures required for all investments, whether short-term or long-term, that are accounted for by the LCM method. These requirements were listed and illustrated in the section discussing short-term equity investments. Exhibit 14–1 illustrates the disclosures for investments in equity securities under the LCM requirements of *SFAS No. 12*.

Investments accounted for using the equity method have a different set of required disclosures, which are detailed in *APB Opinion No. 18:*

1. Disclose parenthetically in notes or in separate schedules:
    a. The name of each investee and percentage ownership.
    b. The accounting policies of the investor with respect to investments in common stock.
    c. The difference, if any, between the amount at which an investment is carried and the amount of underlying equity in net assets, and the accounting treatment of the difference.
2. For those investments in common stock for which a quoted market price is available, the aggregate value of each identified investment based on the quoted market price.
3. When investments accounted for under the equity method are, in the aggregate, material in relation to the financial position or results of operations of an investor, it may be necessary for summarized information regarding assets, liabilities, and results of operations of the investee to be presented.[10]

---

[10] See AICPA, *APB Opinion No. 18,* "The Equity Method of Accounting for Investments of Common Stock" (New York, May 1971), par. 20.

Investments accounted for by the equity method often are a substantial holding for the investor, and as such require the extensive disclosures outlined above. Exhibit 14–3 contains excerpts from the financial statements of The Washington Post Company relating to its investments in equity-based companies.

MARKET VALUE METHOD FOR EQUITY SECURITIES

Yet another method of accounting for marketable equity securities is the **market value method**. It is an option only for those firms whose primary lines of business include investing in the securities of others. Some specialized industries, such as investment companies, stock life insurance companies, fire and casualty insurance companies, and brokers and dealers in securities, are permitted by *SFAS No. 12* to carry equity securities at market with unrealized gains and losses being classified in the equity accounts. This section discusses the accounting procedures of the market value method.

The market value method is fundamentally different from the cost or the equity methods. The market value method is based on the concept of *current value accounting,* not historical cost accounting. Under this method, each individual security investment is revalued at each financial statement date to the current market value of the securities held. The LCM concept is not applied with the market value method.

The market value is summarized as follows:

1. At date of acquisition, investments are recorded at cost in conformity with the cost principle.
2. After acquisition, each individual investment account balance is adjusted at the end of the accounting year to the current market value of the securities held. The adjusted amount then becomes the new carrying value for subsequent accounting.
3. Cash and property dividends declared and paid are recognized by the investor as investment revenue.
4. Increases or decreases in the market value of the equity securities are recognized at the end of each accounting period. One of the following approaches is used:
   a. *Current approach*—The price change during the current period is recognized as investment revenue (or loss) in the current income statement. It would be clearly labeled as the increase or decrease in market value.
   b. *Deferral approach*—The price change during the current period is recorded as a deferred item in owners' equity, labeled as unrealized market gain or loss. When a security is subsequently sold, the difference between its carrying value in the investment account and its original cost must be removed from its deferred status in the unrealized account and recognized as investment revenue or loss. Any additional difference is recognized as gain or loss on sale of investments.
5. At disposal of the investment, the difference between the carrying value at that date and its sale price is recognized as a gain or loss on disposal.

Illustration of Market Value Method for Equity Securities

Current Approach   Assume that on January 1, 1991, Intel Company purchased, as a long-term investment, 1,000 shares of common stock of Decca Corporation for $25 per share. Following the cost principle, Intel would record the investment:

Investment in Decca common stock 25,000
Cash   25,000

At December 31, 1991, assume the market price of Decca Corporation stock is $20 per share, and Decca's reported net income is $80,000. Decca pays no dividends in 1991. Under the market value method, the carrying amount for the investment is increased (decreased) by increases (decreases) in market value of the securities.

EXHIBIT 14-3   Excerpts from Financial Statements of The Washington Post Company Relating to Investments.

Reported on the balance sheet, immediately after current assets:

	1988 (000)	1987 (000)
Investments in affiliates	$163,250	$152,636

Reported on the income statement:

	1988	1987
Equity in earnings of affiliated companies	$19,114	$17,663

NOTES TO CONSOLIDATED FINANCIAL STATEMENTS:

Note A (In Part). Summary of Significant Accounting Policies

Investments in Affiliates. The company uses the equity method of accounting for its investments in and earnings of affiliates.

Note D (In Part). Investments in Affiliates

The company's investments in affiliates at January 1, 1989, and January 3, 1988, consists of the following (in thousands):

	1988	1987
Cowles Media Company	$ 78,399	$ 77,512
Newsprint mills	80,269	68,656
Other	4,582	6,468
Total	$163,250	$152,636

The company's investments in affiliates in 1988 include a 26 percent interest in the stock of Cowles Media Company, which owns and operates the *Minneapolis Star and Tribute* and several other smaller properties. In 1987 and 1988 the company owned a 21 percent interest.

The company's interest in newsprint mills includes a 49 percent interest in the common stock of Bowater Mersey Paper Company Limited, which owns and operates a newsprint mill in Nova Scotia; a one-third limited partnership interest in Bear Island Paper Company, which owns and operates a newsprint mill near Richmond, Virginia; and a one-third partnership interest in Bear Island Timberlands Company, which owns timberlands and supplies Bear Island Paper Company with a major portion of its wood requirements. Operating costs and expenses of the company include costs of newsprint supplied by Bowater Mersey Paper Company and Bear Island Paper Company of $71,400,000 in 1988, $63,300,000 in 1987, and $61,400,000 in 1986.

During 1983 the company acquired interests in several businesses that distribute programming, principally sports events, to pay cable and subscription television subscribers. During 1986 and a portion of 1987, the company's interests included a 33.5 percent partnership in SportsChannel Prism Associates, which operates in the metropolitan Philadelphia area; and 33.3 percent partnership interest in SportsChannel Chicago Associates, which operates in the Chicago area; and a 6.7 percent limited partnership interest in SportsChannel New England, which operates in the New England and upstate New York areas. In August 1987, the company sold its interest in each of the four sports programming businesses.

The company's other investments include a one-third common stock interest in a French corporation based in Paris that publishes the *International Herald Tribune* [the description and information disclosed continues in the same manner as in the above two paragraphs].

Summarized financial data for the affiliates' operations are as follows (in thousands):

	1988	1987	1986
Financial position:			
Working capital	$ 17,185	$100,100	$ 98,485
Property, plant, and equipment	456,160	370,761	380,518
Total assets	694,751	642,374	676,831
Long-term debt	263,773	129,651	155,033
Net equity	226,160	339,905	316,419
Results of operations			
Operating revenues	$662,691	$616,387	$640,353
Operating income	91,957	78,972	81,442
Net income	54,914	53,439	44,356

EXHIBIT 14-3 *(concluded)*

The following summarizes the status and results of the company's investments in affiliates (in thousands):

	1988	1987
Beginning investment	$152,636	$168,421
Equity in earnings	19,114	17,663
Dividends received	(1,803)	(1,638)
Additional investments	599	5,927
Sale of investments	(1,806)	(27,004)
Other	(5,490)	(10,733)
Ending investment	$163,250	$152,636

At January 1, 1989, the unamortized excess of the company's investments over its equity in the underlying net assets of its affiliates at the date of acquisition was approximately $71,000,000, which is being amortized over 40 years. Amortization included in equity in earnings of affiliates for the years ended January 1, 1989, January 3, 1988, and December 28, 1986, was $1,150,000, $1,900,000, and $2,300,000, respectively.

Under the current approach, the change in market value is included in income in the current period. Thus, the entry to be made by Intel at December 31 would record the decrease in market value for Decca:

Investment loss, market price loss on investments
(1,000) × ($25 − $20) 5,000
    Investment in Decca   5,000

Suppose, further, that Decca pays dividends of $1 per share in October 1992. At December 31, 1992, the Decca reports net income of $65,000, and at that date the market price of Decca common stock is $22 per share. Intel must record both the receipt of dividends and the change in market value:

Cash (dividends received) 1,000
    Investment revenue (1,000 × $1)   1,000

Investment in Decca 2,000
    Investment revenue, market price gain on investments
    (1,000) × ($22 − $20)   2,000

Finally, assume Intel sells 400 shares of the Decca common in November 1993 for $26 per share. Since the investment in Decca is currently carried at $22 per share, the entry to record the sale is as follows:

Cash (400 × $26) 10,400
    Investment in Decca (400 × $22)   8,800
    Gain on sale of investments   1,600

Deferral Approach If the deferral approach were used in the above analysis, only the dividends received from Decca would be recorded as investment revenue. The various market value change amounts recorded above as either investment revenue or investment loss would be recorded as unrealized gain/loss on investment, but they would *not* be closed to the income statement. Instead, they would be included in the stockholders' equity section of the balance sheet (called "unrealized market gain/loss on investments"). When the shares are sold, the amount recorded in the unrealized market gain/loss account would be recognized. Thus, when Intel sold the 400 shares in November 1993, the entry to record the sale under the deferral method would be:

Cash (400 × $26) 10,400
Investment loss, market value change 1,200
    Unrealized market gain/loss on investments[11] (400 × $3) . . .   1,200
    Investment in Decca (400 × $22)   8,800
    Gain on sale of investments (400 × $4)   1,600

Both the current approach and the deferral approach result in the same carrying value for the investment. The deferral approach delays the actual recognition of any gain or loss in market value until the securities are sold. That is, the gain or loss is deferred until it is realized.

Some accountants believe that investments in all marketable equity securities, whether short-term or long-term, should be accounted for using the market value method. They contend that market value data:

1. Report the economic consequences of holding the investment.
2. Are more useful to decision makers than cost or equity data in projecting future cash flows.
3. Are objectively determinable for many stocks.
4. Avoid the LCM asymmetric treatment for market when it is above cost.
5. Prevent the opportunity to manage earnings through the sale of selected investments acquired at a low original cost with a high market value, followed later by a repurchase.[12]

Many arguments have been advanced against the valuation of marketable equity securities at market value. The principal arguments cited against the market value method are:

1. It violates the cost principle and places on the balance sheet values that may not be objectively determined and may be temporary.
2. It violates the traditional revenue principle because revenue recognition is based on market value changes rather than on a sale.
3. Because of the volatility of some stock prices, it introduces a vacillating effect on the balance sheet and on reported income.

To summarize, the market value method is not an option for firms other than those in selected specialized industries. It has conceptual appeal to many accountants, but it has been viewed as too radical a departure from the cost principle to be adopted for all marketable equity security investments.

CONCEPT REVIEW

1. How does the market value method differ from the cost method with respect to the carrying amount recorded for the investment? For the amount recorded as investment revenue?
2. Describe the difference between the current approach and the deferral approach under the market value approach.
3. What disclosures are required for long-term investments in equity securities accounted for under the equity method?

---

[11] This is the amount in the unrealized gain/loss account, which is a contra (debit balance) account in shareholders' equity, which relates to the shares sold. The amount equals the current beginning-of-period carrying amount, $22 per share, less the original cost, $25 per share, times the number of shares sold: [($22 − $25) × 400]. The amount of $1,,200 is removed from the holding account and recognized as investment loss since it is realized with the sale of the 400 shares.

[12] Variants of this view are presented by W. Morris and B. Coda, "Valuation of Equity Securities," *Journal of Accountancy*, January 1973, pp. 48-54, and by W. Beaver, "Accounting for Marketable Equity Securities," *Journal of Accountancy*, December 1973, pp. 58-64.

Disclosures of Market Values of Financial Instruments

In December 1990, the FASB issued an *Exposure Draft* that, if issued as a *Statement,* will require additional disclosures about the various investments of a firm. It does not, however, alter the accounting procedures used to account for investments. The proposed *Statement* will require all entities to disclose information about the market value of all financial instruments (with several specific exceptions) for which it is practicable to estimate market values. This proposed statement will significantly affect the disclosures of financial institutions, as these organizations invest extensively in various types of financial instruments.

Definition of Financial Instrument   In addition to cash, a **financial instrument** is defined as either one of the following:

1. Includes evidence of ownership in an entity.
2. A contract that:
   a. Obligates a firm to deliver cash or another financial instrument to a second firm, or to exchange financial instruments on potentially unfavorable terms, and
   b. Conveys to the second firm the right to receive cash or another financial instrument from the first firm, or to exchange instruments on potentially favorable terms.

Evidence of ownership includes all forms of equity securities. The second part of the definition includes all forms of debt securities. Thus, the proposed *Statement* will require a firm to disclose information about the market values of all the investments it holds, assuming it is *practicable* to estimate the market value of the financial instrument. The best evidence of market value would come from quoted market prices. If quoted market prices are not available, management is to develop an estimated market price based, for example, on quoted market prices of a financial instrument with similar characteristics, or estimate the market value using valuation techniques such as those described in Chapter 6. Other possible estimation techniques include the use of option pricing models and matrix pricing models. The proposed *Statement* does state that excessive costs in developing estimates are an acceptable reason for not computing and presenting market values.

The market values of financial instruments for which it is practicable to estimate are to be disclosed either in the body of the financial statements or in the accompanying notes. The result of this proposed *Statement* will be increased disclosure for long-term investments, both in equity and debt securities, of the market values of these investments. For example, the note from The Washington Post Company annual report found in Exhibit 14–3 does not provide information on the market values of the several investments described. If the proposed *Statement* is adopted, it is likely that the firm will have to estimate the market value of these investments in future disclosures.

If enacted, the proposed *Statement* would be effective for financial statements issued for fiscal years ending after December 15, 1991, except for firms with less than $100 million in total assets at the latest balance sheet date. For these firms, the *Statement* would become effective for financial statements issued after December 15, 1992.

SPECIAL PROBLEMS IN ACCOUNTING FOR EQUITY INVESTMENTS
♦

Several special problems relating to the acquisition, holding, and sale of equity investments are discussed below under the following three headings:

1. Investment revenue—cash dividends and interest revenue.
2. Stock split of investment shares.
3. Stock rights on investment shares.

Investment Revenue

Cash dividends on short-term investments in capital stock of other companies are recognized as earned at the time of the declaration of the cash dividend. Cash dividends on capital stock held as an investment are not accrued prior to declaration. Stock dividends are not included as investment revenue.

To conserve cash and still make a distribution to stockholders, a corporation may issue a stock dividend. When a stock dividend is issued, the distributing corporation debits retained earnings and credits the appropriate capital stock accounts. The effect of a stock dividend from the issuing corporation's view is to capitalize a part of retained earnings. Significantly, a stock dividend does not decrease the assets of the issuing corporation.

From the investor's point of view, the nature of a stock dividend is suggested by the effect on the issuing corporation. The investor neither receives assets from the corporation nor owns more of the issuing corporation. The investor merely has more shares to represent the same prior proportional ownership. Thus, the receipt of a stock dividend in the same class of stock as already owned results, from the investor's viewpoint, in more shares but no increase in the cost (carrying value) of the holdings.

The investor should neither make an entry for revenue nor change the investment account other than to record a memorandum entry for the number of shares received. In case of a sale of any of the shares, a new cost per share is computed by adding the new shares to the old and dividing this sum into the carrying value.

Assume XYZ Company purchased 1,000 shares of common stock, par $5, of ABC Corporation at $90 per share. Subsequently, XYZ Company received a 50% common stock dividend. XYZ later sold 200 of the common shares at $75 per share. The entries would be:

At the acquisition date XYZ would record:

Long-term investment in equity securtities, ABC Corp.
(1,000 × $90) 90,000
    Cash 90,000

At date of stock dividend:

Memorandum entry only—Received 50% common stock dividend of 500 shares from ABC Corporation, revised cost per share: $90,000 ÷ (1,000 + 500 = 1,500 shares) = $60.

At the date of sale of 200 common shares:

Cash (200 × $75) 15,000
    Long-term investment in equity securities, ABC Corp.
    (200 × $60) 12,000
    Gain on sale of investments 3,000
(Remaining shares: 1,300 at $60 cost per share).

These procedures are followed for the cost, equity, and market value methods; the only difference in application is the total carrying value (i.e., cost, market, or equity amount). For all three methods, the appropriate total carrying value is divided by the new total number of shares owned to determine the carrying value per share after the stock dividend.

If the stock dividend is of a different class of stock than that on which the dividend is declared, such as preferred stock received as a dividend on common stock, or vice versa, three methods of accounting for the dividend are possible:

1. *Allocation method*—Record the new stock at an amount determined by allocating the carrying value of the old stock between the new stock and the old stock on the basis of the relative market values of the different classes of stock after issuance of the dividend.

EXHIBIT 14-4 Investor Accounting for a Stock Dividend in a Different Class of Stock

Case Data:

1. CD Corp. purchased 100 shares of JKL Company common stock at $75 per share (total cost, $7,500).
2. Some time later, CD Corp. received a stock dividend of 40 shares of JKL preferred stock with a market value of $2,500. At that time, the market value of the common stock was $10,000. Using the allocation method, the cost is apportioned, based on the total market value of $12,500, as follows:

$$\text{Cost allocated to common} = \$7,500 \times \frac{\$10,000}{\$12,500} = \$6,000 \text{ or } \$60 \text{ per share}$$

$$\text{Cost allocated to preferred} = \$7,500 \times \frac{\$2,500}{\$12,500} = \underline{1,500} \text{ or } \$37.50 \text{ per share}$$

Total cost allocated . . . . $\underline{\underline{\$7,500}}$

Entry to Record Receipt of Stock Dividend by CD Corp.:

Investment in preferred stock of JKL Company (40 × $37.50) 1,500
    Investment in common stock of JKL Company 1,500

2. *Noncost method*—Record the new stock in terms of shares only (as a memorandum entry). When it is sold, recognize the total sale price as a gain.
3. *Market value method*—Do not change the carrying value of the old stock. Instead, record the new stock at its market value upon receipt with an offsetting credit to dividend revenue. This method is based on the assumption that stock of a different class received as a dividend is similar to a property dividend.

The *allocation method* is the most consistent with the historical cost principal. The noncost method is considered to be conservative, and the market value method is seldom used. Exhibit 14–4 shows the application of the allocation method, which assigns the original cost to the two classes of stock. This method would be followed for the cost, equity, and market value methods, with the appropriate carrying value being allocated.

Interest receivable and interest revenue on investments in debt securities (e.g., bonds) are accrued at the end of the accounting period with an adjusting entry. Bonds and similar debt securities purchased at a price above par are acquired at a premium; if acquired below par, at a discount. Premium or discount on a long-term investment is amortized. However, on a short-term investment in bonds, the discount (or premium) is not amortized because, by definition, the investment will be converted to cash in the near future.

Stock Split of Investment Shares

Although a stock split is different from a stock dividend from the point of view of the issuer, the two are virtually identical from the point of view of the investor. In both cases, the investor has more shares than before the split or dividend, but with the same total cost as before.[13] To the investor, the accounting for a stock split is the same as for a stock dividend of the same class as already owned. Only a *memorandum entry* is made to record the number of new shares received, and the cost (or carrying value) per share is recomputed.

---

[13] In a reverse split, such as a two-for-three split, the number of outstanding shares is reduced rather than increased. Reverse stock splits are rare.

Stock Rights on Investment Shares

The privilege given stockholders (investors) of purchasing additional shares of stock from the issuing corporation at a specific price (called an *option price*) and by a specified date is commonly known as a *stock right*. The certificate evidencing one or more rights is called a *stock warrant*.

The term stock right is usually interpreted as one right for each share of old stock. For example, a holder of two shares of stock who receives rights to subscribe for one new share is said to own two stock rights rather than one. There is one right per old share regardless of the entitlement of the right. In this case, each right entitles the holder to purchase one half of a share. Rights have value when the holder can buy shares through exercise of the rights at a lower price per share than on the open market. As the spread between the option price and the market price changes subsequent to issuance of the rights, the value of the rights changes.

When the intention to issue stock rights is declared, the stock with the rights sells "rights on." The market price of the share includes the value of the share and the value of a right. After the rights are issued, the shares will sell in the market "ex rights." Also, after issuance, rights usually have a separate market from that of the related stock. They will be separately quoted at a specific market price. After rights are received, the investor has shares of stock and stock rights.

To determine the gain or loss on the sale of either the stock or the rights, it is necessary to allocate the total cost of the investment between the stock and the rights. This allocation usually is based on relative market values; that is, the total cost of the old shares is allocated between the old stock and the rights in proportion to their relative market values at the time the rights are issued.

Example   Assume Garfield Company purchased 500 shares of Franklin Corporation common stock at $93 per share, a total investment of $46,500. The entry to record the investment is:

Investment—Franklin Corporation common stock	46,500	
Cash		46,500

Later, Garfield Company receives 500 stock rights that entitles it to acquire 100 shares of Franklin Corporation common stock at a price of $100 per share. That is, each stock right represents one fifth of a share of Franklin Corporation common stock. At the date the Franklin Corporation common stock first trades ex rights, it had a market price of $120 per share, and each stock right had a market value of $4. To determine the allocation of the cost of the investment to the stock rights and the held common shares, the relative market values are used:

Total market value of common shares held: (500 × $120)	$60,000
Total market value of stock rights held: (500 × $4)	2,000
Total market value of investment	$62,000

$$\text{Cost to be allocated to investments in stock rights} = \frac{\$2,000}{\$62,000} \times \$46,500 = \$1,500$$

$$\text{Cost to be allocated to investment in common shares} = \frac{\$60,000}{\$62,000} \times \$46,500 = \$45,000$$

The cost per share of common stock is now $45,000/500 shares, or $90 per share, and the cost of the rights is $1,500/500 rights, or $3 per right.

The entry to record the receipt of the 500 stock rights for Franklin Corporation common stock is:

Investment—Franklin Corporation stock rights	1,500	
Investment—Franklin Corporation common stock		1,500

Suppose Garfield exercises 400 rights, acquires an additional 80 shares of Franklin at the exercises price of $100 per share, and sells the remaining 100 stock rights for $4.50 per right.

The entry to record the acquisition of these 80 shares through exercising the rights:

```
Investment—Franklin Corporation common stock  . . . . . . . . . .  9,200
        Investment—Franklin Corporation stock rights (400 × $3) . . .      1,200
        Cash  . . . . . . . . . . . . . . . . . . . . . . . . . . . . . .      8,000
```

The entry to record the sale of the 100 stock rights would be:

```
Cash (100 × $4.50)                                               450
        Investment—Franklin Corporation stock rights (100 × $3) . . .      300
        Gain on sale of stock rights . . . . . . . . . . . . . . . . . . .    150
```

The 80 shares of common stock acquired by exercising the stock rights have a total cost of $9,200, or $115 per share. If Franklin Corporation common stock is sold by Garfield, the firm must determine whether the original shares with a cost of $90 per share, or these newly acquired shares with cost of $115 per share, are sold.

If stock rights are not sold or exercised, they lapse. In this situation, a loss equivalent to the allocated cost of the rights should theoretically be recognized by the investor firm. As a practical matter, however, the allocation entry is usually reversed for the portion that lapses, restoring the cost to the investment in common stock account.

ACCOUNTING FOR TEMPORARY INVESTMENTS IN MARKETABLE DEBT SECURITIES

SFAS No. 12 addresses how to account for marketable equity securities but is silent on accounting for marketable debt securities. As a result, *ARB Opinion No. 43* continues as the official guideline for accounting for short-term investments in debt securities. It specifies use of the cost method (not the lower of cost or market) for short-term investments in debt securities. Under this method, investments in debt securities are recorded and carried at acquisition cost in conformity with the cost principle. If the market value of the securities held falls below acquisition cost, there is not a write-down to market (as there is under the LCM method). *ARB Opinion No. 43* does allow for a write-down if the current market value is less than cost by a substantial amount, and if the market value decline is not due to temporary conditions. When both of these conditions exist, *ARB Opinion No. 43* requires that the short-term debt security (on a security-by-security basis) be written down to market value to recognize the permanent impairment of the asset value. There is no direct guidance on how to determine whether the decline in value is a permanent impairment. Changes in value caused by the normal changes in the market rate of interest for debt securities would probably not be viewed as causing a permanent impairment, but a decline in value resulting from a major financial difficulty for the issuer of the debt would more likely be viewed as a permanent impairment. A permanent decline is recorded as a direct credit to the investment account and a debit to a loss (realized) account, such as impairment loss on investments in marketable securities.

Since the issuance of *SFAS No. 12,* an increasing number of firms have adopted the lower of cost or market method for marketable, short-term investments in debt securities. Its application for debt securities is the same as discussed for marketable equity securities—LCM is computed on an aggregate basis, and any unrealized loss at the balance sheet date is charged to the income statement, and a valuation allowance account (a contra account) is credited. The unrealized loss can be recovered in the same manner as that for marketable equity securities. When the LCM method is used, usually a separate portfolio is set up for debt securities, and the LCM method is applied to the portfolio in exactly the same way as illustrated earlier for equity securities. In practice, then, marketable debt securities can be carried either at cost or at lower of cost or market. Since the key characteristic is the same for marketable debt and equity securities (i.e., marketability), it makes sense to account for both using the requirements of *SFAS No. 12.*

The acquisition of a debt security is recorded at cost. However, when a debt security is purchased or sold between interest dates, the accrued interest since the last interest date must be computed and recorded separately from cost. On the next interest date, the new owner of the debt security receives the full cash amount of interest for the interest period. On the transaction date, the buyer and seller agree on the price to be paid for the debt. The amount of cash to be transferred also must include an amount to pay the interest accrued since the last interest payment. This latter amount must be separately recorded in order to determine correctly the amount of interest revenue that the investor will record when interest is received at the next interest payment date.

For example, on May 1, 1992, Laurel Company purchases 100 bonds of Surber Corp. at 96 (face amount $1,000 and stated interest 12%, with interest payable semiannually on July 1 and January 1). Commissions on the purchase are $1,280. Laurel Company will have the following cash outlay:

Purchase price of bonds	$96,000
Commission	1,280
Cost of Bonds acquired	97,280
Accrued interest—January 1 to May 1	
($100,000 × 12% × 4/12)	4,000
Total cash payment	$101,280

To record the above transaction, Laurel makes the following entry:

Marketable debt securities	97,280	
Accrued interest receivable	4,000	
Cash		101,280

When the interest payment is received by Laurel on July 1, the entry to record the interest revenue is:

Cash ($100,000 × .12 × 6/12)	6,000	
Accrued interest receivable		4,000
Interest revenue		2,000

Generally, any discount or premium caused by a difference between the maturity value of the debt security and the acquisition price is not separately recorded because the holding period is short. Any discount or premium is usually not amortized. The investment is carried at cost until it is sold.

When the security is sold, the difference between the carrying amount and the selling price, less commissions and other expenses, is recorded as gain or loss. Suppose that on October 1, 1992, Laurel Company sells its holdings of Surber Corp. bonds at a price of 98 plus accrued interest, and incurs commissions and other expenses associated with the sale of the bonds of $560. The gain or loss is computed as:

Selling price of bonds	$98,000
Less: Commission and expenses	560
Net proceeds from bonds	97,440
Carrying amount of bonds	97,280
Gain on sale of bonds	$ 160

The accrued interest at the disposal date is $100,000 × .12 × 3/12, or $3,000. The entry to record the sale, including recording the receipt of interest revenue for the period July 1 to the transaction date of October 1:

Cash ($98,000 + $3,000 − $560)	100,440	
Gain on sale of bonds		160
Interest revenue ($100,000 × .12 × 3/12)		3,000
Marketable debt securities		97,280

Any gain or loss on the disposition of short-term debt securities is included in the determination of income from continuing operations. If it is determined to be unusual or infrequent, it would be separately identified, but it would not be an extraordinary item.

Accounting for Long-Term Investments in Debt Securities Long-term investments in debt securities are accounted for using the cost method. This topic is covered in Chapter 16, along with accounting for debt by the issuer. Transfers of debt securities from the short-term to long-term classification (and vice versa) are made at the carrying amount at the date of transfer.

Other Types of Investments Generally, investments in securities are the most important item included in the investments account. However, a number of other items can be included under the caption "investments and funds." Most of these investments occur infrequently and are not of a large magnitude. These include special-purpose funds, in which the company sets aside cash or other assets for a special purpose, and the cash surrender value of life insurance on key executives. Also, firms that acquire futures contracts have invested in a form of financial instrument that has the characteristics of an investment. The accounting for each of these types of investments is covered in Appendix 14B.

SUMMARY OF KEY POINTS

(L.O. 1) 1. Firms invest in the securities of other firms either to earn a return on otherwise idle cash or to gain influence, control, or some other business advantage.

(L.O. 2, 3) 2. Investment securities are recorded at acquisition using the cost principle.

(L.O. 3) 3. The four methods of accounting for investment securities are:
   a. The cost method.
   b. The lower of cost or market method (LCM).
   c. The equity method.
   d. The market value method.

(L.O. 3) 4. The LCM method records the investment at the lower of the aggregate cost or aggregate market value of a portfolio of securities. This method is required for short-term and long-term investments in marketable equity securities.

(L.O. 3, 4, 5) 5. The cost method records and maintains an investment at original cost. Only a permanent impairment of value results in a write-down of the cost. Increases in market value above cost are disregarded for accounting purposes. Dividends and interest received from the investment security are recorded as investment revenue.

(L.O. 6) 6. When the application of LCM results in a write-down of aggregate cost to aggregate market for a portfolio of short-term marketable equity securities, the write-down is closed to income during the current period. If this write-down is for a portfolio of long-term marketable equity securities, the write-down is recorded in a contra account in stockholders' equity.

(L.O. 6) 7. For LCM applied to long-term marketable equity securities, any write-down recorded in stockholders' equity can be recovered and recorded in future periods if and when market values increase. The carrying amount of the portfolio can be increased up to its original cost.

(L.O. 6) 8. The equity method must be used to account for long-term investments in voting common stock in which the investor exercises significant influence over the investee. Significant influence over the investee is presumed to exist if the investor owns over 20% or more of the investor voting stock.

(L.O. 6) 9. Conceptually, the equity method is an extension of accrual accounting to common stock investments. Increases and decreases in the net assets of the investee flow through to the investor as they occur.

(L.O. 6) 10. If the investor's initial investment in the common stock of the investee is an amount different from the net book value acquired, the difference must be accounted for as if it were recorded by the investee. Differences between book value as recorded by the investee, and fair market value at the date of acquisition is accounted for by the investor. Any difference not identifiable with specific assets or liabilities is identified as goodwill and is accounted for in accordance with *APB Opinion No. 17*.

(L.O. 6) 11. The market value method of accounting for investments is not in conformity with GAAP except for certain specialized industries. Under this method, investments are carried at market value.

(L.O. 6) 12. Under the market value method of accounting for investment in equity securities, increases or decreases in the market value of the equity securities are recorded each accounting period either currently in the determination of income (the current approach) or as a deferred item in stockholders' equity (the deferral approach). Under the deferral approach, the change in the market value of the securities is recognized as income only when the securities are sold. Dividends received from the investee are recorded as investment revenue by the investor.

(L.O. 7) 13. For each period for which an income statement is presented, an investor firm must disclose the following for its investments in marketable equity securities:
   a. Aggregate cost of the portfolios (short and long term).
   b. Aggregate market value of the portfolios.
   c. Gross unrealized gains and gross unrealized losses.
   d. Net realized gain or loss, the basis for determining the net realized gain or loss, and the change in the valuation allowance that is included in the determination of income.

(L.O. 8) 14. Stock dividends and stock splits are recorded by the investor only as a memorandum entry for the number of shares received. If the stock dividend is of a different class of stock than that on which the dividend was declared, the investor must record the dividend stock in one of three methods: (a) the allocation method, by allocating the carrying value of the old stock between the new stock and the old stock based on relative market values; (b) the noncost method, in which no cost is allocated to the new stock; (c) the market value method, in which the new stock is recorded at its market value with a credit to dividend income (no allocation of the carrying value of the old stock).

(L.O. 8) 15. When stock rights are issued by the investee, the investor must allocate the total carrying amount of the investment between the old stock and the stock rights, usually using the allocation method described for stock dividends.

(L.O. 9) 16. Consolidated financial statements are required when an investor corporation owns more than 50% of the voting stock of the investee corporation. The acquisition can be accounted for as a purchase or as a pooling of interest, depending upon the characteristics of the acquisition.

(L.O. 9) 17. Consolidation results in reporting of the investor and the investee as if they were one firm. Minority interests in the net assets and in the earnings of the investee are recognized in the consolidated balance sheet and the consolidated income statement, respectively.

(L.O. 10) 18. The cash surrender value of life insurance is a form of investment. As insurance premiums are paid on policies that generate a cash surrender value, a portion of the premium is recorded as an investment (rather than as a period expense) such that the investment account reflects the cash surrender value of the policy.

REVIEW PROBLEM
♦

In this chapter, four different methods of accounting for investments in securities were discussed. To summarize and distinguish between them, the following designations are used:

1. *Cost method*—The investment is carried at original cost with no reference to market value even if market value is lower than original cost. Investment revenue includes dividends received from investee.

2. *Lower of cost or market (LCM)*—The investment is carried at the lower of the aggregate cost or the aggregate market value of a portfolio of securities. Investment revenue includes dividends received from investee. Unrealized losses and unrealized loss recoveries flow through the income statement for short-term investments and they are recorded in a contra account to stockholders' equity for long-term investments.

3. *Equity method*—The investment is recorded at cost plus investor's pro rata share of undistributed earnings of investee since the acquisition. Investment revenue includes the investor's pro rata share of the earnings of the investee, adjusted for amortization of goodwill and other adjustments.

4. *Market value method*—The investment is reported at current market value at the end of the reporting period. Investment revenue includes dividends received and change in market value. Use the current approach.

In this review problem, you are to apply each of these methods to an investment. That is, the purpose of this problem is to demonstrate the application of each method to a common set of data. Under GAAP, each method is not an option for the investment described below, but the problem shows how each method would be applied to the data.

Data Assume the following transactions related to investments by Trey Corporation:

Jan. 2, 1991—Trey Corp. acquires 100 shares of Pear Company at a market price of $15 per share, and 200 shares of Apple Inc. for $11 per share. Assume there are no brokerage fees. Also, to simplify the accounting under the equity method, assume the book value of the shares acquired is exactly equal to the price paid for the shares.

Dec. 31, 1991—The two firms in which Trey has invested report the following results:

	Pear Co.	Apple Inc.
Earnings per share for 1991	$2.00	1.50
Dividends per share paid December 31	1.00	.75
Market value per share at 12/31/91	$17	$9.50

Required:

1. Compute the initial investment at cost.
2. Describe how this investment would be accounted for under each of the above four methods. For each method answer the following:
   a. What would be the carrying amount of the investment at December 31, 1991?
   b. What would be the investment revenue recognized in 1991?

SOLUTION
♦

1. Compute the initial investment at cost:

Pear Co.	100 shares × $15/share	=	$1,500
Apple Inc.	200 shares × $11/share	=	2,200
Total investment			$3,700

2. Account for this investment under each of the four methods. For each method compute the carrying amount of the investment at December 31, 1991, and determine the investment revenue to be recognized in 1991.

1. *Cost method.* Investment revenue is the dividends received from the investment securities. In this example Trey Co. would have investment revenue of $250 ($1.00 dividends per share times the 100 Pear shares owned, plus 75-cent dividends per share times the 200 Apple shares owned). The investment on the balance sheet would continue to be carried at the original cost of $3,700.

2. *Lower of cost or market.* Investment revenue includes dividends received as in (1) but it may also be decreased if there is a requirement to write down the investment. To determine whether there is a need to write down the investment, determine the aggregate cost and the aggregate market value at December 31, 1991. The aggregate cost was $3,700. The aggregate market value at December 31 is:

Pear Company	100 shares × $17/share	=	$1,700
Apple Inc.	200 shares × $9.50/share	=	1,900
Total			$3,600

The aggregate current market value has fallen to $3,600, or $100 less than the aggregate original cost. The LCM method requires that we write down the investment to $3,600; thus, investment income is reduced by the write-down of $100. There are unrealized losses of $300 and unrealized gains of $200, which net to the write-down of $100.

3. *Equity method.* The equity method is used only for certain equity investments. Under the equity method, the investing firm reports as investment revenue its pro rata share of the earnings of the investee firm and shows the investment at the original cost plus (or minus) its share of the undistributed earnings of the firm's shares it owns. Thus, the amount that Trey Co. would report as its investment in each investee would be computed as follows:

	Pear Co.	Apple Inc.
Original investment:		
Pear: 100 shares × $15/share	$1,500	
Apple: 200 shares × $11/share		$2,200
Add: Current period earnings:		
Pear: $2.00 per share × 100 shares	200	
Apple: $1.50 per share × 200 shares		300
Less: Dividends received:		
Pear: $1.00 per share × 100 shares	(100)	
Apple: $0.75 per share × 200 shares		(150)
Equity investment at 12/31/91:		
Pear	$1,600	
Apple		$2,350

The total carrying amount for the two investment securities at December 31 is $1,600 plus $2,350, or $3,950. The amount of earnings Trey will report from its investments in these two firms will be its share of each firm's earnings, or $200 from Pear and $300 from Apple.

4. *Market Method.* Under the market value method, using the current approach, investment revenue is the dividends received (or interest income received) plus the increase (or less the decrease) in market value of the investment security. The investment carrying amount is the market value of the investment security. Thus, the determination of investment revenue and carrying amounts for the above example using the market value method would be as follows:

	Pear Co.	Apple Inc.
Original investment:		
Pear: 100 shares × $15/shares	$1,500	
Apple: 200 shares × $11/share		$2,200

EXHIBIT 14-5   Four Methods of Accounting for Investments

	Cost Method	LCM Method	Equity Method	Market Method
Original investment:				
Pear	$1,500	$1,500	$1,500	$1,500
Apple	2,200	2,200	2,200	2,200
Total	$3,700	$3,700	$3,700	$3,700
Investment income for fiscal 1991:				
Pear	$ 100	$ 100	$ 200	$ 300
Apple	150		300	(150)
LCM Adjustment		(100)		
Total	$ 250	$ 150	$ 500	$ 150
Cash received from investment securities:				
Pear	$ 100	$ 100	$ 100	$ 100
Apple	150	150	150	150
Total	$ 250	$ 250	$ 250	$ 250
Change in investment carrying amount:				
Pear	$ 0	$ 0	$ 100	$ 200
Apple	0	*(0)	150	(300)
Total	$ 0	($100)	$ 250	(100)
Investment carrying amount at 12/31/91:				
Pear	$1,500	$1,500	$1,600	$1,700
Apple	2,200†	2,200	2,350†	1,900
Total	$3,700	$3,600*	$3,950	$3,600

* Under the LCM method, the write-down and decrease in carrying amount is computed for the aggregate value of the portfolio of investment securities and is not associated with any one security.

† Assume that the market value of the Apple, which is currently less than the carrying amount shown under this method, is not permanently impaired. If it were determined to be permanently impaired, there would be a write-down to market value.

Compute Investment Income

Add: Dividends received:		
Pear: $1.00 per share × 100 shares	100	
Apple: $0.75 per share × 200 shares		150
Add: Change in market value		
Pear: ($17/share − $15/share) × 100 shares	200	
Apple: ($9.50/share − $11/share) × 200 shares		(300)
Total investment income	$ 300	($150)
Investment carrying amount at 12/31/91		
Pear: $17/share × 100 shares	$1,700	
Apple: $9.50/share × 200 shares		$1,900

Thus, the total carrying amount for the investment at December 31 is $3,600. The investment income for the year totals $150, which equals the $250 in dividends received less the net reduction in market value of the two investment securities of $100.

The results of using the four different methods in this problem are summarized in Exhibit 14–5. There are considerably different results depending on which method is used and on what changes occur in the market values of the investment securities.

APPENDIX 14A: *Consolidated Financial Statements*

This appendix presents the fundamental concepts of **consolidated financial statements**. The complexities involved are deferred to advanced texts that develop this topic. *APB Opinion No. 16,* ''Business Combinations,'' provides the basic accounting guidelines for consolidated financial statements. Consolidation of the financial statements of a parent company and a subsidiary is only a reporting procedure; therefore, it does not affect the accounts of either the parent company or the subsidiary. Consolidated financial statements are prepared only by the parent company, not by the subsidiary.

CONCEPT OF A CONTROLLING INTEREST
◆

When an investor company owns over 50% of the outstanding voting stock of another company, in the absence of overriding constraints, a controlling interest exists. The investor company is called the *parent* company. The second company is called a *subsidiary* company. In a parent-subsidiary relationship, both corporations continue as separate legal entities; therefore, they are separate accounting entities (refer to separate entity assumption, chapter 2). As separate entities, they have separate accounting systems and separate financial statements. However, because of the controlling ownership relationship, the parent company (but not the subsidiary) may be required to prepare consolidated financial statements. In consolidated financial statements the parent and the subsidiary (or subsidiaries) are viewed by accountants as a single economic entity. Thus, the parent company may prepare two sets of financial statements: one set as a separate entity, and another set as a consolidated entity. To prepare consolidated financial statements, the separate financial statements of the parent and subsidiary are combined each period by the parent company into one overall (i.e., consolidated) set of financial statements as if they were a single entity. The income statement, balance sheet, and statement of cash flows (SCF) are consolidated in this manner.

Consolidated financial statements are not always prepared when over 50% of the stock of another corporation is owned because certain constraints may preclude the exercise of a controlling interest. Consolidation as a single economic entity is required by *SFAS No. 94,* ''Consolidation of All Majority Owned Subsidiaries'' (October 1987), which defines control and exceptions:

1. *Control of voting rights*—Control is presumed to exist when more than 50% of the outstanding voting stock of another entity is owned by the investor. Nonvoting stock is excluded from consideration because control is not possible without the vote. However, there is one exception. A subsidiary that is more than 50% owned in certain circumstances and does not qualify for consolidation is called an *unconsolidated subsidiary.* In this case the investment is reported using (*a*) the equity method, if there is significant influence, and (*b*) the cost method if there is neither control nor significant influence.

2. *Exception to the general rule*—*SFAS No. 94* states that '' a majority-owned subsidiary shall not be consolidated if control is likely to be temporary or if it does not rest with the majority owner (as, for instance, if the subsidiary is in legal reorganization or in bankruptcy or operates under foreign exchange restrictions, controls, or other governmentally imposed uncertainties so severe that they cast significant doubt on the parent's ability to control the subsidiary).'' All other majority-owned subsidiaries must be consolidated.

ACQUIRING A CONTROLLING INTEREST
◆

A company accounts for the acquisition of a controlling interest in the voting stock of another company in one of two conceptually different ways:

1. *Pooling of interests*—The parent company acquires the voting stock of an existing corporation by exchanging shares of its own capital stock for shares of the subsidiary. In this case, the parent disburses relatively little cash or other assets and incurs no new liabilities in the acquisition. The owners of the acquiring firm and of the acquired firm become the owners of the combined firm. For example, the 1988 financial statements of Dun & Bradstreet Corporation included the following note (partial):

Note 3 (In Part): Acquisitions

On May 26, 1988, the Company issued shares of its common stock in exchange for all the outstanding shares of IMS common stock. This transaction was accounted for as a pooling-of-interests and, accordingly, the accompanying financial statements relating to prior periods have been restated to include the accounts of IMS.

2. *Purchase*—The parent company acquires the voting stock of an existing corporation primarily by paying cash, transferring noncash assets, or incurring debt. In this situation, the parent disburses a significant amount of resources. The owners of the acquired firm receive cash and other resources; they do not necessarily maintain an ownership interest in the combined firm. For example, the 1987 financial statements of Gerber Products Company included the following note (partial):

On July 31, 1986, the Company, through a subsidiary, Soft Care Apparel, Inc., purchased certain assets of the Baby Products Division of The Kendall Company, a subsidiary of the Colgate-Palmolive Company, for $58,403,000 in cash. The acquired assets include the manufacturing and marketing operations for infant-wear, bedding, sleepers and cloth diapers sold under the Curity label. In fiscal 1987, the Company also acquired six children's centers for cash.

All of the acquisitions have been accounted for as purchases and, accordingly, the consolidated statements of operations include the acquired businesses from their respective dates of acquisition.

ACCOUNTING AND REPORTING

GAAP requires that each subsidiary prepare its own financial statements. However, the parent company is required to prepare consolidated financial statements. These statements include all subsidiaries except those designated as unconsolidated subsidiaries. The parent, not the subsidiary, prepares consolidated statements. Consolidated financial statements include an item-by-item combination (aggregation) of the parent and subsidiary statements. For example, the amount of cash shown on a consolidated statement is the sum of the amounts of cash shown on the separate statements of the parent and the subsidiaries.

While consolidated financial statements are the means by which a controlling interest is reported, the parent company records the investment in unconsolidated subsidiaries using the cost or equity method. The cost method is often used in the accounts because the parent company does not desire to formally enter into its accounts the income, dividend offset, additional depreciation, amortization of goodwill, and so on, required by the equity method.[14] Also, the accounting periods of the parent and the subsidiary may be different. Changes in percentage of ownership complicate the equity method. Frequently, when a company moves from the equity method range (i.e., 20% to 50%) to a controlling interest range (over 50%), it adjusts the accounts from the equity to the cost basis. For practical reasons, the illustrations use the cost method of accounting for the investment.

The consolidated statements are developed using a consolidation work sheet. The consolidation procedures can be adapted on the worksheet so that the results are the same whether the cost or equity method is used in the accounts of the parent company. The consolidated financial statements are prepared from these worksheets.

This section focuses on the preparation of consolidated financial statements. When preparing consolidated financial statements, the method of acquisition—pooling of interests versus purchase—has a significant impact both on the parent company and on the consolidated statements.

Before discussing the pooling of interests and purchase methods, the steps necessary to prepare the consolidation worksheet are discussed. These steps refer to worksheet entries and the resulting consolidated financial statements, not to the journals and ledgers of the separate legal entities involved. These steps are:

---

[14] The equity method is called *one-line consolidation*. Instead of a line-by-line consolidation of the individual accounts, the equity method does the equivalent in a single account labeled "equity in earnings of subsidiaries."

1. Enter the separate financial statements of the parent and each subsidiary on the worksheet, using one column for each entity. Additional column headings are provided for "eliminations" and "consolidated statements."
2. The assets and liabilities of the subsidiary are substituted for the investment account reflected on the books of the parent. This substitution is accomplished on the worksheet by eliminating the owners' equity accounts of the subsidiary against the investment account of the parent.
3. Intercompany receivables are eliminated.
4. Intercompany revenues, expenses, gains, and losses are eliminated.
5. Other intercompany items are eliminated as appropriate.
6. For purchased subsidiaries, adjustments are made on the worksheet to reflect market values that differ from the book values, such as goodwill purchased as part of the cost of the investment in the subsidiary.
7. The remaining revenues and expenses of the parent and subsidiary are combined on the worksheet to derive a consolidated income statement.
8. The assets and liabilities of the parent and subsidiary are combined to derive a consolidated balance sheet.
9. The cash inflows and outflows of the parent and subsidiary are combined on a separate worksheet to derive a consolidated statement of cash flows (SCF).

Consolidated financial statements usually are prepared at the date of acquisition of a controlling interest (balance sheet only) and for each accounting period subsequent to acquisition (income statement, balance sheet, and statement of cash flows). The consolidation worksheet and resulting financial statements are influenced by the way the consolidation is recorded, that is, whether by pooling of interests or by purchase.

Combination by Pooling of Interests

The acquisition of a controlling interest by the parent company in the stock of a subsidiary company by an exchange of shares of stock often occurs because the combination can be effected without the disbursement of cash or other resources by the parent company. The exchange of shares is viewed as the uniting of ownership interests (and not as a purchase/sale transaction) between the parent company and the stockholders of the subsidiary company. Therefore, the recorded assets, liabilities, revenues, expenses, and so forth, for both entities are combined for consolidated statement purposes at their recorded book values. The income of the parent and its subsidiaries are combined and restated as consolidated income. Because a purchase/sale transaction is not presumed when shares of stock are exchanged, market values of the assets of the subsidiary are not used in consolidation on the pooling of interests basis.

APB Opinion No. 16, "Business Combinations" (par. 47), states, "the combining of existing voting common stock interests by the exchange of stock is the essence of . . . [a] pooling of interests." The *Opinion* specifies 12 conditions (not given here) that must be met in order for the pooling of interests method to be appropriate. If they are met, the pooling of interests method *must* be used. Combinations not meeting all 12 specifications must use the purchase method. Because of these 12 conditions, not all pure stock exchanges meet the criteria for pooling of interests.

The general characteristics of the pooling of interests method of preparing consolidated statements may be summarized as follows:

1. The parent company must acquire 90% or more of the voting shares of the subsidiary.
2. The assets and liabilities of the combining companies are reported at the previously established book values of both the parent and the subsidiary. Although adjustments may be made to reflect consistent application of accounting principles, the current market values of the assets of the subsidiary at the time of the combination are not used as a substitute for their book values at that date.
3. No purchased goodwill results from the combination.
4. The retained earnings balances of the combining companies are, with minor exceptions, added to determine the retained earnings balance of the consolidated company at date of acquisition.
5. After combination, comparative financial statements that pertain to precombination periods must be restated on the combined basis as if the companies were consolidated throughout those periods.

Preparing a Consolidated Balance Sheet Immediately after Acquisition—Pooling of Interests Method
Exhibit 14A–1 shows the preparation of a consolidated balance sheet immediately after acquisition. In this case, there was an exchange of shares of a 90% voting interest that qualities as a pooling of interests. Exhibit 14A–1 illustrates the worksheet used to prepare the consolidated balance sheet immediately after the combination.

In Exhibit 14A–1, the worksheet is begun by entering the two separate balance sheets, using *book values* for each company immediately after the acquisition entry. Notice that two account balances on the Company P balance sheet (i.e., the investment and parent common stock accounts) reflect the acquisition entry. The worksheet is designed to provide an orderly procedure for combining the two separate balance sheets into a consolidated statement (the last column). The pair of columns for eliminations is used to prevent double counting of reciprocal items; that is, transactions that are strictly between the two companies must be eliminated because there is now one entity. In this instance, two reciprocal items must be eliminated:

1. The investment account balance reflected on the balance sheet of Company P ($90,000) must be eliminated. In its place, the various assets and liabilities of Company S are added to those of the parent. Similarly, 90% of the common stock reported by Company S must be eliminated. It now is owned by the parent company. Thus, elimination entry (*a*) on the worksheet offsets the investment account balance on the balance sheet of the parent against the capital stock account reflected on the balance sheet of the subsidiary.

2. Intercompany debt—Current liabilities of Company S include a $5,000 account payable owed to Company P; therefore, accounts receivable on the balance sheet of Company P includes this amount. When the two balance sheets are combined, this intercompany debt must be eliminated because it is not a payable or receivable involving the combined entity and an outside entity. Elimination entry (*b*) on the worksheet accomplishes this offset.

After the elimination entries for all intercompany items are reflected on the worksheet, the two balance sheets are aggregated line by line. The 10% interest of the **minority stockholders** of Company S represented by their proportionate share of the stockholders' equity of the subsidiary company is set out separately (denoted by M). Minority interest is a liability for the consolidated entity. The last column of the worksheet provides the data needed to prepare a consolidated balance sheet. The book values of Company S are added to the book values of Company P. The market values do not affect the reporting for a combination by pooling of interests.

Combination by Purchase

The acquisition of a controlling interest by purchase occurs when the combination does not meet all 12 conditions specified by *APB Opinion No. 16* for a pooling of interests. Typically, an acquisition by purchase occurs when the parent company acquires a controlling interest in the subsidiary company by purchasing the voting stock from the subsidiary's stockholders primarily with cash and noncash assets. This situation is viewed as a purchase/sale transaction. Therefore, market values related to the subsidiary must be introduced into the consolidation procedures in conformity with the cost principle. *APB Opinion No. 16* (par 66) states: "Accounting for a business combination by the purchase method follows the principles normally applicable under historical cost accounting to recording acquisitions of assets and issuances of stock and to accounting for assets and liabilities after acquisition." This quote means that, at acquisition date, the parent company must debit the investment account for the market value of the shares of the subsidiary acquired. The parent company pays market value for the investment. The significant implication of this requirement is that in preparing consolidated statements, the assets of the subsidiary (including any purchased goodwill) must be valued by the parent company at their market values at date of acquisition before being aggregated with the book values of the assets of the parent company.[15]

---

[15] In a pooling of interests, book values rather than market values of the subsidiary are used in consolidation.

EXHIBIT 14A-1   Consolidated Balance Sheet, Company P (parent) and Company S (subsidiary), Pooling of Interests Method, Immediately after Acquisition of a 90% Controlling Interest by Company P

1. Company P issues 900 shares of its $100 par common stock to the stockholders of Company S for 900 of the 1,000 outstanding shares of Company S common stock, par $100. This is an exchange of shares (a continuity of the previously existing ownership). Assume that it meets the 12 conditions (specified in *APB Opinion No. 16*) for pooling of interests (including the criterion which requires at least 90% ownership). Company S will continue as a separate legal entity and as a 90% owned subsidiary of Company P. As a result of the transaction, Company P immediately makes the following acquisition entry:

Investment in Company S common stock (90% ownership)* 90,000
    Common stock (900 shares at $100 par)   90,000

   * Because the acquisition under the pooling of interests concept is not viewed as a purchase/sale transaction, it is variously recorded at (*a*) par value of the stock issued, (*b*) the proportionate share acquired of the subsidiary's contributed capital, or (*c*) the proportionate book value of the subsidiary acquired. Some accountants prefer to use average contributed capital per share. This is a minor, but unsettled, issue. In any case, the elimination entry is adapted to attain the pooling of interests results.

2. Immediately after the exchange, the respective balance sheets reflect the following:

	Company P Book Value	Company S Book Value	Company S Market Value	Liabilities and Owner's Equity†	Company P Book Value	Company S Book Value
Assets						
Cash	$610,000	$ 20,000	$ 20,000	Current liabilities	$ 10,000	$ 20,000*
Accounts receivable (net)	10,000*	40,000	40,000	Long-term liabilities	50,000	40,000
				Common stock		
Inventories	20,000	30,000	25,000	(par $100)	690,000	100,000
Investment in Co. S	90,000			Retained earnings	200,000	50,000
Plant and equipment (net)	200,000	110,000	151,000			
Patents (net)	20,000	10,000	14,000			
	$950,000	$210,000	$250,000		$950,000	$210,000

   * At date of acquisition, Company S owed Company P $5,000 accounts payable.
   † S Company liabilities at book value are equal to their market value.

Worksheet to Develop Consolidated Balance Sheet

Account	Balance Sheet per Books Company P	Balance Sheet per Books Company S	Eliminations Debit	Eliminations Credit	Consolidated Balance Sheet
Cash	610,000	20,000			630,000
Accounts receivable (net)	10,000	40,000		(*b*) 5,000	45,000
Inventories	20,000	30,000			50,000
Investment in Company S	90,000*			(*a*) 90,000	
Plant and equipment (net)	200,000	110,000			310,000
Patents (net)	20,000	10,000			30,000
	950,000	210,000			1,065,000
Current liabilities	10,000	20,000	(*b*) 5,000		25,000
Long-term liabilities	50,000	40,000			90,000
Common stock (par $100):					
Company P	690,000*				690,000
Company S		100,000	(*a*) 90,000		10,000M
Retained earnings:					
Company P	200,000				245,000
Company S		50,000			5,000M
	950,000	210,000			1,065,000

M—minority stockholders' 10% interest in Company S.

* Includes effect of acquisition entry of $90,000.

Eliminations:
   (*a*) To eliminate the investment account balance against the stockholders' equity (90%) of the subsidiary.
   (*b*) To eliminate the intercompany debt of $5,000.

Although there are numerous additional complexities in application of the *purchase method,* the general characteristics may be outlined as follows:

1. On the consolidated balance sheet, the assets and liabilities of the subsidiary are reported by the parent company at *cost* on the date of acquisition in conformity with the cost principle. Thus, the investment equals the *market value of the stock acquired.* It also is the cost of the net assets of the subsidiary purchased by the parent.
2. Individual assets of the subsidiary are reported at their individual market values as of the date of acquisition. These include all identifiable tangible and intangible assets (receivables, inventory, land, equipment, patents, etc.). Liabilities of the subsidiary are also reported at their equivalent market values.
3. At acquisition date, the difference between the total purchase cost and the market value of the identifiable tangible and intangible assets acquired (less the subsidiary's liabilities) represents an unidentifiable asset. This difference is reported as goodwill. Goodwill from the acquisition is subsequently amortized as an expense on the parent's consolidated income statement.
4. Immediately after acquisition by purchase, the retained earnings balance of the combined entity is defined as the retained earnings balance of the parent company only. Thus, the retained earnings balance of the subsidiary is eliminated and, as a consequence, is not reported on the consolidated balance sheet.
5. After combination by purchase, comparative financial statements of precombination periods must be reported on a consolidated basis.

Preparation of Consolidated Balance Sheet Immediately after Acquisition, Purchase Method   Exhibit 14A–2 shows the preparation of a consolidated balance sheet on the purchase basis immediately after acquisition. Except for the method of acquisition, Exhibit 14A–2 is based upon the same data for Company P and Company S in Exhibit 14A–1.

In order to prepare the worksheet, the amount of goodwill purchased must be determined. Goodwill is computed as the difference between the purchase price paid by the parent and the market values of the identifiable net assets of the subsidiary. Also, notice that in Exhibit 14A–1, items in (2) have market values different from their book values.

The worksheet shown in Exhibit 14A–2, is started by entering the two balance sheets using amounts immediately after the acquisition entry. Two accounts (cash and investments) on Company P balance sheets reflect the acquisition entry. Also, the middle pair of columns are called "eliminations and restatements" because restatement entries must be made to change the assets of Company S from book value to market value for the proportionate part of the market value purchased by Company P. This is entry (*a*) on the worksheet. Elimination entries must also be made for intercompany items; entries (*b*) and (*c*) on the worksheet. The computations of these amounts are given in Exhibit 14A–2, items 3*a* and 3*b*. The computations indicate that inventories must be reduced by \$4,500; plant and equipment increased by \$36,900; patents increased by \$3,600; and goodwill recorded in the amount of \$40,000. The goodwill amount reflects the excess of cost over market value of each of these items acquired by Company P.[16] The net offset for these amounts is recorded in the investment account as an elimination because that account was debited at acquisition for the market value of the net assets acquired.

The worksheet is completed by extending each item horizontally, considering the eliminations and restatements. The last column gives all of the data needed to prepare a consolidated balance sheet on the purchase basis.

A comparison of Exhibit 14A–1 (pooling of interests) with Exhibit 14A–2 (purchase) reflects three underlying conceptual differences. The first difference is that in a pooling of interests, the book values of the subsidiary are added to the book values of the parent, whereas in a purchase, the proportionate share of the market values of subsidiary assets at acquisition are added to the book values of the parent. The second difference is that goodwill is not recognized in a pooling of interests; in contrast, goodwill usually is recognized in a purchase. The third difference is the treatment of retained earnings in the consolidation. In a pooling of interests, owners before the acquisition transaction continue as owners after the

---

[16] In computing goodwill (see Exhibit 14A–2, case data item 3*a*), if the total purchase cost is less than the parents' pro rata share of summed market values of the individual assets of the subsidiary less liabilities, negative goodwill occurs. Negative goodwill should be allocated to reduce the purchase cost (i.e., market estimates) of the identifiable tangible and intangible assets.

EXHIBIT 14A-2   Consolidated Balance Sheet, Company P (parent) and Company S (subsidiary), Purchase Method; Immediately after Acquisition of a 90% Controlling Interest by Company P

Case Data

1. Company P purchased, in the open market, 90% of the 1,000 shares of outstanding voting stock of Company S for $211,000 cash. Company P recorded the acquisition as follows:

            Investment in Company S common stock (90% ownership) . . . 211,000
                Cash   211,000

2. The balance sheet items of Company S with different book and market values given in 3.*b*. below (first 2 columns). This is the same data given in Exhibit 14A-1.

3. Analysis of the purchase:

    a. Computation of goodwill purchased by Company P:

Purchase price for 90% interest in Company S		$211,000
Market value of 90% of the identifiable *net* assets purchased:		
Total market value of identifiable assets of Company S (Exhibit 14A-1)	$250,000	
Less: total liabilities of Company S (Exhibit 14A-1)	(60,000)	
Total market value of identifiable net assets of Company S	190,000	
Proportional part purchased by Company P	× .90	
Market value of 90% of the identifiable net assets purchased		171,000
Goodwill purchased (90%)		$ 40,000

    b. Proportionate part of each asset of Company S adjusted to market value (i.e., parent's cost) as of date of combination:

	Parent's cost (Market Value)	Subsidiary's Book Value	Proportionate Part of Excess of Cost (Market) Over Book Value
Inventory	$ 25,000	– $ 30,000	× .90 = $(4,500)*
Plant and equipment	151,000	– 110,000	× .90 = 36,900
Patents	14,000	– 10,000	× .90 = 3,600
Goodwill (per above)	40,000	– —0—	40,000
Total (see worksheet entry [*a*] below)			$76,000

* Parent's cost (i.e., market value) is less than subsidiary's book value.

transaction. Therefore, the retained earnings of both companies are combined to derive consolidated retained earnings. In a purchase acquisition, the parent company buys the subsidiary shares, and the prior owners do not continue as owners. Therefore, the consolidated retained earnings are limited to the parent company's retained earnings. This can be observed in Exhibit 14A-1 (retained earnings, $245,000) and Exhibit 14A-2 ($200,000). These three basic differences are maintained in the consolidated financial statements of all subsequent periods.

This appendix provides an introduction to consolidated financial statements. This discussion is important for students who may not take the advanced accounting course on consolidated statements.

Consolidated statements are prepared (by the parent company) when the parent company has a controlling interest in another company (called a subsidiary). A controlling interest exists for accounting purposes when the parent company owns more than 50% of the outstanding voting stock of the subsidiary; the only exception to this basic rule is when control is likely to be temporary or if it does not rest with the majority owner.

Consolidated statements basically involve aggregation on a line-by-line basis of the assets, liabilities, equity, revenues and gains, and expenses and losses of the parent and subsidiary. The manner of acquisition—by pooling (an exchange of shares) or by purchase (using assets to acquire the subsidiary's shares)—has a significant impact on the consolidated statements. Consolidation of the financial statements of a parent company and a subsidiary is a reporting procedure only. This procedure does not affect the accounts of either the parent or the

EXHIBIT 14A–2 (*concluded*)

	Worksheet to Develop Consolidated Balance Sheet				
	Balance Sheet from Accounts		Eliminations and Restatements		Consolidated Balance Sheet
Account	Company P	Company S	Debit	Credit	
Cash	399,000*	20,000			419,000
Accounts receivable (net)	10,000	40,000		(c) 5,000	45,000
Inventories	20,000	30,000		(a) 4,500	45,500
Investment in Company S	211,000*			{(a) 76,000 {(b) 135,000	
Plant and equipment (net)	200,000	110,000	(a) 36,900		346,900
Patents (net)	20,000	10,000	(a) 3,600		33,600
Goodwill			(a) 40,000		40,000
	860,000	210,000			930,000
Current liabilities	10,000	20,000	(c) 5,000		25,000
Long-term liabilities	50,000	40,000			90,000
Common stock:					
Company P	600,000				600,000
Company S		100,000	(b) 90,000		10,000M
Retained earnings:					
Company P	200,000				200,000
Company S		50,000	(b) 45,000		5,000M
	860,000	210,000			930,000

M—minority stockholders' 10% interest in Company S.

* Includes effects of acquisition entry of ($610,000 − $211,000 = $399,000).

Elminations and restatements:

   (*a*) To record the restatement of assets to market value and to eliminate the net effect from the investment account (case data, item 3*b*).

   (*b*) To eliminate the proportionate part of the stockholders' equity of the subsidiary (90%) and to eliminate an equal amount from the investment account (which now must be zero). Entries (*a*) and (*b*) may be combined.

   (*c*) To eliminate the intercompany payable/receivable of $5,000.

subsidiary. Consolidated statements are prepared only by the parent company and not by the subsidiary. This appendix shows typical consolidation worksheets used to prepare the consolidated balance sheets as of the date of acquisition. Preparing consolidated financial statements subsequent to the date of acquisition is beyond the scope of this text. The effect on the income of the parent, however, is the same as that resulting from using the equity method described in the chapter.

APPENDIX 14B: *Other Unusual Investments and Funds*

Appendix 14B covers accounting for several unusual types of investments. These include special-purpose funds, cash surrender value of life insurance, and futures contracts.

SPECIAL-PURPOSE FUNDS AS LONG-TERM INVESTMENTS

Companies sometimes set aside cash and sometimes other assets, in special funds (special-purpose funds) to be used in the future for a specific, designated purpose. Although a special-purpose fund can be a current asset, it is more commonly a noncurrent asset. As such, it is not directly related to current operations. Long-term funds are reported on the balance sheet under the noncurrent classification under the caption "investments and funds."

Funds may be set aside (1) by contract, as in the case of a bond sinking fund; (2) by law, as in the case of rent deposits; or (3) voluntarily, as in the case of a plant expansion fund. The following are typical examples of long-term special-purpose funds:

1. Funds set aside to retire a specific long-term liability, such as bonds payable, mortgages payable, long-term notes payable.
2. Funds set aside to purchase preferred stock.
3. Funds set aside to purchase major assets, such as land, buildings, and plant.

Typically, special-purpose funds are deposited with an independent trustee, such as a financial institution, which agrees to pay a specified rate of interest each period on the balance in the fund. A typical fund is illustrated in Exhibit 14B–1. Special purpose funds are generally disclosed in the notes to the financial statements.

CASH SURRENDER VALUE OF LIFE INSURANCE

Often a firm will insure the lives of its top executives, with the firm as the beneficiary. If the firm should lose the services of one of the insured individuals from an untimely death, it is compensated for having lost one of its valuable resources. There are three types of life insurance policies a firm might acquire on the lives of its executives: (1) ordinary or whole-life, (2) limited payment, and (3) term insurance. Whole-life and limited payment insurance policies build up value while the policy is in force and have stipulated loan values and cash surrender values. Term insurance, however, has no cash surrender value or loan value since the insurance company is not obligated to make payment except in the event of the death of the insured during the term of the policy.

The **cash surrender value (CSV)** of a policy is the amount that would be refunded should the policy be terminated at the request of the insured. It increases over time as the firm pays the insurance premium; thus, it is an asset for the firm. CSV is a form of investment and is usually accounted for on the balance sheet under investments and funds.

The cash surrender value is computed at the end of each year the policy is in force. Each policy contains a schedule that indicates the cash surrender value and the loan value for each policy year. Because a portion of the premiums paid may be returned in the form of the cash surrender value if and when a policy is canceled, only a portion of the periodic premiums are actually expensed. The firm's period life insurance expense is the excess of the premium paid over the increase in the cash surrender value for the period.

To illustrate, assume Zim Corporation took out a $100,000 whole-life policy on its top executive several years ago. In 1992, which is the fourth year the policy has been in effect, the firm pays an insurance premium in the amount of $2,200. The cash surrender value schedule for the policy shows the following:

Policy Year	Premium	Cash Surrender Value
1	$2,200	0
2	2,200	0
3	2,200	500
4	2,200	1,500
5	2,200	2,600

Based on the above information, the premium of $2,200 paid in Year 4 results in an increase in the cash surrender value of $1,000. This portion would be debited to an account called "cash surrender value of life insurance," with the remainder being recorded as expense:

Life insurance expense	1,200	
Cash surrender value of life insurance	1,000	
Cash		2,200

At the end of Year 4, the cash surrender value of the policy totals $1,500, and this is the amount that should appear in the asset account called "cash surrender value of life insurance."

EXHIBIT 14B-1 Accounting for a Special-Purpose Fund: WT Corporation

1. WT Corporation plans to build a new office building five years hence. The plans estimate the total construction cost to be $1,300,000 and a six-month construction period.
2. The company decided to make five $200,000 cash deposits to a special construction fund each July 1, starting on July 1, 1991. The fund will be administered by an independent trustee. The trustee will increase the fund each June 30 at a 10% interest rate on the fund balance at that date.
3. WT Corporation's accounting period ends December 31.
4. The office building was completed on schedule, the contractor was paid $1,300,000 on July 2, 1996, and the fund was closed.

Fund Accumulation Schedule (Annuity Due Basis)

Date	Cash Deposits	Interest revenue Earned		Fund Increases	Fund Balance
7/1/1991	$ 200,000			$ 200,000	$ 200,000
6/30/1992		$ 200,000 × 10% =	$ 20,000	20,000	220,000
7/1/1992	200,000			200,000	420,000
6/30/1993		420,000 × 10% =	42,000	42,000	462,000
7/1/1993	200,000			200,000	662,000
6/30/1994		662,000 × 10% =	66,200	66,200	728,200
7/1/1994	200,000			200,000	928,200
6/30/1995		928,200 × 10% =	92,820	92,820	1,021,020
7/1/1995	200,000			200,000	1,221,020
6/30/1996		1,221,020 × 10% =	122,102	122,102	1,343,122
	$1,000,000		$343,122	$1,343,122	

Selected Journal Entries: First Year and Final Payment

7/1/1991:
Special building fund 200,000
    Cash 200,000

12/31/1991:
Receivable on building fund 10,000
    Interest revenue ($20,000 × 6/12) 10,000

6/30/1992:
Special building fund 20,000
    Receivable on building fund 10,000
    Interest revenue 10,000

7/1/1992:
Special building fund 200,000
    Cash 200,000

7/2/1996:
Cash 43,122
Office building 1,300,000
    Special building fund 1,343,122

Assume that the insured executive dies on April 1, Year 4, after the above premium has been paid and recorded. The provisions of most policies call for the refunding of any premiums paid beyond the life of the insured. Assuming that the policy anniversary date is January 1, and that the $2,200 premium paid on that date was for the entire year, the refund is $2,200 × (9/12), or $1,650. The insurance company makes payment to Zim Corporation of the face amount of the policy ($100,000) plus the refund amount ($1,650). Zim Corporation recognized insurance expense of $1,200 for the year. Since the policy is in effect only three months before the insured dies, the expense recovery is for three-fourths of the year, or $900. A portion of the $100,000 is the payment of the cash surrender value, and the remainder is a gain:

Cash	101,650	
Life insurance expense		900
Cash surrender value of life insurance		1,500
Gain on settlement of life insurance indemnity		99,250

The gain on life insurance is not usually considered to be extraordinary. The cash surrender value of life insurance policies is reported in the balance sheet as a long-term investment. Insurance premiums on which the company is the beneficiary are not deductible for tax purposes. The proceeds received from the policy payout are also not taxable income.

ACCOUNTING FOR FUTURES CONTRACTS—AN INVESTMENT

Business entities and other investors often purchase **futures contracts** as an investment or as a hedge to offset the risks of future price changes. A futures contract is a contract between a buyer and seller of a commodity or financial instrument and the clearinghouse of a futures exchange. Futures contracts vary; however, such contracts have three common characteristics:

1. They obligate the buyer (seller) to accept (make delivery of) a commodity or financial instrument at a specified time, or they provide for cash settlement periodically rather than delivery.
2. They can be effectively canceled before the specified time by entering into an offsetting contract for the same commodity or financial instrument.
3. All changes in the market value of open contracts are settled on a regular basis, usually daily.

SFAS No. 80 specifies two approaches for recording and reporting futures contracts. The two approaches are called the *market-value* approach and the *hedge-deferral* approach. The primary issue in accounting for a futures contract is whether changes in the market value of a futures contract should be recognized as a gain or loss in the reporting period when the market price changes take place, or whether the gain or loss should be deferred to a later date. *SFAS No. 80* specifies two criteria for determining the accounting approach for futures contracts:

1. The item to be hedged exposes the company to market price or interest rate risk.
2. The futures contract reduces that risk and is designated as a hedge.

The market-value approach must be used when the hedge fails to meet both of these criteria. The market-value approach requires that all gains and losses due to market price changes be recognized in the reporting period when the market price changes.

The hedge-deferral approach must be used when one or both criteria are met. The hedge-deferral approach requires that all gains or losses due to market price changes be deferred and recognized at the termination of the futures contract as an adjustment to the cost (or price) in the subsequent terminating transaction.

A simplified futures contract example is used to illustrate these approaches. Suppose the Rye Company is a producer of a grain-based product. The following events occur:

October 1991—The company determined that it needs 10,000 bushels of grain near the end of February 1992. The company expects the current price of $3 per bushel of grain to change. It does not want to assume the risk of such market price changes.

November 1, 1991—The company decides to purchase a futures contract from Chicago Clearing House Inc. to hedge (i.e., shift) the risk of market price changes of grain. The futures contract, which costs $800, provides that the company purchase the grain at the date needed at the then current market price (or pay the equivalent amount in cash if the grain is not purchased). However, between the date the futures contract is purchased (November 1, 1991) and the termination date (when the grain is purchased), Chicago Clearing House Inc. must pay the company cash for all market price increases (from the $3 beginning hedge price), and will collect cash from the company for all market price decreases (again, from the hedge price of $3). Thus, for an $800 fee, the company shifts the risk of market price changes to the clearinghouse. Changes in the market price of grain are settled daily, and each offset is payable or collectible each weekend.

December 31, 1991—At the end of the reporting period for Rye Company, the market price of grain is $2.80 per bushel.

EXHIBIT 14B-2 Illustration of Entries for Accounting for Futures Contract under the Market-Value Approach and Hedge-Deferral Approach

Market-Value Approach		Hedge-Deferral Approach	

November 1, 1991—to record the futures contract:

Prepaid expense, futures contract	800		Prepaid expense, futures contract	800	
Cash		800	Cash		800

December 31, 1991—To record cash payment to clearinghouse because of the market price decrease in grain:

Loss on futures contract	2,000		Inventory cost adjustment, futures contract	2,000	
Cash		2,000	Cash		2,000

The $2,000 is the change in price ($3.00 less the current price of $2.80) times the number of bushels, 10,000. The loss on futures contract is closed to the income statement. The inventory cost adjustment is reported as a deferred charge on the balance sheet.

February 24, 1992—To record the cash payment received from the clearing house due to the market price increase in grain:

Cash	5,000		Cash	5,000	
Gain on futures contract		5,000	Inventory cost adjustment, futures contract		5,000

The payment is computed as the price change since December 31 ($3.30 − $2.80) times the 10,000 bushels covered by the futures contract.

To record the purchase of grain:

Grain inventory	33,000		Grain inventory	30,000	
Cash		33,000	Inventory cost adjustment, futures contract	3,000	
			Cash		33,000

To record termination of the futures contract:

Expenses, futures contract	800		Expense, futures contract	800	
Prepaid expense, futures contract		800	Prepaid expense, futures contract		800

Futures contract results:

Cash inflow	$5,000	Cash inflow		$5,000
Cash outflow	2,000	Cash outflow		2,000
Net gain	$3,000	Net gain		$3,000

In sum, Rye Company has transferred the risk of price changes for grain to the clearinghouse. Under the market value approach, the gain is explicitly recognized, and the grain acquired is recorded at its current cost. Under the hedge-deferral approach, the gain is not explicitly recognized. Rather, the grain is recorded at the cost that was assured by the futures contract, $30,000. In either case the firm is $3,000 better off.

February 24, 1992—At this date (a) The market price of grains is $3.30, (b) Rye Company purchases the 10,000 bushels of grain needed for production at $3.30 per bushel, cash, and (c) The futures contract is terminated.

Exhibit 14B–2 presents the required entries under two cases: (1) neither criterion is met (therefore the market-value approach is used), and (2) one or both criteria are met (therefore the hedge-deferral approach is used).

KEY TERMS

Cash surrender value (740)
Consolidated financial statements (732)
Cost Method (707)
Equity Method (708)
Financial instrument (721)
Futures contracts (742)
Lower of cost or market (LCM) method (697)

Market Value method (717)
Minority stockholders (735)
Pooling of interests method (732)
Purchase method (736)
Realized gain (699)
Realized loss (699)
Unrealized gain (699)
Unrealized loss (699)

QUESTIONS

1. Distinguish between debt and equity securities; also between short-term and long-term investments.
2. What accounting principle is applied in recording the acquisition of an investment? Explain its application in cash and noncash acquisitions.
3. Briefly explain the accounting for short-term investments in equity securities.
4. An investor purchased 100 shares of PO common stock at $20 per share on March 15, 1991. At the end of the 1991 accounting period, December 31, 1991, the stock was quoted at $19 per share. On June 5, 1992, the investor sold the stock for $22 per share. Assuming a short-term investment, provide answers to the following:
   a. March 15, 1991—debit to the investment account, $____ .
   b. December 31, 1991—unrealized loss, $____ .
   c. June 5, 1992—gain or loss on sale of the investment, $____ .
5. On June 15, 1991, Baker Company purchased 500 shares of preferred stock, par $10, at $30 per share. The market value of these shares at the end of the accounting period, December 3, 1991, was $28 per share. Show how this short-term investment should be reported on the 1991 balance sheet.
6. Briefly explain the accounting for short-term investments in debt securities.
7. What is meant by an impairment loss?
8. Explain why interest revenue is accrued on investments in debt securities, but dividend revenue is not accrued on investments in equity securities.
9. Under the LCM method for investments in equity securities, no distinction is made between voting and nonvoting stock, but the distinction is important with respect to the equity method. Explain why.
10. Explain when the LCM method of accounting for equity investments is applicable.
11. Explain how the LCM concept is applied to long-term investments in equity securities. How is cost determined when an investment is reclassified from short-term to long-term or vice versa?
12. Explain the basic features of the equity method of accounting for long-term investments. When is the equity method applicable?
13. Assume Company R acquired, as a long-term investment, 30% of the outstanding voting common stock of Company S at a cash cost of $100,000. At date of acquisition, the balance sheet of Company S showed total stockholders' equity of $250,000. The market value of the assets of Company S was $20,000 greater than their book value at date of acquisition. Compute goodwill purchased, if any. What accounting method should be used in this situation? Explain why.
14. Assume the same facts as in (13), with the additional data that the net assets have a remaining estimated life of 10 years and goodwill will be amortized over 20 years (assume no residual values and straight-line depreciation). How much additional depreciation and amortization expense should be reported by the investor, Company R, each year in accounting for this long-term investment? Give the entries to record additional depreciation and amortization of goodwill.
15. The equity method of accounting for a long-term investment in equity securities usually will reflect a greater amount of investment revenue than the cost method in the same circumstances. Explain why.
16. Explain the basic features of the market value method of accounting for investments in securities. Is it a generally accepted method? Explain.
17. How would the market value method of accounting for investments in securities, in contrast to the cost method, tend to prevent "managed" earnings?
18. Basically, the investor accounts for an ordinary stock dividend and a stock split in the same way. Briefly explain the accounting that should be followed by the investor in these situations.
19. What is a convertible security? Assume an investor has a convertible security with a carrying value of $200,000, which is turned in to the issuer for conversion. The investor receives, through the conversion, common stock with a current market value of $225,000. Explain how the investor should account for the conversion of this long-term investment.
20. What is a stock right (or stock warrant)? If stock rights have a market value, how would the investor account for the receipt of stock rights?

21. Explain the characteristics of acquisition of a long-term investment accounted for by (a) the pooling of interests method and (b) the purchase method.*

22. Contrast the primary effects on the balance sheet of a pooling of interests versus a purchase. Why are the effects different?*

23. Explain why market values are used in the purchase method but not in the pooling of interests method.*

24. Explain why goodwill is recognized in a purchase but not in a pooling of interests.*

* Relates to Appendix 14A.

EXERCISES

E 14–1
Classification of
Investments in Securities
(L.O. 2)

Match the different securities listed below with their usual classification as investments by entering the appropriate letter in each blank space. Usual classification as investments: A—short-term equity investment, B—short-term debt security, C—long-term equity security, D—long-term debt security, E—none of the above.

Typical Securities

___A___ 1. Abbot common stock, nopar; acquired to use temporarily idle cash.
___E___ 2. Land acquired for short-term speculation.
___B___ 3. U.S. Treasury bills, mature in six months.
___A___ 4. GE preferred stock, par $100, mandatory redemption within next 12 months.
___C___ 5. Staufer common stock, par $5; acquired to attain a continuing controlling interests.
___D___ 6. Frazer bonds, 9%, mature at the end of 10 years; acquired for indefinite holding period.
___E___ 7. Foreign Corporation, common stock; difficulties encountered in withdrawing cash earned.
___B___ 8. Certificates of deposit (CDs); mature at end of one year.
___B___ 9. Savings certificate at local Savings and Loan Association.
___C___ 10. Acorn common stock, par $1; acquired as a short-term investment, but now so profitable that management plans to hold it indefinitely.

E 14–2
Short-Term Equity
Investments, LCM:
Entries and Reporting.
(L.O. 4, 6)

On November 1, 1991, Decker Company acquired the following short-term investments in marketable equity securities:

Corporation X—500 shares common stock (nopar) at $60 cash per share.

Corporation Y—300 shares preferred stock (par $10, nonredeemable) at $20 cash per share.

The annual reporting period ends December 31. On December 31, 1991, the quoted market prices were Corporation X stock, $52, and Corporation Y stock, $24. Following is the data for 1992:

Mar. 2, 1992   Received cash dividends per share as follows: X stock, $1; Y stock, 50 cents.
Oct. 1, 1992   Sold 100 of the Y shares at $25 per share.
Dec. 31, 1992 Market values: X stock, $46; Y stock, $26.

Required:

1. Give the entry for Decker Company to record the purchase of the securities.
2. Give any adjusting entry needed at the end of 1991.
3. Give the items and amounts that should be reported on the 1991 income statement and balance sheet.
4. Give all of the entries for 1992.
5. Give the items and amounts that should be reported on the 1992 income statement and balance sheet.

E 14–3
Short-Term Equity
Investments, LCM:
Purchase, Sale, Transfer,
Entries, and Reporting
(L.O. 4, 6)

At December 31, 1991, the short-term equity investments of Vista Company were as follows:

Security	Shares	Unit Cost	Unit Market Price
Preferred stock, 8%, par $10, Knight Corp.	600	$90	$88
Common stock, nopar, Dyer Corp.	200	30	31

The reporting year ends December 31. The transactions which follow relate to the above short-term equity investments and those bought and sold during 1992:

Feb. 2 Received the annual 8% cash dividend from Knight Corporation.
Mar. 1 Sold 150 shares of the Dyer stock at $34 per share.
May 1   Sold 400 shares of Knight stock at $89.50 per share.
June 1 Received a cash dividend on Dyer stock of $3.50 per share.
Aug. 1 Purchased 4,000 shares of Rote Corporation's common stock at $45 per share.
Sept. 1 Transferred all shares of Dyer common stock from the short-term portfolio to the long-term portfolio. At this date the Dyer stock was quoted at $28 per share.

At December 31, 1992, the quoted market prices were as follows: Knight preferred, $98; Dyer common, $28; and Rote common, $44.50.

Required:

1. Give the entry that Vista Company should make on December 31, 1991, to record the equity investments at LCM.
2. Give the entries for 1992 through September 1.
3. Give the entry(s) required at December 31, 1992.
4. List the items and amounts that should be reported on Vista's 1992 income statement and balance sheet.

√ E 14-4
Short-Term Debt
Security, Cost Method:
Entries and Reporting
(L.O. 5, 6)

On September 1, 1991, New Company purchased 10 bonds of Vue Corporation ($1,000, 6%) as a short-term investment at 96 (i.e., $960) plus accrued interest. The bonds pay annual interest each July 1. New paid cash, including accrued interest. New's annual reporting period ends December 31. At December 31, 1991, the Vue bonds were quoted at 95¾.

Required:

1. Give the journal entry for New Company to record the purchase of the bonds assuming the cost method will be used.
2. Give any adjusting entries required at December 31, 1991.
3. Give the items and amounts that should be reported on the 1991 income statement and balance sheet.
4. Give the required entry on July 1, 1992.
5. On August 1, 1992, New Company sold four of the bonds at 96.5 plus any accrued interest. The remaining six bonds were transferred to the long-term portfolio of debt securities. Give the required entry(s).
6. There were no additional transactions during 1992. List the short-term investment items and amounts that would be reported on the 1992 income statement and balance sheet.

√ E 14-5
Short-Term Debt
Security, LCM Method:
Entries and Reporting
(L.O. 5, 6)

On August 1, 1991, West Company purchased for cash four $10,000 bonds of Moe Corporation at 98 plus accrued interest. The bonds pay 9% interest, payable on a semiannual basis each May 1 and November 1. The bonds were purchased as a short-term investment. The annual reporting period ends December 31.

Required:

1. Give the following entries for West Company for 1991, assuming the LCM method will be used:

8/1/1991   Paid $40,100 cash for the bonds including any accrued interest.
11/1/1991   Collected interest on the bonds.
12/31/1991 Adjusting entries (if any). The bonds were quoted on the market on this date at 96.
12/31/1991 Market value, $38,400.

2. Show how the effects of this short-term investment should be reported on the 1991 income statements and balance sheet.
3. On February 1, 1992, two of the bonds were sold for $19,950 cash including any accrued interest. Give the required entry. Assume no reversing entries were made on January 1, 1992.
4. Give the entry for the collection of interest on May 1, 1992.

E 14–6
Basket Purchase of
Securities: Allocation,
Entry
(L.O. 2)

Voss Company purchased stock in the three different companies listed below, for a lump sum of $113,400, to be held as a long-term investment:

N Corporation, common stock (par, $10), 300 shares.

O Corporation, preferred stock (par $100), 400 shares.

P Corporation common stock (nopar) 500 shares.

In addition, Voss paid transfer fees and other costs related to the acquisition amounting to $600. At the time of purchase, the stocks were quoted on the local market at the following prices per share: N common, $100; O preferred, $120; and P common, $84.

Required:

Give the entry to record the purchase of these long-term investments and payment of the transfer fees and other costs. Record each stock in a separate account and show the cost per share.

E 14–7
Long-Term Investments,
LCM: Entries and
Reporting
(L.O. 6)

During 1991, Shale Company purchased shares in two corporations with the intention of holding them as long-term investments. Transactions were in the following order:

a. Purchased 200 of the 10,000 shares outstanding of common stock of T Corporation at $31 per share plus a 4% brokerage fee and a transfer cost of $52.

b. Purchased 300 of 4,000 outstanding shares of preferred stock (nonvoting) of P Corporation at $78 per share plus a 3% brokerage fee and a transfer cost of $198.

c. Purchased an additional 20 shares of common stock of T Corporation at $35 per share plus a 4% brokerage fee and a transfer cost of $4.

d. Received $4 per share cash dividend on the P Corporation stock (from earnings since acquisition).

Required:

1. Give the entry in the accounts of Shale Company for each transaction, applying the LCM method.
2. The market value of the shares held at the end of 1991 were T stock, $34; P stock, $75. Give the appropriate adjusting entry for Shale Company.
3. The market values of the shares held at the end of 1992 were T stock, $36; P stock, $77. Give the appropriate adjusting entry.
4. Show how the income statement and balance sheet for Shale Company would report relevant data concerning the long-term investments for 1991 and 1992.

E 14–8
Long-Term Equity
Investment, Equity
Method: Compute
Goodwill, Entries
(L.O. 6)

On January 1, 1991, JR Company purchased 400 of the 1,000 outstanding shares of common stock of RV Corporation for $30,000. At that date, the balance sheet of RV showed the following book values:

Assets not subject to depreciation, $40,000.*

Assets subject to depreciation (net), $26,000.†

Liabilities, $6,000.*

Common stock (par $50), $50,000.

Retained earnings, $10,000.

* Same as market value.

† Market value $30,000; the assets have a 10-year remaining life (straight-line depreciation).

Required:

1. Assuming the equity method is appropriate, give the entry by JR Company to record the acquisition at a cost of $30,000. Assume a long-term investment.
2. Show the computation of goodwill purchased at acquisition.
3. Assume at December 31, 1991 (end of the accounting period), RV Corporation reported a net income of $12,000. Assume goodwill amortization over a 10-year period. Give all entries indicated on the records of JR Company.
4. In February 1992, RV Corporation declared and paid a $2 per share cash dividend. Give the necessary entry for JR Company.

E 14–9
Long-Term Equity
Investment, Equity
Method: Compute
Goodwill, Entries
(L.O. 6)

On January 1, 1991, Case Corporation purchased 3,000 of the 10,000 outstanding shares of common stock of Dow Corporation for $28,000 cash. At that date, Dow's balance sheet reflected the following book values:

Assets not subject to depreciation, $25,000.*

Assets subject to depreciation (net), $30,000.†

Liabilities, $5,000.*

Common stock (par $4), $40,000.
Retained earnings, $10,000.

* Same as market value.

† Market value $38,000; estimated remaining life of 10 years (straight-line depreciation).

Required:

1. If goodwill is relevant to this investment, show the computation of goodwill purchased at acquisition.
2. At the end of 1991, Dow reported income before extraordinary items, $20,000; extraordinary loss, $2,000; and net income, $18,000. In December 1991, Dow Corporation paid a $1 per share cash dividend. Reconstruct the following accounts (use T-account format) for Case Corporation: cash, investment in Dow Corporation stock, investment revenue—ordinary, and extraordinary loss. Apply the appropriate method of accounting for long-term investments in equity securities, and assume straight-line amortization of any goodwill is over 10 years. Date and identify all amounts entered in the accounts.

E 14–10
Long-Term Equity
Investment, LCM and
Equity Methods
Compared: Entries
(L.O. 3, 6)

On January 3, 1991, TA Company purchased 2,000 shares of the 10,000 outstanding shares of common stock of UK Corporation for $14,600 cash. At that date, the balance sheet of UK Corporation reflected the following: nondepreciable assets, $50,000 (same as market value); depreciable assets (net), $30,000 (market value, $33,000); total liabilities, $20,000; and stockholders' equity, $60,000. Assume a 10-year remaining life (straight-line depreciation) on the depreciable assets and amortization of goodwill over 10 years.

Required:

1. Give the entries, if any are required, on TA's books for each item (*a*) through (*g*) below assuming that the LCM method is appropriate.
2. Repeat 1. above assuming the equity method is appropriate.
   Entries Required and Other Information:
   a. Entry at date of acquisition.
   b. Goodwill purchased—computation only.
   c. Entry on 12/31/1991 to record $15,000 net income reported by UK.
   d. Entry on 12/31/1991 for additional depreciation expense.
   e. Entry on 12/31/1991 for amortization of goodwill.
   f. Entry on 12/31/1991 to recognize decrease in market value of UK stock, quoted market price, $7 per share. Assume this is the only long-term equity investment held.
   g. Entry on 3/31/1992 for a cash dividend of $1 per share declared and paid by UK.

E 14–11
Equity Securities, Market
Value Method: Entries
and Reporting
(L.O. 6)

On January 10, 1991, BT Company purchased as a long-term investment 15% of the 10,000 shares of the outstanding common stock of N Company (par value, $10 per share) at $50 per share. During 1991, 1992 and 1993, the following additional data were available:

	1991	1992
Reported net income N Co. at year-end	$30,000	$35,000
Cash dividends paid by N Co. at year-end	10,000	15,000
Quoted market price per share of N Co. stock at year-end	57	55

On January 2, 1993, BT Company sold 100 of N Co. shares at $56 per share.

Required:

1. Assuming the market value method is used, give all entries indicated in the accounts of BT Company, assuming the company uses the current approach.
2. Prepare a tabulation to show the investment revenue for 1991, 1992, and 1993 of BT Company and the balance in the investment account at year-end 1991, 1992, and 1993. Assume no cash dividends were paid by N Co. during 1993, and that the quoted market price of N Co. common stock was $56 per share at December 31, 1993.

E 14–12
Long-Term Equity Investment, Stock Dividend, Investor's Entries
(L.O. 8)

Each of the following situations is completely independent; however, each relates to the receipt of a stock dividend by an investor.

Case A:
Doe Corporaton had 20,000 shares of $50 par value stock outstanding when the board of directors voted to issue a 25% stock dividend (i.e., one additional share for each four shares owned).

Required:
Van Company owns 2,000 shares of the Doe Corporation stock (a long-term investment) acquired at a cost of $65 per share. After receiving the stock dividend, Van Company sold 200 shares of the additional stock for $70 per share. Give the entries for Van Company to record (*a*) acquisition of the 2,000 shares, (*b*) receipt of the stock dividend, and (*c*) sale of the 200 shares. Assume the LCM method is appropriate for the investor.

Case B:
During the course of an audit, you find two accounts of the investor, May Company, as follows:

Investments in Stock of Yew Company ($100 par value):

Debits

Jan. 1	Cost of 100 shares	$17,500
Feb. 1	50 shares received as a stock dividend (at par $100)	5,000

Credits

July 1	25 shares of dividend stock sold at $125	$ 3,125

Income summary

Credits

Feb. 1	Stock dividend on Yew Company stock	$ 5,000
Aug. 1	Cash dividend on Yew Company stock	3,000

Required:
Assuming the LCM method is appropriate for the investor, restate these accounts on a correct basis. Give reasons for each change.

E 14–13
Long-Term Equity Investment: Cash and Stock Dividends, Stock Split, Entries
(L.O. 6, 8)

PA Company purchased common stock (par value $10, 50,000 shares outstanding) of SU Corporation as a long-term investment. Transactions (which occurred in the order given) related to this investment were as follows:

a. Purchased 600 shares of SU common stock at $90 per share (designated as lot No. 1).
b. Purchased 2,000 shares of SU common stock at $96 per share (designated as lot No. 2).
c. At the end of the first year, SU Corporation reported net income of $52,000.
d. SU Corporation paid a cash dividend of $2 per share on the common stock.
e. After reporting net income of $5,000 for the second year, SU Corporation issued a stock dividend whereby each stockholder received one additional share for each two shares owned. At the time of the stock dividend, the stock was selling at $85.
f. SU Corporation revised its charter to provide for a stock split. The par value was reduced to $5. The old common stock was turned in, and the holders received in exchange two shares of the new stock for each old share turned in.

Required:
Give the entries for each transaction as they should be made in the accounts of PA Company. Show computations. Assume the LCM method is appropriate because less than 20% of SU's voting stock is held by PA.

E 14–14
Long-Term Equity Investment: Stock Rights, Entries
(L.O. 8)

Corporation M issued one stock right for each share of common stock owned by investors. The rights provided that for each six rights held, a share of preferred stock could be purchased for $80 (par of the preferred was $50 per share). When the rights were issued, they had a market value of $7 each, and the common stock was selling at $142 per share (ex rights). Taylor Company owned 300 shares of Corporation M common stock, acquired as a long-term investment at a cost of $22,350. Assume the LCM method is appropriate.

Required:

1. How many rights did Taylor Company receive?
2. Determine the carrying value of the stock rights received by Taylor Company and give any entry that should be made upon receipt of the rights.
3. Assume Taylor Company exercised the rights when the market value of the preferred stock of Corporation M was $130. Determine the cost of the new stock and give the entry to record the exercise of the rights.
4. Assume instead that Taylor Company sold its rights for $7.40 each. Give the entry to record the sale.

E 14–15
Long-Term Equity
Investment: Stock
Dividend, Stock Rights,
Entries
(L.O. 8)

Give entries in the accounts of Cisco Corporation under the LCM method for the following transactions, which occurred over a period of time and in the chronological order shown:

a. Cisco Corporation purchased 100 shares of Bell Corporation common stock at $99 per share as a long-term investment.
b. Bell Corporation issued a 10% stock dividend in additional common shares.
c. Bell Corporation issued rights to current common stockholders entitling each holder of five old shares to buy one additional share of new common stock at $96. At the time, the rights sold for $4 per right and the shares outstanding sold for $116 each (ex rights). Make an allocation to the rights.
d. Cisco Corporation exercised all of its rights and bought new shares.
e. Cisco Corporation sold 120 shares of Bell stock for $100 per share, failing to identify the specific shares disposed of (use FIFO procedures). What is the status of the investment account after this sale (number of shares, cost per share, and total investment amount)?

E 14–16
Appendix 14B:
Special-Purpose Fund:
Accumulation Schedule,
Entries
(L.O. 10)

On January 1, 1991, Koke Company decided to create a special-purpose fund to be identified as the "special contingency fund." The resources in the fund will be used to reimburse employees injured while on the job. The company desires to accumulate a $150,000 fund balance by the end of 1993 by making equal annual deposits starting on January 1, 1991. The independent trustee handling the fund will increase the fund by 9% compound interest each December 31.

Required:

1. Compute the amount of the annual deposits and prepare a fund accumulations schedule.
2. Give the entries relating to the fund that Koke Company should make each year.
3. Assume that on January 2, 1994, the trustee made the first payment from the fund in the amount of $1,000. Give the entry, if any, that Koke Company should make.

E 14–17
Appendix 14A:
Pooling, 100% Ownership:
Consolidation Worksheet
(L.O. 9)

On January 1, 1991, Company A acquired all of the outstanding shares of Company B common stock by exchanging, on a share-for-share basis, 4,000 shares of its own stock. The acquisition qualifies as a pooling of interests. The balance sheets reflected the following summarized data immediately before acquisition:

	Company A	Company B
Assets not subject to depreciation	$200,000	$50,000*
Assets subject to depreciation (net and 10-year remaining life)	120,000	25,000
	$320,000	$75,000
Liabilities	$ 40,000*	$ 5,000
Common stock (par $10)	200,000	40,000
Retained earnings	80,000	30,000
	$320,000	$75,000

* Includes a $5,000 debt owed by Company A to Company B.

Required:

1. Give the entry in the accounts of Company A for the acquisition of this long-term investment.
2. Prepare a consolidation worksheet immediately after acquisition.

E 14–18
Appendix 14A:
Pooling, 90% Ownership:
Consolidation Worksheet
(L.O. 9)

On January 1, 1991, Company W acquired 90% of the outstanding shares of Company X common stock by exchanging, on a share-for-share basis, 3,600 shares of its own stock. The acquisition qualifies as a pooling of interests. The balance sheet reflected the following summarized data immediately before acquisition:

	Company W	Company X
Assets not subject to depreciation	$180,000	$40,000*
Assets subject to depreciation (net and 10-year remaining life)	120,000	$25,000
	$300,000	$65,000
Liabilities	$ 20,000*	$ 5,000
Common stock (par $10)	200,000	40,000
Retained earnings	80,000	20,000
	$300,000	$65,000

* Includes a $4,000 debt owed by Company W to Company X.

Required:

1. Give the entry in the accounts of Company W for the acquisition of this long-term investment.
2. Prepare a consolidation worksheet immediately after acquisition.

E 14–19
Appendix 14A:
Purchase, 100%
Ownership: Goodwill,
Worksheet
(L.O. 9)

In January 1991, Company P purchased, for $149,000 cash, all of the 10,000 outstanding voting shares of the common stock of Company S. The acquisition qualifies as a purchase. Immediately before acquisition, the following additional summarized data were available:

	Company P Book Value	Company S Book Value	Company S Market Value
Assets not subject to depreciation	$410,000	$ 80,000*	$ 85,000†
Assets subject to depreciation (net)	200,000	60,000	67,000‡
Total	$610,000	$140,000	$152,000
Liabilities	$ 40,000*	$ 10,000	
Common stock (par $10)	500,000	100,000	
Retained earnings	70,000	30,000	
Total	$610,000	$140,000	

* Includes a $12,000 debt owed by Company P to Company S.

† Entire market value excess over cost is for short-term investments.

‡ Estimated remaining life, 10 years (straight-line depreciation).

Required:

1. Give the entry in the accounts of Company P to record acquisition of this long-term investment.
2. Compute the amount of any goodwill purchased.
3. Prepare a consolidation worksheet immediately after acquisition.

PROBLEMS

P 14–1
Short-Term Equity
Investments, LCM
Method: Entries
(L.O. 4, 6)

On January 1, 1991, Joy Company acquired the following short-term investments in equity securities:

Co.	Stock	No. of Shares	Cost per Share
T	Common (nopar)	1,000	$20
U	Common (par $10)	600	15
V	Preferred (par $20, nonconvertible)	400	30

Per share data subsequent to the acquisition are as follows:

12/31/1991   Market values: T stock, $16; U stock, $15; and V stock, $34.
2/10/1992   Cash dividends received: T stock, $1.50; U stock, $1; and V stock, 50 cents.
11//1992   Sold the shares of V stock at $38.
12/31/1992   Market values: T stock, $12; U stock, $17; and V stock, $33.

Required:

1. Give all entries indicated for Joy Company for 1991 and 1992. Use the LCM basis. There was no balance in the allowance account on January 1, 1991.
2. Show how the income statement and balance sheet for Joy Company would reflect the short-term investments for 1991 and 1992.

P 14–2
Short-Term Equity
Investment, LCM: Entries
and Reporting
(L.O. 4, 6)

On December 31, 1991, Raven Company's portfolio of short-term investments in equity securities was as follows (purchased on September 1, 1991):

Security	Shares	Unit Cost	Unit Market
BC Corp., common stock, nopar	50	$186	$187
CD Corp., preferred stock, 6% par $40	200	40	35

Transactions relating to this portfolio during 1992 were as follows:

Jan. 25   Received a 6% dividend check on the CD shares.
Apr. 15   Sold 30 shares of BC Corporation stock at $151 per share.
July 25   Received a $45 dividend check on the BC shares.
Oct. 1   Sold the remaining shares of BC Corporation at $149.50 per share.
Dec. 1   Purchased 100 shares of EF Corporation common stock at $47 per share plus a $30 brokerage fee.
Dec. 5   Purchased 400 shares of GH Corporation common stock, par $1, at $15 per share.
Dec. 31   Transferred the CD shares to the long-term investment portfolio of equity securities.

On December 31, 1992, the following unit market prices were available: BC stock, $140; CD stock, $38; EF stock, $51; and GH stock, $14.

Required:

1. Give the entries that Raven Company should make on (*a*) September 1, 1991, and (*b*) December 31, 1991. Use the LCM method.
2. Give the short-term investment items and amounts that should be reported on the 1991 income statement and balance sheet.
3. Give the journal entries for 1992 related to the short-term investments.
4. Give the short-term investment items and amounts that should be reported on the 1992 income statement and balance sheet.

P 14–3
Short-Term Investment,
Debt Securities, LCM:
Entries and Reporting
(L.O. 5, 6)

On April 1, 1991, Lyn Company purchased for cash eight $1,000, 9% bonds of Star Corporation at 102 plus accrued interest. The bond interest is paid semiannually on each May 1 and November 1. Lyn Company's annual reporting period ends on December 31. Lyn Company will use the LCM basis to account for this short-term investment.

On December 1, 1991, six of these bonds were sold for cash at 101½ plus any accrued interest. At December 31, 1991, the Star Corporation bonds were quoted at 97.

Required:

1. Give the entry for Lyn Company to record the purchase of the bonds on April 1, 1991.
2. Give the entry for interest collected during 1991.
3. Give the entry on December 1, 1991.
4. Give any adjusting entry(s) required on December 31, 1991.
5. Show what items and amounts should be reported on the 1991 income statement and balance sheet.

P 14–4
Short-Term Debt
Investment, Cost Method:
Entries and Reporting
(L.O. 5)

At December 31, 1991, the portfolio of short-term investments in debt securities held by Dow Company was as follows:

Security	Par Value	Rate	Interest Payable	Cash Cost*	Date Purchased
X Corp. bonds	$10,000	6%	Nov. 1	$ 9,800	Sept. 1, 1991
Y Corp. bonds	20,000	9%	Dec. 31	20,400	Dec. 31, 1991

* Excluding any accrued interest.

Dow's annual reporting period ends on December 31; the company will use the cost method in conformity with GAAP as specified in *ARB No. 43.*

Transactions relating to the portfolio of short-term investments in debt securities during 1992 were as follows:

June 1 Sold the Y Corp. bonds at 103, plus any accrued interest.
Nov. 1 Collected interest on the X Corp. bonds.
Dec. 1 Purchased $30,000 of Z Corp. bonds at 99½ plus accrued interest. These bonds pay 8% interest, semiannually each March 1 and September 1.
Dec. 31 Transferred the X Corp. bonds to the portfolio of long-term debt securities.

Required:

1. Give the 1991 entries for Dow Company to record the purchase of the debt securities, collections of interest, and all related adjusting entries.
2. Give all of the 1992 entries, including interest collections and any adjusting entries.
3. List the items and amounts that would be reported on the 1992 income statement and the current section of the balance sheet. The Z Corp. bonds were quoted at 99 on December 31, 1992.

P 14–5
Short-Term Equity
Investments, Debt
Securities, LCM: Entries
and Reporting
(L.O. 4, 5, 7)

At December 31, 1991, Piper Company held two short-term investment portfolios as follows:

Description	Quantity	Total Cost	Unit Market Prices
1. Equity securities:			
Damon common stock	50 shares	$2,300	$ 47
Martin common stock	100 shares	2,100	19
2. Debt security:			
Hydro Corp., $1,000 bonds, 9% payable annually on June 1	10 bonds	10,400	103.5

Transactions relating to short-term investments during 1992 were as follows (the annual reporting period ends December 31):

Mar. 1 Sold 30 shares of Damon common stock at $50 per share.
Apr. 1 Sold 70 shares of Martin common stock at $20 per share.
June 1 Collected interest on the Hydro bonds.
June 2 The Hydro bonds were transferred to long-term debt investments; the market price at this date was 103.
Sept. 1 Received a cash dividend of $1 per share on the Damon common stock.
Dec. 1 Purchased 300 shares of ATX common stock at $25 cash per share.

Piper Company accounts for its equity and debt securities at LCM.

Quoted market prices at December 31, 1992, were as follows: Damon common stock, $45; Martin common stock, $21; ATX common stock, $28; and Hydro Corp. bonds, $1,010 per bond (i.e., 101).

Required:

1. Show how the two investment portfolios should be reported on the 1991 balance sheet. Show computations.
2. Give the entries for the 1992 transactions through December 31, 1992.

3. Give the entry(s) to record LCM on the short-term equity securities at December 31, 1992.
4. Give the items and amounts that must be reported on the 1992 income statement and the current section of the balance sheet.

P 14–6
Long-Term Equity Investments, LCM: Entries and Reporting for Two Years
(L.O. 6, 7)

On January 1, 1991, Rae Company purchased 4,000 of the 40,000 shares outstanding of common stock (par $10) of DB Corporation for $80,000 cash, and 3,000 of the 100,000 shares outstanding of common stock (nopar) of CX Corporation for $7 per share cash as long-term investments. These are the only long-term equity investments held. The accounting periods for all the companies end on December 31.

	DB Corp.	CX Corp.
December 31, 1991:		
Income reported for 1991	$40,000	$20,000
Cash dividend per share declared and paid during 1991	1.00	None
Market price per share of stock	15	8
October 20, 1992:		
Sold 1,000 shares of CX stock at $11 per share.		
December 31, 1992:		
Income reported for 1992	50,000	26,000
Cash dividend per share declared and paid during 1992	1.00	.60
Market price per share of stock	17	6
Reclassified the CX stock as a current asset (short-term investment).		

Required:
1. Give all of the entries required for Rae Company for 1991 and 1992.
2. Show how the long-term investments in equity securities and the related investment revenue would be reported on the financial statements of Rae Company at the end of each year.

P 14–7
Long-Term Equity Investments, LCM: Entries and Reporting for Three Years
(L.O. 6, 7)

During January 1991, Poe Company purchased 5,000 of the 50,000 outstanding shares of common stock (par $1) of Styp Corporation at $15 per share cash as a long-term investment (the only long-term equity investment held). The accounting period for both companies ends December 31. During 1991, 1992, and 1993, the following additional data were available:

1. Styp Corporation:

	1991	1992
Net income reported by Styp at year-end	$15,000	$20,000
Cash dividends declared and paid by Styp during the year (total)	6,000	12,000
Market price per share (Styp stock)	6	5

2. On December 31, 1992, Poe determined that the drop in market price was permanent (not temporary) due to unusual circumstances.
3. On January 2, 1993, Poe sold 1,000 shares of the Styp stock at $5.20 per share.
4. On December 31, 1993, Styp shares were selling at $4.75.

Required:
1. Give all of the entries indicated in the accounts of Poe Company assuming the LCM method of accounting for long-term investments in equity securities is used.
2. Show how all of the related accounts and amounts would be reported on Poe's 1991, 1992, and 1993 income statement and balance sheet.

P 14–8
Long-Term Equity Investment, Goodwill: Entries and Reporting for Three Years
(L.O. 6, 7)

On January 1, 1991, Parr Company purchased 30% of the 30,000 outstanding common shares, par $10, of Stub Corporation at $17 per share as a long-term investment (the only long-term equity investment held). The following data in respect to Stub Corporation had been assembled by Parr Company:

1. At acquisition date, January 1, 1991:

	Valued at	
	Book	**Market**
Assets not subject to depreciation	$250,000	$260,000*
Assets subject to depreciation, net (10-year remaining life; straight-line)	200,000	220,000
	$450,000	
Liabilities	$ 50,000	50,000
Common stock (par $10)	300,000	
Retained earnings	100,000	
	$450,000	

* Difference due to inventory, and this inventory is sold during 1991.

2. Selected data available at December 31, 1991, and 1992:

	1991	**1992**
Cash dividends declared and paid by Stub Corporation during the year	$ 8,000	$ 5,000
Income reported by Stub:		
Income (loss) before extraordinary items	24,000	(10,000)
Extraordinary loss	(2,000)	
Quoted market price per share, Stub Corporation stock (December 31)	20	18

3. On January 2, 1993, Parr Company sold 500 of the Stub shares at $18 per share.

Required:

1. Give all of the appropriate entries for Parr Company during 1991 and 1992. Use straight-line amortization of goodwill over a 30-year period.
2. Give the entry required on January 2, 1993.
3. Show what items and amounts based on requirements 1 and 2 will be reported on the 1991, 1992, and 1993 income statements, and 1991 and 1992 balance sheets.

P 14–9
Long-Term Equity Investment, LCM: Cash and Stock Dividends, Split, Entries, and Reporting
(L.O. 6, 7, 8)

Allen Corporation completed the following transactions, in the order given, relative to the portfolio of stocks held as long-term investments:

Year 1991:

a. Purchased 200 shares of MC Corporation common stock (par value $10) at $70 per share plus a brokerage commission of 4% and transfer costs of $20.
b. Purchased, for a lump sum of $96,000, the following stocks of NP Corporation:

	Number of Shares	Market Price at Date of Purchase
Class A, common, par value $20	200	$ 50
Preferred, noncumulative, par value $50	300	100
Class B, nopar common stock (stated value $100)	400	150

Year 1992:

c. Purchased 300 shares of MC Corporation common stock at $80 per share plus a brokerage commission of 4% and transfer costs of $60.
d. Received a stock dividend on the MC Corporation stock; for each share held, an additional share was received.
e. Sold 100 shares of MC Corporation stock at $45 per share (from lot 1).

Year 1993:

f. Received a two-for-one stock split on the class A common stock of NP Corporation (the number of shares doubled).

g. Cash dividends declared and paid:

MC Corporation common stock—$10 per share.
NP, class A, common stock—$5 per share.
NP, preferred—6%.
NP, class B, nopar common stock—$15 per share.

	Year-End Stock Prices		
	1991	1992	1993
MC, common stock	$ 70	$ 40	$ 39.95
NP, class A, common	51	47	24
NP preferred stock	98	95	96
NP, class B, common	140	144	144

Required:

1. Give entries for Allen Corporation for the above transactions assuming the LCM method is appropriate. Show calculations and assume FIFO order when shares are sold.
2. What items and amounts would be shown on the 1991, 1992, and 1993 income statements and balance sheets by Allen Corporation in respect to the long-term investments?

 P 14–10

COMPREHENSIVE PROBLEM
◆

Long-Term Equity
Investment, LCM and
Equity Methods
Compared: Entries
and Reporting
(L.O. 3, 6, 7)

On January 1, 1992, AV Company purchased 3,000 of the 15,000 outstanding shares of common stock of DC Corporation for $80,000 cash as a long-term investment (the only long-term equity investment held). At that date, the balance sheet of DC Corporation showed the following book values (summarized):

Assets not subject to depreciation	$140,000*
Assets subject to depreciation (net)	100,000†
Liabilities	40,000
Common stock (par $10)	150,000
Retained earnings	50,000

* Market value, $150,000; difference relates to short-term investments.

† Market value, $140,000, estimated remaining life, 10 years. Use straight-line depreciation with no residual value and amortization of goodwill over 20 years.

Additional subsequent data on DC Corporation:

	1992	1993
Income before extraordinary items	$25,000	$26,000
Extraordinary item—gain		5,000
Cash dividends declared and paid	10,000	12,000
Market value per share	25	26

Required:

1. For Case A, assume the LCM method is appropriate. For Case B, assume the equity method is appropriate. For each case, provide the investor's entries or give the required information for items (*a*) through (*d*) in a tabulation similar to the one below.

Entries Required and Other Information	Case A: LCM Method Is Appropriate		Case B: Equity Method Is Appropriate	

a. Entry at date of acquisition.
 b. Amount of goodwill purchased.
 c. Entries at 12/31/1992:
   (1) Investment revenue and dividends.
   (2) Additional depreciation expense.
   (3) Amortizaton of goodwill.				

Entries Required and Other Information	Case A: LCM Method Is Appropriate		Case B: Equity Method Is Appropriate	
(4) Additional expense associated with short-term investments (held by DC) for which market value (i.e., purchase price to AV) exceeded book value; these investments were sold during 1992.				
(5) Recognition of change in market value of DC stock.				
d. Entries at 12/31/1993:				
(1) Investment revenue and dividends.				
(2) Additional depreciation expense.				
(3) Amortization of goodwill.				
(4) Recognition of change in market value of DC stock.				

2. For each case, reconstruct the investment, the allowance, and the unrealized capital accounts.
3. Explain why the investment account balance is different between the LCM and equity methods.

P 14–11

Long-Term Equity Investment, Market Value Method: Current versus Deferral Approaches; Entries and Reporting
(L.O. 6, 7)

On January 1, 1991, Taft Company purchased, as a long-term investment, 6% of the 50,000 (par $10) shares of the outstanding common stock of Company S at $11 per share during the years 1991, 1992, and 1993. The following additional company data were available:

End of 1991: Reported net income, $30,000; cash dividends declared and paid, $20,000; market value per share, $15.

End of 1992: reported net income, $25,000; cash dividends declared and paid, $15,000; market value per share, $14.

December 10, 1993: Taft Company sold 200 shares of Company S stock at $17.50 per share.

Required:

1. Assuming the market value method is used, give the entries for Taft Company for each transaction related to the investment, assuming:

   a. Current approach—market changes are reported on the income statement.
   b. Deferral approach—market changes are reported on the balance sheet as a separate element of owners' equity.

2. In parallel columns for each of the above assumptions, show the following at the end of 1991, 1992, and 1993:

   a. Balance of the investment account.
   b. Balance in the unrealized owners' equity each year-end.
   c. Revenue from the investment for each period.

   For this second requirement, assume there were no additional investment transactions during 1993 and the market value of Company S stock was $17.50 per share on December 31, 1993.

P 14–12

Appendix 14B: Special-Purpose Fund: Accumulation Schedule, Entries, and Reporting
(L.O. 10)

On January 1, 1991, Case Corporation created a special building fund by a depositing a single sum of $100,000 with an independent trustee. The purpose of the fund is to provide resources to build an addition to the older office building during the latter part of 1995. The company anticipates a total construction cost of $500,000 and completion by January 1, 1995. The company plans to make equal annual deposits each December 31, 1991 through 1995, to accumulate the $500,000. The independent trustee will increase the fund each December 31, at an interest rate of 10%. The accounting periods of the company and the fund end on December 31.

Required:

1. Compute the amount of the equal annual deposits that will be needed and prepare a fund accumulation schedule through December 31, 1996, for Case Corporation.
2. The total cash outlay by Case will be $_____
   Total interest revenue will be $_____
   The effective interest rate will be _____ %
3. Give the entries for Case on: (*a*) January 1, 1991 and (*b*) December 31, 1991.
4. Give the entries for Case on January 3, 1996 when the addition is completed and the actual cost of $525,000 is paid in full. The trustee paid interest on the fund for two extra days at the fund rate.
5. Show what the 1992 Case income statement, balance sheet, and statement of cash flows should report in regards to the building addition program.
6. Assume the accounting period of Case Corporation ends on October 31 (instead of December 31) and the fund year-end is unchanged. Give any adjusting entry(s) that Case should make at its 1993 year-end.

P 14–13

Appendix 14A:
Pooling, 90%: Worksheet
for Balance Sheet and
Income Statement
(L.O. 9)

On January 1, 1991, Company C acquired 90% of the outstanding common stock of Company D by exchanging 18,000 shares of its own common stock for an equal number of shares of Company D. The acquisition qualifies as a pooling of interests.

After one year of operations, each company prepared an income statement and a balance sheet as follows (summarized):

	Reported at End of 1991	
	Company C	Company D
Income statement		
Sales revenue	$ 630,000	$180,000
Interest revenue	1,000	
Total revenues	631,000	180,000
Cost of goods sold	370,000	98,000
Depreciation expense	37,000	16,000
Other operating expenses	140,000	45,000
Interest expense	4,000	1,000
Total expenses	551,000	160,000
Net income	$ 80,000	$ 20,000
Balance sheet:		
Current assets	$ 560,000	$110,000
Investment in Company D (at cost)	180,000	
Operational assets (net)	360,000	160,000
Total assets	$1,100,000	$270,000
Current Liabilities	$ 70,000	$ 30,000
Common stock (par $10)	940,000	200,000
Retained earnings	90,000	40,000*
Total liabilities and equities	$1,100,000	$270,000

* Company D retained earnings balance at acquisition date was $20,000.

Data relating to 1991 eliminations:

a. During the year, Company C sold merchandise to Company D for $35,000 (at cost); Company D resold the merchandise during 1991.
b. During 1991, Company D paid Company C $1,000 interest on loans.
c. At the end of 1991, Company D owed Company C $20,000.

Required:

1. Prepare a worksheet at the end of 1991 to develop a consolidated income statement and balance sheet.
2. Prepare a consolidated income statement and balance sheet clearly identifying the minority interest.

CASES

Lee Corporation is currently negotiating to acquire Rudd Corporation, a successful enterprise that would complement the operations of Lee. An important factor in the negotiations has been the potential effects of the acquisition on Lee's financial statements. Accordingly, Lee's management has requested that you prepare pro forma (i.e., "as if") balance sheets for the year just ended, under two assumptions—(1) pooling of interests and (2) purchase.

The balance sheets and income statements for the two corporations for the year just ended (prior to acquisition) are as follows:

		Rudd Corp.	
	Lee Corp.	Book Value	Appraised
Balance sheet:			
Cash	$ 485,000	$ 15,000	$ 15,000
Receivables (net)	30,000	65,000	50,000
Inventories	85,000	70,000	70,000
Land	50,000		
Plant (net)	600,000	100,000	230,000
Patents (net)	10,000	30,000	40,000
	$1,260,000	$ 280,000	
Current liabilities	$ 40,000	$ 15,000	15,000
Long-term liabilities	110,000	25,000	25,000
Common stock (par $10)	1,000,000	200,000	
Retained earnings	110,000	40,000	
	$1,260,000	$ 280,000	
Income statement:			
Sales revenue	$6,000,000	$1,000,000	
Costs and expenses (excluding depreciation and amortization)	$5,754,000	$ 967,000	
Depreciation	65,000	10,000	
Amortization of patents	1,000	3,000	
Net income	$ 180,000	$ 20,000	
Market price per share (average shares sold per trading day, 650)	$24.00	Not quoted	

At year-end, Rudd Corporation owed a $10,000 current liability to Lee Corporation. For case purposes, assume that all depreciable assets and intangible assets have a remaining useful life of 10 years from date of acquisition (and straight-line).

Required:

1. Assumption No. 1—At the start of the new year, Lee will acquire all outstanding shares of Rudd by exchanging stock on a share-for-share basis so that the acquisition would qualify as a pooling of interests.
   a. Give the pro forma entry that Lee would make to record the investment.
   b. Prepare a pro forma consolidation worksheet immediately after acquisition.
2. Assumption No. 2—At the start of the new year, Lee will purchase all of the outstanding stock of Rudd for $460,000 cash so that the acquisition would qualify as a purchase.
   a. Give the pro forma entry that Lee would make to record the investment.
   b. Prepare a pro forma consolidation worksheet immediately after acquisition.
3. Which course of action would you recommend to Lee's management? Discuss the primary advantages and disadvantages of your recommendation. Use appropriate data developed for the two assumptions.

ACE Investors Company buys and sells various equity securities. These securities are approximately 90% of their total assets. Because ACE operates in one of the specialized industries permitted to use the market value method, ACE accounts for, and reports, its long-term investments on that basis. Currently, ACE uses the deferral approach to account for, and report, the market value changes in this investment portfolio. The company has decided to reconsider its use of the deferral approach because some major competitors use the current approach. Some of ACE's executives are opposed to changing because they are concerned about its effects on their retirement pay. You have been asked to consult with ACE on this proposed change. Accordingly, you have assembled the following data taken from their records:

a. January 1, 1991—purchased long-term equity securities, cost $50 million.
b. December 31—market value (millions of dollars):

1991, $56.0; 1992, $52.0; 1993, $49.5.

c. Cash dividends received (millions of dollars):

1991, $4.0; 1992, $4.2; 1993, $4.1.

d. December 1, 1993—sold for $6.0 million, 10% of the securities from the portfolio that originally cost $5.0 million; carrying value, $5.2 million.

ACE's accounting period ends December 31.

Required:
1. Briefly explain the difference between the two approaches under consideration by ACE.
2. Give possible reasons why some of the ACE executives are concerned about their retirement pay.
3. (*a*) Which approach would you recommend for ACE? To support your recommendations, you have been requested to provide comparative accounting entries under each approach and to complete the schedule given below.
   (*b*) After completing the schedule, what general conclusions can you draw from it in regard to financial statement effects?
4. What is the fundamental distinction between the two approaches?

Schedule of Comparative Effects on the Balance Sheet and Income Statement

Items	1991		1992		1993	
	Current	**Deferral**	**Current**	**Deferral**	**Current**	**Deferral**
Balance sheet:						
Assets						
Liabilities						
Stockholders' equity						
Income statement:						
Revenues						
Expenses						
Income						

5. Do you see any ethic issues involved in the assignment you have been asked to undertake?

C 14–3
Sherwin-Williams:
Analysis of Financial
Statements
(L.O. 9)

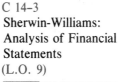

Note 15 to the Sherwin-Williams financial statements provides information on the Sherwin-Williams Development Corporation (SWDC), a wholly owned subsidiary that is consolidated in the financial statements. Summarized data are presented on SWDC.

Required:
1. Suggest some reasons why the FASB would require firms to consolidate nonhomogeneous businesses such as a manufacturer and its finance subsidiary.
2. For the December 31, 1990, financial statements of Sherwin-Williams, by what amount would the following account balances change if SWDC were not consolidated, but rather accounted for as an investment using the equity method?
   a. Total assets
   b. Property, plant and equipment
   c. Long-term debt
   d. Total revenue

   e. Interest expense

   f. Net income

3. How did Sherwin-Williams account for the two firms it acquired in 1990? See Note 4. What was the total purchase price for these two acquisitions? Can you determine approximately what portion of this purchase price was for tangible assets acquired, and what portion was for goodwill? Discuss, using observations of account balances in the financial statements.

Sherwin-Williams
1990 Annual Report

Management's Discussion and Analysis of Financial Condition and Results of Operations

Highlights of 1990

- Effective June 1, 1990, the Company sold Lyons Transportation Lines, Inc. (LTL).

- Effective June 25, 1990, the Company acquired certain assets of the Krylon and Illinois Bronze aerosol paints and coatings businesses of Borden, Inc.

- Effective October 27, 1990, the Company acquired certain assets of the U.S. consumer paint business of DeSoto, Inc.

- During 1990, debt activity included the prepayment of certain outstanding debt with a total weighted-average annual interest rate of 10.04 percent and certain new borrowings that have a total weighted-average annual interest rate of 9.02 percent.

- The Company entered into an agreement with Sears, Roebuck & Co. for the supply of paint products previously supplied by DeSoto.

- New point-of-sale devices were in place in every store.

Earnings Per Common Share
Dollars.

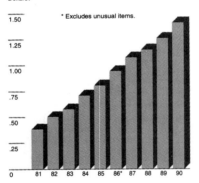

Financial Condition - 1990

Our current ratio dropped slightly, from 2.0 in 1989 and 1988 to 1.9 in 1990, primarily due to a decrease of $103.1 million in cash, cash equivalents and short-term investments as a result of acquisitions ($207.0 million), payments of debt ($33.7 million), and payments of cash dividends ($32.9 million). These decreases in cash were partially offset by proceeds from disposals of assets ($27.4 million) and from issuance of debt ($49.0 million). Accounts receivable ($24.3 million), inventories ($46.9 million), other current assets ($10.4 million), and accounts payable ($26.9 million) all increased primarily due to acquisitions, partially offset by the disposition of LTL. The decrease in the current portion of long-term debt was primarily due to the January 1990 payment of $15.8 million outstanding principal of the 10.50 percent

promissory notes. Other accruals decreased primarily as a result of current year costs and adjustments made to prior accruals.

Working Capital as a % of Sales
Percent

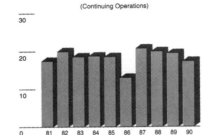

Property, plant and equipment increased from 1989 by capital expenditures of $64.3 million and acquired assets of $9.2 million, partially offset by the disposition of $8.8 million of LTL assets. Capital expenditures represent principally the cost of opening or remodeling paint stores, the installation of point-of-sale devices, and the continued upgrade of equipment at manufacturing, distribution, and research facilities. There were no significant acquisitions in 1989. During 1988, our principal acquisition was the purchase of certain assets of Western Automotive Finishes, Inc., an automotive paint manufacturer and distributor. Capital expenditures in 1988 were principally for the cost of opening or remodeling paint stores and constructing three warehouses to replace the Dayton, Ohio warehouse destroyed by fire in May, 1987. We do not anticipate the need for any external financing to support our capital programs.

The primary impacts on noncurrent assets and liabilities were the acquisitions, debt proceeds and debt repayments. The purchase of intangibles and goodwill accounted for the majority of the $122 million increase in intangibles and other assets. Other long-term liabilities were affected by provisions for the costs of programs related to environmental protection and control in 1990, 1989 and 1988. These provisions were more than offset in 1990 by reclassifications to current liabilities.

Despite the significant cash outlay for acquisitions in 1990, total debt increased by a net of only $15.3 million. During 1990, in addition to prepaying the outstanding principal of the 10.50 percent promissory notes, we exercised our option to prepay $7.6 million of 9.375 percent promissory notes, together representing a weighted-average annual interest rate of 10.04 percent. In October 1990, we incurred long-term borrowings of $12.5 million at 8.861 percent annual interest for 5 years and $12.5 million at 9.478 percent for 10 years under our credit agreement with The Sherwin-Williams Company Salaried

Employees' Retirement Trust. In addition, in December 1990, we completed the sale of $15 million in 8.78 percent annual interest promissory notes which are due in 1993. The new debt, taken as a whole, represents a weighted-average annual interest rate of 9.02 percent. We utilized short-term borrowings for brief periods during the third quarter of 1990, and we may need to utilize insignificant amounts of short-term borrowings briefly during the first half of 1991 to help finance working capital. However, once into the peak selling season, sufficient cash flows should be generated from operations to return to an investment position.

To complement our current outstanding debt, we have arranged significant additional financing flexibility. A shelf registration permits the Company to issue up to $200 million of unsecured debt securities; however, there is no guarantee that an offering thereunder would be successful or on terms acceptable to the Company. During 1990, the Company terminated a subsidiary's commercial paper program and established a similar commercial paper program in the name of the Company in the amount of $280 million. The Company also has in place a $280 million revolving credit agreement with a group of banks. There were no borrowings outstanding under any of these financing arrangements at December 31, 1990, 1989 or 1988. See Note 9 to the consolidated financial statements for a complete description of long-term debt.

Capitalization
Dollars in Millions

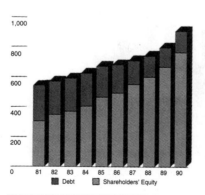

With the net increase in total debt of $15.3 million, we still improved our debt-to-capitalization ratio to 15.6 percent at the end of 1990 compared to 15.8 percent in 1989 and 18.6 percent in 1988. Our debt-to-capitalization ratio has steadily improved since 1978 as a result of increased profitability, planned debt reductions, and the conversion of debentures into common stock.

We acquire our own stock for general corporate purposes and, depending on our cash position and market conditions, we may purchase additional shares of stock in the future.

At a meeting held February 20, 1991, the board of directors declared a quarterly dividend of $.105 per share and a two-for-one stock split. (See Note 2 to the consolidated financial statements.) This dividend represents the twelfth consecutive increase and a compounded rate of increase of 37 percent since the dividend was reinstated in 1979. The 1990 quarterly dividend of $.095 per share marked the eleventh consecutive year that the dividend approximated our payout ratio target of 30 percent of trailing annual earnings.

The jury verdict and judgment for $31.1 million which was entered against the Company during 1989 were withdrawn by the Court in 1990 and the matter was settled for an undisclosed amount. The settlement agreement has been accepted by the Court and is subject to a protective order.

During the period 1987 - 1990, the Company and certain other companies were named defendants in a number of lawsuits arising from the manufacture and sale of lead pigments that were allegedly used in the manufacture of lead paints. It is possible that additional lawsuits may be filed against the Company in the future with similar allegations. The various existing lawsuits seek damages for personal injuries and property damages, along with costs incurred to abate the lead related paint from buildings. The Company believes that such lawsuits are without merit and is vigorously defending them. The Company does not believe that any potential liability ultimately determined to be attributable to the Company arising out of such lawsuits will have a material adverse effect on the Company's business or financial condition.

The Company is presently involved in several proceedings involving potential liability for the clean up of environmental waste sites. The Company continues to assess its potential liability with respect to these sites. This assessment is based upon, among other factors, the number of parties involved with respect to any given site, the nature of the wastes involved and the volumetric contribution which may be attributed to the Company. The Company does not believe that any potential liability ultimately determined to be attributable to the Company will have a material adverse effect on the Company's business or financial condition.

Results of Operations - 1990 vs 1989

Consolidated net sales increased 6.7 percent to $2.27 billion as all segments improved sales during the year. Sales in 1990 were impacted by the acquisitions of Krylon and DeSoto and the divestiture of LTL. Adjusting for these transactions, consolidated net sales increased 5.7 percent. The Paint Stores Segment had a 6.5 percent sales increase, despite economic problems encountered particularly in the northeastern part of the country. Comparable-store sales increased 6.2 percent in 1990. Sales of paint products increased 9.9 percent, while gallons sold increased 7.3 percent. The increase in sales of paint was partially offset by sales declines in wall-covering, floorcovering and window treatments. Sales of the Coatings Segment increased 7.1 percent, primarily in the

Consumer and Sprayon Divisions. The Consumer Division showed strong increases in the Dutch Boy group, as these products were sold nationally in all Sears locations beginning in the first quarter of 1990. The Consumer Division also included two months of DeSoto sales. Sprayon's sales included six months of Krylon sales, which more than offset soft applicator sales. After adjusting for the acquisitions and divestiture made in 1990, the Coatings Segment's sales gain was 4.1 percent. Sales for the Other Segment increased 3.9 percent from 1989.

Sales
Dollars in Millions

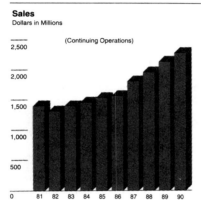

Consolidated gross profit dollars increased 9.5 percent during the year, as we experienced volume gains, price increases and a slowing in the escalation of most raw material costs. Consolidated gross margins were 41.0 percent in 1990 compared to 40.0 percent in 1989. In the last several months of the year, increasing oil prices began creating some raw material cost pressures, particularly in the Automotive, Transportation Services, and Chemical Coatings Divisions of the Coatings Segment. However, given the situation in the Middle East and fluctuating oil prices, we are unable to predict the effect oil prices might have on raw material costs and gross margins in 1991.

Consolidated selling, general and administrative expenses increased as a percent of sales to 32.9 percent from 32.2 percent in 1989. The addition of new stores in 1990 and increased promotional expenses were primarily responsible for the increase in SG&A expenses in the Paint Stores Segment. Amortization of intangible assets and goodwill recorded in the purchase of Krylon was the primary reason for the increase in SG&A expenses in the Coatings Segment.

Consolidated operating profits increased 10.0 percent in 1990. The Paint Stores Segment's operating profits decreased 5.3 percent, primarily due to special credits included in 1989's profits. Adjusting for these special credits in 1989, operating profit of the Paint Stores Segment increased 7.8 percent. The Coatings Segment's

operating profit increased 7.8 percent as most raw material costs began to stabilize. The operating profits of the Other Segment increased due primarily to the absence of provisions established for the disposition of certain unprofitable non-retail properties in 1989. Corporate expenses decreased from 1989 as a result of changes in various provisions and other items which are not directly associated with or allocable to any operating segment. Refer to pages 4 through 9 for a more thorough discussion of Business Segment Information.

Interest expense decreased 17.1 percent during 1990 due to the continued reduction of long-term debt for most of 1990. Interest coverage improved to 18.2 times in 1990 compared to 13.9 times in 1989. Our fixed charge coverage, which is calculated using interest and rent expense, was 3.0 times in 1990. Decreased interest expense and increased profitability more than offset the increase in rent expense, resulting in the slightly higher fixed charge coverage from 2.9 times in 1989. We expect interest expense to increase slightly in 1991 as a result of additional borrowings.

Profits
Dollars in Millions

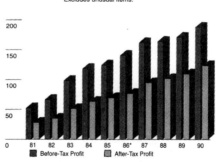

Interest and net investment income decreased 26.4 percent to $10.1 million due to lower investment levels as a result of the use of cash and short-term investments for acquisitions. Other income decreased $2.0 million primarily due to larger provisions for environmental protection and control and losses on disposals of certain assets. These increased expenses were partially offset by a net credit for the disposition and termination of operations as a result of adjustments made to prior accruals. (See Note 6 to the consolidated financial statements.) Net income increased 12.6 percent to $122.7 million and net income per share increased 11.9 percent to $1.41.

Our financial position and results of operations may be affected beginning in 1992 by Financial Accounting Standards Board Statement No. 96, "Accounting for Income Taxes", because of the lower rates adopted in the Tax Reform Act of 1986, and in 1993 by Financial Accounting Standards Board Statement No. 106, "Employers' Accounting for Postretirement Benefits Other than Pensions." The Company has not yet completed all the complex analyses required to estimate the impact of the new Statements. Based on preliminary information currently available, it appears that Statement No. 96 will have a favorable effect on the Company's tax expense by reducing the rate at which deferred taxes are recognized and that Statement No.106 will have a detrimental effect on profits due to the unrecorded liability and expense of accruing for future benefits due employees and retirees.

Return on Sales, Assets, and Equity
Percent

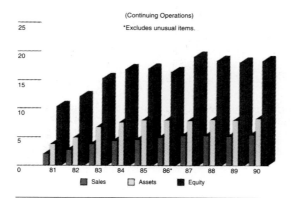

(Continuing Operations)
*Excludes unusual items.

Sales Assets Equity

Results of Operations - 1989 vs 1988

Consolidated net sales increased 8.9 percent. We improved our market share again in 1989 as gallons sold increased at a faster pace than the paint industry in general. The sales increase in 1989 was primarily due to price increases and, to a lesser extent, volume gains. The Paint Stores Segment had a 7.7 percent sales increase, despite continued sluggish retail sales and competitive price pressures. Comparable store sales gains were 7.5 percent. The sale of paint products, due to strong painter and contractor sales, increased 13.6 percent in 1989. Decreased sales of non-paint products, which are primarily retail sales, partially offset the paint products sales increase. The Coatings Segment had an 11.2 percent increase in 1989 sales, primarily in the Consumer and Automotive Divisions. The Consumer Division experienced strong increases in the Kem-Tone® and private label lines, while the Automotive Division showed strong increases in the Sherwin-Williams® product line, along with added sales from Western Automotive Finishes paint products, a company which was acquired in 1988. Sales for the Other Segment were flat in comparison to 1988.

Consolidated gross profit dollars increased 11.1 percent during 1989 as a result of volume gains and price increases. The increase was partially offset by continued raw material cost increases, resulting in gross margins of 40.0 percent in 1989 compared to 39.2 percent in 1988.

Consolidated selling, general and administrative expenses increased in dollars in 1989, but remained flat with 1988 at 32.2 percent of sales. The addition of new stores in 1989 and the annualization of stores opened in 1988, which resulted in additional expenses, along with increased promotional activities in the Paint Stores Segment, were primarily responsible for the increased selling, general and administrative expenses.

Consolidated operating profits increased in comparison with 1988 primarily due to a 30 percent increase in the Paint Stores Segment's operating profits due primarily to a reduction of 1988's profits by provisions established for the closing of certain unprofitable stores. Excluding special charges and credits in 1989 and 1988, operating profits in the Paint Stores Segment rose 7.7 percent for 1989. The operating profits of the Coatings Segment increased only 1.6 percent in 1989 due to the gain realized on the sale of BAPCO in 1988. Excluding the net gain, the operating profits of the Coatings Segment increased over 16.0 percent for the year. Coatings Segment operating profit improved due to price increases implemented during 1989 to cover the increasing costs of certain raw materials, especially titanium dioxide, that had caused lower operating profits in 1988. The operating profits of the Other Segment decreased due to provisions established for the disposition of certain unprofitable non-retail properties. Corporate expenses increased in 1989 when compared to 1988 as a result of changes in various provisions and other items which are not directly associated with or allocable to any operating segment.

Interest expense decreased 7.7 percent during 1989 because of the continued reduction in outstanding long-term debt. Interest coverage improved to 13.9 times in 1989 compared to 12.4 times in 1988. Our fixed charge coverage, which is calculated using interest and rent expense, was 2.9 times in 1989. Decreased interest expense and increased profitability more than offset the increase in rent expense, resulting in a slightly higher fixed charge coverage from 1988's level of 2.8 times.

Interest and net investment income increased 8.3 percent in 1989 to $13.8 million, as the Company had higher investment levels and higher yields than in 1988. Other income decreased $22.7 million due to the absence of gains on the sale of the Company's interest in BAPCO and the realization of certain long-term assets which were recognized in 1988. A reduced income tax rate decreased income tax expense for 1989. Net income increased 7.8 percent to $108.9 million and net income per share increased 9.6 percent to $1.26.

Financial Summary

Millions of dollars, except per share data

The Sherwin-Williams Company and Subsidiaries

Years ended December 31,	1990	1989	1988	1987	1986	1985	1984	1983	1982	1981
Operations										
Net sales	$ 2,267	$ 2,123	$ 1,950	$ 1,801	$ 1,558	$ 1,526	$ 1,454	$ 1,397	$ 1,312	$ 1,399
Cost of goods sold	1,338	1,275	1,187	1,067	922	916	900	897	881	976
Selling and administrative expenses	745	686	629	579	488	464	425	391	356	365
Interest expense	11	13	14	18	19	18	18	16	16	17
Income from continuing operations before income taxes	187	170	163	161	140*	124	118	98	66	52
Income taxes	64	61	62	67	64*	55	55	47	31	24
Income from continuing operations	123	109	101	94	76*	69	63	51	35	28
Net income	123	109	101	97	86*	75	65	55	43	31
Net cash flow provided by operations	155	171	40	85	95	102	126	100	124	51
Financial Position										
Inventories	$ 373	$ 326	$ 323	$ 281	$ 410	$ 367	$ 338	$ 332	$ 299	$ 335
Accounts receivable - net	230	206	196	176	158	155	149	137	131	132
Working capital	392	413	388	373	301	358	336	335	329	297
Property, plant and equipment - net	373	359	333	289	318	291	268	235	246	240
Total assets	1,504	1,375	1,259	1,210	1,207	1,108	1,043	970	902	864
Long-term debt	138	105	130	141	178	191	206	205	209	230
Common shareholders' equity	764	668	601	550	492	465	404	370	334	284
Total shareholders' equity	764	668	601	550	492	465	404	371	349	305
Per Common Share Data (A)										
Average shares and equivalents (thousands)	87,056	86,326	87,830	89,676	91,570	92,444	91,699	95,278	83,613	79,269
Book value	$ 8.77	$ 7.73	$ 6.85	$ 6.13	$ 5.37	$ 5.03	$ 4.41	$ 3.89	$ 4.17	$ 3.85
Income from continuing operations	1.41	1.26	1.15	1.05	.83	.74	.68	.54	.42	.35
Net income	1.41	1.26	1.15	1.08	.94	.81	.71	.58	.51	.40
Cash dividends	.38	.35	.32	.28	.25	.23	.19	.15	.125	.10
Financial Ratios										
Return on sales	5.4%	5.1%	5.2%	5.2%	4.9%*	4.5%	4.3%	3.7%	2.7%	2.0%
Asset turnover	1.5x	1.5x	1.6x	1.7x	1.7x	1.8x	1.8x	1.9x	1.8x	1.8x
Return on assets	8.2%	7.9%	8.0%	7.8%	7.9%*	7.9%	7.5%	6.7%	4.9%	3.7%
Return on equity (B):										
From continuing operations	18.4%	18.1%	18.4%	19.1%	16.4%	17.0%	16.9%	15.3%	12.1%	10.3%
From total operations	18.4%	18.1%	18.4%	19.6%	18.6%*	18.5%	17.6%	16.6%	14.8%	11.6%
Dividend payout ratio	26.8%	27.6%	27.7%	25.7%	26.2%*	28.2%	26.5%	25.1%	25.0%	26.1%
Debt to capitalization	15.6%	15.8%	18.6%	22.2%	27.6%	30.5%	35.0%	37.1%	38.6%	43.6%
Current ratio	1.9	2.0	2.0	2.0	1.7	1.9	1.9	2.0	2.1	2.0
Times interest earned (C)	18.2x	13.9x	12.4x	10.1x	8.5x*	7.9x	7.6x	7.0x	5.2x	4.1x
Working capital to sales	17.3%	19.4%	19.9%	20.7%	13.0%	18.5%	18.7%	18.5%	19.9%	17.4%
Effective income tax rate	34.5%	36.0%	38.0%	41.8%	45.5%*	44.5%	46.9%	47.9%	46.5%	46.5%
General										
Capital expenditures	$ 64	$ 67	$ 72	$ 57	$ 64	$ 75	$ 59	$ 52	$ 48	$ 43
Total technical expenditures	38	37	32	28	26	23	26	23	24	25
Advertising	106	84	84	73	62	62	57	51	42	40
Depreciation and amortization	45	42	37	32	27	24	23	23	22	22
Shareholders of record:										
Preferred	—	—	—	—	—	—	—	40	557	750
Common	12,012	12,230	12,606	12,327	11,936	11,384	9,777	9,641	8,590	8,858
Number of employees	16,397	16,726	16,607	15,901	13,706	12,970	13,092	13,172	14,297	15,879
Sales per employee (thousands)	$ 138	$ 127	$ 117	$ 113	$ 114	$ 118	$ 111	$ 106	$ 92	$ 88
Sales per dollar of assets	1.51	1.54	1.55	1.49	1.61	1.74	1.74	1.83	1.82	1.87

*   In 1986, unusual items, which increased income from continuing operations and net income by $19,595,000 ($.22 per share), are excluded.
    Includes continuing operations only for the years 1981 through 1987.
(A) All common share amounts and per share data reflect the effect of the stock split described in Note 2 to the consolidated financial statements.
(B) Based on common shareholders' equity at beginning of year.
(C) Ratio of pre-tax income from continuing operations before interest expense to interest expense.
This summary should be read in conjuction with the financial statements and notes on pages 16-28 of this report.

Report of Management

Shareholders
The Sherwin-Williams Company

We have prepared the accompanying consolidated financial statements and related information included herein for the years ended December 31, 1990, 1989 and 1988. The primary responsibility for the integrity of the financial information rests with management. This information is prepared in accordance with generally accepted accounting principles, based upon our best estimates and judgments and giving due consideration to materiality.

The Company maintains accounting and control systems which are designed to provide reasonable assurance that assets are safeguarded from loss or unauthorized use and which produce records adequate for preparation of financial information. There are limits inherent in all systems of internal control based on the recognition that the cost of such systems should not exceed the benefits to be derived. We believe our system provides this appropriate balance.

The board of directors pursues its responsibility for these financial statements through the Audit Committee, composed exclusively of outside directors. The committee meets periodically with management, internal auditors and our independent auditors to discuss the adequacy of financial controls, the quality of financial reporting and the nature, extent and results of the audit effort. Both the internal auditors and independent auditors have private and confidential access to the Audit Committee at all times.

J. G. Breen	T. R. Miklich	J. L. Ault
Chairman and Chief Executive Officer	Senior Vice President - Finance and Chief Financial Officer	Vice President - Corporate Controller

Report of Independent Auditors

Shareholders and Board of Directors
The Sherwin-Williams Company
Cleveland, Ohio

We have audited the consolidated financial statements of The Sherwin-Williams Company and subsidiaries listed in Item 14(a) of the Index on page 33. These financial statements are the responsibility of management. Our responsibility is to express an opinion on these financial statements based on our audits.

We conducted our audits in accordance with generally accepted auditing standards. Those standards require that we plan and perform the audit to obtain reasonable assurance about whether the financial statements are free of material misstatement. An audit includes examining, on a test basis, evidence supporting the amounts and disclosures in the financial statements. An audit also includes assessing the accounting principles used and significant estimates made by management, as well as evaluating the overall financial statement presentation. We believe that our audits provide a reasonable basis for our opinion.

In our opinion, the consolidated financial statements listed in Item 14(a) of the Index present fairly, in all material respects, the consolidated financial position of The Sherwin-Williams Company and subsidiaries at December 31, 1990, 1989 and 1988, and the consolidated results of their operations and their cash flows for each of the three years in the period ended December 31, 1990, in conformity with generally accepted accounting principles.

Cleveland, Ohio
January 23, 1991, except for Note 2,
as to which the date is February 20, 1991

Ernst & Young

Statements of Consolidated Income

Thousands of dollars, except per share data

The Sherwin-Williams Company and Subsidiaries

Years ended December 31,	1990	1989	1988
Net sales	$2,266,732	$2,123,483	$1,950,474
Costs and expenses:			
Cost of goods sold	1,337,942	1,275,119	1,186,846
Selling, general and administrative expenses	745,651	685,645	628,574
Interest expense	10,902	13,149	14,253
Interest and net investment income	(10,159)	(13,810)	(12,752)
Other	(4,881)	(6,831)	(29,487)
	2,079,455	1,953,272	1,787,434
Income before income taxes	187,277	170,211	163,040
Income taxes	64,611	61,276	61,960
Net income	$ 122,666	$ 108,935	$ 101,080
Net income per share*	$ 1.41	$ 1.26	$ 1.15

* Per share data reflects the effect of the stock split described in Note 2.
  See notes to consolidated financial statements.

Consolidated Balance Sheets
Thousands of dollars

The Sherwin-Williams Company and Subsidiaries

December 31,	1990	1989	1988
Assets			
Current assets:			
Cash and cash equivalents	$ 95,977	$ 132,214	$ 69,838
Short-term investments	3,000	69,904	84,403
Accounts receivable, less allowance	229,926	205,661	195,726
Inventories:			
Finished goods	317,117	278,220	271,978
Work in process and raw materials	56,221	48,231	51,019
	373,338	326,451	322,997
Other current assets	122,027	111,621	93,174
Total current assets	824,268	845,851	766,138
Deferred pension assets	157,038	142,738	135,821
Intangibles and other assets	149,740	27,541	24,152
Property, plant and equipment:			
Land	41,913	36,748	35,206
Buildings	194,969	191,540	186,721
Machinery and equipment	432,271	404,156	365,834
Construction in progress	18,705	14,294	11,757
	687,858	646,738	599,518
Less allowances for depreciation and amortization	314,508	287,873	266,920
	373,350	358,865	332,598
Total assets	$1,504,396	$1,374,995	$1,258,709
Liabilities and Shareholders' Equity			
Current liabilities:			
Accounts payable	$ 202,855	$ 176,003	$ 160,844
Compensation and taxes withheld	56,477	52,954	49,055
Current portion of long-term debt	2,691	20,492	7,018
Other accruals	145,249	157,829	142,756
Accrued taxes	24,910	26,030	18,316
Total current liabilities	432,182	433,308	377,989
Long-term debt	137,999	104,952	129,604
Deferred income taxes	98,036	93,622	92,242
Other long-term liabilities	72,475	75,480	57,623
Shareholders' equity:			
Common stock — $1.00 par value*:			
86,738,836, 86,253,754, and 86,081,504 shares			
outstanding at December 31, 1990, 1989, and 1988, respectively	48,759	48,482	47,939
Other capital	150,661	142,999	132,621
Retained earnings	712,233	621,750	552,764
Cumulative foreign currency translation adjustment	(15,269)	(14,194)	(13,218)
Treasury stock, at cost	(132,680)	(131,404)	(118,855)
Total shareholders' equity	763,704	667,633	601,251
Total liabilities and shareholders' equity	$1,504,396	$1,374,995	$1,258,709

* Common share amounts reflect the effect of the stock split described in Note 2.
See notes to consolidated financial statements.

Statements of Consolidated Cash Flows

Thousands of dollars

The Sherwin-Williams Company and Subsidiaries

Years ended December 31,	1990	1989	1988
Operations			
Net income	$122,666	$108,935	$101,080
Non-cash adjustments:			
Depreciation and amortization	44,507	41,951	36,865
Deferred income tax expense	(90)	(395)	2,751
Provisions for disposition of operations	(2,221)	7,155	23,316
Funded employee benefits incurred	—	—	6,707
Amortization of intangible assets	7,007	2,299	2,199
Increase in deferred pension asset	(13,798)	(12,695)	(13,872)
Other	5,497	15,831	9,935
Change in current items-net:			
Increase in accounts receivable	(30,632)	(8,432)	(15,293)
Increase in inventories	(7,400)	(799)	(36,577)
Increase in accounts payable	29,511	15,159	2,019
Increase (decrease) in accrued taxes	(1,018)	7,714	(8,535)
Other current items	19,007	7,344	(8,409)
Gains on disposals of assets	—	—	(42,358)
Costs incurred for dispositions of operations	(6,120)	(8,594)	(12,423)
Other	(12,195)	(4,705)	(7,473)
Net operating cash	154,721	170,768	39,932
Investing			
Capital expenditures	(64,351)	(66,933)	(71,551)
Short-term investments	66,904	14,499	53,847
Acquisitions of assets	(207,025)	(4,725)	(18,162)
Proceeds from disposals of assets	27,412	—	55,453
Contribution to employee benefit fund	(467)	(5,432)	—
Other	(1,648)	(2,454)	3,032
Net investing cash	(179,175)	(65,045)	22,619
Financing			
Proceeds from issuance of debt	49,061	2,087	—
Payments of long-term debt	(33,730)	(13,201)	(13,926)
Payments of cash dividends	(32,890)	(30,081)	(27,956)
Purchases of stock for treasury	(1,276)	(12,549)	(25,618)
Other	7,052	10,397	4,507
Net financing cash	(11,783)	(43,347)	(62,993)
Net increase (decrease) in cash and cash equivalents	(36,237)	62,376	(442)
Cash and cash equivalents at beginning of year	132,214	69,838	70,280
Cash and cash equivalents at end of year	$ 95,977	$132,214	$ 69,838
Taxes paid on income	$ 65,720	$ 51,641	$ 62,578
Interest paid on debt	11,015	12,990	14,471

See notes to consolidated financial statements.

Statements of Consolidated Shareholders' Equity
Thousands of dollars

**The Sherwin-Williams Company
and Subsidiaries**

	Common Stock	Other Capital	Retained Earnings	Cumulative Translation Adjustment	Treasury Stock
Balance at January 1, 1988	$ 47,603	$127,164	$479,640	$ (12,689)	$ (92,033)
Treasury stock acquired	—	—	—	—	(25,618)
Stock issued	336	5,457	—	—	(1,204)
Net income	—	—	101,080	—	—
Cash dividends — $.32 per share*	—	—	(27,956)	—	—
Current year translation adjustment	—	—	—	(529)	—
Balance at December 31, 1988	47,939	132,621	552,764	(13,218)	(118,855)
Treasury stock acquired	—	—	—	—	(10,484)
Stock issued	543	10,378	—	—	(2,065)
Net income	—	—	108,935	—	—
Cash dividends — $.35 per share*	—	—	(30,081)	—	—
Unfunded pension losses - net of taxes	—	—	(9,868)	—	—
Current year translation adjustment	—	—	—	(976)	—
Balance at December 31, 1989	48,482	142,999	621,750	(14,194)	(131,404)
Stock issued	**277**	**7,662**	—	—	**(1,276)**
Net income	—	—	**122,666**	—	—
Cash dividends — $.38 per share*	—	—	**(32,890)**	—	—
Reduction in unfunded pension losses - net of taxes	—	—	**707**	—	—
Current year translation adjustment	—	—	—	**(1,075)**	—
Balance at December 31, 1990	**$ 48,759**	**$150,661**	**$712,233**	**$ (15,269)**	**$(132,680)**

* Per share data reflects the effect of the stock split described in Note 2.
  See notes to consolidated financial statements.

Notes to Consolidated Financial Statements

The Sherwin-Williams Company and Subsidiaries

Years ended December 31, 1990, 1989 and 1988

Note 1 — Significant Accounting Policies

Consolidation. The consolidated financial statements include all significant majority-owned subsidiaries. Intercompany accounts and transactions have been eliminated.

Cash Flows. The Company considers all highly liquid investments with a maturity of three months or less when purchased to be cash equivalents. Short-term investments are stated at cost, which approximates market value.

Property, plant and equipment. Property, plant and equipment is stated on the basis of cost. Depreciation is provided principally by the straight-line method. The major classes of assets and ranges of depreciation rates are as follows:

Buildings	2% - 6 ⅔ %
Machinery and equipment	4% - 20%
Furniture and fixtures	5% - 20%
Automobiles and trucks	10% - 33 ⅓ %

Intangibles. Intangible assets, net of accumulated amortization, were $126,976,000, $12,879,000, and $13,909,000 at December 31, 1990, 1989 and 1988, respectively. These assets are amortized by the straight-line method over the expected period of benefit.

Research and development costs. Research and development costs were $19,442,000, $18,058,000, and $16,705,000 for 1990, 1989 and 1988, respectively.

Net income per share. Net income per share was computed based on the average number of shares and share equivalents outstanding during the year after adjustment for the effect of the two-for-one stock split.

Reclassification. Certain amounts in the 1989 and 1988 financial statements have been reclassified to conform with the 1990 presentation.

Note 2 — Stock Split

On February 20, 1991, the Company's board of directors authorized a two-for-one split of the common stock effected in the form of a 100 percent stock dividend to be distributed on or about March 29, 1991, to holders of record on March 4, 1991. Accordingly, all numbers of common shares and per share data have been restated to reflect the stock split. The par value of the additional shares of common stock issued in connection with the stock split will be credited to common stock and a like amount charged to other capital in 1991.

Note 3 — Business Segments

Business segment information appears on pages 4, 5, 6, 7, 8, and 9 of this report.

Note 4 — Acquisitions

Effective June 25, 1990, the Company acquired certain assets of the Krylon and Illinois Bronze aerosol paints and coatings businesses of Borden, Inc. for a total cost, as defined by Accounting Principles Board Opinion No. 16, of $137,510,000. The assets acquired were principally inventory and intangible assets. The excess of the cost over the fair value of the net assets acquired is being amortized over 40 years by the straight-line method.

Effective October 27, 1990, the Company acquired certain assets, primarily property, plant and equipment, and inventory, of the U. S. consumer paint business of DeSoto, Inc. for a total cost, as defined by Accounting Principles Board Opinion No. 16, of $67,940,000. Also effective October 27, 1990, the Company sold certain rights and interests in particular assets of the Chicago Heights, Illinois plant of DeSoto, Inc. for approximately book value.

The Company has accounted for the above acquisitions under the purchase method and, accordingly, the results of operations of the acquired businesses have been included in the statements of consolidated income since the respective dates of acquisition. The purchase price for each of the acquisitions has been allocated to the net assets acquired based on the fair market value determined by independent appraisals.

The following summarized unaudited pro forma financial information assumes the above acquisitions occurred on January 1 of each respective year.

Thousands of dollars, except per share data	Years ended December 31, **1990**	1989
Net sales	$2,475,243	$2,396,974
Net income	$ 110,190	$ 98,681
Income per share	$ 1.27	$ 1.14

The above amounts are not necessarily indicative of the results which would have occurred had the acquisitions been made on January 1 of each respective period or of future results of the combined companies under the ownership and operation of the Company.

During the three year period ended December 31, 1990, the Company purchased various automotive paint distributors, as well as certain paint manufacturers. Assets purchased consisted primarily of accounts receivable, inventory and property, plant and equipment. The results of operations of these businesses since the dates of acquisition were not material to consolidated results.

Note 5 — Inventories

Inventories are stated at the lower of cost or market. Cost is determined principally on the last-in, first-out (LIFO) method which provides a better matching of current costs and revenues. The following presents the effect on inventories, net income and net income per share had the Company used the FIFO and average cost methods of inventory valuation adjusted for income taxes at the statutory rate and assuming no other adjustments. This information is presented to enable the reader to make comparisons with companies using the FIFO method of inventory valuation.

Thousands of dollars, except per share data	Years ended December 31,		
	1990	1989	1988
Percentage of total inventories on LIFO	97%	96%	96%
Excess of FIFO and average cost over LIFO	$81,205	$68,967	$56,138
Decrease in net income due to LIFO	(8,077)	(8,471)	(11,180)
Decrease in net income per share due to LIFO	(.10)	(.10)	(.13)

Note 6 — Other Costs and Expenses

A summary of significant items included in other costs and expenses is as follows:

Thousands of dollars	Years ended December 31,		
	1990	1989	1988
Dividend and royalty income	$(5,975)	$ (6,046)	$ (7,128)
Losses (gains) on disposals of assets	458	(3,299)	(30,179)
Realization of full value of assets	—	(500)	(14,176)
Provisions for environmental protection and control	8,300	5,900	12,000
Provisions for disposition and termination of operations (see Note 7)	(5,430)	3,405	13,716
Equity income	—	—	(3,263)
Miscellaneous	(2,234)	(6,291)	(457)
	$ (4,881)	$ (6,831)	$(29,487)

During the three years ended December 31, 1990, provisions for environmental protection and control reflect the increased cost of continued compliance with environmental regulations. During 1988, gains from the realization of certain long-term assets with little book value and from the sale of the Company's interest in BAPCO, a Canadian partnership, were recognized.

Note 7 — Disposition and Termination of Operations

The Company is continually re-evaluating its operating facilities with regard to the long-term strategic goals established by management and the board of directors. Operating facilities which are not expected to contribute to the Company's future plans are closed or sold.

At the time of the decision to close or sell certain plants, warehouses, stores or other operating units, provisions to reduce property, plant and equipment to their estimated net realizable values are included in other costs and expenses. Similarly, provisions to reduce all other assets to their estimated net realizable values and for the estimated related costs for severance pay, shutdown expenses and future operating losses to disposal date are included in cost of goods sold. Adjustments to such accruals as disposition occurs are included in other costs and expenses.

In 1990, management provided for the closing of certain warehouses and other operating facilities. Adjustments to prior accruals reflect primarily the decreased ongoing costs of certain previously sold facilities, resulting in a net credit to other costs and expenses. The provisions for 1988 included approximately $10,000,000 for the reduction of assets and closing costs of certain unprofitable retail paint stores.

A summary of the financial data related to the closing or sale of the facilities, expected to be completed by 1992, is as follows:

Thousands of dollars	**1990**	1989	1988
Beginning accrual — January 1	$53,812	$55,251	$44,358
Provisions included in cost of goods sold	3,209	3,750	9,600
Provisions and adjustments to prior accruals included in costs and expenses - other	(5,430)	3,405	13,716
Total provision (credit)	(2,221)	7,155	23,316
Actual costs incurred	(6,120)	(8,594)	(12,423)
Ending accrual — December 31	$45,471	$53,812	$55,251
Net after-tax provision (credit)	$ (1,466)	$ 4,772	$15,388
Net after-tax provision (credit) per share	$ (.02)	$ .06	$ .18

Note 8 — Employee Benefits

Substantially all employees of the Company participate in noncontributory defined benefit or defined contribution pension plans. Defined benefit plans covering salaried employees provide benefits that are based primarily on years of service and employees' compensation. Defined benefit plans covering hourly employees generally provide benefits of stated amounts for each year of service. Multiemployer plans are primarily defined benefit plans which provide benefits of stated amounts for union employees.

The Company's funding policy for defined benefit plans is to fund at least the minimum annual contribution required by applicable regulations. Recommended funding for the hourly defined benefit pension plans is actuarially calculated to properly amortize unfunded liabilities during the period of active service to meet the cost of benefits upon retirement. Current benefits paid to retirees primarily offset earnings of plan assets. A change in actuarial assumptions at December 31, 1989 increased the projected benefit obligation, the effect of which is being amortized over future periods.

At December 31, 1989, certain accounting changes were required by Financial Accounting Standards Board Statement No. 87, first adopted by the Company in 1986. The effect of these changes resulted in the recording of a minimum liability for the hourly defined benefit pension plan in long-term liabilities. At December 31, 1990, the minimum liability was partially offset by a noncurrent asset of $844,000.

The pension credit for defined benefit plans and its components was as follows:

Thousands of dollars	Years ended December 31,		
	1990	1989	1988
Service cost	$ 2,934	$ 3,279	$ 2,972
Interest cost	7,940	8,100	7,409
Actual return on plan assets	(14,709)	(24,176)	(14,362)
Net amortization and deferral	(7,934)	1,185	(8,941)
Net pension credit	$(11,769)	$(11,612)	$(12,922)

The Company's annual contribution for its defined contribution pension plans, which is based on a level percentage of compensation for covered employees, offset the pension credit by $14,500,000 for 1990, $13,600,000 for 1989 and $11,650,000 for 1988.

In addition to providing pension benefits, the Company provides certain health care and life insurance benefits under company-sponsored plans for retired employees. Substantially all of the Company's employees who are not members of a collective bargaining unit are eligible for these benefits upon retirement. The cost of these benefits for both active and retired employees is recognized as claims are incurred and amounted to $34,063,000, $29,259,000 and $31,903,000 for 1990, 1989 and 1988, respectively.

There were 13,236, 13,202 and 12,646 active employees and 4,263, 4,217 and 4,240 retired employees entitled to receive benefits under these plans as of December 31, 1990, 1989 and 1988, respectively.

The Company also has a fund to provide for payment of health care benefits of certain qualified employees. Contributions of $25,000,000, $26,000,000 and $18,000,000 were made to the fund in 1990, 1989 and 1988, respectively. Distributions from the fund amounted to $27,290,000 in 1990, $25,930,000 in 1989 and $21,771,000 in 1988.

Based on the latest actuarial information available, the following table sets forth the funded status and amounts recognized in the Company's consolidated balance sheets for the defined benefit pension plans:

Thousands of dollars	December 31,		
	1990	1989	1988
Actuarial present value of benefit obligations:			
Vested benefit obligation	$(86,090)	$ (89,894)	$(63,191)
Accumulated benefit obligation	$(87,255)	$ (91,713)	$(66,005)
Projected benefit obligation	$(99,224)	$(103,457)	$(87,175)
Plan assets at fair value:			
Salaried employees' plans	190,012	183,535	166,879
Hourly employees' plan	52,491	53,264	52,388
	242,503	236,799	219,267
Plan assets in excess of (less than) projected benefit obligation:			
Salaried employees' plans	155,247	143,998	133,533
Hourly employees' plan	(11,968)	(10,656)	(1,441)
	143,279	133,342	132,092
Unrecognized net asset at January 1, 1986, net of amortization	(24,473)	(27,395)	(30,317)
Unrecognized prior service cost	987	502	195
Unrecognized net loss	40,701	40,983	32,901
Adjustment required to recognize minimum liability for hourly employees' plan	(14,724)	(15,294)	—
Net pension assets	$145,770	$132,138	$134,871
Net pension assets recognized in the consolidated balance sheets:			
Deferred pension assets	$157,038	$142,738	$135,821
Minimum liability included in long-term liabilities	(9,448)	(9,516)	—
Accrued pension liability included in current liabilities	(1,820)	(1,084)	(950)
	$145,770	$132,138	$134,871
Assumptions used in determining actuarial present value of plan benefit obligations:			
Discount rate	8.5%	8.5%	9.25%
Weighted-average rate of increase in future compensation levels	5.0%	5.0%	7.0%
Assumed long-term rate of return on plan assets	10.0%	10.0%	10.0%

Plan assets consist primarily of cash, equity and fixed income securities.

The cost of multiemployer and foreign plans charged to income was immaterial for the three years ended December 31, 1990.

Note 9 — Long-Term Debt

Thousands of dollars	Due Date	Sinking Fund/ Interim Payments		Amount in Treasury December 31,			Amount Outstanding Net of Treasury December 31,		
		Amount	Commence	**1990**	1989	1988	**1990**	1989	1988
9.875% Debentures	2016	$5,000	2007	—	—	—	$ 50,000	$ 50,000	$ 50,000
5.45% Debentures	1992	2,000	Payable currently	$ 3,872	$ 2,894	$ 4,894	10,128	13,106	13,106
6.25% Convertible Subordinated Debentures (Convertible into common stock at $2.875 a share)	1995	2,000	Payable currently	9,521	9,521	9,521	341	425	490
9.45% Debentures	1999	2,000	Payable currently	4,909	4,598	4,798	23,091	25,402	27,202
9.375% Promissory Notes	—	—	—	—	—	—	—	7,575	13,425
10.50% Promissory Notes	—	—	—	—	—	—	—	—	18,027
8.78% Promissory Notes	1993	5,000	1992	—	—	—	15,000	—	—
8.861% Promissory Notes	1995	—	—	—	—	—	12,500	—	—
9.478% Promissory Notes	2000	—	—	—	—	—	12,500	—	—
6.25% to 8.31% Industrial Revenue Bonds	Through 2005	Varies	Payable currently	—	—	—	7,175	2,200	2,270
8% to 12% Mortgage Notes secured by certain land and buildings, and other	Through 2005	Varies	Payable currently	—	—	—	6,673	5,312	3,360
Obligations under capital leases — less current portion of $376 in 1990, $423 in 1989 and $471 in 1988							591	932	1,724
				$18,302	$17,013	$19,213	$137,999	$104,952	$129,604

On January 31, 1990, the Company exercised its option to prepay the outstanding principal of $15,768,000 for the 10.50% promissory notes and on December 21, 1990 exercised its option to prepay the outstanding principal of $10,900,000 for the 9.375% promissory notes.

During 1990, the Company completed the sale of $15,000,000 in 8.78% promissory notes due in 1993. The note agreement includes certain restrictive covenants regarding the working capital ratio and net worth.

Under a credit agreement with The Sherwin-Williams Company Salaried Employees' Retirement Trust, the Company may borrow up to the lesser of $65,000,000 or 25% of the assets of the trust until October 9, 1992. Revolving credit amounts outstanding can be converted into five-year term, ten-year term or six-year installment loans at any time. The Company completed a $12,500,000 five-year term and a $12,500,000 ten-year term borrowing under this credit agreement in 1990. The credit agreement includes certain restrictive covenants regarding working capital levels and the working capital ratio.

At December 31, 1990, the Company had no borrowings outstanding under any of the following financing arrangements.

Under a credit agreement with a group of twelve banks, the Company may borrow up to $280,000,000 until June 22, 1992. Amounts outstanding under the agreement may be converted into two-year term loans at any time. The credit agreement includes certain restrictive covenants regarding the working capital ratio. There are no compensating balance requirements.

During 1990, the Company terminated a commercial paper program which had been established for Sherwin-Williams Development Corporation, under which $100,000,000 aggregate principal amount of unsecured short-term notes could be issued, and established a similar commercial paper program in the name of the Company in the amount of $280,000,000.

Under a shelf registration with the Securities and Exchange Commission covering $200,000,000 of unsecured debt securities with maturities ranging from nine months to thirty years, the Company may issue securities from time to time in one or more series and will offer the securities on terms determined at the time of sale.

The Company has sufficient debentures in treasury to satisfy most sinking fund requirements of public debenture issues through 1992. Maturities of long-term debt, exclusive of capital lease obligations and after the above-mentioned reduction for sinking fund requirements to be satisfied from debentures on deposit with the trustee, are as follows for the next five years:

1991—$ 2,315,000
1992—$19,604,000
1993—$12,852,000
1994—$ 3,221,000
1995—$15,783,000

Interest expense on long-term debt amounted to $10,444,980, $12,703,000 and $13,501,000 for 1990, 1989 and 1988, respectively. There were no interest charges capitalized during the periods presented.

Note 10 — Leases

The Company leases stores, warehouses, office space and equipment. Renewal options are available on the majority of leases and, under certain conditions, options exist to purchase properties. In some instances, store leases require the payment of contingent rentals based on sales in excess of specified minimums. Certain properties are subleased with various expiration dates. Property, plant and equipment includes the following amounts for capital leases, which are amortized by the straight-line method over the lease term:

Thousands of dollars	December 31, 1990	1989	1988
Buildings	$ 3,639	$ 4,309	$ 6,001
Machinery and Equipment	404	168	168
	4,043	4,477	6,169
Less allowance for amortization	3,373	3,724	4,987
	$ 670	$ 753	$ 1,182

Rental expense for operating leases was $80,501,000, $78,843,000 and $76,656,000 for 1990, 1989 and 1988,

respectively. Contingent rentals included in rent expense were $7,293,000 in 1990, $7,234,000 in 1989 and $6,659,000 in 1988. Rental income, as lessor, from real estate leasing activities and sublease rental income for all years presented was not significant.

Following is a schedule, by year and in the aggregate, of future minimum lease payments under capital leases and noncancelable operating leases having initial or remaining terms in excess of one year at December 31, 1990:

Thousands of dollars	Capital Leases	Operating Leases
1991	$ 532	$ 51,390
1992	271	44,620
1993	120	36,101
1994	114	29,444
1995	81	21,663
Later years	277	33,255
Total minimum lease payments	$ 1,395	$216,473
Amount representing interest	(310)	
Executory costs	(118)	
Present value of net minimum lease payments	$ 967	

Note 11 — Capital Stock

	$1.00 Common Stock	
	Shares in Treasury	Shares Outstanding Net of Treasury
Balance at January 1, 1988	7,760,248	87,446,120
Stock issued upon:		
Exercise of stock options	88,252	555,298
Conversion of 6.25% Convertible Subordinated Debentures	—	28,506
Treasury stock acquired	1,948,420	(1,948,420)
Balance at December 31, 1988	9,796,920	86,081,504
Stock issued upon:		
Exercise of stock options	140,620	760,396
Restricted stock grants	—	163,000
Conversion of 6.25% Convertible Subordinated Debentures	—	22,254
Treasury stock acquired	773,400	(773,400)
Balance at December 31, 1989	10,710,940	86,253,754
Stock issued upon:		
Exercise of stock options	68,322	455,526
Conversion of 6.25% Convertible Subordinated Debentures	—	29,556
Balance at December 31, 1990	10,779,262	86,738,836

All common share amounts reflect the effect of the stock split described in Note 2.

An aggregate of 6,563,590, 7,117,002 and 4,203,280 shares of stock at December 31, 1990, 1989 and 1988, respectively, were reserved for conversion of convertible subordinated debentures, future grants of restricted stock, and exercise and future grants of stock options. At December 31, 1990, there were 200,000,000 shares of common stock and 30,000,000 shares of serial preferred stock authorized for issuance.

The Company has a shareholders rights plan which designates 1,000,000 shares of the authorized serial preferred stock as cumulative redeemable serial preferred stock which may be issued if the Company becomes the target of coercive and unfair takeover tactics.

Note 12 — Stock Purchase and Option Plans

All common share amounts reflect the effect of the stock split described in Note 2.

As of December 31, 1990, 8,733 employees participated through regular payroll deductions in the Company's Employee Stock Purchase and Savings Plan. The Company's contribution charged to income amounted to $13,519,000, $13,622,000 and $10,048,000 for 1990, 1989 and 1988, respectively. Additionally, the Company made contributions on behalf of participating employees, which represent salary reductions for income tax purposes, amounting to $6,107,000 in 1990, $5,658,000 in 1989 and $5,005,000 in 1988.

At December 31, 1990, there were 12,638,572 shares of the Company's stock being held by this plan, representing 15% of the total number of shares outstanding. Shares of company stock credited to each member's account under the plan are voted by the trustee under confidential instructions from each individual plan member. Shares for which no instructions are received are voted by the trustee in the same proportion as those for which instructions are received.

The Company's stock plan permits the granting of stock options, stock appreciation rights, and restricted stock to eligible employees. Non-qualified and incentive stock options have been granted to certain officers and key employees under the current and previous plans at prices not less than fair market value of the shares at the date of grant. The options generally become exercisable to the extent of one-third of the optioned shares for each full year of employment following the date of grant and generally expire ten years after the date of grant. Restricted stock grants for 163,000 shares were awarded in 1989 to certain officers and key employees which require four years of continuous employment from the date of grant before receiving the shares without restriction. The number of shares to be received without restriction is based on the Company's performance relative to a peer group of companies. Unamortized deferred compensation expense with respect to the restricted stock amounted to $1,783,878 at December 31, 1990 and $2,341,000 at December 31, 1989 and is being amortized over the four-year vesting period. Deferred compensation expense during 1990 aggregated $801,703 and aggregated $460,000 in 1989. No stock appreciation rights have been granted.

	1990 Shares	1990 Aggregate Price	1989 Shares	1989 Aggregate Price	1988 Shares	1988 Aggregate Price
Stock Option Plans:						
Options outstanding beginning of year	2,623,516	$33,798,774	2,932,944	$34,484,313	3,398,808	$36,745,180
Granted	590,400	9,816,200	671,800	9,048,213	348,400	4,674,675
Exercised	(523,848)	(6,112,226)	(901,016)	(8,565,348)	(643,550)	(4,753,719)
Canceled	(73,916)	(1,047,932)	(80,212)	(1,168,404)	(170,714)	(2,181,823)
Options outstanding end of year	2,616,152	$36,454,816	2,623,516	$33,798,774	2,932,944	$34,484,313
Exercisable	1,528,962		1,591,158		1,612,050	
Reserved for future grants	3,829,060		4,345,544		1,100,132	

Note 13 — Income Taxes

Thousands of dollars	1990	1989	1988
	Years ended December 31,		
The components of income before income taxes consist of the following:			
Domestic	$178,647	$159,352	$118,178
Foreign	8,630	10,859	44,862
Total income before income taxes	$187,277	$170,211	$163,040
The components of income tax expense are as follows:			
Current:			
Federal	$52,991	$50,956	$36,777
State and Local	10,000	9,000	8,500
Foreign	1,710	1,715	13,932
	64,701	61,671	59,209
Deferred	(90)	(395)	2,751
Total income tax expense	$64,611	$61,276	$61,960

The Company has recognized the deferred income tax liabilities and benefits resulting from timing differences between financial and tax accounting, relating primarily to depreciation, deferred employee benefit items and other valuation allowances. It is the Company's intention to reinvest undistributed earnings of foreign subsidiaries; accordingly, no deferred income taxes have been provided thereon. At December 31, 1990, such undistributed earnings amounted to $4,705,602.

The source and deferred tax effect of timing differences are as follows:

Thousands of dollars	1990	1989	1988
	Years ended December 31,		
Depreciation	$ 104	$ 3,020	$ 3,425
Dispositions, terminations and other similar items	2,596	(1,954)	(2,630)
Deferred employee benefit items	(745)	5,915	1,419
Other items (each less than 5% of the computed "expected" tax amount)	(2,045)	(7,376)	537
	$ (90)	$ (395)	$ 2,751

A reconciliation of the statutory federal income tax rate and the effective tax rate follow:

	1990	1989	1988
	Years ended December 31,		
Statutory tax rate	34.0%	34.0%	34.0%
Effect of:			
State and local taxes	3.5	3.5	3.4
Other - net	(3.0)	(1.5)	.6
Effective tax rate	34.5%	36.0%	38.0%

Note 14 — Quarterly Data (Unaudited)

Quarterly Stock Prices and Dividends*

1990	Quarter	High	Low	Dividend	1989	Quarter	High	Low	Dividend
	1st	$ 18 ¼	$ 15 ⅜	$ .095		1st	$ 13 ⅞	$ 12 ½	$ .0875
	2nd	20 ⅛	17 ¼	$ .095		2nd	15 ½	13 ⅜	.0875
	3rd	21 ⅛	15 ⅛	$ .095		3rd	17 ⅞	14 ⅝	.0875
	4th	19 ⅞	15 ½	$ .095		4th	17 ½	15 ¾	.0875

Summary of Quarterly Results of Operations

Thousands of dollars, except per share data

Year	Quarter	Net Sales	Gross Profit	Net Income	Net Income Per Share*
1990	1st	$499,460	$193,171	$ 9,995	$ .11
	2nd	611,385	253,215	44,910	.51
	3rd	638,532	263,238	46,746	.54
	4th	517,355	219,166	21,015	.25
1989	1st	$464,781	$176,740	$ 8,810	$ .10
	2nd	583,984	237,620	38,696	.45
	3rd	595,983	240,196	41,598	.48
	4th	478,735	193,808	19,831	.23

* Per share data reflects the effect of the stock split described in Note 2.

1990

Fourth quarter adjustments increased net income by $2,690,000 ($.03 per share). This increase was due primarily to year-end inventory adjustments of $6,906,000 ($.08 per share) and a net credit for disposition and termination of certain operations of $1,466,000 ($.02 per share) which were partially offset by provisions for environmental protection and control and other year-end adjustments of $5,683,000 ($.07 per share).

1989

Fourth quarter adjustments increased net income by $8,250,000 ($.10 per share). This increase was due primarily to a reduction of prior quarters' LIFO expense and year-end inventory adjustments of $15,915,000 ($.19 per share) which were partially offset by provisions of $4,722,000 ($.06 per share) for the disposition and termination of certain operations, and other year-end adjustments of $2,943,000 ($.04 per share).

Note 15 — Real Estate Subsidiary

Sherwin-Williams Development Corporation, a wholly-owned subsidiary, and certain of its affiliates (SWDC) acquire, develop, lease, and manage properties for the Company and others. As required by Financial Accounting Standards Board Statement No. 94, SWDC is included in the consolidated financial statements. Total revenue includes intersegment revenue of $12,663,000, $10,058,000, and $9,575,000 in 1990, 1989 and 1988, respectively, which is eliminated in consolidation with the parent.

Summarized financial data for SWDC is as follows:

	December 31,		
Thousands of dollars	**1990**	1989	1988
Property, plant and equipment — net	$106,768	$99,063	$88,871
Current assets	469	670	1,053
Other noncurrent assets	625	718	817
Long-term debt	58,136	53,225	53,615
Current liabilities	2,652	2,062	3,125
Other noncurrent liabilities	5,676	5,415	4,781
Due to parent	35,286	35,130	19,916
Total revenue	$ 16,678	$14,162	$15,414
Interest expense	5,279	5,306	5,156
Total expenses — net	13,674	11,545	11,191
Net income	1,968	1,714	2,883

Note 16 — Financial Schedules
Property, Plant and Equipment (10-K, Schedules V and VI)

Additions and retirements of property, plant and equipment were as follows:

Thousands of dollars	Beginning Balance	Additions	Retirements	Other Changes	Ending Balance
1990					
Land	$ 36,748	$ 4,470	$ 53	$ 748	$ 41,913
Buildings	191,540	11,574	960	(7,185)	194,969
Machinery and equipment	404,156	43,968	16,319	466	432,271
Construction in progress	14,294	4,339	—	72	18,705
	$646,738	$64,351	$17,332	$ (5,899)	$687,858
1989					
Land	$ 35,206	$ 1,841	$ 307	$ 8	$ 36,748
Buildings	186,721	8,322	1,749	(1,754)	191,540
Machinery and equipment	365,834	54,232	15,870	(40)	404,156
Construction in progress	11,757	2,538	—	(1)	14,294
	$599,518	$66,933	$17,926	$ (1,787)	$646,738
1988					
Land	$ 32,069	$ 3,005	$ 518	$ 650	$ 35,206
Buildings	159,478	22,038	1,632	6,837	186,721
Machinery and equipment	324,498	46,414	12,057	6,979	365,834
Construction in progress	11,663	94	—	—	11,757
	$527,708	$71,551	$14,207	$14,466	$599,518

Other changes consist primarily of acquisitions and dispositions in 1990 and acquisitions in 1988.

Total accumulated depreciation and amortization of property, plant and equipment were as follows:

Thousands of dollars	Beginning Balance	Additions	Retirements	Other Changes	Ending Balance
1990					
Buildings	$ 62,843	$ 7,422	$ 769	$(4,951)	$ 64,545
Machinery and equipment	211,662	37,085	12,302	(845)	235,600
Other	13,368	—	—	995	14,363
	$287,873	$44,507	$13,071	$(4,801)	$314,508
1989					
Buildings	$ 57,638	$ 7,651	$ 1,019	$(1,427)	$ 62,843
Machinery and equipment	190,511	34,300	13,295	146	211,662
Other	18,771	—	—	(5,403)	13,368
	$266,920	$41,951	$14,314	$(6,684)	$287,873
1988					
Buildings	$ 53,665	$ 6,713	$ 1,266	$(1,474)	$ 57,638
Machinery and equipment	166,939	30,152	8,779	2,199	190,511
Other	18,242	—	—	529	18,771
	$238,846	$36,865	$10,045	$ 1,254	$266,920

Other changes consist primarily of dispositions in 1990 and provisions for dispositions in 1989 and 1988.

Note 16 — Financial Schedules (Continued)

Valuation and Qualifying Accounts and Reserves (10-K, Schedule VIII)

Changes in the allowance for doubtful accounts are as follows:

Thousands of dollars	**1990**	1989	1988
	Years ended December 31,		
Beginning balance	$ 2,261	$ 2,737	$ 2,820
Bad debt expense	11,584	9,430	7,535
Net uncollectible accounts written off	(11,362)	(9,906)	(7,618)
Ending balance	$ 2,483	$ 2,261	$ 2,737

Activity related to other assets:

Thousands of dollars	**1990**	1989	1988
	Years ended December 31,		
Beginning balance	$ 27,541	$24,152	$42,153
Charges to expense	(7,007)	(3,822)	(10,595)
Asset additions (deductions)	129,206	7,211	(7,406)
Ending balance	$149,740	$27,541	$24,152

Charges to expense consist primarily of amortization of intangibles in 1990, 1989 and 1988 and funded employee benefits in 1988. Asset additions (deductions) consist primarily of the acquisition of intangibles and goodwill in 1990, the purchase of long-term investments and reclassifications in 1989, and the sale of the partnership interest in BAPCO in 1988.

Activity related to other long-term liabilities:

Thousands of dollars	**1990**	1989	1988
	Years ended December 31,		
Beginning balance	$75,480	$57,623	$42,482
Charges to expense	6,429	14,745	16,378
Accrual additions (deductions)	(9,434)	3,112	(1,237)
Ending balance	$72,475	$75,480	$57,623

Charges to expense consist primarily of adjustments to estimated liabilities and deferred compensation. Accrual additions (deductions) consist primarily of balance sheet reclassifications and adjustments of environmental and other long-term accruals.

Short-Term Borrowings (10-K, Schedule IX)

Thousands of dollars	**1990**	1989	1988
	Years ended December 31,		
Notes payable to banks at December 31	$ 559	$ 431	$ 362
Weighted-average interest rate at December 31	31.5%	28.0%	19.8%
Maximum amount outstanding at any month-end	$ 751	$ 735	$ 484
Average amount outstanding during the period	$ 395	$ 587	$ 284
Weighted-average interest rate during the period	33.4%	21.0%	16.9%

Short-term borrowings are included in accounts payable on the balance sheets. Borrowings for 1990 relate solely to certain foreign subsidiaries at rates prevailing in those countries.

The average amount outstanding is the total of month-end outstanding balances divided by twelve.

The weighted-average interest rate is the actual interest on short-term debt divided by average short-term debt outstanding.

Supplementary Income Statement Information (10-K, Schedule X)

Thousands of dollars	**1990**	1989	1988
	Years ended December 31,		
Maintenance and repairs	$ 25,274	$25,442	$26,351
Advertising costs	106,461	84,465	84,043

Amounts for depreciation and amortization of intangible assets, preoperating costs and similar deferrals, taxes other than payroll and income taxes, and royalties are not presented because such amounts are each less than 1% of total net sales.

Computation of Net Income Per Share (Exhibit 11, Form 10-K)*
Thousands of dollars, except per share data

	1990	December 31, 1989	1988
Fully Diluted			
Average shares outstanding	86,560,437	85,954,145	87,354,494
Options — treasury stock method	503,898	548,504	475,348
Assumed conversion of 6.25% Convertible Subordinated Debentures	132,638	156,146	182,956
Average fully diluted shares	87,196,973	86,658,795	88,012,798
Net income	$122,666	$108,935	$101,080
Add 6.25% Convertible Subordinated Debentures interest net of tax	16	18	20
Net income applicable to fully diluted shares	$122,682	$108,953	$101,100
Net income per share	$ 1.41	$ 1.26	$ 1.15
Primary			
Average shares outstanding	86,560,437	85,954,145	87,354,494
Options — treasury stock method	495,382	372,194	475,348
Average shares and equivalents	87,055,819	86,326,339	87,829,842
Net income applicable to shares and equivalents	$122,666	$108,935	$101,080
Net income per share	$ 1.41	$ 1.26	$ 1.15

* All common share amounts and per share data reflect the effect of the stock split described in Note 2 to the consolidated financial statements.

Business Segments

Millions of dollars

Net External Sales

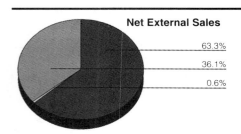

63.3%

36.1%

0.6%

Operating Profits

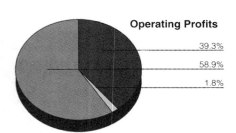

39.3%

58.9%

1.8%

Identifiable Assets

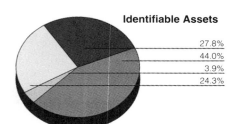

27.8%

44.0%

3.9%

24.3%

Capital Expenditures

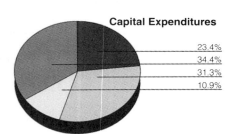

23.4%

34.4%

31.3%

10.9%

Depreciation

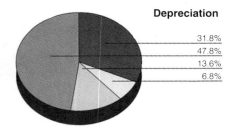

31.8%

47.8%

13.6%

6.8%

Years ended December 31,	1990	1989	1988
Net External Sales			
Paint Stores	$1,434	$1,346	$1,250
Coatings	819	764	687
Other	14	13	13
Segment totals	$2,267	$2,123	$1,950
Operating Profits			
Paint Stores	$ 86	$ 91	$ 70
Coatings	129	120	118
Other	4	(3)	6
Segment totals	219	208	194
Corporate expenses-net	(32)	(38)	(31)
Income from continuing operations before income taxes	$ 187	$ 170	$ 163
Identifiable Assets			
Paint Stores	$ 418	$ 393	$ 426
Coatings	662	480	457
Other	58	49	47
Segment totals	1,138	922	930
Corporate	366	453	329
Discontinued Operations	—	—	—
Consolidated totals	$1,504	$1,375	$1,259
Capital Expenditures			
Paint Stores	$ 15	$ 27	$ 15
Coatings	22	26	39
Other	20	10	8
Segment totals	57	63	62
Corporate	7	4	10
Discontinued Operations	—	—	—
Consolidated totals	$ 64	$ 67	$ 72
Depreciation			
Paint Stores	$ 14	$ 13	$ 11
Coatings	21	21	18
Other	6	5	4
Segment totals	41	39	33
Corporate	3	3	4
Continuing operations totals	$ 44	$ 42	$ 37
Operating Margins			
Paint Stores	6.0%	6.8%	5.6%
Coatings	9.8%	10.0%	10.8%
Other	13.8%	(11.1%)	25.5%
Segment totals	7.9%	8.1%	8.2%

Paint Stores

Coatings

Other

Corporate

Intersegment Transfers

	1990	1989	1988	1987	1986	1985	1984	1983	1982	1981
Coatings	$492	$442	$401	$368	$331	$314	$287	$271	$233	$261
All other segments	15	14	12	7	6	5	4	29	30	35
Segment totals	$507	$456	$413	$375	$337	$319	$291	$300	$263	$296

Years ended December 31,

The Sherwin-Williams Company and Subsidiaries

	1987	1986	1985	1984	1983	1982	1981
	$1,158	$1,009	$ 931	$ 850	$ 724	$ 621	$ 616
	635	544	566	513	485	491	554
	8	5	39	91	188	200	229
	$1,801	$1,558	$1,526	$1,454	$1,397	$1,312	$1,399
	$ 82	$ 91*	$ 64	$ 56	$ 29	$ 14	$ 16
	104	129*	94	77	89	78	57
	5	—	3	10	10	11	8
	191	220	161	143	128	103	81
	(30)	(46)*	(37)	(25)	(29)	(37)	(29)
	$ 161	$ 174*	$ 124	$ 118	$ 99	$ 66	$ 52
	$ 367	$ 303	$ 283	$ 249	$ 197	$ 152	$ 167
	401	351	331	305	300	277	304
	43	46	38	63	67	142	145
	811	700	652	617	564	571	616
	399	257	224	217	203	155	75
	—	250	232	209	203	176	173
	$1,210	$1,207	$1,108	$1,043	$ 970	$ 902	$ 864
	$ 15	$ 12	$ 16	$ 16	$ 7	$ 6	$ 10
	29	21	24	15	12	9	10
	6	13	16	13	22	24	20
	50	46	56	44	41	39	40
	5	4	8	2	2	4	2
	2	14	11	13	9	5	1
	$ 57	$ 64	$ 75	$ 59	$ 52	$ 48	$ 43
	$ 10	$ 9	$ 8	$ 7	$ 6	$ 5	$ 6
	16	12	11	9	8	8	8
	3	2	3	5	8	7	6
	29	23	22	21	22	20	20
	3	4	2	2	1	2	2
	$ 32	$ 27	$ 24	$ 23	$ 23	$ 22	$ 22
	7.1%	9.0%	6.9%	6.6%	4.0%	2.2%	2.6%
	10.4%	14.8%	10.8%	9.6%	11.8%	10.7%	6.9%
	33.9%	(2.4%)	5.9%	10.7%	4.8%	5.0%	3.0%
	8.8%	11.6%	8.7%	8.2%	7.6%	6.5%	4.8%

* Operating profits in 1986 include net credits of $21,179,000 for Paint Stores and $30,023,000 for Coatings and a charge of ($17,417,000) for Corporate from unusual items.

Effect of LIFO

	Year of Adoption	Decrease (Increase) in Income From Continuing Operations									
		1990	1989	1988	1987	1986	1985	1984	1983	1982	1981
Paint Stores............	1980	**$6**	$6	$4	$(2)	$(1)	—	$(1)	—	$2	$5
Coatings	1980	**6**	7	14	3	(5)	$1	4	$(1)	1	13
Other....................	1979	**—**	—	—	—	—	—	(1)	(2)	(3)	2
Segment totals		**$12**	$13	$18	$1	$(6)	$1	$2	$(3)	$—	$20

Notes to Segment Tables

The Other Segment consists of real estate leasing activities which began in 1982, the Chemicals Division which was disposed of in June 1985, and the Sherwin-Williams Container Corporation which was disposed of during November 1983.

Net external sales, operating profits, depreciation, and operating margins include continuing operations only for the years 1981 through 1987.

Operating profit is total revenue, including realized profit on intersegment transfers, less operating costs and expenses. Adjusting for special credits in 1989 and special charges in 1988, operating profit of the Paint Stores Segment increased 7.8 percent from 1989 to 1990 and 7.7 percent from 1988 to 1989. During 1984, a change in intersegment transfer values resulted in increased operating profit for the Paint Stores Segment while the Coatings Segment's operating profit declined due to the effects of the reduced transfer values. Corporate expenses include interest which is unrelated to real estate leasing activities, certain provisions for disposition and termination of operations which are not directly associated with or allocable to any operating segment, and other adjustments.

Identifiable assets are those directly identified with each segment's operations. Corporate assets consist primarily of cash, investments, headquarters property, plant and equipment, and certain property under capital leases.

The operating margin for each segment is based upon total external sales and intersegment transfers. Intersegment transfers are accounted for at values comparable to normal unaffiliated customer sales.

Export sales, sales of foreign subsidiaries and sales to any individual customer were each less than 10% of consolidated sales to unaffiliated customers during all years presented.

Our business segments offer customers quality products such as those bearing the registered trademarks Sherwin-Williams®, Dutch Boy®, Martin-Senour®, Kem-Tone®, Acme®, Rogers®, Western Automotive Finishes , Glas-Clad®, Perma-Clad®, Dupli-Color®, Krylon®, Color Works®, Illinois Bronze®, ProMar® 200, Dutch Boy SUPER®, Dutch Boy DIRT FIGHTER®, and others. Other quality paint products are offered under the trademark of SuperPaint™

INDEX

♦